PRINCIPLES OF ECONOMICS

PRINCIPLES OF ECONOMICS

Roger Chisholm
Memphis State University

Marilu McCarty
Georgia Institute of Technology

Scott, Foresman and Company
Glenview, Illinois
Dallas, Texas
Oakland, N.J.
Palo Alto, Cal.
Tucker, Ga.
London, England

Photograph Acknowledgments

Lawrence Klein: UPI
Karl Marx: Brown Brothers
Simon Kuznets: Courtesy of Harvard University
Wassily Leontief: Wide World
John Maynard Keynes: Radio Times Hulton Picture Library
Paul Samuelson: Wide World
John Law: Brown Brothers
Nicholas Biddle: Brown Brothers
Charles H. Dow: Courtesy of *The Wall Street Journal*
Irving Fisher: Wide World
Milton Friedman: Courtesy of the Hoover Institution, Stanford University
Arthur Burns: UPI
David Ricardo: Brown Brothers
Thomas Malthus: Brown Brothers
W. Arthur Lewis: Courtesy of Princeton University; photograph by Robert Bielk
Alexander Gerschenkron: Courtesy of Harvard University
Jacob Viner: Courtesy of Ellen Viner Seiler
Robert Triffin: Courtesy of Yale University; photograph by Andr**S** Germain
Robert McNamara: UPI
Joseph Schumpeter: Courtesy of Harvard University
Frank Knight: Courtesy of University of Chicago
Thorstein Veblen: Brown Brothers
William Stanley Jevons: Radio Times Hulton Picture Library
Alfred Marshall: Historical Pictures Service, Inc., Chicago
Andrew Carnegie: Brown Brothers
Joan Robinson: Ramsey & Muspratt Ltd.
Paul Sweezy: Courtesy of *Monthly Review Press*
John Kenneth Galbraith: Wide World
George Stigler: Courtesy of University of Chicago
Lillian Gilbreth: UPI
Arthur Okun: Courtesy of The Brookings Institution

Library of Congress Cataloging in Publication Data

Chisholm, Roger K.
Principles of economics.

Also issued in two separate editions under title: Principles of microeconomics and Principles of macroeconomics.
Includes index.
1. Economics.   I. McCarty, Marilu Hurt, joint author.   II. Title.
HB171.5.C63   1978c   330   77-21268
ISBN 0-673-15060-7

12345678910-RRW-858483828180797877

Preface

This text is intended for the one-year principles of economics course. Therefore, it is written for the student encountering economics for the first time. The "usual" subject matter of the first course is treated in a complete and detailed manner. However, this book is not an encyclopedia of economic topics or a grab bag offering far more material than any instructor can cover. Such books advertise their "flexibility," but the result is often that important economic material is never covered by the instructor. The authors of this text believe fewer topics should be covered in a basic course but topics should be explored in greater depth. Stressing a balance between economic theory and real-world examples, chapters are often a couple of pages longer than those found in other texts.

The authors have paid particular attention to the writing style and level. The chapters were reworked and polished many times with this crucial point in mind. The terminology is that of the economist while the language is that of the economic journalist. Thus the writing style is like that found in *Business Week*, *The New York Times*, or *The Wall Street Journal*. The book speaks to today's students in a lively, colloquial fashion without emphasizing current slang or adopting other overly cute devices. It is hoped that such language, besides facilitating learning, will convey the excitement of current economics.

The instructor of economics should have one very important advantage over his colleagues in other social sciences. Many of our world's problems are economic in origin, and many of the major economic problems appear again and again in the headlines of media familiar to the student. Therefore, an economics course should be, for most students, one of their most exciting and relevant courses. The authors believe this text will fulfill this goal.

Special Features

Much effort was directed toward juxtaposing real-world examples and problems with the economic theory and ideas. Three basic issues inserts were employed: Extended Examples, Viewpoints, and Economic Thinkers. The plan was to insert at least one of each in every chapter. However, a few chapters have, say, a Viewpoint and an Economic Thinker. On the other hand, some chapters have seven or eight of these issues inserts.

The **Extended Examples** are just what the title says; they explore some topic from the real world in greater depth and show how it is an example of economic theory in action. In the chapter on Monopoly, there is an Extended Example on "Monopoly in Dolls;" this example describes how a not-so-successful importer of cheap dolls changed marketing strategy and signed up the rights to make dolls of famous personalities like Muhammad Ali. In the chapter on Inflation, we have an Extended Example entitled "Economic Chaos in Argentina;" this example shows how inflation of over 300% per year helped bring on the military overthrow of Isabel de Peron. Another Extended Example, found in the Fiscal Policy chapter, is called "Mr. Carter's $50 Misunderstanding;" it discusses what happened to Carter's proposed $50 rebate and demonstrates some shortcomings of fiscal policy in the real world.

The **Viewpoints** deal with economic controversies and with many of the unsolved economic problems of our times. Quite literally, the Viewpoints are taken from the headlines of newspapers and magazines. The Viewpoints challenge the student to apply the theory he or she has just learned. In fact, many of the Viewpoints are followed by questions asking the student to defend or disagree with the argument. In the chapter on "Big Business and Public Policy," we have a Viewpoint called "Regulation or Strangulation?" which discusses the problems of government regulation; in particular, we note that many trucking companies and airlines *prefer* regulation because transportation rates are kept higher than in a competitive, nonregulated market. In the chapter on "Inflation and Unemployment" we have two opposing Viewpoints, one called "Unemployment Statistics *Overestimate* the Problem" and the other entitled "Unemployment Statistics *Underestimate* the Problem."

Our third issues insert is the **Economic Thinkers**, biographies of great economists, both living and dead. Actually, biographical data are limited to one or two paragraphs. Most of the biography deals with the important economic ideas contributed by that thinker. Some of our Economic Thinkers are Milton Friedman, John Kenneth Galbraith, Marx, Veblen, Keynes, Lawrence Klein, Nicholas Biddle, Sir W. Arthur Lewis, and Alexander Gerschenkron—the list goes on and on.

The average length of these issues inserts is two text columns—or one full page in length. Thus these issues are not intended as diversions; they provide some "meat" for the student.

Other useful pedagogical tools are included. Each chapter starts with a detailed chapter outline. (Learning objectives can be found in the beginning of each study guide chapter.) At the end of each chapter is a summary, a key words and phrases list, and questions for review. The key words and phrases are actually glossaries of all new terms presented in that chapter. In the interests of "pedagogical repetition," some terms appear in more than one glossary. (The Instructor's Manual provides suggested readings from popular magazines for both student and teacher.)

The general organization of the text is fairly traditional. An introductory section of five chapters is followed by the macroeconomic chapters and then the microeconomic chapters. However, any instructor who chooses can just as easily make the jump from the introductory section directly to the microeconomics. The authors wrote the micro and macro portions so that each could stand alone.

There have been a number of new thrusts in macroeconomic thinking in recent years which are not adequately covered in other texts. This text was prepared so that both the Keynesian and monetarist schools of thought are given balanced and positive treatment. This means that aggregate supply receives added emphasis and supply curves are related to changes in the price level. The schools are not set against each other though the differences are explained. No one school is held out as superior or correct. The instructor may wish to do so, of course, but the text is written to prepare the student to follow the on-going debates.

Organization

Some organizational features of this text are standard and usable in a wide range of academic scheduling. Chapters 1 to 5 form the introductory section and lay the groundwork for a basic understanding of the market system in a democratic society. Participants in consumption and production are shown interacting in an environment limited by resource availability and by the actions of government. Besides introducing the concepts of supply and demand, these chapters cover basic microeconomics and macroeconomics. The authors believe a little preparation in micro is needed by students to obtain the most from the macro chapters, and vice versa. At 96 pages, the introductory section is shorter than in many texts and enables the instructor to move more quickly into the micro theory or the macro theory.

The first macro section discusses national income accounting and fiscal policy. National income accounting is covered in Chapter 6. The approach is to show the student the aggregates which will be the subject of the remainder of the text. In many texts this chapter is presented as a necessary evil, a chapter to be endured till we can get on to other matters. In this one, the subject of national income accounting is treated with enthusiasm and clarity. The ties to the rest of the material are constantly kept in the student's attention. Chapter 7 spells out the nature of economic instability. The emphasis is on the problems of uncertainty, inflation, and unemployment.

Chapters 8 through 10 cover the real sector of the economy. The roles of households, firms, and government as actors are emphasized. The aggregate demand and supply chapters show

how the economy reaches the equilibrium level of output. Aggregate supply gets more attention in this treatment than it is given by many authors. Fiscal policy is then shown to be one of the ways to change the level of output and income.

Chapters 11 through 15 explain the monetary sector of the economy. Chapters 11 and 12 explain what money is and how it is created in a modern economy with a fractional reserve banking system. Chapter 14 explains the demand for money as viewed by the classical, Keynesian, and monetarist economists. Chapter 15 returns to the money supply and the actions taken by the Federal Reserve to control the money supply. Monetary policy, from both a Keynesian and monetarist perspective, is explained.

Chapter 13 on Other Financial Intermediaries deserves special mention as it is unique to this book. Most introductory economics texts ignore financial institutions other than commercial banks. Some instructors may feel that since these institutions are peripheral to monetary policy, they shouldn't be discussed. (Those instructors can drop this chapter.) Yet these very institutions will surely have an impact on the economic future of the student. So Chapter 13 discusses savings and loan associations, credit unions, the insurance industry, and stocks and bonds—along with the operations of the securities market and how it affects all of us.

Chapter 16 is also a unique chapter. The dual problems of inflation and unemployment are examined with care. The recent experience with both is explained and related to the student's expected future. The reasons why solutions to the problems are so elusive are discussed at length. The solutions advanced by Keynesians and monetarists are also considered.

Chapters 17 and 18 treat in turn growth and development. The problems associated with growth including the arguments for limiting growth are described. The development chapter emphasizes both the economic and noneconomic problems faced by developing nations. The world energy crisis is also introduced.

The international chapters (Chapters 19–21) develop the basis for trade and the traditional theory of international finance. Chapter 21 brings together the growth and development considerations with the international trade and finance models to explain some of the worldwide problems of famine, war, multinational corporations, and commodity cartels.

The body of the microeconomics section is divided into three parts. Chapters 22 through 26 develop the theory of consumer demand and competitive market equilibrium. Chapter 22 explores the relationship between industry structure and performance. The pros and cons of industrial concentration are discussed. Chapter 23 is unique in economic textbooks in its focus on political economy. Some of the subjects covered in this chapter are: the power elite; the corporate state; how power is wielded *within* corporations and *by* corporations; the use of game theory in both economic and political decision-making; and how wealth corrupts government and government-imposed rules and regulations.

Chapters 24, 25, and 26 construct a micro market of supply and demand. Elasticity of demand is explained along with marginal utility analysis. The concept of marginal utility is extended to current issues involving land use and progressive income taxation. The principles of demand elasticity are applied to marketing, production, and legal decisions.

Chapters 27 through 31 examine costs and pricing within various market structures. Chapter 27 presents cost curves in detail, with short-run economic profit shown as a result of imperfect mobility and knowledge. Chapter 28 completes the process of adjustment to zero-profit competitive equilibrium and outlines the welfare implications. Chapters 29, 30, and 31 explore the pros and cons of market structures outside the competitive ideal.

Chapters 32 through 34 examine resource allocation and income distribution. Understanding marginal productivity theory is the key to this section; this topic is covered in Chapter 32. Chapter 33 then examines how the four factors of production receive payments. Labor is singled out for an extended discussion, including the effects of unions. Chapter 34 covers the important subject of imperfections in income distribution. Poverty and discrimination are treated at some length. Also included here is a discussion of urban poverty and the financial crises of our cities.

Acknowledgments

Naturally, such a major undertaking as writing a basic economics text leaves the authors in debt to many people. First there is the intellectual debt to many economists and other mentors, some of whom the authors have never met. Then there are the many students whose comments and complaints have shaped our teaching of the course.

The authors would particularly like to thank the following professors who offered constructive comments on the manuscript:

Robert Averitt, Smith College
Frank Bonello, University of Notre Dame
Edward Starshak, College of Lake County
Donald J. Yankovic, University of Toledo
Shik Young, Eastern Washington State College

Author Chisholm would like to give special thanks to Rhonda Roseberry, who typed endless revisions of chapters, and to Pam Trask, who asked why college textbooks had to be so dull.

Roger K. Chisholm
Marilu H. McCarty

Contents

Part One
An Introduction to Economics   1

Part Two
National Income and Fiscal Policy 97

Part Three
Money, Banking, and Monetary Policy 209

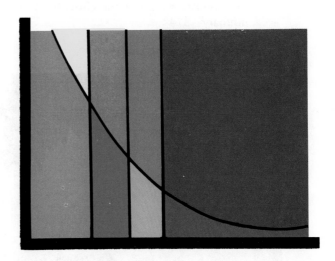

Part Four
Stabilization Policies and Growth   **317**

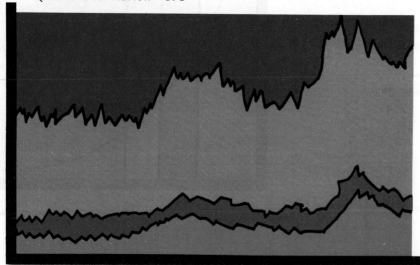

Part Five
International Economics **397**

Part Six
Consumer Behavior and Elasticity 465

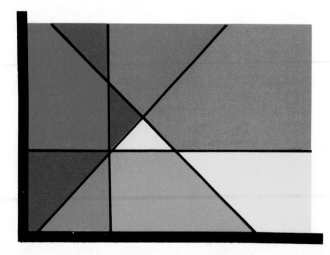

Part Seven
Costs of Production and Product Markets 575

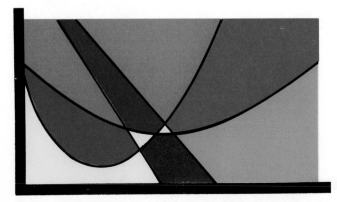

Part Eight
Resource Markets   685

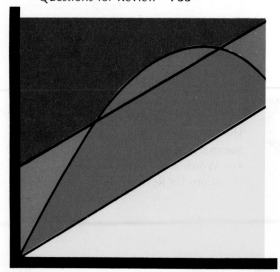

Part One

An Introduction to Economics

1

What Is Economics?

Economics has been defined as the study of how human beings make their living. That isn't a complete definition, as we shall see, but it will do for a beginning. We study economics for a number of reasons. Most of us want to know how we can live better next year than we live now. We want to know what will determine the types and numbers of jobs that will be available to us. We want to know how we can spend so that we will enjoy our incomes more completely. Perhaps we also want to know what the needs of our business will be and how the business can best prepare to meet those needs.

As citizens we want to know how our community will grow and how we can contribute to and benefit from that growth. Our nation's growth and strength are important to us, too, as is the future of the human race. As voters we are concerned about our nation's economic policy. What policies will deal effectively with the problems of inflation, unemployment, and poverty? What taxes are appropriate and how should the tax burden be shared? Should government spend more than it receives? Should we raise tariffs to keep out foreign goods that compete with goods made here? Should we have a minimum wage law? These are only a few of the economic questions that concern us.

What economists do

Most of these questions are not new. In fact, for hundreds of years people have looked for answers to questions like these. *The study of economics developed to explore alternatives, measuring the benefits and costs of policy choices.* Now almost every large corporation has economists on its staff. Many of them work at analyzing prices and production costs. They study the way particular markets function, and how workers, machines, and land are combined to produce goods and services that people will buy. They try to predict the market for Cadillacs and subway trains, soybeans and electric power. They are concerned with acquiring the resources needed for production and with using resources efficiently.

Governments employ economists to analyze these issues as well as broader questions.

Government economists are often concerned with *aggregates* or totals, such as total production, national income, and total employment in the entire nation. They study how the monetary system and the tax structure affect national output and growth. They try to predict the effects of alternative government spending policies on national income and prices and on job opportunities in the future.

Most economists specialize in particular fields. Economists in public finance deal with government budgets: tax revenues and spending appropriations. Monetary economists are concerned with the health of the banking system and its contribution to general economic health. Other economists specialize in international trade, labor relations, agricultural economics, or industrial organization. They may be asked to estimate the effects of higher oil prices or lower tariffs, new labor laws, farm loans or subsidies, and proposed mergers of manufacturing firms.

Understanding how our economy works helps us to plan better. Economic knowledge enables us to make the changes that will help us to live better.

How economists affect our future

Economists are concerned with the social environment: how people live together and the arrangements which help them to live better. Economists observe changes in the attitudes and habits of people and try to explain how these changes affect the economic life of the community. If a definite trend can be identified, the economist may project future problems and opportunities. Plans can be drawn up to deal with future possibilities, and the economist may predict the outcome of various policies. We can better understand how economists affect our lives by examining just one seemingly small part of the economy: the housing industry.

Everyone must have a place to live, so it is important that enough dwellings be produced. Nevertheless, most of us have a rather limited view of housing. We say to ourselves: "I have always lived in a house; all my neighbors for miles around have houses; when the time comes, I too will have a house." The future may indeed unfold in this manner. But ensuring that housing supply meets future demand for type and quantity is not always automatic. In fact, in the mid-1970s there was a shortage of houses, and in some areas, of apartments. What will happen in the housing industry tomorrow? Will there be enough housing to meet everyone's wants? How does the housing industry affect the rest of the economy?

Some definite changes have been taking place in our social environment that will have a major impact on the housing industry in coming decades. Changing trends in population growth will affect the number and kinds of new housing needed in the 1980s and 1990s. Back in the 1950s, the average woman gave birth to 3.8 children. But the fast population growth of that period has now leveled off. Today we are approaching *zero population growth* (that is, the present population will be maintained); only 1.8 children are expected for the average woman of the 1970s.

The post-World War II baby boom from the late 1940s to the early 1950s created a population "bulge" which moves along our age distribution, leading to abnormal demands for certain goods and services. For example, babies born in the 1950s are now beginning to form households and need dwelling places of their own. Traditionally, young adults move first into apartments, then into moderately priced homes. As they approach middle age, many are able to move into more expensive homes, and finally, in old age, they move back into apartments or mobile homes. The age structure of our population at a particular time determines the kind of housing that will be in greatest demand. The bulge of young adults in the 1970s placed heavy demand on apartments, but by the 1980s this group will want single-family homes. About 2.4 million houses will have to be built every year to meet this demand.

Other changes affect the number of total units needed. Rising incomes and growing numbers of "singles" means that more individuals will want separate housing, increasing the demand for apartments. Also, the energy crisis—with the resulting high heating and transportation costs—will probably lead to less emphasis on large suburban homes and greater need for compact, convenient dwellings.

Changes in the homebuilding industry will provide job opportunities for new workers. Moreover, the housing industry uses materials and components from many other industries employing many workers. Careful planning will help young adults to develop the skills needed for employment and to arrange for their own housing needs. Outside the homebuilding industry, other business firms will be watching these trends, too. Suppliers of cement, lumber, roofing material, paint, and electrical and plumbing fixtures must be prepared to satisfy demand. They must develop the productive techniques and accumulate the machines needed for the most profitable lines of building materials. Other business firms will specialize in furnishing homes with furniture, carpets, wallpaper, draperies, and appliances. They must pay close attention to new technology and to changing tastes in home decoration.

Economists collect and interpret information to help individuals and business firms plan their policies for the future. But government also seeks this information because it is interested in the future course of industry development. The homebuilding industry provides jobs for a significant portion of this nation's labor force. So if plentiful jobs are going to be available or, conversely, if construction workers are going to be unemployed, the government recognizes that either has strong effects on the national economy. Indeed, if large numbers of housing and housing-related workers are unemployed, this will affect you, no matter what your profession. If you are in business, you or your company will be losing potential customers. As a taxpayer, you may have to pay more taxes to provide the required unemployment compensation and welfare payments.

Government financial and spending policies are formulated in part on the information gathered and interpreted by economists. If housing production is to continue smoothly, government must ensure ample credit for homebuyers. Government can direct its research and development funds toward more efficient forms of construction, helping to keep building costs down. Government will need to set policies for ensuring the best use of land and for conserving energy resources. Government may want to encourage rehabilitation of existing homes to meet the need for dwellings.

By the 1990s the "babies" of the 1950s will begin moving back into apartments and the building boom may slacken. Jobs in construction and related industries will be cut back. Economists can help government develop new programs to absorb the unemployed workers into new fields. A smooth transition into other employments will preserve workers' skills and maintain total production at a high level. Stable worker incomes will protect living standards for all workers and keep tax revenues flowing into government.

Beginnings: Adam Smith

One of the most famous of all economists was Adam Smith. He is, in fact, often referred to as "the father of modern economics." Adam Smith was a respected professor and scholar during the early years of the Industrial Revolution in England. He was very much aware of the harsh lives of miners and factory workers, the distress of women and young children at heavy labor, the poverty and hopelessness of the masses of people. He wondered how these conditions could be explained and whether they were a prelude to better times.

In Smith's time European economies operated under the economic principles of **mercantilism.** A mercantilist system aimed at increasing national prosperity through favorable trading relationships. By developing its industry and agriculture a nation could trade its valuable output for the gold of other nations. Mercantilism depended on close government regulation of economic activity to ensure the most favorable output of goods for trade.

In 1776, the year of the American Declaration of Independence, Smith published his great work, *An Inquiry into the Nature and Causes of the Wealth of Nations*. In this book Adam Smith described a view of a new economic system that was taking hold in the more democratic new nations of the West. According to Smith, this new form of economy was one in which people were free to decide for themselves what they would produce and how they would spend their incomes. Individual consumers free to express their preferences in free markets, producers free to seek profits by providing goods and services—these were the important actors on the economic scene. Furthermore, the independent choices of individual buyers and sellers would bring about the best results for the community without the need for government regulation or central planning. The community would prosper and grow as if an "invisible hand" were guiding it.

Smith's **"invisible hand"** is one of the most famous phrases in all of economic literature. It describes how competition in free markets would direct production in ways which would increase public well-being. In a system of free markets, producers would compete against each other to sell more goods, forcing prices down to the lowest level at which goods could be produced. If certain goods are scarce, buyers would offer high prices, drawing more producers into industries where the need is greatest. "It is not from the benevolence of the butcher, the brewer or the baker, that we expect our dinner, but from their regard to their own interest. We address ourselves not to their humanity but to their self-love, and never talk to them of our own necessities but of their advantage." Such a system is known as a **market economy.**

From its beginning the United States was one of the few nations that made economic decisions through the free market system. It is appropriate that a nation built on freedom of choice in its political life would also provide freedom of choice in its economic life. Our political democracy is based on the idea that each voter helps to determine government policy. Our **economic democracy** rests on the principle that each dollar spent helps to determine the goods and services that are to be produced. In a free market consumers determine what and how much is to be produced by spending their dollars.

In a world where much of economic activity was and is not free, the market system has been very successful in developing the American economy. More goods have been produced through the market system than through any other system. Nowhere else have average incomes been consistently higher and more community services been provided. Over the years our economy has grown to meet the wants of our people.

Production in the market system may occasionally include some seemingly useless or unnecessary goods and services: Edsel automobiles, palm readings, pet rocks, pornography, and medical quackery. And production may fall short in other needed areas: low-cost housing, long lasting appliances and clothing, tasteful and nutritious food, and inspiring television entertainment. But this is the nature of the market system. Production in the market system is directed mainly by *what consumers want* (and are able to pay for) rather than by what someone decides is "good for" them.

Adam Smith recognized that the ideal results of the market system did not always exist in the real world. He warned that "seldom do people of the same trade ever meet together, even for merriment and diversion, but the conversation ends in a conspiracy against the public or in some contrivance to raise prices." Problems are not always automatically solved when people act in their own self-interest. It is possible to act in self-interest and create problems for others. For instance, some critics have shown that the market system may not distribute output to workers in a way that we feel is fair. Other economists have noted that the market system is unstable, with wasteful periods of unemployment or inflation. Despite its important strengths, the market economy has not been a perfect system.

Issues we face

Because the market system is not capable of resolving all difficulties, many problems remain. Unemployment and poverty stunt the lives of many citizens, large cities face crises of crime and decay, and economic growth has depleted many of our natural resources. Through our legislative procedures, we have modified the free market system in an effort to meet these new problems. Government intervention has placed some restrictions on our freedom of choice.

You will enjoy certain opportunities as a member of a free society, and you must accept certain responsibilities in return. You, the reader, have a stake in our economic system. You must prepare yourself to propose answers to important economic questions, questions involving day-to-day problems and questions involving the health of our productive system in the years to come. How we answer these questions will determine whether there will be a job for you, how much you will earn, what you can buy in exchange for your earnings, and what kind of opportunities you can provide your children. The decisions we make as a nation will affect the quality of life in your community, the taxes you pay, the services you receive, and the health and safety necessary for human growth.

Moreover, all these choices will affect our nation's ability to trade for those goods we do not produce and to defend our national interests when challenged. How we answer economic questions will affect the world's use of resources and the level at which billions of people throughout the world will live for many generations to come.

The scientific method

Do you remember the story of the Greek scientist Archimedes? The King of Syracuse asked Archimedes whether his royal crown was really made of pure gold, as the maker claimed, or whether it was diluted partly with silver. Archimedes was puzzled for an answer until one day, stepping into a bath, he noticed a relationship between the volume of his body and the quantity of water displaced from the tub. It occurred to him that he could find the answer to the King's question if he measured the amounts of water displaced by submerging (a) the crown, (b) and equal weight of gold, and (c) an equal weight of silver. If the crown were made entirely of gold, it would displace an amount of water equal to that displaced by the piece of gold. But if the crown were alloyed with silver, it would displace a greater amount of water. (Archimedes remembered that silver weighs less than gold per unit of volume. He reasoned that an equal weight of silver would require a greater volume, which in turn would displace more water.)

Archimedes was so excited by his discovery that he left the public bath, so the story goes, and ran home through the streets without his clothes, shouting, "eureka, eureka" (I've found it, I've found it!).

Not everyone who runs naked through the streets (or across a campus) has made a scientific discovery. The discoveries of science usually result from years of patient observation and gathering of data, followed by careful testing to make sure that the scientist's conclusion is valid.

Scientists refer to this process as the scientific method of analysis. The earliest use of the scientific method is associated with Francis Bacon in the seventeenth century. The scientific method requires the examiner to gather the important data describing the system under investigation. Data are classified and arranged to allow the examiner to explain the relationships and the forces at work within the system. The first tentative explanation is called a *hypothesis*.

After stating the hypothesis, the examiner must arrange experiments to test the truth of the explanation. Experiments are conducted in laboratories where conditions are controlled. For each experiment the examiner makes a single controlled change in one of the conditions. The effect of each change is noted and compared with the expected effects. Unless the actual change conforms to the expected change, the proposed hypothesis must be rejected as unproven.

The examiner continues to propose hypotheses until the results consistently conform to the proposed explanation. When the hypothesis is finally accepted, it can be stated as a *law* or *principle*. If you have studied one of the physical sciences, you know how carefully each hypothesis must be tested and how precisely each principle must be stated. Centuries of systematic study went into the principles we have learned about physics and chemistry.

Like the King of Syracuse, most of us are perfectly happy to leave physics and chemistry to those who specialize in the field. Perhaps we would like to leave economics to the economists, too, but unfortunately we can't. In our daily lives we must all be involved in economics much of the time. The average family in the United States makes spending decisions involving thousands of dollars a year. Citizens vote for politicians who will spend hundreds of millions, even billions, of dollars. We will all pay taxes, too, and many of us will belong to unions that will bargain with our employers for our wages and working conditions. Some understanding of economics is helpful in making our personal decisions. And some understanding of how economists reason and make decisions will be helpful in evaluating proposals for national policy.

Economics as a science

A science is an attempt to clarify, to understand, to discover. Some sciences are concerned with understanding physical or natural phenomena: physics, chemistry, biology, and geology. In their laboratories physical and natural scientists conduct experiments which help them to understand forces and relationships in our natural environment.

Social sciences are concerned with understanding forces and relationships in our social environment. Along with psychology, sociology, anthropology, and political science, economics is a social science. Like physical sciences, social sciences seek to establish principles that help us understand the world around us.

The first step toward understanding our physical world is to gather and classify information describing a particular part of our environment. Much of this information is measurable. The biologist measures the effect of various nutrients on plant growth; the chemist measures the effect of temperature changes on the behavior of gases. Through repeated experiments, physical scientists gather and classify data describing the situations they are trying to understand. Then they use the data to explain the relationships within the system and to predict the effects of a change in conditions.

Economists work in much the same way as the physical scientists toward understanding our social environment. For instance, economists may be concerned with the effect of higher incomes on total spending in the United States. They may gather data showing that the average automobile assembly-line worker, for example, earns $12,000 per year after taxes. Of this total, $250 goes into a savings account and the remainder is spent. An economist can use the available data and observations of past behavior to predict the change in spending if workers bring home more income, say through a cost of living increase or through a reduction in tax rates.

You can see that numbers are very important in studying these relationships. Any time numbers are used, mathematical relationships are sure to follow. Like other scientists, economists do indeed employ the shorthand of mathematics to simplify and improve understanding.

But economics is much more than the numbers and the unchanging facts of a physical science. Its concerns are *social*—it studies *people*. Economics, like the other social sciences, deals with the relationships among people as they function in society. Sometimes, in fact, the "social" part weakens the "science" of economics. This may happen because people don't always behave in the same predictable patterns associated with a physical science.

The human factor makes economic questions difficult to answer with certainty. Even worse, the social scientist is himself or herself a part of the problem being examined. The economist must be careful to eliminate personal preferences and prejudices and examine the problem on its own merits.

The famous economist John Maynard Keynes called economics "the most difficult of the easy sciences." He meant that many of the ideas and facts themselves are simple. But clear-cut conclusions may be impossible.

Economic models

Examining the social environment may be more complicated than examining the physical environment. Partly this is because the social scientist has no laboratory to test theories of human behavior. The economist's laboratory is the economic system itself. Experiments in the social laboratory would be costly and might unjustly affect the lives of many people. Moreover, experiments in the social laboratory could not be carried out under controlled conditions. Economists usually cannot isolate an economic community and test it for reactions to alternative policies. They can only rely on past observations of economic behavior to predict how people will respond to new policies.

Lacking social laboratories, economists test their theories through the use of models. **Models** are abstractions or simplified views of reality. Models show relationships between selected phenomena occurring in our world; their purpose is to reveal behavior and mak accurate predictions. The selected or significant phenomena are called *variables*. The use of models allows the scientist to observe the effect of a change in conditions on other variables. A model is set up under certain assumed conditions of behavior. Then a single change is made in one of the variables in the system and the resulting total change is noted.

A model is a little like the diagram of a football play. In a football playbook players are represented by circles or X's. A plan is drawn up under the assumption that certain players will behave in certain predictable ways. Movements by offensive players will be countered by predictable defensive moves. Arrows are drawn to show how the play should proceed. On the field the actions probably will not be exactly like the plans developed by the coaches. Too many unexpected events take place and change the outcome. The other team responds in unpredicted ways, new opportunities open up, or mistakes are made. But even when the play doesn't work as planned, the play as diagrammed is still useful.

Economic models relate to the real world in much the same fashion. The model will seldom give exactly the right answer. As economic knowledge advances, some models are discarded in favor of more precise ones. Still, understanding how individual elements behave—the basic function of a model—helps economists to understand the underlying logic of the economy.

Making predictions Once the model is set up, a single change is made in one of the variables and the total result is noted. The result allows the economist to predict how a similar change may affect the real social environment.

For instance, a model may be used to predict sales in the auto industry. It is assumed that growth in sales depends on such things as: the age structure and income of the population; job security and the availability of credit; maintenance and fuel costs; availability of mass transit and imported cars. Sales depend also on price, which in turn depends on union wage contracts, energy and material costs, taxes, and interest on borrowed funds. Price may also depend on volume of autos produced; over some broad range of output more autos can generally be produced at lower costs per auto.

A model may be drawn up to portray these conditions. But because a model is a simplified view of reality it must exclude a variety of other market influences: technological breakthroughs which affect production costs; new consumer attitudes which affect spending; new legislation which affects conditions of buying or selling. Omitting these other influences allows the observer to predict the effect of a single change: an improvement in credit terms, a rise in fuel costs, or a rise in the jobless rate perhaps.

If several economists study the same problem, they may arrive at different predictions. This happens when they build in different assumptions about the behavior of economic variables. They may make different assumptions about consumer response to price changes. They may lack consistent evidence about producer response to changes in demand. Their statistics on past production costs may not apply for future changes. The complexity of the real world can hardly be reflected in a single experiment.

Ceteris paribus In our model of the auto industry, we omitted all influences except the one we were studying. Actually, the economist does not omit the other influences but assumes they are held constant or unchanging. We say that such a model is operating under the conditions of *ceteris paribus*. *Ceteris paribus* is a Latin phrase meaning "all other things remaining the same." The economist uses *ceteris paribus* to help approximate the controlled conditions of a scientific laboratory. Of course, *ceteris paribus* also reduces the realism of our model; it excludes some of the complexity of the real world.

Positive and normative sciences

Besides general differences in subject matter, there is a second important difference between the physical sciences and the social sciences. Scientific analysis generally leads to the formulation of a principle or law that explains the process at work within the system. In the physical or natural sciences, principles can be applied in useful ways to meet the needs of people. For instance, the principle of gas ignition under pressure is used to propel the internal combustion engine. The principle of the growth of antibodies in the bloodstream is used to immunize people against disease.

In many of the social sciences, especially economics, to apply principles often requires political decisions. Economists speaking as social scientists may propose and test economic theories. They may state principles which explain the relationships among economic variables. They may even predict the results of alternative policies based on their investigations. When economists perform scientific investigations, we call it a *positive science*. However, economists often go beyond scientific investigation to suggest policies for curing specific economic ailments. When economists recommend economic policy, we call it a *normative science*.

Economic Thinkers
The Model Builders

Models are simplifications or abstractions of real world complexities. Models are usually set up to illustrate selected principles or parts of the economy. There are models to predict auto sales and models to show the effect of changing tastes on consumer purchases. But some economists have been particularly grand dreamers and thinkers. These economists have wanted a model of the whole national economy, predicting such things as the levels of total output, employment, and price inflation. Such a model could help us visualize how the whole economy works and enable us to predict future economic performance.

The first major model builders of the national economy were the *physiocrats*. These economic thinkers flourished in France during the eighteenth century. The physiocrats were so named because they believed the physical form of a system—be it the universe, society, the economy, or the human body—would govern automatically its actions and effectiveness. They opposed the economic theories of the mercantilists. The physiocrats' position that the economy should not be regulated by the government was quite similar to the views of Adam Smith. In fact, Adam Smith was influenced by the leading physiocrats, when he started writing on economics.

The leading thinker of the physiocrats was, appropriately, a physician, Francois Quesnay. Quesnay summed up the beliefs of the physiocrats in his *tableau economique,* or "economic table." The table illustrated the interrelationships among all the groups in economic society: the consumers and the producers of goods and services, the savers and investors of the nation's productive wealth, the receivers and the spenders of the nation's income. The table resembled a physician's model in which incomes from production flow through the nation from buyer to seller to buyer again—stimulating industry and nourishing the economy like the circulation of the blood. Quesnay's table was the first attempt to visualize the performance of a complex economic system.

As useful as Quesnay's table was in showing how the whole economy works, his model was quite crude. The basic shortcoming of his model was its lack of precision. His model lacked numbers and the mathematics necessary for calculating such items as level of output or production. In fact, it wasn't until this century that we learned how to add up all the diverse things produced in the economy: autos, bubblegum, baseball games, clothing, etc.

Jan Tinbergen was the first modern economist to construct a model of the national economy. He worked in Rotterdam, Netherlands, during the worldwide depression of the 1930s. He was interested in models as means of explaining and dealing with cycles in business activity.

Model building began in the United States after World War II with the work of Lawrence Klein. While at the University of Pennsylvania's Wharton School, Klein performed research on the complex interrelationships among groups in the economy. Then he expressed these relationships in algebraic equations. There were 51 equations describing the effects on income and production when changes take place in any of 50 different variables. The result was a model of the American economy. Such large, mathematical (and computer-based) models are called *econometric models.*

Lawrence Klein's equations mix mathematical measurement of past experience with intuition about future events. True, intuition itself requires detailed understanding of all dependent relationships and of all the political and psychological, as well as economic, forces which influence them. The economist must break down each element and express mathematically all the significant factors that affect it. These include government policies, political pressures, trends in tax revenues, credit policies, vacancy rates in housing, trends in debt obligations, stock and age of consumer durable goods, shifts in consumer tastes, and the age and location of population. Finally, the economist substitutes current economic data in the equations, and a computer is programmed to solve the system of equations simultaneously. The result is a projection of the probable course of the national economy over future months and years.

Because a model is an abstraction from reality, it blocks out many small details in order to focus on the major economic relationships. A test of a model's validity is its ability to forecast and explain reality. Over the 1960s Lawrence Klein's econometric model performed well in predicting economic variables. It predicted the 1969-1970 recession and the timing and dimensions of the recovery. But in 1973 the Wharton model ran into the problem inherent in all abstractions from reality. It could not foresee the *external* shocks from higher fuel costs and higher worldwide food prices. There was nothing in past experience comparable to the massive shocks these events dealt our nation's economy.

This same problem is faced by the other contemporary model builders: Otto Eckstein of Data Resources, Michael Evans of Chase Econometrics, the model builders at the Massachusetts Institute of Technology, and others. All modern econometric models are limited by *ceteris paribus,* the other things which the model holds constant but which go awry in the real world. The model builders must constantly work at revising their equations to reflect more nearly the changing conditions of the real world and to minimize *ceteris paribus.*

More recently, Professor Klein has developed a larger model that links together the models of major countries. Klein's Project Link helps to show how cycles in output and employment are transmitted among trading nations. The global model includes 5,000 equations from 13 Western industrialized nations, from socialist nations, and from less developed nations.

All these models are imperfect. They are subject to the same criticism once made of the physiocrats. Economic reality is too complex to be shown in a simple model, and there are too many unforeseen and unpredictable forces that affect reality. Nevertheless, they represent a beginning effort toward more scientific analysis of the problems and policies that affect our economic health.

Lawrence Klein

While a **positive science** examines *what is,* a **normative science** examines *what ought to be.* Most of our study of economics in this text will be of positive economics. In other words, the emphasis will be on principles and theory. These are the building blocks of any discipline. However, in some chapters we will go further and study normative economics: we will sketch many leading economic issues of our society. Deciding what ought to be is not just an economic function but frequently a political function.

Let's consider an example illustrating this distinction. The question of the *proper* distribution of income is a normative question. Income in the United States is distributed much more equally now than in the early years of our industrialization, but there is still sharp inequality. Today the lowest one-fifth of income earners in the United States receive only about one-twentieth of total national income. What is the proper distribution of income? What income distribution is most healthy in terms of society's other goals? What other goals should be sacrificed in order to achieve the desired level of equality?

As positive scientists, economists have avoided proposing answers to such questions. Instead they try to show the effects of alternative answers. For example, extreme income inequality might be expected to lead to a higher level of saving with greater investment in new productive capital. On the other hand, perfect equality might lead to a higher level of consumer spending, with greater incentives to productivity and growth. Which course should the nation pursue? How much inequality is proper? The question is too complicated to answer with economics alone.

As normative scientists, economists will differ on policy recommendations because each emphasizes different goals. To some economists the goal of maximum individual liberty is more important than equality of income. To interfere with income distribution at all would be an unacceptable interference with individual freedom. On the other hand, other economists feel that maximum individual liberty is impossible if there is extreme

Viewpoint
Economics and politics

"I don't think any man worth a damn can be President of the U.S. unless he understands economics." The man who said that once wanted to be President, the distinguished Senator from Minnesota, Hubert H. Humphrey.

Why is economics so important? It is difficult to name a national problem or issue that is not first of all an economic issue. Our domestic social problems of crime, poverty, illiteracy, and discrimination involve economic questions. Even problems of international relations are primarily conflicts over economic interests.

If economics is so important to our nation's strength, then it would seem that our political leaders would bend every effort toward solving these economic questions. Unfortunately, this is not so easy. It involves policymaking, and policymaking involves normative economics.

Political leaders differ on their approaches to normative questions. Because goals differ, political economy involves advocacy positions. For example, Hubert Humphrey has used his position in the Senate to advocate laws that would increase the role of government in solving economic problems. He has sponsored a proposal to set up an economic planning board in Washington; representatives of business, labor, and consumers would meet with members of Congress to set long-term targets for the proper use of the nation's resources, to coordinate the activities of economic groups, and to suggest broad goals of government policy.

If Humphrey looks to the federal government to solve economic questions, political leaders like Senator Barry Goldwater and Governor Ronald Reagan favor just the reverse approach. They fear the growing influence of Washington and recommend returning economic decision-making to the people themselves. One way to do this would be to eliminate federal economic programs and allow local communities to decide whether or not to continue them, financing them through local tax revenues. Ronald Reagan's campaign for the 1976 presidential nomination involved proposals to abolish the federal role in welfare assistance, education, Medicaid, air-traffic control, postal subsidies, and some other services. In 1964 Barry Goldwater proposed to make the Social Security program voluntary so that individuals could plan their own retirement without federal intervention.

Our leaders differ also in their opinions on government regulation of business activities. President Jimmy Carter, for instance, is confident of the power of a strong national administration to direct the economic climate in which business operates. He objects to government regulation only when it is applied inconsistently or inefficiently. Former President Gerald Ford, on the other hand, has generally favored minimizing the role of government in business affairs. He has opposed government intervention in the private sector, leaving greater decision-making power in the hands of consumers and businesses.

Why is it that intelligent and experienced leaders can disagree so completely on these important questions? Partly, the reason is that they begin with different convictions about the proper goals of our economic system. They have set different priorities among the goals of growth, efficiency, and equality. They are attuned to different sets of information promising to achieve different objectives. And they attract followers who approve of the same priorities and procedures.

The result of our democratic political system is a richly varied array of political opinion with ample opportunity for voters to express their individual economic preferences. Before you can develop your own preferences, however, it is important to expose yourself to a wide range of information. It is dangerous to speak too soon, before you have understood all possibilities.

We think Senator Humphrey's statement should be expanded to "You can't be a good voter and you won't understand the range of policy alternatives and the costs of these policies until you have mastered a few principles of economics!"

inequality of incomes. Severe poverty may prevent some American families from enjoying fully the rights of free people.

When economists are hired by government to evaluate policy alternatives, they usually will be given a set of goals by which to evaluate their recommendations. Other economists working for a firm or an association of firms in an industry will openly advocate policies or goals of the firm or industry. Still others may defend the economic interest of labor unions, educators, environmentalists, and many other nonprofit or special enterprises. All will use the methodology of economics to support their position.

Some economists will associate themselves with a political candidate or political position. They will give lectures and speeches outside the classroom, before audiences composed of people other than students. In so doing they use their personal prestige and expertise and the prestige of their college or university to support and defend a particular solution to economic problems. In so doing, they are engaging in *political economy*. The advocacy role uses the scientific methods of economics to achieve solutions to problems in ways which may favor one group or another. There is a proud tradition of such normative behavior in economics. Adam Smith, David Ricardo, Reverend Thomas Malthus, John Stuart Mill, and Karl Marx all engaged in the practice which survives today.

Try to keep cool

In the scientific approach to the study of economic phenomena, there is no room for personal bias or prejudice. The scientific method requires us to be cool and levelheaded. You will sometimes hear economists calmly discussing questions such as whether a *little* more unemployment must be tolerated to avoid *high* levels of inflation, or whether a slowdown in military spending might be bad for employment. This does not mean that these economists are in favor of unemployment or militarism. It is their responsibility to examine every alternative that presents itself, calmly and objectively.

Personal bias is bad for scientific analysis because it blinds a person to the differences and distinctions which are the basis for intelligent understanding. Emotion charged language should also be avoided and for much the same reason. A word that expresses our feelings may obscure or cover up reality. Those who dislike government-financed health insurance often call it *socialized medicine.* The term "socialized" conjures up an image of the powerful state. Those who favor higher taxes for the rich like to speak of "closing the tax loopholes." They neglect to mention their own middle-class loopholes which they hope will stay open. Precision of language is important to any scientist and particularly to a social scientist.

Some traps to avoid

The failure of language is really a failure in thinking, since words are misused when thought is imprecise. There are other ways of failing to think. One that is well known to economists is the **fallacy of composition**—the assumption that what is true for a part will be true for the whole. If your pay doubles overnight, you will be twice as well off as before. If everyone's pay were to double, probably no one would be any better off. Spending would rise so sharply that prices would double, too!

If you decide to save a larger portion of your earnings, you will probably be able to provide more security for your family. But if everyone should decide to save more, the sharp drop in spending would mean piles of unsold goods. Business firms would cut back production and lay off workers, and all our security would be threatened.

The **false cause fallacy** is another trap for the student of economics. Because economic reality is very complex, the researcher must deal with a multitude of causes. In a controlled experiment, the scientist must keep all variables constant except one and then study the effects of a change in that one variable. This is not generally possible for the economist. Often, too many things are happening in the economic arena to distinguish specific cause-effect relationships. If poverty declines, is it a result of government programs to improve health and education or only a result of normal economic growth? Are rising prices the result of large corporations increasing their profits or of powerful labor unions increasing their wages? Is inflation the result of rising farm prices or of a rapidly growing money supply? It may be that there is not *one* cause but *several.* The economist must try to calculate how much importance to attribute to each of them. Otherwise he will fall into the trap of assuming that because A happens before B, A must be the cause of B. This is known as the fallacy of **post hoc ergo propter hoc** (*after this, therefore because of this*), which is another way of saying that a false cause has been identified.

Using graphs

Economists use graphs to illustrate economic models. Often a picture can clarify basic concepts without using many words. A graph is a line drawing that expresses relationships between numbers. Graphs are helpful because they summarize all relevant information in a simple and concise way. They can be interpreted at a glance and they avoid the need for lengthy explanations. The same information arranged in the form of a table would be much more difficult to interpret.

Most of us are familiar with the use of graphs in our everyday experience. We have used graphs in our school work. We see them used commercially, in advertisements or in reports of sales.

To illustrate the use of graphs, let us suppose you are conducting an experiment with a pair of dice. You throw the dice a hundred times and record the value on the dice each time. It is convenient to record your results on a table like the one shown below. In Table 1 the first column shows the possible value of each throw: two through twelve. The second column shows the number of times each value appeared in your test.

The table is difficult to fully interpret. Plotting the data on a graph will help to display the information more simply.

Table 1
Experiment with Throws of Dice

Value of throw	Number of occurrences
2	3
3	5
4	8
5	12
6	14
7	19
8	15
9	10
10	8
11	4
12	2

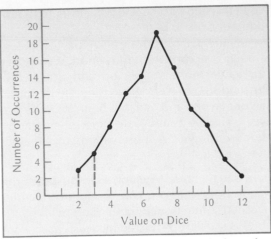

Figure 1 Experiment with throws of dice is shown in a graph. A quick glance reveals the pattern of results in your experiment. Closer examination provides greater detail. There are no points associated with zero and one because those numbers don't occur with two dice added together.

A graph is plotted on two axes, as shown in Figure 1. The *horizontal axis* represents the value shown on each throw. The scale is numbered from 2 to 12. The *vertical axis* represents the number of times each value appeared, from zero to 20.

The value of two appeared three times. To enter this result on the graph, move upward from 2 on the horizontal axis to the value three and place your first point. Similarly above 3 on the horizontal axis, place your second point at five occurrences. Continuing in this way, plot a series of points for each result in your experiment. Connecting the points produces a graph showing the number of occurrences of each value in your test.

What can we learn from the graph? The line reaches a peak at the value of seven, which occurred nineteen times. (If you are a mathematician you understand why seven was thrown more times than any other value.) The values five, six, and eight occurred almost as often, but two and twelve occurred less frequently. The curve helps us to interpret large amounts of statistical information at a glance. We can learn detailed information by examining the graph more closely. For example, the value eleven occurred four times in one hundred throws, or 4% of the time.

In economics we will use graphs to illustrate economic statistics. Graphs will help us to see broad relationships at a glance. Closer examination will provide specific information on particular quantities. Most graphs in economics are either of two forms: time-series graphs and functional graphs.

Time-series graph A graph that shows the value of a particular economic variable over time is called a **time-series graph.** For example, Figure 2 shows the average hourly pay of factory workers in the United States over recent years. We can see immediately that hourly pay rose fairly steadily from $3.95 in January 1973 to $5.30 in September 1976. When we look more closely, we can also see that hourly pay rose faster throughout most of 1974. The rate of increase slowed during the recession of 1975,

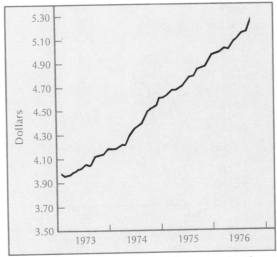

Figure 2 A sample time-series graph. Average hourly pay for American factory workers is shown over four-year period. Overall trend is quickly seen to be upward, though a bit uneven.

when the slope of the line was closer to that of the period 1973.

Figure 3 shows the weekly pay of factory workers over the same time period. Weekly pay fluctuated more sharply up and down. The fluctuations in weekly pay are the result of factory layoffs and variable hours of work per week. Figures 2 and 3 are time-series graphs; they show series of observations of variables over a period of time.

Functional graph A graph that illustrates the relationship between two economic variables is called a **functional graph.** One of the variables is usually considered the *independent variable* and the other the *dependent variable*. A change in the independent variable (cause) is assumed to influence the value of the dependent variable (effect). This kind of relationship is called a *functional* relationship. We say that changes in the dependent variable are a *function* of changes in the independent variable.

Figure 4 shows a hypothetical relationship between the rate of interest on borrowed money and the quantity of business investment spending. In this graph the independent variable, business investment spending, is shown on the horizontal axis. A functional relationship suggests that changes in interest

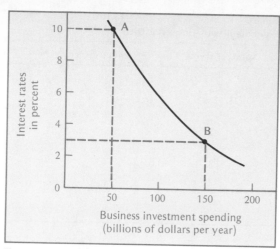

Figure 4 Functional graph: business investment spending as a function of interest rates. If investment spending is indeed a function of interest rates, then statistical data should help to predict investment spending in the future.

rates will affect the quantity of business investment spending.

The graph indicates that an interest rate of 10% will be associated with investment spending of $50 billion a year. But at interest rates of only 3%, investment spending would be $150 billion a year. Follow the horizontal lines from 10% and 3% to points A and B. At point A business investment spending measures $50 billion on the horizontal axis. At point B business investment measures $150 billion. What interest rate would produce business investment spending of $100 billion per year?

The functional relationship of Figure 4 may be stated this way: Investment spending is a function of the rate of interest, or investment equals a function of interest, or $I = f(i)$.

The hypothetical relationship illustrated in Figure 4 is based on past observations and assumptions about business behavior. It is to be expected that high interest charges on borrowed money would discourage borrowing for new investment. High interest costs would reduce the expected profitability of investment, and business firms would be less inclined to invest.

By the same reasoning, low interest charges might be expected to encourage a high level of investment spending. Low interest

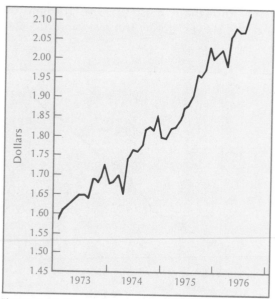

Figure 3 A time-series graph. Average weekly pay for American factory workers is shown over same time period as in Figure 2. Though trend is upward, progress is very uneven. The reason this figure differs from Figure 2 is that this one will show effects of workers being laid off.

costs make new investment projects more profitable, and business firms would be more inclined to invest.

If the assumed relationship between interest rates and investment spending conforms to reality, the economist can use it as a basis for evaluating alternative economic policies. A policy encouraging the banking system to reduce interest rates on bank loans, for instance, will be expected to cause investment spending to increase. The economist can then predict the effects of new investment spending on the level of total spending and employment in the economy.

But remember what we said earlier about the fallacy of false cause. In reality, investment spending is not a simple function of the rate of interest. It depends also on changes in technology that require the purchase of new equipment. It depends on the level of consumer spending and on business expectations of future sales. It depends also on the stock of capital goods already owned by business. In fact, investment spending appears to be influenced more strongly by other factors that cannot be included in a simple two-dimensional model—they were all put aside in *ceteris paribus*. As a result, conclusions and policy recommendations based on this model must be made very carefully.

The use of a graph such as Figure 4 helps in preventing an error which students, businessmen, and even economists often make. The function shows the response of one variable, investment, to another variable, interest. If the rate of interest falls, investment will increase, *ceteris paribus*. In the graph, this would be shown by a movement from point A to point B along the line plotted.

Now suppose one of the *ceteris paribus* conditions is allowed to change. For example, suppose new environmental legislation is passed and antipollution investment is required beyond that which was already planned in many firms. At each and every interest rate, a greater amount of investment is required. This would be shown in a graph such as Figure 4 as a movement of the function to the right. The difference between a movement along a function, such as happens when interest rates change, and a shift in the function is important to economic analysis and policy.

Evaluating the market system

As social scientists we must apply rigid standards of objectivity to our economic analysis. We must be careful to avoid bias that would distort our conclusions. This is true especially with respect to our evaluation of our own market system. We want to understand our system with all its strengths and its shortcomings. Only through objective understanding will we be able to make effective judgments about the economic system that substantially affects our lives.

It will be helpful to establish a list of goals which we believe any economic system should help to achieve. Our goals will be the "performance criteria" by which our market system can be judged and compared with other types of economic organization.

(1) *Productivity and growth.* Probably the first goals of most economic systems would be productivity and growth. Improved *productivity* means greater output from the use of our resources. For example, the phrase "worker productivity" describes the average amount produced by workers in some business or industry. *Growth* of the economy's output is important because it is necessary in order for our living standards to rise. In the past growth has been necessary to sustain a growing population. If the population grows and output does not, then average living standards decline. (Notice that population growth and economic growth are not necessarily tied together.)

In terms of productivity and growth the market system provides strong incentives which seem to encourage greater production. Individual self-interest has seemed to be a stronger motivating force than other motivations such as patriotism, altruism, or the medals awarded in centrally planned economies.

(2) *Economic stability and security.* Two other very important, related goals are economic stability and security. By *economic stability* we mean maintaining full employment and stabilized prices. By *security* we mean providing

the material necessities for those people who can't work or earn enough: the elderly, the sick, the poor, and the unemployed.

In the market system, independent decision-making often leads to periods of instability: rapid growth followed by painful cutbacks in production. Inflation (rising prices) and unemployment plague our market system. Centralized planning would probably improve the performance of the economy in terms of stability and security. But this alternative would mean a drastic reduction in individual liberties.

(3) *Efficiency.* A necessary goal of any economic system is efficiency. We can define *efficiency* as the degree to which an economic system uses its resources to produce the maximum amount of wanted or needed goods. An efficient system would minimize waste. Efficiency is thus closely related to productivity and growth. In fact, for a stabilized labor force increased productivity is probably not possible without increased efficiency.

With regard to efficiency the market system performs very well indeed. The economic theory discussed in this text will show how decentralized decision-making in free markets can help to bring about the most efficient use of our resources.

(4) *Personal freedom and equality.* Finally, we should include the goals of personal freedom and equality. A market system offers maximum opportunity for enhancing and developing the personal dignity and worth of every citizen. There is the maximum freedom possible for pursuing personal goals and lifestyles. Nevertheless, our emphasis on freedom ironically requires a loss in equality. If some individuals are free to succeed spectacularly, others inevitably are free to fail drastically. Other economic systems probably offer greater equality but at the cost of personal freedoms. Some systems, such as that of the Soviet Union, offer neither greater equality nor personal freedom.

Inequality may result not only from the inherent failures of the market system but also from efforts to block the free exercise of individual rights and responsibilities. Discrimination and limitations on opportunity are examples of barriers to equality that need not exist in a market system. Democratic processes provide the means for correcting these inequalities while preserving personal freedom.

Our market system should be judged in terms of these performance criteria. Its strengths and weaknesses should be judged by comparison with the strengths and weaknesses of other systems. As long as its weaknesses represent a smaller cost than the value of its strengths, most of us would hope to maintain the present system. We can use our understanding of goals and performance to help remedy some of its most troublesome weaknesses.

Summary

This chapter has introduced you to the subject matter of economics and the methods used in economic analysis. It describes how economics is similar to, yet different from, other branches of science. We study economics in order to understand the *hows* and *whys* of our efforts to make a living. The hope is that understanding will help us to live and plan better—as individuals, as communities, and as a collection of nations on planet Earth.

The study of economics developed along with the free market system of the Western industrial countries. One of the founders of modern economic science was Adam Smith, who pointed out how free markets link individual self-interest with the common interest. The "invisible hand" of the market guides many of our economic decisions, although government helps to resolve some problems.

We have seen how scientists approach a problem for analysis, and we have learned how economists apply scientific methods in their own field. One limitation of economic analysis is that we usually cannot make controlled laboratory experiments. However, there are ways of getting around this through the use of economic models, or simplified views of reality. Models help to predict the outcome of various economic policy proposals.

Economics is both a positive science, examining *what is*, and a normative science, arguing *what ought to be*. *What ought to be* in economic policy often must be decided by the citizens of a society as a whole through political processes. The economist, like any other scientist, must be careful not to inject bias or false thinking into the problem being examined. The fallacies of composition and false cause should also be avoided.

Graphs are used to illustrate and thereby simplify economic models. Most graphs used in economics are of two types: time-series graphs and functional graphs. In the text to follow you will be using graphs frequently.

We can judge the performance of the market system and other economic systems by the following basic criteria: (1) productivity and growth; (2) economic stability and security; (3) efficiency; and (4) personal freedom and equality.

Key Words and Phrases

- **mercantilism** an economic system aimed at increasing national prosperity through favorable trading relationships.
- **invisible hand** the actions of many independent buyers and sellers to determine a nation's output of goods and services.
- **market economy** an economy which depends on free choice in production and distribution of output and in buying; it is also known as a free market system.
- **economic democracy** dollars spent in the marketplace help "vote" (determine) what is to be produced.
- **self-interest** a condition in which individuals seek to satisfy their own personal desires in the marketplace.
- **scientific method** a systematic procedure for investigating and explaining phenomena.
- **physical science** a science devoted to the study of the physical world.
- **social science** a science devoted to the study of people, especially their behavior and their social institutions.
- **laws or principles** tested explanations of why systems behave as they do.
- **model** a simplified view of reality, useful in testing and explaining economic relationships.
- **ceteris paribus** a Latin phrase meaning "everything else remaining the same."
- **positive science** a discipline that describes and explains a situation as it is.
- **normative science** an attempt to prescribe a means to improve a situation.

- **performance criteria** standards by which to judge an economic system.
- **fallacy of composition** the error in thinking that what is true for the separate parts of a system must be true for the whole.
- **false cause fallacy** the error in thinking that because one event follows another it must be a result of the other.
- **independent variable** a variable whose behavior will influence the behavior of another.
- **dependent variable** the variable that is influenced by another.
- **time series** a series of data measuring some economic variable over time; a time-series graph shows the value of a particular economic variable over time.
- **function** a schedule of data measuring two or more variables where changes in one are associated with changes in the other(s); a functional graph illustrates the relationship between two economic variables.

Questions for Review

1. Outline the steps you would take in investigating a problem in the natural sciences and one in economics. For example, what procedure would be useful in answering each of the following: (a) How are animal feeding habits affected by changes in weather? (b) How are personal expenditure patterns affected by changes in tax rates?

2. Explain the difference between positive and normative questions. Why is goal-setting important and how are political considerations involved?

3. What "performance criteria" are used in evaluating: (a) a track team; (b) a fast-food restaurant; (c) a history term paper?

4. Discuss the following statement: Precision of language is fundamental to economics.

5. Use free-hand graphs to illustrate the following relationships: (a) typical growth patterns of American males; (b) fuel consumption over a year in Minnesota; (c) the effect of telephone usage on a person's monthly bill; (d) the effect of family size on number of meals eaten out. Label axes and curves.

6. Debate the following statement: It is more ethical for people to cooperate than to compete.

7. Define: assumptions, fallacy of composition.

2

The Economic Problem

As you read this you may be wondering how you can arrange the time to finish this assignment, perform a chemistry experiment, write an English theme, and solve some mathematical problems—and pick up your clothes at the laundry! You might enjoy spending a couple of hours at the student recreation center, but that may be farther down your list of priorities. There is so much to do and never enough *time*.

Or your concern may be with other types of needs. You may be wondering how you can make your allowance last out the week: how many dinners can you afford; can you bum a ride to the game or will you have to pay the bus fare; should you buy a Spanish workbook or a pair of gym shoes—can you afford to get your clothes out of the laundry? There is so much you want and never enough *money*.

If you have experienced either of these situations, you will understand a fundamental problem of economics. The fundamental economic problem has two sides: *scarce resources* and *unlimited wants*. As individuals, as business firms, and as a nation our wants are greater than our ability to satisfy them. In fact, every society now and in the past has faced this problem. There are never enough resources to produce all the goods and services a population (especially a growing population) wants.

In 1958 John Kenneth Galbraith published a book titled *The Affluent Society*. He argued that Americans today face problems quite different from those of our ancestors. Our forebears never had enough to go around, he said, but today Americans live in a society rich enough to provide everyone with the basic requirements of life and still have some left over. The phrase "affluent society" has now become a household term. Indeed, there are many extremely wealthy individuals and on the average we do enjoy greater standards of living than most other peoples. We may not always *feel* affluent—there is always some bill waiting to be paid—but as a nation we think in terms of billions and trillions of dollars worth of goods and services. Nevertheless, with all our good fortune there are still many wants left unfilled. With all our affluence there is even a danger that we may lose sight of the basic economic problem: *the problem of scarcity*.

Managing in a world of scarcity

Scarcity is not the same as poverty. Even the rich have to reckon with scarcity. The wealthy individual who can afford to give millions of dollars to a political party or to endow a university with a building that will bear his or her name must still choose among benefactions. For most of us the problem of choice is far more urgent. We schedule our limited time so that each activity yields the greatest possible reward—hours for economics and chemistry and a few minutes for errands. We allocate our limited funds so that our expenditures yield the greatest possible usefulness—gym shoes and bus fare this week, but the laundry will have to wait.

As managers of enterprises, whether business firms or civic clubs, we organize our workers so that their available time and energy produce the greatest possible results. Organizing work for a class project must be done similarly. Students are willing to contribute their efforts toward school projects, but they try to use their resources effectively to produce the best result. Does the class need a parade float, a stage set, a vegetable garden? A few energetic students, some odds and ends, a little money, and a lot of imagination can do the job. There'll be costs, of course—skipped classes and missed meals. For students, time and money are scarce. To use them in one way means giving up something else, so they try to use them carefully.

Most economists, when asked to define their science, say that economics is the study of how individuals and societies organize their scarce resources—how they *choose* among different alternatives and employ their scarce productive resources to provide the goods and services they want most. Choosing is one of the fundamental economic activities.

Kinds of resources

Economic resources have value for us because they are useful in producing goods or providing services. Because they are scarce they must be used carefully. To discourage wasteful use, we set prices which reflect the relative value of each resource and its relative scarcity. This rationing motive is an important part of our market system.

If a resource is so plentiful that it has no price, then we call it a **free good.** At one time our society considered many items to be free goods: air, water, sunshine, etc. But times change. There are few areas in this country where fresh air is a free good. It is certainly not free in the depths of a mine or tunnel where it must be pumped in at some expense, or in a chemical plant where blowers must be operated to filter out pollution. In fact, pollution threatens all of our air and water, and keeping them clean involves costs. Sunlight is normally a free good—but not to Eskimos in their long, dark winters. (If they want to see the sunshine, they must buy an airline ticket south.) Bananas may be a free good to the Jamaican peasant, but they are certainly not free to the Manhattan worker.

Resources used to produce goods or services are called **factors of production.** They are usually classified in four basic groups: land, labor, capital, and entrepreneurship. In our market system all factors of production command a price.

Land

Land consists of all the original and irreplaceable resources of nature. Land includes both the fertile fields and pastures used in agriculture and the urban plots used for skyscrapers. Iron ore, virgin timber, granite, and other minerals are classified as land. The United States is rich in land resources, but even our useful land is limited. For each plot of land, we must choose the type of employment that contributes most toward filling our unlimited wants. We can have a parking lot or tennis courts, but not both, a strawberry patch or a strip mine, saw mills or a wildlife preserve. *Never both at the same time*—we must choose.

Labor

Labor is the purposeful work of human beings. Manual work and brainwork, creative work and routine work, are all classified as labor. Our labor force grows every year, and its quality improves with better health and education. Still, labor-hours must be used wisely to get the maximum benefits from this valuable resource. Moreover, today's labor-hours are available only today. If they are wasted, as when people are unemployed, we sacrifice forever the goods and services they could have produced. Houses won't be built, autos repaired, or dental services performed. We won't have all the things we need.

Capital

Capital is produced means of production. Capital consists of goods we have produced but that we keep aside and use to produce other goods and services. **Capital goods** are thus distinguished from **consumer goods,** which we can use directly. Tools and machines, transportation and communication networks, buildings and irrigation facilities are capital goods. Farmers save a portion of their grain crop to use for seed in the next planting season. Their seed grain is a capital good which allows them to produce more in the future.

Education (including all types of training in useful skills) may be thought of as **human capital.** To build capital requires that we give up something today for something in the future. Like the farmers who give up grain, students give up jobs—and parents give up trips abroad—all for the opportunity to develop a stock of capital. Human capital is an important basis for the growing prosperity of U.S. workers.

The word "capital" is sometimes also used to mean a stock of money, as in **financial capital,** but this is not what we mean when we speak of capital as a factor of production. Financial capital is provided to business firms for construction of real capital goods. This is the way individuals help to save in the current period for the sake of greater production in the future.

Entrepreneurship

The fourth factor of production is more difficult to define, but it is perhaps the most important of all in the market system. This resource is the ability to gather the other resources together into a creative combination for the purpose of production. Economists use a word of French origin for the person who performs this function: the *entrepreneur*. Entrepreneurship implies more than simply managing an ongoing enterprise. That can be done by routine. **Entrepreneurship** requires *initiative* and *willingness to take the risks* involved in doing something new. A person who leaves a comfortable job to go into business is functioning as an entrepreneur on a small scale. Entrepreneurs are exceptional people—outside the usual mold. They don't do things in the usual way—if they did they would not be entrepreneurs. They are the pathbreakers, the creators, the Andrew Carnegies, Henry Fords, and Edwin Lands. The American spirit of individual enterprise encourages the development of entrepreneurial talent.

Production possibilities

We have seen that the economic problem requires us to choose among unlimited wants. Each of us must choose whether to buy stereo equipment, a trip to the beach, or dozens of other things, or whether we should save our money. Sometimes our decisions are made unconsciously, but the result reflects our own individual preferences. We draw up a list of wants according to priorities. Then we allocate our budgets to achieve the greatest benefits. We realize that any choice we make requires a sacrifice of something else; so we choose carefully.

A society, like a person, must choose its priorities within the limits of its resources. A community must choose whether to build a new school or enlarge the old one, to pay off old debts or to reduce taxes, to hire more policemen or more firemen. Our national government collects many billions of dollars in taxes. Still, it must choose—education for toddlers or for space scientists, research into mis-

sile guidance systems or cancer prevention, highway construction or urban mass transit systems.

What are our alternatives and how do we choose? This is part of the subject matter of economics.

We can begin with a simple illustration. We will assume that our community has a particular quantity of productive resources and a particular level of technological development. With the most efficient use of our resources and technology we can produce a given quantity of goods and services.

For this simple illustration we will divide all goods and services into two groups. This is because we can illustrate production of two types of goods and services on a two-dimensional sheet of paper. If it were convenient to illustrate three-dimensionally, we could divide all goods and services into three groups—or even more.

We could name our groups Whatzits and Whozats—or we could classify everything from A to M in the first group and everything from N to Z in the second. It doesn't matter. What is important is to recognize that our resources and technology limit us to some particular total level of production of both groups.

It will be useful to name our groups corn and autos. We may assume that corn represents agricultural products and autos represent manufactured goods. We will use our resources and technology efficiently to maximize the total output from production.

Now suppose that, using all our resources to produce corn, we can harvest 10,000 tons in a year. Of course, this would leave us with zero auto production. On the other hand, using all our resources to produce autos, we can make 4,000 autos a year. Again this would mean a sacrifice of all corn. Our resources are limited.

But there are other alternatives. If our community divides its productive factors between corn and autos, we can produce various combinations of corn and autos, as shown in Table 1. If we are willing to *give up* 1,000 tons of corn by shifting labor into auto factories, we can *produce* 1,000 autos. If we give up 2,000 *more* tons of corn, we could have 1,000 *more*

Table 1
Production Possibilities per Year

	Corn (in tons)	Autos
Combination 1	10,000	0
Combination 2	9,000	1,000
Combination 3	7,000	2,000
Combination 4	4,000	3,000
Combination 5	0	4,000

autos—for a total of 7,000 tons of corn and 2,000 autos. How much *more* corn must we give up to produce 1,000 *more* autos?

Graphing production

Now suppose we plot all possible combinations of corn and autos on a graph, as in Figure 1. The vertical axis shows corn measured in thousands of tons. The horizontal axis shows autos measured in thousands of units. Point A represents the community's decision to specialize completely in corn; point B, a decision to specialize completely in autos. In between are various other alternatives.

Everything *to the right* of our production possibilities curve is beyond our system's current production capabilities. Point C is a com-

bination of corn and autos that is outside the community's possibilities. Our resources and technology do not enable us to produce 8,000 tons of corn and 7,000 autos at the same time. Everything *to the left* of our production possibilities curve reflects unemployment of our resources. Point D represents unemployment of some resources. To produce only 3,000 tons of corn and 2,000 autos would mean sacrificing part of the community's possible output. We would not be using our valuable resources fully to produce the goods we need.

Figure 1 is called a **production possibilities curve**: It shows the existing possibilities and limitations of the community. It illustrates the problem of scarcity and the need to make choices. The curve may change over time as technology changes or new supplies of resources become available, but at present it is fixed. If the community is to get the maximum benefit from its limited resources, it will produce a combination of corn and autos that lies somewhere *on* the production possibilities curve. It cannot presently go beyond the curve to C, and it should not, in its own interest, operate inside the curve at D.

Opportunity cost

The production possibilities curve illustrates the need to make choices. As we move along the curve, we choose among alternative combinations of corn and autos. For any combination chosen, other possibilities must be sacrificed. More corn means fewer autos; more autos mean less corn.

This can be said another way. If we are producing 10,000 tons of corn and zero autos, the cost of producing 1,000 autos would be the sacrifice of 1,000 tons of corn (since the community would have to reduce its corn output from 10,000 tons to 9,000). Economists refer to the value of a *forgone* opportunity as **opportunity cost.** Thus for the opportunity of producing 1,000 autos, we would pay 1,000 tons of corn or an opportunity cost of one ton for each auto. The opportunity cost of the second 1,000 autos is 2,000 tons of corn, or two tons per auto. What is the opportunity cost of producing the next 1,000 autos? What is the opportunity cost per auto? What is the opportunity cost of the last 1,000? What is the opportunity cost per auto?

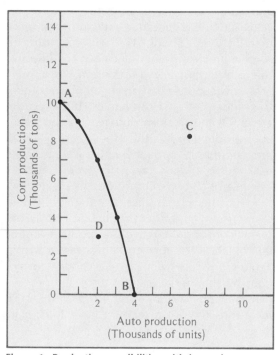

Figure 1 Production possibilities with increasing costs.

We all encounter opportunity costs when we make choices. The diligent student of economics sacrifices the opportunity to read a novel or to play soccer. The buyer of a new stereo tape sacrifices the opportunity to buy a pair of gloves. The school that builds a gym may sacrifice the opportunity to equip a laboratory now.

Making choices based on opportunity costs
Before we can make choices we must understand all our alternatives. We arrange our wants according to priorities. At the top of the list are our most urgent wants. To sacrifice these would involve large opportunity costs. Farther down the list are wants of lower priority and therefore smaller opportunity cost. Most of us make our decisions so that we hold opportunity costs to a minimum. For every possible alternative we calculate the opportunity cost of all the other goods and services we must give up. Then we compare alternatives and select the one with the smallest opportunity cost. In this way we can enjoy the goods we want most at the smallest personal sacrifice.

You followed this procedure, perhaps unconsciously, when you decided to attend college. You compared the opportunity costs of a college education with the opportunity costs of immediate entry into the work force.

The opportunity costs of college are greater than just your tuition. Opportunity costs include the interest your tuition money would earn in some other employment. This is just one of several opportunity costs. For each year you spend in college you sacrifice the opportunity to earn income in some useful work. You have probably sacrificed some personal freedoms if you remain financially dependent. Your total opportunity costs include all the activities you could have enjoyed if you had not chosen to remain a student.

Let's look at the other side of this decision. The important costs of taking a job immediately may not come due until years in the future. Beginning work early in life may mean the sacrifice of opportunities to develop skills for greater long-range productivity and higher income in the future. It may lead to routine work without the challenging experiences that make life interesting.

You will be able to add personal examples of other costs associated with each of these two alternatives. You are willing to pay the tuition costs and to forgo current income and personal freedom for four years, because the opportunity costs of the second alternative are greater. So here you are—at college!

The law of increasing costs

Refer again to the production possibilities graph in Figure 1. Have you noticed that the opportunity cost of producing larger quantities of autos rises as we move along the production possibilities curve? This is a result of the assumptions we made when we drew it. We assumed, first of all, that resources are not equally suited for all types of production. Certain types of land are well suited for agriculture but too remote for manufacture; certain types of labor are well suited for specialized manufacture but relatively useless for heavy physical work. To move all a nation's resources into one type of production would eventually mean smaller gains and higher costs. Secondly, we assumed that some of the community's resources are fixed in quantity and use. The quantity of agricultural land is fixed and suitable only for raising corn. The quantities of factories and machinery are fixed and suitable only for making autos. Other resources can be used to produce either type of output. Labor, for example, can be sent either into the cornfields or into the factories.

Now look again at Figure 1. To move from specialization in corn at point A requires that workers be taken from agriculture and employed in auto production. At first the movement of workers into truck factories may allow factories to operate more efficiently. More autos can be built with a small opportunity cost in corn production. However, as more workers move into the factories, each additional worker has less machinery to work with and becomes less efficient. Fewer additional autos are produced. Meanwhile, as the factories fill up, fewer workers are left to till the fields. Corn production falls by larger amounts as more workers leave corn production. The opportunity cost of producing each additional auto rises as more and more resources are shifted from farms to factories.

The changing pattern of opportunity costs is called the **law of increasing costs:** Opportunity costs increase because the *proportion* of resources used changes.* Total specialization in corn requires an excessive use of labor on a fixed quantity of land. Shifting labor into auto production improves the proportion of labor to land in corn production, and the opportunity cost for each additional unit is low. Continuing to shift labor, however, worsens the proportion of labor in corn and in auto production, and unit costs increase.

Something like this is usually the case in the real world, and that is why the law of increasing costs is important. If it were not so, the production possibilities curve would be a straight line. Then the cost of producing another auto would not increase but stay the same in terms of amounts of corn foregone. Table 2 shows combinations of corn and autos for which the cost of producing more autos is constant at two tons of corn per auto. Figure 2 is the graph of production possibilities under conditions of constant costs.

In the real world, the tradeoff between producing autos and corn will obey the law of increasing costs. Actually, the more similar two goods are in techniques of production, the more likely would the production possibilities curve tend to be straight. For example, the

Table 2
Production Possibilities per Year

	Corn (in tons)	Autos
Combination 1	8,000	0
Combination 2	6,000	1,000
Combination 3	4,000	2,000
Combination 4	2,000	3,000
Combination 5	0	4,000

* We will encounter the law of increasing costs again. It occurs in a slightly different form as the "law of diminishing returns" or the "law of variable proportions." The law of diminishing returns applies to any *one* input when the other factors of production remain fixed or constant. It results from the existence of what we call fixed and variable resources. Using larger and larger quantities of a variable resource (our labor input) with a fixed resource (our fields and factories) will eventually result in smaller gains in output—or stated another way, higher production costs for additional units.

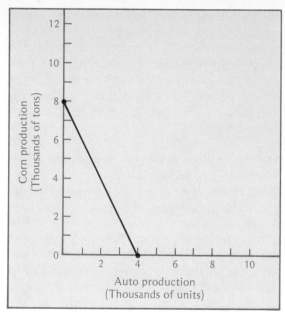

Figure 2 **Production possibilities with constant costs.**

production possibilities curve for producing either soybeans or corn would be close to a straight line. The proportions of land, labor, capital, and entrepreneurship used are roughly the same for producing soybeans or corn. Thus the move from producing one good to another is fairly easily accomplished.

Unemployment of resources

In our discussion of production possibilities we assumed that the resources of the community were being fully and efficiently employed. But it sometimes happens that a society is very far from the full and efficient use of its resources. This would be shown by placing a point somewhere inside the production possibilities curve, say at D in Figure 1. If a society is at D, it can move in several different directions toward the curve by employing idle resources in any of various combinations.

The United States was inside its production possibilities curve during the recession of 1973–1975. Unemployment exceeded 8% of the labor force, or more than seven-and-a-half million workers. As a result, we failed to produce an estimated $226.3 billion worth of goods and services.* The most severe example of unemployment in this century was the Great Depression of the 1930s when the leading industrial countries of the Western world were all inside their production possibilities curves. Not only were there unemployed workers, but factories and land lay unused. The problem was not solved, unfortunately, until the beginning of World War II when all resources were employed to meet the added demand for the production of military goods.

Overemployment and inflation

At other times we have tried to produce outside our production possibilities curve. The most recent example of this situation was the "Guns and Butter" dilemma that faced the United States in the late 1960s.

To illustrate this problem we will name our classifications military goods and civilian goods. On Figure 3 the horizontal axis measures units of military production, that is, military equipment and military services. The vertical axis measures units of civilian production, that is, consumer goods and services and capital goods. In 1965 the United States was operating very close to our production possibilities curve, say at A. But in that year we began our heavy military buildup in Vietnam. Our government began to spend heavily for planes and equipment, pilots and infantrymen for the war.

Increased military production exacted an opportunity cost. To use our scarce resources in this type of production meant foregone opportunities in the production of automobiles, television sets, and new houses. If we were to have more "guns," we would have to give up some of our "butter."

President Johnson's economic advisors reminded him of this. They recommended that consumers be forced to reduce their spending for civilian goods so that resources could move into military production. How could this be

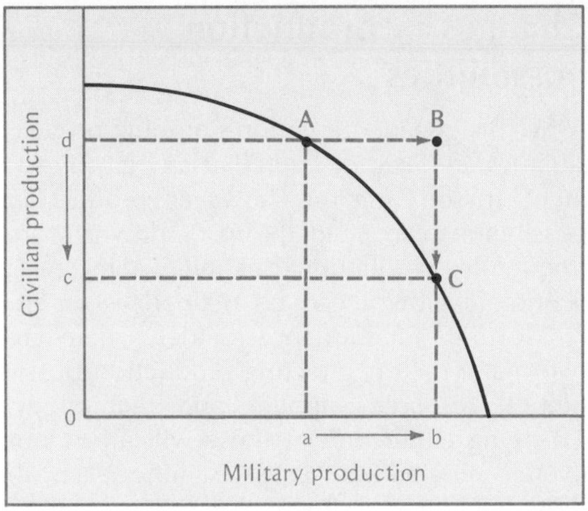

Figure 3 The attempt to produce beyond production capabilities. The quantity ab represents the increase in military production. The quantity cd represents the necessary decline in civilian production.

accomplished? The answer was through higher taxes. But this answer was unacceptable to the President and to Congress. The war was unpopular and taxes were unpopular. Congress and the President were concerned about the reaction of voters, and taxes were not immediately increased.

As a result, civilian spending continued at high levels while military spending rose higher and higher. The economy attempted to move from A to B. But B was beyond our production possibilities.

In fact, more military goods were produced, but civilian production had to fall to C. How was this accomplished without a tax increase? The heavy spending led to rising prices as civilian producers and government bid against each other for the existing quantity of scarce resources. With higher prices the purchasing power of incomes fell. In other words, inflation resulted. The higher prices acted as a tax on incomes, reducing the spending power of families and cutting down their purchases of civilian goods.

We learned about opportunity costs the hard way.

* Production for 1974 and 1975 was $1,407 billion and $1,499 billion, respectively. Unemployment averaged 5.6% and 8.5%. If "normal" unemployment is 4.5%, excess unemployment was 1.1% and 4%. It is estimated that each 1% of excess unemployment reduces output by 3%. Therefore, the loss of output for the two years was:

3(1.1%) × $1,407 =   46.43
3(4%)   × 1,499 = 179.88
                   $226.31 billion

Changes in production possibilities

As we have seen, our nation's production possibilities are fixed or limited at any given moment. In the long run, however, production possibilities can change—up or down. More frequently, production possibilities increase. Economic growth can be defined as an increase in production possibilities. There are two major factors affecting production possibilities: resource supplies and technology. Changing either one of these will affect our overall possibilities. Let's examine each in more detail.

Resource supplies What if the resources available to the economy increase? We assumed that our hypothetical community's supplies of land, capital, and labor were fixed. But population growth will in time add to the labor supply. Moreover, through exploration additional natural resources will be discovered, and better education and health care will improve human capital. The effect on production possibilities is to move the curve outward, as in Figure 4.

Depletion of resources will have the opposite effect. Unless new resources are developed or technological change is great enough to offset the depletion of resources, the production possibilities curve will shift to the left, as in Figure 5. A smaller stock of resources limits a nation to lower total production. The Industrial Revolution that began in the eighteenth century was based largely on energy produced by burning coal. Since then, much of the cheap coal supply of leading industrial countries has been depleted. However, we found important new energy sources in oil, natural gas, and hydroelectric power to help us grow in the first three-quarters of the twentieth century. Now the oil and natural gas are running out and becoming more expensive. Will atomic energy replace them in the future? The search goes on.

An important source of growth in the United States has been the increase in capital resources. Capital investment requires choices and the choices involve opportunity costs. Again the production possibilities curve is useful. This time let us list all goods and services for *current* consumption on one axis; on the other axis we will list all capital goods for use in *future* production. On Figure 6 the horizontal axis represents production of food and clothing, medicine and school books, autos and stereos, and all other consumer goods. The vertical axis represents production of drill presses and lathes, welding torches and assembly lines, power plants and blast furnaces, etc. The capital goods do not provide consumer goods in the current period, but they enable us to produce more in the future.

If an economy is to grow, some resources must be shifted into production of these important capital goods. Capital goods will help to push production possibilities to the right, increasing the quality and quantity of resources. Future production possibilities are increased but only at the expense of current consumption.

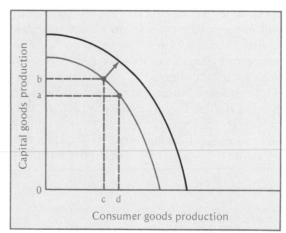

Figure 6 Increasing production possibilities through investments in capital goods. To produce ab, more capital goods, the economy must give up cd consumer goods. But more capital resources will eventually move production possibilities over to the right.

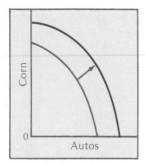

Figure 4 Expanding production possibilities.

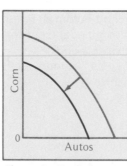

Figure 5 Declining production possibilities.

To use scarce resources in the production of capital goods, the population must be willing (and able!) to give up the opportunity to produce some consumer goods. This is possible only if the people can afford the sacrifice. In many parts of the world, production possibilities are so low that any sacrifice would lead to severe hardships and even starvation. Prospects for economic development are slim—or zero. Growth in production possibilities depends significantly on increasing a nation's stock of capital resources.

Technological advance   Another assumption we made in our discussion of production possibilities was that technology was fixed. The community could not alter its productive methods. In reality, of course, methods of production are changing all the time. Farmers produce many times more corn per unit of land today than they did fifty years ago. Such changes in technology affect the entire production possibilities curve, moving it outward and to the right. Advances in technology are crucial in enabling society to grow and become more productive, that is, to produce more goods with the same amount of resources.

Technological advance involves research, invention, and development or *innovation* (adapting present knowledge to new ends); it may mean the addition of, or improved operation of, physical equipment. In economics, technology also means the organization of production. Better techniques of management, incentive systems to motivate workers, and a healthy climate of enterprise can help to increase production possibilities.

Choosing production

The model of production possibilities shows the limits of production capabilities. Within these limits the community must choose a particular combination of output. Any given choice imposes an opportunity cost in things the community must give up. This means the economy must choose carefully.

Viewpoint
The Opportunity Costs of R and D

There's a story about a famous scientist who worked months on a new invention only to decide finally that the design wouldn't work and should be abandoned. The inventor's assistant was bemoaning the hours and hours of fruitless work in what he saw as a wasted effort. But the scientist corrected him by saying, "But our experiments have not failed. We have succeeded in eliminating one of the ways that won't work. Now let us get busy to eliminate others until we find one that will!"

The scientist was Thomas Edison.

We in the United States have been fortunate in having the creative skills and the liberal business environment which have permitted invention to flourish. We have enjoyed bountiful resources and a favorable climate for producing the goods we need for life. In short, our environment and economic system provided the material necessities of life and an economic surplus to do with as we wanted. As a result we have been able to direct resources toward scientific advance, enabling us to achieve even greater growth in output.

Our fortunate advantages have not been available to many primitive economies where scarcity is a life and death matter. Every action must focus on survival alone. Such nations cannot afford the luxury of failure; thus they cannot enjoy the fruits of success.

Although we have been fortunate in the wider range of opportunities available to choose among, we must not assume that we will always have these advantages. The fortunate circumstances we now enjoy are partly the result of choices made many years ago. Throughout our history American leaders in business and government have chosen to allocate a part of our productive resources toward production of capital resources. These investments in physical and human capital helped to push out the frontier of production possibilities, widening the range of choices open to new generations.

Investment can take the form of new plants and equipment or it can involve *research and development* of new technology (R and D, for short). R and D provides the means to make other resources more productive. Economists estimate that at least one-third of the growth in national output has been the result of technological progress. Growth in the quantity and quality of labor resources and growth in capital investment account for the remaining two-thirds of American economic growth. For the innovating firm, investment in R and D yields about a 30% return over costs, which is about double the return on investment in physical capital.

Both private business firms and government make expenditures for R and D. Over the last two decades total R and D expenditures have averaged about $20 billion annually (when values are corrected for changes in prices). More than half that amount came from the federal government. In fact, from 1953 to 1961 R and D expenditures increased yearly on the average about 14% for government and about 8% for nongovernment. From 1961 to 1967 government R and D increased only 6% a year while private R and D increased 7%. And from 1967 to 1975 government R and D actually shrank 3% a year while private R and D increased about 2%.

How can the relative decline in R and D be explained? In part, the decline is a result of higher costs and scarcity of funds for investment. Government regulation of industrial activity and the high costs of failure are also problems. It may be that the large scale of industrial enterprises discourages invention and innovation. Major innovations often come from outside large established firms; photocopying, computers, hand calculators, and the Polaroid camera are examples. Many large firms are caught in a super-cautious bind which makes them unwilling to gamble on anything short of a sure thing. The magnitude of investment precludes risk-taking. Moreover, today's market pressures have shortened the life-cycle of products 40 to 60% in the last decade. This changes the focus of innovation more toward marketing existing products and refining existing processes rather than breaking new paths.

Government investment in R and D declined because the people and many members of Congress felt there were more pressing needs for funds. In the late 1960s and early 1970s many people became disenchanted with technology. People looked less at (or took for granted) the increased output in agriculture and the abundance of consumer goods and looked more at pollution and the Vietnam War (both were connected to our sophisticated technology).

In the years to come, the result may be a slowing pace of American technological development. Unfortunately, failure to develop new technologies will impair our international competitiveness, slow economic growth, and reduce the number of new jobs available for our growing labor force.

If the potential rewards of expanded productivity are as we have shown, it is critical that we maintain investment at an acceptable level. Our free market system looks to private business firms for the major efforts toward achieving economic goals. We provide tax incentives for investment, but some regard these incentives as inadequate. Federally supported R and D in universities is another way of financing R and D, where the risks are too great for private firms. Whatever the source of R and D funds and whatever the results of R and D activity, there is no real economic gain until the new technology is applied. New scientific processes, new designs, and new equipment must be put to use in some enterprise producing the things people want to buy. And here may lie another explanation for the relative decline in R and D expenditures during the 1970s. The slowdown in consumer spending may have removed the most important incentive for business firms to make the important choice to allocate resources toward increasing productivity. If this is true, then it becomes especially critical to maintain a high level of consumer spending. A high level of demand will convince business firms of the expected profitability and minimize the potential risks of investment spending. A climate of healthy growth is necessary for building confidence and stimulating technological progress.

Specialization

Nearly all the adult citizens of industrialized nations produce goods and services through specialization. *Specialization* means that individuals produce a single or just a few goods or services. That is, few individuals produce all the goods—food, housing, tools, etc.—needed for their existence. The reason we all specialize in some skill is to be more productive and to produce more of that good or service. The wide range of consumer goods and markets—from autos and movies to steel tools and businesses and stores—is only possible with specialization. But specialization means we can't live in isolation. We must, in effect, exchange the goods or services we produce for those produced by others. Specialization inevitably involves exchange and trade. Not only do we exchange or trade with people in our own area, but within our nation different areas tend to specialize in certain products—Detroit in autos, the Carolinas in tobacco, Chicago in electrical goods and candy, Hollywood in movies, etc. And finally, nations tend to specialize, and therefore they engage in international trade.

If a country tends to specialize in a few types of production, that nation will have to depend on trade to exchange its specialty for some of the other goods it needs. A trading nation may emphasize certain goods that employ its unique proportion of fixed resources and labor; it will export these goods in return for goods it can obtain more cheaply abroad.

For example, Denmark's resources are suitable for agricultural production, and Denmark chooses a point on its production possibilities curve nearer the agricultural axis. Then Denmark sells large quantities of bacon to England in return for England's manufactures. England in turn concentrates much of its productive effort on manufactured goods for export. If England tried to produce all the food it needed, it would have to sacrifice manufactured goods, and the opportunity cost would be high. If Denmark were to increase manufacturing, it would have to take resources from the low-cost production of agricultural exports and use them in the high-cost production of automobiles and television sets. Specialization and trade help both countries to enjoy more goods and services, keeping opportunity costs low.

Hypothetical production possibilities curves for Britain and Denmark are shown in Figure 7. For Denmark to increase production of manufactured goods, it would have to sacrifice large quantities of agricultural products. For England to produce agricultural products would mean great sacrifice of manufactured goods.

Guns vs. butter

Many countries are forced to choose between production of military equipment ("guns") and civilian goods ("butter"). If a nation is threatened by enemies it may choose guns over

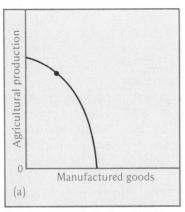
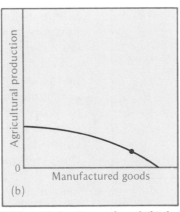

Figure 7 Hypothetical production possibilities: (a) for Denmark and (b) for England. Nations which specialize depend on trade to provide many goods they need. The dot on each curve shows the respective positions of Denmark and England.

butter, as shown in Figure 8. During World War II the United States turned its assembly lines to the production of tanks instead of automobiles, airfields instead of school buildings, and bombs instead of home furnishings. These were the opportunity costs of war.

Citizens willingly made the sacrifices because they knew that military production was necessary for their security. They reduced their consumption of meat, bought fewer pairs of shoes, and drove their automobiles only when necessary. Scarce items were rationed, and saving was encouraged. A democratic society depends on the cooperation of its citizens in times of crisis.

In many nations today the demands of defense industries make heavy inroads upon their citizens' standards of living. When there is no real crisis, citizens must often be coerced into making the necessary sacrifices. An internal police force may be yet another diversion of resources from the production of civilian goods and services.

One important basis for the prosperity of Germany and Japan today is that they were defeated in World War II. Since then they have not had to spend very much on military production and have used their resources to build steel mills, shipyards, and modern manufacturing plants. Their living standards are possibly higher than they would have been if they had won the war!

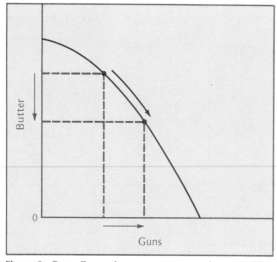

Figure 8 Guns. To produce more guns requires a sacrifice of butter.

Consumption today vs. consumption tomorrow

An even more difficult choice may be the choice between "jam today" and "jam tomorrow." An economy must choose whether to produce *consumer goods* for use this year or to produce *capital goods* in order to be more productive in the next. In some very poor nations the second choice may not be possible. All available resources may be needed just to produce the food and supplies to keep the people alive. In other more prosperous economies, the people may decide to sacrifice production of some consumer goods for the sake of future production. When resources are shifted away from consumer goods industries into the production of capital goods, living standards will be temporarily reduced.

In Figure 6 the opportunity cost of producing capital goods ab is the quantity of consumer goods given up: cd. But the accumulation of capital goods moves production possibilities to the right so that more of *both* goods can be produced in the future.

A nation with many students does this. Students use their energies to develop skills for use in future production. They train as designers, engineers, chemists, managers, and teachers. In the meantime their living standards are relatively low and total production of consumer goods is less than it might be otherwise.

The United States encourages production of capital goods by providing tax advantages to business investors. Moreover, a highly developed system of banks and other financial institutions helps to channel the funds of savers into investment in capital goods. As a result, we have accumulated productive capital and our production possibilities curve has continued to shift to the right.

Other means of accomplishing the same result are used in the Soviet Union. Under the Communists, led by Josef Stalin, the Soviet Union began its first five-year plan in 1928. With enormous sacrifice and hardship the USSR built up its industrial capacity which helped it to withstand the German invasion in World War II. Since the war it has continued its five-year plans and is now in its tenth (1976–1980).

Extended Example
The English Sickness

The United Kingdom of Great Britain was in the forefront of the Industrial Revolution. Eighteenth century Britain had the resources and a highly motivated population to move its economy along a rising curve of production. Profitable growth enabled British entrepreneurs to accumulate savings for investment in capital equipment. The output from factories and machines made possible a naval force essential for controlling its colonial empire.

Gradually, national prosperity and the increasing political power of the masses of working people appeared to change British priorities. More and more resources were channeled to public services provided by government. In the decade 1965–1975 the portion of Britain's output devoted to public spending rose from 45% to 60%. (Actual public spending doubled to $93 billion.) The objectives of public investment have been such important goals as ensuring greater income equality and minimum standards of health, education, and living conditions for every citizen. But there were opportunity costs. The major cost has been a failure to maintain capital investment sufficient for continued economic growth. The attitude of too many British citizens became something like, "Why should I work hard, especially when material rewards are offered tomorrow. I want mine today!" This attitude or condition even had a name among Britain's European neighbors: the English sickness.

As other nations have developed technologically, their productive capacities have surpassed those of Great Britain, leaving the nation behind in its ability to produce material abundance. The high level of government spending and the declining productivity contributed to inflation of 26% in 1975, the highest in the industrial world. British wage earners take home more pay, but their wages are worth less in real purchasing power each year.

Finally, in 1976 the British Labor government called upon the British people to make new sacrifices to cure the nation's ills. Chancellor of the Exchequer, Denis Healey, helped to develop plans for revitalizing British industry. Investment spending was to be allocated toward construction of modern capital equipment. Under the new program the government selected thirty key industries and concentrated aid in those sectors believed to be most favorable for promoting overall growth.

At the same time the British government planned to cut back spending for social welfare programs such as national health care and subsidized housing. Subsidies to government-owned industries were cut also—meaning a loss in jobs and higher prices for these goods and services. Even so, labor unions agreed to cooperate with government's new policy, in view of the growing crisis faced by all. Only time can tell if the people will fully accept these programs.

Illustrate the British dilemma in terms of production possibilities. Do you think the British would have been wiser to extend their production possibilities curve to the right in order to achieve their goals of more equality and higher material well-being for all?

Many other nations have five-year plans: India, the Eastern European countries, and some developing nations. One purpose of the plan is to ensure that resources flow away from the production of consumer goods into the production of capital goods. By contrast, the United States, with its current wants expressed so democratically and effectively by consumers, allocates a much smaller percentage of output to capital goods. Consequently, this has contributed to our growth rate being slower than that of the Soviet Union and some other countries. The premise of the Soviet five-year plan is to deny consumers as much as possible now in order to devote more resources toward catching up with the United States. The Soviets plan at that point to change goals; then their citizens will be able to enjoy as many consumer goods as Americans do.

Private vs. public consumption

Communities must also choose between producing goods and services for private use or goods and services for public use. Public goods include public health and recreation facilities, public education, police and fire protection, social service programs, and defense. The more of its resources a society devotes to production of public goods and services, the less private production it can enjoy. Figure 9 illustrates this choice.

In the United States communities have chosen to use tax revenues for expenditure on public goods and services. Citizens who pay taxes have less income remaining to spend for private goods. Most of us make the sacrifice willingly, but we would like to see our tax money spent wisely.

In China, Russia, Eastern Europe, and a few other countries most workers are employed by the government. Government limits the production of private goods and uses its remaining funds to hire workers in the public sector.

Work vs. play

There is another choice available to prosperous economies. The society may use some of its resources to "produce" *leisure*. As resources are freed from production, the community sacrifices some goods and services they might have

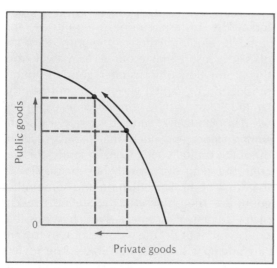

Figure 9   Private goods. To produce more public goods requires a sacrifice of private goods.

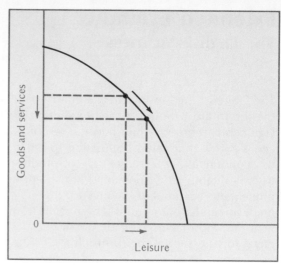

Figure 10   Leisure. To enjoy more leisure requires a sacrifice of goods and services.

produced. The opportunity cost of lazing in the sun is the cabinet you might have built!

Figure 10 illustrates the opportunity cost of leisure. If many people enjoy the simple life, their desire for goods and services may be very small. The economic decision to work or to enjoy leisure is often a cultural one; that is, certain nations at some point in time may place a higher premium on leisure than on work. For example, compared to Americans, the British are renowned for "doing without" or preferring leisure, while the Japanese would rather work and thereby earn and buy more.

How is the choice made?

Societies don't always make their production decisions by conscious choice. How decisions are made depends on the fundamental ideology and institutions that have developed in the community. All these cultural differences affect the incentives of businesses to invest, the efforts of consumers to save, the economic policies of government, and the actions of banking authorities. Many developing countries do not depend on the independent actions of private individuals. They draw up plans for economic growth under the direction of central authority.

The three questions

In making its decisions, every community or society must answer three basic questions. These questions are: *What* is to be produced? *How* is it to be produced? *For whom* is it to be produced?

What? No society can produce everything that all its citizens might want and in the quantities they want. We might all like to live in twenty-room houses with swimming pools and a car for every member of the family, but this is not possible. Somehow the society must decide whether to build twenty-room houses or cluster town houses; swimming pools or cars; schools or airfields; stereos or drill presses; parks or theaters; and it must decide how many resources can be freed for leisure. The answers a community gives to the question *"What"* will determine the quality of life in our society, now and for generations to come.

How? Almost everything can be produced in more than one way. Houses once were made of mud and still are in some countries. In our country they were once made of brick, but real brick houses are rarely built nowadays. It is more economical to build them of plywood and shingles or with a thin veneer of brick on the outside. Many products that once were made of metal or wood are now made of synthetic chemical compounds called plastics.

Communities are endowed with particular combinations of resources which help to determine the way they build and make things. Each community must decide how to use its unique combination of resources in the most efficient way. An abundance of land area would lead to *land-intensive* farming—as in China or the United States. An abundance of labor would lead to *labor-intensive* farming and manufacture—as in the Soviet Union. Plentiful capital leads to *capital-intensive* production—as in West Germany or the United States. It is by finding new ways of doing things more cheaply that productivity increases. If resources are used in ways that are not the most efficient, then society is poorer by the amount of extra output that is given up. The answers a society gives to the question *"How"* will determine the quantity of resources it is able to pass on to coming generations.

For whom? The third basic question to be answered is how society is to divide what it produces among its citizens. Some households receive more than others. Some groups or industries receive more than others. Physicians, for example, usually receive more than farmers or teachers. The system by which society divides its output depends on the value it places on the contribution of each. In the Soviet Union poets and ballerinas tend to receive much more than in the United States. In the United States we reward business executives—and rock stars and quarterbacks. The answers society gives to the question *"For whom"* will provide the incentives for production in the future.

Types of economic systems

As we have already seen, societies and communities usually do not answer these questions by conscious choice. That is, nobody comes to your door and says, "I'm a poll taker. How many cars do you think we ought to produce this year?" But every society does have a system for working out the answers.

Traditional economies

In simpler economies of the distant past decisions were based on tradition. Even today in some societies the three questions (What?—How?—For whom?) are answered as they have been for generations before. Potters provide cook pots, carpenters build dwellings, hunters and gatherers provide food, and tanners prepare hides for clothing. This is the origin of many family names—Farmer, Carter, Miller, Smith, and Taylor, for example.

In primitive societies, following tradition is necessary because there is only a slim margin between life and death. One bad harvest or a disastrous winter can bring ruin. Survival depends on keeping to the ways which proved successful in the past. There is very little *economic surplus* with which to experiment. As a result, there may be few opportunities for economic growth and development. The only hope for such societies may be loans and grants from wealthier nations. Food aid, for example, can provide a surplus which will free some of a country's own resources for the production of capital goods. Construction of industrial capital by foreign firms may also increase productivity and provide the basis for independent growth.

Command economies

In some areas of the world, a favorable climate or fertile land has helped production to grow beyond the amount necessary for survival. Then the choice of what to produce becomes more complex. A prosperous community can choose to use its resources for new types of production. For example, a forward-looking community can decide to build capital equipment for economic growth: factories, simple machinery, roads, bridges. Or an aggressive community can decide to produce military equipment: walls and fortresses to protect it from attack, vehicles and guns to invade other rich areas. Or communities like those of Renaissance Italy can produce luxurious palaces and formal gardens for the ruling class, jewelry and ceremonial robes for priests, or great public buildings and stadiums to celebrate national power.

In such societies the basic economic decisions have often been made by a central authority, such as a king, a dictator, or a central planning board. We call this a *command system*. Command economies tend to develop where it is acceptable to control the use of resources in order to achieve an important goal. To leave production decisions in the hands of many independent individuals may conflict with the national objective. We have seen that in the Soviet Union the objective is to build an industrial base for increasing production in the future. To reach this goal a central planning board was set up to make most production decisions. There are elements of command in other nations where the objective may be capital accumulation, military power, or a luxurious life-style for the controlling elite. Whatever the national goal, a command economy necessarily interferes with the liberties of its citizens.

Economic Thinker
Karl Marx

Karl Marx (1818–1883) was born in Germany and grew up during a time when the Industrial Revolution was reshaping society. The European population was booming and urban slums were growing. It was a time when philosophers were examining the social world around them for explanations of why social systems developed as they did. Marx very early became interested in political conflict and began his career as a political journalist. Then he began to weave his observations about conflict into a major theory of historical change.

Marx's view of history was based on the belief that history moves in stages. History moved from one stage to a higher one because of conflict between competing groups. In each stage one particular class in society would become powerful. But in the meantime another class would be developing whose interests clashed with those of the dominant class. Finally, the new class would overturn the old and set itself up as the newly dominant power. Of course, it would soon be subject to challenge by a still newer class seeking power in *its* own interest.

All this was inevitable. The relative economic positions of classes in any one stage of history determined all the basic arrangements of society: the legal and political arrangements, and even the religion, the social traditions, and the cultural arrangements.

What was the basis by which any class gained power in any particular stage? In Marx's view the basis for control was ownership of the means of production. The groups in society who controlled the means of producing and exchanging goods and services would hold the reins of power.

Marx was able to show how previous history had moved through stages. The first stage in modern civilization was feudalism.

Under feudalism the means of production were controlled by the landed aristocracy. Ownership of the land enabled the nobles of Europe to hold the peasant class in servitude, dependent on landowners for their security and for their means to life. But a new class was developing to undermine the power of the feudal lords. The beginnings of trade opened the way for merchants and capitalists to assert their control over commerce and industry in the new towns. The power of the lords was broken as the peasants flocked to the towns to take jobs in factories.

Under capitalism, ownership of the means of production (capital) enabled the capitalists to drive a hard bargain with the workers. Exploitation of the working class permitted factory owners to assemble even greater wealth and power. A challenge to that power was sure to come. Marx predicted that the "property-less proletariat" (the workers) would rise up in violent revolution and overthrow the dominant capitalist class.

The revolution would come in a nation where capitalism had developed to the fullest. There industry would have become increasingly monopolized by a few large firms. Their monopoly would have enabled them to force wages down and to collect high profits. Misery and unemployment among the working class would finally bring on massive uprisings and the workers would take over the means of production.

There would be two more stages of economic development. Under socialism the nation's productive assets are owned and controlled by the State. During the transition period to the highest stage there would be a "dictatorship of the proletariat." All other classes would be suppressed. Finally, under communism, the workers themselves would own the means of production "in common" and operate them democratically in the interests of all the people. Goods and services would be distributed to all according to their needs. There would be no need for social classes, and eventually government, too, would wither away.

Throughout Marxist theory there is little regard for the power of intellect or free will to affect important events. A society's technical-economic structure or stage is, according to Marx, its most dominant trait. This is both a serious weakness and a real contribution to historical thinking. The idea that human relationships are strongly influenced by the technology and economic development of their age was a new one and has had a major impact on subsequent historical analysis. Not to be overlooked is the religious-like fervor Marx brought to his writings. Marxism offers hope and salvation to millions of our world's people.

Communism Today there are two basic economic systems that rely on command (in full or in part): communism and socialism. **Communism** consists of government ownership of property and the means of production; hand in hand with this centralized economic power is a political dictatorship. In communist nations the government commands what is to be produced. Quotas are set on how many bicycles, radios, autos, washing machines, pairs of pants, etc., are to be produced. Examples of communist nations are the Soviet Union, China, Cuba, Albania, Poland, Hungary, and the other Eastern European countries. However, you should be very much aware that in some of these countries, especially those of Eastern Europe, many small businesses and farms are privately owned.

Socialism Socialism is not as easily defined as communism since it is a word that has become "stretched" in different directions. To some (the followers of Marxist terminology), socialism consists of nations such as the Soviet Union and its Eastern European allies. Such a Marxist definition of socialism allows neither economic democracy nor political democracy.

To others (many people in Western Europe and North America), socialism does not involve the abandonment of political democracy. Under this definition, Sweden, Denmark, and Great Britain are examples of socialism. Sometimes this variation is called *democratic socialism.*

We can, however, note one feature common to any definition of socialism and will use it for our definition. **Socialism** is an economic system where government owns the means of production. Strictly speaking, this means all forms of production. However, we will note that the real world has no country that fits exactly any definitions of communism, socialism, and capitalism. Therefore, we will classify countries like Great Britain and Sweden as socialist, since the major means of production—steel mills, shipyards, railroads, airlines, health care—are owned or provided by the government. These socialist countries have obvious elements of command, since the government sets output or determines the size of these industries. Still, we should not forget that the market functions in other economic areas in these countries.

Market economies

Citizens of democratic societies are allowed greater influence in making economic decisions. Where resources are available for ample production, societies generally turn to the market system to answer the three questions. *What, How,* and *For whom* are decided in the market, where many buyers and sellers compete for their own advantage.

Although no poll taker comes to your door, you do vote your preference for goods and services through the dollars you spend in the market. Nowadays we see many more small cars on the roads than a few years ago. Nobody made a formal decision to produce more small cars and fewer large ones. It has happened because of the purchasing decisions of millions of individual car buyers, and the automobile companies have been forced to respond.

In free markets buyers express their preferences by their dollar expenditures. These expenditures answer the question *What.*

Sellers compete to satisfy buyers by offering the most desired goods at the lowest possible price. They try to use the most efficient technology and the lowest cost resources available. This response to consumer demand answers the question *How.*

Goods and services are divided among people according to their incomes. Incomes are based on the contribution of each to production. We each receive goods equal in value to the resources we contribute to production. This division of goods is the market's answer to *For whom.*

Capitalism Like the word "socialism," "capitalism" is a term that resists an easy, clear definition. *Capitalism* is often used interchangeably with *market economy* or *free markets*, but, strictly speaking, capitalism entails much more. We can define our term by its properties. **Capitalism** is an economic system characterized by the following: (1) private ownership of capital or the means of production; (2) free enterprise, which means the ability to start or dissolve any business; (3) free markets, which means a competitive marketplace (not monopoly nor government) determines supply and demand of goods and services; and (4) freedom of choice for people to buy what they please and to work where they wish. This definition is sometimes known as *pure capitalism.* No nation in the world fits this description, though the United States probably comes closest.

Mixed economy and mixed capitalism Although the United States is mainly a market economy, we retain some elements of tradition in many communities and a degree of command. For instance, we do not leave every decision to individual choice in free markets. We recognize that certain goods and services must be provided outside the market system. Individual buyers and sellers will not be able to arrange for the production of such things as roads and bridges, educational opportunities for all, equipment for national defense, and public buildings. We authorize government agencies to take care of these needs.

We limit the working of the market in other ways: by prohibiting the sale of certain drugs; by restricting gambling and pornography; by regulating certain business practices that are considered monopolistic or undesirable; and by taxing higher incomes more than lower incomes in order to redistribute some of the income from production. This means that our economy is actually a *mixed economy*—primarily a market economy but with some elements of command. (Are there also elements of tradition?)

The United States economy is more accurately described as *mixed capitalism.* All four of the characteristics of capitalism are modified, usually by government. We should notice other modifications in addition to the ones mentioned above. Not everything is privately owned, since our government owns railroad passenger service, research laboratories, and the postal system. Although free enterprise generally exists, the government does regulate some businesses and may even help prevent a business from going bankrupt (as with Lockheed in the early 1970s). Figure 11 shows a schematic summary of the types of economic systems.

In the next chapter we will begin to show how individual buyers and sellers participate in answering the three important economic questions.

Figure 11 **Summary of the types of economic systems.**

Summary

In this chapter we have explored the basic economic problem that every society faces. At any time, every society has limited quantities of resources and a fixed level of technology. Its given resources enable it to produce some quantity of goods and services—its production possibilities. On the other hand, the wants of its people are unlimited.

Economic resources are known as factors of production and are classified as land, labor, capital, and entrepreneurship. Because productive resources are scarce, we must choose carefully how we will use them. Within the limits of production possibilities, any community may choose among alternative combinations of goods and services: total specialization with trade; military equipment or civilian goods; consumer goods or capital goods; private goods or public goods; more goods or more leisure. Each choice involves an opportunity cost in the alternative goods and services given up. Opportunity costs increase as a society moves more resources into the production of certain goods or services. This is because of changes in the proportions of its available resources used in production.

Production possibilities depend on a nation's stock of resources and its available technology. Growth in either of these enables a nation to produce more. Capital is an important resource for growth, but producing capital requires an opportunity cost of consumer goods not produced.

Deciding how to use productive resources requires answers to three questions: What? How? For Whom? Some communities make these decisions by tradition or through the command of a ruling group or party. Some democratic societies decide through the market system. The next chapter begins the explanation of how the market system works to answer the three economic questions.

Key Words and Phrases

- **economic problem** a situation in which resources are limited relative to the wants of the people.
- **free goods** resources which have no economic value (price) because they are in unlimited supply.
- **factors of production** land, labor, capital, and entrepreneurship which are used to produce goods and services.
- **land** the original and irreplaceable resources of nature.
- **labor** purposeful activity of human beings.
- **capital** produced means of production.
- **entrepreneurship** creative activity to combine and use other resources or factors of production.
- **human capital** the developed and refined skills of people.
- **financial capital** money savings which can be used to purchase capital goods.
- **production possibilities** various combinations of goods and services which can be produced with a nation's available resources and technology.
- **opportunity cost** the sacrifice of some good or service given up because of a decision to acquire some other good or service.
- **law of increasing costs** when output of a good is expanded relative to the production of another good, the unit costs of additional units of output tend to increase; opportunity costs tend to increase after some point the more we produce of a good.
- **constant costs** a condition in which expanding output causes no change in the additional costs of producing each unit.
- **specialization** concentrating skills in one type of production alone.
- **consumer goods** goods which are used directly by final consumers.
- **capital goods** goods which are used to produce other goods.
- **private goods versus public goods** goods which are consumed by individuals versus goods which are consumed by the community as a whole.
- **three questions of economic systems** *What, How,* and *For whom* are goods to be produced.
- **traditional economic system** a system in which the three questions are answered in the same way from generation to generation.
- **command economic system** a system in which the three questions are answered by a central authority.
- **market economic system** a system in which the three questions are answered through the independent decisions of the people.
- **mixed economic system** a system in which there are elements of tradition, command, and the market.
- **economic surplus** those goods, services, and resources available after minimum requirements for existence are provided for the people.
- **socialism** an economic system in which the means of production are owned and operated by the state.
- **communism** an economic system in which the means of production and private property are owned and operated by the state; in addition, the state is a political dictatorship.
- **capitalism** an economic system in which the means of production are owned and operated by individual owners, or capitalists.

Questions for Review

1. What are the opportunity costs of becoming a concert violinist? How is a violinist compensated for incurring the costs?

2. How is the law of increasing costs involved in a hamburger stand? a chain of hamburger stands?

3. Draw up a schedule of production possibilities for a hypothetical economy. Classify output as public goods and private goods. Make certain your data confirm the law of increasing costs. Plot your data on a graph and show that additional costs do increase as the economy approaches total specialization.

4. Explain how a nation's goals influence the selection of a point on its production possibilities curve.

5. What are the opportunity costs of unemployed resources?

6. Assume the nation is at full employment and government decides to increase expenditures for programs to provide education and health care for low-income families. What results would you predict: in the immediate period; over the long term?

7. What is the cost to a city of preserving a historic building in the center of town?

8. "You can't have your cake and eat it too." Explain.

9. How does communism differ from socialism? from capitalism?

10. Name five countries that are examples of mixed capitalism.

3

The Free Market:
Supply and Demand

Sam had been in business for many years. He manufactured a beverage known in the mountains as White Lightning, and at his peak he turned out 12,000 gallons a week. His distribution costs were low, and he had no advertising expenses. His price of $4 a gallon brought him a handsome profit. But times change, even in the hills of North Carolina, and things began to happen to Sam's business.

First, his production costs rose. The prices of sugar, rye flour, corn meal, yeast, and coal kept chasing each other upward like dogs going after a coon. Then his equipment began to wear out. Sam's capital goods included a 280-gallon cooker, a 150-gallon barrel, two 55-gallon barrels, 60 feet of copper coil, mash boxes, and a 150-gallon coal boiler. The cost of this equipment almost doubled.

After he raised his price to $6 a gallon, Sam discovered that some of his old customers no longer came around. In fact, a lot of them weren't there any more. They'd moved out of the hills into town and were making enough money to buy legal whiskey instead of moonshine. To cover all his expenses, Sam figured he would have to raise his price to $8 a gallon—but most of his remaining customers couldn't afford that price.

It wasn't the "revenooers" who put Sam out of business—it was the market!

The market: some dimensions

We saw in Chapter 2 that the market is a basic institution of American society. The market decides such questions as what will be produced, how it will be produced, and how society will divide the total product. Actually, there are many markets. There is a market for automobiles, a market for Rembrandt paintings, a market for labor, a market for corn whiskey, and so on. Some markets are concentrated in particular places, like the farmers' markets that we see in many cities during the summer. Other markets are worldwide—for example, the market for grain and the market for motion picture films. A market may be centralized in a particular building, like the stock market, even though buyers and sellers are scattered every-

where. Economists use the term **market** to mean, in Alfred Marshall's words, "the whole of any region in which buyers and sellers are in such free intercourse with one another that the prices of the same goods tend to equality easily and quickly." The market for automobiles has now become practically worldwide. This means that an auto company in Detroit has to think about its competitors in Germany and Japan and elsewhere when it designs and prices its cars; otherwise it may find its customers drifting away like those of Sam the moonshiner.

Demand

Under the market system the question of what will be produced usually is decided by consumers. By **consumers** we mean persons or families who buy goods and services. When they buy, they are, in effect, voting for the kinds of goods and services they prefer. If they prefer smaller cars that use less gasoline, then the message goes back to the auto companies to respond to this preference or face the consequences.

Law of demand

The basic principle underlying consumer preference is called the Law of Demand. The **Law of Demand** states that consumers normally choose to buy fewer units of a good at high prices and more units at low prices. The quantity of a good or service that a particular consumer would buy at various prices can be shown in a *schedule of demand*.

Table 1 shows two such demand schedules for the Smith and Jones families. Each schedule indicates the quantity of ski weekends that the Smith or Jones family would buy per season at various prices. Of course, it is impossible to tell at this point the quantity each family will actually buy and the price actually paid. A demand schedule is hypothetical: it shows what each *would* buy, depending on price. In addition, we must invoke *ceteris paribus* and hold all other factors constant that

Table 1
Demand for Ski Weekend Accommodations

Price	Quantity		
	Smith family	Jones family	Market demand*
$100	0	4	10,000
80	4	6	20,000
70	10	8	30,000
60	18	10	40,000
50	20	12	50,000

*Market demand equals the sum of all individual demand schedules in the market. The Smith and Jones families are, of course, only two of many families in the ski market.

Graphing demand

The market for a consumer good or service can be illustrated by a graph. Figure 1 is derived from the information given in Table 1. The *quantity* of ski accommodations is shown on the *horizontal axis. Price* is shown on the *vertical axis.* Each column under "Quantity" is projected into a separate graph. The quantities for each family in Table 1 appear as a series of points in the graphs of Figure 1. Connecting these points with a line produces what is known as a **demand curve.** Using this procedure, the separate behaviors of the Smith and Jones families can be translated into two demand curves. There will be as many of these demand curves as there are consumers, and the shape of each curve will depend on the preferences of that particular consumer. The Smith curve is flatter than the Jones curve because the Smiths are more responsive to changes in price: if price should fall from $70 to $50, the Smiths would buy twice as many ski weekends, while the Joneses would buy only half again as many. If we add the quantities bought at each price, we obtain a market demand curve, the right-hand curve in Figure 1. The shape of this curve is quite different from the shapes of the Smith and Jones curves. The shape of the market demand curve depends on the shape and position of all individual demand curves. If price should fall from $70 to $50, total quantity demanded would increase by two-thirds.

affect demand. Such factors as consumer tastes, their income, and their expectations are assumed constant for now. Later we will see what happens when any one of these factors changes.

The Smith family are avid skiers, and if the price is $50 per weekend they would buy 20 weekends—representing a total expenditure of $1,000. Their interest would decline, however, if prices were higher, and at $100 they apparently would prefer to spend their money on something else. The Jones family are less enthusiastic about skiing often but like to ski at least a few weekends per season. At a price of $100, when the Smiths would be turned off, the Joneses would still be in the market for four weekends.

The "market," of course, includes many families besides the Smiths and the Joneses. Some consumers would demand more ski weekends than others at a given price. Some consumers would buy at a much higher price than others. The total market demand for ski weekends at each price is shown in the third column of Table 1.

Notice that all three curves shown are *downward sloping*. This characteristic is true of all normal demand curves. This is just a graphical interpretation of the Law of Demand: at

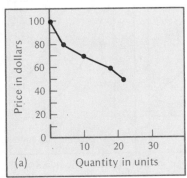

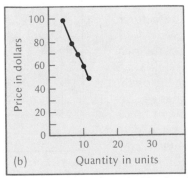

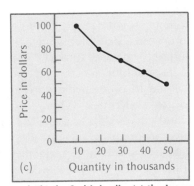

Figure 1 Demand curves for ski weekend accommodations for: (a) total market demand; (b) the Smith family; (c) the Jones family.

lower prices, the quantity demanded of any good would be greater than at high prices (all other factors assumed constant).

Changes in demand

The demand curves in Figure 1 show the relationship between price and quantity for a particular period of time. All other factors which might influence demand are held constant in order to observe the effects of price alone. These other factors are set aside in *ceteris paribus.* They include (1) consumers' tastes, or preferences; (2) their incomes; (3) the number of consumers in the market for a given product; (4) the prices of other goods consumers may choose to buy instead of this product; and (5) what consumers expect to happen to the economy, or to the part of it that concerns them. A change in any of these factors will change the demand for a particular product. An entirely new demand curve must be constructed to show the new quantity that will be bought at every price. Let's consider these other factors one by one.

Tastes Everyone who follows clothing fashions knows that a dress or coat that sold well last year may not find favor at all this year. People still buy clothing, of course, but tastes have changed. Just why tastes change isn't always clear. Sometimes the public seems to fall in love with plaid trousers and Toyota cars and ragtime, and out of love with Beatle records and button-down shirt collars. Producers who are quick on the uptake will try to profit from changes in tastes, either by making a product to suit a new taste or by tying an already existing product to it. For example, the popularity of worn-out blue jeans among the college crowd has led clothing manufacturers to produce new blue jeans with a worn look, and auto manufacturers to upholster their car seats with blue denim. And the nostalgia craze has led to product design reminiscent of the forties and fifties. When tastes change, demand curves shift to show the different quantity consumers would buy at every price level. Figure 2a shows how a specific change in consumer tastes—people don't care for studded jeans anymore—has affected demand for studded jeans.

Incomes Changes in incomes also affect demand curves. When people earn more money, they are likely to buy more goods, particularly things they haven't been able to afford before. We might expect those enthusiastic skiers the Smiths to plan more ski weekends at every price. They will also buy more restaurant meals and perhaps a second car. On the other hand, they may buy less hamburger or cabbage because they will prefer to spend their money on steaks or other higher-priced foods. When large numbers of people experience increases in income, it is safe to predict that sales of luxury goods will increase while sales of some other goods will decrease. Demand curves will shift to show the new quantity which will be bought at every price. Figure 2b shows how rising incomes have affected the demand for tennis rackets.

Prices of related goods The demand for a good may be affected by a change in the price of another good. We would expect the demand for chicken to be affected by beef prices, since people will eat more chicken when beef becomes expensive and less chicken when beef becomes affordable again. An increase in the price of postage stamps is likely to increase the demand for long-distance telephone calls as people turn to calling instead of writing. These are called **substitute goods;** one may be replaced by the other. *An increase in the price of a good will increase the demand for its substitute.* Figure 3a shows how rising coffee prices have affected the demand for tea.

Some goods, on the other hand, go together, like ham and eggs or skis and ski jackets; these are called **complementary goods.** *An*

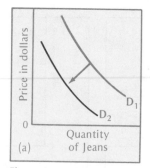 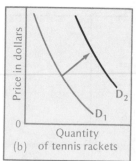

(a) Quantity of Jeans

(b) Quantity of tennis rackets

Figure 2 (a) A change in tastes reduces the quantity of studded jeans consumers would buy at every price level. (b) Higher incomes increase the quantity of tennis rackets that consumers would buy at every price level.

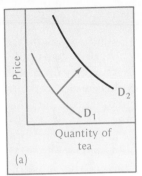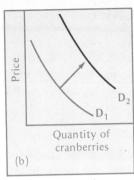

Figure 3 (a) An increase in the price of coffee increases the demand for its substitute, tea. (b) A lower price for turkey increases the demand for its complement, cranberries.

increase in the price of one is likely to be accompanied by a decrease in demand for its complement. Recently in the United States we have seen that a steep increase in the price of gasoline reduces the demand for autos that burn a lot of fuel. The demand curve for substitutes and complements changes to show the new quantities that would be demanded at every price. Figure 3b shows how low turkey prices affect the demand for cranberries.

Number of buyers An increase in the number of customers will ordinarily increase the demand for a product. Such an increase may result from larger families or from improvements in transporting the goods to a greater number of customers. The demand for lettuce in wintertime increased greatly when the California lettuce growers found ways of shipping their product over long distances without spoilage. On the other hand, cigarette manufacturers have worried that the connection between smoking and lung cancer might reduce the number of cigarette buyers. (Apparently their fears were needless, however, as more Americans seem to take up the habit every year.) A growing middle-class population will certainly affect demand; generally, demand will increase.

Expectations Finally, if consumers expect their incomes to increase in the near future, they are more likely to buy expensive items than if they expect their incomes to decline. Much of the

installment buying of consumer durables, such as clothes dryers and TV sets, is done in the expectation of paying for them out of future income. Or if consumers expect the prices of these goods to rise, they may be induced to buy them sooner than they had planned. If consumers expect shortages of a good to develop, they may buy in panic. The resulting demand is so great that the good may be unavailable in the short run. Conversely, if people are afraid of losing their jobs, they are likely to postpone many purchases. Fear of the future was an important factor in the drop in sales of many consumer goods in the 1973–1975 recession: autos, television sets, and kitchen appliances, for instance.

When demand curves shift, the economy moves along its production possibilities curve. A change in consumer tastes may move the economy along the curve away from auto production and toward greater food production. A change toward greater equality of income distribution may mean greater production of buses and fewer Cadillacs. Likewise, changes in relative prices and expectations of changes can cause a movement along a nation's production possibilities curve.

Changes in demand vs. changes in quantity demanded

It is important to distinguish between a change in demand and a change in the quantity demanded. Each of the above five factors can cause a **change in demand**—that is, a change of any of these factors leads to a different level of sales at every price. *Changes in demand cause the demand curve to shift to the right (if demand increases) or to the left (if demand decreases).* You can demonstrate this for yourself in Figure 1 by supposing that the number of ski weekends demanded at each price doubles. The demand curve will shift to the right. Notice that we are talking about *changes in demand.*

A **change in the quantity demanded** occurs *when price changes* but other factors remain the same: *ceteris paribus.* For example, going back to Figure 1 again, if the price of ski weekends should fall from $70 to $60, the quantity demanded would increase from 30,000 to 40,000. If the price should rise from $70 to $80, the quantity demanded would fall from 30,000 to 20,000. Both of these instances involve changes in the quantity demanded. *For changes in quantity demanded, the curve remains the same; moving along the curve leads to a different level of sales at the new price.*

Here are some examples from the real world showing the difference:

1. The number of teenagers in the population increases, and the demand for soft drinks increases. Larger quantities would be bought at every price. This is a *change in demand*, as demand increases and demand curves shift to the right.

2. Falling incomes as a result of the 1973–1975 recession force people to postpone purchases of new household appliances. Smaller quantities would be bought at every price. This is a *change in demand*, as demand decreases and demand curves shift to the left.

3. Higher prices for oil *reduce the quantity demanded* as buyers move up their demand curves. Higher prices increase the costs of manufacturing synthetic fibers, and clothing firms look to cotton as a substitute. There is a *change in demand* for cotton—demand increases.

4. Higher prices for feed grains cause farmers to reduce the quantity used to fatten cattle and hogs. This is a *change in quantity demanded.* Farmers feed their livestock soybeans instead and demand curves for soybeans shift to the right. This is a *change in demand.*

5. Lower prices for stereo equipment lead to larger sales. This is a *change in quantity demanded* as consumers move down their demand curves. Owners of new stereos buy more records, and record demand increases. This is a *change in demand* for records, as demand curves shift to the right.

Supply

Now it's time to look at the other side of the market. We have been studying the behavior of buyers and the reasons for their decisions. For every buyer, of course, there has to be a seller. Sellers decide what to put on the market and how much they will make available at any given price.

Law of supply

The principle underlying sellers' decisions is called the Law of Supply. The **Law of Supply** states that sellers normally choose to provide smaller quantities of a good at low prices and larger quantities at high prices. This is because of the fixed quantity of some resources. A seller's capital goods (plant and equipment) are designed to produce output over some limited range. To push quantity beyond this range is inefficient, involving higher production costs for each additional unit. If suppliers are to be persuaded to produce more, they must be offered a higher price. If price is low, suppliers will reduce their output.

The behavior of sellers can be depicted in *supply schedules* that correspond to the demand schedules of buyers. Table 2 shows supply schedules for two ski resorts at Snowy Mountain: Wonderland and Alpine. The schedules indicate the quantities of ski accommodations that would be provided per season at various prices. Again, it is impossible to tell precisely the quantity each firm will actually supply. A supply schedule shows what each *would* supply, depending on price (all other factors held constant).

If prices are low, Wonderland and Alpine each would provide 400 weekend accommodations. At higher prices, both would manage to find ways of accommodating more people. They would open sooner in the fall and remain open longer in the spring. They would rearrange some facilities to house more people. They might also enlarge their restaurant and entertainment capacity and add more personnel. But all this would be costly and is possible only at higher prices.

Table 2
Supply of Ski Weekend Accommodations

Price	Quantity		
	Wonderland	Alpine	Market supply*
$100	500	600	50,000
80	490	550	40,000
70	475	500	30,000
60	450	450	20,000
50	400	400	10,000

*The sum of all individual supply schedules in the market.

Wonderland appears to be more limited in its ability to vary supply if price changes. Alpine's facilities are more flexible. The final column in Table 2 shows the total quantities of accommodations of all ski resorts that would be supplied at various prices. Figure 4 is drawn from Table 2 and shows the supply curves of Wonderland and Alpine together with the market supply curve. Just as with demand, a **supply curve** plots quantity along the horizontal axis and price along the vertical axis. In general, *supply curves slope upward*. This is because higher prices generally mean larger quantities will be supplied.

Changes in supply

Once again our supply schedule shows the relationship between quantity and price during a particular period of time. We have assumed that other things remain the same—*ceteris paribus*. In time, other things may not remain the same; the supply curve may shift to the right or the left. It will shift to the right if supply increases—that is, if more ski accommodations become available at every price. It will shift to the left if fewer accommodations are available at every price.

A *change in supply* may be the result of several factors: (1) changes in the cost of production (that is, of running ski resorts); (2) changes in the prices of other goods (the other activities arranged by the resort such as snowmobiling and ice skating); (3) changes in the suppliers' expectations about prices; and (4) changes in the number of other suppliers (the other resorts in the business). Let's discuss in turn each of these changes in supply.

Changes in cost of production The cost of supplying a good or service may fall because of technological improvements or because the prices of resources used in production have fallen. If snow could be manufactured by flying over the ski slopes and dropping a few bushels of snowdust, this would certainly move the supply curve to the right. For farmers, cheaper fertilizer would have the same effect on supply curves for wheat and soybeans. A striking example of how a new technology has affected supply is the development of miniature electronic circuits. Miniature circuits have made it possible to produce inexpensive calculators that can be carried in a pocket or a purse. Supply curves shifted to the right as the technology became available to many firms.

The opposite result may sometimes occur: supply may decrease. For example, when energy prices rose sharply in 1974, the supply curve for most industrial products moved leftward, and consumers had to pay higher prices for many goods. Wage rate changes are also an important factor in the cost of supply. If wages increase, then smaller quantities of output can be produced at every price. Supply curves move leftward. The reduced supply of new housing is due in part to much higher wages demanded by construction workers.

Prices of other products Most producers are able to make more than one product. They will naturally want to produce that combination of products that is most profitable for them. If the price of soybeans begins to rise, Illinois farmers may switch some of their land out of corn and into soybeans—thus causing supply curves for corn to move leftward. Many shopping centers

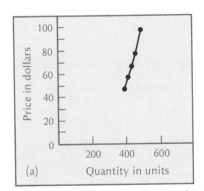

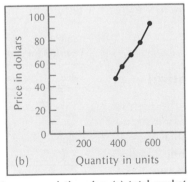

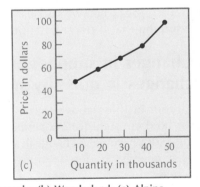

Figure 4   Supply curves for ski weekend accommodations for: (a) total market supply; (b) Wonderland; (c) Alpine.

used to have bowling alleys. As ice skating began to be popular, owners shifted their facilities from bowling to skating. Supply curves for bowling games shifted to the left and supply curves for hockey games shifted to the right.

Expectations   The supply will change if the price of a good or service hasn't risen yet but is expected to in the future. The expectations of suppliers will cause supply to change. For example, farmers may do a bit of hoarding—they may keep some of their soybeans from the last harvest stored in a silo in hope of getting more for their crop later on. Businesses are deeply involved in expectations. They borrow funds and invest in equipment or raw materials on the basis of what they expect to happen over a period of months or years. In the early 1970s many builders invested heavily in vacation homes, and supply curves shifted to the right. The builders expected to earn substantial profits from rising prices of housing. Unfortunately, the recession of 1973–1975 cut into their markets. Many firms were forced out of business and many projects were abandoned. Expectations of hard times ahead will probably hold down the supply of new vacation homes for several more years.

Number of producers   In Figure 4, if ski weekends are selling at $70, the market supply would be 30,000. But suppose the number of ski resorts doubles as many new firms take advantage of expected profitability. If this happens, the market supply will be 60,000 weekends at the same price of $70. The supply curve will have shifted to the right. This is not very likely to happen on such a large scale in any industry, but when we say *ceteris paribus* we are assuming that it doesn't happen at all.

Changes in supply vs. changes in quantity supplied

All four of these above factors are the factors we hold constant (*ceteris paribus*) when drawing a supply curve. A **change in supply** is a result of a change in one of these other factors. When one of these factors changes, we must draw a new curve. Changes in these factors produce changes in the entire supply schedule.

New quantities must be calculated at every price level. *When supply changes, the supply curve shifts either to the left or right.*

Any one supply curve shows the quantities that will be supplied at every price. A change in price brings on a **change in quantity supplied.** If the price of ski weekends rises from $70 to $80, quantity supplied will increase by 10,000 units. If price falls from $70 to $60, quantity supplied will fall by 10,000 units. *A change in price leads to a change in quantity supplied.* The curve remains the same when quantity supplied changes.

Market equilibrium

You're probably unaccustomed to hearing the word "supply" used without any mention of "demand." The two words seem to go together; in fact, economists usually speak of them in the same breath. That is because the interaction of supply and demand is what determines the actual price at which a good will be sold and the actual quantity that will change hands. In Table 3 we have put together the demand schedule for ski weekends (from Table 1) and the supply schedule for ski weekends (from Table 2). The table may seem to be just a collection of numbers, but if you examine it closely you will find that it gives precise answers to the questions: How many ski weekends will people actually buy? What price will they actually pay?

Suppose we experiment by setting the price at $100. Checking the supply column, we can see that 50,000 units would be offered for sale at $100. However, if we look at the demand column we find that only 10,000 units would be purchased at $100. This obviously

Table 3
Demand for and Supply of Ski Weekend Accommodations

Price	Quantity demanded	Quantity supplied
$100	10,000	50,000
80	20,000	40,000
70	30,000	30,000
60	40,000	20,000
50	50,000	10,000

won't satisfy the sellers, who could find more customers if they reduce price. If they come down to $80, they could sell 20,000 units. They would still be left with a surplus, however, so it would pay them to reduce price another notch to $70. At this price they could sell 30,000 units. The surplus has disappeared, because at this price customers are willing to buy the entire 30,000 units.

We can see the interaction more easily in Figure 5. Figure 5 is a graph of the demand and supply schedules in Table 3. If the price is set at $100, there is a surplus. Quantity supplied is greater than quantity demanded. This is shown as the horizontal distance between demand and supply at a price of $100. In the adjustments that follow, sellers try to dispose of their goods by reducing price; they move down their supply curves. Buyers are willing to buy larger quantities as the price falls; they move down their demand curves. Finally, a price is reached that *just clears the market*, that is, where quantity supplied is equal to quantity demanded. At this point we say that the market is *in equilibrium*. **Market equilibrium** occurs where quantity supplied equals quantity demanded.

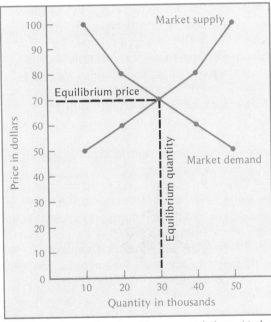

Figure 5 **The market for ski accommodations. Market supply and market demand intersect, resulting in both equilibrium price and equilibrium quantity.**

The same results follow if we begin at the other end of the supply-demand schedules and set a price of only $50. At that price, would-be skiers are willing to buy 50,000 ski weekends, but only 10,000 will be supplied. This time there is a shortage of 40,000 units, shown on the graph as the distance between quantity demanded and quantity supplied at a price of $50. Adjustments follow. Buyers compete with each other for what is available by bidding up the price; they move up their demand curves. Sellers are willing to provide larger quantities at higher prices; they move up their supply curves. Finally, a higher price is reached (in this example, $70) which just clears the market, and we have again reached equilibrium. At a price of $70 quantity demanded is equal to quantity supplied.

The price at which quantity demanded is equal to quantity supplied is called the **equilibrium price.** Only at equilibrium is there no surplus or shortage. At a price of $70 all skiers willing to pay this price will be satisfied. All businesses willing to provide accommodations at the going price will be satisfied. At equilibrium the price tends to stay where it is as long as conditions do not change. This is because all buyers and sellers are satisfied to go on buying and selling at this price.

The term "price system" is often used synonymously with "market economy." Under a **price system,** supply and demand are free to determine prices for all goods and services. The American economy is referred to as a price system, even though (as we shall see) some prices are set outside the market.

Changes in supply and demand

Equilibrium may not last very long in any market. Conditions may change and set forces in motion that disturb it. Buyers and sellers then will adjust to the new conditions, moving toward a new equilibrium price.

One possibility is a change in consumer tastes. Suppose the conviction grows among skiers that skiing is dangerous. Perhaps they have seen too many injured skiers brought down from the slopes by sled. Demand schedules fall, and the market demand curve shifts

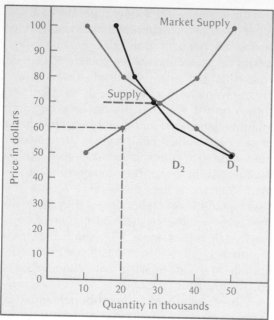

Figure 6 Market equilibrium results with intersection of supply and demand curves. D_1 shows original market demand, while D_2 shows new market demand. Notice the surplus.

to the left. In Figure 6 demand shifts from D_1 to D_2. At the old equilibrium price of $70, supply now exceeds demand. Recreation firms will reduce their prices in an effort to retain customers. They move down their supply curves. When the price has fallen to $60, the market will be in equilibrium again. At this price only 20,000 weekend accommodations will be sold instead of 30,000 as before.

Now let's assume that a change occurs in the number of firms supplying the services. A building boom makes more overnight lodgings available for skiers. The supply curve shifts to

the right. In Figure 7 supply shifts from S_1 to S_2. At the old equilibrium price, supply now exceeds demand. Firms will reduce their prices to capture more customers. As prices fall, buyers will move down their demand curves and buy larger quantities. When prices have fallen to $50, the market will be in equilibrium again. Fifty thousand weekend accommodations will be sold.

The beauty of the graphic analysis is that it helps us to see changes in market equilibrium almost at a glance. For instance, we can see the effect of an increase in demand when supply remains the same. If the demand curve shifts to the right and the supply curve remains the same, equilibrium price and quantity will rise. We are all familiar with the higher prices that are sometimes charged for movie tickets (or even restaurant meals) in evenings and on weekends when demand is greater. Ski resorts also charge higher prices on weekends than during the week, because more people want to go skiing on weekends. We cannot say exactly how high prices will rise in response to an increase in demand without knowing the shape of the supply and demand curves. Still it is very useful to know that the general effect of an increase in demand is to increase both the equilibrium price and the quantity supplied. The general effect of a decrease in demand is just the opposite: if supply remains the same, the equilibrium price and quantity will fall.

The effects of supply changes are also easy to work out. If supply increases and demand remains the same, the equilibrium price will fall but quantity will increase. If supply falls and demand remains the same, precisely the opposite will happen: the equilibrium price will rise and quantity will fall.

When both supply and demand change at the same time, the effects are more difficult to predict. For instance, if supply increases while demand is falling, it's obvious that price will fall. But the new equilibrium quantity will depend on the extent to which the increased supply is offset by the decreased demand. The increase in supply will tend to increase the equilibrium quantity, but the decrease in demand will tend to reduce it. Similarly, if supply

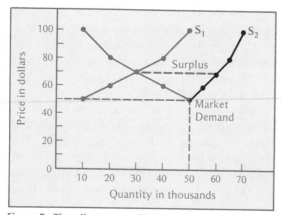

Figure 7 The effect on equilibrium price when supply S_1 increases to S_2.

falls and demand increases, price must rise but the new equilibrium quantity will depend on the relative size of the changes. If the decrease in supply is greater than the increase in demand, the equilibrium quantity will be smaller than before; but if the decrease in supply is less than the increase in demand, the equilibrium quantity will be greater. Can you prove this using graphical illustrations?

It is conceivable that both supply and demand may increase at the same time. In that case, the new equilibrium quantity will obviously be greater than if only supply or only demand had increased. What will be the effect on price? Again it depends on whether the increased demand pulls price up by more than the increased supply pulls it down. Similarly, if both supply and demand fall at the same time, the new equilibrium quantity will be smaller than before, but we can't tell what the price will be until we know the relative sizes of the changes in supply and demand. Figure 8 illustrates a number of recent shifts in market supply and demand. Interpret each in terms of change in price and quantity.

Expectations can make it so

We have suggested that buyer and seller expectations are important in determining demand and supply. If buyers expect prices to fall, they will postpone their purchases and demand curves will shift to the left. Expectations of falling prices can also cause an increase in supply. Sellers throw their stock on the market for what they can get before price falls, and supply curves shift to the right. What is the result? Prices fall as expected!

On the other hand, expectations of rising prices can cause an increase in demand as buyers begin to stock up on a good. Expectations of rising prices can cause a reduction in supply as sellers hold their stocks off the market. What is the result? Prices rise as expected!!

In economics it is interesting that the expectations of buyers and sellers often come true. If they expect prices to rise and behave as if they will rise, they *do rise*.

The search for equilibrium

Market equilibrium is neat and clearly defined on paper. In the real world it may be a different story. In the real world, *ceteris* (everything else) is generally not *paribus* (fixed). Conditions are changing, causing demand and supply curves to shift back and forth. Information may not be quickly transmitted among markets so that there are shortages in some and surpluses in others. By the time all adjustments have taken place, conditions may have changed again and the market will begin to move toward another new equilibrium. In short, the market is *dynamic*; it therefore differs a bit from the *static* market that we assumed. The principles are, however, the same for both. Assuming a static economy enables us to use *ceteris paribus* and analyze the adjustments of the real-world, dynamic economy. Remember that a model is only a simplified version of reality.

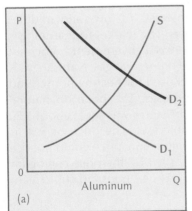
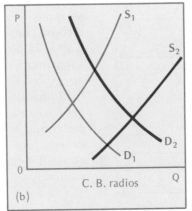
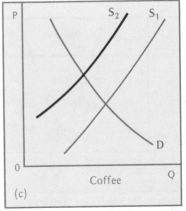

Figure 8 The effect on equilibrium price due to changes in supply and/or demand. P stands for price and Q for quantity.

Price rigidity Another reason equilibrium may not occur is due to *price rigidity,* or *sticky prices.* Prices don't always respond quickly to changing market conditions, especially in the downward direction. Minimum wage laws, union contracts, and monopoly power on the part of the pricing firms can prevent prices from dropping—even when lack of demand dictates that they should drop. This particular situation is all too common and may lead to prolonged periods of *disequilibrium* (lack of equilibrium).

Shortages and surpluses Shortages and surpluses do occur, preventing equilibrium. Large retailers search for equilibrium when they order gift items for the Christmas buying season. Their market researchers study buying habits in past years. They assess the mood of the public and try to predict demand for bicycles, fur coats, electric shavers, and stuffed toys. However, even the most scientific forecasts will leave many stores with a surplus of some gift items and a scarcity of others.

Figure 9 illustrates the market for an unpopular item, say recordings of "Jingle Bells" by a Russian rock group. Equilibrium price for the records would have been $1 each, but price is rigid downward. Why? The retailer has set a price of $5, below which no sales will be made. At the established price there is a surplus of 200 units (and the store's buyer is probably out of a job). After the gift buying season the retailer will announce a Clearance Sale and sell his entire stock for $1 or even less.

The opposite situation can be just as frustrating. A popular gift for Christmas in 1976 was

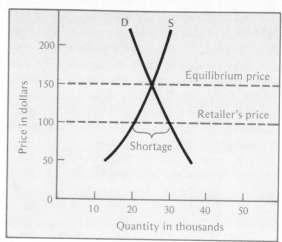

Figure 10 The market for electronic television games. The retailer's price is below equilibrium price. A shortage results.

an electronic game played on an ordinary television set. Figure 10 illustrates larger than expected demand. At the advertised price of $100, ten thousand more games could have been sold. Many customers had to go away angry, and sales people were annoyed about the shortage. It is often impractical to increase price to a level that would "clear the market." The result is that markets cannot reach equilibrium.

Surpluses and shortages are more serious when they involve goods and services that affect the well-being of many people. Occasionally government takes actions which prevent movement toward equilibrium.

Government action in the market For some goods government may set a low price in order to protect the interests of low- and middle-income consumers. The market for natural gas is an example. In 1954 a government agency set a maximum price on natural gas. Natural gas is an important fuel used for heating homes and for industrial purposes. The price on natural gas sold among the states was set at about $.50 per thousand cubic feet. The price of $.50 is called a *price ceiling;* selling price could not rise above the ceiling. (In 1977 the price ceiling for natural gas was $1.44 per thousand cubic feet.)

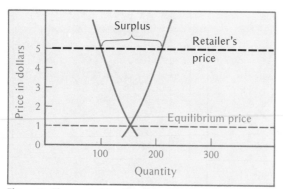

Figure 9 The market for "Jingle Bells" records. Established retailer's price does not reach equilibrium price because of downward rigidity. Here a surplus results.

Over the years population has increased, along with money income, steadily moving the demand curve for natural gas to the right. Figure 11 shows how a shortage began to appear at the fixed price. The problem grew even worse as suppliers cut back production. They were unable to earn sufficient profit at the price ceiling and so they allowed equipment to wear out without replacement. Supply curves began to shift to the left!

The policy was intended to benefit users of natural gas, but the long range result has been serious shortages.

For some goods government may set a high price in order to protect the interests of sellers. The market for certain types of unskilled labor is an example. Congress has passed a minimum wage law that sets a minimum price on hourly workers. In 1976 the minimum wage was $2.50 per hour. The minimum wage is called a *price floor*. Price is not allowed to fall lower than the floor.

Figure 12 illustrates the effect of a price floor. A low demand for unskilled workers and a large supply would lead to an equilibrium price of only, say, $1.50 an hour and 100,000 labor hours would be purchased. At the minimum wage, however, only 50,000 labor hours will be hired. At $2.50 there is a surplus of 200,000 labor hours.

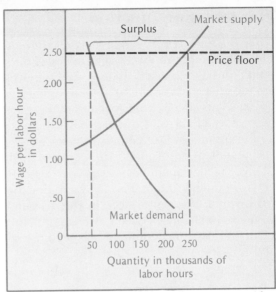

Figure 12 The effect of a price floor is to cause a surplus. Note that equilibrium price is below the price floor. The surplus is difference between where price floor intersects market supply and market demand.

The policy was intended to benefit low skilled workers, but the long range result may have been greater unemployment.

Functions of the price system

Earlier we explored the interaction of supply and demand in a particular market—the market for ski weekends. We've seen that price and quantity tend to adjust so that the amount sellers are willing to supply is equal to the amount customers are willing to buy. If some sellers find the price too low to be worth their while, they withdraw from that particular market and go elsewhere. If some buyers find the price too high for their pocketbooks, they are free to spend their money on something else, or not to spend it at all.

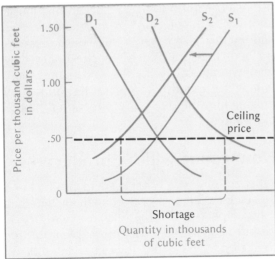

Figure 11 The market for natural gas. Supply decreases from S_1 to S_2 because there is no incentive to produce more. Meanwhile, demand is increasing (from D_1 to D_2) because of ceiling price. Net result of a price ceiling is a shortage.

The rationing function

Prices perform two functions: (1) a rationing function and (2) an incentive function. Prices ration out the available goods and services among buyers according to the amounts each buyer wants and is able to pay for. If Harry wants lots of ski trips, he can have them as long as his money lasts. Others, whose desire is less urgent or whose income is smaller, will receive smaller quantities. Skiers may also arrange their time so that they can go during the week when prices are lower. In this way the price differential between weekdays and weekends encourages a more balanced use of resources.

The incentive function

Prices also provide an incentive for firms to produce more. Where demand is great, prices will rise, encouraging firms already in the industry to produce more and drawing new firms into the industry. Where demand is falling, prices will normally fall, too. Firms will cut back their production, releasing resources for use in other industries where there is demand for them.

Firms are buyers as well as sellers. They buy materials and supplies from other firms, behaving exactly as private individuals do in deciding what to buy and how much. If a new machine promises to cut production costs, or if a certain material can be substituted for another at a saving, a firm will buy the low-cost resources in order to compete with other firms. The economy is tied together by millions of these interactions: linking producers with one another and with consumers, linking one product with other products, and linking every market with other markets. We will discuss this in more detail later when we examine the structure of the whole economy. The important thing to bear in mind is that no person is an economic island, and no business is either. All are interrelated.

It is this interrelatedness that we mean when we speak of the market system. Adam Smith described how individual buyers and sellers in a free market would send and receive signals by means of prices. Prices were the means of communicating society's needs.

Prices helped to ensure flexible adjustment to changing conditions of demand and supply. It is through the market system that our economy answers three basic questions: what will be produced, how will it be produced, and to whom will the output be distributed?

What will be produced

What do American consumers want? Our wants are changing all the time. Thirty years ago we had no television industry. As the first sets were introduced, public interest began to rise and consumers were willing to pay high prices for this new "toy." Resources flowed toward the television industry to take advantage of the profits to be made. Advertisers were willing to pay high prices for the chance to reach a wider and more responsive audience for their selling messages. New stars and new shows were born, and many established performers were drawn from the movies and radio broadcasting into TV. As television expanded, consumers spent less for other forms of entertainment. Movie theaters began to lose money, and many went out of business. Popular magazines like *Collier's, The Saturday Evening Post, Look,* and *Life* found it difficult to compete with television for advertising dollars; they eventually had to stop publication. Radio ceased to be something you stayed home to listen; it became a source of background music and news bulletins and an appendage of the alarm clock. Through it all consumers expressed their preferences by the prices they were willing to pay (by the dollars they were willing to spend). Resources responded by moving into the types of production the people wanted.

How goods will be produced

What resources will be used in production? Most goods can be produced in many different ways, depending on the relative prices of the resources involved. The most plentiful resources may have the lowest prices. But as resources become scarce relative to demand, their prices rise and discourage their use. Furthermore, advances in technology may lead to new lower priced resources for use in production. For instance, the first TV sets were large and heavy, encased in wooden boxes. Now most of them are light enough to carry with one hand. Wood has given way to cheaper plastics made from petroleum. The old vacuum tubes have been replaced by solid-state circuits that never burn out and require much less current to operate. Hand wiring has given way to printed circuits stamped out by machines. And much of the manufacturing is now done in Japan and Okinawa or Taiwan, where skilled labor is available in large quantity and is cheaper than in the United States. These changes were unpredictable. Nobody knew in 1945 that new, strong materials would soon replace wood, or that research and development teams would invent transistors and integrated circuits. Television manufacturers turned to these new technologies because they were cheaper and because competition forced them to.

Who will get the output

Nearly everybody buys TV sets. They are made for mass consumption. But some sets have color; some are built into fumed oak consoles; and some even have screens several feet wide so that Johnny Carson seems to be right there in your bedroom. If we had our choice we would probably all like to have large-screen color sets, but our incomes can't be stretched that far. We buy what we can afford, and for most of us a large-screen TV set would require going without other things we also want (ski weekends, for instance). So the market system rations these TV sets to those whose incomes permit a wider range of choices.

The market system: pros and cons

We don't live in an ideal society. Every day our newspapers tell us of crime, corruption, and poverty. We hear that our air and water are polluted. We see that some people seem to have plenty of income and others not enough.

In describing the way the price system works to guide free markets, we don't want to claim too much. Every economist will agree that our society can stand a lot of improving. Our purpose here is to understand how economic decisions are made and to examine some of the advantages and disadvantages of the system.

Advantages of the market system

The most impressive merit of the market system is the "invisible hand," which turns the private individual's self-seeking to the good of all. We can say this another way: prices in a market economy help us to decide what to produce, how to produce it, and who is to get what. In command economies such as the Soviet Union, most production decisions are made by a central planning board and by political leaders. In recent years economists in those countries have grown concerned about low productivity and low product quality in their system. Some of them have proposed combining central planning with some limited use of the market system. That would take part of the load off the planning authorities and allow some questions to be answered more efficiently by individual buyers and sellers. Hungary and Yugoslavia are now experimenting with "market socialism," and it will be interesting to see how well their version succeeds.

The competitive market or price system, when it really works, is efficient because it channels resources to the places where they are needed most—that is, where they can be most productive and yield the highest returns to their owners. In fact, the market system is probably the *most efficient system* for producing the largest quantity of goods. It does this in response to the wishes of consumers as expressed through their demand for goods and services.

The competitive price system also buttresses freedom, particularly economic freedom, since it leaves the decision-making to market forces rather than to central authorities.

Viewpoint

Should the Free Market Prevail?

If the market system is such a good way of organizing the economy, perhaps we should let it operate more freely than we do. That is the opinion of some economists, including Professor Milton Friedman of the University of Chicago.

Professor Friedman is one of the country's most respected economists. Many economists disagree with him, but they still appreciate the care and precision of his analyses and the consistency of his conclusions. He believes so strongly in the free-market system that he even favors abolishing the public schools and letting people spend the tax money on private schools of their own choice. The role of government, according to Friedman, should be only to maintain peace and security so that individuals can enjoy life, liberty, and the pursuit of happiness. On almost every question of public policy, Friedman asks: Would this matter be handled better if it were left to the workings of the market? More often than not, his answer is yes.

A case in point involves federal compensation for people who have suffered property damage in floods. Friedman maintains that the federal government ought to stop reimbursing flood victims for loss of property. In his view, government intervention leads to the misuse of resources. Here are his reasons:

(1) In a free housing market, people choose their residence after taking everything into consideration, including the danger of being washed out in a flood. This doesn't mean that everyone who buys housing thinks of the danger of floods, but that enough people do so to influence the market price. Safe locations are in greater demand, and their prices are higher than unsafe locations. Greater concentrations of people develop in these safe areas.

(2) Fewer people will settle in unsafe places. Those who do will pay a lower price.

The amount they save may later be used to repair flood damage.

(3) If government assumes the risks and compensates property owners directly for flood damage, more people will find the lower price of unsafe land attractive. They will move into the cheap and unsafe areas. When a flood occurs, the damage will be greater than it would have been otherwise.

(4) The result is a misallocation of resources: using land for purposes for which it is unfit. Once the government starts to intervene it may find reasons for intervening further, such as by requiring people to adjust their living patterns in accordance with government policies on resource use.

What do you think of Professor Friedman's argument? Does it fit the actual circumstances of most flood victims?

Disadvantages of the market system

Critics of the market system say that there is a big difference between the ideal and the reality. One of the greatest shortcomings of the market system is the *unequal distribution* of income and resources. (This seems to be true of any system, but more so regarding the market system.) Capable or rich people are able to use the system more effectively than the weak; the rich grow richer and the poor stay poor. Many inequities of society are transmitted and even magnified through the price system: people with more money get more education and better jobs, which enable them to make still more money and to pass their advantages on to their children. Big companies have advantages over little companies and can sometimes drive their small competitors to the wall—the way the chain stores put many Mom and Pop grocery stores out of business.

This is a way of saying that the market system is far from ideal. There are frictions and obstacles that prevent it from working as smoothly as it seems in theory. Resources don't always flow where they are needed because various barriers prevent them. There are barriers of bigness and barriers of ignorance, as well as a general human reluctance to change. No single American entrepreneur has the resources to start a new auto company to compete with Ford or General Motors. A manufacturer of dog collars may not know that his labor and machinery could be used to better advantage in making harnesses for circus horses. And unemployed workers in Florida don't just jump on a train and head for Texas to look for jobs; they have families and social ties where they live.

Another failing of the market system is that it makes *society as a whole pay for some of the costs of private producers.* The factory that pours out smoke and pollutes the atmosphere creates a social burden that isn't paid for by the polluter. The community pays the costs in terms of illnesses and clean-up expenses. (Of course, command economies have this problem too.) Moreover, the market system when left to itself may fail to produce items that yield benefits to the community as a whole. For example, private firms may produce too little low-cost housing in favor of luxury apartments where profitability is high. Individuals enjoy private benefits, but middle-income neighborhoods may suffer.

Fortunately, we have ways of correcting the most unpleasant results of the free market. Citizens of democratic societies can use their influence as voters to affect government economic policy. For instance, we try to ensure at least a minimum standard of living to all people. Through public welfare programs, food stamps, and public health and education we assist poor families to improve their lives. We provide opportunities for job counseling and training and financial aid for unemployed workers to move to new jobs.

Our income tax and estate tax laws attempt to limit the size of fortunes that can be earned and passed on. And our antitrust laws foster competition and limit the power of large enterprises in order to protect the small operator. When ecological disaster threatened, other laws were enacted to protect communities against the worst results of industrial activity: the pollution, the noise, and the destroyed landscapes.

Our tax revenues are used to provide benefits that the price system overlooks. We subsidize mass transit because private transit systems often cannot operate profitably. We provide parks and recreation centers and we subsidize cultural activities for the enjoyment of the entire community.

We have referred to our market system as a *mixed economy.* We depend primarily on the market, but we modify the results through government action within our democratic processes. We admire the efficiency and the flexibility of the market. We admire the way the "invisible hand" helps to make very efficient decisions for us. But we worry about the problems of inequality and social justice.

These topics are of such vital concern to economists that we will return to them again and again in the text. As you develop further skills in economic principles, the more complicated aspects of market shortcomings will fall under your study and discussion.

Microeconomics and macroeconomics

The study of how the market system works in individual markets is called **microeconomics.** Microeconomics is concerned with the actions of individual firms and households, as well as individual industries and the consumer. It is especially interested in specific markets, such as those for diesel trucks, gypsum, typists, and golf clubs. The distribution of income and resources is part of the study of microeconomics. Other issues examined in microeconomics are: poverty, discrimination, monopoly, agricultural problems, big business and labor unions, and the urban financial crisis.

Macroeconomics deals with the economy as a whole. It talks of *aggregates* and looks at the combination of all markets taken together. It is concerned with such questions as: What determines the total level of production? What is total consumer spendable income likely to be next year? Should the federal government reduce taxes? How do the money supply and banking policies affect the economy? The major areas of study are grouped under *fiscal policy* and *monetary policy.* Some special problems studied in macroeconomics are inflation, unemployment, growth, and international economic relations.

Summary

The market system helps us to answer the fundamental question *what* to produce.

Consumers express their preferences for goods and services through their demand schedules. A demand curve illustrates the quantity that would be demanded at every price. The Law of Demand states that consumers normally choose to buy fewer units of a good at high prices and more units at low prices. On a graph this means demand curves are generally downward sloping.

Other factors such as tastes, incomes, prices of related goods, number of buyers, and price expectations must be held constant when drawing a demand curve. Changes in these factors may lead to a change in demand, causing the demand curve to shift.

Sellers show their selling plans for goods and services through their supply schedules. A supply curve illustrates the quantity that would be supplied at every price. The Law of Supply states that sellers normally choose to provide smaller quantities of a good at low prices and larger quantities at high prices. On a graph supply curves are generally upward sloping.

Other factors such as costs of production, prices of related goods, price expectations, and number of suppliers must be held constant when drawing a supply curve. Changes in these other factors may lead to a change in supply, causing the supply curve to shift.

The actual price and quantity sold depends on the interaction of demand and supply. Market equilibrium occurs at the price at which the quantity consumers buy is just equal to the quantity sellers supply. At equilibrium there is no surplus or shortage and all buyers and sellers are satisfied. Changes in other factors will cause changes in market equilibrium. The market may not reach equilibrium if other factors continue to change or if prices are not allowed to change. Occasionally government intervenes to limit price changes. A price ceiling often leads to a shortage, and a price floor often leads to a surplus.

Prices help to ration goods among those whose desire is greatest. Prices also provide the incentive for producers to expand output or to cut back.

Efficiency is the greatest strength of the market system. Its greatest weakness is probably too great a degree of inequality. But we have developed government economic policies to remedy some of the major shortcomings of our market system. The study of economics is divided into two parts: microeconomics examines how individual markets work and macroeconomics examines the operation of the economy as a whole.

Key Words and Phrases

- **market** an area over which buyers and sellers communicate their purchase and production decisions such that price tends to reach the same level throughout; we may speak of a specific market (for some good) or the whole market (market economy).

- **consumers** buyers of finished goods and services.

- **law of demand** over any single time period consumers tend to buy more of a particular good if its price is low than if its price is high.

- **schedule of demand** data that show the quantity of a good consumers will buy at various prices over a single time period.

- **market demand** the total quantity all consumers will buy at various prices during a single time period.

- **demand curve** a graph which shows the relationship between the quantity demanded and price for a good during a particular time period.

- **substitute good** a good which is easily used in place of another good.

- **complementary good** a good which is ordinarily used together with another good.

- **change in quantity demanded** a movement along a demand curve in response to a change in price.

- **change in demand** a shift of the entire demand curve in response to some other change in the market.

- **law of supply** over any single time period sellers tend to produce more of a good if its price is high than if its price is low.

- **schedule of supply** data which show the quantity of a good sellers will supply at various prices over a single time period.

- **supply curve** a graph which shows the relationship between the quantity supplied and price for a good during a particular time period.
- **market supply** the total quantity all sellers will produce at various prices during a single time period.
- **change in quantity supplied** a movement along a supply curve in response to a change in price.
- **change in supply** a shift of the entire supply curve in response to some other change in the market.
- **market equilibrium** a condition in which the quantity demanded is equal to quantity supplied; there is no tendency for price to change (all other factors held constant); also called just "equilibrium."
- **equilibrium price and quantity** the price and quantity at which the market reaches equilibrium.
- **price system** a market system where supply and demand are free to determine equilibrium prices for all goods and services.
- **surplus** an excess supply greater than demand which occurs when price is higher than equilibrium.
- **shortage** a lack of supply due to supply being less than demand; this condition occurs when price is lower than equilibrium.
- **static versus dynamic models** models which show conditions during a brief period of time versus models which show the effects of some change in market conditions over longer periods of time.
- **price rigidity** a tendency for price to remain constant in spite of the existence of a surplus or shortage.
- **disequilibrium** a condition in which some forces act to prevent the market from reaching equilibrium.
- **price ceiling** a legal limit on how high price can rise.
- **price floor** a legal limit on how low price can fall.
- **rationing function** advantage of the price system in which scarce goods and services are distributed among various uses according to the urgency of wants, as reflected by willingness to pay the price.
- **incentive function** advantage of the price system in which producers are encouraged to produce the goods people want most, as reflected by price.
- **microeconomics** the study of individual markets within the economic system.
- **macroeconomics** the study of how the economy works as a whole.

Questions for Review

1. What determines the "dollar votes" an individual casts in the market place? How does the distribution of "votes" affect a nation's position on its production possibilities curve?

2. Distinguish clearly between a change in demand and a change in quantity demanded. Give examples of both.

3. Indicate whether each of the following is an example of a change in supply or a change in quantity supplied: (a) lack of snow in the Midwest reduces ground water and impairs winter wheat production; (b) removal of embargo against Cuba allows sugar shipments to reach the United States; (c) shortage of coffee leads many consumers to switch to tea and the price of tea rises; (d) slowing rate of population growth causes firms to cut back production of baby foods.

4. How would a government program to purchase food grains affect market demand? Show how changes in government purchases could be used to maintain a stable price in the face of harvests which fluctuate from year to year. Might government sales from accumulated stocks also be useful at some times? Illustrate graphically.

5. What is the significance of a ratio between the value of benefits produced by some enterprise relative to the costs incurred? Give examples of benefit/cost relationships in campus activities or in simple enterprises.

6. Define: market equilibrium, equilibrium price, and price system.

7. In our economy equilibrium is not always reached. What factors may prevent equilibrium?

8. Explain the two functions of prices: the rationing function and the incentive function.

9. Consumer boycotts are often arranged as a means of forcing price reductions for certain items in scarce supply. Sugar, beef, and coffee are recent examples. Explain how boycotts may sometimes have the opposite effect from the one intended.

4

Households,
Business Firms,
and the Circular Flow

Frédéric Bastiat was a French economist who lived in the early nineteenth century. He described a part of the French economy this way:

On entering Paris, which I had come to visit, I said to myself—Here are a million human beings who would all die in a short time if provisions of every kind ceased to flow toward this great metropolis. Imagination is baffled when it tries to appreciate the vast multiplicity of commodities which must enter tomorrow through the barriers in order to preserve the inhabitants from falling prey to the convulsions of famine, rebellion, and pillage. And yet all sleep at this moment, and their peaceful slumbers are not disturbed for a single instant by the prospect of such a frightful catastrophe.

The same could be said of New York City, Des Moines, Iowa, or Kissamee, Florida! Like the inhabitants of Paris, we are all peaceful sleepers most of the time. The market system provides us with the necessities of life and saves us the trouble of thinking about where our breakfasts will come from. But the little market system that each of us inhabits—our local shops, our apartment complex, and our place of employment—is only part of a much larger system, the whole national economy.

The study of the whole national economy is called macroeconomics. Whereas *microeconomics* is concerned with the behavior of buyers and sellers in individual markets, *macroeconomics* is concerned with the behavior of all buyers and sellers in all markets. No matter how well we may be doing in our little individual markets, we are bound to be affected by what happens in the rest of the national economy. The sales of the local hardware store are generally smaller in bad times than in good. This is because the hardware store's customers have less money to spend when times are bad. Some of them have lost their jobs or are working part time. Others, like salesmen, have lost some of their own customers. The sales of the hardware store depend on what is happening to its customers and, in turn, to their customers—many of whom may be far away. Macroeconomics is concerned with everybody's customers, and everybody's employer, and everybody's landlord, all put together—that is, with the aggregates of buyers and sellers in the entire national economy.

Aggregate demand and aggregate supply

Imagine a large arena where many buyers and sellers meet to bargain over goods and services: over ski accommodations, drill presses, doctors' services, pet rocks, life insurance policies—over the entire array of things that are bought and sold. The total demand of all the buyers is called **aggregate demand.** The total supply available to be sold is called **aggregate supply.**

Ideally, aggregate demand would always equal aggregate supply. Everything that is produced would find a buyer. But sometimes demand is too small to purchase all the goods on the market at current prices, and then we are likely to have cutbacks in production and rising unemployment. Sometimes aggregate demand is greater than supply at current market prices; the result may be that the purchasers bid against each other and drive prices up, creating inflation. In 1973–1975, curiously enough we discovered that it is possible to have high rates of unemployment and inflation at the same time. The problems of unemployment and inflation form the core of the study of macroeconomics.

Imagine again the arena where transactions are taking place. Let us try to divide the actors in the arena into two groups: buyers and sellers. We will now discover an important fact that we hadn't noticed before: Most of the people here are involved *both* as buyers *and* as sellers. Most of them are buying from some people and selling to others.

Farmers are buying materials and equipment from manufacturers and selling farm produce to food processors and distributors. Manufacturers are buying materials and equipment from other business firms and selling finished goods to wholesalers and retailers. Even consumers are playing this double game: They buy food and durable goods from retailers and sell their own labor to employers.

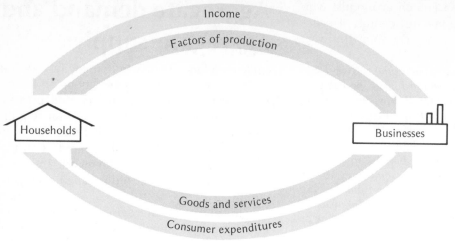

Figure 1 Simplified view of the macroeconomy.

Since buyers are sellers and sellers are buyers, there is a continuous flow of spending among them. The flow of spending is accompanied, in the opposite direction, by a flow of goods and services. We can think of these flows as two loops, one inside the other. At one side of the loops are *business firms*, which receive economic resources and give back finished goods and services. At the other side of the loops are *households*, which receive goods and services and give back economic resources (see Figure 1).

Households

Households are the biggest spenders in our economy, accounting for two-thirds of total spending on output. Furthermore, households are the owners, directly or indirectly, of all economic resources in a capitalist economy. It is households that supply the land, labor, capital, and entrepreneurship to business enterprises and farms. By a household we mean a consuming unit—whether a family, an individual, two or more related persons, or any collection of unrelated persons (such as a commune or a fraternity house) that functions as a decision-making unit.

Households as buyers (consumers)

When households buy goods and services, we call them **consumers.** In ordinary usage the word "consume" suggests eating: We consume beer and pizza, for instance. But in the economic sense we consume everything that we buy for our own use, whether it's an Elton John poster for the wall of our room or a bicycle or a stereo set. The economic action is the purchase. Even if we later throw the item out without using it, we have consumed it so far as the economy is concerned. Purchases for consumption may be divided into three types: durable consumer goods, nondurable consumer goods, and consumer services (see Figure 2).

Durable goods Goods that can be expected to last for a long time, usually for a period of at least a year, are referred to as **durable consumer goods** (or simply **durable goods**). They include automobiles and parts of automobiles, furniture, washing machines, typewriters, and other things we buy to keep and use. In the United States in recent years, spending for durable goods has averaged about one-seventh of total consumer spending. But that is only an average. *Purchases of durable goods can easily be postponed, and when we are short of money or credit we put off buying them.* The old car can be made to go for another year or two. So can the TV set. And we don't really need a microwave

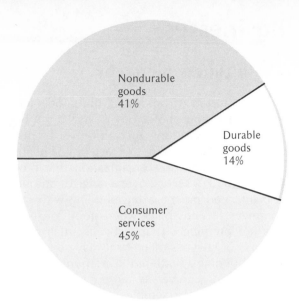

Figure 2 Breakdown of consumer spending for 1976.

oven or a Polaroid camera when times are bad. An important characteristic of durable goods spending is that it fluctuates a good deal, rising during years of prosperity and falling sharply in bad times. It is a key element in the study of business cycles, because when consumers cut back their purchases of durable goods they drive production downward; when they start buying again, they help push production upward.

Nondurable goods Goods that are used up in a short period of time are called **nondurable consumer goods** (or **nondurable goods**). Examples of nondurable consumer goods include food, beverages, clothing, shoes, and gasoline. As our national income has grown, spending for nondurable goods has become a smaller *fraction* of income. The reason, of course, is that our need for nondurables is limited by the capacity of our stomachs and the size of our closets. The same tendency can be seen in other industrialized countries, where spending on nondurables has *declined as a proportion* of total spending. (Of course, total nondurable goods spending rises with a growing middle-class population, but spending on durable goods rises faster.) In the United States nondurables now account for less than half of total spending by consumers. Because the purchase of nondurable goods can't be postponed as easily as the purchase of other things, the demand for them is fairly steady over the course of time, in bad years and good.

Consumer services The fastest growing portion of consumer spending—amounting to more than two-fifths in recent years—consists of **consumer services.** As the name implies, when you purchase a service you get something done to you or for you. Some services are performed by servants—maids, cooks, and cleaning workers. But a ride on a bus or plane, a visit to a movie, a session with a barber or beautician, an appendectomy, or a run down a ski slope also represent the consumption of services. The course in economics you are currently taking is a service, whatever you may think of it; all education, in fact, is services. The provision of shelter is a service also. If you rent, your landlord is providing the service; if you own your own home, you provide the service to yourself.

Economists—especially those studying macroeconomics—often lump all consumer purchases together and call them goods and services. **Goods and services** are just the sum of all durable goods, nondurable goods, and consumer services. Usually goods and services are stated in terms of how much is bought or sold over some time period, like a year.

Households as sellers

The other side of the coin for households is that they sell as well as buy. Even the great army of people who think of themselves as consumers are, in reality, also sellers. Most households own *labor resources* and receive *wages* or *salaries* for selling their labor—the economist's way of saying that they have jobs and go to work. They also own savings which they keep in banks and other financial institutions. Through these institutions the savings are loaned to business for *capital investment;* meanwhile, the households earn *interest* or *dividends* on their savings. Some households own *land resources* for which they receive *rental income.* This may be farmland, mineral deposits, or forest land. Or it may be urban land used for office buildings, theaters, or parking lots. Finally, a smaller group of households own *entrepreneurial resources*—that is, they operate their own business and earn a *profit.* Profit is

Table 1
Households as Sellers

Resource "hired" or provided	Payment
Labor	Wages or salaries
Financial capital	Interest, dividends
Land	Rent
Entrepreneurial resources	Profit

the reward for combining resources into a productive enterprise. Managers and other employees may share in profits through *bonuses*. See Table 1 for a summary of the selling activities of households.

Households usually try to earn as much income as possible with their resources. They look for the best-paying jobs, put their savings where they will earn the most interest, and seek the highest possible returns on their land and entrepreneurial resources. In every case, the return must be high enough to make the undertaking worthwhile. For example, a housewife may decide to go to work if she can earn enough to pay for her clothes, taxes, and carfare with something left over. But if the rewards aren't equal to the unpleasantness of coming home to a messy house with the family to take care of, she may decide to stay home. Or she may decide to rent out rooms instead of taking a job. In that case she will want to receive enough for the rooms to make up for not being able to use them herself. In other words, she will weigh the opportunity costs of her choices. To take still another example, the household may operate its own business, using its labor and entrepreneurial services in return for wages and profit. If, as happens with many small businesses, the returns aren't large enough to compensate for the opportunity costs involved, the household may decide to use its resources in other ways—to sell out and go to work for someone else. The point is that nothing is static or fixed forever. There are always alternative uses for a household's resources, as well as many different ways of spending the income. In our economic system we are constantly choosing among different ways of employing our resources so as to maximize our incomes.

Businesses

The business hierarchy

Plants   The job of producing the goods and services that households buy is carried out by business organizations, in factories or plants. Economists usually refer to a factory as a plant. A **plant** is a compact organization that produces a good or service over a range of output. A plant need not be a big building with tall chimneys. It is any place where goods or services are produced. It may be as small as a doctor's or lawyer's office or it may consist of many buildings scattered over hundreds of acres of land. A university campus is a plant. So is a place that assembles automobiles, or grinds flour, or manufactures shoes.

Firms   Plants are operated and maintained by firms. A **firm** is a complete business organization or enterprise including administration and long-range planning, production, and sales. When people speak of *a business*, they usually mean *a firm*. Consequently, firms are also known as *business firms*. A firm may operate many plants or only one plant. One example of a firm is Standard Oil of New Jersey, which operates many plants for pumping, refining, and distributing petroleum and petroleum products. Another quite different kind of firm is "21" in New York City, which operates a single restaurant for celebrities—and for people who like to watch celebrities.

Industries   All firms producing a particular good or service constitute an **industry.** The petroleum industry includes seven very large firms (often called the Seven Sisters) and many small firms. The telephone communications industry includes one giant (American Telephone and Telegraph Company) and several small independent telephone companies (Winter Park Telephone Company in Winter Park, Florida, for example). The clothing industry and the food service industry include many small and some medium-sized firms.

Industries may be defined broadly as the energy-producing industry, the clothing industry, and the construction industry. Or they may be defined more narrowly as the coal industry, the shoe industry, and the home-building industry.

Sectors A **sector** is a group of industries with some similar characteristics. The manufacturing sector includes all industries engaged in manufacture. Other sectors are the mining sector, the agricultural sector, the service sector, the capital goods sector, etc. (Often it is convenient to speak of the *public sector* and the *private sector* to distinguish activities operated primarily by the government from those operating for private consumption. In addition, economists in macroeconomics like to speak of the household sector, business sector, and government sector.)

Business organization

Business firms differ in form depending on how they are owned and organized. Business firms may be organized in one of three ways: as *single proprietorships*, as *partnerships*, or as *corporations*. These three forms of business firm organization are recognized by the laws of the United States.

The single proprietorship The simplest form of organization is the single proprietorship, owned by one person. The proprietor makes the major decisions. The day-to-day operation may be supervised by a hired manager, or—as is more common—the proprietor may manage the firm personally. The single proprietor usually functions in several capacities, providing not only entrepreneurial services but most of the firm's capital and land resources, and often much of its labor as well. For this reason the proprietor's income usually includes returns for all of these functions: profit for entrepreneurship; interest for the use of financial capital; rent for the land; and wages for the labor (though it will not normally be broken down this way on the firm's expense statement).

Single proprietorships constitute the largest number of United States firms. They are found largely in the services and retail trade, where operations require little capital investment and can be run by a single person. They are the Mom and Pop groceries, the little restaurants, the dentists (some of them), and the shoe repair shops. The single proprietorship offers people the chance to "be their own boss," which is very appealing to anyone who is tired of working as a cog in a big machine.

But the competition is very keen and many of these businesses fail. Furthermore, single proprietorships are subject to *unlimited liability*. The individual proprietor is responsible for settling the debts of the enterprise, even if this means selling his or her personal possessions.

The partnership Sometimes two or more persons may establish a partnership in which they share in the ownership and cooperate in the management. The partnership arrangement enables them to raise more financial capital than they could independently. It may also be a way of combining skills, as when lawyers or doctors with different specialties set up partnerships. This is a common form of business organization in building construction, law, medicine, and financial services. The partnership contract will specify the obligations of each partner, and also what happens if one of them dies or the company goes out of business.

One drawback of the partnership is that each partner is legally responsible for all the debts of the business. In case of failure, the partners' personal assets such as homes, automobiles, securities, and savings accounts may be seized in order to satisfy the obligations of the company.

The corporation To avoid this difficulty, most business firms of any size use the corporation as their form of organization. The corporation is based on the principle of *limited liability*—that is, the owners are liable for the debts of the corporation only to the extent of their stock holdings. If the company fails, the stockholder loses only the amount of money paid for the stock, and the firm's debts have to be paid in other ways if at all (for example, by selling the company's property). In Britain and Canada the word *Limited* or *Ltd.* is added after the name of the firm to show that it is a corporate organization. In the United States we use the word *Incorporated* or *Inc.*

Another peculiar characteristic of the corporation is that, in the eyes of the law, it is a person. It can sue and be sued, and what happens to it in the courts has no bearing on the lives of its owners and managers—unless they themselves have done something illegal. Its owners are the stockholders, who invest their money in return for a share of the profits.

Corporations may issue two basic kinds of stock, *common* and *preferred*. Holders of **preferred stock** are guaranteed a regular, fixed dividend if any dividends are paid at all. Holders of **common stock** are paid dividends only after other obligations (including preferred stock dividends) have been met, and the amount of their dividend usually depends on how well the company is doing. If the corporation is doing very well, the common stock dividends may even be greater than the (fixed) preferred stock dividends. Common stock prices fluctuate widely on the market, depending on present earnings and on what investors think is likely to happen in the future.

Since the holders of both common and preferred stock are legally the owners of the business, they may be entitled to attend stockholders' meetings and vote for a board of directors. The board of directors is responsible for hiring managers to conduct the day-to-day business of the corporation. In theory, common stockholders have the final say on how the business is being run and can vote the directors out if the enterprise has not been profitable. In practice, they seldom take advantage of this right. Most stockholders are too far removed from the operation of the business to have any opinion about it; if they are dissatisfied, the simplest way out is to sell their stock. Holders of large amounts sometimes get together and try to take control of the board, but if the stock is widely held it is difficult for an outside group to get a majority of the votes.

Corporations have other advantages over partnerships and single proprietors. They are continuing operations, unaffected by the deaths of shareholders or changes in stock ownership. And they can more easily raise large sums of money. Money is necessary for capital expansion and for investment in new research and development. A corporation can raise money from (1) its own sales revenues or (2) by borrowing from banks. But the partnerships and single proprietors can also raise money in those two ways. The corporation has a third way: (3) It can issue more shares of stock.

Corporations seldom sell their stock directly to the public. Usually a stock issue will be underwritten by an *investment bank*, which

Viewpoint
Corporate Behavior

The separation of ownership and control provides the strength of the corporate form—and, some say, its potential for harm. Separation allows complete division of labor: stockholders contribute their financial capital when they buy common and preferred stock; managers contribute their special expertise. Because of limited liability, other assets of stockholders are protected from loss in the event of corporate collapse.

Still, the corporate form was slow getting started in the United States. In the early 1800s some states granted corporate charters but placed restrictions on the size and practices of companies. However, with the growth of the railroad, steel, and petroleum industries in the late 1800s, firms sought to expand beyond state lines. New Jersey and Delaware led in chartering enterprises that conduct operations in many states. Both states tried to outdo the other in the leniency of laws regulating corporate behavior. Eventually, New Jersey was earning so much from corporate fees that it was able to eliminate all property taxes and pay off its entire state debt besides. Between 1913 and 1934 almost one-third of state revenues in Delaware came from corporate franchise fees. By 1974, nearly 76,000 corporations were chartered in tiny Delaware; this figure included more than half the nation's largest firms.

Other states have not passed up the opportunity to enrich state revenues through liberal corporation laws. The result has been a wide variety of practices with little consistent supervision of the growth of corporate powers. Furthermore, the theory of shareholder control through corporate democracy has not worked out in practice. Boards of directors are generally composed of corporate executives and others sympathetic to the aims of management. Management's increasing independence from stockholders has produced, in the words of a former corporate board chairman,* "a totalitarian system in industry, particularly in large industry." Corporate behavior came into the spotlight in the mid-1970s with the disclosure of widespread corporate bribery of foreign officials and "customers."

Ralph Nader and the Corporate Accountability Research Group have proposed a remedy to limit corporate power. According to Nader, the solution lies in federal chartering of the nation's largest corporations. Each corporation would still be required to comply with state chartering rules but would be subject to additional federal requirements:

(1) Managers would have to promote corporate democracy by shifting more control to directors and stockholders. Employees and citizens of neighboring communities would be permitted to vote on certain corporate practices.

(2) Firms would be required to disclose practices that are potentially damaging to the environment.

(3) Competition would be strengthened so that consumers might enjoy lower prices, greater product variety, and more innovations.

(4) Consumers, workers, and shareholders would use the courts to protect their rights against unresponsive corporate management.

(5) Finally and perhaps most importantly, the nation's largest corporations would be prohibited from acquiring other firms in highly concentrated industries.

There is precedent for federal chartering of corporations. Banks have been chartered under federal law for more than a century. Federal antimonopoly law would be strengthened by closer supervision of corporate practices. In fact, some restraints on corporate growth might actually reverse current trends toward industrial concentration which, if continued, might lead to complete federal takeover in the future.

Can you think of any arguments against federal licensing of corporations?

* General Robert E. Wood, former Chairman of the Board of Sears, Roebuck and Company.

isn't a bank at all but a company that specializes in marketing new stock issues. The investment bank agrees to take the stock at a certain price and then tries to market it to the public at a profit. Among the chief buyers of new stock issues are insurance companies, mutual funds, retirement funds, and universities which have large sums of money that they want to invest for the dividends they will earn. There is an active market for stocks, especially in years when business is good, because stocks are easy to sell when the holder needs cash. If you put your money into real estate or collections of art, you may not be able to get it out quickly enough. Stocks may also increase in value over a period of years, especially if the firm has been very profitable. When you are able to sell the stock for more than you paid for it, you have made a *capital gain*. Holders of stock can sell through a broker who has a seat on one of the stock exchanges: the New York Stock Exchange, the American Stock Exchange, or a regional stock exchange in one of the large cities.

Circular flow

We have just taken some snapshots of buyers and sellers in the American market economy. Now let's bring them back into the big arena and examine their behavior more closely. It is helpful to view the economy as consisting of flows:

(1) flows of spending from buyers to sellers; and
(2) flows of goods and services from sellers to buyers.

Recall that the "actors" perform both as buyers and sellers. The flows from buyers to sellers and sellers to buyers are continuous and can be visualized as circular. The concept of *circular flow* is a useful aid in analyzing macroeconomic activity (see Figure 3). For example, income is a flow since it is a stream of money received during a period of time, such as a year. The regular appearance of a paycheck is for many people the physical embodiment of the flow. The consumption of goods and services is a flow. Saving is a flow.

Rent, wages, interest and dividends, profit

Resource markets

Land, labor, capital, entrepr.

Households

Businesses

Consumer goods and services

Product markets

Consumer expenditures

Figure 3 The circular flow, emphasizing resource markets and product markets.

Product markets and resource markets

Product markets The chief actors in the arena are households and businesses. The flow of consumption expenditures from households to business firms is shown in the lower loop in Figure 3. The expenditures are tied to a returning flow of goods and services from business to households. The lower loop summarizes the activities in all **product markets** in the economy. It represents the interactions of buyers and sellers in the markets for all durable goods, nondurable goods, and consumer services—for dune buggies, shaving cream, microwave ovens, haircuts, etc. *In product markets, business firms are the important suppliers and households are the important demanders.*

Resource markets But we saw that households are also sellers. They sell their resources to business firms, which buy productive resources of all kinds and pay income for them. The upper loop of Figure 3 shows the flow of productive resources from households to business. Households provide land, labor, capital, and entrepreneurial services to business, receiving in return rent, wages, interest and dividends, and profit.

Where the lower loop represents product markets, the upper loop represents **resource markets.** Economists also call them **factor markets** because resources are the factors of production. The upper loop represents the inter-

actions of buyers and sellers in the markets for farmland, pipefitters, executive vice-presidents, and forklifts. *In resource (factor) markets, business firms are the important demanders while households are the important suppliers.*

Money flows and real flows

At this point we should note that we have been talking about flows of two different things: money on the one hand, goods and services on the other. The outer loop in Figure 3 consists entirely of money payments and is therefore a **money flow.** The inner loop consists entirely of goods and services and resources and so is a **real flow.** The relationships may become clearer if you look at Figure 4. Figures 3 and 4 are simply two ways of looking at the same thing. In macroeconomic analysis we always have these two flows to work with. We must be clear whether we are dealing with the real flow or the money flow. For example, if someone says that the national income has increased by 10% in the last year, does this mean the real flow or only the money flow? If the money flow increases by 10% while the real flow remains the same, we have higher spending for the same quantity of goods. The result is price inflation and few of us are better off. If, on the other hand, the money flow increases by 10% and the real flow by 5%, we still have inflation but we also have an increase in our standard of living. To put this example another way, half of the increased money flow repre-

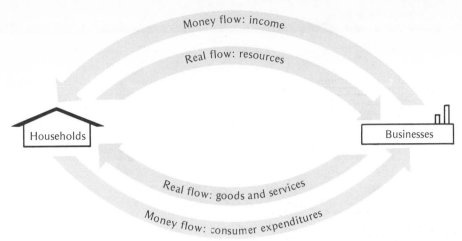

Money flow: income

Real flow: resources

Households

Businesses

Real flow: goods and services

Money flow: consumer expenditures

Figure 4   The circular flow, emphasizing money flows and real flows. Income (shown at top) is the sum of wages, rent, interest and dividends, and profits. Resources (shown near top) are the quantity of land, labor, capital, and entrepreneurship.

sents more real goods and services and half represents only an increase in the price level. We will examine this distinction in more detail later.

Saving and investment

Figure 4 leaves out some important money flows and real flows. Including saving and investment flows will make the circular flow more realistic. Households rarely spend all their incomes. In one way or another they save a portion to be spent later on: for a vacation, perhaps, or a new house or a swimming pool, or for retirement. **Saving** is that portion of income not spent for consumption.

Saving is important to the economy; without it growth would not be possible. If consumers used all their incomes for buying goods and services, we would have a static economy that produced goods only for current consumption. By not spending all their income, households allow some resources to be used for making more capital goods, which will enable the economy to produce more goods and services in the future.

Saving, then, allows funds to be used for investment. **Investment** consists of the funds spent by firms for capital goods. Business firms acquire the investment funds through banks and other financial institutions and use them to hire resources for capital construction—that is, for building new plants and making the equipment to produce new goods. In this way

saving returns to the circular flow in the form of *investment spending*. If all new saving goes into investment, the level of total spending is the same as if all spending had been for consumption.

Thus we have added one more loop to our chart of the circular flow. This can be seen at the bottom of Figure 5, where the stream of household saving flows into the money markets. There is also a stream of business saving, as the chart shows. Like household saving, business saving represents a flow of purchasing power set aside for future needs. In order to make the saving-investment picture complete, Figure 5 also shows the stream of investment spending that flows from the money markets into the business sector.

For total spending in a simple economic system to remain stable, current saving must equal investment spending. Unless all saving returns to the circular flow in the form of investment, the spending flow will shrink. Some goods and services will not be purchased. Production will fall and resources will become unemployed; not all workers, land, capital, and entrepreneurial ability will be put to use. On the other hand, if more investment spending takes place than the current outflow of saving, the entire flow must expand. Spending and production will rise, pressing against the limits of the supply of resources. Such fluctuations in the level of spending and national income constitute one of the major problems of the market system.

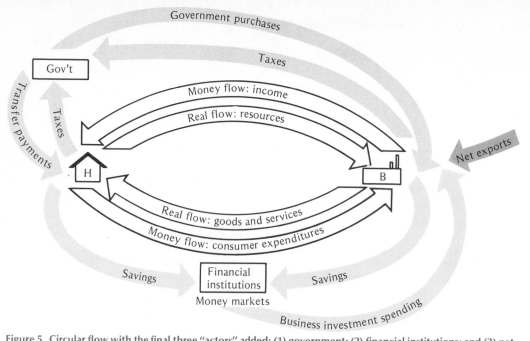

Figure 5 Circular flow with the final three "actors" added: (1) government; (2) financial institutions; and (3) net exports.

Taxes and government expenditures

Let us make one more change in our chart of the circular flow by introducing government activities. Government affects the economy through taxing and spending. As shown at the top of Figure 5, taxes are collected from households and business. Taxes reduce the amounts that households and business have available for spending. But government purchases of goods and services return the spending power to the circular flow. Government uses its tax revenues to buy goods of all kinds, as well as to buy the services of police, firemen, military personnel, education and health workers, agricultural and environmental scientists, and many other workers. In the United States, purchases of goods and services by state, local, and federal governments in 1976 totaled $366 billion, or more than one-fifth of the yearly national output. In Figure 5 government expenditures are shown as an inflow of new spending, increasing aggregate demand. Government expenditures include only

purchases of goods and services from current production. Some government payments are not paid in return for goods and services and are not included. Examples are unemployment compensation, welfare assistance, and Social Security payments. They are called *transfer payments* and are not included in government purchases of goods and services.

As long as government expenditures are equal to tax revenues, there will be no net loss to the circular flow. If government spends less than it collects in taxes, the circular flow will tend to shrink. If it spends more than it collects, the circular flow will tend to expand. We will see later, when we study fiscal policy, that variations in taxes and government expenditures are a means of changing the level of total spending. The influence of government on the circular flow is one remedy for the problems of inflation and unemployment.

Foreign expenditures

One more item needs to be added to our chart of the circular flow. Some spending in the United States economy comes from abroad. Foreigners spend money for such things as

American soybeans, computers, and management scientists. At the same time, Americans spend money for things made in other countries, including cameras, chocolate, automobiles, and ocean cruises.

Exports to other countries mean we must manufacture more goods, and therefore exports increase the flow of spending. Conversely, imports into our country represent goods not being manufactured here, and thus imports decrease the flow of spending. To make things simpler, we will combine these two opposite flows of spending into one flow. We do this by subtracting the outward flow (for imports) from the inward flow (for exports), getting what we call *net exports* or *net foreign investment* (see Figure 5). When the value of imports exceeds the value of exports, net exports are negative. This means that the circular flow shrinks, since purchasing power is leaving the economy. Net exports account for only a small part of spending in the American economy, but our economy is so large that even a small part is important in world trade.

Flows and stocks

We have been describing the movement of goods and services between buyers and sellers as a flow. In more generalized terms, we can define a **flow** as a movement or change over time—including an increase or decrease—of any quantity. Common examples of flows are the flow of water from a faucet or the draining of water from a bathtub or the use of an accelerator pedal in an automobile to control the flow of gasoline to the engine.

Flow problems are very important to economics and are frequently encountered. *Income, an amount of money received in a given period, is a flow.* The regular appearance of a paycheck is for many people an example of this flow. Consumption of goods and services is a flow. Saving is likewise a flow. Depositing savings in a bank or buying United States savings bonds is an example of a saving flow.

It is important to distinguish between a flow of some quantity and a stock. A **stock** is a measure of something which has accumulated, changing only when more flows in or out. The amount of gasoline in an auto tank at any one moment is a stock, as is the amount of water in a bathtub. The amount of money in a savings account is a stock. *Wealth is a total of one's assets and is a stock.* (Notice this distinction between wealth and income.)

Combining the concepts of stock and flow in an example will illustrate the difference. Suppose a worker opens a savings account in January with a $50 deposit and saves $60 per month thereafter. By March $170 has accumulated in the savings account and by June, $350. The original stock grows with each regular monthly flow of $60. The stock is $170 in March and $350 in June. In summary, the stock is the total amount accumulated at any one time, while the flows are the periodic deposits or withdrawals—that is, the movements of money. Stocks and flows are most meaningful when measured. We measure spending flows as an indication of the current level of economic activity.

Changes in the circular flow

Short-term fluctuations

The circular flow provides a means of measuring the level of economic activity. Over short periods of time the activity of buyers and sellers may rise or fall. The result is short-term fluctuations in national income and output around the long-term trend in economic activity. When buying and selling activity falls, employment drops and fewer goods and services are produced. When buying activity rises, sellers attempt to satisfy consumers' growing demands for goods and services. To increase output is only possible if there is excess capacity for use in production. Once all productive capacity is in use, sellers can set higher prices for their limited output and the nation experiences rising prices (inflation).

Short-term fluctuations in the size of the circular flow have characterized the United States economy for its entire two hundred years. Fluctuations in economic activity can mean serious underutilization or overutilization of our valuable resources. Over the long term, however, the trend in economic activity has been upward. Over two centuries we have increased the quantity and quality of productive resources and we have increased the value of production traded in the marketplace.

Growth and the circular flow

Adam Smith saw how a free market system would contribute to growth and help people live better. A primitive economy conducts few activities in the marketplace. Families are largely self-sufficient, producing all their household needs. There is little need for buying and selling. But as an economy grows, certain individuals and groups become specialists in particular types of production. Through specialization and *division of labor* they become more skilled, and total production rises. With their rising incomes these specialists are able to save and invest in capital resources. Total production rises even faster. All this would become possible as markets grow. More buyers in the market made economic activity more profitable for sellers. Then specialization and capital investment could take place. In this view a growing population could help increase production.

A later economist, Thomas Malthus, had a more pessimistic view of growth, especially the effect of population growth. For any nation, certain resources are fixed in quantity. Land is an important resource for many of the activities included in the circular flow; but the quantity of land available for expanding production is fairly limited. As the number of buyers and sellers increased, Malthus predicted that the scarcity of land would restrict growth in production. The level of economic activity could increase only so far; then any further increases in population would mean misery and starvation for some. Malthus felt that even capital investment and technological change could not prevent the inevitable: he predicted that the world's population would finally live under conditions of extreme hardship, war, and starvation.

David Ricardo's view of a limit to growth was similar. Ricardo stressed the importance of capital investment to growth. However, Ricardo felt that capital investment must inevitably decline, causing growth to cease. Why? The increasing scarcity of land would force up land rents and reduce business profits. With declining profits, business could not afford capital investments. Again, the result would be stagnation in production and a natural limit to growth. The circular flow would no longer expand.

Declining profits also provided the basis for Karl Marx's predictions of doom for free market economies. In his view falling profits would lead competitive firms to install labor-saving equipment. In this way they could reduce production costs. But they would also reduce the incomes of wage earners who were expected to buy the output of farms and factories. As buyers disappeared from the circular flow, the level of economic activity would fall drastically. Amid increasing hardship and conflict, the entire system would collapse.

Each of the early economists has something to contribute to current thinking about the problem of growth in economic activity. Analysts throughout the world have expressed growing concern about the problems of population growth, declining capital investment, and insufficient incomes. And we all worry about the effects of economic growth on the world's supplies of critical resources. By studying the various components of the circular flow, we can understand the problems of growth. This will be a subject for macroeconomics.

Business accounting

Business accountants have developed systems for measuring flows and stocks at the level of the individual firm. The firm needs up-to-date information about money flows of receipts and expenditures and real flows of materials and finished goods. The firm is also concerned about the stocks of assets owned by the firm.

Accounting statements for measuring flows and stocks are called, respectively, *Income Statements* and *Balance Sheets*. We will examine each of these statements in some detail. Then we will show how the information contained on these individual statements can be combined to measure flows and stocks for the entire national economy.

The income statement

A firm's **income statement** measures the *flow* of receipts and expenditures within the company. It begins with the gross revenue received (1) and then shows the various costs of production for the period (2). At the end it gives the amount left after all costs have been deducted (3). This is the amount available for paying taxes and for distribution to stockholders. A hypothetical income statement for Wonderland Resort appears as Table 2.

The first item of interest is Gross Revenue from Operations. This represents the total receipts from sales of goods or services. As such, it tells us not only how much money the firm has received but the value of Wonderland's output. Notice that Gross Revenue from Operations is the individual firm's portion of the lower loop of our macroeconomic circular flow.

Most of Wonderland's production costs are out-of-pocket payments made to the suppliers of resources: land, labor, and capital. One important cost is not paid to a supplier in the current period. **Depreciation** on capital represents the estimated cost of the plant and equipment which wears out during each production period. It is a cost of current production even though an out-of-pocket payment is not made. A firm must allow for the fact that machinery, buildings, vehicles, and other capital equipment are used up over a period of years. To do this, the firm assumes that a certain amount of depreciation takes place each year. This makes it necessary to set aside a sum of money each year in order to replace the capital equipment when it is worn out. Firms generally estimate the usable life of each piece of equipment, and then arrive at some reasonable figure to be set aside each year (in this case, one-tenth of the equipment's original cost) for capital depreciation. It is set aside in a special account, thus creating a fund for eventual replacement of the equipment. This is an element of business saving, corresponding to the saving that a household does when it sets aside money to buy a new car.

When total costs including depreciation have been deducted from income, the result is Net Income from Operations or operating profit. In our country, corporations have to pay income taxes just as people do, and the tax bite may be almost 50 percent of profits. Deducting this amount, we are left with Net Profit After Taxes. Part of the net profit goes to stockholders in the form of Dividends (4). How this flow is distributed among stockholders depends on the kind of stock they hold. Preferred stockholders are paid first at a prescribed rate, and common stockholders are paid from what is left of net profits (which may mean that they get more than the preferred stockholders if it has been a profitable year but often means that they get less). Since most common stockholders buy stock with the expectation of partici-

Table 2
Income Statement for Wonderland Resort, Incorporated
January 1, 1978 to December 31, 1978

(1)	Gross Revenue from Operations		$1,000,000
(2)	Operating Expenses:		
	Administrative Salaries	$150,000	
	Wages to Production Workers	425,000	
	Contributions to Social Insurance	25,000	
	Costs of Materials	75,000	
	Property Rentals	23,000	
	Interest on Bank Loans	17,000	
	Total Out-of-Pocket Expenses	−715,000	
	Depreciation on Capital Equipment @ 1/10 ($800,000)	80,000	
	Total Expenses	−795,000	−795,000
(3)	Net Income From Operations		205,000
	Income Taxes Payable (48%)		−98,400
	Net Profit After Taxes		106,600
(4)	Dividends Paid to Stockholders		−50,000
(5)	Retained Earnings: to Surplus		$ 56,600

pating in the profits of the firm, management tries to pay dividends regularly. People sometimes pay more for the stock of firms that pay good dividends; and high stock prices make it easier to raise funds with new stock issues when the company wants to expand.

Not all the firm's profit will be paid out in dividends. The remainder will be held in the corporation as a source of funds for future growth. Stockholders like to see the firm grow, because growth is likely to raise the value of their shares. Good managers, of course, like to be associated with growing firms. Business saving for growth is called Retained Earnings (5) or undistributed profits.

The firm's income statement is a record of flows: flows received from the sale of its output and flows paid for the use of productive resources. The national income statistics published by the U.S. Department of Commerce combine the income statements of all firms producing for final sale, thereby enabling us to see how the whole economy allocates its funds. Since the circular flow is the basis of the whole study of macroeconomics and of national fiscal and monetary policy, understanding income statements of firms is very useful.

The balance sheet

Business firms also use the balance sheet. A **balance sheet** is an accounting statement that measures the value of the enterprise at a certain point in time. In contrast to the income statement, which is a measure of *flows*, the balance sheet is a measure of the *stock* of assets

owned by the firm. It shows the value of all the property of the firm, including land, buildings, equipment, cash, and bank deposits. It is called a *balance sheet* because the total value of assets and the total claims against them must be equal. Table 3 shows a hypothetical balance sheet for Wonderland Resort. The *left side* of the balance sheet shows the value of assets the firm *owns*. The *right side* may be considered the amounts the firm *owes*—that is, the total liabilities or claims (including those of stockholders) against its assets.

Among its assets (1), the value of Wonderland's buildings and equipment is the largest item. The firm also owns a small amount of financial assets in various forms: cash and a checking account for immediate needs and a savings account which can be drawn on for extraordinary needs. The sum of Wonderland's assets is $1,416,000.

Claims against the firm's assets are of two types. Liabilities or debt claims (2) are promises to pay the firm's creditors. They are the firm's IOUs issued to the bank and to suppliers who have delivered food, linens, water, electric power, and other materials for operations. If the firm were to go out of business, it would have to sell its assets and pay all debt claims first before any other claims were satisfied. This action is called *liquidation*. The firm would liquidate its assets and pay the funds received to its creditors. It is important that the value of assets be greater than the value of its debt claims. Otherwise the firm is said to be *insolvent*. Fortunately, Wonderland's debt claims are only $160,000.

Table 3
Wonderland Resort, Incorporated
December 31, 1977

(1) Assets		(2) Liabilities (or Debt Claims)	
Buildings and Equipment	$1,250,000	Bank Loan	$ 150,000
Land	150,000	Accounts Payable to Suppliers	10,000
Cash on Hand	1,000	Liabilities	160,000
Checking Account	5,000		
Savings Account	10,000	**(3) Net Worth**	
		Capital (or Equity Claims)	1,000,000
		Surplus and Reserves	256,000
		Total Net Worth	1,256,000
Total Assets	**$1,416,000**	**Total Liabilities**	**$1,416,000**

The largest claims against the assets of Wonderland Resort are the equity or ownership claims of its stockholders included as part of its net worth (3). When Wonderland began operation, it issued a million shares of common stock at $1 each. The one-million-dollar capital together with a bank loan enabled it to purchase the land and construct its resort facilities. Over the years, operations have been profitable. The firm has gradually reduced its bank loan and has consistently paid dividends to its shareholders. Each year it has set aside an allowance for depreciation and has retained some of its earnings after taxes and dividends. As a result, the total value of the firm's assets has grown to be larger than the sum of its debt and equity claims. The difference between total assets and total liabilities and stockholders' equity appears on the balance sheet as the firm's surplus. Adding surplus to the right side of the Balance Sheet ensures that the total values on each side will indeed balance.

The third group of items on the balance sheet (3) represents a firm's net worth: the net value of its assets after all debt claims have been paid. The **net worth** is the amount which would be available for the stockholders if the firm were to liquidate. The firm's net worth of $1,256,000 would be divided among its shareholders. Each of the one million stock certificates would be worth $1.25 if the firm were to liquidate its assets.

Capital investment Wonderland's balance sheet helps us notice another important business activity. We have used the circular flow to show the flow of money expenditures from households to business and the flow of money income from business to households. We have also shown the real flows of goods and services and productive resources. The balance sheet helps us see how business uses investment funds to expand the stock of capital equipment.

Wonderland has been a profitable enterprise. Ski accommodations are in great demand. The firm meets competition by providing a quality service. It uses the most efficient means available to keep its costs down. It makes interest and loan payments regularly and pays healthy dividends to its stockholders. The profitability of the enterprise leads its management to consider proposals for expansion into new ski slopes higher up the mountain.

The firm's good reputation at the local bank persuades the bank loan officer to recommend a new loan. Bank officials agree to provide $150,000 in new loans for the proposed expansion. An investment bank agrees to sell $500,000 additional shares of stock in return for a small commission. The new loan and stock sales provide $650,000 for investment in new productive facilities: a new modern ski-lift, a clubhouse and restaurant at the summit, and a heated indoor swimming pool.

How does this appear on the circular flow? The savings of households provide the means for bank loans and stock sales. Saving is an outflow from spending as households purchase fewer consumer goods and services. Wonderland's investment is an inflow of new spending—spending for construction and equipment which will make the firm more productive in the future.

As this process is repeated many times in many other industries, the American economy grows. The increase in the stock of capital resources helps move our production possibilities curve out to the right. Households receive greater money income and greater *real* income. Business enterprise grows and provides greater job opportunities for qualified workers entering the job market each year.

Summary

Macroeconomics is the study of the activities of all buyers and sellers together in the nation's economy.

Aggregate demand is the sum of all purchases of goods and services. Aggregate supply is the sum of all final output produced in the economy. Households purchase durable and nondurable consumer goods and services. Households also sell their land, labor, capital, and entrepreneurial resources to business; in return they receive income: rent, wages, interest and dividends, and profit.

Business produces output for sale. Business firms differ in organization depending on how they are owned and managed: a single proprietorship, a partnership, or a corporation. Corporations have limited liability and can acquire investment funds through the issue of new common or preferred stock.

Flows of money expenditures and flows of real goods and real resources are combined in a circular flow. The circular flow represents the sum of all individual microeconomic decisions in product markets and resource markets. The size of the money flow depends on the level of total spending for the economy. The size of the real flow is limited by the nation's stock of productive resources. Some income drains from the circular flow in the form of saving, but it may return as business investment spending. Other income drains out in the form of taxes, but it may return as government expenditures for real goods and services. Foreign purchases also enter the circular flow.

The long-term trend in the circular flow has been upward, but there have been frequent fluctuations above or below the long-term trend. Adam Smith, Thomas Malthus, David Ricardo, and Karl Marx have made predictions about the possible effects of long-term growth and the ultimate fate of our economic system.

A firm's income statement measures the flows of receipts and spending for productive resources. A firm's balance sheet measures the stock of productive capital available at any time. New business investment spending adds to the stock of capital. A consolidated income statement for all firms producing for final sale would show the circular flow of spending and incomes in the macroeconomy.

Key Words and Phrases

- **aggregate demand** total demand for all finished goods and services.
- **aggregate supply** total supply of all finished goods and services.
- **households** arrangements of people, either as groups (families) or as single individuals, who function as a single consuming unit.
- **consumers** people who purchase the nation's output of goods and services.

- **durable consumer goods** goods which are expected to last at least a year.
- **nondurable consumer goods** goods which are expected to last less than a year.
- **service** a useful product of labor which is not tangible but provides some benefit to the buyer; examples are education, a bus trip, a haircut.
- **wages and salaries** payments to households who provide labor for use in production.
- **interest or dividends** payments to households who provide financial capital for use in production.
- **rental income** payments to households who provide land for use in production.
- **profit** payments to households who provide entrepreneurship for use in production.
- **plant** a single productive facility.
- **firm** a complete business organization, including administration, production, and sales.
- **industry** all firms producing a particular good or service.
- **sector** a group of industries with similar characteristics.
- **single proprietorship** a business firm owned by a single individual.
- **partnership** a business firm owned by more than one individual.
- **corporation** a business firm owned by stockholders.
- **limited liability** a condition in which owners of stock are not held liable for the debts of the corporation.
- **preferred stock** a stock certificate which entitles the holder to receive regular specified dividends if any dividends are paid at all.
- **common stock** a stock certificate which entitles the holder to vote in stockholder meetings and to receive dividends at the discretion of management.
- **board of directors** a group of decision-makers decided upon by vote of the stockholders of a corporation.
- **investment bank** a financial institution which engages in marketing new issues of corporate stock.
- **capital gain** an increase in the value of a share of stock from the time of buying to the time of selling.
- **stock exchange** a market for exchange of stock certificates.
- **circular flow** a movement of funds from buyers to sellers and of real goods and services in exchange.

- **product markets** markets for the exchange of finished goods and services.
- **resource or factor markets** markets for the exchange of economic resources for use in production.
- **money flow** the flow of money spending from buyers to sellers.
- **real flow** the flow of goods and services from sellers to buyers.
- **saving** the portion of household income which is not spent for consumer goods and services.
- **investment** business spending to increase the nation's stock of capital goods.
- **taxes** regular payments to government.
- **government expenditures** government spending for the purchase of goods and services.
- **net exports** the excess of foreign spending in domestic markets (exports) over domestic spending in foreign markets (imports).
- **flow** a movement of some economic variable over a period of time.
- **stock** the accumulated value of some economic variable at a particular point in time.
- **income statement** a list of the flow of funds to and from a business firm over a particular period of time.
- **balance sheet** a list of the accumulated value of economic variables within a firm at a particular point in time.
- **assets and liabilities** the value of things the firm owns and the value of things the firm owes.
- **liquidation** a process of selling a firm's assets in order to satisfy its liabilities.
- **insolvent** a condition in which the value of a firm's assets is less than the value of its liabilities.

- **depreciation** the loss in value of an asset (such as a capital good or durable good) as it wears out.
- **net worth** the excess value of a firm's assets over the value of its liabilities.

Questions for Review

1. List the four major components of aggregate demand along with the subcategories of each. Then give examples of each type of spending.

2. How are opportunity costs significant in determining the incomes of the four classes of productive resources?

3. Outline the principal forms of business organization with the advantages and disadvantages of each. Give current examples of each type.

4. Distinguish between capital resources and financial capital. At what point does saving actually become investment?

5. What are "flows" and "stocks" as they are related to economic life? Under what circumstances is it appropriate to measure flows and under what circumstances, stocks? When are capital resources flows and when are they stocks?

6. Show how a firm's Income Statement is similar to statements of aggregate national income. How are they different?

7. Define: investment bank, capital gain, depreciation.

8. The table below lists approximate spending in the United States for selected years. Calculate the relative shares of each group in total spending. Comment on your results.

Year	Total spending	Consumer spending	Business investment spending	Government spending	Net foreign spending
1946	$ 210	$ 144	$ 31	$ 27	$8
1956	421	266	71	80	4
1966	753	465	124	159	5
1976	1692	1077	242	366	7

Note: All dollar figures are in billions of dollars.

5

The Role of Government

Remember the story of Robinson Crusoe? He was the shipwrecked adventurer who washed ashore on a deserted Caribbean island. Through hard work and intelligence, Crusoe fashioned his little island into a virtual economic paradise. He did it almost entirely alone: No one told him when to work, what crops to grow, or how to grow them. Crusoe did as he pleased, when he pleased, with only Nature to obey. Crusoe was an economically and socially free individual.

Economic theory generally assumes that individual buyers and sellers in the marketplace act as freely as did Crusoe on his island. For example, economic theory assumes that when you buy a car, you do so because *you* want to. The salesman sells to you because *he* wants to. No one forces you to buy or him to sell. Economic theory assumes that *all* buyers and sellers act out their economic desires with virtually complete freedom of choice.

Yet this is a most unrealistic assumption! Unlike Robinson Crusoe, we are members of a society. As such, we cannot act—economically or any other way—with complete freedom. As a famous Supreme Court Justice put it: "One man's freedom to swing his fist ends where another man's nose begins." The point is that in society one individual's actions may often affect a neighbor. This is all the more so as populations increase and distances between nations and peoples "diminish." A tension arises, a tension between individual freedom and social responsibility. To regulate this tension we need a powerful force. This force is government.

Government is really no more than a set of rules and the power to see that the rules are obeyed. The rules and power differ among societies and over the centuries. Sometimes kings hold all the power. Sometimes elite committees do. In societies such as ours power is placed in the hands of the voters, who in turn consist of the entire adult society. The elected officials, acting as agents of the voters, wield the power.

The ultimate rule book in our society is the U.S. Constitution. All national laws flow from it. The wonder of the Constitution is its flexibility. Thus old laws may be eliminated or modernized and new laws passed, depending upon what changing circumstances require.

By eliminating, changing, or creating laws, government plays a major role in the functioning of our economy. Sometimes the importance is obvious, as when the government spends billions of dollars to fight a war. Sometimes the importance is subtle, as when laws are passed to regulate working conditions in factories or to restrain environmental pollution.

Economic functions of government

This chapter will examine a number of government's important economic functions. We shall examine some of the things government does and discover how it raises the funds to carry out its responsibilities. Because government plays an important part in the economy's performance, and because our economic lives affect our social, cultural, and political lives, understanding government's economic functions is especially important.

So, let us leave Robinson Crusoe's complete liberty on a tropical island and look into the role of government.

Life, liberty, and property

Our political and economic system rests fundamentally upon the institution of private property. This is an important ingredient of economic freedom. Unless individuals own and control resources, they cannot choose between buying and selling or between producing and consuming. If you don't own your bank account, you cannot choose to purchase a car. If the car salesman does not own the car, he cannot choose to sell it to you.

Therefore, one of the most important economic functions of government in our economic system is to protect property. Government protects individual citizens' property against other citizens who might wish to take it.

You can readily see the importance of this protection. Imagine, for example, how difficult it would be to produce and consume goods and services if bandits and looters were free to steal and ravage. Time and energy which could be used to produce goods would be wasted instead of combating the robbers and looters. (As a leading TV detective said in explaining to a merchant why merchants must pay taxes: "You pay taxes to the bad guys to keep the badder guys off your back." Baretta.)

One important point worth understanding is that property rights are a fundamental and necessary part of any and *all* economic systems. Our system differs from that of Russia and the socialist countries in our greater emphasis on *private property* and *personal freedom* as opposed to *communal property* and *social responsibility*.

In simple societies it is clear what property is. Pigs and horses, beads and bits of gold— such things comprise typical estates in primitive tribes. But in complex societies like ours, property is often symbolized by contracts. *Contracts* are agreements to perform certain activities and to pay specific amounts. The agreement to buy a car on time is a contract. You agree to pay monthly installments; the seller agrees to deliver the car. If either of you violates the terms of the contract, the deal is off.

Laws ensuring the sanctity of contracts are fundamentally laws to protect property. If both parties agree to terminate the agreement, then a satisfactory arrangement must be worked out to protect the interests of both parties. For example, divorce proceedings are terminations of marriage contracts. Lawyers argue to a judge how property of the couple should be divided, and how future commitments are to be met. Neither side may like the judge's final ruling. But a neutral arbitrator is surely preferable to a more violent resolution of a conflict. Once the ruling is made, both parties can turn their minds away from wrangling and towards more constructive activity.

Protection of property extends to transactions even where there is no formal contract. During this century, government in this country has moved to protect property in ways that surely would have seemed strange to earlier generations. Let us mention a few examples.

Product safety   In the early 1900s the meat-packing industry in this country was free to produce virtually any kind of meat products it wanted to. And it was free to produce them any way it pleased. But when investigators discovered that the quality of the products and the production conditions behind them were harmful to the consuming public, government began regulating the meat-packing industry. A regulatory agency was set up to establish product standards and to require that producers clearly state on each product exactly what it contains. Today this governmental body is known as the *Food and Drug Administration* (FDA). It is responsible for protecting the public against all potentially harmful foodstuffs and drugs. More recent examples of government regulation by the FDA are the ban on cyclamates in diet soft drinks and the ban on thalidomide in tranquilizers; both chemicals were found to be potentially harmful. The individual consumer could not have discovered this until it was too late.

There are, however, products other than food and drugs that can be harmful to consumers. So other federal agencies have developed to supplement the actions of the FDA. For example, defective wiring in Christmas tree lights, flammable baby clothing, and unsafe working conditions are just a few of the many areas that come under the review of government agencies.

False advertising   A second example of the need for government action and regulation concerns false advertising. When a zealous manufacturer claims a product is something it really is not and a consumer purchases the product, then the consumer has been wronged. Another governmental agency, the *Federal Trade Commission* (FTC), is charged with seeing that advertisers tell the consuming public the truth about the products they sell. A famous recent case involved advertisements from trade schools. The schools were said to be making false claims about the jobs their graduates could expect to find. In order to protect potential students, the FTC closed down some schools and required the rest to give the true picture of their graduates' employment.

When the government interferes in such cases as food and drug production and advertising, the industries involved may lobby against the new rules. They argue they are free under the Constitution to do and say what they please.

Sometimes they have a point. But as society becomes more complex and as technology improves, individual buyers become generally less qualified to evaluate the products they buy. How can an average consumer judge the effects on the body by cyclamates in soft drinks? How can factory workers be sure the factory's fire escape will work in case of a fire? How can you be sure the water you drink does not contain toxic particles and gases?

Of course, the average consumer often cannot judge. Therefore, governmental agencies—from the Federal Trade Commission to local building inspectors and water commissioners—are established to protect the property of citizens. After all, the human body is the ultimate property!

Money

Our economic system also relies upon the institution of money. Money is the means to accumulate many of the items of property which government protects. Thus the government must establish a system of money which facilitates exchange and provides the incentives to produce. Loosely speaking, we can define **money** as anything that serves as a medium of exchange. Later we will see that money has other characteristics, but exchange is the most important.

Money systems have developed over the centuries to overcome the disadvantages of barter systems. Barter exchange takes place in terms of *physical* goods. Barter requires a "double coincidence of wants." You can exchange an item only if you find your "double" who wants what you have to trade and who has what you want.

For example: You have a car and want a sailboat. You must find someone who has a sailboat and wants a car. And not just any sailboat and car: your double must like *your* car, and you must like *his* sailboat. What if you can't immediately find a "double"? Then perhaps you can find someone who wants your car but has a stereo to trade. But maybe he knows someone who has a sailboat and wants a stereo. Or someone who knows a fourth person who has a house and wants a stereo and. . . . You get the idea how difficult bartering can be. The chances of finding your ideal "double" are very low.

The beauty of money is that money can be used to *symbolize* physical goods. Money is a symbol of value or a store of value. A check for $2,000 can symbolize a sailboat. Or a car. Or a stereo. Or a house. Or any number of things. With money you need no longer find your "double." Rather you must find someone who will pay $2,000 for your car. Then you can find someone with a sailboat going for $2,000.

In a word, money makes trade easier and therefore broadens the areas of exchange. Visit an anthropology museum and you will see some very strange money symbols used in primitive communities. Some societies have used rare shells. Others have used human bones. Still others have employed huge stones. The use of money helped them to avoid the inconvenience of barter.

But money brings with it difficulties, too. The problem with money is that it doesn't work unless it is accepted. What if you traded your car for ten shells, but the fellow who had the sailboat would only accept six giant rocks? You wouldn't be much better off than under a barter system.

To overcome this difficulty, governments have tried to *standardize* their nation's money and establish money symbols that people would accept. Some early standard moneys were precious metals, such as gold or silver. These metals had several advantages: They were not overly abundant, they could be stamped into coins and easily transported, and they could be divided easily into smaller and smaller units. Thus one material—gold or silver—could symbolize many different goods with equal value. But above all, precious metals were widely accepted, not just between town merchants but between countries as well.

Even precious metals have their disadvantages, however. Chief among these was their scarcity. As economies grew, the need for more money grew; but supplies of gold and silver grew more slowly and irregularly. In the 1600s banks began to issue paper money to symbolize gold and silver. As the level of production and exchange continued to grow, governments also issued paper money along with precious metals. With the twentieth century, paper currencies have almost completely replaced precious metal currencies.

And as you might expect, paper money has brought its difficulties. Paper and ink are cheap. Who is to regulate the supply of paper money?

This is the job of government. Government guarantees to citizens that the money in circulation is genuine, and so can be used without fear of fraud. In addition, government decides how much money is to be supplied to the economy and when the supply is to change. By regulating the supply, government helps to maintain the value of money and thus its acceptability in exchange. The entire history and philosophy of money are indeed complex and form an important part of macroeconomics. But one thing is obvious: Government's responsibility to maintain a healthy monetary system is fundamental to our nation's productivity and growth. The regulation of money is one of government's most important economic functions.

Public goods and services

Thus far we have spoken of two basic economic functions of government. These are protection of property and regulation of money. Once these responsibilities are carried out, you might expect that individual buyers and sellers, acting freely in the marketplace, can carry out the task of producing and allocating the goods and services a modern economy needs.

But this is not quite so. There are two categories of goods and services: Private goods and services and public goods and services. The difference is the result of an important fact about consumption: Consumption of some goods and services is exclusive while consumption of others is nonexclusive. **Private goods and services** are usually "exclusive in consumption," that is, they benefit only their possessor or owner. **Public goods and services** are usually "nonexclusive in consumption," that is, they benefit many. For this reason they are sometimes called *social goods and services.* This is an important concept and can best be understood through an example.

Suppose you buy a car. The benefits of ownership accrue to you, exclusively. *You* get the benefits, not your next-door neighbor. Your car is exclusive in consumption. Similarly if you buy a hockey ticket, stereo system, trip to Mexico, and so on, the benefits of the exchange are enjoyed by you. You are willing to pay the price of these items because you are ensured of exclusivity in consumption. As a result, pricing and production of these goods and services are determined in the market. The intersections of many private demand curves with market supply curves determine market equilibrium.

However, you should be well aware that some goods are nonexclusive. For example, suppose you are a sailor and live by a harbor. There is a shoal outside your harbor, around which you must sail without running aground. The shoal is difficult to see at high tide. To remind yourself where it is, suppose you spend your own money and time to build a marker above it. Now you can sail in at day's end, see the marker, and avoid the shoal. You get the benefits of your investment in the marker.

But the benefits are *not* yours exclusively. Soon all the other sailors realize the importance of *your* marker and use it to navigate their own boats. *They* get the benefits, too, even though *you* made the purchase. You cannot stop them from seeing the marker. So you cannot keep the marker's benefits to yourself, exclusively. The consumption of the marker is nonexclusive. It is shared socially. Your marker is a private good, but it might just as well be considered a public good since so many share in its benefits.

The pricing of private goods is a job handled by the marketplace. Buyers and sellers of cars meet and individually agree on a price for cars. You pay the price, you get the benefits. But herein lies the problem of public goods. The whole society enjoys the benefits, and no single individual wants (or is able) to bear the costs. Go back to the example of the marker. One expenditure—yours—provided benefits for all sailors. They got a good deal: Their safety for your money with no expenditure on their part. On the other hand, you got a worse deal: You paid for everyone. The benefits to a single individual may not be as great as the cost of providing the public good. This is where the government enters the picture.

When some goods and services are nonexclusive in consumption, the total benefits to society justify spreading the cost over all citizens. No single individual should be responsible for providing goods and services to be enjoyed by all. Moreover, because no citizen can be excluded from enjoying the benefits, there are no individual demand curves to determine price and output for public goods. In brief, the marketplace cannot determine the price or output of public goods. If the market cannot, who can? The answer, of course, is government. Through our elected representatives we decide on the goods and services we would like to consume as a community. If a local community decides a new water-treatment plant is needed, local officials tax the entire community to pay for the plant. Or if the nation decides collectively that national defense goods and services are necessary, then our Congress taxes all of us to provide the armies and weapons we need. You can think of any number of public goods and services, from fire and police protection to port facilities and city streets. And you can see the price you pay for them when you pay your taxes.

Spending for public goods and services is the way society allocates resources toward the public sector. Through democratic processes we agree to refrain from private consumption by the amount of taxes we pay. Then we agree that these tax revenues will be used for public, not private, consumption. We move along our production possibilities curve toward greater production for the public sector and less production for the private sector.

Social costs

Public goods and services are those whose *benefits* are nonexclusive in consumption. Government takes over production and pricing decisions for these goods and services. *Costs* of goods and services are sometimes nonexclusive also and it is government's responsibility to regulate these costs.

Suppose an oil tanker uses faulty equipment to unload its cargo and spills its crude oil into the waters off your beach. The polluted water is a cost borne by you and all other sailors and swimmers in the area. The cost of the tanker operation, in other words, is nonexclusive.

Some economic costs are imposed exclusively on the producing firm. Suppliers of raw materials, electric power, machines, and labor must be paid at least as much as their opportunity cost. The individual firm pays for each input and in this way compensates for the use of the community's scarce resources.

However, some types of production involve the use of resources which are not exchanged in resource markets. Goods that the individual producer is not required to buy are often called "free goods." Some free goods are fresh air, sunshine, and attractive physical surroundings. When the individual firm uses one of these resources—as, for example, a river to carry away the factory's garbage—that producer is not required to pay for the resource. The community suffers a loss of its resources for which it is not compensated.

This portion of production costs for which the community is not compensated is called **social cost.** Social costs are nonexclusive. No citizen can avoid bearing the cost of foul air and water, destroyed landscapes, and industrial noise. Every citizen must absorb these costs whether or not he or she bought the good or service involved.

It is government's responsibility to deal with these costs. It generally does so in either of two ways. *First, government can simply require the producer to pay for the use of the free good.* For example, if a manufacturer wishes to locate a plant in a community, the local government may simply establish a fee for the air and water that will be used in the production process. Or government may set up standards which require the manufacturer to clean up the air and water used in production. This may mean additional investment in antipollution equipment. Either way the firm must include social costs in total production costs. The manufacturer can then pass these higher costs along to consumers of the final output. All the costs of production are then exclusive. They are paid by the users of the product only.

The second way is for the government to tax goods and services whose production creates social costs. The tax is added to the price of the offending good or service. Buyers pay the cost and government uses the tax revenue to correct the pollution problem. But again the costs are exclusive to those who buy the product.

Whichever method government uses, the important point to remember is that some form of government intervention is necessary to solve the problem of social costs. Because the costs are social, the private marketplace cannot be relied upon to do the job.

Competition, stability, poverty, and discrimination

We have almost completed our basic tally of government's economic functions. But not quite. There are four more broad areas of governmental activity which have important impacts upon our economic system. Table 1 summarizes the economic functions of government.

Regulating and maintaining the competitive marketplace First, government is charged with regulating or policing some activities where operation in the private marketplace had unsatisfactory results. An example of this is the

Table 1
Summary of Economic Functions of Government

Protect life, liberty, and property
    Ensure product safety
    Prevent false advertising
Provide money
Provide public goods and services
Bear or assess social costs
Maintain competitive marketplace
Promote economic stability
Fight poverty
Eliminate discrimination

stock market. For many years stock markets were unregulated. But when the Great Crash of 1929 exposed the effects of fraud and unrestrained speculation, Congress passed legislation providing for regulation of the securities industry. Today, the *Securities and Exchange Commission* (SEC) has broad responsibility to see that the nation's stock markets function smoothly, without fraud or deceit.

Another economic role of government is to ensure competitive markets. When you study market structures later in microeconomics, you will find that monopoly firms tend to produce smaller outputs and charge higher prices than competitive firms. In the late nineteenth century in this country, several huge monopolies (called "trusts") came under attack from economic reformers. These attacks led to important antitrust legislation. Under these laws, the Justice Department has the responsibility to ensure that no single firm can control pricing and production decisions. If there is proof of monopolistic activity, the government can step in and break up the trusts.

Promoting economic stability Another broad responsibility of government is to keep the nation's economic activity as stable as possible. The history of production in the market system shows times of great prosperity, when employment is high and output and incomes are rising. At other times, depressions like the Great Depression of the 1930s have brought widespread suffering. As governments grew to understand the workings of national economies, they developed policies to regulate the level of economic activity. You will learn in macroeconomics how these policies work. The Employment Act of 1946 obligates the federal government to do what it can to maintain reasonably full employment and production.

Fighting poverty The government has also assumed maintenance of individual economic stability. This is to say, it provides welfare payments, food stamps, public housing, low-cost legal aid, and the like to poor families. Another way of stating this is that government has entered the battle against poverty. Government increased its role in the fight against poverty in the 1960s when President Johnson launched the "War on Poverty." The record shows, unfortunately, that we have not been completely successful in eliminating poverty. However, the many income supplements and outright grants of aid have helped lessen the burden of poverty for millions and moved many above the poverty line.

Eliminating discrimination   Finally, there is the matter of discrimination. We generally accept the principle that citizens should not suffer discrimination because of their race, sex, or age. Nonetheless, you need only look into your own life or the lives of friends to discover that discrimination does exist. Women generally find it difficult to find the same jobs—at the same pay—as men. Blacks find less desirable jobs—at lower pay—than whites. The elderly are too often denied jobs even when they can perform them perfectly well.

To guarantee equal opportunity for all citizens in the economy, the government has been called upon repeatedly to fight discrimination. This role took on much greater importance in the 1960s, and statistics now indicate that more and more women and minority groups are finding employment and salary opportunities similar to white males. Although the discrimination picture has brightened in recent years, work remains to be done. One statistic: In 1976 the unemployment rate for adult men was 7.0%; for adult women, 8.6%; for whites, the rate was 7.0%; for nonwhites, 13.1%. These figures suggest that economic discrimination may still exist. How far we want government to go to achieve absolute economic equality is, as we will see later, a very controversial subject. The side-effects are many, including some that are economic.

Levels of government

Government undeniably has a number of important economic functions. To accomplish these tasks and to support a basically democratic philosophy, governmental responsibilities in the United States are distributed among a variety of governmental levels. In general, Americans have avoided placing too much responsibility in the hands of the central gov-

ernment. We have preferred instead to decentralize authority, placing responsibilities in the hands of local governments wherever possible. We believe that local citizens and their elected officials are capable of making many important decisions and of directing important activities for themselves. Still, we recognize the need for a strong central government to protect the interests of all.

For these reasons we have a wide variety of governments. The biggest and most powerful is the central, or federal government. The next level is the state, followed by local government. Local government usually includes towns and cities, and in many regions of our nation, the county or the township.

The relationship between federal and state governments is never placid. It is regulated in part by the U.S. Constitution, the strength of which is its flexibility. Local governments have grown under the regulation of state governments (and state constitutions). But precisely because these relationships are flexible, various levels of governments are continually threatened by the loss of power to other levels. Moreover, whenever local governments look to the federal government for economic assistance, the federal government can impose its will on the localities.

A clear example of this is revenue sharing. In the late 1960s Congress decided that the federal government (U.S. Treasury) would disperse some federal tax revenues to local governments. However, certain grants would be distributed only to local governments which met required standards relating to employment, welfare, and educational practices. Federal funds were not, for example, available to school districts where racial discrimination seemed pervasive. Thus through its controls of billions of dollars in revenue-sharing funds, the federal government reduced the independence of the local levels of government.

It is difficult to say with certainty how the balance of power is shifting between federal and state and local governmental levels. One interesting statistic is that the number of federal government employees increased only 35% between 1950 and 1977, from 2 million to

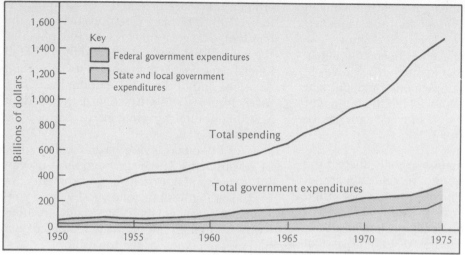

Figure 1 This chart shows federal spending and state and local spending in relation to total spending (by consumers, businesses, government) and total government spending. Notice that in the decade 1965–1975 total spending rose faster than either federal or state and local government spending. (Figures obtained from *Economic Report of the President*.)

2.7 million. But state and local government payrolls *more than doubled,* rising from 4 million employees to 12.5 million by 1977. Figure 1 shows the growth in state and local spending relative to total government spending and to all public and private spending in the United States since 1946. The chart shows little significant increase in federal government spending as a share of total spending since the 1950s, while state and local spending was increasing sharply. Over the period shown federal spending rose by a multiple of 7 and state and local spending rose by a multiple of 21!

These figures do not necessarily mean that state and local governments have wrested power away from Washington. In fact, a good argument can be given for just the opposite case. But the figures do show that a major "growth industry" has been state and local government. Even so, as financially troubled states and cities look increasingly to the federal government for assistance, it is safe to bet that the federal government will continue to usurp power from the state and local politicians.

Government outlays

State and local government

Economists generally lump state and local governments together because the services they offer tend to overlap. Costs of schools, highways, and hospitals, for example, are often shared between state and local authorities. Cities provide local school systems, street cleaning and maintenance, fire and police protection for city residents, water and sewage facilities, parks, and libraries. Counties also provide these services for county residents not served by city governments. In some parts of the United States, townships are important suppliers of some services, particularly education. And there may be broader units of government organized to provide particular goods and services over several counties. Examples are school districts, park districts, and rural water and fire protection districts.

State governments provide a wider range of goods and services. The reason is simply that the state's jurisdiction extends over all the state's residents. Among the services provided by state governments are: agricultural research and information, public colleges and universities, natural resource development, vocational training, treatment for alcoholism and mental disorders, and professional and auto licensing. In addition, state governments may provide local governments with supplemental funds for health, education, and welfare programs. Generally, states will give such assistance in order to standardize the quality of services statewide. If one county has very poor schools, for example, the state may wish to assist that county and bring its educational quality up to a par with other counties. Often, the wealthier counties subsidize such programs by paying higher taxes into state treasuries.

State and local governments are major spenders in the economy. In 1976, for example, these two levels of government combined spent $232.3 billion for goods and services. The federal government spent just $133.4 billion, with most of these purchases going for national defense. The largest single state-local governmental expenditure was for education, which consumed about 38% of the total. Highways ranked second at 10%. Public welfare payments constituted some 12% of state and local expenditures.

State and local government expenditures have exceeded federal spending for ten of the last eleven years. They constitute about 62% of total government purchases and some 14% of all spending for goods and services. In 1940, by contrast, they accounted for just 8% of total spending. Whether state and local financial crises of the mid-1970s will slow this growth in expenditures remains to be seen.

Federal government

Let us now turn from the decentralized governmental units to the central government's spending. Basically there are two uses for its funds. *Purchases* of goods and services and *income-support payments*. The latter are known also as *transfer payments*.

Federal purchases In order to carry out its various responsibilities to the nation's citizens, the federal government must purchase many billions of dollars of goods and services. Total purchases for 1977 were projected at about $166.5 billion. Of that, $101 billion was to be spent on national defense for the nation; $11.3 billion was provided for international affairs

and finance and research and development. Completing the federal government's shopping list were expenditures for agriculture and natural resource development, commerce and transportation, community development, housing, education, and health.

Historians will look upon the first three-quarters of this century as a time when government activity in the economy mushroomed. Total federal purchases have risen from just one percent of total spending in 1929 to 7.9% in 1976. Percentages were higher in war years: 42% in 1944, 16% in 1953, and 11% in 1968. The recent history of U.S. government expenditures is shown clearly in Figure 2.

Why has federal spending expanded in recent years? The development of an active international role on the part of the United States has been a major factor; spending for war and international affairs reflects this historical change. Other factors have been our nation's growing affluence and the demands of the public for more and better services. As the population has shifted from rural farm to urban and suburban living, the demand for governmental services has increased. You may be able to live like Robinson Crusoe if you reside on an isolated farm. But not when you move to a congested city! Finally, changes in age distribution within the aggregate population have stimulated demand for government services. Advances in health care mean more children survive, and so more schools and playgrounds are demanded. At the other end of the spectrum, people live longer, past the time when it is socially acceptable for them to be fully employed. Providing for their needs has further increased the demand for public goods and services.

In a word, society has progressed: We have become more civilized and affluent. And we have paid for this increase in civilization by funneling more of our earnings to the government. The famous Supreme Court justice Oliver Wendell Holmes put it this way: "Taxes are the price we pay for civilization."

Transfer payments The largest group of federal outlays is transfer payments (see Figure 2). **Transfer payments** are "grants" for income maintenance to individuals who qualify under certain government programs. Retired persons receive transfer payments in the form of Social Security checks. The unemployed receive transfer payments as *unemployment* and/or *disability insurance payments.* Welfare, veterans' benefits, and other income-support payments are all examples of transfer payments. These payments are not included in the circular flow until they are actually spent by their recipients.

The growth in transfer payments has been remarkable. In 1949 they were about 20% of total government outlays. By 1977 they were more than 50%. In fiscal year 1977 more than 32 million people collected some $83 billion from the federal government in the form of Social Security benefits. Medicare, medicaid, and other health programs provide $34.4 billion in aid. Another $22.9 billion pays for public assistance, food stamps, and family allowances. Interest on the public debt—the money the government borrows to meet its obligations—is also considered a transfer payment. Because the debt has grown markedly and because interest rates have increased in recent years, interest payments were $45 billion in 1977.

Figure 2 illustrates the sharp increase in U.S. government transfer payments since 1949.

Almost all American citizens receive help from one or more government programs. Millions receive aid under the programs listed above. Others receive benefits from federally subsidized housing, small business loans, college student loans, or GI benefits.

Not only do transfer payments significantly ease citizens' burdens, but they are also important economic stabilizers. Automatic stabilizers help to cushion the effects of abrupt changes in private sector spending. When private spending declines sharply, unemployment usually increases. Then transfer payments to individuals increase, helping to keep incomes fairly stable. On the other hand, when private spending and income rise, the unemployed are rehired and unemployment compensation stops. In both cases, the result is to help stabilize incomes and to moderate changes in the level of economic activity.

By now you are aware that in economics (as everywhere else) even the best programs have their drawbacks. Transfer payments are no exception. Some income-support payments may reduce the incentive to work. Consider: Transfer payments generally are not taxable. Thus in some low-paid occupations an indi-

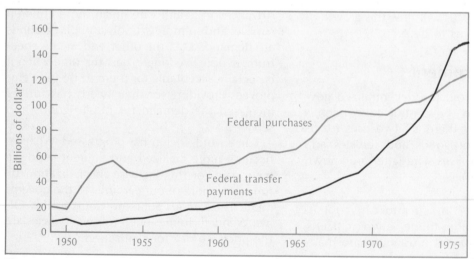

Figure 2 Recent trends in federal government outlays, broken down to (1) purchases of goods and services and (2) transfer payments. Notice that sharpest increases in purchases were during the early 1950s, due to the Korean War, and the mid-1960s, due to the Vietnam War. Also, notice that transfer payments have increased dramatically since the late 1960s. (Figures obtained from *Economic Report of the President.*)

vidual's after-tax income from work may not be much greater than the tax-free income he or she would receive from, say, welfare payments. It is important not to overemphasize this problem, however. The work disincentive is probably rather small simply because the transfer payments are generally rather small. Moreover, the drudgery and humiliation of standing in welfare lines are themselves significant incentives to find a job. If the disincentive problem is real, one solution might be to limit welfare payments to those physically unable to work, and to provide government-sponsored employment to those who cannot find private sector employment. We will consider this subject again in later chapters.

Government revenue and taxation policies

Now that you know some of the things various levels of government do for citizens, you may be wondering *how* they do it. From where, you should ask, come the funds?

Of course, the answer is taxes (and, to a lesser extent, borrowing). All levels of government levy taxes on the citizens within their jurisdiction to provide those citizens with the public goods and services they consume.

State and local government taxation

State and local governments collect a variety of taxes. Their major source of revenue is the **property tax;** it provides about one-fourth of state and local revenues. Property taxes must be paid on residential, commercial, and industrial property. Thus the homeowner pays his property tax directly. The apartment dweller pays his indirectly, through the rent his landlord charges. And consumers pay a good share of industry's property taxes as business firms "build" these taxes into the selling prices of their goods and services.

Then there are **sales taxes.** These are generally levied by state governments, and for a good reason: The sales tax must be uniform throughout the state in order to discourage shoppers from going to another town to avoid

the sales tax. Even though uniformity is desirable, it is not always achieved. In many parts of New York state, for example, the sales tax is 4%. But in New York City, the rate is 8%. Why? Because the state levies a 4% sales tax and the city an additional 4% sales tax of its own. Knowing this, it will come as no surprise to you that not many new cars are sold in Manhattan.

As a group (with many variations from the average), states collected some one-fourth of their revenues from sales taxes in recent years.

Two important additional forms of taxes are **personal** and **corporate income taxes.** These are taxes levied against individuals' incomes and against corporations' profits (that is, after all other expenses have been paid). In the case of individual income taxes, the rate generally increases as the size of a worker's income increases (although many states levy uniform rates). But for corporations the rate is usually a fixed percentage of pretax profits.

Most states have personal and corporate income taxes. These taxes provide less revenue than do the property and sales taxes. The reason is that high income tax rates tend to discourage individuals and businesses from moving into an area. After all, who wants to pay more taxes if it can be avoided? Most states would like to encourage productive individuals and firms to move within their boundaries, and so they try to avoid levying high income taxes. Only about 10% of state and local revenues come from this source.

A few cities have income taxes. But that doesn't mean that only city dwellers pay the tax. New York City, among others, has levied a nonresident income tax which taxes the income of anyone who works in the city—no matter that a worker may *live* in New Jersey. The reasoning is that many suburban dwellers earn their livings in the city and so should contribute to its upkeep.

Yet another one-fourth of state and local revenue comes from the federal government. Federal aid to states was rather small until the 1950s when the federal government began to provide grants for education, social services, and highway construction. Then in 1972 the federal government began its *revenue sharing program* to state and local governments. The amount of funds received is based on a for-

Table 2
Receipts and Outlays of State and Local Governments (1975)

Receipts	Billions of dollars	Percentage of total	Outlays	Billions of dollars
Property taxes	51.5	23%	Education	87.8
Income taxes	28.1	12%	Highways	22.5
Sales, excise, and			Public welfare	28.2
misc. taxes	49.8	22%	All other	91.9
All other	51.7	23%		
Aid from federal				
government	47.1	21%		
Total receipts	228.2	100%	Total outlays	230.4

mula measuring the size of populations and the urgency of need in various locales. The aim is to distribute federal tax revenues among states according to need rather than according to income. It was hoped that federal tax moneys would enable poorer state and local governments to raise the quality of their social programs in accordance with local needs. The alternative was for the federal government to take over the job entirely. See Table 2 for a summary of state and local receipts.

Regressive taxes and state and local government

Taxes can be described as either proportional, regressive, or progressive in their effects. A **proportional tax** collects an equal percentage or share of income from all who pay the tax. A **progressive tax** collects a higher percentage of income from high-income families than from low-income families. A **regressive tax,** by contrast, collects a smaller share of a wealthy family's income than of a poorer family's income. The federal Social Security tax is probably the most regressive tax. However, the majority of regressive taxes are imposed by state and local governments. Sales taxes are regressive. So are property taxes.

Take an example. Suppose a middle-income family earns $12,000 a year and lives in a $35,000 house. A wealthy family earns $100,000 and lives in a $200,000 house. Now suppose the first family pays property taxes of $1,000; the second family pays $6,000 in property taxes.

Why is the tax regressive? To see the answer, compare the amount of each tax with each family's income. For the middle-income family, the property tax bill is 1,000/12,000 = 8.4% of income. For the second family, the proportion is 6,000/100,000 = 6% of income. The regressive tax imposes a higher *percentage* tax burden on low-income than high-income families. The property tax tends to be regressive because: (1) ownership of real property does not always increase proportionately to earnings and (2) tax assessments do not always increase proportionately to prope.ty values.

Sales taxes are usually regressive, too. You might well ask, "If both rich and poor pay the same percentage, how can the tax be regressive?" If the $12,000-year family spends $10,000 on taxable items, and the sales tax is 4%, then the tax bill will be $10,000 × .04 = $400; this is $400/12,000 = 3.3% of the family's income. If the $100,000-year family spends $50,000 for taxable items, its tax bill will be $50,000 × .04 = $2,000, or $2,000/100,000 = 2% of income. Sales taxes are regressive because lower-income families generally must spend a *greater percentage of income* on items like food, clothing, fuel, etc., than do higher-income families.

Some state sales taxes are less regressive than others because some states exempt food and medicine from the tax. The regressive nature of state and local taxes is also offset somewhat by providing more benefits to poorer than to wealthier families. For example, police and fire protection are often required in greater amounts in poorer sections of towns; there may be more violence there. Also, health services are provided to poorer families more often than to wealthier ones. Suffice it to say that calculating the true regressivity of taxes is a complicated task when *benefits received* are considered.

Federal government taxation

If you don't like paying taxes in a particular state or city, you have the option of moving to another. But this option is not true at the federal tax level. If you move from New York to Los Angeles, you will pay the same federal tax in your new setting as you did in your old. (True, you could leave the country. But that is a rather unlikely choice for most of us.) This illustrates an important aspect of federal tax policies: The federal government can use any tax it requires to raise the revenues it needs. It need not fear massive avoidance by people leaving its jurisdiction. The federal government's only tax concern is that very high, "confiscatory" taxation might stifle incentives to produce and therefore reduce the economy's aggregate output.

Politicians know that the public dislikes taxes. As a famous seventeenth century French economist advised the tax collectors: "The art of taxation involves plucking the goose . . . to get the most feathers with the least hissing."

To extract the most revenues with the least hissing from taxpayers, the federal government relies heavily on **income tax revenues** (or income taxes). Federal income taxes are certainly large, and the "hissing" is reduced by having payments withheld from salaries (rather than making one large lump payment). **Personal income taxes** yielded about $154 billion in 1977. **Corporate income taxes** yielded another $56.6 billion or so. Beyond these two income taxes, contributions for **social insurance** (Social Security taxes and unemployment compensation taxes) constituted almost $109 billion. Other federal taxes include excise taxes, gift taxes, estate taxes, gasoline taxes, and customs duties. Since you may pay some or all of these taxes, we will briefly describe each. Then we will consider income taxes and social payments at length. Table 3 summarizes federal government receipts.

Excise taxes Excise taxes are levied against specific goods and services. Occasionally, an excise tax is levied in order to discourage consumption of some commodity, such as liquor or cigarettes. In other cases, an excise tax is applied against items purchased by only a few taxpayers, so as to minimize public opposition. An example of this is the 10% excise tax on most jewelry items.

Gift taxes Gift taxes are levied against gifts to individuals when the gift is of $3,000 or more in a single year. Rates range from $2\frac{1}{4}$% on small gifts to almost 50% on large gifts. Gift taxes discourage wealthy families from passing along wealth to following generations without paying estate taxes at death.

Estate (or death) taxes Estate taxes are levied against the assets of a person who dies. Again, the purpose is to restrain wealthy families from passing their wealth along to following generations. Without gift and estate taxes it would be much easier for the rich to get richer and the poor, poorer. Part of an individual's estate may be passed on to the surviving spouse. As much as half the estate is then exempt from taxes. Tax rates on the remaining value range from 3% for an estate of less than $5,000, to 32.5% on $1 million and 60.9% on $10 million.

Gasoline taxes Next time you fill up your tank, look at the price schedule on the pump. There you will see that several cents of each gallon's price is a federal tax. (In addition, most states—and some cities—charge a tax on gasoline.) Most of these federal tax collections flow

Table 3
Receipts and Outlays of the Federal Government, 1977 (estimated)

Receipts	Billions of dollars	Percentage of total	Outlays	Billions of dollars
Personal income taxes	160.4	40%	Purchases of goods and services	139.4
Corporate income taxes	58.2	14%	Total transfer payments	205.8
Excise taxes and other indirect taxes	24.3	6%	Aid to state and local governments	59.3
Social Security taxes	121.8	30%		
New borrowing	39.8	10%		
Total receipts	404.5	100%	Total outlays	404.5

into highway trust funds, on the assumption that motorists should pay for the construction and repair of the nation's highways. (If you own a boat, you still pay the tax for gasoline. But you can receive a rebate of the federal tax proceeds at the end of the year. The reason, of course, is that boats don't need highways.)

Customs duties or tariffs Many goods and services are cheaper in other countries than in ours. To discourage massive imports of such goods, the government requires importers and American travelers to pay customs duties, called *tariffs*, on the items they bring back into this country when these items exceed a total value of $100.00. Therefore, if you go to Switzerland and purchase some fine wristwatches, be prepared to hand the customs inspector a good deal of money to get your purchases across the U.S. border!

Progressive nature of federal income taxes

As we said above, the federal government relies heavily upon income taxes: both personal and corporate. One important feature of federal income taxes is that they are progressive. Remember that progressive taxes are those which collect a higher percent of taxes from high-income families than from low-income families. Since most taxpayers are not high-income earners, most people approve of the rich carrying a greater burden of the taxes. For the population as a whole, it seems that most people get a better deal. And that is politically popular. (The English liberals are fond of calling this "soaking the rich.")

Here is how the federal income tax works.

The taxpayer is allowed *exemptions* from income for each member of the household. In 1976 the value of each exemption was $750. The family earning $12,000 a year may reduce its taxable income by $750 times the number of persons, say $750 × 4 = $3,000.

Next the taxpayer may deduct certain allowable expenses. These include state and local taxes, interest payments on loans, donations to charitable organizations, some health and medical expenses, and some expenses incurred in carrying on business. Allowable expenses may be itemized precisely or they may be estimated at about 16% of gross income.

When *deductions* are subtracted, the result is the family's taxable income. Table 4 gives hypothetical income tax calculations for families earning $12,000 and $100,000.

Notice that the high-income family pays a much greater percent of its income. This is because the *marginal tax rate* increases as income increases. The marginal tax rate is the rate applied to additional dollars of income. The first one-thousand dollars of a family's taxable income is taxed at the rate of 14%. As Table 4 shows, the sixth one-thousand dollars is taxed at the rate of 19%. The ninety-third one-thousand dollars of income is taxed at the rate of 69%. The highest marginal tax rate is 70%, applied to incomes greater than $200,000. This means that the person earning $200,000 in taxable income is allowed to keep only thirty cents of the last dollar earned.

Of course, in the real world of taxpaying, tax avoiding, and tax-shifting, progressivity loses some of its effect. The Internal Revenue Code is full of ways for wealthier families to reduce their tax bite. They can employ tax accountants and lawyers to advise them on legal deductions from taxable income. Then they can deduct the costs of these accountants and lawyers. Opportunities for reducing tax

Table 4
Hypothetical Income Tax Calculations

	$12,000	$100,000
Gross income	$12,000	$100,000
Exemptions $750	−3,000	−3,000
	9,000	97,000
Deductions (itemized)	−2,000	−6,500
Taxable income	7,000	90,500
Tax: (computations from tax table)	$620 + 19% of (7000 − 4000)	$48,590 + 69% of (93,500 − 90,000)
	= 620 + 570	= 48,590 + 2415
	= $1190	= $51,005
Tax as % of income	$1190/12,000 = 9.9%	$51,005/100,000 = 51%

bills are often derisively called "tax loopholes" by crusading politicians. But reserve your judgment when you hear this word. Some loopholes can benefit you, too. For example, if you are a home owner, you can deduct your mortgage interest payments from taxable income and reduce your own tax bill. The apartment dweller may call your tax break a loophole. You may prefer to call it "encouraging private home ownership."

Advantages and disadvantages of progressive taxes

The reason the tax code has "loopholes" is that there is a serious potential problem with progressive taxes. *The problem is that high tax rates may be a major disincentive to do worthwhile things.* For example, many corporations depend on the sale of stocks and bonds to provide funds for expansion and modernization. Growth in production and creation of new jobs require firms to use savings from many small savers. However, if much of the gains to be made from purchasing stocks and bonds were to be taxed away through a very progressive income tax scheme, the chances are people wouldn't buy them. To overcome this problem, the tax code states that no matter what your income level, capital gains on sales of securities held nine months or longer are to be taxed at a maximum rate of 25%. A *capital gain* is the money earned by the sale of stocks and bonds; it is the difference between purchase price and sale price. *Dividends*, which are the income earned from *holding* stocks and bonds, are considered part of personal income and taxed as such.

There are many, many other examples of "loopholes" in the tax code meant to overcome the problem of tax disincentives. Contributions to religious, educational, or scientific organizations are tax deductible. Tax credits are also available to business firms when they make capital investments or employ welfare recipients.

The progressive tax performs an important function aside from its role as a successful revenue raiser. *This second function is to help provide greater stability in the level of total spending, output, employment, and prices.* Recall our discussion of the circular flow. We showed how independent decision-making might lead to instability as buyers abruptly change their spending plans. A progressive tax structure helps to cushion the effects of abrupt changes in spending, and helps to correct problems of inflation or high unemployment. Here is how it works.

Suppose buyers decide to speed up their spending for consumer goods and services and investment goods. Incomes increase and production expands, pushing against the limits of our productive capacity and creating inflationary pressures. But as incomes increase, families move into higher tax brackets and pay higher marginal tax rates. Unemployed workers are hired and become taxpayers. As a result, tax revenues increase faster than incomes. Larger tax payments drain from the circular flow, limiting the rise in spending and reducing inflationary pressures.

Progressive taxes also help to cushion a sharp drop in spending. If consumers and business firms decide to spend less, income and production will fall. Some workers will lose their jobs and unemployment will increase. But as incomes fall, families will move into lower tax brackets. Unemployed workers will pay no income taxes at all. This time the tax drain from spending will fall faster than income falls. Their lower tax bills will enable families to maintain spending at a somewhat lower level, limiting the drop in production and moderating the decline in employment.

In this way, progressive income taxes help to cushion the effects of independent changes in spending in the private sector. Progressive taxes are an important automatic stabilizer in our macroeconomy. This topic and other automatic stabilizers will be discussed later in macroeconomics.

Social Security taxes

After personal and corporate income taxes, the second major source of federal tax revenue is Social Security. Social Security legislation was passed in the 1930s as a means of providing disability and retirement benefits for workers and their dependents. Employed persons pay 5.85% of their earnings up to $16,500 (1977) to the Social Security Trust Fund. The tax is deducted from paychecks by employers, who contribute another 5.85%. The trust fund is invested in U.S. government securities. Each year 32 million widows, dependents, and retired people receive income-support payments from Social Security.

In recent years Social Security has been changing into a "pay-as-you-go" revenue scheme. This means that tax revenues collected from workers currently in the work force are paid directly to the nation's Social Security recipients. In other words, working sons and daughters pay the benefits to their retired parents (and even grandparents) as the government deducts Social Security taxes from the workers' paychecks. This pay-as-you-go nature of Social Security is now developing into a major problem. Currently, the money paid into the system is barely enough to cover present benefits, which have soared in recent years. The problem is that the number of old people relative to younger workers is expected to increase dramatically within the next 75 years. This means that workers in coming decades will be forced to shoulder an increasing burden of Social Security benefits. One solution would be to increase dramatically the tax rate, but that is hardly politically popular. Another would be to support the Social Security system from the U.S. Treasury. But that would remove the appearance that workers are paying for their retirement through deductions from their working days' paychecks. This appearance was judged to be very important when Social Security legislation was passed in the late 1930s.

Another more immediate problem with Social Security taxes is that they are regressive. Although the same tax rate of 5.85% is charged to all workers, it is applied against only the first $16,500 of income. There is no tax charged on the amount of earnings over this $16,500 ceiling. Income from other sources is not taxed.

To see how this is regressive, consider again the $12,000-year and the $100,000-year families. If we assume the entire income is earned by one member of the family, we have the following data:

Income	$12,000	$100,000
5.85% of first $16,500	$702	$965.25
Tax as % of income	702/12,000 = 5.85%	965.25/100,000 = 0.97%

As in the case of all regressive taxes, the *relative* tax burden is greater on the low-income earner even though the *absolute* tax bill is lower. Because Social Security taxes are regressive, they do not function as economic stabilizers. Furthermore, Social Security tax revenues remain fairly constant even when total income increases.

Evaluating our tax structure

The total tax burden We have shown that state and local governments raise funds primarily through regressive property and sales taxes. Federal tax revenues are collected primarily from progressive income taxes. The effect of all taxes taken together is less regressive and less progressive than either would be alone.

Recall that a tax which takes the same percent of income at every income level is called a *proportional tax*. Over a wide range of earnings, the total effect of all state, local, and federal income taxes is roughly proportional. In fact, in 1971 families earning between $4,000 and $25,000 yearly paid about 32% of their income in taxes. But the effect of total taxes was different at the low and the high extremes of income. Families earning less than $4,000 generally paid a higher percent in taxes, as much as 50% at very low incomes. For this reason, it is said that our tax structure is regressive for incomes less than $4,000. Families earning more than $25,000 also paid a higher percent, again as much as 50% at very high incomes. This makes our tax structure progressive for earned incomes greater than $25,000.

The actual effect of particular taxes is difficult to measure. This is because taxes are often shifted from the person who actually pays the tax. The taxpayer may shift the burden of the tax to another party. For instance, a retailer pays taxes, but the revenue for taxes is collected by increasing the price of the good or service produced. Landlords pay taxes but they collect the revenues in rents their tenants pay. Employers pay taxes but they acquire the revenue by reducing the wages paid to employees.

Consideration of the tax burden must involve tax incidence. **Tax incidence** refers to who actually pays the tax. It is possible to estimate the incidence of taxes, but not precisely.

Net taxes   You may not enjoy paying taxes. But before you grumble too much or too loudly, make sure you grumble about the correct thing: net taxes. We are concerned about net taxes because many families receive *negative taxes*, or transfer payments. **Net taxes** are the amount of actual taxes a family *pays* minus the transfer payments the family *receives*. The net tax structure reflects the real or true tax burden of families at various income levels.

Families at low-income levels generally pay low taxes and receive more transfer benefits. As a result, their net tax rate is very low and may even be negative. Families at higher-income levels generally pay high taxes and receive fewer transfer benefits. Their net tax rate is much closer to their actual tax rate. The effect of transfer payments is to make our net tax structure much more progressive than the actual tax structure.

Summary

While economic theory often assumes a world of completely free economic agents, we have seen that this is not the case in the real twentieth century world. We have seen that governments impose rules and regulations that play an important role in economic activity.

One important economic function of government is to protect property. Laws regarding contracts, safety standards, and product labeling aim at fulfilling this responsibility. Government must also provide a modern, functioning monetary system conducive to stable economic growth and development. In addition, the private marketplace cannot be relied upon to allocate public goods and services and social costs properly because both are nonexclusive. Government must play a role in their production and allocation, too. Finally, the government performs these economic functions: guarantees a competitive marketplace; promotes economic stability; fights poverty; and prohibits discrimination.

State and local governments provide basic services, such as fire and police protection, sanitation, and education. Some revenues are shared within states to equalize the quality of public goods and services statewide. All together, state and local government purchases amount to more than one-half of all government purchases.

Federal government purchases of goods and services include defense spending and community services. Federal spending for social services has increased dramatically in this century because the age mix of the population has changed. Also, we expect more and better "civilization" as our economy grows and prospers.

Transfer payments are more than one-half of all federal outlays. They provide income-support payments, health and nutrition benefits, unemployment benefits, and many other services. There are few Americans who do not benefit from some transfer payment program. Transfer payments, like progressive income taxes, help to stabilize total spending during times of rising or falling incomes.

Local governments raise most of their revenues through property taxes. State governments raise the majority of theirs through sales taxes. Many states (and some cities) also employ income taxes, though rates are generally low. About 25% of state and local government revenues come from federal revenue sharing programs. State and local taxes are generally regressive.

The major sources of revenue for the federal government are personal and corporate income taxes. The income tax is progressive. After exemptions and deductions, higher-income earners usually pay a higher marginal tax rate than lower-income earners do. Highly progressive taxes may stifle incentives to perform valuable services. However, progressive taxes do help to stabilize total spending during periods of rising or falling incomes. And they provide increasing revenues as the economy grows. The Social Security tax is regressive. Social Security revenues do not vary much with income and so this tax is not a good stabilizer.

The total tax burden tends to be regressive at low levels of income, proportional over a wide range of middle incomes, and progressive at higher levels. However, examination of net taxes shows our entire tax structure to be slightly progressive.

Key Words and Phrases

- **contract** an agreement to perform certain acts.
- **barter** exchange of goods directly for other goods without the use of money.
- **money** anything that serves as a medium of exchange for a society; today governments are responsible for issuing money and controlling its supply.
- **exclusivity** the opportunity to enjoy goods and services independently of others.
- **nonexclusivity** the inability to restrict the use of goods or services to a single individual or group.
- **social goods and services** goods and services which are nonexclusive, enjoyed by the community as a whole.
- **private goods and services** goods and services which are exclusive, restricted to the use of a single individual or group.
- **social costs** costs in resource use which are imposed on the community as a whole; pollution is the most common social cost.
- **social benefits** advantages which extend to the community as a whole.
- **transfer payments** payments from government made to persons for which no goods or services are provided in exchange; welfare, unemployment benefits, Medicare, etc., are transfer payments.
- **automatic stabilizers** tax payments and transfer payments which work automatically to moderate changes in consumers' incomes and total spending.
- **property taxes** taxes levied on the value of real and personal property.
- **sales taxes** taxes levied on the price of a good or service and paid at the time of purchase.
- **revenue sharing** a system of intergovernmental transfer of funds, from the federal government to state and local governments.
- **personal and corporate income taxes** taxes levied on the incomes of individuals and corporations.
- **proportional tax** a tax which takes the same percentage from high-income persons as from low-income persons.
- **progressive tax** a tax which takes a higher percentage from high-income persons than from low-income persons.
- **regressive tax** a tax which takes a higher percentage from low-income persons than from high-income persons.
- **excise taxes** taxes levied on particular items, generally considered luxuries.
- **gift and estate taxes** taxes levied on gifts and bequests of property.
- **customs duties** taxes levied on goods brought into a nation from abroad.
- **exemptions** reductions in taxable income based on the number of persons supported by the income.
- **deductions** reductions in taxable income based on certain allowable expenses.
- **marginal tax rate** the percentage tax levied on the last dollar of income.
- **negative taxes** reverse taxes; that is, transfer payments.
- **tax incidence** measurement of who actually gives up purchasing power when a tax is levied.
- **net tax rate** the amount of taxes paid less transfer payments received from government; figured as percentage of income.

Questions for Review

1. What have been the trends in social goods and services relative to private goods and services in the United States? What does this imply about the role of government in our national life? What other circumstances have contributed to these trends?

2. Name the economic functions of government.

3. With respect to the role of government in future years, what do you see as an important basis for greater government influence? What are the opportunities and dangers of this course? What other alternatives to increased government are there?

4. Explain the concept of revenue sharing, showing how it attempts to resolve the conflict between centralization and decentralization of authority. Is revenue sharing necessary?

5. Outline the primary sources and uses of funds for (1) the federal government and (2) state and local governments.

6. Distinguish between government expenditures and transfers.

7. Define regressive tax and progressive tax and give advantages and disadvantages of each. Under what circumstances does a tax serve as an "automatic stabilizer"?

8. Explain how the Social Security tax works. What problem confronts Social Security?

9. Define: incidence of a tax, net tax, exclusivity, and nonexclusivity.

Part Two

National Income and Fiscal Policy

6

National Income Accounting

In previous chapters we have used the term "macroeconomics." It means, you will recall, looking at the economy as a whole. Macroeconomics is concerned with the total of all the goods and services produced by the national economy, or by some segment of the national economy such as corporations or households. (One can also study the macroeconomics of a state or community, of course, but we will confine ourselves in this chapter to the national economy.)

To look at the national economy as a whole we must have some way of adding up all the goods and services produced in it—diesel trucks and schoolbooks, office buildings and the services of typists, etc. The system of adding up all these things is called **national income accounting.** It requires the efforts of large numbers of trained economists and statisticians. In our country the national income accounts are drawn up by the staff of the Bureau of Economic Analysis in the U.S. Department of Commerce. The figures are published on a monthly, quarterly, and annual basis.

Probably the most important and familiar calculation in national income accounting is referred to as *gross national product*. This is a measure of total output or all the production by a national economy. More precisely, **gross national product** (GNP) is the *market value* of all goods and services produced during a given period of time (usually a year). By "market value" we mean the actual market price at which the goods and services are sold. For the United States, the measure is dollars; in other countries, their local currency would be used. (Hereafter we will follow custom and frequently refer to gross national product by its initials—GNP.) Each country, whether it be the United States, France, Nigeria, Egypt, etc., has its own GNP for each year.

When you read in the newspaper that "our GNP rose by 5% last year," it means that the national income economists in Washington have *estimated* that we produced 5% more goods and services (measured in dollars) last year than the year before. *Estimate* does not mean a guess. The work involves sophisticated statistical techniques. However, since each sale of a good or service is not recorded, the total arrived at using statistics must be called an estimate, no matter how accurate. Good data on the economy have been available only in recent years—since the 1940s. The work of developing the data may be traced to economist Simon Kuznets in the 1930s.

The Great Depression of the 1930s aroused people's concern about the state of the economy in a very demanding way. British economist John Maynard Keynes had produced in the early 1930s a new explanation of how the economy operated. Initially his theory was untested because necessary data about the national income were not available. Professor Kuznets and the National Bureau of Economic Research (NBER) began the massive task of collecting the data. The efforts of Kuznets came to fruition in the 1940s. Since then, the kinds of data collected have been expanded. The job is so large the U.S. Department of Commerce does most of it, though the NBER continues to be active in the work.

Some economists feel the development of the means to measure the economy was the most important feat in twentieth century economics. Professor Kuznets received the 1971 Nobel Prize for his effort.

Economists use the data for *many purposes*. The data describe how well the economy is functioning. The data may also be used to construct models of how the economy operates or to test various hypotheses. The data may also be used for analysis of the economy and to support policy recommendations to the political arm of the government. Business firms use them to analyze production and consumption patterns and to forecast sales. Government officials use them to predict tax revenues and also the need for certain expenditures. Military planners use the data to estimate a country's potential to wage war. Thus in less than half a century the data measuring GNP have captured the attention of almost everyone interested in any part of an economy.

The circular flow—once again

We saw earlier (in Chapter 4) that economic activity may be thought of as a circular flow. Resources and output—real goods—move in

Economic Thinker
Simon Kuznets

There are, it has been said, lies, damn lies—and statistics. The witticism is at least partially true, as responsible statisticians would be the first to admit. Statistics are not flesh and blood; they are mere numbers. Mere numbers seldom prove anything—but they can indicate a great many things. Indeed, without valid statistics and the branch of economics that has grown out of application of advanced mathematical techniques to statistics—*econometrics*—economic forecasting which we today take for granted could never have developed.

Simon Smith Kuznets was a leader in the early development of economic forecasting, especially in his work in measuring national income. Measurement of gross national product (GNP) did not spring full grown on the economic scene in the 1940s. Development of this indispensable economic tool was made possible by the painstaking statistical and historical research of scholarly economists like Simon Kuznets.

Kuznets was born in 1901, in Kharkov, Russia. He came to the United States as a young man, receiving his Ph.D from Columbia University in 1926. He taught at the University of Pennsylvania from 1930 to 1954, at Johns Hopkins University from 1954 to 1960, and was also research professor of economics at Harvard University.

Kuznets' most enduring contribution to the advancement of economics was made through his involvement with the National Bureau of Economic Research, where he worked with the Bureau's brilliant director, Wesley Mitchell. The Bureau had been set up to collect statistical data on such items as prices, living costs, interest rates, farm production, and so on. It was designed to be strictly nonpolitical, its members ranging from representatives of the banking community to officers of the left-wing League for Industrial Democracy. The Bureau was interested only in facts and figures, not in political or economic solutions to the problems roused by these facts and figures.

When, in the depression of the 1930s, the government needed information on national income, it turned to the Bureau. Un-fortunately, almost no such usable information was available. Kuznets was brought to Washington to help collect and collate the kind of statistical data needed to measure national income. In 1934, the nation's first national income figures—for 1929–1932—were issued. The work of Kuznets and other economists resulted in data and a statistical methodology that laid the basis for later sophisticated measurement of the nation's GNP.

Kuznets, himself, was quick to point out that his data could only approximate the real world of economics. Certain biases in the data were inevitable. The data could not include, for example, the contribution to national income of the work of housewives, or the value of the products of home gardeners, or the services of householders who made home repairs and improvements. He also pointed out the dangers of using national income data to make comparisons between and among the economies of nations. Cost and availability of goods and services, for example, must be considered along with per capita income in such comparisons.

Kuznets' career has been devoted to refinement of the techniques of research in national product and income. His ability to sift through massive statistical data to provide common denominators useful for economic planning and forecasting has given invaluable impetus to quantitative economic studies. He has written many essays and books on income, productivity, and economic growth, including *National Income and Capital Formation* (1938), *Modern Economic Growth* (1966), and *Economic Growth of Nations* (1971). In 1971, Simon Kuznets was awarded the Nobel Prize in Economic Science.

one direction while a counterflow of income and consumption expenditures—money flows—move in the other direction. Measuring these flows is the way we may add up GNP. First, however, let's reintroduce the "actors" in our economic scene.

Households and firms

Consumption activities may be viewed as carried on by *households*. A household may be an individual, a group of individuals, a family (in one of several forms), a fraternity or sorority, an organization, or a commune. The form of the household is not important. The important thing is that the household makes consumption decisions. The household is also the owner and supplier of the basic factors of production. It supplies labor, management, land, financial capital, and raw materials to the economy.

Production activities are carried out by *firms*. Firms purchase factors of production from households and combine them to produce goods and services which are sold to households, completing the circular flow. In some instances, the difference between the firm and the household may not be very great. In the case of a family farm, the household

consumes some of the produce of the "firm." In other cases, the firm and the people making up the firm are nearly the same. This is especially true for doctors or lawyers in private practice. However, even in these special cases it is possible to separate consumption and production activities. That firms produce and households consume is the important distinction between the actors in the economic drama.

Additional components of circular flow

The description of the circular flow with two actors is not quite adequate to fit the type of economy in which we live. Three other economic actors and activities enter the scene. These are (1) the government, (2) saving and investment, and (3) the rest of the world (meaning the effect of international trade). They are important because they add to and subtract from the circular flow. Figure 1 shows the interrelationships.

Government Local, state, and federal governments enter into economic activities directly as well as by setting the rules for the economic

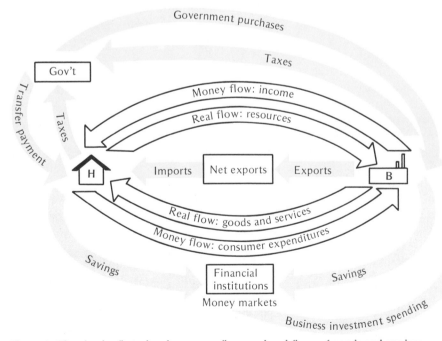

Figure 1 The circular flow showing money flows and real flows of goods and services.

activity of the population. *Governments are treated as consumers in their own right.* They consume everything from paperclips to Saturn rockets. Government expenditures are treated as consumption even though some goods purchased are really used for production. Government consumption is separated from other consumption because it often plays a special role in the economy. In particular, it may be changed from year to year in response to changes in other parts of the economy.

Government not only consumes; it also contributes as a producer to the flow of goods and services. At the state and local level, government provides education, recreation, police and fire services, and sometimes utilities such as water or electricity. At the federal level it produces highways, military research, and postal services among other things.

Saving and investment Actually, saving and investment are activities, not actors like households or firms or government. They are singled out for separate treatment because they play a special part in determining the flow of goods and services.

Saving is the rate at which people try to add to their store of wealth. They do this by refraining from consuming. The flow of goods and services is diminished when they do this. Firms as well as people may practice a form of saving. Saving by firms is that part of profit which is not paid out as dividends and is called *retained earnings*. This diminishes the flow of factors of production and therefore of goods and services. It is important to remember that *saving* is a current activity in national income accounting; it should not be confused with amounts accumulated—known as *savings*—as a result of saving carried out in the past. Saving is a flow while savings is a stock.

Investment, like saving, is a flow concept. **Investment** is the amount added to the stock of capital goods in the economy. You will recall that capital goods are goods used to produce other goods and services. Office buildings, manufacturing plants, machinery, trucks, and private houses are all examples of capital goods. Inventories are also counted as capital. Total investment during a year is called **gross investment.** It includes the replacement of capital goods worn out or depreciated during the year, as well as additions to the stock of

capital goods. **Net investment** is the addition to the stock of capital goods exclusive of depreciation—that is, gross investment minus depreciation:

Net investment
= Gross investment − depreciation.

The word "investment" has other meanings, so it is important to be clear as to what it does not mean for our purposes. It does not mean the purchase of stocks or bonds, even though such purchases may lead to investment expenditures at some time in the future. It does not mean the purchase of land or existing buildings in the hope they will gain in value, or the purchase of paintings, whiskey, wine, antiques, or any of the dozens of other things that people buy in the hope that their prices will rise. Such purchases are called "investments" in everyday conversation, but are not what economists mean by investment. Once again: *investment is the addition to, or replacement of, the stock of capital goods.*

To the extent that investment restores the flow of goods and services, *investment tends to offset the activity of saving.* In a modern economy, different economic actors carry out the activities of saving and investment. There is no assurance that saving will actually lead to investment. Saving is not done for the purpose of investing. As we shall see, this is an important point. The amount of saving relative to investment plays an important role in macroeconomic thinking.

Rest of the world Most economies do not exist in isolation. Most carry on some degree of trade with other economies. The flow of goods and services into or out of the economy has to be included in the national income accounts. Since GNP is supposed to include everything produced by the economy, the outward flow of goods and services sold to people in other countries must be counted in GNP because it is produced by the economy. The reverse holds for imports, which are goods and services produced by other economies but purchased and used in the local economy. *Imports tend to take the place of locally produced goods and services, thus diminishing the flow of GNP.* For instance, if you buy a Volkswagen instead of an American-made car, you diminish the flow of GNP. In national income accounting, imports are subtracted from exports and the difference is called **net exports.** Net exports may be positive or negative, depending on the relative size of exports and imports. If exports exceed imports, net exports is positive and the effect will be to increase GNP; if exports are less than imports, the effect will be to decrease GNP because net exports is negative. Only the *net* effect matters.

Measuring GNP flows: an overview

By the time we reach a diagram such as Figure 1 we can see that the circular flow concept is very primitive. We can also see that the measurement becomes more difficult. A flow may be measured anywhere. Figure 1 is more a maze than a circle. The figure shows only the flows of goods and services. There are, of course, money flows in the opposite direction. The money is used to pay for the goods and services or the factors of production. Measurement becomes complicated.

Not only is measurement complicated by the many things flowing through the economy, but the purpose for which the measurement is to be made may differ for different scholars. In an attempt to bring order out of the chaos, three measurements are used. They all measure the same thing—total economic activity—but measure it at different points in the flow and answer different questions. The three measures are output, expenditures, and income.

Output approach

The output approach measures output of the economy at the sources of production. Recalling our model of the circular flow, we know that goods and services are produced at the following four sources: households, firms, government, and the rest of the world (the net difference between our exports and imports). These economic "actors" are known as *sectors.* When we add up *production* of goods and services in each of these four sectors, we have computed gross national product.

Expenditures approach

Our second point of measurement is suggested when one tries to answer questions about where the production goes. Everything produced in the economy must go somewhere— that is, it must be paid for by somebody who takes possession of it. Households purchase goods and services for consumption purposes. Businesses purchase goods and services for investment. Governments consume some products and services. The rest of the world gets our exports minus our imports. **Gross national expenditures** (GNE) are the sum of consumption expenditures, government expenditures for goods and services, investment expenditures, and exports minus imports. They must equal gross national product:

GNE = GNP.

GNE is GNP broken down by who gets the output.

Income approach

A third point of measurement is often used. For every expenditure, there has to be an opposite money flow. What I pay out, somebody else receives in payment. To produce output, inputs or factors of production are required. The purchase of inputs entails money flows which are of interest since most of us call these payments *income.* They take the form of wages and salaries, rent, profit, and interest and dividends. Adding all these up, adjusting the total for some costs covered by production, and adding in capital goods replacement, we once more obtain an amount equal to GNP. Economists call it **gross national income** (GNI).

We can now show that gross national income is the same as gross national product and gross national expenditures. GNE is equal to GNP as we have seen because both measure goods and services, GNE by who buys them and GNP by who produces them. GNI is equal to GNE because the expenditures are made using the earnings represented by GNI. GNI is equal to GNP because the incomes paid to the factors of production are the costs of producing the GNP. Thus we could write all three in the same equation:

GNE = Gross National Product = GNI.

We can expand this equation by listing the components of GNE and GNI as we described them above:

Flow of Expenditures		Flow of Income
Household purchases of goods and services Government purchases of goods and services Business expenditures on capital investment Net expenditures by foreigners (exports minus imports)	= GNP =	Wages and salaries Rent Profit Interest (and dividends) Other charges or cost of production including indirect business taxes and depreciation.

As we shall see, computing the money flows—GNE or GNI—will ultimately be of great service to us. But first we will show how the output approach is used to arrive at GNP; then we will examine how GNP is added up by totaling either GNE or GNI. The output approach has the advantage as a starting point because it emphasizes the actual goods and services produced as well as where they are produced.

However, before we total up GNP, we want to make sure the market value of our goods and services is measured in *constant* dollars. That is, if GNP rises from one year to the next, we want to know how much of the increase was due to real output increasing and how much was due to inflation.

Real and money GNP

A modern industrial economy produces an almost infinite variety of goods and services. It is impossible to add up all the hamburgers, TV sets, haircuts, and operatic arias unless we convert them into some common unit of measure. Most of us use the same unit—dollars. When someone returns from the store with four sacks of groceries and is asked what they bought, they don't reply by listing all items in the sacks. The answer is usually that they bought $55 worth of groceries. In the same fashion we define gross national product as *the market value* of all goods and services sold to final consumers during a year. The market value of the goods and services produced by our national economy in 1976 was $1,691.6 billion.

Now measuring the quantity of output by its market value raises certain problems. What about inflation—that is, rising prices? Obviously, if prices rise by 10%, we can't say that real output has increased by 10%, even though GNP figures show that it did. It may even have decreased, as happened in 1974 and 1975.

The problem can be simplified by thinking of an economy that produces only two goods, bread and wine. The calculation of GNP for such an economy is shown in Table 1A. This economy produced 1,000 loaves of bread which sold for $0.40 each and 1,000 bottles of wine which sold at $2.00 each. The GNP for that year was $2,400.

Over time, the output of the economy may change. In Table 1B, output has grown to 1,100 loaves of bread and 1,100 bottles of wine. At the original prices, the GNP has grown to $2,640. The increase in output is accurately measured by the increase in its market value. Now look at Table 1C. Another possibility is

Table 1
Calculation of Real and Money GNP

A	B
1,000 loaves bread × $ .40 = $ 400 1,000 bottles wine × 2.00 = 2,000 GNP = $2,400	1,100 loaves bread × $ .40 = $ 440 1,100 bottles wine × 2.00 = 2,200 GNP = $2,640

C	D
1,000 loaves bread × $ .45 = $ 450 1,000 bottles wine × 2.25 = 2,250 GNP = $2,700	1,100 loaves bread × $ .44 = $ 484 1,100 bottles wine × 2.20 = 2,420 GNP = $2,904

Table 2
A Sample Price Index
(1967 is base)

1966	96.7
1967	100
1968	103.1
1969	107.8
1970	114.0
1971	119.5
1972	122.9
1973	126.3
1974	135.1
1975	147.3
1976	154.3
1977	159.1

illustrated here. The output of bread and wine remains the same as it was in the beginning. But the market price of bread has risen to $0.45 and of wine to $2.25. This gives us a GNP of $2,700. Output seems to have increased although we know that it really hasn't. The *money* (or *nominal*) *value* of GNP has risen but *real output* has not.

In fact, neither Table 1B nor 1C comes close to what actually happens over a period of time. Table 1D comes closer to the kind of change that will happen. *Both* output and prices have changed so that the GNP goes up to $2,904. To sort out what has occurred, we must separate the change in output from the change in prices.

The price index

We handle the price change by constructing a price index. A **price index** uses one year—any year—as a base year and computes the prices of other years in terms of the base. The usual practice is to show the base year as 100. Table 2 shows a price index with 1967 as base year. If we desired, we could have shown any of the other years as base (however, recent price indices tend to use 1967 as the base).

The calculation of a price index is shown

in Table 3. To simplify things, we will use only the values from our example above. The output of bread and wine in the base year (from Table 1A) is valued at $.40 per loaf of bread and $2.00 per bottle of wine, giving a GNP of $2,400. The prices rise to $.44 and $2.20 respectively in the current year (from Table 1D); so the *current value* of GNP is $2,640 for the *same output* as in the base year. Dividing the latter GNP figure by the GNP figure for the base year gives us 1.1, or 110, as the index for the current year:

$$\text{Price index} = \frac{\text{Current year value}}{\text{Base year value}}$$

$$= \frac{\$2,640}{\$2,400} = 1.1 \times 100 = 110.$$

We say that prices have risen by 10% over the base year.

The GNP deflator

Now we can use the price index to see how much the output has really changed from one year to another. In Table 1D the GNP was $2,904 after both prices and output had risen. We divide this by 1.1, which is the decimal equivalent of the price index of 110:

$$\frac{\$2,904}{1.1} = \$2,640.$$

The resulting figure of $2,640 is called **real GNP,** which is simply GNP in terms of base-year dollars. Real output has increased from $2,400 in the base year to $2,640 in the current year. Of course, if prices had fallen since the base period, the index would be less than one and the correction needed in order to determine real output would be upward. Since prices have seldom fallen, the correction is usually called deflation. That is, we deflate the

Table 3
Computing the Price Index

Base Year Prices and Output	Current Year Prices Only
1,000 loaves bread × $ .40 = $ 400	1,000 loaves bread × $ .44 = $ 440
1,000 bottles wine × 2.00 = 2,000	1,000 bottles wine × 2.20 = 2,200
GNP = $2,400	GNP = $2,640

current-dollar GNP to obtain real GNP. The national income statisticians refer to the decimal version of the price index as a **deflator.** To calculate real GNP for any year, the calculation is

$$\frac{\text{nominal GNP}}{\text{deflator}} = \text{real GNP.}$$

Let us illustrate the need to deflate GNP to real terms by analyzing U.S. GNP figures for 1974 and 1975. In 1975, GNP was recorded as $1.516 trillion, up from $1.413 trillion in 1974. That represents a 7.3% increase and looks pretty good. However, the deflator, based upon 1972 = 1.00, was 1.164 in 1974 and 1.272 in 1975. The result is that real GNP fell to $1.192 trillion in 1975 from $1.214 trillion in 1974. There was a *decline* in real output of 1.8% instead of an increase. The economy was slightly depressed when measured in real terms.

GNP from the output side

In national income accounting we may treat each of our four sectors—households, firms, government, and the rest of the world—as if it were a business firm in order to measure the output of the sector. An account is drawn up for each showing sales and inventories on one side and costs on the other. The two sides must add to the same amount on the bottom line, following the principles of double-entry bookkeeping. (These accounts are known as *T-accounts,* for obvious visual reasons. See Table 4 for an example.)

The business sector

As we might expect, most of the goods and services of our economy are produced in the business sector. Table 4 presents the data for this sector. The right-hand side shows sales and inventories and the left shows the costs of production. The word "consolidated" in the title indicates that the data represent all businesses in the economy.

Taking the right-hand side first, the largest entry is *sales to ultimate users*—$1,187.8 billion. The users include households, government, and the rest of the world (or exports). The other item on the right-hand side is *gross investment.* Investment is singled out because this expenditure plays a special role in the economy. It is also a rapidly changing item which economists like to study carefully for clues as to how the economy will perform. Remember, investment represents the sale of goods, including raw materials and goods for inventories, within the business sector—not to ultimate users, but for use in future production. It is called gross investment because it includes amounts spent for the replacement of worn-out capital goods, as well as for new additions to productive capacity.

Table 4
Consolidated Business Income and Product Account for the United States, 1976 (in billions of dollars)

Wages and salaries	645.4	Sales to ultimate users			1,187.8
Employer contributions for social insurance	62.1	Gross investment			239.6
Rental income of persons	23.5	change in inventories		11.9	
Interest	82.0	capital goods		227.7	
Proprietors' income	96.7				
Corporate profits and IVA	117.9				
National income originating with business	**1,094.0**				
Business transfer payments	7.1				
Indirect taxes	149.7				
Current surplus less subsidies of government enterprises	−1.2				
Net national product originating with business	**1,247.6**				
Capital consumption allowance	179.8				
Gross national product originating with business	**1,427.4**	**Gross national product of business**			**1,427.4**

Source: *Survey of Current Business,* March, 1977.

Gross investment is divided into two parts: inventory change and capital goods. A firm's *inventory* is the amount of unsold goods on hand. *As such, inventory is a stock concept.* Inventory change, though, is a flow concept: it measures how much is added to or taken away (sold) from the inventory. **Inventory change** is a measure of the amount of goods produced that is not sold but remains in the business sector. Inventories of raw materials and partially finished goods are included here because they will be used for future production. Finished goods in the hands of wholesalers and retailers are necessary for them to perform their services and so are just as properly included here. However, only the *change* in inventory is counted, since this is what comes out of current production.

The inventory change can be found by subtracting sales from additions to inventory. If inventories are increased, current production includes not only what is produced and sold but the addition to inventory. Say a firm had 100 units in inventory at the start of the year. During the year it produced and sold 1,000 units and ended the year with 110 units in inventory. Inventory change was +10 units. Production was 1,000 + 10, or 1,010. Inventory change would be negative if inventory levels are reduced. Suppose a firm starts the year with 100 units in inventory, sells 1,000 units and ends the year with 90 units in inventory. Production was not 1,000 since 10 units were sold from inventory. Inventory change was −10 units. Thus production was 1,000 − 10, or 990 units.

Capital goods include all expenditures for equipment, machines, and furniture used in business, and all construction expenditures. The construction item needs some explanation. A factory, warehouse, store, or office building is intended for use in future production. An apartment house or hotel will provide housing services, and therefore should also be included. The same holds for owner-occupied houses, since a house is not used up immediately but continues to provide services over a long period of time. Residential construction is therefore treated as investment, and the houseowner is thought of as renting the house either to himself or to others.

In summary, the business sector produces goods and services for sale to ultimate users and for gross investment. Adding these together in Table 4, we get the sum of $1,427.4 billion as the contribution of the business sector to gross national product.

The left-hand side of the same account gives the costs associated with the production of goods and services. The first six entries require little comment. *Wages and salaries* and *employer contributions for social insurance* represent the cost of labor. *Rent* is only the payments to persons primarily in the business of renting buildings. *Interest* is the cost of borrowed money, and *proprietors' income* (usually called profit) is the payment to owners of unincorporated business firms. The abbreviation IVA stands for *inventory valuation adjustment,* to cover changes in the market value of goods in inventory. The total of the first six items represents *national income originating in the business sector,* amounting to $1,094 billion.

Several additional costs are listed. *Business transfer payments* include gifts to persons or institutions and also bad debts written off as uncollectible. *Indirect taxes* include license and other fees, customs duties, and sales, excise, and property taxes. *Current surplus less subsidies of government enterprises* includes the earnings of government-owned enterprises such as utilities and transportation systems and the Post Office, minus subsidies paid by the government to farmers, airlines, shipping companies, and its own enterprises. These items, added to the national income originating in the business sector, give us *net national product originating with business.*

The use of the term net national product (NNP) requires explanation. You are familiar with the term gross national product as meaning the total of all goods and services produced by the economy. But some of the capital equipment is used up in production during the year—that is, buildings and machines wear out or *depreciate.* So the statisticians deduct a certain amount from GNP, called the *capital consumption allowance,* which covers depreciation. What is left is called *net national product:*

NNP = GNP − capital consumption allowance.

Table 5
U.S. Government Income and Product Account, 1976 (in billions of dollars)

Wages and salaries	190.7		
Employer contributions for social insurance	4.1		
National income originating with government	**194.8**	Net and gross national product of government	**194.8**

Source: *Survey of Current Business,* March, 1977.

NNP is the output available for use after the economy has replaced the capital goods used up during the year.

The government sector

Governments engage in many activities. Our national, state, and local governments even produce a few goods that are sold in the market. For the most part, however, our government bodies produce services related to health, education, and public safety. These services are not sold in the market and hence the accountants can't add up their prices as is done with the output of the business sector. Instead, the output of the government sector is valued as the total of the wages and salaries of government employees. See Table 5. The net and gross national products of government are identical since there is no capital consumption allowance. The governmental contribution to NNP and GNP (right-hand side of the account) is equal to the *national income originating with government* (left-hand side of the account). In Table 5 the amount is $194.8 billion.

The household sector

Some production of goods and services also occurs in the household sector. The most obvious production is that by domestic servants. This category also includes the output of nonprofit organizations such as the Red Cross and educational institutions. As with government, the cost of the output is measured by the cost of the labor used. The amount given in Table 6 is $56 billion.

The rest of the world

The foreign sector of the economy produces a relatively small part of the output. The amount is measured by the payments made to the resources used to produce the output. Their exact breakdown need not concern us here. The amount given in Table 7 is $13.4 billion.

Summary: GNP by sector of origin

Now we can add up the totals of the four sectors, as is done in Table 8. The business sector produces by far the largest portion of the economy's output, $1,427.4 billion. The government sector produces $194.8 billion. The household sector follows with $56 billion and the rest of the world with $13.4 billion. The total gross national product is $1,691.6 billion for 1976.

GNP from the expenditures side

Table 9 shows how the gross national product is added up on the expenditures side. We are going to meet some new terms here, which have very specific meanings.

Personal consumption expenditures

Personal consumption is by far the largest item in the flow of expenditures. **Personal con-**

Table 6
U.S. Household Income and Product Account, 1976 (in billions of dollars)

Wages and salaries	54.3		
Employer contributions for social insurance	1.7		
National income originating with households	**56.0**	Net and gross national product of households	**56.0**

Source: *Survey of Current Business,* March, 1977.

Table 7
Rest of World Income and Product Account for United States, 1976 (in billions of dollars)

National income originating with rest of world	13.4	Net and gross national product of rest of world	13.4

Source: *Survey of Current Business,* March, 1977.

sumption expenditures are the total of all expenditures by households for durable and nondurable goods plus services. The statisticians are rather arbitrary in defining personal consumption. They assume that everything households buy is consumed the moment it is purchased. Even durable goods such as automobiles and kitchen ranges are counted as personal consumption, though they may last for years. The only exception to this is newly constructed houses, which are treated as capital goods and included in gross private domestic investment (below). Aside from durable goods, personal consumption expenditures include nondurable consumer goods such as food, beverages, cigarettes, etc., and expenditures on services. In 1976 they totaled $1,079.7 billion.

Gross private domestic investment

This is a difficult but precise way of saying "all investment spending by private business firms." *Gross* means that both new investment and replacement investment are included. *Private* means that only the investment of private firms is included, not investment by government-owned enterprises. *Domestic* means that foreign investment is not included. *Investment,* of course, represents goods and services which are to be used for future production (but not durable consumer goods, which as we have

seen are included in consumption). In 1976 gross private domestic investment amounted to $239.6 billion. For our purposes, gross private domestic investment is the same as gross investment.

Gross private domestic investment consists of three broad categories: nonresidential investment, residential construction, and changes in inventories. *Nonresidential investment* includes buildings which are intended for productive purposes, as well as the equipment, machinery, and furniture inside them. *Residential construction* includes all new private housing. If the owner lives in his house, he is considered as renting it to himself. The other element of investment is changes in inventories. If a firm's inventories of unsold goods increase, this is treated as an investment in capital that will yield a return in the future; the firm is viewed as selling goods to itself. Of course, if inventories are reduced during the year, this would be considered negative in-

Table 8
Summary of U.S. GNP by Sector of Origin, 1976 (in billions of dollars)

Business sector	$1,427.4
Government sector	194.8
Household sector	56.0
Rest of world sector	13.4
Total Output = GNP	**$1,691.6**

Table 9
Expenditures Approach to U.S. GNP, 1976 (in billions of dollars)*

Personal consumption			
expenditures			1,079.7
durable goods		156.5	
nondurable goods		440.4	
services		482.8	
Gross private domestic			
investment			239.6
nonresidential		160.0	
residential		67.7	
change in inventories		11.9	
Government purchases of goods			
and services			365.6
federal		133.4	
national defense	88.2		
other	45.2		
state and local		232.2	
Net exports			6.6
exports		162.7	
imports		156.0	
Gross National Expenditures (= GNP)			**$1,691.6**

Source: *Survey of Current Business,* March, 1977.
*Figures may not add up due to rounding.

vestment and subtracted from the total of gross private domestic investment.

Government purchases

This item includes not only federal government purchases but also purchases by 50 states, 3,000 counties, and many thousands of municipalities. State and local government purchases are much larger in total amount than those of the federal government: in 1976 the former amounted to $232.2 billion, as compared to $133.4 billion for the federal government. The figures include all government purchases, but not the total government budget since no transfer payments are included. You will notice that the government doesn't seem to spend anything on capital investment. This is only because the national income accountants prefer to treat capital goods bought by governments as though they were consumed immediately. A government office building, of course, is no different from a private office building and should logically be treated as capital.

Net exports

The final item on the expenditures side is *net exports*, or the difference between exports and imports. Exports represent domestic production and imports represent foreign production. By subtracting foreign production from domestic production, we obtain the net amount contributed to GNP. This is known as net exports even though imports may exceed exports.

GNP from the income side

Now we can turn to the other side of our equation (GNE = GNP = GNI) and see just how all the goods and services that make up the gross national product are distributed in the form of income flows. The various components of GNI are organized into two basic groups: national income and nonincome items.

National income

When analyzing potential spending by firms and households, economists need to know the income of spending units. We need a concept which is closer to what most people think of as their income rather than GNP, which is a measure of the income or production of the economy as a whole. The desired concept is national income (NI), which is the total of all incomes for all factors of production. **National income** consists of all wages, rents, interest payments, and profits received during a period of time (usually a year).

One way to calculate national income would be to accumulate all the national income generated in each sector of the economy. From Tables 4 through 7, we can see the national income by the sector in which the income is formed—that is, as paid by businesses, governments, households, and the rest of the world. In Table 10, the amounts paid by each sector of the economy are summarized showing the total paid to each type of resource. Recall that we discussed each national income component in our output approach to totaling GNP.

Nonincome items

The two nonincome items included in gross national income are payments by business firms: the capital consumption allowance and indirect business taxes. (Actually, there are a few other minor items which we put under "miscellaneous items.") The indirect business taxes include all taxes charged against the

Table 10
Income Approach to GNP, U.S., 1976
(in billions of dollars)

Wages and salaries	$890.4
Supplement to wages and salaries	138.0
Proprietors' income	96.7
Rental income of persons	23.5
Corporate profits	117.9
National interest payments	82.0
National income	**1,348.5**
Capital consumption allowance	179.8
Indirect business taxes	149.7
Miscellaneous items	13.6
Gross national income (= GNP)	**1,691.6**

Source: *Survey of Current Business*, March, 1977.

firm's products. These taxes, which the firm usually calculates as part of its costs, are mostly excise taxes, property taxes, and sales taxes. Corporate income taxes are assessed against a firm's profits and are therefore *not* included here. Recall that the capital consumption allowance is the amount spent for capital goods estimated to have been used up during the year. Businessmen call it *depreciation*. Adding the nonincome items to national income gives us gross national income, which equals GNP.

Related income accounts

The advantage of setting up the income approach to GNP is that it enables us to continue and calculate other useful income concepts. In particular, it is useful to have a measure of personal income and personal saving. Therefore, we start with GNP and work "backwards," breaking it down into its income components.

Net national product We begin by subtracting that part of the GNP that is spent on fixing up the economic machinery so it will keep on producing. In other words, we subtract the capital consumption allowance. What remains is known as net national product (NNP):

$$NNP = GNP - capital\ consumption\ allowance.$$

In Table 11, NNP amounts to $1,511.8 billion for 1976. By having eliminated depreciation (we might call it "yearly replacement costs"), *NNP gives us a measure of all new production.* In much of economics theory, this concept will be very important. Often we will use NNP instead of GNP to denote yearly output of goods and services.

National income We can calculate national income as shown in Table 11. Earlier, in our income approach to GNP, we added up the payments to factors of production to find national income. Working backwards, if we subtract from NNP the items which are not payments to factory of production, we obtain national income (NI). We subtract *indirect business taxes* and *business transfer payments*. Then we add *subsidies less surpluses of government enterprises*. National income is the result. While

Table 11
Relationship of GNP to Personal Income and Saving, U.S., 1976 (in billions of dollars)

Gross national product		**1,691.6**
less Capital consumption allowance		(−) 179.8
equals **Net national product** (NNP)		**$1,511.8**
less Indirect business tax	149.7	
Business transfer payments	7.1	
Statistical discrepancy	7.7	(−) 164.5
plus Subsidies less surpluses of government enterprises		(+) 1.2
equals **National income** (NI)		**1,348.5**
less Corporate profits & IVA	117.9	
Contributions for social insurance	122.8	(−) 240.7
plus Government transfer payments	153.3	
Net interest paid by government & consumers	82.0	
Dividends	35.1	
Business transfer payments	7.1	(+) 277.5
equals **Personal income** (PI)		**1,375.3**
less Personal tax and nontax payments		(−) 193.6
equals **Disposable personal income** (DPI)		**1,181.7**
less Personal outlays		(−)1,105.2
personal consumption expenditures	1,079.7	
interest paid by consumers	24.4	
personal transfer payments to foreigners	1.1	
equals **Personal saving** (PS)		76.5

Source: *Survey of Current Business*, March, 1977.

this is all potentially spendable income, it is still not the same as the amount most people think of as income. To obtain personal income from national income, we have to make additional adjustments.

Personal income National income differs from personal income because we obtain income in other ways than from our services as factors of production or owners of factors of production. Also, part of national income is not available to individuals. In Table 11, *corporate profits* and *inventory valuation adjustment* (IVA) are amounts going to corporations. Contributions for social insurance by both employers and employees also have to be subtracted. Then we add in those payments which are income to some individuals *even though no current production is involved. Government transfer payments* are of this type: Social Security, unemployment compensation, welfare, veterans' bonuses, and other payments which represent a redistribution of income outside of the productive process. *Net interest paid by government and consumers* is also of this type. In 1976 net interest payments amounted to $82.0 billion, meaning that people received more interest than they paid out (or, more precisely, that some people paid out more interest than they received, while other people received more interest than they paid out, the sum total being in favor of the receivers). Since we have just subtracted corporate profits, we must now add back in that portion of them paid out to individuals as *dividends*. Finally, *business transfer payments* are added back in because they represent receipts by persons of spendable income even though no current production may be involved.

After all these additions and subtractions we come at last to personal income. **Personal income** (PI) is therefore the income available to households before they pay taxes. Personal income may be larger than national income. In recession years such as 1974 government transfer payments leap upward and help to increase personal income.

Disposable personal income Not all personal income is spendable. You must pay taxes first. Other things must be paid too: license fees, such as state and local automobile licenses, hunting licenses, and dog licenses; and fines and penalties, such as traffic tickets. What remains of personal income after taxes and fees are paid is known as **disposable personal income** (DPI). It is disposable in any way its receivers choose, or their spouses and families permit.

Personal saving What isn't spent from DPI is saved, according to the national income economists. This income is known as **personal saving** (PS). It may be in people's checking accounts, or lying around their bureau drawers waiting to be spent later, but in an economic sense it is saved. Most of disposable personal income isn't saved in anybody's sense, but spent. In 1976, DPI was estimated at $1,181.6 billion, of which $1,101.3 billion was spent and $80.3 billion saved. Most of the spending was for personal consumption, and a small amount of it for interest payments. A very small amount was sent abroad as gifts to people living in other countries. Small? According to the statisticians, it amounted to $1.1 billion.

GNP counting problems

Avoiding double counting

At this point you may have some reservations about how we arrived at the national product figures we've given above. You may have wondered where the statisticians get their information. For instance, do they ask the auto manufacturers the value of the cars they made last year; and the parts manufacturers the value of the starters or generators they made; and the tire companies the value of the tires; and the steel companies the value of the sheet steel? No wonder the figures are so big, you say. They've counted everything six times over!

The finished car obviously includes all the parts that go into it, you will say. The customer buys the whole thing. That being so, it isn't reasonable to count the output of the parts companies and the tire companies and the steel companies and all the other contributors to the Mobile Monster.

You're right, of course. But the statistics are right too, because they're very carefully put together in such a way that things don't get counted twice. The ways of doing this belong to the art of national income accounting.

The final expenditures method   One way to eliminate double counting is to record output only the last time it is sold. When goods are sold to ultimate users for consumption this works pretty well. Sales to the rest of the world (of raw products, for example) may involve double counting if they find their way back in future imports, but the error will be small.

The value added method   A second way of avoiding double counting is to measure only the value added at each step of manufacture. Consider the sale of a tire to the automobile manufacturer. Instead of counting the entire value of the tire, only the contribution of the tire manufacturer is counted. The manufacturer has added to the value of the rubber he began with by combining it with other materials and processing it. The value added by the manufacturer is found by subtracting the value of the rubber and other materials from the price received for the tire. In the case of the auto manufacturer, the value added is found by subtracting the cost of the tires and other purchased parts such as starters, generators, and steel sheets from the price the manufacturer receives for the car. Another way of measuring the value added would be to sum the payments to factors of production by the automobile manufacturer. If we sum the values added at all the stages of manufacture, they will total the selling price of the finished product.

In practice, both methods are used along with other data. By counting output several ways, it is possible to check the results of one method against those of others.

Things that aren't counted

We've seen that the national income statisticians don't count every transaction involved in the manufacture of a product, because to do so would involve counting some production many times over. Some other kinds of transactions are not counted for quite different reasons.

Illegal activities   No effort is made to count the value of illegal goods and services, even though these are just as much a part of the economy as the others. There are two reasons. First, there is an element of coercion in some illegal matters which is not present in a regular market. Second, the government cannot be in the position of recognizing and measuring activities it is presumably trying to control or stop. The GNP would be a good deal higher if all the graft, gambling, prostitution, illegal drug sales, and other underworld activities were counted. From the economist's point of view the omission of these items is inconsistent. The sale of lottery tickets is included in GNP in states where legal lotteries exist, and so are the revenues of gambling casinos in Nevada. But no accounting is made of the activities of the bookies and the policy operators.

Nonmarket production   Things produced but not sold are left out of GNP. The main reason for not valuing nonmarket activities is precisely that there is no market value to apply to the activity. A meal prepared at home is not counted, although the same meal eaten in a restaurant would be. Likewise with laundry, which is counted if it is sent out but not counted when done in the washing machine in the basement. If large numbers of people turned to do-it-yourself activities they might actually decrease the GNP even though they increased the quantity and quality of goods produced.

There are some exceptions to this rule that things not sold are left out of GNP. As we have already seen, the rental value of owner-occupied houses is counted as production. If a maid or butler receives payment in the form of room and board, or if a farm hand receives perquisites such as housing and farm produce, these things are counted as output. Also, when a farm family consumes some of its own produce, it is counted as output even though no sale occurs. And the "free" checking accounts offered by banks are valued as services in GNP since they are considered to represent a form of interest payment.

Extended Example
My Wife, I Think I'll Keep Her

The television-commercial husband beams fondly at his television-commercial wife. Because she regularly uses the sponsor's vitamin product, she is a first-rate housekeeper and mother. "My wife," says the proud husband, "I think I'll keep her." Leaving aside the male chauvinist flavor of the commercial, the economist, male or female, is likely to retort, "You'd better keep her. She's worth a good deal of money."

Her monetary value, however, is not included in our system of national income accounting. Because she produces things that are not sold, the value of these things are not included in the gross national product. A housewife's work may include washing windows, cleaning and repairing furniture, making and laundering clothes for herself and her family, and any number of other tasks. The value of each of these tasks would be included in national income accounting if it were done by an outsider working for wages or hire. And, of course, the daily meals she prepares are not part of the GNP, although they would be if they were prepared by a restaurant.

What is the real, though uncounted, monetary value of the average housewife's production of goods and services? Recently, the Social Security Administration released figures that throw some light on the situation. Its researchers claimed that, in 1972, the average housewife's economic value was $4,705. The housewife's peak economic value was $6,417, when she was between the ages of 20 and 24. At 35 to 39, it declined to $5,892 and kept declining to around $2,500 for a housewife in her 60s to below $500 for the really elderly.

The researchers also arrived at some interesting figures of comparison between the economic value of housewives and their female counterparts in the labor market. Between the ages of 15 to 19, the housewife's economic value was higher than that of her "working" counterpart—$5,389, as compared with $4,194. For the 20 to 24 age group, the comparison stood at $6,061 to $5,884. As the women grew older, however, the figures began to reverse, with the economic value of housewives steadily declining and that of women in the labor force rising. By age 60 to 64, the ratio was $2,942 for housewives to $7,052 for women in the labor force.

The agency's figures were arrived at by using a market cost system for computing the value of a housewife's services. For example, the value of a home meal was calculated by the minimum wage value of a hired cook, the value of window washing by the minimum wage value of a hired window washer, etc. Researchers found, not surprisingly, that the key variable in computing the economic value of housewives was the number of children needing to be fed and cared for in the household.

The use of minimum wage levels for computing the value of household work has been criticized as too conservative by some economists—and by some women's organizations. The minimum wage may be less than the market price which would actually have to be paid. The lack of market-determined prices is precisely why home-produced output is not included in GNP. The Social Security Administration had to try to overcome the problem and the result is at best an approximation. But many economists laud the attempt to quantify the housewife's value as a step in the right direction toward eventual inclusion of nonmarket production in a broader measure of national output.

Gifts and financial transactions Money transactions are excluded from GNP if they are not related to current production. These include transfer payments such as Social Security payments, veterans' benefits from the federal government, and public welfare of various kinds. Gifts, prizes, scholarships, inheritances, donations, and charities are examples of private transfer payments which are excluded from GNP. The sale of securities such as stocks or bonds is merely a change in the form in which wealth is held and does not represent current production. Also excluded are capital gains or losses which arise from changes in the prices of assets. Of course, the services of a broker in assisting with a financial transaction are considered part of current production and included in GNP.

Used goods Second-hand goods are not part of current output. Their sale is not included in GNP. But second-hand car dealers perform services which are current and must therefore be counted even though the products they handle are not. This same concept applies to all others who sell used goods.

Shortcomings of GNP accounting

You will have recognized by now that national income accounting is imperfect. By this we do not mean simply that it shares the failings of other human activities. It does, of course, but it is also imperfect in another sense. It is an effort to summarize the activities of 215 million people in a few numbers that can be printed on a page. But such numbers can never be more than symbolic of the vast, complex panorama they represent.

Criticisms of GNP accounting can be grouped into three broad categories: statistical difficulties, welfare measurement, and externalities or side-effects. We now discuss each individually.

Statistical difficulties

For an economy as large as the United States, it is readily seen that the job of collecting the necessary data to measure GNP would be massive. It is not possible to count every item produced or to be absolutely sure the item is not resold and therefore double counted. Statistical samples are necessary to measure GNP and any sampling procedure leads to the possibility that errors will creep in. As has already been noted, measurements are made at several points in the flow of goods and services and the results checked against each other. The number of statisticians engaged in the work of measuring GNP is large enough to be measured in its turn as a service produced. Yet the accuracy of the data are still questioned by some.

Proposals for improving data collection are often suggested. In most cases, the proposal involves substantial additional cost. Either households and firms must be required to submit more data at a cost to themselves or the government must increase the number of statisticians employed at an increase in cost. It is difficult in many instances to justify the increase, especially since there are additional criticisms of GNP beyond the statistical problems.

Another statistical problem with GNP is that the data are for the nation as a whole. Presumably an increase in GNP would indicate an increase in output and therefore more goods and services to be consumed. Suppose, however, that during a given year cutbacks in aerospace expenditures result in a substantial decrease in output concentrated on the West Coast and selected cities in Kansas, Texas, and Georgia. If the decrease should be offset by increases in agricultural output in the Midwest, lumber sales in the Northwest, and textile production in the Southeast, then GNP stays the same or may even rise. Does this mean there is no problem? No one questions the benefits of increased production in the areas which experience it but what about the areas suffering from the cutbacks in aerospace? Attention to GNP alone would tend to distract from the problems of selected areas.

Related to the above, another problem is that GNP is not on a per capita basis. Suppose real GNP increases without any problem areas developing. The increase in GNP would seem to indicate that there are more goods and services available for consumption. But, also suppose that population grew during the same period by more than the increase in GNP. Then, on a per capita basis, there would actually be less for each individual to consume. By computing GNP on a per capita basis, it would be possible to say whether the goods and services available for each person had increased.

Welfare measurement difficulties

GNP includes only goods produced and sold in the market. This means that a great deal of production is not measured since it never reaches the market. We have already noted the unrecorded labors of the housewife and the unweighed contributions of the criminal element. Hobbyists and home gardeners may cause GNP to go down if they become so enthusiastic that they generate a lot of non-market production. This is another way of saying that the GNP doesn't measure how well off people are. Initially, GNP was intended as a simple counting measure, not as a gauge of human welfare. But through the years, GNP has come to mean for many people—especially politicians—a measure of welfare or well-being. But is this the case?

For example, a lawyer who lives in Scarsdale drives his car to the station every morning, takes the train into New York City, and catches a subway to his office. His counterpart in, say, Holland rides to his office from home on a bicycle in less time. Other things being equal, who is better off: the person who requires a lot of machinery and time to move him to his work, or the person who wastes less time and pedals there on a bike? The national income statisticians will prefer the American lawyer, of course, because they count only the physical equipment.

In this same vein, GNP fails to measure leisure. Suppose people decide to take more time to enjoy themselves rather than working so hard. Welfare would increase because people chose to relax. GNP would remain the same or perhaps decrease. People would feel they were better off but GNP would fail to measure the increase. It goes without saying that the leisure must be the result of choice and not enforced leisure as a result of unemployment.

Another difficulty is that GNP doesn't measure changes in taste. If the mix of products changes as a result of changes in tastes, the consumer may be better off yet GNP would remain the same. For example, if sugar-free or diet beverages, costing the same as the regular beverages, are sold, people will enjoy them more because they are not getting fat, but GNP will not reflect the increased enjoyment and therefore fails to measure the increase in welfare. New products have the same effect. Digital watches have replaced mechanical watches for a number of consumers. Presumably welfare is increased, but GNP won't necessarily increase.

GNP fails to measure increases in product quality. If cars pollute less as a result of engineering changes, welfare increases though GNP may not. Color television engineering has improved the picture quality and therefore enjoyment, but the price and output of the sets have remained basically the same. Again, GNP would fail to measure the increase in welfare.

Finally, GNP does not measure the distribution of output. If GNP goes up but the goods and services and the income generated go to a small segment of the society, welfare may not increase on balance. This would be especially so if those not receiving any benefits of the increase in GNP were envious of those who had. Again, attention only to the increase in GNP would fail to note that income distribution had resulted in a decrease in welfare. GNP would fail to measure the decrease and in fact would indicate an increase.

Externalities

Economists refer to the side-effects of economic production as **externalities.** An externality might be good or bad, depending on the side-effects. We are concerned now with negative externalities, especially pollution, that aren't included in GNP. Obviously the various types of pollution are overlooked if we consider all increases of GNP to be beneficial.

Some industrial production results in more smoke being poured into the air, while other production results in more waste being dumped into rivers. Some industries accomplish both. In some cases, even if the production process does not create pollution, use of the product may. Discarded cans and bottles are an example. So is the destruction of the ozone layer by propellants used in aerosols.

Another externality is the destruction of resources as a result of production. Strip-mining, deforestation, and depletion of oil and gas reserves are conspicuous examples. Visual pollution which destroys the beauty of an area by putting towers, buildings, or billboards in an area is another example. The increase in GNP as a result would be measured and because of the increase, our society would appear to be better served. However, the cost is high and not measured. In fact, people both now and in the future may be harmed and therefore welfare is reduced.

Some critics would add another negative externality: the effect that a particular product may have on society. Consider, for example, the automobile—that cornerstone of American industrial output. The use of the auto in the urban areas has led to the decline or, in some instances, near destruction of public transportation. This decline may then literally force others to buy autos so they can, among other things, commute to work. The net result has been to increase GNP—but has welfare increased? An even more serious effect concerns the poor. The decline in public transportation is usually accompanied by much higher prices for the rider, so the poor become even poorer. Also, when jobs do follow the auto to suburbia, the poor either lose jobs or have diminished job prospects. The net result is a greater gulf between the middle class and the poor.

Social welfare indicators

Beginning in the late 1960s, several suggestions were advanced for modifying GNP so it is a measure of welfare (rather than production). The methods have been called Net Social Welfare or **Net Economic Welfare** (known as NEW). By 1969, the federal government issued a publication called *Toward a Social Report*. The tentative nature of the title indicated the difficulties involved in developing the measures suggested. As of now, GNP is still with us since it is clear what is being measured.

One thing which should be added to any measure of social welfare is the state of health of the members of the society. However, measures of health are not readily available. The data now being collected measure lack of health. For example, death rates, days lost due to illness, and infant mortality rates are all collected. Of course, health may be presumed to improve when these things are reduced but they do not provide a positive measure of health. Such measures would have to be developed if a total measure of welfare is to mean anything.

The preparation of our society to adapt to conditions as they exist is another measure of welfare. Blind acceptance of all situations no matter how bad is not desirable; so a positive measure of ability to function must be developed. Education is the activity which should produce life-styles appropriate to the world in which a society must live. Data are available as to the number of people educated to a certain number of grades in school or the dollars spent on education. However, there is no good measure of the results of education. Further, some educational activities are aimed at producing basic skills in communication while other educational activities produce job skills. These do not measure welfare even though the absence of these types of education would reduce welfare. Only when education goes beyond the "three R's" does it become a means to greater ability to adapt.

A rather long list of other measures of well-being has been suggested for inclusion in any improved indicator of social welfare. Valuing nonmarket production by the household, especially the housewife's production, and valuing leisure activities would give a closer measure of the actual consumption level of the household.

Several "penalties" to GNP have also been suggested in order to account for society's "bads." The most obvious of these is a penalty for air or water pollution created in the process of making goods and services. If increased

Economic Thinker
Wassily Leontief

During the 1930s, when economists were developing national income accounting, some other economists were exploring different methods to measure the flows of goods and services in our economy. The American economist Wassily Leontief (born 1906) was successful in producing a method that is a useful supplement to national income accounting. His method is now known as *input-output analysis.*

Leontief was born in Czarist Russia and educated in Leningrad and Berlin. As research economist and later as adviser to the Chinese government, he became interested in the flows of resources among a nation's industries. He developed input-output analysis while employed at the National Bureau of Economic Research and at Harvard. His first analysis appeared in 1936. Eventually, Leontief received the Nobel Prize in economics (1973) for this work.

Input-output analysis is based on the use of a large grid. Arrayed along the top and left side of the square grid are the many different industries which operate in an economy. Each entry in the grid shows transactions between two different industries. The sum of all entries should show all production in the economy. Input-output tables for the United States include 78 industrial classifications as well as classifications for nonprofit enterprises, government business, and imports. Broadly speaking, input-output tables are an updated and far more precise version of the *Tableau Economique,* constructed by the physiocrat economist François Quesnay in the eighteenth century.

Input-output tables provide a means for looking beneath the aggregate economic quantities to see what is really happening in particular segments of the economy. These tables are also valuable for studying short-run occurrences and forecasting long-run trends. In particular, the effects of shortages or surpluses of commodities can be studied in detail. If, for example, the output of oil is restricted, the table shows the effect on each industrial entry.

Input-output analysis can be used just as well in command economies or in market economies. Economists in the Soviet Union find an input-output table useful in planning since it shows how much of each input (resource) must be available to every industry in order to achieve the desired levels of output of goods. Firms can plan more effectively to eliminate bottlenecks and avoid surpluses.

Recently, Leontief has turned his attention to a similar analysis on a global scale. He has been especially concerned about the need to preserve the environment upon our spaceship earth. Yet at the same time, we must find ways to achieve economic growth for the less developed nations. In a study published in 1976, Leontief concludes that with proper development strategies our *known* resources should last until 2150 rather than 2075, as had previously been predicted.

output and GNP created smog which led to an increase in lung cancer, an appropriate penalty charge would show that welfare had decreased despite the increase in GNP. The problems posed in the measurement of the penalty charge are rather difficult to solve as it would be very hard to measure the damage done let alone decide which of the many firms actually produced the smoke that caused the cancer.

Another proposal of this type is to separate those consumption expenditures which create satisfaction or welfare from those which are merely necessary in order to survive. Payment of a hospital bill does not create satisfaction but cannot always be avoided unless one considers the alternative of being sick or dead desirable. Once started, this type of calculation is hard to stop. How much of the expenditure for clothing is necessary to protect from freezing and how much creates satisfaction through providing modesty, status, or decoration? Is not the expenditure for food merely necessary to sustain life? It would be necessary to consider all things which contribute to welfare, even if people reacted in opposite ways to the same thing. Then the measurement problems would have to be solved. Beyond that, the weight to be given to each measure in an overall index would have to be decided. The idea of a broader measure of welfare is definitely good. There certainly are problems if only GNP is considered. However, the road to a measure of Net Social Welfare still stretches ahead for a long distance.

A final word on GNP shortcomings

The measurement of GNP is not likely to be abandoned as a result of the criticisms leveled at it. Time has taught many lessons about changes which occur in an economy as GNP changes. The production of goods and services will go on and the output must be measured. At the same time, the criticisms will not soon cease. As long as there are people who realize that the quality of life is not determined by more goods and services regardless of the loss of natural resources or other satisfactions, there will be outcries against the use of GNP as a measure of welfare. However, GNP is still a fair measure of *production.*

Summary

National income accounting is the effort by statisticians and economists to gather data which measure the current production of the various parts of the macroeconomy. The measure of total economic activity is gross national product (GNP), which is the market value of all goods and services produced within the economy for the year. Simon Kuznets was one of the pioneers who developed the methods of measuring GNP.

There are several points in the circular flow of goods and services where measurement of total economic activity may take place. Three basic methods for measuring GNP can be used: the output approach; the expenditures approach; and the income approach. The measurements are equivalent but reveal different concepts in economic activity: gross national expenditures = gross national product = gross national income.

To differentiate between *changes in output* and *changes in prices* in the measurement of GNP, the concept of *real GNP* is used. Real GNP is the current output expressed in the prices of a base period.

Gross national product is the measure of output broken down by the sector of origin. The sectors are business firms, households, government, and the rest of the world.

Gross national expenditures measure the output of the economy categorized by the sectors which purchase the goods and services. The largest expenditure is consumption, which is carried out by households. Investment is the purchase of goods and services by business firms for use in future production. This expenditure receives special attention because it tends to fluctuate. Government expenditures are another sector of demand for goods and services. This expenditure is given special attention because it may be changed as a matter of policy depending upon economic conditions. Finally, expenditures by the rest of the world on our exports minus the amount imported are also a recorded purchase.

Gross national income consists of national income and a few nonincome items. National income measures the payments to the factors of production used in the process of obtaining goods and services. The payments are wages and salaries, rent, interest, and profit.

Net national product (NNP) is GNP minus the capital consumption allowance (which is a measure of the capital goods used up and replaced during the production year).

Other income concepts are derived from NNP. These include national income, personal income, disposable personal income, and personal saving. All of these measure the payments to factors of production and are used to analyze the purchasing potential of households, the ultimate owners of factors of production.

When measuring GNP, national income economists avoid double counting by using the final expenditures method and the value added method. There are four broad categories that aren't included in the measurement of GNP: illegal activities; nonmarket production; gifts and financial transactions; and used goods.

GNP is a good measure of the production of an economy. However, as a measure of the welfare of the members of the economy, GNP has a number of shortcomings. The concept of Net Economic Welfare has been advanced as a means of adding in "goods" and subtracting out "bads" associated with GNP production to measure how well people are doing.

Input-output analysis, developed by Wassily Leontief, is another form of national income accounts. It records all the purchases of inputs by all industries and all sales of output by the industries both to other industries and to ultimate users. The data are presented in tabular or matrix form, which makes them useful for analysis and prediction as well as for recording and describing economic activity.

Key Words and Phrases

- **national income accounting** the process of measuring and reporting by statisticians and economists the dollar amounts of the various flows of goods and services within the economy.

- **gross national product (GNP)** the market value of all goods and services produced during a given period of time (usually a year).

- **household** the consuming unit and also the owner and supplier of resources for production purposes; the *household* rather than the *individual* is used since many decisions are made by collections of people.

- **firm** a complete business organization that makes the decisions in production; the exact form of the firm is not important though it is often treated as though every large corporation were a single proprietorship controlled and run at the direction of one person.

- **retained earnings** that portion of profits which is saved by firms and not paid out as income to the owners of the firm.

- **saving** the act of generating income but not consuming it; saving is a current activity and results in a flow.

- **savings** the accumulation of wealth resulting from past saving; it is a stock concept as opposed to saving, which is a flow concept.

- **investment** the amount added to the stock of capital goods.

- **gross investment** the purchase of new capital goods; this includes not only additions to the stock of capital goods but also the replacement of worn-out capital goods. This term is more precisely called *gross private domestic investment*.

- **depreciation** the amount of capital goods which wear out or are used up during a year.

- **net investment** gross investment minus depreciation; so net investment represents only the *addition* to machinery, buildings, and other capital goods.

- **net exports** exports minus imports.

- **sector** a portion of the economy which serves as a unit in determining production or expenditure within the economy.

- **gross national expenditures** the sum of market expenditures by all sectors of the economy to purchase newly produced goods and services during a period of time (usually a year).

- **gross national income** the sum of all payments to the factors of production used to produce GNP during a period of time (usually one year) plus other charges or costs of production and depreciation.

- **indirect business taxes** these taxes are imposed upon business firms and include license fees, sales, property, and excise taxes, and customs duties.

- **inventory** the stock of raw materials, goods in the process of being made, and finished but unsold goods held by businesses.

- **inventory change** measures the change in inventories during a time period, such as a year.

- **inventory valuation adjustment** adjustment made to inventory figures to separate changes in actual inventory from changes only in the value of inventory because of price level changes.

- **capital consumption allowance** this term is used in national income analysis to refer to *depreciation* but reflects the fact that the accounting concept of depreciation is more sensitive to what the tax laws will allow than the actual wearing out of capital goods.

- **price index** a listing of price values for different years where all the values are given in terms of a base year; the base year is assigned the value 100.

- **money or nominal GNP** GNP valued or calculated at the prices existing at the time the output is measured.

- **real GNP** a measure of GNP which shows the value of output at each time period in terms of the prices of some base year.

- **deflator** an index of price level changes used to adjust nominal or money GNP to real GNP.

- **personal consumption expenditures** the total of all expenditures by households for durable and non-durable goods and services.

- **nonresidential investment** that portion of investment which consists of buildings, equipment, and furniture in the buildings used by businesses for future production.

- **residential construction** all the new housing units constructed during a year.

- **net national product (NNP)** the amount of product available after capital goods used up have been replaced; NNP = GNP − capital consumption allowance.

- **national income (NI)** the total of all incomes of factors of production including wages, rents, interest payments, and profits received during a period of time (usually a year).

- **personal income (PI)** the total of all income and transfer payments actually received by households during a year before any withholding or payment of taxes.

- **disposable personal income (DPI)** the sum of all income and transfer payments received by households after taxes have been paid and therefore available to be used at the discretion of the household.

- **externalities** all the good or bad side-effects of an economic activity; pollution is a "bad" externality.

- **production** any process by which a good is transformed in some way; obvious examples occur in manufacturing, but transportation through distance or storing over time may also be examples of transformation or production.

- **input-output analysis** a system of accounts designed by Wassily Leontief which records all transactions, including the intermediate transactions eliminated from the GNP accounts; the data are presented in tabular or matrix form.

Questions for Review

1. In 1977, a pound of coffee added more to GNP than a pound of beef steak. Since the steak is more nutritional, why should coffee count for more production?

2. Why would an increase in nominal GNP of 5% be misleading as a measure of the increase in output under some circumstances?

3. Look up current figures on nominal and real GNP. Compute the GNP deflator if you cannot also find it in your source of data.

4. Does it really matter that steel production produces smoke and dust when GNP is counted?

5. Since the services of a housewife are not counted in GNP, does it mean that she produces nothing? Why can't her production be added to GNP?

6. What problems exist when we attempt to compare the GNP produced per person in the United States and the GNP produced per person in a country which has not achieved much economic development?

7. What would happen to GNP if we allowed double counting in calculating GNP? How does using value added eliminate double counting in estimating GNP?

8. Which of the following purchases would be included in GNP: (a) 100 shares of IBM stock; (b) a birdcage at a garage sale; (c) a new recording of operatic arias; (d) a used car; (e) a haircut; explain why or why not?

9. If your mother and the lady next door cleaned each other's house for compensation, would GNP be increased over what it would have been if each cleaned their own house? Would production increase? Would welfare increase?

10. If your economics professor marries his housekeeper, what would happen to GNP? What would happen to production?

7

Business Cycles

In the last chapter we looked at the methods the national income economists use to add up all the goods and services produced in the economy. You probably noticed that the totals are never the same from one year to another. Usually they become larger. In some years the GNP grows rapidly, while in other years it grows more slowly. However, there have been years when it declined.

Growth and economic stability

The rate at which the GNP grows is of special interest to everyone. Economists study it to analyze how the economy is performing. Political leaders are responsible for maintaining high levels of economic growth. Politicians are a little like football coaches. Coaches whose teams don't win are likely to lose their jobs, even when it isn't their fault. Politicians tend to lose their jobs when the economy slows down because voters blame them for it.

Most of us want the economy to keep on growing. Our national economic policy is based on growth. A growing economy provides more jobs and higher living standards. The history of our economy is one of quite remarkable growth that transformed a simple frontier society into a cosmopolis of autos, telephones, and moon rockets. But while we want growth, we want other things as well. In particular, we want a stable price level so that the money we save will be worth a little more next year than it is now. If it will buy fewer goods next year because prices have risen, what is the point of saving? We also want the national economy to provide people with jobs and old people with security.

Economic stability: three goals

The ideal economy would do all three things: (1) it would grow steadily over the years, (2) give a job to everyone who wanted one, and (3) maintain a stable price level. There have been periods in our history when the economy almost performed that way, as it did in the 1960s. There have been other periods, as in the 1970s, when it failed on all three counts. In the worst periods we have had widespread unemployment and no growth (or even a shrinking of output). At other times prices have played tricks on us, increasing faster than GNP and faster than our paychecks.

Economists have devoted much effort to finding ways of stabilizing the economy. We even have an act of Congress—the Employment Act of 1946—which states that the federal government has the responsibility to promote maximum employment, production, and purchasing power. Reading these words in the 1970s and 1980s you will certainly be aware that our economists and our government haven't solved the problem of providing jobs and goods at stable prices. You probably know people who have been unemployed for long periods of time—perhaps even to the point of thinking that they will never find jobs again. You've also seen the prices of goods you buy increase faster than the money to pay for them. And you've heard TV newscasters say things like, "This has been one of the auto industry's worst years. Sales of new cars were 2 million less than in 1972."

Why the economy fluctuates

What makes the economy so hard to control? It seems strange that millions of people who want to work and improve themselves should be unable to find jobs. Most puzzling of all, why does the economy go downward when everyone wants it to go upward?

One answer is that a number of different forces are at work in our economy. These forces sometimes work at cross purposes. For instance, the forces that maintain high employment are the same forces that tend to give us higher prices. The forces that counteract higher prices tend to produce unemployment.

Another reason why our economy fluctuates is that certain tendencies are cumulative. If you follow the stock market you will have noticed that when it's on the upswing people start buying because they expect it to rise further. When a turning point is reached and stock prices start to go down, people start selling because they expect the market to keep on falling. After the auto industry has had several bad years, it is likely to have several good ones as customers start replacing their worn-out cars. Fluctuations occur in all parts of the economy. There are seasonal fluctuations, as at Christmas time; there are inventory cycles, when business firms get overstocked and slow down their production or put off buying raw materials (or when they become understocked and start doing the opposite); there are housing booms, when *mortgages* (loans for buying houses) are easy to obtain and buyers are in the market for new houses; and there are many other cumulative movements up and down. We will have more to say later about the different kinds of fluctuations.

Business cycle problems

The question still remains why the play of forces leads to prosperity at one period and to recession or depression at another. Conceivably the different fluctuations could cancel each other out. Or we might have a boom in California and a slump in Delaware, while in Illinois things would be going along as usual. During the 1973–1975 recession, the shortage of energy resulted in Texas and Oklahoma enjoying prosperity while the rest of the country suffered economic hardships. There may be prosperous areas and depressed areas, but on the whole our economy is, like our nation, a single unit despite its many parts. What happens in California is likely to happen in New York as well, though of course each state has its own problems. We are tied together by a common monetary system and by a common national market.

Inflation

We saw in Chapter 3 that if demand rises and the supply of goods and services stays the same, prices will start to go up. But if the economy isn't at the level of full employment yet, the increase in demand will be answered by an increase in supply as firms step up their production. Prices will rise a little, but production will rise a lot. For the readers who remember the conditions of the early 1970s this statement will seem strange. For now, it is enough to

understand that the conditions were not typical of the usual business cycle during the early 1970s. In a following chapter we will look more carefully at the supply curve of goods and services for the entire economy. For now, we may assume that the quantity of goods and services which an economy supplies will generally approach very close to full employment before prices will rise.

As full employment is approached, the prices of many goods and services will start to rise. There may be many reasons. Producers may find it difficult to increase supply any further. Their plants will be operating at capacity, or they may be unable to get materials. If aggregate demand continues to rise, if people still keep spending money, production won't increase much but prices will rise a lot. **Inflation** is the problem of generally rising prices. Inflation always involves a time factor, because price rises can only occur over a period of time. The most common time period cited for inflation is the year, but we could also talk of inflation, or a rising price level, for any given month.

We will come back to inflation—its problems, causes, and cures—in another chapter. We do need to consider some basic causes here to see why inflation is associated with the business cycle. Remember, inflation is a rise in the *level of prices in general*. Some prices may actually fall during inflation, but the main overall direction of movement is upward; some prices will rise more than others.

There are three broad categories of causes resulting in a general price increase. There is one type of inflation called demand-pull inflation. **Demand-pull inflation** results when people want to buy more goods and services than the economy can produce. This is usually called "too much money chasing too few goods." It may be the result of a sudden increase in the amount of money available. Or it may result from a sudden desire to increase expenditures. Examples of such increases are the period when the United States was building canals and railroads in the 1820s and early 1830s or any of the wartime periods we have experienced. We had a strong dose of demand-pull inflation at the end of the Vietnam War. Demand-pull inflation is more of a problem when the economy is near full employment as increases in output are not possible and therefore prices rise. Anytime the economy approaches its production possibilities, demand-pull inflation will threaten.

Another type of inflation is cost-push inflation. **Cost-push inflation** results when "suppliers" are able to raise their prices to other producers who pass along the higher prices to consumers. Our "suppliers" here can be either on the labor side or the business side. Examples of this type of inflation occur when workers are successful in demanding higher wages or if steel producers are successful in demanding higher prices from automobile manufacturers and other steel users. The higher wages and steel prices would be passed along as higher prices for the products consumers buy. In the case of consumer services, such as medical care, education, entertainment, etc., the increase may go directly to the consumer. This happens when barbers raise the price of haircuts or surgeons raise the price of appendectomies. Cost-push inflation may occur whether the economy is at full employment or not. However, when business is expanding, it is easier to increase prices. Thus cost push may be partially related to the business cycle.

The third type of inflation is **structural inflation.** This type is the result of a unique event and is not associated with business cycles. A recent example was the energy crisis created by the shortage of energy sources in the United States and the formation of a cartel by the petroleum-producing countries. The resulting fourfold increase in oil prices led to many rising prices since oil is needed by so many industries. Other examples in recent times were the failure of sugar and coffee crops outside the United States. As a result, not only did sugar and coffee prices rise but so did any goods requiring sugar as a raw product. The drought in the Great Plains in 1976 led to reduced supplies of grain. In turn, grain prices rose. Since grain is needed, for example, for feeding livestock, meat prices rose within a year of the drought. These events can occur at any time and are not related to business cycles.

Regardless of cause, most people dislike inflation. If it creeps along very slowly—say

prices increase at 2 or 3% a year—we may not feel it. But when prices rise at 6 or 8 or 10% per year, as they did in the mid-1970s, everybody feels it and the government will be asked to put on the brakes. There are various methods of putting on the brakes, as we shall see, but they all have the effect of reducing demand. If demand falls too far, the shops will be full of unsold goods. Business firms will cut back their production. Unemployment will start to increase.

Unemployment

Since we are now back at the point of unemployment, let us look more closely at the phenomenon. A few paragraphs back, we said that the goal was to organize the economy so that everyone who wanted a job could find one. However, even at what is known as full employment, not everyone will necessarily be employed at every moment! As we saw in discussing inflation, there may be several types, and such types are also found in unemployment.

Frictional unemployment consists of those who are (voluntarily) between jobs or who are seasonally unemployed. In the United States, many people change jobs for a wide variety of reasons. Sometimes they are trying to find a better job and sometimes they had a fight with the boss. From the time they leave one job until they find another, they are unemployed. Actually, we could amend our definition slightly (with regard to "voluntarily") and include those workers who are fired (as opposed to those *laid off*). Workers who are fired for job-related causes are replaced by others; most usually obtain a new job fairly soon. Frictional unemployment is always present, though in varying degrees. Young people form a disproportionate share of this group since they haven't "settled in" to a profession or desired line of work. Since it is easier to change jobs when times are good, this type of unemployment may even increase as the economy improves. We will simplify matters and say that frictional unemployment is not related to the business cycle.

Another type of unemployment is **structural unemployment,** which is caused by changes in the nature or location of employment opportunities. When the textile industry left New England for the South, many people were not able to follow. When there were cutbacks in the aerospace industry, many people on the West Coast were unemployed. When automobiles replaced horses, harness-makers and farriers were displaced. Relocation and retraining are costly and time consuming. We cannot expect mismatches of jobs and skills to be corrected easily. A ditch digger cannot become an airline pilot or violinist overnight. Nor should we expect a physician to drive a taxi or an engineer to be a short-order cook. Structural unemployment may not be related to business cycles and, therefore, it is not necessarily corrected by expansion of the economy. However, changes come more frequently when the economy is operating well at high levels. Thus, partially, the cycle may influence the level of structural unemployment.

Our third type of unemployment is cyclical unemployment. **Cyclical unemployment** results from decreased aggregate demand and the subsequent cutbacks in production. As firms produce less, they need fewer employees. So when output declines, workers are laid off for no fault of their own. This type of unemployment is called *cyclical* because it is related directly to the business cycle.

To repeat, cyclical unemployment occurs when demand slackens and when production and employment by firms are reduced. It is this unemployment that is the focus of the rest of this chapter.

Our discussion sounds grim, doesn't it? We've gone from unemployment to inflation and back to unemployment in a few short paragraphs. You can see why Thomas Carlyle called economics "the dismal science." It may help if we bear in mind that most of the economy is usually hard at work. Most upswings and downswings increase or decrease GNP by no more than 10% in any one year. The chief exception to this was the Great Depression of the 1930s, when as many as one quarter of the labor force were unable to find work.

What unemployment costs us

When workers are unemployed, our economy is not reaching its production possibilities. Output of valuable goods and services is *not* being produced. Unemployment means that goods and services are being lost forever, because so much of our capital and labor goes unused.

Figure 1 shows that we are still losing some of our potential product. The straight upward-sloping line represents an estimate of what GNP would be if the labor force were fully employed. (The chart defines full employment actually to include about 4% unemployment. The 4% represents people who are between jobs.) The fluctuating line shows actual GNP measured in 1958 dollars. In the lower left-hand corner of the chart, actual GNP is above the amount that would normally be produced in a full-employment economy. That was during the Korean War when the economy was operating full-out to produce goods for the armed forces as well as for civilian consumption. Another such period is shown for the latter part of the 1960s, during the Vietnam War. At other times, however, the actual GNP line dips below the potential GNP line. From the mid-1950s to the mid-1960s actual GNP was below the potential. The lowest points correspond with the business slumps of 1957 and 1960. Another dip came during the 1970 recession. At the upper right of the chart, the sharp falling off in GNP represents the recession of 1973–1975.

There is a hidden cost in business recessions, not shown in the chart. During economic downturns, investment is reduced below what it would otherwise be. Some existing capacity may be allowed to wear out and not be replaced. If investment were not reduced in this way, the line showing potential GNP would rise more rapidly than it does. Had there been no recessions in 1957 and 1960, potential GNP in the 1960s would have been higher than is shown in Figure 1. Thus during economic downturns we not only lose current production; we also lower our future potential as well.

Looking back at American economic history, we see that what took place was a long growth of population, employment, productive capacity, and income. There were occa-

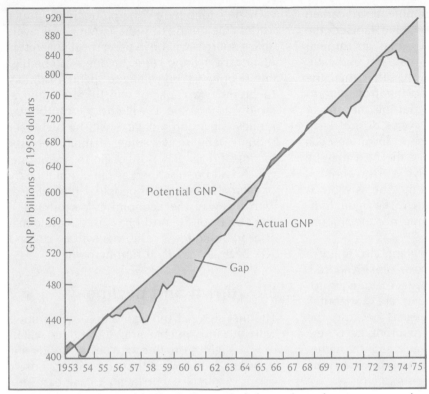

Figure 1 Actual and potential GNP. The brown shaded areas show where our economy has been below our production possibilities. Notice the type of vertical scale used. The distances between GNP values near the top of the scale are smaller than those near the bottom; this was done so that the potential GNP line would be a straight line—easier to use as a reference line.

sional setbacks and many fluctuations, but the main story was growth. In what follows we will be looking at the fluctuations and ignoring the growth. We want to see what the fluctuations have in common; in particular, we want to see what the upswing and downswing of a typical "cycle" look like.

Description of a typical cycle

Economic fluctuations tend to be cyclical. Inflation and price stability, unemployment and full employment, growth and declining output, all tend to recur periodically in some related fashion. These related economic conditions form what is known as a **business cycle.**

Figure 2 is a graph of an imaginary typical business cycle. Probably no cycle or fluctuation will ever be exactly like our imaginary one,

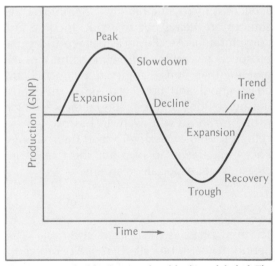

Figure 2 A typical business cycle with phases labeled. The trend line is drawn horizontally to emphasize the cyclical nature of business activity. Actually, due to economic growth, the trend line should slope upward.

but most cycles will resemble it in certain ways. In the diagram, we have labeled the phases of the cycle; most cycles go through these phases. The horizontal axis indicates time. No time scale is given, other than the indication that time is moving from left to right. The reason for not putting months or years on the scale is that cycles do not keep the same schedule. The period from the peak of one cycle to the peak of the next may be three years in one case or five years in another. In the very unusual case it may be as short as two years or as long as fifteen. The figure indicates only the passage of time, not the amount of it.

The vertical axis of the graph also requires some comment. As we have already noted, cycles or fluctuations take place along an upward trend. Very few cycles are horizontal, ending up where they began, because the economy tends to grow. Therefore, each new cycle actually takes place at a slightly higher level of output. In the diagram, however, the trend line is horizontal for simplicity: we are only interested in the up and down movement of the economy.

Expansion

We begin with the economy in the *expansion phase* of the cycle. The output of goods and services is increasing rapidly. Unemployed resources are being put to work. Income and consumption rise. Businessmen consider the prospects favorable and begin to think of expanding their firms. People are willing to purchase goods and housing even if they must borrow to do so. Interest rates increase—which is bad for those who want to borrow but excellent for those seeking to lend their savings. Prices may begin to rise, but the rate of increase is not especially alarming.

Peak

The next phase is the *peak* of the cycle. This period may also be called *prosperity* or even a *boom*. We will leave for later the reasons why the economy peaks rather than just continuing to expand indefinitely. For now we will be content to describe the economic conditions observed at the peak.

The economy will be producing as much as possible during this phase. Almost all available resources will be in use, especially present plant capacity and labor. Incomes will be high and people will be willing to spend. Additions to productive capacity will be attempted as rapidly as possible. It will cost a lot to borrow money, since interest rates will be high even though people save some of their increased income. Prices may now begin to rise at rates which will be described as rapid, inflationary, or even alarming. Most people will be pleased with the way the economy is performing. A few signals of the next phase of the cycle may appear, but in most cases they will be ignored. The peak is actually a turning point.

Slowdown and decline

The first signs of the economy slowing down will not cause much alarm. At first there will be only a slight reduction of sales of goods and services. *Inventories*—the amount of unsold goods available—will begin to increase, but only a little. Some workers who had been working overtime will find themselves working fewer hours each week. Prices may not decline, but interest rates will tend to fall a little. Backlogs of orders will begin to decline as producers catch up with the work to be done. A few more warnings of a potential decline will be noted.

As the decline begins and continues, many things will start to happen. Output and sales of goods and services will decline. Many workers will find that they are no longer needed. Idle capacity will appear in the economy. Inventories will accumulate. Some inventories will be of goods ready for sale but with no buyers appearing. Other goods will be partially finished with no need to complete them. Some firms will have stocks of raw materials which are not needed now for production. Prices may not decline, but there will not be much of a tendency for them to rise either. Interest rates will fall since people will not be inclined to borrow more money in the face of an uncertain economic future. Debts will be repaid where possible, and some people will attempt to save against the hard times ahead.

The decline or contraction may be rapid or slow. Once started, it tends to feed upon itself. As people lose jobs and income they will buy less, which will lead to declining production and put others out of work, who will then buy less. If nothing is done to prevent the continued decline, the economy will sink into a trough.

If the decline persists, it is called a *recession*. Economists are not sure at what point a recession occurs—when a decline becomes something more. One widely accepted criterion is that when the output of goods and services (real output, in constant dollars) declines for two successive quarters, we call it a **recession.** If the recession becomes very severe, lasting longer, and sinking deeper and causing greater economic misery, we call it a **depression.** There is no accepted criterion for saying when a recession has become a depression.

Trough

A recession will continue into, and end in, the trough. The bottom of the cycle is called a **trough.** Graphically, the trough may look like a "V," or it may be flat and broad like the bottom of a pan. Unemployment will be high, which means that large numbers of people who wish to work and be productive cannot do so. This is a real cost to society, since their production is lost forever—it can't be postponed or called upon later; it is something that might have been but will never be realized. Since many people are not working, consumption is reduced. To the extent that unemployment is not equally shared by all groups but instead concentrated in portions of the labor force, such as among young people or blacks, or former aerospace workers, it may lead to special political and social problems.

The other major problem of a trough is that capital goods which wear out may not be replaced. Since excess productive capacity is available, i.e., standing idle, there is no need to replace old equipment. Machines, buildings, and other productive assets may simply be abandoned. To the extent that this happens, the present and future capacity of the economy to produce goods and services will be damaged. Similarly, goods and materials in inventory may deteriorate and be lost. When the

economy begins to recover, business firms will have to replace their inventories; this loss of inventory is a waste.

The only good thing about the trough is that it's a turning point. By the end of the trough, the economy is recovering and expanding.

Recovery

The recovery phase of the cycle will begin when once again productive output of goods and services starts moving upward. Why does it move upward again? In some instances (though this has not been true of recent recessions), wages and prices may fall far enough in the recession so that consumers are able to buy goods even though their incomes have fallen during the decline. Also, the price of borrowed money—the interest rate—may fall and provide a stimulus to industries that are dependent upon borrowed money for much of their demand. Housing, for example, has often led the economy out of a trough, especially since construction uses a lot of labor and therefore leads to higher employment. Housing starts usually depend in part on the interest rate. (The difference between 8% and 10% on a $40,000 house is considerable, amounting to over $24,000 on a typical 30-year mortgage.) Or perhaps scientific discoveries have created a new industry or brought about a need to change the capital equipment being used in some industry. As firms rush to invest in new or different capital goods, the economy will be stimulated. Or perhaps the government will take some action that gives consumers more spending power, such as a reduction in taxes, or spend directly on some large program such as space exploration or defense. Foreign war or the preparation for war has more than once provided such an economic stimulus. All of these reasons play a part in helping turn the economy upward to recovery.

If the economy is successful in beginning to increase output, this may lead to further economic activity. A revival in one area often leads to revival in other parts of the economy, and so the recovery may move ahead to another period of expansion. This brings us back

Viewpoint

Do Business Cycles Occur in a Planned Economy?

Karl Marx argued that business cycles were a natural part of the capitalist system. He said that it is impossible to control or prevent cycles because changing conditions led to responses by capitalists which would always be destabilizing. The alternate boom and bust cycles imposed high costs on workers, who were thrown out of work at intervals. More so than decadence or revolution, economic instability would lead to the downfall of capitalism.

Marx was unwilling to wait until the capitalist economies collapsed from their built-in weakness. He suggested that the economy be run by the state for the benefit of the worker. In a planned economy, business cycles should not occur since they are excluded from the plan. The purpose of planning, after all, is to organize the economy so that only those goods and services that are needed will be produced. The central planning department decides how the economy is to grow, and then sees that production follows the plan. There can be no surplus of unwanted goods, no workers left without anything to do.

Marxist planned economies have now been with us since the 1920s when the Soviet Union moved to a planned economy. The obvious question to ask is has the planned sector of the world economy been free from business cycles? If the capitalist can overinvest or underinvest or invest in the wrong thing, can the central planning committee do any better? Do the economists in Moscow, Budapest, Havana, New Delhi, or Peking have any information which will ensure that just the right kinds and amounts of investment are planned? Do they frequently make errors, for example, by building a service station in the wrong place, perhaps in a Siberian town with no automobiles? Judging in this fashion, central planning does tend to error more frequently than the capitalist countries.

However, suppose we decide to assess the planned economy by its ability to maintain high or full levels of employment. Instead of a multitude of independent businesses making decisions, the central planner can decide precisely what the total investment will be and maintain full employment. After all, if there are not enough useful projects available to employ everyone, perhaps building a railroad through the desert should be undertaken. It may be useful someday. With these advantages, the central planner does indeed perform well in holding down unemployment—at least officially. Planned economies do, however, suffer from a certain, varying amount of *disguised unemployment*. All workers may be employed, but some who arrive at the plant do little or nothing. For reasons of motivation capitalist countries pay unemployment compensation (or welfare to the hard-core unemployed), rather than allow salaries for idleness. Actually, measuring the disguised unemployment makes comparison difficult.

What about the cycle itself? Do planned economies face peaks and valleys in output? Recent history shows that they do. (However, it should be pointed out that there is partial cause from outside those countries: they trade with the capitalists.) Some of the Eastern European countries have had especially difficult times with the cycle. Let's consider Czechoslovakia.

In the 1960s, the planned economy of Czechoslovakia experienced a pronounced recession. It began in 1961 when key industries such as coal, electric power, and steel were unable to meet the production targets set for them. Shortages in these industries soon made themselves felt in other industries that needed their output. In the following year, 1962, the difficulties grew, and now there were shortages in various lines of consumer goods. Finally, the government announced that it was abandoning the five-year plan halfway through its second year. It would be replaced by a one-year plan in 1963 to allow for reorganization, followed by a seven-year plan.

Delays and shortages reappeared in the capital goods industries, leading in turn to underproduction and idle capacity in other industries. To ease matters, the government slashed investments for the interim year of 1963 and trimmed the industrial production target to a mere 1% increase. In the first half of 1963, investment was 17% below that of the same period in 1962. The fuel and power shortage grew because of delays in building the necessary capacity. Things were made worse by a transportation crisis, which in turn held up deliveries of material to the metallurgical and building industries. To these troubles were added a winter of heavy snow and a summer of blistering heat and a drought. Industrial output in 1963 fell below that of 1962. In subsequent years it swung up again.

One could blame the Czechoslovak recession on various things, from bad weather to the mistakes of administrators. A number of Czechoslovak economists laid the chief blame on the planning process itself, which they said had lost touch with realities.

"What good does it do," asked one economist, "if the railroads fulfill all the targets for transport, when the transport of many products is itself unnecessary? What good does it do if productivity is higher in the case of washing machines than of refrigerators, when the stores are full of the former while people are queueing up for the latter?"

to the point in the cycle where we began: expansion. We have described the entire up and down process known as the business cycle as it typically occurs: peak, slowdown and decline, trough, and expansion.

But we haven't described any specific or historical business cycle. In order to get an overview of business cycles as they occur in reality, let us now take a look at recent U.S. economic history.

U.S. business cycles

Figure 3 presents the famous Cleveland Trust Company chart of business cycle movement in the U.S. economy since 1790. The growth of the economy is *not* shown. Instead, a trend line has been drawn, and the movements of the business cycle appear as percentage deviations above or below the trend. To be realistic (i.e., reflect growth), the whole chart should be slantwise on the page, with the earliest years in the bottom left-hand corner and the latest at the upper right. Instead, the upward trend is presented as a horizontal line.

Wars and panics

The captions on the chart indicate some of the characteristics of the times in which cycles have taken place. During the very earliest period, from 1790 to the War of 1812, the changes in economic activity resulted from forces outside the United States. The country was mainly dependent on the trade carried on abroad by its merchant ships. When the ships came and went frequently, the United States experienced prosperity. Many of their customers were European countries engaged in a series of wars. While the Europeans fought, Americans got rich carrying supplies to them. Each of the four peaks prior to 1812 was related to shipping activity.

Bad times, of course, also had their European connection. One of the brief European peaces in 1802 brought an economic downturn for the United States because of a decline in shipping activity. The downturns of 1798 and 1808 resulted from interruptions in trade, though Europe was at war in those years.

The War of 1812 had just the opposite effect on the economy from those of other wars. Most wars have stimulated our economic activity: All available or excess workers are needed by the armed forces; production also increases to generate the needed war materials. But the War of 1812 was fought on U.S. soil; it disrupted the local economy and produced a downswing. After the war, however, the economy swung upward to a peak as people began spending the paper money printed by the government to pay for the war.

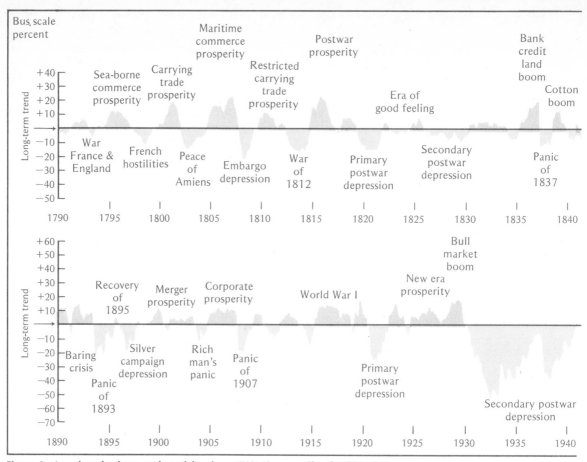

Figure 3 American business-cycle activity since 1790. (Source: Cleveland Trust Company.)

Many of the upswings in economic activity after 1812 were related to wars, including the Mexican War, the Civil War, World Wars I and II, the Korean War, and the Vietnam War. Other upswings were led by developments in a particular product or industry, such as cotton in the 1830s or railroad building in the 1880s. At other times the ready availability of money was a stimulus to the economy, as in the land rush of 1835 and the California gold rush of 1849.

Downswings in business activity seemed to follow wars during the period from the War of 1812 to World War I. Sometimes there would be a short downswing, as happened in the years 1820, 1826–1829, 1865, and 1873–1879. After World War I there was a brief downswing in 1920, but no secondary downswing; instead, the 1920s were a period of prosperity. Some economists believe that the secondary downswing came in the 1930s, the years of the Great Depression.

Other downward movements have originated from purely financial problems called panics. A *panic* happens when people lose confidence in the monetary and banking system. They fear that the banks will fail or that the currency will become worthless, so they rush to convert their savings into something more solid, such as cash or gold. In some cases there is a specific event that sets off the panic. Failure to recharter the Second Bank of the United States set off the panic of 1837. In 1893, a loss of confidence in paper money led to a run on the U.S. Treasury as people tried to convert paper money into gold. Other panics have been triggered by real or imagined shortcomings of the banks; when everybody demanded cash at the same time, the banks failed and this in turn affected the economy.

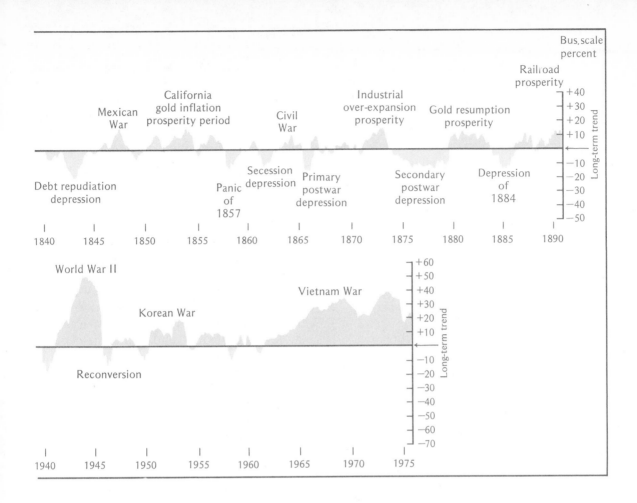

Bus. scale percent

Railroad prosperity

California gold inflation prosperity period

Mexican War

Civil War

Industrial over-expansion prosperity

Gold resumption prosperity

+40
+30
+20
+10

Long-term trend

−10
−20
−30
−40
−50

Debt repudiation depression

Panic of 1857

Secession depression

Primary postwar depression

Secondary postwar depression

Depression of 1884

1840   1845   1850   1855   1860   1865   1870   1875   1880   1885   1890

World War II

Korean War

Vietnam War

Reconversion

+60
+50
+40
+30
+20
+10

Long-term trend

−10
−20
−30
−40
−50
−60
−70

1940   1945   1950   1955   1960   1965   1970   1975

After the 1907 panic, banking reform and the establishment of the Federal Reserve System (our central bank) reduced the likelihood of further panics.

The 1930s

In Figure 3 the decade of the 1930s is labeled the *secondary postwar depression*. It was that, but it was also a great deal more. Nothing like it had ever happened before. *At its lowest point, the unemployment rate reached 25%*—meaning that every fourth person who wanted a job was unable to find one. Many others probably became discouraged and withdrew from the labor force, so the figures underestimate the severity of the problem.

Part of the explanation for the 1930s is to be found in the 1920s. Following the deep but brief downturn of 1921, the remainder of the 1920s was a period of unprecedented prosperity. It was bolstered by a capital spending boom: new plants were built, electric and telephone wires were strung, and highways and railroads were laid down. The period ended with a dizzying speculation in the stock market. The collapse of the stock market was followed by a rapid decline into the depths of the Great Depression.

The economy was not able to sustain the level of capital spending that had prevailed during the 1920s. So much had been built that industrial capacity now exceeded what was needed to produce the smaller amount of goods and services desired in the 1930s. Except for isolated rural areas, telephone and electric lines were everywhere. The country had a large network of highways. Railroads had all the track they needed. And even residential construction had reached a point where it was hard to find people for all the houses. The industries that made these things had to cut back on their production, and this forced other industries to cut back. It is easy to see why large-scale unemployment resulted.

Agriculture was very hard hit during the 1930s. The prices of farm products fell to record lows. Of course, most farmers were able to feed themselves and their families, which was more than the unemployed people in the cities could do. But not all farmers did even that well. *In addition to the depression, drought struck several years in a row;* in the western plains, the drought was so severe that the land was called a "dust bowl." In the crazy world of the 1930s farmers were killing baby pigs because they could not afford to feed them, while people in the cities stood in bread lines to get food.

The burden of debt Adding to the woes of production were a number of financial problems. As a result of the home building activity of the previous decade, *many households had monthly house payments due (the mortgage payments) that were too large for the conditions of the 1930s.* Many had also borrowed to buy automobiles, furniture, and other durable consumer goods. On top of this, many people were speculating in the stock market—that is, buying stocks not for their dividends but in the expectation that they would increase in value. Much of the speculation was done with borrowed money. This enabled people to buy more stock than they could otherwise have afforded; when the market price of the stock went up, they could sell it and pay back what they had borrowed with a profit. As long as the economy was on the upswing, all this indebtedness created no problem. But when the downswing began, people were unable to pay back what they had borrowed. The debts from the 1920s became the burdens of the 1930s. Firms and households alike found that those who had loaned them money wanted to be repaid. Unable to pay because of their declining incomes, debtors turned to the people they had loaned money to and demanded payment from them. Many good loans became bad ones because the national income had shrunk so that there wasn't enough money to pay them all. It's easy to see that with everyone demanding repayment, soon no one would be able to pay anyone.

The crisis in Wall Street The stock market deserves special attention. Most of the speculation was done in 1928 and 1929, the period labeled Bull Market Boom in the chart. The speculation, as we have said, was based on the expectation that stock prices would continue to rise. For a while the expectation helped to sustain itself because people borrowed money on the value of the stock they already owned and used it to bid up prices higher and higher. *By the autumn of 1929, stock prices had gone beyond any relationship to the profits of the companies issuing the stock.* Obviously prices would have to fall eventually to some more realistic level. When people realized that a turning point had come in stock prices, they rushed to sell their stock. In the rapid decline of stock prices that followed, many big investors lost their fortunes. The drop that began on October 29, 1929, signaled the end of the prosperity of the 1920s and the beginning of the downturn of the 1930s.

Table 1 shows an index of stock prices beginning in 1920. The peak year was 1929 and the bottom was reached in 1932. The decline from 1929 to 1932 was 73.4%. A stock millionaire in 1929 would find his fortune worth only $266,333.59 in just a few years.

Many banks were forced out of business within a few years. As the prices of stocks fell, banks found that the loans they had made to

Table 1
Index of Stock Prices and Percentage Change

Year	Index 1941–43 = 100	Percent change
1920	7.98	
1921	6.86	−14.0
1922	8.41	+22.6
1923	8.57	+ 1.9
1924	9.05	+ 5.6
1925	11.15	+23.2
1926	12.59	+12.9
1927	15.34	+21.8
1928	19.95	+30.1
1929	26.02	+30.4
1930	21.03	−20.2
1931	13.66	−35.0
1932	6.93	−49.3
1933	8.96	+29.3
1934	9.84	+ 9.8

people for purchasing stock were not going to be repaid. The stocks that had been pledged as *collateral* for the loans became worthless. Similarly, many mortgage loans became uncollectible, since homeowners no longer had the income or savings to meet their payments. The only alternative the banks had was to *foreclose*—that is, to take possession of the property which had been pledged as security for the mortgage loans. In addition, once a bank was known to be in difficulty, its depositors might come to collect their money. Banks can't pay all their depositors at once.

Banks do not keep all the deposits as cash in the vault. They make loans with the money. The money is safe, generally, but not immediately available. To pay depositors, the banks must first obtain payment on loans outstanding. This is not often possible and is impossible when business conditions are turning sour. Once a bank fails to pay a depositor, others get the word and rush in to get their money before the bank fails. In the early 1930s there were many "runs" on banks, which were then forced to close their doors forever.

With the failure of banks, some of the money available to the economy disappeared. As the economy turned deeper into the depression, neither households nor firms had any desire to borrow money. Interest rates fell, since the demand for loans had declined. At that time, a falling interest rate was taken to be a signal that there was too much money in circulation since interest is the price paid for borrowed money. The monetary authorities acted through the Federal Reserve System to reduce the supply of money. The supply shrank more than it should have, which added to the difficulties of the economy. After 1932 a recovery seemed to be underway, but a second downswing came in 1937. *Probably the main cause of the second downswing was that the money supply had been kept too small for the needs of an expanding economy.* All of these interrelated causes will be studied later.

There are other explanations for the deep depression of the 1930s. Some economists who have made a study of business cycle movements note that the 1929 downturn happened at a time when certain other kinds of economic movements were also heading down. The various movements reinforced each other and carried the economy down farther than a single cycle could have. We will discuss this idea a little later when we come to theories of business cycles. Right now it is enough to say that many forces contributed to the Great Depression.

Eventually, the economy recovered. The administration of President Franklin Roosevelt undertook various programs to relieve the suffering of those who had been hardest hit by the catastrophe. The government also tried different kinds of action to stimulate the economy. But in 1939 the economy was still operating below normal, and millions of workers were being sustained by government make-work programs rather than by private business firms. In the meantime, war had begun in Europe and Asia. *Perhaps more than anything else, U.S. involvement in the war led to the economic recovery of the 1940s.*

The 1940s

The decade of the 1940s must be considered in two parts. The first half was dominated by World War II. In the latter half of the decade, the economy struggled to reconvert to a peacetime basis.

Even before the United States became actively involved, the economy felt the impact of the war. *Expenditures for military purposes had a stimulating effect on many industries.* As incomes rose, people who for years had been doing without a lot of things rushed back into the market. Later, when hostilities began, there were massive increases in outlays for military equipment and manpower.

Unemployment disappeared rapidly. The conscription of able-bodied men into the armed services removed them from the labor force, and soon every available worker was needed in production. Women entered the labor force in large numbers. There was a popular song about Rosie the Riveter, who worked on the assembly line in one of the new aircraft plants. Rosie was real. Many thousands of women moved out of their kitchens and took their places next to men, doing jobs that had previously been thought of as men's jobs.

New investment began on a large scale. Much of the expenditure went to build plants to produce war-related goods, or to convert existing plants for that purpose. Investment for other purposes was postponed until after the war. The production of consumer goods received little attention. For example, new automobiles were not produced during the war, and housing became very scarce.

Wartime price controls Consumers during World War II who wanted to spend their rapidly rising incomes found themselves frustrated in a number of ways. Many goods were simply unavailable. Others were available, but in very small quantities which were sold until they ran out. It was a good idea to be friendly with local merchants, who might be willing to hold some of these items for you. Other commodities in short supply, such as gasoline, sugar, and coffee, were rationed: so much to a person. Along with money, people carried ration stamp books. To purchase a sack of sugar, people paid a price in money and a price in sugar coupons. Both prices were fixed by the government, and could be changed by the price-control board. People who needed sugar to preserve fruits and vegetables were allowed more stamps than those who needed it only to sweeten their coffee. People who needed more gasoline because they used their automobiles in their daily work—for example, doctors— were allowed more gasoline stamps.

Prices did not rise. Considering the scarcity of goods and the vast amount of purchasing power available, they would have risen had not all prices and wages been rigidly controlled. Illegal "black markets" sprang up in which people could buy almost anything for a price several times the legal price. The government cracked down hard on such activities, and issued constant appeals to patriotism to deter people from breaking the law. For the duration of the war these measures succeeded in preventing inflation.

The public was forced to save. *Faced with heavy restrictions on spending, people had little choice but to save a large part of their rising incomes.* This was good, since they were able to lend their savings to the government to help it pay for the war effort. The government had to borrow to finance the war because it had been unable to raise taxes far enough to balance the budget. Taxes at that level might have discouraged people from working as hard as they did. In effect, the public postponed much of its consumption until later. Government bonds—called War Bonds, later Victory Bonds, then Savings Bonds—could be purchased in denominations as small as $25. Children brought their dimes and quarters to school and exchanged them for stamps which they pasted in a book; when the book was filled, it could be exchanged for a $25 bond.

Taxes and savings were not enough to pay for the enormous productive effort of World War II. The government not only taxed and borrowed; it also increased the money supply. In effect, it printed more money. As a result, the money supply grew far faster than the output of consumer goods. In ordinary times this would have led to rapidly increasing prices. But price controls prevented inflation from happening, at least for the time being.

Postwar adjustment When the war ended, a period of great uncertainty began. Many people expected a recession, since previous wars had been followed by recessions. The economy did slow down, and unemployment rose, but not to disastrous levels. During 1945 and 1946, there was a period of reconversion from war production back to a peacetime economy. Factories that had been making carbines and tanks could not turn immediately to producing washing machines and automobiles.

The export sector was strong. Western Europe was rebuilding faster than anyone had expected. Assisted by gifts of U.S. dollars through the Marshall Plan, the countries of Europe bought what they needed to restore their war-ravaged societies.

And then there was the U.S. consumer. Armed with unspent dollars, consumers rushed to buy the goods they had been denied so long. While the demand for newly available housing, cars, and other durables kept the economy from slipping into a recession, it created other problems.

Postwar inflation For one thing, *wage and price controls had been removed shortly after the war.* This released inflationary forces which had been kept hidden during the first half of the decade; all of the price increases that would otherwise have happened earlier now seemed to come at once.

Added to the backlog of accumulated consumer savings was the effect of a rapidly growing money supply. The *national debt*—money borrowed by the government to finance its activities—had grown during the war to a height which seemed staggering by the standards of the period. To keep the cost of this debt as low as possible, the government took measures to hold interest rates down. To accomplish this, it was necessary to keep adding new money to the economy (we will examine the mechanism later on, when we study the monetary system). People used the additional money to bid up the prices of goods and services even further. To make matters still worse, three rounds of nationwide strikes took place, tying up key industries such as autos, steel, coal, and the railroads; the wage increases won in this way added anew to the upward movement of prices.

By November, 1948, the economy was heading down again. The effects of rising prices, the numerous strikes, and the temporary satisfaction of consumer demand seemed to propel the downward movement which reached bottom in October 1949, just as the decade ended.

The 1950s

The decade of the 1950s produced little to detain us here. To be sure, there were three cyclical fluctuations, but the swings in economic activity weren't very wide; in fact, no real recession developed. Prices were fairly stable. Altogether, in comparison with other periods, it was a decade of relative tranquility for the economy.

The first upswing of economic activity, from 1951 to early 1953, came in relation to a war once again. The Korean War put men back into uniform and stimulated production for military use, adding to the normal demands of a peacetime economy.

The second upswing lasted from 1955 through the summer of 1957. This was associated with an expansion in the output of durable goods. Consumers bought houses, cars, TV sets, and other durables. There was also considerable activity in the industries producing capital goods.

The decade ended on a new upswing. It is hard to find any specific cause for this expansion. An automobile strike in 1959 was almost enough to turn the economy around and send it downward, but somehow the shaky expansion continued onward into the next decade.

The first trough of the 1950s was not really a recession, since the real output of the economy did not decline. It was a slowing down in the upturn rather than a real downswing. The Korean War helped the economy recover before an actual recession could develop.

The second downswing began in July, 1953, and bottomed in May, 1954. It was deeper than the 1951 trough, but short-lived. The third dip began in 1957 and hit bottom in 1958. This was the deepest of the three downturns, with unemployment reaching more than 6%—a figure that made some observers begin to think of the 1930s. *The tendency of each downswing to go deeper than its predecessor, with some of the effects persisting into the next expansion, was viewed as a major economic problem during the period.* The economy did not seem to be going anywhere. Its rate of expansion was low, even though the fluctuations were mild.

The boom of the 1960s

The next decade did not start out well. The weak expansion of the 1950s was not sustained, and by April, 1960, the economy was once again headed downward. The decline was not very great, but it started from a rather low peak. Recovery began in February, 1961, and the expansion continued without pause until December, 1969. *This was one of the longest upswings ever observed in the U.S. economy.*

The expansion requires some additional comment. The increasing sluggishness of the economy had been one of the factors leading to the victory of the Democrats in 1960. Under Presidents Kennedy and Johnson a number of measures were passed to deal with specific economic problems. *But the major stimulus to the economic expansion was a lowering of taxes.* There had been little revision in tax levels for some time, and they had become a drag on the economy since they reduced people's disposable income. The investment tax credit of 1962 allowed corporations to write off investment in new capital facilities on their income taxes. And a cut in personal and corporate income taxes in 1964 increased purchasing power and added greatly to the strength of the economic expansion, sustaining it for a number of years.

Then war came again, this time in Vietnam. It was decided not to put the economy on a war footing by cutting back on consumer demand. Instead, the increased military production was added to the growing consumer production, thus further stimulating the economic upswing. Unemployment dipped to 3.5% of the labor force, which is very low for the U.S. economy. With only a very slight slowing in early 1967, the economy was propelled onward and upward.

A new and very difficult problem was developing. As the economy strained to meet the combination of demands put upon it, prices began to rise. The government had chosen not to raise taxes sufficiently to finance the war, and hence had to increase its borrowing. The money supply began to expand at a rapid rate, adding to the upward pressure on prices. By the end of the decade, inflation had become the number one economic problem.

In 1969 the Nixon administration decided to stop the expansion of the money supply, thus removing one of the factors contributing to the inflation. Money soon became very scarce. Conditions developed almost like those of the panics of the last century. Banks in the United States borrowed dollars from European banks at high interest rates in order to provide funds for their business clients. The credit crunch produced a downturn in the economy which began in December, 1969.

The 1970s

The downturn proved to be a mini-recession at worst. Unemployment increased, but the production of goods and services declined only slightly. The strongest effect was in the financial sector. Fearing a deeper recession, with all its political consequences, the administration eased the money supply. By November, 1970, the downturn had ended and the economy headed upward again.

The upward movement was accompanied by continuing inflation. In late 1971, wage and price controls were imposed, with considerable support from most sectors of the public. This support eroded when it was seen that the controls had a distorting effect on the economy, particularly on materials supplies. Soon labor leaders were opposed to the controls because they claimed wages, not profits, were controlled. Finally, the controls were abandoned in stages. The administration turned instead to traditional policies of limiting the money supply. The government also attempted to cut back on spending. The drive against inflation ended by forcing the economy into a new recession. *The recession of 1973–1975 was the worst since the Great Depression;* it was made more serious by *"outside" factors:* shortages of basic raw materials and particularly of energy from oil. The downturn started in the late summer of 1973.

What had been expected to be a slight downturn became much more serious. Unemployment shot up to nearly 10% of the labor force. Real gross national product—the output of goods and services—declined to an extent that had not been experienced since the 1930s. Despite this, inflation continued, reaching more than 12% in 1974. *For perhaps the first time in modern economic history, prices rose during the downturn of a business cycle.*

The bottom of the cycle was reached in March 1975, and a slow, uncertain recovery began that continued through 1977. Inflation continued, however, although at a slower rate.

Theories of the business cycle

We have seen that business cycles are complex happenings. It is clear from the history of U.S. cycles that there is usually more than one cause at work. Even when an upswing or downswing can be attributed mainly to one factor, there are likely to be other influences affecting the outcome. The world of the economist is one of multiple forces that are hard to untangle.

To help them sort things out, economists construct models of the economy and experiment with them. These models may be very simple. The supply and demand curves that we experimented with in Chapter 3 were simple models, showing how a market might behave in response to various changes. We also build models of business cycles. It is possible to build a model of a cycle that has just one cause, say changes in the amount of investment spending by business firms. This doesn't prove that cycles are caused by changes in investment. But it does throw a lot of light on what happens in the course of a typical cycle. A physician treating a patient must know how the heart is related to the kidneys, and how both may affect the functioning of the lungs. If the heart slows down, the kidneys may function poorly, and if the kidneys function poorly the lungs may fill with fluid. Each organ must be understood separately in order to understand how they work together. In like fashion, each component or cause of the business cycle must be studied separately.

Investment cycles and the accelerator

Investment spending is thought to be an important factor in business cycles. It consists of spending on goods and services which will be used to produce more goods and services in the future. But why do businesses undertake investment spending? They do it because they expect the market for their goods and services to increase in the future. They may expect this for various reasons. Perhaps they see the economy starting to move upward, and want to be prepared to meet increased demand by consumers who will have more money to spend. When businesses increase their investment in response to changes in economic activity, this is called **induced investment.** The new investment has been induced by changes in national income and output.

Let us see how this works in the expansion phase of a cycle. As GNP increases, firms begin to find their productive capacity being fully utilized. They need to expand their production lines, plants, and warehouses just to keep up with demand. Investment to meet current increases in demand is one part of induced investment. Second, as production increases businessmen may realize that they will need even more capacity in the future. Thus a second part of induced investment is that designed to meet expected future needs. Third, as GNP rises, profits often rise even faster. Some of the profits may be plowed back into the expansion of the firm. All three of these influences work together during the expansion phase of the cycle, inducing investment

spending above the amount which would have been made if there were no expansion.

Exactly the opposite effects happen during the downswing of a cycle. As output falls, there is less need to provide capacity; there may even be excess or idle capacity. As the decline progresses, business firms become pessimistic about the future. They may even desire to reduce capacity and therefore cancel plans for new investment. Some capital goods may be allowed to wear out and not be replaced. Finally, as production falls, profits fall also and money for investment projects is not as readily available. The decline in GNP has thus caused firms to invest less than they would have if there had been no decline. Induced investment here is negative.

Notice what is happening. Investment is undertaken to create capacity. When investment expenditures are made, they represent an additional demand for output. Thus induced investment causes GNP to rise even faster. The opposite happens during a contraction. When induced investment is negative, it represents an additional decline in demand, causing GNP to fall even faster. In this way induced investment creates what has come to be called the **accelerator effect.** Just as the accelerator on your car makes the car change its rate of speed, the economic accelerator causes the rate of increase or decrease of GNP to be higher than it would have been otherwise.

At the peak and the trough of the cycle, induced investment also plays a role. Toward the end of the expansion phase, most of the desired increases in capacity have been accomplished. Some firms begin to doubt that the good times will continue. Induced investment slowly disappears, and the demand created by it also disappears. The economy starts to slow down. If the slowing continues into the contraction phase, then induced investment will turn negative and the decline will begin.

As the decline continues, induced investment will become less negative. Firms will have decreased their capacity about as much as they feel is advisable. As the pessimism wears off, the economy enters the trough of the cycle. Any stimulus to GNP will then bring about the beginning of recovery. Perhaps investment will provide that stimulus. As additional capital equipment depreciates and has to be replaced, there will be a slight rise in investment. The GNP generated by this will induce more investment. The recovery may start slowly, but when it is well under way the accelerator effect begins to work in an upward direction and expansion proceeds. In this way, it is possible to generate a complete business cycle from the effects of induced investment and the accelerator.

Inventory cycles

Closely related to the investment theory of the business cycle is the inventory cycle. It works in much the same way. In fact, inventories are a form of investment since they consist of goods that are bought or produced for future consumption. *Inventories may be raw materials, partially finished goods, or finished goods kept in stock but not yet sold.* Because of the length of time required to produce a finished product, there must be inventories at all levels of the productive process in order to ensure a reasonably steady flow of goods to final consumers.

Let's begin again with the expansion phase. As GNP increases, sales go up faster than inventories will support. There will be a need to expand inventories, not only to replace what has been sold but also to bring the level of inventories up to that needed for the higher sales volume. The extra production for inventory will have an accelerator effect on GNP. But once inventories reach the new, higher level, production will slow down. Inventories will then appear to be too high, so production will slow even more. Eventually, the economy reaches its upper turning point and starts down. Now inventories appear to be very large relative to sales. Production is curtailed and the negative accelerator begins to work.

When the economy reaches the trough, a further period of time is required to reduce inventories. However, once inventory reaches desired levels or even a little less, the increase in production for inventory will lead to a recovery phase. As the recovery moves on to expansion, the need to build inventories will once again accelerate an increase in GNP.

Here is an example of an inventory cycle. Suppose an automobile company finds that its dealers need 10 cars in stock for each car sold (the customer likes to look at different colors and features for each model). A dealer selling

an average of 10 cars a day will therefore need 100(10 X 10) on the lot. Once the hundred cars are there, only 10 more will be needed each day to replace those sold. But if sales rise to 11 a day, production will have to rise to more than 11 a day. Why? Well, first it will be necessary to increase inventory to 110 cars (10 X 11). Thereafter, 11 a day can be provided. If all dealers experience the same increase in sales, a substantial increase in output to raise required inventories will be necessary. The effect will extend to inventories of parts, to cars moving down the assembly line, and to raw materials such as steel, rubber, plastics, and paint. All will have to be increased. To produce the extra amounts, additional workers will be needed, some of whom will then buy new cars. If car sales rise to 12 cars a day, inventories will have to rise in turn to 120 cars per dealer. We have returned to the beginning of the example, and there is no need to run through the explanation again. Can you show what will happen if sales decline from 10 cars a day to 9 cars a day for each dealer?

The similarity of investment in inventory to investment in productive capacity, from the standpoint of the cycle, should be clear. One reason for thinking about them separately is that economists have done so in the past. But another reason is that changes in inventory levels may appear to firms as an alternative to changes in capacity, especially if the business cycle is mild. Some firms can maintain higher than usual inventories when good times approach rather than having to increase plant capacity. So it is useful then to keep the two concepts separate. In an actual cycle, of course, both kinds of investment may be at work.

Monetary cycles

In describing the above theories, we made no mention of money. The cycles have been described in terms of real variables such as employment, output, and investment. We have not been concerned about the amount of money available. It was assumed that the money supply would adjust somehow without worrying about how the adjustment would come about. If the amount of money did not adjust, there would be surplus money when the economy was in a trough with less being produced and sold. Money would become scarce at a peak as more goods and services are produced and sold. A scarcity of money might even reduce the height of the peak! Thus we want the money supply to adjust so there is always the "right" amount.

Now, let us consider the possibility that the amount of money available may cause business cycles. At the very least, changes in money available may accentuate business cycles, if "cause" is too strong a term. Remember that such changes would arise from the economic forces at work, and not from any deliberate human decision—that is, they would not result from the sort of decision made by the government in 1969 and 1973 to decrease the amount of money in order to prevent the economy from expanding output too quickly.

Let's begin, as before, with the economy expanding. In the expansion phase business firms begin to expect the economy to continue expanding. They see the need to increase their capacity and their inventories. To do so, they go to their banks to borrow money. They feel they can always pay back the loans from the larger profits expected in the future. During the expansion phase, the demand for borrowed money grows.

On the other side of the market, the bankers observe the expansion of the economy and respond to it along with the business firms. They are more willing to make loans during the expansion than at other times, and welcome the new business opportunities. If the banks have idle reserves, they can easily use them to make additional loans. Even if they haven't, they can still increase the supply of credit available to the economy, by a mechanism to be described later. Bank credit is really a form of money. By activating idle money or creating new money, the banks assist in financing the expanding economy. The process cannot go on forever. Eventually, the interest rate—that is, the price of borrowed money—begins to rise. As borrowed money becomes more expensive, business firms revise their willingness to continue borrowing. They will grow concerned about the amount of debt they are going to have to pay back. They may also find that they are attaining levels of productive capacity and of inventory that satisfy them so that they do not wish to expand any further. Finally, at the first hint that the economy is reaching a peak, they become less optimistic about the future. At this point the amount of borrowing by business firms may level off or even begin to decline.

Banks are affected in a similar way. As their ability to make loans reaches its limit, they find that they must raise their prices (that is, the interest rates they charge). They also become less willing to make new loans. They look very carefully at new applicants for loans. The bankers also begin to fear a possible downturn in the cycle, and start to worry about the ability of borrowers to repay the amounts they have already borrowed. Thus the amount of money available to the economy may stop growing, and may even begin to contract.

Once the amount of money borrowed and loaned ceases to grow, the expansion of the economy may slow down. If a slowdown begins, business firms will start to emphasize loan repayment. They will try to reduce the amount of debt they carry so as to avoid being caught with rising borrowing costs at a time when business is declining. Banks will encourage them to reduce their debt burden out of fear that some of the loans may never be repaid. The amount of money available to the economy will begin to decline, adding to the downward tendency.

When the downswing has been reached, some firms may not be able to repay their loans. Some may even be forced out of business, and production will decline still further. If enough firms fail, some banks may begin to fail also. When a bank fails, the amount of money available to the economy declines even more. The contraction of the money supply speeds the contraction of the economy, and so the decline proceeds.

Eventually, the amount of debt will be reduced even though the economy is in a decline. The cycle may enter its trough. Business firms will not desire many new loans at this time, and eventually the interest rate will fall because of the lack of demand for borrowed money. If the interest rate falls far enough, firms will begin to reconsider their need for money. Even though the economy is still in a trough, some capital equipment will have worn out and need replacing. The lower cost of borrowing money makes loans for this purpose attractive even though business is not good.

One industry that often responds to declining interest rates is the home-building industry. Home builders borrow money during the time the house is under construction in order to pay for labor and materials. Potential home buyers also respond to lower rates on mortgage loans. That is why home construction may be one of the first industries to expand in the recovery phase of the cycle. Since home building uses a lot of labor, its expansion has a stimulating effect on demand. This may move the economy from the recovery to the expansion phase.

We have returned to the beginning of the cycle. We have seen how forces operating within the economy have both created and responded to changes in the amount of money available. A complete business cycle has been generated.

Short waves and long waves

Economists studying the business cycle have distinguished cycles of various lengths. There are cycles of three, five, seven, twelve, and fifteen years in length, and even longer ones. Their lengths are determined by measuring the time from the peak of one cycle to the peak of the next. These cycles take place simultaneously. That is, if you sort through the statistical data for a given period, you will find not just one up-and-down movement but several. Sometimes their peaks coincide and reinforce each other; sometimes they occur at different times.

The existence of a number of different cycles has led many able investigators to look for particular causes of some of them. The 15- to 25-year cycles have been attributed to changes in population growth, railroad building, and other factors. The seven-year cycles were once attributed to the influence of sunspots. The reasoning was that changes in sunspot activity affected the weather on earth, and changes in the weather in turn affected the performance of agriculture. Both sunspots and wheat crops seemed to move in seven-year cycles. The agricultural cycles caused the rest of the economy to fluctuate. Nobody holds to this theory anymore, since agriculture has become such a relatively small sector of our economy that it would be like the tail wagging the dog. A Russian professor named Nikolai

Economic Thinker
Nikolai Kondratieff

Born in Russia in 1892, Nikolai D. Kondratieff was an outstanding Soviet economist and statistician of the 1920s. His deep interest in economic planning and agricultural economics coincided with the particular needs and interests of the newly emerging economy of the Soviet Union. In 1920, he founded the Moscow Business Conditions Institute, where, until 1928, he and his colleagues collected important statistical data on agriculture and other economic matters. Kondratieff constructed a series of price indices for Russian agriculture similar to those used in the United States for measuring purchasing power "parity" of American farmers. He also produced the Soviet Union's first five-year plan for agriculture.

Kondratieff's insistence that the welfare of the individual farmer be considered in "farm collective" planning and his refusal to accommodate statistical data to Marxist doctrine when the data showed otherwise got him in trouble with his more doctrinaire colleagues and with the Soviet authorities. He was arrested sometime in the late 1920s or early 1930s and is presumed to have died while imprisoned.

In the West, Kondratieff is best known for his work on business cycles. His *The Long Waves in Economic Life* had appeared in Germany in 1925. His theories of business cycles were brought to the attention of non-Soviet economists largely through economist Joseph Schumpeter in the latter's own work on business cycles.

Statistical data had convinced Kondratieff—as it had other economists—that there were long cycles (or "long waves," as he called them) as well as short business cycles at work in the economy. In fact, short waves had their ups and downs within these long cycles. Statistical data at his disposal from the United States, Great Britain, France, and Germany strengthened his theories, he believed, even though the relatively brief periods covered by available data made absolute proof at least temporarily impossible.

Kondratieff's study led to his dating of these long-wave business cycles: (1) 1780s to 1844–1851, peaking in 1810–1817; (2) 1844–1851 to 1890–1896, peaking in 1870–1875; and (3) a discernible rise from 1890–1896 to 1914–1920, when another decline was very probably scheduled to begin. (A decline, of course, did come—the Great Depression of the 1930s.)

Kondratieff suggested that the long waves were caused by technological innovations (such as railroad building), wars and revolutions, the opening up of new countries, and discoveries of gold. A more recent theory of long waves suggests that they may be caused by certain kinds of decision-making in industry. A 50-year cycle could reflect the amount of time required to form expectations about the future, the amount of time it takes for firms to enter and then leave an industry, and the fact that when capital goods industries undertake to expand their output they must first produce their own capital goods.

The exact predictive quality of long-cycle economic theories is still a matter of conjecture. For what it is worth, however, economists have noted that according to the theories of Nikolai Kondratieff and those who have extended his work, various short cycles within Kondratieff's long wave will tend to reach bottom together sometime after 1980, possibly resulting in another severe depression.

Kondratieff studied very *long cycles* in business activity. He thought the cycles averaged 50 years or so in length. These long cycles are also called *Kondratieff cycles*.

Planned downturns

In our discussion of theories of the business cycle we have not mentioned one cause that has come to be important recently: the planned downturn. The downswings of 1969 and 1973 resulted from deliberate action by the government. It tightened up on the supply of money in order to slow down the inflation. The result was a slowing down of the whole economy. The government has to choose, in effect, between the lesser of two evils: a lot of inflation or a slight drop in production (with an increase in unemployment). However, as we shall see later, planned downturns can easily become too strong. In 1973 the slowing down went much further than the authorities had intended.

Business cycle forecasting

We have now looked at the history of business cycles, considered a typical cycle, and studied some of the possible causes of cycles. One reason for studying business cycles is to try to forecast what is going to happen in the near future. Business executives need to have some foreknowledge in order to make intelligent decisions for their companies. If they expect the economy to expand, they will make quite different plans than if they expect it to contract. That is why large companies employ economists or pay high fees to economic consultants.

So far, nobody has discovered a way of foretelling the future without making mistakes. Economists don't have crystal balls. All they can do is to make educated guesses based on as much evidence as they can muster. Most businesses prefer to use the guesses of economists rather than the guesses of noneconomists. Such an economist will spend the working day looking at the latest statistics of GNP, personal income, housing construction, business investment, prices, employment, department store sales, and so on. Thus it is possible to learn a great deal about where the economy is probably going. The economist may not be able to say when the next upturn or downturn will begin, but he or she can tell you what the present trends are.

The economic forecaster may be able to do better than that. One useful guide to what is coming is other people's expectations. Several agencies, both governmental and private, conduct polls of businessmen to find out how much they intend to spend on capital investment in coming months. On the basis of these polls, it is sometimes possible to estimate whether investment is going to increase or decrease, and by how much. Taken together

Extended Example
Reading the Economic Tea Leaves

Each year, late in December or around the first of January, our economic prophets go to their typewriters or gather in television studios to tell what will happen on the economic front during the coming year. Most of these seers would be quick to tell us also that, despite their computers and sophisticated measurement techniques, economic forecasting is far from an exact science. In truth, it's just the opposite of weather forecasting: it's pretty good in the long term, but in the short term, to be taken with a certain degree of caution. For example, in January, 1975, leading econometricians made their usual predictions for the coming year. Predictions about GNP growth ranged from +2.5% to −3.5%; about price increases, 10.3% to 6.5%; about the unemployment rate, 8.3% to 6.3%. Considering the vast size of our economy, a difference of even a fraction of a percentage point in such economic indicators can be a matter of billions of dollars and millions of unemployed. It is obvious that our economic forecasters cannot always predict with precision. (The actual 1975 figures turned out to be: GNP growth, −2.9%; price increases, 8.4%; and unemployment rate, 9.0%.)

Still, economic forecasting is an indispensable tool for all concerned with economic planning—businessman, banker, government official, and, indeed, almost everyone, because business cycles affect each of us. Any reasonably correct indication of their movements is to be welcomed.

Economic prognosticators and planners depend upon a number of indicators to read the pulse of the nation's economy:

(1) *Unemployment figures* are published monthly by the Bureau of Labor Statistics. They show the number and percentage of workers employed as well as those unemployed. Employment statistics are also given for age, sex, and ethnic groups.

(2) The *Consumer Price Index* (CPI) computes changes in the cost of goods and services and is one measurement of inflationary trends in the economy. The *Wholesale Price Index* (WPI) measures changes in the prices of some 3,000 commodities. Since wholesale prices affect retail prices with a short time lag, this, too, is an important predictor of inflation to come.

(3) The *Industrial Production Index*, published by the Federal Reserve Board, measures physical output of manufacturing, mining, and utility industries. Changes in this index are generally considered indicative of changes in the general economy.

(4) *Retail sales figures* (and *inventory figures*) are compiled to provide sales volume figures of retail stores in the nation. Changes here indicate general changes in the economy and, more importantly, indicate the economic mood of the people. When consumers have confidence in the state of the economy, they tend to buy. When confidence drops, buying lags.

(5) *Interest rate changes* indicate movements in the investment markets and are of great importance to the economic planning of borrowers and lenders. There are many types of interest rates which may be observed. One is the so-called *prime rate*, that charged by a bank for loans to its best commercial customers. The *federal funds rate*, the rate of interest charged for overnight loans between banks, is considered a good short-term indicator of money market conditions. Interest rates on government and corporate bonds are also important.

(6) There are many other indicators of economic conditions. *Foreign trade statistics*, for example, help measure the comparative strength of the American economy with that of other nations. *Stock market indices* such as Standard and Poor's and the Dow Jones averages are good, *long-term* indicators of the economy's health. Most economists, however, pay little attention to the predictive value of short-term stock market fluctuation. (A favorite Wall Street witticism is that the stock market has unerringly predicted nine out of the last three recessions.)

(7) One widely followed indicator of trends in the business cycle is the monthly index put out by the United States Department of Commerce called the *Composite Index of Leading Indicators*. The composite index is especially designed to reflect future

trends in the economy rather than current strengths or weaknesses. It measures monthly changes in 12 different indicators that have been found to be particularly important as indicators of movements in the business cycle. These indicators include figures on average workweek of manufacturing workers, layoffs in manufacturing, price changes in key raw materials, contracts for new plant equipment, prices of 500 common stocks, changes in money supply, and permits for new private housing construction.

All indicators are, of course, just that. They *indicate* rather than *predict*—an important distinction that is sometimes forgotten even by economic experts. At times, the indicators have called turns in the business cycle quickly, with a high degree of accuracy and before the turn of the cycle. At other times, the indicators have not "led" the actual cycle movement by more than a month or so. Imperfect though they may be, however, they can be of very considerable help in managing the economies of individual businesses and industries and the economy of the nation.

with other information, this may be an important clue to the future. It suffers from the drawback that businessmen may be overoptimistic or overpessimistic when they answer the questions of the pollsters. The amounts they actually invest may turn out to be less or greater than they expected.

Consumer expectations are also important. The Survey Research Center of the University of Michigan conducts polls of households to find out what their spending intentions are. In 1973 the Center found consumers to be very pessimistic, and accordingly predicted that an economic downturn was likely—a prediction which proved correct.

Economists also make much use of statistical series called leading indicators. The **leading indicators** represent selected forms of economic activity that move up or down ahead of the economy as a whole. For instance, manufacturers' orders for new equipment can be expected to lead the economy in the upswing. In the same way, a decline in the average workweek in manufacturing may indicate that

a general business slowdown is coming. Figure 4 shows in rather oversimplified form how a leading indicator works. About 40 such series have been identified. The Department of Commerce has selected 12 that make particularly good indicators. It publishes these in a monthly magazine called *Business Conditions Digest*, which can be found in most reference libraries. There is also a composite indicator that combines the 12 leading indicators.

Leading indicators aren't infallible. Even when they turn out to be correct, you can't be sure until afterward. An indicator may turn up one month and down the month after. The forecaster can never be sure whether an upturn in the index for one month is going to be followed by further upward movements in successive months, or whether it will be followed by a plateau or a downturn. His general knowledge of the economy may tell him that one possibility is more likely than another. But the economy as a whole often makes temporary movements in one direction only to reverse them afterward. Or sometimes it hesitates briefly and continues onward as before. Most often the analyst will say something like: "An upswing is due about now. The recession appears to have run its course. That being so, the index of leading indicators suggests that we've bottomed out and may be starting up."

Perhaps we can't hope to eliminate business cycles altogether. In an imperfect world

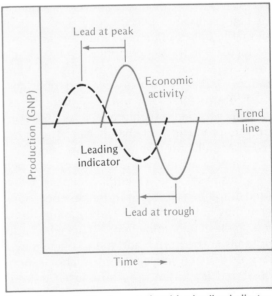

Figure 4 A typical business cycle with a leading indicator.

we must expect the functioning of our economy to be uncertain. Businessmen will make mistakes: they will overinvest from time to time, or produce more than the market can handle. But we should hope some day to eliminate the massive underemployment of resources that occurs during prolonged slumps.

Can this be done in a capitalist economy? To answer this question, we must first become acquainted with some additional tools of analysis. The tools are the subject of the next chapter. The use of those tools in controlling business cycles will be discussed.

Summary

The goals of our economy as embodied in the Employment Act of 1946 are (1) steady and rapid growth, (2) full employment, and (3) stable prices. These goals have each been met in our history, but at times none have been achieved. It may be impossible to simultaneously meet all three at once under most conditions.

The business cycle is a summary of how the economy alternately expands and contracts. The expansion continues till a peak is reached. After the peak a decline or downswing begins which continues till the trough is reached. After the trough occurs, recovery begins, leading to expansion again. A complete cycle may take from 3 to 12 years.

The peak of the business cycle is a period of high economic performance. The peak is desirable unless marred by inflation, which is an increase in the general price level causing a loss of purchasing power to those holding money. Inflation may be demand pull, cost push, or structural. Demand-pull inflation is especially associated with the peak as the economy is producing all that it can. The other forms of inflation may occur at any time.

Unemployment is a problem at the trough of a business cycle. Unemployment is measured as the percentage of those members of an economy in the labor force who cannot find a job. Cyclical unemployment occurs when output falls at the trough and there is generally a lack of demand for labor. Since labor cannot be stored for future use, the unused labor is lost forever to the economy. Thus the loss exceeds the loss of income to the unemployed. Full employment is not at 100% of the labor force as there are always some members between jobs; this type of unemployment is either frictional or structural unemployment.

The U.S. economy has had a series of business cycles since it began. The Great Depression of the 1930s was the deepest and longest trough. Three cycles occurred during the 1950s. There were recent downturns in 1969 and 1973, with the 1973–1975 recession the worst since the Great Depression. Business cycles cost the economy because of lost output during the trough and reduced growth because of low investment and uncertainty.

Business cycles may be caused by changes in investment expenditures. The business community changes the level of expenditures, which changes output and employment. The accelerator effect adds to the instability as increases and decreases in income produce additional changes in the level of investment.

Inventory accumulation is a form of investment. Changes in inventory expenditure may also cause business cycles. Monetary expansion or contraction may also cause business cycles or, at the very least, facilitate business cycles.

Business cycles may be predicted by using leading indicators; the leading indicators are economic data series which serve as a barometer of future ups and downs in business activity.

Key Words and Phrases

- **inflation** an increasing level of prices which persists over a period of time.
- **demand-pull inflation** inflation caused by members of an economy attempting to purchase more than the economy can produce thereby bidding up prices.
- **cost-push inflation** inflation caused by suppliers of basic inputs, intermediate goods, or final goods raising prices even when there is surplus capacity.
- **structural inflation** inflation caused by shifts in demand or supply raising some selected prices without any decline in other prices.
- **level of prices** the general price level is a concept of the average of all prices; it is measured by an index such as the consumer price index.
- **labor force** those members of an economy who

have decided to offer their services outside the household in exchange for money wages.

- **unemployment**   those members of the labor force who are unable to find jobs for which they are qualified and at wages acceptable to themselves.

- **frictional unemployment**   unemployment of a voluntary nature caused by the time required to change jobs.

- **structural unemployment**   involuntary unemployment caused by decline in demand for labor in a particular industry, with a particular skill, or in a particular location; this may occur even though there are jobs open in the economy, because the unemployed are not suited to or not located near the jobs.

- **cyclical unemployment**   general involuntary unemployment caused by a lack of demand such as is found at the trough of a business cycle.

- **business cycle**   a somewhat regular up and down movement in the output of an economy lasting from three to twelve years.

- **recession**   the declining portion or trough of the business cycle—it occurs after a peak; the term is applied to any decline in the output of the economy lasting more than two quarters of a year.

- **depression**   refers to a decline and/or a trough of a business cycle which is especially long and deep.

- **prosperity**   a term describing the peak of the business cycle, indicating high levels of production and income and low unemployment.

- **boom**   a term for the peak of the business cycle which is used when the peak is so high that excesses of many sorts creep into the economy. In particular, there may be inflation, shortages, and mass speculation; oil or gold discoveries often produced boom conditions.

- **inventory**   supplies of raw materials, goods partially finished (such as an automobile moving down the assembly line), and finished goods to be used for future production and sale; inventories are necessary for production and their level may be planned.

- **panic**   a term used when the recessionary period is led by fear in financial matters; people usually sell their securities and withdraw their money from banks.

- **national debt**   the amount of money borrowed by the federal government; there is a great deal more debt outstanding in the U.S., but the national debt refers only to that borrowed on behalf of the people by their government and its agencies.

- **Kondratieff or long cycles**   cycles in business activity which are 40 to 60 years in length.

- **induced investment**   changes in planned levels of investment expenditures which result from an increase in the rate of expansion of the economy; a decrease in the rate of expansion results in negative induced investment.

- **accelerator effect**   the increase (or decrease) in output as a result of induced investment.

- **leading indicators**   a collection of 12 data series which seem to serve as a barometer of economic activity by rising before the economy begins to expand or falling before a recession begins.

Questions for Review

1.   Explain why even the best organized economy would have some unemployment at the peak of the business cycle.

2.   "Inflation is a tax on money held." Why is this statement true?

3.   What are the stages of the business cycle? Explain the economic conditions noted at each stage.

4.   List the things you would consider if you were a businessman planning the inventory you would hold. When you have your list, see how many of the things you have written down would be affected by the business cycle. Would your response to stages of the business cycles tend to smooth out the cycle or reinforce it?

5.   What are the goals of a well-run economy? How may the achievement of one goal interfere with the achievement of either of the others?

6.   What are the problems of being unemployed? How does unemployment affect those who are still employed?

7.   A recovery began in 1975 in the U.S. economy. What is the history of the business cycle from early 1975 to the day which you are reading this question?

8.   What are the three types of inflation? Give the name and a short description of each.

9.   What are the three types of unemployment? Describe each.

10.   Explain how changes in the willingness of business firms to expand capacity may change the need for expanded capacity.

11.   Does your answer to question 10 suggest any way of controlling business cycles?

12.   Look up the latest figures on the Index of Economic Indicators. Is it moving up or down? What does the indicator forecast for the future? Will it be easier or harder for you to find a job when you graduate?

8

Aggregate Demand

In earlier chapters we saw how the output of business firms is regulated by supply and demand. You will remember Sam the moonshine man, who was put out of business when his costs rose and his market dwindled. Now we are going to examine the way in which the whole economy is controlled by supply and demand—only we will call them *aggregate* supply and *aggregate* demand to show that we are talking about the whole national economy rather than an industry or a firm.

We define **aggregate supply** as the value of all the output that is available to be purchased by the national economy at any given time. It is equal to the net national product (NNP), which you will remember is the total of everything produced (GNP) minus what is used up in producing it. We define **aggregate demand** as the value of all the output that consumers, business firms, and other sectors of the economy are willing to purchase at a given time. You might think of the national economy as tending toward an equilibrium point at which aggregate demand and aggregate supply are equal.

Theories of aggregate demand

Classical theory

This way of looking at the economy in terms of aggregate demand is still pretty new. Adam Smith wouldn't have seen the point of it. Neither would other economists before the 1930s, when John Maynard Keynes used this approach as the basis for a new kind of economic theory. Keynes said that the depression of the 1930s could not be explained with the traditional theory. The traditional theory, from Adam Smith and David Ricardo on down to the leading economists of the 1920s and 1930s, had assumed that the national economy was always close to full employment. Whenever it got below the level of full employment, the forces of supply and demand would push it back up again. Of course, the traditional theorists were familiar with business cycles and fluctuations. But they took these to be only temporary disturbances in the flow of production, something like waves upon an ocean.

The attitude of the traditional economists was that since everyone is a part of society, each person's contribution to it is balanced by what each one takes away. The shoemaker exchanges his shoes for the bread of the baker and the meat of the butcher. The worker in an auto factory exchanges his wages for things made by other workers. As the economists put it: "Supply creates its own demand." This came to be known as **Say's Law,** named after the French economist Jean Baptiste Say, who lived in the early nineteenth century. It seemed to make excellent sense because there is no reason why all the members of a society should not be able to contribute something to the common pool of wealth and take away something in return. Just as in a family, where every member contributes a share of the household work and receives food and shelter in return, the members of the national economy were thought of as being interrelated and interdependent.

You may say, "Yes, but society isn't a family. We buy and sell in the market, and when the shoe manufacturer brings his shoes to be sold he can't be sure that there will be a demand for all of them."

The classical economists replied that of course the shoe manufacturer might misjudge his market and produce too many shoes. If he did, he would make fewer of them next time, and try to adjust his output to market demand. If he had more labor and materials than could be used in making shoes, he would look around and find some other market to serve. He would be guided by the price system. In markets where demand exceeded supply, prices would rise so that new producers would be drawn to them and existing producers would expand their activities. Labor and other resources would flow toward such markets and away from markets where supply exceeded demand.

Supply and demand would tend toward an equilibrium in every market, and aggregate supply and demand for all the markets together would also tend toward an equilibrium in which all labor and resources would find employment. A surplus of anything would be reflected in lower prices. Unemployed workers, for example, would be willing to accept lower wages. Lower wages give employers greater incentive to hire workers, and wages would fall until they reached a level at which the quantity of labor supplied would be equal to the quantity demanded. The prices of other unemployed resources would adjust in the same way.

Of course, the system would not always adjust smoothly. Fluctuations and cycles would occur because many producers might overestimate the market at the same time, or underestimate it. External factors, such as wars or new developments in technology, would set off waves in the economy. But these would be temporary disturbances, and the system would tend to return to full-employment equilibrium.

The savings and investment problem

The classical economists were often challenged by critics who found what seemed to be flaws in the theory. The critics were fond of pointing out that some people didn't spend all of their income, but saved it. The income they saved would not be translated into a demand for goods and services. Of course, the savings would be put in a bank or used to buy stocks and bonds—that is, the money would be lent to someone else—and the borrowers would spend it. Business firms borrow money in order to invest in capital equipment, which later is used to make more goods. But what if people save too much, and the goods that are produced cannot all be sold? In the language of economics, what if aggregate demand falls below aggregate supply? Won't this lead to lower production and unemployment?

"No," said the classical economists. "You are forgetting that there is a market for money as well as for goods and services. Those who want to borrow money pay a price for it, called an interest rate. When the demand for money increases, the interest rate will rise and people will be encouraged to save more. When the demand for money falls, the interest rate will fall too; people will want to save less and consume more." The same would hold for business firms: when interest rates were low, they would borrow more funds and invest them in

expansion; when interest rates rose, they would postpone their investment plans and concentrate on paying off what they had already borrowed.

This is a brief summary of what the classical economists called "general equilibrium theory." Many books have been written about this theory. It has also been summarized in equation form for ease of interpretation. For a long time it served well as a means of understanding economic life, and until the 1930s it was the accepted canon of thought in most of the Western world. But it fell upon difficulties during the Great Depression. When a large proportion of the labor force was unable to find work, people turned to the economists and asked them what ought to be done.

The classical economists replied that too much is already being done. Their theory told them that heavy and prolonged unemployment could not happen in a system of competitive markets and flexible prices. It was when business followed policies of keeping prices from falling, and when unions tried to keep wages from falling, that serious unemployment resulted. Matters were made worse, said the economists, when the government tried to interfere with the free market by setting minimum wages and prices. (President Franklin D. Roosevelt's "New Deal" in the early 1930s tried to regulate wages and prevent price-cutting by business firms.)

To many people, the economists seemed to be saying that if the world didn't correspond to their theory it was too bad for the world. This was not a good position for economists to be in. People who run governments and lead public opinion don't like to be told that there is nothing they can do. In Germany at that time Adolf Hitler was demonstrating that unemployment could be cured by producing armaments and building superhighways. In Russia the Communists claimed that a planned economy would end unemployment and poverty forever.

Keynesian theory

At this point Keynes published his *General Theory of Employment, Interest and Money.* He threw aside the classical argument that a competitive economy would tend toward full employment. On the contrary, he said, it might reach equilibrium at considerably less than full employment and stay there. Say's Law was wrong; production did not create its own demand. Keynes argued that in a modern capitalist society the forces governing aggregate supply may not get together in a way that will ensure full employment. This would be especially true if wages did not decline to ensure full employment. If wages do not fall, prices will not fall and surplus goods cannot be sold. Classical economists thought wages would adjust to bring about full employment. If the amount of goods produced at full employment was not the amount demanded, then the interest rate would change. The classical economists also thought that a higher or a lower interest rate would bring about equality between savings and the demand for savings for investment purposes.

Keynes maintained that the interest rate does not always perform the function of equating the supply of savings with the demand for savings. If it does not, then households may decide to save more than business firms want to invest. "What's wrong with this?" you might ask. Plenty! Saving reduces the amount of goods and services in the circular flow (and therefore reduces the number of workers needed to produce the goods and services). However, investment adds to the circular flow because firms buy capital goods—and workers must be hired to produce these goods. So if investment is not at least equal to saving, output may be less than optimum and unemployment will result. In other words, demand does not equal supply at a point of full employment. The economy will contract until it reaches equilibrium at a lower level of income and employment.

Since Keynes wrote his book forty years ago, there has been an enormous amount of discussion and debate among economists as to just why the economy fails to reach full-employment equilibrium, and what ought to be done about it. The theory of these matters has been greatly refined and elaborated. We will examine some of the discussion later. First, though, we will take a closer look at some of the tools economists have developed to handle macroeconomic problems. In the remainder of this chapter we will examine the factors that determine the aggregate demand for goods and services in the national economy. In the following chapter we will study aggregate supply, and how the level of income and employment is determined.

Sources of aggregate demand

In the chapter on national income accounting, we distinguished four sectors of the economy: households, business firms, government, and the rest of the world. We will use these same categories in analyzing aggregate demand, with the slight modification of emphasizing the basic activity of each sector. In this manner, we then identify the four basic determinants of demand: (1) consumption, (2) investment, (3) government expenditures, and (4) net exports (which is the dollar difference of exports minus imports). The reason for choosing these categories is that they correspond to the forces that actually determine the level at which the national economy operates. When households decide to consume more or consume less, they obviously influence the level of aggregate demand. When business firms change their investment expenditures, they also influence the level of aggregate demand. The same holds for changes in the government's purchases of goods and services and for changes in exports and imports.

Consumption (C)

Total consumption by households is the largest segment of demand. Counted among the items of consumption are all purchases of nondurable goods, such as food and clothing, and all durable goods, such as appliances, TV sets, and automobiles. Also included then are purchases of all services: health care, entertainment, haircuts, vacations, restaurant meals, education, and so forth.

Economic Thinker
John Maynard Keynes

Observing the economic scene today, most of us would have difficulty realizing that extensive and open government intervention in the economy is a fairly recent phenomenon. The wide general acceptance of that intervention (even though it may be accepted in more conservative circles only as a necessary evil or even as "the devil we know") owes much to an English economist named John Maynard Keynes. Keynes was not the first economist to promulgate government intervention to cure economic ills. When he conferred with President Franklin D. Roosevelt in Washington in 1934, the American President was already using relatively massive government spending as a device to get the economy out of depression. Indeed, Herbert Hoover, Roosevelt's conservative predecessor, had used similar devices to the same end, although on a smaller scale. What Keynes did was supply the theoretical underpinnings for intervention. He did so in a book published in 1936 called *The General Theory of Employment, Interest and Money*. It proved to be, as Keynes himself had predicted, an economic bombshell. In its own way, it was to become as influential as Smith's *Wealth of Nations* and as revolutionary as Marx's *Das Kapital*.

Keynes himself was a fascinating figure. Economist, financier, philosopher, international diplomatic negotiator, friend of artists and literary greats, it seemed that whatever he did, he did very well indeed. At 29 he was given the editorship of the *Economic Journal*, chief publication of the British economics profession. He wrote books on, among other things, national and international currency and on the economic consequences of war, and had a successful career as teacher and financial adviser to individuals and governments. And, mostly in his spare time, he made a fortune speculating in commodities and in the stock market.

As an economist, Keynes offered new insights into many aspects of economic theory and economic life. It may be said that the entire school of the so-called New Economics had its inception in the work of Keynes.

Classical economists had maintained that in a free economy business recessions, although unfortunate for society, would cure themselves without unduly upsetting the social order. When times were bad, savings would pile up until interest became so low that capitalists would become willing and able to borrow money to build new plants and once again expand the economy. The economy would cure itself.

Keynes, however, concerned with the persistence of the worldwide Great Depression and its propensity toward political and social disorder, looked for other answers to the problem of boom and bust in the nations' economies. One answer he arrived at was almost ridiculously simple: there was, he said, absolutely no assurance that savings would pile up in bad economic times. How can households accumulate savings in a depression, when high unemployment reduces income and saving? Further, Keynes noted that saving would not necessarily reduce interest rates. Investment would depend upon business confidence, which would also be low during a depression (or recession). Thus it was not excessive supply but reduced aggregate demand that caused the depression.

Aggregate demand, then, is a two-sided coin. Consideration must be given to consumption as well as to saving. Since there is nothing inherent in the economy to make investment stimulus automatic, the government must work from the other end if it wishes to increase aggregate demand and end depression. It must stimulate consumption by putting money into consumer pockets through work programs, subsidies, and other "pump priming" devices. Alternatively, the government could directly increase its own expenditures, adding to aggregate demand.

The business and capitalist communities reacted initially to Keynes' theories with outrage. "Socialist" was one of the kinder epithets thrown at Keynes and his followers. Keynes himself, however, was anything but a socialist. He remained, until his death in 1946, a defender of the free enterprise system. To Keynes, government intervention in the economy remained an "abnormal," though necessary, response to "abnormal" economic conditions—a helping hand to be withdrawn as soon as conditions allowed.

The principles developed by Keynes were spread by his followers, known as Keynesian economists. That Keynesian principles have been carried further than Keynes intended is undoubtedly true. Opponents of these principles can point to the growing power of government and to the seemingly ever-present inflationary spiral as indications of fallacy in the economic doctrines of Keynes. Yet there is also no doubt that he spoke to the problems of his time and that his influence will be felt throughout the foreseeable future. Few politicians and economists today would totally disavow the economic theories of John Maynard Keynes.

Consumption vs. saving

A special activity of households that does not come under the heading of consumption is saving. In fact, saving is in some ways quite opposite to consumption and rates its own category. We define saving to consist of income earned but left over after consumption. Income not used for consumption, that is saved, may be held in many forms. It could be held as cash. Some economists term this holding of cash *hoarding* rather than saving. Income saved could be put into checking or savings accounts or into a variety of other securities such as stocks or bonds. It would also be possible to purchase goods not intended for consumption such as gold, diamonds, or real estate.

Since we have mentioned real estate, let us look at the problems raised in deciding whether a household is consuming or saving. Consider what happens when a family purchases a house. A house was at one time listed as an item of consumption. But critics pointed out that, given the long lifetime of a house, its high cost, and its special financing, the purchase of a house actually becomes a form of saving. The long lifetime of a house lessens the impact of depreciation, or wearing out of the house. In fact, in recent years the cost or market value of a "used" house is often more than what the original buyer paid for it. For example, a house that cost $25,000 in 1968 in the Washington, D.C., area sold, on the average, for $50,000 in 1976. This dramatically illustrates the fact that buying a house (or condominium) is a means of saving. The *renting* of an apartment or house can never yield a financial return to the resident. Therefore, rent is a form of consumption.

The issues raised in classifying the purchase of a house demonstrate the potential lack of a clear-cut division between consumption and saving. This division appears increasingly more arbitrary if we reconsider durable goods. Aren't the automobile that we use for four years and resell, the TV set that may last five years, or even more so, the stereo speakers that last ten years somewhat like the purchase of the house—on a reduced scale, of course.

Having raised these problems, we will quickly sweep them under the carpet (and pages). Continuing to label the purchase of durable goods and rare, valuable goods as consumption is admittedly somewhat arbitrary. The durable goods, however, do wear out and we always seem to be buying them. Also, the use of these items is so uneven and a matter of individual circumstances that assessing their value or lifetime is difficult. So we will follow tradition and leave all durable goods and forms of art purchases classified under consumption.

Consumption and income

For now we are interested not so much in total consumption as in how consumers behave. We have all been told from our earliest years that it's good to save some of our incomes and not to spend everything as fast as it comes in. Most of us find this very difficult when we're young and not making much money. There are food bills and clothing bills and rent; there are car payments and doctors' bills. Save? There's just no way. Later, when we have families, it may become even more difficult to save. But not everybody stays poor forever. You may know people among your relatives and friends who have done better and better as the years passed. They go to restaurants. They eat more meat and less of the starch foods; more vegetables; more dairy products. They wear better clothes. They buy home furnishings and take more expensive vacations.

In short, consumption depends on income. As people's incomes increase, they change their consumption patterns in quite predictable ways. For one thing, beyond a certain point they spend a smaller percentage of their income on food and a larger percentage on other things such as housing and transportation. They begin to save a little, though not very much. As their incomes rise further, the *percentage* they spend on basic things such as food, clothing, housing, and transportation becomes smaller and smaller (though of course they may spend more on those things in actual dollars). They spend more and more on recreation, on education for their children, and on dental care. They also save more and more. These patterns of spending have been studied by many economists in the last hundred years.

Table 1 presents some hypothetical income and spending figures for an average American family: the Jones family. As a quick look at the column labeled (1) shows, the Jones family has had its ups and downs. In some years the family income was as much as $13,000. This was when Mr. Jones was working full time and Mrs. Jones had a part-time job. In other years the family income was as low as $5,000 because Mr. Jones could find no steady employment. In the bad years the family actually spent more than its income. This isn't hard to do. The family used up some of its savings, and also took out a loan to buy a car. This is shown in column (3), where the negative numbers appear. When Mr. and Mrs. Jones were both working and the money was coming in, they set aside as much as they could. As their income increased, they consumed more, but they also saved more.

Average propensities to consume and to save

These changes in the way the Jones family consumes at different levels of income are of particular interest. In fact, the relation between income and consumption is designated as the *propensity to consume*. Economists find a special importance for the **average propensity to consume** (APC), which is the ratio of consumption to income:

$$APC = \frac{consumption}{income}.$$

Besides being concerned with the family consumption, the economist is just as con-

Table 1
Income Profile of the Jones Family

Year	(1) Disposable Income	(2) Consumption	(3) = (1) − (2)
1968	$ 5,000	$ 5,500	$ − 500
1969	7,000	7,100	− 100
1970	8,000	7,900	100
1971	6,000	6,300	− 300
1972	9,000	8,700	300
1973	10,000	9,500	500
1974	13,000	11,900	1,100
1975	12,000	11,100	900
1976	11,000	10,300	700

cerned with how the family saves at different levels of income. As you probably would guess, the relation between income and saving is termed the *propensity to save*. Furthermore, we can define the **average propensity to save (APS)** in a fashion similar to above:

$$APS = \frac{saving}{income}.$$

A further look at the Jones family may help clarify these concepts. Table 2 extends our information of the Jones family in two ways. First, notice that the ups and downs of the Jones family income have been smoothed out in the first column of Table 2 by placing the incomes in ascending order (that is, from smallest to largest). Secondly, we have added more columns to the table. In column (4) we have computed the average propensity to consume; we did this by dividing the quantity in column (2) by the quantity in column (1). If you run your eye up and down column (4), you will notice one very special occurrence: *At the lower levels of income, the Jones family has a higher propensity to consume.* At high levels of income, the Jones family has a lower propensity to consume. What this means simply is that the Jones family tends to spend *proportionately* less as its income increases. For example, at an income of $10,000 the Jones family spends $9,500, which is 95% of its income. At $12,000 the Jones family spends more money, $11,100, but this figure is only 92% of its income. So as the Jones family income rises from $10,000 to $12,000, its average propensity to consume drops from .95 to .92.

The average propensity to save has been calculated for column (5) by dividing the quantity in column (3) by the corresponding quantity in column (1). The negative quantities at the top of column (5) indicate that the Jones family is withdrawing money from their savings rather than adding to their savings. Economists call this withdrawal of money a **dissaving.** Dissaving may come from prior saving called *wealth* or by borrowing from others.

If you compare the figures in column (5) with those in column (1), you will notice a basic property of the propensity to save. *As income increases, the average propensity to save increases.* That is, as income increases, so does the percentage of income used for savings. At an income of $8,000 the Jones family saves $100, which is 1% of the income. At $12,000 the savings is $900. What is most striking and important here is not that more money is saved, but rather the rate of saving has increased; at $12,000 the percentage saved is 8%.

Although we have developed the concepts of average propensities to consume and to save independently, the two are related. Since a household like the Jones family can only save or spend its income, the total of saving (S) and consumption (C) in any one year must equal the disposable income (DI) for that year:

$$DI = S + C.$$

We expressed this in slightly different form in

Table 2
The Jones Family's Consumption and Saving

(1) Disposable Income	(2) Consumption	(3) Saving, (1) − (2)	(4) Average Propensity to Consume, (2) ÷ (1)	(5) Average Propensity to Save, (3) ÷ (1)	(6) Marginal Propensity to Consume, change in (2) / change in (1)	(7) Marginal Propensity to Save, change in (3) / change in (1)
$ 5,000	$ 5,500	$ −500	1.10	−0.10		
					.80	.20
6,000	6,300	−300	1.05	−0.05		
					.80	.20
7,000	7,100	−100	1.01	−0.01		
					.80	.20
8,000	7,900	100	0.99	0.01		
					.80	.20
9,000	8,700	300	0.97	0.03		
					.80	.20
10,000	9,500	500	0.95	0.05		
					.80	.20
11,000	10,300	700	0.94	0.06		
					.80	.20
12,000	11,100	900	0.92	0.08		
					.80	.20
13,000	11,900	1,100	0.91	0.09		

column (3) by indicating that saving equals column (1), income, minus column (2), consumption:

S = DI − C.

However, we can also say average propensity to consume (APC) plus average propensity to save (APS) equal one:

APC + APS = 1.

If you think about this for a moment, you might see that it just says the percentage of income consumed plus the percentage of income saved equals one hundred percent— always. A quick check of the Jones family in Table 2 reveals that the sum of any entry in column (4) and the corresponding entry in column (5) does indeed equal one.

How typical is the spending behavior of the Jones family? Well, we did say that it is an average American family. But the average family is not every family. Some like to save more and some less, even in the same financial circumstances. You might in fact be one of those people who would spend every penny no matter how much you earned. However, remember that there are other people who like to save every possible spare penny. So the pattern of spending by the Jones family does represent American families very well. Historically, the average propensity to consume in the United States has been 92% to 95%.* This of course means that the saving rate has been 5–8%. So the APC is useful in analyzing how eager consumers are to spend their money.

Marginal propensities to consume and to save

One of the most useful concepts of consumption involves the effect fluctuations of income have on spending (and saving). If a single family or the nation as a whole increases income by so many dollars, how much of this extra earnings will go to consumption and how much to saving? Economists often attach high

significance to the response of one variable to a change in another. This is called *marginal analysis*. *Marginal* means that a change has taken place; it does not mean something inferior as the term is sometimes used.

Once again let's look at the Jones family. In Table 2, we see, for example, that income changes from $11,000 to $12,000. The Jones family as a result has $1,000 more in income. Of this $1,000, how much is spent, and how much is saved? To see how much is spent, look at column (2). The Jones family moved from spending $10,300 to $11,100; the net result then is $800 of the extra $1,000 was used for consumption. That is, the marginal consumption was $800.

We can use two methods now to find the marginal saving. Continuing by checking column (3), we see the saving figures of $700 and $900; therefore, the amount saved from the extra $1,000 equals the difference between $900 and $700, or $200. A simpler method to find saving here is to subtract the $800 of marginal consumption from the $1,000. This also yields $200 of marginal saving.

We can interpret these findings even further by defining the **marginal propensity to consume** (MPC) as equal to the change in consumption divided by the change in income:

$$MPC = \frac{\text{change in consumption}}{\text{change in income}}.$$

In our example we saw that a change of income of $1,000 led to a change in consumption of $800. So the marginal propensity to consume here equals $800/$1,000 = 8/10 = .80 or 80%.

In a similar fashion economists define the **marginal propensity to save** (MPS) as equal to the change in saving divided by the change in income:

$$MPS = \frac{\text{change in saving}}{\text{change in income}}.$$

For our example above the marginal propensity to save equals $200/$1,000 = 2/10 = .20 or 20%.

* By way of contrast, in Germany the APC is lower, which means Germans prefer, at equal levels of income, to save more than Americans do. This difference in the APC is possibly due to different approaches to buying. Americans prefer to buy on credit while Germans may save their money until they have enough to buy the desired item.

For the moment, a household has only two choices of things to do with income. They may consume or save. Thus, if income rises by $1,000, they may consume $800 and save $200. That means the MPC + MPS = 1. We could calculate MPS as 1 − MPC = 1 − .80 = .20.

In Table 2, column (6) shows the marginal propensity to consume for the different changes in income. Column (7) shows the marginal propensity to save. Notice that in each column the percentages are identical. The Jones family, in effect, consumes the same percentage—80%—of any increases in income. Once again you may ask how does the Jones family compare to other American families? Does the marginal propensity to consume remain a constant figure? For our purposes, we can assume that it does. If we keep the MPC constant, everything will be much simpler. It may be that low-income families have a very high MPC, consuming almost all additional income and saving very little. Very high-income families may have higher MPS and lower MPC than the average family. We will let the Jones family be representative of all families, rich and poor, and use their MPC as if it applied to everyone in the economy.

The concept of marginal propensity to consume becomes of the utmost importance when economists and the President or Congress are trying to determine the level of government spending and tax policy. It may be decided that unemployment is too high and that therefore demand should be stimulated (increasing demand eventually means more workers are needed). If taxes are decreased, most individuals will have more money to spend. (Remember that their consumption is a form of demand.) But our study of marginal propensity to consume has just demonstrated that with an increase in disposable income most people will not spend every extra dollar; some of the money will be saved. So the tax cut has to be formulated on the basis of knowing the national, or aggregate, propensity to consume. At an MPC of .40 the required tax cut would have to be larger than if the marginal propensity to consume were .80.

The consumption function

We have seen that consumption and saving activities of people depend on their income, and that as their income increases people tend to save more and more of it. In addition, we have spoken of the relation between income and consumption as the propensity to consume. There is perhaps a more meaningful way to relate these two concepts. This relationship between income and consumption may also be called the **consumption function.** The word "function" is used in its mathematical sense as meaning a variable whose amount depends on the amount of another variable. Thus we say that the *amount of consumption is a function of the amount of income.*

Let us return to Table 2 to show how a consumption function is derived. In Table 2, the consumption expenditures of the Jones family are shown for each level of income. We can transfer the data to a graph as is shown in Figure 1. The first dot is for consumption of $5,500 at an income of $5,000. The line slopes upward as we go to higher levels of consumption at higher levels of income. Recall that we said the Joneses were a typical family. If there were a million such families in the economy, we could draw the consumption function for the economy simply by multiplying all numbers by 1,000,000. Everything would be the same except all numbers would have six more zeros.

Figure 2 shows a consumption function drawn for the economy as a whole. The verti-

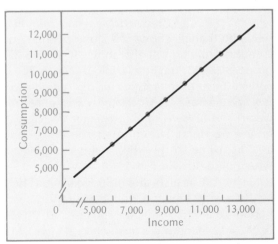

Figure 1 The consumption schedule A for the Jones family.

cal axis shows the amount spent on consumption. The horizontal axis is labeled NNP. You will recall that NNP is the income generated in producing all output minus the amount of goods used to replace the capital worn out during the year. NNP is the income available for use without reducing the stock of capital goods.

The consumption function is an upward-sloping line. It shows the amount of consumption for the whole economy at different levels of national income. As income rises toward the right, consumption rises along with it—but not by as much as the addition to income.

The diagram also contains another line that runs diagonally from the zero point or origin at a 45-degree angle. *This is a reference line put in to show all the points at which consumption is equal to income (net national product).* Points above the line are those at which consumption is greater than income; points below the line are those at which consumption is less than income, and saving takes place. At the point where the consumption function crosses the 45-degree line, consumption equals NNP; at that point saving is zero. Suppose the net national product for a year is $1,333 billion; the vertical line running up from that point on the horizontal axis to intersect the consumption function shows us that consumption is $1,200 billion. The difference of $133 billion represents saving.

We can also see pictured in Figure 2 two other concepts introduced in this chapter. Observe the small triangle drawn just below the consumption function. The horizontal portion of the triangle is labeled *change in NNP.* The vertical portion is labeled *change in consumption.* The triangle shows the slope of the consumption function. It also shows the marginal propensity to consume (MPC). *The MPC is nothing more than the slope of the consumption function showing the amount consumption increases for an increase in income (or decrease, if income decreases).* The consumption function is a straight line so the MPC is the same everywhere along the line.

The APC is also shown in Figure 2. When NNP is $1,333 billion, the consumption expenditure is $1,200 billion. Thus $1,200/$1,333 or 90% of income is consumed. APC is 0.90. However, APC is not constant. Consider what happens when NNP is $1,500 billion. At that

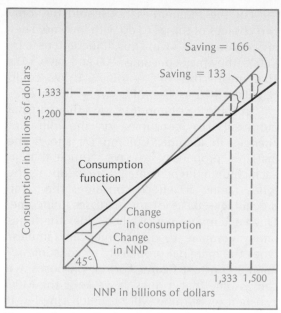

Figure 2 Consumption function for national economy (the sum of all consumers). Points on consumption line below 45° reference indicate saving occurs; points on consumption line above 45° reference line show dissaving occurs.

income consumption is $1,334 billion. APC has declined to $1,334/$1,500, or 0.889. The larger NNP becomes, the lower APC will become. *A constant MPC will result in a changing APC.*

The consumption function shows the planned consumption expenditures at each level of income. It is a demand curve relating consumption to income. It rises as income rises, since we may expect households to increase consumption as income increases. Even if the households do not eat greater amounts of food as increased income permits, they may switch from dried beans and hamburger to artichoke and steak. So consumption expenditures increase.

Nonincome determinants of consumption

Income isn't the only thing that influences the spending of households. You'll recall that when we studied demand, we mentioned various things other than price that might influence demand and cause the demand curve to shift to the right or left, such as changes in tastes or incomes. Similarly, the consumption function may shift up or down because of changes in five factors (other than income): (1) changes in liquid assets owned by households; (2) stock of nonliquid assets; (3) expectations; (4) cultural attitudes; and (5) age of buyers.

Changes in liquid assets owned by households Currency, and things that can be changed into currency very easily, such as bank accounts, stocks, bonds, Treasury bills, and the like, are termed **liquid assets.** If liquid assets increase, their owners will be prepared to spend more at each level of their income than they otherwise would. How can liquid assets increase without income increasing? They won't increase overnight, of course. But such a change occurred during World War II when people weren't able to spend all the money they were making. Consumer durables such as autos and washing machines weren't being produced then. People bought war bonds instead. But after the war all this pent-up purchasing power was released. Many economists had been predicting a serious postwar slump, perhaps even a depression because they had been thinking in terms of the prewar consumption function. But the liquid assets accumulated during the war had the effect of pushing the consumption function upward, and the economy took off.

Stock of nonliquid assets owned by households In the same way, households may hold nonliquid or physical assets. The effect of such assets on consumption expenditures is not clear. Durable goods last longer than a year. The more durable consumption goods, such as cars, TVs, mink coats, and furniture, the family owns, the less they will purchase during any time period. Some nonliquid assets, such as art work, will simply be enjoyed directly with no further expenditure necessary. Still other assets such as gold or diamonds may also appreciate in value leading the family to increase consumption spending. Finally, assets such as real estate may generate earnings which, along with work-related income, will lead to increased consumption expenditures.

Expectations Consumers are sometimes strongly influenced by what they think is going to happen in the near future. Consumer's expectations as to changes in incomes, prices, and supplies of goods affect their consumption. If they think the price of auto tires is about to increase sharply, they're likely to buy a set now for future use. If they expect prices in general to rise, as during the mid-1970s, they will tend to save less and buy more (helping to make the inflation worse, of course). On the other hand, if people are afraid of losing their jobs, they will cut back heavily on their spending. If they expect prices to fall in the future, they will also spend less, since the dollars they save now will be worth more later on.

Cultural attitudes If people place a high value on saving, they will obviously spend less than they otherwise would. Attitudes toward spending and saving don't usually change overnight, but governments in wartime try to encourage thrift—with some success.

State of family life-cycle Some economists list the state of the family life-cycle as a determinant of consumption. Obviously, the consumption pattern of a young family trying to furnish a house and raise children will be different from a retired couple. Much of the change in consumption as it relates to buyer age or family age has already been caught in changes in income since the earning pattern of a family matches the life-cycle closely. Also, while the change in consumption is dramatic for any one family, there is little effect on the economy as a whole. There are always some young families and some old families. However, both the percentages of elderly and of young people in society do change.

The saving function

By now you'll probably have noticed a special relationship between consumption and saving. If there is a consumption function, there must also be a saving function. We may derive the saving function from the data for the Jones family given in Table 2. In Figure 3, the data are plotted in a graph. At an income of $5,000, the Jones family dissaves in the amount of $500. Therefore, saving is shown as −$500. When

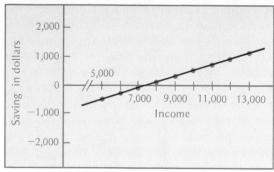

Figure 3 The saving schedule for the Jones family.

income rises to $10,000, saving rises to $500. A line connects all of the other points. As before, we can consider the Jones family representative and simply multiply by the number of families in the economy to obtain the savings function for the economy as a whole.

In Figure 4, we show both the consumption function and the saving function. The upper part of the figure shows the consumption function as it was in Figure 2. The saving function has been added in the lower part of the figure. Since both refer to the entire economy, the vertical axis is the consumption and saving levels for the entire economy. The horizontal axis is NNP.

The amount of saving at point 3 of NNP is S_3, which is equal to the distance from the consumption function to the 45-degree reference line.

As we move to the left or downward along the NNP scale, say to point 2, saving decreases. At point 2, consumption and NNP are equal. All income is consumed and there is no saving. This is the point where the consumption function crosses the reference line and the saving function reaches zero.

As we move farther down or leftward along the NNP scale, consumption exceeds income. At point 1 the consumption function is above the reference line. The distance S_1 measures the amount of dissaving. Any one household may dissave by using up savings (or wealth) accumulated in the past, or by borrowing from another family which is currently saving. A society dissaves by using up inventories and failing to replace capital goods when

they wear out. (It may also borrow from other societies, either through intergovernmental loans or through capital transfers. We will learn more about how this is done when we study international trade and finance.)

What we said earlier about shifts in the consumption function also holds for the saving function, except that if the consumption function shifts upward the saving function shifts downward, and vice versa. This is easy to see. If households decide that they want to consume more (an upward shift in the consumption function), they will save correspondingly less (a downward shift in the saving function). On the evidence, such shifts don't happen very often. The reason we mention them is that they *can* happen, particularly when great changes are taking place in the world as during a war or immediately afterward. In ordinary times, however, the con-

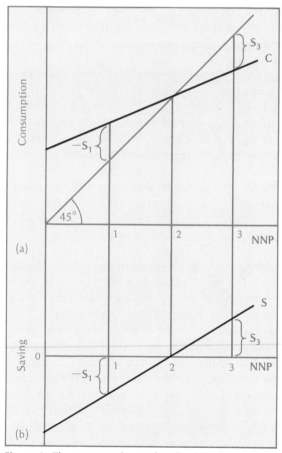

Figure 4 The consumption and saving functions for the national economy drawn together. At point 1 of NNP, a dissaving ($-S$) occurs. At point 2, all income is consumed and none is saved. At point 3, a saving S_3 occurs.

sumption and saving functions seem to be pretty stable. *Changes in spending and saving are governed mainly by changes in income*—movements along the curves rather than shifts.

We can relate saving to consumption by defining saving as the decision to refrain from consumption. This statement is only a variation on our earlier observation that a household either spends or saves its income. So if consumption is a form of demand, then *saving is a reduction in demand*. In summary, the *demand* for goods and services is *reduced* when an individual decides to save. If this saving is not used by someone, say by a businessman who borrows the saving to invest in his firm, then the *output* of goods and services can *decline*. That saving might exceed investment and lay unused is just the problem we mentioned earlier in the chapter. It was an earth-shaking discovery that undermined classical economics.

Figure 4 shows some of these concepts in slightly different form. Recall that in Figure 2 the MPC could be shown as the slope of the consumption function. *The MPS can also be shown as a slope. It's the slope of the saving function in Figure 4.*

Suppose now that NNP increases from point 2 to point 3. With an increase in NNP, saving increases to S_3 from zero. The slope of the saving function shows how much saving has increased. The amount of saving at S_3 is also shown in the upper part of Figure 4. S_3 is the amount from the consumption function up to the 45° line. Notice that in moving from point 2 to point 3, consumption has also increased. The MPC tells us how much additional consumption there will be. The additional consumption plus the additional saving use up all the additional income. Once again, this is another way of showing that MPC + MPS = 1.

In the simple model, APC and APS also add up to one (or 100%). This is easy to see in Figure 4. When NNP is at point 2, consumption is equal to NNP. That is, all income is consumed and none is saved. The APC is equal to 1 and the APS is zero. When NNP increases to point 3, APC is less than one since consumption does not use up all of NNP. However, since the rest must be saved, the APS is now greater than zero and APC + APS = 1.

Investment (I)

We turn now from the study of consumption to another important component of aggregate demand: investment. In formal terms, we define **investment** as the purchase of output (in the form of capital goods) in order to produce additional output in the future. Remember what we said earlier: The economist's definition of investment is somewhat different from our everyday, conversational use of the term. We often speak of investing in stocks or real estate. However, these activities are only variants of storing money, not true investment. To the household or individual, the purchase of capital goods is often remote and may seem unimportant. However, investment is very important to the nation since it enables us to continue our present habits of consumption.

How does the size of investment compare to consumption? Well, in 1976 personal consumption totaled $1,080 billion while investment amounted to $240 billion. One reason for treating investment as a separate component of demand is that it behaves quite differently from consumption. Whereas consumption is relatively stable, *investment is inherently unstable*. For reasons we shall soon see, investment fluctuates from year to year far more than consumption. These changes in the amount of investment have an important effect on the level of demand.

What does the business firm invest in? Economists identify four basic areas of investment: (1) inventory accumulation; (2) business structures—plants, offices, stores, warehouses, hotels; (3) machinery and office equipment and furnishings; (4) construction of new residential housing—apartments, condominiums, and houses. Actually, the investment in houses and condominiums is not done by the firm, but rather by households. *Therefore, the purchase of a new house is both a saving and investment by the household.* (The purchase of an old or used house is not an investment, only a saving.)

Why does a business firm want to invest? There is nothing in the ordinary activity of a firm that compels it to grow bigger, or to go out and buy new capital equipment if the old equipment is still working well. A manufacturer of, say, pencil sharpeners who sells a million sharpeners a year might go right on selling them for quite a while without adding to plant or equipment. Excluding the replacement of worn-out machinery, the firm's only expenditures would be for labor, materials, and other costs of doing business.

But perhaps the market for pencil sharpeners is growing rapidly, and the directors of the firm would like to share in this growth. Or perhaps the directors see a chance to make greater profits in a closely related line of office equipment such as staplers or paper clips. They will decide to increase the existing capacity of the plant, either to produce more pencil sharpeners or in order to add staplers and paper clips to the company's line. In short, they decide to invest because it seems profitable to do so.

To be consistent with the discussion of consumption, *investment must be taken here to mean net investment.* That is, replacement of worn-out capital will not be considered. Only new additions to the capital supply will count as investment. (This is consistent with our use of NNP rather than GNP.) Therefore, in this context, investment is a flow concept, while existing capital supply is clearly a stock. We will now look at those factors that determine the flow of investment.

Determinants of investment

Expectations　A business firm may decide that if current production were greater, its profit would greatly increase. But construction of the new plant and ordering and adding new machinery and equipment take time. The time lag between current needs or possibilities and future business conditions makes investment decisions difficult.

Since the usefulness of the capital goods will only be realized in the future, a firm will undertake investment based upon the expectations of the future. A firm will expand its future profit-making ability only if it is confident that a market will exist. It will try to scale its future operations to the size of the industry and the firm's expected percentage of the market.

So any predictions about investment are quite risky since any two businessmen may evaluate the same circumstances differently. In fact, one of the biggest headaches in economic forecasting comes in trying to predict what business firms are likely to spend in the near future on investment. Both government and private organizations conduct surveys to find out what firms plan to spend on new plants and equipment. But these plans are always subject to change, usually in a downward direction. When business conditions are poor, many plans will be shelved until conditions start to improve. When everyone is feeling optimistic, plans are taken off the shelf and acted on.

Technological change　In its search for increased profits, the firm—usually larger ones, though not always—will have a stake in research and development (R and D) of new products. This R and D is usually a steady form of investment. However, once a firm has developed a new process or new product that could put it a step ahead of its competitors, it will have a strong desire to invest in the capital equipment needed to put it into production. In turn, the competitors will be forced to catch up with some imitation or slight improvement upon the new product; this means they too will have to invest in new equipment for production.

New discoveries and products tend to be unpredictable. In addition, new innovations seem to come in bunches. Once a breakthrough is made, several more follow immediately. Discoveries and advances in solid-state electronics led to large investment in new types of production and equipment in TV sets, radios, stereo components, etc. Integrated circuits became possible as a further development, and new products were digital watches and mini-computers. The computer alone has revolutionized both American business and society. Businesses had to invest in computers in order to survive.

The business firm will also invest to reduce operating costs. The goods or services produced by a firm may remain the same, but the means of production can change by becoming more efficient. Almost always this change involves increased use of technology—often readily available technology. These technological changes are frequently grouped under the heading of *automation*. The result is increased productivity per worker. The business firm may undertake some form of automation simply as part of the ever-increasing quest for more profits. Or the firm may be responding to increased costs. These increased costs could be either more expensive raw products, or more expensive energy sources (such as oil), or, as is often the case, increased wages of the workers. When a firm invests in capital equipment to reduce the number of required workers, we say the firm or industry is moving from being *labor intensive* to *capital intensive*. Although it is often the case, to become more capital intensive does not always imply increased efficiency. The firm must be of some minimum size to support the productive use of its capital. However, a nation or industry with full employment that seeks growth will be forced to become capital intensive—that is, to invest in more capital equipment.

Changes in output   The current levels of business activity will determine the levels of production and inventories. If, for example, the demand for a particular good is expanding, the firm will increase investment in its inventories and perhaps even in new equipment to match the growth. In short, the firm will try to meet the demand for its products, avoiding lost profit opportunities that would result from product shortages.

The level of investment by a firm is linked to the output of the economy by the accelerator effect. As you will recall from the previous chapter, change in the demand by consumers can produce magnified changes in investment. Remember that the investment undertaken in response to changes in output is called *induced investment*.

Government policy and actions   The policy of the federal government affects business investment decisions in two basic ways: (1) levels of taxation and (2) government regulations and standards for an industry. With regard to the first, investment is stimulated by an *investment tax credit* or by a *depletion allowance*, as in petroleum. The investment tax credit is actually a preferential treatment for those companies that are willing to invest a greater amount. Some countries, notably Sweden, offer large investment tax credits in order to nurture the growth of their industries. There are also the

general tax rates. When our government decides on a general tax cut, there is usually one policy for consumers (households) and another for business. A business tax cut is formulated on the basis of deciding how much investment will be stimulated. In addition, state and local governments formulate business taxes with an eye toward stimulating investment within their localities.

Government regulations and standards are a more recent phenomenon in investment. They have resulted from the public's increasing concern with the environment and safety. In some cases the regulation or fear of regulation may depress investment by an industry. On the other hand, some industries may be forced to invest to meet Environmental Protection Agency codes. The clean air and clean water standards force industries either to invest in pollution control devices or to invest in entirely new production procedures. If the Food and Drug Administration bans a given drug or curing agent, then those firms producing it will have to develop substitutes. Occasionally, when some food additive is banned or pollution is barred, the firm will be forced or decide to shut down.

Costs of capital equipment   A critical factor in new spending decisions is the cost of buying new equipment, installing, and operating it. These costs are likely to rise considerably when times are good. In fact, they may be crucial in choking off new investment at the peak of a business upswing. In a recession these costs fall because labor and materials are more readily available.

Interest rate   The interest rate is what financial institutions such as banks and savings and loan associations charge for borrowing money. For example, a simple interest rate of 5% means the customer must pay 5¢ on each dollar borrowed for a year's duration. If, as is the case so often in capital investment and residential construction, it takes longer to repay the money, then obviously the customer will pay more than 5¢ for each dollar.

The interest rate is not only of vital concern to businesses, but perhaps even more so for purchasing residential housing. Both the household desiring to invest in new housing and the business wanting to invest in new capital must pay close attention to the interest rate. Why? Well, because these investments are so considerable that a large amount of money must be committed for a long period of time. If either the household or the firm has the money on hand, the interest rate is a measure of the income they must give up. They could always loan the money out at interest and the higher the interest rate, the more is given up to invest in capital expansion or housing.

More likely, the money will be borrowed; then the interest paid becomes an obvious cost. When the interest rate is high, it costs more to borrow. So a high interest rate is likely to reduce the demand for borrowed money needed for investment. Only the most profitable projects will be undertaken with borrowed money. Conversely, a low interest rate is considered a favorable condition for increased investment.

Why does the interest rate fluctuate? Actually, this is a question to be explored in the chapters on money and banking. But briefly, the interest rate responds to the condition of the economy and may be affected by government action. As it fluctuates, the interest rate also helps stabilize investment. If investment becomes large, it may mean that there are more customers than available money. So a rising interest rate would choke off demand for investment money. A declining interest rate stimulates investment.

Marginal efficiency of investment (MEI)

In the final analysis, firms base their investment decisions on the profit they expect to make from them. Some projects are likely to yield more return than others. Most firms of any size will have a number of investment projects they can carry out when the conditions become favorable. For example, suppose Company X has three projects it could undertake. The first is expected to return 22% on the money invested—that is, for each $100 spent on it, there will be earnings of $22. The second is larger than the first in total amount to be spent, but its expected return on it is estimated at 18%. Finally, there is a third small project, and the return on it is estimated at 4%. These possibilities are shown in Figure 5a, where the vertical axis measures the *rate of return* (ROR) and the horizontal axis measures the investment outlay (I) on each project in dollars. Notice that the curve resembles a series of stair steps.

Of its three projects, which will Company X undertake? Let's assume that the firm has to borrow the funds for all three. If it must pay interest of 8% on borrowed funds, it will probably decide to postpone the third project and carry out the first two since they will return amounts (22% and 18%) well above the interest costs. To determine which investment projects can be undertaken, a firm (or even a nation) is actually seeking to know the rate of return compared to the interest rate. In economics, this rate of return for each level of investment is called the **marginal efficiency of investment,** or MEI.

To see how the MEI applies to the economy as a whole, let's turn to Figure 5b. To get from the investment opportunities of one firm to the investment curve for the entire economy, we add up all the stair steps for all the firms in the economy. The result is the curve shown in Figure 5b. It is called the *marginal efficiency of investment (MEI) curve.* It no longer has stair steps in it because in adding up all the possibilities for all the firms in the economy, the stair steps smooth out. This is because the steps are of different sizes and occur at different places for the many firms.

The MEI curve is the aggregate demand curve for investment goods. If all firms do the same thing as our Company X, then the MEI curve shows the total investment which will be undertaken. Suppose the interest rate (i) is as shown in Figure 5b. All projects out to I_1 are shown as having a higher MEI than the interest rate. Thus they would be profitable and the firms would undertake them. At any other interest rate, we could also read the amount of investment expenditure which will occur. Beyond I_1, the MEI is lower than i and firms won't invest.

Suppose firms are able to borrow at 10% interest. If their marginal efficiency of investment is 12%, it will pay them to borrow money since they will get a 2% net return. If their MEI is only 8%, they will not want to borrow money. In general, *firms will undertake investment as long as the interest rate is below the MEI.*

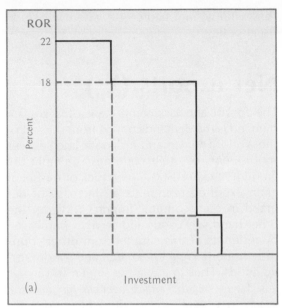
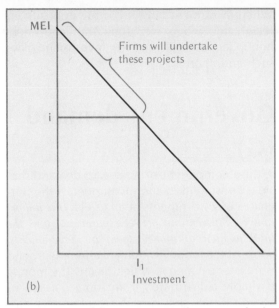

Figure 5 (a) Three investment projects of a firm are shown. The first investment dollars are spent on the most productive project, which yields a rate of return (ROR) of 22%; then investment dollars are spent on the project yielding 18% ROR. The final project considered yields only 4% return. The firm's MEI schedule is shown by the "stair steps" (in brown). (b) The MEI schedule for the national economy. All the "stair-step" functions for individual firms are added together and produce the downward-sloping function. All projects above the interest rate *i* are profitable and will be undertaken.

Even if firms don't have to borrow money and can finance new investment out of earnings on their present operations, they will still pay attention to the rate of interest. If the market rate of interest is 10%, they would be foolish to use the money for a project which will only return 8%. They could put their money to better use by lending it at 10% to other firms that want to borrow it. In other words, *a company will "charge" itself the market rate of interest when it invests its own funds;* that will be the standard by which it judges the profitability of an investment.

This is the concept of opportunity cost which is discussed more fully in microeconomics. Opportunity cost measures cost in terms of what is given up, not necessarily the amount paid.

Notice that a change in the interest rate will cause a change in the amount invested. *If the interest rate falls, the amount of investment will increase. An increase in interest will cause investment to decline.* Changes in the interest rate will cause a movement along the MEI line. The direction of change in investment expenditures is opposite to that of the change in the interest rate.

Remember though, that there are other determinants of investment. Each of these may change. If they do, the MEI line will shift up or down. If businessmen expect higher profits in the future, the curve will shift up producing more investment expenditure at each interest rate. A new technological breakthrough will also produce an increase in investment expenditures because the MEI curve shifts up. An increase in current output will induce additional investment expenditures. Government policy may be changed in such a way that investment will be stimulated. Finally, a decrease in the cost of capital goods will also increase investment. You should go through the list of investment determinants again and make sure you can show how a decrease or downward shift in the MEI curve will be brought about by a change in each determinant of investment.

The principal thing to remember about investment is that it plays a critical part in the fluctuations of the economy. *When investment increases, it stimulates the whole economy to higher levels of income and employment.* Each new investment project means more jobs.

When investment falls, it has the opposite effect. Later, when we study the investment multiplier, we will see why investment plays such an important role.

Government demand (G)

A third component of aggregate demand, besides consumption and investment, is the purchases of governments at all levels. *It is important to differentiate between purchases and the total amount of money spent by governments.* Some of the money which governments spend is transfer payments, which means the money is simply redistributed from some persons to others. Recall that Social Security, veterans' benefits, and welfare programs are examples of transfer payments. Government purchases, however, are a part of demand and as such are of interest to us here. Governments, as we all know, build highways and schools, operate transit systems, and carry on national defense activities among other things. From the economist's point of view, government spending is "autonomous"—that is, it isn't determined by the kinds of factors that determine consumption and investment (which depend on saving, on the interest rate, on expectations, technological change, etc.). Government purchases (G) are larger than investment (I), but less than consumption (C). In 1976, government purchases amounted to $366 billion.

The 50 states, some 3,000 counties, and countless lower levels of governments spend much more together than does the federal government, as we saw in Chapter 5. Their budgets are usually determined by the needs of the people in their jurisdiction. The federal budget is *partly* determined by needs and cannot be changed. *However, the federal government is also required to change its purchases in response to economic conditions.* Government spending is important to the economist because it can be adjusted for economic purposes. It can be used to move the economy out of a recession and to maintain a high level of national income and employment. If, however, government spending is too large for current conditions, it can also cause inflation and unemployment. We will see just how it does these things in Chapter 10, when we study fiscal policy.

Net exports (X_n)

The fourth and last component of aggregate demand is the demand coming from the rest of the world. The demand for goods and services by residents of other countries is simply the amount of exports (X). Every truck or bushel of grain exported represents an increase of demand in our economy. Imports (IM), on the other hand, are goods and services purchased by residents of this country from other countries. Imports are a loss of demand for domestic goods. Thus in a manner similar to savings and taxes, *imports reduce demand for domestic goods.* In general, the amount of imports increases as NNP increases for the same reason consumption increases. With higher incomes, people consume more. Besides consuming various domestic goods, people will consume more Sony stereo equipment, Volkswagens, French wine, European vacations, etc.

We are interested here not so much in exports or in imports, but rather their difference. **Net exports** is the difference of exports minus imports:

$$X_n = X - IM$$

The net exports is the true measure of foreign demand. When the X_n is a positive number, then this country is exporting more goods than it is importing. A positive X_n is added to our other components of demand. However, when this country imports more goods than it exports, the X_n is a negative value. In this situation, we subtract the X_n value from our other components of demand. If imports balance the exports, then there is no net effect on demand.

Within the last twenty years, X_n for the United States has averaged annually about plus $4 billion. The fluctuations have been as high as $11 billion in 1975 and as low as −$6 billion in 1972. So compared with the other components of demand, X_n is quite insignificant for the United States. However, you should realize that the amounts of exports and imports are not insignificant. For instance, in 1976 the X_n was −$5.9 billion. But this figure "disguises" imports amounting to $120.7 billion and exports of $114.8 billion. These trade figures are large and important; only the net effect (−$5.9 billion) on aggregate demand is slight.

Summary

Classical economists believed that the national economy had a tendency to move toward an equilibrium point of full employment. As expressed in Say's Law, the belief was that *supply creates its own demand.* The classical economists also said that investment would equal saving.

Since the Great Depression of the 1930s, most economists have come to believe John Maynard Keynes' theory that the national economy may reach equilibrium at a point well below that of full employment. Keynes also showed investment does not always equal saving.

Present-day economists use the methods of national income accounting to analyze the forces that determine supply and demand. Aggregate demand is made up of four components: the demand of households for goods and services, called consumption; the demand by business firms for goods and services to be used for future production, called investment; demand by government; and net foreign demand.

Consumption is directly related to income. As income increases, so does consumption—but by a lesser amount. Consumption and saving always add up to disposable income $DI = C + S$. An important concept is the marginal propensity to consume (MPC), which is the ratio of an *increase* (or decrease) in consumption to the *increase* (or decrease) in income. The marginal propensity to save (MPS) is the ratio of an increase in saving to the increase in income that led to it. MPC and MPS always add up to 1.

The relationship between income and consumption is also expressed in the consumption function. As income changes, a change in the amount consumed is measured by a movement along the consumption function. The slope of the consumption function equals the MPC. But the function itself may shift up or down because of changes in factors other than income. These factors include: the amount of liquid assets owned by households; the stock of nonliquid assets; expectations about the future; cultural attitudes toward spending and saving; and age of buyers.

The saving function shows the relationship between saving and income. The slope of the saving function equals the MPS. Since consumption is a form of demand, saving is a reduction in demand.

Investment is an important component of aggregate demand. It is much less stable than consumption. It shifts up and down from one year to another in response to the profit expectations of businessmen. The level of investment is determined by a number of factors, including: expectations; developments in technology; changes in output; government policy and actions; the costs of new capital equipment; and the interest rate. The marginal efficiency of investment (MEI) is the rate of return a firm expects to receive on an additional unit of investment. A firm will not invest in projects for which the MEI is less than the interest rate on borrowed funds.

Government purchases (for all levels of government) are another component of demand. Federal purchases can be changed—at least in part—to respond to changing economic conditions.

Our fourth component of demand is net exports, that is, exports minus imports. Compared to our other three components, net exports is insignificant.

Key Words and Phrases

- **aggregate supply** the total value of all goods and services supplied in the economy at a moment in time; it is essentially NNP.
- **aggregate demand** the planned purchases of all members of an economy at any period of time.
- **Say's Law** a statement by French economist Jean Baptiste Say which has come to be quoted as "supply creates its own demand."
- **saving** the act of producing income but not consuming it.
- **renting** purchasing only the service or use of a capital item rather than purchasing the item itself; a form of consumption.
- **average propensity to consume** the ratio of the amount households consume to their income.
- **dissaving** what occurs when the APC is greater than one; consumption either from past accumulation of wealth or by borrowing.

- **average propensity to save** the ratio of the amount households save to their income.

- **marginal propensity to consume** the increase (decrease) in consumption as a result of an increase (decrease) in income; it is the fraction of each additional dollar of income spent on consumption.

- **marginal propensity to save** the increase (decrease) in saving as a result of an increase (decrease) in income; it is the fraction of each additional dollar of income which is saved.

- **consumption function** a schedule which relates the amount of consumption expenditure to income for a household or an economy; the schedule may also be shown as a line on a graph.

- **liquid assets** either money or any item readily converted to money in a short period of time.

- **investment** purchases by firms of newly produced capital goods.

- **labor intensive** a production process which uses a great deal of labor relative to capital and other inputs.

- **capital intensive** a production process which uses a great deal of capital relative to labor and other inputs to produce the output.

- **investment tax credit** a reduction in taxes extended to firms which undertake investment expenditures.

- **depletion allowance** a special tax credit given to those industries such as mining or petroleum which compensates them for using up their natural resources and gives them an incentive to search for more.

- **induced investment** investment expenditures which are the result of changes in output.

- **rate of return** the income generated by an investment project; expressed as a percent per annum of the amount of investment.

- **marginal efficiency of investment (MEI)** a schedule relating the amount of investment per year and the rate of return on each level of investment.

Questions for Review

1. Why do households save? In what form(s) do they keep their savings?

2. A fellow student assures you that she consumes every cent of income she receives. Draw a consumption function and a saving function and show where she is on each.

3. If you did not do so in question 2, draw the consumption function above the saving function. Use Figure 4 as a model. Show the level of income your friend must have. Why is it the same in both the upper and lower parts of your diagram? What is your friend's APC? Her APS?

4. What does the term "marginal" mean as used by an economist? How many different terms are discussed in this chapter using the concept of "marginality"?

5. Suppose you or your family were considering buying a house. How would changes in the interest rate affect your decision? If you were using your own money instead of getting a mortgage, would your answer be any different?

6. How would your optimism or pessimism about the future affect your response to question 5? Why?

7. The previous two questions were intended to get you to think like a businessman in terms of purchasing a house. Can you show why the same two variables, the interest rate and expectations of the future, would affect a business firm as it decides how much inventory to have on hand?

8. Why would a sudden rush to buy petroleum from OPEC nations result in a decrease in aggregate demand in the United States?

9. Complete the following table. The consumption function is a straight line.

Income	Consumption	Saving	APC	APS
$10,000				
11,000				
12,000	$12,100			
13,000	13,000			
14,000	13,900			
15,000				
16,000				
17,000				
18,000				
19,000				
20,000				

10. What is the MPC in the table in question 9? The MPS? Why does the APC change while the MPC stays the same?

9

Aggregate Supply and Equilibrium

In the last chapter we looked at the components of aggregate demand. We saw that consumption, investment, government spending, and net foreign demand are these components and that they add up to net national product.

Now we are ready to see how net national product (NNP) varies from year to year. In order to compute the equilibrium level of NNP, we need first to look at aggregate supply. Most importantly, the intersection of the aggregate supply curve with the aggregate demand curve results in an equilibrium. This equilibrium is just the level of NNP or total new output. So we want to develop a model that shows how to calculate equilibrium. Then we can see how equilibrium levels change, especially as the components of aggregate demand change.

It is useful, however, when studying the performance of the economy to understand not just one, but two basic models showing the levels of national income. The first model we will study is the *Keynesian model*, which tends to stress the importance of real variables in determining equilibrium (i.e., national income and output). A variation of this Keynesian model shows how equilibrium NNP is reached by balancing saving and investment. The second model tends to stress the importance of money in establishing equilibrium. Actually, the two different models resulted because of disagreement among economists as to how the economy behaves. As we shall see, it is possible to look at the same economy and observe different things about it.

A Keynesian model

The classical economists thought that economies tend to move toward levels of output that fully employ all available resources, especially labor. However, as we saw earlier, the Great Depression of the 1930s confounded this view. The Great Depression was characterized by long-lasting and large levels of unemployment which reduced the output of goods and services.

John Maynard Keynes then proposed an economic model that would explain why an economy can remain at such low levels of output (with, of course, the inevitable unemployment). The Keynesian model explains how

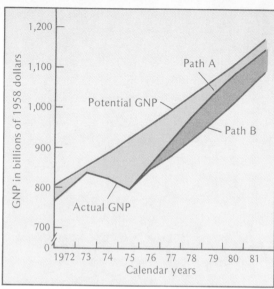

Figure 1 Potential, actual, and projected GNP, 1972–1981. From 1972 to 1975, potential and actual GNP are shown; the recession pushed actual GNP down. At the end of 1975, actual GNP for 1976–1981 was projected as one of two possible paths: path A or path B. Potential GNP is assumed to grow at 3.75% per year. The loss of production is shown by the shaded areas. (Source: Congressional Budget Office.)

an economy very readily can fail to reach its potential for output of goods and services.

Figure 1 shows an application of this model to our own times. Federal government economists produced this chart that shows (1) potential output or GNP, (2) actual GNP through 1975, and (3) two alternative paths of future GNP (the chart was prepared in early 1976). Notice that neither path A nor path B would reach our full potential. Why? To find an answer, we must develop our model.

Balancing aggregate demand and aggregate supply

To introduce the Keynesian model, we invoke ceteris paribus and assume that all prices remain the same: we assume that changes in consumption, investment, and government spending will not change the prices of goods and services. We do this because we are interested in the level of NNP. Recall that NNP is the dollar value of our economy's new output, or NNP equals output times prices. So when NNP changes, we want to know that real output is changing, not prices.

Figure 2a shows the consumption function. This upward-sloping line was encountered in the last chapter. It shows that, as national income increases, consumption increases by a directly related amount. This relationship is just the marginal propensity to consume (MPC). The MPC shows the expected change in consumption for any change in income.

Consumption, you will remember, is the largest single component of aggregate demand. The other three components—investment, government spending, and net exports—can be reduced to two. *To make things simpler, let's forget about net exports at this point.* It is small in magnitude for the U.S. economy (though not for the Japanese or British), and therefore, we can pretend for the moment that it doesn't exist at all. Aggregate demand is then given by the following formula:

$$Y = C + I + G,$$

where Y stands for net national product, C for consumption, I for investment, and G for government purchases of goods and services.

The diagrams in Figure 2 show each of the components of demand separately. For ease of explanation, we will assume that G does not vary with changes in income (Figure 2b). Also, I is determined from the MEI schedule and the interest rate (Figure 2c). Therefore, we can

draw them as horizontal lines for the present. In Figure 3 we combine all three components to obtain the aggregate demand curve, C + I + G. The aggregate demand curve shows the amount of goods and services demanded at each level of output or income. (Remember that we are assuming prices remain constant, so that changes in aggregate demand represent "real" amounts, not money amounts. Later we will bring prices into the picture.) Notice that the horizontal axis of Figure 3 is Y, or NNP, while the vertical axis is the sum of C, I, and G.

Now that we have the demand curve, where is the corresponding supply curve? As such, we do not have a supply curve. We do have the 45-degree reference line. It starts at zero and runs diagonally upward, always the same distance from the horizontal axis and the vertical axis. The amounts of C, I, and G are plotted on the vertical axis. NNP is plotted on the horizontal axis. The 45-degree line shows all the points where C + I + G are equal to NNP. *So our reference line is the aggregate supply curve.*

Consider the point in Figure 3 where the demand curve intersects the 45-degree line. The level of output is shown to be $1,500 billion. The distance from the origin, or zero point, along the horizontal axis represents $1,500 billion. The vertical distance from the horizontal axis to the 45-degree line also represents $1,500 billion. This is shown both by the vertical brackets and by the distance on the vertical axis to the left.

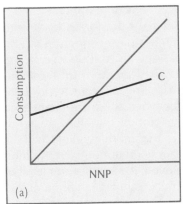 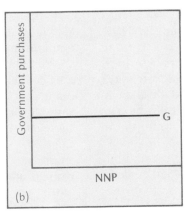 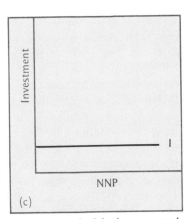

Figure 2 (a) Consumption (C) schedule. As NNP increases, consumption increases. Therefore, the schedule slopes upward. (b) Government spending (G) schedule is likewise horizontal because we are assuming, for the moment, G is not related to income. (c) The investment (I) schedule is shown as a horizontal line because we are assuming investment is not related to income (NNP).

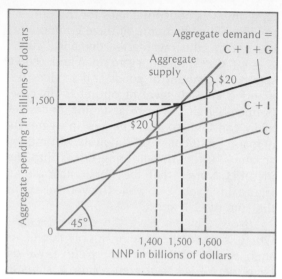

Figure 3 Aggregate demand and the equilibrium NNP. Our aggregate supply curve is the 45° reference line. The aggregate demand curve equals the C plus I plus G curves added together. Equilibrium NNP here is $1,500 billion. At $1,400 billion, demand exceeds supply by $20 billion. At an NNP of $1,600 billion, supply exceeds demand by $20 billion.

The aggregate demand curve crosses the 45-degree line at $1,500 billion. When demand is at the $1,500-billion level, it is equal to the amount of goods and services being produced. The aggregate market is just satisfied. We will assume that the mixture of goods and services is correct. We say that the economy is in an equilibrium. The economy will tend to move toward the $1,500-billion level unless some element of demand is changed. To see why this would be so, suppose output is $100 billion larger, or $1,600 billion, without any change in demand. In Figure 3 the $1,600-billion level is shown.

Remember that G does not change as NNP does so there is no additional demand from the government. Also, I will not change since there is no reason to let the interest rate vary. We do know how C will respond to the change in NNP. If we continue to let the MPC be 0.8, then C will increase by $80 billion in response to the increase in Y by $100 billion. But, NNP has increased by $100 billion; yet the amount demanded will increase by only $80 billion. The amount demanded will be less than the amount available and the aggregate demand curve will be below the 45-degree line.

There is an excess of $20 billion between the amount produced and the amount demanded even though the amount demanded at an income of $1,600 billion is greater than at $1,500 billion. Firms will find that they have more output than they can sell. Their inventories will increase beyond the level at which they wish to keep goods in stock. Accordingly, they will decrease their production until the inventories have been sold off. The economy would tend to move back toward $1,500 billion.

Suppose output is $100 billion less than $1,500 billion, or $1,400 billion. While less is demanded at $1,400-billion income than at $1,500 billion, *the decline in the amount demanded* is less than *the decline in output.*

You should be able to determine why. G and I will remain the same at $1,400 as at $1,500 billion for the reasons given in the previous paragraph. C will change (decrease) by the amount of the MPC times the change in income, or 0.8 × $100 billion equals $80 billion. Thus the amount demanded declines by $80 billion while production declines by $100 billion. As a result, $20 billion more goods and services are demanded than are produced. The aggregate demand curve is thus above the 45-degree line. Firms will find their inventories declining faster than they can be restocked, or there will be lines of unsatisfied customers, or both. Firms will increase their production until output reaches the $1,500-billion level again. Since the economy always tends toward the intersection of aggregate supply and aggregate demand, this level is called an **equilibrium level of output.** This is the Keynesian answer to how the level of GNP is determined.

Table 1 summarizes the forces leading to equilibrium in our simple economy. Only at $1,500 billion does aggregate supply equal aggregate demand. Investment (I) and government purchases (G) are constant. Only consumption changes when there are changes in aggregate supply. Notice that the greater is aggregate supply, the more workers will be employed. At our equilibrium, 91 million workers are employed. An equilibrium level of output does not necessarily mean full employment.

Table 1
Determination of Equilibrium Level of Output and Employment (dollars are in billions)

Aggregate supply = NNP	Consumption, C	Investment, I	Government purchases, G	Aggregate demand = C + I + G	Level of employment (in millions)
1,700	1,120	240	300	1,660	93
1,600	1.040	240	300	1,580	92
1,500	**960**	**240**	**300**	**1,500**	**91**
1,400	880	240	300	1,420	90
1,300	800	240	300	1,340	89

The point of equilibrium for the economy is determined by the position of the aggregate demand curve. If the curve were to shift upward, the equilibrium point would be higher than $1,500 billion. If it were to shift downward, the equilibrium point would be lower than $1,500 billion. Thus there could be any number of equilibrium points, depending on how much spending takes place by households, business firms, and government.

There is nothing either good or bad about an equilibrium. It is simply the level toward which an economy will move. Whether it is good or bad depends upon other things. We will evaluate alternative equilibrium levels later. Let us first see what happens when one segment of aggregate demand changes. Suppose, for example, that businesses decide to change the level of investment expenditures. Will income or output change by the same amount? The answer is no and we will see why. For the moment, let us assume that we are always below potential GNP so that the economy is able to respond to changes in demand.

Saving-investment approach to equilibrium

There is another way developed by Keynes to show how the equilibrium level of NNP is determined. Notice that this is a different analysis but it gives the same result as the above analysis if the economy described is otherwise the same. There is no need to have two approaches to the same problem when both approaches give the same answer. However, sometimes it is easier to analyze a problem using one approach rather than the other.

For just a few paragraphs, let us leave government demand aside. We will add it back in later. If there are only households and firms, we can build a very simple model showing the equilibrium.

Let us start with households. If they receive income, they have essentially two choices of what to do with it as we have seen. They may consume it or they may save it. We could write an equation showing this fact:

$$Y = C + S$$

where Y here is national income for our simple economy. This shows that the income received by households or paid by firms may be either consumed or saved. If it is consumed, there is a demand for more goods and services. If it is saved, there is a loss of demand from households. Thus saving is called a *leakage* from the circular flow. A **leakage** is any activity that diminishes aggregate demand.

Now let's look at the other side of the circular flow. In this simple model, who can the firms sell to? Only households for consumption purposes or firms for investment purposes. We could write an equation which would define the total expenditures or purchases of the simple economy. It would read

$$Y = C + I,$$

showing that NNP would consist of all final sales to consumers and to firms.

Notice now that we have two equations which define the level of NNP. The first showed how households spent the income generated. Saving was a leakage because it represented a loss of future demand for output. But, in the second equation, we see that households are not the only source of demand. They of course determine consumption. Firms, however, determine investment expenditures. Investment is called a **compensating expenditure** (or **injection**). It is an expenditure or demand which offsets the leakage called saving.

The next question should come to mind immediately. How do we know that the leakage, or saving, will be the same as the compensating expenditure, or investment? The answer is, we don't. But if saving is equal to investment, the economy should be in equilibrium. That is, we should be at that level of NNP which will be maintained until either aggregate demand or supply changes.

We already know what the desired or planned level of investment is. The amount was determined by the firms in the economy and is shown in Figure 2c. For now, we may consider the amount of investment to be a constant; so it is shown as a horizontal line since investment does not change as NNP does.

We also know what the planned or desired level of saving is for the economy. It is the *saving function*, which we first encountered in Chapter 8. The desired amount of saving does change as NNP changes. We know that saving increases by the MPS times the change in NNP. Therefore, if we let NNP change, saving will accordingly either rise or fall. In Figure 4a, both the investment and saving functions are shown.

The planned investment level is shown by the horizontal line marked I. The saving function, S, is shown rising as income rises. The slope of the S line is the MPS.

Suppose first that NNP is at $1,400 billion. We see that planned investment is higher than planned saving at that level. The compensating expenditures exceed the leakages. The loss of demand, saving, is more than offset and output would have to rise to meet the demand for goods and services.

Suppose instead that NNP were at $1,600 billion. The level of leakages or saving is now greater than planned investment expenditures. The leakages from demand would not be offset

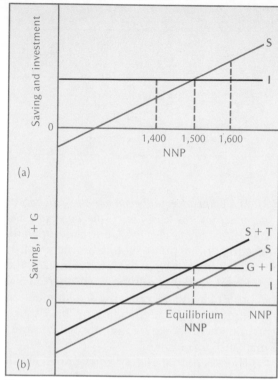

(a)

(b)

Figure 4   (a) Saving and investment schedules for the national economy. Once again, equilibrium NNP is shown as $1,500 billion—this time at the intersection of saving and investment. (b) Government spending is a compensating expenditure and is therefore added to investment. Equilibrium NNP occurs at the intersection of the S + T curve and the G + I curve.

by the compensating expenditures. The leakages would represent goods and services produced but unsold. Therefore, the level of NNP would tend to fall.

Which brings us to NNP at $1,500 billion. Here the planned level of investment expenditures is identical with the desired level of saving. There is no reason to expect the level of NNP to change. The amount of goods and services produced but not consumed is exactly the amount desired by firms for investment purposes. *The level where saving and investment are equal is the equilibrium level of NNP for this simple economy.*

We could show this using the equations from a few paragraphs back. In one case, we said that households used income to either consume or save. That is,

$$Y = C + S.$$

On the other hand, if we look at the expenditures side, the sources of expenditure are consumption and investment, or

$$Y = C + I.$$

We know that the income approach and the expenditure approach must result in identical measures of NNP. In the equations above, if they represent the same economy, the amount Y in one must be the same as the Y in the other. By substitution

$$C + S = C + I.$$

Of course, consumption is consumption whether we look at it as the amount spent by households or the amount of consumption goods sold by firms. The C's on both sides of the equation must be the same so we can cancel them out to simplify the equation. This leaves

$$S = I$$

as a condition of equilibrium. This result is not surprising. We already saw that equilibrium is obtained where saving is equal to investment. In Figure 4a, it is where NNP is at $1,500 billion. At any other level of NNP, planned investment is not equal to desired saving. There will be unplanned changes in inventory or shortages so NNP will change toward $1,500 billion from either side.

We can go one step further at this point. In Figure 2, we saw that government purchases represented a source of demand for goods. In Figure 3, the government purchases were added to aggregate demand. We can do the same thing here. *Government purchases are a compensating expenditure also* since they are a source of demand not dependent upon current income. Since government expenditures are fixed in amount for the moment, we can simply add the amount shown by G in Figure 2b to the amount of I in Figure 2c or in Figure 4a to obtain the G + I line shown in Figure 4b.

The saving function also changes. The government raises part of its revenue through taxes. Taxes are a leakage since payments for taxes mean there is less income for consumption and saving. So the leakages line in Figure 4b consists of saving and taxes, S + T.

Once again, the equilibrium level of NNP is determined where the planned level of compensating expenditures—government and investment expenditures—are equal to the leakages—the desired saving and taxes. The equilibrium level of NNP is marked in Figure 4b.

The equations still work to show the equilibrium NNP though now we must consider that there are three sources of expenditures on goods and services: namely, households, firms, and governments at all levels. Thus the expenditures equation is

$$Y = C + I + G,$$

which is the aggregate demand curve from Figure 3.

The income equation also changes since now income goes for consumption, saving, or taxes:

$$Y = C + S + T.$$

The Y's must be the same for the reasons given, so

$$C + I + G = C + S + T,$$

or since we can still get rid of C from both sides:

$$I + G = S + T.$$

This shows in algebraic form the equilibrium which we derived using geometry in Figure 4b.

The multiplier

A shift in business investment will have a strong effect on aggregate demand. It will increase output by a lot more than the amount of the increase in investment. To see why this is so, let's look at Figure 5. Here we meet our old friend, the upward-sloping aggregate demand curve, with its three components: consumption, investment, and government spending. In Figure 5 we have added them together and shown them as the line C + I + G. The equilibrium point at which aggregate demand and aggregate supply are equal is $1,500 billion. Now suppose there is an increase of $40 billion in demand. Specifically, we will assume that business firms have become more optimistic about the future and

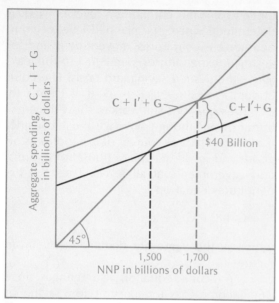

Figure 5 Aggregate demand is increased by $40 billion in investment; the aggregate demand curve shifts upward. Notice the effect on equilibrium NNP. It has risen from $1,500 billion to $1,700 billion.

have increased their investment spending by $40 billion. The demand curve shifts upward, as shown by the dashed line. The new point of equilibrium is at $1,700 billion, as shown by the vertical dashed line. An increase of $40 billion in investment has led to an increase of $200 billion in net national product.

How is this possible? Why should an increase in investment lead to an increase in national product that is five times greater? Is it an optical illusion, resulting from our having drawn the diagram in a certain way? Or have we found a way of adding two and two and getting more than four? Neither. It's not a trick, and it's not magic. In our economy, there is a continuous circular flow of income and expenditure. One person's spending becomes another person's income, which in turn is spent and becomes a third person's income. Not all income is spent, however, since some of it is saved. We saw in the previous chapter how the Jones family (the average family in the economy) spent its income (Table 2 on page 155). When their income increased, they spent 80% of it and saved 20%. In other words, the Joneses' marginal propensity to consume was 80%, or $\frac{4}{5}$. The increase of consumption based on the increase in income leads to a multiple

increase in income as a result of the first increase in investment demand.

Let's return to the increase of $40 billion in investment spending. This immediately becomes $40 billion of income to those who receive it, in the form of wages and salaries, profits, rent, or interest. We will suppose that the marginal propensity to consume of every household is the same as that of our average family, the Joneses—80%. Households will therefore respond to the $40 billion increase in investment with an increase of .8 × $40 billion, or $32 billion, in consumption. They will save the remainder, $8 billion. The second-round spending of $32 billion becomes income for a new set of households, who in turn spend .8 × $32 billion, or $25.6 billion. The repeated cycle of income and spending continues, with the increases becoming smaller and smaller. Table 2 shows the figures for each round through the fifth, and then sums the rest. It can be shown mathematically that the total increase in spending will be $200 billion, of which 80%, or $160 billion, will be spent on consumption and the rest saved. The new equilibrium point will be $1,700 billion in net national product. The total change in NNP is five times greater than the initial change in demand.

The tendency of an increase in expenditure to be multiplied by the flow of income is called the **multiplier effect.** The ratio of the change in income to the initial increase in expenditure is called the **multiplier.** In our example the multiplier was 5. The multiplier

Table 2
The Multiplier Effect Illustrated
(in billions of dollars)

Expenditure rounds	Change in income	Change in consumption	Change in saving
Round 1	$ 40	$ 32	$ 8
Round 2	32	25.6	6.4
Round 3	25.6	20.5	5.1
Round 4	20.5	16.4	4.1
Round 5	16.4	13.1	3.3
All other rounds	65.5	52.4	13.1
Totals	$200.0	$160.0	$40.0

works the same way for a decrease in expenditure. Thus a $40 billion decrease in investment would, in our example, result in a $200 billion decrease in NNP. *The size of the multiplier depends on the marginal propensity to consume.* The greater the MPC, the greater will be the multiplier. This can be expressed in the following formula:

$$\text{Multiplier} = \frac{1}{1 - \text{MPC}} = \frac{1}{\text{MPS}}.$$

The larger MPC is, the smaller will be the bottom part of the fraction (1 − MPC) and the greater the multiplier. Using the value of 80% for the MPC, we can substitute in the formula as follows:

$$\text{Multiplier} = \frac{1}{1 - .8} = \frac{1}{.2} = 5.$$

You should confirm by calculation that if the MPC = 0.5 the multiplier is 2 and if the MPC = 0.9 the multiplier is 10.

This is the simplest version of the multiplier. We have presented it here in order to show how a change in spending may cause a much larger change in net national product.

Other multipliers

Other changes in expenditures would also affect the economy through a multiplier effect. For example, if the consumption function should suddenly shift up or down, the impact on the economy would be the amount of the shift times the multiplier. Consumers can change the level of their income by changing the level of their consumption. We will return to this point when we discuss the paradox of thrift.

Government expenditures also have a multiplier effect on income. Not only will income or output rise to meet the original purchase by the government, but with the respending of money earned, the multiplier effect begins to work. The government multiplier is very important as government expenditures are a matter of policy. That is, we can decide to increase or decrease government expenditures with the expressed intent of changing the level of national income.

Changes in tax levels have very important multiplier effects. An increase in personal income taxes takes purchasing power away from households, and a decrease in the same tax adds to their purchasing power. Changes in business taxes may affect investment. In the early 1960s President Kennedy's economic advisers convinced him that a cut in federal income taxes would stimulate the economy by raising aggregate demand. They turned out to be right. The tax cut (assisted by an increase in military expenditures) set off one of the largest expansions the U.S. economy has ever known. Because the action of tax changes is indirect working through consumption or investment, the equation for the tax multiplier is a little different. We will discuss the tax multiplier more fully in the next chapter.

There are often multiplier effects resulting from changes in exports or imports. We have not considered foreign trade in discussing aggregate demand for the United States since it makes up a very small part of total demand. However, there may be some effects if the change in either exports or imports is large. The impact on the economy is a multiple of the change. An example would be the oil embargo which led to a tripling of the price of imported petroleum. This dampening effect "times" the multiplier led to a decline in demand that was part of the cause of the 1973–1975 recession.

The paradox of thrift

The multiplier can help us illustrate the paradox of thrift. Suppose we return to our initial equilibrium income of $1,500 billion as illustrated in Figure 6. At this level, it is always possible for one household to increase its wealth by increasing the rate of saving. If the saving is used to purchase securities (stocks and bonds), the income from these securities will add to their consumption at a later date. This is desirable both for the household and for the economy.

Suppose, however, that all households try to increase their rate of saving. To increase their saving, they would have to decrease their consumption (C). Suppose the decrease in consumption is $10 billion. Let's label the new

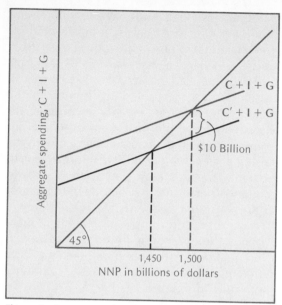

Figure 6 Suppose saving increases by $10 billion. Then aggregate demand falls from C + I + G to C' + I + G. The equilibrium NNP is reduced from $1,500 billion to $1,450 billion (when the MPC = .8).

consumption level as C'. The aggregate demand line will shift down from C + I + G to C' + I + G. We can no longer be at equilibrium at $1,500 billion of income. Production will fall.

We can immediately figure out how much income will fall using the multiplier. As before, let us use MPC = 0.8; so the multiplier is 5. With a $10 billion decrease in aggregate demand, the decline in income will be 5 × $10 billion, or $50 billion. The new equilibrium will be $1,450 billion.

Let us return to our consumers. They willingly reduced consumption by $10 billion to increase saving in order to increase wealth and future income. However, now they find that income is falling—initially by $10 billion. As income falls, they must reduce consumption even more. If the MPC = 0.8, the consumption will decrease by 0.8 × $50 billion or $40 billion. The attempt to reduce consumption and increase saving results in a reduction in income. They therefore move down the saving function to a lower level of saving, in fact, to the original level.

Thus the paradox of thrift returns us to a problem discussed in the very first chapter: the fallacy of composition. One household may

increase wealth and income by saving. All households may not do this, because instead of adding to wealth, increased saving causes a decrease in income! And a decrease in income means decreases in consumption and saving.

Equilibria—good or bad?

We have tried to make clear that the equilibrium level of income is just the level toward which the economy will move. Once there, that level will be maintained till something in the economy changes. The criteria for whether the equilibrium is desirable or not require other considerations. For example, it is very possible to reach an equilibrium point with high unemployment (such was the case in the Great Depression). It is also possible to reach an equilibrium with high inflation. Or we could even reach a point with both. Such equilibria are of course undesirable—they are bad equilibria!

Full-employment equilibrium

Let us begin with the idea of full employment. Full employment is a goal that is often thought to be desirable. Labor cannot be stored. If labor is unemployed, the goods and services which might have been produced are lost forever. The entire economy has lost a chance to benefit from the output and the labor is wasted. On a personal level, much suffering and anguish is caused to those unemployed. Therefore, we don't want equilibria where there is less than potential output and full employment.

Full employment means the number of workers desiring work is the same as the number employers are willing to hire. *Structural and frictional unemployment tend to prevent the economy from reaching really full employment so we can say that 4% of the labor force unemployed is full employment (N*) for our purposes.*

To get back to our aggregate demand diagram, we need to consider what the N* workers can produce. For the moment, there is a fixed amount of machinery, tools, offices, factories, etc., for the workers to use. Also, available technology is not likely to change much over short periods of time. Thus, if we put N* workers to work, there must be a known amount of output produced.

The amount of output produced when the labor force is fully employed is shown in Figure 7. This full-employment level of NNP is Y*. We can define the **full-employment level Y*** as the dollar value of all goods and services produced in one year when the labor force is fully employed. We assign this level a letter rather than a fixed, numerical value because the full-employment level does vary, depending on the potential output (production possibilities) at any given moment. When the labor force and stock of capital goods in use increase, so does Y*.

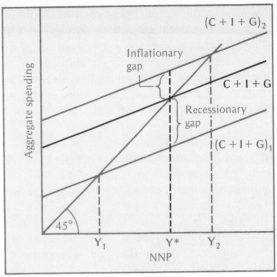

Figure 7 The intersection of C + I + G and the aggregate supply line leads to full-employment equilibrium Y*. When aggregate demand increases to (C + I + G)₂, a new equilibrium Y₂ results and there is an inflationary gap. When aggregate demand falls to (C + I + G)₁, a new equilibrium Y₁ occurs and there is a recessionary gap.

Less than full-employment equilibrium (recessionary gap)

Notice now that Y* is the only level of output which will just ensure full employment. Only one of many possible aggregate demand curves can intersect the 45-degree line at Y*. Obviously, if one did, it would produce a desirable equilibrium since the goal of full employment would be attained.

Consider, however, in Figure 7 the aggregate demand curve labeled (C + I + G)₁. This curve hits the 45-degree line to the left of full employment. Thus the equilibrium level of output is to the left of full employment. We label this level as Y₁. The distance from Y₁ to Y* is the output of goods and services lost because of the lack of enough aggregate demand. This distance is known as a **recessionary gap.** Clearly, Y₁ is an undesirable equilibrium.

Let us consider how we might correct the problem. Obviously, it would be desirable to move toward full employment. There may be automatic forces in the economy to bring about such a movement but we may need to intervene. The "we" here is the federal government. We could attempt to persuade households to consume more, but with unemployment so high, they are not likely to do so. We could also attempt to get businessmen to invest more, but with excess capacity, they will not be interested either.

There are some things which could be done. We could increase government expenditures. This could be done as a matter of policy aimed at restoring full employment. We could also cut taxes, which would lead to more consumption by households and investment by business. Both of these courses of action will be explored more fully in the next chapter.

Inflationary gap

Again using Figure 7, consider now the aggregate demand curve labeled (C + I + G)₂. This curve leads to an equilibrium to the right of, or beyond, full employment. At this point the level of output is still Y*. The economy cannot produce as many goods and services as desired (demanded), because once the full-employment level is reached, output can no longer expand.

Notice that at Y* the aggregate demand curve is above the 45-degree line. People would be willing to buy more than is being produced. How much more is shown as the distance from the 45-degree line to (C + I + G)₂. This distance is labeled the **inflationary gap.** As people try to obtain more goods and services, competition leads to higher prices. This is a true demand-pull inflation situation. It is nobody's fault since each person acts independently and does not recognize his or her contribution to inflation. It is no group's fault either since households, firms, and government are all involved in bidding for the full-employment level of output.

Clearly, the inflationary gap is an undesirable equilibrium. We would want to do something. Once again, there is the need to shift the aggregate demand curve, this time downward. If it is not possible to persuade consumers or investors to reduce purchases, then the policy actions are up to the government. One way to shift aggregate demand down would be to reduce government purchases (G). The other way would be to increase taxes so that consumers and businesses would have less money to spend. We will return to policy actions several times in later chapters since there are many problems to discuss and a few other economic tools which we may use.

Aggregate supply and the price level

For the Keynesian models we discussed, the price level is assumed to be constant. This particular assumption accurately described the times in which Keynes was working out his theories. Remember that Keynes developed his economic model at the time of the Great Depression and when inflation was not a problem. Since prices and wages did not fall much, costs and prices were essentially constant. However, after World War II, rising prices—that is, inflation—became a problem. Keynes had explained demand-pull inflation with his approach. The inflationary gap analysis was developed by Keynes. However, as inflation persisted after World War II, additional models of inflation were developed by economists who were followers of Keynes. Persistent inflation also contributed to the formation of entirely new economic models. A new "school" of economic thought began to emerge.

This new "school" of dissenting economists is known as **monetarist,** because of the importance these economists attach to the amount of money in the economy, and the price level. In the 1950s and 1960s they developed a model that emphasizes the quantity of money in the determination of the equilibrium level of income. The monetarists emphasize an aggregate demand curve that shows the amount of goods and services supplied and demanded at each price level. We will look at the ideas advanced by the monetarists in greater detail when we get to the chapters on money. To understand a little better the determination of prices in both the Keynesian and the monetarist models, let us consider the aggregate supply curve.

Aggregate supply

The aggregate supply curve is illustrated in Figure 8. The horizontal axis measures net national product (NNP), while the vertical axis measures the price level (all prices in general). The level of output that results in full employment is once again shown as Y*. However, for reasons of convenience, we can give Y* a numerical value. Suppose that Y* equals $1,500 billion, the value we were using in the Keynesian models.

In Figure 8, to the left of Y* = $1,500 billion—that is, at lower levels of output than Y*—the *aggregate supply curve* (*AS*) is essentially horizontal. (We will explain why in a few paragraphs.) Since in this range there are unemployed resources, the output of the economy can be increased—and with little or no increase in prices. As the output is increased, we move to the right—toward Y*.

We also should examine what happens to prices when, in this same horizontal part of the supply curve, output decreases. If we decrease output (move to the left on the supply curve), will prices not fall? After all, we are causing resources to become unemployed. If they are not needed, their prices should fall until someone is willing to employ them.

In the past this was true, but the world in which we live has changed. Many prices nowadays are inflexible in the downward direction; instead of falling when there is an excess supply, they remain fixed or even increase. This is true of prices in heavy industry, such as steel or

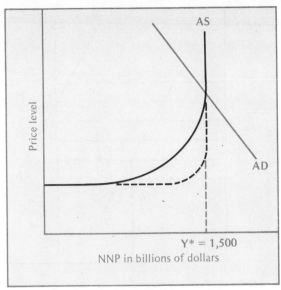

Figure 8 Intersection of aggregate supply (AS) and aggregate demand (AD) curves. The equilibrium shown here is a full-employment equilibrium Y*. Note the shape of the AS curve. No output (NNP) greater than Y* is possible; only the price level will rise (that is, inflation occurs). At the other end of the AS curve, prices are sticky downward.

automobiles, and in those other markets where large corporations dominate. It is also true of wages (the price of labor), particularly where workers are strongly unionized. If prices and wages are rigid and don't fall very readily, the economy won't work the way the classical economists said it should. Economists refer to this rigidity of prices and wages as *stickiness*, especially in the downward direction. Because of this stickiness, the supply curve assumes its somewhat horizontal shape below the level of full employment.

Let's again look at Figure 8, particularly the point marked Y*, which represents the full-employment level of national output. If the economy tries to go beyond that amount of national output, prices will start to rise because no more output can be produced. Employers who try to employ more workers and materials in order to expand their output will have to bid them away from other employers by paying more for them. If these employers get them, other employers will lose them. Prices will rise but total output will remain the same. This is the kind of thing that happens

during wars when the economy is driven beyond its capacity by the government's demand for military supplies, which tends to supplement, not replace, peacetime demand. Thus the AS curve is vertical over the full-employment level. The price level changes but output does not.

One additional comment on the slope of the AS curve is needed here. We have concentrated on the horizontal and vertical portions of the curve in the discussion so far. We need to consider how the curve gets from one end to the other. Consider first the appropriate broken lines as part of the AS curve in Figure 8. The change from horizontal to vertical is rather abrupt. This rapid change was generally the way economists viewed the situation until recently.

Many economists now feel that the AS curve begins to rise long before the economy reaches full employment. Thus there is a decided bend to the AS curve. We will return to this point in a few paragraphs.

Aggregate demand

The aggregate demand curve relates the quantity of goods and services desired by the economy as a whole at each price level. In the earlier discussion, we assumed the aggregate demand (AD) curve was determined without regard to price level. We did this by not letting the price level vary.

We could easily continue to say that the price level does not affect aggregate demand. We could do this by drawing the AD curve as a vertical line in a diagram such as Figure 8. This would show that a particular quantity of goods would be demanded and the price level could be anything. As can be seen in Figure 8, the AD curve is drawn showing that more goods and services will be purchased at lower price levels. In this way, it is similar to an ordinary demand curve which shows that at lower prices, consumers will purchase more of a particular good or service. As prices fall, money becomes worth more in purchasing power terms. Thus, at lower prices, people have "more" money. They can increase consumption of goods and services as their purchasing power increases. Thus, at lower prices, we can expect people will buy more of everything. The AD curve will slope steeply downward.

Equilibrium with sticky prices

Throughout that range of stickiness of prices the economy will obviously behave differently than at the full-employment level. Sticky prices will mean that at some level of prices, there will be many levels of output less than full employment (that is, a horizontal supply curve). As a result, the economy may reach equilibrium at various points below full employment. We can show this by adding a demand curve to the diagram of aggregate supply. In Figure 9 there are in fact two demand curves shown, one intersecting the aggregate supply curve in its horizontal range and the other in its vertical range. There is no magic in having two of them: we are free to imagine any number of AD curves. Each one illustrates different conditions. We can say "What if AD_1 applies?" or "What about AD_2 . . . ?"

The first of our aggregate demand curves, AD_1, intersects the supply curve in the horizontal range—the range of sticky prices. The point of intersection is at a level of prices P_2 and a quantity of output $Y_1 = \$1,200$ billion. If the price level were as low as P_1, suppliers would be unwilling to supply anything at all, though buyers would buy more than Y_1 goods and services. Buyers wanting goods and services would have no choice but to pay at least P_2. The price would not go above P_2 because then suppliers would be willing to supply more output or even operate at the full-employment level of output, Y^*. Only at P_2 can supply and demand be equated. At that price, however, there are potentially a number of equilibrium points possible. Depending on the location of AD_1, there are many levels of Y consistent with price level P_2.

Equilibrium at full employment

A quick look at Figure 9 shows that, at any price level above P_3, there will be no increase in output possible since full employment has been reached. The price level may change but output will remain constant at Y^*. At price levels P_4, P_5, and P_6, suppliers are willing to offer the same amount of goods and services to the market. But at price level P_4, buyers want to purchase more than Y^* amount of goods

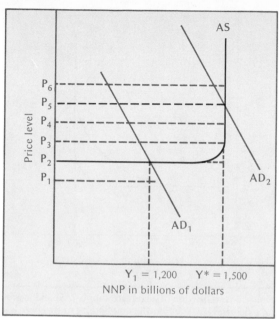

Figure 9 Two different equilibria are shown: one for aggregate demand AD_1 and the other for aggregate demand AD_2. For price level P_2, prices are sticky; the price level won't fall below P_2. There are many equilibria in this price range, of which the intersection of AD_1 and AS is just one. As the economy moves up the AS curve and reaches full-employment equilibrium Y^*, any further movement toward increasing AS will only result in the price level increasing. Notice that there are several possible price levels that result in full-employment equilibrium. However, any equilibrium above price level P_3 is inflationary.

and services. Since Y^* is the limit of the economy's output, attempts by buyers to purchase more than Y^* will only drive up the price level. Let's say at P_6 prices are too high; buyers will not purchase Y^* amount of goods and services at that price, so the price level will decline. Only P_5 is consistent with both equilibrium at Y^* and equilibrium at AD_2.

Equilibrium in the curved area

Now let us return to an AS curve that is more of a true curve rather than two pieces—a horizontal and a vertical piece—with a bend. Such an AS curve is shown in Figure 10. The AS curve shows prices beginning to rise long before the full-employment range.

Consider the aggregate demand curve AD_1. The price level in the economy is P_1. However, output is far below full employment. Consider the economic problem faced by the President in this case. If he does nothing, he will likely lose the next election because of high unemployment. So he may decide to take action to increase aggregate demand to increase output. He may have the government buy things to increase output. Or, he may cut taxes so that households may increase consumption or firms may increase investment. Suppose the increase shifts aggregate demand to AD_2. That is better for employment and output since both are now closer to full-employment levels. But prices have increased from P_1 to P_2. Now he may lose the next election because his economic policy helped cause inflation.

Many economists are concerned that our economy now operates like the AS curve shown in Figure 10. Long before we reach full employment, prices begin to rise. The reasons given usually result from cost-push or structural inflation. As full employment is even approached, workers begin to demand higher wages. Long before capacity is reached, suppliers raise prices. Anticipation of approaching full employment leads everyone to try to get prices up before there is a high increase in prices. The problem of achieving full employment and stable prices is very difficult to solve. We will return to the problems of unemployment and inflation in a later chapter.

Summary

The intersection of the aggregate demand curve with the aggregate supply curve determines the equilibrium level of net national product. Thus the equilibrium level determines the amount of employment as well as the output. Keynes emphasized the role of aggregate demand in a model for the determination of equilibrium NNP. Thus the major components of aggregate demand—consumption, investment, and government expenditures—may be used to determine the equilibrium level of NNP: $Y = C + I + G$. (Net exports is ignored because it is so small.)

Equilibrium NNP means that desired purchases for consumption, investment, and government purposes equal the amount produced. At other levels of NNP than equilibrium, there are economic forces at work to change the level of NNP. If NNP exceeds

equilibrium levels, more is produced than demanded so undesired inventory builds up and NNP falls. If NNP is less than the equilibrium level, more goods and services are demanded than are produced. Thus either inventories are depleted and must be replenished or there are unsatisfied customers. Either way, NNP tends to change. Only at equilibrium are the forces balanced, and the economy will remain there until disturbed.

In graphing aggregate demand we use a 45-degree reference line to show where the NNP demanded is equal to the NNP available. Where the aggregate demand schedule crosses the 45-degree line, the equilibrium NNP is determined.

Equilibrium may also be determined as a balance between leakages and compensating expenditures: that is, between saving and investment.

Because consumption depends upon income and one person's purchases become another person's income, a change in aggregate demand originating in one sector of the economy will have an impact on NNP; this impact

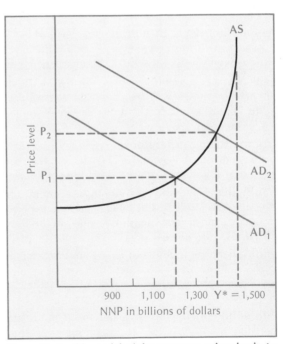

Figure 10 In this model of the economy, prices begin to rise well before full-employment equilibrium is reached. If aggregate demand increases from AD_1 to AD_2, output (and therefore employment) increase as desired; however, the price level rises also, from P_1 to P_2 (i.e., inflation occurs). The economy of the mid-1970s operated much like this model.

is a multiple of the original change in demand. The size of the multiplier depends upon the MPC and is defined for simple economies as 1/(1 − MPC) or 1/MPS.

The paradox of thrift illustrates the use of the multiplier to analyze the effect of an increase in saving. Because of the loss of aggregate demand and the multiplier effect, the attempt to increase saving will be frustrated. The fallacy of composition is also shown since all families cannot save as the one family might.

Equilibria are not necessarily desirable. There may be either a recessionary gap or an inflationary gap for an equilibrium.

We can also show aggregate supply and demand for goods and services related to prices. Aggregate supply may show that increases in output require higher prices even though the full-employment level of the economy has not been reached. Once full employment has been reached, any additional increase in aggregate demand must result in higher prices rather than increases in output.

Key Words and Phrases

- **equilibrium level of output** the level of NNP toward which the economy will move; the level where aggregate supply equals aggregate demand.

- **leakage** an economic activity involving the use of income in such a way that aggregate demand is reduced; saving and payment of taxes are examples of leakages.

- **compensating expenditures** sources of aggregate demand which offset leakages; examples would be investment or government expenditures.

- **multiplier effect** the tendency in an economy for the increase (or decrease) in aggregate demand to produce a larger increase (or decrease) in the flow of goods and services.

- **multiplier** the multiple of change in equilibrium NNP resulting from a change in investment or government expenditures; equal to 1/MPS = 1/(1 − MPC).

- **full-employment NNP** the amount of goods and services produced when the economy is at full employment; because of structural and frictional unemployment, 4% of the labor force may be unemployed.

- **recessionary gap** measured at the full-employment level of NNP, the amount by which aggregate demand is less than full-employment NNP.

- **inflationary gap** at the full-employment level of NNP, the amount by which aggregate demand exceeds the full-employment NNP.

- **monetarists** a "school" of economists who emphasize the role of money as the determinant of output and prices in the economy.

- **stickiness** the tendency of prices to remain at one level; this is particularly true of movements downward as prices fall only slowly if at all.

Questions for Review

1. Calculate the multiplier for: (a) MPC = $\frac{1}{2}$; (b) MPC = $\frac{3}{4}$; (c) MPC = $\frac{9}{10}$. Suppose there is an increase in government expenditures of $10 billion. For each of the three cases, calculate the change in consumption for the first five rounds of expenditures, as was done in Table 2. What is the final change in NNP in each of the three cases?

2. Suppose you believed a depression would begin in a year or so. Should you save your money in order to be ready for it? In what form would you save: bank account; in your mattress; real estate; diamonds? What would happen if everyone agreed with you and everyone tried to save for the oncoming depression?

3. If NNP is greater than the equilibrium level, what are the economic forces that will cause NNP to fall toward equilibrium? If NNP is less than the equilibrium level, what are the economic forces which will increase NNP?

4. An increase in consumption will increase NNP. An increase in NNP will increase consumption. Show each of these changes in a diagram. Why don't consumption and income chase each other constantly like a dog chasing its tail? How is equilibrium ever reached?

5. In previous chapters we saw that inventory accumulation is a part of investment. Yet in moving toward equilibrium, inventory accumulation or depletion led to changes in NNP, not in investment plans. How do you distinguish between these two circumstances?

6. In a pair of diagrams, one above the other, show how the C + I + G approach results in the same equilibrium as the S-I approach.

7. I always seem to spend more than the amount I get in a raise. What does this mean about our MPC? If all families in the economy behaved the same way, what would the multiplier be? What happens to equilibrium with the multiplier you just computed?

8. How does a recessionary gap differ from an inflationary gap?

10

Fiscal Policy

In the previous two chapters, the role of government in determining aggregate demand was mentioned only in passing. In Chapter 8 we studied the major components of aggregate demand: household consumption and business investment. The focus of Chapter 9 was in showing how the economy would reach equilibrium if it operated pretty much on its own. Although we mentioned that government expenditures are a component of aggregate demand, there was no special economic role given to government.

For a given level of aggregate demand, we have seen how an economy would reach equilibrium. However, you should note that an equilibrium position is not a goal in itself. *Any particular equilibrium may be undesirable.* For example, if the economy reaches an equilibrium where demand is far below the capacity of the economy to produce, there will be unemployment and idle factories. Or the equilibrium may be such that aggregate demand intersects the aggregate supply curve in the range where prices must rise. An equilibrium at full employment or beyond will result then in inflation. The equilibrium in both cases is undesirable and should be changed. The part of the economy which acts independently and privately—that is, household consumption and business investment—cannot be expected to change demand on some sort of signal; at least this is true in a market economy. Only command economies can readily dictate consumption and investment. If the equilibrium is to be changed, it must be through a sector which can change demand (that is, change its expenditures) at will and on command. This sector is the public sector, specifically the government.

The government sector includes all levels of government. Many of the government units are small and purchase very few goods and services. There are a lot of these small government units, but together they contribute a substantial amount to total demand. However, from the states on down to the smaller government units (such as cities, counties, etc.), most expenditures are in response to the needs of the people residing in the unit. For example, the bulk of local expenditures are for such essential services as police, fire, sanitation, and elementary and high schools. Changes in local expenditures cannot be made in response to economic conditions that are essentially nationwide. Changes in expenditures in response to economic conditions are appropriately made at the federal level. Expenditures aren't as critical, expenditures are more easily changed from year to year, and decision-making is centralized. We will concentrate on this level of government.

By concentrating on the federal government, we may give the impression that somehow the federal expenditures are greater in size and more important. This is not the case. Together the fifty states and the many smaller government units consume more than the federal government. However, no one state, county, or municipality can do much about the macroeconomy. An economic equilibrium is nationwide. Therefore, economic policy is appropriately adjusted at a national level. In addition, federal spending and decision-making are centralized in one unit rather than split into fifty states, hundreds of cities, and thousands of counties. Unemployment may be greater in some areas than in others. However, it is the federal government which can respond and vary aggregate demand in order to fight inflation or unemployment. The instability created by business cycles is a national problem. Policies must be formulated that have national impact. The federal government is the level that responds to such problems. To see how it responds, let us turn now to an examination of the federal budget.

The federal government budget

The **federal budget** shows all projected outlays and sources of income of the U.S. government. The federal budget is usually stated for a given length of time: the fiscal year. A **fiscal year** begins on October 1 and ends the following September 30; a fiscal year is therefore different from the calendar year. (Previous to 1977, the fiscal year started on July 1 and ended on June 30.)

For many years drawing up the federal budget was a rather haphazard process. The President would send a proposed budget to Congress each January. The various committees of Congress would pass a series of bills appropriating funds for various programs: agriculture, health and education, public housing, defense, etc. There was no system for coordinating spending plans and no effort to relate total appropriations to expected tax revenues.

The economic crises of the 1970s forced a change in budgetary procedures. First, the Executive branch established an **Office of Management and Budget** (OMB) under the President. The OMB receives spending requests from all government agencies. This allows the President to coordinate total spending proposals before submitting them to Congress. The chairman of the OMB meets regularly with the President, the Secretary of the Treasury, and the President's chief economic adviser to review the state of the economy and to evaluate recommendations for economic policy.

In 1974, Congress established a new **Congressional Budget Office** (CBO) to perform similar services for the Congress. The CBO prepares long-range projections of budget estimates. But it is primarily involved in budget analysis for the coming fiscal year. The Office is concerned first with the total cost of new legislative proposals and with the effects of tax policy on inflation and unemployment. It establishes a *ceiling* above which additional spending is not recommended. Specialized divisions within the CBO study legislation in specific areas of government spending: energy, environment, human resources, community development, national security, and international affairs. The aim of the CBO is to keep track of how legislation fits in with the current year's spending ceilings.

For instance, during the recession of 1975 the CBO was investigating the possible effects on employment of public job programs at the federal level and public works grants to states and local governments. The job of the CBO was not to recommend either alternative but to project the effectiveness and the costs of each. Ultimately, however, policy must be made by the Congress (and the President) with the improved information provided by the CBO.

A sample budget

Table 1 shows a sample of a budget: President Ford's proposed budget for fiscal 1977 (October 1, 1976 to September 30, 1977). This budget was sent to Congress by President Ford in January, 1976. Notice that beside the *proposed figures* are the *actual budget* figures for fiscal 1975 and *estimated budget* figures for fiscal 1976. The President submits a proposed budget, but the Congress must approve. There is never any guarantee that a Congress will give the President what he asks for.

The budget for fiscal 1977 is based upon receipts estimated to be over $351 billion. The largest single source is a tax on personal income which will bring in a total of $153.6 billion. Corporate income taxes will bring in $49.5 billion. Another $115.1 billion is received from social insurance taxes and contributions; this is predominantly the Social Security payment that both employer and employee pay. Excise taxes are taxes levied on specific items, such as tobacco, liquor, gasoline, and telephone service. Excise taxes will result in receipts of $17.8 billion. Estate and gift taxes will bring in another $5.8 billion. Customs duties are taxes levied on products which are imported to the United States. Customs duties were a major source of revenue for the federal government when the country was begun but now (in 1977) are slotted for only $4.3 billion in revenues.

The largest single use of funds is the $137.1 billion for *income security*, that is, transfer payments. Military expenditures follow at $101.1 billion. The other cabinet agencies have budget allocations of varying amounts. It is interesting to note that agriculture has a budget of $1.7 billion, one of the smallest amounts. The $3.4 billion budgeted for general government is to cover the cost of running the government. Revenue sharing goes to state and local governments for whatever purpose they desire. The budget for this item is $7.35 billion. In order to service the public debt which is outstanding, $41.3 billion is budgeted for interest payment. Total outlays for the 1977 budget year are projected at $394.2 billion. In addition, President Carter could decide on changes, particularly on the receipts side, and of course, Congressional approval was still required. The latter could result in some changes before the final package is in place.

To visualize the relative importance of the receipts and expenditures, consider Figure 1. The largest source of revenue, as has been noted, is individual income tax. For each $1.00 received, 39¢ comes from personal income tax. Social insurance receipts bring in 29¢ of each $1.00. Corporate income taxes bring in 13¢, excise taxes 4¢, and other receipts another 4¢. In order to meet the expenditures projected, 11¢ will have to be borrowed.

If the budget is specified in terms of who gets the money rather than where it originates (its source), the right side of Figure 1 is ob-tained. The largest piece of each dollar goes directly to people in one form of benefit or another. A total of 40¢ of each federal dollar is spent directly on transfer payments, that is, benefits to people. Defense gets 26¢ of each federal dollar. Since part of the 26¢ goes for salaries, at least part of this amount goes directly to individuals. Grants (revenue sharing) to state and city governments amount to 15¢ of each dollar spent. Government operations use up 11¢ while the interest payments on federal debt amount to 8¢ of each dollar spent.

The *bottom line* of Table 1 shows the *surplus* or *deficit* for the federal budget. For the budget planned for the 1977 fiscal year, the deficit will be very close to $43 billion. This deficit is part of what is known as the *public* or *national debt*; it will be discussed in greater detail at the end of this chapter.

Table 1
Federal Budget: Receipts and Outlays (in millions of dollars) for the Fiscal Year

Receipts by Source	1975 actual	1976 estimate	1977 proposed
Individual income taxes	122,386	130,822	153,641
Corporation income taxes	40,621	40,056	49,461
Social insurance taxes and contributions	86,441	92,571	115,052
Excise taxes	16,551	16,901	17,806
Estate and gift taxes	4,611	5,100	5,800
Customs duties	3,676	3,800	4,300
Miscellaneous receipts	6,711	8,284	7,202
Total receipts	**280,997**	**297,534**	**351,262**

Outlays by Function	1975 actual	1976 estimate	1977 proposed
Military	86,585	92,759	101,129
International affairs	4,358	5,665	6,824
General science, space, and technology	3,989	4,311	4,507
Natural resources, environment, and energy	9,537	11,796	13,772
Agriculture	1,660	2,875	1,729
Commerce and transportation	16,010	17,801	16,498
Community and regional development	4,431	5,802	5,532
Education, training, employment, and social services	15,248	18,900	16,615
Health	27,647	32,137	34,393
Income security (transfer payment)	108,605	128,509	137,115
Veterans benefits and services	16,597	19,035	17,196
Law enforcement and justice	2,942	3,402	3,426
General government	3,089	3,547	3,433
Revenue sharing and general purpose fiscal assistance	7,005	7,169	7,351
Interest	30,974	34,835	41,297
Allowances	—	200	2,260
Undistributed offsetting receipts	−14,075	−15,208	−18,840
Total outlays	**324,601**	**373,535**	**394,237**
Budget surplus (+) or deficit (−)	**−43,604**	**−76,001**	**−42,975**

Source: Office of Management and Budget.

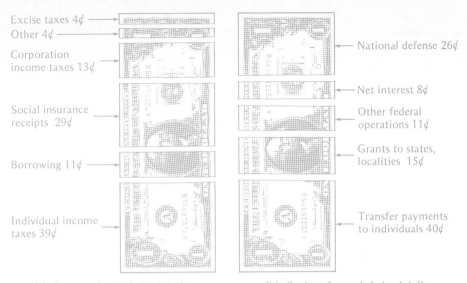

Excise taxes 4¢
Other 4¢

Corporation income taxes 13¢

Social insurance receipts 29¢

Borrowing 11¢

Individual income taxes 39¢

National defense 26¢

Net interest 8¢

Other federal operations 11¢

Grants to states, localities 15¢

Transfer payments to individuals 40¢

(a) Source of each federal dollar   (b) Outlays for each federal dollar

Figure 1 The proposed federal budget for fiscal year 1977. Each dollar spent and each dollar received are broken down into their outlays and sources. (Source: Bureau of the Budget.)

The theory of fiscal policy

The term **fiscal policy** refers to those decisions by government related to expenditures and taxes that most directly affect the level of the economy. Deliberate fiscal actions to remedy immediate economic problems such as inflation and unemployment are called *discretionary.* There are other fiscal actions that aren't deliberate; so we call them *nondiscretionary.* These nondiscretionary actions, such as unemployment benefits and progressive income tax laws, occur automatically because they result from legislation that applies no matter what the immediate economic problems. Since these nondiscretionary policies tend to help the economy (that is, counter the business cycle) automatically, these policies are also called **automatic stabilizers.** We will discuss automatic stabilizers later in this chapter.

Presently, we are especially interested in discretionary fiscal policy: in those changes in government spending and taxing designed to offset economic problems. Changes in the level of government purchases affect the G component of aggregate demand (which equals C + I + G). Changes in government taxing affect the C and I components. Therefore, government spending and taxing policies

ultimately affect the level of NNP. Thus in a decline or a trough of a business cycle, demand from government may be *increased* to offset the loss of demand from other sectors of the economy and to improve overall economic performance. At the peaks, government demand might well be *reduced* in order that existing capacity could be used to produce goods and services for consumption and investment purposes.

As we said earlier, state and local government expenditures are not well suited for purposes of controlling demand in total; their expenditures are for essential services such as public safety, education, and sanitation. These services are not easily changed in response to economic conditions. In fact, when the tax collections are considered, *state and local governments may add to economic instability.* For example, at the trough of the business cycle, state and local tax collections decline as business and individuals earn less (as a group) and so expenditures are reduced also. When tax collections increase at the peak of a cycle, so do state and local government expenditures, adding to the peak. Thus these two lower levels of government are *procyclical* in their response and may reinforce the business cycle. To be sure, not all federal expenditures may be changed either. Some can be, however, and fiscal policy operates directly on these. Expenditures and taxes that represent transfer payments from one segment of the society to another are not considered here, though we will have some additional comments later.

We are left with other expenditures and taxes by the federal government, both of which can be designed to promote economic stability and avoid the worse effects of the business cycle. Both expenditures and taxes may be used to change economic activity. We will consider each in turn.

Government expenditures

Government purchases—be they a missile for defense or a desk for a bureaucrat—represent a demand for goods. By varying its expenditures (i.e., its demand for goods and services), the federal government can affect the economic conditions of this country. The government may choose to pursue an **expansionary fiscal policy,** which means it *stimulates demand;* government expenditures would increase. It does this during a recession, or when output is lagging and unemployment has increased.

Conversely, the federal government may choose to implement a **contractionary fiscal policy,** which means it will *reduce* demand; such a policy would reduce government expenditures. The government usually pursues this policy during periods of inflation (or when inflation is threatening).

Increasing expenditures: the fight against recession and unemployment

If the economy is operating at less than capacity, there are idle resources that could be employed to produce goods and services. Such is the case with a recession. The proper fiscal policy to pursue is an expansionary one. The government must increase demand for goods and services. In order to increase demand, the government increases its purchases (see Figure 2), which increase purchases of goods and services from the rest of the economy. The government may spend more on highways, railroads, national parks, new missiles and

tanks for defense, etc. Depending on how great a stimulation is needed, the government may increase expenditure for all of these things or just a few, or even just one.

In Figure 2 we see the impact on the economy of a change in government demand for goods and services. This means we will leave C and I alone for now. The current level of government purchases is represented by G_1. Thus the current level of aggregate demand is $Y_1 = C + I + G_1$. Now suppose that this level of demand has resulted in a level of output Y_1 with much unemployment. So we want to increase Y_1, knowing that more output will require more workers to be hired. The government economists advise the President to increase government purchases (i.e., raise G_1) in order to expand the economy (i.e., to increase Y_1). *Without a change in taxes,* government purchases are expanded from G_1 to G_2. The increase in government purchases increases aggregate demand. As a result, national income or output (NNP) rises from Y_1 to Y_2. The size of the increase in income depends upon the multiplier (which in turn depends upon the marginal propensity to consume, as we have already seen).

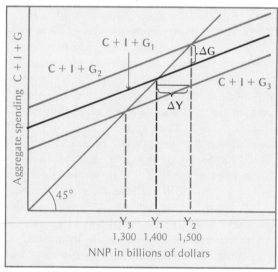

Figure 2 The effect of changes in government expenditures on NNP. Suppose that the economy is in equilibrium at Y_1 with aggregate demand $C + I + G_1$. To increase output, G_1 is increased to G_2. The higher aggregate demand $C + I + G_2$ leads to a new equilibrium NNP, at Y_2. Notice that a change in government expenditures $\Delta G(=G_2 - G_1)$ leads to a change in output $\Delta Y(=Y_2 - Y_1)$. If government expenditures are decreased to G_3, a new equilibrium NNP results at Y_3.

In fact, the government could help expand demand even if it chose to build pyramids throughout the country! Of course, what helps the economy may not contribute much to the improvement of society. So the arguments over the budget aren't only about how much to spend (this affects the economy) but also on what to spend (this affects society). Some critics would go so far as to label defense spending a modern version of the pyramids: advanced missiles and airplanes are built never to be used.

In any event, government expenditures do help increase demand directly and start the multiplier effect in motion. Suppose the government authorizes 1,000 new fighter planes built at one of the aerospace firms. In order to meet this order, the firm may have to expand plant capacity; this entails contracting for builders, plumbers, electricians, etc. Once facilities are available, the firm must hire workers and hire subcontractors for supplying many of the parts needed in the airplanes; so the subcontractors can each hire a few more people. All the newly hired workers earn salaries which they spend: at Sears, at McDonald's, at the local auto dealers, etc. Some of these places will, in turn, need extra workers. So now you can get an idea of how government expenditures have a ripple effect on the economy as demand for goods and services is increased.

Reducing expenditures: the fight against inflation

If the economy is operating at the peak of the business cycle, businesses are operating at or near capacity and unemployment is down. In other words, demand is high, or at a peak. As you will recall, inflation is thus a problem (or soon will be). To reduce demand, the proper government fiscal policy would be a contractionary one. The government should, if possible, cut back on its spending.

To see how a decrease in government demand (G) affects output (Y), look once again at Figure 2. If Y_1 is in the range of increasing prices (that is, output is at a peak), reducing aggregate demand may be desirable. Again, *without changing taxes,* government purchases may be reduced from G_1 to G_3. With less government demand, total demand falls. Thus income falls also from Y_1 to Y_3. Again, the size of

the decrease in Y depends upon the multiplier effect.

With regard to expenditures, a contractionary policy may be more difficult to pursue than an expansionary one. Why? Well, it is always easier to increase spending. Every Congressman has a pet program that he or she would like to see funded. But when government spending is to be cut back, the question quickly becomes, what should be cut? To cut back on spending means to reverse the ripple procedure we outlined in the section above. Basically, federal spending cuts mean some people will be temporarily unemployed. These individuals might be doing their job very well. But if there is no money for funding, these people will soon be seeking employment elsewhere.

In order to cut demand, the government has a second strategy it can follow: increase taxes. We will now discuss federal government tax policies.

Taxation policies

Tax policies are an important tool to be used to change demand for goods and services. The direction of change in taxes is the opposite of the desired impact on the output. To follow an *expansionary fiscal policy,* the government *lowers taxes;* with more money in their hands, both people and businesses will demand more goods and services. For a *contractionary fiscal policy,* government will *increase taxes.*

Increasing taxes: the fight against inflation

As we have seen, the peak of a business cycle means output is at or near capacity and therefore demand is high. Inflation is now either a problem or threatening to be a problem. Increasing the tax rates will remove spending power from the economy, thereby reducing demand and easing inflationary pressure. What tax should be increased? Actually, the government could achieve its goals by increasing almost any of its taxes in appropriate amounts. However, most often, to implement contractionary fiscal policy the government will increase personal income or business income taxes, or some combination of the two. An increase in either has a widespread effect. An increase in personal income taxes will reduce the C component of aggregate demand; an increase in the business income taxes will reduce the I component of aggregate demand.

Decreasing taxes: the fight against recession and unemployment

During a recessionary period—that is, during a decline or at a trough of the business cycle—the idea is to stimulate demand in other sectors. The government can expand demand by reducing taxes (without reducing government purchases). When taxes are reduced, people have more money to spend. Their increased demand for goods and services stimulates the output. In other words, a reduction in taxes will shift the consumption function upward, since there will be less income needed to meet tax payments and more available to spend on goods and services. Also, depending upon the specific business taxes reduced, it may be possible to increase the rate of return on investment projects, increasing the demand for goods and services from firms.

With regard to personal income taxes, a tax cut could be "across the board"—i.e., affecting everyone who pays personal income taxes—or reduced for a single segment of the population: the poor, the middle class, or the rich. Since the poor have a higher marginal propensity to consume (MPC) than the rich, a smaller cut in taxes may be required for the poor than for the rich in order to increase consumer spending by some fixed amount.

Taxes collected vs. tax rate

Total taxes collected make the difference in fiscal matters. Tax collections and the tax rate are not necessarily the same thing. A **tax rate** is the schedule showing how much is to be collected, given certain levels of personal (or business) income and spending. **Tax collection** is the actual total amount collected, given any fixed tax rate. Taxation policies have a goal of either raising or decreasing tax collections. This goal is achieved by changing or manipulating tax rates. When we set out to *change taxes*, we

must make *a change in tax rates* for many types of taxes.

For example, suppose a state had a 5% sales tax as a source of revenue. If taxable retail sales in that state were $100 billion, tax collections would be $5 billion. Suppose the tax rate were increased to 6%, a 20% increase in the tax rate. If the existing level of sales is maintained, tax collections would rise by $1 billion to $6 billion. This would certainly have an impact on total demand. However, the level of sales is affected by changes in tax rates. The people who live in the state will not be able to buy as much with the present level of their income. Thus retail sales may fall to $98 billion. As a result, tax collections will rise to $5.8 billion from $5 billion. The increase in tax collections will be only 17.6% compared with the 20% increase in the tax rate. The restraining influence of the tax increase will be reduced. The same effect will be noted when the income tax rate, an excise tax rate, or any other tax rate is changed. It would be possible in some instances to increase the tax rate and have tax collections decline, depending upon the response of the economy. For the moment, we are interested in the total tax take. Therefore, let us leave to the experts the question of how the tax rates are changed in order to achieve the desired change in taxes collected.

Spending and taxing: a synthesis

Both expenditure changes and tax collection changes could be used concurrently to control economic activity. Sometimes government prefers to change only one. The impact of government expenditures is immediate. The change in demand is felt as soon as the change in expenditures is made. There are two reasons why tax collection changes are less powerful. *First, there is a lag during which the households and firms recognize and adjust to the new level of taxes.* Some taxes are paid infrequently so the effect may not be felt till after the next payment date. *Second, the impact of tax collection change will be less since the consumption function will shift up or down only by the amount of the tax*

Viewpoint
Fiscal Solutions for Unemployment

The Congressional Budget Office made a study of various programs and government fiscal policies available to fight unemployment. The study found that tax-cut policy created fewer jobs than other programs, reduced unemployment least, and was the most costly. The report pointed out, however, that changes in fiscal policies, including tax cuts, could indeed affect employment rates throughout the economy.

Public service employment, the report said, is an effective job-creating device. In addition, it is relatively low cost, since public moneys go mainly to the workers rather than being spent on equipment, which actually may replace low-skilled workers. Antirecession aid to local governments will also increase jobs, although such aid would cost more per job created than public service work. Acceleration of public works programs would also be effective, but would be rela-

tively costly, especially if a good deal of the program's funding were spent on major construction projects—roads, bridges—where expensive machinery must be used.

In terms of cost per job created, tax cuts ranked last. Public service employment, for example, was estimated to supply 80,000 to 125,000 new jobs for an outlay of $615 million to $754 million. A tax cut (one-third corporate and two-thirds personal) would supply 8,000 to 15,000 new jobs at a cost of $960 million to $980 million.

Yet, tax cutting as a fiscal policy to raise employment in a depressed economy remains viable. In fact, it remains one of the most popular among many economists and government officials. Politically, a tax cut will gain votes for the politician. Economically, the effects of the cut are generally felt more quickly *throughout* the economy than many other job-producing stimuli. In addition, and very importantly, jobs created by a tax cut are created in and by the private sector. Money spent for such new jobs goes directly to the worker. Little is spent on administrative costs or is contributed to further swelling of governmental bureaucracies.

---

change times the MPC. Some of the change in taxes will affect saving, which effectively removes part of the impact of taxes on the economy. We will discuss this point in our look at the tax multiplier.

The tax multiplier

In the last chapter we studied the *multiplier* with regard to consumption and investment. In a somewhat similar fashion, the effect of tax collection changes may be calculated through a *tax multiplier*.

Suppose our economy is in equilibrium at an NNP of $1,500 billion and that tax collections from personal income are increased by $40 billion. What will be the change in NNP? Of our three basic demand components— consumption (C), investment (I), and government expenditures (G)—the one which is affected is consumption. (We will consider only personal taxes to avoid confusion—business

taxes would change investment as well.) In fact, if personal income tax collections rise by $40 billion, the disposal income (DI) will decrease by this amount. But recall that DI is used not only for consumption but also for saving. So the amount of decrease in consumption will depend on the marginal propensity to save (MPS). If MPS is .2 (or $\frac{1}{5}$), the MPC is .8 (or $\frac{4}{5}$). So consumption will decrease by .8 × $40 billion equals −$32 billion. (Saving will decrease by $8 billion.) So the decrease in C equals MPC × tax change.

To figure how much NNP will decrease, we will use the multiplier principle as we did in the last chapter. Remember that to calculate the effect of a change in I or C on the level of NNP, we multiply that change by the multiplier, which equals 1/MPS. So a decrease in C will result in the following change in NNP:

$$\text{change in NNP} = C \times \frac{1}{\text{MPS}}.$$

If we substitute our values, we have

$$\text{change in NNP} = -\$32 \text{ billion} \times \frac{1}{.2}$$
$$= -\$32 \text{ billion} \times 5$$
$$= -\$160 \text{ billion.}$$

The NNP will decrease by $160 billion when taxes increase $40 billion. You can see what a strong effect taxes can exert on the economy. Tax cuts can be shown to be just as powerful.

We can combine the two steps we used above and the result will be the tax multiplier. Since C = MPC × tax change and the change in NNP = C × (1/MPS), we substitute to get

change in NNP

$$= (\text{MPC} \times \text{tax change}) \times \frac{1}{\text{MPS}}$$
$$= \frac{\text{MPC}}{\text{MPS}} \times \text{tax change.}$$

The **tax multiplier** equals MPC/MPS. In our example the value of the tax multiplier is

$$\frac{\text{MPC}}{\text{MPS}} = \frac{.8}{.2} = 4.$$

So the multiplier is 5 and the tax multiplier is 4. (Actually, the tax multiplier is −4, since there is a decrease in NNP.)

The tax multiplier could also be calculated by looking at saving instead of consumption. Figure 3 shows the saving function (S) as well as the total leakages, or S + T schedule. It is important to consider the saving function in this analysis. But taxes are also a leakage and must be considered together with saving. Remember that saving is a function of disposable income. A change in tax collections will change disposable income and therefore saving. A change in S will obviously affect the total amount of leakage (S + T).

At the initial equilibrium of $1,500 billion, the saving schedule reflects the level of taxes collected. Adding the taxes collected to S gives us the S + T schedule. When taxes are increased, consumers will adjust both consumption and saving. The saving schedule will shift by the MPS times the change in taxes. Using the numbers we have used all along, the MPS = .2; so .2 × $40 billion = $8 billion. There is a reduction in saving by $8 billion to

accommodate the new level of taxes. Thus the increase in one leakage, taxes, is offset in part by a decrease in the other leakage, saving. The new saving schedule is labeled S′, the lowest line in Figure 3.

The total amount of taxes must now be added to S′, not S. Saving has declined so the increase in taxes is offset in part by the decrease in saving. Suppose T′ = T + $40 billion. Total leakages after the change are S′ + T′, which is higher than S + T but not by $40 billion. T′ is greater than T by $40 billion but S′ is *less* than S by $8 billion. The net upward shift is $32 billion. Therefore, the reduction in Y is

$40 billion times $\left(-\dfrac{\text{MPC}}{\text{MPS}} = -\dfrac{.8}{.2} = -4\right)$

or
$40 billion × −4 = −$160 billion.

The balanced budget multiplier

An intriguing question is what happens if both G and T are increased by an equal amount, say $40 billion. You may have heard some politicians say that expenditures should be raised only when taxes are raised an equal amount. The politicians imply that the two offset one another. However, as we just saw, the answer or implication is wrong: the two do not offset one another. There would be a change in NNP.

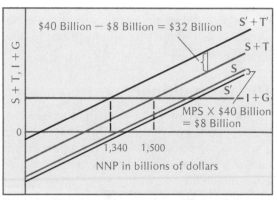

Figure 3 The effect of taxes on equilibrium NNP. The intersection of leakages (S + T) and compensating expenditures (I + G) results in equilibrium NNP at $1,500 billion. Suppose taxes are increased by $40 billion. We can't add this directly to S + T because increased taxes reduce saving S. Saving falls from S to S′; this fall is equal to MPS × $40 billion = $8 billion. So the new level of leakages, which is S′ + T′, has been increased by $40 − $8 billion = $32 billion. However, the new equilibrium NNP is now $1,340. A change of $40 billion in taxes resulted in a change of NNP equal to $160 billion.

The size of the change in NNP relative to the size of the change in G and T is called the **balanced budget multiplier.** Actually, the name is not quite correct. There is no need for the budget of any level of government to be balanced. *What is balanced is the increase or decrease in G and T.* That is, if both G and T are increased by $40 billion, then it is the increases that are balanced, regardless of whether the budget in total was balanced before or after the change.

We have seen in our example above that the government multiplier is 5. The tax multiplier is −4. The balanced budget multiplier is then the sum of the two. In this case 5 + (−4) = 5 − 4 = 1. Algebraically, we can summarize this as

$$\frac{1}{MPS} - \frac{MPC}{MPS} = \frac{1 - MPC}{MPS} = \frac{MPS}{MPS} = 1,$$

regardless of the value assumed for the MPC. In our running example,

$$\frac{1}{.2} - \frac{.8}{.2} = 5 - 4 = 1.$$

This means that if government purchases of goods and services are increased by $40 billion and tax collections are increased by $40 billion, then NNP increases by $40 billion. We can also see that this is so by looking at the effect on each component. A $40 billion increase in G times 5 would result in a $200 billion increase in NNP. An increase of $40 billion in taxes times −4 would result in a decrease in NNP of $160 billion. The net effect on NNP is an increase of $40 billion: $200 billion − $160 billion = $40 billion. *The balanced budget multiplier is always one.*

Budget philosophies

The above discussion did not relate the amount of tax collections to the amount spent for goods and services by governments. Many people think taxes are collected to enable expenditures and therefore there is an immediate and direct relationship. However, if fiscal policy is to be effective, it must be possible to change both expenditures and tax collections to fit the needs of the economy. Thus budget surpluses or deficits are usually required to achieve the economic goals. Some guidelines for budgeting have been developed.

Continuously balanced budget

Sometimes considered a conservative position, many people advocate a budget which is balanced at all times. Few economists support this budget policy. It means that fiscal policy cannot be used to dampen the extremes of business cycles. Expenditures are limited to tax collections and nothing more. Those who advocate this policy do so because they feel that in this way the government is removed from economic activity. But this is clearly not true, *since a continuously balanced budget is procyclical. It increases the forces leading to business cycles.* During a trough, tax collections tend to fall; thus expenditures would have to be reduced, which would reduce demand even more, adding to the depth of the trough. This policy would worsen a recession. At the peak, tax collections rise, allowing greater expenditures that add to demand at the same time demand is rising elsewhere. So this policy could also increase inflation. Instead of controlling the business cycle, government adds to it when a continuously balanced budget is used.

Balance over the cycle

To control the business cycle, it would be necessary to shave the peaks and to fill the valleys. To do this, the budget would be managed to stimulate demand during the trough and to restrain demand at the peak. It follows that the budget would be such that a deficit is observed during the trough. By increasing expenditures, reducing taxes, or both, government expenditures offset the decline in demand from other sectors and prevent the economy from sinking into a recession. To restrain demand at the peak, taxes would be increased, spending reduced, or both to create a budget surplus. If the recognition of the cycle is correct, the budget surplus at the peak would offset the deficit at the trough. *There-fore, in any given year the budget would be unbalanced, but over time the budget would be balanced.* This budget philosophy is also called the *Swedish Budget* since it was popular with Swedish economists for a while. The difficulties involved in using such a budget have prevented adoption by most governments. In order to use a Swedish Budget, the budgetmakers would have to be able to anticipate very accurately the business cycle. They would have to know exactly when the cycle would move up and down and by exactly how much it would move. There would also be restrictions on actions taken. No matter how great the need, no additional money could be spent as the budget deficit would have to be eliminated first.

Fully managed budget

Discontent with any fixed formula led some economists to suggest that the budget position be controlled at all times. Presumably, decision-making at the level of the federal government (including all three branches) would be directed at managing several economic variables. Sometimes called **functional finance,** the budget position would be just one of several tools employed to control not only the level of income and employment but also interest rates, prices, and other variables. During the administration of John Kennedy, the term **fine tuning** was used to refer to this process of monitoring economic conditions closely and applying precise fiscal and monetary policies. At that time, there was much less concern with controlling cycles than with keeping the economy performing at top levels, never allowing problems to develop.

When the economy is operating fairly well anyway, this approach works with great success. The slightest indication that a problem is about to develop brings a response. The difficulty with the approach is that the economic managers of the economy must be extremely watchful. They must be able to detect problems *at once*, diagnose the cause *accurately*, prescribe the *correct adjustment*, and *obtain the approval* of Congress and the President in a short period of time. When many problems

Economic Thinker
Paul Samuelson

Some thirty years ago, Paul A. Samuelson wrote a textbook for the introductory course in college economics. Today there are literally millions of Americans who remember him as the author of the book which introduced them to the subject of economics. Over three million copies of the book have been sold. Samuelson is known to additional millions through his witty and informative regular columns on economic matters in American newspapers and *Newsweek* magazine. It may safely be said that Paul Samuelson is one of the best-known American economists living today. His fame is rivaled, perhaps, only by the University of Chicago's Milton Friedman (with whom Samuelson is often in opposition in economic matters) and the best-selling author and television writer-narrator John Kenneth Galbraith.

Samuelson's fame rests on something more than being a successful writer of textbooks and a gifted popularizer of economic subjects. In 1970, he became America's first Nobel Laureate in economics for "raising the level of scientific analysis in economic the-

ory." His 1947 book, *Foundations of Economic Analysis,* was cited by the Nobel committee as an important breakthrough in the application of mathematics to economic theory, enabling economists to place numerical values on economic abstractions and thus aiding in the application of theory to the real world of economic interactions.

Paul Samuelson was born in 1915 in Gary, Indiana. He did his undergraduate work at the University of Chicago and received his Ph.D. in economics at Harvard University in 1941. He then joined the faculty at the Massachusetts Institute of Technology, where he remains today. He has taught and written in numerous economic areas, including international trade, welfare economics, theory of the firm, monetary and fiscal policies, linear programming, and econometrics. His breakthrough book, *Foundations of Economic Analysis,* was derived directly from his Harvard dissertation, written when he was twenty-three.

Paul Samuelson is a leading exponent of the Keynesian approach to contemporary political-economic problems. Unlike monetarists such as Milton Friedman, he believes fiscal policy to be the key to solving many such problems. He favors active government intervention in the economy whenever necessary—to combat persistent inflation, for example, or persistent unemployment. He was an adviser to Presidents Kennedy and Johnson and encouraged their generally interventionist economic policies. He likewise defended President Nixon's temporary use of wage and price controls to combat recession.

Samuelson's work in applying mathematical concepts to economic theories and his ability to rethink and clarify economic concepts have greatly contributed to contemporary economic thought. His influence is much felt among economists today and will undoubtedly continue to be felt for many years to come.

arise at once or big problems develop rapidly, there may not be readily available solutions to some types of economic problems. Economists may not detect the problem rapidly enough or be able to convince the political arm of government of the desirability of the proposed actions. If the economy is in serious difficulty, functional finance may not be an adequate approach. The frequently serious economic conditions of the 1970s did not allow the successful use of fine tuning.

Full-employment budget

The Employment Act of 1946 makes full employment one of the important goals of economic actions by the government. This has led to the suggestion that a budget be designed and balanced at the full-employment level. Tax collections and expenditures would be set at a position needed to achieve an aggregate demand consistent with full employment. Instead of balancing the actual budget, a budget is developed which would be balanced at full employment. If the economy is not at full employment, the actual budget position would not be balanced. In this case the budget should be in deficit to stimulate the economy. If the economy is operating at greater than the full-employment level, the budget would be in surplus to reduce inflationary pressures and capacity problems.

By placing the emphasis on full employment, this budget may fail to meet other needs. There are other budget concerns not related to full employment which might have to be left unsolved because of the need to balance the budget at full employment. For example, there may be costly health care needs which would have to be removed from the budget to obtain balance. Also, it is possible to disagree about the level of unemployment that can or should be obtained. (Remember that even at "full employment," frictional unemployment is always present.) If both inflation and unemployment are problems (as was the case in the mid-1970s), it may be desirable to tolerate some unemployment. Why? Well, if we try to remove the unemployment, we should increase demand. But increased demand is an inflationary pressure and will at this point only worsen inflation. So to improve unemployment a little bit we would obtain a lot more inflation. So full employment isn't always the wisest immediate goal. And once again, the problems of knowing the level at which the economy will operate, the level at which full employment is reached, and the difference in the budget between the full-employment and actual levels all work to make this budget process somewhat imprecise.

Automatic stabilizers

Very few people would suggest that fiscal policy consists only of discretionary tools. When fiscal policy is discussed, automatic stabilizers are seldom mentioned precisely because no direct action is required. Many of the automatic stabilizers act in such a way that they tend to offset business cycles.

Automatic stabilizers are *automatic* in that they act on the economy without any intervention by economic policy makers. They are *stabilizing* in that they tend to create budgetary deficits when a recession begins; and they also create budget surpluses at full employment when inflation threatens.

There are three basic automatic stabilizers: (1) progressive tax structures; (2) unemployment insurance and welfare benefits; and (3) agricultural price floors and ceilings. (Actually, there are several other automatic stabilizers that are more limited in impact.) Recall that progressive taxes are those that take a greater percentage of income from the high-income citizens and a smaller percentage from the poor. The most important progressive taxes are personal income taxes. The number of people receiving unemployment and welfare benefits increase during hard times (in a recession) and decrease in good times. The U.S. government helps American agriculture by buying up surpluses and thereby keeping prices up. It is of further aid to the American economy by selling the surpluses during years of poor harvests; this helps keep prices from rising too high. All three of these programs were passed to help individuals in need. They have a residual benefit to the whole American economy by affecting aggregate demand. To see how they work consider Figure 4, which shows in slightly different fashion data we have seen before: the receipts and expenditures of the federal budget.

On the receipts side of the budget, many of the sources of funds are sensitive to changes in employment and economic activity. When a recession begins, sales of goods and services and employment start to decline. As a result, corporate income taxes, Social Security contributions, and excise taxes all decline immediately. The personal income tax is even more powerful. If a worker who had been fully employed starts working part-time, he pays taxes on a smaller income. Because of the nature of

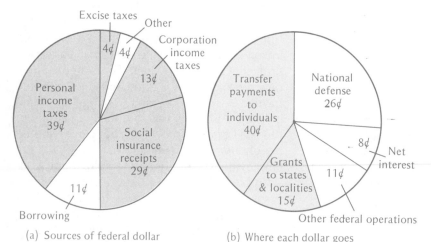

(a) Sources of federal dollar   (b) Where each dollar goes

Figure 4 (a) On the receipts side of the federal budget, automatic stabilizers are shown as shaded areas. The personal income tax is particularly effective as an automatic stabilizer. (b) On the expenditures side of the federal budget, the automatic stabilizer is shaded. Unemployment payments, Social Security benefits, and various welfare benefits—i.e., the types of transfer payments—are automatic stabilizers; for example, they all increase when the economy slows down and people are out of work.

income taxes, he may fall into a lower tax bracket. If so, he pays taxes at a lower tax rate on a smaller income. His taxes fall by a greater proportion than the income declines, which is the same as an automatic cut in taxes. Of course, if he becomes unemployed, his income stops and he pays no taxes at all. So as demand decreases, tax collections automatically decrease. Decreased tax collections allow more consumer spending, and therefore more demand, than would otherwise occur.

At the peak of the business cycle, the reverse occurs. As income increases, excise, corporate income, and social insurance tax collections all increase. Personal income taxes may increase even more rapidly. If a worker finds a better job, gets a pay raise, or gets a lot of overtime pay, he may end up in a higher tax bracket. If so, his taxes go up faster than his income. The increases in tax collections act as a force in creating an automatic budget surplus. In other words, the increased taxes automatically lessen demand and ease inflationary pressures.

Figure 5 illustrates the phenomenon. Government expenditures are held constant in the diagram, though we shall see in a moment that expenditures also respond to economic conditions. Let us say that the budget is balanced at full employment, which is Y*. If demand increases beyond Y*, taxes (T) will increase rela-

tive to government expenditures (G) and tend to reduce demand, helping to lessen inflation pressures. If a recession develops so that income falls below Y*, T becomes smaller than G, creating a budget deficit that stimulates the economy toward full employment. All of the changes in tax collections happen without any change in legislation. Changes in the economy result automatically in changes in tax collections. The policy measures occur and are directed in the proper direction without conscious action.

Return to Figure 4 to see that there are items such as transfer payments (unemployment and welfare benefits) that also tend to stabilize the economy. When a recession begins, benefit payments rise immediately and automatically. The greatest increase would be in payments under unemployment insurance. Social Security and other benefits also increase. Payments under various agricultural programs increase as do various veterans' benefit payments. The grants to states and communities also find their way through general assistance programs to people who are suffering as a result of the recession. All of these programs help raise demand when it is low by providing people with money to spend on the necessities of life. The reverse happens as the economy moves toward full employment or beyond.

While automatic stabilizers will help prevent business cycles, their beneficial forces are quite mild. If cycles are more severe (as they often are), the automatic stabilizers will not give adequate control. Discretionary fiscal policies are usually required to "aid" the automatic stabilizers. Over time, the entire system of automatic stabilizers may operate to create problems. During the late 1950s, income was rising, lifting families to higher tax brackets. With no increase in government expenditures, the tax burden increasingly depressed the economy. This effect is called **fiscal drag.** The fiscal drag of the 1950s was remedied by the tax cuts in the early 1960s.

The public debt

At the beginning of this chapter we looked at a sample budget of the U.S. government. We saw that the bottom line of receipts and expenditures showed a projected deficit—that is, more

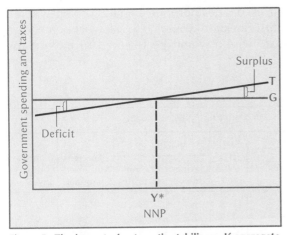

Figure 5 The impact of automatic stabilizers. If aggregate demand increases beyond Y*, taxes increase; the budget surplus reduces aggregate demand. If demand falls below Y*, taxes decrease; the resulting budget deficit stimulates demand back toward Y*.

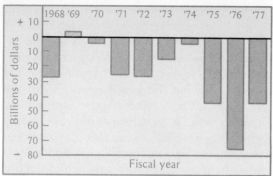

Figure 6 Annual federal surpluses and deficits are shown for 1968–1977 (years 1976 and 1977 are estimates). The last year our economy had a surplus was 1969. (The deficits are shown below horizontal line while the surplus is above the line.)

was to be spent than received (see Table 1 again). We also saw that the use of fiscal policy would result almost always in deficits and surpluses. Rarely would we have a balanced budget in any single year. With some luck we might balance the budget over a period of several years.

Figure 6 shows surpluses and deficits over the last decade. Notice that there have been many more deficits than surpluses. The last year we had a surplus was in 1969.

Since the beginning days of World War II up to now (nearly 40 years), we have had many more deficits than surpluses. In fact, the federal government has accumulated a deficit of $553.6 billion (as of September, 1975). This accumulated government spending deficit is known as the **public debt** (or **national debt**). (Thus the public debt differs from *private debt*, which is the accumulated debt of all individual

American consumers and firms.) The budget deficits are debts because the government has borrowed all that money—just as you or I incur debts by borrowing.

It is interesting to note who lends the government all that money. Surprisingly, the government itself lent part, since $142.3 billion came from various agencies and trust funds and $87 billion came from the Federal Reserve Bank. (See Table 2 for a breakdown of debt in recent years.) The remaining $324.4 billion came from outside the federal government. As one would expect, banks, insurance companies, and other corporations did some of the lending. Lower levels of government loaned $32.2 billion to the federal government. Various individuals loaned a lot of money; through the purchase of the $25, $50, $100, and other denomination savings bonds, people loaned their government $66.5 billion. Most readers will be familiar with savings bonds and some will be familiar with other kinds of bonds sold that net an additional $23.0 billion. Only $65.5 billion is owed to lenders who are not residents of the United States. This last amount is the most likely to cause difficulties since it is owed to others who might like to receive payment at some point in time.

Debt in itself is neither good nor bad. It is always necessary to consider (1) the ability to repay that debt, even if the debt is never to be repaid, and (2) the purpose for which the debt is used. The appropriate analysis to answer the first question would be to ask what percentage of income would be required to pay off the

Table 2
Ownership of Public Debt (in billions of dollars)

End of period	Total gross public debt	Held by—		Held by private investors							
		U.S. Govt. agencies and trust funds	Federal Reserve Banks	Financial corpora-tion*	Other cor-porations	State and local govts.	Individuals		Foreign and inter-national	Other misc. investors
							Savings bonds	Other securities		
1968	358.0	76.6	52.9	78.2	14.2	24.9	51.9	23.3	14.3	21.9
1969	368.2	89.0	57.2	67.5	10.4	27.2	51.8	29.0	11.2	25.0
1970	389.2	97.1	62.1	73.2	7.3	27.8	52.1	29.1	20.6	19.9
1971	424.1	106.0	70.2	75.4	11.4	25.4	54.4	18.8	46.9	15.6
1972	449.3	116.9	69.9	77.7	9.8	28.9	57.7	16.2	55.3	17.0
1973	469.9	129.6	78.5	69.6	10.9	29.2	60.3	16.9	55.6	19.3
1974	492.7	141.2	80.5	64.2	11.0	29.2	63.4	21.5	58.4	23.2
1975	553.6	142.3	87.0	90.0	15.0	32.2	66.5	23.0	65.5	32.3

Source: Federal Reserve Bulletin.
*These financial institutions are commercial banks, mutual savings banks, and insurance companies.

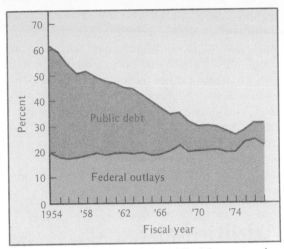

Figure 7 Federal outlays and the public debt expressed as percentage of GNP.

debt. Figure 7 illustrates the relationship. In 1954, both the debt and GNP were smaller than at present, but the debt was over 60% of production at that time. Over the years, the debt grew but income grew faster; so that by 1974, the debt was somewhat below 30% of current production. This represented a much more tolerable level of debt than was present earlier. Most of the present debt was the result of the necessity of fighting two World Wars. In the years since World War II the growth of public debt has been rather modest. Most of the deficits since 1960 occurred due to the use of fiscal policy and, later, the Vietnam War. Since 1974, the debt has been increasing relative to income. By 1977, it was over 30% of income again. In part, the reason for this was the deep recession of 1973–1975, which caused income to grow less rapidly.

This is not to say that the debt does not have to be handled with care. Management of government debt is an important aspect of fiscal policy. It is important that interest costs of the debt be kept as low as possible without unbalancing other parts of the economy. The size of the debt relative to income should be kept in balance. The debt should not be handled in such a way that it creates inflationary pressures.

However, the potential for difficulty is not an argument against public debt or private debt. It makes no more sense to say that a government should never borrow than it does to say that firms or individuals should never borrow. Firms borrow money for productive purposes and pay both the loan and the interest through their productive activities. People borrow money for consumption purposes. Many people have borrowed money to buy a house or car. When you pay for something with a credit card you are borrowing money also. Governments borrow for both production and consumption. That they do so wisely is important. The difference is that firms or people may have difficulty repaying the loan. A national government may not have to worry about repayment. One way the federal government could repay the debt is to print as much money as needed to pay off its creditors. At an extreme, the government could simply refuse to pay. Of course, the result would be to undermine the confidence of everyone, resident or not, in the integrity of the government. However, our debt is presently nowhere near so large as to even consider such extremes.

Some criticisms of the public debt

Over the years many worries have been expressed about the trouble that the public debt causes. Some of these worries are unfounded and others are potential problems only if the debt is handled recklessly. Let's consider the major criticisms of the public debt.

(1) *Can we go bankrupt from too much internally-held government debt?* Probably not, since the public debt is owed to the American public, not to any foreign nation. The debt need not be *retired* (paid off); the government only has to "roll over" the debt (that is, pay back bond cost plus interest each time a particular bond issue comes due). If the debt were owed to foreigners, then inability to pay could be a problem. It is possible to mismanage the debt. In such circumstances, the amount of money in the system could grow rapidly. The resulting inflation would be a serious problem. The difficulty is not the debt itself but the inflation created.

(2) *Does the debt shift the burden through time?* The question is usually asked in the form of, "Aren't we mortgaging our grandchildren?" Again, the answer is negative. The burden is borne by those who must give up goods and services. Since most of the debt is related to war, the choice for the federal government was to borrow to win the war, or to lose. Ultimately, the people who gave up the goods and services to fight the war bore the burden. They were denied consumer goods in order for the government to produce war supplies, and at that point the cost was incurred. The additional burden of inflation, when it occurs, is usually borne within a few years of the deficit(s).

(3) *Does the debt redistribute income?* In principle it could, but it is not clear that it does. The image of wealthy bondholders earning income from interest while not working at the expense of a poor working-class taxpayer is widely held but probably untrue. The studies have shown that taxpayers and bondholders are the same people for all income brackets. In fact, government bonds tend to be owned by relatively poor people with taxes paid by relatively wealthy people and corporations. Therefore, if anything, there is the possibility that income is shifted from high-income to low-income families by the debt.

(4) *Does government borrowing crowd out borrowing for capital investment?* This question came to be asked in the mid-1970s, when the public debt increased due to the recession. Since the government does borrow from many of the same sources as do private businesses, this could happen. However, it appears to be possible only after a long or deep economic downturn. There was a slight shortage of capital in the mid-1970s because the 1973–1975 recession was the worst recession since the Great Depression.

Advantages of the public debt

Is there any advantage to the debt? There are several things which may be said in favor of the debt. (1) The debt serves as basis for much of the money supply. Without it, there would be a great deal less money available, as will be seen in later chapters. (2) Many people are willing to lend to the government in order to make a "sure" profit. The bonds serve as an important asset for people who want more than savings account earnings but who are unwilling or unable to pursue income in the stock market or other riskier asset markets. The wealth held in government bonds enables many families to get through periods of economic hardship. (3) Ultimately, if it were not possible for the government to borrow, it would not be possible to undertake fiscal policy, and the economic instability would impose very high costs on our society.

Additional fiscal policy problems

What to do with a surplus

Both deficits and surpluses create problems. It would seem that a surplus is not serious, but there are difficulties. In the first place, it is difficult to achieve a surplus. It takes substantial will power to run a surplus budget position. A surplus would place a lid on economic prosperity. During a business cycle peak, people would want to benefit from the good times and would not be pleased to see their government put a damper on economic activity. Surpluses are indeed dampers. In the second place, if government policy is such that a surplus is accumulated, the best thing to do with it is keep it. Once again, people would not like to see their government building up piles of money when they would like to spend it themselves. It is very hard to convince people that the taxes being collected but not spent are really beneficial to the taxpayer.

It would seem reasonable to suggest that the surplus be used to retire government debt. However, it is not clear that households and firms that own government bonds would be willing to give them up. In fact, if economic conditions are good, people may be trying to buy more bonds in order to have a reserve against potential hard times ahead. If people are trying to loan their government money

Extended Example
The Great Shortfall Mystery

"Smoking Found Boon to Health." "Hell Frozen Over Says Exorcist." If you were to awake to such headlines some morning, you would probably rub your eyes to be sure they weren't deceiving you and then respond with an incredulous "So *what?*" In the fall of 1976, Americans awoke to news almost—some would say equally—as startling: the government was having great difficulty spending the taxpayers' money! Government experts were complaining that they had been unable to spend 2% of the projected budget, or $7.5 billion, originally scheduled to be spent in the first six months of the year. From July to September, the underspending problem had grown even worse. The total spending shortfall came to over $15 billion. This reduced aggregate demand and had a definite effect on slowing the economic recovery that had begun in the previous year.

How had the government's fiscal policy come to jump the tracks? The experts are still not sure. When they first became aware that spending was lagging behind budget predictions, they tended to believe the shortfall was the result of changes in government bookkeeping. Previously, the fiscal year ended on June 30, at which time all government agencies rushed to spend all their remaining funds before the deadline. In 1976, the government changed its fiscal year to end on September 30. Government officials figured that the usual end-of-fiscal-year spending bulge was merely being postponed from June to September. They were wrong. The expected bulge did not occur.

Another theory was that agency heads padded their budget estimates more than usual in fear of cutbacks by the conservative Ford administration. Another was that budget directors had allowed for more inflation in the economy than actually occurred. Another explanation was that there had been unusual delays in getting government contracts for spending outlays through the maze of bureaucratic red tape. The conspiratorial-minded suggested that administration officials, true to their pledge to hold down spending, were deliberately holding up expenditures already budgeted. There was, and is, no evidence that this was so.

The mystery remains a mystery. The cause of the shortfall may have been any one of those suggested, a combination of them—or, none of the above. Fiscal policy in our vast economy as administered by our vast governmental bureaucracy is a statistically imperfect albeit a potent tool. Even when it goes awry, it can have important effects. In the elections of 1976, Jimmy Carter defeated President Gerald Ford by the narrowest of margins. Who is to say that the spending shortfall of that year and its contribution to the recovery slowdown had nothing to do with Carter's victory?

(which is, in effect, what they are doing when buying savings bonds), the government may have trouble trying to pay back loans and retire debt. More importantly, it may be counterproductive fiscally to do so even if it is possible to retire debt. With regard to fiscal policy, the purpose of the surplus is to diminish total demand. Debt retirement would place the money back in the hands of consumers and investors; so this action would thwart the intended fiscal effect of the surplus.

What to do with a deficit

A government has the same problem as an individual when a deficit results. It must borrow to pay its bills. Unlike households or firms, a government, if its credit is good, may have more options. A government may borrow from other governments. During World War II, the United States loaned money and goods to other governments to conduct the war. A government may enter the market and borrow just as you and I do. If people are saving, there will be a market for government bonds. Of course, since consumers and investors are also trying to borrow, the government borrowing could divert goods and services from private uses.

During a trough of the business cycle, there may be no private demand and so savers would welcome the opportunity to buy government bonds. The deficit so financed would then stimulate the economy.

A national government has yet another alternative. The government may borrow by simply creating money. In the United States the Congress could authorize printing of money through Treasury Notes ("Greenbacks"). More likely, the new money would be created by selling government bonds to the Federal Reserve System. In exchange for the bonds, the Federal Reserve could give the government credit in a bank account or, if cash were required, issue new Federal Reserve Notes. Federal Reserve Notes are money or currency. Take a dollar bill from your wallet and you will see that it says Federal Reserve Note across the top. The mechanics of creating money through government borrowing will be outlined in detail in the next few chapters, which are on money.

Three problems in using fiscal policy

There are still difficulties involved in using fiscal policy. However, an imperfect tool may be better than none. Some of the problems relate to the timing of fiscal policy changes.

Accurate data *First, it must be possible to determine the need for fiscal policy changes.* Data become available only with a delay. Minor fluctuations in economic activity may be confused with major business cycle movements. It may not be clear to anyone that a change is needed for some time. By then, the size of the policy change may have to be larger than would have been required if the need had been detected earlier. Accurate assessments can be a further problem. For example, fiscal year 1975 was approached with a *proposed budget* that was to be $9.4 billion in deficit. On a high-employment basis this eventually turned out to be $11 billion too little; it was too restraining and added to the recession. As a result, this led to increased unemployment; so increased benefits under unemployment compensation pro-

grams added $6.5 billion to the deficit. Also in reaction to the recession, veterans' benefits were increased, adding another $4.4 billion to the deficit. These two unexpected increases plus many more resulted in a $20 billion increase on the expense side and a $14 billion decrease on the receipts side. The originally projected deficit of $9.4 billion quickly became a $43.6 billion deficit. Ironically, had the government budgeted a bigger deficit for fiscal stimulation, the actual resulting deficit might have been less.

Time lag *The second problem is the delay or time lag that results inevitably from a massive decision-making unit.* The Congress, President, and the large staffs of both need to coordinate. The exact plans for an expenditure or tax change must be worked out, debated, passed as law, and the appropriate changes conveyed to the responsible agencies for action. By this time the action may be too little and too late. In addition, even after the fiscal policy change is made, there are response lags in the economic system itself. If expenditures are increased, it may take the production system some time to begin producing the additional output. Tax changes may take longer to work through to changes in expenditures by firms and households.

Political problems *The third problem is probably the most serious: political difficulties.* It is not always possible to simply increase or decrease governmental expenditures. Certain firms or industries may benefit if expenditures in a particular area are increased. A cut in expenditures may result in plant closings or military base closings with resulting economic chaos in the communities affected. Taxes are not cut across the board. Which taxes or whose taxes are cut becomes the issue. Even personal income tax cuts may have different impacts. If a person is so low on the income scale that no taxes are paid, a tax cut is of no concern. Tax cuts may mean less to a household with a lot of deductions. Tax cuts may be only for certain income brackets. Thus the political arguments, especially in an election year, may hold up an otherwise agreed-upon policy move. Worse yet, political moves may prevent any change or result in expansionary policy when restraint is required.

Extended Example
Mr. Carter's $50 Misunderstanding

A tax rebate is an immediate, one-time transfer of funds to taxpayers. Usually, it is a fixed amount, although it could be scaled according to the tax bracket. A tax rebate to stimulate the economy and create jobs in a sluggish economy is often referred to as a "quick fix." Like a cut in tax rates (which operate more slowly than a rebate and over a longer period of time), a rebate is intended to put money into the pockets of consumers, who will spend it quickly, thus creating more demand for goods and services and consequently additional jobs. Sometimes, however, the quick fix can take too long to be approved, and by then, economic conditions have changed.

In January of 1977, newly elected President Jimmy Carter proposed a $50 rebate to all taxpayers as part of his fiscal policy to stimulate the economy. (Later it was adjusted to all taxpayers earning under $25,000 per year.) He lobbied hard for his proposal, telling Congressional leaders that the working people of the country would suffer if the rebate were denied. Then, in April, President Carter did a complete turnabout. The rebate, he said, was unnecessary and inflationary. In fact, if Congress passed any kind of a tax cut at all, he would veto it.

Why this sudden change in the nation's fiscal policy? According to the President and his spokesmen, economic conditions had changed so rapidly since the rebate plan's inception that it was no longer necessary. Almost every economic indicator was now pointing upward. Inflation, not recession, was now the enemy. A $11.4 billion across-the-board rebate would fuel additional inflation and higher unemployment. The quick fix could turn out to be a dangerous overdose.

All of which was probably true. The tax rebate plan had never had wide support. Economists who early on had read the signs of approaching recovery and business leaders who feared its inflationary potential rallied against the proposal. (Big business did not, however, oppose the investment credit plan which was part of Carter's stimulus package.) Big labor was also opposed. Some segments of the economy opposed the rebate as being too small to have much effect, and, indeed, the small size of the proposed rebate may have accounted in some degree for general lack of support for the plan among the public at large. So the rebate "died" that April.

In many ways, President Carter's decision concerning the $50 tax rebate was almost the exact mirror image of President Ford's similar flip-flop in the first days of Ford's administration. Ford started out with a "Whip Inflation Now" campaign, which included calling on Congress to raise taxes. But Congress postponed action, and in a few months, as the recession deepened, the President was calling for a tax cut. He got the cut, which undoubtedly contributed to moving the economy out of the recession.

A final note: Some waggish economists have suggested that President Carter's handling of the $50 tax rebate proposal in early 1977 was really a brilliant economic ploy. Because people were led to expect the rebate, they rushed out to spend the money before they had it in hand—in the grand old American tradition of buy now, pay later. Consequently, the economy boomed, and the rebate was no longer necessary.

Summary

An economic equilibrium may be undesirable: there may be either too much unemployment or too much inflation. Any equilibrium can be changed by *fiscal policy:* that is, by adjusting government spending and taxing policies.

The federal budget is a device for planning federal expenditures. Thus it can help plan fiscal policy. OMB and CBO work together to coordinate the massive federal budget. The budget is proposed by the executive branch and approved by the legislative branch. A budget covers the federal fiscal year from October 1 to September 30.

The largest source of federal revenue is personal income taxes. The largest spending category is transfer payments to individuals.

Discretionary fiscal policy is the change in the budget balance (or imbalance) to stimulate or restrain the economy by changing private demand for goods and services. A budget deficit will stimulate the economy by increasing the private demand for goods and services.

Nondiscretionary fiscal policy relies upon measures which operate to unbalance the budget in response to changes in the economy rather than the result of conscious budget action. These measures are called automatic stabilizers and include such things as unemployment compensation and the progressive personal income tax.

Fiscal policy may be accomplished by changing tax collections while holding federal government expenditures constant. Conversely, fiscal policy may require a change in expenditures holding tax collections constant. Both expenditures and tax collections may be utilized together.

Stimulating the economy means increasing aggregate demand; this increase can be accomplished by either a tax cut or an expenditure increase. Restraining or dampening the economy means decreasing aggregate demand; this can be done by a tax increase or an expenditure decrease.

Tax collections refer to the dollar amount collected. The tax rate is the proportion of income or purchase which is collected in taxes. Tax collections can usually be changed by changing the tax rate. Therefore, fiscal policy may require a change in the tax rate, but whether tax collections change as well depends upon what happens to the value of the item taxed.

Multipliers may be used to calculate the effect on the economy of a change in fiscal policy. The government expenditures multiplier is the same as the investment multiplier, namely 1/MPS. The tax multiplier is smaller; it is equal to MPC/MPS. A change in taxes has a strong effect on the economy. However, a change in expenditures has a stronger effect than a tax change (for an equal amount). This difference is reflected by the balanced budget multiplier. The effect that equal increases (or decreases) in expenditures and taxes have on NNP is always in favor of expenditures. The balanced budget multiplier is always 1.

There are a variety of budget philosophies. These include the continuously balanced budget, the Swedish Budget (or budget balanced over the cycle), the fully managed budget, and the full-employment budget.

Automatic stabilizers help lessen the effects of the business cycle. There are three basic automatic stabilizers: (1) progressive taxes; (2) transfer payments; and (3) agricultural price floors and ceilings.

If a budget deficit occurs, the amount of the deficit must be borrowed. The total amount of such borrowings is the national debt. Our present level of national debt is about 30% of current production (GNP).

If the national debt were mismanaged, it could undermine our monetary system and cause a great deal of inflation. Deficits could also pose a problem if the borrowing by government crowds out borrowing by private firms; in such a case a capital shortage would occur.

The national debt has three advantages: (1) it serves as a basis for much of the money supply; (2) in the form of savings bonds, it helps poor and middle-income people earn more money than they could with bank accounts; (3) it enables the continued use of fiscal policy for lessening the effects of the business cycle.

Key Words and Phrases

- **federal budget** a complete listing of all sources of revenue and the amounts of each outlay for the federal government (and many of its agencies).

- **fiscal year** a year for which a budget is planned; it may differ from a calendar year. For the federal government it runs October 1 to September 30.

- **Office of Management and Budget (OMB)** an organization in the executive branch of the federal government which assists the President in planning federal expenditures and in managing the operations of the government.

- **Congressional Budget Office (CBO)** a parallel organization to OMB in the legislative branch of the federal government; this office assists the Congress in planning, funding, and analyzing various spending and taxing proposals.
- **ceiling** a maximum level for spending or debt.
- **actual budget** the budget after the actions of the Congress have been completed; the actual budget isn't known until the end of the fiscal year.
- **proposed budget** the budget figures that are submitted by the President to the Congress for approval and action.
- **fiscal policy** decisions of the federal government on the use of tax collection policy or spending policy to stimulate or restrain the economy.
- **discretionary fiscal policy** policy actions taken in response to specific economic problems such as inflation or unemployment.
- **nondiscretionary fiscal policy** changes in tax collections or government expenditures which result automatically from changes in the economy.
- **automatic stabilizers** the group of legislated economic programs which respond to changes in the economy without conscious action to dampen the business cycle; these programs include unemployment compensation, Social Security, graduated personal income tax, and various subsidy programs.
- **expansionary fiscal policy** increases in federal government expenditures or reduction in tax collections designed to offset a recession by increasing the demand for goods and services.
- **budget deficit** a situation where government expenditures exceed tax collections.
- **contractionary fiscal policy** decreases in federal government expenditures or increases in tax collections designed to offset inflation at the peak of the business cycle by reducing demand for goods and services.
- **tax rate** the percent or proportion of income or expenditure which is collected for tax purposes; sales or excise taxes are expressed as a certain percent of the selling price and personal income tax as a percent of income.
- **tax collections** the dollar amount of taxes collected; the amount collected depends upon the tax rate and the value of the income or purchase taxed.
- **tax multiplier** a number which may be multiplied times the change in tax collections to determine the change in the equilibrium output of the economy; in the simple economy, it is MPC/MPS.

- **balanced budget multiplier** when government expenditures and taxes are increased equal amounts, equilibrium NNP increases by an amount equal to the expenditures; thus the balanced budget multiplier is always 1.
- **continuously balanced budget** a federal government budget which is always in balance regardless of economic conditions. This budget philosophy leads to a budget which is procyclical; that is, it adds to the business cycle.
- **Swedish Budget** a philosophy which has the budget in balance over the business cycle but which is in deficit during the decline and trough phases and in surplus during the expansion and peak stages.
- **budget surplus** a situation where tax collections exceed the expenditures.
- **fully managed budget** a budget philosophy which says the budget should be either balanced, or in surplus, or in deficit depending upon the needs of the economy and the stage of the business cycle.
- **fine tuning** the close monitoring of changes in the economy and the precise application of the correct fiscal and monetary policies.
- **full-employment budget** a budget concept which adjusts expenditures and tax collections so that aggregate demand is always at a level that would maintain full employment.
- **fiscal drag** the tendency of automatic stabilizers to prevent a high-employment economy from reaching its full growth potential; as national income rises, many people move into higher tax brackets, and these increased tax collections create unplanned surpluses.
- **national (or public) debt** the accumulated federal budget deficits; the debt results from federal government borrowing.
- **private debt** the amount owed by firms and individuals on their own behalf.

Questions for Review

1. Describe each of the budget philosophies. What is meant by the statement that "a continuously balanced budget is procyclical"?

2. If unemployment is "too high" to be politically acceptable, what fiscal policy should be followed? Why?

3. If inflation threatens, what fiscal policy would you recommend to the Congress and President? Why?

4. What powers do you attribute to the OMB and CBO? How are they different?

5. Find a present copy of the federal budget. Is it in deficit or surplus? What is the total amount to be spent? How much will be spent on education?

6. To increase income by $50 billion, would you use an increase in government expenditures or a tax cut? Why? Which would require the smaller increase in the deficit?

7. What is the role of the MPC in determining the effect of fiscal policy? Is it different for taxes than for expenditures?

8. With high unemployment, hiring unskilled workers to level the southern Appalachians and fill in the Gulf of Mexico would be desirable. Why or why not?

9. Suggest ways the national debt can be harmful to the economy.

10. Does the balanced budget multiplier apply if the budget is not in balance initially?

11. Start at full employment with the federal budget in balance. Show why it must go into deficit if a recession begins.

12. Suppose the fiscal policy-makers offer a tax credit to businesses if they increase investment expenditures. What will happen to the federal budget? What will happen to the expenditures of both the public and the private sectors?

Part Three

Money, Banking, and Monetary Policy

11

Money and the Banking System

We now turn to discuss what many people would call their favorite item or label as a modern-day magic wand: Money. If you possessed enough of it, you could have leisure time, be able to travel everywhere, and own or buy everything you wanted. To obtain money, people have lied, cheated, robbed, and killed. So it comes as no surprise that some people believe money to be "the root of all evil," or a taint corrupting all of society. Certain self-sufficient communes set up in the early 1970s tried to do without money.

The economist's view of money is much more tempered. Money is seen neither as a cure-all nor as the root of all evil. To understand the role of money in society, we will first look at how the need for it developed. The conditions requiring the use of money tell us a lot about its functions.

Aspects of money

Primitive societies: life without money

Our earliest, primitive ancestors were part of an atomistic society. That is, their level of organization was no larger than the individual family or very small group. There was no need for money because each family met all of its needs. There were few worries as to the difference between needs and wants. The major task of these early people was survival, to supply basic needs: food, clothing, and shelter. These early families hunted or gathered their own food, provided their own clothing, and built or found their own shelter. We might even say the lives of these individuals were very similar to the situation of a Robinson Crusoe.

At some point in human history, various groupings of these early peoples started to *differentiate tasks;* there developed a small degree of specialization. One individual might be a hunter, another a farmer, another a medicine man, another a leader or chief, and another may have become a craftsman. We describe this type of society and economy as ruled by *barter.* Money still wasn't needed because people exchanged what they had for what they wanted—that is, they bartered. Those who fashioned tools, weapons, and ornaments traded with the farmers and hunters for food. The medicine man offered protection from evil spirits, thereby ensuring favorable conditions for a good harvest; so the farmers would each contribute a certain amount of food to this protector.

It is not too hard to see that as primitive society became more highly organized and specialized, the barter system would start to prove quite cumbersome. Suppose a farmer brings his freshly harvested artichokes to town. If he wants a new pair of overalls, he must look for a clothier or tailor who wants to dine on artichokes. This is called a *double coincidence of wants.* A great deal of time could be spent matching up people with other people who want to make an exchange. Another time waste in barter would be the haggle over the exchange rate. How many artichokes to a pair of overalls. The answer would depend on how well the harvest went, the distance the artichokes were transported, how much fabric is available, etc. So the rate may have to be decided anew at every exchange. Clearly we have reached the point where money must be (and was) introduced into the economic system. Having looked at what would happen without money, we are now prepared to look at money for what it does or why it is desired.

Functions of money

One way of looking at money is to consider the functions it performs. We have seen how hard it is to organize a modern economy without money. Therefore, we should be able to do things with money that we could not do when there was none. In fact, there are four basic things that money does for an economy and the people in it.

Medium of exchange The main function of money is to avoid the necessity of finding the double coincidence of wants. If anyone makes a product, they sell it for money. The farmer need not find a clothier who also likes artichokes. He sells the artichokes for money. In fact, he need not even find the consumer of his produce. The farmer will sell his product for money to someone who will find artichoke eaters. The pants, insecticide, or space-shuttle manufacturers can sell their product for money. Similarly, those who perform services may do so for money. The physician, lawyer, musician, or computer programmer performs the service in exchange for money. This function of money is called the *medium of exchange*.

Unit of account Money solves another problem. If artichokes sold for forty cents and a pair of overalls for twelve dollars, then it would be easy to decide how many artichokes would exchange for a pair of overalls. The clothier may sell more than overalls. If he also sells shirts and socks, we may want to know how much he sells in total. We could report how many shirts, socks, and overalls were sold. With money, we could simplify and summarize what he sold by reporting the money total. This function of money is called the *unit of account*.

Standard of deferred payment Suppose a computer programmer needed his appendix out immediately but did not want to pay for it right now. Without money, it would be difficult enough to arrange an exchange of surgery for a computer program at a moment in time. It is even more difficult to talk about surgery now in exchange for a computer program two years from now. With money, the physician does not have to anticipate his needs two years from now. He merely expresses a price in terms of money. The price stated may be higher compared with the price at the moment because of the delay in payment. However, a money price is readily stated. This function of money is called a *standard of deferred payment*.

Store of value Finally, suppose the farmer does not have any immediate needs. He would be forced to hold his artichoke crop if there were no money. He would have to protect them from the weather, insects, spoilage, and theft. There would be substantial difficulties encountered in doing so. The situation is even worse when services are involved. The physician cannot perform surgery today and then put the operation on the shelf until he is ready to convert it to money. In both cases, it is better to sell immediately and hold money until an expenditure is necessary. Money is not the only thing that they could hold. They could

have bought diamonds or art work and held them. Also, money may not be a perfect way to ensure the ability to purchase at a later date. If prices change, the goods or services you can purchase may increase or decrease. Yet, money is still a very good way to produce and sell something now even though a purchase will not be made until later. This function of money is called the *store of value*.

Money then is anything which can adequately perform the above functions. As a *medium of exchange*, it facilitates transactions involving goods or services. As a *unit of account*, money allows comparison of very different things or literally allows us to add apples and oranges. A *standard of deferred payment* means that money may be used to separate in time the exchange of a good or service and the payment for that good or service. Working the other way, money serves as a *store of value* which enables us to receive payment at the moment and postpone a purchase until a later time.

Demand for money

Another way of defining money is in terms of the *reasons money is desired*. At first, it would seem obvious that money is desired because it performs the functions just mentioned. Of course, that is a correct response. There are, however, times when looking at the motives for holding money gives a different perspective than studying what money does. Different problems require different approaches. The approach which looks at the reasons for wanting money arrives at three categories or motives.

Transactions

The most obvious reason for holding money is to spend it. Most expenditures can be planned, if not in detail, at least by broad general type. When you leave the house in the morning, you know you need bus fare to and from work or classes. You also need lunch money. Since you don't know what will be on the menu, you cannot know for sure how much money but you can estimate an amount. Thus *planned transactions* will require that money be available.

Most people in our society receive money at intervals. Usually, the receipt is because of a paycheck received weekly, biweekly, or monthly. For students, the receipts may come only once a semester or infrequently in letters from home. The idea is to stretch the money until the next receipt. Figure 1 shows the typical time pattern. The receipts are shown at regular intervals. Immediately after the receipt, money holdings are high. However, as transactions are made, the balances decline. Most people have experienced the necessity of stretching a few dollars to the next payday.

Precautionary

Most people also have some money in reserve for unplanned expenditures. It is essentially "mad money." The difference in the type of transaction is only a matter of degree. Lunch is planned at least in general. *Precautionary balances* are sums of money which are available for those situations which we all know happen but which are not planned. We tend to think of such events as bad. The necessity of fixing a flat tire or paying a traffic ticket are examples. There are also happy events. Precautionary balances may be used to take advantage of a sale at the record counter of your favorite store.

Speculative

The third motive for holding money is called the *speculative motive*. Money held for this purpose is held as an asset rather than as something to be spent. The speculation is on the price of stocks and bonds. If you expect the prices of stocks and bonds (securities) to fall, then you will hold money until they actually decline. Then the purchase is made. Money becomes one of several assets that may be held because of its future value. Money in your pocket does not earn interest, but its price in terms of money never changes. Other assets such as stocks and bonds pay interest but their price may also change. The person holding money has to decide which way the price of securities will move. If the price appears low, the money holder may expect the price of securities to rise. In this case our "speculator" would no longer hold money; the securities would be bought and held. The speculative motive relates the demand for money to the movement in prices of the securities and the earnings possible.

It may not be possible to go through your wallet and decide why you are holding each piece of money you find there. For most students, the little bit that is there is soon to be spent. The transactions motive dominates the others. The luckier ones will be able to hold some precautionary balances. Speculative balances are probably absent. Even if an individual does not know why he or she is holding each piece, the idea of the three motives is useful when studying why money is used.

What has served as money

Commodity money

Whether an economist concentrates on the functions money serves or the reasons for holding money, the things which may serve as money are quite diverse. Many items or commodities have been used. As people went from barter societies to more advanced economies, money had to be invented. At first some forms of money were related to something useful. Arrowheads were used in some early societies.

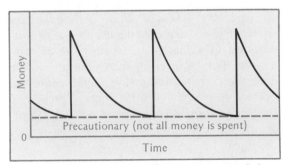

Figure 1 Level of money holdings over an extended period of time. The broken line represents precautionary balances, which means not all money is spent.

They were fairly standard items and, in a pinch, could always be used on an arrow. They easily served as a medium of exchange. Because they required effort to manufacture, they could also serve as a store of value. Unless someone could find a quick and easy way to make arrowheads, they would never fall in value.

Not all primitive moneys were hard or durable. Hides served as money in some instances. In the frontier period, the beaver skin was often the money used. As settlements developed, the hides were not used directly. Trappers would place their hides in a warehouse. Only the warehouse receipt was actually passed around. Being smaller, lighter, and less smelly than hides, the receipts were readily acceptable. They were a simple form of paper money.

Not all early moneys were necessarily useful. The strings of beads, known as wampum, used by Indians could serve as decoration but had no other immediate use. Wampum served very well as money. While anyone could make wampum, it was not easy to do so. The right stones and shells had to be found, polished into beads, drilled, and strung on the sinews. If wampum was in short supply, an Indian would gladly make more since it would exchange for deer meat or whatever he wanted advantageously. If wampum were plentiful, it might be easier to shoot the deer rather than go to the effort of making wampum. There was a tendency for the amount of wampum to be self-regulatory so it was always in adequate supply but not overabundant.

Not all products used for money were quite so difficult to produce in abundance. In the early days of Virginia, tobacco leaves served as money. They were a consumable product. However, the farmers quickly realized that they would be better off if they planted tobacco which grew tall and rank. They could also add as much manure as they could find. The tobacco plants would produce a lot of large leaves and do so quickly. The only difficulty with this was that the British soon complained that the tobacco was totally unfit to smoke.

Some money has no practical usefulness at all. You may have heard of the residents of an island in the South Pacific who use huge stones as money. The stones are carved in the shape of a doughnut. They may be six feet in diameter and weigh a great deal. They obviously do not circulate in the usual sense for it is nearly impossible to move them. They remain in one place at all times. If a transaction occurs, ownership of the money changes but it does not move. The society is such that all members are aware of who owns which pieces of money and when the ownership changes.

Commodity money can develop during times of severe crisis. For example, in post-World War II Germany, cigarettes served as money for the first couple of years.

Coins

Coins are actually a form of commodity money, since the substance from which a coin is made has been, until recently, a valuable commodity. As early as the sixth century B.C., the idea of coins began to develop. The larger ingots of metal were cut into smaller standard weight pieces that could easily be passed from hand to hand. One early society cast the metal into animal shapes which denoted the value of the coin. Later, a more practical wedge-shaped piece was used; the word "coin" derives from the Latin term meaning "wedge." Coins eventually were made (we say "struck" or "minted") by placing the metal on an anvil and striking it with a hammer and die which imprinted the coin on one side only.

Various metals have been used for coins by differing societies. Gold, silver, copper, and bronze have been preferred. There were two reasons for using these metals. *First, they are relatively soft and thus are easily worked by primitive methods.* For example, these metals could easily be formed into tokens and marked so that all would know which king had issued the coin. *The second reason for preferring these metals, especially gold and silver, is that they are relatively scarce and are valuable for use as commodities.* If the metal was worth more as commodity than as a coin, many people would melt the coin to obtain the metal. More importantly, scarcity of the metals prevented the king from easily expanding the supply of money and thereby making the money worthless.

The practice of *milling the edges* of coins (that is, making the little ridges) was adopted to prevent people from shaving away part of the coin. The term "debasing a currency" arose from the practice of adding base metals such as lead or iron to the gold or silver in order to make existing stocks of the valuable metal into increased numbers of coins.

Coins now are essentially tokens and do not take their value from the metal contained in the coin. For example, Canadian coins are made of aluminum. In the United States there is almost no nickel metal in the five-cent piece, though we still call it a nickel. Coins from a dime to a half-dollar are made of layers of several metals. Except for the difficulty of converting all coin-operated machines, a practical suggestion would be to make coins of plastic. Many people, however, fear this action because it would be very easy to expand the number of coins indefinitely or at least until the plastic was more valuable than the face value of the coin.

Paper money

Paper money probably had its origins in various warehouse receipts. When people took their gold to the goldsmiths they got a receipt for it. Since the goldsmith had to have a vault for his own gold, he often kept gold for other merchants or individuals. After a while, people would simply exchange the receipts rather than bothering to go to the goldsmith and claim their gold. The goldsmiths eventually made out the receipt in such a way that whoever was holding it could claim the gold. However, since the paper was more convenient, almost no one ever actually wanted metal.

Other receipts also circulated, as has been noted. Warehouse receipts for furs were widely circulated in frontier America. In some instances a farmer would receive a credit for produce sold to a merchant. The receipt could also be used for money since it could always be turned in at the store for desired goods.

When governments got in the business of issuing paper money, it was often in the form of a receipt for metal, especially gold and silver. The paper money was more convenient so it circulated rather than the metal. Sometimes paper was used only for large amounts. For example, there was a time when a $5.00 bill was the smallest paper bill available. Coins were used for smaller amounts. At other times, paper has been used for very small amounts such as dimes and quarters. Federal paper money (our "greenbacks") was first issued in the United States in 1861: $5, $10, and $20 notes appeared.

The type of paper money we have been discussing was backed by something of value, like gold. However, there were times when governments issued paper with nothing more than faith in the government for backing. The use of such money is often associated with periods of stress, such as a war. The Continental Congress issued paper notes; these notes were issued in such great numbers that they were the source of the phrase "not worth a continental." Treasury notes were also used in the War of 1812 and the Civil War. The issues of the Confederacy were of the same type.

Definitions of money today

The heading of this section implies that money can be easily defined. Certainly when you reach in your pocket and pull out a coin, you *know* what money is. This part of money is what everyone agrees is money. However, most people—and nearly all economists—are inclined to include more than coins in the definition. Exactly how much more is included is subject to some disagreement. The disagreement is resolved (in part) by offering more than one definition of money!

Currency

Our first component of money is currency. **Currency** consists of both coins and paper money. Probably no one would dispute that currency is money. In December, 1975, we had $73.7 billion in currency (see Table 1). Of this sum, $65 billion was in paper money and almost $9 billion in coins.

Today in the United States paper money consists entirely of Federal Reserve Notes. These notes are also referred to as *fiat money*. That is, the notes are money because the law says they are money. However, paper money does have "backing." At one time our paper money was backed by gold. Since the 1930s, though, paper money in the United States has not been backed by gold. Instead, the backing for paper money consists of a number of items known as *collateral*, which is held by the Federal Reserve System. We will discuss collateral for paper money later in this chapter.

Until recently, the Treasury used some silver in coins. Also, small bills called silver certificates were in use for a while. Then in the early 1970s all silver was withdrawn from the minting of coins. The Treasury still provides coins, but they are made of less costly metals.

Demand deposits

The next component of money is **demand deposits.** *Demand deposits are the amounts that people and firms have in their checking accounts.* This is the largest segment of the money supply. At the end of 1975, the total amount of demand deposits was $221.3 billion. Money in demand deposit form is very convenient. When you make a transaction, you write out a check for the exact amount. There is no need to make change. You also have a record of the purchase. Some may question whether a check is as acceptable as currency. In most cases it is, at least with proper identification. In fact, currency is not always acceptable either. Try to ride a bus in most cities and make payment with a very good $10 bill. Acceptability is not everything when defining money.

Narrow money, M_1

The two items just mentioned, currency and demand deposits, make up the money supply. This definition of money is called **narrow money,** or M_1:

M_1 = currency + demand deposits.

Notice that only those forms of money which do not pay interest are included. Neither currency nor demand deposits pay interest to the owner. As can be seen in Table 1, the total amount for M_1 is $295 billion as of December, 1975. Of course, this is the sum of the columns showing currency and demand deposits.

Near-moneys: other definitions of money

Table 2 shows other definitions of money. M_1 was called narrow money. It is the least inclusive definition. Sometimes economists like to include other assets in the definition of money, since these assets are a store of value. These other assets pay interest to the owner but are so much like money that they are included in the definition of money. These broader measures of money are known as **near-moneys.** Which definition is used may depend upon the problem being analyzed. We will look at the definitions first. The need for different definitions of money will become clearer in the next few chapters.

M_2 In Table 1, time deposits *at commercial banks* are shown. **Time deposits** include the familiar passbook savings account. This may be the regular account or one of the several special accounts that most banks offer. Time deposits also include the *certificates of deposit* (CD's). (For the moment, we are interested only in the smaller certificates; that is, the certificates less than $100,000 in size.) The total of savings deposits and CD's in commercial banks was $368.3 billion in December, 1975.

Returning to Table 2, we see that the next definition of money is called M_2. This definition of money adds the savings or time deposits at commercial banks to M_1:

$M_2 = M_1$ + time deposits
   = currency + demand deposits +
                          time deposits.

The total was $663.3 billion at the end of 1975. Thus M_2 is currency, demand deposits, and time deposits at commercial banks.

M_3 The next broadest definition of money is M_3. In Table 2, we see that this amount was $1091.9 billion at the end of 1975. To see how

Table 1
Components of Money Stock Measures (in billions of dollars, seasonally adjusted*)

| Time period | Currency | Demand deposits | Commercial banks | | | Nonbank thrift institu- tions |
| | | | Time deposits | | | |
			CD's	Savings accounts	Total	
1972 (Dec.)	56.9	198.4	43.6	270.0	313.6	319.6
1973 (Dec.)	61.5	209.0	63.5	300.9	364.4	348.0
1974 (Dec.)	67.8	215.3	89.8	329.3	419.1	369.2
1975 (Dec.)	73.7	221.3	82.9	368.3	451.2	428.6

Source: Federal Reserve Bulletin.
*Seasonally adjusted: Some data series have regular patterns of change which are associated with the season of the year or the calendar. By statistical analysis, this pattern may be identified and removed. Then it is possible to see how the data are really changing without the confusing movements caused by the seasonal pattern.

we extend money to this definition, look at the column headed "Nonbank thrift institutions" in Table 1. In December, 1975, this portion of M_3 was $428.6 billion. Included in this total are all deposits at savings and loan associations, mutual savings banks, and credit unions. The grounds for treating these entries as money are strong, since people have ready access to their deposits. In some instances, they can make automatic transfers to their checking account so these balances are very much like money. Thus M_3 is money defined as currency, demand deposits, time deposits at commercial banks, and deposits at nonbank thrift institutions:

$$M_3 = M_2$$
$$+ \text{ deposits at nonbank thrift institutions.}$$

A final word on money definitions There are broader definitions of money that are sometimes used. Economists go on to define M_4, M_5, etc. These definitions include large certificates of deposit and some of the near-moneys which

exist. These near-moneys are usually rather short-term securities. Included would be the 90-day notes on bills issued by the Treasury Department. These securities are almost money because they are so **liquid;** that is, they can be turned into other forms of money almost instantly. While these near-moneys are important in some cases, we run the risk of not knowing where to stop. There are many assets which are close to being money. Stocks and bonds are quite easily marketed. Some goods or commodities are easily exchanged. Should all these be called money? We must stop somewhere.

So for our needs M_3 is a sufficiently broad definition. In fact, unless otherwise indicated, *our use of the word "money" will be limited to M_1, narrow money.* We now turn to those institutions responsible for creating and managing the money supply in the United States: the commercial banking system and its regulator, the Federal Reserve System.

Commercial banks and money

The money used in the United States is dependent not upon gold or valuable metals but upon a highly organized banking system. **Commercial banks** are privately owned, profit-making firms dealing in service-oriented activities. Because they handle the community's

Table 2
Measures of Money Stock
(in billions of dollars, seasonally adjusted)

Period	M_1	M_2	M_3
1972 (Dec.)	255.3	525.3	844.9
1973 (Dec.)	270.5	571.4	919.5
1974 (Dec.)	283.1	612.4	981.6
1975 (Dec.)	295.0	663.3	1091.9

Source: Federal Reserve Bulletin.

Economic Thinker
John Law

Like prophets, economists are sometimes without honor in their own country. Born in 1671 in Edinburgh, Scotland, John Law was to have his economic theories rejected in his native land. They were, however, later taken up by the French government. Law himself was to become the leading financier and one of the most powerful men in France—until bad luck and overexpansion brought his financial enterprises to an end.

In 1694, Law killed a man in a duel and fled, under sentence of death, to Amsterdam, where he studied banking. He returned to Scotland in 1700 and, in 1705, published *Money and Trade Considered*. He proposed plans for revenue and trade reforms and for establishment of a national bank. Parliament rejected his proposals and Law went to France, hoping he would be better received in that financially troubled country.

King Louis XIV had recently died and French finances were in critical condition. After some struggle and disappointments, Law succeeded in interesting the new regent, Philippe II, in his proposals for saving France from economic ruin.

Law believed that expansion of credit and issuance of paper money would stimulate trade and commerce. Law argued that paper money was vastly superior to coin as a medium of exchange. It was easier to produce, cheaper to move and store, and was readily divisible into any needed amount for individual transactions. Law also argued for establishment of a private bank empowered to issue paper money in order to stimulate the economy.

In 1716, Philippe II chartered to "Mr. Law and Company" a private bank permitted to issue paper currency. Two years later, the bank was made the Royal Bank of France, with its paper notes guaranteed by the state. Bank paper was accepted by the state as tax payments and soon the use of the bank's paper money was prevalent throughout all France. Law's economic policies served the nation well. Unemployment dropped, inflation was curbed, and investment prospered. Law was appointed state controller general of finance.

In 1717 Law had formed a company to acquire monopoly rights to all commercial trade in the new world's Louisiana Territory, which at that time belonged to France and was known as "Mississippi." Based on monopoly of the territory's manufacture and export of tobacco, Law's company prospered. It bought out other international trading companies and became the Company of the Indies. Law merged his company with the Royal Bank and took over most of France's public debt and the administration of public revenues.

Law sold shares in his huge company to the public. The public bought the shares in a frenzy of speculation. Men fought publicly for the privilege of buying shares. Almost everyone in France except the utterly destitute rushed to invest in Law's company. Law assured investors that investment in his company would bring them great wealth, not only through monopoly of commerce but also through mining of the Louisiana Territory's fabulous store of gold and precious stones.

For a time, it looked as if Law was right. Company profits soared, and the value of its shares rose fiftyfold in two short years. Fortunes were made overnight. But the bubble was soon to burst. The Louisiana Territory was not nearly as rich in resources as Law had thought. It was certainly not rich enough to return a profit to each of the thousands of people who had invested their francs in Law's company. The value of its shares began to fall.

Despite Law's brilliance as a financier, there was one major flaw in his thinking. He believed that stock shares were basically currency and could be manipulated as such. He

tried to stabilize the value of his company's stock in much the same way that currency value may be stabilized. He put a fixed value on the shares, to be supported by the treasury of the Royal Bank of France. When investors began to trade their stock for bank currency, the nation's money supply grew rapidly and inflation grew apace. Law then made a great blunder. He chose to deflate the value of his stock and the value of the nation's currency in an effort to combat inflation. A financial panic ensued as investors rushed to sell their shares in fear that inflated prices and deflated currency would soon make their investment worthless.

Law and the French government did their best to stem the tide. At one point, the government even rounded up hundreds of beggars, gave them picks and shovels, and marched them through the streets of Paris. It was hoped that the people would believe the beggars were actually a band of eager emigrants off to the new world to mine the riches waiting there. But the value of Law's company shares continued to fall. And, since the value of currency was tied to the value of the stock, currency value also fell. The French economy sunk further into depression. Eventually, the King removed the Royal Bank's support of the stock in an effort to restore the value of French currency. But to no avail. Soon the value of the stock and of paper currency fell to zero. The nation returned to gold as the only viable medium of exchange. Law's monetary system had collapsed. In December, 1720, he fled the country in disgrace. In 1729, Law died in Venice, where he had been able to support himself by his prowess as a gambler.

Ultimately, John Law was a failure, but a magnificent one. The collapse of his system did much to discredit, at least temporarily, the concepts of national banks and paper currency. Nevertheless, his policies had worked well for a time. In a few short years, he succeeded in raising the French economy from depression to prosperity and in establishing much-needed tax and monetary reforms. Most importantly, perhaps, Law was, in a sense, a prophet of a newly emerging system of economics—the system we today call capitalism. Financier, entrepreneur, risk-taker, he was a forerunner of many like-minded capitalists who would help to develop that system in the years to come.

money, commercial banks need the trust of the community. (As a result, many banks engage in public relations activities such as providing meeting rooms and other services to the community to keep as much good will as possible.)

Most people look to a commercial bank as a place to keep money and other valuables. Some people keep various valuables locked in a safe-deposit box in the bank vault. More often, however, money is deposited in an account at a commercial bank. If the money is to be used soon, the owner will probably have a **checking account,** which means that money may be obtained or used by writing an order to the bank to transfer funds to another person or firm. This "order" for transfer of funds is a **check.** If the money is to be kept for longer periods, the deposit will probably be kept in a **savings account.** Commercial banks pay interest on the deposits in savings accounts as an inducement to customers to place their money and leave it in the bank.

The commercial bank does not make any money directly from its checking or savings deposits. Why does the commercial bank encourage customers to make deposits then? Well, because the commercial bank does not simply hold money for its customers, but uses the deposits to earn income. One basic source of income is to use deposits to buy income-earning assets. Chief among these purchased assets are bonds issued by the government (state, local, and federal). The other basic source of income is to make loans and charge the borrowers a fee called the *interest rate*. For example, a commercial bank that pays a 5% interest rate to its savers may charge a 9% interest rate to its borrowers who obtain loans. Roughly speaking, the bank retains the 4% difference for profit and to cover costs.

With regard to the national economy, the most important activity of banks is making loans available for business investment, *mortgages* (loans for purchasing houses), and other individual needs. Part of this money for loans comes from savings accounts and part comes from the ability of commercial banks to create money. (The next chapter will explore in detail how banks create money.) By using the money of *savers* for the needs of *investors*, commercial banks perform a vital service for our economy.

Recall that saving reduces the circular flow and aggregate demand. But commercial banks make this money available for investment spending, which thus offsets the reduction in aggregate demand.

Commercial banks are called **financial intermediaries,** since they perform the go-between task of "mating" savers and investors. However, people may find their needs best filled by other financial intermediaries, such as savings and loan associations, insurance policies, credit unions, mutual savings banks, etc. These other financial institutions will be discussed at greater length in a later chapter.

To increase its earnings, a commercial bank will try to make more loans. However, there is always some risk that a loan will not be repaid or not be repaid on time. Thus there is a conflict between profit-making through loans and safety for the depositors (who have their money in savings and checking accounts). To increase income, bankers may be tempted to expand loans beyond the point of safety. Indeed, in the past, commercial banks were opened which began making loans before receiving any deposits! Also, some commercial banks have been in the position of loaning out nearly all of their deposits; when the depositors sought their money, they found that they were out of luck, that the bank had gone out of business without repaying depositors. During *panics* some banks have been able to repay only part of the deposit, say, one dollar for every three that were deposited. So to control and assist the commercial banks, there is the need for a central bank. In the United States the central bank is called the Federal Reserve System.

The Federal Reserve System

The Federal Reserve System was created in 1913 under the Federal Reserve Act. At the time, there was a need to regulate the commercial banking industry and to establish order in the money system. Most nations have a central bank which regulates money and banks. The central bank is a bank for the government and for other banks. The organization in the United States is somewhat different.

Nominally, the United States has twelve central banks. In practice, they all operate pretty much in accord.

The operation of the Federal Reserve System

Figure 2 shows the organization of the Federal Reserve System. At the top of the chart is the *Board of Governors*. The Board is composed of seven members and is located in Washington, D.C. The members are appointed by the President for a 14-year term, with each appointee to be confirmed by the Senate. The terms are arranged so that a new member is appointed every other year. The members are often well known as bankers. This has caused some people to wonder how well they can do as regulators of banks. Occasionally, the members are from other businesses and once in a while an economist is appointed. At least two of its present members are economists: Arthur Burns and Henry Wallich.

In addition to regulating the banking industry, the Board is required to operate the entire Federal Reserve System. It also has the responsibility of setting and implementing monetary policy. It does this through the Open Market Committee.

Figure 2 Schematic diagram of the Federal Reserve System.

Open Market Committee There are numerous committees and organizations which operate under the Board. They perform a variety of tasks related to the operations of the System. Some conduct research for the Board. One of the important committees is the Open Market Committee. The members of this committee include the members of the Board plus five presidents of the district Federal Reserve branches. The Board must decide what monetary policy to take. The problem the Board tries to solve is how much money to provide the economy in order to keep it operating as well as possible.

District Federal Reserve Banks There are twelve federal districts and each one has a bank which may have one or more branches. The districts are shown in Figure 3 by location of the district bank. The map in Figure 3 locates each bank. Some districts are small in area but are densely populated. Others spread over a large area. District 6 at Atlanta covers much of the Southeast and has branches at Birmingham, Jacksonville, Nashville, and New Orleans.

It is possible that the various district banks could act independently. Usually, they act to-

gether to implement decisions made by the Board. One or two of the districts have sometimes delayed a day or two in making policy changes, to let the Board know they did not necessarily agree with the policy change.

The Federal Reserve banks do not serve the general public directly. The System is not a federal government agency either. Actually, it is a privately owned organization. However, it is not really a profit-making organization even though it does have sources of revenue. Earnings up to 6% annual return are paid out to the stockholders; anything above that goes to the U.S. Treasury. The purpose of the System is not to earn money, but to stabilize American banking and to decide and carry out monetary policy.

Member banks How does the Federal Reserve System interact with the commercial banks; or more specifically, how does it interact with the bank in which you have your checking or savings account? Well, there may be no direct connection.

This country's roughly 14,000 commercial banks can be identified as either state banks or national banks. They are all privately owned

- ● Reserve bank cities
- • Branch bank cities
- ▬ District boundaries
- ── Branch territory boundaries
- ✳ Board of Governors of the Federal Reserve System

Figure 3 **Locations and territories of the Federal Reserve Banks and their branches. (Alaska and Hawaii are in the 12th district.)**

and profit making, but those chartered by the states are called **state banks** and those chartered by the federal government are called **national banks.** All of the roughly 4,700 *national banks must be members of the Federal Reserve System.* The state banks have the option of joining or not. Nearly 1,100 state banks (out of around 9,300) have joined the System. So in total, about 40% of all banks in this country are members. Because all of the larger state banks are members, a significant portion of all banking business is carried out by members. In fact, since nearly 80% of all the demand deposits are in member banks, the Federal Reserve System has a strong direct influence on American banking.

To join the System, the bank must be approved for membership. In doing so, the bank agrees to abide by regulations. It must also become a stockholder in its district Federal Reserve Bank. The System needs the member banks to operate. The banks are regulated by the System and receive benefits from it. The operations of the System are described below.

What the Federal Reserve System does

Some of the functions of the Federal Reserve System have already been mentioned. We will go back over some of these in greater detail. The function we think of as most important, monetary policy, will be discussed last. In order to carry out monetary policy, the Federal Reserve needs the help of other members of the economy. Part of the explanation must therefore be left to other chapters.

Supervision   The function of regulating banks in their operations is very important. As was noted, not all banks are federally chartered though some state chartered banks are members of the Federal Reserve System. If a bank wishes a federal charter, it is approved and issued by the Federal Reserve.

Once in operation, a commercial bank is regularly examined by the Federal Reserve. The books and records of a bank are regularly *audited*. In addition to such obvious matters as detecting errors or embezzlement, the auditors also check for sound management practices. This means checking to see that the bank is not making loans that are too risky or making too

many loans of the same type. Preventing losses is very important.

Other activities of banks will also be regulated. If a bank wants to build a branch, the action must be approved. The Federal Reserve also oversees the sale of a bank, the formation of a new bank, or the merger of existing banks. The Federal Reserve also looks into other businesses that banks may pursue. The varieties of special accounts offered, credit cards, and other services are scrutinized. Among services that banks offer include computer services, trust departments, tax services, mutual funds, agricultural management services, travel agencies, and real-estate investment. As of early 1976, it has been suggested that banks be allowed to enter into raising capital for business by assisting in the issuance of corporate stocks. All of these activities by member banks are (or would be) regulated under the Federal Reserve.

Bank of federal government   The Federal Reserve System acts as a bank for the federal government. The government has its bank accounts with the Federal Reserve. When payments are received, the deposit goes into the system and checks are written against these deposits. If you receive veterans' benefits or benefits under Social Security, the payments are made with checks drawn on accounts at the Federal Reserve. The Federal Reserve does for the government nearly all those things which your friendly local bank does for you.

There are additional services performed by the Federal Reserve for the government. These are services similar to those provided by banks for corporations but seldom for individuals. The Federal Reserve System helps the U.S. Treasury sell bonds or notes. If there are bonds to be sold, the Federal Reserve carries out the sale. As we will see later, some securities may be purchased by the Federal Reserve. The Federal Reserve also arranges for payment of interest on the government bonds and redeems them when they are mature.

Check clearing   The Federal Reserve System assists the commercial banks in their check-clearing operations. **Check clearing** means that the checks are sent to the banks on which they are drawn for payment. Through the use of accounts that commercial banks maintain at the Federal Reserve, this is accomplished with greater speed than would be possible otherwise.

If you write a check to a company at a distance from your home, they deposit it in their bank where they are located. If there were no clearing mechanism, their bank would have to send the check to your bank for payment. Presumably, the money would not be available to the company until the check was paid by your bank. (However, even before the Federal Reserve, the deposit was often made immediately.)

Now the process is much faster. The company deposits the check and gets immediate credit. The bank sends the check to the District Federal Reserve Bank and in turn receives immediate credit. It is then up to the Federal Reserve to present the check to your bank and collect the payment. In practice, there may be checks sent both ways so they are balanced and very little money actually moves.

Providing currency The bills which you carry in your pocket and recognize as money say "Federal Reserve Note" on the top. These notes are issued by the Federal Reserve System. These are simply noninterest-bearing notes of the System. When you hold one, you are holding nothing more than an IOU from the Bank. Unlike other securities of a corporation or government, it pays no interest to its owner. You hold it not because of the high-quality paper or the pretty engraving. It also says on the face that it is *legal tender* for all debts public and private. That is the legal term which says it

is money because the law says it is money. You hold it because it meets your transaction, precautionary, and speculative demands for money. You can use it in exchange because others will accept it. If you present a Federal Reserve Note to a commercial bank or to a Federal Reserve Bank, you could get another one just like it.

The Federal Reserve sends out notes in whatever quantity the general public wants. If, for example, the need for more currency in daily transactions was great, the Federal Reserve could double the amount of currency in circulation. Since most money is demand deposits anyway, the System allows individuals and firms to change from demand deposits to currency at will. There are times of the year when more currency is needed. These times usually coincide with major holidays, like the Christmas season. People are buying more and so need more cash. The Federal Reserve System supplies the bills as needed. If you look at a bill, you will see which District Bank issued it. After the holiday, many of the bills find their way back to the Bank. They are kept until needed again or destroyed if worn or dirty. The Federal Reserve also decides the *denominations*, or sizes (1, 2, 5, 10, 20, etc.), of the bills. For example, in April of 1976, a new note of the $2.00 size was issued after a ten-year period in which bills of this denomination were not in existence.

Table 3 shows a typical Federal Reserve chart indicating the Federal Reserve Notes outstanding and the **collateral**, which is the backing that the System holds against the notes. Not all of the notes are in circulation. There is more collateral than immediately nec-

Table 3
Federal Reserve Notes and Their Collateral (in millions of dollars)

Notes and collateral	Wednesday					End of month		
	1976				1975	1976	1975	
	1/28	1/21	1/14	1/7	12/31	1/31	12/31	1/31
F.R. notes outstanding (issued to Bank)	81,328	81,557	81,778	81,871	81,877	81,228	81,877	74,538
Collateral held against notes outstanding	83,608	83,608	83,608	83,608	83,408	83,608	83,408	76,217
Gold certificate account	11,596	11,596	11,596	11,596	11,596	11,596	11,596	3,207
Special Drawing Rights certificate account	302	302	302	302	302	302	302	93
Acceptances								425
U.S. Govt. securities	71,710	71,710	71,710	71,710	71,510	71,710	71,510	72,492

Source: Federal Reserve Bulletin.

essary. Notice that the *gold warehouse receipts* represent a very small portion of the collateral. The rest of the collateral consists of part of the national debt. That is, the Federal Reserve System guarantees the debt to you with a debt to it from the federal government. *Special Drawing Rights* represent money borrowed from the International Monetary Fund (this topic will be discussed later in the chapter on international finance).

Banker's bank The "Fed," as the Federal Reserve is commonly known, also serves as a bank for the commercial banking system. In doing this, the Fed makes loans to the banks. On occasion, a bank will need cash for reserves or even to meet withdrawals. The bank may use loans it has made as security and borrow, at interest, from the Fed. As we will see, the interest rate charged by the Fed is used in conducting monetary policy.

Controlling money supply *By far and away the most important task of the Federal Reserve is controlling this country's money supply.* The Fed, acting as the agent of the U.S. government and working through commercial banks, is the only institution that can expand (i.e., create) or contract the total amount of money available to the U.S. economy.

The reasons for wanting or needing to manipulate money supply are tied intimately to the evils that plague an economy: inflation, unemployment, and stagnation of economic output. Recall that earlier we described demand-pull inflation as basically "too many dollars chasing too few goods." So by controlling money supply, the government has a strong tool for dampening inflation or stimulating employment and economic growth. In short, *the control of money supply can be used to moderate the effects of the business cycle.*

The various policies and alternatives available to the government for controlling money supply are referred to as **monetary policy.** The methods, philosophies, and difficulties of implementing monetary policy will be discussed in Chapter 15.

Summary

Life is possible without money, but money eases most economic activities. Use of money eliminates barter and the double coincidence of wants. Money serves four functions; it's (a) a medium of exchange, (b) a store of value, (c) a unit of account, and (d) a standard of future payment.

Money may also be defined in terms of the demand for it. The transactions demand is the desire to hold money for use in future planned expenditures. The precautionary demand is the desire to hold money against future unplanned expenditures. The speculative demand for money is the desire to hold money while waiting for the price of other securities, such as stocks and bonds, to fall.

The earliest forms of money were probably different commodities. At various times throughout history, arrowheads, wampum, stones, tobacco leaves, beaver pelts, cigarettes, and many other items have served as money. Coins are actually a form of commodity money, though today coins are no longer made of valuable commodities. Paper money originally developed from warehouse receipts. Since 1933, American paper money has not been backed by gold.

Presently in the United States, any definition of money would include currency and demand deposits. Currency consists of coins and paper money; currency is also known as fiat money since its value comes from legislation rather than from the metal or paper backing. Demand deposits are checking account balances in commercial banks. They are called demand deposits because they may be transferred at the written order of the owner; the written order is called a check.

Narrow money, also known as M_1, consists of currency and demand deposits; this is the most common definition of money. There are broader measures of money known as near-moneys. M_2 consists of M_1 plus time deposits at commercial banks.

Commercial banks are privately owned, profit-oriented firms offering a variety of financial services. The services include safekeeping of valuables, savings accounts, checking accounts, the making of loans, credit cards, and other financial services. Commercial banks are important to our economy because they are financial intermediaries. That is, they "mate" savers and investors; they make savings available for investment, which helps increase the circular flow.

The Federal Reserve System exists to regulate the banking industry and establish some order in monetary matters. The "Fed," as it is called, consists of twelve district banks which are nominally separate but usually act in harmony.

The Federal Reserve System is directed by a Board of Governors consisting of seven persons appointed by the President of the United States. The board members serve for fourteen years. The Open Market Committee is the other important group in the management of the Fed. This committee is directly responsible for buying and selling securities in order to regulate the money supply.

Commercial banks may be chartered by the federal government and belong to the Federal Reserve System or they may be chartered by state government. Some state banks belong to the Fed also.

The Federal Reserve System supervises member banks, serves as banker for the federal government, clears checks for the banking system, provides currency by issuing notes, controls the money supply, and serves as a bank for the commercial banks.

Key Words and Phrases

- **barter**   direct exchange of a good or service for another good or service.
- **double coincidence of wants**   the coming together of two persons each of whom has something the other wants or can do something for the other so that a trade may take place.
- **medium of exchange**   anything which may be used to facilitate trade since it is nearly universally acceptable.
- **unit of account**   a standard which may be used to add together many different types of items.
- **standard of deferred payment**   anything which may be used to accomplish a transaction at present while settlement is delayed.
- **store of value**   anything which may be used to keep wealth intact.

- **transactions demand**   money *used* for expenditures over some time period.
- **precautionary demand**   money held because it *might be* spent.
- **speculative demand**   money held as an asset.
- **currency**   coins and paper money.
- **fiat money**   anything which is considered money because legally it is declared to be money even if the money has no, or very little, intrinsic value.
- **demand deposits**   accounts at commercial banks which must be paid when the owner requests payment. The order to do so is called a *check;* thus they are checking accounts.
- **narrow money** M_1; the definition of money which is most restrictive. It includes currency and demand deposits only.
- **near-moneys**   definitions of money that are broader than M_1: definitions of money that include accounts or items drawing interest.
- **M_1**   currency plus demand deposits.
- **M_2** M_1 plus time deposits at commercial banks.
- **M_3** M_2 plus time deposits at nonbank thrift institutions.
- **time deposits**   deposits at commercial banks which are supposedly subject to withdrawal only after 30 days notice (though in practice paid immediately) on which interest is paid by the bank.
- **liquid**   the condition that an asset may be turned into money quickly and easily without a loss in value.
- **commercial bank**   a privately owned firm which provides a variety of services relating to the holding and transferring of money and closely related financial assets.
- **checking account**   an account at a commercial bank subject to transfer on order of the owner; money in a checking account is known as *demand deposits.*
- **savings account**   an account at a commercial bank which pays interest and is not generally subject to transfer on order; often the owner has a small book called a *passbook* in which the records are kept. The money in savings accounts is known as time deposits.
- **mortgage**   the legal agreement between lender and borrower with some sort of real estate securing the loan; usually refers to a loan for buying a house.
- **financial intermediaries**   any institution which collects money from savers or depositors and lends it out to those who need it.
- **state bank**   a commercial bank chartered by the state government.

- **national bank** a commercial bank chartered by the federal government and regulated under the Federal Reserve System.

- **check clearing** the process of crediting a bank where a check is deposited and returning the check to the bank of the check writer so the account may be reduced by the indicated amount.

- **legal tender** the phrase which is used to make something—our "greenbacks"—serve as money; this phrase means that we may pay or discharge debts by using the "money" even though it is only a token, such as a piece of paper.

- **collateral** anything which is held as security on an agreement; with regard to money, it is the backing for Federal Reserve Notes (our money).

- **monetary policy** the various philosophies and methods available to the government for controlling money supply.

Questions for Review

1. What makes money valuable?

2. Why do we continue to use metal coins when plastic ones would serve as well? What "backing" is there for our coins?

3. Does money always serve as a store of value? When does it serve well and when poorly?

4. Would paper money be worth more if there was gold backing it up?

5. Look up the current amount of money available. Try to find the amount of M_1, M_2, and M_3. (Use the *Federal Reserve Bulletin.*)

6. How does the Federal Reserve interact with commercial banks? What functions does the Fed perform?

7. Why are commercial banks important to the American economy?

8. What is the collateral for Federal Reserve Notes?

12

Commercial Banks and the Creation of Money

We have outlined briefly the role of the Federal Reserve Bank in the American banking system. We saw that Federal Reserve Banks are essentially bankers' banks. We turn now to a discussion of *our* banks—in particular, the approximately 14,000 *commercial banks* set up to provide us with services without which our economy could not function.

We do have other kinds of firms providing financial services—savings and loan associations, for example. We also have other financial institutions, such as the insurance industry and the stock market, which provide us with other important financial services. In the next chapter we will discuss some of these institutions. But we start with commercial banks because these banks have one tremendously important function that no other financial intermediary has: *commercial banks can actually create money*. (The Federal Reserve can control the amount of money commercial banks create.)

Before we discuss this important function of commercial banks, however, we will first present a brief sketch of the development of banks and banking services in general. We will also discuss the nature of the United States banking system: how it operates and the services it provides.

Historical development of banking

Banking institutions have been in existence since ancient times. Keepers of the ancient temples of Greece and Babylon lent out at interest the precious stones and metals entrusted to their safekeeping. And many of us are familiar with the Biblical account of the expulsion of the money changers from the Temple of Jerusalem. The money changers were, in effect, using the Temple as a place for banking business rather than for worship. They were exchanging (for a profit) coins of visiting pilgrims for money that could be spent locally.

Forerunners of our modern banking system began to develop in the late Middle Ages. At first, banks were usually related to some other form of business. For example, one such type of bank was essentially a warehouse for money. People who sought protection for their valuables looked to businesses that used vaults in their own day-to-day dealings. They would leave their excess money with a jeweler or goldsmith, who already had vaults available and who would for a fee store money for others.

In a time when distant communication was not easily established, international merchants were able to provide another kind of banking service. For example, if a resident of London had to make a payment to a Paris businessman, he had the choice of either making the long trip to Paris or arranging for a messenger to carry money, usually heavy gold coins, to Paris. How much easier if he could find an established merchant in London who had an agent in Paris who could make the payment for him. The London resident could give the money to the local merchant. For a small fee, the merchant would guarantee that actual payment would be made in Paris from the merchant's French assets. (In addition to the fee charged for the service, the merchant might hope to make additional gain as a result of changes in the value of French versus English money during the time the order-to-pay notice was in transit from London to Paris.) Such transactions were not necessarily international in scope. Merchants could be of service between cities within the country. In any event, payment to distant areas, using an instrument much like a check or *money order* (an order to pay), was a banking service offered first by firms primarily in some other business.

Another type of banking service evolved from firms which were essentially brokers for loans. These firms specialized in bringing borrowers and lenders together, for a fee, of course. It was a natural development for these firms to accept money from lenders and hold it until borrowers could be found. They became depositories of money for lending.

It was inevitable that as banks became distinct businesses in their own right, they would tend to offer both storage and lending services. These operations led to the use of "instruments of credit." (Instruments of credit are merely pieces of paper saying "I owe you something of value" or "you owe me something of value.") This, in turn, led to the development of paper money. How did the development come about?

Let us say you left a bag of gold in a sixteenth century bank. The banker would give you a receipt for the gold—a piece of paper saying the gold was on deposit and that it was yours whenever you wanted it back (minus the fee he charged for keeping your gold safe). Later, you decided to spend the bag of gold for a new suit of armor. You could go to the bank vault, present your receipt, pick up the gold, and give it to the armorer. But why bother? Why not just give the armorer the receipt, and let *him* pick up the gold? The armorer, in turn, might decide that he needed a bag of gold's worth of metal. So why should he bother to pick up the gold? Instead, he passes your receipt along to his metal supplier. Let *him* pick up the gold if he wants to. Or leave it in the vault if he wishes. The receipt itself is as good as gold. In short, your receipt—an instrument of credit—was "assigned" to the armorer, and he in turn "assigned" it to the metal supplier.

Much more convenient all around. But still not as convenient as it might be. Each time the receipt changed hands, it had to be signed over—*reendorsed*—to the new owner. So why not simply make the original receipt "payable to bearer" instead of to one specific person?

But there was another problem. Your original receipt was for a bag of gold. But suppose you wanted to buy a locket for your lady—a nice locket, but not worth a full bag of gold. You would have to go to the vault, draw out part of your gold, and get a new receipt for the remainder. A nuisance. So why not have the banker give you several receipts for your gold in the first place, each for a fraction of the gold's full value? That way you could make small purchases as conveniently as large ones.

Eventually, receipts for deposits became instruments of credit, or paper money. This development led to another: the issuance of *bank notes*, another form of paper money. Bankers soon noticed that only a portion of the gold in their vaults needed to be kept on reserve to give to receipt-bearers who came in to ask for their money. Each day, withdrawals would be made. But each day, also, deposits would be made. It was very unlikely that on any given day *everyone* would ask for their gold back and *no one* would bring in new gold for deposit. There was always some gold idle in the vault.

So why not lend this idle gold out at a profit? True, the gold did not, strictly speaking, belong to the bankers. But since no one was using it, why not let it gather interest rather than dust? Better still, why bother with the gold itself? Why not just issue pieces of paper saying the bearer could come and get the gold if he wished or use this paper as if he were the actual owner of the gold?

Thus bank notes, as these pieces of paper came to be called, came into existence. (In the United States, until relatively recent times, banks were allowed to issue this kind of currency on the same basic principle as did their medieval forebears.)

It did not take long for the early banks' depositors to conclude that they, too, were entitled to a piece of the action. After all, the money being lent out was theirs in the first place. So, and because banks were competing among themselves for the community's available gold supply, bankers began paying interest on deposits, rather than demanding a fee for their safekeeping. The bankers, of course, passed this cost along to borrowers in the form of added loan interest.

It was but a short step from the development of instruments of credit and paper currency to the development of checks. To pay a bill, for example, a depositor merely had to write out an order—a check—instructing his bank to transfer money from his account to the account of the person to whom the money was owed. Before this service came to be used by individuals, it was used only by commercial enterprises. Banks that provided the service came to be known as "commercial banks." The term is still used today, as a glance at the title of this chapter will attest. Of course, many individuals now use the services of commercial banks.

Banks in the United States

Because of its democratic origins, the United States from its earliest days feared the development of an aristocratic moneyed class. The Bank of the United States, founded by Alexander Hamilton in 1791, was this country's first central bank, but it lasted only until 1811.

Economic Thinker
Nicholas Biddle

The struggle to maintain the value of the American dollar and to control its supply through a strong central banking system began with the birth of the Republic. The end of the Revolutionary War brought economic crisis as well as freedom from British rule. Debtors were in control of most state legislatures and were quite happy to pay these debts with near-worthless currency issued by local banks. Alexander Hamilton attempted to restore financial order. He insisted on the federal government's taking responsibility for the nation's war debt and established the Bank of the United States (in 1791) to help stabilize currency value. In a few years, America's credit, at home and abroad, was once again "as good as gold."

The first Bank of the United States acted as fiscal agent for the federal government, but was privately owned and operated. Throughout its existence it was well managed and prosperous. Its conservative stance, however, and especially its conservative policies on lending and on currency issuance, antagonized more expansionist-minded businessmen, especially in the West, and agrarian debtors, especially in the South. These interests succeeded in blocking the bank's recharter in 1811. Lack of a central bank made financing of the War of 1812 extremely difficult, and by the end of that conflict, the nation's finances were once again in chaos. A second Bank of the United States was chartered (for 20 years) in 1816 to help deal with the situation.

Nicholas Biddle was appointed a director of the new bank by President James Monroe in 1819 and became its president in 1823. The bank grew in power and prosperity under his management. But the tide of history was running against the belief of Biddle and other conservative Eastern financiers that a central bank was essential to stabilize the currency and control inflation. The coming "Age of Jackson" was to bring down the bank and leave the nation without a central banking system until the establishment of the Federal Reserve System more than seventy-five years later.

Nicholas Biddle was born in Philadelphia, in 1786, the son of one of the "old" aristocratic families in the new Republic. He attended Princeton University, where he became an accomplished linguist. He was appointed secretary to the United States ambassador to France and later served in the same capacity to James Monroe in England. Back in Philadelphia, he practiced law and, in 1810, was elected to the Pennsylvania House of Representatives. Biddle was also a man of letters, contributing verse and short stories to literary journals of his day. In addition, he prepared and edited for publication the manuscript journals of the Lewis and Clark expedition to the Pacific Ocean, one of the great travel narratives of all time.

When Biddle was appointed to the board of the Bank of the United States, he was already fairly well versed in economic theory and was especially drawn to the work of Adam Smith and David Ricardo. His continued study in economics reinforced his belief that conservative banking policies were essential to the nation's prosperity.

Biddle's Bank of the United States was not a government bank. Like the first Bank of the United States it was a private, commercial bank. It was chartered in Philadelphia and had branches in 16 cities, its "western" branches being in Kentucky, Ohio, Louisiana, and in the "western" city of Pittsburgh. In many ways, however, it functioned as a central bank in today's sense of the word. It handled federal revenues, for example, and received deposits of federal tax moneys.

Most importantly, the bank was expected to control the paper money issued so

abundantly by state banks and establish order in the financial markets. Under Biddle's management, the bank endeavored to ensure the value of paper currency in circulation throughout the country. Whenever possible, it retired currency issued by other banks in favor of its own or of currency issued by other banks known to be solvent. Periodically, it would demand payment in gold for currency in its vaults that had been issued by other banks. Consequently, the tendency of some banks to issue more currency than their assets allowed was at least partially checked.

The Bank of the United States became a profitable business under Nicholas Biddle. One reason was its conservative loan policies. The bank eagerly made loans to prosperous and well-established businesses in the East. It was not so eager, however, to make risky loans to new businesses in the West or to plantation owners or farmers in the South and other sections of the country who needed help in hard times. Many disaffected Westerners and Southerners became disenchanted with Biddle's Bank of the United States.

In 1828, Andrew Jackson became President of the United States. Jackson, from Nashville, Tennessee, was a sworn enemy of the patrician Easterners. Men like Biddle, he believed, had victimized the South and the West for their own personal gain and for maintenance of Eastern industrial prosperity. Also, Jackson did not like the fact that so many foreigners were stockholders in the bank. Jackson sincerely—and tragically—believed the bank's main purpose was to earn money for its owners and to prevent the West from growing, not to help the United States bring order to its monetary system.

The Bank of the United States became a central issue in Jackson's 1832 campaign for reelection to the presidency. Jackson had, in the same year, vetoed a bill to recharter the bank. Upon his triumphal victory over his probank opponent Henry Clay, Jackson promptly removed government money from the Bank of the United States and deposited it in favored state banks, where he hoped it would be used more equitably among the various sections of the nation.

The Bank of the United States was mortally wounded; its charter as central bank expired in 1836. Nicholas Biddle continued to operate the bank as a totally private concern until it collapsed in 1841 as a result of the business panic of 1837. Biddle's Jacksonian enemies brought charges of financial fraud against him, but he was subsequently acquitted of all such charges. He died, defeated but respected, in 1844.

Western and agrarian interests complained that it catered only to the rich mercantile class. These complaints brought about its closing. The second Bank of the United States was founded in 1816. Once again the complaint was heard that the Bank favored what might today be called the Eastern establishment. President Andrew Jackson, the champion of Western and agrarian interests, in 1832 vetoed rechartering the Bank and it expired in 1836. It was not until 1913 that a central United States banking system again came into existence. That system, as we know, is called the Federal Reserve System and is still in operation.

The democratic origin of U.S. banking led to a system mostly of unit banks. **Unit banking** is a banking system of separate, locally maintained banks, i.e., a series of individual units. Unit banking differs from **branch banking,** which consists mainly of a few large banks with many branches. Most European countries rely on branch banking. The United States today has a dual system, with some states allowing branch banking and others prohibiting it.

Bank charters in the United States

Just as many Americans were suspicious of the power of a central bank, they were also suspicious of the power of individual banks. Federal and state governments used the device of bank charters to help control this power. **Bank charters** are simply governmental permission to operate banks, according to certain guidelines. With this permission go restrictions on the chartered bank—regulations concerning the bank's financial backing, the kinds of loans it may or may not make, the number and locations of branches it may operate, the services it may or may not provide, and so on. Charters also set up regulatory bodies to see that provisions of the charter are complied with.

At first, charters were issued only by specific legislative action. That is, if someone wanted to open a bank, a special law had to be passed either in Congress or in the state legislature. In 1883, however, New York state passed a Free Banking Act. This allowed almost anyone to open a bank as long as they complied with certain minimum charter conditions. Free Banking Acts soon spread to other states. Before long, all banks became state institutions.

Laxity and abuse of state regulation soon began to create havoc in the economic community. As noted above, banks had the power to issue currency against the value of their deposits. Some state-chartered banks, especially in the Western states, began to issue worthless or near-worthless currency and to engage in other unsound if not illegal practices. The activities of these so-called **"wildcat" banks** gave rise to a federal system for chartering banks. The term "wildcat" was used because it was said that these banks were located in such remote places that only wildcats could find them. The new system gave federally chartered (national) banks the right to issue currency. It also placed a high tax on state bank notes in an effort to drive this kind of currency out of the marketplace.

Consequently, most banks took out national charters. But banks of deposit, which did not issue bank notes, were unaffected by the new tax. Many of them remained under state charters. Thus today the United States has a dual banking system. We have both national banks and state banks.

The Federal Deposit Insurance Corporation

As we have seen, charters and government regulations help police the banking system and ensure its orderly functioning. Such devices have also served to protect the bank's customers from undue risk and loss. One such consumer-protection instrument is the Federal Deposit Insurance Corporation (FDIC).

The problem of banks not being able to repay customers their deposits recurred frequently in early American history. These bank collapses often occurred in clusters due to **banking panics**—people running en masse to withdraw all their money. Even a financially sound bank can't supply the money immediately if all its depositors want their money at once. So panics are an unfortunate problem of customer confidence. The start of the Great Depression in the early 1930s caused many banking problems and a few panics. In 1933, to protect deposits of customers, and more importantly, to shore up public confidence in banks, the U.S. Congress passed a banking act creating the Federal Deposit Insurance Corporation (FDIC).

The FDIC was established to make sure that depositors in any bank which is a member of the FDIC would not risk losing their deposits. Member banks pay a small percentage of the value of their deposits to the FDIC as a kind of insurance premium. In return, the FDIC guarantees that the bank's customers will not lose their deposits even if the bank itself fails. Over the years, the size of the account that could be insured has risen with expansion of the economy. Today it is $40,000.

The FDIC, like the Federal Reserve System, state regulatory agencies, and the Federal Controller of the Currency (for national banks), has the power to police bank operations as well as insure deposits. Almost all commercial banks belong to the FDIC. The FDIC membership notice on the facade of a bank is a welcome reassurance to all depositors that their money is protected from bank failures.

Bank expansion

There are no true monopoly banks in the United States. Charter provisions and other regulations restricting number and location of

Extended Example
Bank Failure Without Panic

In the period 1974–1976, bank failures in the United States rose to record levels. In 1975, for example, 11 banks failed, the highest number of failures since 1942, when 23 banks went under. (In the deep depression year of 1937, there were 83 failures.) The rash of bank failures in the mid-1970s was in large part due to unwise real-estate and building-construction loans, especially loans to real-estate investment trusts (REITs). REITs were highly favored investments in the pre-recession 1970s, and many banks rushed to cash in on the building boom by lending money to these trusts. Economic conditions worsened, however, and the boom ended. Many real-estate investment trusts, finding themselves stuck with hundreds of unsold condominiums and partially finished construction sites, were unable to repay their loans. The lending banks found themselves in stormy weather, and not a few of them failed to weather the storm.

Despite the seriousness of this situation, there were no depositor panics such as often characterized bank failures in earlier times. No crowds stormed the tellers' cages of the affected banks. And panic did not spread from weaker banks to stronger ones, causing the latter to lose deposits as often happened in previous times. Relative calm prevailed, due in no small part to the soothing presence of the Federal Deposit Insurance Corporation (FDIC). Depositors knew that their savings were safe, insured by the federal government up to $40,000 against loss.

But the role of the FDIC in dealing with troubled banks goes deeper than merely guaranteeing against loss of depositor savings. Although the FDIC does not have regulatory power over the nation's larger banks, only over its smaller ones, it is responsible for the orderly liquidating of the affairs of all failed banks. It may, for example, pay off insured depositors and then sell the bank's assets to other banks. Or it may finance the merger of a failed bank with a sound bank, guaranteeing the sound bank against excess losses due to taking over the failed bank's liabilities. In 1975, FDIC funds were used to finance five such mergers of insolvent banks with sound ones. In three cases that year (in Chicago, Houston, and Algoma, Wisconsin), FDIC funds were used to help create entirely new banks to take over the obligations of failed banks.

The FDIC may also step in to prevent bank failure. In November, 1975, for example, it made a $10-million loan to the Southeast Banking Corporation to finance a merger plan with (and head off the probable failure of) Florida's Palmer First National Bank.

The Federal Deposit Insurance Corporation is also empowered to set up its own bank to replace a failed bank if the local community has no other institution available for banking operations. Such Deposit Insurance National Banks (called "Dinby" for short) are allowed to operate for a period of only two years, during which time the local community is expected to organize a new private bank to replace the failed institution. The Swope Parkway National Bank in Kansas City, Missouri, for example, failed in January, 1975. The bank had been owned and operated by blacks to serve the local black community. The FDIC opened a "Dinby" to serve this community and to give it time to set up a new minority-owned bank before final disposition of the original failed bank's liabilities and assets.

The FDIC, then, provides not only insurance against loss of deposits, but also assurance to business and financial interests that bank failures will not be allowed to wreak havoc throughout the economy if such havoc can be prevented. In 1974, for instance, the FDIC (and the Federal Reserve Bank) spent $2.7 billion to bail out the huge Franklin National Bank of New York. It then placed advertisements in newspapers throughout the country to reassure the public, and especially the financial community, that the FDIC was ready and able to deal with any possible future bank failures, large or small. The general public and the financial community were duly reassured. The large number of bank failures that followed in 1975 gave rise to considerable national concern, but never to nationwide alarm and panic.

branch banks prohibit growth of such a monopoly. Nevertheless, banks have grown in size and economic power. Bankers, like their counterparts in other businesses, recognize the advantages of "economies of scale." That is, some operations are more efficient when done on a large scale. Like other businessmen, they wish to maximize profits. Therefore, they seek legal ways to avoid restrictions on their power to do so.

Several recent developments have led to the retention of a unit form of banking while allowing substantial centralization of ownership and control. One is the formation of **holding companies,** which are private businesses whose sole purpose is to buy banks. A holding company with several banks is in substance a single bank with several branches. Because the holding company is not itself a bank, it can often do things a bank cannot, such as sell insurance or invest in real estate.

More recently, banks have utilized electronic equipment in an effort to expand their business into areas where they are not allowed to open branches. For example, some banks have set up machines in the railroad stations and airports of their own or neighboring towns. These machines offer at least simple banking services such as check cashing and deposit receiving.

Such electronic devices, the banks argue, are not truly branches. However, in 1976 the Supreme Court upheld a Chicago Appeals Court decision that such devices were in fact branches. They were declared illegal where states forbid branches. New charter provisions and changes in state and federal regulations will undoubtedly have to be developed to deal with the business of "electronic banking." Let us close our general discussion of the development of the banking system with a closer look at this relatively recent development.

Electronic banking: toward a "checkless society"

It is evident that the banking business has become a prime user of modern computer technology. All government and most corporation checks now bear the tell-tale perforations that show they will be processed by computers. Your bank statement and the checks furnished by your bank bear computer code numbers. Your bank itself may now have a computer terminal on its premises for your personal use. On it you may check your bank balance, your loans outstanding, and/or the date on which your last check cleared for payment. Computers are also being used extensively to facilitate consumer borrowing through the use of bank credit cards. (Many other businesses, of course, have moved to computer technology for debit and credit record keeping—department stores, retail gasoline outlets, large supermarket chains, to name just a few.)

There is nothing very mysterious or even unusual about this trend toward electronic banking. It is a natural development of the trend we have already noted in our historical sketch of the business of banking. The trend has been toward efficiency and convenience. Our economic system has progressed from the use of product barter, to the use of precious metals, to the use of paper instruments of credit—all in the name of convenience and efficiency. Electronic banking is merely the latest step in that direction.

Electronic banking is now moving toward what bankers call the "Electronic Funds Transfer System" (EFTS). This is a plan to reduce the use of paper money (and checks) by moving funds between and among financial institutions via computer. For example, Social Security recipients may now, if they wish, have their monthly payments transferred directly to their bank accounts. No actual check is needed. Soon all of the government's Civil Service payments will be handled this way. In 1977, New York state began to pay its pensioners via computer-deposit to their bank accounts, rather than mailing individual checks. Many businesses now give their employees the option of computer deposit. Salaries may be transferred directly into the employee's bank account. No payroll check need change hands.

Aside from convenience and efficiency, EFTS has the potential for cutting down the expenses of the banking system (and of all other businesses having credit and debit operations). The estimated cost of processing a bank check is around 35 cents. To process a bank credit-card transaction costs about 55 cents; a cash transaction costs 15 cents. Millions of such transactions occur every day. EFTS is still too new for bankers to be certain how much of these vast costs can be saved by computer transactions. But indications are that the savings will be considerable.

Of course, electronic banking has drawbacks. Complaints have been made about bank failure to credit receipt of computer funds promptly and failures to notify recipients that the funds are available. There have been complaints about faulty computer programming resulting in embarrassing "bouncing checks." (As programmers are fond of reminding us, computers are, after all, only human.)

Electronic banking has even given rise to a new type of bank bandit. Jesse James has put away his six-shooter and enrolled in a school of computer technology. Fraudulent transfer of funds via computer is a new threat to bank security. New methods for circumventing such frauds have had to be devised. Whether these security precautions can ever be one-hundred percent successful is still a matter of debate among computer technicians.

Regardless of temporary drawbacks, however, electronic banking is undoubtedly the wave of the future. Silicone chips and magnetic tapes are rapidly replacing paper checks as the method of choice for transferring money from one person to another. Yet, complete reliance on electrical devices will probably never be a reality. Some transactions take place in locations distant from any connection to computers. Very small transactions such as candy vending machines or parking meters will still be handled with coins. There are many problems to be solved where records of a transaction are necessary. Finally, there are some transactions which people do not want recorded and prefer to use cash. This is obviously true of illegal activities, but is also true of the husband who does not want his wife to know of the women "friends" he takes out to lunch.

The business of commercial banking

We have referred to banks as financial intermediaries. This is to say that banks function as intermediaries, or go-betweens, between borrowers and lenders. Put simply, their essential function is to take in money from lenders and give it to borrowers. The lender becomes the bank's *creditor;* the borrower becomes its *debtor.*

A commercial bank provides many services as it goes about its business of bringing creditor and debtor together. We shall discuss some of these services in a moment. First, however, let us take a look at the items to be found in a balance sheet of a typical commercial bank. An understanding of the assets and liability items of a bank can serve as an entry into our discussion of how commercial banks operate. Remember, a commercial bank is a business. Its business is to take in money to lend or invest at a profit. Like all other businesses, it has assets and liabilities which must be kept in balance.

The balance sheet of a commercial bank

Let us now look at Table 1. First, note the asset column. Cash or currency is obviously an asset. The cash item will include money actually in the bank's vault, the bank's money that happens to be on deposit in the vaults of other banks, and bank money on deposit at the Federal Reserve Bank. These latter two items are included as bank cash because they can easily be converted to actual vault cash if the bank needs to do so.

The second asset item is investments. As we have noted, banks are in business to make a profit. One way they can do so is to invest in securities. They may purchase short-term securities, which pay relatively small returns but are easily turned into cash. Banks may also hold long-term securities, such as bonds issued by corporations and federal, state, and local governments. These securities pay larger returns, but must be kept for longer periods for

Table 1
Simplified Balance Sheet for a Typical Commercial Bank

Assets	Liabilities
Cash	Deposits
Investments (securities)	Capital
Loans	

full profitability. Whether short- or long-term, securities represent an asset to the bank.

The largest asset of a commercial bank is likely to be loans. The bank, of course, profits by the interest it charges on loans. The loans themselves represent assets because the money lent out still "belongs" to the bank— even though it may be temporarily in someone else's cash drawer.

On the liabilities side of the balance sheet, deposits are the major item. Deposits represent a liability because this money does not really "belong" to the bank. They belong to the depositors. The bank is the debtor; the depositors are creditors. Theoretically, all the creditors could at one time demand that the debtor (the bank) pay up. But as we know from our earlier discussion of the development of banks, this does not happen. (The fact that it does not is the foundation stone of the entire banking system.)

The capital item in the liability column represents the value of the stock sold to finance the setting up of the bank. It is a liability because, theoretically, the people who bought the stock could all at one time reclaim their money. As is the case with depositors, however, this is not likely to happen.

The balance sheet we have been describing is, of course, vastly oversimplified. Aside from actual monetary amounts, a real balance sheet would contain many more items. For example, the physical plant itself is an asset to a bank. Presumably it could be sold for cash. Profits on a bank's capital that have not yet been paid out to shareholders would be listed as a liability in a real balance sheet.

Let us now take a closer look at the two principal items of a commercial bank's balance sheet: the liability called deposits and the asset called loans. We will take the liability first, for without it there would be no assets.

Deposits

Deposits are of two basic types: *demand deposits* and *time deposits.* These terms refer to the kinds of banking accounts we are all familiar with: checking accounts and savings accounts. If you lend your money to a bank in the form of a checking account, you can get your money back any time you want, or demand, it. You present a check to the bank's teller (the bank gives you a supply of checks when you open your account) drawn for any part or all of the amount in your account. If you wish to pay a bill, you make out a check for what you owe to your creditor. He then will present it to the bank and receive his (your) money. You can see why checking deposits are called **demand deposits.** The account money must be paid on demand.

Savings accounts are known as **time deposits.** Legally, banks have the option of placing restrictions on how soon after depositing your money in a savings account you may draw it out. Banks, however, will almost always allow you to draw on your ordinary passbook savings account on demand. So, in this respect, an ordinary savings account is similar to a checking account. You cannot, however, write checks on a commercial bank's savings account—to pay bills, for example.

The bank pays interest on the money you put in a savings account. It will pay you a higher interest rate if you agree not to withdraw any of your money for a certain period of time—six months, perhaps, or one year, or five years. The longer you agree to leave your money, the higher rate of interest you will receive. These long-term accounts often involve an instrument of credit called a "certificate of deposit." You may buy a certificate from the bank for $1,000 and agree to keep it a year, say, or perhaps five years before cashing it in.

Loans

Deposits, whether demand or time, are the source of the bank's principal asset: its loans. Banks make two major types of loans: commercial and consumer.

Commercial banks make loans to all types of commercial enterprises. Farmers, for example, may need money for farm equipment or to tide them over until crops are harvested. Business firms may need money to develop a new product, or to meet a payroll during a period when receipts are low, or to buy wholesale products to sell at retail, or to expand a production facility. The list of possible commercial needs for ready money is almost endless.

Extended Example

Borrowers, Please Apply

We all know the cartoon stereotype of the large-bellied banker sitting comfortably on his money bags and refusing to part with his golden horde, despite the plaintive pleas of would-be borrowers. The truth is, however, something far different. Profit from loans is the lifeblood of the banking industry and bankers more often than not actually seek out borrowers—sometimes with a singular lack of success.

In 1976 and early 1977, for example, banks had considerable difficulty in putting their assets to work. Loans to business firms were in a downturn that had begun some two years previously. Corporations were not inclined to borrow to increase their inventories; inflation had slacked off and businessmen saw no reason to stock up now on raw materials and supplies as a hedge against rising prices. Also, an economic recovery was in progress and many corporations were using their increased revenues to pay off their present bank debts rather than adding new debts to company liabilities. Nor were most companies interested in borrowing for expansion of their productive capacities. True, the economy was getting better, but the rate was slow and extent of recovery was still a question mark. Most corporations preferred to take a wait-and-see attitude toward borrowing for expansion.

Bankers were sitting on their money bags all right, but with a plaintive plea of their own—please come and get it!

When commercial banks find themselves awash in money they are unable to lend out for low-risk profit, they are likely to seek out borrowers who represent a somewhat higher risk of being unable to pay back the loans—at least on time. Ordinarily, and providing the loans are not too much of a risk, this is a sound business practice as far as the banks are concerned. In addition, it may contribute to the well-being of the economy by funding risk-taking, but basically sound, enterprises. In the 1976–1977 period, however, commercial banks were more than usually reluctant to reduce their idle assets

through such loans. Many of them had just been badly burned by higher-risk loans that went unpaid. In fact, the entire banking industry had come under a cloud because of unsound loan policies; that is, they loaned to too many high-risk borrowers. (In addition, the recession of 1973–1975 caused many small businesses to go bankrupt—with loans unpaid.)

In the optimistic conditions of the late 1960s and early 1970s, commercial banks made a great many loans they came to regret. Corporations (and many foreign countries) were scrambling for capital funds and quite willing to pay high interest rates. More than a few banks were temporarily blinded by the lure of these high rates to the financial soundness of the loans themselves. A large number of loans turned bad when the economy sank into the deep recession of 1973–1975. In September, 1976, the American Bank and Trust Company of New York collapsed. Three even larger bank failures had occurred in the previous three years. In 1976, too, the First National City Bank and the Chase Manhattan Bank—second and third largest in the country—were designated by the Comptroller of the Currency as "troubled" institutions, meaning that the Comptroller's office was carefully monitoring their lending policies and other operations.

By mid-1977, the nation's commercial banks—many with more than a little help from their friends at the Fed and in Congress—had weathered the storm, but the sour taste of bad loans lingered on. Bank money lay idle as low-risk borrowers stayed away from the market and banks themselves exercised extreme caution in lending to higher-risk enterprises. In late 1977, the picture began to change as more low-risk corporations and industries began once again to borrow from the banks for expansion and other activities. In addition, consumer loans, which had actually increased during this period of low commercial borrowing, continued to increase in volume. The business of banking began once again to increase its profitability in line with the growing economic recovery. It is well to remember, however, that our cartoon banker seated on his money bags is not always comfortable and of large belly—he oftentimes bears a lean and hungry look.

Commercial banks also make loans to consumers—that is, to you and me. Or, as economists call us, households. You may go to your commercial bank and, assuming the bank thinks you're a good credit risk, get a loan to purchase a bike or even a Buick. You may take out a loan to build a new room on your house, or to take yourself and your family on vacation. Or you may borrow from the bank to pay a medical bill, or your taxes. Again, the list of possible consumer needs for loans is practically endless.

A relatively recent consumer credit device is the bank credit card. Made possible by the development of electronic computers, credit cards are used to make small and frequent loans to consumers. The loan is made when the consumer uses the card to charge a purchase at a merchant's place of business. The bank, rather than the consumer, initially pays the merchant. It charges the consumer interest for this service. It also collects a percentage fee (around 2%) from the merchant who receives the price of the purchase from the consumer. The interest on such loans is relatively high, but consumers seem willing to pay for the convenience. Most merchants are willing to pay a fee to the bank for the increase in business the cards bring them. The two most widely used bank credit cards are "Master Charge" and "Visa." There are, however, many other bank credit cards in existence.

Another recent form of consumer borrowing is "overdraft" or "ready-credit" loans. The bank "credits" a customer's account with a designated sum over and above the customer's checking account balance. The customer may draw on this credit when and if he wishes a consumer loan. No loan-application form need be filled out once the credit is given. No interest is charged unless the customer actually uses the credit.

Most consumer bank loans are for relatively small amounts. Nevertheless, they are an important source of revenue for commercial banks. Also, they may serve as a buffer for the bank when commercial loans (the bulk of a bank's lending) lag. Business loans are inclined to peak and fall with the business cycle. The volume of consumer loans is somewhat less responsive to this cycle.

For example, aggregate commercial bank business loans at the end of 1974 were $129.5 billion, up from $88.7 billion in 1972. In August, 1976, however, they had fallen to $111.1 billion. On the other hand, consumer loans *rose* more than $2 billion from their 1974 peak to $37.2 billion in August, 1976. Even so, business loans are about three times the volume of consumer loans at any given period (see Figure 1).

Other commercial banking services

As businesses, banks are competitive with one another. They actively seek time deposits (which the banks use to earn income) by offering competitive interest rates. They compete for demand deposits by offering convenient checking accounts and convenient ways of making transactions. For example, they may provide no-waiting-in-line deposit service, outside computer terminals for deposits and withdrawals during nonbanking hours, and so on.

Aside from accepting deposits and offering loans, commercial banks provide many other services for profit. They may sell federal savings and other forms of government bonds. Foreign currencies may be purchased at commercial banks. So may traveler's checks. Banks may manage the financial affairs of their customers. Through their trust departments, they

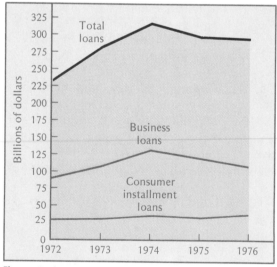

Figure 1 Loans at commercial banks. (Source: Federal Reserve Bulletin.)

may manage stocks and bonds of a customer's estate. They may also set up mutual funds or real-estate trusts in which the bank's customers may participate.

Banks may rent out their computer services to corporations for record-keeping or payroll processing purposes. For individuals, they may offer Christmas Club savings plans and safety deposit vaults for storage of valuables. Banks may even serve as outlets for state lottery tickets and subway tokens.

All of these services, plus many more, are intended to increase the profitability of the commercial bank. The essential economic function of the bank, however, and its basic source of income, is its service as intermediary between lender and borrower.

Commercial banks and money creation

We said at the outset of this chapter that commercial banks have a function that belongs to no other financial intermediary: *commercial banks can create money.*

Keep in mind, however, that when we say commercial banks can create money, we do not mean they actually create new currency. That, as we have learned, is the job of the Federal Reserve System. But money is more than just the bills in our pockets or purses. To the economist, money (M_1) equals currency in circulation *plus* demand deposits. Demand deposits consist of money we have entrusted to banks and which banks must return to us immediately on our demand. Since these deposits are so readily available for circulation, economists include them in their definition of money. As we shall see below, it is through manipulation of demand deposits that commercial banks create money.

Bank reserves

Banks earn a profit by investing in money-earning properties and securities and by making loans. The money they use for investments and for loans is supplied by the deposits they hold, both demand deposits and time deposits. Since these deposits may be withdrawn as needed by the depositors, the banks must keep a certain amount of cash available for ordinary withdrawals. Therefore, not all of these deposits can be used for earning a profit.

How much money must a bank reserve for deposit withdrawals? State and federal regulations set formal schedules for such reserves. Bank **reserves** include cash held in its own vault and money on deposit at the Fed. For example, a member bank of the Federal Reserve System *must* maintain a specified amount of money on reserve for withdrawals. This sum is called a bank's **required reserves.** These required reserves consist of fixed percentages of a bank's actual or total reserves; that is, fixed percentages of demand deposits and time deposits must be held at all times. As the volume of deposits (i.e., total reserves) change, the amount of required reserves will also change.

In 1975, a commercial bank belonging to the Federal Reserve System had to hold required reserves on its demand deposits amounting to $7\frac{1}{2}\%$ of the first $2 million, 10% of the next $8 million, 12% of the next $90 million, 13% on the next $300 million, and $16\frac{1}{2}\%$ on everything else above this level. (Time deposits have their own schedule of required reserves.) The percentages are also called **reserve ratios.**

According to these requirements, a bank with $10 million in demand deposits would be required to hold the following reserves:

$7\frac{1}{2}\%$ of $2 million + 10% of $8 million
$$= \$150,000 + \$800,000$$
$$= \$950,000 \text{ total required reserves.}$$

So the required reserves for this bank must be *at a minimum* $950,000. Not all of this amount, or of any bank's required reserves, are held on the premises as cash on hand. In fact, most of the required reserves are held at the regional Federal Reserve Bank.

Required reserves cannot be used by the bank for loans and investments. For this purpose, banks call on their *excess* reserves. **Excess reserves** consist of all deposits held by the bank over and above the amount needed to cover required reserves. Another way of expressing this is:

excess reserves
$$= \text{(total) reserves} - \text{required reserves.}$$

You will have seen by now that reserve requirements are yet another device for protecting consumers of bank services. Reserve requirements make it almost impossible for a bank not to have your deposit money ready for you when you want it. Reserve requirements also serve as a means of controlling the nation's money supply, as you will see when we come to our discussion of the Federal Reserve System and monetary policy in Chapter 15. Reserves are an important factor in the money-creating function of commercial banks.

Money creation by a single bank

We are now ready to see how banks actually do create money. To help us understand the process more easily, we will begin by looking at a single bank, rather than at the banking system as a whole. Our bank is, of course, fictitious and its balance sheet as shown in Table 2 is simplified for purposes of illustration. Further, we will concern ourselves only with what happens when a single new deposit is made at our hypothetical bank, the First National Bank.

Let us suppose that our sample bank receives a deposit of $1,000. At the moment of deposit the bank's balance sheet (disregarding all other assets and liabilities) would be as shown in Table 2.

The deposit is deemed a liability because it still belongs to the depositor and must be returned to him at his demand. But as long as it remains in the bank, it is also an asset. It is part of the bank's "cash in hand" and it is available for loans or investments. We call this cash in hand a bank's reserves. (Actually, all reserves need not be, and for the most part are not, on hand. They may be on deposit at the Federal Reserve or some other bank. The important thing is that they are immediately available if the bank needs them.)

Table 3
First National Bank—Ready for Action

Assets		Liabilities	
Required reserves	$100	Deposits	$1,000
Excess reserves	900		
	$1,000		$1,000

But, as we have seen, a bank cannot spend all of its reserves. By law, it must keep a percentage of its reserves on hand to pay those depositors who may, at any given time, want to withdraw their money from the bank.

Let us say that the Federal Reserve Board requires the bank to keep 10% of its deposits in reserve. For our First National Bank, this means that 10% of the $1,000 deposit (that is, $100) must be put aside as required reserves. The cash it has available for lending purposes is its excess reserves, which here amount to $1,000 − $100, or $900. Table 3 shows how this is reflected in the balance sheet.

The First National Bank can use the excess reserves it now has to make a loan as long as it keeps $100 (10% of the deposit) in reserve. Suppose one of its customers comes in and wants some help to purchase a new garden tractor she saw at the hardware store that morning. She needs $900 to buy it. First National makes the loan. Let us assume the customer already has a checking account at the First National. The bank merely adds the $900 to her present account, which will allow the customer to pay for her tractor by check. The balance sheet for First National will now be as shown in Table 4.

First National Bank has added $900 to its liabilities—the money it has added to the customer's deposit account. But it has also added $900 to its assets—because the money still "belongs" to the bank, even though it is tem-

Table 2
First National Bank—Upon Deposit of $1,000

Assets		Liabilities	
Reserves	$1,000	Deposits	$1,000
	$1,000		$1,000

Table 4
First National Bank—After Loan Is Made

Assets		Liabilities	
Required reserves	$100	Deposits	$1,900
Excess reserves	900		
Loans	900		
	$1,900		$1,900

porarily in the customer's pocket (her checking account).

Take another look at Table 4. Something very strange has happened. We started out with $1,000 in cash. No further cash has come into the picture. Yet, lo and behold, the bank's balance sheet shows assets and liabilities of $1,900. The First National Bank has created money—$900 worth of money.

How can this be? Actually, the answer is fairly simple. Recall what we have already learned about money. A nation's money, we know, is defined as currency in circulation *plus* demand deposits (because these deposits can readily become cash). We also know that money is a medium of exchange. It is something of value that can be exchanged for something else of value.

The bank lent its customer $900, certainly something of value. In exchange, it received the customer's promise-to-pay, which is also something of value. To the bank, this promise-to-pay is worth $900. This IOU has, in effect, become a medium of exchange worth $900 (plus interest, but we will ignore that for the present). The bank has turned the IOU into money, as money is defined by economists.

The economist's definition of money is no mere fanciful theory. The money so defined is real money that is used in exchange for real goods and services. In fact, it is through commercial banks acting as intermediaries between lenders and borrowers that most of the money actually used in our economy is created.

Now let us return to our First National Bank. As we said, the bank's customer wishes to pay for her new tractor by check. She does so, and eventually the check comes back to First National for clearance. When it is cleared, First National's balance sheet is as shown in Table 5.

The bottom line for liabilities and assets is now back to what it was in Tables 2 and 3—$1,000. The nine hundred created dollars have "disappeared," so far as First National Bank is concerned. It is evident, then, that a single bank making a loan equal to its excess reserves can indeed create money, *but only temporarily.* How, then, are commercial banks able to create enough money to service almost all of the needs of our economy? We shall see how in the following section.

Multiple-bank deposit expansion

The simplicity of the First National Bank's operation ($900 in, $900 out) and the fact that all of the transaction took place within a single bank soon brought its money creation to a halt. The banking system as a whole, however, can create money and continue to create it far beyond the capacity of a single bank. It can do this through a process called *multiple-bank deposit expansion.*

Let's continue from where we left off with the First National Bank. The customer wrote a check for $900 payable to the hardware dealer. The dealer then deposited this check at his own bank, say the Municipal Bank and Trust. When the check is processed, the balance sheets of the two banks will be as shown in Table 6.

The First National Bank is back where it was in Tables 2 and 3. The $1,000 in new deposits is balanced by $900 in loans and $100 in reserves. However, Municipal Bank and Trust now has reserves of $900 because it has received a deposit of $900. The economy's money supply has increased by $900. The $900 created by the First National Bank has not

Table 5
First National Bank—After Check Clears

Assets		Liabilities	
Required reserves	$100	Deposits	$1,000
Loans	900		
	$1,000		$1,000

Table 6
First National Bank—After Check Clears

Assets		Liabilities	
Required reserves	$ 100	Deposits	$1,000
Loans	900		
Total	$1,000	Total	$1,000

Municipal Bank and Trust—With New Deposit

Assets		Liabilities	
Reserves	$900	Deposits	$900
Total	$900	Total	$900

really disappeared. It has simply gone to another bank. From there, as we shall see, it will in turn create money of its own.

Let us say that the Municipal Bank and Trust is ready and willing to use this new $900 deposit to turn a profit. It can do so by lending out the money. But, like the First National Bank, it must keep 10% of the deposit on reserve, that is, 10% of $900 = $90 as reserves. It has, therefore, $810 ($900 − $90) to lend out. Suppose now that a customer came in seeking a loan of $810 to buy, say, a motorcycle he has seen on sale. He gets the loan and has the money deposited in his Municipal Bank and Trust account. He then goes to the dealer, gives him a check for $810, and rides off on his new bike.

The dealer banks at a firm called the Bank of Commerce and Industry. He deposits the check in his account at this bank. When the check arrives at the Municipal Bank and Trust for clearance, the balance sheets of each of our three banks are as shown in Table 7.

Note that our original $1,000 has already added $900 + $810, or $1,770, to the assets of the banking system. The commercial banking system has created $1,710 worth of new purchasing power through loans.

If the Bank of Commerce and Industry wished to continue the loan process, it would have to keep $81 as required reserves (10% of $810 = $81) and would have $729 ($810 − $81

required reserves) with which to make loans. By now, you should be able to draw your own new balance sheet for the Bank of Commerce and Industry when the $729 is loaned out. In the process, you would gain evidence of further creation of money by the commercial banking system.

Surely there must be an end to this process. If not, the economy would soon be awash in money. There *is* an end, there must be an end. Note that our demand deposits, loans, and the required reserves have been getting smaller in each round. Each of these will continue to decrease as the money-creating process continues. To see what will finally happen, look closely at Table 8. Table 8 is a simulated combined balance sheet for the entire banking system as our original $1,000 moves through it. To simplify further, the last several banks in our fictitious system are represented merely by dots. Names are not important here.

Table 8 is merely an expanded illustration of the same principle illustrated by our tables for individual banks. That principle, as noted at the outset of this section, is called the multiple expansion of demand deposits. Table 8 illustrates just how far our original $1,000 deposit can go in the banking system. That is, it shows the *maximum* amount of new money it can create.

Note that the First National Bank lent out $900 of the original $1,000 demand deposit. The Municipal Bank and Trust lent out $810 of that $900 when the money arrived there as a demand deposit. And so on. By the time the $1,000 had gone through the entire system, it had generated $9,000 in total loans. That is, the system had *created* $9,000 *new* money ($9,000 worth of purchasing power).

But at this point Table 8 indicates that the money expansion finally stops. Why? Loans, as we have learned, are made from a bank's excess reserves. The loan column in Table 8 also represents the total amount of excess reserves generated by the original $1,000. Now look at the required reserves column. By the time our excess reserves have been used up (the $9,000 point), the banking system's required reserves have reached a total of $1,000.

Table 7
First National Bank—After Check Clears

Assets		Liabilities	
Required reserves	$ 100	Deposits	$1,000
Loans	900		
Total	$1,000	Total	$1,000

Municipal Bank and Trust—After Check Clears

Assets		Liabilities	
Required reserves	$ 90	Deposits	$900
Loans	810		
Total	$900	Total	$900

Bank of Commerce and Industry—After Deposit

Assets		Liabilities	
Reserves	$810	Deposits	$810
Total	$810	Total	$810

Table 8
Combined Balance Sheet—Entire Banking System

Assets			Liabilities		
Required Reserves			Deposits		
First National Bank	$ 100		First National Bank	$ 1,000	
Municipal Bank and Trust	90		Municipal Bank and Trust	900	
Bank of Commerce and Industry	81		Bank of Commerce and Industry	810	
Farmers and Mechanics Bank	72.90		Farmers and Mechanics Bank	729	
Planters' Bank	65.61		Planters' Bank	656.1	
⋮ ⋮ ⋮	⋮ ⋮		⋮ ⋮ ⋮	⋮ ⋮	
Total required reserves	$1,000				
Loans					
First National Bank	$ 900				
Municipal Bank and Trust	810				
Bank of Commerce and Industry	729				
Farmers and Mechanics Bank	656.10				
Planters' Bank	590.49				
⋮ ⋮ ⋮	⋮ ⋮				
Total loans	$9,000				
Total assets		$10,000	Total liabilities		$10,000

Remember, we said at the outset that each bank in the system had to keep 10% of its deposit on hand as a reserve required by law. The sum of these reserves has now reached $1,000 or the legally required 10% of the total assets of the system ($1,000 required reserves plus $9,000 in loans). There is no money left to put into the required reserve account. As our original $1,000 went through the banking system, each bank had to keep a portion of it in reserve. Now the $1,000 is used up.

By the same token, each bank was able to lend out 90% of its demand deposit—its excess reserve. Our original $1,000 spawned a total of $9,000 in excess reserves throughout the system. The system's total assets are now $10,000 (required reserves, $1,000, plus loans, $9,000). There are no more excess reserves left to allow further expansion of the original $1,000. Note that the liabilities column in Table 8—deposits generated by our original $1,000—has also reached $10,000. The system as a whole is now in balance. The money-creation process so far as our original deposit is concerned must now come to an end.

To sum up, recall that the money-creating process in our single bank illustration stopped as soon as that bank's excess reserves ($900 of the $1,000 deposit) were deposited in another bank. And indeed, each of the other banks in our illustration went through the same process.

That is, it created money, but stopped doing so as soon as it used up its excess reserves. *The commercial banking system as a whole, however, continued on with money creation*—until it, too, had exhausted all its excess reserves. The process continued just as long as excess reserves remained anywhere in the system. When they dried up, the process stopped.

It might be well to remind ourselves once again at this point that banks do not create money only in theory. They do in fact turn IOU's or promises-to-pay into real money. The multiple expansion of bank deposits gives the economy new medium of exchange that can be traded for real goods and services. Our hypothetical tractor plowing in the home garden and the motorcycle speeding down the highway represent tangible evidence of this real-world fact.

The deposit expansion multiplier

As we have now seen, although excess reserves can be lost to individual banks, the system as a whole may still retain them. The system, as we have also seen, is able to lend money by a certain multiple of these reserves. This multiple depends on the amount of reserves the system is required to maintain.

The number of times the demand deposits are expanded is called the **deposit expansion multiplier,** or more simply, the **deposit multiplier.** The deposit multiplier offers a shortcut for calculating the maximum net increase in demand deposits; that is, it enables us to compute quickly the *maximum possible increase* in the money supply after excess reserves are raised.

The deposit multiplier is equal to the reciprocal of the reserve ratio requirement:

$$\text{Deposit multiplier} = \frac{1}{\text{reserve ratio}}.$$

In the example above, the reserve ratio was 10%, or .10. Substituting into our formula, we get

$$\frac{1}{.10} = 10 = \text{deposit multiplier.}$$

To calculate the increase in money supply (demand deposits), we multiply the initial excess reserve by the deposit multiplier. Once again using our example, we have

$$\$1,000 \times 10 = \$10,000.$$

This value of the total money supply is equal to what we calculated earlier using Table 8.

The reserve requirement determines the multiplier and therefore how much the commercial banking system can expand the reserves to get the total possible money supply. For example, had the reserve requirement been 20%, the First National Bank would have been limited to an $800 loan out of the $1,000 deposit. The multiplier would be $1/.20 = 5$. Thus the $1,000 in new reserves for the banking system as a whole would have supported at most only $5 \times \$800 = \$4,000$ in loans and would have led to $5 \times \$1,000 = \$5,000$ increase in the money supply. By controlling required reserves, the Fed can exert control on the money supply.

Other limits on actual deposit expansion

As we have noted, the deposit expansion multiplier calculates the money creation at a given reserve ratio maximum. That is, for a 10% reserve ratio, a tenfold expansion of money is the *most* that can occur. In practice, *the expansion is considerably less than its possible maximum.* Why?

First, there are *cash leakages* from the system. Not all borrowers will deposit their money in the bank as a demand deposit. Some will want cash—either part or all of the sum. For example, let us return for a moment to Table 6 above. Here we assumed that the hardware dealer deposited the $900 check he received in payment for his garden tractor in his account at Municipal Bank and Trust. The result was then shown in Table 6 as an immediate increase in the money supply by $900. Suppose, however, he needed $600 of this sum in cash and therefore cashed the check and deposited only $300. Then we would have a balance sheet as shown in Table 9. The money supply would have increased by only $300 instead of $900. The subsequent increases in money supply would therefore have been also comparatively reduced.

A second reason why expansion may be less than maximum is that *banks might not choose to loan out all excess reserves.* They may want to keep extra cash on hand as a buffer against unexpected withdrawals. In addition, business conditions influence lending. When business is bad, firms may not wish to invest in new plant facilities, for example. Therefore, they won't borrow from the banks. Consumer

Table 9
First National Bank—After Check Clears

Assets		Liabilities	
Required reserves	$ 100	Deposits	$1,000
Loans	900		
Total	$1,000	Total	$1,000

Municipal Bank and Trust—After Deposit but with Cash Leakage of $600

Assets		Liabilities	
Reserves	$ 300	Deposits	$ 300
Total	$ 300	Total	$ 300

loans can also drop during hard times. Even in boom times, borrowers may hesitate to borrow, perhaps because of high interest rates. They may decide to wait for interest rates to drop. So both at the peak and trough of the business cycle borrowing may not keep pace with the banking system's supply of excess reserves. In short, financial conditions and the attitudes of consumers can cause leakage from deposit expansion.

Recall that we said the Fed set reserve ratios in the $7\frac{1}{2}$% to $16\frac{1}{2}$% range in 1975. Corresponding maximum multipliers for this range would be around 6 to 12. In practice, the multiplier was and is in the range of 2 to 3. In fact, the multiplier in the United States has been declining recently. It was approximately 2.5 in early 1975. Thus the reserves provided by the Fed were expanded two-and-one-half times to obtain the total money supply. The multiplier declined to less than 2.5 in 1976. The banking system is not expanding its reserves as much as it had. Borrowers are not borrowing and the multiple expansion does not proceed as far as it had earlier.

Money contraction would also occur as a multiple if the banking system loses deposits. You should be able to go through the argument beginning with the withdrawal of the original deposit from the First National Bank.

Summary

Banks have been in existence, in some crude form, since ancient times. Modern banking originated with the goldsmiths in Europe in the Middle Ages. Banks were first storehouses of money (for safekeeping), then they paid bills over long distance through their branches, became lenders of money, and issued "instruments of credit" (an early form of paper money).

Banking began in the United States soon after the settlers arrived. Alexander Hamilton founded the first central bank in 1791, which lasted only twenty years. American banks are chartered to do business by either a state or the federal government. Some states had free banking laws in the past which allowed anyone to open a bank. This contributed to the formation of "wildcat" banks, which were primarily schemes to get rich quickly by printing paper money.

The Federal Deposit Insurance Corporation (FDIC) was formed in 1933 to insure the deposits of banks. The bank buys the insurance but it is the customer who is protected since the insurance guarantees return of deposits even if the bank fails.

Where branch banking is not allowed, bank holding companies are often formed which own several banks and may do other financial business as well. Increasingly, computers are used by banks to do many tasks. Computers have enabled the Electronic Funds Transfer System (EFTS) to be established. EFTS means funds are transferred between accounts without using checks or paper money.

The commercial bank accepts deposits—both demand and time deposits—and transfers money on order. The chief liabilities of a commercial bank are its deposits and its capital. The assets of a commercial bank include cash on hand, securities owned, loans made, and the bank building and real estate.

The commercial banks are so named because they initially made loans only to businesses. Consumer credit has been a fairly recent development. Credit cards are an even more recent development. Banks provide numerous other services including time deposits, sale of government bonds, sale of foreign currencies, computer services, sale of traveler's checks, and management of estates.

Bank reserves consist of cash in the vaults and money on deposit at the Federal Reserve or at other banks. Banks are required to keep a specified fraction of the deposits as vault cash or on deposit at the Fed; this money is known as required reserves. The money not held in required reserve may be held as excess reserves. Most of the time, banks use the excess reserves to purchase securities or make loans.

Since the loan of one bank may become a deposit in another, the banking system can expand any deposit by some multiple. This means of creating money is known as multiple-bank deposit expansion.

The size of the deposit multiplier depends upon the reserve requirement. The lower the reserve requirement, the larger the multiple expansion of deposits. The multiplier is 1/reserve ratio.

The actual deposit multiplier is less than the theoretical maximum, because (1) cash leakages occur and (2) banks may not choose or be able to loan out all excess reserves.

Key Words and Phrases

- **unit banking**   a system of separate, locally maintained banks; no branches are allowed.
- **branch banking**   a system containing a few large banks with many branches.
- **money order**   an instrument used for the transfer of money. The person wishing to send money purchases one for the face amount plus a small fee; the order directs payment to the recipient.
- **bank note**   paper money issued by a particular bank.
- **bank charter**   the legal papers establishing a banking business.
- **"wildcat" banks**   banks of dubious integrity formed to issue money which would never be redeemed. The phrase originated from the fact that these banks were "located so far back in the woods that only 'wildcats' visited there."
- **banking panic**   a loss of confidence in the banking system or in one or a few particular banks causing depositors to attempt to withdraw all their money.
- **holding companies**   firms set up to own banks in states which do not allow branch banking; the holding company may also provide financial services which the bank(s) it owns are prohibited from doing.
- **Electronic Funds Transfer System**   the transfer of funds from one institution (bank) to another via computer; eliminates need for checks and currency.
- **creditor**   one who loans money or extends credit.
- **debtor**   one who borrows money or goes into debt.
- **reserves (total reserves)**   cash in vault and money on deposit at the Fed.
- **required reserves**   cash in vault or deposits by a bank at the Fed which the Fed requires the bank to maintain; the amount is set as a fraction of deposits in the bank.
- **reserve ratio**   the proportion or fraction of the bank's deposits which are required reserves.

- **excess reserves**   cash in the vault or deposits at the Fed which a bank maintains above the amount required; equals total reserves minus required reserves. These are the reserves used by banks to earn profits.
- **multiple-bank deposit expansion**   the creation of demand deposits in our banking system.
- **deposit multiplier**   the maximum number of times the demand deposits can be expanded by commercial banks.

Questions for Review

1.   Is your money safe in a bank? Why or why not?

2.   How do banks get away with keeping only a small fraction of their deposits on hand? What would banks be like if they had to keep everything deposited in them?

3.   With your book closed, use the banks in your area to build an example of what happens when one of them gets $1,000 of new deposits.

4.   If the reserve requirement is increased by 50%, what happens to the deposit multiplier? What happens to the amount of money available? Why?

5.   Why is the actual deposit multiplier less than the theoretical maximum?

6.   Since a bank cannot have more assets than liabilities, how can they create money unless they are counterfeiting?

7.   "Let me see the color of your money" used to mean more than simply prove you are ready to enter a transaction. Why?

8.   In St. Louis during the frontier period, furs often served as money. Yet many of the furs were stored in warehouses. How would people carry out transactions?

9.   Is your state a unit or branch bank state?

10.   Obtain a copy of an annual report from a local bank. Or, use one of the quarterly statements of condition published in the newspapers. What are the principal liabilities listed? What are the assets of the bank?

11.   From an advertising brochure or newspaper ad, find out how many services your local bank offers.

12.   Will EFTS ever eliminate the use of paper money? Explain.

13

Other Financial Intermediaries

In the previous chapter we discussed the role of commercial banks in bringing lender and borrower together. There are, however, other financial intermediaries that play an important part in this process. Such intermediaries range all the way from large savings institutions, through finance and personal loan companies, to the neighborhood pawnbroker. The more important of these intermediaries are major adjuncts to the nation's commercial banking system. And it is most likely that in the course of our lives each of us will have personal contact with one or more of these institutions.

Let us now consider at some length three major financial intermediaries that are at work in our economy: thrift institutions, the insurance industry, and institutions dealing in stocks and bonds.

Thrift institutions

The most important thrift institutions in our economy are (1) savings and loan associations, (2) mutual savings banks, and (3) credit unions. Of these three, savings and loans and mutual savings banks most closely resemble regular commercial banks. They offer many of the same services offered by commercial banks. The imposing bank building down your street, busily offering banking services to the general public, might well be the home of one of these institutions rather than a commercial bank. (One tip-off that it is not a commercial bank is likely to be the use of the word "savings" in the institution's name.)

Savings and loan associations

In the United States, associations for the collection of savings for the express purpose of financing home ownership began to spring up in the 1930s. Savers in such associations could either accumulate enough money to buy homes or could borrow mortgage money from the association to finance home ownership. Today, savings and loan associations (often called "S & L's" for short) still function as intermediaries between savers (lenders) and those who wish to borrow money to finance home building.

Comparison with commercial banks In terms of assets, the savings and loan industry is about one-third as large as the commercial banking industry, as may be seen in Table 1. However,

Table 1
Total Assets and Deposits of Commercial Banks and Savings and Loan Associations, Selected Years
(billions of dollars)

(a) Commercial Banks

Year	Total assets	Total loans	Business loans	Consumer loans	Total securities	U.S. treasury	Government agencies	Demand deposits	Time deposits
1950	199	60.3	—	—	96.6	—	—	90	36
1967	487.7	282.0	—	—	117.1	—	—	141.9	202.8
1970	576.2	313.3	109.6	203.7	147.8	61.7	86.1	142.5	178.8
1974	919.5	500.2	183.3	316.9	190.2	50.4	139.8	272.3	322.9
1975	964.9	496.9	176.0	320.9	224.2	79.4	144.8	281.8	338.7
1976	1010.8	576.0	176.2	379.8	244.5	101.2	143.3	318.4	494.0

(b) Savings and Loan Associations

Year	Total assets	Mortgages	Government securities & cash	Time deposits
1967	143.5	121.8	12.6	131.6
1970	176.2	150.3	16.5	146.4
1974	295.5	249.5	23.2	243.0
1975	338.4	278.7	30.9	286.0
1976	391.9	323.1	35.7	336.0

Source: Federal Reserve Bulletin.

all the deposits at S & L's are time deposits or shares. Commercial banks have both demand and time deposits. Notice that in 1950 demand deposits were almost three times as large as commercial bank time deposits, but by 1976, time deposits were almost twice as large as demand deposits. This probably indicates the increase in affluence of Americans.

There is a major difference in the types of loans made also. *The S & L's make mortgage loans almost exclusively.* In fact, in 1970 and 1974 the amount of mortgages was even greater than deposits, meaning the S & L's had to find the money somewhere else! A few government bonds are owned and some cash is also held by S & L's. Commercial banks, by contrast, own sizeable amounts of securities, about one-third of which are government bonds and the rest are bonds issued by government-related agencies. Loans of various sorts are most important among the earning assets of commercial banks. One-third of the loans are to businesses and the rest are mostly to consumers; small amounts are lent to other banks.

How S & L's Operate Almost all savings and loan associations are "owned" by their depositors. The actual operation of the association, however, is really done by salaried managers. When you open an account at an S & L, you technically become a "shareholder" in the institution. The income you earn on your deposit is called a "dividend," rather than interest. (Basically, however, there is no real difference here.) Your savings are credited to your account in the form of an entry in your passbook. Your dividends are also credited to you in the same way, generally every three months.

By regulation, you must notify the S & L a certain number of days beforehand if you intend to withdraw any or all of your savings. In practice, however, withdrawals from regular savings accounts are generally made upon demand and without notice (just as they are with a commercial bank's savings account).

The principal incentive for you to save at a S & L is that the association is generally allowed to pay a higher interest rate (dividend) on your savings than is a commercial bank. This interest rate differential varies from time to time, depending on the state of the economy and the Federal Reserve System's activities in setting commercial bank interest rates. It may also vary from area to area and even from bank to bank. Neither commercial banks nor thrift institutions always pay the maximum allowable interest rate on savings accounts. Rates may depend on how aggressively bank managers seek savings accounts in a given area or in a given economic situation. A typical allowable differential between commercial bank and thrift institution interest rates is shown in Table 2 (these values applied in 1976).

Besides regular passbook accounts, savings and loan associations offer so-called "certificates of savings" accounts at higher rates of interest (as do commercial banks). Depending on government regulations, you may usually purchase such certificates in the amount of $500 or up, with the stipulation that the money must stay on deposit from a minimum of ninety days up to a designated number of years. (For wealthy individuals and corporations, S & L's may offer up to $100,000 certificates of savings at very favorable rates and time terms.)

If you should decide to withdraw your savings before the certificates mature, you generally will be allowed to do so. Certificates are issued for a fixed time period and **maturity** refers to the date they expire. However, you will then forfeit the higher dividend (plus a certain amount of regular dividend) that you would have gained by keeping your savings on

Table 2

Typical Interest Rate Differential Between Commercial Banks and Savings and Loan Associations (1976)

Type of account	Maximum allowable savings rates	
	Commercial banks	Savings and loans
Regular (passbook)	5%	5.25%
90-day (passbook)	5.5%	5.75%
One to two-and-a-half years (certificate)	6%	6.5%
Two-and-a-half to four years (certificate)	6.5%	6.75%
Four to six years (certificate, minimum $1,000)	7.25%	7.5%

Source: Federal Reserve Bulletin.

deposit until maturity. Of course, if you have a four-year certificate and do not want your money when it matures, you can always purchase another one and leave your money on deposit.

Like commercial banks, savings and loan associations are chartered by either the federal or the state government. About one-third have federal charters.

All federally chartered S & L's are members of the **Federal Home Loan Bank** system (FHLB). Some states require their state-chartered associations to belong to the system. Other states give their associations the option to join if they wish. Actually, over 90% of all S & L's belong to the FHLB.

The Federal Home Loan Bank system was set up in the early 1930s to help deal with association failures spawned by the Great Depression. The system is patterned after the Federal Reserve System, which helped deal with commercial bank problems during the same period. Like the Fed, the FHLB has regional banks serving as "bankers' banks" for local associations. Although the FHLB does not control the business operations of S & L's in the same manner as the Fed controls commercial banks, it does provide assistance to associations and acts as a kind of watchdog over operations. Local associations are encouraged to maintain deposits at their regional Federal Home Loan Bank as security against loans. Or a regional bank may sell some of its own assets to raise cash for an association temporarily in need of it.

Also in the 1930s, and for much the same reasons as the FHLB was set up, the **Federal Savings and Loan Insurance Corporation** (FSLIC) was created. Like the Federal Deposit Insurance Corporation (FDIC) set up to protect commercial bank depositors, the FSLIC provides insurance against loss of personal savings because of association failure. Each S & L pays a small percentage of its savings deposits as a premium for the service. The FSLIC sign on the facade of a savings and loan association building gives the same reassurance to association customers as does the FDIC insignia on commercial banks. (State-chartered associations not covered by FSLIC are required by state law to insure deposits with private insurance firms.)

A savings and loan association must retain a margin of assets in excess of the value of the claims represented by its deposits. This margin, depending on government regulation, runs around 10% of the association's investment earnings. The margin is a buffer against unusual drains on the association's assets. It is not, like the reserve of a commercial bank, an asset in itself (although the margin is often termed a "reserve"). It is not available for lending. It is, rather, similar to the capital account found in a commercial bank's balance sheet.

Mutual savings banks

Almost everything we have said above about savings and loan associations applies also to mutual savings banks. Both types of institutions are engaged primarily in the business of supplying mortgage loans. They both serve as intermediaries between lenders and builders.

Mutual savings banks—or just *savings banks* as they are generally called—are found in the Northeastern states. The preponderance of them are in Massachusetts, New York, and Pennsylvania. They are not prevalent in newer sections of the nation. In these newer areas, the development of commercial banks and savings and loan associations made them unnecessary. There are, in fact, about ten times as many savings and loan associations in the nation as there are savings banks.

Table 3 shows that the savings bank industry has total assets of $130.6 billion, which is about one-third as large as the S & L industry. Savings bank deposits are all time deposits. There are some differences in the loans made between savings banks and S & L's. Savings banks make mortgage loans, but their mortgages in recent years total only about half of the deposits in the banks. Personal loans are made by some savings banks and the rapid growth of these loans may be seen in Table 3 (in the column "Other loans").

Savings banks purchase government securities which they hold for the interest earnings. From 1960 to 1970, the holdings of government securities declined but then began increasing again. Savings banks also own corporate stocks

Table 3
Total Assets and Deposits of Mutual Savings Banks (billions of dollars)

Year	Total assets	Mortgages	Other loans	Government securities*	Corporate securities	Cash	Time deposits
1960	40.6	26.7	0.4	6.9	5.1	0.9	36.3
1965	58.2	44.4	0.9	5.8	5.2	1.0	52.4
1970	79.0	57.8	2.3	3.4	12.9	1.3	71.6
1975	121.0	77.1	4.0	6.3	28.0	2.4	109.8
1976	130.6	79.8	5.2	8.1	32.3	1.6	118.2

Source: Federal Reserve Bulletin.
*Federal, state, and local government securities.

and bonds. There has been a rapid increase in their holdings of corporate securities from 1960 to 1976.

Unlike savings and loan associations, mutual savings banks are all state chartered and are hence regulated by state bodies. About 60% of them come under some federal regulation, however, through membership in the Federal Deposit Insurance Corporation, the same body that insures commercial bank deposits. Savings banks not holding FDIC insurance are covered by state or private insurance plans.

Like S & L's, savings banks are "mutually owned." That is, there are no outside owners of bank stock, as there are with commercial banks. Legally, however, savings banks are not really "owned" by their depositors or by anyone. They are controlled by trustees appointed by the state. Like S & L's, they are required to keep a designated margin of assets over debt claims held against them by depositors.

Savings banks and savings and loan associations both provide many banking services aside from their prime function of financing home ownership. They provide almost all the services offered by commercial banks—from traveler's checks and holiday savings funds to individual retirement accounts and investment advice. They provide for electronic transfer of funds among their branches and between themselves and commercial banks. They sell low-cost insurance and provide trustee accounts for estates. Savings banks in New York now may even provide personal consumer loans (up to a maximum of $1,000), a service heretofore confined to commercial banks.

Only commercial banks are allowed to provide demand-deposit checking accounts. But aside from this very important distinction and a few others, the line between services offered by savings institutions and commercial banks is rapidly being blurred.

Credit unions

A third important thrift institution is the credit union. A **credit union** is a cooperative savings association formed by members of some recognized group. Most often, the association embraces all employees of a particular firm or all members of a labor union or of a professional organization. In some areas, a geographic boundary may define who can belong to the association.

Members of a credit union join by purchasing shares in the association. Shares are valued at a fixed amount, usually $5.00. But fractional shares may be purchased, and savings of amounts as low as a quarter per month may be allowed. Withdrawals legally require 60 days' prior notice but in practice are paid on demand. Depositors are the owners of the credit union.

Credit unions are very low-cost operations. Often, the employer or other sponsoring group provides offices and other necessary facilities. The officers and directors, as members of the group, serve without pay. Members may volunteer their services in the day-to-day activities of the union. Larger credit unions, however, may pay salaries for needed services. Credit union profits are usually exempt from income taxes. For these reasons, successful credit unions are able to pay members dividends that are somewhat higher than those paid by S & L's or banks.

Credit unions can offer their member-owners readily accessible loans at very reasonable rates. Loans are typically small, perhaps from $300 to $1,000. The purpose of the loan may be almost anything the borrower desires. Above $300, a cosigner on the loan, usually a fellow member, may be required. Of course, the member may secure the loan by pledging his shares in the union as collateral. Members of a group may join its credit union to obtain a loan without a prior purchase of shares. For employee groups, repayment is usually made by payroll deductions that go directly to the credit union.

Credit unions, like S & L's, may be chartered by the state or by the federal government. Slightly more than half of the credit unions are federally chartered. Like other thrift institutions, they are subject to reserve regulations and other rules and restrictions. However, depositors (share owners) are not insured against loss. But regulations require that excess reserves be kept in insured banks, and the credit union's investment of its excess funds is restricted to low-risk securities. Credit union failures have been very infrequent. Conservative lending policies and group loyalty of credit union members serve to keep loan losses at a minimum.

Unlike savings and loan associations and mutual savings banks, credit unions act primarily as financial intermediaries between lenders and *consumer*-spenders. Most loans are for purchases of consumer items such as cars, boats, TV sets, or other such products, or perhaps for minor home repair needs. Since loans are for relatively low amounts, the total money involved in credit union loans is comparatively small. For example, total assets of credit unions were $45 billion in 1976, which is approximately one-eighth of the total assets of savings and loan associations. However, in 1976, credit unions financed almost 99% of all nonautomobile installment credit.

The number of credit unions is large—nearly 23,000—and so are the number of members—34 million. Credit unions have expanded past their original role—to provide low-income loans to factory workers who couldn't get commercial bank loans. Credit unions now embrace middle-income and some upper-income workers. In fact, credit unions are presently the fastest growing financial intermediary. So their role as financial intermediary in the nation's economy is by no means insignificant.

Economic impact of mortgage money

Earlier in this section, we touched on the role of savings and loan associations and savings banks as intermediaries between lenders and those who wish to borrow for home construction and home ownership. Let us now consider in somewhat more detail the importance of this mortgage-money function to our economy.

Approximately 85% of the assets of a typical savings and loan association will be in first mortgage loans. That is, 85% of its loans will have been made for the purpose of home construction and home ownership. Sixty percent of the loans of the typical mutual savings bank are made for the same purpose. Savings deposits are the principal assets of savings and loan associations and savings banks. The long-term nature of these deposit accounts provides a stable source of assets for lending. The stability of these assets makes them an ideal source of funds for long-term financing of home buying and home construction.

It is difficult to overestimate the importance of home construction in our economy. Nationally, 111,000 houses were being completed each month in 1976. In addition, approximately 20,000 mobile homes were shipped each month. Residential construction resulted in $59 billion of expenditures. The effect of all this may be better likened to a wave than a ripple. First, of course, are the vast number of jobs involved in the construction industry itself—jobs for carpenters, bricklayers, electricians, glaziers, plumbers, architects, to name just a few. And, to back up a step, there are the jobs for people who work in plants providing materials and finished products that go into home construction—plants that produce cement, bathroom fixtures, furnaces, air conditioners, and so on.

Then there are the vast number of jobs and products involved in furnishing and maintaining a finished home. A myriad of industries and workers are likely to be involved in the economic life of a home—from producers of cups to producers of carpets, from purveyors of garbage disposals to purveyors of grass seed. The list could go on and on.

Statistics on "housing starts" are a common ingredient of the monthly economic news mentioned by the media. Such statistics are a vital indicator of the health of a nation's economy. The thrift institutions that function as a principal conduit of the mortgage money behind these statistics are indeed important to the nation's economy.

When people fail to add to their savings or even withdraw their savings from the savings and loans and mutual savings banks, the impact on new housing construction is often very dramatic. During periods of unemployment, people cannot add to and may draw from their deposits. If interest rates or earnings opportunities are better elsewhere, say in bonds or stocks, people do not place their money in the S & L's or mutual savings banks. When the deposits fail to grow or even decline, the major sources of mortgage money soon dry up. As a result, construction soon declines since few people are able to arrange the necessary financing for new houses. The supplying industries may also be affected. In addition, sales of home furnishings and appliances decline and workers may be laid off. The effects go far beyond the construction industry to reach many parts of the economy.

The insurance industry

The concept of insurance (sometimes called *assurance*) goes back to ancient times. Babylonian traders "insured" their caravans against loss. They financed them with loans that had to be repaid only if the caravans arrived safely. The rate of interest on the loans depended on the risk involved in the caravan journey. The Greeks applied a similar practice to their seaborne trade. Romans developed burial clubs to provide funeral funds for members. Later, the clubs provided benefits to survivors of the deceased—the rudimentary beginnings of life insurance.

By the Middle Ages, *marine insurance* (insurance against loss at sea) was common in all the maritime nations of Europe. The most famous of all marine insurance companies—

Lloyd's of London—was founded in the late seventeenth century. It was named after a coffeehouse where merchants and shippers gathered to conduct business. Today, Lloyd's will insure almost anything—from a professional soccer player's legs to good weather for a public celebration.

The first insurance company in what is now the United States was established in 1735, in Charleston, S.C. Fire insurance companies were established in New York in 1787 and in Philadelphia a few years later. The first life insurance company in America was established by Philadelphia Presbyterians in 1759 for the benefit of ministers and their families. Burglary insurance came into being in 1885; this type of insurance was strictly an American development. Health and hospital insurance only appeared in 1929.

Today in the United States, the institution of insurance touches our lives from cradle to grave. The majority of us have life insurance policies which pay money to our heirs when we die. Most of us hold one or more other kinds of insurance—health and hospital, fire, theft, automobile liability, to name just a few possibilities. Even if we do not directly hold insurance policies, we are still very likely "covered" by some aspect of the insurance system. Government insurance such as Social Security and unemployment compensation provide protection for almost everyone. *Liability insurance* held by others protects us from financial hardships caused by accidents. If the stairs of old East Wormwood Hall finally collapse beneath your feet, for example, the school's insurance company will come to your financial rescue (and protect the school from your lawsuit).

What is the basic principle behind this financial institution we call insurance? *All financial intermediaries deal with risk.* Bank loans may go unpaid, for example, and loan interest rates must be set high enough to compensate for this risk. *Insurance companies, however, actually profit on the concept of risk.* They are, so to speak, in the risk business. Through dealing in risk they are able to amass vast sums to lend to borrowers. How is this possible?

Each day, each of us faces the possibility of two main kinds of loss—loss of life (or loss of health, a "partial loss of life") and loss of property. You may suddenly die. Your property may be stolen, or go up in flames. Now, it is impossible to say for sure that you will die a week from Thursday or that your home will burn down two years from the day you built it. Such events are unpredictable. But they are unpredictable only individually. *For large groups of people and houses, they are highly predictable.*

Beginning in the seventeenth century, statisticians have been able to work out tables that compute the actual probability of such events happening in a given group. Working from recorded data, they have found that although *you* might not die a week from Thursday (or at some other particular time), *someone* in your group (your age, occupation, or geographic group, for example) will. They know, likewise, that it is highly probable that *someone's* house will burn down within a given period of time.

Loss of life or property means financial loss. Obviously, most individuals cannot put aside enough money to compensate themselves or their families for such loss. What they can do is join together in groups to protect against risk. Each individual can contribute a small amount of money to a pool, out of which the members of the group who actually suffer loss will be compensated. Since statisticians are able to tell the group the probability of loss, the group knows how much money it must keep in the pool to compensate potential victims of loss. Each member risks a small loss—the money he or she pays into the pool—to avoid the consequences of a greater loss—loss of life or property.

Insurance companies are basically agents for such groups. They collect the individual's small contribution to the pool and pay out larger sums to victims of loss. The contributions are called **premiums.** The sums paid out are called **benefits.**

The insurance company provides this service for profit. It must take in more than it pays out. Consequently, it sets premium rates according to its probability tables. Also, it puts restriction on its coverage. It will not insure against chance events for which there are no statistical data. (Try as you may, you cannot get insurance against being kidnaped by visitors from outer space.) Insurance companies will not insure against catastrophic events such as war damage, which would present losses far too extensive for their pool holdings. And they are reluctant to provide coverage for other events that might prove too great a drain on their holdings—flood insurance, for example, or burglary and theft insurance in high-crime areas.

The establishment and operation of insurance companies are regulated by various governmental agencies and commissions. There are, for example, regulations governing the amount and kinds of investments insurance companies may make. These regulations are designed to ensure that enough funds are on hand or readily available to pay claims. Originally, insurance companies were regulated only by state agencies. Since the mid-1940s, however, the federal government has also been involved in such regulation.

Let us now take a brief look at some of the more important types of insurance prevalent in our society.

Life insurance

Life insurance is designed primarily to compensate the *dependents* for any financial hardship caused by the *insured person's* death. As such, it may be term insurance or straight life insurance.

Term insurance There is a policy by which a person contracts to pay periodic premiums based on the amount of death benefits designated and the current probability of the policy-holder's death. This is term insurance. The premiums (but not the benefits) rise as the insured person gets older. This is because death rates increase with age. However, premiums on term life insurance generally start at a low rate.

Straight life insurance The policy by which a person contracts to pay the same annual premium throughout the life of the policy is called straight life insurance. In the early years, the holder is actually paying a premium higher than that called for by the mathematical probability of his death. This enables the company to collect more money than it would with term insurance. Out of these additional funds, the insurance company, in effect, contributes the extra money needed for rising premiums as the insured person gets older and the probability of death increases. In this manner the policy-holder pays out the same premiums throughout his life or the life of the policy.

In addition, higher premiums are a kind of forced savings. The reserve money that is built up by high payments belongs to the policy-holder in that he can borrow on it during the life of the policy. Of course, if he dies while the loan is outstanding, the amount of the loan will be deducted from the money paid to his beneficiaries. (The receiver of a policy's benefits is called *beneficiary*.) Also, the policy-holder can cancel the policy and have the reserve returned to him.

Annuity and endowment policies Life insurance coverage is provided by annuity and endowment insurance policies. The primary intent of these policies, however, is to provide future financial security. Premiums on such policies may be quite high, depending in part on the amount the holder (or his heirs) expect to receive at some designated time in the future. A proportion of the premiums is kept in "reserve" for this purpose. (Actually, the premium payments are invested by the company in securities, bonds, or some other income-producing activity.) A common procedure is to have the policy cancelled in old age, say at retirement, at 65. The amount of money built up by this time may run into the thousands of dollars. The money can be paid in a lump sum, or in monthly payments at a fixed rate for the rest of the policy-holder's life (once again, the statisticians can find an average age of death). This is a popular life insurance plan. (Of course, the amount of money the policy-holder receives is considerably less than if the money used for premiums were paid or deposited directly in a commercial bank or thrift institution.)

Pension plans

Pension policies (or pension insurance plans) are specifically intended to provide income upon the holder's retirement from active labor. Most policies provide income until the death of the retired person. Many continue payments to widows and dependent children of retirees.

They are closely akin to annuities and endowments in purpose but much wider in extent.

It has been said that life insurance provides protection if you die and pensions provide it if you live too long. Be that as it may, pension plans provide a convenient method for saving for your later years. As such, they have become an important segment of the insurance industry and an influential source of investment funds.

The bulk of pension insurance policies today are those covering a specific group of employees or professional people. Many are funded by contributions of management and/or labor within individual companies, or by professional societies and/or their members.

Pension policies may be written and pension funds managed by regular insurance companies, insurance companies specializing in pension operations, or by investment departments of banks.

Noninsured pension plans We should note here that many pension plans operate outside the insurance industry. These "noninsured" programs are often managed by the owners of a company or the directors of the group involved. For a long time there was little outside regulation of such plans. Their success and solvency depended primarily on the business sense, good will, and honesty of the plan's managers. In 1975, however, a Federal Pension Law was passed to help control and supervise such plans. In addition, many noninsured plans are managed by trust departments of commercial banks, which all but guarantees their successful operation.

State and local governments may also operate pension plans outside the insurance industry. If they do not call upon private companies to handle their pension plans, they may set up their own agencies to handle them. They may also turn to commercial bank trust departments. The United States government itself operates the largest "pension plan" of all—the Social Security system.

Health and hospital insurance

Health and hospital insurance is intended to pay, or help us pay, our medical expenses. It is available from the insurance industry either on an individual or group basis. Through statistical probabilities, insurance companies know that someone in your "group" is likely to get sick at some particular time, is likely to run up x number of dollars in doctor bills, and is likely to spend y number of days in the hospital and use z number of hospital services. Consequently, the companies are willing to insure you against medical expenses in return for a regular contribution (your premium payment) to a fund set up to pay such expenses.

You may purchase a health and hospital policy that will reimburse you for every conceivable medical service you may be unfortunate enough to need—including services for catastrophic illness. Or your policy may have an upper limit on reimbursement for services—for example, just so much toward the cost of your hospital room, just so much for a given surgical procedure, just so much for doctor bills. Also, your policy may cover hospital expenses only, or doctor bills only. Some private insurance health and hospital policies are automatically cancelled when you reach a certain high-risk age. Others remain in force throughout the holder's lifetime. Naturally, the extent and quantity of coverage you receive depend on the amount of premiums you (and/or your employer) pay.

Private insurance companies also offer *disability insurance*, often in connection with regular health and hospital policies. If you purchase such a policy, the company will pay you a designated "maintenance income" up to a given length of time should poor health or physical disability prevent you from earning a living.

Noninsured health and hospital plans As with pension plans, health and hospital plans may operate outside the insurance industry. Health insurance may be obtained from various non-profit, so-called "prepayment" plans. The best known of these is the one most of us are familiar with—Blue Cross-Blue Shield. As do private insurance companies, Blue Cross-Blue Shield bases premium rates on the extent and type of coverage offered. Like private compa-

nies, it offers coverage on an individual or group basis. Benefits are usually paid directly to the hospital or physician that provides the medical services covered by the policy.

Government also plays a major role in health and hospital insurance outside the insurance industry. Workmen's compensation, Medicare, Medicaid, veterans' hospitals, and other governmental institutions provide health services and compensation for physical disability to millions of Americans. The "premiums" paid to provide these services are, of course, contributed by the nation's taxpayers.

Property insurance

Just as you may insure your life or your health, you may also insure your property, including your financial assets. Insurance statisticians know the probability of your being burglarized, sued for damages, or having your home or place of business burned down or damaged by a tornado. Consequently, they are willing to assume the risk of such events in return for your payment of a designated premium.

You may insure your household or business property against almost any contingency—fire, theft, wind storms, and so on. Businessmen may insure safe transit of their products on land, sea, and in the air. Car owners may insure their vehicles against accident damage. Store owners may insure against breakage of the plate glass windows of their establishments. The list is almost endless.

As with life insurance, the premiums you pay for property insurance will depend on the amount and extent of coverage you purchase. And, as with other insurance, it will also depend on the risk involved. Fire insurance premiums, for example, will be influenced by the structure (wood? concrete?) of the building involved, and perhaps even by the quality of available fire-fighting services. Premiums for insurance of a ship's cargo may vary with prevailing weather conditions.

Liability insurance

Insurance against property may also take the form of insurance against loss of financial assets due to damage you may cause to other persons' lives or property. *Casualty* or *liability insurance* may be purchased to cover such loss. *One form of liability insurance most of us are familiar with is automobile insurance.* Most states require such insurance for licensed vehicles. If you hold such insurance and have an accident, your insurance company will pay for the damage caused to other people or their property. The extent of the damage it pays will depend on the type of policy you hold.

There are many other types of liability insurance. Individuals and business firms may insure against injury-causing accidents that occur on their property. Businesses may insure against the possibility of damage being done by their products—perhaps a supermarket's assignment of canned fish may spoil in transit, for example, and be inadvertantly sold to the public. Storekeepers may insure against the possibility of a store sign falling on a customer or against the possibility of a passerby being injured by splinters from a shattered storefront window.

Of course, there must be an element of negligence involved if the injured party is entitled to damages. But negligence may be difficult to prove or disprove. (Was the shattered window caused by the wind? Or was it poorly installed in the first place?) Most businesses are happy to purchase liability insurance and let the insurance company fight such matters in court.

Professional people such as physicians and surgeons may also insure against injury being caused by negligence in the course of their professional activities. Such liability coverage is commonly referred to as *malpractice insurance.*

Economic impact of the insurance industry

It is obvious even from our brief discussion of the insurance industry that a vast amount of savings accrue to it through premium payments. In 1976, for example, life insurance companies alone totaled approximately $300 billion in assets. Where and how the industry invests these assets is of prime importance to the economy.

Life insurance companies are likely to invest in long-term, low-risk securities and in relatively safe financial enterprises. *Their need for cash is fairly predictable because of their reliance on proven probability tables. They do not need to hold substantial liquid assets.*

They invest heavily in commercial mortgages. That is, *they supply money for the building of commercial enterprises such as manufacturing facilities, office buildings, and apartment houses.* They may make mortgage loans directly to builders. They may also purchase mortgages from other financial institutions that specialize in lending mortgage money. If state regulations allow, they may even directly enter the real estate market. They may finance, build, and maintain hotels, commercial recreation areas, apartment complexes, and even shopping centers.

Life insurance companies also invest heavily in government bonds and low-risk corporate bonds. They thus contribute to the smooth flow of the nation's governmental services and to the expansion and stability of the nation's corporate economy. (In 1977, mortgages and corporation bonds accounted for about three-quarters of the life insurance industry's assets.)

Property insurance companies are more likely to invest in common stocks than in bonds and mortgages. Although the companies operate on the basis of tables of probability, the nature and extent of property damage is less predictable than the probability of death and ill health. Who could foresee with any great degree of certainty, for example, the collapse of a dam or the destruction of a whole town by tornado? Consequently, property insurers need ready access to cash should such catastrophes occur. Common stock provides a source of such liquid assets.

Thus fire and casualty insurance companies have their greatest economic impact in the stock market. Their heavy purchase of common stocks supplies needed money for new businesses and for expansion of existing ones.

Extended Example
The Rising Cost of Liability Insurance

You have probably not worried about rising insurance costs, with the possible exception of automobile insurance (which is a form of liability insurance). However, in the mid-1970s, liability insurance costs became a disaster area—indirectly affecting even you. Costs for malpractice insurance and product liability—both forms of liability insurance—doubled, tripled, even quadrupled within one- and two-year periods. Since doctors pay malpractice insurance and manufacturers pay product liability insurance, you might say "Why should I worry?" Because you pay indirectly for this insurance when costs are passed on to the consumer!

Consider the problem of malpractice insurance. In 1975, the generally steady rise in premium costs of medical malpractice insurance coverage took an astounding leap forward—premium costs rose as much as 500% in that year alone. Why? Because the courts started awarding greatly increased payments for medical negligence and because lawyers and patients followed by increasing the law suits. Hospitals and medical practitioners complained they could not afford the expense of rising insurance, and insurance companies threatened to withdraw from the medical malpractice business if premiums were not raised even higher.

The crisis was well publicized and the evening television news documented more than a few unedifying instances of doctors going on strike to protest rising insurance costs. State legislators and medical societies stepped in to try to deal with the crisis, the former to provide arbitration panels to hear malpractice suits and to dampen down excessive awards to complainants, the latter to form their own doctor-owned insurance companies to write malpractice insurance. The health-care industry, unfortunately, had one of the highest rates of inflation among all American industries in the 1970s. The average worker's paycheck did not increase anywhere as quickly as did hospital and doctor bills. Malpractice insurance costs contributed in part to the inflated bills.

When doctors started countersuing patients and winning the suits, the number of malpractice suits in the courts declined. The problem of high malpractice insurance costs remains, however, and some observers feel that the only long-run solution lies in federal government involvement in subsidization of medical malpractice insurance, as it is now involved in flood insurance and burglary insurance in high-crime localities.

A less well-publicized, but even more serious crisis is shaping up in another area of liability insurance—product liability. Here, too, premiums are zooming, and at roughly $1.5 billion a year the premiums are approximately twice the total paid for medical malpractice insurance. For some companies, premium costs have risen from less than 1% of sales revenue to as high as 15%, thus threatening to wipe out product profitability entirely. Hardest hit have been makers of industrial machinery and industrial chemicals and manufacturers of high-risk consumer goods such as medical devices, car parts, and drugs. And again as with malpractice coverage, insurers are threatening to discontinue writing product liability insurance unless higher premiums are paid.

Rising product liability costs harmed more than just manufacturers, who had reduced profits. Some small firms went out of business. In the drug industry, for example, firms cut back on the development of new drugs and vaccines. The drug firms reasoned, "Why develop a new product when a few users who contract negative side effects can sue and win large sums of money?" (Human biology being as it is, when a large number of people use a drug—any drug—some few will develop negative side effects.) Eventually, many firms in diverse industries—toy manufacturers and electrical appliance makers, for example—started raising their prices to consumers to offset insurance costs.

The immediate cause of soaring product liability rates is fairly evident: increased complexity and injury-risk of many new products whose existence was undreamed of a generation or so ago and increased consumer awareness of the right to redress against injury. The long-term cause, however, and the one possibly more amenable to change, seems to lie in the court system developed over the years to deal with product liability cases.

In the 1970s, the courts moved toward a position where the maker of a product is responsible for any product defect that causes injury—and this for the full life of the product. For example, it has been estimated that one out of every five claims for injuries suffered on the job involves a machine over thirty years old and 75% of all such claims involve machinery over ten years old. The employers who purchased and use these machines are totally without responsibility for injury claims even though the machines may have been allowed to deteriorate through employer negligence.

Neither is the employee likely to be held responsible for his or her own negligence. Recently, for example, a miner crippled on the job was awarded $500,000 to be paid by the maker of the coal shuttle car that injured him, even though his fellow workers testified he had been improperly trained by his employer and was not operating the car correctly. In automobile-part failure cases—brake failure, for example—the fact that the operator of the vehicle may have been drunk at the time of the accident would very probably be inadmissible as evidence in a court suit for redress against injury.

Most observers agree that reinstatement of the principle that *contributory negligence* can be a defense against sole responsibility of the manufacturer for product injury is a necessary first step toward solving the product liability crisis. In addition, it is widely felt that legislation should be developed to put some limit on the amount of money that can be awarded in specific product liability cases, especially on so-called *punitive damages* over and above actual economic loss caused by the injury. Insurance sources estimate that in the average bodily-injury suit, victims (or survivors) are awarded $9.00 in tax-free cash for every $1.00 of economic loss (loss of wages, medical expenses, and so on).

All observers agree, however, that the right to be redressed for injury from defective products must not be undermined. In today's society, such protection is an imperative consumer right. (It is true that state workmen's compensation laws provide some protection against outright destitution brought about by on-the-job injury, but such compensation is more often than not inadequate. In Massachusetts, for instance, loss of an entire hand is valued at only $5,250.) Nevertheless, consumers must also realize that there is a price to pay for this necessary right—in higher product prices and sometimes in complete product loss if premium costs become unacceptable. How much are consumers willing to pay for how much product safety and for how much protection against product defect? The correct answer to that question should be the concern not just of insurers and product manufacturers, but of all of us.

The securities market

Institutions dealing in the buying and selling of securities are another major financial intermediary in our economy. As do banks and insurance companies, they help bring together lenders and borrowers. They do this by dealing in **securities,** which is the general term we use for *stocks* and *bonds*.

Stocks and bonds are simply printed pieces of paper saying that the owner of the paper has a claim against whoever issued the paper. They are just another form of promise-to-pay agreements (IOU's if you wish) that we have discussed previously. If you buy new-issue stock in a company, you are in effect lending money to it. In return, the company promises you a "share" of its profits. If you buy a bond, the bond issuer promises to pay back the price of the bond (your loan to the issuer) plus a designated amount of interest. In either case, you have a credit claim against the borrower.

Theoretically, the owner of a company that needs a loan (perhaps to develop a new product) could come knocking at your door and ask if you had some spare cash to lend him. But that's not how it happens in our vast economy. Instead of coming to you directly, the company that needs a loan goes to the securities market. There it issues (prints up) promises-to-pay and waits for someone to come around and purchase them. We are oversimplifying things, of course, but that is what basically happens in the financial intermediary we call the *securities market*.

The securities market goes by many names (some of them unprintable when the market "goes sour," as it sometimes does). It is referred to as the *stock exchange*, or simply *the exchange*, as Wall Street, or simply the Street. If we are interested only in bonds, we may refer to it as the bond market. Whatever we call it, the securities market is nothing more or less than certain financial institutions—investment companies and brokerage houses, for example—set up to buy and sell securities. We will consider the actual day-to-day operations of these institutions in some detail later on in this section. But first, let us consider the two major credit instruments they deal in: stocks and bonds.

Stocks

As noted above, if you buy stock in a company, you are entitled to a share in the company's profits. You have, in effect, become part owner of the company. The number of shares you buy determines how much of the company you own and your share of the company's profits. But what if there are no profits? Then your investment earns you nothing. Indeed, the company may lose money or even fail completely. Then the value of your loan to the company (the price of your shares) falls, or even becomes worthless. That is the risk you take (and one reason why money invested in securities is called "risk capital").

There are two major types of company (corporation) stock: preferred and common.

Preferred stock If you buy preferred stock in a corporation, your investment is subject to less risk. The corporation promises to pay you a fixed amount each year out of its profits (if there are profits). It further promises to pay you this amount before other stockholders get their share of the profits.

For example, let us say that a corporation has 1,000 shares of preferred stock outstanding. Each share originally represented a $100 loan to the corporation, for a total of $100,000. The corporation promised to pay a 5% dividend each year on each $100 share. (Interest on stock loans is called a **dividend**.) Let us say that the profits turn out to be $5,000 for one particular year. The holders of the 1,000 shares of preferred stock would receive their promised $5.00 for each share. But, as you can see, that takes care of the profits. Owners of nonpreferred stock would likely receive nothing that year on *their* investment.

Preferred stock has other advantages which need not concern us here. Suffice it to say, that these advantages are primarily in the "less risk" category. For example, if a corporation goes bankrupt, preferred stockholders would have some priority to claims on its remaining assets.

Common stock Stock which carries no debt claim preference of any kind is called common stock. Perhaps it should be called the "not-so-common stock," since it is the foundation stone of securities investment. It represents the ownership of our corporate economy. Calling it "common" does not imply that it is undistinguished. The common stock of a corporation is the "paper proof" that the corporation is owned "in common" by all its shareholders.

As already noted, stock shares in a corporation entitle the holder to a share of the corporation's profits—if any. Shareholders receive their share of these profits in the form of "dividends."

The dividend is generally paid in cash, in which case it is called a "cash dividend." If business has been especially good, the corporation may pay out its regular dividend plus an extra dividend.

Sometimes a corporation will pay a "stock dividend." It may have cash profits to distribute, but prefers to use this cash for further expansion. It will then give the stockholder additional stock in the company instead of cash. If, for example, a 3% stock dividend is declared, a holder of 100 shares of stock would receive three additional shares to add to his portfolio. (The total stocks and bonds held by an investor is called his **portfolio.**)

Sometimes a corporation may declare a *stock split*. For example, it may declare a two-for-one split. If you owned 100 shares of such stock, you would now have 200 shares in your portfolio. But this would not be a dividend. If each of your 100 shares was worth $100 before the split, each of your 200 shares after the split would be worth only $50. As a stockholder, you have gained nothing (except, perhaps, 200 pieces of prettily-printed paper). A corporation does not split its stock to directly reward its stockholders. Its primary purpose is to lower the stock's price per share. At a lower market price, more investors are more likely to invest in the corporation's stock, which will result in a higher value assigned to the corporation.

We have noted that common stock represents ownership of a corporation. We have also noted that stock represents a share in corporation profits. But common stock (unlike preferred stock) does not *guarantee* a fixed percentage of the profits. In fact, it does not guarantee that the holder will get any of the profits at all. The corporation may decide that all the year's profits should be spent on productivity expansion. Or perhaps that they should be put aside for some financial emergency the company anticipates for the following year. Or, as we have seen, the company may pay in corporation stock instead of cash.

But you, as a stockholder, are part owner of the corporation. Don't you have anything to say in the matter? Well, yes and no. As an owner of the company, you get a vote in the election of its board of directors—one vote for each share you own. You also get to vote on various other corporation matters. But the directors remain in control of the corporation's day-to-day operations. They make the decisions, including the matter of dividend payments. You can readily see why this must be so. Thousands of stockholders, scattered all over the country (and indeed the world), could not possibly operate the corporation's business.

However, as a stockholder, you are not without influence. You do help elect the company's officers. Consequently, these officers want to keep you happy. They will try to run the corporation at a profit and to pay out dividends whenever they reasonably can. If they displease enough stockholders often enough

and long enough, some or all of them could be voted out of office. (By law, the corporation must each year mail official election ballots to each of its stockholders.)

In recent years, some stockholders have attempted to put representatives of public interest groups on the board of directors of their corporations. These stockholders feel that the directors of large corporations should include, say, an environmentalist to ensure that profits do not come at the expense of pollution. Or, perhaps, that the board should include a minority race member to ensure equal opportunity in employment. Such stockholders' efforts have as yet met with minimum success, but they can be expected to continue.

Value of stocks Stocks are said to have three kinds of value: *book value, par value,* and *market value.* **Book value** is the value of corporate stock according to the corporation's bookkeeper. The accountant adds up the company's assets, subtracts its debts, and divides the result by the number of shares outstanding. This gives the book value of each share of stock. **Par value** is simply the amount printed on the stock certificate when it was first issued by the company. It indicates that this is the minimum price that the corporation may legally accept for each share of stock. It generally is set low and is meaningless except to fulfill certain legal requirements.

Neither book value nor par value is very important to most investors. Market value, however, is another kettle of fish. **Market value** is the price at which stocks are bought and sold on the securities market. Market value changes from day to day and even from hour to hour and minute to minute. Market price of a stock fluctuates with the current fortunes of the company involved and with its prospects for the future. It fluctuates also with the "psychology" of the market—the fears and hopes of the people involved in buying and selling stocks.

Types of securities markets To understand this fluctuation we must understand that the securities market is really two markets. The first is called the **primary market.** The primary market deals in "new issues." When a corporation wishes to raise money, it generally works through an investment company or *investment* *bank* that specializes in this process. The investment company acts as intermediary between the borrowing corporation and those who are willing to lend it the money it needs. This is the main function of the so-called primary market. It is the secondary market, however, that most of us are familiar with. The **secondary market** consists of buyers and sellers of securities that have already been issued. *When we speak of market value of a stock (or bond), we mean its value on the secondary market.*

Why is there a market for these securities? Why are people interested in buying and selling them *after* the original transaction between borrower and lender? Remember, stocks (and bonds) are instruments of credit—promises to pay. As such, their value can change as the ability of the debtor to pay changes.

For example, let us say you bought one share of a drug company's profits. The share cost you $50. The company does reasonably well and pays you several dollars each year in dividends as your share of the profits. Then one day the company's researchers discover a cure for the common cold. Profits soar and your share of them grows apace. Your dividends grow to, say, $50 a year.

Very nice indeed. Now let us say you happen to need a few hundred dollars in a hurry. Can you raise it by selling your share in the drug company? You certainly can. You can go to the securities market and sell your $50 share for, perhaps, $300! You will have made a profit of $250, plus the dividends you have already received. (This $250 gain on your original investment is called a *capital gain.*)

But why should someone pay you $300 for a credit claim against the drug company that cost you only $50? Simple enough. The buyer has $300 ready money that he is more than happy to invest in a stock share he expects to pay $50 a year in dividends. That's a lot more than he could ever expect to get from, say, a $300 savings account.

Unfortunately, this is the kind of stuff dreams are made of. It's not really likely that your company will discover the cure for the common cold. Chances are your $50 share in the company will, with luck, go on paying just a few dollars in dividends per year. The value of your share on the securities market will likely not grow very much, nor very quickly.

And even if the dream were true, it could change to a nightmare. Suppose the cold cure turns out to have a nasty, unforeseen side effect. It causes baldness or ingrown toenails, or whatever. Your corporation is dragged into court and goes broke paying damage claims. Your $50 share of the profits becomes a $50 share of nothing. The stock is worthless.

Our example is, of course, fanciful. But from it you can get an idea of what is meant by a stock's market value. The secondary securities market—the stock (and bond) market we are most familiar with—is where the action is. Here, pleasant dreams and nightmares may both come true.

Bonds

As we have noted, a stockholder owns a share of the corporation that issues the stock. His share of the profits depends on the profitability of the corporation itself. Consequently, the value of his stock can fluctuate widely in the securities market. A bondholder, on the other hand, is not an owner of the entity that issues the bond. The purchase price of his bond represents a direct loan to the issuer. He can demand repayment of the debt (the bond's "face value") at a specified time (the "maturity" date of the bond). He also receives a specified yearly interest on his loan throughout the bond's lifetime. Since return on investment does not depend primarily on the issuer's profits and losses, bonds are a less risky investment than stocks. Corporations and governments both issue bonds as a means of borrowing needed capital.

Corporate bonds Bonds issued by corporations represent a debt of the corporation. As such, the payment of both principal and interest is an item of cost in the firm's balance sheet. The **principal** is the amount borrowed (i.e., the cost of the bond), while **interest** is the cost of borrowing (i.e., the amount to be earned by the bond holder). Both principal and interest must be subtracted from income before profits are determined. Only then may dividends be paid to stockholders. Interest on bonds is a legal debt of the corporation. It is required to pay this debt just as it is required to pay wages and salaries to its employees.

Bonds are usually issued at relatively high face values. The minimum denomination is usually $1,000. Bonds may *mature* (the face value becomes due) in anywhere from five to forty years, and sometimes even up to and beyond a century. Such bonds can be bought and sold on the secondary market well before reaching maturity. Because of their original expense and long-term maturity, corporate bonds are not likely to be purchased by the average security buyer. Most of them are purchased for the portfolios of banks, insurance companies, and other large financial institutions.

Bonds may be *secured* (their value backed) by something owned by the corporation. For example, **mortgage bonds** or **indentures** may represent a claim against real estate owned by the firm. Similarly, equipment trust bonds pledge the value of machinery owned by the firm as security for the loan (bond). Railroads often use such bonds when borrowing money to buy rolling stock. Collateral-trust bonds are bonds backed by securities owned by the corporation and held by a trustee. Other bonds are protected only by the credit-worthiness of the corporation and backed only by its income. Such bonds are called **debentures.**

Besides lower risk, corporate bonds have other advantages over stocks as investments. Some corporate bonds, for example, may be converted to (exchanged for) the corporation's common stock. This right of exchange is called **convertibility.** Let's say you buy a $1,000 bond issued by the drug company we spoke of earlier. To help convince you to lend the company this $1,000, it made you an offer you didn't want to refuse. It said that you could at some future date trade your bond for twenty shares of common stock if you wish. So you bought the bond and sat back to enjoy the security of your investment and its regular interest payments. Then came the cold cure. The company's common stock jumps to a market value of $300 a share. Your bond, as promised, can now be converted into twenty shares of common stock. Since each share is worth $300, your $1,000 bond is now worth $6,000. (Not bad at all. But remember, it's only a dream.)

On the other hand, most corporate bonds carry a provision that they may be "called" after a certain period of time. That is, the corporation may elect to pay back their face value *before* the debt is due. This corporate right is known as **callability.** As a bondholder, you get your original investment back more quickly than you had expected. But interest payments also stop. Why should this concern you? Because corporations generally "call in" their bonds only when interest rates throughout the economy are low. They "retire" the bonds they sold when interest rates were high. They then issue new bonds on which they will have to pay only the current lower rate. Fine for the corporations. But if you wish to stay in the corporate bond market, you will have to be satisfied with a lower rate of interest on your new bond investment.

Government bonds As do corporations, governments also need to borrow money, either for current needs or for expansion of public services. To do so, they issue bonds. Bonds are issued by the federal government and by state, city, and other governmental bodies. United States government securities (including bonds and other promise-to-pay debt issues) are truly secure investments—as no-risk as any investment could possibly be in this uncertain world. (After all, the federal government owns the press that prints the nation's money.)

State and local government bonds are also generally considered very low-risk investments. Unlike the federal government, state and local governments cannot print money. But, like the federal government, they have the power of taxation to back up the value of the bonds they issue. It is true that some large urban centers (notably New York City) have recently found themselves in financial difficulty. But government default on its debts (total refusal to pay off its bonds) is not a likely occurrence. Even during the Great Depression, almost no governmental bodies defaulted fully on their securities.

The United States government issues a variety of bonds and other types of credit instruments. The most familiar are United States savings bonds. These are issued in small denominations, beginning at $25. Other popular denominations are $50 and $100. The purchaser of the bond pays less than face value;

the bond matures (to its face value) in ten years. The bonds are redeemable at almost any time, at the option of the holder. Since they may be cashed in at any time, they are, in effect, like money in the bank. Of course, the longer the holder keeps the bonds, the more interest is earned.

The federal government also issues bonds of higher denomination and longer maturity. *Treasury bills* are short-term bonds, usually maturing in 91 days. They are issued in denominations of $1,000 to $1,000,000. *Treasury notes* are intermediate-term loans to the Treasury, maturing in about three to five years. *Treasury bonds* are issued for longer periods of time, from about twenty to thirty-five years.

In addition, the federal government borrows money through bond issues for a variety of special purposes. For example, it issues securities to raise money to lend to savings and loan associations for the building of homes. It issues bonds for money to lend to farmers to buy seed, machinery, livestock, and farm land. It also issues securities in order to make loans to foreign, especially developing, nations.

Local governments also issue bonds for a variety of reasons. Bonds may be issued to build schools, parks, and roads. They may be needed to build a bridge or build housing for the poor. Almost any type of public service may need funding by bond issue.

State and local bonds are classified by their source of money for payment of principal and interest. There are two basic types of state and local bonds: general obligation bonds and revenue bonds. **General obligation bonds,** or "full-faith and credit" bonds, are funded from the regular tax revenue of the issuing agency or government. If tax revenues are adequate, these bonds will be paid by the issuing agency. **Revenue bonds** are paid for from revenues raised by the project funded. These are usually used for transit and toll collection facilities such as bridges, tunnels, and highways.

Mutual funds   Another important dealer in securities is the *mutual fund investment company.* Mutual fund companies purchase stocks and bonds for their own portfolios. They then sell shares in these portfolios to the public. In effect, these companies sell shares in themselves. An investor may buy these shares outright. He may also contribute a designated amount each

month to the fund. The amount contributed determines the number of shares or partial shares he will own in the fund.

Mutual funds are particularly attractive to small investors and to other individuals who wish to turn over their investment decisions to the "professionals" who manage the funds. In addition, the investor holds a portion of the many stocks that are in the fund's portfolio. His money is not tied up in the fortunes of one or just a few corporations. Also, the investor may at anytime "redeem" his investment. The fund company will buy back his stock at a price determined by the company's current assets.

Mutual funds offer many kinds of investment packages. Most funds concentrate on purchasing common stocks for their portfolios. Some hold a mixture of so-called "growth" stocks—stocks that the managers expect to grow quickly in market value. Some concentrate on less risky stocks that can be expected to pay regular if relatively low dividends. All mutual funds charge a small commission to handle the investor's money. In addition, some funds "load on" a certain percentage to the purchase price of shares to cover management expenses. Others are so-called "no load" funds. Here management costs are extracted from the general earnings of the fund.

Closely allied to mutual fund companies are *closed-end investment companies.* These firms also buy stocks and bonds to resell proportionally to investors. Once they are sold, however, the opportunity to buy new stock in the fund is closed. The shares then go on the market to be bought and sold just like any other secondary security issue. Their market value will then depend on supply and demand. The issuing company will not "redeem" them by buying them back.

Closed-end investment companies usually hold diversified portfolios, including bonds and preferred stocks. Some, however, specialize in the securities of a single industry. Funds specializing in real estate were especially popular in the late 1960s and early 1970s. These *real-estate investment trusts* (REITs) prospered during the building boom of that period. After

1973, however, many REITs began to show losses, and some failed completely. Their popularity soon waned. In the mid-1970s, "unit trusts" became investment favorites. *Unit trusts* are corporate and government bond packages sold to investors on a proportional share basis. Packages containing municipal bonds are particularly popular because income from such bonds is tax exempt.

Value of bonds The value of bonds, like the value of stock, may fluctuate. Hence, like stocks, bonds are bought and sold on the market. We have seen why the market value of stocks fluctuates. Why does the value of bonds do likewise?

Bonds go on the secondary market for the same reasons stocks do. Their holders may wish to trade them for needed cash. Or perhaps the bondholder becomes worried about the financial stability of the corporation he has invested in. Corporate bonds are less risky than stocks. But this does not mean there is no risk at all. A bond as well as a stock can become worthless if a corporation's finances go *all* the way down the drain. The prudent bondholder may decide to take his money and run. The market value of a bond may fluctuate with the fortunes of the corporate issuer.

Bonds are issued with a nominal or face value, usually $1,000 each. However, the bond may not sell for $1,000. Depending upon many things, the price may be less than $1,000 or more than $1,000. If there is doubt the issuer can meet principal and interest payments, the bond may sell for much less. If interest rates fall, the price of the bond may rise.

But the main reason for fluctuations in the market value of bonds is interest rates. Let us say you bought a $1,000 corporate bond paying 7% interest. If interest rates in the general economy remain at about this rate, you could probably sell your bond for about what you paid for it, give or take a bit. But if general interest rates rise to 8%, you may have some trouble selling your 7% bond. Why should someone give you $1,000 for a bond that will pay him $70 a year interest? There are now $1,000 bonds for sale that pay 8% interest, or $80. If he does buy your bond, he will surely demand that you sell it to him for something less than you paid for it. On the other hand, if interest rates go down to, say, 6%, your bond will be more attractive. The potential buyer may then be willing to buy it at more than its original price. In brief, other things being equal, *the market value of bonds moves up if general interest rates fall and moves down if general interest rates rise.*

So then, the market value of bonds may fluctuate. But because bonds are less risky investments than stocks, their value fluctuates much less drastically.

Table 4 compares the interest yields on several different securities which are generally held for longer periods of time. The shorter-term securities generally yield less since the money is not tied up for long periods of time. All interest rates have moved somewhat together. They moved upward until 1969 or 1970

Table 4
Selected Bond and Stock Yields, 1966–1976

Year	U.S. government bonds	State & local government bonds	Corporate bonds	Corporate stocks, preferred	Corporate stocks, common
1966	4.66	3.90	5.34	4.97	3.40
1967	4.85	3.99	5.82	5.34	3.20
1968	5.25	4.48	6.51	5.78	3.07
1969	6.10	5.73	7.36	6.41	3.24
1970	6.59	6.42	8.51	7.22	3.83
1971	5.74	5.62	7.94	6.75	3.14
1972	5.63	5.30	7.63	7.27	2.84
1973	6.30	5.22	7.80	7.23	3.06
1974	6.99	6.19	8.98	8.23	4.47
1975	6.98	7.05	9.46	8.38	4.31
1976	6.81	6.67	8.96	8.00	3.75

when a decline set in. The decline lasted until 1971 or 1972; then an increase began. Another peak occurred in 1974 or 1975 with rates generally lower in 1976.

Interest yields on state and local government bonds are generally lower than bonds issued by the federal government. This is possible because the interest is not taxed as income by the federal government; so the interest paid can be less and yet yield spendable income comparable with other bonds. Corporate bonds yield more than government bonds because there is greater risk. Stocks generally yield less than bonds issued by corporations because people hold stocks in anticipation of price increases. This is especially true of common stocks.

However, the expectation of price changes may be frustrated. Table 5 shows the movements of the Standard and Poor's index over an eleven-year period. There are gains but there are also losses. There is a drop from 1968 to 1970 and another from 1972 to 1974. There may be a long-term upward trend but nothing is certain from one year to the next. Of course, the yearly averages hide the day-to-day movements of stock prices. Many people try to guess the direction of movement not only of the general level of stock prices but of the prices of individual stocks. This is much harder, but large amounts of money may be made (or lost)!

The data from Table 5 are shown in Fig-

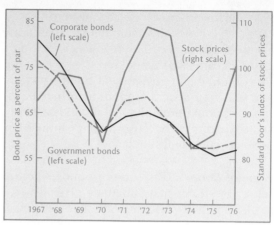

Figure 1 Stock and bond prices, 1967–1976. Notice how widely stock prices fluctuate.

ure 1. The up-and-down movement of stock prices is very obvious. Stocks purchased in 1967 or in 1972 would have been a bad buy. Of course, purchases in 1970 and 1974 would have turned out to be good buys. These years were recession years, however, and few people had money to buy. Bond prices show a generally downward trend, corresponding to the upward movement of interest rates. Figure 1 emphasizes the point that bond prices tend to fluctuate less than stock prices.

How the securities market operates

Exchanges The securities market provides a convenient, centralized location for trading (selling and buying) the stocks and bonds that finance American capitalism.

Our nation's securities market originated under a tree on New York's Wall Street. Here, in 1792, a small group of merchants began to meet daily to buy and sell company shares. These early traders were, if nothing else, bright enough to come in out of the rain. They soon moved into a coffeehouse tavern to do their "exchanging" of securities. From this humble beginning grew what we now know as the *New York Stock Exchange*—the nation's largest.

The second largest exchange is the *American Stock Exchange.* It too had its start out-

Table 5
Stock and Bond Prices, 1967–1976

Year	U.S. government bond prices	Corporate bond prices	Standard & Poor's index of stock prices (1941–1943 = 10)
1967	76.55	81.8	91.93
1968	72.33	76.4	98.70
1969	64.49	68.5	97.84
1970	60.52	61.6	83.22
1971	67.73	65.0	98.29
1972	68.71	65.9	109.20
1973	62.80	63.7	107.43
1974	57.45	58.8	82.85
1975	57.44	56.2	85.17
1976	58.66	57.7	101.77

Source: Federal Reserve Bulletin.
Bond prices shown as percent of par.
Stock prices are Standard & Poor's index of 425 stocks.

doors, in the 1840s. But it was not until 1921 that it moved indoors into a building in downtown New York. Until 1953, it was called the *New York Curb Market*, since it was on the street's curbs that most of its business was transacted. Although it is now known as the American Stock Exchange (Amex, for short), it is sometimes still referred to as "the curb."

Today the securities market also includes "regional" exchanges. For example, there are exchanges in Boston, Detroit, Pittsburgh, and some other large cities. There is also a Midwest Stock Exchange and a Pacific Coast Exchange. These exchanges originally traded only in stocks of local companies. Today, however, they also trade in the same securities that can be bought and sold on Wall Street.

In addition to the regular exchanges noted above, there is also an *over-the-counter market*. Originally, business in this market was conducted across a counter, hence its name. Today, however, it might better be called "over-the-telephone." Its transactions are now carried out by telephonic communication. Here you may buy and sell securities not available on the regular exchanges. The over-the-counter market trades in the stock of many small corporations. But it also trades in the stock of some major companies, including banks and large insurance companies. Most bonds, corporate and government, are traded in the over-the-counter market.

Brokers If you wish to invest your money in securities, you ordinarily do so through a *stock-broker*. You open an "account" with your broker in much the same way you open a bank account. You are likely, however, to do business over the telephone rather than visit your broker personally.

Let us say you wish to buy 100 shares of Common Cold Cure Drug Company at $50 per share. Your broker will take your order by telephone. His representative at the exchange on which your company's stock is traded will be notified. The representative will find someone there who wishes to sell 100 shares. The deal will be made.

In a few days, you will receive a notice that 100 shares of Common Cold Cure Drug Company have been purchased for you. And please send $5,000 plus a *commission* for your broker's services. When your money is re-

ceived, the stock is credited to your account. If you insist, the broker will actually send you 100 pieces of printed paper representing your ownership of 100 shares in the drug company. Actually, you will likely leave the shares with your broker. There they will be safe from theft or other possible loss.

When and if you wish to sell your shares, you merely telephone your broker and order them sold. His representative at the exchange will find a buyer. In a few days you will receive notice that the transaction has been completed. Your broker will send you the money at which he was able to sell your shares, minus his commission. Or, if you wish, you may leave the money in your brokerage account. (You may want to use it soon to purchase some other stock.)

As long as you keep the stock, your broker will send you the dividends, if any, that your stock earns for you. Or, if you wish, he may just credit them to your account. In the meantime, however, you will be interested in the market value of your stock. If its value rises, each share is worth just that much more should you decide to sell it.

How do you keep track of its value? Easy. You just check the financial pages of your daily newspaper. There you will find a listing of securities, including yours. After the name of each stock you will find various information about it, including, for example, how many of its shares were traded that day, what its highest and lowest prices were, and what it "closed at." The latter figure is the current value of each share. For example, if your $50 stock closed at $52, you would have a $2.00 "capital gain" on each share (at least on paper). On the other hand, if it closed at $48\frac{1}{2}$ you would be out $1.50 per share.

As noted earlier, market value of stocks may change from day-to-day and even minute-to-minute. As with other things of value, the price depends on supply and demand. If your drug company really did discover a cold cure, you can be sure many investors would want to buy shares in the the company—your shares if you wanted to sell them. Demand would push up the price.

Periodic price changes are shown on the *ticker tape* found in brokerage houses and other investment outlets. (Actually, the ticker tape is now figures flashed electronically on a screen.) If you follow the fortunes of your drug company on the screen, you will note that its price changes by eighths. One moment it may be selling at $50, the next at $50\frac{1}{8}$, $50\frac{1}{4}$, and so on, up—or down. (This way of counting is a throwback to the old "pieces of eight" of pirate days.)

Stocks are frequently sold in lots of 100 shares. A lot of 100 shares is known as a **round lot.** A round lot priced at 50 would mean $5,000 was invested ($50 × 100 = $5,000). Similarly, $50\frac{1}{8}$ is $5,012.50, $50\frac{1}{4}$ is $5,025, and so on. Of course, it is possible to purchase only a single share of stock; any sale or purchase of 1 to 99 shares is called an **odd lot.** There are firms that specialize in handling odd-lot transactions.

The prices of securities in the over-the-counter market are shown differently than exchange prices. Over-the-counter prices are indicated by how much is bid and how much is asked for each share. A "bid" of, say, $20 means a potential buyer is willing to pay $20 for a share of a particular security. An "ask" of, say, $22 means a potential seller wants $22 for each share he has to sell. The actual trading price will come out somewhere around these two figures.

Securities may also be bought and sold through agencies other than stock and bond brokers. Government bonds and other such securities may, for example, be purchased through banks. *Investment banks* (which are not really banks at all) specialize in selling new issues. Investment banks give the issuing company the money it wishes to borrow. In return, it receives the newly issued stock and attempts to sell it at a profit to individuals and institutions with money to invest.

Regulation of the securities market

As we have seen, the Great Depression spawned government regulation of the nation's financial institutions. The securities market was no exception. In 1934, the Securities and Exchange Commission (SEC) was formed. The SEC is composed of five commissioners appointed by the President of the United States for terms of five years each. Its principal job is to protect investors from unscrupulous operators and to help ensure the functioning of the market as a financial intermediary.

Before a corporation can borrow from the public by issuing stocks or bonds, it must register with the Securities and Exchange Commission. It must issue a "prospectus" telling the public its exact financial status and how it intends to use the money raised. Other pertinent data must also be made public.

SEC regulations prohibit persons connected with the securities market from putting out false information about the securities in which they deal. Most security institutions, including brokerage houses, investment banks, and investment counseling firms, are required to register with the SEC. Information about their business operations must be made available to the commission.

In addition, as we have already noted, commercial banks are forbidden to act as investment banks or investment companies. And, the Federal Reserve Board has the power to regulate the amount of stock that can be sold *on margin* (that is, on credit).

In 1970, Congress passed a Securities Investors Protection Corporation bill. It provides insurance coverage for brokers' accounts similar to that provided for bank and S & L accounts under FDIC and FSLIC. Securities and money deposits left with brokers are insured up to $50,000 against possible business failure of the brokerage firm.

In addition to government regulation, the securities market has its own rules and regulations administered through professional associations of its members—the Securities Industry Association, for example. The boards of governors of the various stock exchanges set up standards for who may be admitted to trade on the exchange and the financial status of companies that may be listed for trading.

An unofficial but important "regulator" of the securities market is the media—both the general media and specialized financial publications. Wide dissemination of news about securities and business corporations does more than help investors choose their investments

Economic Thinker
Charles Dow

In late 1976, stockbrokers had reason to be happy. They pointed with glee at the *Dow Jones industrial averages,* which had broken the 1,000 mark, signaling a "bull market." By the late spring of 1977, however, Wall Street smiles had turned to worried frowns. The "Dow" was down to 918.88, a 15-month low. The stock market's most closely watched barometer was signaling stormy financial weather.

The man who gave his name to this business indicator was Charles H. Dow, born in Connecticut in 1851. He became a journalist and in 1880 came to New York to work for a financial news service. In 1882, with a partner named Edward D. Jones, he founded Dow Jones & Company, a messenger service which delivered financial news bulletins to Wall Street brokerage houses. In 1889, the company began to publish a business affairs newspaper that was the forerunner of the *Wall Street Journal.* Today, the *Journal* is perhaps the most influential, certainly the most widely read, of all American publications specializing in financial news.

Early in the *Journal's* career, Charles Dow began compiling surveys of stock-price averages as a barometer of the investment climate and, thus, an indicator of business conditions in general. Today, the "Dow," or the "Dow Jones" as it is more formally called, is the best-known index of stock-market activities. (Similar indices, such as Standard and Poor's "500" and the Value Line Index, are also widely used by the business and financial communities.)

Actually, the Dow Jones average is four separate averages. There is one for industrial securities, one for rails, one for utilities, and a composite average intended to reflect conditions in all market segments. The Dow averages have come to be accepted generally over the years as sound indicators of market health. Typically, the index turns upward around six months prior to a business cycle upturn and downward around three to six months before a downturn. Recently, there has been criticism of the Dow compilations, especially of the Dow Jones industrial averages. They have been criticized for reliance upon too few stocks for averaging—less than 10% of the actual number of stocks traded each day—and for too much attention to the stock of giant, firmly established companies rather than giving consideration to the stock of less well-known concerns. Nevertheless, Dow Jones averages have managed to retain their eminence as popular indicators of stock-market conditions.

Charles Dow has also given his name to a widely known theory of market action—the so-called Dow theory. Simply put, Dow theorists maintain that stock-market prices move in three basic ways, something like the way the waters of the earth move. The primary movement is similar to a tidal action. This is the long-term trend. The short-term trend is like waves moving in the opposite direction—if the long-term trend is upward prices, the short-term is downward prices. Day-to-day market fluctuations are like ripples on the water—not important in themselves but, in accumulation over time, indicators of direction of tidal action and waves.

Dow theorists claim that their formula, originated by Charles Dow and refined by others over the years, can forecast significant changes in stock-market performance. The Dow theory has been credited with predicting the market crash of 1929 and the beginning of recovery in 1933 as well as with forecasting other movements. Other theorists and analysts dispute the predictive value of the Dow theory, preferring other forms of market analysis to aid them in their decisions to buy and sell securities. Nevertheless, Dow theorists remain prominent among Wall Street's crystal-ball gazers and investment counselors.

wisely. Would-be financial manipulators are restricted by the glare of publicity. And even honest money managers and financiers are less likely to stretch the rules when they know their business operations are being watched by the public.

The *Wall Street Journal* is perhaps the best known of the many news publications that specialize in financial information. Government publications and industry journals provide a constant source of financial data. Industry and corporation information is available from investment counseling and rating firms such as Value Line, Standard and Poor's, and Moody's. And corporations themselves provide information to the public through their required "annual reports" to their stockholders.

Bonds and preferred stocks are periodically "rated" as to their value by Standard and Poor's and Moody's. The best quality, based on the current credit-worthiness of the issuer, is given ratings from triple A to one A. Securities rated B are less desirable; C or D ratings may mean the issuer of the security is in serious financial difficulty that should be corrected.

The economic impact of the securities market

When we consider the economic impact of the securities market as a financial intermediary, we are speaking primarily of the new-issues market. As we have seen, it is here in this "primary market" that borrowers seek lenders and lenders seek borrowers. Purchasers of new-securities issues become creditors of the corporations (and governments) that issue them. Corporations (and governments) become debtors to the securities-holders.

Each year, vast sums of money are passed between borrowers and lenders through the securities market. Corporate and government bonds supply a huge amount of funds toward maintenance and expansion of thousands of the nation's corporations and businesses.

The secondary market that deals in stocks and bonds after they are originally sold is not truly a financial intermediary in the sense we have used the term throughout this chapter. It does not bring borrower and lender together. Nevertheless, it has an effect on the primary market.

Extended Example
Of Blueberries and Bonds

We all know that if for some reason the nation's blueberry crop is overly abundant, the price of blueberries will plummet. Bad news for the growers, good news for lovers of blueberry pie, but, by itself, not all that important to the nation's general economy. We sometimes forget, however, that overproduction can cause trouble in the capital market as well as in the produce market. And in the capital market, it can raise general economic havoc.

The year 1976 had been called the best bond market year in history. It produced a high-volume, high-value spurt of bond and other debenture selling and buying. In January, 1977, however, the spurt became a torrent. Corporations and businesses rushed to market $2.7 billion of bonds and debentures to help expand their productive capacities. This was some $900 million more than market traders had expected. In addition, the Treasury Department announced that it intended to issue securities to borrow over $82 billion, compared with the $65.6 billion it had raised in 1976.

A bond glut was obviously just over the horizon. The price of bonds in the market fell, since traders knew that if the market was not already oversupplied, it soon would be. Large investors in bonds, such as insurance companies, rushed in to pick up bargain bonds already in the market. The volume of money available to purchase new issues was drastically reduced.

Companies wishing to borrow money for new expansion found themselves in an unpleasant bind. In order to compete in the capital market, they were forced to offer higher interest rates than they had anticipated to prospective buyers. Some companies resigned themselves to lower profits and/or less expansion than they had planned for. Some reacted by raising the prices of their products, thus contributing to the economy's inflation. Many companies took a third route. They withdrew their bond offerings from the market and gave up for the time being their plans to invest in expansion and hire more workers. The economic recovery that had been advancing steadily in previous months became stalled, with the ill effects of the slowdown being felt throughout the economy.

The bond market recovered in subsequent months as oversupply gradually diminished. Its temporary weakening, however, is evidence that, along with blueberries and practically everything else that is bought and sold in the open market, bonds and debentures are also subject to the law of supply and demand.

Prices on the secondary market (what we ordinarily call the stock exchange) influence the prices of new issues. If the value of a corporation's stock already on the exchange is high, it will be able to borrow new money (issue new stock) easier, and at a higher price per share. New companies and new business ventures will also find it easier to raise money when the secondary market is "bullish." (A *bull market* means stock values are growing higher. A *bear market* means values are falling.) In addition, stock exchange and over-the-counter facilities give "liquidity" to securities. Investors are more likely to lend money through purchase of securities when they know their stocks and bonds can easily be exchanged for cash on the secondary market.

Both the primary and secondary securities markets are important to our economy. The first functions as a direct financial intermediary in the raising of capital for economic expansion. The second supports and facilitates this function.

Summary

There are numerous financial intermediaries other than banks organized to allow persons to save their money safely while earning interest on the amount saved. These particular intermediaries are known as thrift institutions. We are interested in three thrift institutions: savings and loan associations, mutual savings banks, and credit unions.

Savings and loan associations accept savings deposits and make mortgage loans. They are relatively new, dating from the 1930s. They are owned by their depositors. They pay slightly higher rates of dividends on the deposits compared with commercial banks. S & L's are chartered by either the states or the federal government. The Federal Home Loan Bank serves the S & L's in much the same way the Fed serves commercial banks. The FSLIC insures the deposits of the S & L's.

Mutual savings banks are very similar to S & L's. They are very old in concept and are concentrated in the Northeastern states. The subsequent development of commercial banks and S & L's made them unnecessary in the newer parts of the country. They are owned by their depositors and make mortgage loans and some consumer loans. They are chartered and regulated only by the states. Control of the mutual savings banks rests with a state-appointed board of trustees. The savings banks may provide all the banking services offered by commercial banks except checking.

Credit unions are saving organizations formed by a recognized group of people—often employees of a corporation, members of a particular profession or union or other group. The credit union is owned by the depositors, usually operates at very low cost, and makes relatively small, consumer-oriented loans.

Insurance is a means of using the law of large numbers to deal with risks. Firms are formed which, in exchange for a small known fee (premium), make payments (benefits) that help reduce the loss of death, injury, or other disaster.

Insurance companies may be mutually owned by the insured or may be profit-oriented firms owned by shareholders, not necessarily the insured.

Marine insurance is one of the oldest forms of insurance where ship and cargo are covered in case of shipwreck. Fire insurance protects buildings against fire. Other disaster losses may be insured. The principle is the same. Only a few ships sink or buildings burn.

All insured pay a small amount even though they lose nothing. The insurance firm may use the money to make investments so additional funds are available to pay out if a loss is sustained by one of the insured.

Life insurance, really death insurance, compensates for the loss of life. Payment is made to a beneficiary, usually the family of the insured. Life insurance is of many types, including term, straight life, and annuities.

Pension plans are designed to continue income after retirement. They are a form of saving for old age. Health and hospital insurance pays medical costs if the insured is sick or injured. Disability insurance continues income if the person loses earning capability. Prepaid medical plans are not insurance as such, but rather members contribute a small fixed amount in exchange for payment of hospital or medical expenses.

Liability insurance protects the insured person from legal action if something he does or has charge of causes injury to another. Malpractice insurance is a form of liability insurance used by doctors to protect themselves from lawsuits brought by their negligence.

Insurance firms have money to be invested and often purchase large amounts of long-term securities such as mortgages, bonds, common stocks, and corporate loans.

The securities market relates to the sale and purchase of stocks and bonds.

Stocks are shares in the ownership of a corporation. They are bought and sold on stock exchanges or in the over-the-counter market. The share represents a fractional ownership of the corporation. A share is usually common or preferred. Preferred stock has a set dividend payment which is paid before dividends on common stock. Common stock has no set dividend. The payment may be nothing or it may be very large. A share of stock has: (1) a *par value*, which is the face value of the stock; (2) a *book value*, which depends upon the assets of the firm; and (3) a *market value*, which is the amount it sells for on the stock exchange.

Bonds are debt instruments—the bondholder lends money to the seller of the bond. The principal is the amount borrowed and the interest is the annual payment in return for the loan. The face value of the bond means almost nothing and the price it sells for determines its value. There is an inverse relationship between the selling price and interest rates.

Bonds may be issued by corporations. Indentures are bonds backed by real assets. Debentures are bonds backed only by the (expected) profits of the firm. Some bonds are *convertible* to common or preferred stock. Some bonds may also be called in before they mature.

Governments at all levels issue bonds. The bonds may be *revenue bonds* in that the revenue earned from the project repays the debt or they may be *general obligation bonds*, which means the tax revenues of the government repay the bond. Government bonds may be called bills, notes, or bonds; bills are short-term and bonds are long-term instruments.

Mutual funds are firms which manage securities portfolios and sell their own shares to persons with small amounts of money to place in the securities market. REITs do the same except they purchase real estate.

Bonds have a face value and a market value which need not agree. Both bonds and stocks have a primary and secondary market. The primary market is where the newly-issued securities are sold by the firm or government to raise money. The secondary market is the resale market where bonds and stocks are exchanged among people with money to lend. The stock exchanges—for instance, the New York Stock Exchange and the American Stock Exchange—are examples of secondary markets. Bond prices tend to fluctuate less than stock prices; bonds are a lower-risk purchase than stocks.

The sale of securities is usually accomplished by a stock broker, who serves to bring buyers and sellers "together." The securities markets are regulated by the Securities and Exchange Commission (SEC).

Key Words and Phrases

- **maturity** the date upon which a security becomes due or expires.

- **savings and loan association** a thrift institution that accepts time deposits and that makes mostly mortgage loans.

- **Federal Home Loan Bank** the equivalent of the Fed for the savings and loan associations.
- **Federal Savings and Loan Insurance Corporation** the agency which insures deposits in the savings and loan associations.
- **savings banks** mutual savings banks; they are found in certain regions of the country. They are owned by the depositors and make mostly mortgage loans.
- **credit union** an organization owned by the depositors, all of whom are members of some recognizable group. The shares are usually sold in fixed amounts with fractional shares possible. The loans are made only to member-owners and are typically small and consumer oriented.
- **liability insurance** insurance purchased to pay the injured should an accident of some sort occur.
- **premiums** the fees paid by the insured to the insurer to purchase insurance coverage.
- **benefits** the payments from the insurance company to the person who has had an accident or is the one named to receive the payments.
- **beneficiary** the receiver of an insurance policy's benefits.
- **life insurance** policy providing payments to dependents (the beneficiary) in the event of insured person's death.
- **term insurance** a simple form of life insurance which runs for a period of time; premiums increase with the age of the insured. It is financial protection for the insured person's beneficiary with no cash value built up; as a result, it is often inexpensive.
- **straight life insurance** for fixed premiums, the insured buys coverage on his life. The policy builds up a cash value which may be borrowed at any time.
- **annuity or endowment** provides insurance on the life of the insured but is mostly a saving instrument as the intent is to provide future financial security in the form of annual payments or a lump-sum withdrawal.
- **disability insurance** a form of insurance which makes income payments if the insured person is disabled.
- **health prepayment plans** hospitalization coverage which is not insurance but which works in similar fashion in that payments are made to the plan in return for payment of hospital and doctor bills should the need arise.
- **malpractice insurance** insurance purchased by physicians or other professional persons to cover losses resulting from being sued for errors in their work.
- **securities** stocks and bonds; actually, a term which has broad application to a variety of financial instruments.
- **stock** refers to the share and the piece of paper representing the share of ownership in a corporate enterprise.
- **bond** a piece of paper which shows ownership of a portion of the debt of a corporation or government.
- **stock exchange** a place where stocks are bought and sold. The best known are in New York but there are others in cities across the U.S. and in other parts of the world.
- **dividend** the amount of the profit of a corporate enterprise paid to a shareholder; also, the interest earned at S & L's is called a dividend.
- **portfolio** the collection of securities and assets of all types owned by an individual; refers to the contents (and not literally to the container).
- **stock split** an action taken by a corporation which increases the number of shares of stock it has issued.
- **book value** the value of a corporation obtained from adding up the assets of the firm as measured by the accountants.
- **par value** the amount printed on the face of a share of stock which is often set very low to meet legal requirements but in general bears no relationship to any meaningful value of the company.
- **market value** the price a share of stock sells for determined by supply and demand for the stock on the stock exchange.
- **primary market** the market for newly-issued shares of stock either by a new company or by an existing company trying to raise additional capital.
- **secondary market** refers to the market for the resale of securities. The trade is between two individuals; the issuing entity is not involved except to keep records of the exchange.
- **principal** refers to the amount borrowed on a loan or in the sale of a bond.
- **interest** the cost of borrowing in that it is the annual payment necessary to service a debt brought about by a loan or sale of a bond.
- **debentures** a bond backed only by the earnings potential of the issuing company.
- **indentures or mortgage bonds** bonds backed by the real assets of the issuing company.

- **convertibility** the privilege attached to some bonds of converting the funds on prearranged terms to shares of stock at some time in the future.
- **callability** the right reserved by a company to pay off a debt or bond before it comes due.
- **Treasury bills** securities sold by the U.S. Treasury with short lives, such as 91 days.
- **Treasury notes** securities sold by the U.S. Treasury with maturity some three to five years from date of issue.
- **Treasury bonds** securities sold by the U.S. Treasury with maturity dates beyond five years from the time of issue.
- **general obligation bonds** bonds issued by government units which are to be paid from the general tax revenues of the issuing unit.
- **revenue bonds** bonds issued by governments which are to be paid for by revenues raised by the project for which the bonds are issued. An example might be bonds issued to finance construction of a toll bridge; the principal and interest on the bonds are to be paid from the tolls collected.
- **over-the-counter market** the market for shares of stock of small corporations. The trades are not conducted at any one place but by telephone between the brokers, one of whom serves as the marketplace for that stock.
- **stockbroker** a firm or member of such a firm which buys and sells shares of stock for individuals representing them and carrying out the trades on the stock exchanges.
- **round lot** a group of 100 shares of stock which are sold together.
- **odd lot** any amount of shares less than 100 which are bought or sold.
- **mutual fund** a firm formed to manage an investment portfolio, its shares being sold to people who would like to buy stocks but have only small amounts of money or little knowledge of the market.
- **real-estate investment trust (REIT)** a firm which specializes in owning real estate. Its shares are sold to persons with small amounts of money to invest in real-estate developments.
- **margin** the purchase of a security on credit. The margin is the amount paid by the purchaser; the rest of the money is loaned by the brokerage firm.

Questions for Review

1. Identify the savings and loan associations in your home town or college location. How are they like banks? How do they differ?

2. If you live or go to school in an area where there are mutual savings banks, list those you know about. How do they differ from commercial banks? How do they differ from S & L's?

3. If you are a member of a credit union, what group of people are its owner-depositors? If you are not, locate one. (Some student groups have one as do some faculty groups.) What group of persons does the credit union serve? What kinds of loans does it make?

4. How does insurance work? Why do people insure? Why not self-insure?

5. One of the largest prepaid health plans is very well known. See if you can identify it. How does it differ from health insurance?

6. How many stockbroker firms operate in your home town or the town where your college is located? Pick one and visit it to see the services it performs.

7. While at the brokerage firm, watch the "ticker tape" for a while. What is the current price of IBM? Xerox? GM? Exxon? (If you cannot go to a broker, check the listings on the business page of your local paper or the *Wall Street Journal*.)

8. What is the current level of the Dow Jones index? If it moves upward, what will happen to the price of a particular stock?

9. Pick the stock of a company. Pretend you purchased it today. How much money would you have paid? Follow the stock for a week. Sell. Did you make or lose money?

10. Why would the market value of a stock differ from the book value? What is a corporation worth?

11. Who owns the government debt? What would happen if it were paid off?

12. Suppose a bond is issued with a face value of $1,000 and an interest rate of 8%. If the bond sells on the market for $800, what is the interest rate? If the interest rate drops to 6%, what would the bond sell for?

14

Demand for Money

Prior to the 1930s and the writings of John Maynard Keynes, most economists would have agreed that the total amount of money available in the economy had a great effect on prices but very little or no effect on the quantity of goods and services the economy produced. It was Keynes who noted that not all money available necessarily would be used for purchases of goods and services. Additional money might be used to purchase securities instead. Then the amount of money would affect interest rates. Keynes also showed that under deep depression conditions, the amount of money may not even affect interest rates as additional money will just be held.

For several decades after World War II, the writings of Keynes had a profound influence on economic policy in the United States. However, from about 1960 on, there was a growing number of economists who began to see things differently. These economists are often called *monetarists* because they place primary emphasis on the quantity of money available to the economy. Money to them is not merely a facilitator of exchange, but a valuable good which people demand the same way they demand food or clothing. When money is held, it is an item of wealth the same as a stock or bond, a diamond, or a Rembrandt painting. Money performs a service when it is used. Other goods and services are given up when money is held; so money is a good with a price like any other good. In the monetarist view, we must have a demand for money balances. Let us look at the demand for money as the ideas developed over time.

The equation of exchange

One way of understanding the impact of money supply on the economy is to refer to something economists call the *equation of exchange*. The equation of exchange was developed by the American economist Irving Fisher. This equation has been an integral part of economic thinking since then. Some economists believe that it represents a true statement of how our economy functions. Others say it is little more than a mathematical restatement of conditions which may be explained in other ways. In any event it is still useful to economists today. Simply stated, the equation holds that the total amount spent by buyers equals the total amount received by sellers. The **equation of exchange** is stated mathematically as

$$MV = PQ.$$

Here is what the letters stand for:

M = money supply. The **money supply** is simply the total amount of money available in dollars or whatever currency is used in the economy.

V = velocity. **Velocity** is the rate at which money moves as it carries out its functions. *It is the number of times an average dollar changes hands during a given time period.* For example, let us say the time period is one year. Say you spend $10 on January 1, for a textbook. The bookstore owner uses your $10 to pay a store clerk for his part-time work. The clerk, being a frugal fellow, hangs onto the $10 until Christmas time. He then uses it to buy earrings for his girl friend. The jewelry-store owner places the $10 in his cash register. Presumably, he will eventually spend the money. But it is now December 31—our time is up. Your original $10 has changed hands three times. Its velocity in terms of transactions is 3.

P = price. This is the aggregate or general price at which all goods and services produced in the nation are sold. *We might also consider P as a price level.*

Q = real output of goods and services. Q is a measure of quantity. We cannot, of course, add textbooks to store-clerk work to earrings, any more than we can add apples and oranges. An "appleorange" does not exist. But this is an accounting problem and need not concern us here. For economic purposes, differing goods and services can be added up to give us a total. (Recheck the national income accounting chapter to see how this is accomplished.)

Thus $P \times Q$ is simply the money value of all goods and services produced and sold. As noted earlier, the product of $P \times Q$ is called gross national product (GNP). So we could state our equation as

$$MV = PQ = \text{GNP}.$$

It may be helpful to think back to the concept of the circular flow presented in the national income accounting chapter. The right-hand side of the equation of exchange is simply the flow of goods and services measured in money terms which flow around the circle. The left-hand side of the equation is simply the money flow which moves around the circle in the opposite direction. If $M = \$250$ billion and each dollar averaged 4 trips around the circle each year, then the money flow would be $1 trillion. Income velocity of money, or V, would be 4 and the flow of goods and services (or GNP) would also be $1 trillion.

The classical view
The equation of exchange as demand for money

The equation of exchange emphasizes the role of money in expenditures, not saving. The equation is always true. Think of the circular flow. The equation says that the flow of goods and services—GNP—in one direction must be equal to the amount of money flowing the other way around. Economists prior to Keynes—the classical economists—used the equation to explain the demand for money. By implication, money is used for little else than spending. The only reason people would hold money would be to smooth out the differences between the times when money is received and the time it would be spent. If everyone's timing was perfect, the money held would last until just before the next paycheck was received. Remember, this is known as the *transaction demand* for money. Of course, a miscalculation could result in too much money left at the end of the month.

To see how the demand for money may be derived, start with the equation of exchange:

$$MV = PQ.$$

To get the desired amount of money, divide through by V, giving

$$M = \frac{1}{V}PQ.$$

The classical view of money velocity is that it is unchanging or constant over long periods of time. So the classical economists let $1/V = k$. The letter k stands for constant and is just a shorthand form for $1/V$, which we are assuming to be constant. So the equation is now

$$M = k \cdot PQ.$$

In this form we see that the amount of money demanded is a proportion k of PQ or GNP. The proportion held is the inverse of velocity. To return to our earlier example, if GNP is $1 trillion and the velocity is 4, then desired cash holdings are $\frac{1}{4}$ (25%) of GNP. The amount of money demanded is $250 billion.

Figure 1 illustrates the demand for money. The horizontal axis shows GNP and the vertical axis the amount of money demanded. The demand curve has a slope of $k = 1/V$. If $V = 4$, then for an increase in GNP of $4, the amount of money demanded is $1. When GNP is $1,000 billion, the amount of money demanded is $250 billion. If GNP increases to $1.2 trillion, the amount of money demanded will be $300 billion. The amount of money demanded is directly related to the spending involved in GNP and no other use is made of money.

The interest rate and the equation of exchange

You may have noticed that we have been talking about money and the demand for money and have not yet used the words *saving* and *interest rate*. Surely not all money goes for ex-

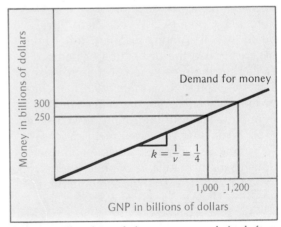

Figure 1 The demand for money, as derived from $MV = PQ$. Velocity is assumed constant; thus $M = k \times PQ$, where $k = 1/V$. The constant k equals the slope of the triangle, which here is 1/4. When GNP $(= PQ)$ is known, we can easily find the amount of money demanded (shown on the vertical axis).

Economic Thinker
Irving Fisher

Irving Fisher was a mathematician, statistician, businessman, inventor, reformer, public health advocate, and one of the most important economists of his day. He authored 28 books and almost countless articles on subjects ranging from mathematics, statistics, and economics to health fads, human breeding (eugenics), and prohibition of alcohol. He invented a rotary card-filing system, which he later sold for a not-so-small fortune. In the boom times of the 1920s, he parlayed his fortune into a much larger one in the stock market. Unfortunately, he could see into the economic future no better than more ordinary mortals. Just one week before the stock-market crash of 1929, Fisher announced publicly that the American economy was surely on a "permanent plateau" of prosperity. Within a very short time, Fisher's fortune, along with that of many thousands of others, had disappeared.

Fisher was born in 1867, in Saugerties, New York. He entered Yale in 1884 to study mathematics. Under the influence of William Graham Sumner, the great sociologist and economist, he combined economics with his study of mathematics and received his Ph.D. in 1892. He taught mathematics at Yale until 1895, when he transferred to Yale's economics department. He remained active at Yale until 1935, some twelve years before his death in 1947. Among his many other honors, Fisher had the distinction of being elected to the presidency of the professional societies representing three main branches of economic scholarship: the American Economic Association, the American Statistical Association, and the Econometric Society.

Irving Fisher made valuable contributions to mathematical economic theory and to statistics. His work helped combine these two disciplines into the single discipline known as econometrics.

Fisher also adapted for modern economics the classical theory of interest rates. Fisher postulated two types of interest: the real interest rate and the market interest rate.

The market rate of interest is the "money rate" as reflected in the market place. Five percent market interest rate, for example, means that five dollars in interest is paid annually for every $100 one borrows. The real rate of interest is something different. Real interest is measured in terms of the amounts of capital goods or in terms of the goods given up when interest is paid. Any difference between the two rates represents changes in the purchasing power of money or of imbalances in supply of and demand for money. Fisher maintained, as do present-day classical theorists, that, historically, prices go up when interest rates go up and come down when rates come down. Price stability, therefore, is more related to interest rates and money supply than to demand and production factors.

Fisher's concern with theories of price stability led to a book published in 1911 which he called *The Purchasing Power of Money*. The work was a detailed study of the problems of money and purchasing power. In it he revised the classical theory of money and prices in a formula that came to be known as the Fisher Equation: $MV + M'V' = PT$. (M represents the quantity of money in circulation; V represents its circulation velocity; M' and V' represent the quantity of time deposits and its circulation velocity; P represents the average price level

of goods sold; and T represents the number of transactions or total quantity of goods sold.) A shortened version of the Fisher Equation is $MV = PT$, with M representing both money in circulation and time deposits. This equation has since been adjusted to the equation $MV = PQ$.

Fisher's equation has been attacked by later economists in that it ignores variables found in mixed economic systems and assumes the actual existence of the free market ideal. His dictum that any increase in money supply must result in a proportionally corresponding increase in prices is, they say, far from certain. Nevertheless, variations of his equation have become important working tools in the study of money and purchasing power as the monetarist economists see the economy. And his inclusion of instruments of credit and bank time deposits in the concept of "money in circulation" is, in itself, an outstanding contribution to economic theory.

An economist in the classic mold, Irving Fisher in his early career was a firm opponent of government intervention in the economy. Controls on business, he believed, and welfare measures such as workmen's compensation could only lead to socialism and economic slavery. In his latter days, however, he began to oppose pure laissez-faire policies, advocating control of corporate trusts and heavy inheritance taxes to help redistribute the nation's wealth.

Table 1
Some Important Interest Rates and a Sample of Their Fluctuation

	Interest Rates	
	1974 High	1977 (Jan.)
Federal Reserve discount rate	8.0%	5.25%
Prime rate	12.0%	6.25%
90-day Treasury bills	9.9%	4.3%
Long-term Treasury bond	7.4%	6.4%
Corporate bond, top grade	8.7%	7.9%
36-month new-auto loan, national average	11.6%	11.0%
Mortgage on new home, national average	9.4%	9.1%

rates. One that you frequently hear mentioned in the media as it fluctuates is known as the prime interest rate. The **prime interest rate** is the interest charged by commercial banks to their best customers. In the next chapter we will learn about the *discount rate*, which is the interest rate charged by the Federal Reserve Bank for borrowing by its member banks.

Almost all of these various interest rates are tied together—even if the connection is a loose one. For example, as the prime rate changes noticeably, many of the other rates will change also in a similar manner. So for this reason and for convenience we will continue to speak of "the" interest rate as the representative or average interest rate.

With what we already know, it does seem that the amount of money demanded should be affected by the interest rate. Not in the classical system! The equation of exchange was the demand for money, and the interest rate was determined elsewhere. Figure 2 shows how the interest rate was thought to be deter-

penditures; some is saved and some is borrowed. Here the interest rate must matter. If you borrow money, interest will be paid. If you place money in a savings account, interest is received.

We often refer to the interest rate as "the" interest rate—as if the economy operated with only one interest rate for all dealings. However, as you already know, interest rates on savings accounts vary (depending on the institution and the length of deposit). In addition, the interest rate on a savings account at a commercial bank is less than the rate charged to customers who borrow from the bank (the difference goes toward the bank's profit). Actually, there are many more interest rates. See Table 1 for some of the more important interest

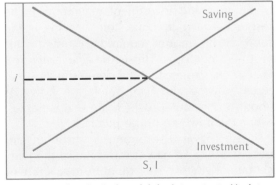

Figure 2 In the classical model the interest rate i is determined by the intersection of saving (S) and investment (I).

mined in the classical system. The interest rate (*i*) is shown on the vertical axis. Both saving and investment are plotted on the horizontal axis. The curves labeled *saving* and *investment* relate the amount of each to the interest rate.

The investment schedule is the same as we have seen in previous chapters. Investment is carried out by firms. It represents expenditures for brick and mortar, plant and equipment which will be used for future production. The most productive investment expenditures will have a high rate of return. As more investment is carried out during a period of time, less productive projects will be included. These projects will be profitable and undertaken only if the rate of return is sufficient to cover the interest cost of borrowed money. At lower interest rates, more investment will be profitably undertaken. Thus the economy will have low investment at high interest rates and greater amounts of investment at low interest rates. Figure 2 reflects this: the investment curve slopes downward.

Saving is forgone consumption. People would ordinarily not give up present consumption unless they had an incentive to do so. It is assumed that people are impatient and would prefer to consume now. However, if they receive interest payments for their saving, they are offered greater future consumption in exchange for the forgone present consumption. The higher the interest payment, the more present consumption will be given up. In Figure 2 the saving curve slopes upward showing more saving at higher interest rates.

By saving, households make available the resources required by investors. At a given interest rate, the classical economists maintained that saving and investment are equal. (We saw in Chapter 8 that Keynes eventually showed that saving and investment may differ.) The resources freed by households' saving is the same as the amount required by firms for investment purposes: This is the *equilibrium real interest rate*. Notice that it is determined by real forces. Saving and investment are flows of goods and resources which are real variables. Money is nowhere in the picture.

The classical economists distinguished between the real rate of interest and the market rate of interest. The **equilibrium real rate of interest** is that rate toward which the economy

naturally tends when prices are stable. The **market rate of interest** is that rate which occurs at any given point in time. As such, the market rate does fluctuate frequently.

In the classical view the interest paid for money borrowed or lent will be very close to the real rate of interest. The market interest rate for money may for short periods of time be something higher or lower than the real rate. However, it must surely return to the level of the real rate. Thus saving and investment determine the interest rate independent of monetary conditions. The equation of exchange explains the demand for money based upon expenditures and the velocity of money.

Keynes and the demand for money

Keynes introduced the idea of three motives for holding money. We have examined these earlier. They were *transactions, precautionary,* and *liquidity* or *speculative* motives. The transactions motive was really the only motive for holding money if the classical view were correct. Money was only demanded for spending purposes. Keynes recognized that money was held for other reasons, particularly the precautionary and liquidity motives. Some money might just be held. Thus the velocity, as Keynes went on to show, is not constant since some money might not circulate. Money would be held as an asset, a noninterest-paying asset, and as such would substitute for other securities such as savings accounts, stocks, and bonds. When money is held as an asset (i.e., for speculative demand), velocity is affected and tends to change.

The price of securities

In the microeconomic world, the price of substitute goods affects the demand for the given good. For example, suppose we have two substitute goods: Coke and Pepsi. The price for one can't rise too much above the other because most people would substitute (choose) the much cheaper drink. This concept is true for money as well. As a medium of exchange, there is no true substitute. Being a medium of exchange is one of the characteristics that defines money. However, as a store of value, money has many partial substitutes. One substitute that is particularly close is the wide variety of securities. (Other, more distant substitutes are precious stones, fine paintings, real estate, etc.)

For the sake of simplicity, imagine that all securities in the economy are of one type bond. In the securities market, money is, in effect, borrowed; the *borrower* issues the securities to the *lender* (the purchaser of securities). A security is thus a kind of IOU. Assume (which is generally true) that the lender of the money is interested in earning a stream of income from loaning money to other people (that is, from holding the securities). If the rate of interest in the economy is very high, relatively little money will have to be loaned out to obtain any level of income. In other words, the amount that the lender (purchaser) will have to *pay* for a security which will yield a specific number of interest dollars will be smaller than would be the case if the interest rate in the economy were low. The high interest rates mean the security holder will earn more money.

Suppose the securities (IOU's) remain outstanding until repurchased by the borrower. In some cases they may never be repaid; the borrower simply makes the annual interest payment. In this case there is a very simple formula which tells you how many dollars you must invest (the dollar value of securities that must be purchased) in order to earn the annual interest income. As you might guess, the sole determinant of this IOU price will be the rate of interest in the economy. The price (P_{sec}) of the securities times the interest rate (i) equals the annual interest receipts (R):

$$iP_{sec} = R.$$

In order to find out how much is to be invested (purchased) to earn interest receipts, we restate the equation as

$$P_{sec} = \frac{R}{i}.$$

Now suppose every security paid $1 per year: $R = \$1$ per year. Then the price of the security would be

$$P_{sec} = \frac{\$1}{i}.$$

Remember that P_{sec} represents the average price of all securities prices. A rise in its price or a fall in the interest rate means all securities prices rise and all interest rates fall. Suppose the interest rate were 10%. The price of a security would be

$$P_{sec} = \frac{\$1}{.1} = \$10.$$

Suppose now that the interest rate falls to 5%. The price people would be willing to pay for a $1 per year income stream would be

$$P_{sec} = \frac{\$1}{.05} = \$20.$$

Thus the price of the security rises.

We can use this result to show a demand curve for money. Suppose people are initially in balance as to money holdings, securities, and income. With income held constant, let the interest rate increase. That is, the price of securities falls. People suddenly find they have "excess" money in the sense that the higher earning, bargain-priced securities are more desirable. They prefer the substitute for money, namely, securities. They are willing to hold more securities and less money. In Figure 3, this might mean a movement from point A to point B. The people have rearranged their securities portfolio to include less cash, a non-interest-bearing asset, for more securities, which we have just said started paying a higher rate of interest.

The same thing happens if interest rates decline. Start with everyone content at point A. Let the interest rate decline, or what is the same thing, the price of securities rise. Since securities are higher priced, people will be willing to hold more money and may even sell some securities. The movement would be from point A to point C.

Remember now, income has not changed so the amount of money held for transactions and precautionary purposes has not changed.

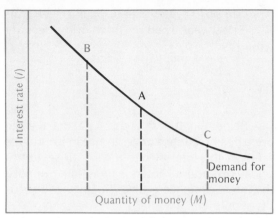

Figure 3 The Keynesian model shows a relationship between the interest rate and the demand for money. At high interest rates—say at point B—the demand for money declines because people want to hold more securities. At low interest rates—say at point C—the demand for money increases.

We are looking at the speculative motive for holding money. In this case money is one asset and securities represent others. As the price of securities changes, people hold more or less money as an asset.

If the price of the substitute goes *up*, the quantity of the given good demanded (money) tends to go *up*. If the price of securities goes *down*, money demanded can be expected to fall. This makes perfect sense when you think about it carefully. If the price of a security goes down, the amount of money demanded would be expected to *fall* because the substitute is a better bargain. The price of an IOU going down means that the interest rate in the economy has *risen* ($1/i$ is smaller, hence i is greater). With higher interest rates the *opportunity cost* of holding money is *larger*. More potential interest income is forgone by hanging on to cash. *The security prices decline and interest rates rise when the money supply decreases (all else constant).*

The interest rate and money supply

Of course, the demand for money by itself does not tell us what the interest rate will be. We need to examine the interaction of supply of and demand for money to see what the result will be.

In Figure 4, the demand curve for money as an asset is once again shown. A supply curve is also shown. The supply and demand curves must both be understood as not being total money supply and demand; from both, the money needed for transactions and precautionary balances has been subtracted. Also, the supply curve is drawn as a vertical line. It is drawn this way because we are letting the Federal Reserve determine what the money supply will be. In reality, the supply curve may have some slope (upward and to the right) but we do not have to consider that possibility now. Furthermore, a sloping supply curve would not change the results of our analysis.

Figure 4 shows that M' amount of money has been supplied in excess of transactions and precautionary balances. Will people be willing to hold that much money? Most students will answer that people will always be willing to hold that much money and even more. But that is not the truth for all of the economy. Not everyone is as poor as most college students. Some people get to choose how much they will hold. Suppose the interest rate is i_1. People would like to hold more than M' as is shown in Figure 4. They experience a "shortage" of money as an asset. To overcome this shortage,

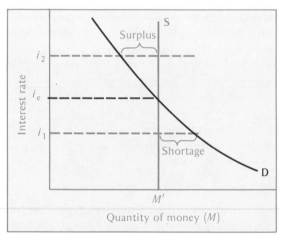

Figure 4 In the Keynesian model, the interest rate is determined by the intersection of the supply of and demand for money. The money supply and demand curves shown here are for *speculative* money balances. The equilibrium interest rate (i_e) will eventually result. If the interest rate were too high—say at i_2—a surplus of money would result. This money surplus will bring the interest rate down to i_e. The reverse happens if the interest rate is too low—say at i_1.

they could sell some securities. However, if several persons sell securities all at once, securities prices will fall and the interest rate will rise. When securities prices fall far enough that interest rates rise to i_e, the economy will be in equilibrium with respect to its money holdings and the interest rate.

Suppose in Figure 4 the interest rate was at i_2. After obtaining enough money for transactions and precautionary balances, people would discover that M' was more than they wanted to hold as an asset. There is a surplus of money available. People would prefer to exchange noninterest-bearing money for interest-earning securities. One person could do this easily but if many people enter the securities market, the price of securities would rise and the interest rate would fall. When the interest rate has fallen to i_e, the economy would again be in equilibrium, for the given level of income, with respect to the interest rate and the supply of money.

The interest rate and an increase in the money supply

We are now ready for the next step. Suppose we start in Figure 5 with income determined (and therefore transactions and precautionary balances determined), the money supply at S_1, and the interest rate at i_e. People would be content with the amount of money M'. Then suppose the Fed increases the amount of money, shifting the money supply curve to S_2.

The increase in money must be held by someone. At the old interest rate, i_e, the additional money is viewed as surplus. People do not want to hold it as an asset so they convert it to securities. However, this action bids up the price of securities, as we have seen. The increase in the price of securities results in a fall in the interest rate. When the interest rate reaches i'_e, the system is again in equilibrium since people are now willing to hold the amount of money available.

Velocity once again

We can now see how the Keynesians view velocity. Recall that the classical economists viewed velocity as constant, and therefore, an

increase in the amount of money would increase either output or prices or both. The speculative or liquidity demand changes this conclusion in the Keynesian view.

Increase in money with income constant When income is held constant, transactions and precautionary balances will also remain the same. So with an increase in the money supply, the result is the one we reached in Figure 5: The "extra" money is not needed for spending purposes, and thus we may expect all of it to be held as an asset. The interest rate will fall, and people will hold the money. The word "hold" is the key to what happens to velocity. Money being held is not circulating at all. The entire increase of money has a velocity of zero. Therefore, the average velocity of the entire money supply must be pulled down. If we use the equation of exchange ($MV = PQ$), the increase in M must be matched by a decrease in V since we have assumed the other side of the equation does not change.

Increases in money if income changes We do not need to assume that income cannot change. In fact, we might expect that it will change if the interest rate changes. Recall that the interest rate is one of the things businessmen consider when they plan their investment expenditures. As the increase in the amount of money begins to result in lower interest rates,

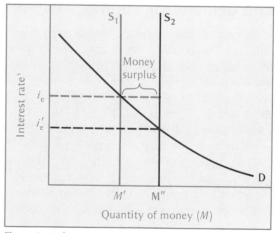

Figure 5   A change in the money supply affects the interest rate. If money supply increases from S_1 to S_2 (all else constant), the interest rate falls: the equilibrium interest rate moves down from i_e to i'_e.

there may be an increase in investment expenditures. Through the usual multiplier effects, income and output will rise. If income rises, some money will be needed for transactions purposes. The Keynesian conclusion then would be that an increase in money would be partially spent and partially held in asset balances. Both income and interest may change, the interest rate falling and income rising. Some of the money will circulate and some will be held. The velocity will change but by not as much as we concluded when income is held constant.

So the Keynesian view of velocity is quite different from the classical view. While the classical economists assume velocity is constant over long periods, the Keynesians say velocity not only can change but is inherently unstable.

The demand for money: the monetarist view

The monetarist economists differ from the Keynesians in that they do not try to establish motives for holding money. The monetarists derive a demand function for money. However, they do indicate that there are a number of variables which influence the amount of money demanded. Let us examine each of the variables in turn.

The demand for money balances

How can we talk about a *demand* for money? After all, the demand for money would seem to be infinite, or almost so. To the extent that people *want* more and more goods, they will want more and more money with which to buy those goods. From the beginning of this chapter we have said that money is a *good*. It is a good because the quantity supplied is limited. This implies something must be forgone, given up, for the privilege of having money. If money is *held*, goods can't be bought. Remember, in this discussion we are talking about the amount of money *at any given moment in time*. For right now, the discussion is *not* concerned with the cost of having a dollar now versus having a dollar one year from now (which involves inflation and interest rates), though we will return to this point later.

It may be a good idea to reexamine the concept of *price*. Price is something that can be calculated and is meaningful. It is the amount of one good that has to be given up or forgone for *one unit* of the alternative. The price of any good can be calculated in this manner even though most prices are measured in dollars.

The price of money But now comes the question of the *price* of the very thing we have been using to measure the prices of all other goods—the price of money itself. Conceptually, this is an easy matter though the actual measurement may be difficult and full of problems. For now, consider all of the output of the economy being produced at a given moment in time. Put all of this output into conceptual "marketbaskets"—a kind of *average* set of purchases for the *average* buyer all of which is of *average* quality and *average* cost of production. A lot of averages to be sure! But in dealing with aggregates we can make these assumptions accurately. This sort of a marketbasket is estimated for the whole economy as well as for various groups within the economy (capital goods, farm goods, etc.). A dollar value is obtained representing the average purchases of the average user of dollars or, what is the same thing, a dollar cost per marketbasket. In equation form, the price of marketbasket (P_{mb}) is so many dollars *per* marketbasket:

$$\text{Price}_{mb} = \text{dollars/marketbasket.}$$

In effect, we have the price of one good—our marketbasket—in terms of another good—money.

For the moment, we will consider two more common goods and how the price of one is expressed in terms of the other. If there were only two goods in the world, once we had the price of one good in terms of the other, then automatically we have the price of the other in terms of the first.

For example, suppose that 25 pounds of food is equivalent to 5 cords of firewood. Then the price of firewood (P_w) becomes

$$P_w = \frac{25f}{5w} = 5 \text{ pounds of food } per \text{ cord of wood,}$$

where f stands for food and w for firewood. Given this figure, the price of food (P_f) in terms of wood is also set. It is simply the reciprocal of the first:

$$P_f = \frac{5w}{25f} = \frac{1}{5} \text{ cord of wood } per \text{ pound of food.}$$

We have exactly the same kind of problem with dollars *per* marketbasket. Once this number is estimated, finding the *price of dollars* is nothing more than taking the reciprocal of the marketbasket price. In other words, the price of dollars is the fraction of a marketbasket that must be forgone *at any instant in time* to hold on to one dollar.

What possible meaning can the price of money have other than a dull piece of arithmetic? The *price of money* is another way of saying *purchasing power! The price of a dollar is the same thing as the purchasing power of that dollar.* In the wood/food example, the *price* of food equaled $\frac{1}{5}$ cord of wood per pound of food. But this price is also the *purchasing power* of one pound of food. It would *buy* $\frac{1}{5}$ of a cord of wood. If the price of food went up, its purchasing power went up. Higher-priced food meant that one pound of food *cost* more wood, but would also *buy* more wood were the trade the other direction.

Notice that we are talking about the price of money at any given point in time. We are *not* (at least directly) talking about the price or cost of money between time periods, which is the interest rate. We will consider interest later but before we do, one more simple definition may be derived from the present discussion. The price of all marketbaskets is a **general price level** (GPL) for the economy. A general price level is useful to see what's going on in the economy as far as *changes* in the average prices. The same thing applies if you talk about the *absolute* price of money. The absolute price is not very meaningful, but change in the *relative* price of money (purchasing power of money)

is something that we are all interested in. Both the general price level and its reciprocal, the purchasing power of money, are normally expressed as *index numbers*. If some year is arbitrarily given a base value of 100, the other years are indexed—that is, are assigned numerical values—that reflect the changes in the price level or purchasing power of money.

The demand function for money   The monetarists assume demand for money is based upon its usefulness (1) in assisting transactions and (2) in storing value. At any moment in time, the people in an economy have the choice of holding all of their wealth in cash (only a theoretical possibility) or holding no money whatsoever, of spending every cent the instant they lay their hands on it. But the important question is now, "How much money will people want to hold at any given moment?" In other words, we need a demand function for money.

A demand function states that the *quantity* of a good demanded is an inverse function of its *price*, all other things remaining the same. The quantity of money demanded in the economy (M_d) is an inverse function of the price of money (P_m), everything else being equal. Basically (if everything is equal), monetarists assume people will demand quantities of money sufficient to keep their *total purchasing power* constant. People really hold money to spend and so will keep enough money to carry out their spending plans. If the *per dollar* purchasing power of money falls, people will demand enough extra dollars to maintain their *total* purchasing power. If they get *more* dollars than this amount, they will try to buy more goods and *not* hold the excess money. If they have too little money for the economic conditions, then their demand for alternatives to money such as goods and perhaps financial assets will fall.

Before explaining the demand function which we have just described, it may be well to explain those variables which determine the demand for money. These are the things which must be held constant as we consider the quantity of money demanded at each price level.

(1) *Income.* Money is a good which will be held in greater quantities as income rises.

(2) *Price of securities or interest rate.* Securities are close substitutes for money. As the price of securities rises or interest rates fall, people may substitute money for securities as a means of holding wealth.

(3) *Expected price changes.* If people expect prices to rise or rise more rapidly, they will buy now, reducing the amount of money held. If prices are expected to decline, people will wait till the decline occurs to buy, increasing money held.

(4) *Institutional variables.* Various institutional arrangements allow people to match up their receipts of money with their expenditures. Paying bills by check once a month rather than paying cash reduces the amount of money held. Similarly, widespread use of credit cards reduces the need for cash balances.

We will return to some of these points later, but for now these variables are being held constant while we examine the quantity of money desired at each price level.

In Figure 6, a demand for money curve is presented. Here the price of one unit of money (P_m = 1/general price level = 1/GPL) is plotted against the quantity of money demanded. With the assumptions just made, this means that along the *demand function M_d* (with all of the other variables affecting money demand held constant), *the quantity of money demanded*

multiplied by the purchasing power (*price*) of each of those dollars will be such that the total purchasing power of the money stock will be constant.

Suppose the general price level is low (this is the same as the price of money being high). A high money price is P'_m. Using the M_d curve, we see that people will want to hold M' amount of money. Suppose the price of money falls to P''_m. Money is cheaper relative to other things so more of it may be held. How much more money is held can be easily seen if we remember that we are assuming people try to hold the same purchasing power at all times. The decline in the price of money to P''_m from P'_m means the general price level has risen. People must hold more money to purchase the same goods as before. Thus the increase in the quantity of money held from M' to M'' just offsets the rise in the price level (fall in price of money from P'_m to P''_m).

Another way of looking at the change in the quantity of money held is to consider the rectangles drawn under the M_d curve in Figure 6. From geometry, we know that the area of the rectangle is the product of the price of money, P_m, and the quantity of money, M. The area is simply the purchasing power of money. The money demand curve, M_d, is drawn so the purchasing power of money is the same at each price level. The area of the rectangle at the higher price level is $P'_m \times M'$. The area of the rectangle in the second instance is $P''_m \times M''$. In both cases, the area is identical. The increase in money held is equally proportional to the price decline, so they are precisely offsetting. If the price of money fell to P'''_m, then M''' would be such that $P'''_m \times M'''$ would be the same as the other two areas. *The percentage increase* (decrease) *in money held would be the same as the percentage decrease* (increase) *in the price of money.*

Changes in money supply Examine Figure 7 to see what happens *if the quantity of money available changes,* all other variables held constant. Suppose initially that the money supply is S_0. As we did before, the money supply curve is drawn as a vertical line. We do this because we are assuming the Fed is able to say what the money supply will be and that the supply is not affected by such things as the interest rate or price level. Say the quantity available is M'.

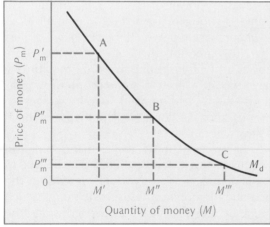

Figure 6 In the monetarist model, the demand for money is shown as a function of the price of money (that is, the general level of prices). At a high general price level (that is, low price of money), say at P'''_m, the quantity of money demanded is high—M'''. When money is more expensive (at P'_m), the quantity of money demanded is low.

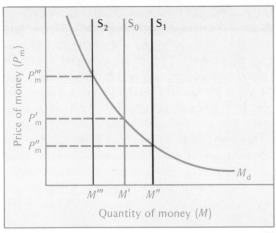

Figure 7 Changes in money supply (all else constant) will affect the price of money (and thus the general price level). When money supply increases (from S_0 to S_1), the price of money declines (from P'_m to P''_m). When money supply decreases (from S_0 to S_2), the price of money rises (from P'_m to P'''_m).

The price of money at which M' will be held is P'_m. Thus the general price level is determined.

Now suppose the money available is increased to S_1, resulting in M'' dollars being available. People will hold the quantity M'' at a lower price of money P''_m. But a lower price of money means a higher price level ($P_m = 1/GPL$). *The increase in the quantity of money has resulted in a higher level of prices.* Similarly, suppose the money supply had been reduced to S_2 with a quantity of dollars available equal to M'''. The smaller quantity of money would cause the price to rise to P'''_m. The rise in the price of money is the same as a decline in the price level. *Reduction in the quantity of money causes the price level to fall.*

Changes in money demand We can also consider *a change in the demand for money* (see Figure 8). Suppose we hold M_s constant with M' dollars available; initially, the demand for money is M_{d_1}. The resulting price of money is P'_m. The decline in demand may come in several ways. We could let people simply change their feelings about money, deciding they want to hold less of it. Or we could let one of the variables we have been holding constant change. For example, if people felt prices would be higher in the future, they would spend some of their holdings of money now. We could also imagine an increase in technol-

ogy which would enable us to make all purchases by simply inserting a card in a slot at the store. Again, demand for money would decline.

Let the demand for money fall to M_{d_2}. The price of money would fall to P''_m, which means the price level would rise. It is interesting and a little amusing to consider the implications of the things we have just said. If people decide they like money less, their attempts to get rid of it only drives up the general price level till they need the same amount as they previously had. Or the fear of inflation in the future becomes a self-fulfilling prophecy. By trying to get rid of the money now before it decreases in value they bring on the very price increase they fear!

Money demand, securities prices, and interest rates

We have seen that *the price of money is a variable which affects the quantity of money demanded.* Another variable which affects the quantity of money demanded is the price for close substitutes for money. These substitutes are such things as savings accounts, stocks, and bonds.

The principle is the same as was given before in the Keynesian demand for money. If securities prices fall, securities become a good buy and money will be exchanged for securities. *The quantity of money demanded will fall as*

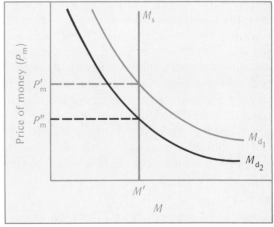

Figure 8 Changes in the demand for money (all else constant) will affect the general price level (and the price of money). If the demand for money declines (from M_{d_1} to M_{d_2}), then the price of money declines (from P'_m to P''_m). Remember that a decline in the price of money means a rise in the general price level.

securities prices fall. The opposite happens if securities prices rise. *As securities become expensive, people simply hold money and the quantity of money demanded increases.*

As was shown above, the price of securities moves in opposite directions to the interest rate. *A rise in securities prices is the same as a fall in the interest rate.* We could therefore look at the interest rate. *An increase in the interest rate* (fall in securities prices) *would result in a smaller quantity of money demanded* since people would convert money to securities to obtain the higher interest earnings. A decline in interest rates (rise in securities prices) means the alternatives forgone by holding money are less attractive so people simply hold money. *At lower interest rates, more money is held.*

Other variables in money demand

There are three other variables or groups of variables (besides the price of money and the interest rate) in the demand for money. They are: (1) real income; (2) expectations; and (3) institutional variables. The relationships between these variables and the quantity of money demanded is strong and direct.

Real income Real income is, in effect, the total amount of goods and services available to the economy. The greater amount of goods and services available, the more of everything may be demanded, including money. In this sense, money is a very superior good since the quantity demanded will rise as income goes up (production and flow of goods rise) and will fall when income goes down (the production and flow are reduced). These statements assume that all other factors influencing the quantity of money demanded are held constant. Essentially, this total production also accounts for the "size of market" which indicates who the potential demanders may be. "Tastes" also are captured in some fairly subtle ways by the income variable.

Expectations In much the same manner that expectations affect the demand for goods and services, so do the expectations of people affect the demand for money. In general, if people think that the price of a good is going to be cheaper in the near future they hold as

little of that particular good as possible in favor of something else that they hope will maintain its value. If people think that the price (purchasing power) of money is going to fall, this is the same thing as saying they expect the price of other goods and services to *rise*. Everything else being equal, they will try to hold a minimum amount of money and speed up anticipated purchases as much as possible. On the other hand, if the expectation is for falling prices in the goods and services department, this means expected increases in the purchasing power of money; hence don't buy now, buy later.

Institutional variables Institutional variables also affect the demand for money by affecting the velocity at which money circulates. Money being held has a zero velocity. *So the more that people hold on to money, the lower is the velocity.* Remember that expenditures and velocity are related flows. If money is "spent faster"—if it performs more transactions in any given period of time—it is almost the same thing as having more money in the economy. The existing supply is being used at a higher rate and therefore is in one sense more efficient. *If the velocity of money rises, then the quantity of money demanded at any given level of price falls (all else being constant).* Conversely, if the *velocity* of money *falls*, then a larger quantity of money will be required to perform a given level of transactions at a given level of prices; so *demand for money rises.*

There are many economic institutions that influence velocity and money demanded. A few examples can be mentioned, though you should easily be able to suggest others. How often people are paid is one factor. The longer the period between paydays, the more money must be held from one payday to make it to the next. The use of checks reduces the need for cash. The speed with which banks clear checks determines how much money is held in checking accounts. The use of bank credit cards reduces the need for money. If credit cards could be used for every purchase, no one would ever hold cash and checking account balances would be reduced by every purchase. Thus a variety of economic arrangements influence money holdings.

In conclusion

We have come to expect that arguments have a resolution. Our thinking tends to follow the thesis-antithesis-synthesis pattern. The first idea—the thesis—is expressed and accepted for a while. The very expression of the first idea is enough to call forth the expression of the counterstatement—the antithesis. Finally, after a struggle, a resolution or synthesis will occur. Our presentation of classical, Keynesian, and monetarist models resembles this approach.

However, the money models of the various schools of economists remain an area of controversy. *The synthesis has not occurred.* We may show the impact of money in each of the models, but the discussion goes on among economists and others.

Classical (or pre-Keynesian)

The classical economists viewed the equation of exchange as a theory. However, in their theory, money did not matter—at least not as far as any real variables such as output, employment, and the interest rate were concerned. Velocity was thought to be a constant over long periods of time. The level of real output was determined in the labor market since full employment was obtained through flexible wage rates. The interest rate was determined by saving and investment. That left money as a variable on one side of the equation and prices as a variable on the other. The influence of money was only on prices. We might show it this way:

$$Money \longrightarrow Prices$$

Keynesian

In the Keynesian model money does not matter very much either though there can be some effects on real variables depending upon the response of the economy. In the Keynesian model, there is greater interdependence and money has an indirect impact on spending and income. The transmittal mechanism is illustrated by the diagram below. If the money supply is increased, people find they have too much money at existing interest rates and income. Except in the special case where money does not affect interest, we would expect people to convert the excess money to securities, bidding up the price of securities or lowering the interest rate. The higher prices for securities (or what is the same thing, the lower interest cost of borrowing money) will stimulate firms to issue securities to undertake investment projects. The spending on the investment projects through the multiplier process eventually increases all output or income. Since Keynes was concerned about less-than-full-employment problems, the resources were thought to be available to increase income without any upward pressure on prices.

$$Money \longrightarrow Interest \longrightarrow Investment$$
$$\longrightarrow Output \text{ and } employment$$

Monetarist

The monetarist position emphasizes the impact of money on spending. If the amount of money is increased without any corresponding increase in output, people will attempt to get rid of the excess by spending it. This does not seem an altogether unreasonable position. The additional spending may have several effects. If the economy is at less than full employment, the additional spending will stimulate production and employment. If income is already at or near full employment, then spending will tend to bid up prices (that is, cause inflation). The rise in income and/or prices will continue until the quantity of money demanded increases by the same amount as the increase in supply. The monetarist position that money matters most may be diagrammed as follows:

$$Money \longrightarrow Spending \nearrow \begin{array}{l} Output \text{ and} \\ employment \end{array}$$
$$\searrow Prices$$

Summary

The equation of exchange expresses a relationship which is always true and under special conditions it becomes a theory. The equation, $MV = PQ$, says that the GNP, the right-hand side, is equal in value to the amount of money times the velocity of circulation of that money.

The classical model of the economy converts the equation of exchange to a theory of demand by assuming velocity to be constant and showing the money demanded to be dependent upon economic transactions.

In the classical model, the interest rate is a real variable being determined by the interaction of saving and investment. The market rate of interest may be different from the real rate for short periods of time. Money only affects the price level.

The Keynesian model of the monetary sector emphasizes the transactions, precautionary, and speculative (liquidity) demands for money. The transactions demand is the same as the classical concept—money used for spending. The precautionary demand is for money held against contingencies.

The speculative demand is for money as an asset. Money is a noninterest-bearing asset. Other securities bear interest. There is an inverse relationship between the price of securities and the interest rate.

Asset owners will generally hold a portfolio of different securities, one of which will be money. At very high interest rates, the portfolios will contain more interest-bearing securities and less cash. At lower interest rates, the portfolios will contain less interest-bearing securities and more cash. The speculative demand for money therefore is an inverse relationship between interest rates and money.

In the Keynesian model, an increase in the money supply may be expected to lower interest rates as people rearrange their portfolios. The additional money will be used to buy securities, bidding up the price of securities and lowering interest rates. If the lower interest rates stimulate investment spending, then through the multiplier process, income and output will be increased.

In the Keynesian model, velocity is not a constant since an increase in money will result in lower interest rates and more money held in idle speculative balances.

The monetarists emphasize the role of money in spending. Thus the quantity of money determines the price level and, in part, production and employment. The demand for money depends upon several variables. (1) One variable is the purchasing power of money, which is inversely related to the price level. More money is needed as the price level rises to keep purchasing power constant.

Other variables affecting the amount of money demanded in the monetarist model include (2) the level of income, (3) the price of securities or the interest rate, (4) the expected direction and rate of price level changes, and (5) a variety of institutional variables determining the ways in which we use and receive money.

Key Words and Phrases

- **monetarists** a "school" of economists who assign to the quantity of money the primary cause of fluctuations in the economy.
- **equation of exchange** $MV = PQ$.
- **money supply** the total amount of money available to the economy. The definition may be M_1, M_2, etc., depending upon the problem being studied (throughout this chapter, we use M_1).
- **velocity** the rate at which money circulates; expressed as the number of times an average dollar changes hands during a year.
- **prime interest rate** the interest rate charged by commercial banks for loans to their most creditworthy business customers.
- **equilibrium real interest rate** the interest rate which occurs when saving and investment are equal. Since saving and investment are expressed in terms of the goods and services used, the interest rate is real rather than monetary.
- **market rate of interest** the rate of interest actually resulting from borrowing and lending money (actually there are many market rates of interest).
- **borrower** a person or firm obtaining money on loan; the issuer of securities such as bonds or notes.
- **lender** the person or firm providing money on loan; the purchaser of securities such as bonds or notes.
- **general price level** a measure of the overall level of prices in an economy; the average price of an average item purchased.
- **price of money** the purchasing power of money; inversely related to the general price level.

Questions for Review

1. Can you identify the transactions balances in your pocket, wallet, or purse? How about the precautionary balances? Does this mean that the concepts are faulty? Or only that there is no money in your pocket, wallet, or purse?

2. Which is most important in determining your demand for money—your income, prices, interest rates, inflation, or when you last were paid? Which is least important?

3. Suppose interest rates on savings and loan or mutual savings bank shares went to 10%. How would you decide to shift money to them from other sources?

4. How would you find the real interest rate? Look up the current rates on Treasury bills, Federal Funds, AAA corporate bonds, and long-term government bonds. Are any of these related to the real interest rate?

5. Assume you are a classical economist. Trace the effects of an increase in money using your model.

6. Now assume you are a Keynesian economist. Use your model to analyze the impact of an increase in the amount of money. (Because of the interrelatedness of your model, comment on the expected change in prices, interest rates, employment, investment expenditures, and output.)

7. In your answer to question 6, what happened to velocity as you applied your model? What happens in the Keynesian model to velocity as money is increased?

8. Would people always want to hold more money? If you spread money over the countryside from an airplane, would people always pick it up? Why or why not?

9. "If inflation is expected to increase, you should try to get your hands on as much money as possible." Agree or disagree? Why?

10. If V is constant, what happens to GNP if money increases by 6%? Suppose real output grew only 3%. What was the rate of price increase?

11. Suppose a bond is issued at $1,000 face value, and it pays $50 per year in interest. What is the interest rate? If the bond sells for $900, what is the interest rate? Would people be more inclined to buy the bond at $1,000 or $900? Why or why not?

12. Why hold money instead of bonds when money pays no interest?

15

Money Supply and Monetary Policy

In earlier chapters we defined money and "near-moneys" (certain assets which can easily be converted into money). We noted that a definition of money included currency plus demand deposits (checking account money). We saw that currency is government-created money, and that demand deposits are bank-created money. We also discussed the uses of money. And we talked about the dynamics of changing demand for money within an economy.

We come now to a discussion of money supply and how it affects the performance of the economy. Since our money supply—both currency and demand deposits—is determined by the Federal Reserve System, our discussion will center on what the Fed does. We have learned that its most important function is to control and respond to periodic rise and fall in the economy's demand for money. We shall now see how the Fed carries out this function.

We will discuss the money problems involved in controlling the supply of money. We will see that sometimes the Fed is successful in solving the problems—and that sometimes it is not so successful. The **monetary policies** of the Fed—that is, the policies it adopts to control money supply—can have considerable impact on the nation's economy. Monetary policy does have an impact on the pocketbooks of students and senior citizens, and on each and everyone of us in between.

It almost goes without saying that an important economic policy tool such as control of a nation's money supply will be a subject of controversy. Some economists believe control of supply should be left to reliance on a fixed standard of value, something like the gold standard of earlier use. They feel the use of monetary policies to expand money supply in hard times only leads to too much money and hence inflation.

Other economists believe the Federal Reserve System should be used to control money supply, but that the system has flaws that should be taken into account. Others believe that fiscal policies (government manipulation of tax and spending powers) are a better means of control than monetary policies. In this chapter we will also take a closer look at these areas of disagreement about the Federal Reserve System's monetary policies.

Monetary policy and $MV = PQ$

We saw in the last chapter that the equation of exchange, $MV = PQ$, is a very simple representation of how money works in the economy. The Keynesian and monetarist economists have added significant parts to the equation. However, we may find that the simple model is a good way to understand monetary policy. Monetary policy consists of actions taken by the Fed to change money supply M. To keep things very simple for the moment, let us assume that velocity or V will not change.

If V is constant, then any change in the money supply M must produce a change in PQ. Often we cannot say for sure which will change: whether price level P will change or output Q will change. In fact, both usually respond to a change in M. But we are now ready to reconsider two important economic problems discussed earlier—unemployment and inflation. We will now discuss how monetary policy (making changes in money supply) may be useful in solving these problems.

The trough and unemployment

Recall from the chapter on business cycles that the trough (or low point) of the cycle means greatly reduced output of goods and services. The usual side effect of reduced output is unemployment. When demand slackens for goods, demand for workers to produce those goods obviously decreases also.

Suppose that we want to relieve unemployment, as we often do. What course of action should we pursue? Well, a first step is to increase the amount of goods and services produced. Increased production requires additional workers. In short, we want to increase Q.

A further observation about the trough (a recession period) is that inflation—that is, an increase in P—is usually not then a problem. Inflation is usually related to excessive demand for goods and services. Inflation is generally a problem at the peak of the cycle.

So, returning to our equation $MV = PQ$, we now have a situation where both velocity, V, and price level, P, may be assumed to be constant. So a change in M must result in a nearly corresponding change in Q. If we increase money supply M during a recession we can be fairly certain that output Q will also increase. (Fairly certain, not entirely certain, because as we shall see, although an equation is simple, people are not—especially when it comes to money.) And remember that as output increases, unemployment will decrease.

When the money supply expands, banks will have more money in their vaults and will be more willing to make loans, whether to consumers to buy new cars or to businesses for investment purposes. At first only some people will have more money. But as they buy goods and services, the money is passed on to others. More people now find they have extra money available. Consumers use some, if not all, to purchase additional goods and services which they would otherwise not have bought. Businesses use the money to purchase more raw materials to expand or modernize their firms. *Thus the increase in the money supply succeeds in increasing Q and filling in the trough of the cycle.*

The peak and inflation

At the peak of a business cycle, output Q is high and unemployment is low. Businesses may not be able to produce enough to meet demand. Demand will grow as producers hire more workers to increase production. These workers will demand more goods on which to spend their wages. Shortages may result, and prices most surely begin to rise. So our problem at the peak is inflation, or a rising price level, P.

In this situation, we can assume Q is fairly constant since, as we have just said, output is at or near a peak. (When the active labor force is at work, the economy is said to be at its *full-employment level.*) Since velocity, V, and output, Q, are not going to change much, M and P are of increasing interest.

The problem here is the rise in the price level, P. If P is to be brought under control, that is, reduced, monetary policy may have to be used to decrease money supply, M. In our equation, a reduction in M will produce the desired fall in P. Once again, if money is restricted in its availability, people will be less willing and able to buy. Prices will go down. (Since we are holding Q constant, we are in effect saying that everything being produced at the full-employment level will be sold. In practice, however, the reluctance to buy may also affect output, Q, but for now we will ignore this in order to concentrate on the effect of M on price.) *Thus money supply is reduced or tightened to fight inflation.*

To bring P down, actual *reduction* of M may not be necessary. Instead, the *rate of its growth* may simply be reduced. M will continue to grow, but more slowly. P will fall, but, again, more slowly.

Money supply and the Federal Reserve

The Federal Reserve System has been previously described. We discussed the many functions of the Federal Reserve and indicated that its important function is the determination of the nation's money supply—its monetary policy. We will now examine how the Federal Reserve carries out this function. First, let us examine the balance sheet of the Federal Reserve Bank.

Balance sheet for the Federal Reserve

Assets of the Banks The Federal Reserve Bank has a consolidated balance sheet for all the District Banks showing the total assets and liabilities. At the end of January, 1977, the Federal Reserve System had assets and liabilities totaling $124 billion. Let us look closely at this balance sheet, as shown in Table 1.

The first two assets listed—gold certificates and Special Drawing Rights—are important for international transactions with the central banks of other nations. The *gold certificates*, totaling a little over $11.6 billion, are represented by gold owned by the U.S. Treasury. (While we may think of gold as being stored in Fort Knox, actually much of it is in the

Table 1
Consolidated Statement of All
Federal Reserve Banks, January 31, 1977

Assets	$ Millions
Gold certificates	11,658
Special Drawing Rights	1,200
Loans and securities	633
Government and government agency securities	100,924
Buildings and equipment	366
Other assets	9,138
Total assets	124,019

Liabilities	$ Millions
Federal Reserve Notes outstanding	81,198
Deposits	
Member banks	23,411
U.S. Treasury	11,397
Other	1,025
Capital and surplus	2,495
Other liabilities	4,493
Total liabilities	124,019

Source: Federal Reserve Bulletin.

District Federal Reserve Bank in New York.) Since the gold represents less than 10% of all the assets of the Federal Reserve, it is of little importance to *domestic* money creation.

The *Special Drawing Rights* or SDRs are called "paper gold." They give their holders the right to draw currency from the International Monetary Fund. The main use of both real and paper gold is to settle accounts in international trade. Should the United States buy more goods and services from other countries than it sells to them, the difference must be paid for. SDRs, the International Monetary Fund, and other matters of international finance are discussed in Chapters 20 and 21.

Another asset is *loans made to member banks*. These are short-term loans requested by member banks so that they may maintain or increase their reserves. The item is an asset to the Federal Reserve Banks since it is in effect an IOU from the commercial bank. For example, if you lend a friend $100, you would still include that $100 in figuring your total worth. The money is still yours. (It's merely— and hopefully temporarily—in your friend's pocket.)

The biggest single asset and perhaps the most important is *U.S. government and government agency securities*. As of January 31, 1977, the Federal Reserve Banks held $100.92 billion

in such securities. This represents United States notes and bonds and other promise-to-pay paper that the government has sold to pay its debts. The holder of this paper has, in effect, lent his money to the government. The government has, in turn, promised to return the money, plus interest, by a certain date. The Federal Reserve Banks may lend their money to the government directly and thus directly receive the notes or bonds to add to the Fed's assets. Or the Fed may buy them on the open market from commercial banks or from individuals. (We shall learn more about open market operations of the Fed later on in this chapter.)

As of January, 1977, the total debt of the federal government was $653.9 billion. Of this amount, the federal government itself owned approximately 22% and the general public had loaned the federal government about 63% of the total. The proportion lent by the Federal Reserve is about 15% of the total. As we shall see, these government securities may be used by the Federal Reserve to control the amount of money available in the economy.

The Fed has other assets as well. As is true of any firm, there are the buildings, vaults, computers, furniture, etc., owned by the Fed. Physical assets amount to approximately one-third of a billion dollars. The remaining assets include checks in the process of being presented to the writers' banks for payment. In all, the Fed has assets of slightly more than $124 billion.

Liabilities and capital account of the Banks
The liabilities side of the account for the Federal Reserve is also interesting. The first item is *Federal Reserve Notes*. The amount of these notes in circulation at the end of January, 1977, was nearly $81.2 billion.

As we noted in Chapter 11, almost all United States paper money in circulation is Federal Reserve Notes. When these notes are in circulation, they represent a claim against the assets of the Federal Reserve Banks that issued them. Theoretically (but not actually), you could take the Federal Reserve dollar bill now in your pocket to the nearest Federal Reserve Bank and demand a dollar's worth of the bank's assets. Hence such notes are a liability to the bank.

Member bank deposits totaled $23.4 billion at the end of January, 1977. This is the amount of cash reserves that member banks keep on deposit at the Federal Reserve. They *must* keep a minimum amount. They *may* keep more. These reserves are a liability to the Federal Reserve Bank because they really belong to the member banks. But, as we shall see, the Federal Reserve can manipulate these reserves to help control the amount of money in the nation's economy.

The next liability consists of deposits in the Bank by the U.S. Treasury. The $11.4 billion on deposit in January, 1977, represents the receipts of the Treasury from taxes, loans, or other sources which it needs to pay its current bills—your tax refund, for example. It is the checkbook balance of the federal government. There are other deposits of approximately $1 billion.

Note, too, the item called "Capital and surplus." Recall that Federal Reserve Banks are privately owned, though government controlled. They are owned by the member banks, who purchased shares in the Federal Reserve when they joined the system. "Capital" represents the value of these shares. "Surplus" represents the profits the Federal Reserve Banks make on their capital investments. These profits are limited by law. The total capital and surplus is $2.5 billion. Other liabilities total $4.5 billion. The total liabilities come to slightly more than $124 billion, which just matches the total assets.

Monetary policy activities and goals

We have looked at the assets and liabilities which the Federal Reserve System can manipulate to achieve monetary policy changes. The Fed cannot control the effects of monetary policy entirely by itself. As we will see, *the actual filtering of the policy through the economy can be aided or retarded by the commercial banks and the general public.*

The Fed must first, of course, decide whether a policy change is required. If so, it must then decide what change is required and what method to use.

Stimulation The Fed may decide it is necessary to stimulate the economy. *Stimulation of the economy* means increasing or expanding the supply of money. It therefore sets in motion certain policies it expects will increase the amount of money available. In our equation ($MV = PQ$) an increase in M will increase Q. Some economists emphasize that an increase in the money supply will increase consumer spending, which in turn will cause an increase in output and employment. Other economists emphasize that an increase in money makes it easier and cheaper for investors to increase borrowing. In either case, the increase in consumption or investment, through the multiplier process, will increase output and employment. Stimulation is expected to pep up a lagging economy. This kind of action is also known as *expansionary monetary policy.*

Restraint The Fed may decide it is necessary to restrain the economy. Restraint may be required when the economy is booming too rapidly. Then it would be desirable to reduce the money supply to reduce the upward pressure on prices. In our equation a decrease in M will decrease P. Again, economists disagree on precisely how this reduction in money supply works through the economy. Some emphasize that less money makes it harder and more expensive to borrow money; this reduces consumption and investment, and output falls. Others maintain that a decrease in the money supply causes consumer spending to decline. In either case, a decrease in the money supply will decrease prices and employment. When the Fed acts to restrain the economy, it is said to have a *tight money policy.*

Monetary policy tools: quantitative controls

Suppose the Fed has decided to make a policy change. It has three major tools and a variety of minor ones at its disposal. Of the three major tools, called **quantitative controls,** two are not used very often. Let us begin with these two, coming to the most important one last.

Reserve ratios

In the balance sheet of the Federal Reserve Banks we noted on the liability side that one large item is the member bank reserves. The amount of reserves each member must hold at the Fed or as cash in their own vaults depends on the amount and kind of deposits held by the bank. Time deposits (savings accounts) have lower reserve requirements than demand deposits (checking accounts). This is because time deposits are left in the depositors' accounts longer than demand deposits. The reserve requirement also depends upon the size of the bank. Those with larger deposits must keep proportionately more on reserve as their deposits grow. Table 2 shows Federal Reserve requirements for member banks.

Suppose a bank had $5 million in demand deposits. As Table 2 shows, it would have to maintain minimum required reserves of $7\frac{1}{2}$% on the first $2 million (or $150,000) and 10% on the remaining $3 million (or $300,000). This means it would need a total of $450,000, either in the vault as cash or on deposit at the Fed.

Now suppose the Fed increased the reserve ratio to 10% on the entire $5 million. The bank would have two choices. It could remove $50,000 from excess reserves (money available for lending) and move this amount to the required reserves; this way the required reserves would be $500,000. Or it could reduce its demand deposits to $4,500,000, so that the existing required reserves would be adequate. In either case, money—demand deposits and currency—would be removed from the economy and placed on deposit in the Fed or the vault of the member bank. *Increasing reserve ratios is one way the Fed can contract the money supply* (i.e., reduce M).

To expand the money supply, the Fed can reduce reserve requirements. In our example, it could make the requirement $7\frac{1}{2}$% on the entire $5 million. The required reserve would then be only $375,000. Since the bank had $450,000 on deposit, it could now draw out $75,000 and use the money to lend at profit. Or it could simply leave the whole $450,000 in its reserve and expand its demand deposits to $6,000,000. In either case, more money would flow into the economy.

The Fed does not often use changes in reserve requirements to affect money supply. The method can be *too* effective. Table 2 shows very few changes in reserve requirements between 1972 and 1976. And some of the changes applied only to certain banks or certain types of deposits. The reason for this is that small changes in reserve requirements produce very large changes in the amount of money. In our example of contraction the bank with $5 million went to $4.5 million, a 10% contraction. In the expansion example, the increase was from $5 million to $6 million, a 20% increase. When you consider that a change in reserve requirements affects all member banks, the total change in money supply due to the money expansion (or contraction) multiplier can be massive. Thus the Fed tends to use this powerful tool sparingly.

Table 2
Reserve Requirements on Deposits of Member Banks
(Deposit intervals are in millions of dollars. Requirements are in percent of deposits.)

							Time deposits					
							Other time					
							0-5 million, maturing in—			Over 5 million, maturing in—		
Effective date	Demand deposits					Savings	30-179 days	180 days to 4 years	4 years or more	30-179 days	180 days to 4 years	4 years or more
	0-2	2-10	10-100	100-400	Over 400							
1972—Nov. 9....	8%	10 %	12 %	$16\frac{1}{2}$%	$17\frac{1}{2}$%	3%		3 %			5 %	
1973—July 19....	8	$10\frac{1}{2}$	$12\frac{1}{2}$	$13\frac{1}{2}$	18	3		3			5	
1974—Dec. 12....	8	$10\frac{1}{2}$	$12\frac{1}{2}$	$13\frac{1}{2}$	$17\frac{1}{2}$	3		3		6		3
1975—Feb. 13....	$7\frac{1}{2}$	10	12	13	$16\frac{1}{2}$	3		3		6	3	1
Oct. 30....						3	3		1	6	3	1
1976—Jan. 8....	$7\frac{1}{2}$	10	12	13	$16\frac{1}{2}$	3	3	$2\frac{1}{2}$	1	6	$2\frac{1}{2}$	1

Source: Federal Reserve Bulletin.

Extended Example
The Cost of Federal Reserve Membership

About 40% of all banks in the nation are members of the Federal Reserve System. All national banks must be members. State banks may be members if they wish, and although the majority of state banks are nonmembers, the largest ones are. Thus, as we said earlier, about 80% of all the nation's demand deposits are in member banks, giving the Fed a powerful influence over the money-creating capacities of the nation's commercial banking system.

The percentage of total commercial bank deposits that is held by Federal Reserve member banks has, however, been steadily decreasing in recent years. More and more of the banks which have the option of doing so are choosing to drop out of the System. From 1971 through 1976, for example, more than 200 banks with about $10 billion in deposits withdrew from the System.

Belonging to the Federal Reserve System has definite advantages. Member banks have access to the Fed's fast and convenient check-clearing system, for example, and access to the Fed's "discount window" if they need to borrow short-term reserves. There are other advantages also, including the added security against bank failure provided by the Fed's function as a watch dog over banking procedures. Why, then, are some banks choosing to withdraw from the system? The answer is that some banks feel their profit margins are cut too drastically by the restrictions of membership.

How does membership cut into a bank's profitability? The Fed insists on higher reserve ratios—that its member banks maintain reserves of, say, around 7% to $16\frac{1}{2}$% of demand deposits, depending on the total amount of these deposits in the member bank. State regulations about reserves vary, from requiring none at all in Illinois to requiring the same as the Fed requires in many others. In states requiring less reserves than does the Fed, banks are free to use this extra money to lend out at a profit. In addition, the Fed counts only cash and noninterest-bearing deposits from commercial banks in regional Federal Reserve Banks as reserves. Many states, however, allow banks to count interest-bearing municipal bonds and government securities as reserves. These securities earn money for the bank while being held in reserve. Obviously, nonearning reserves of banks that are members of the Reserve System are less desirable than earning assets. It is not too difficult to see why some banks, faced for one reason or another with decreased profitability, consider membership in the Federal Reserve System a luxury they can no longer afford.

What does this problem of banks opting for nonmembership mean to the system itself? Experts disagree, but the Fed is clearly worried and concerned about further erosion of its membership. Such erosion, the Fed contends, reduces its ability to monitor the nation's money supply. Member banks must report their deposits weekly; nonmember banks report only once every three months. The more banks that are outside the system, the more difficult it is to keep close tab on the supply of money in the economy. The Fed also says that membership erosion reduces its actual capacity to control the money supply by raising or lowering required reserve ratios. The less the total amount of deposits involved in this procedure, the less potent this important monetary tool becomes. So monetary policy itself is jeopardized as an effective economic policy.

The Fed, meanwhile, is doing what it can to counter the effects of its membership drop. It is, for example, currently sponsoring federal legislation that would allow it to impose reserve requirements on all banks, members and nonmembers alike, thus lessening the profit motive as a spur to a bank's decision to withdraw from the system. Actually, this problem of strong central bank controls and weaker state controls is very similar to the problem faced by Nicholas Biddle's Bank of the United States with state banks; in the era of President Jackson, state banks achieved their goal of being loosely regulated—the central bank dissolved.

Also, *the Fed's attempt to increase M by reducing reserve requirements may not always work.* As we noted, if reserve requirements are reduced, the bank could withdraw reserves or increase demand deposits. But there is another course of action possible to the bank. It does not have to do anything! If the demand for loans were slack, it might do just that. Only if the bank wants or needs the extra money will it go into circulation. If the bank does not use it, *M* will not increase.

Discount rate

Banks, even as you and I, borrow money. In fact, most banks borrow quite frequently. They may need money to meet their reserve requirements which the Fed insists they do each Wednesday. Or they may wish to borrow to increase their loan capability. Commercial banks sometimes find they need increased funds to meet short-term needs of their customers. For example, banks serving farm areas may need a large supply of cash in early summer to lend to the surrounding farm community until farmers are ready to harvest and sell their crops. A city bank may have to dip deep into its reserve to accommodate a corporate depositor who suddenly wishes to transfer a huge deposit to a bank in another city. Sometimes the banks do what everyone else does. They go to another bank with extra funds to borrow the money needed. The interest paid on such loans is the *federal funds* rate. If they can't find a bank willing to lend or the cost is too high, they must find the money elsewhere. In such cases, the commercial bank may borrow funds from its district Federal Reserve Bank.

Again even as you and I, commercial banks must pay interest on such loans. The interest on money borrowed from the Fed is called the **discount rate.** This term means simply that the amount of money the borrower (member bank) receives is "discounted" by the amount of the interest. The interest is paid at the time the loan is negotiated, rather than when it is repaid. In other words, interest on the loan is paid "up front."

Commercial banks may pay this discount rate (interest) by giving the Federal Reserve Bank some of the secured promissory notes (most likely government bonds) they are currently holding.

At one time, commercial banks used their customers' promissory notes for this purpose. These notes had already been "discounted," of course. The borrowers had paid the interest "up front." The notes were then "rediscounted" by the Fed. Commercial banks no longer use this method, but the term "rediscounted" still hangs on; in some instances, people still speak of the Federal Reserve discount rate as the *rediscount rate.*

By changing the discount rate, the Fed may encourage or discourage banks to borrow. *A higher discount rate means less borrowing from the Fed and less money available for loans to consumers and investors.* Thus raising the discount rate may serve to lower aggregate demand and cut inflation. By the same token, a lower discount rate might be expected to stimulate the economy, expanding output and employment. It should also be noted that a change in discount rates to commercial banks tends to create a corresponding change in interest rates throughout the economy.

The total amount of money borrowed by commercial banks in any given period is comparatively small. Banks are rather actively discouraged from "using the discount window." Thus the importance of the discount rate as a means of monetary control is limited.

Some economists feel the discount rate changes come only after interest rates have changed in the general economy. It is thus only a signal to the economy that the Fed is aware that interest rates have changed and is now ready to follow the general trend. Others feel the discount rate is a valuable indicator of monetary policy, even though it is not quantitatively very important. It is a means by which the Fed can give the public a clear signal of current economic trends. Some policy changes are not readily perceived by the general public. For example, if reserve requirements are decreased, only bankers really know about it. However, a change in the discount rate is noticed and reported in the press. A drop in the discount rate is a signal to the economy that banks now have more money to lend. The economy needs a boost.

Table 3 shows the discount rates in effect on February 28, 1977. Notice that the St. Louis District Bank delayed four days in setting its

Table 3
Federal Reserve Bank Discount Rates, February 28, 1977

District Bank	Rate for government securities	Rate for other securities	Rate charged nonmembers on government securities	Effective date
Boston	$5\frac{1}{4}$	$5\frac{3}{4}$	$8\frac{1}{4}$	11/22/76
New York	$5\frac{1}{4}$	$5\frac{3}{4}$	$8\frac{1}{4}$	11/22/76
Philadelphia	$5\frac{1}{4}$	$5\frac{3}{4}$	$8\frac{1}{4}$	11/22/76
Cleveland	$5\frac{1}{4}$	$5\frac{3}{4}$	$8\frac{1}{4}$	11/22/76
Richmond	$5\frac{1}{4}$	$5\frac{3}{4}$	$8\frac{1}{4}$	11/22/76
Atlanta	$5\frac{1}{4}$	$5\frac{3}{4}$	$8\frac{1}{4}$	11/22/76
Chicago	$5\frac{1}{4}$	$5\frac{3}{4}$	$8\frac{1}{4}$	11/22/76
St. Louis	$5\frac{1}{4}$	$5\frac{3}{4}$	$8\frac{1}{4}$	11/26/76
Minneapolis	$5\frac{1}{4}$	$5\frac{3}{4}$	$8\frac{1}{4}$	11/22/76
Kansas City	$5\frac{1}{4}$	$5\frac{3}{4}$	$8\frac{1}{4}$	11/22/76
Dallas	$5\frac{1}{4}$	$5\frac{3}{4}$	$8\frac{1}{4}$	11/22/76
San Francisco	$5\frac{1}{4}$	$5\frac{3}{4}$	$8\frac{1}{4}$	11/22/76

Source: Federal Reserve Bulletin.

rate to the level prevailing at the other 11 District Banks. Presumably, they could all set different rates but in fact they usually work together.

Open market operations

The Fed's activities in buying and selling United States Treasury bills and bonds on the open market is its most potent weapon in the control of money supply. **Open market operations** consist of buying and selling such securities. The Fed's customers are commercial banks or the general public. These transactions are very important in regulating money supply because of the flexibility they offer. The changes in money supply may be in almost any amount or in either direction. They may be quickly reversed if the policy seems unwise after the fact. The Open Market Committee of the Federal Reserve System makes the decision as to which securities to buy or sell and in what amounts. The Federal Reserve District Bank in New York is the hub of open market operations.

Let us say the Federal Reserve System wishes to increase the nation's money supply through open market operations. In an attempt to do so, it will buy Treasury securities. Let us say it buys these securities from commercial banks. As we have seen, banks sometimes want or need to increase their liquidity—that is, they want or need cash. Most likely, they want the cash to lend at a profit to investors and consumers.

When the Fed buys securities from a commercial bank, it pays for them by depositing their dollar value in the commercial bank's reserve account. Assuming that the member bank has enough in its reserve account to meet legal requirements, it now has extra reserves to lend to the public. And, as we have seen in our discussion of how banks create money, the bank may be able to increase the overall money supply by many times the amount of the added reserves. So if the commercial banks choose to use their added reserves—and they may choose not to do so—there can be a substantial increase in the nation's money supply.

The Federal Reserve System may also purchase Treasury securities from the public. In all probability, they will be purchased from a bond dealer, who has such securities in his inventory. If so, the bond dealer receives a check from the Fed which he deposits in his commercial bank account. That bank now has a new liability—the demand deposit credited to the dealer's account. The money supply is immediately increased by this amount. When the check gets to the Fed for clearance, the bank has an asset, an addition to its reserve. The added reserves again may be loaned to the public, resulting in even more money in the economy. So then, *whether the Fed buys Treasury securities from the commercial banks or from the public, money supply increases.*

Now let us say the Federal Reserve System wishes to reduce the nation's money supply through open market operations. It then begins to sell its Treasury securities. Commercial

Extended Example
How Open Market Committee Changes Money Supply

Fed assets		Fed liabilities	
	$ billion		$ billion
Government securities	+$1.0	Member bank reserves	$1.0
Totals:	+$1.0		+$1.0

Suppose the Federal Open Market Committee (FOMC) decides to use monetary policy to expand the money supply of the nation. The members of the FOMC meet in secret so people will not be able to profit by their decisions. They carry out their transactions on behalf of the various Federal Reserve District Banks, but most of the actual purchases or sales are made in New York by the New York branch.

Given that a decision to stimulate the economy has been taken, the idea is to put more money into the system. The way to do this would be to purchase government securities such as Treasury bills or longer-term government bonds. Let us say they decide to purchase $1 billion of government securities.

The people charged with conducting the transaction will go to the various securities dealers. These are the large banks and a few dealers who specialize in selling government securities. The buyers for the Fed will purchase the $1 billion in securities from whoever is interested in selling. The sellers will be anyone with bonds to sell, such as individuals, commercial banks, insurance companies, other firms, and maybe even the dealers trading on their own account.

The Fed will pay for the bonds with a check on itself. If the seller is a commercial bank, the Fed may simply credit the bank with additional reserves. Otherwise, the seller will eventually deposit the check in his own bank. The bank will then have additional reserves in the form of deposits, some of which must be deposited at the Fed. Suppose, for simplicity, the purchase is made entirely from the member banks with payment made with credits to the commercial banks on the books of the Fed. The balance sheet of the Fed will change as follows:

Thus the Fed's accounts still balance.

Of course, the member banks are in business to make money. They cannot make money if they keep all those reserves on deposit at the Fed. They need to make loans which will earn interest income. At least they need to purchase some more interest-bearing assets. If the reserve requirement is 20%, the banking system collectively can use the $1 billion reserves as backing for a total of $4 billion in new loans or investments. Thus they can begin to be aggressive in making loans or in purchasing bonds.

The money loaned will be deposited in a bank somewhere in the system. Similarly, the sellers of securities to the banks will eventually deposit the checks in their own banks. As we have seen, an increase in reserves with a 20% required reserve rule will result in a fivefold increase in demand deposits and hence in the money supply. We can summarize the changes in the member banks collective balance sheet as follows:

Member bank assets		Member bank liabilities	
	$ billion		$ billion
Reserves at Fed	+$1.0	Demand deposits	$5.0
New loans and investments	+$4.0		
Totals:	$5.0		$5.0

To be sure of your understanding, consider a sale of government securities by the Fed. Can you work through the balance sheets and the explanation? Using the equation of exchange, show how the change in M can have an impact on the rest of the economy.

banks may have more cash in their vaults, including their reserves held by the Federal Reserve Banks, than they can presently use. Buying Treasury securities will put their idle money to work drawing interest. When commercial banks buy securities from the Federal Reserve, the process noted above is reversed. The price of the securities is withdrawn from the commercial bank's reserve account held by the Fed. The commercial bank's cash reserve dwindles. It now has less money to lend to investors and consumers. The nation's money supply also dwindles.

Further, a commercial bank may wish to purchase the Federal Reserve's securities without dipping into its reserves. Perhaps its reserves are not all that plentiful. Perhaps they are even below the required limit. In that case, it may refuse to grant extensions on loans it has made to the public. It may demand immediate payment of existing loans. Thus it will have cash to purchase the Fed's securities. Getting this cash directly from the public causes the money supply to decrease very rapidly.

If the Fed sells directly to the public, the purchaser presumably pays by check. The check is drawn against his account with a commercial bank. The bank's liabilities are decreased as the purchaser's money is removed from his demand deposit account. But the bank's reserve account is depleted by a corresponding amount when the check reaches the Fed. The commercial bank now has less money in its reserve account to spend. Again, whether the Fed sells its Treasury securities to banks or to individuals, the nation's money supply can be expected to decrease.

As we shall see below, the Federal Reserve System's open market operations are somewhat more efficient in lowering money supply than in increasing it.

Other policy tools: qualitative controls

There remain a few other methods which the Fed has at its disposal to produce desired changes in the economy. **Qualitative controls** are a type of monetary fine tuning. Their overall effect is slight compared with the potentially large changes that can result from the use

Economic Thinker
Arthur Burns

Mostly he was called simply "The Chairman." Officially, he was Chairman of the Federal Reserve Board. As such, Arthur F. Burns was one of the most important and powerful men in the economic life of the nation. When "The Chairman" spoke, people did indeed listen, including bankers, businessmen, and powerful politicians.

And they did not always like what they heard. Some complained that Burns (and the Fed) moved too slowly in increasing the nation's money supply to combat recession. Others complained that Burns' monetary policies were too expansionist, thus inflationary. He was attacked from the right by economists such as Milton Friedman, who believed that on-again off-again increases of the money supply had a destabilizing effect on the economy and caused lack of confidence in the business community. His policies were attacked from the left by economists such as Paul Samuelson, who believed his power was too absolute and that it should be checked by officials responsible to the nation's electorate. Through it all, however, Chairman Burns remained more or less unflappable. The autonomous power of his office and his own scholarly personality kept him in the Washington hierarchy. Indeed, it has been said that the awe in which he was held was second only to that accorded the President.

Arthur Burns came to America as a young man from Austria, where he was born in 1904. He taught economics at Rutgers University (where Milton Friedman was one of his pupils). Later, he taught at Columbia University. Burns made his reputation as an economist with his work in identifying and measuring business cycles. He explored the subject in depth in his 1946 book, written with Wesley Mitchell, *Measuring Business Cycles*. In 1953, Burns left Columbia to be-

prices. The Keynesian cure for unemployment—increasing the total demand—no longer works. It merely brings a new disease—inflation.

Burns' critics contend that experience, even in recent years, shows the continued value of Keynesian principles. Cutting taxes and increasing government spending still make the economy run faster. The reverse still slows it down. The real problem, they say, is knowing when to stop. They contend, for example, that the Keynesian policies of the Nixon administration and of Burns' Fed did lead to economic recovery in 1972. But inflation developed because the policies were applied too strongly (1972 was an election year). In 1973–1975, on the other hand, the government, and the Fed, did far too little to support the economy. The result was a deep recession.

Burns' views led to a certain amount of conflict between himself and the Congress during the first year of Carter's administration. He was in disagreement with some of the stimulative policies desired by the Democratic Congress. He was willing, however, to have government be "the employer of last resort," a position favored by Carter's economic advisers. He also favored experimentation with government programs of wage and price stabilization, believing that such a policy is probably necessary and inevitable in a modern industrial economy.

Throughout his public life, Arthur Burns has been an outspoken adviser to, and sometimes self-appointed teacher of, the business and political sectors of the nation. His legally mandated reports to various Congressional committees often evolved into something closer to professional lectures to students than to reports of Federal Reserve activities. He advised politicians and financiers on everything from fiscal policies to unemployment problems, incomes policies, international problems, and conservation of energy. He insisted always, however, on the independence of the Federal Reserve Board and, as Chairman of the Board, on his own independence in setting the nation's monetary policy.

come Chairman of the Council of Economic Advisers under President Eisenhower. In 1970, he was appointed Chairman of the Federal Reserve Board. His term as chairman expired in January 1978. As a governor of the seven-man board, his appointment runs for a term of 14 years. He may, if he wishes, remain on the board until 1984.

As Chairman of the Federal Reserve Board, Burns steered a generally conservative course. The hyperinflation of the post-World War I Austria of his youth made him deeply wary of expansionary monetary policies. His position in this respect was generally favored by the banking and business community. He was also suspicious of government fiscal policies intended to fight recession by force-feeding consumption. He was not, however, a dogmatic anti-Keynesian. He believed that Keynesian principles had worked well enough in the twenty years or so after World War II. In recent times, however, the situation had changed; Burns contends that the fact that unemployment and inflation are experienced together in today's economy calls for something other than simple Keynesian cures. Demand can be reduced to fight inflation and increased to fight unemployment, as the Keynesians say. But it cannot be simultaneously increased and decreased to fight both recession and high

of quantitative controls. Qualitative controls consist of three possible courses: moral suasion, selective credit controls, and selective interest controls.

Moral suasion

A less formal term for moral suasion is "jawboning." The Fed "jawbones" the economic community when its spokesmen make speeches, give newspaper interviews, or make appearances before Congressional committees. It may advocate less spending by consumers. It may advocate energy conservation to conserve the money supply that would otherwise move to oil-producing countries. It might ask bankers to make more loans in order to stimulate the economy. It might warn the banking community that excessive loans are dangerously heating up the economy. There may be an implied threat in the last type of jawboning. The Fed has the power to examine its member banks at any time to make sure their loans are aboveboard and not excessively risky.

Jawboning is, at times, an effective tool. But its effectiveness really depends on the response of bankers and the public. As we shall see below, if bankers do not wish to expand loans, it is almost impossible for the Fed to force them to do so. Likewise, the business community and the public can not be forced to borrow against their will.

Selective credit controls

The Federal Reserve System has at times used credit controls to channel spending in certain directions. Special legislation has been enacted to allow the Fed to control credit and hence control money supply. The Fed may discourage consumers by requiring the purchaser to make a larger down-payment and by shortening the repayment period. For example, if you can buy a car for $1,000 down and $100 a month for three years, you may decide to buy it. Ordinarily, market forces determine the terms of such loans. But if the Fed compels the banker to insist upon $2,000 down and repayment over two years, you may refuse (or not be able) to buy. The loan you do not take out means that some money may remain idle in the reserves of the bank. Thus the money supply grows less rapidly than it would have if you

had taken out the loan. Of course, if the Fed makes it even easier for you to purchase a car, you, and presumably many other potential buyers, will contribute to a rise in the prosperity of the auto industry—and thus the economy.

The Fed may also use credit controls to limit stock market transactions. It may set "margin requirements" on stock purchases. *Margin rate* is the amount of money a purchaser must put up if he wants to buy stock on credit. What he does not pay out of his pocket, he must borrow from a bank or from the brokerage house that handles his transaction. High margin rates will discourage stock market transactions and hence loans. Low margin rates will encourage such transactions. They will thus increase loans.

Margin rates also affect the price of stocks, and hence the amount of money in circulation throughout the economy. When people can easily obtain money to buy stocks, and want to buy them, stock prices will go up as demand increases. If money is hard to come by, the converse will happen.

Selective interest controls

The Federal Reserve has the power to set interest rates commercial banks can pay on time deposits. It can use this power to effect changes in the economy. The principal way it does this is by shifting money from one sector of the economy to another.

For example, let us suppose that the monetary authorities believe that the construction industry is overbuilding. Too many office and apartment buildings are going up. The market may soon be glutted. Construction is largely financed through mortgage loans from savings and loans and mutual savings banks. Remember, the Federal Reserve has no authority over interest paid by these institutions. It can not require them to lower the interest they pay on the deposits of their customers and thus discourage further deposits. Yet it is these deposits which the institutions are lending to builders to fuel construction expansion.

What can the Fed do? It can raise the level of interest *commercial banks* are allowed to pay *their* depositors. This will make commercial banks more competitive and help syphon money supply away from the savings and loan associations and mutual savings banks to commercial banks. There it will be loaned out to another sector of the economy, perhaps to consumers or to investors in capital goods.

Remember, though, construction is a very labor-intensive industry. Slowing it down could result in an unwanted increase in unemployment. The Fed must tread carefully when it walks in the tangled forest of our national economy. In fact, during the mid-1970s, the construction industry, especially housing, was quite depressed. So the Fed made sure commercial banks paid less on their deposits than did the savings and loan institutions. This way savings and loans would attract money from new depositors that could be made available for mortgages. The interest paid out by commercial banks will have some bearing on the interest charged to borrowers. If interest paid out increases, then unless volume of deposits increases greatly, banks may feel compelled to raise the interest rate on borrowing. However, because banks and other thrift institutions like savings and loans compete with one another, the interest paid out cannot differ too widely. If it did, the institution with the much lower interest rate on deposits would not attract new depositors and would even have difficulty holding current depositors. Such an institution would be in serious financial difficulties.

Evaluating monetary policy

Monetary policy of the Federal Reserve System is only one of many economic policies used to change the direction of, or stabilize, a nation's economy. It is used in conjunction with other policies, especially fiscal policy. Hence it is difficult to be sure of its degree of effectiveness. In truth, there is much controversy among economists about the use of monetary policy.

There would seem to be a kind of fashion swing in the popularity of monetary policy. From the creation of the Federal Reserve System in 1914 until the late 1930s, the use of monetary policy was a dominant force in controlling the American economy. For the next twenty years or so, fiscal policies (taxing and

spending by government) were dominant. In recent years, monetary policies have again come to the fore. But there are now indications that the popularity of fiscal policies may be once again on the rise. Keep in mind, however, that monetary and fiscal policies are not necessarily mutually exclusive. They are more often than not used in tandem to affect the economy. The problem, of course, is to strike the right balance between the two approaches.

Now let us take a look at some of the pros and cons of the controversy surrounding monetary policy.

The pro arguments

Flexibility and speed The Board of Governors of the Federal Reserve System can act quickly when problems appear in the economy. It can, for example, raise or lower reserve requirements almost overnight. It can enter the open securities market whenever it wishes. Furthermore, policies can be quickly changed, implemented, or even reversed.

Fiscal policies, on the other hand, can seem to take forever and a day—first to decide on them and then to put them into action. For example, Congressmen must carefully consider the conflicting interests of the nation's voters before it passes a tax bill. Deciding priorities for government spending is likewise time consuming. Congressmen don't determine monetary policy; the Federal Reserve Board does.

Nonpolitical and politically acceptable By Congressional dictate, the Federal Reserve System is free from political interference. Its governors can make decisions purely on economic lives of a change to a tight money policy, for example. They are, however, immediately aware of a tax law that puts money in their pockets or takes it out. Consequently, Federal grounds. Further, decisions of the governors do not have immediate, direct impact on the consciousness of the people. Most citizens are not immediately aware of the effect on their Reserve decisions are more politically acceptable. What people don't know won't cause a political fuss.

Neutrality Changes brought about by monetary policy affect the entire economic community. Quantitative controls do not directly discriminate against or favor any single sector. Changes that do result occur within the framework of the free market. Free market competition, not the policy itself, engenders whatever discrimination occurs.

Fiscal policies, on the other hand, are not neutral. Large expenditures for arms or highways, for example, discriminate directly in favor of military suppliers and highway contractors. Since there is only so much money in the budget, such expenditures directly "discriminate" against other segments of the economy—mass transit, for example, or education.

The con arguments

Economists differ in their attitude toward monetary policy. Broadly speaking, we can group economists in two opposing factions: Keynesians and monetarists. The Keynesians not only stress the importance of fiscal policy; they also advocate the use of monetary policy. To be sure, they feel fiscal policy is much more important and useful than monetary policy. When handled properly, however, monetary policy is an effective supplement to fiscal policy.

The monetarists are not too enthusiastic toward the use of either fiscal or monetary policy. They believe that changes in the money supply have too powerful an effect to apply as fine tuning. Monetary policy has tended to magnify economic problems rather than solve them. Therefore, the monetarists argue that the best way to handle the money supply is to let it grow at the same rate the productive capacity of the economy grows. Once the growth rate of the money supply is established, it should be maintained. If the increase in money is a little more or less than the economy is expanding, it does not matter since people can adjust to the difference without too much difficulty.

Though not the only critic, the monetarists are probably the most severe critics of the Federal Reserve's monetary policy. Partly they feel the Fed cannot in any event do the right thing if they actively pursue a policy that involves changing the rate of growth of the

Extended Example
The Fed Shoots at a Moving Target

One of the main functions of the Federal Reserve System is to conduct monetary policy, primarily through controlling the rate of growth of the money supply. This variable in the economy is an important one to businessmen and investors as they plan their financial activities. If money is "tight," the supply growing at about 3% a year or less, investors can expect the cost of borrowing for expansion (interest rates) to be relatively high. If money is "loose," the supply growing at about 6 to 8% or even more, borrowing costs will be lower, at least for a while. In either case, investors and financial institutions can make their plans accordingly.

But can they? Critics of the Fed contend that its control of money supply is far too unpredictable. In 1975, Congress passed a joint resolution requiring that the Federal Reserve Board publicly state its target for money growth throughout the economy every four months, in the expectation that such disclosure would increase predictability and lessen short-term fluctuations of money supply (and also force the Fed to be more open about its monetary policies). The resolution, however, would seem to have had little effect.

In 1976, for example, the Fed declared its target for money growth between the third quarter of 1975 and the third quarter of 1976 to be 5 to 7½%. The yearly growth rate was within this target, but short-term fluctuations in 1975 ranged from a high of over 18% in June to about 2% in July and back up to about 14% in November. Despite stated targets, short-term fluctuations in money supply remained as erratic as ever, much to the annoyance of "strict monetarists" such as Milton Friedman, who advocate predictably steady growth.

But Arthur Burns, Chairman of the Federal Reserve Board during this period, contended that such fluctuations were not necessarily harmful, but, indeed, were sometimes needed. Burns declared himself willing to live with mandated targets as something to shoot at in the long run but reserved the right to change short-term targets at any time the economy seemed to call for such change. There can be no magic number for money growth such as the strict monetarists advocate, said Burns. "Our objective in life is not to hit the target, but the best possible performance of the economy."

Not all the blame is to be laid on the Fed, however. The general public has something to do with it also. People can, to a considerable extent, offset the actions of the Fed. Suppose the Fed is trying to restrict the growth of the money supply. But, at the same time, people are moving deposits from their savings accounts to their checking accounts. No one person would have much effect but if a lot of people do it, the money supply may actually increase (due to different reserve ratios).

So, despite disclosure of money-growth targets, the Fed's control of money supply remains relatively uncertain and unpredictable. The targets will probably continue to be movable ones, and what they should be and how they should be defined will undoubtedly continue to be the subject of argument among economists and money market professionals.

money supply. And finally because so many variables, in their view, affect the demand for money, the Fed cannot be sure that the economy will react as the Fed intended. Let us look at the major criticisms of monetary policy.

Politics and imprecision Critics complain that in the past, monetary policy has often been used to fulfill political ambitions of the party in office. The President can affect the decision of the Federal Reserve through the appointment of board members and through "jawboning." So in the past, the incumbent administration has acted to have the Fed stimulate the economy during the election year, even at the risk of the more pressing problem of inflation.

More importantly, critics complain of incorrect or imprecise actions on the part of the Fed. The governors of the Federal Reserve are as prone to error as lesser mortals. For example,

restraint in money supply in the 1930s reinforced the Great Depression. In the post-World War II era, excessive expansion of the money supply fueled inflation.

Monetarists say that the Fed's best intentioned money managers also have the problem of choosing how much stimulus or restraint to use. If the Fed is conservative and initially makes a small change, there may not be any visible result; so a larger change is apparently needed. By the time the larger change is implemented, the economy has made the necessary adjustment. So the second (large) policy action is no longer needed and perhaps is now in the wrong direction, given the recovery of the economy.

Time lags Connected with problems of imprecision are various time lags. Because monetarists look at time specifically, they emphasize a series of lags which will make it difficult to adjust the money supply. The first is a *recognition lag*. Forecasting in economics is imperfect, small changes in the data available may or may not indicate a major economic change, and data available refer to several months back. All of these factors combine to make it difficult to decide when monetary changes are necessary. *Administrative lag* arises because it takes time to adjust institutional arrangements. Money managers may be able to respond within a relatively short period of time. If more complete changes, such as changing the federal budget, are required, it would take a full budget year to make the necessary changes.

Results lag refers to the time it takes for the economy to respond to the change in either monetary or fiscal policy. The monetarists argue that when all the lags are taken together, the expansionary measures taken to relieve the last recession may take effect during the following recovery or boom, adding to the potential for inflation.

Conflict with government policies The United States government is perhaps the all-time big spender. To help finance this spending, it sells promissory notes—government bonds—on the bond market. It naturally wishes to pay as little interest as possible to the people who buy these bonds. Total interest in this case is likely to be huge. Even a very small rise in the rate will cost the government—that is, its taxpayers—billions of dollars. Yet the Federal Reserve may want to raise interest rates to dry up loan-money supply and thereby lessen inflation. If it does this when the government is seeking loans (selling its bonds) to pay off its debt, the increased interest rate can send the cost of raising this money quite high. For example, the total federal debt outstanding at the end of fiscal year 1976 was approximately $635 billion. Interest payments on this debt amounted to about $34.6 billion. This is an average interest rate of 5.45%. Suppose this rate were to rise to 6%. Total interest paid would rise to $38.1 billion or $3.5 billion more interest paid for an increase in interest rates by 0.55%. Such conflicts have arisen in the past. The Federal Reserve and the United States Treasury have pledged to avoid them in the future. But there is no guarantee that they will.

Neutrality more apparent than real Even though no segment of the economy is directly favored or hurt by monetary policy, there may be considerable impact on certain segments. The impact is not lessened because it happens indirectly rather than directly. Also, interest rates will be affected within a short period of time by changes in monetary policy. Those people who receive interest income will gain or lose depending upon the direction of movement of the interest rate. Also, certain industries are more dependent on borrowed money than are others. (Recall our discussion above about the effects of interest rates on the construction industry.) Furthermore, changing the terms on which firms enter capital markets affects investment expenditures. For example, high loan costs will soon have a depressing effect on the durable goods industry.

Inability to affect nonmonetary inflation Monetary policy is often used to fight inflation. However, some inflation is not monetary in origin. Prices and costs may rise even if employment is down and the money supply is not increasing. In terms of the equation of exchange ($MV = PQ$), P increases without a corresponding change in M. (As we shall see later in our chapter on inflation, the increase may be due to cost-push inflation. Business and labor monopolies may be able to raise prices regardless of the laws of supply and demand.) If prices go too high, Q (real output of goods and services) will begin to decline. The Federal Reserve will then step in to stimulate the economy. It will increase M (money supply). But more money, in this case, merely feeds inflation. The Fed will, in effect, be reinforcing inflation. If it does *not* act to stop the decline in Q, it may be accused of fostering a recession. Nonmonetary inflation is a no-win proposition for the Fed.

Inability to predict how people will react Bankers, businessmen, and John Q. Public have minds of their own. The Fed can lead them to water, but it can't make them drink. Let's look at $MV = PQ$ once again. For purposes of simplification, we assumed V (velocity) remained unchanged. Actually, V—the number of times a given amount of money changes hands in a given period—does change. Sometimes it changes quite rapidly, at least for short periods of time. (Overall, there has been a rather steady increase in our economy's money velocity in the past 30 years.)

If the Federal Reserve increases interest rates, V may quicken significantly. Money will move around faster as people step up their investments in interest-bearing bonds and securities.

But the idea behind higher interest rates is to lessen M (money supply) and thus lessen P (price) and Q (quantity). However, if V increases while M decreases, the total value of MV remains pretty much unchanged. Thus there is little or no effect on PQ. (Remember, the two sides of this equation must balance.) It's merely a stand-off.

Consider what happens at the trough of a business cycle. As business declines, there is less need for money for business transactions. Some money may be converted to other assets such as time deposits or securities. Other money, especially currency, may become idle in bank vaults. Thus not only does the rate of circulation decline but some money disappears as well since vault cash is not part of the money supply. Therefore, M drops and V drops with it. Now suppose the Fed increases M by increasing its member banks' reserves. Banks now have money to lend. Borrowers rush in to borrow it for production and consumer spending. Business begins to boom again.

Or does it? Not necessarily. Times are hard, and bankers may be cautious about lending money. They may believe borrowers will not be able to pay back the loans promptly. So bankers sit on their new reserves. Even if the banks take a come-and-get-it attitude, perhaps few customers will. Borrowers may decide this is no time to take on extra debt. Hard times have already put them deep enough in debt. Because people refuse to allow banks to put their new reserves into circulation, the Fed's attempt to increase M is thwarted. And V continues to fall. Thus P and Q may continue to fall or certainly do not improve.

At the peak of a business cycle, the Fed may reduce M to cool the expanding economy. But V may continue to grow anyhow. Times are good, so people are not afraid to lend, spend, and borrow. Banks continue to make loans.

In 1969, for example, when the Fed tightened money supply, banks got around the restrictions by borrowing United States dollars from foreign financial institutions. And the general public had ways of its own to beat the system. It used credit cards, installment loans, and other substitutes for circulating cash. V continued to rise. Then the Fed tightened the money supply even further. It cut M more deeply, and finally did succeed in stopping the increase in V. MV fell and so did PQ. But the fall was so severe that sources of credit dried up. This "credit crunch" led to a recession that lasted into 1971. The impact of the Federal Reserve tight money policies to restrain the economy also contributed to the deep recession of 1973–1975. (In this instance, however, faulty fiscal policies probably helped foster economic decline, aided by the energy crunch, high prices of raw products (due to drought or other shortages), and other economic difficulties.)

Inability to deal evenly with the business cycle As we noted above, Federal Reserve monetary policies can indeed restrain the economy. If the Fed acts firmly enough, it can completely dry up member banks' reserves. Loans from foreign banks cannot possibly compete with the Fed's massive power to withdraw money from the economy. So far as bankers are concerned, the Federal Reserve ultimately holds the whip hand when it comes to decreasing the nation's money supply. Its policies may well be effective at the peak of the business cycle.

The trough of the business cycle, however, is an entirely different situation. Again as noted above, the Fed cannot force us to spend our money if we don't want to. No matter how high the reserves, banks cannot be forced to lend it out. And people cannot be forced to borrow or spend it. *Thus Federal Reserve monetary policies are more effective in restraining the economy than in stimulating it.*

Monetarist prescription for money supply

Monetarists argue that monetary policy has done the wrong thing. If managed correctly, there are positive benefits. "Correctly" in their view means that the money supply grows at a constant rate which is close to the growth of real output.

Monetary policy can reduce some economic uncertainty about the future By announcing the rate of increase in the money supply, the money managers reduce the uncertainty surrounding future monetary conditions. This is especially important in borrowing or lending. If the lender knows what to expect concerning prices and interest rates in the future, he will be more willing to make loans. It is the uncertainty about future changes in monetary conditions which lead to a reluctance to make loans and higher borrowing costs.

Monetary policy can prevent major economic changes Sometimes conditions are so extreme that monetary changes are required. Monetarists would allow discretionary monetary policy in these circumstances. An example would be a war. In the past, war has usually brought a rapid expansion of the money supply and very high rates of inflation. Monetarists would urge restrictive monetary policy to control the inflation. Of course, this would make the cost of the war more immediately apparent since the civilian population and the government would face higher interest rates and also higher taxes. This might make leaders more reluctant to pursue war.

Economic Thinker
Milton Friedman

Milton Friedman, winner of the 1976 Nobel Prize in Economic Science, is one of America's best known economists. He is also one of the most controversial. He speaks out regularly and with gusto, in essays, interviews, and in his widely read *Newsweek* articles, for conservative economic policies. He readily admits to being a political conservative also. He was an adviser to conservative Republican candidate Barry Goldwater in the 1964 presidential election and, later, to President Richard Nixon. He insists, however, that economic theories and systems can and should exist free of partisan politics. He further insists that his own particular theories—no matter that they are likely to comfort economic and political conservatives and outrage liberals—are free from such bias. (True to his principles, Friedman broke publicly with Nixon in 1971, when the President instituted a government wage and price freeze to fight the current inflation: "Price window dressing," said Friedman, "which will do harm rather than good.")

Milton Friedman is a firm believer in Thomas Jefferson's precept that the best government is the one that governs least. He would abolish just about every government regulation of the marketplace now in existence. He favors abolition of Social Security and all welfare programs, which he would replace by a "negative income tax" or direct money payment to the truly needy. He would abolish the corporate income tax and also all government subsidies to business. He would introduce a voucher system providing direct payments to parents so they could send their children to the private schools of their choice rather than to tax-supported institutions. Above all, he would cut government spending to the bone and resist all further growth of government bureaucracy. America's tax burden, he maintains, is far greater than the amount paid as "taxes." In a 1977 interview with *U.S. News & World Report,* Friedman commented, "If the Federal Government spends $460 billion in fiscal 1978, which is roughly what the President (Carter) proposes, and takes in something like $400 billion in taxes, who do you suppose pays the other $60 billion? The tooth fairy?" There is no economic tooth fairy, says Friedman. The people pay in the form of the hidden "tax" of inflation or in the form of future higher taxes to pay interest and principal if the government borrows the extra $60 billion.

Milton Friedman was born in 1912 in Brooklyn, New York, the son of immigrant parents. He worked his way through Rutgers University. He received a master's degree in 1933 from the University of Chicago and a Ph.D. from Columbia University in 1946. He then joined the faculty of the University of Chicago, where he remained through early 1977, the leading exponent of the so-called "Chicago School" of economic thought, which includes an abiding faith in the virtues of the free market system.

When Milton Friedman was awarded the Nobel Prize, singled out for praise was his work on consumption analysis—that is, the relationship of consumption to income. Friedman attacked a problem in the Keynesian model which said that the more income people have, the larger proportion they will save and the smaller proportion they will

spend. Friedman's analysis led to the conclusion that consumption is a constant fraction of the consumer's "permanent income" (income level expected over long periods of time), regardless of the size of permanent income. If the ratio of consumption to permanent income is largely unaffected by the amount of income, so too is the ratio of saving to income. Everyone except the utterly destitute could and in theory did save, especially when they faced uncertainty about the future. Friedman's permanent income theory undermined some earlier economists' justification for inequality in distribution of wealth—that is, that there must be many poor people in a society so that the few rich people can be rich enough to save more money and invest it in economic growth.

Friedman also attacked the Keynesian notion that the economy could be stabilized by sharp increases and decreases in the money supply. In his *History of Money in the United States, 1867-1960*, he contended that such efforts at "fine tuning" the economy resulted in business uncertainty and actual destabilization of the economy. Friedman's views on government monetary policies have often led him to open conflict with the governors of the Federal Reserve Board and especially with its former chairman, Arthur Burns, Friedman's one-time teacher at Rutgers.

Friedman believes that instead of periodic increases and decreases in the money supply, the Fed should move gradually toward expanding the money supply at a rate roughly equal to the long-run increase in economic output. This, he believes, would eliminate the tendency toward inflation in a growing economy. Once rough equilibrium between growth in the money supply and growth of economic output is reached, Friedman would like the Fed to continue increasing the money supply by a constant rate from month to month. The rate of increase would be in line with anticipated growth in the overall economy, somewhere between 3 and 5% per year. The free market, not politicians, financiers, and central bankers, would control the growth of money supply.

Friedman has also applied his free market ideals to the international monetary area, favoring freely floating exchange rates over fixed rates. The 1975 decision of the International Monetary Fund to let currency values fluctuate in the open market was undoubtedly influenced by Friedman's theories and those of his supporters. Friedman has also been credited for gaining national support for the idea of an all-volunteer army by his vigorous public support of that policy. In addition, much of the push toward current efforts to deregulate certain businesses—airlines and trucking, for example—in the interests of competition and lower prices can be traced to Friedman's influence.

Milton Friedman is a distinguished scholar and economic activist. He believes that the free and open market is the testing ground not only of economic practices but also of ideas and theories. The seven judges of Sweden's Royal Academy of Science who named him a Noble Prize winner were not, he told a reporter, the ultimate judges of his economic career. Final judgment would be made over time in the free marketplace of ideas.

Monetary policy need not add to economic problems Properly managed, the money supply will be neutral, argue the monetarists. By maintaining a constant growth rate, monetary managers will stop looking at the wrong targets and avoid the problems of not acting in time and then responding with too much in the wrong direction, too late.

Monetarists: what monetary policy cannot do

Monetary policy cannot permanently reduce unemployment The monetarists insist that the unemployment rate is determined by conditions in the labor market which are structural in nature. There are conditions which prevent the labor market from reaching full employment. Of course, the monetary authorities could temporarily reduce unemployment by stimulating the economy with an increase in the money supply. The reduction can occur only if the workers do not anticipate the change. The reason for the temporary change is that rising prices make the workers temporarily cheaper for employers to hire.

Once workers begin to anticipate the increase in prices, they will adjust their wage requirements to protect their purchasing power. Unemployment will return to the former level even though there is a higher rate of inflation. Any attempt to reduce the inflation rate will result in much higher rates of unemployment until workers are convinced that the inflation rate will fall.

Monetary policy cannot permanently reduce interest rates It would seem that increases in the supply of money would result in lower interest rates. From the money demand curve, we know that excess money will be used to buy securities, bidding up the price of securities and lowering the interest rate. However, we also know that excess money may be used for spending, which may increase prices.

Finally, there is the third variable called expectations. Once people expect inflation, there may be further adjustments. We may analyze the situation in three stages.

First, the initial effect of an increase in money may be to increase the price of securities and lower interest rates. The money is excess and can be converted to interest-bearing substitutes for money.

However, the second stage is reached where some people, noting the higher value of their securities, will feel wealthier and increase spending. As full employment is reached, prices may begin to rise. With rising prices, another effect is noted on interest rates. The interest rate is the compensation to the lender for giving up money now for future repayment and the cost to the borrower of money now for the right to make payment later. Since the lender will not be able to spend his money until later, he will need protection from the increase in prices. Otherwise, the money he gets back will buy less than the money he loaned. Thus he will charge more. The borrower will be willing to pay more. For a consumer, higher prices mean higher income for him and he will be able to pay more. For a businessman, higher prices mean higher profits

so he too can pay more for borrowed money. Thus rising prices can mean interest rates will move back toward the original level.

Since the intent was to lower interest rates, a larger increase in the money supply may now be tried. This leads in turn to temporarily lower interest rates but later to rising prices and interest rates returning to former levels. If the money supply again is increased, the third effect comes into play. Both borrowers and lenders begin to expect continuation of increases in the money supply and higher prices. The lender, to protect his purchasing power, will build in not only present inflation but expected future inflation; so the lender will insist on higher interest rates. The borrower will be willing to pay higher rates for the same reasons as before. Therefore, when expectations come into play, the interest rate may end up even higher than it was before the money managers attempted to lower it.

Some final questions about Federal Reserve policies

Now that we have discussed how the Federal Reserve System carries out its money supply functions and the pros and cons of its effectiveness, it is time to ask some further questions.

Is the System really free to pursue the policies it wishes to pursue? As we have already noted, it cannot always count on the economy to respond to its policies. The public and the banks are free to go their own ways. They can thwart these policies, at least for awhile.

But our question implies another, more fundamental query: Can the Fed function independent of outside government and financial interests? Again as we have already noted, government has indeed at times interfered in the System. We saw that the massive federal debt run up during World War II prompted the government to enlist the aid of the Fed to keep interest rates low. It convinced the Fed to expand money supply, even though business was enjoying a postwar boom. High inflation was the end result.

How free is the Fed from outside financial and political interference? When the System was set up, much care was taken to be sure the Fed was free from such influence.

Extended Example
Shadow over the Open Market Committee

The economists and financiers on the Open Market Committee of the Federal Reserve Board are a potent force in regulating the amount of money in the nation's economy. They make the decisions as to buying and selling United States Treasury bills and bonds on the open market. When they buy these instruments, from commercial banks and the public, the money paid for them becomes almost immediately available throughout the economy for purchase of goods and services. When they sell these instruments, the money paid for them is withdrawn from the economy. The Committee, consequently, is a natural target for pressure from various economic and financial groups who either wish to see money supply grow or wish to see it slacken. And whatever the Committee does, it's almost certain to be criticized—either for doing too much or for not doing enough.

The Open Market Committee even has a so-called "shadow open market committee" looking over its shoulder. The shadow committee is a group of conservative monetarists who not only hold the monetarist doctrine of the importance of money supply to the economy (rather than tax changes and government spending), but also believe the money supply should be allowed to grow only very slowly. Even when the Federal Reserve Board is keeping money growth at a level that draws criticism from expansionist-minded economists, the shadow committee is likely to contend that the level should be lower still. In any case, the shadow committee closely monitors the Board's handling of monetary policy and consistently warns against the pleas and threats of those—usually Congressmen and their committees—who seek faster growth of the nation's money supply.

In 1977, for example, the Federal Reserve Board set a target rate of money growth at 4.5 to 6.5% for the year—too low to suit many expansionist-minded economists. Not low enough, however, for the shadow open market committee. At its semiannual meeting in March, 1977, the shadow comittee recommended that 4.5% be the *maximum* growth rate target rather than its minimum.

True to its conservative instincts, it further warned that President Carter's plans to stimulate the economy, while it might lead to reduced unemployment in 1977, would surely lead to higher prices and fewer jobs in 1978 and 1979. It also criticized the administration's efforts to get other industrialized Western countries—West Germany and Japan, for example—to stimulate faster rates of economic growth. "Production of money," said the shadow committee, "is no cure for shortfalls in the production of goods."

Just what influence the shadow committee has on its real counterpart, the Open Market Committee, and on the monetary policies of the Federal Reserve Board in general is open to question (as is the influence of pressure groups seeking greater expansion in money supply). In this case, not even the "shadow" really knows. Nevertheless, the shadow committee believes it does have some influence over the deliberations of its counterpart and intends to continue monitoring the Fed's monetary policies and to keep it firm in the faith that slow expansion of the money supply is the infallible way to prosperity in the modern economy. As one member of the shadow open market committee put it after the March, 1977, meeting: "We must be as conservative as possible so that Congress will think (the Fed) is being liberal by comparison."

The power of the banking industry to interfere was restricted by the System's organization. The industry owns the stock of the Fed (member banks must buy the stock in order to join the System), but policy is made by the Fed's governing boards. And the boards can act without stockholder approval. Also, bankers are a minority on the boards of District Banks. The Fed controls appointment of the majority of board members.

So far as political interference is concerned, this, too, was restricted at the outset. The President of the United States does appoint the Board of Governors. However, terms of service on the Board are staggered so that it is impossible for his appointees to comprise a majority for any great length of time. Also, the Senate must confirm Board appointments. Although the Fed must keep Congress informed of its plans and policies, the Congress has no direct strings on the Fed's budget. And no member of Congress can be appointed to the Board.

Despite these safeguards, the possibility and threat of interference does exist. Board members, and especially its chairman, are subject to public criticism, as are all public officials. Politicians may, and do, attack their policies publicly. Such attacks may have subtle but real influence on their decisions—as, of course, may public praise. Board members, after all, are only human.

More serious is the political threat of legislation to change the Fed's original charter or even to abolish it altogether. The threat is not entirely idle. Officials of the Fed and officials of the government consult and cooperate with one another, despite periodic differences about what is best for the economy. But irreconcilable differences may arise. If they do, legislation created the Fed and legislation could wipe it out. This threat may ensure that the Federal Reserve System will seldom be more than a thorn in the side of the political process.

As to interference by the banking industry, the situation is similarly clouded. There are restrictions on the contributions of bankers to policymaking. As we have seen, bankers are a minority on the boards of the District Banks. But the majority members are seldom unfriendly to the banking industry. They, too, are financiers. They are likely to have had close ties with banking interests in their personal business dealings. It is a fact of life that the various boards and committees of the Fed will likely be dominated by persons with money-market ties and interests. Although the Fed may, and certainly has, instituted policies unpopular with the banking community, bankers are well and powerfully represented in the System.

Yet, special interests have generally been kept at bay in the functioning of the Federal Reserve System. Reasonable men may disagree as to the exact effectiveness of its policies. The correct mix of monetary and fiscal policies that is best for the economy may be subject to serious debate. All in all, the Fed has functioned reasonably well as the nation's central bank and arbiter of its money supply.

Summary

Monetary policies are the actions taken by the Federal Reserve System to increase or decrease the rate of growth of the money supply in order to stimulate or restrain the economy.

The intent of monetary policy may be illustrated using the equation of exchange, $MV = PQ$. For the illustration, we may assume V (velocity) of circulation is a constant.

At the peak of the business cycle, Q (output) is at the maximum and P may be rising as inflation threatens. A reduction in M would be expected to produce a reduction in P. Thus a reduction in money supply reduces inflation.

At the trough of the business cycle, Q is lower than desired and high unemployment exists. An increase in M may be expected to result in increased spending, which would increase Q without much upward pressure on prices.

The Federal Reserve System is the ultimate source of our money supply. The assets of the Fed are the backing for the money. Eighty percent of the backing is from government securities. Gold represents less than 10% of the backing for money.

The Fed issues its own notes called Federal Reserve Notes that we recognize as our paper money. The rest of the money supply consists of demand deposits.

The Fed has three major policy tools; they are known as quantitative controls. One is the amount of required reserves which the commercial banks must keep on deposit with the Fed or as vault cash. The larger the required reserves, the more restrictive is monetary policy and vice versa.

The second policy tool is the discount rate. The discount rate is the interest rate charged commercial banks when they borrow from the Fed. A lower discount rate encourages borrowing and is thus an expansionary monetary policy.

Open market operations are the third monetary policy tool. The Fed may purchase or sell government securities in exchange for currency or bank deposits, that is, money. A sale of securities results in less money in the hands of the public or banks.

There are a variety of lesser monetary policy tools—known as qualitative controls—including moral suasion, selective credit controls, and selective interest controls.

Monetary policy is relatively flexible and speedy compared with fiscal policy. Monetary policy is supposedly nonpolitical in its conception. It is also neutral in that it operates economy-wide in its effects.

However, critics of monetary policy argue that the Fed is not free of political considerations. Also, the on-again, off-again policies leave a pattern of imprecision in actual performance.

There are other shortcomings of monetary policy. There are time lags in monetary policy corresponding to recognition, administrative, and response lags. Monetary policy may be in conflict with government fiscal policy. The neutrality of monetary policy is not actual since there is greater impact on those sectors of the economy which are dependent upon borrowed money. Monetary policy is unable to deal with inflation other than demand-pull inflation fostered by excess amounts of money. Monetary policy is also weakened since the general public can thwart the actions of the Fed by changing velocity. Finally, monetary policy has been criticized for being less effective against recession than against inflation.

The monetarists are a group of economists "led" by Milton Friedman. They argue that money is very important and that the money supply should increase at the same rate as real output. If the money supply grows at the same rate as output, monetary policy will reduce economic uncertainty about the future, and will not add to economic instability. The monetarists argue that monetary policy cannot permanently reduce unemployment or cannot permanently reduce interest rates.

Finally, the Fed is a creation of the political process and as such must not get too far out of line with the desires of Congress and the President or the political process could presumably dismantle the Fed.

Key Words and Phrases

- **monetary policy** actions of the Federal Reserve designed to increase or slow up the expansion of the money supply in order to stimulate or restrain the economy.
- **expansionary monetary policy** the monetary policies designed to increase the growth rate of the money supply in order to stimulate the economy.
- **tight money policy** reduction of money supply to restrain the economy and fight inflation; also known as contractionary monetary policy.
- **discount rate** the interest rate paid by member banks when they borrow from the Federal Reserve; sometimes known as rediscount rate.
- **open market operations** purchases or sales of U.S. government securities designed to implement monetary policy.
- **quantitative controls** major monetary policy tools; consist of reserve ratios, discount rate, and open market operations.
- **qualitative controls** policy tools for monetary fine tuning; consist of moral suasion, selective credit controls, and selective interest controls.
- **recognition lag** the time it takes policymakers to perceive a change in the economy after the change has actually begun to take place.
- **administrative lag** follows the recognition lag and refers to the time required for policymakers to decide to take action, to determine what that action should be, and then to carry out the change in monetary policy.
- **results lag** the time required for a change in monetary policy to have an impact on the economy.

Questions for Review

1. If a commercial bank, say the one in which you have an account, does not have enough reserves to meet its required reserves, what must it do? List as many actions as you can which your bank can take to acquire adequate reserves. Could any of these affect you directly?

2. If we switch to using credit cards and electronic transfer of funds, what happens to velocity? How would this affect the Fed's control of money supply?

3. Some economists have suggested that banks should have a 100% reserve requirement. That is, all deposits would have to be kept in the vault. How would this action affect the economy? Would such an action be desirable?

4. List the ways the Fed can increase the money supply. Can it decrease the money supply by reversing the actions? Why or why not?

5. Can the general public change the money supply? How?

6. Why is it easier to contract the money supply than to increase it?

7. What are the assets of the Federal Reserve? What are the liabilities?

8. Why is the Fed independent of political activity? How is the Fed kept free of political entanglements? Do you feel the Fed is really apolitical? Why or why not?

9. Why is a government security a reserve for the Fed? How can debt be something desirable?

10. What are the principal shortcomings of monetary policy?

11. What are the proper goals of monetary policy according to the monetarists? What will be the desirable results of achieving the goals? What cannot be done using monetary policy according to the monetarists?

Part Four

Stabilization Policies and Growth

16

Inflation and Unemployment

If our economy had to choose one dragon to be slain, most economists would probably agree that its name is inflation. Unfortunately, like most legendary dragons, this one does not kill easily. Lop off its head and it fairly soon grows another, blazing nostrils and all. No St. George has arisen from among economists to slay the monster once and for all. Most likely, none ever will. Economists generally agree that the best we can do is to try to tame it, cage it, and learn to live with it.

You need not be a monster buff or even an economics student to be aware of this particular dragon. All you need do is take a shopping trip to your supermarket, your department store, or wherever you go to buy the things you need. Or read the political and economic columns in your newspaper or news magazine. Or tune in on the evening TV news program. The dragon is fairly certain to be mentioned, at least once a month.

In short, inflation is a very real problem in our economy. Inflation means higher prices for the things you buy. Specifically, **inflation** is a *dynamic* process with the general price level moving upward *over a period of time*.

There is, unfortunately, a stabilization problem that is nearly as bad as inflation: it is unemployment. Some economists would in fact argue unemployment is a greater problem because those affected suffer so much.

The seriousness of unemployment as a social problem can be emphasized in thousands of little stories as each individual is affected. For example, the day before election day in November, 1976, word got out in Detroit that Cadillac would be handing out job applications. There was no guarantee that an applicant would get a job. People lined up the night before. One woman fainted in line. A fight broke out among workers waiting for a chance to apply. The only notice officially given had been small bulletins posted within the plant. The only source of information was from workers already employed. Through word of mouth, 5,000 people learned there might be a job and came to apply. Cadillac employs about 9,000 blue-collar workers and another 2,000–3,000 salaried workers. To handle job-seekers, company officials had set up five desks, which proved to be far too few. Company management said afterwards that they really did not expect such a crunch of people.

Why do we group such different problems as inflation and unemployment in one chapter? Well, economists have learned that a battle against inflation will also very likely entail an eventual battle against unemployment, and vice versa. Our economic St. Georges have not one but two dragons to slay. And they have found that the closer they come to dealing a death blow to one of the beasts, the more rambunctious the other is likely to become.

So we will discuss the problem of inflation first and then study unemployment. We will summarize what we know of fiscal and monetary policies as they are used to fight both inflation and unemployment. Finally, we will consider the Phillips curve, which shows direct links between our "dragons."

Rate of inflation

Inflation is a long-term rise in the general price level of goods and services. The opposite trend, a lowering of the price level, is called *deflation*. Deflation can also cause grave problems in an economy. However, persistent deflation is an unusual phenomenon. It is not presently a problem in most modern economies, nor is it likely to become one soon. Consequently, we will concern ourselves here only with inflation.

Inflation may be categorized by the speed with which it develops—*the rate of inflation*. This rate is expressed as the percentage of increase from one year to the next. For example, the government may announce that the inflation rate over the past year is 6%. This means that the level of prices is 6% higher than it was for the same point in time last year.

This 6% inflation rate does not mean that the price of each and every good and service rose 6%. The prices of some goods and services may not have gone up at all. Some prices may have even come down. Others may have risen by a greater amount, say 10%. Still others by a smaller amount, say 2%. However, the overall rise, on an average, was 6%.

Measuring the inflation rate

The common way of measuring the rate of inflation is to use a price index. A **price index** measures the *relative* changes in prices of selected items from one year to the next. The index specifies the price level for one year as a *base*, which is denoted as 100. All the other years in the index are stated in terms of the base year.

The two most commonly used price indices are the Consumer Price Index (CPI) and the Wholesale Price Index (WPI). The **Consumer Price Index** consists of an average of prices on a selected group of goods and services that are presumably bought by the typical consumer. The **Wholesale Price Index** measures selected prices on key industrial and agricultural products, such as steel, copper, sugar, coffee, etc. Because the WPI deals in raw, unfinished products, the WPI tends to measure prices *before* the CPI does. However, the CPI more accurately reflects the prices paid by consumers. Neither the CPI nor WPI measures all prices in the economy. This contributes to

some statistical inaccuracies in either price index. The practical effect of this is that small changes are usually meaningless. The indices are not sophisticated enough to measure small changes in inflation. Figure 1 shows graphs of the CPI and WPI over the last 25 years. The degree to which they differ means in practice neither is exactly precise.

Table 1 shows the CPI for 1966 to 1977. Notice that 1967 is used as the base and is therefore 100. To find the increase in prices in 1976 we divide the value for 1977 by the value for 1976:

$$\frac{182.4}{170.5} = 1.069.$$

This figure means prices rose .069, or 6.9%. So we can say that inflation for 1976 was *roughly* 6.9%.

Remember that a decrease (or increase) in the level of prices does not mean that *all* prices have declined (or risen). For example, the level of prices may decline if *some prices fall* and

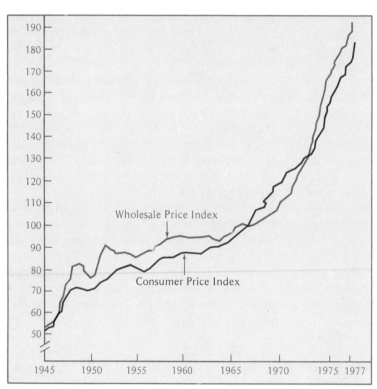

Figure 1 Consumer price index and wholesale price index since 1945; the base is 1967 = 100. Notice the high rate of inflation since 1970, as measured by either index. (Source: *Economic Report of the President.*)

Table 1
The Consumer Price Index

Year	Consumer Price Index
1966	97.2
1967	100
1968	104.2
1969	109.8
1970	116.3
1971	121.3
1972	125.3
1973	133.1
1974	147.7
1975	161.2
1976	170.5
1977	182.4

some prices rise. All that is needed is for more prices to fall than to rise, or for the declines to be larger in magnitude than the increases, or some combination of the two.

Creeping inflation

Inflation rates may range from mild, through serious, to extremely severe. There is no hard and fast rule for gauging the exact percentage point at which the rate changes from mild, say, to serious, or from serious to severe. However, economists are in general agreement as to what rates are acceptable and not acceptable in the economy. For example, an inflation rate of 1–3% is generally considered mild. Such a low rate is called **creeping inflation.** Most economists would agree that this type of inflation is acceptable (some would say inevitable) in modern economies.

Double-digit inflation

On the other hand, an inflation rate of 10% or above is generally considered unacceptable socially and politically. This so-called **double-digit inflation** is a clear signal that the value of a nation's unit of money is eroding much too rapidly. Inflation has become a serious economic drain on the nation's economy.

Actually, of course, there is little significant difference between a 10% (double digit) rate and, say, a 9.5% (single digit) rate. Both are relatively high. But the term "double-digit inflation" has taken on a psychological importance. It has become more than an economic signal. It has become something like a warning siren to the public and to the economic community. In the early 1970s, for example, the United States inflation rate reached double-digit proportion. There then developed considerable increase in media and public concern about the inflation problem. When inflation finally slipped below the 10% figure, the nation breathed a collective sigh of relief.

Hyperinflation

But double-digit inflation is not the worst that can happen. Economies can also suffer *hyperinflation.* Inflation rates may run 100% or even much higher.

In Germany after World War I, for example, inflation ran rampant. Between 1919 and 1923, the price index rose from 291 to 142,905,055,447,917! Such a figure is so high as to be almost incomprehensible to most of us—like the almost infinite number of light years required to reach a far-distant planet. But for the German people, the inflation itself was all too real. Money was next to worthless. Workers demanded their pay every few hours, at which time they would rush out to spend it before prices went even higher. They would then return to their jobs, work a few hours, and rush out again to repeat the process. What was the use of keeping money when its value was shrinking by the minute? Also out of hyperinflation Germany came stories of people returning empty beer bottles and collecting more marks for the empties than they had paid for the full bottles only hours before. And stories were told of people needing to carry two or more shopping bags stuffed with money to the grocery store to purchase a half-bag of groceries.

Hyperinflation has also ravaged economies in more recent times. Prices in Japan, for example, were astronomical during World War II years and for some years after. In Chile in the 1950s, the inflation rate ran between 40 and 70% yearly. Some underdeveloped nations today are suffering from hyperinflation, even as they seek to industrialize and build up their economies.

Extended Example
Economic Chaos in Argentina

Almost everyone in the United States today has had personal experience with the difficulties of coping with rising prices. When our inflation rate hits the double-digit mark—10 or 11%, as it did in the mid-1970s—we are duly alarmed, since we know such coping will become even more difficult. And most of us would find it almost impossible to contemplate what an inflation rate of, say, 30 or 40% would mean to our social and economic well-being.

At just about the same time our inflation rate was hovering near the low double-digit figure, Argentines would have happily traded their rate for the one that was causing us so much concern. In January, 1976, Argentina's Ministry of Economy announced that prices had gone up 20% in the single month of December and that the inflation rate for the year 1975 stood at 335%.

The Argentine peso had been for many years among the most stable of currencies, and millions of immigrants had come from Europe to work for and to save this strong currency for investment. But, by the mid-1970s, inflation and consequent devaluation of the peso had taken a terrible toll. In 1950, the Argentine peso traded at 4 to the dollar. In 1976, it traded at 14,000 to the dollar! As the government was reduced to printing currency to pay its own bills, the amount of paper currency in circulation soared—in December, 1975, at a rate of 2 billion pesos a day. As one South American editorialist put it, "The Argentine economy now requires increasing doses of new money to keep on functioning, the same as a drug addict consumes increasing quantities of the poison that is killing him."

The huge inflation rate affected everything Argentines bought and sold. In one week in December, the price of a small glass of cheap wine went from 7 to 10 pesos and the price of cigarettes doubled. An interior decorator told a newspaper reporter that at current prices it was cheaper to paper walls with 100-peso notes than with wallpaper.

Businessmen found it impossible to plan ahead, as costs and prices outraced projections. The concept of saving (and subsequent investment) was eroded. Banks offered 70% annual interest for savings accounts, yet savings declined. Why bother with 70% interest when prices were going up more than 300%?

The Argentine government of this period, headed by President Isabel de Peron, tried, of course, to stem the inflationary tide. New tax measures were put through in an attempt to cut down government deficits. Such measures failed, however. Labor unions pressed for higher wages to meet each increase in the cost of living, which in turn increased the government's deficit as it sought to meet the higher costs of the services provided to the populace. In addition, more tax revenue was lost as many Argentine producers smuggled their products and commodities out of the country to sell for currency other than the devalued peso—especially for American dollars. Inflation continued to rage.

When a nation suffers from the kind of inflationary economic chaos suffered by Argentina in the mid-1970s, civil strife becomes a more likely occurrence. It is no small coincidence that in early 1976, the government of Mrs. Peron was toppled by a right-wing military coup, bringing with it the usual social disruption, bloodshed, terrorism, and political repression attendant upon such violent changes in government.

Clearly, hyperinflation is unacceptable. It can lead to the total collapse of a nation's monetary system. A nation's citizens may be forced to revert to primitive barter as their money becomes worthless. It can lead to severe economic disruption. It can also lead to a breakdown of a nation's social and political order. There were, of course, many complex reasons for the rise of Adolf Hitler and the horrors of World War II. But most historians would agree that the disruption of German society by post-World War I hyperinflation was one of the important precursors of that international tragedy.

Causes and types of inflation

Why does inflation happen? Economists have identified three basic causes of inflation. Inflation may be caused by (1) demand-pull factors in the economy, (2) cost-push factors, or (3) structural maladjustments. It may be caused by any one of these, or by any combination of them. Let us look at each of them in turn.

Demand-pull inflation

Demand-pull inflation is the traditional and most common type of price rise. **Demand-pull inflation** is often and accurately referred to as "too much money chasing too few goods." As sellers perceive that people want more goods and services than sellers can provide, they readily increase the price charged. In effect, consumers compete against one another and bid up the price of goods and services. When the sellers, in turn, try to increase output to meet increased demand, they bid up the price of the things they must buy in order to do so: labor and raw materials, for example. This rise in incomes gives people the ability to make more purchases, bidding prices up still higher. The process moves from demand for goods and services to rises in prices and incomes. It is therefore referred to as demand-pull—demand pulls up prices.

Economists may agree that a particular inflation is chiefly demand pull in origin, but there are two different schools of thought about the origins of the demand that generates the price increase. The argument follows along the lines of the two principal theories of modern economics discussed in earlier chapters: Keynesian and monetarist.

Those economists who are philosophically related to *Keynes and his disciples tend to emphasize aggregate demand (total demand for goods and services) as the source of demand pull.* At full employment, any increase arising in any sector of aggregate demand will lead to upward movements in prices. There may be more than one source of demand. Consumers may desire more goods and services for consumption purposes. Businessmen may desire more output for plant-investment purposes. Increases in government expenditures on goods and services for military or any other use will lead to increased demand and higher prices. Increased exports to other countries may be another source of upward pressure on prices.

Keynesians tend not to be very concerned about money supply as a source of, or cure for, demand-pull inflation. They recognize that an extreme shortage of money could prevent inflation from getting started. They know, also, that an extreme surplus could cause runaway inflation. But since neither of these extremes is likely in a modern economy, Keynesians concentrate on aggregate demand as the source of demand-pull inflation. They believe, for example, that the American economy's upward price drift over the years (its creeping inflation) is mainly caused by heavy government demand for goods and services in both the military and public sectors.

Monetarists, on the other hand, emphasize the role of money as a source of demand-pull inflation. If money supply increases beyond that amount which households and firms want to hold, the monetarists say, they will spend it. Spending will result in the purchase of more goods at constant prices or the same goods at higher prices or some combination of both. Suppose the available goods and services are increasing at a rate of 3% per year. There will thus be 3% more goods and services available for purchase each year. However, suppose also that the amount of money available is growing at 7% per year. If households and firms wish to, they can use this additional money to purchase available goods and services. However, since the goods and services are increasing at a rate of only 3%, only 3% of the money increase can be spent on them. This leaves a 4% increase in the money supply as excess. But it will not stay idle long as the best use of money in this case is to spend it. It soon will "start chasing" available goods, and force up the price of these goods. Total spending will increase by the total amount of the money increase: 7%. Of this, 3% will represent the real value of the goods and services purchased. The remaining 4% will represent demand-pull price inflation. Thus, say the monetarists, excessive growth of the money supply, not aggregate demand, is the chief source of demand-pull inflation.

Whatever the theoretical or actual source of demand-pull inflation, its practical workings are perhaps best illustrated in war and postwar periods. War is fertile ground for demand-pull inflation. As a nation gears for war, the need for producing military goods—guns, bullets, ships, planes, tanks, clothing, food supplies, etc.—crowds the production of consumer goods. Any idle plants or unemployed workers are quickly absorbed into the economic system to meet the military's needs. As a result, employment, wages, and profits soar. However, the production of consumer goods is no longer large enough to meet demand. Aggregate demand rises as people seek to spend their high incomes. Money supply increases apace as economic theories bow to the pressing reality of a nation's victory or defeat in battle.

Demand-pull inflation would, in fact, always run rampant in wartime if strong measures were not taken to restrain it. A nation at war will submit to economic restrictions that it would probably rebel against in peacetime. Rationing is used to dampen consumer spending. Limits may be put on wages and profits. Such measures help mitigate some of the serious effects of wartime demand-pull inflation. Similar measures, plus smooth and fast reallocation of production to consumer goods, may also help dampen postwar inflation.

The wartime economy presents a classic illustration of demand-pull inflation. And it is well to remind ourselves that cold-war economies also have built-in tendencies toward this type of inflation.

Cost-push inflation

Cost-push factors in an economy are another cause of inflation. **Cost-push inflation** occurs when wages or profits rise faster than productivity. For example, a labor union may have enough power to force a firm to raise wages higher than warranted by the workers' productivity. This larger cost per unit of productivity will then be passed along to the firm's customers. Or the firm may be powerful enough (because it holds a monopoly or near-monopoly in the marketplace) to raise the price of its product with little or no regard to the competitive pressures of the market. The powerful firm's customers will then pass along this added cost to its own customers.

Whether the price rise is due to an unjustifiable wage increase or to an unjustifiable profit increase, the rise is inflationary. It represents no real gain in productivity or value. And, in both cases, one price rise leads to another. There is a snowball effect, leading to what is sometimes referred to as the "cost-price spiral." Once the process is underway, each industrial user of the product adds the new cost (plus a bit more for added profit on his added cost) to the price of his own product. The spin of cost-push inflation continues merrily on and on.

Many economists try to use a more specific description than cost-push inflation. When the costs rise due to labor demands and wage hikes, they refer to the result as **wage-push inflation.** Similarly, when the costs rise due to monopoly-type pricing by firms, they call this **price-push inflation.** However, we will continue to use the more inclusive term, cost-push inflation.

Structural inflation

When prices of products rise rapidly because the products are in drastically short supply, the price rise is said to be structural. **Structural inflation** is caused by the temporary structural shortages in the economy, rather than by demand-pull or cost-push factors. The severity of this kind of inflation depends on the number of goods and services facing shortages and the degree to which a good is central to the operation of an economy. For example, at the close of World War II, the American people had accumulated large amounts of money that they had not been able to spend because of lack of goods or government restrictions on purchases. So now they entered the market seeking automobiles, washing machines, and many other consumer products. However, it was not possible for the industrial economy to change over from the production of war materiel quickly enough to supply this pent-up demand. The "structure" of the economy itself had to be changed before the goods in demand could be produced. Until a complete changeover could be accomplished, structural inflation caused a steep rise in prices.

Of course, not all inflation-causing shortages are due to the structure of the economy. Shortages may also be caused by circumstances over which the national economy has little or no control. Agricultural commodities such as sugar, wheat, or coffee may come into short supply because of crop failures. Or nations which export critical commodities may keep them off the market for their own economic or political purposes. For example, commodity-producing nations may form cartels to keep their product off the market until high demand allows them to sell it at an inflated price.

Of course, a nation like the United States, with its large and vigorous economic base, can take most such commodity shortages in stride. We can, for example, cut down on our use of sugar if necessary without drastic effect on the economy. Nevertheless, even the United States will suffer some inflationary pressure from such a shortage.

Consider, for example, what happens when sugar prices suddenly soar because of a temporary supply shortage. Sugar is used in the production process of many industries—in the production of industrial alcohol, for example. Such industries will, of course, raise the price of their products to compensate for the higher cost of sugar. The "ripple" effect of a sugar shortage on food prices can be dramatic. Thousands of the processed food items you buy contain sugar, even if only in small amounts. Other items, such as pastries and soft drinks, are very high in sugar content. In all cases—from corned beef to candy bars—the prices of such products rise when a sugar shortage develops.

When a commodity that is truly vital to a nation's economy comes into short supply, the effect can be devastating. Consider, for example, the inflationary pressures on the United States economy which came with the 1973 cutoff of oil supply from the oil-producing nations. Further cost-push inflationary pressure came with the subsequent fourfold increase in the price of petroleum products. And, of course, the price of domestically produced energy commodities rose to meet the price of foreign petroleum.

The high cost of gasoline was merely the most evident result. Almost everything a modern economy produces depends on oil (and other energy-producing commodities) somewhere in the production process. The inflationary effect of high oil prices was felt immediately throughout the entire economy. It is still being felt today.

Effects of inflation

We are often told that inflation hurts everyone. The implication is that everyone gets hurt equally. As with most such generalizations, the facts are otherwise. It is true that our inflation dragon breathes its fire upon us all, the just and the unjust alike. But some of us it merely scorches, some it badly burns, and some it may not only leave unharmed but may even warm with its glow.

Redistribution of income

Inflation (like unemployment and taxes)—especially when it is unanticipated—redistributes income. It takes from one consumer and gives to another. It takes from one producer and gives to another. For example, it takes from you when you buy skis at an inflated price and gives to the sporting goods store owner. But the owner is also a consumer. Inflation takes from him when he pays the electric bill for his store. The electric utility, a producer, gains. But the gain is soon taken away and given to another producer, the coal mine operator, for example. And so on and on.

But some of this inflation money does stick somewhere along the line. This, in itself, is not necessarily bad. As we have seen, the fact that some of the money circulating in the economy "sticks" in the form of wages and profits is what keeps the economy going. The trouble with inflationary redistribution, however, is that it is haphazard and may consequently be socially disruptive.

Consider, for example, the plight of older people on fixed retirement income. There is little or nothing they can do to increase money income in order to meet increased prices. The stories we hear of old people buying dog food for their own consumption may not always be true; but they reflect a grim reality for some that is all too true. Consider, also, the poor, the ill, and the handicapped. Their real incomes, most likely low to begin with, may be even more tragically diminished by inflation.

In short, for some of us, inflationary redistribution is all take and no give. Some of us, on the other hand, will be less injured or even helped by inflation. Part of this discrepancy depends upon whether or not the inflation is anticipated. Knowing that an inflationary trend is in progress or that it will soon be can affect the way we do business with one another.

For example, unanticipated inflation redistributes income from creditor to debtor, that is, from those who loan money to those who borrow. Because of the increase in the price level, the debtor is able to repay the loan, both principal and interest, throughout the term of the loan with money which does not buy as much as the money originally borrowed. Thus, if the loan was for the purpose of buying a car, the borrower gets the car sooner and cheaper, because he has repaid the loan with money which has gradually become so devalued that it would no longer buy the same car. If inflation is anticipated, however, the lender may not make the loan at all. More likely, however, the lender will make the loan, following one of two possible strategies. First, the period of time for the loan to be repaid may be shortened. Alternatively, the interest charge may be increased. If the lender would ordinarily make the loan at 4% interest but expects 5% inflation, he will charge at least 9% interest on the loan to protect against inflation. Perhaps a numerical example would help. If a lender loans $100 at 4% interest, he will be repaid $104 at the end of a year. If prices are stable, this repayment would be considered adequate compensation for the loan. However,

if prices rise by 5% during the year, the $104 will purchase only as much as $98.80 would have purchased when the loan was made. Thus the lender has lost money. Of course, if he expects the 5% rise in prices, he can protect himself by charging an additional 5% interest. If he charges 9% interest, he will receive $109 at the end of the year, which will prevent the loss of purchasing power. Unanticipated inflation redistributes income away from lenders toward borrowers. Anticipated inflation redistributes it away from borrowers to lenders.

The net effect of the creditor-debtor redistribution is hard to predict. If lenders are high-income, high-saving persons and borrowers low-income, low-saving persons, then actual spending may be increased by unanticipated inflation. However, if borrowers and lenders are all pretty much the same, then there is no net effect on total spending. Some are gainers and some are losers, but all are part of the system. However, in most modern economies, the government is a net debtor relative to the people governed. What is more, the government is often able to determine by itself what amount of debt will be in existence. Thus, with inflation, the creditor-to-debtor redistribution results in goods and services being transferred to the government from the people. Inflation works just like a tax and is sometimes called the "cruelest tax" as it sneaks up quietly and falls most heavily on those least able to pay. The weaker the government, the more likely inflation is to be used instead of legislated taxes. Some countries like Argentina and Italy have a difficult time collecting taxes from their citizens; these countries also have had high inflation. Part of this high inflation has been due to government debt and demand. Of course, in a representative democracy, the government is not an outside force as it is in a dictatorship, yet the transfer still occurs.

Reduced saving

Inflation has other effects on the economy. We have already seen that investment is important because it helps expand our stock of capital. It helps a country and its output grow. *When inflation is high, interest rates rise to high levels.* High interest rates lead to reduced borrowing and choke off investment.

Remember, also, that the most important source of investment is bank savings—especially the personal saving of consumers. *Inflation can lead people to reduce savings in commercial banks.* Why hang on to money when its purchasing power gets lower by the day? For example, suppose a savings account yields 6% interest. That 6% is money earned. But if inflation is 5%, the true earnings are only 1%. If inflation goes up to 8%, then the saver is actually losing 2% per year of his purchasing power. This saver will likely decide to spend his money immediately and enjoy its present purchasing power unless the inflation generates uncertainty as well. When uncertainty occurs, people may hang on to their money even in inflationary periods.

Wealthier people may turn to speculation rather than investment. They may purchase gold, silver, diamonds, art works, and other items that they hope they can easily sell later at prices that have at least kept pace with inflation. Or investment money may be transferred out of the country, finding productive use in a less inflated economy. Thus inflation can help lead an economy into recession and depression as investment sources dwindle.

Fighting inflation

In modern economies, as we have previously noted, inflation probably cannot be entirely eliminated. The economy can, however, be manipulated to control the effects of inflation when its rate becomes unacceptable. First, of course, there must be a general consensus that the rate of inflation is indeed unacceptable. Then the cause, or causes, of the inflation must be identified, a difficult task in itself. Finally, a course of economic action must be put into effect. The problem is agreeing on the right course to take. As we shall see, here as in other economic matters, economists find plenty of room for argument.

When does the rate of inflation become unacceptable? In part, the answer to this question may be quite relative, dependent on the country and the particular era. In the late 1960s in the United States, 5% inflation would have been classified as unacceptable. By the mid-1970s, however, after this country had experienced double-digit inflation as high as 12%, a level of 5 to 6% was not considered so intolerable by many. Nevertheless, many people still feel that a 5% inflation rate is a reasonable danger point: 5% or above is generally considered unacceptably high. At this point, many on fixed incomes are feeling the pinch and are facing the possibility of being unable to afford necessities. Also, at this level many people become disinclined to save.

In order to reduce inflation, the economist must first try to identify the cause and then prescribe a course of action, just as a doctor must try to identify the cause of a patient's ailment before he writes a prescription. Whether inflation is demand pull, or cost push, or structural will determine, in part, the type of fiscal or monetary action that will most likely control it. But we have another problem. Just as a number of diseases and ailments have the same symptoms, so too the cause of inflation is not always easily identified or recognized. In fact, as we have previously noted, inflation often develops from a combination of sources, particularly combinations of demand-pull and cost-push factors. For example, the Vietnam War greatly increased demand and led to a strong demand-pull inflation. When this inflation persisted over a couple of years, the expectations of both labor and business were altered. This led to cost-push inflation, as labor wage demands and business pricing practices were escalated to anticipate expected inflation.

Fighting demand-pull inflation

As we have seen, excess demand is the source of demand-pull inflation. Any policy aimed at fighting this type of inflation must necessarily be aimed at reducing excess demand. How this is done will depend in part, at least, on which economic philosophy is in ascendency: Keynesian or monetarist. The Democrats often follow Keynesian policies, while Republicans *tend* to follow monetarist policies. (However, it should be noted that Republican Nixon called himself a Keynesian while Democrat Carter has been accused of being conservative like the monetarists.) As noted above, Keynesians emphasize aggregate demand as the source of demand-pull inflation. Monetarists emphasize money supply as the source. Naturally then,

Keynesians emphasize fiscal policies—tax changes, government spending policies, and so on—to lower excess demand. Monetarists, on the other hand, emphasize a "stabilized" money supply to do the trick.

Using fiscal policy Recall that aggregate demand includes consumption (C), investment (I), and government expenditures (G). (Aggregate demand equals C + I + G.) Keynesians would be inclined to directly attack these components, individually or in combination, in order to reduce demand-pull inflation.

For example, *government expenditures could be reduced.* Highway construction, aid to education, military spending, and a host of other government activities could be curtailed. The government demand for goods and services would thus be reduced, decreasing overall demand in the economy.

However, as we saw earlier, there are drawbacks to trying to reduce government expenditures. Human nature being what it is, reduction in government spending will be strenuously resisted by affected segments of the public. The defense department, public assistance supporters (for welfare, medical aid, poverty alleviation), the scientific community, the construction industry, and other pressure groups all have one thing in common: they want government spending in their fields to increase, not decrease.

In addition to this political pressure, reduction in government expenditures has another drawback. The process is necessarily slow. Drawing up of government budgets and their subsequent Congressional approval takes a good deal of time. The impact on the economy of reduced government spending is subject to comparatively long delay.

The *consumption component of aggregate demand may also be attacked (reduced).* This may most easily be done through raising taxes. Higher taxes take money from the consumer and thus diminish demand for (ability to purchase) goods and services. As consumer demand weakens, high prices (inflation) also come down. The effects of tax policy changes are quickly felt throughout the economy.

However, again there are drawbacks to this policy. Changes in tax policies may not always be just and equitable. Pressure groups will be alert to protect or enhance their special interests when tax changes are under consideration. A simple surtax on incomes is perhaps the easiest and least politically disruptive method. In 1968, the Johnson Administration imposed a 10% tax surcharge. All personal income taxes were automatically raised by 10%. It was hoped that this could reduce the high demand for consumer products being fed by government expenditures for the Vietnam War. At that time, the American public in general had not repudiated the nation's military involvement in the war. The surtax met little political opposition. In fact, many economists felt that the additional tax was long overdue.

Nevertheless, under most circumstances any tax rise—no matter how much some economists may think it necessary to fight inflation—is a political hot potato. The votes are gained in lowering, not raising, taxes. For example, President Ford suggested an antiinflation tax rise in 1975, but retreated from this position when the political flack started to go up along with the unemployment rate. In the presidential campaign of 1976, Democrats and Republicans alike vowed to lower taxes, not raise them.

However, increasing taxes can help to control inflation. It is a weapon that has been used in the past. Given the right political and economic conditions, it can be so used again.

The third component of aggregate demand, *investment, may also be reduced in the fight against demand-pull inflation.* This, too, can be done through the tax structure. For example, a higher tax could be placed on business profits. This will reduce the amount of money available to industry to invest in new plants and in other expansionary activities. Investment demand for goods and services will decrease. Demand-pull inflation will also decrease.

Another way to reduce investment involves the money supply. If interest rates rise, money becomes tight and borrowing for investment decreases. Earlier, we mentioned that during periods of anticipated inflation, banks will raise interest rates for borrowing. This happens because banks and other financial intermediaries try to guarantee that money made from loans is not lost as inflation. However, these interest charges do vary among banks. A stronger measure for raising interest rates is to have the Federal Reserve raise its discount rate to banks. This increase will almost surely be passed on to the borrowing public. As a result, with many people and firms reluctant to borrow, investment declines.

Politically, a policy of reducing investment is often acceptable because its negative side effects do not emerge immediately. Unlike with tax increases and reduced government spending, the voter and consumer are less likely to notice this action. However, reduced investment can be a drastic measure with long-run consequences since future output will almost certainly decline (or be less than it otherwise would have).

Using monetary policy Although Keynesians minimize the importance of the money supply as it affects inflation, they certainly do not ignore it. They do, in fact, believe it can be used as an aid to fiscal measures in fighting inflation. We can illustrate monetary policy for a simple economy with the equation of exchange. Recall that $MV = PQ$, where M is money supply, V is money velocity, P is price level, and Q is output of all goods and services. To reduce inflation (that is, lower P), we want to lower M. Our assumption of the previous chapters concerning V still holds: V is assumed constant in the short run. So as money supply (M) is reduced by the Fed, P will decline. The only drawback to this strategy is that output Q could decline, even if not as rapidly as P falls.

The monetarist approach If the Keynesians believe that the manipulation of money supply should be used to fight inflation, where does this leave the monetarists? Remember, we said earlier that the monetarists believe excessive money supply is the most important cause of demand-pull inflation. In fact, monetarists feel that money supply has such a powerful effect on the economy that economists should not try fine tuning; that is, economists should not tamper with or manipulate the money supply for treating short-run ailments like inflation or unemployment. Monetarists would not try to fine tune the economy by resorting to sudden changes in fiscal policy or monetary policy. Such changes, they say, are disruptive and, because of time lags in implementation, even counterproductive. Instead, they are likely to

take the long-run view. *Monetarists advocate stabilizing and controlling the money supply growth rate so that it matches the growth of the economy.*

For example, if the output of the economy is growing at the rate of 3% per year, money supply should grow at the same rate. If money increases at 3% per year, spending will grow at 3% per year. (The change in M will equal the change in Q.) Prices will not increase because available goods and services are increasing at the same rate as the money to purchase them.

If money supply is carefully controlled, say the monetarists, any demand-pull inflation that arises will be temporary. If control of money supply remains on target, inflation will gradually disappear. This is true, but such a policy would leave us with no tools to fight short-run disruptions.

Fighting cost-push inflation

Cost-push inflation, you will recall, is not, like demand-pull inflation, a case of too much money chasing too few goods. Its source, as we have noted, is so-called "market power." Some industries and some labor unions have the power to raise prices or increase workers' wages with scant regard to supply and demand conditions or productivity per worker. The wage-price—or if you wish, price-wage—spiral goes into effect. Costs push prices up and up.

Under these circumstances, money supply is not the problem. MV may be considered fairly stable in cost-push periods. Consequently, when P rises, there is no obvious response from the left side of the equation. The equation of exchange does not work well to explain cost-push inflation. In cost-push inflation prices rise almost independently. If M is lowered to fight inflation, Q will drop even faster and farther. The result will be an unemployment rate too high to be accepted. Monetary policies, then, are of little use in fighting cost-push inflation. Fiscal policy is similarly ineffective. An increase in taxes or a decrease in government expenditures will reduce aggregate demand and create unemployment. But cost-push inflation is not caused by excess demand; so reducing demand will have little effect on the increase in prices.

So what can be done? Not much, really, short of changing our economic system. Some steps, however, can be taken to lower such inflation. The government can employ **incomes policies,** where incomes are kept stable by freezing or fixing both wages and prices in some fashion. There are two types of incomes policies: wage-price guidelines and wage-price controls.

Wage-price guidelines When the government sets up **wage and price guidelines** (or guideposts), it is asking industry and labor to stay within set limits in their price and wage policies. Since the goal is to keep wages and prices from rising too high, the government will formulate percentage increases for both labor and business. For example, the government might determine that 5% increases are a reasonable limit for both wage hikes and price increases. Increases can be less than 5%, but they should not exceed it. In order to enforce them, the government might then go to the people and try to rally public opinion against those who violate the guidelines.

Sometimes this policy is successful, at least for a while. President Kennedy's Council of Economic Advisers had some success back in 1962 with this policy. It worked by using "jawboning." Kennedy's own pungent if not very gentlemanly reference to steel operators as S.O.B.'s during his fight to roll back steel prices was received with approval by the general public. The steel companies then lowered prices back to their previous level. Other firms were thus very cautious in raising prices.

However, there is a very basic shortcoming of guideposts: adherence to them is voluntary. The economy cannot be forced to respond— and frequently it does not. President Ford's 1975 "WIN" (Whip Inflation Now) buttons quickly wound up in more trash cans (and button collections) than they did on lapels.

Since there are few alternatives to wage-price guideposts, they are worth trying. This is particularly true in the view of some economists who believe the greatest economic problem of the 1970s is inflation—specifically cost-push inflation. President Carter's economic advisers would probably agree, since the President tried guideposts with some success. For example, when in May of 1977, Republic Steel and Youngstown Sheet and Tube—the fourth and eighth largest steelmakers—announced price hikes of 6.8 to 8.8%, U.S. Steel Company (the largest producer of steel) followed a week later with only 6% price hikes. This forced the steelmakers to roll back price hikes to 6%. Why did U.S. Steel not follow the early hikes? Because of the pressure from the Carter Administration. In addition, through jawboning, Carter's Budget Director, Bert Lance, stopped some big banks from raising their prime interest rate, which would have choked off investment (and eventually output) and revived expectations of more inflation.

Wage-price controls The government can go beyond the use of guideposts to fight cost-push inflation. It can implement **wage and price controls,** which prevent any wage and price increases. This strategy will, in fact, stop any type of inflation. However, it represents a drastic change in our economic system. When wage and price controls are employed, the market economy ceases to exist. The economy becomes in effect a command economy, with all the attendant problems of black markets and resource allocation decisions. The government is consequently reluctant to take such action unless an extreme emergency exists.

Wartime presents one such emergency. Wage and price controls (along with other economic measures such as rationing) are more readily acceptable in wartime to help deal with shortages and inflation. Recall that one of the chief functions of price fluctuations due to supply and demand is allocation of resources and scarce items. When prices fixed by government are below prices determined by supply and demand, black markets can result. On a black market, people are willing to pay more for a scarce item than the legal price, because at the legal price there isn't enough of the item to satisfy demand. In wartime, however, the government can appeal to the patriotism of people and ask them to refrain from buying on black markets. It does work—at least for a while.

Wage and price controls may also be invoked when a nation is not officially at war. President Nixon, for example, did so in August, 1971, in order to lower inflation. The country generally accepted the measure, although labor complained that the administration's new policies would control wages more stringently than profits. In any case, the controls were soon phased out (by early 1973).

There is no doubt that wage and price controls will lower or even completely halt inflation. But, as we have noted, if our economy is not to be drastically changed, such control can only be temporary. When controls are lifted, the basic cause or causes of the inflation remain. So inflation will resume. In fact, inflation could worsen as people expect further controls and therefore get a jump on them by jacking up prices even more. This happened after the wage-price controls of 1971–1973 were lifted.

Antitrust action   Eventually, in order to stop cost-push inflation, it may also be necessary to attack the ability of various segments of the economy to increase and pass along increases in prices. This means a direct move against economic power, which may be difficult without the use of considerable political power. It is generally suggested that more vigorous enforcement of antitrust laws may reduce economic power and therefore the ability to raise prices at will. Extension of the antitrust laws to labor unions has also been advocated so that the power of organized labor to raise wages may also be reduced. Making the economy more competitive may help prevent cost-push inflation, but bringing about increased competition has proven to be difficult.

Fighting structural inflation

The only cure for structural and other inflations caused by shortages is time. In the short run, people must simply adjust to the current reality and new structure. Eventually, the economy will regear itself to produce the product that is in short supply. Eventually, abundant crops will replace crop failures. Prices of such products and commodities will come down as the items come into greater supply.

It is possible, of course, that cartels or other economic and political restrictions will keep a product in short supply over a lengthy period of time. The economy may then be forced to put up a more active fight against shortage-based and price-fixing inflations.

One possible strategy to lessen the effects of structural inflation is to *stockpile* key raw materials like oil, uranium, coal, copper, cobalt, etc., and even some agricultural products like grain. Actually, our government does do some stockpiling of many of these materials for reasons of national security; during a war, the supply could be cut off. However, an expanded program of stockpiling could accomplish at least one thing in the fight against inflation: it could provide time before the effects of a shortage would occur.

As we noted earlier, the effects of the energy-shortage crisis of the early 1970s are still with us. Indeed, most economists would agree that the crisis itself is still on-going. In any case, the American economy and the economies of other nations have taken various measures to cope with the problem and thus keep inflation under control. The United States has developed new sources of oil supply in the state of Alaska and in the seabeds off the Atlantic and Pacific coasts. Great Britain and the Scandinavian countries have found and are pumping oil from the North Sea. Research is being stepped up in the use of solar energy and in nuclear reactors for energy production. Measures to conserve energy—restrictions on gasoline consumption, better insulation techniques for buildings, more efficient use of electricity, and so on—have been inaugurated.

Whether America or other like-situated nations will soon or ever become "energy independent" is problematical. But a vigorous economy can at least take measures to cushion the shock of sudden basic commodity shortages. Such measures help to prevent the resulting inflation trend from leading to runaway cost-push inflation.

The problem of unemployment

The labor force of the United States includes all those people who (1) are 16 years of age and over and (2) are willing and able to work and are either employed or actively seeking employment. This means that there are many people over 16 not included in the labor force: those institutionalized in either school, hospitals of various sorts, or jail. Those who are retired do not belong to the labor force. However, many individuals who are over 65 either never retired or have come out of retirement; they are part of the labor force. A mother with young children may find it difficult to enter the labor force. Those women who choose to be full-time housewives are not included in the labor force. There is also a statistical group known as the hard-core unemployed; if they give up looking for work, they are not considered part of the labor force. Finally, there are a few other individuals who are not part of the labor force because the wages available are not high enough to compensate them for their trouble.

All the members of the labor force who are out of a job are considered unemployed. The Bureau of Labor Statistics issues monthly figures on both employment and unemployment. The figure we are most familiar with is the percentage of the labor force unemployed. Figure 2 graphs the history of unemployment in the United States by year since 1930. Notice how the Great Depression years of the 1930s stand out, followed by the year 1975. Notice that the low points for unemployment were the first half of the 1940s, the early 1950s, and the mid-1960s—all war years.

Figure 3 shows the growth of employment through the same time period. A 5% unemployment rate today would mean many more

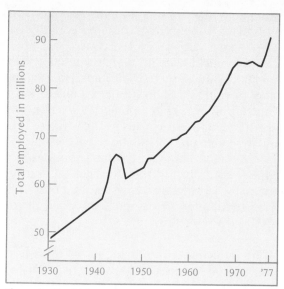

Figure 3   The history of employment since 1930. The biggest jumps in employment occurred after World War II, at the end of the Korean War (1954), and in the last few years (1976–1977). (Source: U.S. Department of Commerce.)

people are unemployed than a 5% unemployment rate for 1950. Why? Because the labor force is larger today.

The unemployment percentage rate is a true *aggregate* value. It disguises many "micro" aspects of unemployment and many of the trends. It doesn't tell us how many minorities, women, and teenagers are unemployed. The federal government does, however, issue separate figures for these groupings. Actually, these three groups contribute a disproportionately large share to the unemployment rate. In addition, the unemployment rate doesn't tell us how many people are *underemployed*—those who work part-time jobs or who are only able to work part of the week or who work jobs that don't use that person's training. (A space engineer working as a waiter at a hamburger joint is underemployed.)

Unfortunately, the effects of unemployment are not confined to those who are unemployed. If there is 8% of the labor force unemployed, the other 92% cannot be smug in their employment. There are those among that 92% who are not likely to become unemployed and who see the threat of unemployment as a useful device to control those they supervise. This is shortsighted at best. The existence of unemployment may improve behavior and reduce demands for higher wages on the part of existing employees. But, employers and employees alike lose from unemployment. The

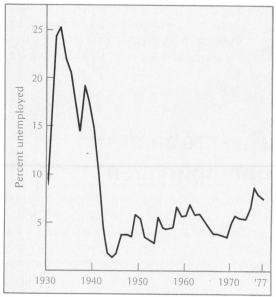

Figure 2   The history of civilian unemployment since 1930. (Source: U.S. Department of Commerce.)

failure to employ all of the labor force means that there will be fewer goods and services to consume. Under mid-1970s conditions, the loss reached $40-50 billion each year in things everyone could enjoy. In addition, all American workers and taxpayers bear the burden of providing funds for unemployment compensation and welfare programs.

Estimates of the cost associated with unemployment when its rate is above 4% have been made by the Congressional Budget Office. As of late 1975 or early 1976, each increase in the unemployment rate by one point, say from 5% to 6%, adds *$16 billion* to the government deficit. Of this, $2 billion represents benefit payments to the unemployed workers and the other $14 billion represents *taxes not paid* by the workers and their employers. If the workers could be put back to work for less than $16 billion, the government would be ahead. However, the job creation problem is difficult since each percentage point on the unemployment rate represents almost 1 million workers (based on the number of workers employed in the late 1970s).

Types of unemployment

In an earlier chapter, we saw that there are essentially three types of unemployment. These are frictional, structural, and cyclical unemployment. Let us refresh our memory about these types of unemployment.

Frictional unemployment This form of unemployment results because it takes time for job-seekers and jobs to match, even when the labor market is working well. Some people who lose their job may require a lot of time to find a new one. Even when the labor market is improving, many people must leave their present job in order to seek a better one. During the search period, they could be unemployed. These job-changers make up the greatest part of the 4–5% of the labor force which will be unemployed even at "full employment."

Structural unemployment Structural unemployment results from a mismatch of the supply and demand for labor. Even though the labor market may have otherwise "cleared," there is a certain amount of unemployment reported which is the result of structural problems. There may be a mismatch of skills such

that the unemployed are not capable of filling vacant jobs. There may be geographical concentrations of unemployed workers with the vacant jobs in other parts of the country. Or there may be vacancies in traditional women's jobs such as nurses, telephone operators, or maids while the unemployed are men. In each case there exists both unemployed and jobs, but the problem is not so much the overall supply and demand as the inability to quickly match up the unemployed with the jobs. To eliminate the unemployment would require relearning of skills, relocation of families, or changes in social values. Entire generations may be required for adjustment. Structural problems contribute to unemployment even at "full employment" and are not relieved simply by increasing overall demand for labor.

Cyclical unemployment This name is slightly misleading. The name suggests that such unemployment is the result of being in the trough of the business cycle. The slack demand for goods and services during a downswing *is* certainly a cause of unemployment. However, there are periods of slack demand that may persist for a long time. These periods of slack demand are not truly cyclical in nature but they do cause unemployment. If demand is reduced either by the stage of the cycle or by some persistent cause, the unemployment created is called cyclical unemployment.

Defining full employment

If there are three types of unemployment, how then do we define full employment? In our discussions in earlier chapters, we mentioned the full-employment level. The implication of that phrase seems to mean that every person desiring employment at that level of real wages would be employed. Yet you are probably aware that our economy seldom reaches levels of unemployment even close to zero. Look at Figure 2 to see how frequently our economy has been below the 4% level. At present, there is disagreement as to whether we should consider 4% or 5% as the full-employment level.

When we say that the labor market *clears*, we mean that at some level of real wages there are enough jobs for all those seeking employment. In the real world, there are some types of unemployment which are not related to the failure of the market to clear. All frictional unemployment fits in this category. Some structural unemployment must be included also since only major social upheavals would result in the reduction in the number employed. There is no possibility that a change in the real wage would ever reduce unemployment below these levels. We consider about 4 to 5% of the unemployment in the U.S. labor market to be "normal"; thus 95 to 96% of the labor force employed represents "full employment."

Economic policy and employment problems

Much of the discussion of employment problems has been related to unemployment. Unemployment is certainly a serious and costly problem. However, it is also possible to have excess demand for goods and services, which leads to demand-pull inflation. This is also an employment problem; the need here is to increase the number of workers employed to improve the productivity of all workers and to use the workers as effectively as possible. It is also necessary to make sure workers are kept working and producing rather than spending time on strike trying to protect their income levels or looking for higher-paying jobs. The solution of employment problems may be attempted through economic policy. Both fiscal and monetary policy may be used. Monetary policy would mean that the money supply would be used to attack employment problems. Fiscal policy would mean that the federal budget would be used to change conditions in the labor market; both purchases and tax collections of the government could be used. Let us look at each policy in turn.

Unemployment and fiscal policy

Suppose we have a high level of unemployment, say $7\frac{1}{2}$%, and we wish to reduce it using fiscal policy. What actions can we take? Well, recall that unemployment means there are idle resources and that goods and services are not being produced. The economy must be *stimulated* by increasing demand for goods and

services and, thus, for labor. We may do this directly by increasing government demand; the government increases its demand by expanding its purchases. To produce the goods and services demanded, more people would have to be employed. Remember, there is a multiplier effect for government purchases so the net impact on the economy will be greater than the increase in government purchases.

A second action in fiscal policy to stimulate demand is to cut taxes. A tax cut, expenditures remaining the same, will mean that other sectors of the economy will have more to spend. If personal taxes are reduced, consumption will increase, leading to an increase in demand for labor. Business tax cuts will result in greater profits now and the expectation of profits in the future. Thus investment expenditures by firms may increase. Present profits make it possible to increase productive capacity through investment. The expectation of future profits makes the investment expenditures desirable. Investment expenditures increase demand for labor both to produce the investment goods and to operate the new investment already in place. The multiplier effect works with tax cuts also. As we have seen, the multiplier is smaller for tax changes than for changes in government expenditures (demand).

Problems in using fiscal policy

Fiscal policy should be as direct as possible in its effects. To wipe out unemployment, the expenditures should be designed to employ as many persons as possible. So the government has a problem: it must decide where to spend its money. Increasing purchases from industries which use large amounts of labor would be far more effective than the same amount purchased from a capital-intensive industry. Construction, especially housing, is labor intensive so spending for construction would stimulate the growth of jobs. If the government increases the defense budget, this will result in more jobs for mostly high-skilled workers, such as engineers. However, if most of the unemployed are unskilled or semiskilled workers, then these individuals will probably remain unemployed. So fiscal policy must try to be attuned to the types of unemployed rather than just an aggregate number or undifferentiated mass.

Tax cuts may be similarly related to the creation of jobs. The investment tax credit is designed not only as a general stimulus to the economy but also as an incentive to increase capacity and potential employment. Firms are also given tax reductions if they provide jobs or training for the unemployed.

Another problem in using fiscal policy to stimulate the growth of jobs is deciding whether the private sector or public sector should have the new jobs. Most of the policies we mentioned above—such as increasing government expenditures or using tax cuts—have the effect of creating jobs in the private sector. Most people, including Congressmen, believe this is proper. Private sector workers are considered more efficient and the jobs potentially more permanent. However, there are many unemployed who are so unskilled that they have little chance of finding lasting employment in the private sector.

Some economists and politicians have suggested that the government become the employer of last resort. The federal government would directly hire unemployed workers, particularly the unskilled. These public sector jobs would be used for large projects of national undertakings, such as laying new railroad beds (which are now mostly worn out), repairing highways, cleaning up the environment, and other large projects whose need arises.

Many people criticize the growth of public sector jobs as contributing to the bloated growth of big government. They feel such actions would undermine the market economy. In addition, many people feel government workers are less efficient and productive than their counterparts in the private sector. Defenders of the government as employer of last resort argue that such jobs would not be permanent. Those workers who are cyclically unemployed could be employed until jobs appeared again in the private sector. The hard-core unemployed—those who are illiterate and unskilled—might need longer employment by the government. But even these workers might learn skills while on the job.

Another possibility of using fiscal policy in the public sector would be to set up government training programs. The advantage of such programs is that they could improve the working of the market, particularly the labor market. The government did this with some success when Lyndon Johnson was President. His administration set up the Job Corps to train inner-city young people. However, as the government cut its spending during the Nixon years, the Job Corps lost much of its funding. Actually, one of the greatest criticisms of government training programs is that they are expensive, with cumbersome administrative costs.

There is another problem using fiscal policy to eliminate unemployment. Tax changes and government expenditure changes will certainly cause changes in total or aggregate demand. But their usefulness is limited. The first problem has to do with the length of time before the correct policy is implemented. There will be a period of time before the economic problems are recognized and there is general agreement that something ought to be done. In addition, the federal budget is set once a year; however, unemployment may vary within that time period. Therefore, it is not possible to change fiscal policy every time the unemployment rate moves up or down.

There must be some recognition that a recession is developing or that the labor market is at a point where prices won't rise when demand is increased. Once the problem is recognized, the legislative process is also slow. Tax cuts or expenditure cuts cannot be legislated immediately. Even after the law is changed, some time may pass before the actual change in taxes or expenditures may come about. When President Carter was inaugurated in January, 1977, a tax cut (in the form of a tax rebate) was one of his highest priorities in order to reduce the high level of unemployment. By March, the tax cut had not yet cleared the Congress. By April, the economy was recovering, unemployment was dropping sharply, inflation was increasing—and the President decided to abandon the idea of a rebate.

Unemployment and monetary policy

Monetary policy may also be called upon to reduce unemployment. It can be used alone or in harmony with fiscal policy. *To increase the number of jobs the proper strategy is to increase the money supply.* There are two different explanations as to how the money supply affects employment levels. (1) The monetarist economists would emphasize that more money leads to a direct increase in spending. (2) Keynesian economists would be more likely to suggest that the increase in money supply would lower interest rates, which in turn would make investment more attractive. As investment projects are undertaken, more workers are required. For our purposes, we need only know that an increased money supply does stimulate the growth of jobs by stimulating output.

To increase the money supply, the Fed would use one of its three tools. The reserve requirement could be reduced. Or the discount rate could be lowered. Finally, and most likely, there could be open market purchases of securities. In each action, the money supply would increase as long as there was enough demand for loans to get it into circulation.

Once into circulation, money could stimulate spending, which would increase output and employment. Or, if the money is converted to other interest-bearing securities such as bonds and stocks, the price of the securities rises and the interest rate falls. The lower interest rate *should* stimulate investment spending. Making the investment goods would require labor as would the operation of the plant and equipment after it is in place. Thus unemployment would be reduced or eliminated.

Monetary policy is by its nature very widespread in its effects. A reduction in the money supply will quickly be felt in almost all parts of the economy. An increase in the money supply is less likely to be spread so evenly, however. It may be wise to consider ways to send the increase in money in directions where employment effects will be greatest. For example, we have said that building houses requires a lot of labor. If the money supply is increased, it may be worthwhile to increase the amount of money available for mortgages. This may be done several ways. One is to allow savings and loan associations and mutual savings banks to offer higher interest to attract more savings. These institutions make most of the mortgage loans. Another way would be to make it easier to borrow under Veterans Administration or Federal Housing Authority terms. Finally, the Federal Home Loan Banks can purchase existing mortgages making cash available for more loans. If mortgages become cheaper, home building will be increased. Thus increasing the money supply in *selected areas* of the economy such as agriculture, consumer credit, or mortgages may have a more direct and immediate effect on unemployment than a general increase in the supply of money.

Unemployment in the 1970s

Figure 4 shows the unemployment rate for the period of 1969–1977. In 1969, the unemployment rate was low with a sharp rise during 1970. During 1971 and 1972, unemployment was fairly steady. By the very end of 1972, there was some improvement which lasted through 1973. Shortly after the beginning of 1974, the unemployment rate shot up, reaching peak levels in early 1975. These mid-1970s years witnessed the highest unemployment since the Great Depression. From the peak, slow improvement continued into 1977, though by mid-1977 the unemployment rate of 7% was above the levels in 1973 and much above the levels of 1969.

Figure 4 also shows the unemployment rate for *heads of households*. Working wives and teenagers are *not* included in this measure. The only women included here are those who head households (which includes, of course, single women). Notice the gap between this measure and the one for all unemployment; the gap averages roughly two percentage points though it has widened over the period shown. Many economists and politicians claim that the rate of unemployed household heads is now a better measure of the severity of the unemployment problem. They argue that the overall unemployment rate now reflects changing cultural values rather than economic

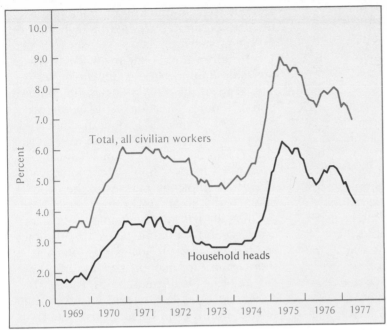

Figure 4   Recent unemployment rates for all civilian workers and heads of households. Notice the increasing gap between the two rates. At the beginning of the period, the gap was about 1½%; at the end of the period, the gap was close to 2½%. (Source: U.S. Department of Labor, prepared by the Federal Reserve Bank of St. Louis.)

difficulty. During the 1970s, literally millions of housewives entered the labor force to become working wives; this changeover has been due to the further "emancipation" of women.

High unemployment groups

We said earlier that three overlapping groups have especially high unemployment: women, teenagers, and blacks. The unemployment problems associated with these three groups are mostly *structural* problems. The high unemployment levels of the 1970s have been concentrated in these groups; so let's look at each in turn.

Unemployment among women   The unemployment rate for women workers has remained higher than the unemployment rate for men. There are several reasons for this. One, which we just mentioned, is the very rapid increase in the number of women seeking jobs. Other reasons include the lack of enough traditionally female jobs and the remaining resistance to women in traditional male jobs.

Since some women are *secondary wage earners* (that is, they have working husbands), the unemployment rate probably does not show the true extent of unemployment among women. Married women are more likely to withdraw from the labor force rather than remain unemployed for long periods even though they would like to work.

The entrants to the labor force are women in the 25-to-44-year age bracket. These are women who in earlier periods would have been at home caring for children. In 1970, 43.2% of the women over 16 years of age were in the labor force. By 1977, the proportion had reached 48% and, by the 1980 census year, may reach one-half of all women of working age. In 1960, only one-third of the work force was female. By 1970, the proportion was 38.1%. The percentage topped 40 by 1976, almost a decade ahead of the time earlier projected. What are the reasons for 4 out of 10 workers being women? There are many.

Income is the main reason women enter the labor force. For many, low-income potential for their husband led them to seek a second salary. In a study done in 1973, half of the

Viewpoint
Unemployment Statistics Overestimate the Problem

During the presidential campaign of 1976, the unemployment rate hovered around 8%. In previous campaigns, a jobless rate that high would have meant real trouble for the incumbent, conjuring up the vision of bread lines and industries shut down. Yet, although the incumbent, Gerald Ford, lost the election, it is doubtful that the unemployment rate had very much to do with his defeat. In fact, both candidates, although not neglecting the unemployment issue, concentrated their economic promises and prognostications during the campaign on the issue of inflation rather than on unemployment. Both camps sensed that unemployment, even at the 8% rate, was not a burning issue among the majority of the electorate.

Why not? Many experts would argue that the answer lies in the unemployment statistics themselves. They do not say that the statistics are necessarily distorted or manipulated. They do contend, however, that unemployment figures may be seriously misleading. Why? Because while the figures may show unemployment to be at a high level, the percentage of population *employed* may also be at a high level. The number of people working in recent years, for example, has risen far faster than the population. Today's rate (1977) of teenage unemployment is extremely high (estimated at about 18% and about 36% for minority teenagers). Yet more teenagers are working today than ever before. The unemployment rate for adult women is also high. Yet the percentage of working women is also at an all-time high. Unfortunately, say these critics, economists tend to concentrate on the unemployment figures and ignore the employment numbers. Unemployment figures may supply politicians with campaign rhetoric, but unless employment figures are also taken into consideration, they can be a misleading indicator of economic health. The majority of the American electorate in 1976, these experts

contend, sensed this fact and therefore refused to be unduly aroused by high unemployment statistics.

How can the unemployment rate rise at the same time that the employment rate rises? Part of the answer lies in the composition of today's labor force. Today, the percentage of women and young persons in the labor force is much higher than in previous eras. (Women, who made up 33% of the work force in 1960, now account for over 40% of all employed persons in the economy.) And women and young people have traditionally had high unemployment rates, even in good economic times, because they are generally freer to leave their jobs and shop around for new ones than, for example, adult heads of households. Part of the answer, too, lies in the rapid growth of the service industries in recent years—retail trade, health care, education, recreation facilities, and so on—which traditionally have high personnel turnover rates, and, indeed, often hire on a seasonal or part-time basis. Workers in these areas, more often than not young people and women, enter and leave the labor force more frequently than adult males and are consequently more frequently counted among the unemployed.

In the 1950s, when employment rose, unemployment usually fell by about the same number of jobs. In the two-year recovery from the 1949 recession, for example, every additional job removed one worker from the unemployment rolls. In the 1970s, however, the two-year recovery from the 1970 recession saw about three million new jobs created with a reduction in unemployment of a mere 3,000! Obviously, many of these new jobs were not taken by the unemployed. They were taken by new entrants into the labor force, often younger men and women, but even more often by adult women entering the labor force for the first time. Before the "sexual revolution" and the rising inflation rate that compels many families to seek a second income, most of these adult women would have remained full-time housewives and outside the labor force.

Unemployment statistics as an indicator of economic health may also be distorted by the increase in "transfer payments"—unemployment compensation, Social Security, and other welfare payments. From 1966 to 1976, the number of persons employed increased from 72.9 million to 88.4 million. Yet, during this same period, transfer payments increased from $44.7 billion to $196.7 billion. It is not unreasonable to suppose that such cushions against poverty may also provide disincentives to work and thus increase the unemployment statistics without greatly decreasing the overall well-being of the economy.

Critics of the unemployment statistics as a valid economic barometer do not suggest that such figures should be abandoned by economic planners. They do say, however, that unemployment statistics are not sufficient unto themselves. Employment figures, changes in the work force, changes in the economy, and welfare payments must also be considered. If such matters are taken into account, they say, 2 to 2.5 points could be taken off the current unemployment rate as far as its real effect on the economy is concerned. Most economists agree that the mid-1950s, when unemployment stood at about 4%, was the golden age of employment. However, if current unemployment statistics are adjusted by this 2 or 2.5 points, current "real unemployment" is seen to be not so far above the golden mean of 4% as to cause undue alarm in a growing economy.

white women seeking a job were married to a man who made $9,000 or less. For black women, half had husbands earning $7,000 or less.

For middle-income families, a second income was necessary to defend their standard of living. Inflation had wiped out any gains made. In other cases, a special project was the reason for the second income. Sending children to college or buying a second home, a boat, or a recreational vehicle were reasons for the second job and income.

Another reason women are entering the labor force is that more women are heads of households. In many instances, college-educated women are choosing careers over marriage. Also, the divorce rate has risen; so women, many with children to support, are of necessity entering the labor force.

Finally, the entire psychology of the women's role in the labor force is changing. "Women's lib" probably had something to do with it. Effective birth control also made it possible to limit family size. The role of the housewife is no longer held in high esteem. Women are more inclined to work simply as an outlet for creative energies.

All of these factors combine to lead to high unemployment among women. The American work force has changed as a result of the entry of women. The American job market is still trying to cope with the resulting situation of high unemployment as the decade of the 1970s comes to a close.

Teenage unemployment Teenage unemployment has been especially serious in the 1970s. The unemployment rate has always been high for teens. Figure 5 compares unemployment for the 16–to–19-year age group with that of adults—both male and female. Prior to 1970, when adult unemployment was below 5%, teens faced unemployment rates between 10 and 15%. After 1970, teenage unemployment dipped below 15% only in 1973. From 1974 on, the rate has been hovering around 20%: One in five people aged 16 to 19 has been unable to find employment. Lack of jobs often interferes with education as the young person cannot afford to stay in school. Lack of income postpones or prevents normal family formation as the young people cannot afford to marry. Finally, idleness leads to a search for other activities. These activities may often be illegal, leading to an arrest record and problems for future employment at any age.

There are numerous reasons for high unemployment among teenagers. Primarily, there are so many of them. While most of the "war babies" are beyond the teenage years, birth rates remained high in the 1950s. So there are still large numbers of young people around.

Many young people are still completing their education. Thus they have special job requirements. The need to work when they are not in school limits the times of day and amounts of time a teenager may work. Employers are often not flexible enough to allow erratic working hours. Part-time jobs are especially scarce.

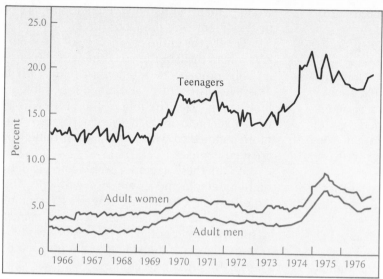

Figure 5 Teenage unemployment rate compared to that for adults. (Source: U.S. Department of Labor.)

A young person's age works against him in finding a job. There are specific prohibitions in the law preventing a teenager from working around dangerous machinery. Employers are often reluctant to hire those whom they consider too immature, especially if the job involves contact with the general public.

Many adults have openly or at least implicitly conspired to protect their own jobs from the younger workers. There are numerous ways this may be done. Requirements of a high school or college degree, even if it is not needed to do the job, prevent young people from obtaining the job until they complete their education. Similarly, some jobs require licenses to do the work. The licensing agency is usually composed of adults who impose high requirements on those seeking the license.

Additional restrictions may be imposed if union membership is required to obtain a job. Often it is hard to enter the apprentice program if a family member is not already a member of the union. Then, a long apprenticeship at low income works an additional hardship on young people. Finally, the minimum wage is high enough that employers cannot put young people to work in jobs which otherwise might be open.

Viewpoint
Unemployment Statistics Underestimate the Problem

Of the 7.8 million people statistically listed as unemployed in 1975, 3.6 million were between the ages of 16 and 24. In other words, although such persons constituted only a quarter of the labor force, they accounted for nearly half of the unemployed. It is estimated that workers over 25 now have an unemployment rate of about 6%, persons between 20 and 24 a 13.5% rate, and persons 16 to 19 an 18% rate.

For blacks and other minority young people, the figures are even more depressing. Unemployment for young blacks, for example, has always been high, but it has recently reached proportions not seen since the Great Depression of the 1930s. In 1977, U.S. Labor Department figures showed that about 36% of blacks between the ages of 16 to 19 who wanted to work could not find jobs. This was about five times the national rate of joblessness, and over twice that of white teenagers. For blacks between 20 and 24, the unemployment rate was over 20%, also more than twice that of the comparable white age group. Even these figures may not show the full dimension of the problem. Some experts point out that the statistics do not take into account the many thousands of young blacks, especially in urban ghettos, who have simply given up seeking seemingly nonexistent jobs. Nor do they count young blacks working part-time because they cannot get full-time employment. If such persons were taken into account, black teenage unemployment might well be nearly 70%.

No economist, sociologist, psychiatrist, or other social scientist can accurately measure the devastating effect that being unable to earn a living has on an individual—be the person black or white, old or young. Society can only guess at its true effect and take note of its material manifestations when they erupt in society.

Juvenile crime, for example, has risen to levels unprecedented in United States history according to most law-enforcement officials. Some of this rise is probably due to loosening of family ties and other cultural factors, but it is certain that idleness among teenagers is an important contributory factor. Juvenile crime and early postjuvenile crime is especially prevalent where the jobless rates are highest. Murder, for example, is the leading cause of death among black men between the ages of 16 and 25.

Experts have pointed out the increasing number of idle urban youths—many but by no means all minority youth—who have taken up an underworld fringe existence to survive—pushing dope, male and female prostitution, and so on. Again, societal factors are undoubtedly involved in this growing phenomenon, but joblessness must certainly be a major contributory cause. And again, no one can calculate the personal cost to the young people involved in such activities, let alone the cost to society in increased law-enforcement costs, increased

costs to crime victims, and increased loss of valuable human capital.

Young people are not, of course, the only ones who suffer a personal price for unemployment. Who can estimate the personal anguish of the adult "unemployment statistic" who cannot properly feed, clothe, and shelter himself or herself or provide these necessities for his or her family?

A Congressional study released in late 1976 gives some indication of the effects of unemployment on the well-being of individuals. Experts involved in the study found a direct link between fluctuations in unemployment and illness and criminal behavior. No similar correlation was found between such matters and inflation or real per capita income.

The study noted that in 1970 the unemployment rate increased 1.4%. The overall rate for that year was 4.9%, considerably less than in subsequent years. Yet, according to the study, that 1.4% increase cost American society about $21 billion in lost income, increased mortality among the unemployed, and increased incarceration in jails and mental institutions. In addition, it accounted for about 1,540 suicides, nearly 6% of the total; about 5,520 hospital admissions, 4.7% of the total; about 7,600 state prison admissions, 5.6% of the total; and about 1,740 homicides, 8% of the total.

Unemployment statistics, the study concluded, are more than mere numbers on an economic barometer. At best they represent personal misfortune. At worst they represent personal anguish and even individual tragedy.

How would you reconcile this Viewpoint with the previous one?
Are they contradictory? Is it possible both are true?

Of course, the lack of a job while young means that the person will never get the work experience needed to get a job later on. The result of teenage unemployment is that the worker of, say 25, is just getting an entry level job which he could have done a decade earlier. Thus teenage unemployment has implications which follow the worker throughout his working life.

Black unemployment Unemployment among blacks and other minorities remains a serious problem. Figure 6 shows how the unemployment rates of blacks and other minorities compare to the rates for whites. In all cases, the actual rate may understate the unemployment problem. The reason that the measured unemployment rate understates the true magnitude of unemployment includes *disguised unemployment.* That is, many blacks work at part-time rather than full-time jobs, work at jobs below their skill level, or have withdrawn from the labor force. The latter are called *discouraged workers* because they have faced frustration for so long that they have stopped looking for work even though they would like to be employed; these workers no longer show up in the unemployment statistics.

The reasons for high black unemployment are many. Despite changes in the laws, job discrimination still exists and works against the black worker and workers from other minority groups. Lack of job skills may result as blacks move from rural to urban areas. Lack of job skills remains a problem for young blacks since there seems little reason to acquire skills with most of their neighbors out of work. Inability to acquire the first job leaves younger blacks without work experience and unemployable as they grow older.

Many blacks found jobs in manufacturing in cities during the post-World War II era. However, these jobs are disappearing— replaced by capital-intensive plants or "relocated" overseas because of cheaper costs. The jobs available are of a different type and generally located in suburbs, away from the inner city where many blacks live. Lack of housing and/or transportation makes it difficult to reach the jobs which are available. Thus very high unemployment among blacks remains a problem.

Other problems of structural unemployment

In November, 1975, the unemployment rate was greater than 8% yet more than a million unfilled jobs existed. If the unemployed could be used to fill the jobs open, a full percentage point could be chopped off the unemploy-

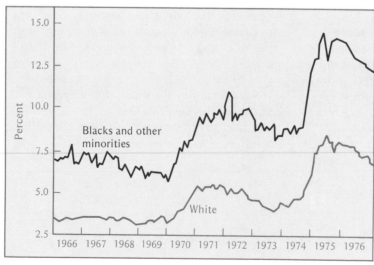

Figure 6 Unemployment rate for blacks and other minorities compared to that for whites. (Source: U.S. Department of Labor.)

Viewpoint
Structural Solutions to a Structural Problem

Typically and traditionally, economists (and the general public as well) have looked at unemployment as a kind of aggregate problem: a particular percentage of the aggregate (total) labor force accounting for an aggregate x millions of persons out of work. Typically and traditionally, also, solutions to the unemployment problem have tended toward the aggregate. Monetary and fiscal policies are used to increase employment by increasing aggregate demand for goods and services. Therefore, changes in money growth, interest rates, government spending, and taxes have been considered the most productive approach to the unemployment problem. Historically, this approach has been more or less effective in dealing with the problem. In the 1970s, however, its effectiveness has seemed to be rather less than more. High unemployment has remained a persistent, nagging problem throughout most of the decade.

Many economists have now come to believe that unemployment is a structural rather than an aggregate problem in today's economy and that its solution must be approached from a structural point of view. They believe we must look at the various components (the structure) of the unemployment rate and devise plans to deal with these specific components rather than concentrate entirely on policies to deal with the overall unemployment rate.

Government figures in January, 1977, showed that 7.3% of the nation's labor force, or 6,958,000 men and women, were out of work. This aggregate figure, however, may be far less significant than the figures for the individual components of the unemployment figure. Male heads of household, for example, had an unemployment rate of 4.3%; white-collar workers a rate of 4.5%; whites a 6.7% rate; and female heads of household, 7.0%. All of these components were below the aggregate 7.3% unemployment rate. On the other hand, the rate for nonwhites was 12.5%; for white teenagers it was 18.1%; and for nonwhite teenagers it was 36.1%.

Monetary and fiscal policies seemed to be working fairly well for some unemployment components—male heads of households and white-collar workers, for example. But it was very obvious that the unemployment problem among blacks and young persons, for example, was not being solved by traditional policies alone. Economists and other concerned citizens have consequently begun to call for more specific solutions to this dilemma. They are looking for more efficient ways to fit job-seeker and job together through training and education and to eliminate barriers to employment caused by rigidity in union and minimum wage scales and other restrictions on free competition in the labor market.

(1) One solution that has been offered is that the government set up some kind of a national youth service program, administered at the local level, to train young people and other unemployed persons for specific jobs available in the local community. Proponents of such a program point out that unfilled jobs are available, even in urban ghetto areas, and that more such jobs can be made available through proper economic planning. The problem is that far too many young persons are ill-equipped or even totally unequipped to fill such jobs. Special training should be available to the unemployed, especially vocational training and training for employment in the growing service industries. More advanced skills should also be taught for jobs available in local technical industries. The essential ingredient of this kind of program is that training be for specific, available jobs. Too often in the past, special training programs have resulted in newly qualified workers unable to find jobs in their home communities and hindered by poverty or prejudice from finding them elsewhere.

(2) A variation on this plan is a program that would tie training more closely to the local business community. Once workers are brought to a basic level of competence through government-sponsored institutional training, they would move to on-the-job training in local business and industry. Some

sort of tax incentive or voucher system would be used to compensate the employer for hiring and training inexperienced or partially qualified personnel.

(3) Some economists feel that although education and skill development are basic to solution of structural unemployment, modification of the minimum wage law is also required. They point out that many of today's youngsters and less-skilled workers are simply not worth the $2.30 per-hour minimum in terms of what they can produce. If the minimum were reduced for such people, more would be hired. To counter the argument that this would result in a kind of slave labor, it has been suggested that the government pay a subsidy to the worker to bring the pay scale up to a minimum.

(4) Other economists believe the unemployment compensation system should be adjusted to make it less of an incentive to remain unnecessarily jobless until benefits run out—perhaps by taxing such benefits, which now are tax free.

None of these plans is the perfect solution to the problem of structural unemployment. We probably need several of these plans working together at one time. Economists and other experts disagree on the feasibility of the various programs that have been suggested. Most, however, would agree that all such plans are at least on the right track—much unemployment in today's economy is structural and calls for structural solutions.

ment rate. Why the simultaneous existence of jobs and unemployed? There seem to be three major reasons.

First, most of the jobs were in the industrial areas of the Northeast and around the Great Lakes. However, the population movement is toward the South—in the Sunbelt from Florida to California. There was little desire among workers to go to the areas where jobs were available. This was true of workers in the immediate area of the jobs as well as those already located in the warmer areas of the country.

Second, many of the jobs are simply too unattractive to find applicants. Many workers are not interested in jobs on the night shift or at low pay. The openings are often in entry-level jobs with little chance of advancement. The jobs may also be in traditionally low-paying industries such as textiles and garment making.

The third problem is at the other extreme of the range of skills. Many of the job openings require special skills which are in short supply. Machinists, mechanics, welders, and secretaries are needed in many areas of the country. Doctors, nurses, other health-care specialists, and engineers with specialties or managerial skills are all in great demand. In Maine, lumberjacks are imported from Canada to fill positions. Of course, the unemployed could be trained or retrained to fill the positions but it will take time. Thus there is no immediate matching of the unemployed with available openings.

The paradox of growing employment

We have already seen that the number of jobs available and filled has been growing. Oddly enough, job totals were growing fastest when unemployment was above 7% and declining only slightly. For example, from April of 1975 to June of 1976, the number of jobs filled grew by 3.8%. Only once since World War II has the number of jobs grown that fast and that was a 4.3% increase which began in 1954. In the one month from June to July of 1976, 400,000 more people went to work. That made 3.6 million more people employed in the fifteen months since the trough of the business cycle in April, 1975. The economy has been capable of growth and of responding to fiscal and monetary policy.

One of the reasons the unemployment rate has not declined is that the labor force has grown so rapidly. Workers previously withdrawn from the labor force and new workers have entered at very rapid rates. The new jobs are filled and some workers remain unemployed. For example, when the number of jobs increased by 357,000 from October to November of 1976, the number of workers grew by 557,000 over the same period. Therefore, 200,000 remained unemployed, and the decline in unemployment was only 157,000. So the unemployment level remains high.

The Phillips curve: the big tradeoff

Students of economics have long been aware of the existence of a relationship between the rate of inflation (price instability) and the rate of unemployment in an economy. In the late 1950s, an economist named A. W. Phillips "formalized" this relationship. Using historical economic data from his home country, Great Britain, he developed an econometric device to measure the relationship. The device is in the form of a curve and is now called the **Phillips curve.** Each nation and each time period of a nation has its own Phillips curve. Figure 7 shows a *hypothetical* Phillips curve.

Each point along the curve shows a different combination of inflation and unemployment. For example, Figure 7 shows that if inflation is running at 10%, the unemployment rate will be 2%. If inflation is 3%, unemployment will be 8%. As you move along the curve, you will note that a reduction of unemployment corresponds with a rise in inflation and that a reduction of inflation comes at the expense of a rise in unemployment. In other words, *according to the Phillips curve, there must be a tradeoff between inflation and unemployment.* There is no underlying reason why the Phillips curve should exist. If there is a rationale at all, it is that as unemployment declines and we approach full employment, both cost-push and demand-pull forces work more powerfully leading to greater rates of inflation. Inflation may be brought down to low levels only at the cost of high unemployment.

If this is so, society can choose a point along this curve at which it believes it will operate at the greatest good for the greatest number of its citizens. For example, according to Figure 7, if a nation is unwilling to accept an unemployment rate higher than 5%, it must not try to push inflation below 5%. That is, the economy must tolerate 5% inflation. If a nation chooses an inflation rate of 3%, it must be willing to accept an unemployment rate of 8%. In this instance, since few nations will tolerate an unemployment rate of 8%, it will have to learn to live with more inflation than it would like.

Keynesians and the Phillips curve

As noted above, Phillips based his measurements on data from the British economy. Data from the American economy in the 1960s seemed to correspond rather closely with the British model. See the lower curve in Figure 8. In the late 1960s and in the 1970s, however, new data began to emerge. The curve seems to have shifted upward (see alternative 1 in Figure 8). There is still a tradeoff between unemploy-

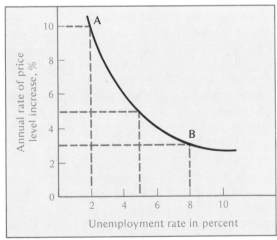

Figure 7 A hypothetical Phillips curve. Point A shows high inflation with low unemployment. Point B shows low inflation and high unemployment.

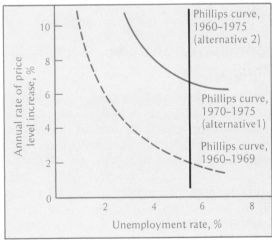

Figure 8 The Phillips curve with U.S. data, 1960-1975. If the data are taken over the whole period from 1960-1975, alternative 2 results—which means there is no tradeoff between unemployment and inflation. If the data are broken into two periods—1960-1969 and 1970-1975—then two Phillips curves are shown. Alternative 1 shows the curve for the 1970s period, which reveals high levels of both inflation and unemployment.

ment and inflation, but unemployment and inflation are both at higher rates than on the earlier curve.

Some Keynesian economists argue that this upward shift in the Phillips curve is more apparent than real. They point out that the data include the abnormal effects of the Vietnam War and oil price hikes. Economic conditions in these years (high inflation *plus* very high unemployment) distort the curve. Further data, they believe, will correct the curve.

The Phillips curve indicates *that a lower curve is better than a higher one for the economy as a whole.* We have seen that we can lower inflation rates by lowering demand for goods and services. In other words, we can choose an inflation point on the Phillips curve. But must we be satisfied with the high unemployment rate that may go along with this inflation rate? In other words, the correct economic policies would lower the curve for a more favorable tradeoff, rather than simply trying to find the "best" combination of inflation and unemployment.

Some of the policies suggested to shift the Phillips curve down or to the left include improving the workings of the labor market by increasing information available about job openings, increasing training of labor for skills in short supply, easing the pain and cost of changing jobs, reducing the minimum wage, and reducing the bargaining strength of labor unions.

Monetarists and the Phillips curve

The monetarists take an even more radical view of the Phillips curve. They say the tradeoff is a short-run effect. To see the longer-run effect, the inflation and unemployment data must be examined from 1960 to 1975. The long-run Phillips curve is vertical—that is, there exists no long-run tradeoff (see alternative 2 in Figure 8). In other words, there is no *direct* relation between inflation and unemployment. They maintain that for whatever reason 5 to 6% unemployment now appears "natural" for the U.S. economy. This natural rate may be changed by the same policies suggested in the previous sections of this chapter. However,

given any structure of the economy, the natural rate of unemployment will prevail.

The short-run Phillips curve then will reappear if economic policy is used to try to change the rate of unemployment. If the economy is stimulated to reduce the unemployment rate, an initial reduction in unemployment would result with only a slight increase in inflation. However, workers would soon recognize that inflation had increased. They would bargain for higher wages to protect their purchasing power. The higher wages will increase unemployment back to the natural rate. Only now, the rate of inflation will be higher. We have returned to the vertical long-run Phillips curve at a point higher than the one from which we started.

Inflationary recession

Figure 8 indicates that in the American economy inflation and unemployment seem to be growing apace. But, as we have seen in our previous discussions of free market economic theory, this is not supposed to happen. Price rises are supposed to help lift the economy toward full employment, not drag it down. An "inflationary recession" would seem to be a contradiction in terms. Perhaps it is. A new word was coined for this condition—"stagflation." **Stagflation** indicates an increase in inflation with a simultaneous decrease in productivity and employment. The word probably was a media creation rather than economic in origin. Whether the concept will survive in economics is questionable. However, the dual problems of inflation and unemployment were present in the mid-1970s and the word was used in some circles to describe the condition.

How can high inflation and high unemployment go hand in hand in the economy? Actually, we have already partially answered this question in our previous discussion of types of inflation and methods for fighting them. Market power would seem to be a basic cause of this phenomenon.

As we have seen, some firms and industries are powerful enough to raise prices almost regardless of the competitive market system. Some labor unions are powerful enough to dictate wage increases not based on increased productivity. This results in a wage-price inflation spiral—a cost-push inflation. These economically unjustifiable increases in prices and wages do not lead to higher employment, as justifiable increases might.

Another cause of inflationary recession lies in the changing nature of the American labor force. More inexperienced and part-time workers are coming into the labor force. Untrained and unskilled teenagers find it difficult to find work in an economy dependent upon skilled labor. More women are entering the job market, either as primary wage earners or, more often, as second-income workers. For example, in 1976, women constituted 40% of the United States labor force. The labor force itself has increased in size and volatility, thus leading to "structural unemployment." The economy cannot easily and at once absorb all the potential workers seeking employment.

Another source of the problem lies in government regulations. Minimum wage laws are designed to protect workers from being exploited. But they may also contribute to unemployment by discouraging employment of young and unskilled workers. Employers may be reluctant to pay the legal minimum rate for certain kinds of menial and unskilled labor. Consequently, such jobs may remain unfilled. Other government regulations, such as farm-price supports, transportation rate regulations, tariff regulations, and so on, also contribute to high prices.

Fighting inflationary recession What can be done to fight the economic trend toward inflationary recession? In short, what can be done to lower the Phillips curve?

One answer, obviously, is to reduce the market power of giant industries and big labor. New antimonopoly legislation or more vigorous enforcement of present laws may be brought into play. Labor itself might be subjected to certain restrictions of the antimonopoly laws. Collective bargaining might be confined to the local level rather than be carried out at the national level. This might help lessen the inflationary impact of wage increases. Or, of course, strict controls on wages and prices might be enacted by government decree.

We have already discussed some of the problems inherent in wage and price controls. Antimonopoly restrictions on business and labor also have drawbacks. For example,

breaking up large industries could lead to a loss of economy of scale in such industries. This, in turn, could lead to lower productivity and loss of jobs. Curtailment of the power of labor could lead to excessively low wages and longer working hours. This could lead to excessively low purchasing power and high unemployment. Local-level collective bargaining could lead to local "wildcat" strikes and chaotic national labor-management relations. If such devices are used at all, they must be used with a great deal of discretion.

Other devices have been suggested to deal with the problems of government regulations and the changing labor force (structural unemployment). Government price-fixing regulations could be redrawn to prevent rather than encourage excessive price rises. The labor force problem might be attacked directly by manpower-training programs designed to develop skills needed in modern economies. Transportation might be improved to facilitate access to job-producing areas. Tax incentives might be given to business and industries for job-producing expansion and on-the-job training. The government itself might become the employer of last resort.

Cushioning the effects of inflation

As we have noted, the causes of inflation and stagflation are varied and complex, and often overlapping. As we have also seen, the fight against them requires measures, monetary and fiscal, that are likewise varied, complex, and overlapping. We have speculated that the fight will never be completely won. But we have seen that the economy must continue to endeavor to check inflationary pressures. Runaway inflation can destroy the economy and perhaps society itself.

In fact, persistent, high inflation is possibly the leading economic problem of the 1970s. Figure 9 shows the CPI and WPI for the period 1969 to April, 1977. There has been a continual rise in prices during this period. The WPI rose at a 3.9% rate from January of 1969 to October, 1972. The rapid rise began in October and

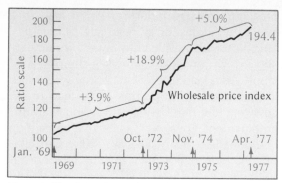
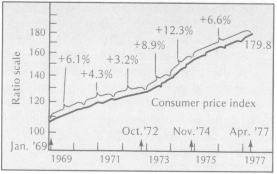

Figure 9 The CPI and WPI shown for a recent period, 1969–1977 (where 1967 = 100). Percentages are annual rates of change for periods indicated. Note very high rates of inflation in 1973–1974. (Source: Federal Reserve Bank of St. Louis.)

lasted a little over two years to November, 1974. The inflation rate was 18.9% as measured by the WPI. After November, the inflation rate fell to 5.0%.

The consumer price index followed a similar pattern. From 1969 to the end of 1972, the rise in the CPI varied from 3.2% to 6.1%. During 1973, the inflation rate reached 8.9% and in 1974, double-digit inflation was reached with a 12.3% rise in prices as measured by the CPI. From the end of 1974, the price increase has been 6.6%.

Inflation rates in the second half of the 1970s were lower than in the first half. After all, 5% inflation as measured by the WPI or 6.6% as measured by the CPI seems tame after 12 to 18% earlier. However, even these rates of inflation can result in large price changes if allowed to persist. Consider Table 2, where prices are measured in 1977 and again in the year 2022 with a 5% inflation during the entire 45-year period. A loaf of bread which costs 25 cents in 1977 would sell for $2.25 in 2022. A $35,000 house would sell for over $300,000. A small car selling for a little over $3,000 would carry a price tag of $28,527 in 2022, enough to buy a luxurious customized car in 1977. Even at 5% inflation can erode purchasing power unless incomes rise as well.

As we know, the effects of anticipated inflation can be mitigated by manipulation of terms of loans between borrower and lender. The effects may also be cushioned by investment in commodities which are likely to in-

crease in value faster than the rate of inflation. For example, you might gamble on hoarding gold, or dash out and purchase a Rembrandt or two. For most of us, however, such devices are something less than realistic.

Table 2
Projection of 5% Inflation over the 45-Year Period 1977–2022

Item	Beginning level*	After 45 years
Grocery Items		
bread (1 lb. loaf)	$ .25	$ 2.25
2% milk (1 gallon)	1.39	12.49
A-large eggs (1 dozen)	.85	7.64
ground beef (1 lb.)	.99	8.90
whole fryer (1 lb.)	.49	4.40
round steak (1 lb.)	1.49	13.39
cabbage (1 lb.)	.33	2.97
potatoes (1 lb.)	.13	1.17
canned tomatoes (16 oz.)	.35	3.14
peanut butter (28 oz.)	1.35	12.13
butter (1 lb.)	1.25	11.23
Clothing		
man's suit	$ 85.00	$ 763.73
man's coat (all weather)	60.00	539.10
man's dress shoes	25.00	224.63
woman's slacks	14.00	125.79
woman's dress	30.00	269.55
woman's coat (all weather)	39.00	350.42
woman's dress shoes	16.99	152.66
Housing		
new house	$34,980	$314,296
1 bedroom apartment	135/ month	1,213/ month
Automobile		
Pinto	$ 3,175	$ 28,527
Malibu coupe	4,588	41,223
regular gas (1 gallon)	.599	5.38

*St. Louis prices in early 1977.
Source: Federal Reserve Bank of St. Louis.

Viewpoint
Inflation in the 1970s

In 1972, the inflation rate in the United States was 3%. In 1973, it jumped to 9%, and in 1974, to 12%. More recently it has fallen from its 1974–1975 double-digit figure, but it is still well above the 1972 level. Why has it been so difficult to deal with inflation in the 1970s?

Many economists suggest that one reason for the difficulty is that the inflation of the early and mid-1970s was not really home grown. They point out that the usual domestic causes of inflation—big federal deficits, loose money policies, wages rising faster than productivity, and unwarranted price increases—were only part of the reason. The $14 billion deficit in fiscal 1973, for example, was large but not monstrous. Money growth was 9%—high but not unreasonably so. Wages actually lagged behind price increases, and corporate profits were by no means excessive.

The major causes of the inflation of this period, say many economists, are to be found in the international sector, not the domestic. First, of course, was the unprecedented quadrupling of world crude oil prices. All fuel-related prices had subsequently to be increased. Also, there was a vast increase in world demand for food. American surplus food stocks, especially grain, were quickly exhausted (in addition, the American harvest of 1974 was one of the worst in years), thus putting increased pressure on domestic food prices. A third international factor was the 1971–1973 dollar depreciation, which increased the cost of imports and the demand for exports—both of which contributed to higher domestic prices.

In the later 1970s these international factors disappeared or became less significant. But their legacy lingers on as inflationary pressures persist throughout the economy. These international factors led to a cost-push spiral: wages seeking to "catch up" to an inflation they did not cause and from prices continuing to rise to compensate for increased costs initiated by world economic conditions.

Economists also point out that inflation in the 1970s is difficult to deal with because, domestically, its major source is cost push, not demand pull. Fiscal and monetary controls on demand have little effect on cost-push inflation. In fact, stringent fiscal policies in the form of wage and price controls were tried in 1971–1973 and failed to do much to stem the inflationary tide. Recent economic trends in the United States have led many economists to conclude that slack demand—even a recession—whether or not due to government intervention in the economy has very little effect in checking wage hikes and holding down general prices.

To deal with the kind of cost-push inflation prevalent in the 1970s, some economists advocate a stick approach, others a carrot. Some advocate a penalty if a company raises wages or prices by amounts exceeding national guidelines. Beyond a certain point, a percentage of its wage costs would not be tax deductible. The higher the wage costs go, the higher would go the nondeductible percentage, which would soon make it impracticable for the businessman to pass along the higher costs in the form of higher prices for his products.

Other economists would enforce wage and price guidelines through incentives rather than penalties. Employers who stayed within nationally set guidelines would have their Social Security payroll tax reduced by a certain percentage, with taxes from general revenues being used to reimburse the Social Security system. Employees of such firms would also pay reduced Social Security taxes. The government would guarantee that if inspite of this voluntary staying within set guidelines the consumer price index rose above a certain percentage, the participants in the plan would receive a tax rebate.

Other schemes for dealing directly with cost push have been advanced ranging from stockpiling of raw materials to various other combinations of tax incentives and penalties. All such plans, of course, face formidable political and economic obstacles. The most important thing, however, is that economists are now coming to see that inflation in the 1970s is not simply or wholly the same as earlier inflations. When even recession, the traditional if extreme cure for inflation, fails to work, new solutions must be sought. We learned in the 1970s, for example, that recession causes much more loss in productive output than gain in price stability.

Indexing A more formal and realistic device to cushion the effects of inflation is the use of indexing. *With a system of indexing, all prices and wages would be adjusted at frequent intervals to account for changes in the price level.* In this way no one would gain or lose from inflation.

A partial system of indexing is the use of so-called "escalator clauses." Many labor contracts have such clauses and they are known as Cost of Living Adjustments (COLA). They call for automatic wage increases as prices increase throughout the duration of the contract. Some lending institutions tie loan payments rates to price-level changes throughout the term of the loan. Pension benefits and insurance dividends may also be tied to a cost of living index. It has been suggested that Social Security and welfare benefits also be indexed.

Presently, all of these payments are fixed in dollar amounts. Loan repayments are made in a series of pre-agreed payments. Pensions and Social Security pay so much per month. If the general price level rises, the fixed amount per month purchases less and the recipient suffers. Therefore, an index such as the consumer price index would be used to adjust the payment. If the CPI increased by 5%, the monthly benefit would increase by 5% also. The labor contracts with COLAs already do just that.

Some economists have suggested that indexing should be expanded to all segments of the economy. Many feel that some sort of indexing system should be applied to at least the large and vital industries. Much of the economy's wage rate would then rise or fall according to the rise or fall in the cost of living index or some other agreed-upon measurement.

There have also been suggestions for tying the economy's tax structure to some comprehensive measure of living costs. When costs rise, the tax rate would automatically be lowered. As we have seen, government spending contributes greatly to inflationary pressure. The threat of lower tax income might act as a restraint on government spending, according to proponents of indexing, and thereby cushion the effects of inflation.

Summary

Inflation and unemployment are two forms of economic instability which may be interrelated in such a way that solution of one problem makes the other problem worse.

In order to measure and calculate inflation rates, prices in general are represented by a price index. A base period is chosen and prices relative to the base period make up the index. Two widely used indices are the consumer price index (CPI) and the wholesale price index (WPI).

Inflation is a continuing rise in the general level of prices. Inflations are categorized by several schemes. One is by the speed of the price increase. Creeping inflation represents very slow increases such as 1 to 3% annually. Double-digit inflation refers to inflation rates of 10 to 99% annually. Hyperinflation refers to very rapid rates of price increase.

Inflation may also be categorized by its causes. One type of inflation is demand-pull inflation. Demand-pull inflation is caused by the members of the economy trying to purchase more than the economy can produce, thereby bidding up prices.

Cost-push inflation is caused by the ability of monopoly suppliers of factors of production raising their prices, which increases costs; the result is higher prices to the consumer.

Structural inflation is caused by shortages in selected markets due to problems related primarily to that particular market.

Inflation is undesirable in that it redistributes income unfairly. The redistribution is in favor of debtors at the expense of creditors (when unanticipated), in favor of producers at the expense of those on fixed incomes, and in favor of the government at the expense of almost everyone. Inflation often leads people to reduce their savings and spend now—before their purchasing power is eroded.

Demand-pull inflation may be countered by reducing the excess demand. This may be done by reducing the money supply or by using a restrictive fiscal policy position.

Cost-push inflation is more difficult to overcome. It would be desirable to reduce monopoly power so that costs cannot be increased. Alternatively, either of two incomes policies could be used: (1) wage-price guidelines or (2) wage-price controls, which is a very drastic step.

Structural inflation will eventually work itself out. Stockpiling of key raw materials could lessen the effects. If the problem is long term, such as the energy problem, additional efforts to solve the problem may be required.

Unemployment results when a person is in the labor force but is unable to find employment in jobs at his skill level.

Frictional unemployment results when people are in the process of changing jobs. They are between jobs, sometimes voluntarily.

Structural unemployment results when there is a mismatch between the jobs available and the persons available for work. There may be geographical, skill, age, or sex reasons for the persons not being suited for the jobs.

Cyclical unemployment results when there is a general lack of demand such as occurs at the trough of the business cycle.

Full employment does not mean that all members of the labor market are employed since there will always be some frictional unemployment in even the smoothest running economy. Thus 95 to 96% of the labor force employed represents "full employment."

Expansionary fiscal policy—that is, increased government spending or decreased taxation—may be used to reduce unemployment of a cyclical nature. The lags in implementing fiscal policy may restrict its use to more severe cases of cyclical unemployment.

Expansionary monetary policy may serve to reduce the amount of cyclical unemployment.

The Phillips curve shows the tradeoff between inflation and unemployment. High rates of inflation and low unemployment are associated and vice versa. The monetarist school of economists points out that the long-run Phillips curve may be vertical above a natural rate of unemployment—that is, there is no true tradeoff.

Stagflation is a term applied to the simultaneous existence of inflation and cyclical unemployment—it could also be called inflationary recession.

Indexing is a means of cushioning the problems of inflation without getting rid of the inflation. Indexing would allow the prices stated in long-term contracts to be adjusted as inflation proceeds.

Unemployment in the 1970s has not fit the Phillips curve hypothesis. There has been an expansion of jobs available but the labor force has grown very rapidly. As a result, joblessness remains high, especially among specific groups such as women, teenagers, and blacks. Some economists say that the high unemployment of the 1970s is deceptive; the rate of unemployment for heads of households is not excessively high.

Key Words and Phrases

- **inflation**   a long-term rise in the general price level of goods and services.
- **deflation**   a lowering of the general price level; the opposite of inflation.
- **price index**   a number computed to measure the change in the overall level of prices; one year of the index is chosen as base 100.
- **consumer price index**   a measure of the level of prices for a fixed market basket of goods and services thought to be purchased by a typical working-class American family.
- **wholesale price index**   an index used to show the level and changes in the level of prices for a selected group of basic commodities at wholesale.
- **creeping inflation**   a rise in the general price level at very low rates such as 1 to 3% per year.
- **double-digit inflation**   a rise in the general price level at rates greater than 10% per year but less than 100% per year.
- **hyperinflation**   a rise in the general price level at extremely rapid rates; any rate above 100% per year would certainly be called hyperinflation.
- **demand-pull inflation**   a rise in the general price level caused by purchasers trying to obtain more goods and services than the economy is capable of producing.
- **cost-push inflation**   a rise in the general price level caused by increases in the costs of production passed along as higher prices.
- **wage-push inflation**   a rise in the general price level caused by wages rising faster than labor productivity, thereby increasing costs which are passed to consumers as higher prices; a form of cost-push inflation.

- **price-push inflation** a rise in the general price level caused by suppliers using monopoly powers to raise the cost of raw materials and intermediate goods, whose costs are passed on as higher prices; a form of cost-push inflation.

- **structural inflation** a rise in the general price level caused by shortages in some areas of production with resulting higher prices.

- **incomes policies** nominally, a cooperative effort by employers, labor, and government to reduce cost-push inflation by matching wage increases to productivity increases; usually, the term becomes another name for wage and price controls.

- **wage and price guidelines** a voluntary program to hold wage and price hikes within some specified guideposts; a form of incomes policies.

- **frictional unemployment** unemployment, often voluntary, which results when a worker leaves a job or a new worker enters the labor market; it lasts until a new, perhaps better job is found.

- **structural unemployment** unemployment which results when one industry, one occupation, or one region of the country faces declining demand even though the economy as a whole is operating close to full employment. Structural unemployment may persist due to discrimination, immobility of the labor, or the need to retrain labor.

- **cyclical unemployment** unemployment resulting from a general loss of demand for output and therefore for labor. The name derives from the idea that the trough of a business cycle produces this kind of unemployment.

- **Phillips curve** a curve which relates the rate of inflation to the level of unemployment. The relationship is inverse—meaning that high rates of inflation are associated with low unemployment and vice versa.

- **stagflation** a term coined by the press rather than economists which refers to the simultaneous presence of unemployment and inflation, a condition previously thought impossible; inflationary recession.

- **indexing** a system used to adjust agreements or contracts involving money so that the payment rises as the general price level rises.

- **underemployed** the condition where a person holds a job with requirements that are far below the level of skills of that person; a brain surgeon driving a taxi would be an example.

Questions for Review

1. Why does frictional unemployment remain at about the same level at all times? Why does the level of cyclical unemployment change?

2. How can monopoly power raise prices?

3. Does the level of prices affect the distribution of income? How?

4. Why is it hard to have both stable prices and full employment?

5. Suggest some ways to shift the Phillips curve downward.

6. Why are we less concerned about unused land or idle machinery? Why the concern about unemployed labor?

7. List the three types of unemployment. How would you attack each of them?

8. Can you think of some ways to reduce structural unemployment? Would your suggestions be likely to be enacted into law by Congress?

9. Would price controls prevent inflation? Why or why not? What would happen with controls in force?

10. What is an incomes policy? Why are wage-price guidelines suggested by some economists?

17

The Theory of Growth

The importance of growth to a nation's economy is almost self-evident. With economic growth a nation can provide employment for its labor force and an increased standard of living for all its people. Without growth, a nation's economy may eventually stagnate, and its people will more likely suffer social and economic poverty.

In this chapter we will take a close look at the phenomenon of economic growth. We will see how economists have developed various theories to explain growth. We will discuss the various determinants of economic growth. And we will see that although growth is beneficial to a nation's economic health, it also entails economic problems to be solved and, sometimes, a social price to be paid.

Defining & measuring economic growth

We can define **economic growth** as the increase over a period of time in an economy's total production possibilities for generating goods and services. Notice that our definition says *production possibilities* rather than *actual production*. There is a good reason for this: an economy recovering from a business cycle trough (a recession) will greatly increase its output of goods and services. But this is not economic growth. To qualify as economic growth, an economy's capacity—that is, its production possibilities—must expand.

More specifically, economic growth is the increase at full employment in economic output as measured by the economy's gross national product (GNP). For ease of measurement, growth is therefore the dollar value of the nation's total output of goods and services.

However, when we use GNP as a measure of growth, we must note that we are speaking of *real* GNP, not *money* GNP. Recall that $GNP = PQ$, where P is the price level and Q quantity of output. If inflation occurs, P may increase enough to raise GNP even though Q remains constant or even decreases. This represents a rise in money GNP, not real GNP. Real GNP measures goods and services produced and is not affected by inflation. If money GNP

increases one year by 4% over the previous year, and if inflation has also increased prices by 4%, then real GNP has not increased at all.

Some economists prefer to define economic growth as *the increase in real GNP per capita*. Per capita GNP means that the economy's gross national product is measured in terms of the number of people participating in the economy. For example, if the value of a nation's GNP is X number of dollars, that X would have a much different meaning for a nation of ten million people, say, than a nation of one-hundred million people. The per capita GNP of the smaller nation would be ten times as great as that of the larger nation, even though the actual dollar value GNP was the same for both nations. To put it another way, if the population of a country increases faster than does its output of goods and services, its per capita GNP and standard of living will decline. The output (GNP) may increase, but there will be more people sharing the increase; therefore, per capita GNP will actually decline.

Growth measured as increases in real GNP is quite adequate for measuring an economy's ability to expand. Growth measured by per capita increase in GNP, however, is a better guide to understanding a nation's standard of living and for comparing it to that of other nations.

Figure 1 illustrates some important points about economic growth. Suppose a nation produces two kinds of products, manufactured and agricultural. The production possibilities frontier is the curved line showing the maximum amount of both products the economy can produce. Suppose that initially the production frontier is as shown in curve 1 in Figure 1. This curve shows the maximum output of the economy at a given time for any and all combinations of agricultural and manufactured products. If growth occurs, the production frontier shifts outward—that is, to the right on the graph to curve 2. The economy can now produce more agricultural products or more manufactured products or more of both. There is an increase in potential GNP.

But suppose the economy is operating at point A, below the initial production frontier. The economy is not producing all that it

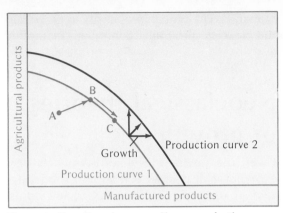

Figure 1 Growth only occurs if our production curve moves outward to the right. Point A shows underemployed resources; however, a move from point A to point B is not growth, because a movement from less than full employment to full employment is not growth. Also, a movement from point B to point C is not growth; it is only a change in our "production mix." Growth only occurs when a new production possibilities curve (such as curve 2) can be drawn farther to the right.

can—it may be in a recession. There are unemployed resources. More goods and services will be obtained if the economy moves from point A to point B. However, this is not growth since all that is happening is that idle resources are being used. Real economic growth can occur only if the economy is already operating at full capacity.

Consider also movement from point B to point C. The economy is operating at full employment at both points. In moving from point B to point C, there is merely a change in the product mixture to include more manufactured goods and fewer agricultural goods. There is a shift of resources from agriculture to manufacturing. However, since the maximum output of the economy has not changed, there has not been any real economic growth. We sometimes confuse either a return to full employment or a change in the product mix from agriculture to manufactures with growth.

Classical theories of growth

Three British economists, Adam Smith (1723–1790), David Ricardo (1772–1823), and Thomas Malthus (1766–1834), were the principal contributors to classical theory of economic growth. Basically, all three of these men viewed society's potential for economic growth as limited. Each felt that economic growth had natural boundaries beyond which society could never evolve. These limits were based on three of the four inputs to production: labor, capital, and natural resources (land).

Adam Smith

For Adam Smith, natural resources determined the limit of economic growth. Until resources were depleted, growth would occur through the processes of *division of labor* and *specialization*. That is, output per worker would increase as workers specialized in making various segments of products rather than in producing a complete product. As productivity increased to meet expanding markets, wages and profits would rise and economic growth would continue until raw materials were exhausted.

David Ricardo

For Ricardo, economic growth was limited by the concept of *diminishing returns*. Each nation has a fixed amount of land to draw on for its wealth. As more work units are applied to the land, more production is drawn from it for distribution among the population. But after a certain point, each additional work unit applied to the land produces less income per unit than did each of the earlier (fewer) units. The law of diminishing returns sets in to limit economic growth. Figure 2 illustrates the effect of diminishing returns on production frontiers. Successive addition of labor causes outward shifts in the production possibilities curve, but the size of the shift gets smaller and smaller.

Ricardo also stressed the importance of *capital accumulation* (savings for investment) to economic growth. The capitalist must accumulate large sums of money from his profits to invest in capital so that production possibilities increase. But this too, according to Ricardo, was subject to the law of diminishing returns. At first, each unit of invested capital would produce a given amount of profit from the land. But as more and more capital units were invested, each additional unit would begin to

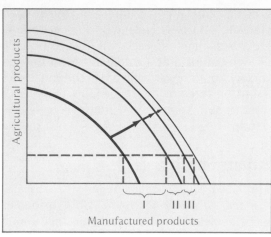

Figure 2 Growth with diminishing returns. Each increase is smaller than the last: I > II > III > . . . Eventually, there is little or no increase.

return a smaller profit. Just as additional workers on the land caused output per worker to decline, so additional investment would cause profit per investment unit to decline. As output per worker (and hence wages) and profits continued to decline, a point would be reached where incentive to work and invest would entirely disappear. Economic growth must inevitably cease because of the law of diminishing returns.

Thomas Malthus

Malthus was even more pessimistic about the possibility of continued economic growth. For him, the forces of obstruction against growth were at work even before the law of diminishing returns sets in. Because the initial stage of prosperity caused wages to rise, workers tended to have more children at this stage of the cycle. They thus added more and more workers to the land, hastening the onset of diminishing returns.

But this was not all of the problem. Malthus believed that food production grew in an *arithmetic* series—1 unit, 2 units, 3 units, 4 units, and so on. Population, however, grew *geometrically*—2 people, 4 people, 8 people, 16 people, and so on. In other words, food production cannot (after an initial prosperity period) keep up with population growth. War, famine, and disease may temporarily check population growth, but eventually poverty must be the condition for the majority of

humanity. The human propensity to propagate the species prohibits continued economic growth.

Neoclassical theories of growth

Given the pessimistic views of the classical economists, it is little wonder that economics came to be known, in Thomas Carlyle's words, as "the dismal science." But the economic expansion of the Industrial Revolution gave rise to a more hopeful view of economic potential. By around the 1870s, economists began to see evidence that the classical theories of growth (and decline) had been perhaps unnecessarily pessimistic. The Industrial Revolution had brought sustained growth to industrial economies, despite normal depletion of resources and high rates of population growth. A new group of theorists, today known as the neoclassical economists, arose to explain this unexpected phenomenon. Their theories emphasized two growth factors generally neglected by the classicists: the *role of technology* and the *role of savings*.

Technology and savings

Technology—new inventions that increase labor output—helped hold at bay the law of diminishing returns. Adding to the labor force did not necessarily mean that there would be more and more people competing for a piece of a limited economic pie. Technology would increase the size of the pie itself. More people, true. But a bigger pie to share, thanks to production-increasing inventions.

In addition, because increased production means higher wages, more people come to earn wages in excess of their need for present consumption. They are able to save money and invest it in further facilities for production. And investment is a prerequisite of economic growth. Thus capitalists and workers alike contribute to capital accumulation for investment. Increased investment and new technology go hand in hand to sustain economic growth.

Business cycles and growth

Of course, the neoclassical economists were aware that even a sustained growth economy did not work perfectly. There were still business cycles to contend with. Periods of economic instability were bound to occur. But, in general, the neoclassicists considered business cycles as self-correcting adjustments to the process of economic growth. Economic instability did, in turn, serve to reduce economic growth.

Joseph Schumpeter (1883–1950) developed the idea that economic growth caused economic instability in the form of business cycles. (Karl Marx had said much the same thing about 75 years earlier.) Schumpeter thought inventions happened on a fairly regular basis. However, new inventions could not always be readily put to use. Usefulness was developed through *innovation*, which took known inventions and made them practical. Schumpeter thought that innovation would tend to be bunched in time since one development in technology led to another. During a period of innovation, the economy would operate at full speed as everyone rushed to utilize the new technology. However, once this rush was over, there would be little to stimulate the economy till the next innovative period would arrive. Thus there would be a recession or depression between the peaks of investment activity. The innovations would lead to growth, but also to ups and downs in the economy.

The theory of secular stagnation

The Great Depression of the 1930s brought with it a prolonged no-growth economy. A group of economists, led by Alvin Hansen of Harvard University, advanced a new theory to explain this phenomenon—the theory of *secular stagnation*. Hansen and his colleagues believed that the disappearance of America's western frontier, our relatively low population growth, and the fact that science and technology were not producing new ideas had caused the economy to stagnate. People, they said, must learn to live without a constantly expanding economy. They must learn to accept low growth or even no-growth, not just as a possibility but as an inevitability. Joseph Schumpeter further added that the role the

entrepreneur could play was shrinking as people changed their values. As the entrepreneur "disappeared," growth would decline.

Ultimately, John Maynard Keynes provided an alternative, accurate explanation of why economic growth ceased during the 1930s. The Great Depression started out as an economic downturn into a trough of a business cycle. As output declined, the level of income fell. Consumption and saving also fell, since low income, not the high interest rate available, was the more compelling force in the consumers' view. With saving reduced, funds for investment became scarce. The only way out was to increase income directly. Since neither the unemployed consumer nor the profitless businessman was in a position to increase spending and output, someone else, perhaps the government, would have to increase expenditures. But the Great Depression lasted so long because government policies were such as to reinforce the trough, rather than lift up the economy. When the government did step in with increased fiscal expenditures, it wasn't enough. The depression ended when World War II began, because then the government did greatly increase its expenditures—on military equipment.

Eventually, World War II also acted as a spur to further innovation. The age of atomic energy, jet propulsion, and television began. A decade later saw such innovations as the transistor, satellites and space rockets, and the computer. *The years from 1946 to 1970 were marked by the greatest economic growth in Western history.* Much of this growth was provided by a multitude of innovations, which originated mostly in the United States. The theory of secular stagnation was buried! Tables 1 and 2 summarize the development of growth theories.

Table 1
Summary of Growth Theory Contributions

Component aiding growth	Contributor
Natural resources & labor	Predecessors of Smith
Division of labor & specialization	Adam Smith
Capital accumulation	David Ricardo
Technology & innovation	Neoclassical economists
Saving	Neoclassical economists

Table 2
Summary of Barriers to Growth

Barrier	Contributor
Natural resource limits	Adam Smith
Diminishing returns	David Ricardo
Expanding population	Thomas Malthus
Economic instability	Classicists; Karl Marx; Joseph Schumpeter
Demise of entrepreneur	Joseph Schumpeter

Full-employment growth

As we have noted, economic growth involves an increase in output at the same time that the economy is fully utilizing its resources. One of the key resources is, of course, labor. Our real-growth economy should also be a full-employment economy. Furthermore, modern economists are particularly concerned with constructing a model for full-employment growth without resorting to stimulating the economy through war or government intervention. Both of these recourses are too inherently unstable. Some data for such a hypothetical economy are shown in Table 3.

Suppose we start out with full-employment output (GNP) equalling $1,000. Historically, about 5% of income is saved. That is, the average propensity to save (APS) is .05. During the first year in our example, this would result in saving of $50.00 for the economy. Let us assume that all saving is invested; therefore, $50 in new capital is created. To see how much growth occurs as a result of the new capital, we need to examine the *capital/output* (*K/O*)

ratio, which is the ratio of capital required to produce a unit of output. This ratio is usually stated as approximately three-to-one for the United States. That is, three dollars of capital is required to produce one dollar of output. In other words, the $50 of new capacity will produce about one-third as much new income, or $16.67. The dollar amount of growth is $16.67. Therefore, the potential GNP for the next year is $1016.67.

If growth is sustained, this output will generate saving in the amount of $50.83. To maintain full employment, investment must also increase to $50.83. But suppose businessmen decided to invest the same as last year, only $50.00. This would mean less than full employment, since saving (income not spent) would exceed investment. What is more, the problem the following year would be worse, since the $50 would add to capacity even though there is unemployment. Businessmen would see no need to invest even more during year 3, because unemployed workers are not able to buy their products and there is already excess capacity.

We are now ready to see what is required to maintain a stable full-employment growth path. The rate of increase in the potential output must be matched by the rate of increase in investment. This we may call the full-employment growth rate:

$$\text{Full-employment growth rate} = \frac{\text{APS}}{\text{K/O ratio}}.$$

Using the numbers in our example, full-employment growth rate = .05/3 = 1.67%. Thus we see that if potential output increases by 1.67% each year, investment and actual demand must grow by 1.67% also or full employment will not be maintained without intervention by government. If investment and demand increase appropriately, by the sixth year potential GNP will rise to $1086.14.

This simple model does not tell us *how* or *why* businessmen would increase investment. (Nor does it consider noneconomic or a large number of other economic variables which may affect growth.) It does illustrate the *compound nature* of growth. Growth may proceed at a constant 1.67% rate, but the amount of increase is larger at each round. Look again at

Table 3
Hypothetical Economy Growing from Initial GNP of $1,000

Year	Full Employment Output	Saving = Investment = Increased capital (APS = .05)	Increase in output because of increase in capital (K/O ratio = 3)
1	$1000.00	$50.00	$16.67
2	1016.67	50.83	16.94
3	1033.61	51.68	17.22
4	1050.83	52.54	17.51
5	1068.34	53.41	17.80
6	1086.14	54.30	18.10

Table 3. The increase in potential income between years 1 and 2 is $16.67. From year 5 to year 6, the increase is $17.80. The 1.67% is applied to income of $1068.34 to obtain $17.80 after year 5. Because income in year 5 is larger, the increase is larger even though the growth rate remains the same.

Suppose we have two economies, both initially identical in terms of GNP. However, one is growing at 3% annually while the other is growing at 4% annually. The first would double in size in 35 years. The second would double in size in only 18 years and would double that level again by the time the first had doubled in size only once. Or consider a very large economy such as that of the United States growing at 3% annually while some small economy is growing at 5%. The small economy's GNP would soon reach and then surpass that of the United States.

Determinants of economic growth

In our discussion of various theories of growth, we have paid passing attention to the major sources of growth: human resources (population); capital accumulation for investment; changes in technology and economic structure; natural resources; and economic stability. Let us now take a further and more detailed look at these sources.

Human resources

Population quantity The size of a nation's population can itself be a source of economic growth. All else being equal, the greater the population—or more precisely, the labor force—the greater will be the nation's productive capacity. More workers means more production—and more capacity to consume production.

In the United States, for example, immigration and a growing native population greatly contributed to the nation's economic growth. A large and growing population was needed to exploit our vast expanse of unused land and natural resources. The economy grew apace with the westward expansion of the nation's labor force. And, of course, as the labor force grew, so did the "nonproductive" population—that is, children, the elderly, and other members of the population who may be said to consume more than they produce. In the United States, increased output through specialization of labor and ready access to natural resources kept pace with the expanding population and kept the economy growing.

But, as we have seen, more labor added to a fixed amount of land and capital will sooner or later reach the point of diminishing returns. Even the United States, with all its vast resources, is not immune to this economic phenomenon. What can be done to counteract this tendency toward diminishing returns in labor productivity? One important answer lies in the improvement of population quality.

Population quality Education and health are the two major determinants of population (labor) quality. Investment in education and health is investment in the basic source of all wealth—*human capital*. None of us is born knowing how to make a living. We must be educated and trained in the skills necessary for us to contribute to the economy's productivity and hence to partake of its goods and services. Whether a person learns through formal education or on-the-job training or a combination of both, it is evident that a skilled worker will outproduce an unskilled worker. A nation's growth depends not only on the quantity of its labor force, but equally or even more on its quality. Quality can be obtained and maintained only if a nation invests and continues to invest in the education and training of its people.

The law of diminishing labor returns can also be kept at bay by investment in the health of a nation's labor force. A healthy worker will outproduce a sickly worker. Investment in good nutrition and prevention and control of disease will produce dividends in greater output per worker and, of course, in the social stability of the nation as a whole. The good health, physical and mental, of an economy's work force—laborer and executive alike—is a prerequisite for sustained economic growth.

Capital accumulation

The accumulation of capital for investment in the economy's productive capacity is impera-

Economic Thinker
David Ricardo

In the years following publication of Adam Smith's *The Wealth of Nations*, most economic and social thinkers were convinced that this was the best of all possible worlds, or, despite the poverty they saw around them, soon would be. Socialist utopians and conservative industrialists were alike in these beliefs that reason and the natural laws of economic progress would prevail in an ever-growing spiral of economic bounty for all. Then along came two hitherto unknown gentlemen who would forever shatter this general innocence. One was Thomas Malthus, the theorist of population growth. The other was his contemporary and friend, David Ricardo.

Ricardo was born in England in 1772, of Dutch-Jewish parentage. His father was a broker on the London Stock Exchange and young David followed him into the brokerage business. By the time he was 25, he had amassed a fortune large enough to enable him to devote most of his time to the study of economic theories and their application to the England of his time. In 1817, he published his *Principles of Political Economy and Taxation*. In this monumental work he set forth the principles and theories that were to become almost synonymous with what has today become known as the classical school of economics.

But Ricardo's theories did not lead him to the optimistic conclusions of Adam Smith. Ricardo posited an "iron law of wages" which purported to show that, all economic and social factors considered, no matter how prosperous the economy, wages could never rise above a bare subsistence level. Workers would never earn more than just enough to put roofs over their heads and food in their bellies. At this point they would fall prey to "the delights of domestic society," by which Ricardo meant they would sleep with their wives and produce children who would grow up to swell the ranks of workers and force wages down. Ricardo devoutly wished that workers, for their own welfare, would exercise "moral restraint" in such matters. But he was far too wise to believe that they would.

Capitalists, aside from the not inconsiderable fact that they lived better than wage earners, were not, in the long run, all that much better off. Their lot was to spend their days accumulating wealth to invest in further wealth-producing facilities to keep wage earners at least at a subsistence level. Competition would keep the capitalist's nose to the grindstone, and wage payments would forever cut into the capitalist's profits.

The landlord, for Ricardo, was the only real beneficiary of the prevailing law of economics. The landlord's income—rent—was not subject to competition. There is a finite amount of arable land, and the value of highly productive land does not compete with that of less productive land—it drives the value of the latter upward. The value of land, and hence the cost of food produced on the land, increased automatically. Workers must be paid enough to buy their necessary "crust of bread," the rising cost of which came out of the capitalist's profits. In the long run, only the landlord could truly inherit the earth.

Ricardo blamed no one for this state of affairs. Landlords were no more greedy than anyone else. They just happened to be the system's natural beneficiaries. But it is not surprising that Ricardo himself became the hero of Britain's rising industrialists. With the help of Ricardo's theories, and of Ricardo himself, they eventually succeeded in bringing about repeal of England's "Corn Laws," which had kept grain prices artificially high by high tariffs on imported grain. (Lower grain prices meant that lower wages could be paid for the subsistence of workers.) Thus Ricardo's theories became an important weapon in the fight for free trade among nations.

Ricardo carried on lively arguments with his good friend Thomas Malthus, with whom he disagreed about almost everything except his theories of population growth, and continued to expound his theories and conjectures until his death in 1823. His writings and the urbane and pleasant personality of the man himself did much to popularize the study of what was called in his day "political economy." His success in drawing theory from the economic world he saw about him and in applying theory to that world have led some to call him the father of modern economic studies. Most would agree that his work and its long-lasting influence place him among the greatest of economists.

tive to economic growth. Even the most skilled worker can produce little with bare hands. The need for tools and machines is obvious. And capital is needed to produce tools and machines.

Capital accumulation comes from that portion of a society's wealth that is saved—that is, the portion that is not spent on immediate consumption of goods and services. In the days of David Ricardo, capital accumulation came from the capitalist's profits. Today capital accumulation also depends on a nation's aggregate savings. The problem, of course, is how to accumulate enough savings to invest in economic growth.

A nation may attempt to force its citizens to save for capital investment. It may force reduction of immediate consumption by lowering or eliminating production of certain consumer products. Or, through monetary and fiscal policies, it may make the cost of such goods prohibitive. But such measures are difficult to take and enforce, especially in democratic nations. In poorer countries, consumption may already be so low that further reduction could result in starvation. Even in advanced industrialized economies, a certain level of consumption must be maintained as an incentive to produce. In general, all nations try to avoid forced saving for capital investment except as temporary expedients to meet temporary crises—for example, in wartime.

Capital accumulation may be increased by raising interest rates to encourage people to save. Here, too, however, caution is necessary. High interest rates to savers also mean high interest rates to those who borrow this money for capital investment. If rates rise too high, investment may become too costly for profitability. Investment may cease and economic growth come to a halt.

Government may take certain actions to help increase capital accumulation for investment. For example, it may offer tax incentives to those who invest. The device of tax reductions on corporate profits used to invest in new production capacity has been a powerful stimulant to capital accumulation in the United States and other industrial economies. The government may also channel tax funds directly into capital investment to maintain or increase economic growth. It may build roads, bridges, and other public facilities, for example. Or it may directly subsidize expansion and development of private industries. The government may simply attempt to stabilize the economy in order to reduce the risk to those who undertake capital formation.

An economy may also accumulate capital from outside sources. That is, it may borrow from foreign governmental or private sources. Of course, such funds must eventually be repaid and repayment may then contribute to a slowdown in economic growth. Sometimes, a nation may receive outside capital as a kind of donation. The donor country may wish to "buy" the political goodwill (and possibly the military assistance) of the recipient nation. In

Viewpoint
Government Ambush at Capital Gap?

Between 1965 and 1974, the United States economy witnessed an almost incredible capital accumulation of $1.6 trillion needed to turn out the goods and services demanded by the public. It is estimated that between 1975 and 1985, we will need the truly mind-boggling sum of $4.5 trillion to accomplish this task.

Where will this vast amount of money come from? For the most part, it will have to come from what have always been the principal sources of investment capital—the savings of the American consumers and the profits of American business.

What will happen if capital accumulation falls considerably below the needed sum? Some very unpleasant things, say most economists. The financial markets would be unable to finance the economy's expenditures at interest rates low enough to make expansion possible or even to maintain present growth rates. The economy would suffer from shortages and inflation, since business would not have enough capital to produce sufficient goods and services at reasonable prices. Because only the very strongest companies would likely win out in the struggle for scarce capital, smaller businesses would fail or be gobbled up by the giants. Social disorder would intensify because overall gains in the economy would be too thin to meet the needs and expectations of most of the general public.

Most economists agree that generating sufficient capital accumulation in the next ten years will be a formidable task. Many believe that the chief obstacle to such accumulation is unwarranted growth in government borrowing and government spending. Big-spending governments, they say, are the chief potential danger, the bad guys who, unless they are cut down to size, will prevent the good guys from passing safely through treacherous "Capital Gap" into the land of economic plenty. Contemporary research, say these economists, has shown that throughout the industrialized world overall growth is lowest in those countries where government spending in the public sector is largest.

How does government spending cut into capital accumulation for expansion and economic growth? There is a long-term relationship between an economy's stock of capital goods and the amount of output it can produce. A certain proportion of total production must be periodically invested in new capital goods if economic growth is to take place. If, for example, it takes $3 worth of capital investment to produce $1 worth of goods per year, 12% of each year's net national product will have to be earmarked for new capital investment if the economy is to grow at a 4% annual rate. But if government spending rises to such a high level that taxes to pay for this spending make it impossible to set aside 12% of net national product for investment, the growth rate will fall below 4%. "Spend and tax, spend and tax" may not only lead to slowing of economic growth but eventually to economic stagnation.

Many of those who see government spending as the chief villain in the struggle for economic growth are, naturally, opposed to any increases in this spending—especially for creation of jobs in the public sector of the economy. Creation of jobs, they say, should be the business of the private sector. Private-sector jobs make a far greater long-term contribution to real economic growth than make-shift and unwarranted public employment. Some economists suggest that government should not even attempt to be the employer of last resort. And, of course, they call for changes in the tax structure to provide greater incentives for savings and investment—particularly a cut in the corporate tax rate so that more money will be freed for accumulation of investment capital. They also call for a reduction in the federal capital gains tax, pointing out that since 1970 the top bracket for ordinary income has dropped from around 70% to 50%, while the capital gains tax bracket has risen from a maximum of 25% to a maximum of over 35%.

Not all economists, of course, are convinced that government spending is the chief obstacle to capital accumulation and economic growth—or, at least, certainly not the only one. They note that in recent years savings have been flowing into fewer and fewer hands. Deposits in the largest banks in the United States, for example, rose from 20% of total bank deposits in 1962 to 33% in 1975. Money held by large pension funds has more than tripled since 1962 and mutual-fund assets have doubled. Yet the number of individuals holding shares in American enterprise has declined sharply.

The problem, some economists suggest, is not that government is siphoning off money needed for investment, but the allocation of such money. Too much of it is concentrated in large banks and other financial institutions that are by their very nature conservative in their approach to risk-taking when it comes to capital investment! The danger, these experts insist, is not that investment capital for economic growth in the next decade will not be available. The danger is that smaller and more adventurous economic units will not have access to this capital and will thus be unable to contribute to the economic growth of the nation.

other cases, the donor country may act out of more altruistic motives—to prevent starvation, for example.

Advances in technology

Technological progress is another important determinant of economic growth. Such progress involves the development and use of new knowledge and skills to increase economic output. New knowledge and skills may be applied to existing resources to obtain their more efficient use—more efficient oil-drilling methods, for example, or better dams to harness water power. Technological advances may also entail productive exploitation of newly discovered resources—electric power, for example, or atomic energy. New discoveries and inventions often entail growth in capital goods formation and hence add further to economic growth. For example, the development of jet engines required construction of new types of aircraft for their utilization. The development

of electronics brought with it the need for vast capital investment in new computer systems and other electronic devices.

But technological advances entail more than new knowledge and inventions. Such progress also involves advances in business methods and management. Entrepreneurs seek ways to apply new technology and invest risk capital to do so. They also continually search for better marketing techniques and better methods for distributing the products of economic growth.

Efficient transportation techniques, for example, are a prerequisite for continued economic growth. Good roads and fast ships and cargo planes are needed to open new markets and sustain existing ones. For example, America's railroads contributed mightily to our industrial growth in the nineteenth century. Without them, the pace of western expansion would have been severely limited. Today, our vast system of interstate highways helps keep our economy growing by providing quick intercity shipping and ready access from remote farming areas to big cities.

Measuring technological progress For purposes of measurement, economists include with technology "all other growth factors" except growth in the size of the labor force and growth of capital accumulation. All "other" factors include such things as advances in business methods and improved labor skills. The true dollar value of technology's contribution to a nation's real GNP is, therefore, impossible to ascertain with accuracy.

Instead of trying to measure it directly, economists first determine what portion of growth can be attributed to labor force growth and capital growth, factors which can be statistically measured. Whatever portion of growth remains unaccounted for after these calculations is contributed to technological progress. For example, if real GNP grows at a rate of 5% and labor plus capital can be shown to have provided 4% of that growth, the remaining 1% is attributed to progress in technology. Suppose that GNP is $1,000. Growth of $50 then occurs. That represents a 5% increase. Growth of the labor force and capital goods is known to account for 4% or $40 of the increase. The remaining $10 is thus the result of technological progress.

Division of labor and economy of scale

As noted previously, classical economists, especially Adam Smith, emphasized the importance of specialization and division of labor to economic growth. Specialization leads to greater output per worker. For example, if one worker specializes in making tires for an automobile, another in blowing glass for windshields, another in grinding pistons, and so on, far more automobiles will be produced than if one worker does all of the tasks necessary to build a simple automobile.

Division of labor generally also leads to economies of scale. As more workers are added to the building of automobiles, for example, the size of the plant expands. *Economy of scale* begins to operate—that is, cost per unit of production decreases and efficiency increases as the size of the plant increases. Less hours are required for each car produced, thus freeing skilled labor for use in other areas of a growing economy.

Specialization and economies of scale are not just determinants of economic growth. They are also the results of growth. And they entail fundamental changes in the structure and organization of a growth economy.

Natural resources

Natural resources are an obvious source and determinant of economic growth. An economy with access to abundant resources—farmland, minerals, timber, water supply, and so on—has a ready source of economic expansion. The United States, for example, has been particularly fortunate in this respect. Our vast geographic expanse with its abundance of resources necessary for industrial growth has been a mainstay of economic growth throughout our history as a nation.

Many other nations, especially underdeveloped countries within arid geographic boundaries, have not been so fortunate. But there is a limit to natural resources, even in nations such as the United States. Rivers may go dry or their waters may be spoiled by pollution. Timber may be overcut and mines and oil wells may be depleted. (Our current shortage of domestic sources of oil is a good example of natural-resource depletion.) Continued eco-

Extended Example
Economic Growth and the High Cost of Energy

No one will ever count the millions upon millions of words written and spoken concerning the nation's first comprehensive energy program promulgated by the Carter administration in 1977 and later amended and passed into law by Congress. As America listened to the flow of words—about taxes and rebate of taxes on energy consumption, solar and nuclear energy generation, gas guzzlers, the plight of the auto industry, the virtues of home insulation, and so on and so on—it is understandable that they paid attention to only those words most likely to affect their own economic and personal prospects. Many economists, however, believe these millions of words might better be boiled down to the formulation of one fundamental economic principle: the effect of high energy costs on the economic growth of the economies of the entire world.

Ever since the Industrial Revolution, rapid economic growth has depended to a very great extent on readily available, inexpensive energy. Ever since Watt's steam engine replaced the windmill and water wheel, energy-intensive production has led the way to increased economic growth, from the gasoline engine to electrical power. First coal and then mostly oil have fueled this growth for the last two hundred years, cheaply and abundantly. Now, we are told bluntly and brutally, the days of cheap and abundant energy are over. A new economic age frought with dangers never before faced has come into being.

Experts may disagree about the exact dimensions of the world's remaining supply of its most important fuel—oil. But they all agree that it is finite. Experts may also disagree as to the relative importance of the various causes of the current high price of energy—cartels of oil-producing nations; national and international monopolies of production, refining, and distribution; natural shortages; the quantum leap in energy consumption necessitated by rapid industrialization and advanced technologies; and so on. But the high cost itself is all too evident.

By 1977, three years after the oil-producing nations (OPEC) had raised the price of crude oil from $2.75 a barrel to almost $12.00, oil-consuming nations had paid out an additional $225 billion for their oil and have lost an estimated $600 billion in economic output. Less developed nations alone have gone $170 billion into debt.

The United States, powerful though its economy is and one of the nations least dependent on foreign crude oil, has been estimated to have lost in 1976 alone more than $60 billion in gross national product and more than 2 million jobs because of increased energy costs. In addition, the American economy has been further depressed by tight money policies intended to fight inflation induced by high energy costs.

Many economists contend that the world will never again see the kind of rapid economic growth which characterized most industrial nations in the past, especially since World War II. The growth rate of capital-intensive production as replacement for labor-intensive facilities is necessarily slowed as capital-intensive facilities become more expensive because of high energy costs. There is, after all, only so much financial capital to go around. What is spent on energy cannot be spent on expansion and consequent economic growth. This, they say, may well account for the lamented lack of capital investment in the world economies that has prevailed for the past several years. Capital-intensive production now contributes not nearly as much to capital formation for investment as it once did. The rate of economic growth in industrial nations must perforce be slowed.

The less developed nations present an even gloomier picture. Deficits in balance of payments for all the underdeveloped nations are now running $40 to $60 billion a year, largely because of high energy costs. International financial experts agree that there is grave danger to the entire international economy if such deficits continue. International financial institutions may come to their aid with loans, but eventually these loans too must be paid. If the less developed countries drastically restrict their imports and increase their exports, they could well invite economic retaliation by better developed and industrialized nations struggling against the high cost of their own energy consumption. In short, the problem of high energy prices and economic growth is a worldwide one. Price restraints, conservation, and development of new energy sources may alleviate the problem. Whether they, and other measures, can solve it, only history will say.

nomic growth requires constant vigilance against loss or depletion of an economy's natural resources. Nature's bounty has its own natural limits.

Economic stability

As noted above, economic stability is a source of economic growth. Only where the general economy is making full use of its *existing* capacity to produce does it have the potential for growth. Thus a stable economy is itself a source of growth, since prosperity ensures capital accumulation for expansion.

On the other hand, radical fluctuations in the economy, such as severe changes in the business cycle, tend to limit growth or even bring it to a stop. During recessions, savings fall along with incomes. Capital accumulation dries up. Investment in new capital goods is retarded because existing productive capacity is itself lying idle. A portion of the economy's productive capacity may be allowed to wear out and not be replaced. Production thus lost may never be regained, nor may the lost production of unemployed labor.

Inflation is another form of economic instability that retards growth. Investors are reluctant to risk their capital in periods of high inflation. They will hesitate to invest in new productive capacity when their real profits on such investments are likely to be eroded by rising prices. Instead, they will be more likely to seek quick profits on more speculative investments. Or they may put their money in land, precious metals, art, or other nonproductive items whose value may be expected to *appreciate* (gain value) at a rate higher than the current inflation. If inflation is extreme and localized, investors may seek out more stable, foreign economies in which to invest their savings.

It is imperative, then, that both government and the business community work to keep the economy stable in the interest of continued economic growth. As noted above in the section on capital accumulation (and, as you will see, in many other parts of this text), government is taking an increasingly direct role in planning for and sustaining economic growth. Government, even in mixed economies, is becoming more and more active in promoting growth through developing human resources and in providing the economy with capital goods and services. It actively engages in monetary and fiscal policies intended to keep the economy stable and thus promote economic growth.

The case for economic growth
Improvement in living standards

That economic growth is beneficial to a nation and its people would seem to go without saying. First and foremost, growth means more abundance for more people. Without growth there can be no increase in a nation's standard of living. Indeed, as population increases, some growth is essential just to maintain human life and sustenance.

Growth helps satisfy humanity's unlimited wants. As an economy grows, additional wants and changing tastes of the populace can be met. Increased productive capacity eventually enables wider consumption of the fine arts or even things that are purely frivolous. Economic growth also provides the resources to meet such problems as pollution and disease eradication. In addition, we should note that Mother Nature never rests; she keeps growing: new diseases and crop blights emerge every year or two. Human society—even advanced

countries—must keep growing to respond to nature's challenge. An economy of no growth is like a swimmer trying to remain at one position in the Pacific Ocean by treading water; the lesson is clear: either swim now or drown later.

Redistribution of income

Economic growth serves social, as well as the material, needs of the nation. It provides the resources to help deal with pressing social problems. For example, in most economies, not all members share equally in the output of the economy. There always exist poor people who not only want more, but need (and deserve) more. Without growth, it is necessary to attempt to take from some in order to eliminate poverty. With economic growth there is more for everyone. If those who already have a goodly share of goods and services see that they will get more, they are willing to let a somewhat larger share of the increase in income be diverted to those who have less. So the larger the economic pie, the more there will be to provide for programs intended for the benefit of society as a whole. Growth then may help redistribute a nation's income to the benefit of all its citizens.

U.S. growth history

Blessed with abundant resources, an energetic and intelligent labor force, and a large market for goods, the U.S. economy has been able to grow ever since the first explorers landed on our shores. This growth has not been without interruption. Figure 3 shows the path of GNP since 1890. The actual data include some movements other than growth, such as the movements from A to B or B to C in Figure 1. The general trend of GNP, especially from peak to peak, represents growth. There was a mild decline in GNP about 1895 and another about 1909. In 1921, right after World War I, there was a considerable drop in income; beginning in 1929, the Great Depression appears as a steep decline in GNP. Since then, except for a slight

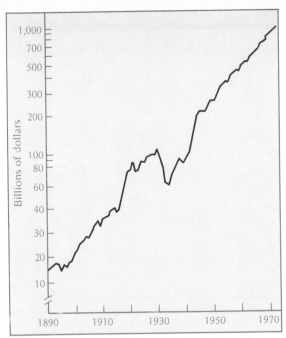

Figure 3 Growth of GNP from 1890–1970, shown in current dollars (that is, GNP is not deflated for changes in the price level). (Source: U.S. Department of Commerce.)

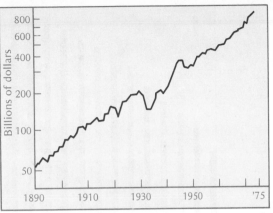

Figure 4 Growth of real GNP from 1890–1975 (shown in 1958 dollars). (Source: U.S. Department of Commerce.)

relapse in 1937, only slowdowns in the expansion are noted. Figure 3 shows changes in nominal or money GNP. Therefore, both price and output changes are recorded. To examine more closely economic growth, we need to look at changes in output alone.

Figure 4 shows real GNP, or GNP measured in prices which do not change. Therefore, any up or down movement reflects a change in the production of goods and services. Figures 3 and 4 are drawn so we can compare them directly. It is easy to see that real GNP has expanded less rapidly than GNP, which has price increases built-in. Some of the decreases in output become more apparent. This is especially true of the mild recession in 1915 and of the 1921 post-World War I recession. A much greater difference is noted after 1945. In Figure 3, only a slowdown in growth is noted between 1944 and 1950. However, in Figure 4, it is apparent real output declined from 1944 to 1947 and did not recover till 1950. These departures from growth slow down the actual expansion of the economy.

It is a little tricky to summarize the growth of the U.S. economy as it is shown in Figure 4. Different methods give slightly different results. However, we may look at the line as it is drawn and see several distinct periods. For example, from 1890 to 1907, the growth rate was 4.4 to 4.6% compounded annually. This was a period of rapid growth. From 1907 to 1929, the growth rate was much lower, about 2.7 to 2.8%. The Great Depression and World War II make our calculations less certain, but for 1929 to 1965, growth occurred at a rate of 3.1 to 3.9%. From 1965 to the present, the growth rate has been dropping, in part because of the recessions of 1971 and 1975. The average growth rate from 1965 to 1975 was 2.5%.

After 1975, the increase in GNP was greater than 6%. Not all of this was real growth. Some of the increase in output was of the sort illustrated by a move from A to B in Figure 1, while some is growth in the sense of increased population potential.

U.S. growth compared

It is interesting to compare the growth of the United States with the Soviet Union. The comparison is made difficult because the concept of GNP and pricing in the two economies is quite different. However, experts have made some estimates of the performance of the Soviet economy. In Figure 5a, it may be seen that the GNP of both countries has grown from 1950 to 1975. The GNP of the U.S. remains ahead of the U.S.S.R.

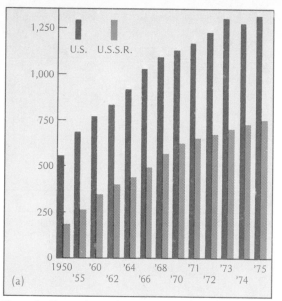
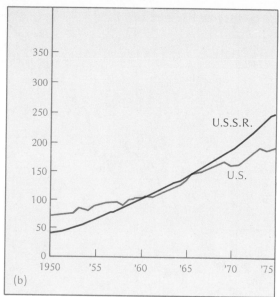

Figure 5 Comparison of American and Soviet growth: (a) GNP (in billions of 1973 dollars); (b) industrial growth (1960 = 100). (Source: Central Intelligence Agency.)

However, the Soviet economy is carefully planned. Thus the growth of the economy is much smoother. The decline in output experienced in the U.S. in 1974 was not seen in the Soviet economy. Plans in the U.S.S.R. are set for five years unless something, such as World War II, interrupts the plan. The U.S.S.R. is now in its tenth economic plan. The ninth was supposed to deliver more consumer goods but crop failures in 1972 and 1975 prevented attainment of the goals. The goals have been set for 35 to 50% increases over the five years, or 5 to 8% per year. The goals for heavy industries have been higher than for consumer goods in most years.

The result may be seen in Figure 5b. Industrial output of the U.S.S.R. was below that of the U.S. in 1950. However, with higher growth of industrial output, the U.S.S.R. passed the U.S. by 1960. The U.S. pattern shows not only slower growth over the fifteen-year period but the ups and downs of the business cycle. The U.S.S.R. has maintained steady as well as higher growth of industrial output. The consumer in the U.S. is still much better off than his counterpart in the U.S.S.R., but the increase in industrial production has allowed the U.S.S.R. to increase military capacity at the present and to increase the potential for future consumer goods.

The case against economic growth

Since the benefits of economic growth are so self-apparent, it would seem that no one could possibly argue against it. Yet in recent years many economists and other social scientists have come to question growth as an idea in itself. A few such thinkers even argue for the total elimination of growth, or *zero economic growth* (ZEG). This radical approach is rejected by most students of the matter. But that it is advocated at all is a measure of the seriousness of the questions being raised.

The majority of social scientists do not question the potential benefits and economic necessity of growth. Many, however, do question the concept that growth is a plus in itself—regardless of its cost. In other words, they recognize that there *is* a cost to be paid for economic growth. They are concerned that society be made aware of this cost and that it make wise choices when it is forced to choose between growth and possible adverse effects of growth. *Bigger*, they warn us, is *not* always and automatically *better*.

Growth and social ills

Growth critics question whether growth actually contributes to solution of social problems. Or, more precisely, they maintain that although growth may alleviate some social problems, it also adds new ones. Look, they say, at our inner cities. Despite economic growth, the poor are still with us—and finding it ever more difficult to escape from the economic and social decay of our urban centers. True, growth has brought a larger economic pie, but there has not been much change in the relative shares of the pie allotted to the various segments of society. Poverty is still prevalent and it is still as degrading as it ever was—even if few are actually starving in this country.

Growth, these critics argue, must be guided by society. Industrial expansion that serves only the affluent suburbs, say, and leaves the core cities to decay is not real growth at all. It only adds to social ills. Growth must serve all the people. It must not become an end in itself.

Growth and the quality of life

Growth critics point out that there is an intangible but very real cost of growth that may be even more important than its material costs. Unchecked economic growth, they say, has distorted and sometimes even destroyed our quality of life. Human values have become subservient to economic goods. "Things," as Thoreau said many years ago, "are in the saddle and ride mankind."

Growth has indeed brought each of us more material goods. But it has not enhanced the quality of our lives. The products of our economic growth are as likely as not to be shoddy ones. Obsolescence is purposely built into them to increase demand for product replacement. Consumer satisfaction must be sacrificed to the god of economic growth, from whom all material blessings flow.

And, to keep this god happy, each of us must spend our days earning and spending, earning and spending. When economic growth becomes an end in itself, obtaining and consuming the products of that growth also become ends in themselves. Economies of scale and specialization enable us to build millions of automobiles and television sets, for example. But the cost is millions of hours of mind-dulling labor on assembly lines. Surely the human spirit pays a price for this kind of labor—and for that of executives who become slaves to the corporations for which they toil.

It is argued that growth has added to our feelings of insecurity and alienation by rendering obsolete many workers' job skills. Growth is fine if you have a skill that is needed before, during, and after the growth process. However, as we have seen, growth often involves new products for new markets and capital accumulation with new technology. As a result, a college graduate may be obsolete five years after graduation.

The growth process accelerates job skill obsolescence. We have more to consume, but we have more people being replaced. The additional output may compensate for the actual cost of retraining and reemploying a person. However, there is no way to fully compensate for the loss of identity which is involved in changing occupations. Many people introduce themselves by their occupations. Many surnames such as Smith, Baker, Miller, and Cooper originally identified the person by trade. This loss of identity is not offset by more consumption. That growth is destructive of human security is the complaint against growth.

Economic growth and population

As noted above, obtaining and maintaining a proper balance between the benefits and "disbenefits" of economic growth is not a simple task. Critics and proponents of growth alike, however, agree that population control is an important key to the problem.

Advocates of zero economic growth take a very dim view of the population problem. As they see it, in about fifty years or less, per capita output of agriculture and industry will reach its peak. After that point, the earth's resources will rapidly become depleted. Population, however, will continue to increase, at least for a few decades. This is a modern version of Malthus' theory. Starvation and poverty

Economic Thinker
Thomas Malthus

Like his friend David Ricardo, Thomas Malthus was destined to shatter the complacency and optimism of the economic world of his day. Like the Deists of his time, who believed God had created the world much as a watchmaker creates a fine watch and left it to its own mechanistic devices, Malthus posited a natural preordained system in which economics, like all else, must necessarily function. But observation of the world around him convinced Malthus that the Creator's "watch" contained within it a time bomb—an inevitable population explosion. His theories were to bring bitter denunciations and lend credence to the belief that economics was indeed "the dismal science." They have come down to us, however, as still cogent and applicable to many portions of the modern world.

Thomas Malthus was born in 1766. His father, Daniel Malthus, was a friend of the English philosopher David Hume and an admirer of the French philosopher Rousseau. The elder Malthus was sympathetic to the optimistic theories of the English utopians who foresaw a rational, bountiful society within reach. His son Thomas, now an English clergyman, was not so sure that peace and prosperity were at hand. To convince his father to the contrary, he wrote his objections down on paper. His father was impressed by Thomas' arguments and suggested they be published. Thus was born, in 1798, Malthus' *An Essay on the Principle of Population As It Affects the Future Improvement of Society*. In this book, Malthus demolished once and for all the notion that humanity is preordained to progress upward and onward merely by virtue of its innate nature and the goodness of nature's God. On the contrary, said Malthus, left to their own natural devices, people are destined for an impoverished future and perhaps even for extinction.

Land, said Malthus, is finite. New discoveries may add to the bulk of productive land and new techniques may add to its productivity. But the process is slow and, ultimately, must come to an end. Land cannot breed. But people can. Malthus conjectured that human beings tend to double in number every 25 years. In time, it was inevitable that population would outstrip the earth's capacity to sustain human life. Land productivity, said Malthus, could at best increase only arithmetically—1, 2, 3, 4, 5, and so on. Population, however, increases geometrically—2, 4, 8, 16, 32, and so on.

The conclusion was as dreadful as it was inevitable: most of humanity was condemned to live in misery and poverty. The bounty of the earth would go mainly to the strong. There could never be enough for all. Wars and human vice would serve to slow the growth of population but not to stop it. "Sickly seasons, epidemics, pestilence, and plagues," said Malthus, will also take their toll. But, in the end, to no avail. Only gigantic famine will be left to return the world to a population level suitable for survival.

It is understandable that for many of his high-minded and humanitarian contemporaries, the Malthusian theory of population growth was a devilish brew and, for some, Malthus himself the devil incarnate. Yet Malthus was a devout clergyman, a gentle and kindly person whose students fondly called him "Pop" outside his hearing. Malthus, like his friend Ricardo, was not a defender of the status quo. Nor did he see his population theories as justification for exploitation of the weak by the strong. He was a scholarly student of economic trends and population growth. His conclusions seemed dreadful to all who considered them carefully, including, we may safely assume, the Reverend Malthus himself.

Malthus made other contributions to economics, but he is, of course, remembered primarily for his contribution to population-growth theory. His warnings of the dangers of unchecked growth impelled economists and other social scientists to seek solutions to problems outside the framework of an assumed preordained progress. The accuracy of his predictions of doom may be faulted, since he did not foresee the extent of improvement in agricultural techniques nor could he know of the tendency of highly industrialized societies to produce fewer children than the societies with which he was familiar. His basic premises, however, remain valid and a challenge to concerned thinkers throughout the crowded world of today.

are inevitable for the majority of the human race unless resources are conserved now through zero economic growth.

These latter-day "dismal scientists" are, however, in the minority. Most thinkers look to *zero population growth* (ZPG) rather than to ZEG for a solution. They too believe that the world's population cannot continue to grow indefinitely. They believe, however, that steps can, and indeed must, be taken to limit population growth. Contraceptive techniques and family planning must be developed and used, with zero population growth the ultimate aim. Continued economic growth is feasible only if the limits of the earth's resources are countered by control of population growth.

Attainment of zero population growth will not be easy. Some societies, for social, cultural, or religious reasons, find it more difficult than others to control population growth. Some poorer nations even fear that population control may merely be a device to ensure their continued domination by richer countries. They feel that a large population is necessary to their economic and military power vis-à-vis nations. And it is not just poorer nations that

have expressed reservations about zero population growth. For example, in late 1976, the government of France called for an increase in population if France were to continue as a first-rate world power. Other nations have argued against ZPG on economic grounds. It is feared that a static population will, because of advances in medical science, result in an increasing proportion of older people dependent for their sustenance upon the economic productivity of a decreasing number of young people.

Nevertheless, it is generally conceded that economic growth cannot continue if population growth is not checked. Population growth, fortunately, has already slowed markedly in most industrial nations and in many underdeveloped countries. In 1976, for example, the population growth rate for the United States was 1.3% annually. Japan had a growth rate of 1.1%; the Soviet Union 1.0%; Brazil 2.9%; China 2.4%; and India 2.6%. Four countries, Barbados, Britain, Austria, and Malta, had achieved zero population growth. Portugal and West Germany both had actual population declines. Thus population control, though difficult, would seen to be a feasible alternative to drastic reduction in, or elimination of, economic growth.

Growth and the ecology

Post-World War II industrial expansion has caused increasing concern about environmental consequences of economic growth. This concern with the environment led to interest in the science of **ecology,** which is the study of relationships between living organisms (plant and animal) and their environment. Critics of growth point out that waste from our overuse of combustion engines, our chemical industries, our factories, and so on are fast making vast areas of our nation unfit for wildlife and, in some instances, even human habitation. Our rivers and streams, the very air we breathe, have become cesspools of pollution. What is more, environmentalists point out, industrial pollution is really cost-free garbage disposal for the people who profit most directly by increased production. This garbage disposal is paid for by society at large and not just by those who make the products and those who can afford to consume them.

The damage to the environment is one argument which has been used most effectively to limit growth. Yet there is a dilemma. *Only a growing economy can effectively divert resources to the preservation of the environment.* Let us examine in greater detail the costs and benefits of growth as they relate to the environment.

The arguments against growth result from a rapidly deteriorating environment. The list of problems is very long. Many are familiar but others are less well known.

Air pollution Air pollution is a problem, especially in urban, manufacturing areas. Air pollution is of at least two kinds. First, there is particulate matter. This refers to dirt, dust, and solid waste thrown into the air. Some of the solid stuff is more annoying than serious. After all, white curtains at the window are not necessary if the window is too dirty to see through. Other chemicals in gaseous form are also discharged. These are more harmful to people, animals, and plants. Some are directly poisonous such as carbon monoxide, which, by the way, is also produced by automobiles driven by consumers. Other gases produce still other harmful effects. Some hydrocarbons are changed by sunlight into the air pollutant we call *smog*. Those fluorocarbons used as propellants in spray cans are thought to damage the ozone layer of the atmosphere which protects us from ultraviolet rays from the sun. It does little good to point out that volcanoes produce many of the same pollutants naturally or that pollen is a natural particulate pollutant. Economic growth adds a great deal to air pollution.

Water pollution Water pollution is similarly a result of economic growth. Flushing waste down the sewer is the cheapest way to get rid of it. Thus, water, especially in economically developed areas, is soon fouled. Lake Erie was once thought to be without any living creatures or at least no desirable water animals or fish. The Detroit River was thought of as a very large sewer. The Chicago River was reversed so it would carry waste away from Lake Michigan rather than into it. Lake Michigan is the water supply for many cities, yet it was so polluted that for many years some beaches were closed to swimmers.

Other environmental problems Economic growth creates other environmental problems. Land may be cleared of natural plant growth. Wildlife destroyed or driven off can never return to its natural areas. Other resources may be depleted. Natural gas and crude petroleum are in short supply. Even if the resource is not depleted, getting it may leave scars on the landscape. Strip-mining is an example of such activity. Some chemicals such as pesticides, herbicides, fertilizers, and others may do damage in unsuspected ways or there may be toxic residues. Heat, light, and noise produced by firms and households may also harm the environment. Ultimately, some pollutants may result in death of humans or, at least, cancer, birth defects, or genetic mutations.

Awareness of pollution Concern about environmental issues is one of the things which comes with wealth. The concern increases more rapidly than income as economic growth proceeds. The poor nations and poor people in rich nations have little concern for environmental issues. The jobs and products of economic growth are too important to worry about dirt or anything else. Belching smokestacks are desired for the income which is earned. It is only the affluent nations such as the United States which are in a position to want to preserve the environment. To do so, we must have sufficient income to be willing to expend part of it on cleanliness.

There is, unfortunately, a tendency to connect the smoke and dirt with economic activity. One business reporter, stationed in an industrial town by his newspaper, developed his own system of measuring economic activity. He would open his front door and peer out. If he could see only his front fence, he would report that business was booming. If he could see the house across the street, business was reported to be so-so. If he could see all the way to the corner, business was terrible and a recession was reported as underway.

In many cases, those who benefited from economic growth also paid the price. The employees who worked in a plant often lived nearby. Therefore, they were the ones who suffered from the dirt and polluted air. The toll on health often was enormous. Some of the heaviest industry and the most polluted air is found in the Ohio River valley between Ohio and West Virginia, just west of Pittsburgh. Two towns were studied to see the effects of the pollution. One town had 31% and the other had 59% more heart disease than was found in the rest of Ohio. The death rate from bronchitis was higher than observed in other parts of Ohio, an industrial state; in one town, 145% higher and the other, 372% higher. The pollution in the area is the cause. In Chicago, the coroner used to be able to tell if a body had been a person who had lived in Chicago a long time by the amount of black soot in the lungs. The beneficiaries of economic growth often carried marks of which they were not aware.

The big clean-up Much has been done to clean the environment. In fact, the 1970s will probably be viewed as the decade in which we turned the corner in our battle against pollution. Water resources have been cleaned up or are being cleaned up. In some cases, there is only a timetable for cleaning up but progress is being made. There are now fish in the Detroit River. Commercial fishing may return to Lake Erie. There is still a lot of silt in the Missouri and Mississippi Rivers, but pollution is way down. It has been a long time since the Des Plaines River near Chicago or the Cuyahoga River in Cleveland have caught fire. And the boast by one steel firm that the water they dump into Lake Michigan is cleaner than that they take out is more difficult to believe every day. Of course, the expense was tremendous, with about $18 billion being spent by the federal government between 1972 and 1977. Much more was spent by other governments and by businesses.

Air pollution has also been reduced. Automobiles are much cleaner in 1977 than they were in 1967. At one time, a motorist could solve his problem of what to do with exhaust gases by running them out the exhaust pipe. Of course, the smog created imposed a high cost on those who had to breathe. Now, the cost is imposed on the motorist in terms of pollution-control equipment and lead-free gasoline. As a result, carbon monoxide and other hydrocarbons are released at only 15% of the levels a decade earlier. And the nitrogen oxide exhaust has been cut in half. Eighty-five percent of the major polluters such as factories, electric utilities, or incinerators are either clean or on a schedule which will clean up the air. Smoke, soot, and dust have been reduced by 14%. Sulfur dioxide, the compound which makes eyes water, has been reduced 25%.

Another important area of improvement has been the handling of solid waste. Many governments have found new ways of handling trash. Open dumps and burning garbage are no longer used in many areas. The garbage may be burned, but the incinerator is now clean and the heat from the garbage is used to make steam, which turns generators or heats buildings. Some areas separate the trash and metal and glass and reclaim iron, steel, aluminum, and glass as well as paper. One chemical company now claims that it is processing waste materials to recover chemicals it formerly discarded. For some materials, such as silver, the recovery process is highly profitable.

The cost of cleaning up The improvements have not been easy and the cost of cleaning up has been high. The benefits have been noticed everywhere in an improved environment. More money must still be spent. But the peak expenditures have passed and smaller sums will be spent in the future. The iron and steel industry spent $350 million in 1976 and will still be spending more than $300 million per year through 1979. The automobile industry spent $160 million in 1974 and will now spend only about $50 million per year through 1979. The paper industry spent close to $400 million in 1975 and will still be spending $200 million per year as of 1979. Petroleum will be spending only $400 million per year in 1979 after a peak expenditure of almost $800 million in 1975.

The critics of the attempts to clean up the environment are not only the businesses which must spend a great deal of money. This is not to excuse those businessmen who do not like being told to clean up and complain about the cost. The critics are responsible people who point out that the efforts to clean up the environment require investment which does not increase output. In fact, it may decrease output. The reduction in fuel economy of automobiles is only one example. There are jobs created in firms producing the equipment which is used to reduce pollution. But, the industries installing the equipment are using funds to reduce pollution which might otherwise be used to expand productive capacity and create jobs. The clean air or water is not part of the product they sell. Thus output and future capacity may be reduced by the clean-up effort.

The concern for loss of jobs may be overstated in some cases. The Environmental Protection Agency (EPA) of the federal government has reported only about 75 plants closing as a result of inability to meet the regulations. Since these were generally old and small plants, the loss of jobs has only been about 16,000. State and local regulations are another matter; some state standards are tougher than those set by the EPA. If one state or city tries to really get tough, they may simply drive industry to nearby areas which have less difficult standards. The jobs are not lost but workers bear the burden of moving or loss of jobs to workers in other areas. Some cities have decided to limit growth to preserve open space and natural resources. This idea is good for the people who live in the houses already built but makes it difficult for those who would like to move to the city and for those employed in the construction of new housing.

New directions Zero economic growth has been proposed to preserve the environment. Those in favor of ZEG argue that we should not try to coax any additional production from our spaceship earth to preserve the resources we still have. The problem with this concept is that population keeps growing. With more people and the same output, the standard of living must fall. Without also controlling population growth, ZEG will not be a very satisfactory solution.

Finally, only a growing economy can really do anything about pollution. In a growing economy, there is enough produced to provide for current use and provide the materials needed to control pollution. Resources must be used wisely. Replaceable resources must be replaced. Depletion of others must be prevented. The old technology with its dirt and pollution must be changed. It is often easier to build a factory which is clean than to modify an existing one. The simple answers to environment problems probably do not work. It is not possible nor desirable to stop producing everything. Nor is it wise to avoid growth. For only persons with enough to eat and adequate shelter will be able to turn their attention to controlling pollution. Paradoxically, our economic growth is probably a necessary condition to continue the fight against pollution and other damage to the environment. As pollution standards get tighter, more products will have to be discarded; industry will have to develop replacements.

Summary

Economic growth is the process where an economy increases its productive potential over time. The results of economic growth are measured by increases in real GNP. In some cases, economists prefer to use increases in real GNP per capita to define growth.

The production possibilities curve or production frontier is used to show the maximum output of the economy. Moving along the frontier changes the combination of products produced but yields no growth. Growth implies that the curve shifts upward.

Classical economists were concerned about economic growth but were pessimistic as to how far economic growth could proceed. Adam Smith saw growth arising from division of labor and specialization of function until natural resources were depleted. David Ricardo saw growth limited because of fixed resources and diminishing marginal productivity of the other factors of production. Thomas Malthus raised the spectres of pestilence, famine, and disease because population would grow much more rapidly than output.

The neoclassical economists used similar models of economic growth but were interested in the rapid economic growth of the period after the U.S. Civil War. They noted that workers did not consume all their income but saved some which led to capital accumulation and greater productivity of labor. Also, the role of invention and innovation in the creation of technology was seen as contributing to greater productivity of all resources and growth.

After the period of growth, the Great Depression brought no-growth and the theory of secular stagnation, which said developed economies could achieve neither full employment nor growth.

Modern models of economic growth point out the dual role of investment expenditures, in that investment both creates the productive capacity and ensures adequate aggregate demand to maintain full employment.

Some of the other determinants of economic growth are: (1) human resources including the number in the labor force and the quality of their training; (2) capital accumulation; (3) technological progress; (4) economies of scale; (5) natural resources; and (6) economic stability.

Growth is desirable because it allows the improvement in living standards and a wider distribution of the benefits of economic activity.

The U.S. economy has grown a great deal though there have been periods where growth has been reduced or even stopped. The growth rate was around 4.5% from 1890–1907; around 2.7% from 1907–1929; and about 3.5% from 1929 to 1965.

There are some critics of economic growth. They argue that more goods and services do not necessarily mean better living. What is more, the abundance may be misleading for the goods are often of lower quality. Some critics argue for zero economic growth (ZEG).

Others argue that we could improve living standards by reducing population growth while keeping economic output at present levels. These critics call for zero population growth (ZPG).

Concerns with a deteriorating ecology have also raised questions about continued economic growth as we use up natural resources too fast.

Key Words and Phrases

- **economic growth** the increase at full employment over a period of time in an economy's potential output of goods and services.
- **production possibilities** the maximum output of different combinations of goods and services which an economy can produce.
- **division of labor** breaking up the productive process into a sequence of tasks.
- **specialization** the process where each worker or machine becomes or is designed to do one of the sequence of productive tasks and do it very efficiently.
- **capital accumulation** the process of converting saving to investment goods to expand future output.
- **technology** knowledge applied to the productive process which increases the productive potential of other factors of production.
- **innovation** the process of applying new inventions to practical production problems; the creation of technology.
- **secular stagnation** a condition in which an economy has persistently low levels of investment causing depression and no economic growth.
- **capital/output ratio** the amount of capital needed to produce a unit of output; the ratio is used in two ways: an average concept which shows what the capital already in place is capable of producing and a marginal concept which gives the capital necessary to increase output by some amount.
- **economy of scale** as the size of a plant increases, cost per unit of production decreases; increased efficiency resulting from large size.
- **ZEG** zero economic growth.
- **ZPG** zero population growth; a solution to economic growth problems advocated by some.
- **ecology** the science that studies relationships between plants and animals and their environment.

Questions for Review

1. If people must become more productive to have growth, in what sense are they better off with growth?

2. Suppose you read that the economy of a recently independent nation in Africa or Asia is growing more rapidly than that of the United States; would you be surprised? Why or why not? What would happen if the relative growth rates lasted for 20 years or more?

3. Can you compare the standard of living of a resident of Chicago or Atlanta with the standard of living of a resident of a small town in another state? How?

4. Extend the analysis of question 3 to compare your own standard of living with a resident of a poor nation of Africa, Asia, or South America. Do additional problems arise? What ones? Are you better off than someone in a less developed nation with an annual income of $300?

5. If natural resources become scarce, what would happen to the price of the resources? To the rate of economic growth? What would people do if the price rises? If it doesn't rise?

6. You are presumably creating human capital as you study this material. What is the cost of your investment? What return do you expect? Studies are showing little return to investment in a college education in the 1970s. Why are you still in school? Does your education do anything directly to improve your quality of life?

7. There is some recent evidence that Thomas Malthus may yet be correct. Why is this so? Would ZEG help? How about ZPG?

8. Suppose new technology came along which allowed the economy to produce the same output using fewer resources. Would this still be considered growth? Why or why not? Would the residents of the economy be better off as a result of the technology?

9. Explain how capital accumulation aids growth. How is capital accumulated?

10. Have you benefited from economic growth? How? Are your parents better off than your grandparents? Are you in any way worse off? Are any of these arguments for stopping economic growth?

11. "Mechanization costs jobs and is bad for the economy." Do you agree or disagree? Why? Suppose we had to build the interstate highway system with crews of people using hand tools and shovels. What would happen to employment in the United States? To the cost of the highways?

12. How do we value an animal or plant species which will be wiped out by economic growth? Is it infinitely valuable? Can we compare the loss of species with the benefits of economic growth?

18

Growth and Less Developed Countries

Scarcely more than a hundred years ago, our country asked itself a fearsome question: Can a nation exist half slave and half free? The answer was no. But a terrible war had to be fought before we could come to terms with this fact.

Today, the question is a global one: Can the world exist with some of its people living in relative prosperity while the rest of its people live in abject poverty? Most of the world's thinkers believe the answer is again no. Something, they agree, must be done to narrow the social and economic gaps between the *have* and the *have-not* populations of the globe. If the economic gap is not narrowed, great social and political upheavals are in store. No nation, no matter how rich, is secure from the effects of such upheavals.

In the previous chapter we discussed the sources and effects of economic growth. Our discussion centered mainly around the Western, industrialized nations. Historically, it is in these nations that the theories of growth have been most applicable and its effects most manifest. We turn now to the economics of the less developed nations of the world. What are the sources of their relative poverty? What can they do to improve their economic condition? What can other nations do to assist them in this process? In short, what can be done to bring the benefits of economic growth to all nations?

Characteristics of developing nations

It matters little what nomenclature we use to refer to the so-called "have-not" countries of the world. "Developing nations" or "less developed nations" seem to be the currently favored references. They have also been, and still may be, referred to as "emerging nations," "impoverished nations," "underdeveloped nations," "nonindustrial countries," "Third World countries," and "nonaligned nations." Sometimes the grouping connotes military and political interests as well as economic conditions ("nonaligned nations" is a case in point). But, in general, the terms noted above are used for nations in a low stage of economic development, regardless of their particular political

institutions or military alliances. There are somewhere between 75 and 100 such nations. For the most part, they are located in the Southern hemisphere—in Asia, Africa, and Latin America. Although they represent very diverse societies and cultures—some relatively new, some dating back to antiquity—they do share certain general characteristics.

Poverty

The most common characteristic of the developing nations is the grinding poverty of the great majority of their people. In the United States, annual per capita income is about $6,000. Most of Western Europe and countries like Canada, Israel, Japan and Australia have per capita incomes well above $3,500. Per capita income of Eastern Europe and the Soviet Union is estimated at about $1,500. The developing nations, with about two billion of the world's population, have an annual per capita income of less than $500—one-twelfth of that of the United States. See Table 1 for a GNP comparison of selected countries.

Table 1
GNP per Capita for Selected Countries in 1974

Country	GNP	Country	GNP
United States	5,979	Jordan	286
Afghanistan	81	Kenya	172
Angola	492	Luxembourg	5,377
Australia	4,184	Mexico	870
Austria	3,858	Nepal	90
Belgium	4,873	Netherlands	4,557
Burma	82	Nigeria	250
Cambodia	81	Norway	4,872
Canada	5,487	Pakistan	126
Costa Rica	775	Portugal	1,339
Denmark	5,364	Spain	1,728
Finland	3,770	Sudan	135
France	5,002	Sweden	6,379
Germany (West)	5,615	Switzerlnad	6,297
Greece	1,691	Turkey	604
Iceland	4,930	Uganda	161
Ireland	2,174	United Kingdom	3,129
Israel	2,732	Venezuela	1,357
Italy	2,609	Zaire	147
Japan	3,687		

Source: *Statistical Abstract of the United States, 1975;* data from *Organization for Economic Cooperation & Development* and *World Almanac for 1976.*

Startling as such figures are, they are mere approximations and more meaningful to economic theorists than to the human beings who live with them. How, for example, do we compare the value a dollar has for you with the value it may have for an Indonesian peasant? To the peasant, it may mean the difference between living and dying. And what does $500 per capita income mean to a farmer in a country where almost all of the annual $500 winds up in the hands of wealthy landowners? (Remember that "per capita" is an average.)

The real poverty of millions of people who share our globe can scarcely be imagined by those of us living in more affluent societies. Even the most impoverished of our cities live a life of relative comfort when compared with the daily lot of the truly poor in nations like Bangladesh or Ethiopia. The closest most of us will ever come to such poverty are television images of the dull eyes and swollen bellies of starving people who happen to be currently of some news interest.

Worldwide concern about the poverty of less developed nations is not new. Especially since World War II, much effort has gone into alleviating this problem. Some progress has been made. But the economic gap between the rich and poor nations is actually growing rather than diminishing. As we shall see below, population growth is a major factor in this regression in the comparative economic growth of less developed nations.

Overpopulation and lack of human capital

Most less developed countries suffer from high rates of population growth. Even though they may experience some increase in economic growth, the increase in population cancels out its benefits. The economic pie becomes larger, but not large enough to satisfy the needs of the growing number of people who must share in it.

As we noted in our discussion of growth theories in the previous chapter, economic growth itself contributes to overpopulation—which in turn steals away its benefits. Economic growth generally means better living conditions and improved health care. More children survive to breed more children. Death

rates of adults also decline, thus adding to the size of the population. Birth control and family planning, as we have already pointed out, would seem to be imperative to solve this economic and social problem. Some developing nations, notably India and China, have taken strong measures in this direction.

In addition to overpopulation, however, there is the problem of "population quality." (We are speaking here, of course, of the "economic" quality of a people, not of its human and cultural quality.) Most developing nations lack or are meagerly supplied with human capital. Their people are generally without the educational advantages necessary to develop skills needed for a viable and growing economy—especially a modern industrial economy. Literacy, without which very little human capital can be developed, is itself a pressing problem in many developing nations.

Figure 1 shows the relative increase in population for the richest and the poorest countries. For the ten highest per capita GNP countries the population growth rates are all fairly low—many less than 1% per year for the period 1960 to 1972. What is more, the average growth rates for 1965 to 1972 are actually lower for many of the countries. Thus those with low population gains are slowing the increase even more. Canada and Australia have the highest increase. The United States and Switzerland tie for third fastest population gains among the rich nations. Most of the other top ten countries in income are in Western Europe. These countries have much lower population gains than the United States.

The poorest countries all have very high population increases. Almost all of the thirteen poorest have population growth rates greater than 2% per year. Their populations are growing more than twice as fast as those of the rich countries. Only three of the thirteen countries shown were able to reduce the rate of population growth during the late 1960s and early 1970s. The rest were only able to hold the increase to the same rate and a few actually saw growth rates increase. Pakistan, not the poorest of the group, had the highest rate of

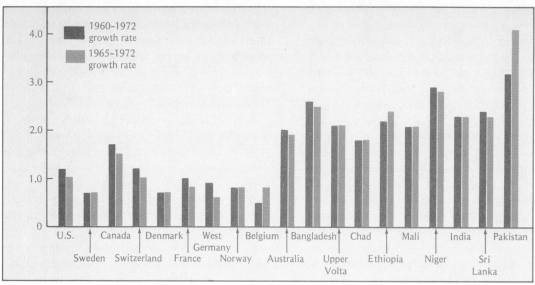

Figure 1 Comparison of population growth rates for the richest and poorest nations. (Source: NASA, *Outlook for Space.*)

increase and the rate of growth was also going up. At the growth rates experienced in Pakistan, population would double four times in a century. For every person living in Pakistan today, there will be 16 in 100 years (if the current growth rate is maintained).

Lack of capital

A third characteristic common to most developing nations is lack of capital formation. As we know, economic growth is impossible without capital goods such as factories and machinery. As we also know, the funds for such goods come from investment of an economy's savings. But people can save only if they have more than enough income to meet their day-to-day needs. How can people accumulate capital for investment in the tools of economic growth when they can barely meet their own subsistence needs? The answer is, of course, that they can't.

It is true that a few developing nations have little or no natural resources on which to base economic growth. Most, however, do have such resources—land expanse for agriculture, for example, or timber lands or valuable minerals. The problem, however, is that often these resources remain untapped or only partially tapped because of lack of capital for proper exploitation.

In many less developed nations, population is so great that agriculture cannot possibly provide savings for investment in capital goods. Everything that is produced—food and timber from the land, fish from the streams—is immediately consumed just to keep the population alive. There is no surplus production to save for investment in nonagricultural goods.

Some developing nations have natural mineral resources to help them toward economic growth. But there, too, lack of capital goods is likely to hinder full exploitation of the resource and thus prevent capital formation. In addition, many such minerals—tin, bauxite, and even gold, for example—face a world demand that is not favorable to the developing nations. The world markets can absorb only so much of these products. If production is increased to a point where capital accumulation becomes feasible, the price of the product on the world market will fall. Increased production may actually result in less income—and no possibility of saving for investment in further productive capacity.

The vicious circle of underdevelopment

The economic bind in which developing nations too often find themselves may be thought of as a kind of vicious circle. Figure 2 illustrates the concept. Start where you will in such a circle, there seems to be no way out of it.

For example, start at the upper right hand of the illustration—a generally undeveloped economy. Such an economy probably has a population which has few job-market skills. This economically backward population means that the economy will remain less developed. This constitutes a circle in itself. If we consider rapid population growth which increases the population, we see that the situation gets worse. Underdevelopment makes it impossible to train the rapidly increasing population. Growth comes from a number of sources, as we saw in the last chapter, particularly from capital accumulation. Tracing the rest of the loop in Figure 2 illustrates capital cannot easily be accumulated in developing nations. An economically backward population is a low-productivity economy. Low productivity leads to low per capita income. Low per capita income means that it is difficult to

buy much and essentially impossible to save anything. Low savings rates mean that little or nothing is available for investment in capital goods or in human capital. Lack of capital returns us to low productivity and low productivity is assurance of an underdeveloped economy. We are back where we started from. The vicious circle remains unbroken.

Barriers to economic growth

The adverse economic conditions of most of the developing nations present a challenge that must be met if a stable world society is to endure and prosper. Gloomy as the situation may be, despair is not the answer. Of course, some of us fortunate to live in affluent societies may take the I've-got-mine-Jack, and-to-hell-with-everybody-else attitude.

A few social scientists actually do argue for a kind of "life boat" ethic with regard to world food problems. The life boat of the world, they say, is filled to capacity. No one else can be allowed in lest everyone drown. Food should not be given to starving nations. Let famine and disease reduce their populations to an economically viable size. To feed the hungry is only to reduce the survival chances of the well fed and to postpone inevitable further famine among the poor.

But most of us would be repelled by such an approach. We agree almost intuitively with the poet that no man is an island. And, by extension, most of us have come to realize that no nation can ever stand entirely aloof from the other nations that share our world. Whether nations act out of moral or humanitarian principles or out of self-preservation, they have come to see that the world is bound inextricably together by modern instant communication techniques and almost instant methods of transportation. What diminishes one people diminishes all people.

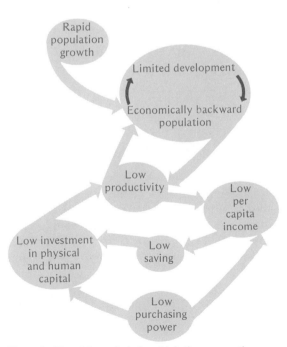

Figure 2 The vicious circle in which the poor nations are often trapped.

What, then, can be done to solve the problems of economic growth in developing countries? Let us take a closer look at these problems and examine some of the ways they may be solved or alleviated. The solutions, as we shall see, must come from two basic sources: *through internal changes in the developing nations and through assistance from nations whose economies have already advanced.*

Mention of outside assistance, which we will discuss in detail later in this chapter, brings up a point that should be noted now. It is true that the developed nations have, so to speak, been through the mill of economic growth. They have faced and solved many of the problems now facing less developed countries. But this is not to say that all the developing nations need do is follow the leaders. Economic and social conditions have changed over history. All cultures are not the same. All nations are not born equal. For advanced nations to tell poor nations to "do as we did" is not only insufferably smug; it may also be totally impossible for the poor nations.

As an obvious example, we may take the case of economic growth in the United States. It developed from a position of great land expanse and bountiful natural resources. It had the advantage of a skilled native labor force and ready access to the skills of millions of immigrants when they were needed for further economic expansion. It had the advantage of a culturally mixed population not bound by social or religious taboos against certain prerequisites of economic growth, such as an achievement-oriented population (which produces entrepreneurs) and labor mobility. Overpopulation was never a problem. And it had the advantage of a political system that emphasized individual freedom to achieve the benefits of a growing economy. Other now industrialized and advanced nations had similar if not identical advantages. No developing nation today is in such an enviable position.

Population problems

As already noted, unchecked population growth is a powerful deterrent to economic growth. For example, even though India doubled its agricultural output between 1945 and 1976, its economic gains from this advance were practically wiped out by a doubling of the population in the same period. We have also noted that economic growth itself contributes to population growth.

Some nations have made a direct attack on the problem. Family planning and birth control information is widely disseminated. Birth rates are coming down in some of the less developed nations. But more and faster progress needs to be made and many barriers to this progress remain. For example, low-literacy levels often hinder dissemination of family-control information through the printed word. Lack of trained manpower and poor transportation facilities may obstruct attempts at personal instruction. Deliverance of chemical and medical means of contraception may be hindered by lack of adequate funds. In addition, a people's religious or cultural heritage may cause resistance to contraceptive methods and techniques. Even economic considerations may enter the picture. In some underdeveloped agricultural countries, children are looked upon as a source of economic security—that is, a source of unpaid farm labor to provide family sustenance.

Whatever the obstacles, however, it is clear that the less developed nations must continue to work toward an economically acceptable reduction in population growth. Without such reductions vigorous economic growth will be virtually impossible.

Employment and human resource problems

Employment problems in developing nations are often of a different nature than employment problems in more advanced economies. In Western nations, when aggregate demand falls, workers are "laid off" and remain idle until demand quickens. In developing countries, however, the problem is not so much idle labor as unproductive labor. Such economies suffer from what is called **disguised unemployment.** Most of the labor force may be hard at work. Workers may toil more and much longer than in Western nations. But they produce much less per labor unit. Much of the working labor force is actually "unemployed" even though it is at work. For example, while the labor force is "working," it may not be producing much or much of anything which the market values. Thus, while energy is expended by the workers and they manage to work up a sweat, they might as well be idle for all the good that their effort does.

Most of the labor force in developing nations is engaged in production that is *labor intensive;* that is, in production that relies heavily on human labor inputs rather than on the labor-saving devices we call capital goods. Agriculture, for example, is very labor intensive, especially in nations lacking modern farm equipment and farming methods. And the economies of many developing nations are primarily agricultural. We know from our study of the law of diminishing returns that, after a certain point, adding more labor to a given amount of land results in less production per worker. Unfortunately, the traditions and culture of many underdeveloped nations contribute to overemployment (disguised unemployment) in agriculture. In many societies, if a father is a farmer, it is almost unthinkable that his sons will be anything other than farmers also.

Figure 3 shows what happens when agri-cultural output grows about the same rate as the labor force. In both developed nations and underdeveloped nations, agricultural output has increased a great deal. Both areas of the world reached 130% of their 1961–1965 levels by 1974. Yet in the less developed nations, most of the increase came from more people, almost all of whom were employed in agriculture. Thus per capita output remained nearly constant, and hunger is not overcome.

Of course, lack of other productive work also contributes to overemployment in agriculture. Many developing nations have little or no other industry to absorb their labor force. And what industry is available is itself likely to be labor intensive—and thus readily subject to the law of diminishing returns. Owners of industry are likely to substitute human labor for investment in capital goods when labor is plentiful and cheap. Quick and high profits are the result—along with little or no real growth in GNP.

In other words, even though labor-intensive industries may provide much needed employment in overpopulated countries, such industries are necessarily low in productivity. More and better capital goods would seem to

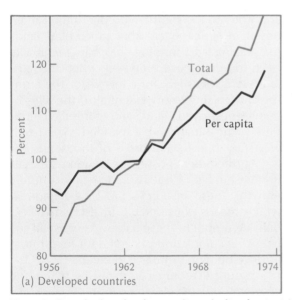

(a) Developed countries

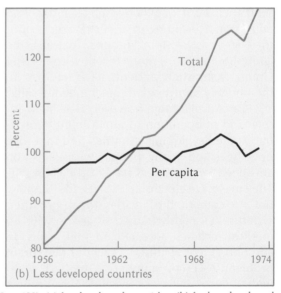

(b) Less developed countries

Figure 3 Growth of total and per capita agricultural output (1963 = 100): (a) for developed countries; (b) for less developed countries. Total growth rates for both rich and poor countries have been similar percentage increases. But the large population growth of the less developed countries has held back per capita food growth. (Source: NASA, *Outlook for Space.*)

be called for. But even here caution is needed. Sudden influx of labor-saving capital goods, though good in the long run, may result in immediate and severe unemployment. India, for example, could obviously use more capital goods. But many of India's labor unions have fought introduction of certain labor-saving industrial improvements on the grounds that they would cause unemployment among India's vast urban population.

There is a further dimension to the problem of employment in developing nations. As noted above, the quality of the labor force is likely to be poor because of lack of health care and education. There is a lack of people with entrepreneurial, supervisory, and other skills needed in a modern industrial economy. The general shortage of people with entrepreneurial skills is particularly troublesome. Unless someone is willing to take the risks involved in investment, there will be no capital formation and no jobs for others. Lack of entrepreneurship hinders economic growth.

Many less developed nations have attacked this human resource problem by attempting to improve their educational and health facilities. But this is difficult to do when so much of the economy's output is needed for immediate life subsistence. Often, they send their most qualified younger citizens to educational facilities in industrialized countries, such as Western European nations, the United States, and, more recently, the Soviet Union. Many such students have returned to their home countries with much needed skills.

Careful planning, however, is needed for this kind of operation to attain its full potential. Some developing countries find that they now have too many people with skills too advanced for the actual state of the economy. They may have electronic experts, for example, but no computer capacities to absorb their expertise. Or highly trained surgeons, with no medical facilities adequate to their skills. In addition, there is the so-called **brain drain problem:** A certain number of the best qualified students will elect to remain in the host country, because the opportunities for personal achievement are greater there than at home. Also, some countries like India and the Philippines churn out college graduates in such large numbers that many never find appropriate jobs, because industries and technology have not grown fast enough to provide jobs for skilled labor. This latter problem shows that some sort of overall planning is probably needed.

Natural resource problems

Some developing countries have a scarcity of natural resources to add to their economic difficulties. They may, for example, be burdened by lack of arable land, poor climate, lack of waterways, and absence of mineral wealth. Little can be done to overcome such handicaps except to see that what resources the nation does have are used efficiently.

Modern technologies suitable to nations with abundant resources may not be applicable in countries with less natural endowments. Mining techniques that bring quick profits but are wasteful of the commodity being mined could be disastrous to a country with very limited mineral resources. Drainage and irrigation techniques that work well in moderate climates may actually deplete agricultural resources in countries subject to severe weather extremes. For example, during years of favorable rainfall the people of the Sahel—those countries on the southern border of the Sahara desert in Africa—were able to develop lands for grazing and farming that had previously been too dry to use. However, when the rainfalls were very slight for a few years, the farming and grazing—now essential to the lives of many—destroyed land and turned it into desert (the Sahara thus expanded). The result was starvation for hundreds of thousands.

Further, mere possession of adequate natural resources is no assurance of economic growth. These resources must be exploited, which means considerable investment in expensive production capacities. As we shall see below, accumulation of capital for investment in developing countries is difficult.

A further complication arises when the economy of a developing nation depends primarily on a single natural resource, or even on relatively few resources. World technological changes may suddenly lessen or even wipe out the values of such commodities. Synthetic fibers, for example, have cut drastically into the market for hemp products. The development of synthetic rubber and plastics has severely damaged the value of natural rubber, which is grown mostly in less developed nations.

On the other hand, some nations have moved rapidly out of the underdeveloped category through exploitation of a single natural resource. The rapidly growing prosperity of some oil-producing nations is graphic evidence of such a possibility. It should be remembered, however, that, given the overwhelming need of industrial nations for energy, this particular situation is somewhat unique in world economic history.

Technological problems

As we know, technological advances are an important component of economic growth. As a general economic rule, progress in technology occurs along with capital investment, which is needed to develop and utilize the new technology. But, as we have also seen, developing countries have particular difficulties in raising capital. However, the picture is not all dark. Fortunately, the cost of research and development of much new technology has already been met by the industrialized nations. It is available for use or adaptation by developing nations.

In addition, some advances in technology can be used with little or no need for increased capital goods. Technology can be adapted to or used to replace, for example, the crude axe of native use and result in increased timber production. A gasoline-powered chain saw would do better. Modern developments in agricultural methods and fertilization can easily be substituted for more primitive farming practices for increased food production. It is important to remember, however, that the situation may call for *adaptation* rather than *adoption*. Highly efficient methods for growing certain grains, for example, may actually be counterproductive if the grain does not answer the nutritional traditions of the populace.

As the economy of a developing nation grows, more of the available technologies will come to be used, which in turn will foster further growth. *Such nations, however, are forced to be more selective in their choices of technology than are the developed countries.* Technology in industrialized nations tends to be labor saving and capital consuming. In developing nations, labor is plentiful and capital scarce. Often, developing nations must be content with technology that increases productivity and organizational efficiency but may add little to existing capital goods—new complex machinery, for example, or new factories. Advances in technology mean slow and steady economic progress for developing nations. They cannot, overnight, become industrialized giants on the Western model.

Social capital problems

Many developing nations are lacking in the economic "infrastructure" essential to economic growth. That is, they lack public services, known as *social capital*, that we in industrialized nations take almost for granted. We take them for granted despite the fact that approximately half of our investment capital is used for expenditure on these services. To obtain such essential services for themselves, many developing countries would have to spend an even higher percentage of their total capital investment.

What is social capital? It is the communication network and public social services without which modern economies cannot function. It is paved roads, railways, airways, telephones, post offices, and mail services. It is electric generators and other energy-producing facilities. It is schools, hospitals, sewage plants, and housing. The list could go on and on.

Developing nations are likely to have a shortage of social capital—and few ways to obtain it. Yet, as we have said, social capital is essential to vigorous economic growth. The problem is further complicated by the fact that social capital is seldom immediately productive. The temptation is to neglect accumulation of social capital in favor of more immediately profitable investment in capital goods. The dilemma is that both types of investment are needed simultaneously.

Government and economic growth

The role of government in developing countries is of great importance to their economic growth. It is historically true that government intervention in the economic growth of most Western nations started at a relatively low level. But, as we have seen throughout this book, that intervention has grown with economic growth itself. And, it is obvious that government intervention in the economic life of developing nations is today at least as prevalent as it now is in developed nations—and in many underdeveloped countries, much more so. Leaving aside the pros and cons of such intervention—its potential for loss of personal freedoms, for example—why is the role of government so important to the growth of underdeveloped nations? The basic answer would seem to be that there is no other institution present to do the job. The characteristics necessary for a viable market system to work its Western economic wonders are absent.

For example, only government can deal with the basic problem of overpopulation in developing nations. Only government can launch a contraceptive campaign massive enough to have any real effect. Government is the only institution that can even begin to provide the social capital necessary for economic expansion. And only government can impose monetary and fiscal policies to guide the economy toward a pattern of economic growth.

It is imperative then that the government of a developing nation be honest, stable, and strong enough to fulfill these functions. Unfortunately, some developing countries lack the political and social traditions necessary to this kind of government. Others, because of internal and external pressure, find such a government difficult to maintain. Such problems can only be solved with time—and perhaps by humanity's instinct for social as well as self-preservation.

Given an able government, what can the leaders of developing nations do to promote economic growth? In some situations, government may only need to ensure basic conditions conducive to growth—social stability, for example, or an orderly business climate. In other cases, more positive intervention is needed.

Government may engage in long-range economic planning. It may inaugurate five-year or ten-year plans to coordinate growth to the benefit of all sectors of the economy. It may take positive steps to deal with overpopulation, train its citizens in industrial and business skills, and provide necessary social capital.

Government may also dictate land reforms and other economic reformations to increase savings for investment in growth capacity. Proper land reform would eliminate the holding of large farms by absentee landlords who "rent" parcels of land to a large class of peasantry. Such reforms could make farmers more productive and hence give them a potential for saving. A farmer, or anyone else for that matter, is more productive and works harder when working for himself than when working for others. Tax incentives may be used to induce the wealthy to invest in the nation's needed capital goods. The power of taxation may also be used to redistribute the nation's wealth more equally and toward investment in the nation's general welfare. If the nation's level of sustenance is high enough, government may tax all its citizens to decrease immediate consumption in favor of capital investment.

Caution is in order, however. Too harsh and arbitrary use of government power can easily become counterproductive. An overtaxed citizenry may lose incentive to produce or to sacrifice for the common good. Capital may flee the nation for more permissive and profitable economic climes. To avoid such possibilities, and for other political and economic reasons, some developing nations resort to inflationary policies to enhance growth. They simply print more money to pay for ongoing needs. This kind of "taxation" falls most heavily on the nation's already poor or near-poor and will ultimately destroy economic growth.

In addition, the governments of less developed nations must be careful not to try to do too much, not to overregulate the economy. Such actions could stifle initiative and slow growth.

The problem of capital accumulation and investment

Each of the challenges to economic growth in developing nations that we have enumerated above is related in one way or another to perhaps the most important challenge of all—the problem of how to accumulate capital for investment in growth. We know that most developing nations are woefully weak in the productive facilities—factories, heavy machinery, and so on—necessary for economic growth. And we have seen that the basic poverty of the economy and its people is the root of the problem. An economy that barely provides enough for its citizens' sustenance of life cannot hope to accumulate savings for investment in capital goods.

The situation is not a great deal better for developing nations with somewhat more advanced economies. Although some domestic saving may occur, it is likely to be slight. It may not be enough to give the economy the kind of boost it needs to begin and maintain the process of capital accumulation. Investment in capital goods increases production, which in turn increases capital accumulation. If original investment is too meager, the process may never really be set in motion. The economy cannot break out of the vicious circle of underdevelopment.

A shortage of savings is not the only unfortunate characteristic of capital accumulation in less developed countries. The investment process itself has problems peculiar to or aggravated by social and economic conditions in many such countries.

In the first place, wealthy citizens of developing nations may hesitate or refuse to invest their savings in domestic capital goods. Wealthy landlords, for example, may prefer to spend these profits on purchasing more land or on grandiose consumption. Or savers may not wish to risk their money by investing in an undeveloped domestic economy.

What profit will there be, for example, from investing in a shoe factory if the population is too poor to buy shoes? Lack of domestic market is a disincentive to investment. Or why should people invest in a steel mill, say, in a country with no railways and few roads to bring iron ore to the plant and to distribute the plant's production, or where facilities to produce the plant's raw material are poorly developed? Lack of social capital and of complementary industries is a further disincentive to invest.

Furthermore, most developing nations lack educated workers. They also have a lack of managerial talent. Under these circumstances, success of a new business enterprise may be a risky proposition. In addition, investors in the domestic industries of less developed nations may face crippling competition from the products of the already industrialized nations.

Cultural and political problems

The cultural and political forces can indeed be powerful barriers to economic growth. Political and economic institutions and cultural-religious value systems are intertwined to such an extent that it is often impossible to tell where one begins and the others leave off. Economic growth can be hindered.

One example is the influence of Marxist economic theory on an economy. Capital is not deemed productive in Marxist theory and the decision-makers are not allowed to use a rate of return or rate of interest calculation when deciding how to allocate capital resources. As a result, resources are often misallocated. The use of quantitative and qualitative targets sometimes has disastrous results.

Another example includes a cultural aversion to giving up family land in order to move where the modern jobs are located. Traditions dictate that successive generations should live on the family land, which would preclude following the market forces to more productive jobs. The response to market conditions with desirable economic gains is blunted by the deeply rooted cultural values.

The influence of the socialist ideology is felt in two ways. First, and most obvious, is the reluctance of both natives and foreigners to invest in a country which they feel will limit their rate of return. At best, it may be below what they could obtain elsewhere. At worst, the local government might ultimately seize

Economic Thinker
Sir W. Arthur Lewis

W. Arthur Lewis is a gifted economic scholar and humanitarian who has been a pioneer in the study of economic growth and development. Born in 1915, in the British West Indies, he was educated mainly in England. He taught at the London School of Economics and at the University of Manchester and served as Vice Chancellor of the University College of the West Indies. He served as economic adviser to the British government, concentrating on the problems of economic development in his native area, the Caribbean. He has also been an economic adviser to the government of Ghana and a special adviser to the Prime Minister of the West Indies. Lewis has been active in the field of international banking, especially as it relates to the problems of developing nations, within the United Nations and, among other positions, as a director of the Industrial Development Corporation of Jamaica and President of the Caribbean Development Bank. In 1963, Lewis was knighted by the British government. He is currently at Princeton University, in the United States.

W. Arthur Lewis set forth his theories of economic development in *The Theory of Economic Growth,* published in 1955. In it, he began with a fundamental question: Is growth ever and always a desirable social goal? Perhaps it is, answered Lewis, but only perhaps. Growth does indeed bring positive good: it limits disease and famine and increases the range of society's control over our physical, social, and economic environment. But proponents of growth must remember that there is a price to be paid. Growth may bring unwanted disruption of a nation's culture. Its social values may fall prey to aspirations for individual wealth and power. Above all, growth may bring the urban blight that is a curse and characteristic of industrialized nations. Still, says Lewis, these costs may be as much a result of *too rapid growth* as of growth itself. If reason prevails, growth can be guided in such a way that the worst of industrial blight and disruption may be avoided.

What is the role of capital in the economic growth of underdeveloped countries? Studies have shown that for advanced nations, an investment of 10% of annual output yields a 3% growth rate of income. For underdeveloped nations, however, a much higher investment would be necessary to achieve 3% growth per year. Capital must first be invested in nonproducing "social overhead capital" such as educational facilities, transportation networks, and communications systems. Only when these things are in place can the economy grow at a rate relatively comparable to that of advanced nations. Lewis' pioneering work in the theory of economic growth laid to rest the notion that development was a simple process, the same for all countries and in all times. His *Theory of Economic Growth* and his later *Development Planning* showed that economic growth is a complex and dynamic process and that its effectiveness depends upon maintaining a rational balance among the numerous factors contributing to it.

Lewis has argued for land reform, land reclamation, rural development, sound international currencies, and, if necessary, direct government intervention to promote economic growth in underdeveloped nations. Many of his theories have been put to practical use throughout the world.

their entire investment. Second, and less obvious, is that the socialist or welfare state orientation of the governments leads them to provide social security, unemployment benefits, or public housing by taxing away the funds which would otherwise go for real investment or economic "infrastructure." They often try to provide benefits that the developed countries did not even contemplate until their economies were much larger and self-sustaining.

For these reasons, and for others touched upon in this chapter, developing nations face formidable obstacles in accumulating investment capital from domestic sources. Obviously, the vast majority of them need outside aid if they are to lay the necessary groundwork for economic growth. Fortunately, they have access to such aid through investment of foreign private capital and aid from foreign governments.

Foreign investment in developing nations

Foreign private capital investments

Historically, foreign private investments have been important sources of capital for developing nations. Until comparatively recent times, such aid was more often than not primarily for exploitive rather than developmental purposes. Colonialism was the order of the day; the bulk of the underdeveloped nation's wealth was extracted for the benefit of foreign, more "advanced" countries. Today, such blatant economic colonialism is almost entirely a thing of the past. *Nationalism*—a sense of country and culture—has all but wiped it away.

Private foreign capital no longer "follows the flag." That is, it is for the most part truly private. Investors who risk their savings in foreign lands no longer do so with assurance that their profits are more or less guaranteed by the military might of their industrialized homeland. It is worth noting, however, as we shall see below, that rumblings of "economic imperialism" are still heard, especially in developing nations heavily infiltrated by investments of multinational companies.

The operations and the pros and cons of multinational companies will be discussed further in the section on international economics. Suffice it to say here that the multinationals have been an important source of capital investment for many developing nations. And, although the growth of multinational companies has recently slowed, they will undoubtedly continue to contribute to such nations' economic growth for some years to come.

Private capital investments from foreign sources may take the form of money investment in an already established business or industry. Or the money may be used to set up a new firm, with as much managerial responsibility as possible being given to local residents. Sometimes, capital goods are sent directly to a developing nation, along with personnel to operate machinery and/or to train local people to do so.

A flow of private foreign capital may bring important peripheral benefits to less developed nations. Most such nations welcome private aid and are willing to do all that they can to encourage its continued flow. To encourage private foreign capital they know they must provide social capital and a stable political and economic climate. A stable economy and government and a satisfied citizenry mean higher productivity. Domestic economic growth feeds on foreign capital and engenders further capital flows from foreign sources. Growth feeds on growth to the benefit of all.

Foreign private capital investment, however, is not the perfect solution to the problem of capital accumulation in developing nations. Such investments also bring problems. Although political colonialism is more or less dead in our times, various forms of economic colonialism are still a possibility. Developing nations often find there is conflict between their own national interests and the profit-motivated interests of the suppliers of capital.

In a few cases the conflict is stark and obvious. If the emerging nation is weak enough and its need for capital particularly pressing, foreign investors may come to dominate the nation's economy. They may exploit the nation's natural resources in much the same manner as did the earlier colonialists.

This is particularly true when the developing nation has a so-called "plantation economy" base. Foreign capital may be used to extract more minerals or agricultural products from the land. But the work is done at the same low wages and in much the same manner as before infusion of the new capital. The native labor force learns no new skills, production per worker is not greatly increased, and almost all additional profits accrue only to the providers of the capital. A favored few may share in these profits, but in some cases the profits are not reinvested; instead the profits are shifted into other countries for investment. The nation as a whole eventually may suffer from depletion of its resources. In such a case, new capital has a negative effect on the nation's economy. It makes real economic growth more difficult than ever.

In most cases, however, problems arising out of foreign capital flows are more subtle and complex. Even when the developing nation and the foreign providers of capital attempt to strike a balance between their sometimes conflicting interests, problems may still occur. Too often the operation and maintenance of capital goods bought with foreign capital become the prerogative of foreign managers and workers. Local labor is employed only for low-skill and dead-end jobs. Little or no attempt may be made to train and educate the local labor force and thus contribute to long-term economic growth of the developing country.

Also, foreign investors are likely to seek out established and profitable industries in which to put their capital. Often such industries are geared to products exported by the host country. Increased dependence upon export industries conflicts with the developing nation's wish for independence from the economic and political pressures of the more advanced nations who are consumers of their exports.

Problems of foreign capital investment may also arise from the attitudes and actions of the host country. As we have noted, the power of taxation may be used to increase capital accumulation in underdeveloped nations. But it may also be used to discriminate against the legitimate profit expectations of foreign investors. Host countries sometimes erect obstacles to the interests of foreign investors in the form of regulations that inhibit good business practices or restrict the flow of profits earned by foreign investments. Some developing nations may deliberately lag in supplying social capital necessary for profitable investment. In addition, there may be the problem of official graft and corruption to add to the difficulties of doing business in foreign lands. And, of course, there is always the threat that the host nation may *nationalize* (take over, sometimes with little or no recompense) the property of foreign investors.

The actual barriers to foreign investment may not be as high as businesses think. But, if investors think there will be problems, the barriers may be "real" because investment will be reduced.

Foreign government investment

In the interest of world order and in their own self-interest, foreign governments also contribute to the social and economic capital accumulation of the developing nations. The United States, for example, gives aid in the form of low-cost loans and outright grants to many developing nations. Food is sent to poorer nations in on-going programs and in particular emergencies. Loans for capital improvements and technical assistance are made through our *Agency for International Development* (AID). These are very long-range, low-cost loans. In point of fact, the loans are often more like grants than loans. The receiving nation is seldom pressed for repayment, and sometimes the loan is repaid in the overvalued currency of the developing country.

As with private foreign capital, the contribution of foreign governments to capital accumulation presents problems for the developing nation. First, of course, there is the danger of political or military domination by the donor nation. In addition, foreign capital may be used unwisely and thus not contribute to domestic savings necessary for growth. Or it may be wasted on grandiose projects—monumental government buildings, for example—that contribute little to economic expansion. All too often developing nations devote too much of foreign aid to building up military forces.

Finally, the developing nation may find itself so debt ridden that its dream of economic growth is shattered in the cold dawn of near or actual bankruptcy.

In addition to acting as suppliers of capital for developing nations, foreign governments play a vital role in an important aspect of their economic growth we have only touched upon in this chapter—foreign trade, as it relates to the economic well-being of developing nations (and of all nations). (In the next few chapters, we will discuss the theory of trade and barriers to world trade such as tariffs and quotas.)

Most foreign aid, however, is administered on a more business-like and international basis. For example, the *International Bank for Reconstruction and Development* was formed in 1944 at a conference of world leaders. Commonly called the **World Bank,** it operates in a manner similar to commercial banks but for the express purpose of lending capital to underdeveloped nations to stimulate economic growth. The five largest contributors of funds, or shareholders in the bank, are the United States, Great Britain, France, West Germany, and India. Other shareholders represent various blocks of nations throughout the world. Because of sound management and its large initial funding, the bank is able to borrow funds from world money markets at a low rate of interest. It passes these funds along to needy nations at a lower rate than they could likely receive elsewhere or if they tried to borrow directly from the money markets.

The World Bank also operates the *International Development Agency* (IDA). IDA loans are made to needy countries that have little or no short-range means of repayment. The loans extend for 40 years, with no repayment necessary at all for the first 10 years. There is a nominal service charge for the loan, but no interest charge. The World Bank, through its affiliate, *International Finance Corporation* (IFC), also makes loans to private industries within developing nations for expansion beneficial to the economic growth of the nation.

World Bank loans are used for building social capital in the developing nation—for education, health services, roads, airfields, energy generators, and so on. Or, among many other purposes, they may be used for industrial development, especially in mining, iron, and steel manufacture. Or for flood control and irrigation projects to assist agricultural production.

However, there are problems with such loan policies. The World Bank has noted that even though the growth capacity has increased in those countries where loans are made, the very poor often are not really being helped. The increased wealth is not spread evenly; because of power and ownership, the upper classes (even in socialist-oriented developing countries) manage to net nearly all of the gains. So in 1977, World Bank President Robert McNamara announced a shift in direction. The Bank would start instituting a *basic-needs policy* with loans partially contingent on the loans being used for projects that redistribute wealth to those suffering abject poverty. More loans would be made for projects that improved the health, food, housing, and education of the poor.

Stages of economic growth

The growth models of the last chapter apply to any economy which is expanding productive capacity. When we deal with less developed nations, the problem is that growth has failed. Thus we are in a position of needing to transform the economy so growth can begin and continue. The transformation process may just happen or we can seek to bring it about. The process of economic development is something more than economic growth because of the other conditions which must change. We can view the growth process as a series of plateaus or stages; we will discuss each stage in turn.

The following model was developed by Walter W. Rostow. It has been criticized as being only descriptive. Indeed, it is even hard to bring about growth by taking each step in turn. However, each step seems essential and must be taken by an economy if it is to grow and develop. This is true whether the growth is centrally planned as it is in a communist society or whether growth is left to the operation

Economic Thinker
Alexander Gerschenkron

Economic historians are interested in the process by which nations develop economic institutions for deciding economic questions. They explore the characteristics which distinguish traditional economies from command economies and command economies from market economies. Of course, it is always risky to generalize on the basis of historical evidence; there are more differences in this world than there are similarities. Still, a look at how nations have developed economically may be helpful in evaluating policies for the future.

An important economic historian is Alexander Gerschenkron (born 1904). Gerschenkron specializes in the study of economically underdeveloped countries. He has examined traditional economies of the past as they have attempted to achieve industrialization. He has looked for similar characteristics and differences among nations and analyzed the process of change in each. The result is a model of development: a description of the common stages through which underdeveloped nations must pass along the way to modern economic development. The significance of Gerschenkron's model today lies in his conclusions about the dangers of lingering backwardness. In fact, he makes some gloomy predictions about the failure to develop a nation's resources.

All nations were backward once. To move from primitive economic arrangements to a modern industrial society required a sharp break with the past. Many Western nations experienced these changes at roughly the same time; the United States, Germany, Great Britain, and France achieved at least partial industrialization during the first half of the nineteenth century.

The process of change was more difficult for many nations that were to reach industrialization later. Gerschenkron identified common characteristics of nations on the brink of development. First, there is a sufficient supply of resources on which to base production. Although there may be some scarcities and some obstacles to development, these are not so serious as to rule it out entirely. Second, the potential benefits of industrial development are beginning to be understood among the population. There is a substantial group of people who are actively seeking new opportunities for greater prosperity. Finally a "tension" arises between the existing economic institutions and the groups who would install new and progressive arrangements.

The tension is greatest in nations which came late to economic development. This is because the existing economic relationships are extremely backward relative to those of more modern nations. Moreover, the opportunities available are much greater when late developing nations can take advantage of technological discoveries made in other nations. Dealing with the extreme tension in these backward nations requires bold movements in many directions at once, if the nation is to overcome the obstacles and enjoy the benefits of growth more quickly.

Gerschenkron pointed to Czarist Russia as an example of extreme backwardness relative to the industrialized West. Russia began its industrial development late in the nineteenth century and had to overcome serious obstacles to change. The old institution of serfdom had kept Russia's economy exceptionally primitive; there was no trained industrial labor force, there was little basic industry, and there were serious shortages of industrial capital such as power facilities, transportation and communication systems, urban housing, and public services. The extreme backwardness produced severe tension that could be broken only through abrupt and massive moves to create totally new institutions. As in so many backward nations, the only force strong enough to make these bold moves was the central government. In addition, Russia had a long tradition of strong rulers, or czars, and so it became a command economy.

Government had some advantages in the push for growth. Massive industrialization required sacrifices from the people: incomes had to be used for capital investment rather than for consumption; small family plots had to be consolidated into larger and more efficient farms; workers had to move into crowded cities close to factory jobs. Only government could impose these sacrifices. The result was oppression of personal freedom and generally a militant character to Russia's economic development. The sacrifices of the people were said to be necessary because of a supposed military threat from abroad. Their sense of national pride and patriotism and the promise of better times to come led the Russian people to submit to the sacrifices necessary for growth. Growth proceeded faster along those lines that would enhance the military power.

This is where Gerschenkron draws some gloomy predictions about the future. Severe tensions between backwardness and the urgency of development may require that a strong government enforce the necessary changes in economic institutions. The Russian experience suggests that extreme backwardness may lead inevitably to some sort of dictatorship as the society adopts a command economy. Then dictatorship may lead inevitably to war as the government uses external threats as justification for internal oppression.

If Gerschenkron's generalizations are valid, the industrial nations of the world cannot afford to ignore backwardness, wherever it exists. Nations like China, Cuba, and Chile may provide further examples of how economic distress may lead to loss of personal freedom. Many nations of Africa and South America also face the disruptions of development. Whether they choose a command economy or a free market economy may have a real bearing on the future peace of the world.

of an impersonal market in a capitalist society. Both not only must accumulate capital and technology but they must organize it effectively.

Traditional society

This is the condition of the undeveloped economy. The forces which have kept the economy from growing are still in control. The production of the economy is primarily agricultural. The crude technology used is not adaptable to modern, industrial production. The social organization of the system is dominated by traditions, taboos, customs, and roles which prevent change and inhibit economic and social mobility. The people may be very well adapted to local conditions, but they are not in a position to change.

Preconditions for growth

During the preconditions stage, the traditional economy breaks down and is replaced by other forms. The usual example of this stage is the collection of changes which occurred in Europe at the end of the Middle Ages. First, and maybe most important, *there must be a rapid increase in the productivity of agriculture.* Food production must grow faster than population so that *agricultural surpluses* are available. These surpluses are important since they enable the nation to start investment in capital goods. New technology must be adapted to one or more industries during this stage. Finally, entrepreneurs must appear who will put everything together and direct the development of the economy.

Takeoff

This is a critical stage if growth is to occur. If the takeoff is not achieved, the preconditions will not lead to growth. The chains are finally broken and the economy begins to grow. The most important event is the increase in the rate of saving. From a traditional rate of 5%, there is an increase to about 10%. This increase in saving adds to the productive capacity of the country. The rapidity of change produces social and political changes which break down the rest of the traditional economic system.

There is a sort of peaceful revolution. This stage is estimated to last 25 years.

Drive to maturity

This stage lasts some 60 to 100 years. A very high rate of saving continues. As much as $1 of every $5 of income may be saved. Output and income grow very much more rapidly than population. During the early years, heavy manufacturing and transportation industries will predominate. As the stage progresses, new industries will appear. Toward the end of the stage, production will increasingly include goods and services aimed at a growing number of very wealthy people.

High mass consumption

At this stage, emphasis shifts to providing high levels of consumption for all members of the economy. Manufacturing is less important than provision of services. Restaurant service grows while food consumption actually declines. The United States since World War II and Japan and Western Europe in recent years typify this stage.

Decline and fall?

The original discussion of the stages of economic growth did not spend much time on the possibility or necessity of a decline. Continued growth of the mass consumption society was foreseen. It may be that the Roman Empire was an early-day example of things to come. We have few modern examples to consider. It is interesting to speculate about the U.S. economy in 2000 or 2025.

In conclusion

It is easy to see the problems faced by nations which have not yet achieved economic development. With movies and television, the people are aware of the advantages of the developed nations and their own poverty. They are often insistent upon sharing in the economic benefits. They are also prey for almost any scheme which offers economic gain.

In a few cases, social revolution or military adventures may be the only course of action. The countries lack any of the prerequisites for growth. Additional territory, additional resources, or a redistribution of the resources in existence seem to offer the only hope—even if the hope proves illusory.

In other cases, economic development is possible but the delay seems intolerably long. Must each stage of the development cycle be experienced or may some be shortened or skipped altogether? This is the question posed by the people of the less developed nations to their leaders. The leaders turn to economists of developed nations and find that they really have little to offer. Yet, the wealth of the developed nations is both coveted and despised by those who are the "have-nots." The differential between the "haves" and the "have-nots" is great. It is difficult to build a peaceful world when such great differences exist. So far, only small wars have resulted—in Ireland, in the Mideast, in Africa—but how much longer the world has to solve the development problems before major wars develop is not clear. The problem of economic development will occupy economists for a long time to come.

Summary

Lack of economic development in some nations while others enjoy great wealth places social and political strains on all nations of the world. There are certain characteristics common to all less developed countries.

(1) Poor nations suffer most from their *poverty*. The level of income is low and the distribution of the income is generallly very inequitable. (2) A large and rapidly *growing population* often presses on the poor nation's resources. There is little human capital in the form of education and training. (3) *Physical capital* is also lacking. The low level of income makes it difficult for the poor nation to accumulate capital from saving of the local population. A vicious circle of poverty develops which means that low income leads to low saving which leads to more poverty.

Development may become an important political goal of a nation. But a developing nation faces several barriers or challenges that it must overcome to grow.

(1)   Controlling population growth is one method attempted to achieve economic development.

(2)   Building skills in the population is another. Employing existing skills effectively may require relocation of the population or better flows of labor market information. Before development is achieved, a brain drain may develop which will cost the economy some of the badly needed human resources.

(3)   Natural resource problems are difficult to overcome since an economy cannot create natural resources where there are none. Selling the primary products directly may lead to entering a world market which will absorb additional quantities of the commodity only at very much reduced prices.

(4)   Technology is not always the answer. If technology is to be employed, it must first be adapted to local conditions. The technology of advanced nations is seldom immediately useful. In addition, the local population must be trained to use and accept the new technology.

(5)   Social capital is often lacking in a less developed nation. The economy is not strong enough to produce such items and there is no market incentive to provide such capital. Yet without roads, airports, postal services, hospitals, and schools, the economy will have trouble developing beyond the present stage.

(6)   Governments may have to play a greater role in the economies of developing nations if the process of development is to be speeded along. In some instances, government may only have to provide social stability and an orderly business climate. In most cases, however, government must undertake a more active role, providing long-range economic planning and land reform.

(7)   Capital accumulation is often difficult for developing nations. Capital may be taken out of the country by the few wealthy residents. Investment by foreigners may be resisted on cultural or ideological grounds. A poor economy with all its problems is not a likely place for investment in any event.

(8)   Cultural and political barriers may have to be overcome for growth to occur.

Direct aid or investment by foreign sources is possible through (1) foreign private capital investments and (2) foreign government assistance. Foreign private investment is useful when it helps build capital in the host nation. Much of this private capital is provided by multinational companies. In the past, multinational firms have unfortunately been able to dominate the economies of small host nations.

Foreign governmental aid can be administered either (1) *directly* through grants or low-cost loans or (2) through *intermediary institutions* like the World Bank.

The developing economy may have to proceed through a series of stages which include the traditional society, the precondition for growth, the takeoff, the drive to maturity, the high mass consumption stage, and perhaps the final stage of decline.

Key Words and Phrases

- **disguised unemployment**   a situation where workers report to their job and do either no work or little useful work.

- **brain drain problem**   a condition faced by many less developed countries of the world where the highly trained people, badly needed for economic development, leave for more developed areas at higher income levels.

- **adaptation (of technology)**   the process of taking highly developed technology from advanced areas and amending it to make it useful in less developed areas.

- **adoption (of technology)**   the acceptance by producers of a new technology.

- **social capital**   the collection of various capital goods which may be publicly or privately owned but which serve in the broad areas of education, health, transportation, communication, and energy.

- **World Bank**   formally, the International Bank for Reconstruction and Development; funded by the industrialized nations, it loans money out at low rates for specific projects in developing nations. Through subsidiaries, it may make loans directly to governments of needy nations or to private developers with plans for investment in a poor nation.

- **nationalize**   government takeover of private firms; sometimes the firms are compensated by the government, other times they receive little or no payment.

- **agricultural surplus**   the food left over after a nation's people are fed; some economists feel that such a surplus is a key ingredient for economic growth, since it can be sold to provide capital goods.

Questions for Review

1. How great a difference between rich and poor will be tolerated in the U.S.? How great a difference in wealth will the world tolerate between the U.S. and some of the poorest nations? Can you say how you came to believe as you do?

2. Suppose we shipped a number of our large agricultural tractors to farmers in India or China to use to plow their rice paddies? Would rice production rise? What would the result be?

3. Would you suggest to residents of poor nations that they simply move to developed areas? Why or why not? What would the problems be? the results?

4. Why are birth rates high in poor nations? Can lower birth rates bring economic development? After economic development, why do birth rates fall? Can you list some countries which have set out to lower birth rates? How did they do it? How did they deal with religious beliefs?

5. Why does aid from developed countries often fail to produce development in the poor nations?

6. Suppose a poor nation has one natural resource—a metal ore, petroleum, or an agricultural product such as coffee, chocolate, or jute. Should the country expand production of the product and sell it on the world market in order to get rich?

7. Farmers in some poor nations plant crops because their fathers and grandfathers planted those crops. Suppose the product is no longer desirable. How does the farmer find out? If and when he does, how does he go about changing his production pattern? Can the United States help him?

8. How does a poor nation without natural resources get them?

9. What are the stages of economic growth? Can any economy skip a stage? Can we hurry up the process? How?

10. Explain how the World Bank operates.

Part Five

International Economics

19

International Trade

Sometimes very old words are useful for describing very new phenomena. "Synergism" is an old word used to describe a process which produces more output than the sum of its inputs. Medical science uses the word to describe how two drugs interact to produce a greater total effect than the sum of the two used separately. Managers of enterprises use it to describe how cooperative effort can yield greater output than individuals working alone. In both cases, synergism is the process by which the whole becomes greater than the sum of its parts. The concept of synergism is especially useful for describing economic phenomena.

In this chapter we will explore the synergistic effects of world trade. Trade is synergistic because its total benefits are greater than the sum of the individual benefits enjoyed before trade. When individuals trade, the total utility of all goods and services received is greater than the utility or satisfaction given up. Synergism has taken place.

Trade between nations is synergistic, too. The people of a trading nation receive more additional utility per dollar from consuming goods produced in another country than they give up in the goods they exchange.

As trade grows to include many nations, the synergistic effect increases. Trade permits each nation to *specialize*—that is, to do what it does best. Each nation tends toward a *division of labor* that allows workers to develop great skill in making the products in which it specializes. Specialization and division of labor result in improved technology and greater productivity throughout the world. When nations trade freely, all peoples enjoy higher standards of living and a greater variety of social and cultural opportunities. And the total improvement is greater than the sum of improvements each country would have achieved without trade. Synergism is at work.

Trade, then, bestows benefits on the trading nations. It also bestows power. The United States, because of its climate and land mass, has been able to develop a highly efficient agricultural technology. We are able to feed one-fourth of the world's population. Our high productivity in agriculture also frees our energies for the production of high-value manufactured goods. We can produce many more of such goods than we need for our own use. But other nations need and want these goods. The United States thus has great power—leverage, you might call it—in the economic and political world.

The oil-producing nations of the Middle East enjoy the power associated with their wealth of energy resources. As global requirements for fuel increase and as alternative sources are gradually depleted, their power to withhold supplies and set prices lends much weight to their political and economic demands.

Other nations and blocs of nations exercise the power of trade. Some have strong trading capabilities and hence much power. Some have relatively less. Some Third World nations, for example, have little or no influence in world decision-making. They lack materials and goods for trade. Therefore, they lack the power to command goods and services to expand their production and raise their standards of living. Trade is power.

Beginnings of trade

Early primitive tribes recognized the benefits of trade. Without trade, each extended family group within the tribe had to produce its own requirements of food, shelter, and decorative ornaments. Eventually, family groups began to specialize—some in food gathering, some in weapons production. Some even specialized in performing rituals to placate tribal gods. Such goods and services came to be traded within a single tribe.

Later, some isolated groups expanded their trade to include other tribes. They were cautious at first. In remote areas of Africa, northern Russia, and the southern Pacific a form of silent barter developed. A member of one tribe would approach a familiar trail crossing and deposit items for trade: beads, clay pots, and dried fruits, for example. Then the primitive merchant would retreat to a nearby sheltering bush to watch.

Soon a trader from another tribe would approach and deposit other goods believed to be acceptable in exchange: cloth, a tool, and perhaps a goat. He likewise would disappear into the bushes.

The first trader would return and, if the offering was acceptable, take it and leave. If the offering was judged inadequate, the trader might remove one item from the first pile. If the second trader found the exchange agreeable, the trade would be complete. The fine art of haggling has a long history!

The pure theory of international trade

The pure theory of international trade has microeconomic and macroeconomic implications. Its microeconomic aspects refer to the interaction of demand and supply in individual markets. As in domestic markets, trade establishes an *equilibrium* price and quantity for traded goods and services. When markets are linked through trade, equilibrium occurs at the intersection of *global demand* and *global supply*.

The macroeconomic aspects of international trade refer to the effects of trade on a nation's output, income, and employment. Growth in aggregate global demand can stimulate greater production and help to relieve problems of domestic unemployment. Excessive global demand can push a nation beyond its normal productive capacity and lead to inflation. An even more important macroeconomic aspect of international trade is the growth in production possibilities that results from specialization and international division of labor.

Micro aspects of international trade

We will begin with a look at the microeconomic aspects of international trade and show how trade affects equilibrium price and quantity of traded goods.

First, let us suppose the world is composed of only two nations. Citizens of both nations must consume certain quantities of food and burn certain quantities of fuel. Their demand curves for food and fuel are shown in Figures 1 and 2. Demand curves are downward sloping. This shows that some quantity must be used regardless of price (everyone has to eat) and that larger quantities will be consumed at lower prices. The curves are drawn identically to simplify the explanation.

Now suppose that country A is uniquely situated to produce fuel and country B to produce food. A's resource capabilities make its costs of producing fuel very low and its cost of producing food high. This means that A's short-run supply curve for fuel will lie low and to the right, suggesting low unit costs for fuel production. A's supply curve for food will lie high and to the left, suggesting high unit costs for food production. Conversely, B's short-run supply curve for fuel will lie high and to the left and its supply curve for food will lie low and to the right.

Without international trade, domestic demand and supply alone will determine the

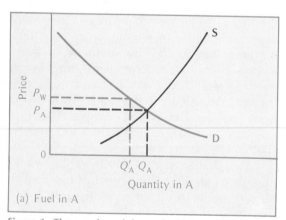

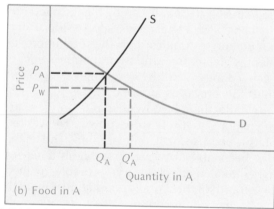

Figure 1 The supply and demand within country A: (a) for fuel; (b) for food. Notice that fuel is more plentiful. P_W is the world market price and Q'_A is country A's output at world price.

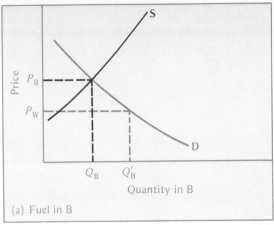

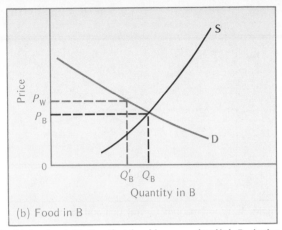

Figure 2 The supply and demand within country B: (a) for fuel; (b) for food. Notice that food is more plentiful. P_W is the world market price and Q'_B is country B's output at world price.

equilibrium price and quantity for both commodities in both markets. Fuel will be abundant and cheap in A and food scarce and expensive. In B, fuel will be expensive and food cheap.

Citizens in both countries will expand consumption of both food and fuel as long as they feel the use of each adds more to their well-being than they must give up to purchase the food or fuel. The well-being or utility contributed by the last unit consumed is called *marginal utility*. Because of the low price of fuel in A, fuel consumption is expanded to a large quantity OQ_A. So much fuel is used that the last unit provides little additional utility, by the principle of diminishing marginal utility. (This principle states that, after some point, as more units of a good are acquired, each additional unit adds less utility than the one before.) In B, the higher price restricts the quantity of fuel consumed to OQ_B. Consumption is limited to the small quantity by the high price. As a result, the utility of the last unit consumed will be very high.

Differences in marginal utility of consumption between nations open the possibility for trade to enhance global welfare. Total world utility will be increased if fuel is transferred from regions where its marginal utility is low to regions where its marginal utility is high. To transfer a unit of fuel from country A would cause only a small loss in total utility. The gain in utility in B would be comparatively much greater.

The same generalization applies to the marginal utility of food in the two countries. Trade permits citizens of A to trade fuel, for which their marginal utility is low, for food, for which their marginal utility is high.

How will trade affect price and quantity?

Let us suppose *free trade* is opened between countries A and B so that their goods are traded in a single combined market. For simplicity, we will assume there are no transport costs. The combined world markets for fuel and food are shown in Figure 3. Global demand for fuel is the sum of demand of A and B. Similarly, global demand for food is the combined demand of A and B.

With trade, A may now specialize in the production for which its resources are best suited—fuel. A's short-run supply curve then becomes the world supply for fuel. With total specialization, A can avoid wasting resources on food production. As a result, its supply curve for fuel will lie farther to the right than before trade. B will use its resources only in food production. Its short-run supply curve becomes the world supply of food. Total specialization will also move B's supply curve farther to the right than before trade.

Compare OP_A and OP_B in Figures 1 and 2 with OP_w in Figure 3.

don't use utility, inter product, inter personal & inter personal comparison — prod u instead (handwritten)

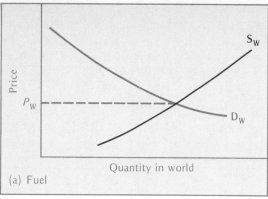

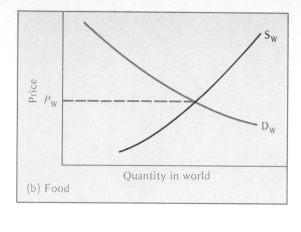

Figure 3   World markets for: (a) fuel and (b) food.

The new equilibrium price for fuel is now greater in A and lower in B than before trade. Citizens of A move up their demand curves for fuel until marginal utility is sufficient to justify the new higher price. Citizens of B move down their demand curves for fuel until marginal utility is consistent with the new lower price. Citizens of B gain utility which is greater than the utility given up by citizens of A. Verify that this is true by comparing purchases in each country at the new world price (Figures 1 and 2). Show that in each case the utility gained in the importing nation is greater than the loss to the exporter.

At equilibrium, the utility of the last unit of fuel used is the same in both countries. There can be no further benefit through shipment of fuel from one nation to the other. Fuel consumption is now greater in B than before trade and lower in A.

Similar results occur in the world microeconomic market for food. The new equilibrium price equates marginal utilities worldwide so that no further benefit can be made from trade in food. At equilibrium, food consumption is greater in A than before trade and lower in B.

But note that *total* consumption of fuel and food worldwide may actually be greater than before trade. With specialization, producers of the two commodities may achieve cost savings allowing them to produce a larger total supply.

What are the benefits of specialization?

As nations specialize, resources move into particular kinds of production and short-run supply curves shift to the right. Greater specialization may involve lower unit costs, the same unit costs, or rising unit costs. The effect of specialization on unit costs depends on the availability of particular resources needed for production.

Rising unit costs occur when an industry uses a particular resource which is in short supply. If many firms begin production, they will bid up the price of the scarce resource. Even the United States can not fulfill *all* the world's food needs. To do so would require plowing up city streets, marshes, and mountains, and costs would rise prohibitively. Even plentiful Arab oil resources are not unlimited. At some point oil deposits will become depleted and recovery costs of petroleum will rise.

When particular resources are limited, unit costs will eventually rise with expanded production. At first specialization will cause short-run supply curves to shift rightward; but resource scarcity may finally prevent further increases at the same cost. The result of specialization may be an increase in world prices.

Falling unit costs occur when the increase in production brings on technological progress. For instance, labor skills may grow with specialization. The entry of many new firms into an industry may make specialized transport or power facilities practical. Large industry

Economic Thinker

Jacob Viner

Jacob Viner was born in 1892, in Montreal, Canada. He came to the United States in 1914, and received his Ph.D. from Harvard in 1922. He became a citizen of the United States in 1924. Soon after his arrival here he became associated with the University of Chicago and remained on its faculty until 1946. He then became professor of economics at Princeton University. Viner was consultant to the United States Treasury Department from 1935 to 1939 and to the State Department from 1943 to 1952.

Jacob Viner's interests were wide ranging, both within the field of economic theory and in other areas such as the history of religion and of British social thought. His principal contribution to economic theory, however, was in international trade. In 1937, he published his *Studies in the Theory of International Trade*, a monumental review and evaluation of the subject. His work was to serve as a model for many of his economic peers and for those who later came to serious study of international trade. Viner was particularly interested in measuring gains from international trade. Building on the work of earlier theorists, he argued for the usefulness of "partial equilibrium analysis" as an economic tool. That is, he emphasized the study of "representative firms" to throw light upon the broader aspects of economic systems. Viner's approach provided great impetus to empirical research into the complexities of international economics.

Viner was also interested in the newly emerging study of monopoly or imperfect competition. In a famous essay on cost and supply curves in 1931, Viner helped to clarify for American economists the concepts of a young Italian economist, Piero Sraffa, whose brilliant work helped open this area to economic analysis.

Jacob Viner was a prolific writer. In addition to his own books and numerous articles, he edited the *Journal of Political*

Economy for more than fifteen years, contributing greatly to the scholarly excellence of that journal. Some 2,000 manuscript pages of his own works in progress were being readied for publication at his death in 1970.

requirements for raw materials or component parts may lead to economies of scale in their production. Specialization in coffee production has enabled Brazil to develop technological aids which reduce unit costs. Specialization in electronics has permitted Japan to focus its research and development energies in this industry. Other examples come to mind: meat from Argentina, aircraft from the United States, precision instruments from West Germany. Specialization and large-scale production of these goods for export have permitted technical cost advantages.

Whenever technical progress accompanies specialization, unit costs will fall. Short-run supply curves will shift rightward by larger and larger amounts so more units can be produced with fewer resources. *World prices will fall with specialization and trade.*

Constant unit costs are the result of offsetting changes in resource costs and technical advances. Specialization will cause short-run supply curves to shift rightward moderately as more units are produced at the same unit costs.

To the extent that unit costs are constant or falling, the world will enjoy the greatest gains from trade. When unit costs increase, specialization and trade may result in rising world prices. But still costs will generally be lower than without specialization.

How will international trade affect incomes?

Changing price patterns have further effects which benefit the citizens of trading nations. In our hypothetical example, we assumed that different resource advantages brought on the cost advantages which stimulated trade: an abundance of fuel-producing resources in A and an abundance of food-producing resources in B. Without trade, A's plentiful fuel-producing resources would command a low price. This is because a plentiful supply relative to domestic demand means a low equilibrium price.

Without trade, Japan's skilled labor force would command low wages; Japanese consumers could not possibly purchase all the cameras and electronic equipment they produce. Without trade, Kansas wheat fields would be worth much less and farmers' incomes would be lower. When particular resources—including land, labor, capital, and entrepreneurship—are plentiful relative to the *derived demand* for their services, incomes will generally be low. (Recall that derived demand is the demand for a resource that results because of the demand for the goods the resource can produce.)

The reverse is true when resources are scarce relative to domestic demand. In our hypothetical example, scarce food-producing resources command high incomes in country A. Supply is low relative to the demand for output. Wheat-producing lands in Canada and mineral deposits in Japan are real-world examples of resources which are in short supply relative to derived demand. Without trade, their incomes would be very high.

Trade narrows the gap between earnings paid to a region's various productive resources. Trade raises the derived demand for the fuel-producing resources of A. The rise is reflected in higher returns for oil fields, drilling and refining equipment, and pipelines. In B, trade increases the derived demand for food-producing resources. Wage rates rise for farm laborers and rents rise on farmlands. Entrepreneurs receive higher profits for production of agricultural equipment. The United States resembles country B with regard to the benefits of trade to farmers. Sales of grain to Russia in the mid-1970s enabled American farmers to enjoy higher incomes. The benefits of this trade also provided the extra income needed to buy new farm equipment.

With free trade, resources in both nations are employed in industries for which they are best suited. Resources receive incomes according to the value of their output in *total world markets*. Higher return to resources encourages greater productivity and provides funds for new capital investment. Research and development efforts can focus on technical progress in the region's specialty. As a result, production may take place at even lower unit costs, further enhancing the basic benefits from international trade.

Trade reduces the derived demand for high-priced resources and products that are not a nation's "speciality." Resource owners complain of cheap foreign imports cutting into their domestic market and reducing their incomes. Workers complain about the possibility of losing their jobs or having to learn a new trade. The fact that overall and in the long run *everyone* will be better off will not comfort them. As we shall see in Chapter 21, powerful voices have been raised throughout modern history to restrict international trade. They are still being raised. And they are still powerful.

Macro aspects of international trade

The macroeconomic aspects of international trade include the broad national and world aggregates in economic activity: the levels of output, income, and employment; resource allocation and income distribution; and growth in production possibilities.

National income and trade

For some nations international trade represents a major part of total production. Production for export has long been significant in Belgium and the Netherlands where exports represent more than one half the gross national product (GNP). Other European nations export large percentages of their national output to pay for necessary imports of food and raw materials. Table 1 shows the relationship between imports and exports and total output for selected countries.

In the United States our large and varied land mass provides most of the food and materials we need. And a large domestic consumer market provides outlets for our manufactured goods. Therefore, imports and exports represent only about 8% of United States GNP. However, the United States is the world's largest trader. In 1976, imports amounted to nearly $121 billion and exports nearly $115 billion.

The strength of demand for foreign goods is reflected in a nation's computation of aggregate demand. *Aggregate demand* is the sum of consumption expenditures, business investment, government purchases, and net exports. In mathematical terms,

aggregate demand $= C + I + G + X_n$.

Net exports are the excess of foreign sales over purchases from foreign sources:

X_n = value of exports − value of imports.

Note that X_n can be a positive or a negative number. What nations in Table 1 enjoyed a positive value for net exports in 1974? What nations had a negative value?

If the value of imports exceeds the value of exports, X_n becomes a negative number. The result is a decrease in the value of a nation's aggregate demand and a fall in national output, income, and employment. Spending for imports is a "leakage" from aggregate demand. For an economy at full employment, a fall in aggregate demand may mean the loss of jobs.

Table 1
Trade as a Percentage of GNP for Selected Countries, 1974

Country	GNP (in millions of dollars)	% Imports	% Exports
Argentina	81,385	2.7%	4.0%
Australia	55,300	20.0	19.5
Austria	29,100	31.1	24.6
Belgium	47,700	62.3	59.3
Brazil	77,220	16.3	10.3
Denmark	27,700	36.4	34.1
Finland	17,060	42.3	34.1
India	71,000	6.7	5.5
Israel	8,950	62.4	19.2
Italy	138,270	29.6	21.9
Japan	405,300	15.3	13.7
Mexico	48,650	13.4	7.0
Netherlands	61,700	54.8	54.4
Nigeria	14,802	18.5	64.6
Norway	18,750	44.9	33.5
South Africa	26,125	27.6	19.1
Spain	63,500	24.1	11.1
Switzerland	40,900	35.3	28.8
Turkey	23,700	15.7	6.5
United Kingdom	175,500	30.9	22.0
United States	1,406,900	7.8	8.0

It may also mean a failure to employ scarce resources efficiently.

If the value of exports exceeds the value of imports, X_n will be a positive number. The result is an addition to aggregate demand. This means an expansion of output, income, and employment. For an underemployed economy, a rise in aggregate demand can give a welcome boost to output. But for an economy already at full employment a rise in aggregate demand can also produce inflation and distortion in the use of scarce resources. Table 2 shows the components of U.S. exports and imports for selected recent years. What has been the trend in these values? What commodities seem responsible for changes in the flow of trade?

Figure 4 shows how shifts in X_n affect an economy. An increase in X_n is shown in Figure 4a. An increase in X_n may be caused by an increase in exports or a decrease in imports. The diagram is drawn with a parallel upward

Table 2a
U.S. Exports—Each Given as Percent of Total Exports

Item exported	1960	1971	1974
Food and live animals	13.2%	10.0%	14.4%
Beverage and tobacco	2.4	1.6	1.3
Crude materials, except food & fuel	13.7	10.0	11.3
Mineral fuels and related materials	4.1	3.4	3.5
Chemicals	8.7	8.8	9.1
Machinery and transportation equipment	34.3	44.7	39.3
Other manufactured goods	18.7	16.4	17.0
Total Value of exports	$20,408m.	$43,493m.	$97,143m.

Table 2b
U.S. Imports—Each Given as Percent of Total Imports

Item imported	1960	1971	1974
Food and live animals	19.9%	12.1%	9.3%
Beverage and tabacco	2.6	1.9	1.3
Crude materials, except food & fuel	18.3	7.4	5.9
Mineral fuels and related materials	10.5	8.2	25.1
Chemicals	5.3	3.5	4.0
Machinery and transportation equipment	9.7	30.4	24.5
Other manufactured goods	30.3	32.8	27.2
Total value of imports	$15,073m.	$45,563m.	$100,972m.

shift in the aggregate demand curve. At less than full employment the increase in X_n may be a welcome change. At full employment the increase may be inflationary.

A decrease in X_n is shown in Figure 4b. The decrease may be the result of a decrease in exports or an increase in imports. At full employment or below, the decline in X_n will mean a disturbing loss of jobs. But if the economy is suffering from inflation, the decline may assist in controlling the inflation.

The foreign trade multiplier

Changes in consumption, investment, and government purchases (C + I + G) are known to have a multiple effect on national output, income, and employment. Changes in these components of total spending produce *multiple changes* as incomes are spent and respent throughout the economy—much like ripples in a pond. The total change in income is a result of this *multiplier effect*.

Changes in net exports (X_n) produce similar results. The **foreign trade multiplier** is a measure of the change in output, income, and employment that results from a change in net exports. The size of the foreign trade multiplier depends on the response of a nation's economy to change in the level of foreign spending. Compare the small change in X_n in Figure 4 with the greater change in national income and output. The greater change is a result of the foreign trade multiplier.

The foreign trade multiplier in action World War I brought economic dislocation to the warring nations and a collapse of world trade. When peace came, nations tried to rebuild domestic industry by discouraging imports.

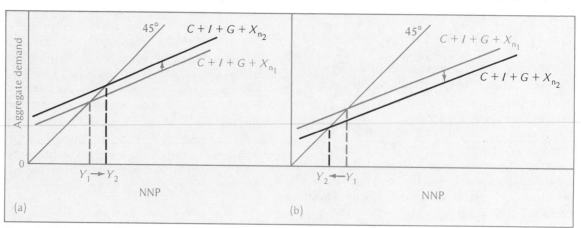

Figure 4 (a) An increase in net exports (from X_{n_1} to X_{n_2}) causes an increase in aggregate demand, which leads to an increase in NNP (if Y_1 is not at full employment). (b) A decrease in net exports reverses the process. Aggregate demand falls and so does output (NNP) and employment.

Every import was seen as a threat to jobs at home. Trade was blocked by tariffs in order to protect local industry from international competition. But a restriction in one nation's imports is necessarily a restriction on another's exports. If country A will not buy food from country B, then B cannot buy fuel from A. International trade collapsed. The X_n component of aggregate demand fell to zero, or below, in many nations.

With the drop in export sales, Western nations experienced sharp declines in output, income, and employment. The drop in aggregate demand culminated in the Great Depression of the 1930s. Other factors contributed to this great decline in economic activity, of course. But the loss of foreign markets was a serious problem in many nations. Recognition of the bad effects of tariffs led to more enthusiastic support for free trade in later years.

Resource allocation

Regions differ in their resource endowments. Products differ in their resource requirements. A region with plentiful labor and little capital may be characterized as labor abundant and capital poor. Recall that products requiring much labor are characterized as *labor intensive*, while those products requiring much capital are called *capital intensive*. It is reasonable to assume that labor-abundant regions will specialize in labor-intensive production.

In the early years of our history, the United States was land abundant but labor and capital poor. This allowed us to export the raw products of our mines, forests, and farms. But we had to import labor- and capital-intensive manufactured goods. As our population grew and we acquired more capital, we increased production of goods requiring more labor and capital: textiles, machinery, automobiles, and aircraft. In recent years our population growth has slowed. But high productivity and high incomes have enabled us to save and invest in larger quantities of capital. We have been able to continue to increase our specialization in capital-intensive goods for export—aircraft, for example, and power plants.

Our growing stock of capital has enabled us to produce some goods generally associated with other countries. For generations the abundance of labor in certain Oriental countries enabled them to export fine carpets to the United States. In recent years, however, we have developed computerized looms for duplicating Oriental rugs at much lower unit costs. The carpet industry has become more capital-intensive, giving our carpet exports an advantage over labor-intensive carpets produced abroad.

Not all capital is material. In addition to machinery and equipment, we have invested in *human* capital. Investment in labor skills enables us to produce goods which are labor saving, land saving, and *material* capital saving. Many United States exports should be characterized as human-capital intensive.

A high level of human capital is required in the production of chemicals, data processing equipment, and precision instruments. Even agricultural products are human-capital intensive in so far as specialized education and scientific research have enabled the American farmer to outproduce other farmers. For example, American rice producers use advanced knowledge and scientific techniques to plant, wash, and process rice. Productivity is thus vastly superior to that of the rice paddies of Southeast Asia. We also export human-capital-intensive *services*. Business and technical consulting, insurance, and financial services require highly trained human capital.

Production possibilities & absolute advantage

A nation's particular combination of resources enables it to produce particular kinds of output. To demonstrate the relationship between resources and output, we will construct models of production possibilities for two nations with different resource endowments. As in our previous model, we will assume that all possible output for each country can be classified as either fuel or food. We will combine productive resources into homogeneous lumps in each country. Each "resource lump" includes the nation's particular combination of land, labor, capital, and entrepreneurship. Because labor constitutes the most plentiful resource, we will call a lump of resources a *labor hour*. We will assume each nation owns one-hundred resource lumps, or labor hours, to use in production.

Comparing productivity

Table 3 below shows the quantities of food and fuel which can be produced per labor hour in the two countries. Each labor hour in country A can produce either 10 units of fuel or 5 units of food. In country B each labor hour can produce 2 units of fuel or 6 units of food. A's resources are more suited for the production of fuel and B's for the production of food. This can be seen two ways: by comparing productivity in the two countries and by comparing costs for the two commodities.

To compare productivity, read the columns vertically. Reading from top to bottom, it can be seen that A outproduces B ten-to-two in fuel production. But A's productivity is only five-to-six in food production. Reading from bottom to top, we see that B outproduces A six-to-five in food production. But B's productivity is only two-to-ten in fuel production.

The relative productivity per unit of resource in two nations is called a **productivity ratio.** A's productivity ratio is greater in fuel ($\frac{10}{2} = 5$) and B's is greater in food ($\frac{6}{5} = 1\frac{1}{5}$).

With each labor hour, country A can produce five times as much fuel as country B. Stating this relationship differently, country B produces only $\frac{1}{5}$ as much fuel as country A. However, country A can produce only $\frac{5}{6}$ as much food as country B per labor hour. Country B produces $1\frac{1}{5}$ as much food as country A per unit of resource.

The *absolute costs of production* are the quantities of resources given up in the two countries. Each unit of fuel costs $\frac{1}{10}$ labor in A

Table 3
Production per Labor Hour of Resource

	Units of fuel	Units of food
Country A	10	5
Country B	2	6

Table 4
Production Costs in Labor Hours

	Fuel	Food
Country A	$\frac{1}{10}$	$\frac{1}{5}$
Country B	$\frac{1}{2}$	$\frac{1}{6}$

and $\frac{1}{2}$ labor hour in B. Clearly, fuel production is less costly in A. Each unit of food costs $\frac{1}{5}$ labor hour in A and $\frac{1}{6}$ labor hour in B. Food production is less costly in B. Table 4 shows production costs in A and B for fuel and food.

Country A requires fewer labor hours per unit of fuel produced than country B requires. But country B requires fewer labor hours per unit of food produced than country A.

The principle of absolute advantage

Refer again to Table 3 showing production in countries A and B. In A, the use of a single labor hour is more productive in fuel production. Moreover, to produce each unit of fuel uses fewer productive resources in A than it does in B. We say that A's resources have *absolute advantage* in the production of fuel. B's resources are more productive in food production. To produce each unit of food uses fewer productive resources in B than it does in A. B has absolute advantage in the production of food.

The **principle of absolute advantage** can be stated simply:

Whenever a nation can produce a particular good or service more cheaply than another nation in terms of resources used, it is said to have absolute advantage in production of that good.

For example, the character of its natural resource endowment gives Spain absolute advantage in cork production, Sweden absolute advantage in lumber, Norway in seafood, Denmark in ham, and the Netherlands in cheese. In addition, specialized capital resources in these nations have enhanced their absolute advantage as they concentrated their energies on developing these particular industries.

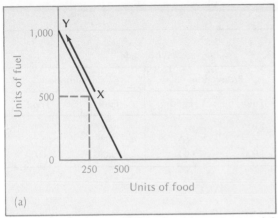

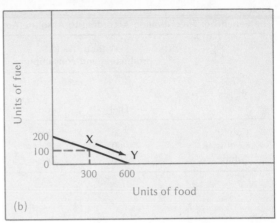

Figure 5 Production possibilities for: (a) country A and (b) country B. Notice that country A is able to produce more fuel than food, while B can produce more food than fuel. Before trade, each nation must be self-sufficient; production and consumption are shown at point X. With trade, nations specialize according to absolute advantage; production is shown at point Y.

Production possibilities Now let us look at A and B's total production possibilities. Assume that each nation has one-hundred labor hours for use in production. Total production possibilities are shown in Figure 5. A's resources and technology enable it to produce more fuel. B's enable it to produce more food. Using all its resources, A could produce either 1,000 units of fuel, 500 units of food, or any combination shown on its production possibilities curve. Using all its resources, B could produce either 200 units of fuel or 600 units of food.

For simplicity, the production possibilities curves have been drawn with a constant slope. The constant slope assumes constant opportunity costs in the production of food and fuel. As A moves resources from production of fuel into food production, each additional unit of food requires the same opportunity cost in fuel not produced. The constant opportunity cost for producing a unit of food in A is two units of fuel. Similarly, to move resources from food production to fuel production in B requires a constant opportunity cost of 3 units of food.

Trade among nations is often based on the principle of absolute advantage. The principle of absolute advantage allows each nation to specialize in the production for which its resources are best suited. Using the production possibilities curves for A and B, let us compare production and consumption before and after trade begins.

Without trade, A and B must produce their entire requirements of both goods. Suppose each nation decides to allocate half its labor hours to food and half to fuel. A can produce and consume 500 fuel units and 250 food units. B's production and consumption are 100 fuel units and 300 food units. Move along each nation's production possibilities curve to point X, where each is self-sufficient in food and fuel production. Total production in the two nations is 600 fuel units and 550 food units as shown at the left in Table 5.

If trade opens between A and B, total production and consumption will increase. Trade permits both nations to use their resources most effectively. Each nation can specialize in the production in which it has absolute advantage. Move along each nation's production possibilities curve to point Y, where each specializes according to absolute advantage. In A, specialization in fuel will yield total production of 1,000 units. In B, specialization in food will yield 600 units.

Dividing output in half and trading will provide both nations more total units than without trade. Check Table 5 to see that this is true. When countries A and B were not trading, each consumed what it produced; total consumption was 600 units of food and 550 units

Table 5
The Benefits of Specialization According to Absolute Advantage

	Without trade, production and consumption		With trade			
			Production		Consumption	
	Fuel	Food	Fuel	Food	Fuel	Food
Country A	500	250	1,000	0	500	300
Country B	100	300	0	600	500	300
Total	600	550	1,000	600	1,000	600

of fuel. When they decided to trade, they specialized and increased production. In our example, they decided to trade one half of food output—500 units—for one half of fuel output—300 units. They could have decided a different ratio of trade—say, perhaps a unit of food for a unit of fuel. As Table 5 shows, the final result here was that each country was able to consume more after trading. The total consumed becomes 1,000 fuel units and 600 food units.

At the beginning of this chapter we used the term "synergism" to describe the gains from trade. From the discussion above, you can see that, in economic terms, a whole can indeed become greater than the sum of its parts.

Absolute advantage of individuals and among nations

Like nations, some individuals enjoy absolute advantage in the production of certain goods and services. Their superior productivity encourages them to specialize and to earn large returns from their specialty. Reggie Jackson earns substantial returns from his skill as a homerun hitter, Joan Sutherland for her operatic voice, and Dr. Christiaan Barnard for his surgeon's skills. The world economy would have suffered if they had used their resources in mining, weaving—or teaching economics. Their specialization according to absolute advantage enables the rest of us to enjoy the benefits of their talents.

It is generally assumed that modern industrialized nations have absolute advantage in manufactured goods and that less developed nations have absolute advantage in basic

materials. The assumption is that costs of producing basic materials are lower in less developed countries. In actual fact, industrialized countries rather than developing countries have absolute advantage in production of most raw materials.

For example, the less developed countries produce only 28% of world mineral products. Free market economies produce 45% and command economies 27%. Less developed countries do produce as much as 90% of a limited list of commodities: coffee, cocoa, tea, jute, hard fibers, and natural rubber, for example. Specific geographical features give them absolute advantage in the production of these commodities. Such commodities, however, are few. Moreover, the actual marketing and transporting of these commodities often depend on the resources of the industrialized countries. Among less developed countries, resource endowment and absolute advantage are unevenly distributed. Only a few have the capacity to produce and export large quantities of minerals.

What can we conclude with respect to absolute advantage among nations?

We must acknowledge that some nations—the industrialized nations—may possess absolute advantage both in manufacturing and in the production of basic materials. If this is true, does this contradict the pure theory of international trade? Will only favored nations benefit from trade? No, the benefits of trade do not depend on the existence of absolute advantage. Even nations without absolute advantage in any production at all may still gain from world trade. The world economy will benefit and their producers will benefit when such nations specialize according to *comparative advantage*.

Comparative advantage

Thus far, our trading model has been unrealistic. There may be some commodities in which neither country A nor country B enjoys absolute advantage. Resource costs of production may differ from our simple model. Still, specialization and trade will permit more effective use of resources and greater total production of most goods.

In Table 6, output figures have been changed so that A and B are equally efficient in the production of fuel. However, A outproduces B five-to-two in the production of food, giving A absolute advantage in food production.

Opportunity costs

This time, specialization will depend on the principle of comparative advantage. The *principle of comparative advantage* is somewhat more complex than the principle of absolute advantage:

Whenever a nation can produce a particular good or service at lower cost stated in terms of *other goods*, it is said to have comparative advantage in producing that good.

Comparative advantage is based on a comparison of production costs in terms of other goods. *Comparative cost ratios* express the *opportunity cost* of producing one good instead of another and are read horizontally in Table 6.

Reading horizontally shows costs of producing food and fuel in the two nations. The opportunity cost to A of producing 10 units of

Table 7
Opportunity Costs

	Fuel	Food
Country A	$\frac{1}{2}$ food unit	2 fuel units
Country B	$\frac{1}{5}$ food unit	5 fuel units

fuel is the five food units which a labor hour could have produced. The cost per fuel unit is $\frac{5}{10}$ or $\frac{1}{2}$ food unit. Similarly, the opportunity cost to A of producing 5 units of food is 10 fuel units or 2 fuel units for each food unit. In B, the cost of producing 10 fuel units is the 2 food units which a labor hour could have produced, or $\frac{1}{5}$ food unit per fuel unit. B's cost of producing 2 food units is 10 fuel units or 5 fuel units for each food unit. Opportunity costs are shown in Table 7.

A's opportunity cost is lower for food production and B's is lower for fuel production. Each unit of fuel requires a smaller opportunity cost in B. We say that B has comparative advantage in the production of fuel. Similarly, A has comparative advantage in the production of food.

Again, specialization and trade will increase total production. Without trade and using half their resources in food and half in fuel, the two countries produce the quantities shown at the left in Table 8. With specialization and trade based on comparative advantage, total production is shown at the right. Total world output is increased when nations specialize according to the principle of comparative advantage.

Table 8
The Benefits of Specialization According to
Comparative Advantage

	Production without trade		Production with trade	
	Fuel	Food	Fuel	Food
Country A	500	250	0	500
Country B	500	100	1,000	0
Total	1,000	350	1,000	500

Table 6
Production per Labor Hour

	Fuel	Food
Country A	10	5
Country B	10	2

Extended Example
A Trade Secret

Absolute or comparative advantage can come about in strange ways. Maybe the strangest was a result of a discovery in China almost 3,000 years before Christ. As the story goes, the young empress Si Lin Shi was strolling in her garden and absent-mindedly picked a cocoon from the branch of the mulberry tree. Later she dropped it into a cup of steaming water and a new industry was born! For the cocoon began to unwind into a shimmering thread, strong enough for weaving into lustrous and durable cloth.

For thousands of years the secret of silk production remained in China and the Chinese enjoyed a monopoly of this valuable export. Their resources were particularly suited for cultivating mulberry trees, and their plentiful labor soon learned the skills needed for this careful work. Moreover, as they specialized, the Chinese developed technologies for improving the production of silk fabric. China prospered through export sales of this valuable product. It was not until the twelfth century that silk began to be made in Italy and 500 years later in France. Even today China is the generally recognized leader in production of fine silk, enjoying not only comparative advantage but also continuing absolute advantage.

Several attempts were made to establish silk production in the United States but they were never successful. During the colonial period, the British attempted to establish silk manufacture in Georgia, but the land and climate were never exactly suitable and the industry was short-lived.

What exactly is silk? Actually, it constitutes the home of a moth worm, strings of protein containing some fats and even a little fluorescence. Some silk threads are "bumpy" because of an unknown defect in the worm-builder. But even bumpy silk threads can be woven into the very beautiful fabric, silk shantung. Silk garments have always been prized by members of the social aristocracy, and silk furnishings have often adorned the homes of the wealthy.

What other secrets wait to be discovered in trading nations of today's world?

Combined production possibilities

Production possibilities curves show the benefits of specialization according to comparative advantage. Without trade the two nations must be self-sufficient, allocating half their resources to the production of each commodity. Consumers are limited to the combination of goods available on their own production possibilities curve. The curves for A and B are shown in Figure 6.

Using one-hundred labor hours, A can produce 1,000 units of fuel or 500 of food. B can produce 1,000 units of fuel or 200 units of food.

Again the production possibilities curves are drawn as straight lines for simplicity. Movement from total specialization in fuel to 500 units of food requires opportunity cost of 2 fuel units in A and 5 fuel units in B for each food unit produced. Each curve has been drawn with a constant slope, but the steeper slope for B indicates B's higher opportunity cost for food.

Without trade and with national self-sufficiency, the nations produce and consume at the level designated by point X.

Now suppose the economies combine production possibilities through trade. Total production possibilities are shown in Figure 7. Global specialization in fuel would yield 1,000 + 1,000 = 2,000 fuel units, as shown on the vertical axis. Global specialization in food would yield 500 + 200 = 700 food units.

However, if A specializes in the production of food and B in fuel, total yield is 1,000 fuel units and 500 food units. Movement from global specialization in fuel requires an opportunity cost of only two units of fuel per unit of

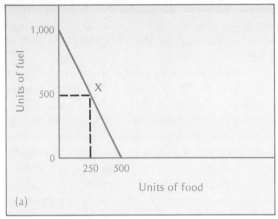

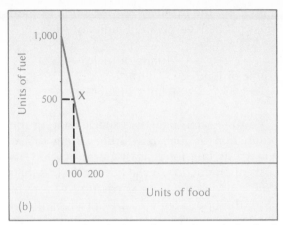

Figure 6 Production possibilities for: (a) country A and (b) country B. Country A has absolute advantage in producing food, while B has comparative advantage producing fuel. If they do not trade, each must be self-sufficient—at point X. Total output without trade is 250 + 100 = 350 units of food and 500 + 500 = 1,000 units of fuel.

food. This is because of A's comparative advantage in the production of food. Movement of A's resources into food production requires sacrifice of only two units of fuel until A is finally fully specializing in food. (To move beyond this point would require the use of B's resources in food production at an opportunity cost of five fuel units for each unit of food.)

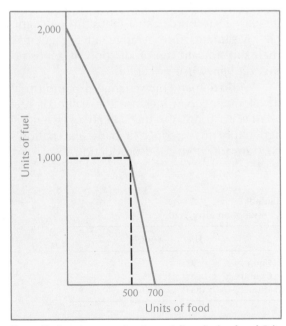

Figure 7 Suppose country A specializes in food and B in fuel and that both trade. The world is better off because now 1,000 units of fuel are produced and 500 units of food are produced. The world now has 150 more units of food through specialization.

The rate of exchange on traded goods

With combined production possibilities, A and B can produce and consume a larger total. Again compare production after trade with production before trade in Table 8. Specialization and trade yield an additional 150 units of food. How will the larger total output be distributed between the two nations?

The answer depends on exchange rates. **Exchange rates** measure the relative value each nation places on the goods exchanged in international trade. The relative value is based on the strength of demand in each country and on the supply costs of production.

First, let us assume that consumer demand for the two goods is identical in both nations. This allows us to compare their production costs independently.

Refer back to Table 7 once again for opportunity costs in the two countries. Assume that A specializes in the production of food, where its opportunity cost is lower. A's food is exchanged for B's fuel output. A will be willing to exchange food for at least 2 units of fuel, its costs of production. A will not accept fewer than 2 units. B will be willing to pay up to 5 units of fuel, the opportunity cost of producing food domestically. B will not pay more than 5 units. Thus the *exchange rate* for a unit of food must fall between 2 and 5 units of fuel:

$$1 \text{ unit of food} = \begin{array}{c} 2 \text{ units of fuel} \\ \text{to} \\ 5 \text{ units of fuel.} \end{array}$$

At the same time, B is specializing in the production of fuel. B will be willing to exchange its fuel for at least $\frac{1}{5}$ unit of food, its costs of production. B will not accept less than $\frac{1}{5}$ unit. A will be willing to pay up to $\frac{1}{2}$ unit of food, the opportunity cost of producing fuel domestically. A will not pay more than $\frac{1}{2}$ unit of food:

$$1 \text{ unit of fuel} = \begin{array}{c} \frac{1}{5} \text{ unit of food} \\ \text{to} \\ \frac{1}{2} \text{ unit of food.} \end{array}$$

The exact value of the exchange rate is determined by the strength of demand in the two nations. If food is the more essential good, its price, or exchange rate, will be higher. The exchange rate will lie near the upper limit of the acceptable range:

1 unit of food = 4 units of fuel.

The price, or exchange rate, for fuel will be lower. It will lie near the lower limit of the acceptable range:

$$1 \text{ unit of fuel} = \frac{1}{4} \text{ unit of food.}$$

When food is the more highly valued good, the nation producing food will enjoy a larger portion of total production. A's producers will receive four units of fuel for each unit of food they export. When fuel is less highly valued, producers of fuel in B will receive a smaller portion of total output. Producers of fuel in B must give up more units of fuel for each unit of food they import.

Even so, consumers in both nations will benefit from trade. Refer again to Table 8 showing production before and after specialization. Assume that B's fuel is to be exchanged for food at an exchange rate of 1 fuel unit = $\frac{1}{4}$ food units. In order that B's consumers enjoy the same level of fuel as before trade, we will allow them to keep 500 units and trade the

remaining 500 units. Exchanging four fuel units for one food unit yields a total of 125 food units, 25 more units than B consumed before trade.

A must pay only $\frac{1}{4}$ food unit for each fuel unit received. To receive 500 fuel units, A pays a total of 125 food units. This leaves A with 375 food units, 125 more than A consumed before trade. Table 9 summarizes these results and shows consumption by each nation after trading. Compare this with Table 8, which shows consumption without the benefit of trade.

Specialization increased total production by 150 food units. Of the greater output, 125 additional units were consumed in A and 25 additional units were consumed in B. Both nations gained. A's gain was greater because A's resources are more productive in the more highly valued commodity. A's gains from trade will enable it to expand production, focusing research and development efforts on technical progress in food production.

B's gains are not as great. But any gain is a plus. Furthermore, world economic conditions are constantly changing, altering the structure of gains from trade among nations. Cost relationships change as natural resource endowments are depleted. A nation's comparative advantage may shift as certain types of production become more costly. Or a nation may increase its resource capabilities through capital investment. Comparative advantage may then shift toward the production of goods requiring heavy use of capital.

World demand may change also. Industrial development may increase the value of fuel relative to food. Or the spread of scientific agriculture may reduce a particular nation's cost advantage in food production.

Table 9
Consumption after Trade

	Fuel	Food
Country A	500	375
Country B	500	125
Total	1000	500

Changing world conditions may gradually alter trading relationships, shifting the benefits of trade from one nation to another. New conditions may provide nations with incentives for industrial development that were previously lacking.

So the benefits from trade need not be equally divided. The world will still be better off with trade than without it.

In the real world, there are more than two trading partners and more than two products traded. Clearly, this makes the results more complicated. But the principle of comparative advantage still applies. For example, the United States and Brazil both trade with many other nations. The United States and Brazil also trade food with each other. However, the exports of Brazil to the United States are coffee, cocoa, and bananas, in which Brazil has both an absolute and a comparative advantage. The United States in turn sends Brazil wheat, rice, and tobacco, which the United States produces with comparative, but not an absolute advantage.

Changing terms of trade and national power

As we have pointed out, an exchange rate is the measure of the relative value nations put on the goods they exchange. The actual ratio of these values determines a nation's **terms of trade**—that is, how many units of product must be given up to receive a unit of product from another country. If the terms of trade are favorable, a nation gives up fewer units of product than it receives. *Favorable terms of trade depend on the market value of the goods traded.* Put simply, if there were more demand for apples to keep the world from starving than for gasoline to keep it on wheels, nations with apple trees would enjoy more favorable terms of trade than nations with oil wells.

Favorable terms of trade enhance national power. Unfavorable terms of trade may condemn a nation to prolonged backwardness. Many less developed nations need capital equipment to build an industrialized economy. They complain that the cost of such equipment has soared. Manufacturing nations, they say, have the power to force them to pay high prices because their need is so desperate.

Manufacturing nations demand more and more units of their raw materials in exchange for fewer and fewer units of machines as the needs of the less developed nations grow.

Manufacturing nations say this is untrue. A thorough analysis of price trends, they say, shows that the terms of trade have not shifted in this manner. Improved technology and vigorous competition in the manufacturing nations may have actually reduced prices of capital equipment relative to prices of raw materials.

Be that as it may, the argument goes on. And there can be no doubt that many of the commodity-producing nations are among the most backward in the world.

What can such nations do to prevent deterioration of their terms of trade? Or to change the terms in their favor? They can band together to form a cartel to increase their economic power in the world. A **cartel** is an international monopoly that sets prices and allocates output. The Organization of Petroleum Exporting Countries (OPEC) is an outstanding example. The economic power of OPEC is evident to drivers of cars and users of other petroleum products throughout the world. Coffee-producing nations of Latin America have entered into similar agreements to restrict output and raise prices—though they are not as effective as the OPEC cartel. Third World producers of bauxite have also combined their interests for economic advantage. They produce one-half the world's supply of this commodity. Banded together, they can exert considerable economic power.

Still, for many nations of the Third World, specialization in commodities has great risks. If world demand changes suddenly, a nation may not be able to sell its specialty. Moreover, advanced nations may develop a cheap synthetic to compete with its natural resources and undercut its entire market. Or the raw commodity itself may gradually disappear from the nation through continued exploitation. The east African nation of Kenya has been threatened by this very result. For many years, a major export was animal products: wild animal skins, tusks,

Viewpoint
The North-South Dilemma

Rising energy costs and the worldwide recession of the 1970s were especially damaging to the less developed countries, known as LDCs. While import bills were rising, demand for their commodity exports fell off. The result was increasing indebtedness, falling real standards of living, and a reduced capacity for economic development.

Something had to be done.

Most of the LDCs fall in the Southern hemisphere. The widening gap between their incomes and those of Northern industrialized nations led to demands for new trade policies. The problem was brought before the Conference on International Economic Cooperation in 1977 with the goal of easing North-South tensions through new international agreements.

Discussion centered on the terms of trade between LDCs and industrialized nations. Representatives of commodity-exporting nations pointed to the wide fluctuations in prices of raw materials they sold in world markets. In the case of many raw commodities, price changes have little effect on the quantity supplied; supplies of sugar, rubber, and sisal, for instance, are not very responsive to changes in price. The result is widely fluctuating prices. In years of high demand relative to supply, prices rise sharply, raising production costs for manufacturing industries of importing nations. Because prices of manufactured goods seldom fall, the effect is a permanent inflationary trend in the prices of manufactured goods traded. On the other hand, years of low demand relative to supply mean falling commodity prices and reduced purchasing power among the LDCs.

Widely fluctuating incomes have produced other harmful effects.

The risks associated with resource development have slowed capital investment in the LDCs and kept resource costs higher than they might be otherwise. Their representatives argue that price stability in commodity exports would help to smooth out this worldwide "stop-go" cycle in trade. Furthermore, greater stability would help to moderate inflation, and it would encourage investment in LDCs. These nations want agreements which would help to smooth the flow of their commodity exports and keep their revenues more stable.

Some commodity agreements have been in effect for years. They involve mainly food and fiber exports and basic industrial materials. The oldest formal agreement is the International Tin Agreement established in 1956. Members are the seven leading tin producers, which include Malaysia and Bolivia (the largest producers) and some importing nations. Exporting member nations contribute to a fund which is used to purchase tin in years when private demand is less than supply at current prices. Without the fund, prices would fall and revenues of the exporting nations would suffer. The fund gradually accumulates a buffer stock of tin to be sold in years when private demand is greater than supply at current prices. Without the buffer stock, prices would rise and contribute to world inflation.

The buffer stock of tin is now about one-tenth world annual sales. The fund is used to buy tin when price falls below an established floor; sales are made when price rises above an established ceiling. The result of purchases and sales is a profit for the fund. Average earnings for exporters have not changed, but cyclical fluctuations have levelled off. Other agreements in coffee and cocoa have been less effective in recent years because of poor harvests. There are proposals to purchase buffer stocks for sugar, copper, cotton, rubber, tea, jute, and sisal.

Other proposals are being discussed which would set up broader arrangements under the United Nations Conference on Trade and Development (UNCTAD). A common fund would be used to accumulate buffer stocks of many commodities.

Many economists doubt the wisdom of any such restrictions on free trade. Price guarantees could lead to inefficiency in resource allocation and higher production costs throughout industry. There is the suspicion that poor nations are more interested in price *increases* than in price *stabilization;* if that is the case, any future attempt to hold prices *down* would lead to resistance. Furthermore, the cost of storing buffer stocks adds to the price of all consumer goods produced.

There is another element which bears on this question. In many LDCs pressure is building to establish more complete control of supplies—following the example of the OPEC petroleum cartel. Commodity agreements could be a first step in that direction. On the other hand, they could be a means of forestalling that kind of pressure and for redistributing some of the world's income in favor of poor nations.

Probably the best hope for the LDCs lies in fundamental changes in production processes around the world. Developed nations are beginning to experience serious shortages of energy and other materials and they are becoming more concerned about industrial pollution. Many LDCs have vast potential for hydroelectric power and are hungry for industrial development. They have the labor and the energy for manufacture. Moreover, processing and manufacturing near the source of raw materials may turn out to be more economically efficient, producing gains for the LDCs. Regrettably, development of industries such as these is often restrained by restraints on imports into industrialized nations.

and carcasses. Little by little, trade was depleting Kenya of an important resource that attracted tourists to the country. Finally, in 1977 the government imposed a ban on further shipments of animal products. In the future Kenya would like to specialize in providing services to tourists, rather than in exploiting its valuable resource.

Diversification may be one answer to the risks involved in specialization. Third World nations might divert more of their export earnings toward building an industrial economy. They might increase government spending for public health and education. This, in turn, could lead to increased work skills and technological know-how within their borders. *A diversity of exportable products is a good hedge against unfavorable changes in terms of trade.*

The United States is not immune to the ups and downs of changing terms of trade. The flow of many of the products we once made for our own use and for export has been slowed. Changing world conditions have altered our areas of specialization.

You have only to look at the brand names of your TV set, your phonograph, and your tape recorder to know this is true. Changing terms of trade have caused us to import many of these products from West Germany or Japan. Brazil, with cheap hides available from cattle herds of the pampas, sells the United States millions of leather shoes a year. And the sneakers you wear more likely come from Taiwan than from Massachusetts (which, at one time, produced nearly all the shoes sold in this country).

This does not mean that the United States has become a have-not nation. Our resource capacity is vast. We are able to alter our areas of specialization to meet changing trends. Our technology and our investment in human capital allow us to export sophisticated computer equipment, aircraft, nuclear power plants, and other goods and services. Breakthroughs in agricultural technology—complex planting and harvesting devices, techniques for fast freezing of perishable meal and poultry—enable us to help feed the world.

The United States will continue to trade on favorable terms if we maintain our ability to react constructively to changing trends. Our technical superiority and our material and human resources can give us the power to export our products on favorable terms. They can also enable us to import the foreign commodities and consumer goods we need and enjoy.

Summary

This chapter describes the "synergistic" effects of world trade: the growth in benefits nations enjoy from specialization and exchange. The microeconomic aspects of trade involve supply and demand in domestic markets. Without trade, equilibrium price and quantity depend on production costs in separate national markets. In any single nation, scarce, high-priced goods will be consumed in small quantities and their marginal utility will be high. Plentiful, low-priced goods will be consumed in larger quantities and their marginal utility will be low. Trade among several nations enables exchange of goods (providing low marginal utility) for other goods (which provide higher marginal utility). Total world utility is increased.

Specialization yields further benefits when improved methods of production lead to falling unit costs. Moreover, specialization and trade help to adjust incomes worldwide, raising incomes for resources used in a nation's specialty and reducing incomes for others. The total benefits of added production are greater than the loss of income to those displaced by foreign competition.

The macroeconomic aspects of trade involve the relative value of total exports and imports. Net exports are included in aggregate demand and help to determine the level of output, income, and employment: $C + I + G + X_n = GNP$. Changes in X_n produce multiple effects on output in both an upward and a downward direction. A decline in trade after World War I contributed to the severity of the Great Depression among Western industrialized nations.

A nation's resource allocation helps to determine its specialization. The United States has changed from a land-abundant nation exporting raw materials to a capital-abundant nation specializing in capital-intensive products for export. Some important exports are characterized as human-capital intensive.

When a nation produces a particular good or service more cheaply than another in terms of resources used, it is said to have absolute advantage in production. When two nations specialize according to absolute advantage and engage in trade, total production possibilities are increased. Modern industrialized nations actually enjoy absolute advantage in production of both manufactured goods and raw materials. Developing nations have absolute advantage in only a narrow range of commodities for export.

Lacking absolute advantage in production, a nation will still enjoy comparative advantage. Comparative advantage exists when production costs are lower in terms of other goods which could have been produced instead: the familiar opportunity costs. Again, specialization according to comparative advantage increases total world output.

Comparative costs of production and the strength of demand among nations determine the exchange rates on traded goods. In turn, the exchange rate determines the units of exports a nation must give up in order to receive a unit of imports: its terms of trade. Favorable terms of trade enhance a nation's wealth and power and enable it to accumulate productive capital.

Key Words and Phrases

- **synergism** a condition in which the total result of some activity is greater than the sum of individual activities taken separately.

- **specialization and division of labor** concentrating efforts on the production of certain goods and services; the opposite of self-sufficiency.

- **marginal utility and total utility** the gains in satisfaction and the total satisfaction enjoyed from the purchase of additional units of a good or service.

- **derived demand for resources** the demand for resources which results because of a demand for the goods or services they can produce.

- **foreign trade multiplier** the multiple effects on output, income, and employment a nation enjoys when it is able to sell goods abroad.

- **productivity ratio** the relative productivity per unit of a resource.

- **absolute advantage** a condition in which a nation produces some good or service using fewer resources per unit of output than other nations.

- **comparative advantage** a condition in which a nation produces some good or service at a lower cost in terms of the opportunity cost of other goods which could have been produced.

- **exchange rate** the ratio between units of goods traded for units of other goods.

- **terms of trade** the relative quantities of imported goods received relative to quantities of exports.
- **cartel** international monopoly that allocates output and sets prices for some good (usually a raw material).

Questions for Review

1. In our discussion of the microeconomic aspects of trade we assumed no transportation costs. How would including transportation costs affect the conclusions we reached? How does this help explain why food is more expensive in the Bahama Islands than it is in Florida?

2. Explain how specialization may cause unit production costs to fall. What circumstances would cause unit production costs to rise with specialization?

3. How can specialization and trade reduce incomes for some groups? In what way is this an advantage to the world economy?

4. Are there other disadvantages of specialization and division of labor? Cite current examples.

5. How would you describe Brazil's absolute advantage in the production of coffee? What are the resource costs of coffee production? Does Brazil also have comparative advantage in coffee production? How would you describe the cost of coffee production in terms of computers not produced?

6. Explain how comparative advantage is related to opportunity costs. How are opportunity costs reflected on a nation's production possibilities curve?

7. Explain what happens when the foreign trade multiplier takes effect. Use an example from current news: increased oil imports from OPEC nations, reduced coffee exports from Brazil, increased television sales from Japan, revival of tourism in Cuba.

8. The hypothetical data below show the quantities of fuel and food which can be produced in country A or country B per unit of resource. Which nation has absolute advantage in fuel production? in food production? Which nation has comparative advantage in fuel production? in food production? What is the opportunity cost of fuel in terms of food in A? in B? Assume each nation has 100 resource units. What is the change in output following specialization if we assume resources were formerly equally divided between the two goods? How does this example differ from the example given in the text? Why?

Output per Unit of Resource

	Fuel	Food
Country A	5	8
Country B	4	6

9. There's an island off the Florida coast named Cedar Key because of the great cedar trees that once grew there. There was also a flourishing pencil factory, and the natives grew prosperous from the sale of the island's product. Today there is very little industry and the inhabitants are no longer prosperous. Can you speculate as to what went wrong?

10. American aluminum companies buy bauxite from Jamaica for $25 a ton (1974). The cost to produce aluminum from low-grade clay in the U.S. is $40 a ton. How does this information help to determine the exchange rate for bauxite? What other circumstances are involved in determining a nation's terms of trade?

20

International Finance

We have discussed the pure theory of international trade. We have shown how specialization according to the principle of comparative advantage permits trading nations to enjoy higher standards of living. We might say that trade substitutes for resource mobility. We cannot move a mine or a factory from one country to another. But we can move the products of such resources. This allows the fullest use of different resource endowments. Finally, we have seen how trade helps to equalize prices and income shares within nations.

Thus far, our discussion has focused on *real flows* of commodities. In our hypothetical model, the exchange of food for fuel depended on exchange rates *between the two goods*. We were not concerned with the money value of the goods. The terms of trade in food and fuel were expressed as a barter arrangement between countries A and B.

Only in very simple economies is barter an acceptable means of exchange. Barter is difficult and time consuming. Exchange is more efficient when money is used as a standard of value and a medium of exchange. This is particularly true for trade among nations. A universally accepted medium of exchange permits a nation to sell its goods in one market and use its earnings to buy goods in another. Total benefits from trade are enlarged as many nations specialize according to comparative advantage and participate in world trade.

Our discussion of international finance will now focus on the *financial arrangements* by which nations pay for the goods exchanged in foreign trade. In this chapter we will be interested in *money flows* rather than in the flow of goods themselves.

A look at the past

Marco Polo, who lived during the thirteenth century, may perhaps be called the father of international trade. He was not, of course, the first to trade across national boundaries. In fact, his father was a trader-explorer before him. But Marco Polo's written account of his journeys in the Orient caught the imagination of Europe. He wrote of the existence in Asia of things like asbestos, coal, and paper currency.

Such things were almost unheard of in Europe and the Mediterranean nations of the Middle East. Soon, caravans of traders were carrying Oriental tapestries, spices, rare woods, honey, and precious stones to Europe. Subsequent opening of ocean lanes increased the barter exchange of goods between areas. Eventually, exchange through barter gave way to exchange based on gold.

For hundreds of years gold served as the primary medium of exchange in international commerce. Gold brought its holders command over other nations' productive resources. These resources could then be used for conquest, bringing in new supplies of captured gold. A growing stock of gold ensured a nation economic power, regardless of its own resource endowment.

Lacking domestic supplies of gold, European nations sent adventurers out across the Atlantic. They returned with gold from the Incan and Mayan civilizations in South and Central America and from other areas.

Not all the gold was the result of conquest, however. Gold could be *earned* through trade. Traders from Italy, England, France, and Spain served as middlemen, financing the building of ships, planning voyages, and marketing the goods of productive peoples throughout the world.

Mercantilism

Emphasis on accumulation of gold led to a trade policy called *mercantilism,* from the word "merchant." The term reflects the importance of merchants in building a nation's domestic economy. Just as a merchant profited by taking in more money than he spent, so a nation would profit by exporting more than it imported. **Mercantilism** was an economic policy based on building and continuing a *favorable balance of trade*—an excess of exports over imports. The mercantilists believed national power would increase as a nation acquired gold in trade.

Mercantilists, however, tended to ignore an important truth. It is that over the long term, a nation's trade balance must come to an equilibrium, since sales (exports) cannot *forever* exceed purchases (imports). Nor can purchases exceed sales forever for a single nation. This would eventually deplete all other nations of everything of value they own. Eventually, sales must come into balance with purchases. Otherwise trade would stop altogether.

Mercantilists gave little thought to the necessity of a balance between imports and exports. They sought to achieve a *continuing excess* of sales over purchases. An excess of sales would allow one nation to collect more for its exports than it paid for its imports. The extra earnings would be accumulated in the form of gold, which would then increase a nation's command over resources of many other nations.

The mercantilists also failed to heed another important fact. To continue accumulating gold in this way requires citizens of the exporting nation to reduce their standards of living. As they continue to export vast portions of the products of their farms, mines, and factories, they are left with fewer goods for their own enjoyment. Unless they import a similar quantity, they are poorer than before. A nation's growing stock of gold provides no immediate creature comforts for its people. Under mercantilism, the accumulation of gold gave a nation great power. But gold was not food to feed a child. Nor fuel to warm a peasant's house.

The mercantilists had forgotten that the goal of production is consumption. If all peoples are to realize the benefits of trade, goods and services must flow in both directions. Gold, like the currencies that later came to replace it, is only a *means* of facilitating the flow. It is not an *end* in itself.

Gold in international trade

Gold was useful in international trade for several reasons. It could be made uniform in value. It was durable. It would not spoil in transit or melt in the sun. It was malleable, yet it held its shape—qualities which made it suitable for stamping into coins.

Gold and other precious metals, particularly silver, continued to be used as a medium of exchange for many years. But metal is cumbersome to handle in large amounts. Banking systems were developed. With banks it was not always necessary to transport gold in payment for traded goods. If a nation's imports from one country were offset by its exports to that country, the value of the gold used in the exchange could be shifted from one country's *account* to the other's and back. The gold itself stayed put.

However, the use of metal money remained a barrier to the expansion of trade. As trade among nations increased, it became more and more inconvenient. Nations turned from gold bullion and coins to paper currencies as a medium of exchange.

The first paper currency was still evaluated in terms of gold. In fact, from 1837 to 1914 the United States dollar was equivalent to 23.22 grains, or about $\frac{1}{20}$ ounce, of gold and the British pound to 112.78 grains or about $\frac{1}{4}$ ounce. One British pound was almost 5 times as valuable as one United States dollar. So one pound would exchange for about 5 dollars.

The value of a nation's currency was maintained by its government's willingness to exchange gold for money at the established exchange rate. Thus the United States government would stand ready to purchase gold—either newly mined or coined gold—at the official price of $20.67 per ounce. Newly mined gold could be presented to the Treasury and paper money issued to the seller in exchange. Or paper money could be presented to the Treasury to be redeemed in gold.

The promise to convert paper to gold acted as a restraint on the tendencies of governments to print too much money. **Currency convertibility** (giving gold in exchange for paper money) meant that a nation's gold stock could be rapidly depleted if too much convertible currency should be presented to the Treasury for redemption. It would be risky to print money without gold to back up its value. Of course, if a nation's gold stock grew, its power to create money would grow also.

Large quantities of money were needed to finance rapid industrial growth of the nineteenth century. Fortunately, gold discoveries in California, South Africa, Alaska, and Siberia became available to fuel this industrial expansion. But the growth in supply of new gold slowed in the late 1800s, and the supply of new currency slowed also. Limited supplies of currency began to hold back the growth of industrial production. Governments dealt with the shortage by issuing new money for domestic use to stimulate full capacity production. But when the new money entered international trade, other nations often presented it for redemption in gold. Expanding nations whose earnings from sales abroad were too low to pay for their purchases of foreign goods lost gold as foreigners demanded conversion of paper money to gold.

In recent times, most nations have removed the relationship between their currency and gold. Gold is now just another commodity that is traded regularly, like soybeans or cotton. (But remember, gold is still a very valuable commodity.) The currency of a nation no longer gets its value from gold. Currency is worth what it exchanges for in world currency markets—its exchange rate. These markets and the ways in which money reaches them are discussed below.

The balance of payments

A nation's international transactions are recorded in its annual **balance of payments** statement. *Outpayments* for a nation's imports are shown as negative values. *Inpayments* from its exports are shown as positive values. The sum of outpayments relative to the sum of inpayments determines the net flow of currency. An excess of outpayments produces a negative balance because more currency flows out than is returned. We say a nation is experiencing a *deficit* in its international payments. An excess of inpayments produces a positive net balance. We say a nation is experiencing a *surplus* in its international payments.

The balance of payments statement may be divided into three major parts. The three parts are (1) current transactions, (2) capital transactions, and (3) official settlement transactions. Table 1 is a simplified balance of pay-

Table 1
United States Balance of Payments (in millions of dollars)

Current account	1960	1968	1974
Merchandise:			
Exports	19,650	33,626	98,309
Imports	−14,758	−32,991	−103,586
Net balance of trade	4,892	635	−5,277
Military transactions	−2,753	−3,143	−2,158
Investment income	2,287	4,004	10,122
U.S. grants and other payments	−2,652	−2,800	−6,044
Balance on Current Account	1,774	−1,313	−3,357

Capital account			
Long-term capital flows	−2,985	−944	−7,344
Short-term capital flows	−1,132	3,483	−2,394
Errors and omissions	−1,060	415	4,798
Net capital account	−5,177	2,954	−5,040
Balance on Current Account and Capital Account	**−3,403**	**1,641**	**−8,397**

Official settlement transactions*			
Changes in liabilities to foreigners	1,258 (increase)	−761 (decrease)	9,831 (increase)
Changes in U.S. official reserve assets	2,145 (decrease)	−880 (increase)	−1,434 (decrease)

*The sign of Official Settlement Transactions (net) must be the reverse of Balance on Current and Capital Account. Thus an excess of merchandise imports over exports (−) must be balanced by *increased* liabilities to foreigners (+) or by a *loss* of *reserves* (+). As a result, the balance of payments is always "in balance."

ments statement for the United States for selected years.

The balance on current account

Most current transactions are those involving purchases and sales of goods and services in trade. For example, purchases by United States citizens of Volkswagens, Nikons, Irish sweaters, and Norwegian luxury cruises are recorded in the United States balance of payments statement as negative quantities, or outpayments. Sales of aircraft, grain, agricultural equipment, and Hollywood films are recorded as positive quantities, or inpayments. The difference between the value of current imports and exports is the **net balance of trade.**

Currency flows for imported and exported goods and services constitute the largest part of the current account. However, there are also the earnings from United States *investments abroad.* Hilton Hotels, General Motors assembly plants, and Gulf Oil rigs and wells, for example, earn incomes for their American owners. These incomes are shown as positive values in the current account. Conversely, income to foreigners who have investments in America are shown as negative values.

Included in the current account transactions are some **unilateral flows**—one-way flows for which no goods or services are exchanged. Most unilateral flows appear in the form of *U.S. government grants* or aid to other governments—for example, gifts of food or medicine or even outright dollar gifts. But they also include pensions, for instance, paid by companies to retired workers living abroad. The current account also includes *military transactions,* such as military aid to other nations. Current transactions even include the check you might send to your cousin in Manila at Christmas time.

At the end of an accounting period, total outpayments from trade, unilateral transfers, and investment income are compared with total inpayments. The net *balance on current account* may be either positive or negative.

Study of the United States balance on current account over time shows the growing competitiveness of United States industry relative to industry abroad. In the early years of our nation, industry was poorly developed. We needed to buy many goods from abroad. In return, we sold relatively low-valued items like tobacco, hides, and silver. For much of our early history, the United States balance of trade was .negative. More dollars flowed out than returned through trade. As our manufacturing capacity developed, however, we were able to supply more of our needs locally. Moreover, we were able to increase our sales abroad and thus to increase the inflows of currencies. In the twentieth century the destruction caused by two World Wars retarded the growth of European industry; this gave added advantage to United States agriculture and manufacturing. Our trade balance has been positive for most of the years for which data are available.

In recent decades, however, European and Asian recovery from the war years has brought new competition to world markets. Foreign steel, automobiles, and electronic equipment have begun to displace United States products, both in this country and among our former customers abroad. Commodity-producing nations have raised prices for their petroleum, cocoa, coffee, and copper. Rising world prices and larger quantities of imports have aggravated the outflow of U.S. currency for purchase of foreign-made products and commodities. These and other problems produced a negative balance of trade in 1971, the first since 1893.

After a few years of negative balances, our balance on current account again turned positive in 1975. One reason was our strength in agriculture; the United States is uniquely equipped to supply much of the world's food needs. Another is our technological know-how. Our sales of food and sophisticated modern equipment have helped to bring in foreign currency and restore the balance. Another reason was the recession of 1973–1975, which sharply curtailed demand for imports in the United States.

Our balance of trade was negative again in 1976 and 1977. One major reason for this was our recovery from the 1973–1975 recession. This recession was worldwide—though its effects elsewhere were a little later. The United

States led the world recovery. American consumers had money to spend on imports whereas foreign consumers still lacked the money to spend on our exports. But another major cause of the deficit was the cost of imported Arab oil (our imports of it increased as the economy recovered). This was considered quite ominous since our dependency on foreign energy sources threatens to worsen.

What determines the flows of payments? Flows of payments are based on the market value of traded goods and on the principle of comparative advantage. Manufacturers trade for raw materials which have the greatest value in production. Consumers seek goods which provide the greatest utility or satisfaction in consumption. Some traded items are of value both in production and consumption. For example, soybeans are useful in consumption. They provide utility as a substitute for meat in many countries. Soybeans are also useful in production. They are a protein source for livestock.

The usefulness of a good depends also on its quality. The quality of fine textiles from the Orient or precision instruments from West Germany provides added value in consumption and production. The superior quality of Swiss watches and the purity of Libyan petroleum enhance the value of these products.

The cost of traded items is also a factor in world demand. Cost depends on local resource endowments and on the technology of production. A wealth of natural resources or an abundance of capital equipment keeps production costs low.

Wealth of resources has often permitted United States producers to undersell producers in other nations. For example, many countries produce wheat. But our favorable climate and abundant land resources allow us to sell wheat at a cheaper price than wheat supplied by most other countries.

Furthermore, the health and skills of our labor force, together with high productivity, have helped to keep labor costs per unit, and hence cost to consumers, low. Productivity has grown with advancing technology. Investment in research and development has helped to

give the United States a comparative advantage in many industries: for example, in satellite communications and in sophisticated weaponry.

For these and other reasons, the value of United States products has been high relative to price. This has encouraged exports and helped our balance of trade. We have readily found buyers for our farm machinery, computers, and tobacco products, to name just a few. Continued trade benefits in the future depend on continued improvements in the quality of our manufactures, careful management of valuable resources, and close attention to production costs.

The capital account

What happens if the United States trade balance becomes negative over a long period of time? Dollars will pile up in the hands of foreign producers as they sell more goods to us than they buy from us. What can foreigners do with the dollars they accumulate through sales to the United States? One way of spending the dollars is through purchases called *capital transactions*.

Capital transactions are the second of the three major parts of a nation's balance of payments statement. **Capital transactions** represent investment by citizens of one nation in the productive capacity of another. Foreign investors use their funds to purchase claims against some portion of the receiving nation's capital. These investments, or claims, may be *long term* or *short term*. The long-term investor expects to wait a comparatively long time before settling the claim and collecting the hoped-for profit. The short-term investor expects the claim to be redeemed more quickly.

Long-term capital investment may be *direct* or *indirect*. United States firms such as IBM, Ford, and Exxon have made *direct investments* in foreign nations by acquiring production facilities there. Foreign firms such as Sony, Nestlé, and Volkswagen have invested directly in facilities here.

Extended Example
International Lending and Debt

Borrowing within a nation is fairly simple to arrange. The borrower prepares a loan application stating the purpose of the loan and establishing the borrower's credit-worthiness. The lender keeps a close eye on the enterprise so as to ensure the safety of the loan. Regular payments of interest and principal are made as the project begins to be profitable.

Borrowing between nations is more complex. A nation's balance on current account shows the relationship between its purchases and sales abroad. An excess of purchases leads to an outflow of currency or of claims to the nation's wealth. The balance on capital account shows the relationship between its private lending and borrowing transactions abroad. A nation may borrow short-term to finance an excess of foreign purchases; or it may borrow long-term to finance major development projects which are not expected to become profitable for a number of years. Credit transactions with private lending institutions are "hard currency" loans; that is, they are expected to be repaid with stable currencies whose value is ensured.

In the 1970s, banks in the United States and Western Europe had dollars to lend for long-term development projects. The chief borrowers were the communist members of Comecon—the Council for Mutual Economic Assistance. Comecon is the Eastern European counterpart of the Common Market and includes the Soviet Union, East Germany, Poland, Bulgaria, Czechoslovakia, Hungary, Mongolia, and Cuba. In the past, communist nations had been reluctant to borrow from Western institutions, because they did not want to reveal the details of their construction plans. But in 1975 their borrowing from Western banks reached $2.5 billion, and in 1976 was rising still further. Total Comecon indebtedness was about $32 billion, one-third borrowed by the Soviet Union.

Most of these loans were *syndicated*. That is, large banks in several countries participated in providing the financial capital. U.S. banks provided about 15%, the principal lenders being Chase Manhattan, Citibank, and the Bank of America. The interest rate was based on London's interbank borrowing rate on Eurodollars. The rate for an individual Comecon member was set at between .5% and 1.75% above the London rate. Loans were made to finance projects like a chemical complex in Poland and a truck plant in the Soviet Union.

By 1977, the large size of the debt was beginning to cause concern. Some banks had reached their limits on lending to individual institutions. The limit on loans to any single borrower is set at 10% of reserves and capital. Fears of default began to be expressed.

Probably such fears are unjustified. To default on a loan would close off the borrower to the Western technology needed for development. Also, the Soviet Union, in particular, has vast resources available for paying off its indebtedness. It is the world's largest oil producer and the second largest producer of gold. Even exceptionally large imports of grain ($4 billion in 1975) should not seriously affect the Soviet Union's ability to pay. Moreover, command economies are able to divert resources freely into those areas believed to be most favorable for national growth. The result has been an excellent payments record for communist borrowers.

Less developed countries face a more difficult problem. Lacking a strong industrial capacity, they are often unable to borrow from private financial institutions. They must finance their foreign purchases with loans from international lending institutions. Their official borrowing is shown on the third part of the balance of payments and is often characterized as "soft-currency" loans. A soft-currency loan can be repaid in the nation's own currency, which may decline in value relative to other currencies.

International lending institutions provide *short-term* loans through the International Monetary Fund and *long-term* development loans through the International Bank for Reconstruction and Development (World

Bank). Many less developed countries were forced to increase their short-term borrowings in the 1970s in order to finance their rising oil bills. Their lack of important goods for export led many nations deeper and deeper into debt. By 1977, they were asking that the International Monetary Fund provide debt relief: postponement of interest and rescheduling or even cancellation of regular loan payments. Otherwise there were threats of bankruptcies with no repayment at all.

The member nations of the International Monetary Fund considered the request, but most were opposed. Even some of the borrowing nations were opposed. They felt that the best way to ensure continued financial and technical aid was to fulfill their obligations to lending institutions. Furthermore, the eventual recovery from worldwide recession was expected to increase their sales of raw commodities and to raise their export prices. Development of their export potential should help them to meet debt repayments and to maintain their good credit ratings.

Direct investment has advantages. A company may save on transportation costs by operating a factory close to its foreign markets. It may be able to operate more cheaply near certain resources it needs for production. And, as we shall see when we come to our discussion of multinational companies, direct investment may offer tax breaks and hedges against tariffs and other trade restrictions.

But some long-term investors are unwilling to assume the risks and responsibilities of complete ownership of facilities in other countries. They may prefer *indirect*, or *portfolio*, *investment*. They invest in the stocks and bonds of foreign companies. Or they lend money to a foreign government by buying some of that government's bonds.

Short-term investments are claims which are due to be paid off within a year. For example, a short-term investor may lend money to a foreign borrower by buying a short-term promise-to-pay note. The foreigner is expected to repay with interest within a year. Or the investor may "lend" money to a foreign bank by opening a passbook account that pays interest. Or the investor may buy a short-term "certificate of deposit" from the bank. The claim will be satisfied with interest at the end of a stated period of time.

The *total* outflow of long- and short-term capital investment determines a nation's *balance on capital account.* Again, this balance may be positive or negative. *Often, the sign of the balance on capital account will be the reverse of that on the current account.* This is because an outflow of payments from a nation with excessive imports will leave its trading partners with more of the importing nation's currency than they need. The currency outflows give other nations the opportunity to purchase productive facilities in the importing nation. In effect, the importing nation must "sell" its productive assets in order to pay for its excess imports.

In the early years of our nation, the United States balance on capital account was generally positive. British, Dutch, and German investors used their earnings from trade to invest in developing American industry. Railroads, canals, roads, and factories were financed with foreign funds. More financial capital came into the country than left it.

As our own exports increased, however, a positive balance on current account enabled United States investors to invest in other nations. United States firms acquired bauxite mines in Jamaica, factories in Taiwan, and hotels in Hong Kong. Our multinational corporations invest capital in other nations. Our investors now send capital out in order to profit from the growth in economic activity in other parts of the world. In short, our capital account is now often negative.

What other factors affect the balance on capital account? International capital flows respond to the same incentives as domestic capital flows. In general, investors choose to invest their funds where they expect the greatest net return. Financial capital usually flows from areas where it is abundant into areas where it is scarce. This is because earnings on capital are likely to be small wherever it is abundant. Financial capital flows into capital-poor areas because earnings there are likely to be great. Capital-poor areas are willing to pay dearly for capital because they need it badly.

Inflows of financial capital during our early history were in response to high expected earnings. Our more recent outflows have been in response to profitable opportunities elsewhere. The free flow of financial capital contributes to economic efficiency. It sends investment funds to areas of greatest need.

International capital flows may not distribute capital resources perfectly, however; the flow may rise or ebb or even be temporarily dammed up. Economic and political conditions within each country affect the flow of investment capital. In particular, direct investment in a foreign country may be risky. A company, Ford, for example, will build a plant in a foreign country only if it is assured satisfactory operating conditions in that country. To show a profit, it may need a pool of relatively low-paid labor. It may need easy access to the country's resource materials and to its transport system. It may need a low tax rate from the host country. If it is assured of such things, it will build. And capital will flow from where it is abundant to a foreign country where it is more needed.

But what happens if conditions in the host country change? The labor force may be siphoned off to some newly developed industry. The host country's transport may be disrupted by war. It may raise its tax rates or restrict the free trade of Ford's foreign-made products. The flow of capital will slow or even stop altogether.

Ford, of course, will have anticipated such possibilities. But in its view, the risk was not high enough to keep it from building the foreign plant. If Ford had decided the risk was too high, the flow of capital would never have begun at all—no matter how much capital was available or how badly it was needed abroad.

Indirect capital investment is also affected by economic and political conditions. In theory, people will be eager to invest their excess capital in foreign countries where capital is in short supply. Such countries will pay high interest on investment capital, and money will flow to where it is needed. But famine, war, or other disasters may strike capital-poor coun-

tries. The value of foreign-owned securities may fall. The countries may find themselves unable to pay interest on their loans. Again, capital flows from capital-rich areas to capital-poor areas will slow or even stop entirely for a time.

Despite such interruptions in the long run, capital tends to flow from where it is less needed to where it is more needed.

The basic balance The balances on current account and long-term capital are combined to provide a nation's **basic balance** (*not* shown in Table 1). The basic balance will be negative if some of its currency remains in the hands of nonresidents at the end of the accounting period. The balance will be positive if a nation draws more of its currency back through trade, investment income, and long-term capital investment than it pays out. The sign of the basic balance and its amount determine the net flow of funds which must be settled by international balancing transactions.

Official settlement transactions

Whether the balance on current and capital accounts is positive or negative, there must be a way to settle the remaining outstanding claims held by citizens of one nation against citizens of another. These outstanding claims are settled by official settlement transactions. Official settlement transactions constitute the last of the three major parts of a nation's balance of payments statement. **Official settlement transactions** are those transactions necessary to balance all remaining claims after current and capital transactions are complete. Official settlement transactions are of two kinds: monetary transactions and credit transactions.

Monetary transactions involve the transfer of currency in settlement of claims. A nation's central bank holds reserve currencies of many different countries. These foreign exchange reserves constitute an asset for the central bank. A net outflow of domestic currency may require the central bank to give up its own foreign reserve holdings in exchange for the money held by foreigners. The result will be a loss of reserves and a reduced ability to buy foreign goods.

In the past, monetary transactions often involved the transfer of gold. An excess of its currency in the hands of foreigners would require a nation to redeem its currency in gold. However, monetary gold has not moved in international trade for several years. In 1971, in fact, the United States government announced it would no longer ship gold to balance international accounts. Foreign holders of dollars must now use them in trade or for capital investment. Or they may exchange them for other national currencies.

Credit transactions include international lending among central banks or through international credit organizations. The most significant international credit organization is the International Monetary Fund (IMF). The IMF was established after World War II to help arrange conditions favorable for rebuilding world trade. The actual operation of the Fund will be discussed more fully in the next chapter.

What determines the flows of balancing transactions? The size and the direction of balancing transactions are based explicitly on the size and direction of the current account and the capital account. Balancing transactions are necessary to offset these "independent" flows in the private sector. But the fundamental determinant of "independent" flows is the purchasing power of a nation's currency relative to currencies of other trading nations.

Foreign exchange rates

The purchasing power of a nation's currency is reflected in the price it commands in world currency markets. The *price of a currency* is its **exchange value** (or **exchange rate**). In free international markets currency values are based on the interaction of supply and demand.

We seldom think of money as an item to be bought and sold. It must be, of course, or international trade would halt. Suppose you had a thirst for French wine. You might mail ten dollars to a grower in France who would then ship you the wine. But the French dealer would have difficulty spending your dollars at the local bakery. Dollars are a nuisance when everyone else is using francs to buy and sell. If you continued your ten-dollar purchases, your French wine dealer would probably ask you to stop. Handling your foreign dollars would mean too much of a daily hassle in trying to spend them.

It would be another story if there were a "money store" down your street. Then you could go there and buy francs to send. Actually, there is such a money store. Or, more precisely, a money supermarket. It's called the **foreign exchange market.** Unlike a supermarket, however, it does not exist in one place. Many banks and other financial institutions buy and sell foreign currency—or pieces of bank paper that substitute for currency.

When wholesale sellers of French wine export their product to the United States, they wish to be paid in francs. American importers could go to the foreign exchange market and actually buy francs to pay for the wine. In practice, however, it is simpler to send a check in dollars drawn on the local bank. Sellers in France will present the dollar-check to their own banks. The French banks will exchange the dollars for francs and deposit them in the exporters' accounts. The banks will charge for the service, of course. And when someone in France, perhaps a Frenchman traveling to America, wants dollars, banks will have dollars to sell. Again for a fee.

So then, when consumers want foreign currency to make purchases, they go to the foreign exchange market. Actually, it is their agents, the importing businesses, who enter the market to exchange domestic currency for the currency of a particular exporting nation. Toyota dealers, for example, go to the market to buy Japanese yen. They create the market demand for yen. *Thus the demand for a nation's currency reflects the demand for its products in consumer world markets.* In world capital markets, it may also reflect the attractiveness of a nation's investment opportunities. Like consumers, investors must have foreign currency if they wish to invest in foreign economies.

The demand curve for foreign currency is downward sloping, as are demand curves for most goods. If the price of yen is very low, Toyota customers in America will want large quantities of yen—and ultimately large quantities of Toyotas. At high yen prices, consumers will want fewer yen and fewer Toyotas. If the price of yen became very high, many United States auto buyers would shift to Fords or some other "dollarmade" product.

Figure 1 represents a foreign exchange market. For simplicity it portrays demand and supply for currency in a two-currency world: yen and dollars. The demand curve for yen shows the quantities demanded at various prices, when price is stated in terms of dollars. It is the sum of all worldwide demand for yen. The demand curve has a downward slope to show some consumer responsiveness to yen price changes. If a certain quantity of Toyotas were judged necessary for import because U.S. buyers would accept no other car, the curve would be steeper and less responsive to yen price changes.

Yen are supplied to foreign exchange markets by holders of yen. Some holders are Japanese citizens who offer to exchange yen for dollars to use in trade. Thus the suppliers of yen are also demanders of dollars. Other holders of yen may be business firms and financial institutions in nations other than Japan. They may have received yen in return for sales of their goods or services to Japan. Or perhaps a firm or bank received a loan payment in yen. Often these holders are seeking dollars to settle their own debt obligations in, say, Germany. Or they may want to invest at interest in a third country. When business or financial holders of yen offer it on the market, they become suppliers of foreign exchange. Thus the supply of a nation's currency reflects the desire of holders to exchange yen for other currencies.

Figure 1 also includes a hypothetical supply curve for yen. It is the sum of the quantities which would be supplied by all international holders at all possible prices. Again, the supply price for yen is measured in terms of dollars. The supply curve for a currency slopes upward. This is because holders will normally offer a larger quantity at high prices than at low prices.

Market equilibrium (the point at which supply and demand are equal) occurs at the intersection of the supply and demand curves. For the period covered by this hypothetical model, the equilibrium price of yen in dollars is $.003 or $\frac{1}{3}$ cent and the equilibrium quantity is 100 million. (The 1977 price of yen on foreign exchange markets was about $\frac{1}{3}$ cent, or about 300 yen to the dollar. Demanders of yen paid $\frac{1}{3}$ cent per yen.) In effect, demanders of yen are at the same time suppliers of dollars at a price of 300 yen per dollar.

The value of a nation's currency in terms of other currencies is critical to its balance of trade. High yen prices, for example, mean that fewer yen will be bought on the foreign exchange market. Fewer foreign consumers will want yen for purchasing Japanese products. To foreign buyers, the price of Japanese exports will seem too high. Japanese export manufacturers will be forced to cut back on production. Unemployment in Japan might grow.

Japanese consumers, however, could benefit. Their yen would be worth more in foreign currency. They could sell yen at the high price and increase their own buying power. They could import more goods for their own use from abroad. The end result of high yen prices

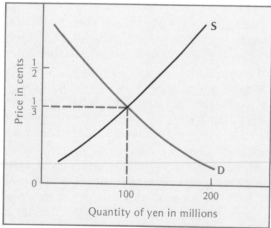

Figure 1 The foreign exchange market for yen in terms of dollars. The price of yen is determined by supply and demand. The demand for yen reflects foreign demand for export products made in Japan. The supply of yen reflects the willingness of yen-holders to exchange yen for other currencies, like dollars. A high level of supply suggests great import demand (imports into Japan).

would probably be a deficit in Japan's balance of trade. More currency would flow out for imports than would return for exports.

A very low yen price would have the opposite result. Low-priced yen would be in great demand for purchase of Sonys, Toyotas, and Nikons. Japanese export industries would flourish. But Japanese consumers would receive fewer units of foreign currency for each yen. Their buying power would fall and import purchases decline. The result of low yen prices would probably be a surplus in Japan's balance of trade. More currency would flow in from exports than would flow out for imports.

The extent to which high or low yen prices would produce a deficit or a surplus depends in part on the responsiveness of buyers to price changes for the products being traded. A really determined Toyota buyer would not be discouraged by high-priced yen. To the extent that Japan's customers continue to buy regardless of higher yen prices, Japan's deficit would be reduced. On the other hand, Japanese requirements for U.S. soybeans may not fall even when yen prices are very low. Soybeans are a vital source of protein in Japanese diets. To the extent that Japan's consumers continue to import, regardless of low-priced yen, Japan's surplus would decrease or even disappear.

International trade equilibrium

A few summarizing statements may be helpful here. The value of a nation's imports and exports of goods and services—its current account—will rarely balance. Neither will its imports and exports of capital—its capital account. In order to make them come out even in a nation's balance of payments statement, certain balancing transactions are necessary— the official settlements transactions. These transactions are simply statements of the amount of imbalance and how the nation goes about correcting it. The statement itself is simple. But the reality behind the transactions is complex and very important to a nation's economy.

How does a nation "balance its books" in international trade? Where does it get the money to pay its creditors if its basic balance is negative? It does what you and I do when we owe money. It dips into its reserves—its savings account, so to speak—to pay its bills. If its reserves are low, it may borrow from other nations. In both cases, the balance of payments statement is brought into balance.

Small shifts from deficit to surplus to deficit are considered healthy and normal. But a continued excess of outpayments over inpayments or inpayments over outpayments reflects a fundamental *disequilibrium* in a nation's international economic relationships. Fundamental changes must be made in the nation's economy in order to bring accounts back into balance. Changes may be needed in the ratio of domestic prices to foreign prices. The nation's level of income may be too high or too low. Changes in the level of production and employment may be necessary to correct a payments disequilibrium.

Throughout much of history, nations have dealt with disequilibrium in either of two ways: (1) they have allowed exchange rates to fluctuate freely according to supply and demand or (2) they have allowed the automatic adjustments of the gold standard to affect the domestic money supply.

Correcting disequilibrium through flexible exchange rates

In a free market, exchange rates are determined by demand and supply. Changes in international demand and supply produce changes in currency values, just as changes in demand and supply in product markets cause changes in their prices. When the exchange rate is allowed to fluctuate, consumers will adjust their purchases to correct disequilibrium.

A surplus in international payments may be the result of an increase in a nation's exports. Foreigners demand more of a nation's currency to pay for their purchases from that nation. This increase in demand is reflected in a rightward shift in the currency demand curve and an increase in price. The higher price, however, discourages foreign consumers from using that currency to buy a nation's exports. Thus the surplus of inpayments will be limited by a rise in the currency's exchange rate. *After a nation's currency rises in value, its exports cost more.* Its exports then fall and the surplus drops or disappears.

Moreover, the higher price or exchange rate for the currency stimulates an increase in imports as domestic holders of the currency seek to take advantage of its higher value. They supply more domestic currency in exchange for foreign currency in order to increase their purchases of foreign imports. The supply curve shifts to the right and currency flows out, again reducing the surplus in international payments.

A deficit in international payments may be the result of an increase in a nation's imports. As foreign holders of the currency put increasing amounts of it into foreign exchange markets, the greater supply forces its value down. An excess of supply is shown as a rightward shift in the supply curve with a fall in its equilibrium price (see Figure 2). *When the value of a nation's currency decreases, its exports cost less.* Exports increase and the deficit is reduced or eliminated.

Figure 2 represents the foreign exchange market for United States dollars. The value of United States dollars is expressed in terms of West German marks. The equilibrium price of dollars before the excess supply was four marks. Germans desiring to buy United States

goods paid at the rate of four marks for each dollar. When the excess supply of dollars forced their value down to two marks, German importers could purchase United States goods for the price of two marks per dollar.

Sales of American made goods are likely to increase as Germans compare the low mark price of dollars with, say, the high mark price of yen. The resulting increase in U.S. exports will help to increase the inflow of currency from Germany, and, of course, from other nations with which we trade. It will sop up dollar holdings abroad and help keep our international payments in equilibrium.

There are some disadvantages, however, to this solution of a nation's trade equilibrium problem. *An important disadvantage is the effect of a low-price currency on the price of imports.* If the mark price of dollars falls from four marks to two marks per dollar, for example, American importers will have to pay twice as many dollars for each foreign item purchased. For example, the dollar price of German beer selling for ten marks in Germany would rise from $2.50 to $5.00 per six-pack in the United States:

Before Change *in Exchange Rate*	*After Change* *in Exchange Rate*
4 marks = 1 dollar	2 marks = 1 dollar
10 marks = $2\frac{1}{2}$ dollars	10 marks = 5 dollars

Most of us would waste little sympathy on drinkers of foreign beer. They can easily shift to domestic brands. After all, we know that a reduction in imports is necessary to reverse excessive outflow of dollars. But many imports are essential to United States national output. Bauxite and copper are important ingredients in many industries. Crude oil is a necessary source of energy. A falling dollar exchange rate increases the price of such commodities and thus increases costs of production in the United States. And paying more dollars for these important imports will worsen the outflow of our currency.

Allowing currency values to fluctuate in response to changes in demand and supply has another disadvantage. *Sudden shifts in market demand or supply can cause broad and sudden changes in currency values.* Trading can be risky when the future value of a currency is uncertain.

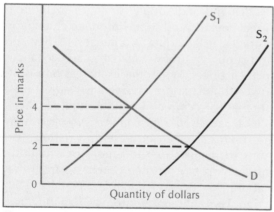

Figure 2   An increase in imports in America increases the supply of dollars in foreign exchange markets. The supply curve shifts to the right and the price of the dollar drops in terms of other currencies, such as marks. With S_1, the dollar equals 4 marks; with increased dollar supply S_2, the dollar drops to only 2 marks.

For example, suppose a United States importer contracts to buy a Toyota at the current exchange rate of 1 yen = $\frac{1}{3}$ cent. A 1,500,000-yen Toyota would be expected to cost $5,000: 1,500,000 yen = (1,500,000) $\frac{1}{3}$ cent = 500,000 cents = $5,000.

By the time the Toyota is delivered the actual price of yen might be either $\frac{1}{2}$ cent or $\frac{1}{5}$ cent because of fluctuations in the exchange rate. If the price is $\frac{1}{2}$ cent, the buyer would be charged 1,500,000 ($\frac{1}{2}$ cent) = $7,500. The buyer might be unwilling to pay $2,500 *more* than he had expected to pay. On the other hand, if the yen price falls to $\frac{1}{5}$ cent, the buyer would pay 1,500,000 ($\frac{1}{5}$ cent) = $3,000, a much better deal. But this time the Japanese seller might be unwilling to accept $2,000 *less* than he expected.

Fluctuating exchange rates may thus act as a deterrent to international trade. Buyers and sellers may be unwilling to risk sudden and substantial changes in the prices of traded goods.

Forward exchange Foreign exchange risks can be minimized by dealing in the *forward markets.* Toyota dealers can purchase a forward contract for yen at its current price. A **forward contract** entitles the holder to receive a certain quantity of currency at a given time in the future and at exchange rates specified in the contract. The currency dealer selling the forward contract would agree to provide 1,500,000 yen at the current value of $5,000 when payment is due on the Toyotas. The currency dealer charges a fee for the service, which is high enough to offset the net cost of acquiring the yen and making them available on time. He is also gambling that if the yen's value does fluctuate, it will do so in his favor.

Correcting disequilibrium under the gold standard

Although trading nations no longer adhere to the gold standard, it once was an effective means of correcting a fundamental disequilibrium in a nation's basic balance. Under the **gold standard,** a nation's money supply was based on its holdings of gold. Gold "backed"

the nation's paper currency, and the currency was convertible to gold. Paper money used in foreign trade was also convertible. As we noted earlier in this chapter, a nation's gold stock limited its ability to issue large quantities of paper currency.

Under the gold standard, a heavy outflow of dollars for imports led to adjustments which reversed the currency flow. An excess of imports would cause a nation's currency to pile up in the hands of foreigners. Under the gold standard, much of this currency was returned to the nation's treasury for conversion to gold. Gold stocks would decline, reducing the gold reserves held as backing for its currency. The money supply would then have to be reduced to a level consistent with the smaller gold stock.

With less money in circulation, spending and incomes would decline. Merchants would reduce prices to capture the dwindling market. Workers would accept lower wages, reducing costs of production. But lower costs and lower prices would attract foreign buyers. Lower incomes would have the effect of reducing foreign purchases. As a result, inpayments would increase and outpayments fall, and a nation's international payments would move back toward equilibrium.

The gold standard also helped to correct disequilibrium because of its effect on interest rates. A shrinking money supply caused interest rates on loans to rise, as domestic borrowers competed for limited funds. Foreign investors would then find it increasingly profitable to lend their money to the deficit nation at high interest rates. Currency would begin to flow in to increase the nation's money supply. The nation's international payments would move back toward equilibrium.

There were disadvantages to this system, however. First of all, it was slow acting. Administered prices (prices set without much attention to the laws of supply and demand) and the power of labor unions often kept prices and wages higher than they needed to be. Costs fell very slowly, as did prices, and exports were slow to increase. Foreign currency did not flow in, it trickled in. The nation's people had to suffer a prolonged period of high unemployment and low consumption. Eventually, the gold standard system could be expected to reverse these economic misfortunes. But in the meantime, the people suffered grievously.

Secondly, high interest rates tended to retard a capital-poor nation's economy. Local firms often could not afford to borrow the funds necessary to keep production going. Construction of new productive facilities ground to a halt. Reliance on the gold standard eventually brought the nation's economy back to normal. But, again, the nation's people had suffered lost income and lost production opportunities.

We may conclude that the gold standard provided automatic means of adjustment to restore equilibrium to trading nations. But we must acknowledge that adjustment often brought considerable pain to the deficit nation. A continuing outflow of currency was corrected, but the costs were lower output and employment in domestic industry, higher interest rates, and slower economic growth.

Recent monetary history

The collapse of the gold standard

More and more, democratic governments of the early 1900s became reluctant to impose the harsh remedies of the gold standard on their citizens. They looked for other means to correct a fundamental disequilibrium in international payments.

World War I had aggravated the payments deficits of Western nations. Imports necessary to fight the war had depleted national gold stocks. After the war, nations tried to recoup their wartime losses of gold reserves. They levied high tariffs to restrict imports and to stop the outflow of currency. A vicious circle developed: as nations cut back their purchases, other nations were unable to export. More tariffs were levied in more nations, and trade in the industrialized world slowed to a trickle.

The macroeconomic effects of reduced trade were smaller aggregate demand, reduced output, and growing unemployment. The Great Depression of the 1930s was partly a result of restrictive tariffs.

During the Great Depression, many nations went off the gold standard. President Franklin Roosevelt announced in 1933 that the United States would no longer redeem its currency in gold. Other nations took the same step.

Bretton Woods

The problems of international balance continued to build during the years between World War I and World War II. As World War II drew to a close, finance ministers of the allied powers met in Bretton Woods, New Hampshire, to plan the restoration of trade when peace came. They agreed to establish a gold-exchange standard for international trade; this system was a modification of the old gold standard.

Under the **gold-exchange standard,** nations could hold as reserves both gold and foreign exchange. Foreign exchange reserves included the currencies of trading nations, chiefly that of the United States—the dollar. Other national currencies were to be pegged in value relative to the dollar. The dollar itself was pegged to gold, at $35 an ounce.

The new system was expected to have certain advantages over the old gold standard. It would allow nations to avoid some of the pain of adjustment under the old system. When a nation's currency outflows were excessive, other nations would agree to support the currency at the pegged rates. Instead of allowing an excess supply to push down the value of a currency, the new system authorized central banks to buy the currency at its pegged rate. Central bank purchases would absorb the excess currency and keep its rate from falling. Currencies would be held in bank reserve accounts until needed to purchase other currencies.

Pegging the values of currencies allowed nations temporarily to spend more for imports than they earned for exports. But deficits were not expected to continue indefinitely. It was expected that a continuing disequilibrium would be dealt with by reducing excess spending abroad. Otherwise it would be necessary eventually to reduce a currency's pegged

Economic Thinker
Robert Triffin

A scholar and teacher, Robert Triffin is nevertheless no ivory-tower economist. Throughout his career he has been an active participant in the practical application of economic theory to the real world—especially in the areas of international trade and balance of payments. His ideas and his activities have had a major impact on the economies of many nations throughout the world.

Triffin was born in Belgium in 1911. He attended the University of Louvain there and came to the United States, to Harvard University, to obtain his doctorate degree. His dissertation was published, in 1940, as a book entitled *Monopolistic Competition and the General Equilibrium Theory.* Triffin taught at the University of Louvain and at Harvard. In 1951, he joined the faculty of Yale University.

Triffin's doctoral study was a pioneering effort in the study of monopolistic economies. Triffin contended that market forms are more varied than shown in earlier economic models and that these varied forms could be studied empirically. Many later studies in economic monopoly were built upon Triffin's work—although it was sharply attacked by the neolibertarians of the Chicago School, who felt competitive economies were the only proper subject of economic theory.

Triffin's main interest, however, was in the economics of international trade and international finance. His interest led to his appointment as the first chief of the Latin American Section of the Federal Reserve Fund. He was appointed to a task force set up by President John Kennedy to study balance of payments problems. He later served on Kennedy's Council of Economic Advisers. Triffin has directed a number of monetary and banking innovations in various Latin American countries and helped establish the Central American Clearing House, which functions as a kind of common market apparatus for member countries. Triffin has also acted as adviser for the Organization for European Economic Cooperation and for the United Nations. He is the author of many books on international finance, including *Europe and the Money Muddle, Gold and the Dollar Crisis, The World Money Maze,* and *Our International Monetary System.*

For many years, Robert Triffin was connected with the International Monetary Fund, in which he was active almost from its inception. He was a strong critic of the gold-exchange standard. Early on, he proposed that a reserve unit be created by the Fund to replace gold and/or the dollar and pound sterling as an international reserve. In effect, the Fund would become the bank of last resort for troubled economies of the world. In 1967, Triffin's plan became one basis for a general international monetary reform which saw the creation of Special Drawing Rights—so-called paper gold—as a source of reserves for nations temporarily without funds needed for international payments.

value. Thus the Bretton Woods system allowed a nation to postpone the painful price and income adjustments that had been necessary under the gold standard.

During the almost thirty years of the Bretton Woods system, the U.S. dollar was often a surplus currency. It was planned that way. The world stock of gold and other national currencies was not enough to finance the expected growth of peacetime trade. The United States provided dollars in aid and loans to European nations. And our government's policies encouraged imports and payments deficits in order to provide these dollars. Dollars were in great demand abroad because of the need for imports by nations whose industries had been devastated during World War II.

The collapse of the Bretton Woods system

But conditions changed and new arrangements had to be made to deal with them. By the 1960s European economies had recovered from the war and needed fewer imported goods from the United States. Moreover, their rebuilt and modernized industries were often able to undersell U.S. manufacturers in world markets.

U.S. deficits continued to pour dollars into foreign exchange markets as our imports grew faster than our exports. A "dollar glut" characterized the late 1960s. Foreign nations no longer needed our dollars. The excess supply of unused dollars would normally have pushed down the price. Under the old gold standard, a lower price for dollars would have set in motion all the painful adjustments described earlier. But under the Bretton Woods agreement nations were bound to support the dollar's price. Central banks continued to buy dollars at the pegged rate to keep the exchange rate from falling. The United States continued to have a fundamental disequilibrium in its international payments.

The result was growing distortion in the world economy and growing dissatisfaction among the finance ministers of our trading partners. In Germany, for example, the *Bundesbank* was obliged to buy dollars at the price of four marks per dollar. To issue four marks for each dollar flooded Germany with marks, worsening the risk of inflation. Germany and other nations demanded that the United States stop the outflow of currency and correct our balance of payments disequilibrium. The high pegged value of the dollar allowed U.S. customers to buy at a low price many goods and services from abroad. In addition, U.S. tourists could afford to visit Europe in great numbers. But more important, the dollar's artificially high value enabled U.S. investors to make direct investment in the capital assets of many other nations. French and Latin American governments demanded that we correct the conditions which gave American investors unfair advantage over their own citizens.

How was this to be done?

One possibility would have been to restrict imports into the U.S. by levying new tariffs. The result would have forced American consumers to reduce their purchases of foreign goods. This action would restrict the flow of outpayments and correct our deficit problem. But the United States and other Western nations had seen the results of tariff wars in the past. We were convinced of the benefits of trade and committed to greater freedom of trade through regular tariff reductions.

Another possibility would have been to restrict imports by policies aimed at reducing growth in national income and employment: in particular, contractionary monetary and fiscal policies. Slower money growth, higher taxes, and reduced government expenditures would reduce all spending, including purchases from abroad. This would restrict the flow of outpayments. Furthermore, contractionary policies would hold down U.S. prices and encourage foreign spending in the United States. Contractionary monetary and fiscal policies could also be expected to push up interest rates, attracting short-term foreign loan currency into the U.S. economy.

Contractionary policies were rejected also, since our government was committed to rising production and high-employment levels. In addition, the Vietnam War required large output of both military and civilian goods.

A third possibility was rejected by European governments. Our balance of payments deficits could be brought under control, we said, if European nations would agree to change the pegs which tied their currencies to the dollar. The German mark, for instance, could be pegged at two marks to the dollar instead of four. The mark's higher price would encourage German citizens to buy from the United States, bringing surplus dollars back. And the higher priced mark would discourage U.S. purchases abroad, further reducing our deficit.

To increase the mark's value in this way is called **revaluation.** European governments resisted major revaluation of their currencies because of the effect on their own economies. To revalue their currencies significantly would increase their own imports and reduce exports. This would cause a fall in their own domestic output and employment. Therefore, the European governments rejected this possibility.

A fourth possibility would have the same results, however, and it was finally decided upon. If European governments refused to *revalue* their own currencies *upward*, the United States would unilaterally *devalue* the dollar downward. **Devaluation** is an act of government to *decrease* the value of its currency. In 1971 the United States government announced a change in the dollar's value. The value of a dollar was reduced from $35 per ounce of gold to $38 per ounce. In effect, a dollar was worth about 8% less in international trade than before devaluation. At the same time President Nixon announced that the dollar would be convertible to gold only to foreign central banks and not to individuals or businesses.

Unfortunately, the deficits continued and a second devaluation was necessary in 1973. The value of a dollar was reduced from $38 per ounce to $42.22 per ounce of gold. This amounted to an additional 10% devaluation. At the same time the "gold window" was closed. President Nixon declared that the United States was suspending convertibility of the dollar to gold altogether.

To devalue the dollar was a drastic step. The United States government had hitherto avoided devaluation because of the effect on foreign holders of dollars. Central banks, business firms, and trusting individuals abroad were holding dollars as financial assets. To reduce the dollar's value by almost one-fifth—as the two devaluations did—wiped out a large part of their holdings. Such an action is not likely to instill confidence in a nation's ability to manage its financial problems.

Devaluation helped increase U.S. exports by providing more dollars for each unit of foreign currency exchanged. American goods became less expensive for foreigners to buy. However, devaluation cut U.S. imports by requiring more dollars for each unit of foreign currency used in trade. Foreign goods became more expensive to buy. The increase in exports relative to imports helped to bring surplus dollars back. It helped move the nation's international payments back toward balance, thus helping to correct its fundamental disequilibrium.

Floating currencies

In 1973, finance ministers of major trading nations met to seek acceptable solutions to new trading problems. An important change in currency relationships was the result.

The nations agreed to allow their currencies to "float." **Floating currency values** are determined solely by the interaction of demand and supply. Central banks would no longer purchase foreign currencies to maintain an established peg. Figure 3 shows how several currencies have fluctuated in value against the dollar.

It was hoped that floating currency values would correct payments imbalances. A temporary outflow of currency would hit foreign exchange markets as excess supply. The excess supply would force its value down. At the lower price, foreigners would demand more of the currency to spend in the deficit country. Thus the outflow would be reversed and payments would come back into balance.

Managed floating

Modifications were later made in the currency float concept. Currency relationships among major trading nations are now controlled by "managed floating." Currency values are allowed to fluctuate with market demand and supply. But *wide fluctuations* are prevented by central bank intervention. If greatly increased demand threatens to raise a currency's value sharply, the central bank enters the market to

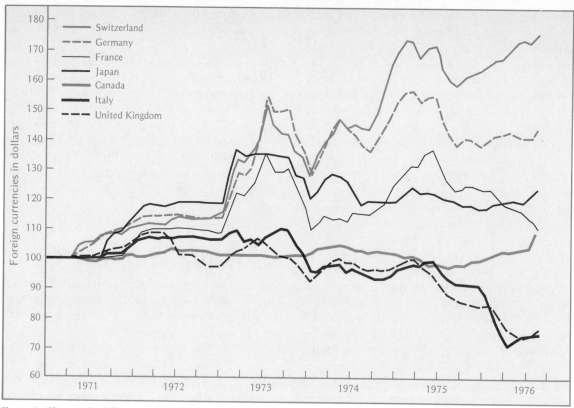

Figure 3 Changes in dollar cost of foreign currencies. The cost of these currencies is expressed as an index (where January, 1971 = 100).

sell that currency. In effect, it offsets the increased demand with new supply. By preventing a sharp increase in the price of its currency, a nation can protect its exporters from a severe drop in sales.

On the other hand, if greatly increased supply threatens to depress a currency's value sharply, the central bank enters the market to buy that currency. In effect, it offsets the increased supply with new demand. By preventing a sharp drop in the value of its currency, a nation preserves the purchasing power of its currency in the market for imports.

Managed floating has helped keep currency values fairly stable. However, nations sometimes intervene in the foreign exchange markets to achieve unfair trade advantage. They may violate international agreements so as to increase their exports at the expense of other countries. In 1976, Japan was criticized for such intervention. It was accused of pre-

venting the yen from floating upward within the managed float. Keeping the yen cheap helped to protect Japanese manufacturers from foreign competition. Harley-Davidson, the American maker of large motorcycles, complained that it had lost much of its American market because of artificially undervalued yen. Some nations feel that the managed float system is not a fair or effective control for their currency in the international trade market. Other nations allow their currency to float within the system but depend also on other arrangements for controlling its exchange value.

Viewpoint
Problems with Floating Exchange Rates

"If it ain't broke, don't fix it."

Sometimes tinkering with something that works reasonably well may end up causing it not to work at all. At least this is the opinion of some analysts of international exchange relationships. In the debate over fixed versus floating exchange rates, this group favors a minimum amount of central bank tinkering with national currency values.

Western trading nations adopted floating exchange rates in the early 1970s, when the United States devalued the dollar and suspended currency convertibility. For years, some economists had been recommending an end to the system of fixed exchange rates. They looked to market forces to determine international values, much the same as they would rely on free market forces to establish prices in domestic product markets. Any government tinkering with the free market was seen as a dangerous interference with healthy adjustments between buyers and sellers. Unwarranted meddling would likely create greater problems than those it was intended to solve.

Back in the eighteenth century, David Hume had explained how international gold flows would lead to automatic adjustments healthy for international trade. When a nation spent too much abroad, it would suffer a balance of payments deficit. The outflow of money would reduce the domestic money supply, putting downward pressure on prices and employment, cutting imports, and stimulating exports. The result would be a continual movement toward equilibrium: *external* equilibrium as the flows of trade brought payments back into balance; and *internal* equilibrium as domestic spending adjusted to noninflationary full employment in all trading nations. Automatic stabilization through the free market would relieve government of the responsibility to intervene when the system "ain't broke."

In 1975, member nations of the International Monetary Fund met in Jamaica and agreed on a policy of nonintervention in international currency markets: only the absolute minimum central bank intervention would be used to stabilize currency values. The prices of currencies were left to fluctuate according to fundamental economic factors such as domestic economic growth rates, interest rates, and price trends, as well as expectations about the future course of these variables. Exchange rates were expected to move opposite to domestic price levels, so as to offset different inflation rates among nations. Floating rates would have an important advantage in terms of internal stability; they would remove from government the obligation to use contractionary fiscal and monetary policies to restrain domestic inflation. Champions of the free market cheered the changeover to a policy of minimum government intervention in internal and external markets.

What have been the actual results of floating exchange rates? By 1977, the results were becoming especially painful for the world's less developed countries (LDCs). Floating rates were supposed to lead to external and internal balance; but in actual fact the float was worsening these nations' problems of balance.

Their problems stemmed first of all from their efforts to industrialize. Imports of industrial equipment and materials, particularly fuel, were becoming more costly while revenues from commodity exports were fairly stable or even falling. Rising import prices were worsening domestic inflation, already aggravated by heavy development spending at home. In theory, rising domestic inflation should be offset by falling exchange rates. The lower exchange rate on domestic currency would then stimulate export sales, bringing in the foreign currency needed for the nation's imports of industrial capital.

Unhappily, these automatic adjustments did not come about. For floating rates to do their job, it is necessary that buyers respond to price changes by altering the quantities they buy. Demand must respond to price changes: lower currency values must encourage foreign buyers to purchase the nation's exports and discourage domestic buyers from purchasing imports. In actual fact, however, many demand curves in international trade are highly unresponsive to price changes. Domestic firms must purchase equipment from abroad if industrialization is to proceed; lower currency values required a greater outflow of currency to pay for the same necessary quantity of imports. Moreover, foreign firms were in no rush to increase their purchases of commodity exports; this was particularly true when many exporters actually raised their prices to compensate for the lower currency exchange rate.

Instead of offsetting price trends in the domestic economy, floating rates appeared to be reinforcing them. Once a nation began to experience a decline in currency values, the problem seemed to snowball. The chain of events was: (1) international payments deficit, (2) declining exchange rate, (3) higher priced imports, (4) domestic inflation, (5) loss in international competitiveness in export markets, (6) more severe international payments deficit, and so on.

The LDCs were not the only ones in trouble. By 1977, severe inflation and collapsed currency values had also afflicted Great Britain, Italy, and France. Figure 3 shows how these currencies nose-dived in 1975 and 1976. All were also experiencing inflation in the double-digit range.

There is another problem with the present system of floating exchange rates: Unfortunately, some nations don't play by the rules when it is to their advantage not to do so. In theory, a fortunate nation experiencing a payments surplus should find its exchange rate rising. The result would be rising prices for its exports, declining sales, and smaller inflows of currency. Thus floating rates would help to move the surplus nation back to equilibrium. In practice, however, the automatic adjustment is not always welcome because of its contractionary effects on domestic employment. To avoid this result, a nation may refuse to let its currency float. The float gets "dirty" when a nation continues to intervene in currency markets to prevent its own currency from rising in value.

During 1976, it appeared that Japan was guilty. Japan's central bank was buying up surplus foreign currency to prevent an increase in the exchange rate for yen. The yen's artificially low price fueled Japanese exports and stimulated a strong recovery from recession—at the expense of Japan's trading rivals. Other industrialized nations were unable to compete with Japan's low-priced exports, and their industries remained depressed.

Such violation of international agreements is not likely to be tolerated for long, particularly when national governments must answer to voters concerned about unemployment at home. Unless peaceful solutions are found, the likely response would be new tariffs to exclude imports and a general slowdown in international trade. The world economy would suffer as a result.

To avoid this, some analysts have recommended establishing a range within which each nation's currency would be allowed to float. Governments would be expected to use conventional fiscal and monetary tools to correct internal inflation or recession. But they would also be permitted to intervene temporarily in currency markets to keep currency values within the prescribed range.

Optimum currency areas and the European snake

Sometimes nations peg their currencies fairly close to each other in value. They hope to enjoy greater benefits from trade because of intergroup currency stability. Nations which form a single geographic trading bloc find stable rates especially helpful. Such groups of nations are called **optimum currency areas.**

One optimum currency area is a group of European nations who manage their currencies within a narrow band of fluctuations. In 1976, the group consisted of West Germany, Belgium, the Netherlands, Luxembourg, Denmark, Norway, and Sweden. The chief currency in the group is the West German mark. The mark may rise or fall in value with respect to other world currencies. But as it rises, other nations in the group intervene in the market to raise their currency values also. Likewise if the mark falls, other nations in the bloc supply more of their own currencies to bring the value down. Because these currencies move up and down together, much as a moving reptile undulates, the group has been called the *European snake*. When the currency of a bloc nation is traded outside the group, its value is controlled by the managed currency system.

Petrodollars and balance of international payments

Sharply increasing prices for OPEC oil have presented the trading world with a serious international payments problem. The problem affects deficit nations and surplus nations alike, but it is especially damaging to deficit nations of the Third World. These are the poor nations which have fallen behind the rest of the world in industrial development. They desperately need funds for capital investment and energy for growth.

Heavy importers of Arab oil have already paid out most of their reserve holdings of foreign exchange. For many Third World nations lacking valuable exports, this has meant heavy borrowing to finance their petroleum imports. The United States has been less seriously affected than other nations because earnings from agricultural exports have kept our reserves of foreign currency relatively stable.

The problem concerns us deeply, nevertheless. Historically, petroleum prices have been set in terms of dollars. Oil importers throughout the world have therefore been paying for their purchases in dollars. As a result, oil-exporting nations are acquiring large reserves of U.S. currency. This large overhang of Arab *petrodollars* has led to fears of how the money might be used in the international trading market.

Should Arab nations suddenly throw their dollars on foreign exchange markets for conversion to marks, yen, or some other currency, the value of the dollar could fall sharply. Flows of international payments throughout the world could be disrupted.

Extended Example
Arms Sales

While the United States has been losing its comparative advantage in some manufactured exports, it has gained advantage in at least one other. Sales of military equipment were about $10 billion in 1975, comprising a major part of our trade balance. Foreign orders are predicted to continue increasing, so that by 1980 one-fifth of U.S.-made military equipment will be sold abroad.

McDonnell Douglas Corporation is an important exporter. In 1975, McDonnell Douglas earned $419 million on sales of their F-4 fighter plane and A-4 attack aircraft. Boeing's airborne warning and control system (AWACS) aircraft is another big seller. Boeing expects to earn $3.5 billion on foreign contracts over the next five years (1977–1982). Grumman's F-14 airplane, Textron's helicopters, and Raytheon's missiles are also earning valuable foreign exchange. Northrop Corporation has been exporting an unusual product; it trains pilots and builds air bases for the Saudi Arabian government.

United States arms exports have gone primarily to Iran, Israel, and Saudi Arabia. Heightened international tensions in these areas led at first to some Congressional opposition to military sales. Nevertheless, as our customers switched from credit to cash, opposition faded rapidly. The nation's economy benefited richly from the multiple effects of military sales; the newly developing areas of the U.S. South and West enjoyed particular prosperity.

Still, there are worries associated with U.S. arms sales. Is it wise to provide the means for military aggression in other parts of the world? Will our deadly exports ever be turned against us? On the other hand, if we refuse to sell, won't other nations grab the opportunity to supply the market? These are important questions which will continue to face citizens of the United States.

Ideally, petrodollars would be recycled back into international finance with as few disruptions as possible. In fact, many petrodollars have returned to the United States through expenditures for capital equipment. Arab countries have become customers for United States firms building schools, hospitals, factories, and even entire towns. As still developing nations, their need for capital goods is great.

Arab investors have also used petrodollars to purchase capital assets in the United States. Their aim has been to accumulate income-earning assets against the time when their oil resources are fully depleted or in case the demand for petroleum slackens. Arab investments have included direct investment in hotels, resorts, and banks. Portfolio investment in United States corporate stocks and bonds have been popular, too. Petrodollars have also been recycled through Arab investments in other nations, particularly in England and West Germany.

But the problem of redistributing the huge sums of dollar currency suddenly flowing into Arab oil-producing nations is still with us. The ultimate effect of this economic phenomenon on world payments remains to be seen. We will discuss the problem further in the next chapter when we take up the subject of international movements of capital in general.

Summary

Barter is especially difficult in international trade. Therefore, nations have developed monetary standards for exchange of goods. During the eighteenth century, emphasis on accumulating gold led to the philosophy of mercantilism with a stress on exports relative to imports. Mercantilism ignored the need for balance in the flows of traded goods.

Trade was made easier through development of banking and the use of paper currencies convertible to gold. The slowing rate of growth of gold production finally made currencies inconvertible.

A nation's balance of payments statement shows the amounts of outpayments and inpayments from trade. Current transactions include merchandise trade, unilateral money flows, and income from investments abroad.

The balance on current account may be positive or negative, depending on the relative values of these inpayments and outpayments. The United States balance on current account was largely negative until this century when it has generally been positive. In recent years, expanding technology abroad has reduced our positive balance and occasionally produced a negative one. Maintaining a high quality of output and low production costs is essential for increasing United States sales abroad.

Capital transactions on the balance of payments statement include investors' claims against the assets of another country. Long-term capital investment may be direct—in productive facilities—or indirect—in securities or bank accounts. The balance on capital account generally bears the opposite sign from the balance on current account. This is because net outpayments for trade generally return in the form of capital investment, and vice versa.

The net flow of capital depends also on the expected earnings from investment in areas of capital abundance and areas of capital scarcity. Sometimes economic and political conditions make direct foreign investment risky, and capital flows dry up. Similar risks also impede indirect investment and short-term investment. Combining the balance on current account and the balance on long-term capital produces a nation's basic balance.

The size of the basic balance and its sign determines the net flow of funds which must be settled by international balancing transactions. Balancing transactions are called *official settlement transactions* and require either a transfer of foreign currency reserves or borrowing through international credit organizations.

The flow of international payments is fundamentally a result of the relative purchasing power of different currencies. The exchange rate for currencies is determined by demand and supply in foreign exchange markets. A high-valued currency may lead to a deficit in a nation's payments and a low-valued currency to a surplus.

A continued and prolonged imbalance in a nation's international payments reflects a fundamental disequilibrium and must be corrected. Flexible exchange rates will help to bring imports and exports into balance, but they increase the risks of trade. The old gold standard would automatically adjust exports and imports by changing the domestic money supply. Both solutions impose hardships on deficit nations, however.

After World War II at Bretton Woods, trading nations established a gold-exchange standard. The dollar became the world's most important trading currency. Nations agreed to preserve fixed exchange rates by purchasing and selling currencies in foreign exchange markets. Eventually, the artificially high value of the dollar had to be corrected through devaluation. Now currencies "float" within broad bands.

In recent years the most serious balance of payments problems have involved OPEC holdings of petrodollars. The problems are particularly severe in less developed countries which need petroleum imports and lack valuable exports.

Key Words and Phrases

- **barter** exchange of goods for other goods without the use of money standard of value and medium of exchange—the functions of money in facilitating trade.
- **mercantilism** a national policy favoring exports (and the accumulation of gold) over imports.
- **exchange rate** the price of one national currency in terms of another.
- **currency convertibility** the ability to exchange paper currency for a stated amount of gold.
- **deficit** an excess of outpayments over inpayments in international trade.
- **surplus** an excess of inpayments over outpayments in international trade.
- **current transactions** international payments for purchase of goods and services, as income for investments, or as unilateral payments.
- **unilateral flows** payments for which no good or service flows in exchange.
- **balance of trade** the net flow of payments for exchange of goods and services.
- **capital transactions** international payments for investment in productive assets of another country.

- **long- or short-term capital flows** international capital transactions for investments maturing after more than a year or in less than a year.
- **direct and indirect capital investment** purchases of productive assets in another nation and purchases of securities or share accounts in productive assets.
- **basic balance** the net flow of funds between nations for current transactions and long-term capital transactions.
- **official settlement transactions** balancing transactions which offset the net flow of payments for current and capital transactions.
- **foreign exchange market** the worldwide market for exchange of national currencies.
- **fundamental disequilibrium** a condition in which a nation's net flow of payments is consistently in one direction; that is, a consistent outflow (deficit) or a consistent inflow (surplus).
- **flexible exchange rates** an arrangement in which prices of currencies are established by demand and supply in free markets.
- **forward exchange** purchase of a contract guaranteeing delivery of foreign exchange at a specified price at some time in the future.
- **gold standard** an arrangement in which international gold flows offset the net flow of paper currency; the paper currency is backed by gold.
- **Bretton Woods** the site of international agreements to stabilize exchange rates through central bank purchases and sale of currencies.
- **gold-exchange standard** an international system in which the value of currencies was "pegged" to the dollar and the dollar was "pegged" to gold.
- **revaluation or devaluation** changes in the fixed value of a currency in an upward or a downward direction.
- **floating currencies** currencies whose value is set by the free movement of supply and demand.
- **managed floating** an arrangement in which central bank purchases of currencies help to keep their value within an established range—within this range supply and demand determine currency values.
- **optimum currency areas** groups of nations which agree to maintain the value of their currencies in some established relationship with each other.
- **European snake** a group of European nations whose currencies are held to some established value relative to each other.
- **petrodollars** dollars paid for petroleum imports and held by petroleum-exporting nations.

Questions for Review

1. What advantages did the policy of mercantilism convey to a nation? What disadvantages?

2. How did currency convertibility reduce the risks of trade? Did it also act as a restraint on trade?

3. Explain the purpose of the threefold division of the balance of payments statement. How are the signs of the three accounts related? What are the typical trends in the signs of the accounts over time? What fundamental factors determine the size and direction of a nation's inpayments and outpayments?

4. Distinguish between direct and indirect capital investment. What are the advantages and disadvantages? Why is it customary to distinguish between flows of long-term and short-term capital? How does borrowing on the third part of the balance of payments differ from borrowing on the second part?

5. In 1977, Egypt reduced the dollar price of its pound from $2.56 to $1.42 for foreign investors. What would be the desired result? Describe the process which would be expected to follow.

6. What are some disadvantages of a general devaluation of a nation's currency? What are the disadvantages of a revaluation?

7. Under what circumstances would the gold standard fail to bring about the adjustments in income and prices necessary to correct a balance of payments disequilibrium?

8. What specific problems under flexible exchange rates and the gold standard was the Bretton Woods system designed to correct? What other problems did it create? Why did other nations resist efforts to change the system?

9. Distinguish among: fixed exchange rates, floating exchange rates, and managed floating.

10. In 1977, a scarcity of coffee put sharp upward pressure on prices. In a few months coffee prices rose by one-third and U.S. consumers cut back purchases by 17%. What would be the effect of these changes on the balance of payments between the United States and Brazil?

21

International Commercial Policies and Institutions

The pure theory of international trade explains the benefits nations enjoy when they trade freely according to the principle of comparative advantage. Unhappily, we do not achieve all the benefits possible under ideal conditions—for conditions are seldom ideal. Consequently, trading nations have developed policies and institutions to deal with problems actually encountered in international trade and finance.

For descriptive purposes, these problems can be characterized as problems of internal or external balance—though both are intimately connected. *Problems of internal balance* involve the short-run effects of trade on domestic output, income, and employment. These short-run effects lead, in turn, to the long-run problem of a nation's potential for economic growth.

Problems of external balance focus on the economic relationships among nations. Prolonged deficits or surpluses can produce serious problems for trade relationships. External problems also include changing power relationships among nations. Relationships change with changes in comparative advantage and in relative growth rates among nations. Changing power relationships are especially critical for the nations of the Third World.

This chapter will examine the policies and institutions which have been established to deal with problems of internal and external balance.

Policies of internal balance: protectionism

Internal balance is critical to a nation's output, income, and employment. Aggregate demand is the sum of all spending for goods and services and determines the level of economic activity. For a healthy economy, aggregate demand should be neither so great as to produce inflation nor so low as to produce unemployment. Net foreign spending is an important component of aggregate demand in many nations. A sound trading policy aims at regulating net foreign spending in the interests of internal economic stability.

Tariffs

Nations have often tried to "protect" their domestic economy through the use of devices that restrict free trade. They have resorted to a policy called **protectionism.** Protectionist devices include tariffs, quotas on imported products, and even outright prohibition of imports. Nations with command economies often use the foreign exchange market to restrict imports. As we shall see below, they may refuse to provide foreign currency to their citizens for buying foreign goods.

The most common protectionist devices are tariffs—a form of tax on imported goods. They may be *revenue tariffs* or *protective tariffs.* **Revenue tariffs** are not designed to hamper free trade; they are designed only to secure revenue for the importing nation. Therefore, the tariff rate must be low enough not to discourage imports. In the United States, revenue tariffs (custom duties) accounted for most of the government's revenue until introduction of the income tax in 1913. (Long before that, a revenue tariff on tea led to a party in Boston Harbor that helped change world history.)

Protective tariffs are designed to raise the cost of imported products. The nation's consumers will consequently buy fewer of these products and more products produced by domestic industries. Sometimes the tariffs are set so high that they become "prohibitive." No purchases of foreign-made goods can be made at all. Protective tariffs may also be "preferential." That is, they impose a lower rate on the products of one nation than on those of another. Blocs of nations often use such tariffs to favor members of the group.

Figure 1 illustrates the effect of a tariff in internal markets. The model shows domestic demand for a foreign good, in this case, Japanese motorcycles. Before the imposition of a tariff, the supply curve is as shown by S. At equilibrium, i.e., the intersection of supply and demand curves, easy riders will purchase 1,000 units per month at a unit price of $2,000.

But cycle imports reduce the X_n component of aggregate demand and threaten unemployment in domestic industries. (Remember that X_n equals the value of exports minus the value of imports.) Consequently, the importing

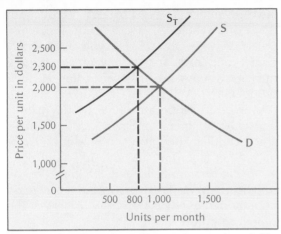

Figure 1 **The effect of a tariff on an imported good, like Japanese motorcycles. A $500 tariff adds $500 to the supply cost of each motorcycle. So the supply decreases from S to S_T. The equilibrium price rises $300, from $2,000 to $2,300. Quantity sold falls from 1,000 to 800.**

nation may decide to levy a tariff to reduce cycle imports and raise X_n.

A tariff of $500 per unit shifts the supply curve upward by $500 at each quantity, as shown by the curve S_T. Equilibrium price and quantity after the tariff are shown at the intersection of demand (D) and S_T. Only 800 units will be bought at a price of $2,300. Of this unit price, $500 is collected by customs officials and $1,800 is paid to the Japanese manufacturer.

American consumers must pay a higher unit price and will also enjoy fewer units of the imported item. But the X_n component of aggregate demand will rise with the fall in imports. Furthermore, many buyers will shift their purchases to American-made cycles, raising income and employment in the domestic economy.

Final results are not always as planned, however. Restrictions on U.S. imports also restrict the export sales of foreign producers. Workers in foreign nations will lose jobs. To avoid loss of jobs and a general decline in economic activity, other nations may retaliate by imposing tariffs of their own.

Retaliatory tariffs will restrict U.S. sales to foreign consumers. A drop in U.S. export sales will cause a decline in net exports. The X_n component of aggregate demand shifts downward, with multiple contractionary effects on domestic output and employment. It looks as if the only real beneficiaries of the tariff are U.S. motorcycle manufacturers!

It is easy to see why protectionism is called a "beggar thy neighbor" policy. It is also clear that thy neighbor can just as easily beggar thee. If tariffs are likely to produce these unfavorable results, why are they ever used? There are some fairly persuasive arguments in favor of tariffs.

Philosophy of Tariffs

The infant-industry argument One argument in favor of tariffs is that they can protect new domestic industry. Without a tariff, established competitors in other countries would undersell a beginning industry and prevent it from ever reaching efficient operation. Supporters of infant-industry tariffs want to exclude import competition until the new industry gets on its feet.

Such tariffs were useful during our own early years as a nation, when our industries were just beginning to develop. And tariffs are generally tolerated in developing nations of today. Many developing nations employ tariffs to protect their young industries. Successful industrial growth will help these nations to diversify their economies.

But a disadvantage of infant-industry tariffs is the industry's unwillingness ever to see the tariff removed. After years of a protected domestic market, producers are often reluctant to move out into the real world of free competition. Infant-industry protection may have other unhealthy effects on productive efficiency. The exclusion of competition may discourage technical development and reduce efforts to cut production costs. The infant may never grow up. The end result of infant-industry tariffs may be slower economic growth, a lessened ability to compete in world markets, and higher domestic prices.

The strategic-industry argument The objective of some tariffs is to protect an industry that produces goods vital to a nation's defense. In the case of a strategic industry, productive efficiency relative to that of other nations may not be an important consideration. The domestic industry may require protection because of its importance to national defense:

oil, natural gas, shipping, and steel, for example. Without protection, such industries might be weakened by foreign competition. Then in an international crisis the nation might find itself in short supply of products essential to its national defense.

The argument for a strategic-industry tariff seems reasonable on first hearing. However, it is difficult, if not impossible, to determine precisely which industries are essential to a nation's defense. Almost all industries would be able to come up with pretty good reasons why their products are "essential" to the defense effort.

In any case, economists generally recommend policies other than tariffs to protect domestic producers of strategic goods or materials. *A tax-supported subsidy* may accomplish the desired results. A subsidy is a direct payment for a specific objective. It can be made subject to strict control and quick termination. It is also subject to periodic review by Congress. Consequently, it is a more flexible form of industrial support than a tariff.

In the United States, subsidies are awarded to the merchant marine industry to overcome its cost disadvantage relative to foreign shippers. Tariffs and quotas have been used to protect domestic producers of essential energy supplies. As a result, prices are higher for some products than they otherwise might be. But producers are expected to use some portion of their profits for industry expansion. In this way, the nation will have a ready supply in case of national emergency.

The production-costs argument A common complaint of U.S. producers—especially back in the 1950s and 1960s—was that the wage rates of American workers were too high. The resulting high production costs, it was argued, called for a tariff to raise the price of foreign products and prevent the loss of sales for domestic goods. Proponents of this argument classify this as a "scientific" tariff. Supposedly, it is calculated to bring production costs in line worldwide.

An obvious criticism of this argument involves the fundamental basis for trade. Trade is possible and beneficial because of *different* production costs in different countries. Different production costs are the basis for comparative advantage. To equalize costs throughout the world would eliminate trade altogether.

High wage rates for U.S. workers generally reflect our comparative advantage. In free markets workers are paid according to their productivity. Well-paid U.S. workers receive this high reward because their productivity is high. Our unique combination of resources and technology permits us to produce a larger output per labor hour. As a result, labor costs *per unit of output* may actually be lower for the American worker. If this is so, no price increase on imported goods is necessary to protect the American producer.

This does not mean that all United States industries and jobs are secure against competition from low-cost foreign-made products. It is true only in industries where U.S. resources possess comparative advantage. Where productivity of *foreign* workers is greater and unit costs lower, the principle of comparative advantage dictates a shift of U.S. resources away from that industry.

U.S. textile manufacturers have been experiencing such a shift. Foreign producers have undercut markets for certain types of textiles. Jobs have been lost, factories closed, and returns on investment capital have dropped in the United States. The adjustment has been painful for many individuals and communities.

But long-range benefits can accrue to the economy as a whole. The movement of U.S. resources away from this industry (and others like it) frees resources for employment in industries in which we enjoy comparative advantage. In another industry workers might well produce relatively greater output per unit of resource—in electronics, chemicals, and transportation equipment, for example. U.S. income and total world output will be increased as resources shift from industries in which their productivity is low to industries in which their productivity is high.

The terms-of-trade argument The terms-of-trade argument for tariffs is often voiced by nations producing low-value commodities for export. Their export earnings on raw commodities may be insufficient to finance imports necessary for economic growth. They must solve their balance of payments problems. To do so, they say, they must impose tariffs to improve their terms of trade.

Figure 2 illustrates how a tariff can improve their terms of trade. A tariff on imported manufacture will shift supply curves (S) up by the amount of the tariff. Equilibrium price before the tariff is imposed is OP and quantity is OQ. The tariff ac shifts supply up to S_T. Equilibrium price rises to OP_T and quantity falls to OQ_T. At the new equilibrium quantity, unit cost to the foreign producer is measured along the supply curve S at Q_Ta. The importing nation pays out a smaller price for each unit of manufactured goods imported and the remainder is collected as tariff.

With the tariff, the amount foreign producers receive for their product is lower by the distance ab. In effect, foreign producers pay ab of the tariff tax to customs officials. The remainder of the tariff tax, bc, is paid by local buyers in the form of the higher total price they pay for imported manufactured goods. The terms of trade are said to be more favorable because a smaller quantity of raw commodity exports must be paid out for each unit of manufactured imports.

As noted above, the terms-of-trade argument for tariffs is often made by developing countries. Yet tariffs can be particularly damaging to a developing nation. Its import needs are often necessary for industrial development and for the material needs of its people. With the tariff, the domestic cost of its imports will increase, raising the cost of economic development. Furthermore, a retaliatory tariff on the developing nation's commodity exports would aggravate the problem even more.

Actually, a tariff may not improve a nation's terms of trade at all. If domestic demand for imports remains high despite the higher price, the entire burden of the tariff can be shifted to local buyers. Outpayments will remain high as before, and the domestic economy may be starved for funds.

Each of the arguments favoring tariffs is plausible. *But each has the effect of encouraging and prolonging inefficiency in the allocation of scarce resources.* Because of the harmful effects of tariffs, most economists recommend monetary and fiscal policies to correct short-run problems of internal balance. Appropriate expansionary policies can produce healthy changes in output, income, and employment. They need not produce the economic distortions and the retaliatory measures likely with a tariff.

Other barriers to trade

Quotas Tariffs are the most common form of trade restriction, but there are others. An especially damaging trade barrier is the quota. **Quotas** set limits to the quantity of imported goods. In the United States, quotas have been used to limit imports of certain kinds of domestic steel, petroleum, textile products, and other goods. In 1959, for example, quotas were placed on Arab petroleum imports into the United States.

Figure 3 illustrates the effect of a quota on the domestic market for steel beams. Demand, D, is the sum of United States industrial demand for steel, whether produced domestically or imported. Supply, S_D, is the sum of supplies offered for sale by domestic producers alone. Total supply, S_Q, is equal to domestic supply plus the import quota. Without a quota, foreign producers would supply a larger quantity, making total supply S_F.

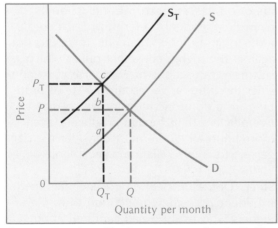

Figure 2 Use of a tariff to improve terms of trade. Tariff ac moves supply from S to S_T. The new equilibrium price is P_T and the new equilibrium quantity is Q_T. Producers receive Q_Ta of the higher price. The tariff ac is shared by consumers and producers; consumers pay bc and producers pay ab.

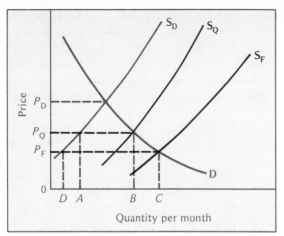

Figure 3 A quota affects supply. S_D is domestic supply; S_Q is the sum of domestic supply and the amount supplied by the quota; S_F is what the supply would be without a quota. The quota permits an imported quantity of only AB. Without a quota, quantity imported would be larger, DC, and price would be lower P_F. Notice effect of quota on domestic production: with a quota, it is OA; without a quota, it falls to OD.

At an equilibrium price of OP_Q, the quantity OA is supplied by domestic producers. The quota AB is supplied by foreign producers. Steel prices are lower (at OP_Q) than they would be without trade, at OP_D. But without a quota, foreign supply would be larger and price even lower, at OP_F. Moreover, the quota places limits on the increase in supply if demand should increase. As industrial needs grow, additional supply must be met from local sources alone at higher prices. Foreign firms are unable to increase their sales in the protected market.

In spite of the damaging effects of a tariff, it at least enables quantity to increase. Buyers who are willing to pay the tariff are able to increase their purchases without restrictions. For this reason, a tariff, while objectionable, is still preferable to a quota.

Export duties and subsidies Other trade barriers are export duties and subsidies. **Export duties** are taxes paid by exporters on goods shipped abroad. *The objective is to reduce the profitability of export sales in order to retain goods for domestic markets.* Governments occasionally impose export duties to avoid loss of valuable commodities.

Extended Example
Pressure for Protection

The 1950s and 1960s were prosperous decades for the industrialized nations. Broad, worldwide reductions in tariff barriers played a large part in stimulating production and employment and increasing real incomes. Regrettably, the 1970s brought a whole new set of economic circumstances. Rising OPEC oil prices shoved many nations into international payments deficits. Recession with persistent unemployment and staggering inflation led to calls for new trade policies.

National political leaders tend to seek policies that will improve their own nation's economic position. Interest groups at home apply pressure for policies that favor their particular industries. Labor unions lobby for policies to preserve jobs. Some of the loudest calls for selected protectionist barriers have been occurring here in the United States. The greatest pressure for protection has been in some of the following industries: steel, electronics, sugar, and shoes.

United States trade policy is proposed by the International Trade Commission and the U.S. Treasury under the Trade Act of 1974 and within broad guidelines set through membership in the General Agreement on Tariffs and Trade (GATT). The President must approve recommendations for tariffs or quotas, subject to Congressional overrule. President Carter must balance off industry and union arguments for protection against the higher consumer prices which result from restrictions on trade. He must consider the long-range resource costs of propping up a domestic industry which may be less efficient than foreign producers. Even more importantly, he must consider the dangers of foreign retaliation against United States exports.

Steel Domestic steel producers have been experiencing rising competition from foreigners who by 1976 had captured about one-fifth of the market for basic steel; on the West Coast, Japanese manufacturers were supplying one-third of the market. In 1976 voluntary quotas on certain steel imports were arranged with Japan and were enforced also on the Common Market, Canada, and Sweden. Quotas are permitted under United States trade law under its "escape clause" if imports can be shown to have injured domestic producers. The clause has been used only in the case of stainless or specialty steel. Although quotas are illegal under GATT, they can often be agreed to "voluntarily" among nations.

Imports of other low-priced steel have forced price reductions for domestic steel and cut profits, already low because of the recession. United States steel producers contend that low import prices are actually a result of tax rebates paid foreign producers by their governments; that is, the low prices result from a form of export subsidy. They accuse other governments of attempting to export their unemployment—increased their own sales at the expense of American workers. The steel producers have asked our government to impose "countervailing duties" to offset this price advantage.

Electronics Until recently, the United States has hesitated to regard rebated taxes as export subsidies, but pressure is building up to do so in electronics as well as steel. Imposition of countervailing duties will have particular impact on Japanese and Common Market sales in the United States. An estimated 60% of radio sales and 70% of television sets are imported. Probably 100,000 U.S. jobs in this industry alone have been lost through imports in the 1970s. In April, 1977, a New York Customs Court ruled that Japanese tax rebates were in fact export subsidies and clamped duties of roughly 15% on imports. The ruling was appealed and overturned, but in the meantime Japan agreed to cut its shipments of television sets to the United States by almost one-half.

Sugar Export subsidies may also be a problem in the sugar trade. United States cane and beet sugar producers have been supplying more than half the domestic market. But in 1977, export subsidies abroad had reduced the world price of raw sugar below United States costs of production. To allow collapse of domestic production would severely damage the economies of agricultural regions in the United States and leave us open to

unreasonable foreign price demands in the future. But to protect inefficiency would be costly and would invite competition from corn-based sweeteners, produced largely in Japan. In this case President Carter decided on a subsidy to local growers of up to 2¢ a pound when the world price falls below U.S. production costs.

Shoes A classic problem in trade and tariff policy is the one facing United States shoe manufacturers. The shoe industry began in New England more than a century ago. Because production used minimal capital and cheap labor, it was ideal for a primitive stage of industrial development. Today these same qualities make shoe manufacture attractive to nations like Italy, Spain, Taiwan, Brazil, and South Korea. Their cheap labor has enabled these nations to undersell United States producers. During the first half of the 1970s, more than one-half of the remaining United States shoe manufacturers went out of business. By 1975, almost half of U.S. sales were imports; domestic production and employment had fallen by one-third. The U.S. International Trade Commission recommended quotas and high tariffs on imports greater than the quota, but President Carter rejected the request. Instead he proposed some voluntary quotas and increased aid for workers displaced by foreign competition.

Under present laws, workers displaced by foreign competition may receive up to 70% of earnings for as much as a year, plus training in new job skills, allowances to search for work in other cities, and partial payment of moving expenses. In the two years after the law went into effect (1975–1976), almost 200,000 workers received benefits, although most did not need the full amounts available. During the period, technical assistance and low-interest loans were also provided to 63 companies threatened by foreign competition.

Evaluate overall United States trade policy. What are the important arguments pro and con for present policy? Evaluate specific solutions in the problem industries discussed. Consider other industries facing foreign competition: autos, for example. What solutions would you suggest to their problems?

Export subsidies have the opposite effect. They are payments to exporters for goods sold abroad. In effect, a portion of the production cost of an exported good is returned by government to the producer. This allows local producers to reduce their prices in foreign markets and undersell their competition. Nations may subsidize their national airlines—Air France, for example, or British Airways. In the United States, privately owned airlines complain that this gives government-owned airlines abroad an unfair advantage in international transport competition.

Governments of importing nations are usually aware of the use of subsidies to reduce import prices below domestic competitors. When possible, these governments impose "countervailing duties" on the import. Countervailing duties add a local tax to bring the final selling price in line with domestic prices. The result is to capture the subsidy for the local government.

Some nations impose **quality standards on imports.** The effect is to protect local manufacturers without imposing quotas or duties of any kind. In the United States, for instance, imported automobiles are required to have antipollution equipment and to meet other design and safety specifications. Some quality specifications may be difficult for foreign producers to meet. They may even lack the facilities to meet them altogether. Thus such restrictions may effectively limit a nation's imports.

Foreign exchange controls Perhaps the most serious *long-run* interference with free trade comes with **foreign exchange controls.** This policy is possible only if the national government has control of all currencies used in foreign exchange. Foreign trade dealings are then conducted through a nation's central bank or some other government agency. In effect, the nation controls its traders' purse strings. For example, a trader in a country with such a managed economy may wish to import American cement. The nation may feel that its own cement-makers need protection from foreign competition. It does not have to use tariffs or other such devices to limit the import. It merely denies the trader the dollars necessary to make the trade. For cement purchases, the foreign exchange window is closed.

The nation may close its foreign exchange window for import of luxury items such as jewelry or automobiles. But it may open it for items such as industrial machinery or food needed for economic development.

This type of control is sometimes an advantage to a developing country. It enables government to exercise control over its international trade as a means toward economic growth. But it has the same disadvantages as other barriers to free trade. It may inhibit the workings of comparative advantage. It may limit the long-run benefits derived from free international trade. Additionally, it may easily result in collusion between government officials and business interests. Bribes may open the foreign exchange window to favored traders. The nation's overall plans for economic development may thus be frustrated.

In some nations exchange controls lead to a system of **multiple exchange rates.** Exchange rates may be set very low on imports of capital equipment and high on luxury imports. This helps to conserve foreign exchange for purchases which contribute to economic growth.

Strict control of foreign exchange is practiced by the Soviet Union. The Soviet government controls all trade and is able to manipulate all exports and imports according to national goals.

Boycotts and embargoes The most extreme forms of interference with international trade are devices such as boycotts and embargoes. A **boycott** is a refusal to deal with particular nations, and an **embargo** is a refusal to ship certain goods. Such devices are used to halt trade altogether. They are normally used in wartime, since a nation at war does not trade with its enemy. But they are also used in peacetime, sometimes for political reasons. Often they are used for both political and economic reasons.

The United States, for example, has invoked "trading-with-the-enemy" laws to boycott American trade with Cuba and North Korea. In 1973, Arab oil-producing countries placed an embargo on oil shipments to the United States. These countries were not at war with America. The embargo was placed to protest against and perhaps reduce United States support to Israel against Egypt and Syria. For many years Arab nations have had a boycott in effect against the goods of foreign companies who trade with Israel.

Occasionally nations use such devices, rather than less-restrictive import and export quotas, to protect their domestic economies. In 1973, domestic shortages forced the United States to place embargoes on the export of soybeans and forty other commodities. It was felt that United States domestic needs at the time were simply too great to allow free trade in these products.

In 1975, a temporary embargo was placed on shipment of United States grain to the Soviet Union. Russia had recently bought huge amounts. Consumer and other interest groups felt the depletion of our grain stock would lift grain prices too high. This would cause unacceptable increases in the cost of food at home. The embargo was soon lifted. But the government persuaded U.S. grain companies to accept a **moratorium**—a temporary embargo—on grain shipments to world markets. It also entered into an agreement with the Soviet Union whereby Russia agreed to limit its 1976 purchases of American grain to 17 million tons. The Soviet Union also agreed to buy at least 6 million but not more than 8 million tons each year until 1982.

Devices such as boycotts and embargoes may be temporarily justifiable to protect a nation's vital political interests. They may be necessary to prevent domestic shortages and harmful distortions of a nation's internal economy. Nevertheless, they are barriers to the full benefits to international trade.

The United States experience with trade restrictions

As we have shown, free international trade can provide benefits to the economies of all nations. Why, then, do nations put up barriers to free trade? Governments are subject to many pressure groups who clamor for protection of their immediate interests. Organized business groups may want special advantages for their products in order to increase profits. Organized labor may support tariffs in order to keep wages high or to prevent layoffs in affected industries. Politicians are naturally swayed by the people whose votes and financial support help keep them in office.

From enactment of the so-called **Tariff of Abominations** in 1828 until 1934, the overall trend in the United States was toward high tariffs. In 1930, the **Smoot-Hawley tariff** (named for the men who sponsored the bill in Congress) brought the highest rates ever imposed. Average duties amounted to 60% of the value of the imports covered by the legislation.

In 1930, remember, the United States was sinking into the depths of the Great Depression. By 1934, it was seen that high tariffs were no real answer to the great economic decline, which by then had spread throughout the world. In that year, Congress began the long process of dismantling our high-tariff structure. It passed the **Reciprocal Trade Agreements Act.** The act called for reduction of United States tariffs as foreign nations reduced their own. The reductions could be as high as 50% of the existing rates for cooperating nations.

The act periodically comes up for renewal and changes. In 1962, President Kennedy began the **Kennedy Round** of negotiations among the world's ministers of trade with the aim of continuing the trend toward lower tariffs. In 1975, trade barriers were reduced further.

In 1975, however, the United States was suffering another period of economic decline. Recession losses prompted a clause in the act calling for government financial aid for United States industries hurt by lower tariffs. The act called for aid to retrain and relocate workers in these industries. It also included *"escape clauses."* One such clause called for imposition of higher tariffs whenever an import reached a certain percentage of its total domestic sales—its *"peril point."* Another clause called for "countervailing duties" when other nations officially subsidized their export sales to the United States. Some analysts regarded such provisions as a potential step backward toward protectionism. They could conceivably be used ·to postpone painful—though necessary—adjustments required by the principle of comparative advantage.

In the late 1970s some analysts began to question the entire concept of international trade economics. The benefits of free trade have not been challenged. But, these analysts say, the old concept of "free trade versus protectionism" is outmoded. New developments, such as the spread of managed and controlled economies which can interfere at will in international trade, have changed the rules of the game. Furthermore, they say, America has exported its technology along with its products. Thus comparative advantage now shifts too suddenly and drastically from nation to nation. Immense United States investments in the economies of other nations and the growth of multinational companies operating across national borders have further complicated the situation. Because of such developments, new concepts may be called for. In any case, the free-trade-versus-protectionism fight is far from over.

The General Agreement on Tariffs and Trade

Reciprocal trade agreements are two-nation agreements. A broader approach is needed if trade barriers are to be reduced worldwide. In 1947, the **General Agreement on Tariffs and Trade** (GATT) came into being. It was signed by 23 countries, the United States included. It now has more than 80 member nations, including some communist countries.

Members of GATT participate in multinational negotiations to resolve trading conflicts and to plan freer trade policies. Negotiations have led to percentage reductions of tariffs in broad product categories. Moreover, all tariff reductions are applied according to the *most-favored-nation principle*. That is, any tariff reduction is extended on nondiscriminatory terms to all *members* of GATT. The agreement also prohibits most import quotas.

Trade and long-run economic growth

If a nation is to continue to enjoy the benefits of trade, it must maintain a comparative advantage in production of certain goods demanded in the world economy. A favorable trading position depends on production of high quality goods and services at low cost, in order to attract consumer spending in a foreign market. Nations strive to develop resources and expand technology so as to improve their productivity and to reduce costs. Success in these efforts determines a nation's area of specialization and affects its terms of trade. Governments, therefore, are very active in such endeavors.

Government-subsidized research, for example, has contributed to technical advance in United States industry. Although most research funds have focused on military development, the results have often been applicable to industrial processes and consumer products. Tax credits to businesses for investment in expansion have also been used to spur productivity increases.

In 1971, a new device was set up to help U.S. manufacturers increase their competitiveness abroad. Business firms were encouraged to establish **Domestic International Sales Corporations,** or DISCs, to handle their export business. As a DISC, a company producing at least 90% of its output for foreign markets is allowed certain tax advantages. It is allowed to deduct any taxes paid to foreign governments from its U.S. tax bill. It is also excused from all U.S. income taxes until its profits are returned to this country. In effect, this amounts to an interest-free loan to the exporting firm.

The **United States Export-Import Bank** is another device to encourage this country's foreign trade. It finances a variety of trade between the United States and the rest of the world. The goal is to increase world and especially U.S. trade by providing low-cost credit to countries buying our exports. In effect, the funds are actually received by the U.S. supplier. Eventually, the foreign country makes payment plus interest charge to the Bank.

Some nations have attempted to spur industrial growth by establishing **free trade zones.** Zones are established into which imported materials and components can be shipped duty-free. These goods are then processed or assembled and exported without being subject to any kind of local tax. One result of free trade zones has been more efficient utilization of a nation's labor resources.

Policies for external balance

Problems of external balance involve economic relationships among nations. As the world becomes increasingly interdependent, nations are faced with an increasing number of trade problems. Just as no man is an island, no nation is insulated from the effects of the internal policies of its trading partners. Internal policies to expand domestic economic activity can cause unwanted increases in spending and inflationary pressures throughout the trading world. In effect, one nation can export its own inflation to other nations. Internal policies to contract domestic economic activity can have undesired impact on other economies also. One nation can export its own unemployment to others.

A healthy economic environment calls for some international coordination of internal policies to minimize these disruptions and distortions. Economic cooperation requires consultation and compromise in order to serve the interests of all parties.

Frequently, multinational conferences are held to seek compromise solutions to common problems. Compromise sometimes reduces a nation's freedom of action. But trading nations have generally been willing to accept minor loss of national sovereignty because of the long-range benefits of cooperation. International policies and institutions have been developed to deal with exchange rate problems, to accommodate short- and long-term credit needs, and to remove barriers to intraregional trade.

Exchange rate policies

Cooperative attempts to deal with exchange rate problems in international trade were discussed in the last chapter. There we learned that for many years the gold standard regulated the flows of international expenditures, helping to balance external accounts. But the gold standard forced painful adjustments in a nation's output, income, and employment.

The international conference at Bretton Woods was an attempt to deal with this problem. It changed the *gold standard* to a *gold-exchange standard.* Under the new system, central bank intervention in foreign exchange markets helped to postpone and smooth out these painful adjustments. Currency values were "pegged" to prevent exchange rate fluctuations.

But, as we further learned in Chapter 20, the real value of a nation's currency depends on its supply and demand in the world market. Despite pegged currency exchange rates, changes in supply and demand began to put pressure on the prices of some currencies.

In part, the reason was different rates of growth among trading nations. Different growth rates meant differences in the supplies of various currencies in foreign exchange markets. Slow-growing nations suffered a worsening outflow of currency. Some wealthy industrialized nations enjoyed an inflow. Recall that under the gold-exchange standard a nation's currency is convertible to gold. This can cause problems for nations whose currency is widely held in world markets. Foreign holders, such as banks, might fear a loss in value as the excess supply grows. They dump their holdings on the market, increasing its supply still further. This could bring on the feared decrease in price of the currency. Even worse, foreign holders may present currency to the nation's treasury for conversion to gold. In the early 1970s, for example, the U.S. dollar was in excess supply and pressure was building for a decrease in its price. Foreign holders turned in dollars for gold, and by 1973 the U.S. gold stock had fallen to $11 billion, from $20 billion in 1960.

The excess currencies held in bank reserve accounts contributed to the collapse of the Bretton Woods agreement. In 1973, nations agreed to allow exchange rates to fluctuate according to market demand and supply. Central banks would no longer buy up and hold excess foreign currencies. It was hoped that the shift to flexible exchange rates would help to correct currency relationships and to restore balance to international payments accounts.

A few nations, notably France, still look back with approval on the automatic adjustments under the gold standard. And some economists agree that payments deficits and surpluses should be dealt with through fixed exchange rates and prompt international adjustments in output, income, and employment. In any case, the world economic recession of 1973–1975 diverted attention from any further cooperative attempts to deal with problems caused by shifts in exchange rates among trading nations.

International credit organizations

As part of its efforts to stabilize exchange rates, the Bretton Woods conference established an international body to provide short-term loans to nations experiencing balance of payments deficits. This organization is known as the **International Monetary Fund** (IMF) and now includes 128 member nations. Its representatives meet yearly to plan international credit and exchange policy.

Members of the IMF contribute gold and national currencies to the Fund depending on their national income and their participation in international trade. In years of payments deficits, member nations are permitted to draw on these funds to settle their international accounts. However, long-term borrowing is discouraged. A continuing need for loans suggests a fundamental disequilibrium that needs to be corrected. The borrowing nation may be required to make certain fiscal and monetary arrangements as a condition for receiving a new loan.

For example, continuing deficits in balance of payments may imply rampant inflation in the borrowing nation. Consumers may be using their inflated incomes to purchase too many low-priced imports from producers abroad. Domestic producers may be unable to sell their high-priced goods abroad, thus aggravating the currency outflow. Before an IMF loan is made in this instance, the borrowing nation may have to agree to impose contractionary fiscal and monetary policies to correct its inflated economy.

The IMF may also influence the policies of nations with a surplus trade balance. Such nations accumulate currency reserves as their exports rise relative to their purchases from abroad. When reserves pile up, a nation may be urged to adopt expansionary monetary and fiscal policies. Expansionary policies raise domestic incomes and stimulate purchase of imports from other nations. For example, as the recession of 1973–1975 drew to a close, deficit nations were urging the United States, Japan, and Germany—the three largest economies of the free world—to expand their economies and speed their own recovery. It was hoped that higher incomes would stimulate import demand and contribute to economic expansion in the deficit nations of the trading world.

The IMF is also involved in preventing or alleviating shortages of currencies used in trade. Severe shortages may cause a "liquidity crisis." The word "liquidity" is used to refer simply to the availability of ready money. Lack of liquidity in one or more nations can stifle trade throughout the world.

To meet such a shortage, the IMF created a new form of currency which it called **Special Drawing Rights** (SDR). SDRs (sometimes called "paper gold") are guaranteed rights to borrow. They are issued by the IMF according to a nation's reserve holdings in the Fund. (The value of an SDR unit is a weighted average of sixteen trading currencies. In 1977, it was about $1.25.)

When a member nation needs funds to finance a deficit, it can exchange its holdings of SDRs for equivalent amounts of the foreign currencies it needs for trade. Then these currencies can be used to settle its accounts. There are some restrictions on the use of SDRs. The restrictions are intended to prevent nations from becoming too dependent on credit and to encourage them to employ internal policies to correct their payments problems.

It has been suggested that the allocation of SDRs among member nations should be based on need rather than on the amount a nation contributes to the Fund. The original plan, in effect, rewards nations which have already achieved success in production and trade. The richer they are, the easier it is for them to borrow through SDRs. The new proposal would link borrowing privileges to the *lack* of success. It would provide international credits to nations in greatest need of machinery and equipment for developing their economies. It would thus enhance world trade and development.

Economic Thinker
Robert McNamara

Not too many years ago, Robert McNamara was much in the news. As one of the new breed of post-World War II managerial "whiz kids," he had risen rapidly in the executive hierarchy of the Ford Motor Company to become, in 1960, its first president who was not a member of the Ford family. He held this position only for a month. President John Kennedy, impressed by reports of McNamara's success in applying "scientific management" techniques to the production of automobiles, called him to Washington to become Secretary of Defense. There his battles with the Pentagon establishment and his controversial policies of "a bigger bang for a buck" soon brought him national attention and general acclaim in the public press. More recently, Robert McNamara has served quietly and effectively as president of the International Bank for Reconstruction and Development, popularly known as the World Bank. There the decisions he makes and the policies he directs have far greater impact on far more of the world's people than ever before during his stormy career as civilian boss of the American military establishment.

Robert McNamara was born in San Francisco, in 1916. He graduated from the University of California in 1937 and received his Master's of Business Administration at Harvard. He joined the Army Air Force in World War II. After his career at Ford and his appointment to Defense by President Kennedy, he remained as Secretary under President Lyndon Johnson. He resigned the position in 1968 to become president of the World Bank.

When the World Bank was established in 1945, one of its principal objectives was to supply money to develop "social capital" in needy nations. Money was lent for investment in power facilities, transportation systems, and other such elements of a nation's economic infrastructure. As expected, economic growth followed. But the further expectation that economic benefits would spread to the majority of the people was not realized—at least not to the extent that had been hoped. Economic benefits went disproportionally to people already at higher income levels. Unemployment, illiteracy, and malnutrition too often remained the lot of much of the population. To stem this tide, McNamara introduced new grass-roots investment policies. The World Bank now gives greater attention to loans for improvement of small agricultural enterprises, development of basic industrial skills, health and educational facilities, and population control.

The World Bank has remained solvent and has grown in financial esteem and effectiveness under the leadership of Robert McNamara. Stormy times are undoubtedly ahead for the bank, as the aspirations and power of needy countries rise with the success of the bank (and other similar financial institutions) in meeting the purposes for which it was formed. At the 1976 meeting of the International Monetary Fund (to which all members of the World Bank must belong), representatives of less developed nations were asking for a very substantial increase in the bank's lending capacity, much of which would come from the United States in the form of trade credits. By 1977, loans were pouring from the World Bank at an annual rate of almost $6 billion, with the need for even more credits growing apace. Economic difficulties and the rise of new trade barriers among the wealthier nations, including the United States, have added to the bank's problems. In addition, there is the tremendous problem of the effect of rising energy prices on the economies of rich and poor nations alike. All indications are, however, that the World Bank, under the steady tutelage of Robert McNamara, will weather the economic and political storms of the 1980s, as it has those of previous decades.

Developing nations support this proposal enthusiastically. They would like to draw SDRs in amounts based on the GNPs of the nations contributing to the Fund's reserves. That is, the higher a nation's GNP, the greater its contribution of SDR loans to developing nations. Developing nations also wish to use SDRs to restructure the massive debt accumulated through their necessary imports of high-priced oil.

In 1975, the IMF agreed to begin to sell off one-third of its gold holdings (totaling 17.5 million ounces) and distribute half the proceeds of the sale to poor nations. The profit on these gold sales was projected to be about $1.6 billion by 1979. Half of this would be allocated to nations having per capita incomes of less than $400. Unfortunately, this amount is small relative to the total deficits in these countries. In 1975, the deficits totaled around $34 billion.

Developing nations have another source of long-term credit. **The International Bank for Reconstruction and Development** (IBRD) was established in 1945 as a companion organization to the International Monetary Fund. It is often called the **World Bank.** The purpose of the World Bank is to provide long-term loans for construction of industrial capital in developing nations. Transportation and communication facilities, power plants and irrigation facilities, steel mills, and furniture factories have been built in developing nations through low-interest IBRD loans.

Intraregional trading organizations

Much of the phenomenal growth of the U.S. economy may be attributed to our large internal free trade area. An important part of our Constitution was the prohibition against barriers to trade between the states. This encouraged movement of resources and products throughout the nation. As a result, regions were able to specialize according to comparative advantage. The South, for example, could take advantage of its favorable land and climate for cotton production. It could then ship cotton to the North, where factories were waiting to process it into clothing and other products. Similarly, the North's industrial capacity enabled it to sell machinery and other industrial products to consumers in the South.

Extended Example
George Marshall and the Marshall Plan

The program was known as the "Marshall Plan." It is an irony of history that perhaps the greatest mass economic undertaking of all time should properly bear the name not of an economist but of a Five-Star General of the United States Army. It is also ironic that just a few years after he had stepped down from his leadership of America's military might throughout the carnage of World War II, this man of the sword was to be awarded the 1953 Nobel Peace Prize. Ironic, yes—but such honors were richly deserved.

George Catlett Marshall was born in Uniontown, Pennsylvania, in 1880. A graduate of Virginia Military Institute, he served in the United States Army for 43 years. He served as a staff officer in World War I and was later an aide to General Pershing. In 1939, he was appointed Army Chief of Staff and in late 1944 was made General of the Army. Marshall's scheme for the conquest of Nazi Germany was adopted by the allies, but his wartime duties were not confined strictly to military matters. He also took part in numerous wartime diplomatic conferences. At war's end, President Harry Truman appointed Marshall Ambassador to China. In January, 1947, he was recalled to Washington to become Secretary of State. He resigned from that post in 1949 because of ill health, but was called from retirement the following year to serve as Secretary of Defense. Marshall died in 1959.

When World War II came to a close in 1945, the economy of Europe was in ruins. Before the war, Germany had been the major industrial nation on the continent. But war's destruction had left the country unable even to feed itself, let alone produce goods to fuel its own economy and that of less industrialized European nations. The economies of other European nations, winners and losers alike, were in similar disarray. Of all the major powers, only the United States had escaped economic disaster. The task of preventing total economic and social collapse of Western Europe fell to America. By 1947, the United States had spent $23 billion on international relief and reconstruction. But it was soon realized that a better organized, more integrated aid plan was needed if the economic horrors of post-World War I were to be avoided and, indeed, if the seeds of World War III were not to be sown.

On June 5, 1947, Secretary of State George C. Marshall delivered the commencement address at Harvard University. He outlined a plan for European aid that would come to be known as the European Recovery Program or, more popularly, the Marshall Plan. The plan called for cooperative economic action among the nations of Western Europe. The intent was to distribute material and financial aid from the United States on a broad scale for greater efficiency in promoting economic recovery. In 1948, the countries participating in the plan—Austria, Belgium, Denmark, France, Germany, Great Britain, Greece, Iceland, Italy, Luxembourg, Netherlands, Norway, Sweden, Switzerland, Turkey, and the United States— established the Organization for European Economic Cooperation to coordinate the aid program. (Eastern European nations were invited to join, but the Soviet government, fearing economic and political dominance by the Western bloc, overruled expansion of the plan to its satellite nations.)

In the following three years, the United States sent about $10 billion in aid to Europe, almost all of which was in outright grants. Many American advisers and coordinators went to Europe to screen requests for funds, supervise spending, and help reshape the European economy. The Marshall Plan helped rebuild Europe's industries; it aided in the necessary scrapping of obsolete production methods and in the rapid introduction of new technical devices and business methods. Production of basic commodities—food, coal, iron and steel, electric power, and transportation services—was restored. Barriers to international trade were reduced wherever possible and national currencies were stabilized in value (primarily through the World Bank) in order to facilitate productive trade among these nations. By 1951, European industrial production was

41% above its *prewar* level, combined gross national product was 15% higher in real terms, steel production was 20% greater, and electricity output had doubled. It is worthy of note that after World War I, it took seven years for Europe to reach just its prewar level of production.

The Marshall Plan was, in short, a spectacular success. In addition, it marked a high point in American social idealism. National self-interest was, of course, also involved. Collapse of the European economy would have had damaging effects on the American economy. Economic collapse would have engendered social and political unrest harmful to the democratic governments of Europe and, perhaps, helpful to dictatorial governments. Nevertheless, in 1950 not one cent of the plan's funds was spent on military items. The money was spent entirely in a sincere effort to repair the ravages of war and to better the lot of the people of Western Europe. And, although it never succeeded in establishing a truly integrated Western European economy, the plan laid the groundwork for international economic cooperative efforts that continue today.

Most of us are inclined today to take our internal free trade for granted. But imagine what our lives as consumers would be like if this trade were severely restricted. What if Detroit could not easily sell cars to consumers in Kansas City or St. Paul? What if Florida's oranges were not allowed easy entrance into New Jersey or Illinois? What if California's food products were forbidden to consumers in New York City or in Baltimore? Our lives and the economic life of our nation would be drastically different.

Customs union Following World War II, a momentous step was taken toward achieving some of the same benefits for the nations of Western Europe. Belgium, the Netherlands, and Luxembourg joined together in a customs union known as *Benelux*. A **customs union** is an agreement to eliminate tariffs within the member countries. Elimination of tariffs enabled the three small nations of Benelux to exchange freely the materials and components needed for their developing industries.

The success of Benelux led to its expansion. West Germany, France, and Italy joined the bloc. It became known as the **European Economic Community** (EEC). In 1973, Great Britain, Ireland, and Denmark were admitted to the EEC. The EEC is now generally called the **Common Market.**

In addition to the elimination of internal tariffs, *a customs union establishes a common external tariff.* This means that producers in the United States and elsewhere are subject to import duties on their sales to Common Market countries, while local producers have a substantial advantage.

The coordination of trade policies within the common market suggests future coordination of other policies as well: domestic fiscal and monetary policies to maintain similar growth rates and similar levels of inflation or unemployment; external political strategies to enhance their strength as a bargaining unit; and possibly a common currency to give further stimulus to the free movement of resources and goods. There is even effort being made for a common passport for EEC citizens.

Free trade area   Some other European, Latin American, and communist nations have also formed trade blocs. A common form of such cooperation is a **free trade area.** Members of a free trade area remove most internal tariffs within the trade bloc. But there is no common external tariff. Administrative problems may arise in free trade areas when foreign producers export to the lowest tariff member and then reship freely within the free trade area. This makes it difficult if not impossible for the importing countries within the bloc to collect the actual tariff rate they have imposed on trade from outside the bloc.

Free trade areas of the world include the Latin American Free Trade Area (LAFTA), the European Free Trade Area (EFTA), and the Eastern European Council for Mutual Economic Assistance (Comecon). In the mid-1960s, Bolivia, Chile, Colombia, Ecuador, Peru, and Venezuela formed a Latin American common market. This bloc is generally known as the Andean Pact nations. (Chile withdrew in 1976.)

Cartels   Commodity-producing nations of the Third World have also formed trading organizations to stabilize prices for their exports. These blocs often take the form of cartels. **Cartels** are marketing organizations established to purchase and sell commodities for the group as a whole. Coffee producers, for example, would suffer a sharp decline in export earnings when world coffee prices fall. Under a marketing agreement, coffee-producing nations contribute to a fund to buy coffee when an excess supply threatens to drive prices down. The marketing organization holds the coffee until market conditions are more favorable for selling. Commodity purchases and sales by marketing boards can provide some assurance to commodity producers of a stable price for their output. Other developing nations have entered into similar arrangements for the sale of commodities such as cocoa, tin, wheat, and sugar. OPEC—the oil exporters—is the most successful cartel.

Internal capital movements

Freer trade relationships have increased the flows of capital among nations. The United States, for example, sends vast quantities of its currency abroad to pay for its purchases from foreign nations. As we saw earlier, these flows increased during the late 1960s because of the boom in economic activity in many parts of the world, especially in Europe.

Eurodollars   One result of the burst in international capital flows from the United States has been the appearance of so-called Eurodollars. **Eurodollars** are dollar balances owned outside the United States, mostly in Europe (hence the name). They may be deposits in European banks, United States banks, or European branches of United States banks. Eurodollars result from the export earnings of European firms, from U.S. investment abroad, and from other transfers of U.S. dollars, such as American tourist spending abroad. As United States importers pay for their purchases, foreign producers deposit their dollar receipts in their bank accounts. These dollar balances provide foreigners with a source of interest income. And they provide foreign banks with additional cash reserves to lend to creditworthy customers.

Depositors typically seek the highest interest income on Eurodollar balances, and banks seek the highest interest on loans. As a result, Eurodollar balances are subject to frequent shifts among banks and even among nations as holders seek investments that will pay them high incomes. Such sudden shifts can lead to drastic changes in a nation's money supply and uncontrolled disruption of a nation's economy.

By the mid-1970s, many Eurodollars were owned by Arab nations. Exports of high-priced oil to the nations holding Eurodollars had caused a shift in these dollars to the bank accounts of Arab oil producers. Eurodollars in the hands of Arab nations became known as "petrodollars." The situation grew more complex in the 1970s as Eurodollars were joined by Euroyen, Euromarks, and any number of other currencies. The term **Eurocurrency** has been coined to include all national currencies on deposit outside the domestic economy.

As we have seen in our discussion of banking systems, a nation's central bank can regulate the nation's currency supply. A central bank cannot, however, control its currency outside its borders. Central bankers are working together trying to devise instruments for regulating Eurocurrency. However, the problem is not yet sufficiently understood to permit clearcut solutions.

Multinational corporations Another result of plentiful international capital has been the phenomenal growth of multinational corporations. **Multinational corporations** are large firms having extensive production or distribution facilities in more than one nation. Most large United States corporations are now multinationals.

Direct investment in a foreign country allows a company to avoid tariff charges. Multinational corporations have other advantages. Firms engaging in many operations can plan production on the basis of different resource costs in their several locations. Labor-intensive processes can be performed in nations where wages are low. Investment capital can be borrowed in nations where interest charges are low. It is even possible to shift profits to countries with low income taxes. This is done by setting the prices of components produced within the company according to the various tax rates.

For example, suppose a corporate division in England produces electronic circuits to be used for communication equipment ultimately assembled and sold by another division in Switzerland. Charging a low price for the circuits would shift taxable income to Switzerland; a high price would retain income in England. The choice of strategy would depend on which country had the lower tax rates.

At first, multinational firms were welcomed in the host nations. They brought capital investment, provided jobs, paid taxes, and contributed to rising incomes and output. Eventually, the climate of acceptance began to change. Host nations came to resent the profits accumulated by foreign firms, profits which were often sent back to the country of ownership. They came to resent the avoidance of full tax payments. And they were fearful of the alien political power that might result from heavy foreign financial involvement in their economies. For example, the interference by ITT in Chilean politics in the early 1970s frightened many nations where multinational corporations were active. They began to wonder if the multinational companies in their midst might someday contribute to the overthrow of *their* governments.

Some multinational investments have been nationalized by host countries. Owners are usually paid a portion of the value of the investment. In other nations, foreign governments have insisted on 51% of share ownership. Saudi Arabia, for example, took ownership of 25% of Anglo-American oil concessions in 1970. It also stipulated that its share was to rise year by year until it reached 51% in 1981.

The great size and potential economic and political power of many multinational firms raise serious questions about their proper international control. Coherent policies for dealing with this kind of international power are still to be developed. Such policies may entail some form of supranational organization on the order of regional or world government—not a likely prospect in the near future.

Summary

Nations do not always enjoy the full benefits of international trade. Trade may create problems of internal balance involving domestic output, income, employment, and growth. Or trade may create problems of external balance. Problems of external balance involve international economic relationships, including changes in comparative advantage and relative growth rates among nations.

Internal problems of unemployment are often dealt with by imposing tariffs on foreign imports. Supporters of tariffs claim they are necessary: to protect infant industries, to encourage development of strategic industries, to offset lower wage costs in other nations, or to improve the terms of trade between raw commodity exports and manufactured imports. Opponents of tariffs point out the higher prices and smaller quantity of goods traded under protectionist policies; they advocate subsidies and monetary and fiscal policies to accomplish desired goals without interfering with efficient resource allocation.

Quotas limit the quantity of certain imports and keep prices above the lowest free trade price. They also prevent quantity from increasing fully when demand curves shift.

Export duties make exported goods more expensive to foreign buyers and reduce their sales. Export subsidies make exported goods cheaper and more competitive in world markets. However, importing nations may impose "countervailing duties" to offset this advantage. Another means of protecting local production is through quality standards on imports. Control of foreign exchange and multiple exchange rates help to limit imports to only essential items. Boycotts and embargoes are more restrictive barriers to trade, set up for political or economic reasons.

The highest United States tariff rates were levied under the Smoot-Hawley Act of 1930. Since 1934, the United States has engaged in reciprocal tariff reductions with our trading partners. The recession of 1973–1975 led to changes in American tariff laws, calling for special aid to domestic industries harmed by imports. The General Agreement on Tariffs and Trade (GATT) is a multinational organization for extending tariff reductions according to the most-favored-nation principle. Governments have encouraged productivity growth and trade through subsidized research, tax credits, Domestic International Sales Corporations, the Export-Import Bank, and free trade zones.

External problems of international payments deficit or surplus have been dealt with through the gold standard, the gold-exchange standard established at Bretton Woods, or more recently through freely fluctuating exchange rates. To help finance deficits, the International Monetary Fund (IMF) was set up to provide short-term loans to members. The IMF adds to total world liquidity by issuing Special Drawing Rights (SDRs). The International Bank for Reconstruction and Development, or World Bank, provides long-term loans at low interest, primarily for development projects in less developed countries.

Some neighboring nations have formed customs unions or free trade areas to liberalize trade among members. Other commodity-producing nations have formed cartels to raise and stabilize prices of their commodity exports. Freer trade has increased international capital flows; large holdings of Eurocurrencies threaten to disrupt monetary policy in some nations. Also the size and power of multinational corporations may present some problems in the future.

Key Words and Phrases

- **internal balance** a condition in which the domestic economy enjoys favorable levels of output, employment, and income.
- **external balance** a condition in which a nation enjoys rough equality in international inpayments and outpayments.
- **protectionism** policies of trade restriction aimed at protecting domestic producers.

- **revenue tariffs** import duties designed to collect revenue.
- **protective tariffs** import duties designed to restrict imports.
- **infant-industry tariffs** tariffs to protect young industries from more established foreign competitors.
- **strategic-industry tariff** a tariff to protect domestic producers of products essential to a nation's security.
- **production-costs tariff** a tariff to equalize low costs of production abroad with higher domestic costs of production.
- **terms of trade** the quantity of goods which must be exported per unit of goods imported.
- **quotas** legal restrictions on the quantity of a foreign good which can be imported.
- **export duties** taxes on exports designed to discourage sale abroad of certain domestically produced goods.
- **export subsidies** payments to domestic producers which enable them to sell abroad at lower prices.
- **countervailing duties** taxes placed on certain imports to offset export subsidies paid the foreign sellers by their government.
- **quality standards on imports** legal standards on goods which often exclude foreign-made products from domestic markets.
- **foreign exchange controls** government control of foreign exchange markets for the purpose of determining how foreign exchange is spent.
- **multiple exchange rates** prices for foreign exchange which differ according to the proposed use of foreign exchange.
- **most-favored-nation principle** an agreement to extend any trade advantage equally to all parties to the agreement.
- **Smoot-Hawley Tariff Law** tariff legislation including the highest import duties in United States history.
- **Reciprocal Trade Agreements Act** legislation providing for mutual reduction and eventual elimination of tariffs.
- **General Agreement on Tariffs and Trade** international agreement governing trade policies favoring freer trade.
- **Domestic International Sales Corporation** subsidiary of a domestic firm, set up to facilitate sales in another country.

- **Export-Import Bank** primarily a United States credit facility set up to provide trade credits for foreign purchases of American goods.
- **free trade zones** areas where foreign materials may be processed and exported without becoming subject to domestic tariffs.
- **International Monetary Fund** international organization for helping to solve payments and liquidity problems.
- **liquidity** availability of sufficient currencies for trade.
- **Special Drawing Rights** unlimited rights to borrow currencies for use in trade.
- **International Bank for Reconstruction and Development** the World Bank for extending long-term loans for economic development.
- **customs union** a group of nations having no internal tariffs and a common external tariff.
- **European Economic Community** the customs union consisting of most Western European nations and known as the Common Market.
- **free trade area** a group of nations having no internal tariffs and no common external tariff.
- **Eurocurrency** currencies owned by persons or institutions outside the issuing nation.
- **multinational corporation** a business firm with subsidiaries in more than one nation.
- **cartel** international monopoly that allocates output and sets prices for some good.

Questions for Review

1. Outline the most persuasive arguments in favor of protectionist/tariff policies. Point out the weaknesses of each argument. Suggest other approaches to minimize the internal problems associated with trade. In what ways are quotas even more damaging than tariffs?

2. Distinguish between export duties and export subsidies. What are the objectives of each?

3. What are the usual justifications for foreign exchange controls? for multiple exchange rates?

4. List significant legislative events in United States tariff history together with the approximate dates of each. What have been the recent trends in trading relationships?

5. Explain how a nation can "export inflation." How can it "export unemployment"?

6. What are the chief objectives of Domestic International Sales Corporations? of free trade zones? Distinguish between free trade zones and free trade areas.

7. How would a "liquidity crisis" affect trading nations? What has the International Monetary Fund done to help forestall such a crisis? How do the credit policies of the World Bank differ from the IMF?

8. Describe the origin and historical development of the European Common Market. What future developments are possible?

9. What are the major problems associated with the growth in Eurocurrencies?

10. What are the advantages and disadvantages of multinational corporations?

11. Zaire produces more than half the world's cobalt, with Zambia and Morocco supplying most of the rest. Suppose the three countries combined to control supply and raise price. What circumstances would determine the benefits to producing nations?

Part Six

Consumer Behavior and Elasticity

22

An Overview of American Market Structure

Our market system is based upon the freedom of buyers and sellers to pursue their own interests. This fundamental principle was first spelled out by Adam Smith. Smith argued that a system of free markets would permit buyers and sellers to pursue their own interests and benefit not only themselves but all of society. On the surface this seems strange. If I'm selling shoes I will find it in my interest to seek the highest price possible, won't I? How can that be of benefit to society?

Later we will see just how the pursuit of self-interest promotes the benefit of all. Of course, we are talking about legal and ethical market activities. Muggers and con artists were not the subjects of Adam Smith's *Wealth of Nations*. Freedom to pursue one's self-interest is not a license to exploit and plunder.

First we must assume that people behave rationally: they consider carefully the benefits and costs of their economic decisions. Each person chooses among alternatives, selecting the one alternative that will provide the most satisfaction at the lowest cost, given each's own circumstances. It can be shown that when all buyers and sellers do this, the market will usually come as close as possible to satisfying everyone's individual wants. As Adam Smith wrote, in pursuing individual interests each person "is led by an invisible hand to promote an end which was no part of his intention." Smith added:

By pursuing his own interest he frequently promotes that of the society more effectually than when he really intends to promote it. I have never known much good done by those who affected to trade for the public good.

The freedom of each participant in the market is limited by the freedom of all the others. When all citizens seek to increase their benefits and reduce their costs in every individual transaction, their total benefits are maximized and their total costs are minimized.

Other economic systems are based on other types of motivation. In some societies religion plays an important role in everyday economic activities. The Christians and Moslems of the Middle Ages devoted their economic resources to the service of their religious faith. In those societies people were not al-lowed to act according to individual preferences; important economic questions were decided by guilds or by religious authorities. In other societies the political creed dictates what people do in the economic sphere. In communist countries of the present day, for instance, most economic decisions are made by planning boards, following the orders of the political leaders.

Even market economies do not always rely completely on self-interest to guide economic activity. We allow government to regulate pricing and output in certain strategic industries: communication, transportation, and electric power are examples. Moreover, in wartime citizens will be asked to give up temporarily the right to make consumer choices freely and to sacrifice individual self-interest for the sake of the national good. During World War II, the U.S. government set rigid controls on prices and asked the public to observe them. Not everyone complied, as the existence of a "black market" showed, but most people put their country first and refrained from buying at illegal prices. Modern psychology has shown that people are motivated not only by self-interest but by idealism. They want to think well of themselves and to be respected by others in the community.

Efficiency and equity

When we criticize our economic system, we are likely to argue that it doesn't work as well as it might or that it doesn't distribute rewards as fairly as it should. Many of the laws passed by our federal and state governments are intended to change the economy in one of these two respects—that is, to make it work better or to make it function more fairly. We label these two goals *efficiency* and *equity*. Quite often these two goals are in conflict with each other.

We may define economic efficiency very broadly as getting the most output from our resources. Any change that increases total output without increasing the amount of resources used may be said to increase economic efficiency. A change that diminishes the output per unit of resources decreases economic efficiency.

Remember that our economic resources are the factors of production: land, labor, capital, and entrepreneurship. All are limited. More formally, we can define **efficiency** as the degree to which an economic system allocates and utilizes its limited resources in an optimal (best) way. The concept of efficiency is important today more than ever before because our nation is growing more concerned about the problems of poverty and shortages of raw materials. While some resources are becoming increasingly scarce, we are finding more and more things that we want to do with them. If we are to continue raising the living standards of all our people, it will be necessary to improve the efficiency of our economy.

In theory, as the next few chapters will show, a free market system is the most efficient way of running an economy. But actual market systems in the world today are not like the one that Adam Smith wrote about. We will examine the ways in which the American economy differs from Adam Smith's model of the economy. We will see how monopoly, monopolistic competition, and oligopoly affect the efficiency of the market system.

A second important basis for judging the performance of an economy is **equity**—the extent to which the economy rewards people fairly for their efforts. *We must distinguish between equity and equality. Equity* implies fair (but usually unequal) shares, while *equality* implies identical shares. No industrial society—market system or communist—distributes output equally among all its citizens. Some degree of inequality is believed to be fair. Most people consider it fair for the president of a company to be paid more than the janitor. The principle of equity does not require that rewards be equal. On the other hand, equity does involve relative earnings. How much more should the company president receive than the janitor? Twice as much? Three times? Four times as much? How much inequality is fair?

Most people also feel that it is fair to help those at the bottom of the income pyramid, particularly those who are unable to support themselves. We expect our government to transfer income from those who are better off to those who are poor. It does this through income taxes, unemployment benefits, public welfare assistance, and in other ways. So while we don't think income must be distributed equally to all, we do feel that justice requires us to adjust the distribution of income that the market system provides—to smooth out the peaks and valleys. In this way we help to make our unequal distribution of income fairer or more equitable.

If perfect equality were the only concern, we could change the distribution of income even more than we have already. We could take more from those who are better off and give more to the rest of the population in the form of benefits: health insurance, higher pensions, cheaper transportation, and more public services such as parks and museums. But at some point greater equality would interfere with economic efficiency. If rewards were equal, it would no longer be in anyone's interest to work hard and save for the future. The result would be a slower rate of economic growth. Equal rewards would damage our system of economic incentives. Production would not be as high as it might, and total income would be lower.

For these reasons, greater efficiency may require less equality, as when a company improves its efficiency by laying off its slowest workers. Or greater equality may mean some loss of efficiency, as when high corporate taxes discourage business from investing in new, more productive equipment.

It appears that some inequality is necessary to encourage greater productivity. At the same time, extreme inequality may discourage productivity. Poor rewards at the bottom of the range do not offer much incentive for achievement, since people have little hope of improving their standard of living. And excess rewards at the top of the range may also stifle initiative and reduce effort.

Thus we are safe in assuming that both too much equality and too much inequality would impair the efficiency of our economic system.

We may decide to sacrifice a certain amount of efficiency in order to achieve greater equality. It is not for economists to make a final decision about the proper level of equality. Economists have studied the effect of income distribution on production. They have also studied efforts to change the income distribution by such means as minimum wage laws, income taxes, inheritance taxes, and labor unions. Economists can estimate what the effects of more equal distribution are likely to be. But it is up to the voters to decide how much equality we want—based on considerations of efficiency and equity.

From structure to conduct and from conduct to performance

Efficiency and equity depend strongly on the *structure* of industry in our economy. The structure of an industry involves the arrangement of firms. Structures range from a single firm producing the entire industry output to many firms, each producing only a small portion of the total. In the United States most industries fall somewhere between the two extremes.

Industry structure is important because it may influence the *conduct* of firms in the industry. A firm's conduct depends to a large extent on whether it is the only firm in the industry or whether there are many rival firms. Its conduct with respect to efficiency and equity is important to all consumers.

If industry structure leads to particular types of conduct, then conduct is important in influencing the *performance* of firms in an industry. *Performance* refers to the ability of firms to fulfill the long-range goals of the community. We have seen that a major goal of the community is efficiency in the use of its scarce resources. Industry structure should contribute to efficient and stable growth in production. In this way it will enhance the security of the community and establish the basis for equity in the distribution of output. Industries may be judged on their performance relative to these important goals.

Four product market structures

In this chapter we will summarize the working of *product markets* in the United States. We will be studying the structure, conduct, and performance of product markets. Recall that product markets are concerned with how all our goods and services are provided. Buyers of finished goods and services meet sellers in product markets where price and quantity are determined. *Resource markets* operate similarly to product markets. In resource markets buyers of land, labor, capital, and entrepreneurship meet with sellers and determine price and quantity of resources.

We will see that there are differences in the way product markets operate in different industries. We will analyze four different market structures: perfect competition, monopoly, monopolistic competition, and oligopoly. Most industries fit into one of these categories, depending on how large the firms are relative to the industry and how the firms set their prices. For instance, if one firm controls all the production in an industry it is said to be a *monopoly*. At the other extreme, if there are many small firms producing the same kind of product, we call this structure *perfect competition*. Between these two extremes we will describe *monopolistic competition* and *oligopoly*.

The reason for classifying industries in this way is to make it easier for us to understand how firms operate in different situations. For example, if many individual farmers have difficulty selling all their pigs at the going price, they may decide to get rid of them at a lower price. On the other hand, when an auto manufacturer's sales drop off, the auto company may raise its price! You may say that the pig farmer is weak and therefore can't charge enough while the auto manufacturer is strong and can charge higher prices. There is some truth in this but not enough for a satisfactory explanation. If we observe that the pig farmer operates in a competitive industry while the auto manufacturer is in an oligopoly, and that each is responding rationally to the structure of the industry, we are much closer to an understanding of their behavior.

In studying the different market structures, we will try to make comparative judgments. We will base our judgments on those important performance criteria: efficiency and equity.

Perfect competition

The kind of market structure described by Adam Smith was essentially what modern economists call *perfect competition.* Since nothing in this world is perfect, we should not expect to find many actual markets that conform precisely to the theory. If markets were perfectly competitive, the following four conditions would have to be true.

Four basic conditions

(1) *There must be many small buyers and sellers in the market.* All buyers and sellers must function economically: That is, they must *rationally* seek their own self-interest by weighing the costs and benefits of each alternative action. Buyers must seek their own self-interest by demanding the maximum quantity of useful goods and services for every dollar spent. Sellers must seek their own self-interest by producing goods and services with the least amount of scarce resources. When many small buyers and sellers behave in this way, no single individual or group has the power to influence the behavior of the market. The actions of one are balanced by the actions of others; what happens in the market is not the decision of any one person.

The pig farmers mentioned above cannot control the selling price for pigs or the buying price for farm equipment and supplies. Pork prices depend on consumer demand and on the total number of pigs brought to market. When the price of pork is rising, a single farmer may decide to produce more pigs in expectation of higher prices. Of course, if all pig farmers decide to do the same, they may produce so many pigs that the market price will fall. Then some farmers may have to sell their output at a loss. In competition, prices are the result of the decisions of all buyers and sellers in the market.

Not many industries have so many buyers and sellers as this. Markets for most products are generally too small for many buyers and sellers to operate. Independent food service establishments and retail stores in large cities may come closest to the competitive model.

Some types of farming are still carried on by many small operators selling to many small buyers. As long as there are many small buyers, no single buyer can force price down by refusing to buy. And with many small sellers, no single seller can force the price up by refusing to sell at the market price.

(2) *A second necessary condition for perfect competition is that the products of the industry must be all alike—that is, homogeneous, identical, or indistinguishable.* The automobile industry would not meet this condition, since nobody is likely to confuse a Ford with a Toyota. The retail coffee industry wouldn't meet it either, since the coffee makers try very hard to persuade people that Brand X is different from Brand Y. The products of every seller in an industry must be equally acceptable to buyers if the industry is to qualify as a perfectly competitive one. If a product is unique in any way, it may be able to attract buyers even when its price is higher than competing products. Its seller becomes the *single* supplier, thus breaking the first condition that there be many sellers. If all the sellers are selling an identical product, no one of them has an advantage over the others. Most pig farmers would meet this qualification.

In most industries, competitors seldom sell identical products. Most products differ in color, taste, design, or function. Others may look alike and may even be chemically identical, but in some way they appear to the buyer as different. Advertising often creates the illusion of differences among products. Bayer Aspirin is more acceptable to many buyers than are similar brands, even though Bayer may cost more. Most shops and stores are unique in particular ways. One may provide services that competitors do not, such as delivery service, easy credit, or more friendly sales people. Farm products, such as sweet corn, wheat, or tomatoes, may appear identical to the average person's eye and are therefore often cited as examples of homogeneous goods. But even farmers may provide unique delivery services or grow specialty fruits and vegetables that command premium prices.

(3) *A third condition for perfect competition is that buyers and sellers must have complete knowledge of market conditions.* Buyers must understand what products are available, how they are to be used, and what their prices are throughout the market. Complete information allows

shoppers to buy the most wanted goods in markets where they are most plentiful and are selling at the lowest prices. Sellers must also have complete information about prices and production costs throughout the market. This allows sellers to supply goods to markets where they are scarce and selling at the highest prices. Under perfect competition, producers have complete information about different ways of making their products. This allows them to use low-cost production techniques and low-cost resources. All competitors must understand conditions in the market. Better information would give one competitor an advantage over others. (However, obtaining the information is a cost to both buyers and sellers.)

Modern communications help to speed the flow of information throughout an industry. But technology changes fast, and those who have the newest methods try to keep them secret from their competitors. Sometimes the battle for control of information goes to great lengths. Companies install security precautions such as identification badges, guards, and combination locks. Their competitors hire spies. There is even counterespionage: companies hire counterspies to find out who is leaking information to their competitors. One of the best-known kinds of espionage is carried on by large retail chains; often they employ comparison shoppers to go around and find out what their competitors are selling, and for how much. Occasionally, a disloyal employee who has access to vital information will sell it to other companies. When new autos are being tested on the proving ground, competitors have been known to hire airplanes to fly over with high-power cameras and radar gear. Patent laws are one way of protecting information. They entitle an inventor to a monopoly on the use of a new process or product for a period of time, ensuring an advantage over competitors. Thus patents prevent condition (3) of perfect competition from being satisfied.

(4) *Access to information would be useless without the fourth condition for perfect competition: mobility.* Buyers and sellers must be able to react quickly to news of market conditions. Buyers must move to areas of abundance where prices are low, while sellers must move to areas of scarcity where prices are high. Production must be carried on in places where resources are plentiful and costs are low. Any obstacle to movement raises costs of production above their lowest possible level. Since conditions are always changing, it is important that buyers and sellers be able to move as freely as possible in order to make the most of new possibilities.

In the short run, mobility is always limited. Restaurants cannot move quickly to new locations. Manufacturing firms cannot move quickly into production of new goods. Farmers cannot quickly become dentists, nor can school buildings become oil tankers. Workers' skills are fixed, and they require retraining before a change of occupation. Moreover, the lingering effects of educational and job discrimination restrict the mobility of some groups into industries where their skills are needed.

The theory of perfect competition requires smooth, costless, and almost instant adjustment to changes in the economy. Resources must flow smoothly from one location, product, or occupation to another. The ultimate mobility would be the instant creation of companies to meet new demands and the instant disappearance of companies that are no longer needed. In reality it takes time to create a new firm and begin operations. It even takes time—a few months perhaps—to dissolve a firm, as we saw in the mid-1970s in the case of the W. T. Grant variety store chain. There are always many legal claims to settle and much physical property to dispose of.

Putting the conditions together

We have seen that a perfectly competitive market must meet four conditions: it must have (1) many small buyers and sellers (2) of a homogeneous product, (3) who have complete information and (4) who are completely mobile. Let's put these conditions together and see what they mean in terms of economic efficiency.

We have described a mechanism that will respond immediately to changes in demand. If the demand for pigs increases, it will be felt as an increase in the price received by farmers. This will cause pig farmers to increase their output in order to increase their incomes. The news of this opportunity will spread like wild-fire, and other farmers will start producing pigs. Every farmer is under pressure to adopt new methods of production in order to produce still more pigs at an even lower cost. Competition will drive prices down to the minimum for which pigs can be produced. Farmers whose costs are higher will be forced out of the industry. Surviving farms must operate at their most efficient level of output (i.e., most profitable volume) in order to achieve lowest unit costs of production.

Without even thinking about it, consumers will have voted to have their economy produce more pigs and a little bit less of something else—corn, or chickens, or whatever else farmers could have produced. So far as this industry is concerned, consumers are getting maximum output at the lowest possible cost. Competition *forces* firms to operate efficiently.

One result of vigorous competition may be less favorable for consumers, however, over the long term. Where price is forced to the very minimum necessary to cover costs, firms may never be able to accumulate funds for investment in new research and development. A small competitive firm may be unable to bear the risks associated with development of new products or processes. And it may fear that any successful innovation would be rather quickly copied by its rivals. In these circumstances, strong competition may discourage the search for new technologies that ensure the growth of the U.S. economy.

Demand curves in perfect competition

The assumptions of perfect competition may be unrealistic, especially in industries outside agriculture, but they give us a starting point from which to explore how things actually work. Let's think for a moment about the demand curve in a perfectly competitive industry. Remember, from Chapter 3, our model of the market for ski weekends? We added all consumer demand curves to arrive at total demand in the market as a whole. The market demand for the industry was shown as a downward sloping curve. This was because at lower prices there were more customers for ski accommodations. Likewise, the market supply for the

entire industry was shown as an upward sloping curve—because at higher prices more ski accommodations would be offered for sale.

The model of the market for ski accommodations is shown again as Figure 1. Table 1 lists the data on which the curves are based. The equilibrium price is $70. That is the price at which the demand for ski weekends and the supply of ski weekends are equal. A total quantity of 30,000 ski weekends will be sold at that price.

Figure 1a shows the market demand curve. But this is not the demand curve facing an individual firm. When there are many firms in a competitive industry, the equilibrium price is the result of decisions of all buyers and sellers. This means that each individual firm is faced with a single price at which it can sell its output. Even though the demand curve for the industry is downward sloping, the individual firm faces a horizontal demand curve drawn at the level of the market equilibrium price. This is because in a competitive industry no individual firm is strong enough to affect market price. A horizontal demand curve is included in Figure 1b at equilibrium price of $70. This is the demand curve facing Wonderland resort. Figure 1b also shows Wonderland's individual supply curve, drawn from data in Chapter 3.

Refer to Table 1. At the equilibrium price of $70 Wonderland must decide on a level of output. It has no choice as to price. If there is perfect competition, no single firm can charge a price higher than equilibrium. This is because there are (1) many other small sellers who are (2) selling identical products and have (3) perfect information and (4) ease of mobility into this market. Under these conditions Wonderland will decide to provide 70 units of accommodations, as shown in Figure 1b. Refer to Figure 1c to determine the quantity supplied by Alpine resort.

Table 1
Demand for and Supply of Ski Weekend Accommodations

Price	Quantity demanded	Quantity supplied
$100	20,000	50,000
90	25,000	40,000
70	30,000	30,000
60	35,000	20,000
50	40,000	10,000

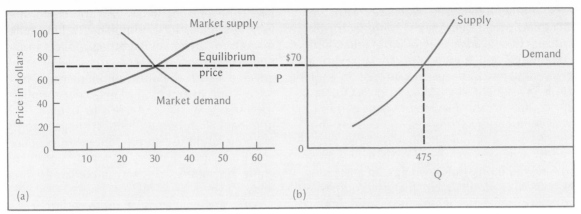

Figure 1   (a) Competitive market for ski accommodations; supply and demand determine equilibrium
price, $70. (b) At $70, Wonderland Resort supplies 475
accommodations. (c) At $70, Alpine Resort supplies 500
accommodations.

We say that the individual companies in
this situation are "price takers." Price is set by
the interaction of decisions of many buyers
and sellers, each too small to affect price. This
is true only when there is perfect competition
or a situation very close to it. In other market
structures, we will see that price and output
decisions are made differently.

Monopoly

The model of perfect competition illustrates
one extreme market structure. Now we will
look at the opposite extreme, the model of
monopoly.

Single seller

The monopoly model requires only one assumption: that of a single seller. In a monopolized industry, one seller supplies the industry's
entire output. The single seller may achieve its
monopoly position through the absence of any
one of the other three conditions that characterize perfect competition. That is, it may provide a unique good or service, it may have
information that is not available to other firms,
or it may be taking advantage of a lack of
mobility.

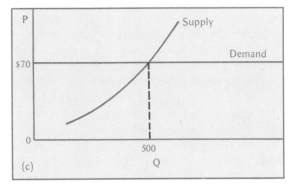

A unique good or service   The product of the
monopoly firm is different from the products
offered for sale by all other firms. The monopoly is the only firm in its industry. Buyers can't
buy the product anywhere else. As the only
supplier of the good, the monopoly firm has
the power to set price anywhere on its demand
curve.

Information barrier   The monopoly firm may
have information that is not readily available to
other firms wanting to enter the industry. This
could be information necessary in production.
Or it might be knowledge of particular geographic markets where sales are greatest, or
knowledge of strategic resources, formulas, or
designs. Without information, rival firms are
unable to enter the market, and the monopoly firm can control the total output of the
industry.

Lack of mobility Finally, difficulties of movement may prevent new firms from entering the industry to take advantage of profitable conditions. Many industries require very large capital investment just to begin operation. If an enormous investment is required in order to start up production, this may be a serious barrier to new competition. Moreover, the existing monopoly may enjoy economies of large scale; that is, it spreads its capital costs over a large volume of output, thus keeping unit costs low. A new firm would have higher production costs and could not compete.

Another barrier to entry may be the high expenditures necessary to advertise the new product. The monopoly may be so well established that no other firm can afford to challenge it. If a new firm is to capture part of the market, it must provide buyers with information about its product and incentives to buy. Heavy advertising expenses may make its costs too high to compete.

An example of lack of mobility can be seen in the U.S. automobile industry. While the industry is not a monopoly, the four U.S. firms are so thoroughly entrenched that they need fear no *domestic* rival. The costs required to challenge General Motors would be too great, and so would the risks. Only foreign manufacturers with established plants, ample financial assets, and secure market were able to expand slowly into the American market.

Methods of monopoly

Back in the late nineteenth century, some U.S. firms used ruthless methods to acquire market positions close to monopoly. Sometimes they did so by driving rival firms out of business. Or they forced small firms into mergers with the dominant firm. They did this in one of several ways. One way was to engage in *predatory price cutting.* In areas where there were competitive firms, the dominant firm would reduce its price far below costs, making up the loss by setting higher prices in areas where it faced no competition. In this way a "robber baron" might force rival firms to sell out.

Another strategy was the *squeeze operation.* Suppose a giant firm bought raw materials from many small suppliers and sold its finished output to many small buyers. As the largest buyer of materials, the firm could offer very low prices to its suppliers; lacking other markets for their materials, the suppliers would be forced to accept. As the largest seller of the finished good, the firm could demand high prices from its buyers; lacking other suppliers, the buyers would be forced to comply. The dominant firm would collect large profits, which it could use to buy out small suppliers and purchasers. Finally, it would control the entire operation from raw materials to final sales.

Through tactics like these a firm (or a group of firms) might secure control of production in an industry. Once a monopoly position was sure, then the firm could raise price above its full production costs and cut back quantities offered for sale. With control over market supply, the monopoly could collect monopoly profits without fear of competition. Of course, having a monopoly on a product doesn't guarantee profits. There must be *demand* for the monopoly product.

Monopoly is *less efficient* than perfect competition. We have already seen that perfect competition is ideal from the standpoint of efficiency: it produces maximum output at the lowest possible cost. In contrast, the final result of monopoly may be less output of a good or service than would be provided by competition. Once the monopoly position is secure, price may rise above the competitive price. After years of assured operation free from competition, production costs may also rise. This is because the monopolist is not forced by competition to produce at lowest cost. Furthermore, a secure monopoly firm is under little pressure to develop and apply new production techniques. For all these reasons, monopoly firms may not be forced to operate efficiently.

Few pure monopolies actually exist in the United States. Some firms may enjoy small and temporary monopolies. A restaurant or shop may dominate a local market area. But as population grows, there is room for competition, and rival firms will move in. Even a single railroad may not monopolize transportation services between two cities. When traffic builds up, buses, airlines, and trucking firms will enter the market and provide competition. A single electric power company may monopolize the supply of electricity in an area, but it will not monopolize the supply of all energy; the local gas company will provide some competition. For many decades the American Telephone and Telegraph Company (AT&T) has provided most of the nation's telephone communications. But in recent years other firms have begun to supply some communication services that were formerly in the exclusive hands of AT&T. How an industry is defined also affects the degree of monopoly. When an industry is narrowly defined, one firm may be dominant; for example, single firms provide Atlanta-to-New Orleans passenger railroad transportation, telephone service in Winter Park, Florida, and custom-made hiking boots. However, when industries are defined more broadly, as transportation, communication, or recreation equipment, it is difficult for a single firm to control supply.

Growing markets provide opportunities for competitors to invade the area of a monopoly and reduce its power. As substitutes become available, the monopoly firm loses its power to set prices. Substitute forms of transportation, energy, and communication develop as an economy grows. New supplies of strategic resources or synthetic resources reduce a monopoly's hold on factors of production. Research and development programs create new products and new production techniques to undermine the monopoly's power.

Monopolistic competition

We have discussed the basic assumptions of models of two extreme types of market. They are extreme because neither perfect competition nor pure monopoly occurs very often in American industry. In between them, we find most American markets; these markets may be classified into two other types: *monopolistic competition* and *oligopoly*. These market structures contain elements of both competition and monopoly, and they reflect more nearly the conditions of actual markets.

Monopolistic competition is similar to perfect competition in one respect: there are many small buyers and sellers. But monopolistic competition is similar to monopoly in another respect: the goods or services sold are not homogeneous. Monopolistic competition can never become true monopoly because capital requirements are generally so low that many small firms can enter the industry. But even though there may be many firms, each still tries to distinguish its product from those of the others. It does this in order to attract buyers to its product and keep them. Pete's Barber Shop is a good example of a firm in monopolistic competition: once you've met Pete and sat in his chair and listened to him talk baseball, you'll never confuse him with any other barber. If you like his work, you'll stick by him through the years. You'll pay his prices, too, even if he does charge a little more than the barber down the street.

A firm in monopolistic competition may give uniqueness to its product in two ways: (1) through design or service features that improve the usefulness of the product, or (2) through appeals to buyer psychology that give the *appearance* of greater usefulness. This process of creating uniqueness is called **product differentiation.**

Product differentiation allows a firm to establish some monopoly control over price. In monopolistic competition, some buyers will remain loyal to a particular brand even if the price is slightly higher. For this reason the firm in monopolistic competition is not forced to produce and sell at the very lowest cost. And by the same token it faces less pressure to employ newer and cheaper production techniques.

Where do we find monopolistic competition? Almost everywhere. Grocery stores, restaurants, dry cleaners, stationery stores, book publishers, and most small shops are monopolistic competitors. In manufacturing, we find monopolistic competition in industries where there are large numbers of small firms: women's clothing, shoes, wood furniture, men's and boys' suits and coats, among others. Firms engaged in monopolistic competition tend to be limited to local, rather than national, markets.

Under monopolistic competition it pays to advertise, but often on a limited scale. Since most of the firms are small, they can't afford lavish expenditures. Their ads appear in local newspapers, not on national TV. They use direct mail. Sometimes they buy spots on local radio and TV broadcasts.

There are seldom too few firms in this type of market. On the contrary, monopolistic competition tends to draw more firms than necessary to satisfy market demand. This is because it is so easy to enter the field and because the business appears so profitable. Every year thousands of shops and small businesses are established, and every year thousands fail. In a new and expanding industry with a growing consumer market, profits will be adequate for the first firms to enter the industry. But the profits will soon attract competition, each new firm supplying a good or service somewhat different from the others. The new firms must often set lower prices to attract a share of the market. Competitive price cutting will cut into the profits of all. Finally, many firms will share a market that isn't quite large enough for them all, each charging a price that just covers its full costs of production and no one collecting substantial profits.

It may appear that these results are the same as the results under competition. But this is not the case. In perfect competition there are only enough firms to supply the entire market at lowest costs of production. Each firm produces enough output to achieve minimum costs and maximum efficiency. In monopolistic competition there are too many firms. Each has a smaller share of the market than would be true under perfect competition. The existence of product differentiation enables them to charge their customers a little more than a firm under perfect competition could charge. Each monopolistically competitive firm will produce too little output to enjoy minimum costs. Their prices must cover their higher production costs and also the cost of advertising. Product differentiation interferes with competition, so that firms in these industries operate at less than maximum efficiency.

Extended Example
How to Be Successful in Monopolistic Competition

Find a product that can be sold through food and drugstore outlets, that is purchased primarily by women, that sells for less than $3, that can be easily and distinctively packaged, and for which there is at least a $500 million market not already dominated by one or two producers. Then take aim and fire.

That is how Hanes Corporation broke into the consciousness of American women with L'eggs, the cleverly packaged pantyhose that captured 13% of the market in its first five years. By 1976 the company was already looking for new worlds to conquer in men's socks and underwear. According to its president, Robert Elberson, "The only way we can continue to grow in women's hosiery is to continue to take away from somebody else. And that gets progressively tougher and more expensive."

In its invasion of the women's hosiery field, Hanes spent heavily on advertising. Previously it had been an apparel manufacturing company, but in 1969 management decided to become a consumer goods marketing company. It hired experts from companies like Procter & Gamble, General Mills, and R. J. Reynolds—firms which also stress the importance of marketing. The marketing approach begins with the customer rather than the product. Hanes starts by finding out what consumers dislike about existing goods or about the way they are merchandised. Once it spots an opening, it develops an approach to fill it. That is followed by test marketing to see how the public reacts and finally by planning sales and distribution methods. Between 1969 and 1975, Hanes raised its advertising budget from 5% of sales to 13%.

In the crowded market for consumer goods the motto seems to be: If you can't be new, then be different.

Oligopoly

Oligopoly differs from monopolistic competition in that there are fewer firms. The word *oligopoly* means "few sellers." There may be as few as two, or there may be a fairly large number, say 30, with just two or three dominant firms. These are the glamorous companies of American industry, with the executive suites and the company airplanes. Their production is carried out on a large scale. Their sales efforts are usually nationwide. Often they produce standardized industrial commodities where product differentiation is not practical: steel, aluminum, copper, and petroleum are examples. However, the oligopolies we are most familiar with are those producing goods with some product differentiation: automobiles, TV programming, cigarettes, cereals, classical records, movies, and tires.

Oligopoly firms tend to grow through *merger*, as small firms combine to enlarge their market share or are absorbed by bigger firms. They have high overhead costs for plant, equipment, advertising, and executive salaries; but their greater volume permits large firms to spread their costs over a larger number of units, keeping unit production costs down. Even so, their market power enables oligopoly firms to keep prices higher than costs of production.

Firms in oligopoly know each other and are quick to meet each other's challenges. If a particular firm were to shave its prices in order to undersell the industry, its competitors would react at once by reducing prices all around. Since no single firm can hope to maintain a price advantage and since all firms lose profits if price falls, there is a tendency to move together. One or two firms may be the leaders; when they raise or lower their prices the others follow. This makes for *price rigidity*, a common characteristic of oligopoly which distinguishes it from competitive industries. This is why automobile prices fluctuate much less than the price of pork. When consumer demand falls in an oligopoly, price is likely to stay the same. It may even increase so as to cover the higher unit costs at reduced volume. During inflation, oligopoly prices generally rise together—but in spurts. These coordinated price increases protect each firm's market share while keeping total industry output fairly stable.

Oligopolists find other ways of competing than through price. Aggressive selling and advertising are important *nonprice methods of competition* in oligopoly. The Bic pencil company sells ballpoint pens shaped like bananas and has advertised heavily on TV. In the American automobile industry, four oligopoly firms compete by emphasizing superficial differences in design. Product differentiation is less important for oligopoly firms that sell homogeneous materials such as steel, cement, or aluminum. Among these firms, nonprice competition takes the form of service or credit arrangements on behalf of customers. There may be "institutional" advertising to inform buyers about the industry as a whole and the nice people who work in it. In some cases such as drugs or chemicals, firms may run informational advertising in which highly technical messages are aimed at specialists who use the product. Oligopoly firms may also compete through expenditures for research and development, the source of many new products. Everyone is familiar with the advances made in industries producing office equipment, cameras, calculators, and electric toothbrushes. These advances required enormous investment and the mobilizing of scientific and technical skill.

In general, the closer an industry in oligopoly is to the consumer, the more advertising and product differentiation it will have. Automobiles have already been mentioned. But consider the aspirin tablet. Although all aspirin is identical in substance, one would scarcely be aware of this from the TV ads. Similarly, automobile rental firms rent the same kinds of cars but plug their services relentlessly on TV.

Oligopoly prices are higher than they would be under perfect competition, and they tend to be rigid. To the extent that firms coordinate their policies, the harmful results of monopoly will follow. Output is lower than in competition and production costs may not be pushed to the minimum. When competition is weak, firms may not be forced to operate efficiently.

Moreover, if an oligopoly firm's market position is secure, it may hesitate to undertake the risks and costs of investing in new products and processes. The firm may invest instead in competitive advertising. Competitive advertising to expand one firm's market share at the expense of another's may produce no real benefits to the economy—except in terms of employment of artists, composers of jingles, and rising television performers, and perhaps more excitement and variety in our life-styles.

Summary of the four market structures

In the chapters that follow we will examine in greater detail what economic theory has to say about the four market structures. In particular, we will study how pricing and output decisions are made under perfect competition, monopoly, monopolistic competition, and oligopoly. We will also try to appraise the performance of firms in each market structure in terms of two important considerations: efficiency and equity.

Let us now recall our general conclusions about pricing and output under each of the four market forms:

Perfect competition

(1) large number of buyers and sellers
(2) competition to increase output at lower prices
(3) each surviving firm producing at lowest cost
(4) rapid communication of information about processes and markets
(5) fast response to changing market conditions
(6) ease of market entry and exit
(7) a scarcity of funds for research and development

Monopoly

(1) a single firm producing too little output compared to production from many competitive firms
(2) higher price and often higher production costs than under competition

(3) less pressure for technical advance, although sufficient funds for R&D may be available
(4) slow response to changing market conditions

Monopolistic competition

(1) ease of entry because of low capital requirements
(2) too many firms, relative to the size of the market, producing differentiated products
(3) less than maximum output for each firm, so that unit costs are higher than at greater volume
(4) higher prices than under competition
(5) heavy use of resources for product differentiation, including advertising

Oligopoly

(1) high barriers to entry based on capital costs and access to technology
(2) a few large interdependent firms, spreading their high capital costs over a large volume
(3) little price competition and rigid prices so as to cover full production costs
(4) coordination among firms in setting market shares
(5) higher prices than under competition
(6) nonprice competition, through advertising, service, or credit arrangements.

Evaluating market structures

Efficiency and market structure

We have been using the model of perfect competition as a standard with which to compare other market structures. Perfect competition provides the most favorable environment for economic efficiency. (Remember, we defined efficiency as the maximum output of desired goods from any quantity of resources.) To the extent that an industry is monopolistic or even oligopolistic, it will be less efficient than perfect competition. Scarce resources will be producing less output, and unit costs of production may be higher.

Viewpoint
Advertising in the Professions

"Upper and lower dentures: half price, this week only."
"Year-end sale—divorce proceedings handled cheap."
"Lost our lease—appendectomies performed at cost."

These advertisements are only imaginary—and frankly ridiculous. But it was partly to prevent such appeals that professional associations have generally prohibited advertising among their members. The public, it is said, does not have the necessary knowledge to evaluate the quality of professional services. Therefore, it is argued, professional people must follow a rigid code of professional ethics in order to protect consumers from incompetent practitioners. Professionally determined standards of excellence in every field prevent the entry of those who might lower the quality—and the price—of medical, dental, or legal services.

These views are coming under attack in the current climate of rising consumer action and accelerating prices for professional services. In many communities young doctors, dentists, pharmacists, and lawyers are challenging the rules prohibiting advertising. They are opening "clinics" in which a large volume of professional services can be handled at low unit cost. They want to provide basic services to a wider range of urban low- and middle-income consumers. A high volume of service output depends on advertising to get the word out.

However, enterprises like these have run afoul of state licensing boards, which are composed entirely of members of the profession. It is not surprising that these boards have used their power to restrict entry to the professions and to prevent the sale of services through new high-volume, low-cost methods. They want to reserve for professionals the right to perform even simple routine services that could easily be performed by lower cost paraprofessionals.

Monopoly in the professions may be largely responsible for their sharply rising prices. Price inflation is most notable in the health services. In 1976, while the consumer price index for other services was rising at an annual rate of 7.7%, health care costs went up 10.3%. The President's Council on Wage and Price Stability attributed the price rise to the physician's power to determine the scope and method of care provided. Lacking incentives to improve efficiency and install cost-reducing innovations, the professionals constitute, in the words of George Bernard Shaw, a "conspiracy against the laity."

The legal profession has prohibited advertising among lawyers since 1908. However, recent Supreme Court rulings have declared that professions may not form monopolies and that the First Amendment protects the right to advertise. Some lawyers argue that advertising will raise the price of legal services, give large firms an advantage over small ones, and perhaps even persuade customers to buy services they don't need. Furthermore, advertising may destroy traditional lawyer-client relationships and encourage the growth of prepaid services. Others say that advertising might provide the incentives for improved efficiency. Meaningful advertising would provide a responsible method of communicating price. (In states where pharmaceutical advertising is permitted, average prices of drugs and eyeglasses have fallen significantly.) Misleading advertising is already prohibited by existing laws.

The Federal Trade Commission, the Justice Department, and private individuals have brought suit against state professional codes and trade practices that restrict competition. In years to come, we are likely to hear further debate on this important issue.

We must remember that very little perfect competition exists in our economy today. However, as we shall see, the model of perfect competition is a very useful tool of analysis. If we were to try to change our economy so as to make it perfectly competitive, we would have to return to a much simpler way of life. It would be impossible to have perfect competition among our modern large-scale industries; they would not fit the four fundamental conditions we described above. Perfect competition would mean no automobiles, no electricity, no household appliances—in fact, hardly any of the conveniences of modern life. Perfect competition would mean no product differentiation, with all the opportunities for variety in consumption we enjoy. Obviously, we aren't about to do away with these advantages just for the sake of increasing competition. Our economy will continue to have important elements of monopoly and large sectors of oligopoly in it. A practical goal will be to maintain competition as much as possible within oligopoly and monopolistic competition and to prevent firms and industries from moving toward monopoly pricing. In a later chapter we will discuss public policies toward big business which aim to improve the efficiency of our actual market structures.

Even if monopoly and oligopoly aren't as efficient as perfect competition, are they *much* less efficient or only a *little bit* less? Some economists believe that our economy functions very nearly the way the theory of perfect competition says it should. Over a period of time it responds to changes in demand by allocating resources fairly quickly to new uses. Labor and capital move out of old, declining industries into new, expanding ones. Also, prices and output change when technology changes.

Some economists have even argued that monopoly and oligopoly have some desirable features. Even though prices may be higher, market power may also result in greater industrial research and product development. One of the best-known proponents of this view was Joseph Schumpeter (1883–1950). Schumpeter argued that economic growth and technical progress are brought about not through perfect competition but through large firms struggling to keep ahead of other large firms. He held that

firms turn to monopolistic practices in order to protect themselves in the risky business of introducing new methods and new products.

An example occurred in the period 1959–1964. This was a time of fairly stable prices for the economy as a whole, but prices were actually falling in some industries where technical improvements caused a decline in production costs: computers, plastics, tires and tubes, household appliances, synthetic fibers, rubber products, and aluminum. These industries are oligopolies in which the market is dominated by only a few very large producers.

There is no consensus among economists as to whether firms must be very large in order to take advantage of improved technology. Some, like Schumpeter, have opposed breaking up industrial giants into small competitive firms. Others have argued that small firms can also be progressive. They point out that small firms carry on research and have introduced many of the major inventions of recent times. If this is so, we don't need to have industrial giants in order to have rapid technological change. We will have much more to say about this subject later.

Equity and market structure

From what we have just said, it is obvious that efficiency isn't the only thing we want to consider when we compare the four different market structures. A perfectly competitive economy might be the most efficient, but it wouldn't deliver all the goods we want. Nobody wants to disconnect the electric lights or give up our wide range of consumer choice.

Much of the same can be said of equity. Remember that equity doesn't necessarily mean equality. Income may be distributed unequally and still be distributed fairly. If income is distributed too unequally, however, it may also be inequitable.

Which of the four market structures distributes income most fairly? If we think that fairness means rewarding people according to their contribution to production, then we can argue that the more competitive the economy

Economic Thinker

Joseph Schumpeter

One of the recent giants of economic theory was Joseph Schumpeter (1883–1950), who was born into the Austro-Hungarian Empire in Triesch, Moravia. Schumpeter grew up in Vienna, Austria, taught at a number of European universities, and eventually emigrated to the United States in 1932 to teach at Harvard University, where he remained until his death. He was reputed, early in his teaching career, to have fought a duel with the school librarian in order to enable the students to have wider access to the library. Although he worked most of his life as an academic, Schumpeter was a dynamic man who also labored occasionally in politics and business. He served as the Minister of Finance for a year in the new Austrian Republic which was created at the end of World War I. As a bank president in 1924, he lost his private fortune in a financial crisis that ruined his bank.

It is understandable that Schumpeter would focus his professional attention on the causes of business cycles. Cycles in the level of spending and production had caused much hardship in his native Austria. According to Schumpeter, business cycles were the natural result of a dynamic economy. The key to economic growth and change was the entrepreneur-innovator—the creative individual who would take the risks and apply the technologies to stimulate economic development. But because innovative activity took place irregularly, the economy would expand irregularly. Spurts of vigorous activity would be followed by collapse and crisis.

Schumpeter's most famous work—and one of the great economics books of the twentieth century—is *Capitalism, Socialism and Democracy*. His interest in the innovating entrepreneur became both the center and the point of departure for this book. Although Schumpeter was an ardent supporter of capitalism, in this book he predicted its eventual downfall and the rise of socialism. Ironically, the doom of capitalism and the free market system would be more the result of its successes than its failures.

As capitalist economies grow prosperous, said Schumpeter, they will become less driven to innovate. The innovating entrepreneur, who is the vital catalyst of capitalism, will be phased out by corporate bureaucrats. The growth of large corporations, the result of business successes, will bring on bureaucracies and planning by routine. Why would corporations grow static in this way? Because new processes and products undermine the existing capital structure of the firm. If new technology is to be introduced it will mean the destruction of old technologies. Schumpeter believed "creative destruction" was necessary for growth, but it would be resisted by those in control.

Paralleling the demise of the entrepreneur would be a growing intellectual hostility to capitalism and a more active role by big government. Both would result from the shortcomings of capitalism. Schumpeter felt the intellectuals of the universities and media would focus more on inequality and other shortcomings rather than on the material and social successes of capitalism. Government would be encouraged to expand its economic activity, eroding market freedom and the freedom of entrepreneurs.

Today some economists would say that recent trends in the United States bear out this prediction. They go further and single out Great Britain, where capitalism is quickly disappearing, much as Schumpeter said it would.

is the fairer it will be. Under perfect competition, resources are rewarded according to what they contribute to production. Workers who have important skills generally receive more than the unskilled; the owners of valuable land receive higher rents than the owners of poor land; expanding industries pay more for resources than declining industries. The principle here is not equality, you will notice, but one's value to the productive process. A poor widow with six children, forced to support herself by scrubbing floors, would receive less than the career woman with no dependents. Competition may distribute income fairly while distributing income unequally.

Under oligopoly the widow may still be scrubbing floors, but her pay may be higher. Oligopoly is able to charge higher prices and get a higher return, which can then be distributed to the resources it employs. Income may be based more on market power than on actual contribution to production. Examples of this can be seen in the pay levels of U.S. industry. In oligopolies such as steel or automobiles, wages tend to be higher than in more competitive industries such as clothing manufacture. The difference cannot be attributed to labor unions because all three industries have strong unions. But the manufacture of most clothing is carried on in small competitive shops that require relatively small amounts of capital. Entry into the industry is much easier than in steel or automobiles, and the returns to resources employed in it are generally lower.

While resources may be paid more in monopolistic or oligopolistic industries, the level of output and employment is lower. More workers are left to seek employment in lower paid competitive industries. The result may be both less equity and less equality. Furthermore, to the extent that monopoly and oligopoly add to price inflation, *all* workers receive lower *real* incomes.

Equity, as well as efficiency, seems to favor perfect competition over the other market forms. To the extent that industries lack competition, resources will not flow freely from one to the other. Incomes will fail to reflect the value of a resource in production.

Industrial concentration in the United States

We said earlier that there is very little perfect competition in U.S. industry. In the area that we think of as "big business," most industries are oligopolies. In order to get a picture of the degree of oligopoly in various industries, economists use a measure known as the **concentration ratio.**

A concentration ratio measures the importance of the largest firms in an industry compared to all the firms taken together. Thus if the four largest firms account for 90% of an industry's sales, we can say that the industry is highly concentrated. If the four largest firms account for only 2% of the sales, the industry is not concentrated at all. Concentration ratios are usually calculated for the four largest and eight largest firms in an industry. They may measure sales as a percent of total sales, productive assets as a percent of total industry assets, or value added in production as a percent of total value added. *Value added* is the difference between the dollar value of a firm's output and the amount paid to other firms for inputs such as materials, parts, and energy.)

For example, a concentration ratio for the cigarette industry in 1975 is calculated as shown in Table 2. The four largest firms were R. J. Reynolds (32.5% of total sales), Philip Morris (23.8%), Brown and Williamson (17.0%), and American Brands (14.2%). Together they accounted for 87.5% of the industry's sales.

Table 2
Concentration in the Cigarette Industry

Company	Sales (billions of cigarettes)	Market share (percent of total sales)
R. J. Reynolds	193.6	32.5%
Philip Morris	141.7	23.8
Brown and Williamson	101.3	17.0
American Brands	84.5	14.2
Total industry sales	596.0	
Concentration ratio		87.5%

Extended Example
Concentration in the Aluminum Industry

Efficient markets depend on price flexibility. Changes in demand are communicated to producers as their stocks pile up or are depleted. Competing firms react by changing their prices. They reduce prices to avoid accumulating unwanted stocks. Or they raise prices to ration their limited stocks among their most urgent buyers. When markets are free and competitive, prices serve as incentives to increase or decrease output in line with the changing needs of the economy.

When competition is weak, the automatic adjustment of output to demand works less efficiently. Large firms in concentrated industries can avoid price cuts without worrying about losing sales to rival firms. They all need a steady flow of high sales revenues if they are to maintain and expand their large capital investments.

The aluminum industry provides a recent example. Aluminum has been the miracle metal in the postwar economy. Made from bauxite extracted from clay, this lightweight metal conducts heat and electricity well, reflects light and heat, and resists corrosion. It is an important input for cans, appliances, autos, and building construction.

Over recent decades aluminum production in the United States has become concentrated in three large firms. Together Alcoa, Reynolds, and Kaiser account for about 70% of the nation's capacity for producing aluminum.

The recession of 1973–1975 hit hardest at firms producing durable goods and housing—two of the principal users of aluminum. Demand curves for aluminum shifted to the left. A competitive industry would have reacted by reducing prices, with the expectation that lower prices would increase sales. But the president of one of the three major firms revealed, "I don't think I'd sell one extra pound of metal if we cut the price." Apparently, aluminum producers believed that buyers would not respond to a price cut by increasing orders. Thus a price cut would reduce revenues for all the firms rather than expand sales. The firms reacted to the fall in demand by a series of price increases amounting to more than 50% in 1974 (from 25 to 39 cents per pound). By early 1975, sales had plummeted by 40% and firms cut operations to about 73% of productive capacity.

Policymakers in the national government grew concerned about the rising unemployment in the aluminum industry and about its contribution to inflation. They saw that high aluminum prices were causing higher production costs in many other industries. Their higher costs meant even more price increases, lower sales, and lower employment. Concentration in the aluminum industry seemed to be aggravating both inflation and unemployment throughout the economy.

With recovery from the recession in early 1976, demand for aluminum began to pick up. This time it was *higher* demand which became the motivation for higher prices. Ingot prices rose to 48 cents a pound, a further increase of about 20%.

In the long run it is likely that high prices will affect the shape of demand curves for aluminum. The development of substitutes will increase user resistance to higher prices, and demand curves will become flatter. Already plastics are filling many uses and other users are turning to steel. Competition from other materials may prove to be the important force for holding down materials prices in the future. But for the immediate period concentration in this and other basic industries probably worsened the nation's economic problems.

What elements of this account are relevant to microeconomics and what elements are relevant to macroeconomics?

Table 3
Ratio of Assets to Total Assets of All
Manufacturing Corporations

	1947	1967
50 largest	31%	38%
100 largest	39	49
200 largest	46	60

Table 4
Ratio of Sales to Total Sales of All
Manufacturing Corporations

	1947	1967
50 largest	22%	30%
100 largest	29	40
200 largest	36	50

There are certain difficulties with the concentration ratio. *First, what is an industry and who belongs to it?* Does a company making floor tiles belong to the tile industry or to the floor covering industry or to the home products industry? If the firm is thought of as belonging to the tile industry, it may have a large share of the market. But if it is thought of as part of the floor covering industry, it may be far less important.

A second problem is that we calculate a concentration ratio only for the largest four or eight firms. It doesn't give us a picture of the whole industry. For example, a study in the 1960s showed sales concentration ratios of 70 for the tire and tube industry and 31 for the meat packing industry. The ratios suggest that tires and tubes is the more concentrated industry. But the figures conceal the fact that in tires and tubes there are only 105 firms while in meat packing there are 2,833. So in the meat packing industry the four largest firms are very large compared to the other 2,829 and therefore command much greater market power.

Finally, a concentration ratio doesn't show the actual level of competition in small local markets. It usually is calculated for the country as a whole. In any particular locality or region, one or two firms may have overwhelming market power because other firms are too far away to compete with them. This would be the case in such industries as sand and gravel, hardware supplies, plant nurseries, supermarkets, and mobile homes.

Aggregate concentration ratios

One way to escape the limitations of the industry concentration ratio is to include all industries in a single ratio. The **aggregate concentration ratio** measures the level of concentration in the economy as a whole. It can be used to compare the importance of big firms over time. The aggregate concentration ratio is usually calculated for the nation's 50, 100, and 200 largest firms.

An important study published in 1972 reported significant changes in aggregate concentration ratios over the past several decades. The data showed that the share of productive assets owned by the 50 largest U.S. firms grew from 31% of total manufacturing assets in 1947 to 38% in 1967. The data for the 50 largest, 100 largest, and 200 largest firms are summarized in Table 3.

Concentration ratios expressed as shares of total manufacturing sales also increased over the period (see Table 4).

Finally, a similar change took place in concentration ratios expressed as shares of total value added (see Table 5).

The complete report shows that the greatest growth took place during the postwar boom from 1945 to 1958. The largest firms continued to grow over the last half of the period but at a slower pace. The evidence also shows that newcomers to manufacturing tended to grow faster than established firms.

Table 5
Ratio of Value Added to Total Value Added in
Manufacturing Corporations

	1947	1967
50 largest	17%	25%
100 largest	23	33
200 largest	30	42

Table 6
Ratio of Profits to Profits in All Manufacturing Industries

	1947	1971
50 largest	26%	43%
100 largest	34	50
200 largest	41	64

Occasionally, we want to know the share of the largest firms in total profits. Again, the evidence points to greater profitability among the largest firms (see Table 6).

The rise in concentration was more noticeable in the decade 1947–1958 and slowed in recent years.

Market structure and macroeconomics

The study of industry markets and structures of markets belongs to microeconomics. That is because in our discussion of market structure we are primarily concerned with the behavior of buyers and sellers in particular markets. But market structure is also related to macroeconomics. This is because the structure of industry influences the performance of the whole economy. Our description of market structures suggests that the closer an industry is to perfect competition, the more efficient it is. By the same token, the more competitive the economy as a whole, the more efficient it will be. The more competitive the economy as a whole, the more easily it will respond to changing conditions. Resources will earn incomes that reflect their real contribution to output. And they will move more easily from one sector or industry to another. Prices will be more flexible, and costs may be lower.

In the chapters that follow, we will study the four structural models in greater detail.

Summary

Microeconomics is the study of buying and selling in individual markets. There are four basic kinds of product markets, distinguished by the kinds and amounts of competition in them. To describe them we have used economic models or simplified pictures of the real world.

The model of perfect competition assumes that there are many small buyers and sellers who buy and sell a homogeneous product, with perfect information and ease of mobility among markets. Under perfect competition, firms are "price takers." Price is set in the market by the interaction of many buying and selling decisions.

The monopoly model has only one seller. Monopoly may result from uniqueness of the product or from restraints on information or mobility. A monopoly firm is a "price maker." If it chooses, it can set its price to yield maximum total revenue from sales. The price generally is higher than under perfect competition, and the quantity of output is lower. Monopoly power may be the result of large initial capital requirements and higher costs for new entrants. Or the monopoly firm may have forced its rivals out of business through "predatory price cutting" or "squeeze operations" or through selling a better product at a lower price.

Under monopolistic competition there are many small firms, but each sells a differentiated product. Advertising and brand loyalty are important in monopolistic competition. Price is generally higher than under competition and firms produce less than their optimum output.

The oligopoly model includes a few large firms whose product may be homogeneous. Initial capital costs are high, making large volume necessary for lowest unit costs. Because oligopoly firms are interdependent, they often coordinate their price and output plans. Price is generally rigid and higher than it would be under competition.

The goal of efficiency is best served when markets are competitive. Equity may also be greater under competition if equity is defined to mean basing rewards on actual contributions to output. Incomes received depend on the quantity and quality of resources an individual owns. This means that income would be distributed unequally even under perfect competition.

Some evidence suggests that industrial concentration has grown in the United States. The rate of growth in concentration has probably slowed, however, in recent years. A high level of concentration may mean lower output and lower real incomes for the economy as a whole.

Key Words and Phrases

- **efficiency** using resources so as to achieve maximum output per unit of scarce input.

- **equity** distributing benefits and costs from production in a way that society regards as fair.

- **structure of industry** arrangement of firms in an industry according to size and market power.

- **conduct of firms** behavior of firms with respect to competition.

- **performance of firms** the result of a firm's behavior with respect to efficiency and equity.

- **perfect competition** a condition in which many independent buyers and many independent sellers operate in the marketplace.

- **monopoly** condition in which a single seller controls the entire output of an industry.

- **monopolistic competition** a condition in which many small sellers compete to sell differentiated products.

- **oligopoly** a condition in which a few large producers control most of the output of an industry.

- **homogeneous products** products which are indistinguishable.

- **product differentiation** creating product uniqueness (a Chinese meal differs from, say, an Italian meal) or the appearance of uniqueness (as with advertising).

- **nonprice methods of competition** advertising, special services, credit arrangements, research and development of new products.

- **concentration ratio** the percentage of industry output supplied by the largest four or the largest eight firms.

- **aggregate concentration ratio** the percentage of our economy's output supplied by the largest firms—either the largest 50 or 100 or 200.

Questions for Review

1. Explain why the concepts of structure, conduct, and performance are critical to a study of industrial activity in the United States.

2. During what stage of American economic development did monopoly occur, and how was it achieved?

3. What types of industries are most often characterized by oligopoly and monopolistic competition?

4. Outline the most significant arguments against, and in behalf of, oligopoly and monopolistic competition.

5. What are the limitations of the concentration ratio as an indicator of market power?

6. Discuss the effects on the national economy as a whole of concentration of market power. How are efficiency and equity affected by industry structure?

7. Consider the fundamental economic circumstances that often underlie industrial concentration. Can you project any trends in these circumstances for the future? What do your predictions imply about market power and the future role of government in the economy?

8. On the basis of the following concentration ratios, how would you describe trends in the beer industry?

| Year | Percent of total shipments | | |
	4 largest	8 largest	50 largest
1958	28	44	88
1963	34	52	94
1967	40	59	98
1972	52	70	99

9. Define: homogeneous products, product differentiation.

23

Economics and Power

In the preceding introductory chapters, we have discussed the basic components of the study we call economics. We have noted that economists use graphs, charts, and models to help us understand how economic forces operate. But it is important to keep in mind from the outset that graphs and charts and models are not entirely accurate. They are, at best, representations of human relationships in the economic marketplace.

Economists are, of course, aware of this fact. They know that the early scholars who studied how human physical needs were supplied did so almost entirely in the framework of political and social relationships. In fact, economics was known as "political economy" at first and this term is being dusted off and used more often in the 1970s. The idea is that economics is a valid study only within the context of the "political" life of human beings. It implies consideration of ethical and sociological relationships—the way people actually *behave* in the marketplace.

However, as the study of economics progressed, as more sophisticated measuring tools were developed, economics became more "scientific." Economic facts can be multiplied, subtracted, added, and so on. They can be turned into statistics and mathematical formulas—and, in our day, fed into a computer. However, not all behavior lends itself to this kind of mathematical manipulation. Consequently, a tendency developed to concentrate on the marketplace itself, rather than try to "figure in" the interactions of the people who operated in it. Models were developed to illustrate economic phenomena—unemployment, inflation, supply and demand, for example—with little or no attention to the "variable" known as human behavior.

Such models were and are useful to the study of economics. Indeed, they are indispensable to an understanding of the complexities of economic life. But it is important to recognize that, in real life, people have the power to interfere with and alter the theoretical results of these models.

For our purposes, **power** may be considered the ability to exert a desired outcome or action or to increase the chances of an outcome. We need not get in a tangle over words: *Power, influence,* and *control* mean the same thing.

Many modern-day economists have, in a sense, returned to the concern of their earliest predecessors—a concern with human behavior. They have become particularly interested in how people organize to exert pressure on the marketplace and how other people organize to exert counterpressure. They are also interested in the power of politics and political events to influence economic outcomes. So in this chapter we will consider some of the principal ways people gain, use, and maintain economic and political power to influence the theoretically "pure" functioning of the marketplace.

Market models and countervailing power

The concepts of power which economists have traditionally studied are related to the marketplace. The market is the arena in which economic problems are solved. As we saw in the previous chapter, there are market models which range from perfect competition to monopoly, with oligopoly and monopolistic competition in between.

Perfect competition, at one extreme, is a model of a market where buyers and sellers have no power except their economic response to market conditions. Where markets are perfectly competitive, no one firm has any market power; price is determined by supply and demand. Under perfect competition, markets are regarded as giving desirable answers to the questions of *what, how,* and *for whom* to produce. The existence of market power is undesirable and will result in a deviation from the optimal situation. Firms with power can reduce output and set higher prices. Varying degrees of market power produce distortions in market performance. The economic questions are not resolved in the best manner when compared with the situation of no power.

Monopoly is at the other extreme, where a single firm has considerable power in its market to set output and price. In between are oligopoly and monopolistic competition. Under all three of these models, firms have power and can, in varying degrees, reduce output and set higher prices. These market models, along with perfect competition, will be discussed in much greater detail in later chapters.

There are other instances of power in the economic world. These are scattered and relate to market power in selected markets. Labor unions in the factor market would be a specific example. Long enough ago to be considered traditional (in the early 1950s), the economist John Kenneth Galbraith coined the term **countervailing power.** Countervailing implies a balancing of forces. Since market power exists, it is wise to attempt to neutralize it with an equal power called countervailing power. In the example of labor unions, the workers form a monopoly on the supply side to balance the power of employers. Farmers may form cooperatives and other organizations to gain market power back from both their suppliers and the processors to which farm products are sold. Grocery chain stores operate as consumer cooperatives to gain power in dealing with monopolistic suppliers.

Government also plays a role. Through government, consumers or other groups may gain elements of countervailing power. The government may assist passively by not opposing the formation of a countervailing power. Or more actively, the government may become the countervailing power through its own antitrust legislation and regulatory agencies.

Organization theory: a study of power

Economists are interested in power as it manifests itself in organized groups. It is mostly through group action that individuals affect the marketplace economy. People who seek economic power organize to do so. They form corporations, labor unions, consumer and political organizations, and so on. Consequently, economists are interested in learning how organizations themselves function. They have turned to a study of "organization theory" to see how organization power operates.

One source of organization power is obvious. There is power in numbers. One unit of individual power added to another unit gives us two units, and so on. In addition, if some or many of the members bring a great deal of individual power to the organization, the total sum of power will be considerably increased.

But studies have shown that there is much more to organization power than this. The real power of an organization derives from the *interplay of power between and among individual members of the group.* Further, in this dynamic process, *power is transferred to the organization itself.* The organization takes on a life—and a power role—of its own. And, indeed, its power becomes greater than the sum of the power of its individual members.

Personal power

Since organizations consist of individuals, let us turn first to a consideration of individual or personal power. Every individual has a certain amount of power to influence events in his or her own life or in the lives of others. The amount of such power varies enormously from person to person. All else being equal, a physically attractive person will probably exercise more personal power over others than an unattractive individual. One endowed with brain power will likely have more influence over events than a dullard. A pleasant personality enhances one's power. An unpleasant one is likely to diminish one's influence. A person with a certain amount of wealth will have more power over events than a pauper. A person with status (which is not necessarily the same as wealth) has more power than "one of the crowd." Many other factors help determine the power of an individual—some of them the result of the individual's own efforts, some a matter of luck. (As has been said, all men are created equal, but some are created "more equal" than others.)

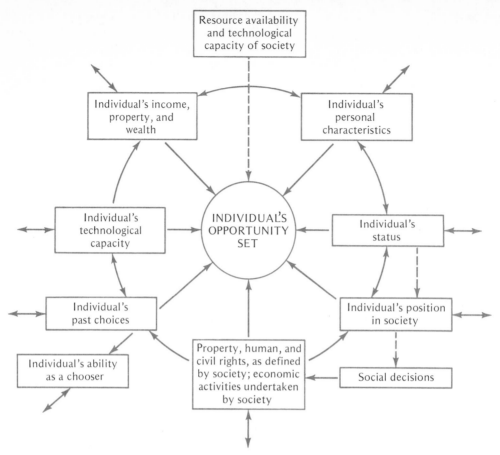

Figure 1 An individual's opportunity set at a given moment. (From Randall, Alan, "Information, Power, and Academic Responsibility," in *American Journal of Agricultural Economics,* Vol. 56. Copyright 1974 American Agricultural Economics Association.)

Individual power can of course only be exercised in a "social setting," whether on a one-to-one basis, in a group, or in an entire society. The setting itself may enhance individual power or, on the other hand, nullify it completely. If society glorifies wealth and property over human dignity, the wealthy person has more power than the social reformer. If Albert Einstein had been born in the tenth century, the true power of his brain probably would have been diminished in a scientifically primitive society.

Figure 1 illustrates some of the principal factors that may enhance or limit individual power. It shows what is called an individual's "opportunity set." An **opportunity set** represents the collection of actions open to an individual in a given social group (or organization) at a given time in the individual's life and in

the life of the organization. The surrounding characteristics determine what the person can do and who he can influence. For some, the opportunity set is small and those individuals may be essentially powerless.

Personal power within the organization

Power within an organization is usually wielded through (1) direct control of members of the group, (2) control of the administrative and productive facilities of the organization, and/or (3) control of communications among members of the group and between the group and external organizations.

Leaders of the organization are most likely to exercise direct control over other members. In a corporate group, for example, the president of the company and a few other officials have the power to hire and fire, reward and punish whomever they will. Wages may be raised or lowered. Working conditions may be made pleasant or unpleasant. The countervailing power of unions modifies and curtails this power somewhat. Thus executive members of the organization have direct power over other members. The higher the member in the corporate hierarchy, the more direct power he has over other members.

But power may also be exercised through control of the organization's facilities—the so-called "instrumentalities" of the organization. For example, the operator of a machine essential to the profits of a corporation may wield considerable power. If the operator would be difficult to replace, even a corporation executive might be reluctant to challenge that member's power. A tool-room supervisor may exercise power over his peers because of his control over who gets which tools to perform functions within the organization. Even the copy machine operator or the typist in the typing pool is not without power. Control of the group's copy machine and typewriting instrumentalities gives one the power to reward other members with fast and accurate work, or punish with work that is slow and inaccurate.

Control of communications within an organization is a very important determinant of individual power. Communication is the life blood of any organization. Without its free flow the organization will sicken and ultimately die.

Corporations, for example, are especially vulnerable to the power of its members who control communications within the group. Corporation executives may issue orders designed to enhance the organization's profitability. But such orders are useless if they are not communicated to those charged with carrying them out. The power of the executives to make policy may be thwarted by the power of organization members who control communications within the group. Someone quite low in the chain of command may prevent the organization from acting simply by failing to transmit the order from his superiors. Or, members low in the ladder of organizational positions may be able to influence the actions of the organization by transmitting inaccurate, manufactured, or false information to those in charge. The organization may fail to take advantage of an opportunity because the leadership is prevented from learning of its existence.

Organization power

As noted earlier, the power of an organization may become greater than the sum of the power of its individual members. Individual power exercised *within* the organization is ultimately transferred *to* the organization. The organization takes on a life of its own. *It* wields the real power.

The original purpose of the organization is to increase each member's power. And, in most cases, that is what it does. The economic power of members of a corporation, for example, will ordinarily increase with an increase in the corporation's power. More profits will mean higher salaries and other economic benefits.

But there is a price to pay. The more power that accrues to the organization, the less effective each member's individual power becomes. If the organization becomes powerful enough it may ultimately wield its power regardless of the will of its members, or even against its members' interests.

Evidence of this phenomenon is all around us. "Don't blame me; I just work here" is a signal that a group member is powerless (or is claiming to be) because of the power of the organization to which he belongs. War criminals commonly plead that the organization of which they were a member—the military or the nation itself—rendered them powerless *not* to commit atrocities. In the Watergate scandals, some trial defendants maintained that their crimes were not crimes at all. They were not crimes because the deeds were done to maintain the power of a political administration, not in the interest of their own power within that administration.

In 1974, a Turkish Airline DC-10 crashed, killing 346 people. Investigation showed that a faulty cargo door had blown out and caused the tragedy. Further investigation revealed that the American corporate builder of the plane and the government office charged with air safety were both previously aware of the DC-10's faulty cargo-door design. In the economic and political interests of the organizations to which they belonged, individual members of both groups had minimized the danger of the design error. As individuals, none of these persons would have endangered the life of any human being. They would never knowingly have used their power in such a manner. But the organizations of which they were members did so. The *organizations* decided the faulty design was an acceptable risk. The *organizations* had the power to enforce their decision. The "system" made it impossible for even the conscientious individuals to head off a disaster. Bureaucracies wherever they are found protect individuals from wrong decisions but in turn control the actions of the individual members.

Maintaining organization power

For the most part, membership in an organization is voluntary. Individuals willingly sacrifice some of their personal power in order to obtain greater power through the organization. But the organization must itself pay a price for this transference of power. It must use part of its energies (or wealth) to keep its members willing to remain in the organization. Sometimes, as we have noted above, it must be able to keep its members even in the face of organizational activities that are contrary to the wishes and seeming best interest of its members. How do organizations achieve this end?

People become members of an organization in order to gain certain advantages, personal or economic. Most of them will remain with the organization if it continues to provide these advantages. Members of a consumer group, for example, will likely remain in it as long as it protects consumer interests. Workers will continue to form unions as long as the unions help provide good wages and good working conditions. Employees of corporations will be inclined to remain with an organization that offers them good salaries and other economic benefits.

Human nature itself also helps provide organizational stability. Once we join a group, most of us are reluctant to leave it without very good cause. Belonging becomes a habit. Inertia contributes to our willingness to stay with the organization. As employees, we may be hesitant about leaving our jobs for the uncertainty and upheaval of finding work with another organization. (When employees are handicapped by age, by excessive debts, or by possession of nontransferable skills, the power of the organization to keep them in the group is almost unlimited.)

Organizations have, in fact, many means of retaining the individuals upon whom their power is based. These methods are powerful because they are as much psychological as they are material. In Japan, for example, many large corporations aim deliberately at lifetime employment for their workers. Corporate policy calls for the company to become a substitute, or second, family to its employees. The company provides services ranging from medical care of expectant mothers to burial services for deceased employees. Children of employees are trained to enter the corporation when they become old enough to do so. Birthdays and other family holidays are celebrated on company time and at company expense. Family meals may be served on company premises. Free entertainments and full recreational services are provided for employees and their families. In return for such benefits and for the security of life-long employment, the corporation gains membership stability and almost perfect loyalty.

United States corporations employ similar methods to maintain group membership. Here, however, attempts to retain organization members are not likely to be so extensive or all-inclusive. Group loyalty may be fostered by holding sales meetings and conventions in luxurious surroundings. Blazers with company insignia may be provided for office wear. Company picnics aid the organization's morale. Group-singing of corporate songs may be provided for the entertainment—and edification—of employees. In recent years, some firms have experimented with group psychology sessions to reinforce company loyalty. Others have taken to showing films containing subtle and not so subtle illustrations of the dire results to employees of possible corporate failure to achieve its aims.

Whatever incentives are employed, the aim is to maintain and increase the organization's power. To do so, the organization seeks to get its members to identify with the group in furtherance of group objectives. All of this is perfectly proper and well and good—if the objectives themselves are well and good and if the members retain their own identity. But power, especially organization power, can corrupt. The so-called "organization man" may be tempted to exchange all his individual power for the benefits of belonging to the organization. He may, in effect, lose his identity to the organization. If the organization becomes corrupt in its pursuit of power, the organization man may become the war criminal or the Watergate criminal in the dock.

Games economists play

Another tool that economists use to study how power is obtained and used is *game theory*. **Game theory** consists of a group of mathematical theories developed jointly by a mathematician, John von Neumann, and an economist, Oskar Morgenstern. The logic of these theories is applied to alternative strategies that are available to solve problems—particularly economic and military problems. If one chooses the strategy that is statistically advantageous, according to game theories, one usually wins the game. The object of the game is to gain economic (or military) power.

The game can be very complex, with many players and many actions and outcomes to be considered. When computers are used, an almost countless number of factors may be written into the rules of the game. For our purposes, however, let us look at two simple illustrations of game theory. One illustration is concerned with direct economic power. The

other is an illustration of political power—which is itself an important factor in economic power.

Consider the following examples. If there is only one store in a town, it does not matter much where the store is located. The owner will get all the business. If there is only one candidate for a political office, the candidate may be an extreme liberal or an extreme conservative. Either way, he will be elected. Suppose, however, that there are two participants in each of the above situations.

If there are two stores in a town, both will try to be near the center of town. If one is located near the center of town and the other is not, the central store will get more customers. Locating anywhere but near the center would be a losing strategy as the probability of obtaining customers is reduced. With two candidates in a political process both will be forced to choose a moderate stance on most issues if they wish to win the game. If one candidate takes an extreme position, a left-wing position say, his adversary will probably win, because he will get all of the middle-of-the-road votes and the right-wing extreme as well. (Something like this happened in the presidential campaigns of Barry Goldwater in 1964 and George McGovern in 1972. One was successfully identified in the eyes of the voters as a right-winger and the other as a left-winger. Each lost by a landslide.)

When many participants enter the game, strategies can change radically. If there are many stores, it may be preferable to desert the central district. It may be better to seek a high proportion of the residents of one part of town as customers than to take a chance in the center of town where there are more potential customers but more stores bidding for their trade. Political strategies will also change with the number of game participants. If there are many candidates, one might win by deliberately taking an extreme political stance. One might get only 30% of the vote. But the remaining 70% might be distributed more or less equally among three or four middle-of-the-road candidates.

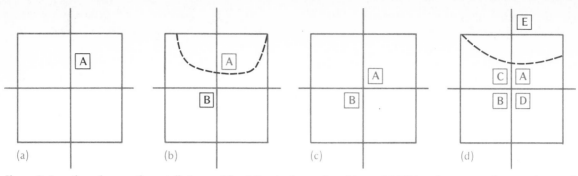

Figure 2 Location of competing retail stores with relation to the center of town. (a) With only one store in town, it gets all the business no matter where it locates. (b) With two stores, the one in the center will probably receive more business. (c) Two stores in the center of town will tend to split business. (d) With many stores in the center of town, the store on the fringes may now be able to receive the largest share of business.

Figure 2 illustrates game theory at work in our retail store example. The situation in which only store A exists is shown in (a). The store is located away from the center of town. If the alternative for the town's citizens is a lengthy drive to a neighboring town, store A will get all or almost all the business. Suppose now that retailer B enters the scene. Wisely, B chooses a site near the main crossroads. For a while, store A may keep an advantage because of customer loyalty and habit. After a time, however, B will gain the economic advantage. Store A will attract business mostly from north of the dotted perimeter shown in (b). B will be left with a larger share of the population as potential customers.

If A responds by moving to the crossroads also, then the situation will be as shown in (c). Store A will have a chance of regaining old customers from the south end of town. They will not now have to drive past B to get to A. Each store will now have an even chance of obtaining new customers.

We can analyze the game with five players, which may be the case after the town has grown. We can further assume that the roles of A, B, C, D, and E were chosen by lot. It is true that at first A had all the economic power—the only store. As B, C, and D come along, their positions were taken near the center. However, E wisely chooses the edge of town as is shown in Figure 2d. Store E will get few customers from the south edge of town but may get almost all of the people living north of the dotted line. This leaves A, B, C, and D to fight it out for the rest. Shopping centers have suc-

cessfully followed the strategy of E—moving into the suburbs or periphery of the city.

A political game theory is illustrated in Figure 3. In (a), the candidate has chosen to present himself as moderate with somewhat conservative leanings. The line labeled "extreme liberal–extreme conservative" represents the broad political spectrum along which the candidate can take his stand.

In (b), candidate B enters the picture. As you can see, he has chosen to appeal to the most conservative voters. Candidate A thereupon moves closer to the middle of the spectrum. In a two-candidate election, B has chosen a losing strategy. B will certainly get the 20 to 30% of the votes of the most conservative members of the electorate. But by taking a moderate position, candidate A will get the support of most voters to the left of B on the political spectrum. This vote will include not only moderates and liberals. Even extreme liberals may vote for A. Their only other option is not to vote at all. Not voting will entail the risk of electing B, who is totally unacceptable to them.

The strategies usually employed by political game theorists is shown in (c). Both candidates wisely stake out positions near the middle and near each other. Candidate A is reasonably assured of getting the votes from those to his left on the political spectrum. Similarly, B should capture most of the spectrum to his right. Winning the election (and the game) depends upon capturing the middle ground. By reducing the number of voters in the middle, the job of campaigning is reduced. However, this strategy does lead to some frustration as one voter once expressed with the phrase "There isn't a dime's worth of difference among the lot of them!"

In each of the games above, the general idea was to gain political or economic power through choosing the correct strategy. Since the rules were simple, the results were fairly predictable. The players were free to make simple choices. In real life, however, and in complex game theories, choices may not be simple or free. If a candidate's position is controlled by a party or by a pressure group, then the player's road to power is clearly restricted. If the location of stores is predetermined by a planning board, then the player's choice of location is restricted by the actions of the board.

Also, the power of an individual player may not depend entirely upon his or her own skill or game assets. We may suppose that each player comes to the game with some "ability to play" and thus some power entirely his own. However, to get more power and influence the result of the game, he may have

to join with some of the other players in a coalition. A **coalition** is not a formal organization; rather, it is a loosely formed group which will disappear after the outcome is decided. The player's power is determined by what he contributes to the coalition, not by what his individual power is.

Game theory and political power

Game theory applied to politics can be particularly informative about how power is gained and exercised. For example, most of us would agree that the principle of one-person one-vote is a sound and democratic one. But is one person's vote really equal to every other person's? Game theory shows us that one vote does not necessarily have the same power to influence results as another vote.

To illustrate, consider the following situation of three players in a voting game: let there be one voter with six votes, a second voter with three votes, and finally a voter with only one vote. Is the second voter three times more powerful than the last? The answer is no. Actually, neither the second nor the third voter has any real power. Together they control 40% of the vote, but even together they cannot affect the result; they are powerless, both individually and together. Once the voter with six votes has voted, the result is determined. All power rests in the six votes of the first voter.

When votes are equally distributed among the players, the power of each depends upon his ability to join a coalition or group of other voters. Acting alone he is powerless. (Some coalitions are also powerless, as we saw in the case of the second and third voters above.) The power of a voter depends upon whether or not he joins a coalition that can move into the winning position. His power will be enhanced if his vote is the swing vote, the vote that brings victory. Having joined a coalition, the threat to withdraw may also add to a voter's power. If his vote is important, the rules of the game may offer him certain advantages to remain in the coalition. Also, a voter may gain power by joining a "blocking coalition." Such a coalition can not win the game, but, as long as it stays in existence, it can prevent any other coalitions from winning.

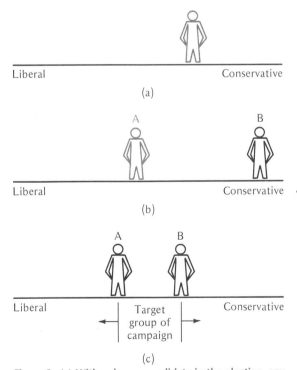

Figure 3 (a) With only one candidate in the election, any political stance will win. (b) With two candidates, the one who adopts an extreme position will probably lose. (c) In most elections with two candidates, both will try to move toward center and attempt to push the other further left or right.

Economic Thinker
Frank Knight

Among economists, Frank Knight (1885–1972) is known as more the philosopher than the scientist. Born in rural McLean County, Illinois, Knight attended Cornell University intending to pursue a Ph.D. in philosophy, but switched his major interest to economics. Soon after receiving his doctorate in economics, he went to the University of Chicago as an instructor. There, in 1921, he published his most famous book, *Risk, Uncertainty and Profit.* This study marked the beginning of his reputation as a proponent of the theory of pure economic competition. In it Knight distinguished between risk and uncertainty: risk is insurable, while uncertainty isn't. Profit is thus the reward to businesses for facing uncertainty in their decisions.

His writings and teaching at the University of Chicago, along with those of Henry Simons and Friedrich von Hayek, helped establish that institution's reputation as a citadel of neoclassical, libertarian economics. The "Chicago School of Economics," as it is known, is the foremost advocate of free enterprise and the greatest opponent of government "interference" in the market. That tradition is carried on today by Milton Friedman, George Stigler, and many others.

Knight recognized that the economic model of perfect competition is only an ideal. He was well aware that the marketplace is subject to the irrational application of power by individuals and groups and that this power distorts the free enterprise ideal. Nevertheless, to Knight, unbridled free enterprise was the only true economic wisdom. Economists, social scientists, and governments must not interfere with this ideal by trying to change social institutions through regulations and control. Such interference can only lead to revolution and dictatorship.

Knight's preoccupation with the virtues of free enterprise led him to the conclusion that the only economic models worth attention by economists were models based upon the ideal of perfect competition. Models and theories based upon the possibility of monopolistic interference with the marketplace were unproductive. If such monopolistic tendencies did exist, they would correct themselves in time. If there were imperfections in the free market system, such imperfections were caused by the ignorance of consumers, often influenced by advertising. Labor unions, with their great power to influence costs and prices, represented a dire threat to the free market system. On the other hand, corporate power, because it was subject to the uncertainty and risk of profit making, could not in the long run permanently disrupt the free market.

Despite his defense of the free enterprise system, Knight saw that the greatest enemies to the free market were some of those who argued for it. In *The Ethics of Competition,* a collection of his essays written between 1921 and 1935, he criticized free market arguments designed solely to

defend the special interest of those who profited by the existing social and economic order. Knight argued that there was nothing ethical about competition that resulted in unfair distribution of productive resources and monopolistic ownership of property and productive capacities. A truly free economic system must not be corrupted and abused by power-seeking individuals and institutions.

Knight, however, did not consider this possibility an economic or even a social problem. The problem is a moral one. Science had destroyed religion as a moral force, but had left nothing in its place. The danger existed that humanity would now turn to government to solve its problems. That road, Knight argued, could only lead to dictatorship and loss of freedom. The tendency of power to corrupt the free enterprise system must be checked by a common morality based on freedom to seek out the truth and on honesty and mutual respect.

Although firm in his insistence that the ideal of pure competition represented the best of all possible economic worlds, Frank Knight was equally insistent that all dogmas should be challenged. Generations of his students were taught to distrust all authority—even his. The quest for truth, he argued, in economics as in all else, must be an unending one if society is to remain free.

In the real-life political situation of 1976, members of a blocking coalition had very evident political power. Noncommitted delegates to the Republican national convention were publicly courted by the contenders for presidential nomination—Gerald Ford and Ronald Reagan. They were wined and dined by the Reagan campaign and flattered by invitations to the White House from the Ford staff. The race for nomination was expected to be close. The votes of the noncommitted delegates could not win the nomination for either man. But they could block the victory of either. Each such voter, therefore, held considerable power and was consequently wooed publicly by both contestants. Delegates already committed received much less attention.

Voting, of course, is not the only way political power is gained or used. As noted above, many other factors may be written into the rules of the game. The factors are not inventions of the game makers, as are the rules and hazards built into commercial games, such as Monopoly. Game theory factors represent real happenings in the real world.

For example, voting power itself is subject to events prior to voting. The power to pick who shall run for office may well be more important than the power of the voters who actually put the candidate in office. And once the candidate is in office, he may have the power to thwart the voters whose power put him there.

On the other hand, the people themselves may thwart or limit the political power of their elected representatives. For example, racial integration in the public schools is mandated by the power of law. Yet this power has been limited by that of groups acting outside the official political process. Public protests and disruptions, plus setting up new nonintegrated private schools in certain communities, have brought an outside power to bear on the situation. For a less serious instance of limitation on the power of elected public officials, consider our speed laws and the growing use of citizens band radios. Drivers often use their radios to warn of the presence of police officers charged with enforcing traffic laws.

Deciding what issue will be voted on is important. Even the wording of the question to be voted upon is important as conductors of public opinion polls well know. Consider, for example, the following question of an economist's survey: "Do you *plan* to buy a new car during the next six months?" If you have not made specific plans to do so, you would respond "no." However, your present car may be in very poor shape and about to collapse. You therefore feel that it will have to be replaced soon, even though you have settled on no set date. If the question had been "Do you *expect* to buy a new car in the next six months?" the answer may have been "probably," which is in the affirmative. The questions look almost identical, but the word "expect" is broader than "plan."

The factors built into political game theory must also include the real-life potential that the *objectives* of political power may be altered by the formation of special-interest coalitions. The only bonds between members may be that they agree strongly on some issue. For example, until the late 1960s an objective of the United States government was to prosecute and win the war in Southeast Asia. Gradually, however, many people came to believe this policy was wrong. The number of votes they could cast was far from a majority. So they formed protest groups to express their strong feelings in the media and in the streets. The protests culminated in a huge peace march on Washington in November, 1969. How much effect this and earlier protests actually had on the decision of the government to change its policy can not be known. But that it had some effect can not be doubted. The objective of government policy was eventually changed from prosecuting the war to ending it. The real-life antiwar players had ultimately wielded more power than they could as voters. Of course, the protests were more costly than merely voting. By undertaking the cost of the march, the protestors demonstrated the depths of their passion. A vote is a vote whether the voter feels strongly or not about the issue or candidate. Power may require strong feelings or commitment—feelings strong enough to form coalitions.

Politics, wealth, and economic power

We all know that wealth means power. If you are flat broke, you are likely to feel powerless. You can go almost nowhere and do almost nothing. A few dollars in your pocket and it's a different scene. You have regained your power to go places and do things. And your power grows as your dollars grow. With great wealth, your power can become enormous.

Economic Thinker
Thorstein Veblen

Thorstein Veblen (1857–1929) was probably America's greatest political economist. Sharp and incisive, he said much about contemporary economics that angered and upset his academic colleagues. To many, his views represented a total rebellion against the "given economic wisdom" of his day. Veblen, however, was never bothered by the hostile reception of his ideas, but delighted in disturbing the intellectual peace of his time.

Born in 1857 of Norwegian immigrant parents, Veblen spent his boyhood in rural Wisconsin. He studied at Carleton College, Johns Hopkins, Cornell, and Yale University, where he received his Ph.D. in economics. He taught at Chicago, Stanford, and Missouri universities, and, in his later years, at the New School for Social Research in New York. Never a popular instructor—his students complained that he mumbled rather than lectured—his teaching career was undistinguished. His unconventional social behavior and maverick ideas also contributed to his lack of professional success. He died, alone and impoverished, in 1929.

Veblen's best-known work, *The Theory of the Leisure Class,* was first published in 1899. In it he coined the still widely used term "conspicuous consumption." The phrase refers to how "the leisure class" tends to spend its wealth on unproductive goods and services designed solely to impress others. Vulgar ostentation becomes the road to social acceptance. Whenever possible, the middle class, and eventually even the poor, imitate the wealthy by also spending money wastefully in the illusory hope of becoming true members of the leisure class. Such behavior, Veblen contended, disputes the notion of diminishing marginal utility, which is a basic cornerstone of microeconomics. Diminishing marginal utility holds that the more an individual has of some good, the less satisfaction is provided by additional amounts. Thus diminishing marginal utility supports the law of

ethics of the jungle. In such an economy, the hands-off theories of the classical economists were, to Veblen, an invitation to social disaster. The power of the community at large must be brought to the marketplace to counter the power of the trusts and monopolies. Technology, Veblen believed, could bring about necessary political, social, and economic reform. But the people must have social control over technological change to prevent its being used to further enhance the power of the profit seekers.

Veblen wrote many books attacking the economic and social institutions of his day. Institutions themselves, he said, were little more than widespread habits of thought. They were not fixed in place for all time as many economists of his day and earlier seemed to believe. They were, instead, subject to evolutionary change in a constant power battle between those who wished to reform them and those who sought to keep them unchanged. Among such institutions, he said, were the universities. Universities had evolved into fiefdoms of administrators more concerned with intrigues and conspicuous extracurricular activities than with scholarship. The "captains of industry" wielded the real power through endowments and governing boards. Scholars had to defer to this power in order to maintain their positions. What was taught in the universities was what the business leaders wanted to be taught—conformity to accepted social behavior and to the "given wisdom" of economic thinkers who considered contemporary capitalism a near-perfect system. Veblen argued this position in a book called *Higher Learning in America* (1918). It is interesting to note that he chose as subtitle for the book "A Study in Total Depravity." Although he later dropped this subtitle, its uncompromising tone is a measure of the uncompromising and hard-hitting nature of Veblen's criticism of the social fabric and institutions of his day.

demand. However, Veblen said that more goods might be sold at higher than at lower prices when "conspicuousness" replaced value as the criterion for purchase; this could undermine many economic theories.

Veblen believed that the evolutionary process in the United States had brought about an economic system motivated solely by profit. Its ultimate object was to produce gain, not goods. When the captains of industry found they had produced too many goods and services to maintain their profit margin, they used their power of monopoly or near-monopoly to restrict production. If necessary, they would use the power of their wealth to maintain profits through unproductive military expenditures and even war.

Profit seeking produces a predatory economy in which the power of profits takes precedence over the production of goods and services—no matter what the cost to society. The ethics of the marketplace is the

Wealth as a source of power

The relationships between wealth and power are many. One of the more frequent, simple, and apparently harmless forms of linking wealth to power is through "conspicuous consumption." By spending money in a conspicuous or showy fashion, the wealthy individual calls attention to himself or herself as someone special: special only because of wealth. Money may be lavished on personal grooming, clothing, large automobiles, and big houses. Obvious leisure can be a sign of wealth. Credit cards or accounts at expensive, fashionable stores and restaurants are visible signs of wealth. The very rich may vacation at some exotic place—not isolated but in the company of other obviously wealthy individuals. Even contributing to, or raising funds for, charities and other worthy projects may be undertaken with an eye for publicity or the society page of a newspaper.

Conspicuous consumption is based on the premise that most members of our society automatically and tacitly assume the wealthy individual is successful and hence powerful, or has the potential of power. The display of money is, in effect, a display of power. As crude and vulgar as these conspicuous spending activities are, they are apparently effective. Conspicuous consumption is indeed so effective that the lower middle class and poor often imitate the rich in this way. Secretaries may vacation where their bosses do—on a less frequent basis, of course. Some of the poor may spend what little they have on flashy or expensive clothes and autos. "Keeping up with the Joneses" is a syndrome based to a certain extent on conspicuous consumption.

These activities are a further concern to the economist when they become a poor allocation of society's scarce resources or when they are undertaken at the expense of future consumption and growth.

Voting, candidates, and wealth

Great wealth can be particularly vexing with regard to its impact on our society's basic political institution: democracy. It is no secret that it takes money, often a great deal of money, to be elected to political office. And it is no secret that people who finance political campaigns expect to gain or maintain power—often economic power—by doing so. There is nothing necessarily sinister about this. Wealth may be used in political campaigns to foster the good of society. The well-financed candidate may truly be the best individual for the job.

Nevertheless, the fact remains that wealth, especially great wealth, can, and too often does, unduly influence the political process. "Power corrupts," said the British historian Lord Acton, "and absolute power corrupts absolutely." It is against this innate tendency toward corruption that democracies must be constantly on guard. When economic and political power are joined together, the tendency toward corruption is vastly increased.

Our history is replete with examples of the corruption of political institutions by economic power. We have all heard about political "bosses" and other politicians who used their political power to gain economic power for themselves and their friends. New York's nineteenth-century politician Boss Tweed is a prime example. He succeeded in robbing the public treasury of millions of dollars before he was brought to justice. We know, too, how early American financiers J. P. Morgan, Jay Gould, John D. Rockefeller, and others used venal politicians to further their financial empires. In our own day, it is not exactly uncommon to learn of bribery and payoffs between politicians and persons of wealth. And, of course, criminal collusion between politicians and wealthy campaign contributors was a basic factor in the Watergate scandal that toppled the administration of Richard Nixon.

Many more such historical examples might be given. And, human nature being what it is, it can be expected that they will continue to occur. Such illegal uses of economic and political power can only be dealt with by the countervailing powers of an alert electorate, a free press, and the legal system. But there are also perfectly legal ties between politics and economics in our democracy. The student of economics should at least be aware of their existence within the complexities of our economic system.

Regulatory agencies Volumes could be and have been written about the ties between business, wealth, and politics. We can scarcely do more here than what we have already done: point out their existence. But perhaps a brief look at government regulatory agencies will be instructive.

Governments, especially the federal government, abound with agencies and commissions intended to oversee and regulate certain segments of our economy. The Food and Drug Administration, for example, is intended to ensure that the food we eat and the drugs we take for our health will not poison or otherwise injure us. The oil industry, the natural gas industry, the banking industry, the aviation industry—to name just a very few—are likewise subject to agency regulation.

The work of such agencies is vital to the welfare of society. Without them, such industries might be even further removed from our ideal state of perfect competition. It is the regulatory agency's job to check this power. The problem arises with who is to be appointed to make policy in these organizations.

Often, perhaps far too often, the people appointed to run such agencies are drawn from the industry being regulated. An executive from Shell Oil is appointed to the agency regulating the oil industry, for example. Or a Dow Chemical executive goes to the Food and Drug Administration. When their terms of office expire, they frequently return to the payrolls of their industry. Now this does not mean that such appointees will not serve the public interest in their agency jobs. But certainly there would be a temptation to promulgate economic and social policies favorable to the industry one was once a part of and to which one expects to return.

This so-called "revolving door" staffing policy of regulatory agencies has been the subject of much criticism. In the election of 1976, both presidential candidates pledged to correct the situation. Some progress has been made in this direction. For example, some federal regulatory agencies now require that appointees from the regulated industry agree not to return to that industry for a stipulated number of years after leaving the agency. But the problem remains. People with expertise about an industry are difficult to find outside that industry. The power of an industry to see to it that its interests are *overrepresented* in the regulatory agency is difficult to check.

The Campaign Funding Law In 1975, Congress passed a Campaign Funding Law designed to counter the power of wealth in presidential campaigns. The law provided that the major presidential candidates could finance their campaigns from public funds. Each candidate receives $21.8 million for this purpose. Candidates are forbidden to spend more, even from their own personal funds. The money itself comes from the taxpayers via a voluntary $1.00 checkoff on personal income tax. (After paying out a total of $72.3 million for the 1976 primary and presidential campaigns, the fund still had a surplus of $23 million.)

The law also provided for public funding of congressional elections, but this particular provision was invalidated by the Supreme Court.

The funding law proved to be a considerable success in the 1976 presidential election. Some flaws became evident as the campaigns progressed, but legislation has been proposed to correct them. Certain loopholes in the law are to be closed and other imperfections corrected. Most importantly, efforts are being made to meet the Supreme Court's objections to public funding of congressional elections in the original law.

The Campaign Funding Law of 1975 and its revisions will not eliminate the power of great wealth to influence political institutions. But the cumulative weight of millions of one-dollar individual contributions provides a much needed public counter power to the power of wealth in the political process.

Extended Example
Lobby Power

A lobbyist is one who attempts to bring about government decisions favorable to "special interests." Sound sinister, perhaps even subversive or illegal? Not at all. Lobbying is an accepted and perfectly legal exercise of individual or group power. In a sense, it supplements representative government. Your Congressional representative, for example, represents all the people in your district. But it may happen that you wish your representative to favor (or not to favor) a law that is of special concern to you or to a group whose aims are in accord with yours—a law concerning legalization of marijuana, perhaps, or water pollution by the chemical industry. So you sign a petition or write a letter to your representative. You become, in effect, a lobbyist for a "special interest."

Lobbying is, of course, much more than a simple matter of letter writing or petition signing. It is also a highly sophisticated and high-budgeted process practiced by well-organized special-interest groups. Lobbying groups representing corporations, banks, consumers, organized labor, education, medicine, farming—to name just a few—spend large amounts of money to influence legislation and government regulations. Public-interest groups such as Common Cause and Ralph Nader's organizations fight for government legislation favorable to what they see as the public welfare. Lobbying groups maintain permanent, government-regulated organizations in Washington and in most state capitals in order to bring group power to bear on legislation affecting their political and economic interests.

One such group, as yet little known outside business and economic circles, is the Business Roundtable. It was formed in 1972 to counter the atmosphere generated by critics of business. With its membership now including chief executives of major businesses and corporations, its influence as a pro-business lobby is growing rapidly—perhaps at the expense of more traditional business groups such as the United States Chamber of Commerce and the National Association of Manufacturers. As might be expected, the Roundtable group worked closely with the Republican administrations of Presidents Nixon and Ford in helping to formulate laws and regulations conducive to business interests. It now works equally closely—but perhaps a little less easily—with the Democratic administration of President Carter.

One reason for the Roundtable's growing success as a lobbyist for business power (aside from its large budget, around $2.5 million in 1977) is its willingness to move with the times. For example, when the Labor Department was drafting regulations for business to follow in hiring minorities, old-line business lobbyists, in time-honored fashion, denounced the whole idea of government acting as an agent of social change. Hands off the free enterprise system was the cry. Roundtable spokesmen, on the other hand, accepted the idea in principle and asked only that regulations for minority hiring be drawn with the least possible disruption to established business practices. Many of the guidelines suggested by the Roundtable were later accepted by the Labor Department. A similar approach was used when Congress was drafting a bill to control industry's use and manufacture of toxic substances. The Roundtable did not rant against government interference in the "business of business." It was not unalterably opposed to such legislation. Instead, it lobbied for a control law that it could live with.

Of course, other lobbying groups, such as Common Cause or the AFL-CIO, might argue that, despite its seeming reasonableness, the Roundtable wields more business influence over government than is warranted or wanted. But that is the name of the lobby power game. Such other groups also have their organized lobbies to make sure their voices are heard in the domestic, political and economic arena.

Foreign governments and foreign interests also maintain lobbies in an attempt to influence United States laws and international activities. Perhaps the most famous (or infamous, depending on one's point of view) was the so-called "China Lobby." For years following the Communist victory, Nationalist Chinese in exile on Taiwan and their American sympathizers lobbied for United States aid to China's defeated leader, Chiang Kaishek, with a view to his ultimate return to the mainland as conqueror of the Red regime. The China Lobby made its influence felt in United States foreign and domestic politics until very recent times. More than one American politician was elected or defeated on the basis of support or lack of support from the lobby. Military appropriations and foreign alliances were more than a little influenced by its interests and wishes. Indeed, it is not too much to say that our military involvement in Southeast Asia was partly a result of the China Lobby's contribution to the American mind-set of the times.

The main impetus for the China Lobby was ideological—that is, the concept of "democracy" versus "communism." Other foreign lobbies are more attuned to economic concerns. For example, the price of sugar is of great concern to the economies of the Dominican Republic and the Philippines. The price of coffee is important to Brazil, as is the price of tin to Bolivia, or, indeed, the price of the Volkswagen to West Germany. Lobbyists from these (and from other similarly concerned countries) actively seek to influence legislation that has bearing upon what Americans will pay for such products. These lobbyists also argue against imposing tariffs and quotas on imported goods.

Such lobbyists are seldom content with presenting their viewpoints to American legislators. More subtle persuasion is also prevalent. *Junkets* (free and often luxurious trips, generally to the lobbyist's homeland) are offered to legislators and their families so that, ostensibly, the situation can be studied firsthand. Lavish parties may be given for key legislators. Gifts and favors, sometimes illicit if not illegal, may likewise be offered and accepted.

As might be expected, the line between legality and illegality in this kind of exercise of power can sometimes become blurred. Do gifts and favors from lobbyists "buy" votes favorable to the economic interests of foreign governments? (Or, for that matter, votes favorable to the economic interest of domestic lobbyists?) To take a bribe, whether from a lobbyist or any other source, in return for a vote is definitely against the law. But who is to say that a junket, or an invitation to a party, or a free ski resort weekend was the deciding factor in a government official's decision to support or not to support a piece of legislation or a proposed regulation? In most cases, the verdict would have to be something equivalent to the Scottish judicial outcome called "not proven."

Sometimes, of course, lobbyists overstep the bounds of propriety into blatant illegality. In 1976, for example, Washington was shaken by revelations about attempts by South Korean businessmen to influence legislation through illegal campaign contributions and other payments to members of Congress. Over $1 million per year to scores of Congressmen was said to have been involved in this illegal application of lobby power.

For the most part, however, lobbyists operate well within the law. Campaign contributions from domestic sources are legal. Short of complete public financing of elections, they are also necessary. Business lobbies such as the Roundtable, public service lobbies such as Common Cause, or labor lobbies such as the AFL-CIO are not out to buy votes. They are out to influence legislation. They do so by rewarding their friends and punishing their enemies—particularly through legal campaign contributions.

That organized lobby groups have considerable power and are adept at its exercise is a fact of economic life. In an open society, however, lobbies are properly subject to public scrutiny. Hopefully, under such scrutiny, competing interests of the nation's various lobby groups will serve as checks and balances, one against the other, much as the Constitution provides for checks and balances in government itself.

Organizations banding together for power

The individual may do well or poorly in the struggle for power. We have seen how individuals may acquire power to influence others. We have examined the quest for power through organization. The individual loses power to organizations. Yet some individuals have power within the organization. The analysis need not end here. We may ask if the limit of power is set by the organization. The answer is no. Organizations may get together to increase their power even more. The combination of organizations may be a formal grouping or linking or it may be a rather casual arrangement. We will examine three models which attempt to explain the phenomenon of multi-organization power. The first, *interlocking directorates*, deals with purely economic organizations. The second, the *corporate state*, deals with combinations of economic, political, and other organizations. Finally, *multinational firms* show how economic and political organizations may go beyond national boundaries.

Corporate power and interlocking directorates

Wealth is generated through control of productive assets, and wealth generates power. In our economy, this kind of power is usually exercised through the business corporation. The bulk of this power is in the hands of the corporation's board of directors. Sometimes the power is fairly evenly divided among the board members. Often, however, the board itself is controlled by one or a few members who happen to own the lion's share of the company's stock. For example, the business publication *Fortune* estimates that at least 150 of the nation's 500 largest corporations are controlled by one individual or a few members of a single family. Since the wealth of the nation's large corporations is vast, it follows that they have the power to influence and control many outcomes in the marketplace.

The power of a corporation's directors and hence of the corporation itself may extend well beyond a single corporation. One firm may associate itself with one or more other corporations in order to enhance its power. It is not necessary to acquire another firm or to merge with it (although this is one method a corporation may use to increase its wealth and power). Instead, a corporation may use the device known as an *interlocking directorate*.

An **interlocking directorate** (or **"interlock"**) means that directors of one corporation may also be directors of other closely allied corporations. A director of a computer-producing corporation, for example, may also sit on the board of a company that supplies certain computer components. Or a director of the component-supply company may also be an official of a chemical company that produces the metal alloys used in making computer components. It is easy to see that cooperation between and among such corporations would be likely to enhance profits and hence enhance the power of each corporation to influence the marketplace.

Figure 4 shows how a group of United States petroleum companies are actually interrelated with each other and with other interdependent firms. The names of the petroleum companies are pointed within six-sided symbols. The names of the other firms are shown within circles. Links between and among the corporations are represented by a line connecting the firms. Members of the boards of directors of the various companies are identified by a number. Some members are listed only once, as they link only two firms. Others may serve on several different boards. For example, number 38 is on the board of Cities Service as can be seen at the left edge of the figure. That same number also appears on the boards of Hewlett-Packard, Colgate Palmolive, Mutual Life, and Chemical Bank of New York.

Note that there are no direct ties between one petroleum company and another. *Antitrust prohibits direct interlocks between firms in the same industry.* It thus prevents complete and direct control of industry-wide product prices. But note that there are many cases where only one firm intervenes between one petroleum firm and another. This link is often a financial institution such as an insurance firm or a bank. Such links may be very significant in the wielding of corporate power.

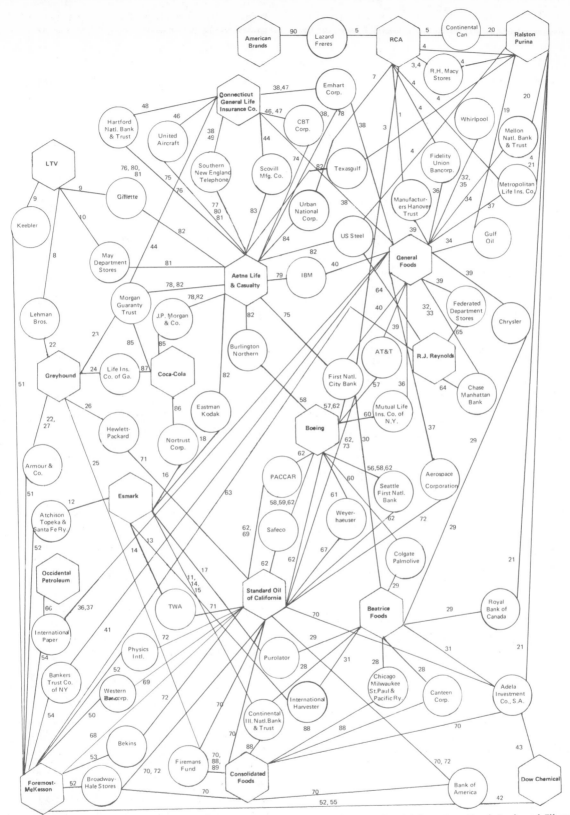

Figure 4 Interlocking directors of oil companies. (This chart is taken from a "Special Report on Food, Fuel, and Fiber," prepared by the Institute for Southern Studies, in *Southern Exposure*, Fall, 1974, published at Box 230, Chapel Hill, North Carolina 27514.)

Organizations Banding Together for Power 505

For example, banks make loans to petroleum companies, and petroleum companies maintain large deposits of money in banks. It is very useful to the oil company to have a friendly member on the bank's board of directors when the firm applies for a loan. Likewise, the bank is happy to have one of its own people sitting on the firm's board when the firm is deciding where it wishes to deposit its cash.

There is nothing illegal about all this. But clearly, the economic power of the cooperating institutions is enhanced by such arrangements. The power of the corporation is increased because of its increased ability to obtain capital for maintenance and expansion of production. In addition, its power may be increased because of the reluctance of interlocking banks to lend capital to competing petroleum firms outside the interlock. The bank's power is, of course, increased by the addition to its deposits.

Interlocking insurance companies play much the same role. When petroleum companies wish to obtain long-term loans, perhaps for construction of complex drilling machinery that may take many years to prove profitable, they often turn to insurance companies. (The assets of life insurance companies are well-suited for long-term lending.) As with banks and oil companies, when directors with mutual interests sit on the boards of interlocking petroleum and insurance companies, the power of each is greatly enhanced. The petroleum company has a ready source of long-term loans so that it can grow. The insurance company may also experience increased sales perhaps by using the credit card system of the petroleum company to reach and sell to more customers. Both may act together to influence legislation which will improve the business climate.

Interlocking directorates can increase corporate powers in many ways other than the examples noted above. To give but one further example: suppose a corporation wishes to raise money by issuing stocks or bonds. The corporation does so through a financial institution called an *investment bank*. It borrows the money from this institution. In return for the money, the investment bank reserves securities (stocks or bonds) which represent assets and/or potential assets of the company. It then sells these securities, mostly to other large financial institutions such as banks and insurance companies.

If such institutions are already linked to the borrowing corporations, they are more likely to purchase the securities. If the investment bank is linked to the corporation, it is more likely to "underwrite" its securities (lend it the money) in the first place.

The power of a corporation is measured by its wealth. When access to new financial capital (new wealth) is made easier through business links with lending institutions, its power is increased.

The corporate state

Economic organizations and political organizations may also combine to gain power. The growth of large corporations in this century has been paralleled by the growth of the executive branch of government—the power of the presidency and the President's many appointed offices (especially in the Cabinet). The two are related. Some have called the symbiotic situation of corporate and executive power the **corporate state.**

Earlier we mentioned how regulatory agencies and the industries to be regulated exchange personnel. In the corporate state, the large corporations and the executive branch trade people back and forth. The same people make decisions in both spheres. Both political and economic power are concentrated in a group of people—called a **power elite**—who can decide who else will be admitted to the "club." For example, the President may choose Cabinet members or other high posts within each department from available company presidents. When these members' terms are over, they will often return to industry, sometimes with the same firm, sometimes as a consultant. Other groups, such as universities or labor unions, may be tapped by the executive branch from time to time. John Kenneth Galbraith has called this process **bureaucratic symbiosis.** This is, while the bureaucracies do not formally merge, by exchanging "parts" they create a climate more favorable to each other.

Though it may be inevitable that such exchanges occur in the search for the "best qualified individual," there is obviously much room for abuse.

Examples of this interchange of people may be found in the formation of his Cabinet by President Carter. The Secretary of Defense and Secretary of Commerce were respectively a university president and vice-president. The Secretary of the Treasury was president of a large bank. The people chosen are undoubtedly very able. They need not show any special favoritism for the organizations they left. Yet, by a series of decisions, there are subtle changes made which improve the power position of both organizations, perhaps at the expense of the individual members.

There are few people who dare to challenge the power elite, once it's in a position of power. As long as people feel secure and have at least certain levels of consumption now and in the predictable future, most people do not even care who is making the decisions. There may be no spokesman for the general public interest. This does not mean that a challenge could not be mounted. It would be possible to form a voting bloc consisting of small businessmen, small farmers, urban liberals, conservatives everywhere, racial minorities, and blue-collar workers. The power could be shifted to a different set of leaders. But unless such a dramatic shift does occur, it is clear that the government's ability to control large corporations is impaired.

Organizations are bound together by a general interest or ideology and by an internal government. There is generally a set of rules or laws which members are to observe. There are also officers charged with exercising not their own power but that of the group against the members of the group. The form of government varies as much among organizations as it does among countries. In form, the government may be centered in one or a few people or it may be quite democratic. The government may be benevolent or despotic.

Organizational governments interact with political governments, power groups, or other organizational governments. Larger organizations or corporations may transcend city and even state governments. Large organizations may relate to the federal government in the same way a state government does. The corporate government controls the members of the organization the same way a state does. To change governments, an individual must change organizations or change their state of residence. The cost is unevenly distributed since it costs the state or organization little or nothing to substitute one person for another. For the real person to change states requires an expensive move. Power distributes the burden to those least able to bear it.

Multinational corporations and power

As we have seen, political power and economic power often go hand in hand. We may examine the case where there are multiple sovereign states as well as economic organizations. Multinational corporations are particularly instructive in this regard. **Multinational corporations** are companies which operate extensively in other countries in addition to the one in which they are based. Most large United States corporations are multinational. They do business, either directly or through wholly owned subsidiaries, in many countries. At least 20% of the total assets of such corporations come from operations in foreign countries. The percentage is a good deal higher for some corporations, especially those dealing in the commodities of foreign lands, such as rubber and oil.

Table 1 shows the total production of goods and services of some of the world's largest countries along with that of some of the largest multinational corporations. Of the forty-five largest producers on the list, fifteen, or one-third, are multinational corporations. Five of the fifteen corporations are not based in the United States. One firm, Exxon, produces more goods and services than do fifteen national economies on the list. Russia and China undoubtedly outrank Exxon, but data were not available and so they are not included in Table 1. We must proceed with some care in making the comparison since the GNP data for

Table 1
Total Output for Largest Economies and Largest International Corporations (1975)*

Country of firm	Billions of dollars	Country or firm	Billions of dollars
1. United States	1294.9	24. Iran	25.6
2. Japan	413.1	25. **Texaco**	**24.5**
3. West Germany	348.2	26. **Ford**	**24.0**
4. France	255.1	27. Turkey	22.0
5. United Kingdom	174.8	28. **Mobil**	**20.6**
6. Italy	138.3	29. **National Iranian Oil**	**18.9**
7. Canada	118.9	30. Norway	18.8
8. Brazil	77.2	31. **British Petroleum**	**17.3**
9. India	71.0	32. Finland	17.1
10. Spain	60.2	33. **Standard Oil of California**	**16.8**
11. Netherlands	59.7	34. Greece	16.3
12. Australia	52.2	35. Venezuela	16.1
13. Sweden	50.1	36. Indonesia	15.4
14. Mexico	48.7	37. **Unilever**	**15.0**
15. Belgium	45.7	38. Nigeria	14.8
16. **Exxon**	**44.9**	39. **IBM**	**14.4**
17. Switzerland	40.9	40. **Gulf Oil**	**14.3**
18. **General Motors**	**35.7**	41. **General Electric**	**13.4**
19. **Royal Dutch-Shell**	**32.1**	42. **Chrysler**	**11.7**
20. Argentina	31.4	43. New Zealand	11.7
21. Austria	27.9	44. **International Tel & Tel**	**11.4**
22. Denmark	27.4	45. Portugal	11.2
23. South Africa	26.1		

*Russia, China, and Eastern European nations data not available. Also, sales data of firms may include double counting of intrafirm sales, which are eliminated from GNP data.
Source: for countries, *World Almanac*, AID supplied; for companies, *Fortune*.

a country are not quite the same data as net sales for a corporation. However, the point remains that the multinational corporations are quite large.

It is not difficult to see how a powerful multinational corporation can gain political as well as economic power in a host country. The simplest method, of course, is outright bribery of the country's leader. Prior to the mid-1970s such bribery was generally thought to be confined to operations in underdeveloped countries, and not all that important to the host country's political life. A few gifts to the local sheik, a few machine guns to help a local governor keep law and order in his province, perhaps a discreet contribution to a local leader's favorite "charity"—such activities were generally considered little more than a slight addition to the cost of doing business in a foreign country.

True, the American public was vaguely aware that in some areas the economic power of American companies (and that of the corporations of some other developed nations)

was closely allied to the area's political power. For example, the power of United Fruit Company over the political life of Central and South America's so-called "banana republics" had been widely publicized. But such countries were, after all—well, just banana republics. Did it really matter that economic and political power were virtually indistinguishable in such places?

Then in the mid-1970s came the shocking revelation of far more extensive international corporate bribery than had been thought. And it was revealed that the corruption of host-country political leaders was not confined to underdeveloped nations. Multinational corporations were revealed to have bribed the leaders of highly developed nations in their efforts to gain economic power through control of political power. The scandals resulting from

Lockheed Aircraft's bribery toppled the government of Japan and disgraced the royal family of the Netherlands. In Italy, the scandal contributed to the growing strength of the Italian Communist Party in that nation's elections.

But the power of multinational corporations does not depend on bribery. The true power of multinational corporations derives from prevailing economic circumstances and perfectly legal business procedures.

In many cases, the host country of a multinational corporation is quite willing—in some cases, desperate—to trade some of its political power for the economic advantage offered to the nation by the corporation's willingness to locate there. The corporation will perhaps help the country to develop its resources. The multinational firm may provide the capital to mine or harvest basic commodities. The firm may train the citizens in modern business and industrial techniques, thus developing the nation's human resources. Most importantly, it will provide jobs and purchasing power for the nation's people.

Consequently, the host nation is ready to offer incentives to the corporation. It may provide low tax rates on the company's profits, for example, or see to it that the company has easy and free access to the country's rivers and roads for transportation of its products. It may restrict the power of its citizens to protest ecological or personal disruptions caused by the plant's facilities. It might prohibit formation of labor unions whose demands could limit the corporation's profits.

In general, the weaker the host country's economy is, the greater the corporation's power to influence its political (and social) life. If a government believes the corporation's benefits are essential to its economy (and perhaps even to its survival), it will offer many incentives to the corporation. If the corporation is powerful enough, it may gain almost complete political control of the country. The French economist Servan-Shreiber has argued that in some circumstances the host country can become a virtual colony of the corporation and, by extension, of the corporation's home country. In truth, something like this did happen in Central and South America's "banana republics" in the early twentieth century. And it happened elsewhere in earlier periods, particularly with trading companies formed by colonial powers such as Spain, Great Britain, and France.

But countervailing power can be brought against multinational corporations. Once the corporation's facilities are in place, they may become a source of power to the host country. There is always the threat that they can be taken over (*nationalized*) by the government. Also, what the government has given, it can take away. For example, favorable tax rates can suddenly become less favorable, which in effect becomes a countervailing power against that of multinational corporations.

Because of such pressures and because of changing national and international economic conditions, American and European multinationals have in recent years begun to limit their foreign operations.

We have gone into considerable detail about the use (and abuse) of power in our economic system. Yet we have barely touched the surface of this interesting and complex subject.

Almost any one of us could add to the story: the economic power of the small-factory owner in your home town, perhaps. Or the power of your labor union to control your livelihood. Or the power of government or defense industries to influence the policies of your college or university through grants of research money. All such exercises of power, and many, many others, are constantly acting and interacting in our dynamic economy.

As we study economics, it is well to keep in mind that our market economy is guided not only by the "invisible hand." The fist of power is also in the game.

Viewpoint
The Invisible Hand in Your Pocket

In the mid-1970s, the nation was hit by a series of scandals involving big-business bribery. First came the Watergate scandal, which included stories of illegal contributions to the 1972 campaign of President Nixon by some of the largest corporations in America. These contributions were, in effect if not in law, payment of bribes in return for expected preferential treatment of these corporations in the coming administration. Senator Frank Church of Idaho, for example, reported that a former Grumman Aircraft official said he had been solicited for a $1 million campaign contribution by a Nixon aide in return for assistance in landing a contract to sell planes to Japan.

Then came revelations by a Senate subcommittee that American multinational corporations had been paying huge bribes to businessmen and officials of foreign countries to facilitate selling their products. Lockheed Aircraft Corporation, it was revealed, had paid out $24.4 million in bribes to help sell its planes to foreign countries, particularly in Japan, the Netherlands, and Italy! Reports soon followed of other multinationals—most but not all in the business of selling military hardware—being heavily involved in overseas bribery.

Once the initial public shock wave over such revelations had passed, the big-business community reacted to restore its image. Its answer to the charges was simply that "everybody does it." If American companies did not pay bribes, they would be at an economic disadvantage with their foreign competitors. There was no law against such bribes, and, according to Commerce Secretary Elliot Richardson, any such law would be "unenforceable." In addition, the State Department warned against public discussion of bribes paid to foreign officials lest it damage our relationships with the countries involved.

In short, bribery by American multinational companies should not be a matter for public concern. It is an accepted application of big-business power and, as such, is strictly an internal business matter. But is this all there is to it? Aside from the question of ethics and the very real foreign policy problem of American corporate interference in the sovereign governments of other nations, there are also economic factors to be considered. Can anyone doubt that bribery dollars will *not* come out of company profits? Or that they *will* come out of the pockets of American consumers of the bribe-giver's products? The American economy (and also the economies of affected foreign nations) will ultimately pay the bill—either through higher prices for consumer goods sold by the corporation or through higher taxes to pay for higher priced military goods.

Among those who most staunchly defend bribery as necessary for overseas business may also be found the staunchest defenders of the free market economy ideal. Nowhere is it written, however, that the invisible hand Adam Smith postulated to guide such an economy was intended to pick the pockets of its consumers.

Business bribery and related practices on the domestic scene have also reached alarming proportions. The United States Chamber of Commerce estimates that the cost of so-called white-collar crime in the United States is a staggering $40 billion a year! Such crime ranges from corporate embezzlement to employee rip-off of office machinery and supplies. Bribes and kickbacks alone add about $7 billion to the cost of doing business in the American economy.

One focal point of business bribery is the company officials charged with purchasing goods and services. Far too often, graft and bribe-taking are considered a way of life among some such employees. The mode of operation is generally simplicity itself. A purchasing agent buys supplies with the tacit understanding that part of the cost of the supplies will be "kicked back" to the agent. Few industries or businesses are immune to this kind of bribery. It is estimated, for example, that in New York's second largest industry, printing, one out of every eight dollars goes to bribery or other forms of graft. Purchasing agents are not, of course, the only people involved in illegal business gratuities. Many other company officials are subject to the temptation and taint of business bribery. One case in point is the recent "payola" scandals involving disc jockeys who took payment in cash, and sometimes in narcotics, in return for plugging the records of certain recording companies.

One reason for the high incidence of bribery and other white-collar business crime in the American economy is that the penalty for such crime is slight—assuming that the culprit can be found out and is prosecuted. Bribery, unless it involves an elected official, is classed as a misdemeanor in the states where the bulk of American businesses have their headquarters. In New York, the maximum prison term on conviction for bribery is three months; in New Jersey, one year. Illinois merely levies a fine not exceeding $5,000. Some states, Ohio, California, and Massachusetts, for example, have no specific laws at all against commercial bribery. In addition, there is the tendency of judges to be very lenient with nonviolent criminals who, perhaps like themselves, are known as family men and upstanding pillars of the community.

Stronger laws against business bribery are undoubtedly necessary. In addition, the business community itself must take increased measures to police its operations if the drain on the economy from business crime is to be stopped. In the meantime, it must be recognized that domestic bribery and other forms of business crime have a potent effect on the economy of the nation. In the end, and as with overseas bribery, it is the public that pays for business crime—in disruption of the marketplace and in higher prices for goods and services.

Summary

The 1970s have seen economists become more interested in political economy. Economists are also making great efforts to understand economic behavior of people that isn't well described by present models. Such efforts have led economists to study how power affects economic outcomes.

In the product markets, the ideal and desired situation is perfect competition, where no power is exerted. In monopoly, oligopoly, and monopolistic competition, firms have power and can reduce output and raise prices. This market power is acceptable only when it is balanced by a countervailing power.

Every individual has a certain amount of power; the factors that determine the amount of this power can be shown by an opportunity set. Personal and economic power can increase in organization with other people.

The power of an organization may be greater than the sum of power of its members. As organization power increases, many individual members find that, although the economic benefits increase, they lose personal power and identity. Organizations maintain their power by trying to ensure the loyalty of members (employees) by offering personal benefits like insurance, medical benefits, credit unions, and by holding conventions, picnics, and group discussions.

Game theory is used to select the most statistically favorable strategy for gaining economic power or profit. In a "game" with two players, the player closer to the center of business or the political spectrum increases his chances for "winning."

There are many connections between power and wealth. A common connection is conspicuous consumption. Wealth is also used to increase power by contributing to the selection of political candidates. Wealthy individuals can corrupt our political institutions in order to earn special favors. Government is entrusted with the power to regulate many industries. However, all too often the "regulators" are drawn from industry and return to industry jobs. The Campaign Funding Law of 1975 has helped reduce the power of the wealthy in presidential elections.

Corporations can band together for mutual economic gains through interlocking directorates. The growth of government executive power and corporate power to serve mutual interests is called a corporate state. The corporate state is run by a power elite through a process of bureaucratic symbiosis. Multinational corporations often wield great power in the host nations.

Key Words and Phrases

- **power** the ability to exert a desired action or to increase the chances of an action.
- **countervailing power** a power used to neutralize some existing power; unions may act as countervailing power to business power.
- **opportunity set** the sum of actions open to an individual at some given time.
- **game theory** the use of mathematical probabilities to make economic decisions in certain situations.
- **coalition** a loosely formed group to help bring about some outcome, after which it dissolves.
- **interlocking directorate** a situation where some members of the board of directors for one company are also board members of closely allied companies.

- **corporate state** a political condition where centralized executive power (presidency) is tied to, and serves the best interests of, large corporations.
- **power elite** a group of individuals who shuttle between high-level corporate and government jobs and who hold political and economic power.
- **multinational corporations** large corporations that operate in more than one country.

Questions for Review

1. What is countervailing power? Cite three examples of countervailing power.

2. What attributes affect an individual's power?

3. How is power wielded in an organization?

4. The "organization man" might say "Don't blame me." Explain how this attitude evolves.

5. Explain how the power elite functions through bureaucratic symbiosis.

6. What methods can multinational corporations use to gain power over host nations? What methods have host nations adopted to curtail multinational power?

7. Explain how the interlocking directorate operates to gain and maintain power.

24

Consumer Demand and Utility

"Let your fingers do the walking through the Yellow Pages," runs the advertising slogan. Most of us do just that, once we have decided what we want to buy. Knowing what we want must come first. How do we decide?

A glance at the Yellow Pages of any phone directory will show that the variety of goods and services available is far greater than the capacity of our pocketbooks. In fact, we are confronted every day with a bewildering array of prices and qualities of goods and services, even among those necessary for life. At the supermarket we find hundreds of food items to choose among, while in a large department store there are enough goods to furnish almost anybody's life-style. We usually manage to choose among all these things (though later we sometimes wish that we had chosen differently).

Economists have a theory of how we do this. It is called the *theory of consumer choice*. The theory is important because it helps to explain how individuals express their preferences in free markets. Then the decisions of millions of consumers, made in thousands of stores and shops, must somehow influence production of all the goods and services we want.

If we look closely, we find common patterns in the way consumers make their choices. These patterns apply to fur coats and beer, dental care and hockey tickets, copper tubing and laboratory technicians. The principles that explain consumer choice are fundamental to the competitive market system. It is consumer choice that guides the decisions of producers on *what* is to be produced, *how* production is to be carried out, and *for whom* output is to be provided. Without knowing it, consumers send signals to the producers of the goods and services they buy (or don't buy), telling them how to allocate scarce resources among different productive uses.

Suppose this were not so. If there were no competitive market, decisions would have to be made in some other way. In a centrally planned economy, for example, the planning board would have to create a list of directives to replace the market. The plan would specify how much of what kinds of goods to produce, for whom to produce the goods, and how to combine resources in production. Everything would have to be planned so that the right inputs would arrive at the right places at the right time. Planning production would be enormously complicated. In a free market system these decisions are made independently by producers and distributors in response to the signals of consumers.

Of course, the market system isn't quite as simple as we've made it sound. Because of the time required to produce some things, their production has to be planned in advance. This may lead to overproduction or underproduction of some items. A real-estate developer may build a hundred $60,000 houses only to find that he can't sell them all at that price. Or an apple grower may plant trees and discover several years later that there are too many apples. Sometimes a producer may market an entirely new good or service in the hope of eventually persuading people to buy it. In all these cases the initial decision is made by the producer, but it is up to the consumer to determine whether it was the right decision.

In the chapters that follow we will describe the behavior of consumers in free markets and present the theory that explains their behavior. Later we will look at the market system as a whole and evaluate how well it meets the needs of society. We will also explore some proposals that have been made for improving it.

The demand for goods and services

Let's suppose we decide to buy a hamburger. We go to the Golden Arch or the Jolly King and ask for a Super de Luxe Cheeseburger with Everything. While we're waiting for our order to be filled, we reflect on what we've done. We find that we've already made a number of choices. We've chosen to buy a hamburger—not just any hamburger but a Jolly King burger; furthermore, we've selected their biggest, with melted cheese and mustard and onions and relish. If the chef were to bring us a plain hamburger we'd be highly annoyed, even though the plain hamburger would satisfy our hunger and might even be more nourishing. We didn't ask for something to satisfy our hunger; we asked for a very specific combination of *characteristics*.

If we pursue this a little further, we'll see that what we are really buying in many of our purchases is a bundle of properties or qualities. For instance, we don't buy bread, we buy thin-sliced rye bread without caraway seeds, or Mrs. Porter's cracked wheat bread with molasses. We all want different combinations, of course. Some of us want plain white bread and others want raisin bread. Because we want different things, we may react quite differently to the same thing. Status seekers may be willing to pay the high price to buy a Cadillac. Others, who are able to pay the price, may refuse to buy a Cadillac because they feel that seeking status through a car is ridiculous. One person will buy an apple pie, while another person will be turned off by the very thought of all those calories.

Characteristics

Not every possible property of a good or service is necessarily relevant to a decision to buy it. A bottle of fine wine probably has certain disinfectant qualities, but a consumer seldom considers this while choosing fine wines. A lawyer may be a champion handball player, but this has nothing to do with the legal service rendered. It is not necessary to consider all properties. Only those which affect the consumer's decision need be considered. The collections of properties that may possibly affect a particular consumer choice are called **characteristics.**

Since characteristics are those properties which lead consumers to desire a good or service, it is possible that some things might have no characteristics. Of course, people would not choose such a product and so it would not be a salable commodity. Some goods or services may have only a single characteristic. For example, the several brands of aspirin tablets basically all have one characteristic: they provide five grains of acetylsalicylic

acid, which works to kill pain. Even if the consumer thinks of the compound in terms of "it makes the headache go away," there is only the one basis for choosing aspirin—it is a painkiller. One function of advertising is to make the consumer believe that a particular firm's product has some *other* characteristic that the consumer needs. The fact that consumers do buy expensive name-brand aspirins proves how well advertising adds *salable characteristics.*

The vast majority of goods and services have more than one characteristic. A hamburger has certain characteristics such as protein, vitamins, fat, and calories. These and other chemical properties produce the characteristic known as flavor or taste. Likewise, a car provides transportation services, status, shelter from the weather, and comfort. An article of clothing may retain body heat, provide stylishness in dress, meet needs of modesty, and decorate the person as well; these properties are the characteristics of clothing.

Choice of characteristics

The decision to buy goods is the result of choosing a particular package of characteristics. Choosing proceeds in two steps. First the consumer evaluates the kinds and amounts of characteristics provided by various goods and services. At this point the role of information becomes vitally important. The consumer can evaluate all the characteristics only when provided with all relevant information. For example, two small jars of jam may contain more jam than the large jar of the same brand and *cost less*. But some consumers might buy the large jar because they are deceived by visual comparisons or because the labels fail to inform them (or both). When enough information is provided, the selection of each characteristic becomes an objective process.

As a second step in choosing, the consumer decides whether to buy one collection of characteristics or another. Although the characteristics themselves can be objectively measured, the consumer's reaction to characteristics is highly individualistic. For example, one brand of stereo speakers might be more suitable for listening to rock music while another might be better for classical music. The consumer must choose accordingly the desired characteristic for his or her own purposes. Ann may love apples and Joan may hate them. Why? For the same characteristic—the apple's flavor.

Since most goods and services contain a bundle of characteristics, the consumer buys a certain good or service because it has the particular mix of characteristics desired. No one would buy hamburger if it did not first have nutritional value in the form of protein and calories. To obtain more calories and less protein, you could buy a loaf of bread instead. To obtain more protein, some (few) consumers might buy cottage cheese. Thus goods and services are purchased only to obtain particular characteristics, and the demand for goods and services depends upon the ability of each to provide characteristics.

Presumably consumers will try to obtain as much as possible of each characteristic which they desire. They will be limited by their incomes, of course, unless they use some of their accumulated savings. No two consumers will try to consume precisely the same bundle of characteristics, but they will try to consume as much of the desired characteristics as their incomes allow. The collection of actual goods and services purchased will vary even more. Different consumers may obtain necessary protein from fish, chicken, steak, hamburger, or even soybeans. They may maintain health by regular visits to a physician, chiropractor, acupuncturist, or even a faith healer. Different strokes for different folks!

The first step then is to choose a collection of goods which contain the characteristics desired. The second is to obtain as much of the characteristics as possible within a person's limited income (and accumulated wealth).

In summary, goods and services are not desired for themselves. Instead, consumers look at the characteristics of the goods and services and try to obtain as much as possible of the characteristics they desire within the limits of their income (and maybe wealth). Characteristics are those observable, measur-able, objective properties of goods which are relevant to the choice of the good or service for consumption. To be a "good," a commodity or service must have at least one characteristic. Most goods have more than one characteristic and goods are distinguished by the different combinations of characteristics embodied in them.

The utility of goods and services

We buy goods and services because we enjoy the particular characteristics they provide. Characteristics are desirable for filling our basic wants or because they provide enrichment to life.

Economists compare the desirability of goods and services by comparing their utility. **Utility** is a measure of the satisfaction obtained from a purchase. All consumers are alike in one respect: they try to obtain as much utility (that is, satisfaction) as they can from the goods and services available to them.

The utility of owning an item involves more than its usefulness. Some of the things we buy are not strictly useful in the sense that they are not absolutely necessary for life. They provide satisfaction of another sort, and the satisfaction is different for different owners. *Utility is a very subjective matter, varying with the individual.* But we can say—and this is true of everyone—that the amount of added utility we get from anything tends to diminish as the amount of the good or service we have increases. In fact, economists have developed a theory of consumer choice based on *diminishing marginal utility.* The total quantity of food and clothing we have provides some total quantity of utility. But if we have plenty of food and clothing for a particular period of time, the additional utility we get from having one more can of beans or another T-shirt will be small. Likewise the total amount of recreational activity we enjoy provides some total quantity of utility. But again, over a particular period of time even the most enthusiastic TV viewer or ice fisher will eventually grow tired of the activity. The marginal utility of recreation tends to diminish.

Notice the emphasis here is on each additional consumption of a good. Economists have a word to describe the increment or most recent addition to a quantity: **marginal.** A marginal purchase is the last purchase, or the additional purchase within some period of time. "Marginal" differs from "total," which is the sum of all amounts within some time period.

The structure of human wants has been compared to a pyramid turned upside down. The small layer on the bottom represents basic food, clothing, and shelter that we need to keep us alive and protect us from the weather. Once those needs are provided for, we move up to a larger layer of wants—furniture, appliances, more colorful clothing, automobiles. But this is not the end. When these wants are satisfied we look for services that make life healthier and more pleasant. We want medical care, education, recreation, and cultural enrichment. Each layer is larger then the one before. Each includes a wider range of wants and provides a wider range of satisfactions.

Unfortunately for the purposes of our theory, utility cannot be measured. An individual can say, "I would prefer to have a new jacket rather than a third chair for my apartment." But economists can't say just how badly the individual wants the new jacket. There is no real unit of measure to describe the satisfaction consumers gain from the things they buy. Right now we will ignore this problem and proceed as if it were possible to measure utility. We will assign values to each purchase as if each buyer's utility were known and measurable.

Marginal utility

Tables 1 and 2 are utility schedules for a Miss Jones and a Mr. Smith. The tables show the quantities of satisfaction each gets from owning additional opera tickets and stereo tapes during a particular period of time. The quantities of satisfaction are measured in *utils*. Of course, *the util is imaginary*. There are no instruments for measuring utils; we couldn't say, for example, that we get 20 utils from eating a porterhouse steak. Why do we use this imaginary measure? Because it is useful in constructing our theory of consumer choice. *Remember that although the unit of measurement is imaginary, the satisfaction derived from consumption is not imaginary*. The tables of consumer preferences that we construct using utils are models of the way each consumer makes choices.

As Table 1 shows, Miss Jones receives 10 utils from owning her first opera ticket and 9 utils from the second. Mr. Smith is as enthusiastic as Miss Jones about his first visit to the opera, but his enthusiasm starts to wane after that. His interest in a third visit is zero, and he would have to be dragged kicking and screaming to a fourth performance.

Now look at Table 2. It shows that Miss Jones attaches a high degree of utility to the purchase of her first stereo tape but considerably less to the purchase of additional tapes. Mr. Smith, on the other hand, keeps getting satisfaction from additional tapes, though in lesser amounts.

Tables 1 and 2 show what we call the *marginal utility* obtained from opera tickets and stereo tapes. **Marginal utility** is the utility gained from owning or consuming an *additional* unit of a good or service during a particular period of time—paintings, apples, autos, pet rocks, or what you will. It is important to remember that marginal utility refers to the change in total utility resulting from an additional unit of consumption. For Miss Jones, the fourth opera ticket *adds* seven utils to her util-

Table 1
Utility Associated with Purchases of Opera Tickets
(one season)

	Miss Jones	Mr. Smith
1st purchase	10 utils	10 utils
2nd purchase	9 utils	5 utils
3rd purchase	8 utils	0 utils
4th purchase	7 utils	−5 utils
5th purchase	6 utils	−10 utils

Table 2
Utility Associated with Purchases of Stereo Tapes
(one year)

	Miss Jones	Mr. Smith
1st purchase	12 utils	10 utils
2nd purchase	8 utils	8 utils
3rd purchase	4 utils	6 utils
4th purchase	0 utils	4 utils
5th purchase	0 utils	2 utils

Extended Example
The Marginal Utility of Cleanliness

The air hung heavy in the big cities, laden with soot and chemicals. The rivers and lakes were dying. The country seemed to have become a vast machine for turning nature into pasteboard, plastic, and smog.

That was how many Americans felt in 1970. Decades of industrial growth had contaminated many streams, scarred landscapes, and fogged the skies. In response to public concern, Congress set up the Environmental Protection Agency (EPA) to try to reverse the trend.

Success came easily at first. The fish began to return to Lake Erie. New automobiles were designed with emission controls that kept most of the hydrocarbons out of the air. Trash was turned into electricity and steam or recycled for future use. The EPA made itself felt. In the course of its cleanup campaign it forced the closing of 75 plants costing the jobs of 16,000 workers. At the same time, however, the EPA spent a lot of money ($16 billion in 1975) and probably created more than a million jobs in combating pollution.

Complaints began to be heard that the agency was going too far. Critics pointed out that while pollution has its costs, so do the measures taken against it. They asked, how much pollution do we really want to do away with? As the costs of combating pollution rise, isn't there some point at which the benefits of still more cleanliness are lower than the costs?

Suppose, for example, that the industrial town of Miasma pours its wastes into a river. People who live downstream from Miasma complain that the river is so polluted they cannot go swimming or boating. A canning factory downstream is about to close because the water isn't clean enough for its operations. The state legislature passes a law requiring the factories in Miasma to reduce their discharge of pollutants to zero. The factories call in some economists who study the costs involved and report that it will cost $20 million to reduce the pollution by half, $40 million to reduce it by three-quarters, $70 million to reduce it by 90%, and $250 million to eliminate it entirely. The Miasma chamber of commerce urges the state legislature to change the law and allow the factories to clean up just 90% of the pollutants. The factory representatives say they are eager to do their share toward reducing pollution, but that the cost of reducing their discharge of pollutants to zero is too great for them to absorb. They will have to raise the prices of their products to a point where they will lose most of their customers. The river is perfectly able to absorb a certain level of pollution, they argue. The question is, how much can the community live with?

We have here an example of the principle of diminishing marginal utility. Everyone wants clean water, particularly those who live downstream from an industrial town. But too often we forget that obtaining clean water involves social costs—costs in terms of higher prices and lost jobs. It is reasonable to assume that the marginal utility of cleaner water downstream from Miasma will start to diminish beyond some point and will keep on falling, while expenditures for pollution control increase. To continue to push for completely pure water in the river will not provide added benefits equal to the additional sacrifices required.

Unfortunately, it is difficult to measure the benefits of such things as clean water and air. They are not sold in the market, and there are no dollars-and-cents measurements for their marginal utility. We can estimate roughly the benefits of protection from chemicals that cause cancer. But it is much more difficult to set a value on less airport noise or on lower emissions from motorcycles.

Another problem is that in trying to clean up our environment we may cut down the production of things we need. Food is an important example. America's agriculture depends on the use of large amounts of chemicals in fertilizers, weed killers, and insecticides. Some of these chemicals wash off the fields and pollute our rivers and lakes. If we prohibit the use of certain chemicals in agriculture, this may reduce our food output. How much food production are we ready to give up in order to reduce the pollution of our streams? This is an even more difficult question to answer if the food we produce is to be eaten by peoples in other countries while the cost of water pollution is to be borne close to home.

A similar question arises in the field of nuclear energy. The United States now gets almost a tenth of its electricity from nuclear power plants, and in the future the proportion is likely to increase. One by-product of modern power plants is radioactive material that is dangerous to life and must be disposed of carefully. There is also the danger of accidents that could injure people living in the neighborhood of a nuclear plant. How do we balance the marginal utility of electrical power with the marginal hazard of atomic radiation?

ity, while for Mr. Smith the fourth opera ticket actually *decreases* his total utility by five utils.

In general, we can say that marginal utility declines as more units of a particular good or service are consumed within the time period. That is, each good or service provides **diminishing marginal utility.** The first apple we eat in a single day contributes a great deal to our utility. A second apple is still good but less enjoyable than the first. If pressed, we can probably get a third one down, but we'll wish we were eating something else. Almost all the pleasures of life seem to diminish as we indulge them.

Total utility

Marginal utility declines—but what about total utility? We define **total utility** as the sum of the utilities provided by all the units of a good or service that we have purchased within the time period. As long as marginal utility is positive, total utility increases with each additional purchase. It increases more and more slowly, of course, because each new purchase adds less utility than the previous purchases. Marginal utility diminishes. At some level of purchases, marginal utility may even become negative. When this happens, further purchases will cause total utility to decline. This must be true for everything we purchase, because sooner or later a large amount of anything gets to be a nuisance. The most avid moviegoer would find it inconvenient to visit the theater ten times a day. The most ardent collector of old autos will eventually run out of space for storing them.

Tables 3 and 4 show the amounts of total utility that Miss Jones and Mr. Smith get from their purchases of opera tickets and stereo tapes. Total utility is calculated by adding the marginal utility associated with each additional purchase within the time period. Compare Tables 3 and 4 with Tables 1 and 2 to see that this is true. For Miss Jones, total utility increases with each purchase of opera tickets over the range shown. It increases by smaller and smaller amounts, however, because her marginal utility diminishes with each purchase. For Mr. Smith, the total utility of opera tickets reaches a peak very soon and then stops rising. Total utility starts declining when his marginal utility becomes negative (on the fourth purchase). This is because the suffering that Mr. Smith must endure when he attends the fourth opera offsets the pleasure he got from the first two. For Mr. Smith, four operas provide less total utility than to attend two or three.

Table 3
Total Utility Associated with Purchases of Opera Tickets (one season)

	Miss Jones	Mr. Smith
1st purchase	10 utils	10 utils
2nd purchase	19 utils	15 utils
3rd purchase	27 utils	15 utils
4th purchase	34 utils	10 utils
5th purchase	40 utils	0 utils

Table 4
Total Utility Associated with Purchases of Stereo Tapes (one year)

	Miss Jones	Mr. Smith
1st purchase	12 utils	10 utils
2nd purchase	20 utils	18 utils
3rd purchase	24 utils	24 utils
4th purchase	24 utils	28 utils
5th purchase	24 utils	30 utils

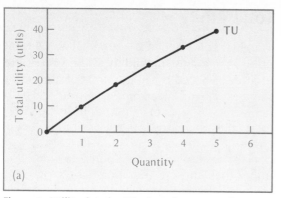
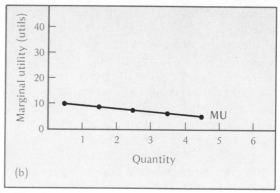

Figure 1   Utility data for Miss Jones' opera purchases: (a) total utility; (b) marginal utility.

Graphing utility

It is easier to see the relationship between marginal and total utility if we use graphs. The utility data for Miss Jones and Mr. Smith are graphed in Figures 1 and 2. The points for marginal utility are plotted *between* the numbers on the horizontal axis because utility increases during the process of adding another unit. Figure 1 shows Miss Jones' marginal and total utility curves for opera tickets during the current season. Notice that the line of total utility (TU) continues to rise over the entire range. But the line of marginal utility (MU) continuously declines. This suggests that eventually the marginal utility of opera tickets may become zero even for Miss Jones, and that the total utility line may therefore reach a peak. In other words, at some point further visits to the opera during a single season may provide no additional satisfaction even for so avid a fan as Miss Jones. Mr. Smith, you will remember, reaches that point early in the season. His total utility curve (Figure 2a) looks like the roof of the Astrodome, and his marginal utility curve (Figure 2b) slopes downward very steeply.

The structure of utility

Let's sum up what we have learned about utility curves thus far. First, we have noted that marginal utility tends to decline as additional units are consumed during a single time period. Eventually, for most goods and services marginal utility will fall to zero and may even become negative.

Total utility is the sum of the utilities gained from all purchases of the good or service during the relevant time period. It can be calculated by adding the marginal utilities of each unit purchased. Thus total utility for three units is represented by the height of the utility curve at point 3 in Figure 1a. It is the sum of the marginal utilities of the first three units shown in Figure 1b. As long as marginal utility is positive, the purchase of another unit *increases* total utility. When marginal utility starts to decline, total utility still increases but by smaller amounts. We say then that the total utility curve is rising at a decreasing rate.

At some point, marginal utility may become zero. Adding another unit during a particular time period adds nothing to total utility. Then the total utility curve levels off, at least

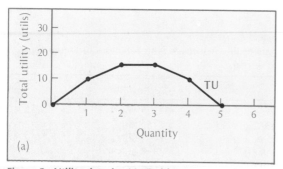
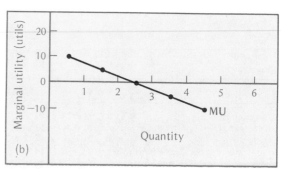

Figure 2   Utility data for Mr. Smith's opera purchases: (a) total utility; (b) marginal utility.

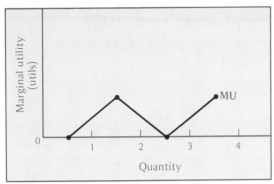

Figure 3 A sample marginal utility curve. Notice that marginal utility here is not decreasing, but rather vacillating.

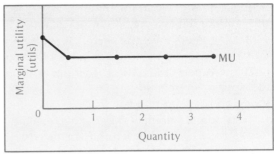

Figure 4 Another sample marginal utility curve. After initially declining, the marginal utility levels off and remains constant (at least through first four purchases).

briefly. Should marginal utility become negative, total utility will start to decline. The purchase of another unit *decreases* total utility. Total utility may remain positive, but each additional unit purchased pulls the curve down a little more.

Examine Figures 1 and 2 again to make sure this is true. Then look at the marginal utility curves in Figures 3 and 4. Can you determine the shape of total utility based on the shapes of the marginal utility curves shown?

Marginal utility and consumer demand

Thus far, our discussion of marginal utility has omitted an important factor involved in consumer choice. Before we can calculate consumer demand we must know something about relative prices and the amounts consumers have to spend.

As a consumer you may imagine a multitude of marginal utility curves associated with the things you buy. There is a curve for automobiles, motorcycles, and bicycles; for coats, shoes, and shirts; for steaks, cans of soup, and pizzas. Over any particular time period the additional utility associated with owning an automobile may be much greater than that to be gained from another pizza. Yet you buy a pizza rather than an automobile. Why? Of course, it is because of price.

Table 5 shows hypothetical marginal utility schedules for autos, shirts, and pizzas for a particular time period. Marginal utility (MU) is measured in utils as before. The price (P) of each item is listed also. Including prices enables us to measure the marginal utility gained per dollar spent on any one of the items.

We can see from Table 5 that the purchase of an automobile would add substantial utility. However, because the price of autos is high, the value of marginal utility per dollar (MU/P) spent is very low. For the first auto purchase it

Table 5
Hypothetical Marginal Utilities per Dollar of Expenditures (over one month)

	Autos			Shirts			Pizzas		
	MU_a	P_a	MU_a/P_a	MU_s	P_s	MU_s/P_s	MU_p	P_p	MU_p/P_p
1st purchase	100	$100	1	50	$25	2	25	$5	5
2nd purchase	50	100	0.5	40	25	1.6	20	5	4
3rd purchase	−100	100	−1	25	25	1	15	5	3
4th purchase	−200	100	−2	10	25	0.4	10	5	2
5th purchase	−500	100	−5	0	25	0	5	5	1
6th purchase	−1000	100	−10	−5	25	−0.2	0	5	0
7th purchase	−2000	100	−20	−10	25	−0.4	−10	5	−2
8th purchase	−3000	100	−30	−15	25	−0.6	−20	5	−4

is only one util, while for the first shirt it is 2 utils and for the first pizza, 5 utils. Column 3 in each schedule shows the marginal utility per dollar of each purchase: MU/P = utils per dollar of expenditure. The subscripts indicate the specific purchase, "a" for autos, "s" for shirts, and "p" for pizzas.

Consumers normally plan their expenditures so as to achieve what they believe to be the greatest marginal utility per dollar of expenditure. For the consumer in Table 5, the most desired expenditure would be for a pizza. This is because pizzas offer the greatest marginal utility per dollar of expenditure—greater than the consumer could obtain from shirts or autos. Notice that this is the case for our consumer's second pizza as well; MU/P is 4 utils compared to only 2 for the first purchase of a shirt or 1 for an auto. Even a third pizza would be preferred to shirts and autos in this consumer's utility schedule.

The consumer is said to be in equilibrium when purchases *within a single time* period are arranged so that the marginal utilities per dollar spent on every item are equal. This is called the **equal marginal utility principle.** It can be stated in symbols as

$$\frac{MU_a}{P_a} = \frac{MU_s}{P_s} = \frac{MU_p}{P_p} = \cdots = \frac{MU_z}{P_z}.$$

That is, the marginal utility per dollar of expenditure on autos equals that for shirts, pizzas, and so on for all goods. When the consumer has chosen correctly, all the goods in the particular collection purchased should yield the same marginal utility per dollar. It is easy to see that this is true by considering what would happen if the ratios were not all the same. Suppose, for instance, that the purchase of another pizza would yield more MU/P than the last purchase of a shirt. The consumer would increase total utility by purchasing more pizzas and fewer shirts. But as more pizzas are bought, the marginal utility of further purchases of pizzas would decline. The consumer would continue purchasing more pizzas relative to shirts until MU_p/P_p is finally equal to MU_s/P_s. At this point the consumer is in equi-

Extended Example
The Marginal Utility of Urban Land

Among the duties of city planners is that of deciding what will be done with the community's land. How much of it should be zoned for commercial and industrial use, how much for houses and apartment buildings, and how much for parks, schools, and roads?

From the city's point of view, commercial and industrial properties have a great deal of charm: they pay taxes. They also provide jobs for local residents, who then pay taxes themselves. Houses and apartment buildings provide tax revenues too, but not to the same degree. Parks and roads do not pay taxes at all, but they help to attract new residents and businesses that will. The problem is how to strike a balance among these different uses of land.

If the city wanted to be as rich as possible in terms of tax revenues, it would zone most of its land for industrial and commercial uses. But we may assume that each kind

librium, purchasing autos, shirts, and pizzas in the correct proportions for achieving maximum total utility.

But this isn't the whole story. The condition that MU/P be the same for all goods and services only tells us what *proportions* of products will be consumed. We also want to know precisely *how much* of each item is consumed. A wealthy person may consume a larger collection of all goods than a person of modest means. The *relative* amounts in each collection are determined by the ratios mentioned above, but the wealthy person will have more money to spend and will therefore purchase a larger total collection. We need to know the size of the consumer's budget.

In our example shown in Table 5, the consumer will begin by purchasing three pizzas. This is because the third pizza yields more marginal utility per dollar of expenditure than

of land use is subject to diminishing marginal utility. The first thousand acres of industrial property have much greater utility than the second or the tenth. The same is true of residential property and of parks.

The community has an MU/P for land use just as individual consumers have for the things they buy. There are benefits in terms of the additional utility gained and costs that must be paid. The cost is the services the city must provide for each category of property. The cost of providing services for office buildings (highway and street maintenance, police, garbage collection, etc.) will be greater than providing the same services for residential areas. While the cost of maintaining parks is probably least of all, the cost of parks includes the *opportunity cost* of the taxes which would have been received had the land been used for office buildings and parking lots. By comparing the MU/P of land use for different kinds of property, city planners are able to decide how to allocate land resources. Where MU/P is greater for, say, industrial use, more land should be zoned for it. When the MU/P is equal for all categories of land, the city will have reached its point of maximum total utility.

a single purchase of shirts or autos. But if the consumer's budget permits, the next purchase will be one shirt. With a more substantial budget, after acquiring a number of pizzas and shirts, the consumer may reach a level at which the purchase of an auto is possible.

With a budget of $45 per time period, the consumer in Table 5 would choose one shirt and four pizzas, receiving a marginal utility per dollar of 2 for the fourth pizza and the first shirt: $MU_s/P_s = MU_p/P_p = 2$. Total utility would be 120 utils (the sum of the marginal utilities of four pizzas and one shirt). This is the maximum amount of utility the consumer can get with a budget of $45.

Suppose the consumer's budget increases to $200 per time period. The consumer maximizes utility when

$$MU_a/P_a = MU_s/P_s = MU_p/P_p.$$

Looking at Table 5 we see that the consumer maximizes utility with a purchase of:

1 auto ($100)
3 shirts ($75)
5 pizzas ($25).

Marginal utility is equal for all items:

$$\frac{100}{\$100} = \frac{20}{\$20} = \frac{5}{\$5} = 1.$$

Total utility is calculated thus:

auto (100)   = 100 utils
shirts (50 + 40 + 25)   = 115 utils
pizzas (25 + 20 + 15 + 10 + 5) = 75 utils
                                          290 utils.

This is the maximum utility possible with a budget of $200.

The demand curve

We have been able to determine the quantity of each item purchased because we knew the prices of all the goods, the amount of money the consumer could spend, and the consumer's preferences among goods (marginal utility schedule). Recalling the earlier discussion of supply and demand (Chapter 3), we can think of each quantity purchased as a single point on the consumer's demand curve. That is, given a certain budget it is the quantity of pizzas, shirts, and autos the consumer will buy at a particular price during a particular period of time. Now let us suppose that prices change. Suppose, for instance, that the price of owning an automobile falls to $25 in a given time period while the price of a pizza rises to $10. There will be a change in the marginal utility per dollar (MU/P) of each item. As P_a falls to $25, MU_a/P_a rises. As P_p increases to $10, MU_p/P_p will fall. Consumers will adjust their purchases to conform with the new MU/P's. In short, within consumers' budget limitations, they will tend to purchase more autos and fewer pizzas until MU_a/P_a and MU_p/P_p are again equal.

The price change has enabled us to plot a second point on the consumer's demand curves. A lower price for automobiles is associated with larger MU/P and larger quantities purchased. A higher price for pizzas is associated with smaller MU/P and smaller quantities purchased. In this way it is possible to visualize an entire demand schedule. Within their individual budget limitations, consumers will allocate their spending so as to achieve maximum total utility. *Higher-priced items will generally be associated with relatively low MU/P*, and smaller quantities of them will be purchased. *Lower-priced items will generally be associated with higher MU/P*, and larger quantities of them will be purchased. By plotting the quantities of an item that would be purchased at different prices, we can obtain the consumer's demand schedule. The market demand schedule for an item is the sum of all individual demand schedules, which in turn are derived from utility schedules such as those in Table 5.

Using the marginal utility of money to plot demand

We have seen that people's purchases of goods and services vary according to the marginal utility that goods and services provide. But money can also be said to have marginal utility. We don't like to spend all our available funds; we prefer to have a little cash on hand, and perhaps even a sizable bank account to tide us over in case of emergency. For some of us the marginal utility of money is greater than it is for others. Whatever it may be, when we are in equilibrium the marginal utility of money held ($MU_\$$) must be equal to the marginal utility per dollar spent on goods and services:

$$\frac{MU_a}{P_a} = \cdots = \frac{MU_z}{P_z} = MU_\$$$

As with other commodities, it is sometimes assumed that money provides diminishing marginal utility. The more we have of it, the less eager we are to have still more. (This may not hold true for everyone; some people find money endlessly attractive and just can't get too much of it. But don't most of us spend more recklessly on payday than just a few days before payday?) It seems safe to say, as a rule, that persons with very small budgets probably attach a high MU to the last dollar available for spending while persons with large budgets

Extended Example
Marginal Utility and Income Taxes

Government policymakers consider marginal utility when they establish income tax rates. Most income tax rates are *progressive*—that is, they are proportionately greater for higher incomes. Figure 7 presents marginal utility schedules for money for opera fans Miss Jones and Mr. Smith. The schedules are based on the assumption that the marginal utility of income diminishes in much the same way as the marginal utility of goods. Miss Jones earns an income of $200 per week and Mr. Smith earns $150. We assume that equal amounts of income provide equal utility to both taxpayers. This means that the 200*th* dollar received by Miss Jones yields less utility than the 150*th* dollar received by Mr. Smith. Miss Jones achieves total utility equal to the entire area under her marginal utility schedule, up to an income of $200. Similarly, Mr. Smith receives total utility equal to the area under his marginal utility schedule up to an income of $150. The total utility of the community is the sum of the utilities enjoyed by Miss Jones, Mr. Smith, and all the other citizens.

Now suppose that the government imposes an income tax. It plans to collect revenues averaging $10 per taxpayer per week. How should the tax bill be shared?

First, suppose that the tax bill is shared equally by all taxpayers. Miss Jones and Mr. Smith each pay $10, making their disposable incomes $190 and $140, respectively. The total utility of each is reduced by the appropriate area under each marginal utility curve. But the payment of $10 involves a smaller sacrifice for Miss Jones than for Mr. Smith, as indicated by the heights of the two areas. Under our assumptions, citizens with higher incomes lose less utility than citizens with lower incomes because of the diminishing marginal utility of income.

If we want to impose more nearly equal sacrifices upon Miss Jones and Mr. Smith,

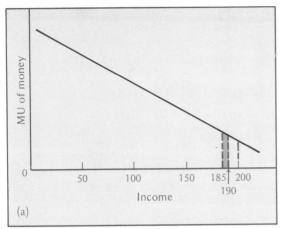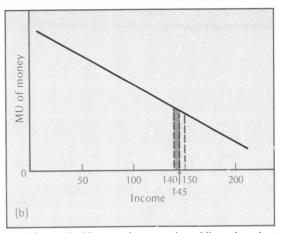

Figure 5 Marginal utility of income schedules for (a) Miss Jones and (b) Mr. Smith. Areas between dotted lines show lost utility due to taxes. Notice that area between $190 and $200 for (a) is less than area between $140 and $150 for (b). The assumption of equal marginal utility of income supports arguments in favor of progressive income taxes.

we must tax them differently. Suppose tax rates are set so that Miss Jones must pay $15 per week and Mr. Smith only $5. The additional $5 tax for Miss Jones reduces her after-tax income to $185. Total utility *declines* farther by the shaded area in Figure 7a. But the additional $5 in spendable income for Mr. Smith increases his disposable income to $145. As a result, his total utility *increases* by the shaded area under his MU function (see Figure 7b). The gain to Mr. Smith is greater than the loss to Miss Jones because his MU function is higher at this level of income. Thus the extra sacrifice imposed on Miss Jones is less than the satisfaction gained by Mr. Smith. His additional spendable income adds more to his total utility than her loss subtracts from hers.

Supporters of progressive taxation argue that community welfare is increased when higher income earners bear a larger portion of the tax burden. Their argument rests upon the assumption that all citizens have the same marginal utility schedules for income. This would mean that all citizens have the same capacity for enjoying the things that money can buy. Critics of this argument say, "How do you know? It may be that individuals differ in their enjoyment of goods and services. Miss Jones may require a weekly trip to the opera to keep her happy, while Mr. Smith may obtain his satisfaction by sleeping ten hours a day."

However, suppose Mr. Smith enjoys the simple life; he prefers to consume more goods and services that are produced outside the market—perhaps he raises his own food, builds his own furniture, sleeps more. His spending is limited to the bare necessities of life.

It's possible that Miss Jones' marginal utility of money at a weekly income of $200 is much higher than Mr. Smith's at a weekly income of $150. To tax Miss Jones more heavily would involve a greater loss in total utility than to tax them both equally. According to this view, the progressive income tax could mean a greater loss of utility to the community than would an equal tax on all income earners. Of course, there is no scientific solution to this controversy. Utility cannot be measured, and so the argument for equalizing tax burdens cannot rest solely on the basis of diminishing marginal utility.

There is still another question. We cannot be certain that the marginal utility of income declines at all. Perhaps an extra dollar is just as precious to a rich person as to a poor one. If so, then someone with a high income may miss the dollar paid in taxes just as much as someone with a small income. However, most people seem to agree that the rich can afford to carry more of the load than the not-so-rich. It seems ridiculous to argue that a dollar means just as much to the millionaire in his mansion as it does to a poor man struggling to feed his children.

Marginal Utility and Consumer Demand 525

probably attach a lower MU to the last dollar. Additional purchases will be made as long as the MU/P associated with an item is greater than the MU of money.

We can illustrate this with the example shown in Table 6, which gives the MU/P for successive purchases of pizzas. Columns 4 and 5 are the $MU_\$$ for consumer A and consumer B. Money provides greater marginal utility to consumer A because consumer A's income is low. The last dollar available for spending is 4 times as valuable to consumer A as to consumer B. This means that A must receive 4 times as much marginal utility in the collection of goods purchased as B.

How many pizzas will consumer A purchase? Behaving like our previous consumers, A will equate marginal utilities per dollar for money and pizzas: $MU_\$ = MU_p/P_p = 4$. The number of pizzas providing a marginal utility per dollar of 4 is 2. Suppose price falls to $2.50. Then MU/P for the first pizza will rise to 10, for the second pizza to 8, for the third to 6, and for the fourth to 4. Therefore, consumer A will buy a total of four pizzas at a price of $2.50. If the price should rise to $6.25, consumer A will buy only one pizza. Can you show why?

By equating MU/P with $MU_\$$ at various prices, we are able to plot consumer A's demand curve for pizzas. Now, turning to consumer B, we can do the same. Remember that consumer B has a larger budget and a lower MU for money. Consumer B can continue to spend as long as each additional purchase provides MU/P greater than 1. At a price of $5, how many pizzas will consumer B purchase? Table 6 shows that the answer will be five, because then $MU_p/P_p = MU_\$ = 1$. If the price of pizzas were to rise to $10, consumer B

would purchase four pizzas. Can you show why? Figure 6 illustrates demand curves for pizzas for consumers with different money incomes and different $MU_\$$'s.

Marginal utility and consumer's surplus

One interesting characteristic of the downward-sloping demand curve is that it gives the consumer a sort of bonus. If Miss Jones is prepared to buy eight opera tickets at $10 each, we know that the eighth ticket provides the same marginal utility per dollar as would any other purchase—say, a new hat or dinner in a good restaurant. But we also know, from the principle of diminishing marginal utility, that the eight tickets she buys provide greater total utility than the $80 she is actually paying for them.

For Miss Jones the marginal utility of the eighth opera ticket is equal to the marginal utility of its $10 price. We know this because of the equal marginal utility principle. In equilibrium consumer purchases are arranged so that

$$\frac{MU_a}{P_a} = \frac{MU_b}{P_b} = \cdots = \frac{MU_z}{P_z} = MU_\$$$

Substituting,

$$\frac{MU \text{ of } 8th \text{ opera ticket}}{\$10} = MU_\$$$

or

$$MU \text{ of } 8th \text{ opera ticket} = \$10 \times MU_\$$$

The eighth ticket gives Miss Jones precisely as much additional utility as she gives up. But the principle of diminishing marginal utility reveals that each of the first seven opera tickets yields equal or greater utility than the eighth. The cost of each ticket is the same—$10—but marginal utility is different. Each previous purchase added more utility than the next one. Therefore, the total utility of eight tickets must exceed their total cost. The difference between total utility and the utility of the amount spent is called **consumer's surplus.**

Table 6
Hypothetical Marginal Utilities for Pizza and Money

| | For Pizzas | | | For Money | |
| | | | | Consumer A, $MU_\$$ | Consumer B, $MU_\$$ |
	MU	P	MU/P		
1st purchase	25	5	5	4	1
2nd purchase	20	5	4	4	1
3rd purchase	15	5	3	4	1
4th purchase	10	5	2	4	1
5th purchase	5	5	1	4	1

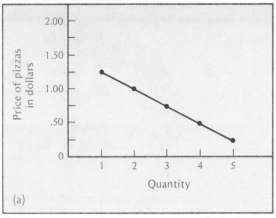

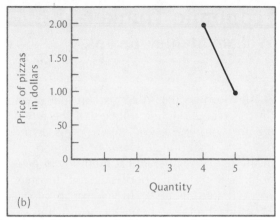

Figure 6 Consumer demand curves for two individuals purchasing pizzas: (a) consumer A; (b) consumer B. Consumer B has a larger budget than consumer A. The larger income allows consumer B to purchase a greater quantity at every price. This is because of the lower marginal utility of money at higher incomes.

We can show this graphically. Figure 7 shows the demand curves for Miss Jones and Mr. Smith. In Figure 7, the downward-sloping lines are the demand curves for opera tickets, showing the quantities of tickets that will be purchased at various prices. A horizontal line has been drawn at $10 to show the fixed price. Miss Jones' total expenditure is calculated by multiplying price times quantity: P × Q. Price and quantity are measured by drawing lines from the demand curve to the vertical and horizontal axes. The values on the price and quantity axes form the sides of a rectangle Oab8. Because the area of a rectangle is the

product of its two sides, Miss Jones' total expenditure can be represented by the area of the rectangle Oab8:

$$\text{Total expenditure} = P \times Q = Oa \times O8$$
$$= \text{area of rectangle Oab8.}$$

Miss Jones' expenditure appears as a rectangle formed beneath her demand curve. But her total utility from the purchase of tickets is shown by the entire area under her demand curve for the quantity purchased. This is because total utility is the sum of all marginal utilities associated with additional purchases of an item. The sum of all the values under Miss Jones' demand curve is the entire area: Ocb8. Miss Jones would have been willing to pay more for the first seven tickets because they provide greater MU/P. The difference between her total expenditure and her total utility is the triangle acb, which represents consumer's surplus. For Mr. Smith, whose utility schedule is lower, the triangle is smaller, but even for him there is a consumer's surplus.

Using marginal utility: some applications

Who thinks about marginal utility? Aside from economists, practically nobody. If you were to ask a friend to compare the marginal utility per dollar of a new sweater with that of a hockey ticket, you would get only a puzzled look. Even

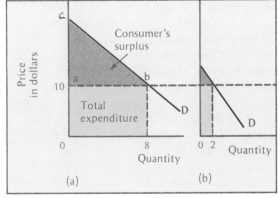

Figure 7 Demand curves for (a) Miss Jones and (b) Mr. Smith showing consumer's surplus. Both shaded areas under the demand curve constitute total utility. Subtracting utility for total purchase price (bottom shading) leaves consumer's surplus. Notice that important factors determining the consumer's surplus are (1) number of purchases—the horizontal length—and (2) the slope of the demand curve.

Economic Thinker
William Stanley Jevons

Stanley Jevons (1835–1882) is considered one of the great economic thinkers of the nineteenth century. He was known in his own day as an economic "scientist," pioneering in the use of mathematical methods in economics. Born in Liverpool, England, Jevons concentrated his early studies in natural sciences like biology, chemistry, and metallurgy. However, he soon became interested in understanding the poverty he saw in London (where he attended school) and started writing on political economy. Jevons' knowledge of economics was gained entirely through readings outside his formal schooling.

Today Jevons is esteemed for his major contributions to modern utility theory, in particular the marginal utility of income from work. He was the first to show that consumers would increase purchases of a good until the marginal utility gained from a small additional quantity would be equal to the marginal utility of its price—the familiar $MU_a/P_a = MU_b/P_b \cdots = MU_\$$. The marginal utility theory of pricing was in conflict with Marx's *labor theory of value,* which claimed that price is the value of the labor "embodied" in a good. Followers of Marx believed that a good is valuable only because labor is used to make it. Jevons turned this around and proved that a good is valuable only if it provides utility. Then labor becomes valuable when it is used to produce the good. Jevons showed how labor is not the only valuable factor of production; therefore, workers are not exploited, as Marx had maintained.

Jevons accepted a job in Australia in 1853 and lived there for six years. Experience in the Australian mint led to Jevons' studies of the determinants of the value of gold and of the effects of gold discoveries on the general price level. He was particularly interested in the social consequences of a change in the value of money. He wrote an early textbook on money in which he illustrated dramatically the disadvantages of barter. He played a major role in the development of monetary theory.

Jevons made other important contributions to economic theory, particularly on fluctuations in spending that lead to business cycles. His father had been a successful iron merchant until the depression of 1848 left him bankrupt. His grandfather was also bankrupt through a run on his bank in 1816. Both events stimulated Jevons' interest in business cycles. He applied the techniques of a natural scientist to investigate the causes of cycles, developing statistical series of prices and production in Great Britain back into the 1700s. Because of the regular appearance of economic depressions every ten or eleven years, he associated their occurrence with regular sunspot activity and the effects of weather on agricultural production. Later he changed this view to include many other causes.

Jevons' most famous work is his *Theory of Political Economy* (1871). His family had long been interested in social problems, but Jevons was himself opposed to public charity for the needy. He felt that social programs rendered the poorest classes dependent on the rich when they should be encouraged to provide for themselves.

Viewpoint
Precision and Utility Analysis

Marginal utility analysis is a way of comparing benefits with costs. Most of us are accustomed to making these comparisons among goods when we allocate our budgets (though we don't call these comparisons marginal utility analysis). For instance, we subjectively compare the utility gained from additional purchases of articles of clothing. A Perma-press shirt may be expected to yield greater additional utility than a 100% cotton shirt. The Perma-press shirt does not require ironing and it remains crisp and fresh throughout a day's wearing. Furthermore, price comparisons often favor the Perma-press variety. Perma-press fabric is made from fibers produced synthetically from petroleum. Until 1973, relatively low-cost Arab oil helped to keep petroleum prices low and reduced the cost of producing synthetic fibers for clothing. We might purchase a Perma-press shirt for $10, whereas a shirt made of more costly cotton fiber might sell for $20.

The result of our comparison would appear as follows:

$$\frac{\text{Marginal utility}}{\text{Price}_{pp}} > \frac{\text{Marginal utility}}{\text{Price}_{cot.}},$$

where pp stands for Perma-press and cot. for cotton. Therefore, the consumer would increase purchases of Perma-press shirts until the MU/P is equal for all purchases. In this fashion society would gain the greatest amount of utility from all shirt purchases. Right?

Wrong. The biologist Barry Commoner suggests that we should look more closely at the costs involved in producing these two items. To produce fibers for cloth requires the use of energy. Production of cotton fibers uses energy from the sun, converting the chemical content of air and water to long strings of molecules in a form of congealed solar energy.

On the other hand, production of synthetic fibers uses energy to heat petroleum, to break it apart, and to combine it again into long strings of molecules. The raw materials are oil and natural gas, with natural gas used to provide the necessary heat. The chemical industry now accounts for about 7% of the nation's annual fuel consumption.

When we Americans indulge our preference for Perma-press over cotton shirts we are encouraging the use of a nonrenewable resource (oil and gas) rather than a constantly renewable one (sunlight). Moreover, we are losing unused energy to the environment and creating additional pollution in the process.

How can we include these considerations in our benefit/cost comparisons? Can we adjust our strictly economic calculations to include all these secondary costs?

First we must make sure we have correctly evaluated the utility gained from each product: the comfort and appearance of the fabric itself; the durability of the garment; and, of course, the increased leisure for the laundry-person!

Next we must include in costs the total cost of a decision to purchase a shirt. To the purchase price we should add the cost of environmental pollution and the replacement cost of the energy used in production. To develop replacements for a nonrenewable resource will require substantial investment in new research and technology. Including all secondary costs might yield an entirely different relationship:

$$\frac{\text{MU}}{\text{Full cost}_{pp}} < \frac{\text{MU}}{\text{Full cost}_{cot.}}.$$

When the economy as a whole allocates its spending according to full costs and benefits, the result may be greater conservation of our nonrenewable resources.

Thus the tools of economic analysis are useful not only for evaluating strictly economic alternatives. They are equally suitable for the many complex questions we must consider when we establish priorities for using our scarce resources.

economists aren't really interested in measuring the additional satisfaction to be obtained from making another purchase.

But the *concept* of diminishing marginal utility is of great importance nevertheless. Even though we aren't aware of it, we all consider marginal utility in making many of our daily choices. We have a limited budget which we try to spend in ways that will give us the greatest total satisfaction. When we go through a cafeteria line we make a whole series of utility comparisons: Shall we get soup and a hamburger, or a chef's salad? Which combination will provide the greatest total utility per dollar of expenditure? Will string beans add enough utility to justify their price? Will the tremendous satisfaction of chocolate layer cake be worth the high price? We make these choices without consciously thinking about marginal utility.

Sometimes our choices involve time rather than money. When time is limited, we must decide how to use it so as to receive the largest total benefit. We still use the principle of MU/P in allocating our time constraint, but now P represents a quantity of time spent rather than money. For example, students must decide how to allocate their time among various campus activities: studying for a history exam, performing an experiment in chemistry lab, and practicing for a tennis tournament. The utility gained from each activity is the growing competence of the student. But as more units of time are consumed in any activity, the marginal utility gained will decline. Beyond a certain point, further study or practice within a particular time period adds little or nothing to the student's competence.

Expressing it in symbols, we say that the MU/P of study is MU/hour. Students will allocate their study time so that the MU/hours of every activity are equal: that is, so that the utility added by the last hour is the same for history, chemistry, and tennis. For one student the combination that maximizes total utility may be three hours for history, five hours for chemistry, and two hours for tennis. For another, the same ten hours of time may be best distributed so as to allot two hours to history, two to chemistry, and six to tennis.

Summary

The theory of consumer choice explains how consumers help to answer the question *What?* Consumers demand goods and services which provide certain desired characteristics. The satisfaction derived from these characteristics is called utility. Consumers try to maximize total utility within their limited budgets. As more units of a good are purchased in a single time period, each additional unit tends to provide diminishing marginal utility. Changes in marginal utility determine the total utility gained from consumption of all units owned. The consumer's budget limits the number of units he or she can buy. However, within each consumer's budget, the greatest utility is achieved when units are purchased so that marginal utility per dollar is equal for all goods and for money: $MU_a/P_a = MU_b/P_b = \cdots = MU_z/P_z = MU_\$$. When all consumers observe the equal marginal utility principle it is possible to plot points on consumer demand curves.

Because marginal utility diminishes, some units of a good will provide greater utility than the utility of the money paid. The excess of utility is called consumer's surplus.

The equal marginal utility principle is used to allocate personal budgets, time, and even urban land.

The theory of diminishing marginal utility of money is an argument made in support of progressive income taxes. High income receivers are assumed to sacrifice less in utility when higher tax rates are levied on their higher incomes. Diminishing marginal utility is also a way of comparing the added benefits against the costs of antipollution legislation.

Key Words and Phrases

- **characteristics** properties of a good or service that affect consumer choice.
- **utility** satisfaction obtained by a consumer from purchasing a good or service.
- **marginal** the increment or addition of something.
- **marginal utility** the additional satisfaction (utility) that results when an additional unit of a good or service is comsumed (purchased).
- **diminishing marginal utility** when additional units of a good are acquired, each additional unit adds less utility than the one before.
- **total utility** the sum of satisfaction provided by the total quantity of a good or service purchased.
- **equal marginal utility principle** the consumer is in equilibrium when the marginal utilities per dollar spent on all purchases are equal.
- **consumer's surplus** total utility of a purchase minus the utility of the amount spent; surplus results because purchase prices are equal for all quantities of the good while utility declines to level of last purchase.

Questions for Review

1. Explain the relationship between total and marginal utility. Show the effects of diminishing marginal utility on total utility. Demonstrate arithmetically and graphically.

2. What are the important characteristics a consumer would look for in each of the following consumer goods: a fishing boat, a pleasure boat, a TV dinner, a jogging suit?

3. How is it possible to get around the problem of measurement in evaluating the utility of an item? Describe how a typical consumer might decide on a particular combination of purchases within a fixed budget.

4. Using the consumer preferences of Table 5, graph the marginal utility and total utility for purchasing shirts.

5. True or false: Higher-priced items usually have a (relatively) low MU/P.

6. Under what circumstances might consumer's surplus be quite large?

7. The great architect Frank Lloyd Wright once said: "Give me the luxuries. I can do without the necessities." How would you describe his marginal utility functions? How would you describe your own?

8. Suppose you are packing a knapsack for a weekend camping trip. Describe how marginal utility analysis helps to decide the items to include. What is the cost of including each item? What corresponds in this problem to the consumer's budget in the text?

9. Define: diminishing marginal utility of income.

25

Elasticity and Demand

Would you pay $3,000 for a picture of Honus Wagner?

Wagner played shortstop for the Pittsburgh Pirates in the early 1900s and led the National League in batting for eight years between 1900 and 1911. He was one of the five original members of the Baseball Hall of Fame. Given all this, is a 65-year-old photo of Wagner swinging a bat worth $3,000?

There are some who would answer yes. This is because Mr. Wagner's picture was distributed with other baseball cards in packages of caramel candy around the year 1910. For collectors of baseball cards, it's a real rarity, and the owner will be wise to store it in a bank vault along with the Abraham Lincoln autographs or the diamond tiara.

To an economist, Honus Wagner's picture has whatever value people choose to place on it. Someone must be willing to pay the price. Some of us want to own baseball cards while others prefer stamps or coins or paintings or recordings. Some of us want sports cars, and others want boats or motorcycles; some want baby kittens, and others want trips to far away places.

The characteristics of all these goods differ, but they have one thing in common: they provide utility for someone. As we have seen, utility is the basis for all demand. The utility added by one more unit of a good, whether a baseball card or a kitten or a motorcycle, together with its price and the amount of money we have to spend determine how much of it we will buy.

The demand curve again

We have seen that our demand for a good or service can be drawn in the form of a curve, showing how much we would buy for different prices during any given time period. Figure 1 is a typical demand curve. The quantity purchased is shown along the horizontal axis of the graph. The price per unit is shown on the vertical axis. Like most demand curves, this one slopes downward from left to right. Consumers would buy less at higher prices and more at lower prices.

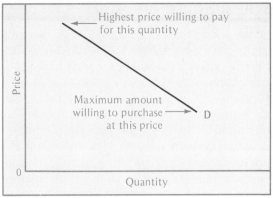

Figure 1 A typical demand curve.

For any particular period of time, the demand curve shows how consumers would behave in response to a change in price. It shows, at one end, the largest quantity that consumers would purchase if the price is very low, and at the other end the highest price they would pay to get any of the product at all. We assume that consumers always buy as much as they want at any particular price—that they are always on the demand curve rather than below it. Likewise, we assume that they never go above it, because, given their limited amount of money, they prefer to use their purchasing power in other ways.

The central idea of the demand curve is that, as the price of a good or service declines, more of it would be bought. In general, demand curves slope downward. They need not be shaped like the one shown here; they may level off at the ends, or they may not curve at all but be straight lines. Most slope downward. Why? One reason we have already studied is diminishing marginal utility. The more we have of something, the less urgent is our current need for more. If we have no bread, we may be willing to pay a dollar a loaf. But after our first purchase the utility of bread falls rapidly. As our supply increases, we think of other things we want. Diminishing marginal utility means falling marginal utility per dollar (MU/P). If we are to buy more units, price must also fall to bring MU/P in line with the MU/P's of other goods we buy. Beyond some quantity, MU falls so low that we wouldn't buy more for our own use even if price falls to a penny a loaf.

The substitution effect

Some goods have consistently high marginal utility because they are easily substituted for other goods in a consumer's market basket. For useful substitutes a fall in price may mean a substantial gain in marginal utility per dollar. Consumers can increase their total utility by buying more of this good and buying less of other goods with similar characteristics. If the price of chicken falls, we tend to eat more chicken and less beef or lamb. If the price of beef rises, its MU/P will fall relative to substitutes for beef. We will buy less beef until its MU/P is as high as that of pork or seafood. When the **substitution effect** is working, price and quantity purchased move in opposite directions. Consumers buy more at lower prices.

The income effect

Finally, demand curves slope downward because of the effect of price changes on our incomes. If the price of a good falls, we have more income to spend on all the things we buy. It's like having an increase in pay. If the price of beef falls we will have more to spend for everything—and that includes steaks! This effect on the consumer's purchasing power of a change in the price of a good is called the **income effect.** For some goods the income effect may work in the opposite direction from the substitution effect. Bread is an example. If the price of bread falls, the consumer who buys a certain number of loaves a week will have income left over for spending on other things. The consumer can choose to spend the additional purchasing power for (1) more bread, (2) a more expensive kind of bread, or (3) some other commodity, such as cake or fruit. The lower price for bread may make the consumer so much better off that he or she may buy *less* bread than before, perhaps eating out more often instead.

We have a name for those goods that people buy more of when the income effect gives them more spending money than before. These are called **superior goods.** Those that people will buy less of are called **inferior goods.** The distinction has nothing to do with

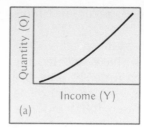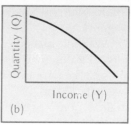

Figure 2 Engel curves for (a) superior good and (b) inferior good.

the quality of the goods concerned. It is simply that as people's incomes rise they tend to buy more of the goods for which they have a higher preference.

Consider the consumption of protein. We can obtain protein from many sources. At low levels of income, people obtain protein from rice, beans, cheese, and cereals. As their incomes rise, these foods tend to be phased out of many diets in favor of meat. In fact, as income increases, the consumption of meat rises even more rapidly than income. Meat is a superior good, while other sources of protein are generally inferior. Likewise, some kinds of meat are preferred to others. In America steak is a typical superior good. Hamburger is an example of a good that falls into both categories—it is superior for some consumers and inferior for others. As people first begin to switch away from vegetable sources of protein, hamburger is a superior good and its consumption rises rapidly. As people's incomes increase further and they begin switching to steak, hamburger becomes an inferior good.

To offer another example, cloth coats are inferior goods—not because they lack warmth but because they do not contain enough of the other characteristics people desire in coats. Wool coats are superior goods for those in the lower ranges of incomes, but they become inferior goods for people in higher ranges. Fur coats may not be warmer than wool or cloth coats, but they are superior goods for those in upper income brackets.

The relationship between income and the quantity of a good or service consumed is shown by the curves in Figure 2. These are called **Engel curves,** after the German mathematician/economist who first wrote about them. The upper curve in Figure 2 is that of a superior good. Notice that the quantity purchased increases faster and faster as income (Y) increases. The lower curve, for an inferior good, shows the opposite relationship: the quantity purchased decreases at a faster and faster rate as income increases. These curves are drawn smoothly, but in reality they need not be smooth at all. They may have bumps or flat places on them. For instance, if groups of consumers shift suddenly away from an inferior good, as sometimes happens, the curve will drop sharply.

It's fun to classify various goods or services as inferior or superior. Bus transportation is inferior, since people use cars whenever they can afford them. Peanut butter used to be an inferior good, at least for adults, until Jimmy Carter was elected President. Psychiatric counseling seems to be a superior good, and so are winter vacations in Mexico.

The income effect always works together with the substitution effect. *The income effect will reinforce the substitution effect in the case of a superior good.* As price falls, the consumer has more purchasing power and may decide to buy more of the superior good. But at the same time the lower price may encourage substitution of that product for other goods. The shopper who finds a welcome price reduction for shirts may use the additional purchasing power to buy more shirts instead of sweaters.

For an inferior good, however, the income and substitution effects are likely to work against each other. For some inferior goods the income effect is more powerful than the substitution effect. As price falls, the consumer has more purchasing power and may decide to buy less of the inferior good. In cases like this the demand curve will slope upward. As price falls, the increase in purchasing power will cause people to buy less of the good. On the other hand, a price increase will reduce consumers' income and lead them to buy more. Such goods are called **Giffen goods,** after Sir Robert Giffen, a Victorian economist. They are mostly an intellectual curiosity since there are very few real-world examples to be found.

Elasticity of demand

We have seen some of the factors that cause people to buy more or less of a good when its price changes. Purchases of some goods change much more than the purchases of others when their prices rise or fall. For instance, a price reduction for monogrammed T-shirts is likely to increase sales substantially. On the other hand, a price reduction for calculus textbooks is not likely to have much effect on students' purchases. Economists say that the demand for T-shirts is more *elastic* than the demand for calculus textbooks.

Elasticity measures the response of quantity demanded to a change in price; the price can increase or decrease. *Elasticity is just a convenient, shorthand way of expressing the important relationship between price and quantity demanded.*

Using the concept of elasticity, we can answer such questions as:
(1) Which is more responsive to price changes, foreign demand for U.S. aircraft or our demand for imported whiskey?
(2) Will a price reduction for Honda 150's attract enough new customers to make up for the lower price each customer pays?
(3) Will a higher price for theater tickets encourage consumers to take up bowling instead?

More precisely, **demand elasticity** is the percentage change in quantity demanded for some good relative to the percentage change in price for that good. This relationship is described by the simple equation

$$\text{elasticity} = \frac{\%\text{ change in quantity demanded}}{\%\text{ change in price}}.$$

Elasticity is a number without units. It doesn't tell us the level of price or quantity but shows the responsiveness of demand to changes in price. For example, if the price of peaches falls from 30 cents a pound to 15 cents, we can assume that consumers will increase their purchases considerably. But sometimes we want to know more precisely what their response will be. Perhaps we know that in the past when prices fell by half, consumers doubled their purchases. We can put this information into our equation as follows:

$$el = \frac{\% \text{ change in quantity}}{\% \text{ change in price}} = \frac{100\%}{50\%} = 2.$$

If we are in the fruit business this information may be very useful to us in pricing our product. Suppose we have an oversupply of peaches and need to get rid of them quickly before they spoil. If we know the elasticity of demand for peaches, we will have a better idea of how much we need to cut our price.

The interpretation of elasticity

The demand for a particular commodity is said to be **elastic** if the percentage change in quantity demanded is larger than the percentage change in price: consumers will respond to price changes by changing their purchases significantly. If the price is reduced by 1%, the quantity sold will increase by a larger percentage, say 2% or 3%. In the example of the peaches above the demand was elastic. Demand is said to be *elastic* for any value of elasticity greater than one (written $el > 1$).

Demand is said to be **inelastic** if the percentage change in quantity is smaller than the percentage change in price: consumers will respond to price changes by changing their purchases very little, if at all. If the price falls by 1% the quantity sold will increase by a smaller amount, say .7% or .5% or perhaps as little as .2%. The elasticity therefore will be less than one. Demand is said to be *inelastic* for any value of elasticity less than one (written $el < 1$).

A special case worth noting is that of **unit elasticity:** This occurs when the percentage change in price and the percentage change in quantity are the same. A 5% increase in price brings a 5% decrease in quantity sold. In mathematical form this condition is $el = 1$.

We can get a better understanding of elasticity if we apply our formula to a typical demand curve. Table 1 shows demand data in columns (1) and (2). For every price there is an accompanying quantity: at $12 one unit is sold, at $10 two units, etc. In column (3) are the elasticities, calculated from the formula we developed in the Extended Example.

To calculate the elasticity of a price drop from $12 to $10, we begin with the values 12 (P_1), 10 (P_2), 1 (Q_1), and 2 (Q_2). We substitute these values in our equation and solve:

$$\text{elasticity} = \frac{1 - 2}{1 + 2} \div \frac{12 - 10}{12 + 10}$$
$$= -\frac{1}{3} \div \frac{2}{22}$$
$$= -\frac{1}{3} \times \frac{22}{2} = -\frac{22}{6}$$
$$= -3.67$$

Repeating this for all the values in columns (1) and (2), we obtain the elasticity values in column (3).

You may have noticed that our values are negative, while those in Table 1 are not. Actually, *price elasticities of demand are always negative* since either the numerator or the denominator of the equation must be negative: either the price change is negative or the quantity change is negative. By tradition, however, economists ignore the minus sign, being interested only in the magnitude of the figure.

You will notice that the demand schedule has different elasticities at different points. In the $10–$12 price range elasticity of demand is very high: 3.67. Elasticity falls as we go down the demand schedule—to 1.0 in the $6–$8 price range and to only .27 at the lowest price where demand is very inelastic. For most goods, consumers are relatively insensitive to price changes when price is very low. Table 2 summarizes the values obtained from Table 1.

Table 1
A Demand Schedule Showing Elasticities

(1) Price	(2) Quantity	(3) Elasticity
$12	1	
		3.67
10	2	
		1.8
8	3	
		1.0
6	4	
		.56
4	5	
		.27
2	6	

Extended Example
Calculating Elasticity

We noted that the demand for peaches was elastic because the price fell by half and the amount sold doubled. But the formula we used had a flaw in it. Using simple percentages, you will get different answers depending on how you do your arithmetic. We figured a price change from 30 cents a pound to 15 cents a pound as being a 50% decrease. But suppose the price went the other way, from 15 cents to 30. That would be a 100% increase. Similarly, the change in quantity would be, instead of a doubling, a halving. Putting these figures into the equation we would get:

$$el = \frac{\text{\% change in quantity}}{\text{\% change in price}} = \frac{50\%}{100\%} = .5.$$

The elasticity seems to have changed from 2 to .5. Which is right? We can't have it both ways—either the demand for peaches is elastic or it's inelastic.

We avoid this flaw in the simple percentage formula by using average values as the bases from which to figure our percentage changes. The percentage change in quantity can be stated as

$$\text{\% change in quantity} = \frac{\text{change in quantity}}{\text{average quantity}}.$$

while, in like fashion,

$$\text{\% change in price} = \frac{\text{change in price}}{\text{average price}}.$$

Now we can restate our equation as

$$\text{elasticity} = \frac{\text{change in quantity}}{\text{average quantity}} \div \frac{\text{change in price}}{\text{average price}}.$$

It will make things easier if we substitute the letters P for price and Q for quantity in the formula, and number them so we won't mix them up:

P_1 = old price
P_2 = new price
Q_1 = old quantity
Q_2 = new quantity.

Then we can write the change in price as $P_1 - P_2$ and the change in quantity as $Q_1 - Q_2$. Since the average of two numbers is their sum divided by two, we write

average price = $(P_1 + P_2)/2$.
average quantity = $(Q_1 + Q_2)/2$.

Substituting these expressions into our previous elasticity equation, we now have

$$\text{elasticity} = \frac{Q_1 - Q_2}{(Q_1 + Q_2)/2} \div \frac{P_1 - P_2}{(P_1 + P_2)/2}.$$

and cancelling the two's,

$$\text{elasticity} = \frac{Q_1 - Q_2}{Q_1 + Q_2} \div \frac{P_1 - P_2}{P_1 + P_2}.$$

Let's return to our example of the peaches and substitute in the equation as follows. When the price of peaches rises from 15 cents a pound (P_1) to 30 cents (P_2), consumers reduce their purchases from 200 pounds (Q_1) to 100 pounds (Q_2):

$$\frac{200 - 100}{200 + 100} \div \frac{15 - 30}{15 + 30} = \frac{1}{3} \div \frac{-1}{3} = -1.$$

When the price of peaches falls from 30 cents a pound (P_1) to 15 (P_2), consumers increase their purchases from 100 pounds (Q_1) to 200 pounds (Q_2):

$$\frac{100 - 200}{100 + 200} \div \frac{30 - 15}{30 + 15} = \frac{-1}{3} \div \frac{1}{3} = -1.$$

Notice that, figured this way, elasticity is the same whether we're increasing price or decreasing it.

Special kinds of demand curves

If we were to draw the demand curve for Table 1, we would have a straight line sloping down to the right. This is the typical demand curve that economists think about when they speak of demand curves. Such demand curves are called *linear* (straight) and are used in books like this quite often because they are easy to draw and they make explanations easier. Economists often apply them to the study of real problems because the statistical procedures used lend themselves to straight-line relationships, and because the results aren't too far from reality. In mathematics, an equation that fits this kind of demand curve is called a *linear function.*

Vertical demand curves   If we tilt the linear demand curve until it becomes vertical, we have a curve with zero elasticity throughout its length. Such a demand curve implies that consumers insist on a certain quantity of a good whatever its price. They won't take more of it or less of it, regardless of how low or high the price. Few real commodities fit this case, though some may come close to it under certain conditions—perhaps tickets to the Superbowl or to a very popular rock concert. (Ticket scalpers work on the principle of zero elasticity. They might be able to get almost any price for a pair of Superbowl tickets after all the seats have been sold out.) Such a demand curve is shown in the top diagram of Figure 3. Notice that the quantity sold is always the same. This makes $Q_1 - Q_2$ equal to zero no matter what happens to the price. The numerator of the fraction measuring elasticity will thus be zero,

Table 2
Types of Elasticity

Random elasticity values	Interpretation (type)	Condition
3.67	elastic	el > 1
1.8	elastic	el > 1
1.0	unit elastic	el = 1
.56	inelastic	el < 1
.27	inelastic	el < 1

and the fraction itself will be zero (since zero divided by any number is still zero). Economists call this demand curve **perfectly inelastic** or **absolutely inelastic.**

Horizontal demand curves   At the other extreme is the horizontal demand curve shown in Figure 3b. This is important in economic theory because it is the demand curve of a firm selling in a perfectly competitive market. It implies that the firm is able to sell any quantity at the price indicated but is unable to charge a higher price because of competition. Along this demand curve, price does not change regardless of what happens to quantity. Therefore, $P_1 - P_2$ is zero everywhere. This means that in the formula for elasticity we must divide the numerator by zero. We may think of this as representing infinity, since such a fraction is infinitely large. We say that this demand curve has **infinite elasticity.**

Demand curves with constant elasticity   It is possible to draw a demand curve that has the same elasticity everywhere along it. One such curve is shown in Figure 3c. It is not, as we have already seen, a straight line but what

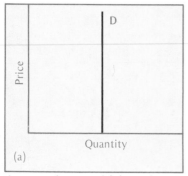

(a)

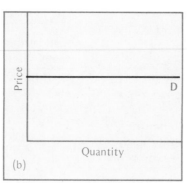

(b)

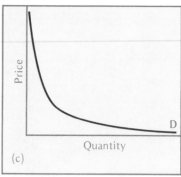

(c)

Figure 3   Three special demand curves: (a) perfectly inelastic; (b) infinitely elastic; (c) unit elasticity everywhere.

Extended Example
Elasticity and Parking Fees

Sometimes we find that the price of a good or service varies greatly depending on where we are or what time of day it is. The price of parking space in cities is an example. Parking fees seem to be cleverly arranged to hit our pocketbooks hardest when we most need to find a place to park. This is because prices are set to take advantage of different elasticities of demand.

During the main part of a business day, demand for parking is high and inelastic. Many drivers must visit urban offices even if it costs more. Owners of parking garages can charge high prices and still expect to fill all their spaces.

In the evening and on Sunday, offices are empty. Restaurants and shows attract fewer drivers relative to the available parking. Some spaces will remain unfilled, and parking rates are likely to reflect the lower and more elastic demand. Figure 4 shows the demand curves for parking during the day and at night.

Sometimes drivers are allowed to park free. This only happens, however, where there is plenty of space and demand is highly elastic. Suburban shopping centers are glad to provide free parking in order to attract drivers who can readily move from one shopping center to another unless convenient parking is available. In the cities, some restaurants and shops will pay part of their customers' parking fees. In effect, they are subsidizing their customers to persuade them to do business with them.

mathematicians call a rectangular hyperbola. Economists say it has *unit elasticity*. Elasticity is equal to one everywhere along the curve. This means that the percentage change in quantity is the same as the percentage change in price for any pair of reasonably close points on the curve.

Elasticity of demand and a firm's revenue

Business firms are concerned with the elasticity of demand for their products. They must try to estimate the effect of a price change on sales. An increase in price will reduce the quantity sold, but by how much? If demand is elastic, we can expect that a higher price will cause a substantial drop in sales, reducing the firm's total revenue. But if demand is inelastic, sales will drop off by a smaller proportion than the price change. Total revenues will increase even though the number of sales falls.

To illustrate, let's take the demand schedule of Table 1. You will recall that elasticity varies over the length of that schedule. At high prices demand is elastic. In the middle price range elasticity falls to unity. At very low prices demand is inelastic. These differences in elasticity as we move along the demand schedule are shown on the curve in Figure 5.

Total revenue

The data underlying this demand curve are given once again in the first three columns of Table 3. Column (4) shows the effect of elasticity on a firm's total sales revenue. We calculate *total revenue* (TR) at every point on the demand curve by multiplying price times the

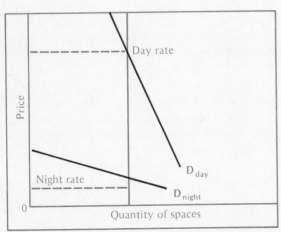

Figure 4 Demand for parking spaces during the day and at night. The demand curve for day parking is steeper, that is, more inelastic.

quantity sold: P × Q = TR. Total revenue may be represented by the area of a rectangle formed by horizontal and vertical lines drawn from any point on the demand curve. The dashed lines in Figure 5 form such rectangles. Notice how the rectangles vary in size as we move down along the demand curve.

Total revenue is greatest at the point where elasticity is equal to one. At that point the area of the rectangle under the demand curve is also greatest. Within the price range of $8 and $6, the percentage change in quantity is equal to the percentage change in price. A 1% increase in price leads to a 1% drop in quantity; thus there is no change in total revenue. Likewise, a 1% decrease in price leads to a 1% increase in quantity; again there is no change in total revenue.

Table 3
Hypothetical Data for Market Demand

(1) Price	(2) Quantity	(3) Elasticity	(4) Total revenue	(5) Marginal revenue
				$12
$12	1		$12	
		3.67		8
10	2		20	
		1.8		4
8	3		24	
		1.0		0
6	4		24	
		.56		−4
4	5		20	
		.27		−8
2	6		12	

What happens to total revenue outside this middle range? Look first at the higher part of the demand curve where elasticity is greater than one. In this range there will be a greater percentage change in quantity than in price. Within the range of $8 to $10, a 1% increase in price leads to a 1.8% decrease in the quantity sold. The larger percentage drop in quantity means a reduction in total revenue. In the range from $10 to $12 elasticity is even greater. A 1% increase in price will bring a 3.67% decrease in the quantity sold, and the reduction in total revenue will be still larger. On the other hand, if the firm reduces its price by 1%, its sales will increase by 3.67% and thus total revenue will increase.

At the lower end of the demand curve, elasticity is less than unity. This means that the percentage change in quantity will be less than the percentage change in price. In the price range from $6 to $4, a 1% decrease in price leads only to a .56% increase in quantity. The firm will reduce total revenue if it cuts price.

We have drawn Figure 6 immediately below Figure 5 to show how total revenue varies with changes in price. The two graphs have the same horizontal scales. Notice that total revenue increases as we reduce price, and keeps increasing until we reach the point on the demand curve where elasticity is equal to one. Beyond that point, total revenue decreases as we reduce price, even though the volume of sales is greater.

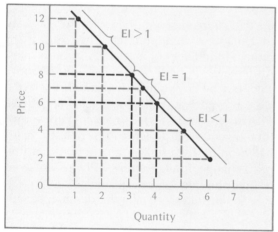

Figure 5 A hypothetical demand curve broken down showing the ranges of varying elasticities. At high price, demand is elastic here; at low price, demand is inelastic.

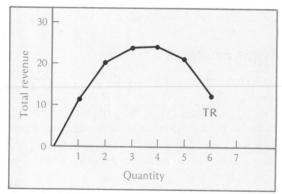

Figure 6 A total revenue (TR) curve. This curve is calculated from Figure 4, using the formula TR = P × Q. TR is greatest where elasticity equals one.

Extended Example

Monopolistic Competition in Ladies' Apparel

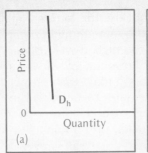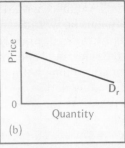

Figure 7 A clothing retailer sets two markets: (a) high-fashion clothing; (b) ready-to-wear clothing.

The ladies' apparel industry is described as a fragmented industry: it is broken into many small producers, each supplying a small fraction of the market. Initial capital costs are low, encouraging entry of new firms and increasing competition among them. Not only must firms compete among themselves for customers; they also must compete for sales against the customer's existing wardrobe!

As a result, the apparel industry reflects all the characteristics of monopolistic competition. There are many firms, each producing a smaller volume at higher prices than under perfect competition. Firms differentiate their product through design changes and heavy advertising, making profit margins very slim.

In order to increase demand and make demand curves less elastic, the industry must constantly create new fashions. New fashions render the customer's existing wardrobe out-of-date and shift demand curves to the right. New fashions create urgency in the mind of the fashion-conscious consumer and tilt demand curves up. In the area of high fashion clothing, firms are often able to sell more units at higher prices.

In recent years fashion-conscious Americans have been urged to emulate the Argentine ranchero, the guerilla fighter, the Indian peasant, and the Russian street sweeper. Often consumers have gone along with current fads, willingly paying the higher prices and discarding last year's clothes. But occasionally, they have rebelled. In the early 1970s American women refused to accept the maxi-skirt and clothing manufacturers lost millions of dollars.

If the maxi-skirt was the Edsel of the clothing industry, the pantsuit was its Mustang. Once American women grew accustomed to its comfort and wearability, they could not be persuaded to discard it completely in favor of new dresses. To the extent that consumers regard pantsuits as acceptable substitutes for skirts, demand curves for dresses will remain more elastic.

The apparel industry provides another example of using knowledge about demand to increase revenues. High-fashion design firms sell their "original" creations to wealthy women for as much as $5,000 a garment. At that price, volume is so low that profits are minimal. Therefore, the same firms market a separate line of ready-to-wear at much lower prices. See Figure 7. Total market demand is the sum of the two curves, and there are two prices instead of one. Total revenue is the sum of two rectangles formed beneath the two demand curves (see Figure 8).

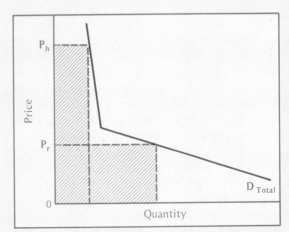

Figure 8 The separate market demand curves shown in Figure 7 are combined to give total market demand. Total revenue is sum of the shaded areas.

A retailer would not use the term elasticity, but he would say the same thing in different words: "If price is too high, it will discourage sales and keep total revenue low. If we cut price, volume will increase more than proportionately and our total sales revenue will increase. At some point, however, further price cuts will lead to smaller proportionate increases in volume. Then total sales revenue will begin to fall."

If a firm wanted to maximize its total revenue, it would sell its product at the price at which the elasticity of demand is equal to one. At that level of price and output, no change in price can produce a larger total revenue.

Marginal revenue

In making its pricing decisions, a firm isn't as concerned with total revenue as it is with marginal revenue. Management wants to know what will happen if it changes the price just a little and sells just a little more or less. **Marginal revenue** is the *change* in total revenue that results from a unit change in quantity sold. In Table 3 we show marginal revenue in column (5). It is calculated by figuring the differences between total revenue in column (4) for each change in price. As price is reduced from $12 to $10, total revenue increases by $8. Further reductions in price increase total revenue, but the increments are smaller each time and eventually become negative. This is shown graphically in Figure 9. The curve of marginal revenue slopes downward until it plunges through the zero level and becomes negative. At that point, reductions in price still increase quantity sold but they reduce total revenue.

Compare Figure 9 with Figures 5 and 6. Notice that over the price range where demand is elastic, price reductions yield greater total revenue. For each additional unit sold marginal revenue is positive. Now look at the price range where demand is inelastic. Over this range, price reductions yield less total revenue. For each additional unit sold marginal revenue is negative. Maximum total revenue occurs at the price where elasticity of demand is equal to one. This is also the price where marginal revenue is zero. *If a firm wants to maximize total revenue, it will set price so that marginal revenue is equal to zero.*

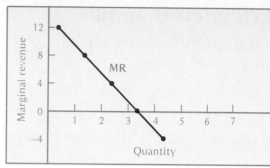

Figure 9 Marginal revenue curve for data presented in Figure 5. Where marginal revenue is zero (between 3 and 4 in quantity), total revenue is greatest.

This can be stated another way. If the firm is operating in a price range where marginal revenue is positive, it should reduce price for greater total revenue. If the firm is operating in a price range where marginal revenue is negative, it should increase price for greater total revenue.

Changing elasticity to increase total revenue

Many firms attempt to increase demand for their products in order to increase total revenue. Graphically, this means that demand curves shift to the right. If a firm's customers can be persuaded to purchase more units at every price, total revenue will increase. Another way is to make demand curves less elastic. If customers can be persuaded not to reduce their purchases proportionately when price increases, total revenue will increase. The firm can continue to raise price over the range of inelastic demand until it reaches the point of unitary elasticity.

Many companies have managed to tilt their curves so as to make them less elastic at every price level. One way of doing this is to make sure the consumer thinks of the product as uniquely desirable. It is not just any loaf of bread, but it is Mother Porter's Cracked Wheat Bread with Molasses. Consumers are less sensitive to price changes for products that they identify through brand names. Advertising is a

way of intensifying this attachment to a particular brand. Chemists tell us that there is no
difference between ordinary aspirin and the
well-known brands that are advertised on TV
and radio, but the demand for advertised
brands is less elastic. Manufacturers can raise
price significantly without suffering a great
drop in sales.

The results of a successful marketing campaign are illustrated in Figure 10. This firm has
tilted its demand curve from D_1 to D_2. The
shaded area shows how it has narrowed the
range through which sales volume can move
and how it has widened the range over which
price can be changed. With curve D_1 small
changes in price could cause sales to fluctuate
over almost the whole distance from O to Q.
With the new curve, D_2, the range is reduced
to about a third.

Once the demand curve is set, a firm must
decide on a particular price and quantity. If the
firm wants to maximize its revenue, it will set
its price at a point on the demand curve where
elasticity is equal to one. Figure 11 shows two
curves of quite different slope and the point of
maximum revenue or unit elasticity for each. In
each case, the revenue-maximizing firm will
sell Oa units at a price Ob. Total revenue is the
area of the rectangle under the curve. At any
other price on these demand curves total revenue would be lower, and the area of a rectangle formed under the demand curve will be
smaller. Try it.

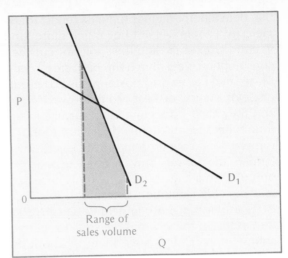

Figure 10 Demand for a product increases from D_1 to D_2.
Range of sales volume has declined. The firm can offer
much less of an item to get equal total revenue.

Revenue problems in agriculture

A highly inelastic demand curve (i.e., a steeply
sloping demand curve) is an advantage for a
business firm that wants to be able to increase
its prices freely without reducing its sales volume very much. For farmers, however, inelastic
demand curves often produce quite different
results. As a rule, farmers have little control
over their prices. When crops are good, the
large volume of farm products on the market
can cause prices to fall abruptly. When crops
are bad, the scarcity of farm products can
cause prices to shoot sky high. This is because

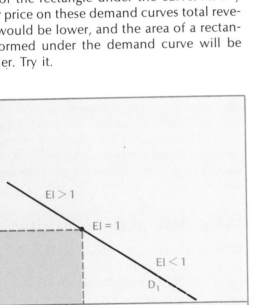

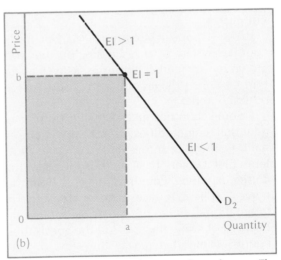

Figure 11 Two different demand curves. The shaded areas are respectively the maximum total revenues for each curve. The
point of unit elasticity (El = 1) determines the maximum total revenue.

the demand for farm products tends to be inelastic. People will not buy much more food in good crop years, and they will not cut their consumption very much in bad crop years. Meals aren't as easy to postpone as is the purchase of a house or a car or a microwave oven, and they can't be accumulated for use in the future. Because the demand for farm products is inelastic, a large drop in price is necessary if farmers are to sell only a small increase in output. And a large price increase is necessary to reduce consumption when food is scarce.

Farming is highly competitive. Because it is the industry that comes closest to perfect competition, farmers can't do much about the prices the market sets. An abundant harvest can be an advantage to consumers who can buy larger quantities at sharply reduced prices. The consequences for farmers are less pleasant. The revenue they receive may fall below the outlays they have to make for machinery, fertilizer, and household supplies.

Governments have tried various ways of stabilizing prices in an effort to keep farmers' incomes from falling sharply in good crop years. In the United States, from the 1930s to the beginning of the 1970s, the federal government kept the prices of a number of farm commodities above a certain level by purchasing surplus farm output. The Department of Agriculture also tried to limit the production of some crops through restrictions on the acreage that could be planted. In 1973, Congress ended the policies of buying surplus output and restricting acreage for many farm products (but not all).

The European Common Market has a complex system of *price supports* on the crops grown by its member countries, as well as import controls to keep out farm products from other countries.

Some countries specialize in exporting agricultural commodities or raw materials. As nations, these countries have the same problems that farmers have as individuals. When coffee-exporting countries have a bountiful harvest, they may face national disaster. The international price of coffee will plummet downward, while the prices of the goods these countries import may stay the same or even increase. A bad year, on the other hand, may bring prosperity to some farmers because the smaller quantity can be sold at premium prices. In 1976, frost in Brazil damaged much of the coffee crop. Prices soared in 1976 and 1977, enabling surviving producers to collect substantial revenues for their exports.

The problems of the raw material-producing countries have been the subject of many international conferences and of many schemes for regulating the prices of commodities in international trade. With the exception of the Organization of Petroleum Exporting Countries (OPEC), not much progress has been made in setting up arrangements to maintain high prices.

Elasticity of demand: some special features

Behind the downward-sloping demand curve lies the principle of diminishing marginal utility. As consumers get more and more of a good during any time period, the additional utility from owning still more units declines. Therefore, if consumers are to be induced to buy more, price must be reduced. A lower price is necessary to bring MU/P into equality with the MU/P of other purchases.

We have used the concept of elasticity to measure the responsiveness of consumers to price changes for various goods. Now we see that elasticity is a way of comparing the diminishing marginal utility of various kinds of purchases. *When marginal utility declines sharply with additional purchases, we may expect the quantity demanded to fall sharply.* A substantial price reduction is necessary to encourage consumers to buy more, and we say that demand is inelastic.

What determines elasticity?

What makes marginal utility fall faster for some goods or services than others? Four important factors may be cited. These are (1) the availability of substitutes, (2) whether a good is a necessity or a luxury, (3) the proportion of consumers' incomes devoted to the purchases, and (4) the length of the time period involved in drawing the demand curve.

Extended Example
Monkey Business

Some products are in demand not chiefly for their use by consumers but because they contribute an important function in industry. Would you believe—monkeys?

Monkeys are an example of a good with particular characteristics needed for scientific research. University and public health research organizations purchase monkeys imported from India, Brazil, and Peru. Because their biological systems are so close to humans, monkeys react similarly to disease and to medicinal drugs. For example, the South American marmoset monkey is vital to experiments involving the liver disease, hepatitis. Squirrel monkeys are useful for testing vaccine for swine flu. Owl monkeys are vital to malaria tests.

These special properties of monkeys make the demand curve highly inelastic and enable suppliers to raise prices freely. In 1970 foreign suppliers cut their shipments drastically and raised price to $45, five times the previous price. With transportation and maintenance costs the final cost is about $200 per animal.

Exporters of monkeys claim they were forced to reduce shipments in order to conserve their monkey population. But U.S. buyers suspected the reduced supplies were actually the result of conscious decisions to exact higher prices for a product with inelastic demand.

Buyers have been willing to pay the price because (1) there are no suitable substitutes, (2) monkeys are essential to laboratory research, and (3) their cost still represents only a small part of a total research budget. The fourth determinant of demand elasticity (4) is time. It takes time to develop substitutes and during short periods of time demand is inelastic.

American biologists are already at work on the problem. To deal with the high price of imported monkeys, scientists are encouraging development of domestic supplies. The costs of breeding monkeys locally are high because of the necessary controlled conditions and because of the high mortality rate of the infant animals. Current costs are estimated at about $1,200 each. Experience—and cooperation from the monkeys—should soon bring down that figure, however. In that case there will soon be substitutes for foreign monkeys and demand for imports will become more elastic.

Availability of substitutes The most important factor in determining the elasticity of demand for a good is the availability of substitutes for it. If the consumer can buy something else that will serve the same purpose, a very small change in price may bring a large change in the quantity purchased. For instance, if the price of one brand of cola drink were to increase by a nickel a bottle, a lot of cola drinkers would switch to competing brands; the demand would be quite elastic for that particular brand. If prices for all cola drinks were to rise by a nickel a bottle, however, there might be very little decline in sales.

At the other extreme are goods and services which are absolutely unique. When there is no substitute for a thing, buyers must purchase it without regard to price. The demand for the services of a kidney dialysis machine is quite inelastic for a patient whose kidneys have failed. Other goods and services with few substitutes include salt, insulin, and dental services. For these items demand is relatively inelastic with respect to price changes. A certain quantity is quite necessary, but beyond this amount marginal utility declines sharply.

Necessity or luxury Some goods—like many food stuffs—are necessary to life; such goods have few substitutes, and we would expect the demand for them to be relatively inelastic. The substitution effect for luxuries is stronger. Demand for luxuries will be relatively elastic because consumers will substitute among them as their prices change.

In general, luxuries can be classified as superior goods. Earlier we defined superior goods and showed how demand for these goods increases when lower prices increase consumer purchasing power. We called this the *income effect*. As prices fall, consumers have more spendable income and will use the extra income to buy larger quantities of goods they regard as superior. As incomes rise, the consumption of luxuries will rise more rapidly than the consumption of necessities. The income effect, added to the substitution effect, increases the elasticity of demand for luxuries relative to demand for necessities.

Proportion of income spent The elasticity of demand for a good is directly related to the portion of the consumer's income spent on it. When the price of candy bars went from a nickel to a dime many years ago, that was a price increase of 100%. But the demand proved inelastic; the quantity purchased declined little if at all. This was because the increase made practically no difference in relation to the income people had to spend. In contrast, a 100% increase in the price of automobiles would reduce sales drastically.

Time Another factor that is closely related to the two forgoing factors is the length of the time period covered by the demand curve. If the time period is short, there will be less opportunity to find a substitute than if the need can be postponed a while. If we have a flat tire on the highway and need to replace it, we will buy a new one at the next gas station even though the price may be high. For a short time period its marginal utility is great enough to justify its high price.

For longer time periods, consumers can adjust purchases more freely in response to price changes. In the case of new products, for instance, consumers may have to learn to use them. Until this happens, the marginal utility of a new product is very low. Over time the demand for microwave ovens or hand calculators responds more readily to price changes as people become accustomed to the new products. It even takes time for consumers to adjust their life-styles to enjoy new luxury products. Over longer time periods, the income and substitution effects mean greater elasticity of demand for luxuries.

Extended Example
Loss Leaders in Retail Stores

A marketing expert's version of Parkinson's Law might read:

Expenditures rise to absorb the capacity of the pocketbook.

At least that's what happens when many of us visit retail shops or supermarkets.

How often have you gone shopping for the "advertised special" and ended by filling your cart with a dozen other items you hadn't really planned to buy? This is precisely what the retailer expected you to do!

Retail shops and supermarkets often advertise a particular item with the hope of attracting customers. The item is called a "loss leader" because it may be sold at a loss. Nevertheless, the low price is expected to generate enough new sales for other higher priced items to more than offset the loss on the "bait."

Deciding on a loss leader involves consideration of demand elasticities. If demand is elastic, a very small change in price will elicit a great change in volume. Store traffic should rise and sales of other items increase in some proportion. If demand is relatively inelastic, store volume probably won't increase very much. Check your newspaper for the weekend specials. Very likely the advertised items will be characterized in the ways we have described goods in elastic demand:

(1) There are many substitutes. Customers can substitute the advertised product for other higher priced goods: economy-size bottles of soft drinks, chicken.

(2) For most people they are luxuries—fruits, ice cream, etc.—rather than essentials. Consumers who are undecided about indulging themselves will give in when price is reduced.

(3) They may even be items which involve a relatively large portion of a consumer's budget. This way a price reduction will make a real difference in purchase plans.

Items for which demand is inelastic are not likely to be advertised as a "come-on." For these items consumers purchase the quantities they require regardless of price. And few buyers are likely to respond to a special price when the need is not urgent. Some items in relatively inelastic demand might be the following: lampshades, auto repairs, diamond engagement rings, salt. Can you suggest others?

Items in inelastic demand provide an important part of a retailer's strategy in another way. Once the customer has taken the bait, prices for items in inelastic demand can be raised. It is assumed that customers will buy these items in roughly the same volume, and a higher price will raise total store revenues. The store comes out ahead.

Think about this the next time you shop for notebooks at "$\frac{1}{3}$ off regular price" and buy, in addition, toothpaste or shaving cream at a substantial mark-up.

Manufacturers use the same principle to boost their revenues. This is possible when a single firm produces several items to be used together. Examples are cameras and film, razors and blades, and even electric stoves and electric power.

A manufacturer of cameras, razors, or stoves has many competitors. This means there are close substitutes for the product and demand for a given brand is elastic. However, once a particular item has been selected, the consumer is locked into the purchase of the necessary complementary good. Demand for film, blades, and electric power becomes highly inelastic.

The clever manufacturer will take advantage of the difference in elasticities among the various goods produced. Price is generally reduced to the absolute minimum on the good for which there are rival producers. In fact, it may even be given away. The manufacturer can afford to take a substantial loss on the razor, knowing that price can be raised sharply for blades!

In the early 1970s the rising cost of sugar raised the cost of producing many soft drinks. For the Coca Cola Company the cost of producing Cokes rose sharply relative to the cost of producing its sugar-free diet drink. Yet the prices were raised for both! Can you explain this in terms of elasticity?

The income elasticity of demand

We have been talking about the relationship between changes in price and changes in the volume purchased. Economists call this the *price* elasticity of demand to distinguish it from other kinds of elasticity. The concept of elasticity may also be applied to changes in purchases that result from changes in income. This is called **income elasticity of demand,** and the basic formula is

income elasticity

$$= \frac{\% \text{ change in quantity demanded}}{\% \text{ change in income}}$$

As with price elasticity, we transform this formula into one based on averages:

income elasticity

$$= \frac{Q_1 - Q_2}{(Q_1 + Q_2)/2} \div \frac{Y_1 - Y_2}{(Y_1 + Y_2)/2}$$

$$= \frac{Q_1 - Q_2}{Q_1 + Q_2} \div \frac{Y_1 - Y_2}{Y_1 + Y_2}$$

where Y_1 is the old income and Y_2 is the new income.

For most goods, rising consumer incomes lead to larger total purchases. We have classified steak and fur coats as superior goods. An increase in income leads to an increase in quantity purchased. For superior goods calculations of income elasticity involve the same sign for the numerator and the denominator. *Thus income elasticity is positive for superior goods.*

Inferior goods are those whose purchases decline as incomes rise. Potatoes, chicken, and bus transportation are often classified as inferior goods. An increase in income leads to a decrease in quantities purchased. *For inferior goods income elasticity of demand is negative.*

Income elasticity equal to one signifies equal percentage changes in income and purchases.

The value of income elasticity reflects the effect of changes in income on consumer demand. Long-range trends toward higher incomes in the United States have sharply increased purchases of autos, vacation homes, and home recreation equipment. For these goods income elasticity of demand is high and positive. Income elasticity is lower for most food items and basic clothing.

Short-range fluctuations in income also affect demand. Periods of recession or prosperity cause changes in sales, depending on income elasticities for various goods. Declines in income lead to sharp reductions for many durable consumer goods: appliances, furniture, and automobiles. Production and employment in these industries fall sharply during short-range declines in income and rise during periods of prosperity. These industries were hard hit during the recession of 1973–1975 and were slow to recover. In contrast, spending for nondurable consumer goods remained fairly steady.

Cross elasticity of demand

Another kind of elasticity involves the demand for two related goods. For example, paint and paint brushes are related goods. If the price of paint rises, we may expect that less paint is sold and therefore fewer paint brushes will be sold. The higher cost of painting discourages remodelling, and thus the demand curve for brushes shifts to the left.

We define **cross elasticity of demand** as the percentage change in quantity demanded for one good relative to the percentage change in price for another:

cross elasticity

$$= \frac{\% \text{ change in quantity of good A}}{\% \text{ change in price of good B}}$$

The calculations for cross elasticity of demand are similar to those for price elasticity and income elasticity. But in this case the two parts of our fraction refer to different goods:

$$\text{cross elasticity} = \left\{ \frac{(Q_1 - Q_2)}{(Q_1 + Q_2)} \right\}_A \div \left\{ \frac{(P_1 - P_2)}{(P_1 + P_2)} \right\}_B$$

In the case of paint and paint brushes, mentioned above, the cross elasticity of demand was negative. The increase in paint prices led to a decrease in demand for paint brushes. But cross elasticity of demand is not always negative. Higher paint prices may lead to an increase in sales of wallpaper. We would then say that the cross elasticity of demand for wallpaper when paint prices increase is positive. By the same token, a decline in wallpaper prices will probably lead to a decline in the demand for paint. Since the quotient of two negative numbers is positive, the cross elasticity will again be positive.

Complementary goods We may characterize paint and brushes as *complementary goods:* they usually are used together. An increase in the price of paint reduces the demand for its complement, paint brushes. *Thus when two goods are complementary, the cross elasticity of demand has a negative sign.*

Another example of complementary goods is biscuits and jam. What makes them complementary is that they are more desirable together than separately. One may, as any child knows, eat jam all by itself out of the jar. One may also eat biscuits by themselves. But putting the jam on the biscuits heightens the enjoyment of both. That is why a decline in the price of biscuits could easily lead to increased sales of jam, as well as of biscuits.

Shirts and neckties are obviously complementary. If the price of shirts falls, more shirts may be purchased and probably also more ties. But complementarity doesn't always work both ways. The price of ties would probably have to fall a great deal in order to bring about greater sales of shirts.

Substitute goods Some goods replace others. Paint and wallpaper can be used in place of each other, and therefore we call them *substitute goods. When two goods are substitutes, their*

Extended Example
Cross Elasticity and the Law

The question of relatedness among goods and services is of more than textbook interest. Decisions of the U.S. Supreme Court have turned upon the measurement of cross elasticity. The Clayton Antitrust Act prohibits mergers of companies in the same industry if the effect would be to reduce competition. But what is an industry?

Defining the industry was an important consideration in a Court decision in 1964. The second largest U.S. manufacturer of tin cans had purchased the third largest U.S. producer of glass containers. The companies claimed that each produced different goods; therefore, the merger did not reduce competition in the two separate industries. The court decided differently, and the decision was based on the cross elasticity of demand. The Justices felt that users of cans and bottles could substitute between the two products fairly readily. With a high positive cross elasticity of demand, the two goods were part of the same industry. To allow the merger would be to increase the tendency toward monopoly in that industry. The expanded firm would control a substantial part of the market for containers and might increase price. For this reason the merger was not allowed. (But the Court was not in complete agreement. Two of the Justices issued a dissenting opinion in which they held that glass and metal containers were two separate industries, rather than one, and that both were in competition with plastic, paper, foil, and other kinds of containers.)

Another very famous decision involved the production of cellophane. A single firm produced almost all the nation's output of cellophane which it sold at prices as much as seven times the prices of other types of wrapping material. The producer of cellophane claimed that all wrapping papers, such as wax paper and brown wrapping paper, were essentially part of the same industry. That is, they were good substitutes for each other, and their cross elasticities were positive and large. Under this definition cellophane constituted only a small portion of industry output and there was no monopoly in the industry. Would you agree that the cross elasticities among these products are high? The courts did. The case was decided in favor of the manufacturer of cellophane.

cross elasticity of demand is positive. An increase in the price of one increases the demand for its substitute.

Substitutes have roughly similar characteristics. Whether they really replace each other depends on the individual consumer. For some people Bourbon would be an acceptable replacement for Scotch, while for others it would do only as a last resort. Margarine and butter are very close substitutes for most of us. The various cola drinks are also very close. Slightly more distant substitutes for a cola are other soft drinks such as root beer or orange soda. More distant still are milk, coffee, orange juice, beer, wine, or—when we're desperate—water.

Cross elasticity is a useful measure of the *relatedness* of different goods and services. High cross elasticity indicates a close relationship: a change in the price of one has a significant effect on the demand for the other. See if you can decide whether the following are close complements or good substitutes: tables and chairs; Scotch and soda; Coke and Pepsi; movies and plays; pretzels and popcorn.

In theory, any good may be related to any other good, if only distantly. To say that the cross elasticity of two commodities is zero is to imply that there is no conceivable relationship between them. If the price of skis rises, we wouldn't expect the demand for country-fried chicken to be affected at all. But we can't be certain of this. Remember the substitution and income effects. If the price of skis rises, consumers will be less well off and may have to restrict other purchases. The effect on country-fried chicken will depend on whether it is a superior or an inferior good. If it's superior, less will be purchased when the real income of skiers falls. If it's inferior, perhaps more will be purchased. The actual effect, of course, may be too slight for us to detect. It is best not to worry about this. For practical purposes we can think of some goods as being essentially unrelated in consumption and as having a cross elasticity of zero.

Summary

Demand curves show the quantity of a good that would be purchased at every price during a certain time period. Demand curves slope downward for three reasons: (1) there is diminishing marginal utility for additional purchases of a good; (2) at lower prices consumers will *substitute* more of the lower priced item for higher priced ones; (3) lower prices increase consumers' *incomes* and allow them to purchase larger quantities of superior goods. Some goods are inferior; a lower price increases consumers' incomes and enables them to reduce their purchases of inferior goods.

Demand may be characterized as elastic or inelastic depending on the responsiveness of consumers to a price change. Demand elasticity is defined as the percentage change in quantity relative to a percentage change in price. Vertical demand curves are perfectly inelastic: $el = 0$. Horizontal demand curves are infinitely elastic: $el = \infty$. A rectangular hyperbola has constant or unit elasticity throughout: $el = 1$. Most curves show variation in price elasticity from elastic ($el > 1$) at high prices to inelastic ($el < 1$) at low prices.

Total revenue is represented by the area of a rectangle drawn beneath demand at the market price. Maximum total revenue is achieved when $el = 1$: a percentage change in price produces an equal percentage change in quantity purchased.

Marginal revenue is the change in revenue which results from a change in price. When $el > 1$, marginal revenue is positive: a percentage decline in price produces a greater increase in quantity, and total revenue increases. When $el < 1$, marginal revenue is negative: a percentage decline in price produces a smaller increase in quantity, and total revenue decreases. When $el = 1$, marginal revenue is equal to zero: a percentage change in price produces an equal change in quantity, and total revenue is unchanged.

Advertising campaigns may help to shift demand curves to the right and to make them less elastic. The result may be greater pricing freedom and larger total revenue. Alternatively, inelastic demand may mean very low prices when quantity is ample, a frequent problem in agriculture.

Elasticity of demand depends on (1) the substitutability of the good or service, (2) whether the item is a necessity or a luxury, (3) the proportion of income spent for the item, and (4) the length of time for which the demand curve is drawn.

Income elasticity measures the percentage change in quantity relative to percentage change in income. Superior goods have positive income elasticity of demand and inferior goods have negative income elasticity of demand. Cross elasticity of demand measures the percentage change of quantity of one good relative to the percentage change in price of another. Complementary goods have a negative cross elasticity of demand, and substitute goods have a positive cross elasticity of demand.

Retailers and manufacturers use elasticity to set price, reducing price where demand is elastic and raising price where demand is inelastic.

Key Words and Phrases

- **substitution effect** lower prices for a good encourage a consumer to substitute the low-priced good for other higher-priced ones.
- **income effect** lower prices for a good increase a consumer's purchasing power and enable him or her to purchase more of certain goods.
- **superior goods** goods whose purchase increases when consumers' incomes increase.
- **inferior goods** goods whose purchase declines when consumers' incomes increase.
- **Engel curves** graphs which show the quantity of a good purchased at various levels of income.
- **Giffen goods** goods whose purchase increases at higher prices, often because of their "snob" appeal; Giffen goods have upward-sloping demand curves.
- **demand elasticity** the percentage change in quantity demanded of a good relative to a percentage change in its price.
- **elastic** a condition of demand where the percentage change in quantity demanded is larger than the percentage change in price.
- **inelastic** a condition of demand where the percentage change in quantity demanded is smaller than the percentage change in price.

- **unit elasticity**   a condition where the percentage changes in price and quantity demanded are the same.
- **linear function**   any function or equation that fits (or describes) a straight line.
- **perfect inelasticity of demand**   a condition where a percentage change in price brings on no change in quantity demanded.
- **infinite elasticity of demand**   a condition where infinite changes in quantity demanded take place with no change in price.
- **total revenue**   the product of price times quantity sold.
- **marginal revenue**   the change in total revenue that results from a unit change in quantity sold.
- **income elasticity of demand**   the percentage change in quantity demanded relative to a percentage change in income.
- **cross elasticity of demand**   the percentage change in quantity demanded of one good relative to a percentage change in price of another.

Questions for Review

1. Give examples and explain the effect of price change on quantity demanded when (a) the income and substitution effects work in the same direction; and (b) the income and substitution effects work in opposite directions.

2. Draw a typical linear demand curve. Then draw a second curve which lies exactly half way between the demand curve and the vertical axis of your graph. This curve is your marginal revenue curve. Use the marginal revenue curve to explain changes in total revenue which would result from changes in price.

3. Use the following hypothetical data to compute the price elasticity of demand for goods produced by firms A and B.

Firm A		Firm B	
Price	Quantity	Price	Quantity
100	5	100	11
80	10	80	13
60	15	60	15
40	20	40	17
20	25	20	19

What pricing policies would you recommend for maximizing total sales revenue?

4. Compare elasticity of demand for each of the following pairs. In every case consider the four determinants of elasticity and discuss the significance of each for the particular good.
(a) a new auto—auto repair service.
(b) newspapers—*New York Times*.
(c) food—clothing.

5. What types of goods would be expected to have negative cross elasticity of demand? Explain.

6. How do the income and substitution effects interact for: (a) an inferior good; (b) a superior good?

7. Define: income elasticity of demand, Giffen goods.

8. How have high oil prices affected demand for propane gas? How has the fast-food trend affected supermarket sales? What effect did high building costs have on the demand for mobile homes? Give other examples of interaction between markets.

9. Recent weather changes have damaged crops in many parts of the world and raised prices of basic foods. How is the income effect demonstrated in the effect of higher food prices on certain food purchases? What is the income effect of excise taxes? What type of industries are harmed most?

10. Large industrial users of electric power are often charged at a lower rate than residential users. This is in part because capital costs are lower when a large volume of service is provided one single user. When fuel costs rose in the 1970s, however, the greater cost increase was passed on to large industrial users. Explain why.

11. Soaring coffee prices in the winter of 1977 discouraged consumption. What effect did this have on demand for muffins and donuts? Explain in terms of elasticity. What effect did this have on the demand for waitresses?

12. What is the mathematical shorthand for demand that is: (a) unit elastic; (b) inelastic; (c) elastic?

13. Ice skating rinks must often operate 24 hours a day in order to cover their high costs. However, skating fees vary throughout the period and on different days of the week. Explain in terms of elasticity.

26

Supply and Elasticity

Whenever consumers demand a good or service, someone will generally be willing to supply it. This is true even if the item is illegal, immoral, or fattening—and especially so.

Most of us are, or will be, suppliers of some sort. We will seek out consumer demand and try to fill it. We will sell insurance policies, auto repairs, industrial designs, fast foods, or tap dancing skills. Few of us, however, will imitate those ambitious entrepreneurs who sought to supply Colombian grass to the nation's pot smokers by using parachute drops. Evidently, it was worth someone's efforts in 1976 to hire old World War II cargo planes to cruise low over the Georgia hills, dropping bales of illegal greenery to "salesmen" waiting below.

This chapter will examine supply curves with the same attention we have previously given to demand curves. We will use the concept of elasticity to describe and compare supply curves. Then we will show how elasticity affects economic policy in particular markets.

In the chapters to follow, we will look more closely at the way firms make their production decisions. Our investigation will enable us to construct supply curves under various market conditions.

Supply curves: a review

We saw earlier how supply curves reflect the output decisions of producers. In general, producers would be willing to supply larger quantities at higher prices and smaller quantities at lower prices. If the price of tennis shoes is high, it would pay firms to operate their plant and machinery more intensively. They would hire more labor and purchase more materials with the object of meeting the demand and thus increasing their profits. If the price of tennis shoes should fall dramatically, then firms would operate their plant and equipment less intensively, hire fewer workers, and cut back their orders for materials. By reducing production, firms would seek to reduce their expected losses from low selling prices.

Drawing the supply curve

Figure 1 shows a typical supply curve drawn for some good or service over a given period of time. The upward slope shows that higher prices would mean higher production and lower prices would mean lower production. We say that there is a *positive* relationship between quantity and price. Larger values on the horizontal axis are associated with larger values on the vertical axis.

The points along the supply curve indicate the largest quantities that would be produced at every price level over a certain time period. There is another way of saying the same thing: *the supply curve shows the lowest price for which a firm would be willing to produce a given quantity.* Producers would not supply output below or to the right of the supply curve because the price would not be high enough to make it pay. They would, of course, be glad to produce any quantity at prices above or to the left of the curve, but this is not likely to happen in competitive markets. Rivalry among firms would force the price down to the lowest level at which the producers will accept orders.

Elasticity of supply

The concept of elasticity is useful in describing supply, just as it is in describing demand. We saw that demand elasticity measures the response of quantity demanded to a change in price during a particular time period. The

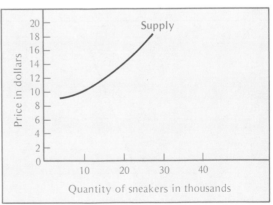

Figure 1 A typical supply curve is upward sloping.

changes are stated in percentage terms, and we calculate elasticity by dividing one percentage by the other. If the result is greater than one, we say that demand is elastic: quantity responds by a greater percentage than the price change. If elasticity is less than one, we say that demand is inelastic: quantity responds by a smaller percentage than the price change. Elasticity of supply is calculated in the same way.

When we drew the supply curve, we pointed out the positive relationship between price and quantity supplied. An increase in price would lead to larger quantities and a reduction in price would lead to smaller quantities. For this reason our elasticity figure will be a positive number. The numerator and denominator will have the same sign, and the quotient of two numbers with the same sign is always positive.

To illustrate elasticity of supply, let us look at two hypothetical markets for shoulder bags. Table 1 supplies the price and quantity data for two kinds of shoulder bags: hand-tooled leather bags and machine-made vinyl bags. The quantities shown are the numbers of bags which would be produced for sale in a particular market in a given period of time. The table also shows the elasticities of supply for the two goods.

We have drawn the supply curves for leather and vinyl shoulder bags in Figure 2. As we know from Table 1, the supply of hand-tooled bags is inelastic at all points on the curve. The supply of machine-made vinyl bags is elastic, reflecting the ease with which factory

Table 1
Supply Data for Shoulder Bags (one month)

Price	Quantity of leather bags	Elasticity	Quantity of vinyl bags	Elasticity
$50	28		9000	
		.33		1.125
40	26		7000	
		.28		1.167
30	24		5000	
		.22		1.25
20	22		3000	
		.14		1.5
10	20		1000	

output can be stepped up to meet an increase in price. An interesting characteristic of these curves is that if we extend them as shown in Figure 2, the inelastic supply curve cuts the horizontal axis to the right of the origin of the graph, while the elastic supply curve cuts the vertical axis above the origin.

Perfect inelasticity

Some goods and services are fixed in supply, and no increase in price will bring forth a larger quantity. There will never be more Rembrandt paintings than exist now or another genuine 1926 Model T Ford. The supply curve for a good that is fixed in supply is shown in Figure 3a. It is drawn as a vertical line because the quantity remains the same at all prices. Because the change in quantity is zero, the value of elasticity in this case is also zero. (The numerator of the fraction measuring elasticity will

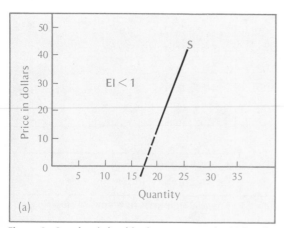

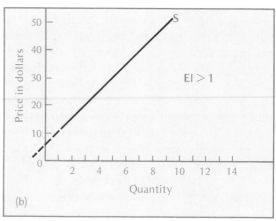

Figure 2 Supply of shoulder bags per month: (a) hand-tooled leather bags; (b) machine-made vinyl bags.

Extended Example
Calculating Elasticity of Supply

If the price of hand-tooled leather handbags rises from $40 to $50, encouraging producers to make 28 bags instead of 26, what is the elasticity of supply?

We use the same formula that we developed in the chapter on demand elasticity. The change in quantity is expressed as

$$\frac{Q_1 - Q_2}{(Q_1 + Q_2)/2}$$

and the change in price as

$$\frac{P_1 - P_2}{(P_1 + P_2)/2}$$

Dividing the two percentages and cancelling the 2's leaves:

$$\text{Elasticity of supply} = \frac{Q_1 - Q_2}{Q_1 + Q_2} \div \frac{P_1 - P_2}{P_1 + P_2}.$$

Using the values given above, P_1 is $40 and P_2 is $50. Likewise, Q_1 is 26 and Q_2 is 28. Substituting in the equation, we have:

$$\frac{26 - 28}{26 + 28} \div \frac{40 - 50}{40 + 50} = \frac{-2}{54} \div \frac{-10}{90}$$

$$= \frac{-1}{27} \times \frac{-9}{1}$$

$$= \frac{1}{3} = .33.$$

This means that, at this point on the supply curve, a 1% change in the price of leather bags will lead to a change in supply of only .33%. Thus we can say that the supply of leather bags is inelastic. At other points on the supply curve, supply is even more inelastic as we can see from Table 1.

Table 1 also provides price and output data for machine-made vinyl bags. If their price rises from $40 to $50, the number supplied will increase from 7,000 to 9,000. Substituting in the formula, we have

$$\frac{7,000 - 9,000}{7,000 + 9,000} \div \frac{40 - 50}{40 + 50} = \frac{-2}{16} \div \frac{-10}{90}$$

$$= \frac{-1}{8} \times \frac{-9}{1}$$

$$= \frac{9}{8} = 1.125.$$

The supply of machine-made bags is more responsive to price changes; supply is elastic over the price range shown.

---

be zero; hence the fraction itself will be zero.) Supply curves for which elasticity is equal to zero are said to be **perfectly inelastic.**

Infinite elasticity

At the other extreme, the supply of some goods and services can expand to any amount with no change in price. There is no human-made good with such a flexible supply, but pencils probably come as close as any other manufactured good. The supply curve for pencils may be said to have practically infinite elasticity. Referring to our formula, we see that this time the denominator will be zero since there is no change in price. A number divided by zero is infinitely large. Supply curves for which elasticity is infinitely large are said to be

infinitely elastic. Infinitely elastic supply curves are drawn as horizontal lines at whatever happens to be the established price for the good or service (Figure 3b).

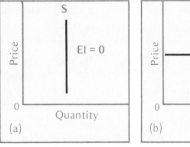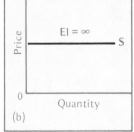

Figure 3 The two extremes in supply curves: (a) perfectly inelastic supply; (b) infinitely elastic supply.

Elastic vs. inelastic supply curves

Classifying supply curves as elastic or inelastic enables us to say certain things about the nature of supply. We can say, in general, that *inelastic supply curves reflect a relatively small response by producers to change in price.* For some reason producers are unable to take full advantage of price increases by expanding their output in equal proportion. On the other hand, when price falls, producers are unable to make sharp cutbacks in their output. Perhaps the best example of this type of producer is a farmer who decides on production at the beginning of the growing season and can't change production plans until the following season. Whether farmers plant too many watermelons or too few, they have to live with their decision for that growing season.

Elastic supply curves reflect a relatively greater response to price changes. Producers are able to take on more workers and open more production lines when prices are rising, and to cut back when prices are falling. Supply tends to be fairly elastic in manufacturing industries. In many services it is highly elastic, particularly those employing unskilled labor.

What determines the elasticity of supply?

Suppose Pierre, the French baker, makes a batch of pastry. He puts the pastry in his window, and toward the end of the day there are a dozen unsold. He has a choice of eating them himself or marking down the price in hopes of selling them before closing time. He won't make a profit selling them at half price, but he will get back some of his expenses. His supply curve for that batch of French pastry is perfectly inelastic; he won't make any more apple tarts or chocolate eclairs that day even if someone were to offer him double the usual price, but he is willing to sell what he has at any price.

There are three important factors affecting the elasticity of supply: (1) time; (2) technology; and (3) expectations of supplies. Let's look at each in turn.

Time

Our example of the French baker illustrates a very important point about supply: Time is important in determining elasticity. If we make the time period short enough, almost every supply curve becomes inelastic. There aren't enough materials, or enough workers, or enough machines, to increase the quantity supplied any further during a very short time period. On the other hand, if we make the time period long enough there is almost no limit to the possible increase in quantity supplied. Economists customarily distinguish three time periods when analyzing the behavior of supply. There is the *immediate time period*, in which the baker can make no more pastry because work is over for the day. There is the *short run*, in which the baker can increase output up to the limit of the existing plant—that is, by hiring more workers and putting in more hours a day making apple tarts and chocolate eclairs. Finally, there is the *long run*, in which the baker can move to a larger plant, put in more ovens, and perhaps be faced with competing bakers who are attracted by the expected profits.

Figure 4 shows three supply curves illustrating the immediate or momentary period, the short run, and the long run. Supply in the momentary period is perfectly inelastic: bakers can't increase their quantity supplied no matter what price is offered. Therefore, the supply curve is vertical. The example most often given to explain momentary inelasticity is the farmer who comes to market with his crop and has to sell it at whatever price the market offers. Often the product is perishable, like tomatoes or lettuce, so the farmer can't take it home and wait for a better price. And a farmer can't bring more if the price is high, because the entire crop has been harvested.

But over a period of a year or more the farmer's supply curve will become more elastic, like the short-run curve in Figure 4. If prices are favorable, the farmers grow more tomatoes and lettuce with their existing land and equipment. Bakers produce more pastry with their existing plant. As the upward-sloping curve shows, supply is responsive to a higher price.

Extended Example
Gum Drops and Beer

Many common household and industrial products require a little-known ingredient supplied from Sudan, south of Egypt. The rare ingredient is gum arabic, the sap of the acacia trees found growing wild in this African nation. In 1968, production of 61,545 tons was used in the manufacture of candies, ice cream, beer and wine, dietetic foods, adhesives, rubber, ceramics, fertilizer, explosives, hair sprays, lotions, ointments, and detergents. Although there are substitutes, none has the special characteristics required in these uses. As a result, the derived demand for gum arabic is rather inelastic.

In late 1968 the Sudan was hit by a drought which lasted six years. Farmers and nomads moved out of the region, and production of gum arabic dropped to a low of 21,194 tons in 1973. Supply curves shifted to the left and the market equilibrium price rose.

The nation is now attempting to regularize supplies of this valuable export. Farmers are now cultivating acacia trees in small plantations. Cooperatives have been formed to organize production and credit is being extended to encourage capital investment. Transport companies have been formed to provide dependable freight service from the producing areas. Potential production is estimated at 100,000 tons annually.

What is the shape of the long-run supply curve for gum arabic?

If sales continue to grow and prices continue to rise, in the long run, farmers and bakers will add to their productive resources. Farmers will buy more land and equipment; bakers will enlarge their bakeries. If, on the other hand, they face declining prices, some of them may leave their industry and try to make a better living elsewhere. In the long run, supply curves will become still more elastic, since quantity may expand or contract to almost any extent; they will approach infinite elasticity, as in Figure 4. (Supply curves may not reach infinite elasticity, however, if higher-cost resources must be used. Thus if farmers have to buy more expensive land, or if the greater demand for fertilizers causes fertilizer prices to rise, farmers will have to charge a bit more for their vegetables and the supply curve will not be completely horizontal. We will explore this possibility in more detail later.)

Technology

In an earlier example, we found that the elasticity of supply for hand-tooled leather bags was less than one (inelastic) while that for machine-made vinyl bags was greater than one (elastic). At any particular time it will be much easier to expand the supply of machine-made bags than that of hand-tooled ones. To produce more hand-made bags it will be necessary to find more skilled workers and set them to work. In contrast, the obedient machines

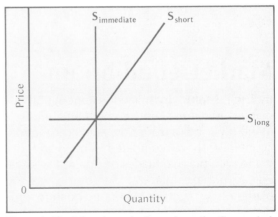

Figure 4 Elasticity of supply depends on the time period. Each of the three time periods may have different supply curves and therefore different elasticities.

stand ready at any time to labor a little harder or a little longer. Obviously, some technologies are more flexible than others in terms of volume of output. An even better example is the automobile industry, where wide swings in production may occur from one year to another or even from one month to another.

Along with the technology of production, we may include differences in the availability of resources used in particular industries. When resources are plentiful, the quantity of output is generally more responsive to price changes than when necessary resources are scarce. If in order to expand output, producers must mine an inferior vein of coal or develop new and more expensive ways of purifying ores, then an increase in supply may require a substantial increase in price.

Expectations

Business firms are run by human beings, not machines, and changes in supply may depend on how people feel or think about the future. The fact that prices have increased may not be enough to start the wheels turning unless those in command think the higher prices will continue. A sudden drop in prices may not discourage production very much either, unless business firms expect prices to remain low. The producer of hand-tooled shoulder bags may not want to train additional craftsmen and set them to work unless the increase in demand is expected to continue. Thus business firms do not always adjust their production to market signals, rightly or wrongly. When they don't, supply may remain inelastic for some time.

Market equilibrium

By itself, supply doesn't tell us enough about markets. We must know something about demand if we are to learn how markets function. Economists have compared supply and demand with the two blades of a pair of scissors. The action takes place at the point where the blades come together. When the quantity producers are willing to supply is just sufficient to meet the demand of those who are willing to buy, we say that the market has reached equi-

Extended Example
The Green Revolution

We have shown how supply curves become more elastic as producers adjust their output to accommodate the demands of buyers. Over time, supply curves may tilt from perfectly vertical to perfectly horizontal or, in terms of elasticity, from perfect inelasticity to infinite elasticity. The slope of the supply curve depends on the response of producers to price changes.

When producers are *responsive*, we consumers are able to enjoy larger quantities of goods and services without having to pay higher prices. Is it possible, you may ask, for producers to be *so responsive* that we consumers might enjoy larger quantities at even lower prices? In other words, is it possible for supply curves ever to slope *downward?* In one sector of the U.S. economy conditions have been such as to bring about this pleasant result, largely because of the work of scientists like Norman Borlaug.

In 1970, Norman Borlaug received the Nobel Peace Prize. The unusual thing about this award was that Norman Borlaug is a botanist. Why should a *botanist* be awarded the *Peace* Prize?

More specifically, Borlaug is a plant geneticist. He specializes in plant mutations, plants which are superior to their ancestors in such things as protein content, fertility, and resistance to disease.

Borlaug was instrumental in changing wheat from a tall, fragile plant which would collapse in bad weather to a more stable, shorter variety. The resulting wheat plant converts water and fertilizer into a larger kernel of grain, rather than into useless straw. Furthermore, the new plant is resistant to wheat rust and other plant parasites and can be grown over a wide range of climatic latitudes.

Borlaug's work began in Mexico where crops had been regularly decimated by wheat rust. The research was long and painstaking. It involved months of careful work followed by more months of patient waiting for new plants to develop. Plants of desirable characteristics had to be cross pollinated with other plants to produce new seeds. Then Borlaug and his team of scientists would plant by hand 4,500 to 5,000 new varieties of wheat—about a million and a half seeds. From dawn to dusk the planting had to be done quickly, for then the first young sprouts had to be inoculated twice with a hypodermic solution of wheat rust. Plants that survived were retained for developing rust-resistant strains; they were further adapted to prepare them for the land and climatic features of particular countries.

Borlaug is in the forefront of a worldwide movement financed by U.S. foundations. The purpose is to provide the collective wisdom and experience of American farmers to countries struggling with the problem of too little food for their growing populations. Borlaug's new seeds helped to make Pakistan self-supporting in wheat and put India on the road to self-sufficiency. His goal was always to increase a nation's wheat production by at least 100% in the first year of experimentation. The goal was psychologically important for generating local government support for his project and for convincing native farmers to adopt his techniques.

World population is now about four billion. It is presently increasing about 2% annually; if it continues at this rate, population will reach about eight billion within 35 years. Demand curves for food are shifting to the right, and it is important that supplies of food grow at least as fast. For the past two centuries the application of technology to agriculture has accomplished sufficient growth to prevent mass starvation. Further improvements in productivity will be more difficult. This is because there is less tillable land remaining for cultivation and because costs of chemical fertilizers have been rising. Scientists are seeking new ways to expand agricultural output, but they worry that the world may be approaching absolute ceilings of production.

Unhappily, research and development spending in agriculture has declined (when measured in real terms). Currently, scientists are working on projects to:

(1) improve plant use of carbon dioxide for producing carbohydrates and for creating their own fertilizer, nitrogen, within the plant itself;

(2) produce improved plant strains in the laboratory rather than through the time-consuming process of crossbreeding;

(3) increase output per acre through use of high-yield planting techniques;

(4) increase beef and egg production through animal hormone treatments;

(5) fatten cattle on a diet of garbage. Failure to continue technical advance in these and other areas will slow the growth of food supply and increase prices over the globe.

What are the implications of rising market prices for food? A larger portion of consumer budgets will have to be allocated toward purchase of basic needs. Other consumer goods industries will suffer a decrease in sales as consumers cut back other spending. Incomes to resource owners will change and resources will shift among industries according to changing consumer spending. The adjustments within food-producing nations like the United States will be gradual, but there will be some disruptions nevertheless. Those who are harmed by the changes will demand government action to protect their interests. For instance, consumers may demand government imposed embargoes on food exports and price controls on food. Food producers in this country and food importers abroad will resist these policies. Other nations may retaliate with embargoes on shipments of their basic raw materials to U.S. industry. The benefits of international trade will be replaced by the trauma of international conflict, possibly leading to outright war.

For these reasons we should recognize and encourage the work of "Peace" scientists like Norman Borlaug.

librium. The *equilibrium price* is the price which brings buyers and sellers together in the right numbers to clear the market. It is the price at which the quantity suppliers want to sell is just equal to the quantity consumers want to buy.

Not everybody will be happy with the equilibrium price. Some producers may find that they must accept a lower price than they had hoped to get; their alternative is to hold off and wait for a better day. Some would-be consumers may find that the price is more than they had wanted to pay; their alternative is to refrain from buying.

Figure 5 shows three different equilibrium positions in the same market over a period of time. The *immediate period* supply curve S_1 represents the limited quantity of a good available at a particular moment (Q_1). Buyers must pay price P_1, which is determined by the intersection of the demand curve with S_1. Those who don't want to pay that price must go without. But sellers are aware of the unsatisfied demand and, as quickly as possible, take steps to increase supply. Their response to the high price is shown by the *short-run* supply curve S_2. At the new equilibrium point, determined by the intersection of the demand curve with S_2, a larger amount, Q_2, will be sold. Purchasers willing to pay price P_2 are able to buy. There are still potential customers, however, and supply eventually increases still more. The *long-run* supply curve is S_3, and the long-run market equilibrium point is at the intersection of demand with S_3. As producers adjust production over longer time periods, equilibrium price falls to P_3 and quantity increases to Q_3. More customers are satisfied and more goods are available at lower prices.

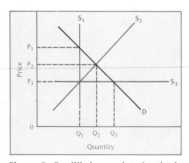

Figure 5 Equilibrium points for the immediate period, the short run, and the long run. Notice that equilibrium price declines from P_1 in the immediate period to P_3 in the long run.

What difference does elasticity make?

Understanding elasticity helps us to understand price behavior. As supply becomes more elastic, consumers benefit from greater output and prices become more stable. Increases in consumer demand will encourage the proper response from suppliers. Not all firms will be equally responsive to an increase in demand. Some firms have already reached their limits and for one reason or another cannot expand any further; others may go on growing, and some new firms may appear. These differences in the way firms respond also exist among industries, as we shall see.

Microeconomic adjustments The process of adjustment to a change in demand can be looked at from two points of view. One is the *microeconomic* point of view, examining the way in which individual firms respond to change. When the industry is competitive, firms will adjust more rapidly, increasing or cutting back their production when demand rises or falls. If conditions require it, new firms may enter the industry or old firms may drop out. Firms must react quickly to avoid losing out to competitors. A quick response is possible only if technical information is readily available to all firms and if capital and labor can move freely among industries.

Macroeconomic adjustments Another way of looking at the process of adjustment is from the *macroeconomic* point of view, which concerns the general price level. Here again the adjustments will take place more quickly in competitive industries. If factors such as monopoly or lack of mobility or governmental restrictions slow down the adjustment process, prices may remain higher or lower than they otherwise would. For example, if the government puts a tariff on silk scarves to keep out low-priced scarves from abroad, producers of scarves in this country will be protected from competition. They may not take steps to expand short-run supply, and they will be able to charge higher prices than if there were no tariff. High-cost producers will be able to stay in business, and others will earn higher profits because their foreign competitors have been

Extended Example
Macroeconomics and Supply and Demand

We have examined the microeconomic effects of changes in demand, but demand has macroeconomic effects as well. Shifts in demand cause price changes and signal business to adjust output to the needs of consumers. Increases in demand cause price increases and provide the incentives to expand production. Employment and incomes rise as the economy enjoys greater output of goods and services.

One type of demand has particularly important implications for macroeconomics. It is business investment for inventories. On the average, business firms attempt to hold inventories equal to about two months of sales. When sales increase, inventory orders must often increase by *twice* as much in order to maintain this ratio. Of course, the reverse is also true. When sales fall, inventory orders are cut by a larger amount.

Inventories include raw materials used in manufacture, unfinished goods, and goods ready for final sale. Increased inventory demand can cause demand curves for industrial materials to shift to the right. In the short run prices will rise; over the longer term the high prices will serve as an incentive to expand output of industrial commodities.

Inventory demand can send the wrong signals to producers and severely damage the economy. This was the case during the recession of 1973–1975. Shortages of industrial commodities had built up during the previous years; oil and grain were the most notable, although there were also shortages of lumber, steel, copper, and other industrial materials. Business firms sought to build up their inventory stocks as protection against future shortages. The immediate effect of the shift in demand was sharply rising prices for industrial commodities.

Rising prices added a second reason for inventory building. Expectations of still higher prices in the future persuaded business firms to try to beat the price rise, and demand curves shifted even further.

Production increased, and higher prices encouraged many suppliers of industrial goods to expand productive capacity. Unfortunately, they were responding to faulty signals. By the time productive capacity increased, demand had shifted back to the left and prices began to fall.

The drop in demand was the result of several causes. First, consumer spending had declined as a result of the recession. The high unemployment and threats of layoffs held down consumer spending and producers moved to cut back inventories. Second, many orders for industrial materials were made in duplicate so as to ensure delivery. When the goods were received, the duplicate orders were cancelled. Finally, interest charges rose sharply in 1974, making borrowing for inventory purchases especially costly. Business demand was cut back sharply.

Inventory buying is subject to abrupt periods of expansion and contraction, leading to severe pressures on suppliers. When supply is inelastic, prices rise and the nation experiences inflation. Over the longer term, producers expand their capacity and supply becomes more elastic. Prices should fall. Often, however, prices are rigid downward and the higher price is built into prices of finished goods. One reason prices don't fall is the cost of the added productive capacity. The cost must be spread over the number of units produced by the expanded plant. If demand should fall, this cost is spread over a smaller quantity of output and prices must rise further. The costs of inventory accumulation probably contributed heavily to price inflation in 1973–1975.

Unemployment was also a problem during those years. Again, inventory demand was a factor. The overinvestment in inventories in previous years left firms with excess stocks, particularly in view of declining consumer spending. Orders were cut back drastically so that firms could work off the excess. Reduced inventory buying led to cutbacks in employment and ultimately to further drops in consumer spending.

fenced out. Inelastic supply may lead to unusually low prices in other markets. In rural areas wages are sometimes low, because the workers who live there cannot easily move. They cannot respond quickly to low wage rates by reducing supply. Thus they work for sub-normal wages, while employers and consumers reap an advantage.

Prices that are rigidly high or low cause a transfer of income into some industries and away from others. In some industries fewer goods are produced than consumers would buy if prices were lower; in others, costs and prices are kept artificially low and resources are misallocated to products of low value. In the examples given above, fewer silk scarves are produced than consumers might buy if there were no tariff restrictions, while rural areas turn out more low-cost products than consumers would buy if labor moved into better paying jobs and prices were raised.

Since 1954, the U.S. government has kept natural gas prices from rising freely. Price controls have interfered with long-range adjustment to increased demand for natural gas. Producers have not increased short-run supplies significantly, nor have they invested in new exploration to increase long-run supplies. Low prices have transferred income away from this industry and resources have flowed out. If Congress finally decides to lift price controls on natural gas, the equilibrium price will probably rise sharply to reflect the growing demand relative to highly inelastic supply.

When government sets prices

The price system, as we have seen, is a useful means of guiding production. Changes in prices signal changes in consumer demand. Higher prices indicate that more is demanded, leading producers to expand output. Lower prices lead them to cut back. Market forces help to direct productive resources in order to satisfy changing consumer tastes.

Sometimes governments seek to interfere with the adjustment process by controlling prices. In time of war when resources are needed for war production, it is necessary to hold down the production of consumer goods. To prevent their prices from rising, the government may decide to set maximum prices (called *price ceilings*) on various commodities so that consumers will not bid up prices.

At other times, for other reasons, governments may decide to set minimum prices (called *price floors*). Both kinds of price controls have far-reaching economic consequences.

Price ceilings and shortages

Maximum prices set by government are called **price ceilings.** Because a price ceiling is almost always set below the equilibrium price, in effect it places a lid on the price of a good. Price ceilings are necessary when it is felt that the equilibrium price would be undesirably high. In time of war, prices are controlled to prevent inflation and to enable lower-income consumers to buy their share of goods.

During World War II, gasoline supplies were needed for the U.S. war effort. Fuel was needed for planes, ships, and tanks, with little remaining for civilian drivers. At the same time, rising incomes earned in war production had put greater purchasing power in the hands of consumers. Inflation was a real threat.

Figure 6 shows what might have happened if market forces had been allowed to work. The supply curve is vertical to show that the amount of gasoline available for civilian use is fixed. In the absence of price controls, the equilibrium point would be at the intersection of the supply and demand curves; price would be P_e. The ceiling imposed by the government reduces the price to P_c. At this price the demand for gasoline is Oa, which is much greater than the actual supply Ob. There is a *shortage* equal to ab. People don't have to pay as much for gasoline as they would if there were no price ceiling, but only the first comers will be served.

Thus price ceilings normally create shortages which must be corrected through **rationing:** rationing means to allot scarce items among buyers, generally on the basis of need. During the war, the U.S. government set up rationing boards to help distribute scarce items equitably among consumers. The boards issued coupons that had to be used when buying rationed commodities. Every household

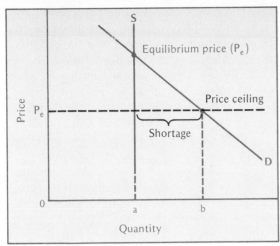

Figure 6 A price ceiling is set; it is usually below equilibrium price, as shown in the figure. When the price ceiling is below the equilibrium price, a shortage *ab* results. Often, the supply *Oa* will be rationed.

received coupons according to the number of members and their occupational needs. Doctors, for example, received more gasoline coupons than most other people. Large families received more coupons for sugar, meat, and shoes than smaller families. No purchase could be made without the proper coupon. Purchases required both money and coupons; neither one alone was enough.

Another form of rationing is simply to let people stand in line. The British call this "queueing." Those first in line have first chance at whatever there is: first come, first served. In wartime many British people often stood in line throughout the night for the chance to buy sugar or meat, just as today people stand in line for World Series tickets.

In some countries you can still find people standing in queues to buy consumer goods that are in short supply. The command economies of the Soviet Union and most of the East European countries have fixed ceiling prices for food and other commodities. Sometimes these consumer goods run short, with the result that lines often form outside shops before daylight.

A modification of the queue is the system of allotting scarce parking spaces at the curb in most U.S. towns and cities. The motorist drives around looking for a vacant space, then parks

and puts money in a parking meter. Usually there is a one- or two-hour time limit, after which the driver is expected to move on and let someone else use the space. Some drivers try to circumvent this by simply putting more money in the meter, but the time and trouble of returning every hour or two for this purpose discourages most of them. Parking space is rationed by inconvenience!

Scarcity and rationing sometimes lead to growth of a black market. A **black market** is an illegal market in which goods are bought and sold outside the normal channels of distribution at prices above the legal ceilings. Sellers in the black market manage to acquire items that are scarce and sell them at whatever the traffic will bear. During World War II, anyone willing to break the law could buy tires, gasoline, and quality cuts of beef on the black market. In the Soviet Union today the black market is so extensive as to constitute a complete counter-economy to the state-controlled economy. It is not confined to consumer goods but includes industrial raw materials, personal services, and anything else that can be traded outside the legitimate channels.

Price ceilings can be effective for short periods, holding down prices even when demand is great. This is particularly true in wartime when the public is ready to support government controls wholeheartedly. But if price ceilings remain in effect over a long period, they may actually force prices to rise. Since a price ceiling limits profits in the controlled industry, firms are discouraged from investing in new productive facilities in order to expand their output. Instead, productive resources flow away from that industry to others where the rewards are greater. Output in the industry declines as the old productive facilities wear out. Shortages worsen. Eventually, when the price controls are taken off, prices may rise more sharply than if there had been no controls. Many economists believe that something like this actually happened in 1971–1973, when the federal government clamped a lid on prices to hold back inflation. Shortages built up in some of the raw material industries, and when the controls were lifted there was a bulge in prices. That is why governments generally prefer to allow prices to be set in the market, except during periods of national emergency.

Viewpoint
Rent Control

There are few public issues related to economics that are debated more hotly than price controls. Many buyers vigorously defend ceilings on the prices they pay; sellers just as strongly demand price floors as a means of maintaining their incomes. Many economists hold that prices should be determined by market demand and supply alone.

Government must evaluate the total benefits and costs of nonmarket pricing and make the correct decision. Unfortunately, a correct decision at one point in time may result in policy that lingers beyond the point when new conditions require a change. One single interference with the market may lead to reactions in the private sector which reduce the benefits and increase costs. This leaves government with a more complex set of circumstances to evaluate. As time goes on, it becomes more difficult to measure precisely the gain or loss from any decision. Moreover, interest groups on both sides harden their positions, increasing the political difficulties of any government decision.

Rent controls are a prime example. Controls in the form of price ceilings were imposed on apartment rentals in New York City during World War II. The high wartime demand for housing and the limited supply would have sent rates skyrocketing. The usual market response would have been for resources to move into the housing industry to take advantage of economic profits. But labor resources, raw materials, and power were critically needed for military production. Furthermore, higher rents would have pushed up living costs for workers, adding to their wage demands and aggravating inflation. Rent controls were supposed to be only a temporary measure to prevent these types of crisis.

The temporary expedient has lasted more than thirty years and has precipitated other crises not foreseen at the time. Nevertheless, despite their questionable value, controls are proving virtually immune to efforts to remove them. To make matters worse, the issue is closely tied to other economic problems of New York City.

Rent control has succeeded in protecting middle-income residents from rent increases but only at a tremendous cost to landlords and mortgage lenders. Low rents have reduced funds for maintenance and capital improvements. Thus the cost of rent control is reflected in decaying and abandoned dwellings. Ceilings on the profitability of investment have produced a general disincentive to invest more capital within the city.

To remove controls entirely is not a practical solution either. If rents were allowed to rise to market levels, the higher living costs would drive more of New York's middle-income taxpayers to lower cost housing outside the city limits. The loss of tax revenues would aggravate the city's already serious financial problems.

Decontrol has begun gradually to affect rents. About a million and a half apartments are under control by New York State or City rent programs. Some rents have been allowed to increase by up to 7.5% a year. But most rent increases are permitted only when apartments change hands. This means that apartments which have remained in the same hands for many years rent at substantially below market rates. These apartments are generally in the more stable and more desirable neighborhoods, and their tenants are upper-middle-income families. Decontrol would bring the greatest rent increases in these areas, with the most serious disruptions among these more affluent taxpayers. They are the citizens New York cannot afford to lose. In addition, New York has a large population of elderly, many of whom live in inexpensive rent-controlled apartments. If rents rose suddenly, as they would if controls were abandoned, many elderly could not afford any housing. Rapid decontrol could lead to some difficult social problems.

All this brings to mind the statement once made by a prominent scientist: It is never possible to do *just* one thing. The scientist was referring to nature's ecological balance and the ripple effects any one action will have on every other life form in the system. But the statement is equally true about a market economy and government actions to control it. An action designed to accomplish one small result for a definite period of time will set in motion a whole series of reactions, some useful and some not so useful. Once the balance is destroyed, it becomes increasingly difficult to correct the situation. New York has been trying for thirty years and the end is not in sight.

Price floors and surpluses

Governments sometimes try to prevent unusually low prices by setting minimum prices. A government imposed minimum price is called a **price floor.** Price floors are used in sectors of the economy where incomes are believed to be too low, notably in agriculture.

Demand curves for agricultural products tend to be inelastic. People consume a fairly stable quantity of food regardless of prices. Supply curves are also inelastic in the very short run. Their position depends on growing conditions during the year. Since growing conditions change from year to year due to weather, supply curves may shift left and right as agricultural output changes. The result is that prices tend to fluctuate widely from one year to another.

In the milk industry, price floors are used in an effort to stabilize prices and incomes for dairy farmers. Milk producers throughout the country are permitted to form associations or cooperatives that set prices. The object is to restrict output and to keep prices from falling too low. Such agreements are illegal in most of U.S. industry, but milk-producing cooperatives are exempt from the price-fixing laws. The result is illustrated in Figure 7. The demand curve is highly inelastic. Milk producers are willing to sell quantity Oa at the cooperative's price floor, P_f. But at that price consumer demand for milk is less than the amount supplied. There is a *surplus* of ab, the distance between demand and supply at the fixed price floor.

If milk producers were to compete freely for sales, price would be forced down to the equilibrium price. If the price is to remain at P_f, some way must be found to dispose of the surplus. In the years when the federal government was supporting prices for a number of farm crops, the Department of Agriculture bought the surpluses and stored them. Now milk cooperatives get rid of their large supply by selling "excess" at lower prices to manufacturers of milk products—cheese, condensed and powdered milk, butter, and ice cream. The manufacturers' demand for milk is more elastic than consumers' and therefore they will buy the remaining supply if the price is low enough. The cooperative maximizes its revenue by selling for a high price in the inelastic milk market and for a lower price in the elastic milk-products market.

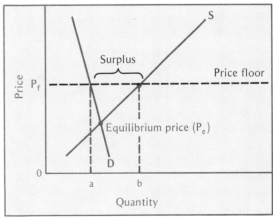

Figure 7 The effect of a price floor for milk is shown. A price floor is usually above the equilibrium price. As a result, a surplus ab results.

Extended Example
Peanuts and Price Supports

Who would have thought that advances in scientific agriculture would virtually bury the United States in peanuts? In the last 35 years new fertilizers, herbicides, and pesticides have increased peanut production in the Southeast from 700 pounds to 2,500 pounds per acre. Under acreage allotment laws, farmers are allowed to plant 1.6 million acres and that's a lot of goobers!

Twentieth century technology of food production has helped to shift supply curves to the right, often faster than demand has increased. The result has been falling market prices and lower incomes for farmers. American consumers buy only about two-thirds of our annual peanut output. Under farm price-support laws the remaining surplus is bought by the government at prices almost double the market equilibrium price. The surpluses acquired by government must then either be sold on the world market at a loss or donated to domestic and foreign food aid programs. The cost to American taxpayers runs between $125 and $150 million each year.

The peanut problem has not escaped notice of the Department of Agriculture. Efforts are under way there to increase consumer and industrial demand for peanuts. There is some natural growth in demand as population grows. Average consumption is about $7\frac{1}{2}$ pounds per person each year; but unfortunately, weight-conscious Americans are becoming increasingly concerned about the high calorie content of peanuts. The trend toward smaller families is certain to reduce demand for peanut butter, which accounts for about half the peanuts sold. Still, peanuts contain more protein, minerals, and vitamins per pound than beef and are a valuable, cheap food for poor people. Peanuts are potentially an important source of nourishment for a world plagued by food shortages.

To attempt to stimulate the demand side of the market is politically more acceptable than to tamper with supply. To correct supply problems would require massive cutbacks in production so that supply would come into equilibrium with demand at a market price acceptable to farmers. Before this could happen there would have to be an end to government price guarantees to farmers. If Congress repealed its price-support law, farmers would be forced to sell their surplus peanuts on world markets at market equilibrium prices. Many would go out of business entirely. Others would cut back peanut production severely.

How would this affect American consumers? Shifts in supply would finally yield a market equilibrium price. At equilibrium, quantity supplied would be just sufficient to satisfy market demand. At the equilibrium price there would be no surpluses and no shortages. Furthermore, price would be just high enough to cover all costs of production; otherwise farmers could not remain in the peanut business. Last and most importantly, the nation's scarce resources would be allocated toward producing the kinds of goods people want to buy.

How does this article illustrate the three important questions of the market system? How has government interfered with the market's answers to the three questions. Does the high fixed price serve a rationing function or an incentive function? Explain. What are the opportunity costs of peanut surpluses?

In general, a price floor guarantees profits to firms in the industry concerned. But is has other consequences. The artificially high price encourages firms to expand their production; resources will move into the industry. Price floors tend to encourage a growth in output and to create unsold surpluses. This is a misallocation of resources, since it doesn't reflect what consumers want.

Thus government efforts to control markets are likely to result in shortages (with price ceilings) and in surpluses (with price floors). The government takes these measures for short-range political reasons—to shelter the public from inflationary forces or to help farmers stabilize their incomes. The long-range problems that may result are less important to governments elected for only four-year terms.

Agriculture and supply elasticity

We have already seen that supply is more responsive to price changes over a long period of time than it is at any particular moment. In agriculture time plays a greater role in supply elasticity than in most other industries. The growing cycle for plants and animals makes supply highly inelastic over the time necessary for crops to reach maturity. The supply of any farm commodity is the result of decisions made many months before and of changes in climate during the growing period. An unusually large harvest of eggs, strawberries, or calves' liver may cause prices to fall sharply. This is because demand is also inelastic and consumers will not stuff themselves with eggs simply because they are available.

These price changes may lead to new production decisions, however. Farmers will shift their resources where they can get better prices. Over the long run, supply will become more elastic. Throughout the twentieth century, U.S. agriculture has responded to price changes by massively increasing output. This response has been made possible by technological advances. Hybrid seed and new varieties of livestock, chemical fertilizers and pesticides, machinery and scientific feeding processes have helped farmers to increase out-

put enormously with very little increase in price. What has happened is summarized in Figure 8, where long-run supply has become infinitely elastic (as indicated by the horizontal supply curve).

This long-run elasticity of supply has been a great boon to the U.S. standard of living. It has enabled American families to live well while spending a much smaller proportion of their incomes on food than is the case in other countries. We enjoy a greater variety of food and more protein than most other people. We supply our food requirements and contribute heavily to supplying the rest of the world, while employing only about 5% of our labor force in farming. This allows us to devote most of our resources to the production of other goods and services.

While it is an advantage for consumers, the long-term elasticity of supply has been a serious disadvantage for many farmers. For them relatively low farm prices have meant falling incomes. To make matters worse the prices of manufactured goods essential to farming have risen. Farmers have often felt squeezed between the lower prices they receive and the higher prices they must pay. Many have been forced to leave farming altogether.

Moving people out of farming was necessary for economic progress. Falling farm prices were a signal that supply was more than adequate to meet demand, and that farm labor

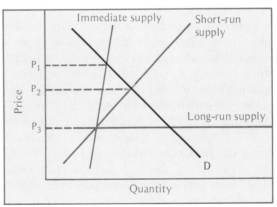

Figure 8 Elasticity of supply is shown for farm products for different time periods. Notice that in the long run the supply is infinitely elastic, so price (P_3) doesn't rise as supply increases.

and capital could be put to better use elsewhere. But Americans have always felt an affection for the "family farm," partly because so many of us were born on farms or had ancestors who were farmers. We have been reluctant to see people forced off the land when they would prefer to remain there. Also, farmers have always had an important voice in national affairs through their elected representatives in Washington.

There have also been strategic and economic reasons for government intervention to keep resources in agriculture. Strategically, we recognize the importance in world affairs of a strong agricultural economy. Our farmers provide many poor nations with the means of survival. Our farm exports help to earn foreign currencies to exchange for other needed imports. Over the next century the ability to supply food may be a decisive factor in global strategy.

Economically, low food prices have helped to keep down wage demands. Our low living costs relative to those in other countries have helped to keep our costs of production lower. Thus our goods are more competitive in world markets, and our own standards of living are higher than they would be otherwise. Furthermore, to encourage farmers to leave agriculture might have dangerous consequences in years to come. Our abundant farm surpluses have provided a cushion against climatic disasters or other food crises. A severe drought or flood, an invasion of plant blight, a world war, or a collapse of world trade could bring starvation unless we encourage surplus production in good years.

For these and other reasons, the federal government has intervened over the years to prevent (or at least slow) the drift of people from farming. It has used tax revenues to supplement the incomes of farmers. It has provided extensive research services to improve farming methods. It has financed education and job training in rural communities. It has tried to encourage industry to move into rural areas where there is surplus farm labor. The "farm problem" has not been completely solved, as any working farmer will tell you. But much has been done to cushion the impact of economic forces upon the farmer.

Elasticity and taxes

No field of economics is more controversial than the economics of taxation. What is the best (most efficient, most equitable) way of paying for government? One mark of a successful tax is that it collects the maximum amount of revenue with the least disturbance to the economy. That is, it does not greatly change the allocation of resources among industries.

An important source of tax revenues is sales and excise taxes added to the purchase price of a good or service. When demand is inelastic, consumers will buy roughly the same quantities regardless of price. When supply is inelastic, producers will supply roughly the same quantities regardless of price. A sales or excise tax will raise the selling price of such goods, but it will have little effect on the quantities produced and sold. Government will collect its revenue, and production will continue much as before.

Results are different if demand and supply are elastic. Consumers will reduce their purchases when a tax is added to the price of a good in elastic demand. Government won't collect as much revenue as it would if demand and supply were inelastic, and the level of economic activity will decline.

A successful sales or excise tax will tax those goods characterized by inelasticity of supply and demand. We will examine this principle in greater detail below.

Specific and ad valorem taxes

A **specific tax** is a tax that raises the price of a good by a *fixed* (specific) *amount* per unit. Each unit is charged the same tax. For example, some taxes on cigarettes are specific taxes. A state may charge, say, 10¢ per pack sold.

A specific tax shifts the supply curve upward by the amount of the tax. The new supply curve is parallel to the old, as shown in Figure 9a.

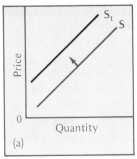
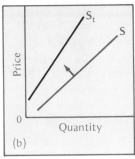

Figure 9 The effect on the supply (S) of a good by imposing: (a) a specific tax; (b) an ad valorem tax. S_t (supply after tax) is parallel for a specific tax and diverges upward for an ad valorem tax.

An **ad valorem tax** varies with the price of the good. This is because the tax is imposed on the value of what is sold, according to a *fixed percentage*. For example, a tax of 10% of the value of a good will increase as price increases. At low prices the tax raises unit price by a small amount. At high prices the tax raises unit price by a larger amount. Sales taxes and property taxes are ad valorem taxes and so are most import duties. An advantage of ad valorem taxes is that government revenues automatically increase as prices go up. Of course, they also have the disadvantage that revenues fall if prices ever go down. Figure 9b shows the effect of an ad valorem tax. The supply curve tilts upward by larger amounts at higher price levels. As a result, supply curves become less elastic when ad valorem taxes are imposed.

State and local governments collect much of their revenues from taxes on consumer purchases, both specific and ad valorem. The most commonly taxed goods are liquor, cigarettes, and gasoline. These are preferred sources of revenue because the demand for them is inelastic, and the tax will have less effect on production.

Taxes where demand is inelastic The effect of a tax on commodities for which demand is inelastic can be seen from Figure 10, using cigarettes as an example. The demand curve is steep, since the response of cigarette smokers to price changes is relatively low. Most nicotine users will continue buying about the same quantity even if prices rise substantially.

Suppose the original market price is $3.00 per carton. At this price 1 million cartons are sold per time period. Now the government imposes a specific tax of $.50 on each carton sold. Market supply shifts upward by $.50 at every quantity. What will the tax revenue be? After the tax, consumers move up their demand curves and purchase only .9 million cartons. Tax collections will be $.50 × .9 million = $.45 million, or $450,000.

Taxes where demand is elastic The demand for many consumer goods is more responsive to price changes than that for cigarettes. Figure 11 illustrates what happens when a tax is imposed on a good for which demand is relatively elastic, such as cheese. Cheese is a good for which there are many substitutes. Most cheese fanciers would have little difficulty breaking their cheese habit if prices rose significantly. Suppose at a price of $3.00 per pound, they buy 1 million pounds per time period. When a tax of $.50 per pound is imposed, market supply shifts upward as before. But with elastic demand the quantity sold falls sharply to .3 million pounds (that is, to 300,000 pounds). The government collects a tax revenue of $.50 × .3 million = $.15 million, or $150,000. The higher price has turned off so

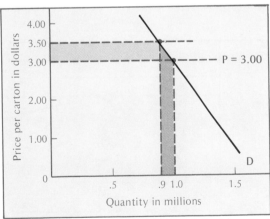

Figure 10 The effect of a tax on a commodity (cigarettes) for which demand is inelastic. A $.50 tax on cartons of cigarettes causes price to increase to $3.50 per carton and demand to fall from 1.0 to .9 million cartons sold. Tax revenue ($.50 × .9 million) is shown in the brown shaded areas. The total revenue lost to the cigarette industry is shown in the blue shaded area.

many cheese consumers that tax collections are much lower than when the same tax is imposed on cigarettes. In addition, the cheese industry is now quite upset at the loss of customers and sales.

Who pays the tax?

When we see the tax on our sale slips, it seems obvious that we consumers are paying it. From the standpoint of economics, however, the matter isn't that simple. The incidence of a tax—that is, the relative shares paid by the buyer and the seller—depends on the elasticities of demand and supply.

The first thing that the tax does is to increase the price of the product. We can think of this as an upward shift in the supply curve, since a higher price will be required to induce producers to supply any given amount. This is shown graphically in Figure 12, where S is the supply curve after a $.50 tax has been imposed. Given the supply curve, the incidence of the tax will depend on the elasticity of the demand curve. In Figure 12a demand is relatively elastic and consumers are able to substitute other products for the one taxed. Quantity purchased falls substantially, and the equilibrium price only rises from $3 to $3.10. Of this price, producers receive $2.60 compared to $3 before the tax; the remaining $.40 is their contribution

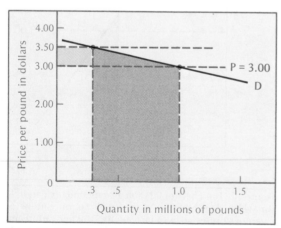

Figure 11   The effect of a tax on a good (cheese) for which demand is elastic. A $.50 tax on a pound of cheese causes price to increase to $3.50 per pound and demand to fall from 1.0 to .3 million pounds sold. Tax revenue is shown in the brown shaded area, while total revenue lost to the cheese industry is shown in the blue shaded area.

to the tax. Producers pay most of this tax, while consumers pay only an additional $.10.

When demand is less elastic than supply, as in Figure 12b, the opposite happens. Consumers continue to purchase roughly the same quantity, while selling price increases by almost the entire amount of the tax. The effect of inelastic demand is to shift the greater part of the tax burden to the buyer. Price rises to $3.40, of which the seller keeps $2.90. Forty cents of the $.50 tax is paid by the buyer and only $.10 by the seller. You can visualize from the diagram the effect as demand becomes more or less elastic over the relevant range. *When demand is elastic, the increase in price is less;* consumers pay relatively less of the tax while producers pay more of it. *When demand is inelastic, price rises by almost the full amount of the tax;* consumers pay more of the tax and suppliers less.

Taxes on imports: the case of oil

In 1973, oil-producing nations stopped their shipments of oil to the United States and other industrialized countries and then resumed sales at much higher prices. In response, the U.S. government imposed a $1 tax on each barrel of imported oil. It was thought that the higher price would discourage consumption and encourage production of domestic oil. This would make us less dependent on imported oil and less subject to the demands of foreign producers. What actually happened?

Consumer demand for oil was relatively inelastic in the short run. Americans were accustomed to having lots of gasoline available, to wearing synthetic fibers made from petrochemicals, and to using oil-based fertilizers in agriculture. There was no time to develop substitute goods or to find substitute raw materials.

The supply curve, on the other hand, was relatively elastic. The oil-producing countries had markets throughout the world; they were not limited to the U.S. market. For that matter, they could afford to leave their petroleum in the ground where its value would increase over time. Their small economies generally could not spend vast earnings all at once.

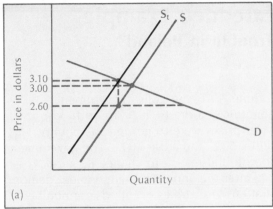

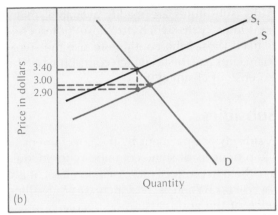

Figure 12 Tax incidence depends on elasticity of supply and demand. The effect of a $.50 tax is shown when: (a) demand is more elastic; (b) when supply is more elastic. When demand is elastic, producers pay more of the tax ($.40 of the $.50). When supply is elastic, consumers pay more of the tax (also $.40 of the $.50).

We have already seen that when demand is less elastic than supply, the greater part of a tax will be shifted to the consumer. That was what happened in the case of the tax on imported oil. Moreover, the quantity purchased fell very little, in spite of the tax. The net effect was to channel heavy tax revenues to the federal government. Consumers had less spendable income for other purchases. This had a contractionary effect on other sectors of the economy, causing cutbacks in production and employment and contributing to the serious recession of 1973–1975.

Taxes and disincentives

Taxes present difficult problems for governments. Taxes are needed in order to pay for public services, but the wrong taxes may discourage economic activity. There is a thin line between satisfying the needs of government and doing injury to the economy.

Governments sometimes overlook the negative effects of taxes, with unhappy results. An example can be found in the recent history of New York City. In 1975 the city government levied a tax on its best known industry: the sale of stocks and bonds in the New York securities markets. A transfer tax of $.25 was imposed on each $1,000 sale of securities.

The transfer tax might have succeeded in raising revenues if demand and supply had been inelastic. Unhappily for New York, secu-

rities buyers found they could trade just as easily in neighboring New Jersey where there was no transfer tax. Securities dealers moved across the Hudson and set up offices in New Jersey. What little was added to the city's revenues by the tax was more than offset by the emigration of business from the city. The result was to aggravate the Big Apple's financial troubles.

This disincentive effect of taxes is particularly harmful in the case of ad valorem taxes such as sales taxes, excise taxes, and property taxes. Consumers will, if possible, make their purchases elsewhere. When Cook County, Illinois (which includes Chicago and many suburbs) imposed a tax on liquor sales, this was a bonanza for stores just across the county line; many people living in Chicago's suburbs transferred their liquor purchases to escape the tax.

Property taxes may have especially serious consequences, due to disincentives. Because property taxes increase with the value of the property, landlords may avoid improving their buildings, thus encouraging the spread of slums.

Sometimes a tax is imposed with the *intention* of creating a disincentive. An example of this kind of tax is one placed on styrofoam drinking cups. Styrofoam is not biodegradable; unlike paper it does not break down when exposed to weather. The heavy use of styrofoam cups leads to littered roadsides and recreation areas, requiring expensive maintenance at public expense. Imposing a tax on these cups raises their price to consumers. Because paper substitutes are readily available, many consumers will switch to these other containers. Those who continue to use the styrofoam cups pay the tax which contributes to the expense of cleaning up.

Subsidies

A **subsidy** is a payment by the government to the producers of some commodity to encourage them to produce more of it. In effect, it is a reverse tax. Whereas a tax increases the selling price of the good, a subsidy decreases price, allowing producers to sell more units. A subsidy may be a *specific* amount returned to the producer for each unit sold or an *ad valorem* payment based on price.

The payment of a **specific subsidy** to a producer shifts the supply curve down by the amount of the subsidy at every price level. An **ad valorem subsidy** shifts the supply curve down by larger amounts at larger volumes and thus makes supply more elastic.

The purposes of a subsidy are (1) to reduce the price of a good or service and/or (2) to increase the supply of it. The second objective is generally more important. State and local governments often give subsidies to attract business firms in order to make jobs for their people and to increase tax revenues. These subsidies often take the form of property tax reductions, cheaper land, or the chance to borrow money at low rates of interest.

Remember that taxes disturb production less when demand and supply are inelastic. *Subsidies affect production more when demand and supply are elastic.* This is because the quantities produced and sold will be more responsive to a change in price. If supply is elastic, the quantity produced will increase substantially in response to the subsidy. If demand is elastic, consumers will buy larger quantities when price is reduced by the subsidy.

An industry may be subsidized because it is felt to be vital to the nation's security. In the United States, agriculture was subsidized for many years by means of price supports. Transportation industries are often subsidized, as the U.S. airlines used to be and as the airlines of other countries continue to be. Many for-

Extended Example
Trouble in Poland

In June, 1976, the Polish government announced a drastic increase in food prices. Meat prices were to go up 69%, poultry 30%, butter 50%, and sugar 100%. The government soon found reason to change its mind. The day after the announcement, violent demonstrations and strikes occurred in a number of Polish industrial centers. Workers tore up railroad tracks outside of Warsaw, stopping the international express from Paris. In Radom, demonstrators set fire to the Communist Party headquarters. Premier Piotr Jaroszewicz rushed to the television cameras and declared that the matter deserved further thought. The government had received a number of new proposals, he said, and several months would be needed "to reexamine the matter and work out a proper solution."

The Communist government was understandably nervous. Twice before, in 1970 and 1956, top leaders had been given the ax when workers rioted over prices and living conditions. The trouble this time was not unique to Poland. It stemmed from inflation—the same illness that was afflicting the capitalist countries of the West.

Inflation was a problem not only in Poland, but in Hungary, Czechoslovakia, and other East European countries. Ceiling prices in these centrally planned economies are fixed by the state, but that did not prevent production costs from rising. Price pressure in Poland came from several sources. The prices of goods that Poland imported from Western countries had gone up in the previous two years, adding $7.4 billion to the import bill. At the same time, Poland's exports to Western markets had dropped by about $1 billion because of the recession.

What did this have to do with food prices? Poland, after all, is an agricultural country and doesn't have to import its food. The crux of the problem lies in the way the centrally planned economy sets its prices. Most of the food bought by workers in the cities is marketed through state purchasing agencies. Farmers in Poland sell their produce to the state, which then distributes it to city consumers at a fixed price. The state was taking a loss on this transaction. In short, it was *subsidizing consumers by running large deficits* which had to be made up from other sources. The deficits had a tendency to grow because there was an upward drift in wages and industrial costs that were also being subsidized. The subsidies were paid from funds that might otherwise have been invested in factories and other productive facilities, or in housing and schools.

The losses in foreign trade meant that the government had to choose between cutting back its investment program or reducing its subsidies to consumers. Put simply, if economic growth was to continue, consumers would have to pay more for pork chops. Even a centrally planned economy cannot shelter its citizens indefinitely from the play of economic forces.

In Poland the solution was postponed, but time would only make it more difficult. The Hungarian government went ahead and increased its meat prices, while in Czechoslovakia consumers were told they could expect a "restructuring" of wholesale prices at the end of the year.

eign airlines are owned outright by their governments and operate consistently at a loss. This raises problems for competing U.S. airlines that must operate without a subsidy.

Some countries subsidize their export industries. Without a subsidy these industries might not be able to compete in the world market against the established industries of other countries. A subsidy enables an industry in a developing country to meet world prices and earn the foreign currency needed to pay for the nation's imports.

Like taxes, subsidies may have harmful effects on incentives. A subsidy makes life easier for the firms receiving it. Subsidized firms may grow dependent on their government revenues and allow their productivity to slip. Subsidies may also encourage too many firms to enter the industry, thus attracting resources that could be used better elsewhere.

Summary

Supply curves show the quantity producers will supply at various prices over a certain period of time. Price elasticity of supply measures the percentage change in quantity supplied relative to the percentage change in price. When producers are unable to respond to price changes by changing quantity, we say that supply is perfectly inelastic: el = 0. When quantity can be changed infinitely without a price change, we say supply is infinitely elastic: el = ∞.

There are three factors that affect elasticity of supply. (1) Elasticity of supply is strongly affected by the time period for which the supply curve is drawn. In the immediate time period supply is often highly inelastic. In the short run, supply is more elastic and in the long run, supply may approach infinite elasticity. (2) Technology of production affects elasticity by limiting the substitutability or availability of resources needed for changing the quantity of output. (3) Business expectations also affect the readiness to respond to price changes.

Over time, changes in elasticity of supply will affect the equilibrium price of goods and services. Smooth adjustment of production to consumer demand helps to keep prices stable and ensures that resources are used for kinds of production consumers want. Occasionally, government intervenes to prevent price adjustments, in the interests of particular groups. Government ceiling prices protect consumers from price inflation but generally lead to shortages and rationing. Government price floors protect farmers from falling incomes but often lead to surpluses. Farm surpluses reflect a misallocation of productive resources, but at the same time serve other political and strategic purposes.

A mark of a good tax is that it collects sufficient revenue without significantly altering production patterns. This result is achieved best by taxing the sale of goods and services with inelastic demand and supply. A specific tax raises price by a specific amount, while an ad valorem tax raises price by a certain percentage. The less elastic is the demand for a good, the more revenue a tax will collect.

The incidence of a tax refers to the relative sacrifice borne by the buyer and the seller. If supply is more inelastic than demand, the greater sacrifice is borne by the seller. If demand is more inelastic than supply, the greater sacrifice is borne by the buyer. When supply and demand are elastic, a tax can result in a disincentive to produce or to buy the item, and low tax revenues will be the result.

A subsidy is a reverse tax. Subsidies can also be classified as specific or ad valorem. A mark of a successful subsidy is that it alters production patterns in certain intended ways. This result is achieved best by subsidizing production of goods and services with elastic demand and supply. Subsidies interfere with free competition by favoring particular industries or sectors.

Key Words and Phrases

- **perfect inelasticity of supply** a condition where no change in supply is possible regardless of the change in price.

- **infinite elasticity of supply** a condition where infinite changes in quantity supplied can take place with no change in price.

- **immediate time period** the short time period during which supply is inelastic.

- **short run** a longer time period when supply becomes more elastic.

- **long run** a much longer time period when supply approaches infinite elasticity.

- **price ceiling** a maximum price for a good set by government.

- **black market** illegal trading in goods at prices higher than the fixed price ceiling.

- **rationing** allotting an item in scarce supply among buyers; often accomplished by coupons assigned by need or through queueing (first come, first served).

- **price floor** a minimum price for a good set by government.

- **specific tax** a tax of a specific amount regardless of the value of the good.

- **ad valorem tax** a tax which is based on the value of the good; a fixed percentage tax.

- **subsidies** payments from government to encourage particular types of producton.

- **specific subsidy** subsidy of a fixed amount.

- **ad valorem subsidy** subsidy based on the value of the good or service; a fixed percentage subsidy.

Questions for Review

1. Show how changes in the time period covered by a supply curve cause changes in the shape of the curve. Explain the process by which price changes serve as incentives to adjust output.

2. Use the hypothetical data below to calculate price elasticity of supply for firms A and B. Will the curves cut the horizontal or vertical axis?

How would you characterize the two firms on the basis of the important determinants of supply elasticity?

3. Describe the conditions which would give rise to market disequilibrium. Are there current examples of industries in which government has intervened to prevent equilibrium? What have been the results?

4. Demonstrate the effect of subsidies on supply curves. Explain why subsidies are most effective when supply is elastic.

5. Why are taxes more effective when demand is inelastic?

6. What are the macroeconomic benefits of smooth adjustments of supply over the long run? Cite specific industries in which supply has been slow to adjust and point to the problems this creates for the macroeconomy.

7. Define: rationing, black market.

8. What are the purposes of a subsidy?

9. How can a tax "kill the goose that lays the golden egg"?

10. Various government policies were proposed in 1977 to deal with the nation's growing energy problems. Evaluate each of the following, showing how the policy would affect supply curves in particular markets: (a) a tax on heavy "gas-guzzling" automobiles; (b) a subsidy on home insulating devices; (c) relaxation of environmental regulations in the coal industry.

Firm A		Firm B	
Price	Quantity	Price	Quantity
100	45	100	35
80	35	80	30
60	25	60	25
40	15	40	20
20	5	20	15

Part Seven

Costs of Production and Product Markets

27

Perfect Competition:
Costs and Production Decisions in the Short Run

The summer Alfred Wunderkind graduated from high school, he opened his own business. He established the "Your Place" Auto TuneUp Company. He rented a van and equipped it with rented tools and materials for performing engine tune-ups in parking lots while the owners were at work. He printed circulars for distribution at office buildings and factories.

At the end of the summer Alfred had lost $550. His rental fees had run $1,300 for equipment and $1,500 for the van. He had performed 75 tune-ups at $30 each for total receipts of $2,250. He had also devoted several hundred hours to the enterprise, for which he received nothing. And he was left with unused spark-plugs and a closet full of advertising circulars. In fact, Alfred had lost much more than $550—he had lost a summer.

Alfred decided to give up the business and go to college.

Later in this chapter we will examine some of the reasons Alfred's business went wrong. Mostly we will explore the ways in which successful business firms make their decisions about what to produce. We will show how the self-interest of business managers helps to promote the efficient use of resources. We will see how profit serves to guide production according to consumer preferences. And we will also show how the existence of competition in free markets contributes to growth of output, lower prices, and higher standards of living.

To make things simple at first, we will assume that the economy is perfectly competitive. The theory of perfect competition, you will recall, makes certain assumptions about the economy:

(1) There are many sellers, none of them very big, and there are many buyers.

(2) All the firms in an industry produce an identical product, so that one company's product is no more different from another's than Farmer Smith's oats are different from Farmer Brown's.

(3) Information is equally available to all firms; knowledge about production techniques and market conditions gives all producers equal advantage.

(4) There are no barriers to new firms wishing to enter the industry and there are no obstacles to prevent firms from leaving it. As market demand increases, new firms will be drawn in; when it decreases, firms will leave.

The four characteristics of competition ensure that no single firm is able to influence market price by changing the amount it sells. To managers, price seems to be determined by the forces of supply and demand in the market rather than by their own decisions.

This chapter is concerned with short-run decisions of the firm in competition. We distinguish between the short run and the long run because firms behave differently in these time periods. In the **short run** a firm makes decisions on the basis of its existing stock of capital equipment. If Mother Muffin finds that she can sell more pies at a profitable price, she will hire more workers and run her existing equipment harder. If, on the other hand, pies aren't selling well, she will cut back on the operations in her plant. Whatever the level of demand, however, the firm's production plans are limited by its stock of fixed resources in the short run.

Over a longer period, Mother Muffin may decide to expand operations by installing more ovens or perhaps moving to a larger building. Or she may decide that there is no future in this industry and go out of business entirely. In the **long run,** then, a firm can decide to expand or contract its capital stock. We will describe the process of long-run decision-making in the next chapter.

How we measure costs of production

If a firm is to succeed, it must provide something the public wants. And it must do so without losing money. Otherwise, like Alfred Wunderkind's tune-up business, it is wasting resources. Its workers, its managers, and its plant might better be used in some other way.

Companies are always thinking about costs and prices. If a firm is of sufficient size, there will be employees whose job it is to analyze the data on money paid out and revenue taken in. On the basis of this information, management will evaluate the firm's performance.

There are two approaches to this task of measurement. One is that of the *accountant* and the other is that of the *economist*. The accountant is mainly concerned with seeing that the firm meets its financial obligations—that it pays its bills on time and stays out of trouble. The economist is more concerned with the way the firm uses its resources—that is, with its performance in terms of economic efficiency. Because accountants and economists measure costs in different ways, they often reach different conclusions about the health of the firm and the value of its operation.

Accounting costs: the bottom line

A firm must meet its **accounting costs** if it is to remain in business. Accounting costs are also called *explicit costs* or *historical costs*. Every month revenues must be accumulated and paid out to the resources used in production. Each resource must be paid at least as much as its opportunity cost: the going rate for its employment. It is the accountant's job to prepare a statement comparing the firm's income with its expenses for that month. A hypothetical Income and Expense Statement is shown in Table 1.

The first item shown is income from sales of $8,500,000. Below this the accountant lists the necessary expenditures for the month. Total current expenses are $7,800,000. But these are only the firm's out-of-pocket costs. Over

any production period the firm also incurs other obligations that must be paid eventually. It is appropriate to include in expenses all amounts which are accrued during the month but not paid until a later time.

One kind of accrued expense is *depreciation* on the firm's plant and equipment. A firm's capital stock gradually wears out as it is used in production. The cost of capital depreciation should be included along with other production costs. One way of doing this is to set aside each year a certain proportion of the price of each piece of capital equipment. For example, if a machine is expected to last 20 years, the firm may set aside $\frac{1}{20}$ of the machine's value every year. This is a form of business saving which helps to replace equipment when it is worn out.

Another kind of accrued expense is taxes. The firm does not pay all its taxes on a monthly basis. Some taxes are paid quarterly. Therefore, its accountants set aside a certain amount each month to cover *accrued tax liability*. This helps to ensure that funds to cover the taxes will be on hand when needed.

Net income is shown on the bottom line in Table 1. This is what is left after all deductions have been made. **Net income,** or **profit,** is the amount available for distribution to the owners of the business—that is, to the sole proprietor if there is one, or the partners, or the owners of stock in the corporation. Eventually, the owners expect to receive at least some gain to compensate them for putting their savings into the company or for devoting their energies

Table 1
Income and Expense Statement, December, 1977

Gross income from sales		$8,500,000
Expenses:		
Rent on office space	$ 400,000	
Wages and salaries	2,000,000	
Interest on loan	200,000	
Materials	5,000,000	
Utilities	200,000	
Total current expenses	7,800,000	
Depreciation	100,000	
Total expenses		−7,900,000
Net income from operations		600,000
Accrued tax liability		−300,000
Net income after taxes		$ 300,000

to the business. Otherwise it would pay them to use their resources in some other firm. The firm will usually not pay all its profits to the owners. It will retain a portion of earnings for future needs: as a reserve against a temporary decline in income or for potential expansion (another form of business saving).

A successful firm will show a large amount on its "bottom line" and one that grows from year to year. If the amount gets smaller or is negative, the firm is in trouble. A negative figure for net income means that the firm's costs are greater than its income from sales. If it continues to lose money, drastic changes will be necessary. That is why the firm's monthly Income and Expense Statement (sometimes called Profit and Loss Statement, or "P and L" for short) is of critical interest to managers and owners.

Economic costs: efficient resource allocation

When economists speak of costs, they are likely to be thinking of something more than the costs we have been discussing. Economists are concerned with full *opportunity costs*—the cost of using resources for one purpose rather than another. When Alfred Wunderkind spent his summer in the auto tune-up business, he figured his net loss at $550. But $550 represents only his loss on explicit costs. Actually, his total loss was much greater than that. If Alfred had spent his time painting houses for $5 an hour, he might have earned, say, $2,000. His real loss, therefore, was $550 plus $2,000, the *implicit* cost of *his own* labor. The unpaid work of performing engine tune-ups cost Alfred $2,000 in forgone earnings.

In economic life, production decisions must be based on the opportunity cost of all resources, whether purchased from other resource owners or supplied by the business firm itself. The costs of resources held within the firm are called **implicit costs;** although they may not actually be paid out, still they reflect the income a resource could be earning in

another employment. If a firm rents a piece of land for parking its trucks, the firm will have to pay at least as much as the owner could get by renting the land to an amusement park or a vineyard. But even if the firm owns the land itself, the firm must figure this rent expense as part of its full opportunity cost. Similarly, all workers must be paid as much as they could earn in some alternative employment, from hired technician to chief executive. Lenders of financial capital must be paid at least as much interest as they could earn on other investments of equal risk. But the firm must also *pay itself* for the use of its own financial capital. These are the full opportunity costs of productive resources. Gross income from sales must be great enough to cover the opportunity costs of *all* resources used in production: the explicit costs paid to other resource owners and the implicit costs of using the firm's own resources in some way. If sales revenue fails to cover full costs, then it would be wiser to use the resources in alternative employments where income is greater.

Explicit costs and implicit costs

Have you considered the total costs of your college diploma? Probably you are aware of the money outlays, the costs we have called the **explicit costs:** tuition fees, the cost of books, dormitory rents. But there are other costs. While you are busy attending classes, you may be sacrificing opportunities to earn an income. If so, the full cost of your education includes the forgone income from that job you didn't take. (This may explain why golf pros, opera singers, and Hollywood stunt men don't find it practical to pursue advanced college degrees.)

What are the total costs of strawberries grown in your neighbor's yard? They include the explicit cost of seed, fertilizer, and garden tools. But suppose your neighbor is a respected lawyer whose time is valued at $100 an hour. Each hour spent tending strawberries adds an implicit cost which reflects the most productive use of your neighbor's own labor. Thus the full opportunity cost of those strawberries from the garden may be substantially higher than the supermarket price!

Many less developed countries face important decisions involving full opportunity costs. Often their resources are severely limited, and it is important to use them in the most productive way. The resources may seem much cheaper than they are because their explicit costs are low. But to use those resources unproductively will mean large implicit costs. If land is used for parade grounds instead of for farms, the full opportunity cost will include the agricultural production forgone. If strong young men are made to walk around carrying guns, their labor power is lost to manufacturing industry. If funds are used to build magnificent office buildings or sports stadiums, the country will be poorer for the power plants that might have been built instead. Each of these examples of patriotic display involves a heavy opportunity cost which must be borne by the nation's people.

Defining profit

Normal profit   When a firm's implicit costs are considered, the effect may be to reduce the final profit figure shown on the Income and Expense Statement. An important implicit cost is the cost of using the firm's own entrepreneurial resources. *Economists regard profit as the opportunity cost of entrepreneurship.* Just as land, labor, and capital must earn, respectively, rent, wages, and interest, the entrepreneur must also earn a return. For the entrepreneur, the necessary return is called **normal profit.** Normal profit enables those who provide entrepreneurial ability to continue to use their resources in that particular way.

Normal profit is treated by economists as part of the opportunity cost of production. In looking at the Income and Expense Statement, we would subtract normal profit from net income in order to evaluate the performance of the firm. Total revenue must be enough to cover all costs, including rent, wages, interest, and normal profit, if the firm is to remain in business. (Many economists would also consider dividends paid to stockholders a part of normal profit. Often payment of dividends is a necessary inducement to ensure that a firm's stock is attractive to savers.)

Economic profit   If normal profit is treated as part of costs, what do we call the firm's earnings above that amount? We have another term for these. When total revenue exceeds total cost (including normal profit), the firm is said to have made **economic profit.** *Economic profit is a return to the entrepreneurial resource over and above the necessary normal profit.* Later we will see that in perfect competition firms will not make economic profit in the long run. This is because competition from other firms will reduce market price to the point at which each firm covers only its full opportunity costs (including normal profit).

In the short run, economic profit may result from abnormally high demand or from restrictions in supply. For instance, if a firm introduces a new product and captures the entire market, it may be able to set price well above its total costs of production. It will earn large economic profits. This will last until other firms succeed in marketing a similar product at a lower price. Eventually, competition will drive price down; economic profit will decline and perhaps disappear. Something like this happened in the pocket calculator industry in the mid-1970s. The price of the first simple calculators fell as competing firms struggled for a share of the market. Then more complex calculators were introduced at higher prices and another round of competition began.

Economic profit serves two important functions in the market system: (1) *It is a reward* for firms that satisfy rising consumer demand by developing new products and by developing technical processes which reduce production costs. (2) *It is an incentive* for firms to move into expanding industries, aiding the growth and technical development of U.S. industry.

What if economic profit is negative? This happens when Income from Sales is not enough to pay all production costs, including normal profit. Negative economic profit can be considered the penalty for producers who make mistakes. It is their punishment for being wrong about the profitability of new products and methods. (Alfred's lack of experience may excuse his mistaken expectations about the tune-up business. However, in business as in life it is often true that experience is the best teacher. His $550 "lesson" may have prepared him for more correct decisions in the future.)

Resources in the short run

We have already distinguished two time spans for making economic decisions: the short run and the long run. They differ because of the character of resources available to the firm. During the short run, a firm will have a certain stock of **fixed productive resources:** a plant with machinery, an office building, and salaried administrative personnel. These resources are fixed in the short run because plant and equipment cannot be increased or decreased very quickly, and because a salaried staff is hired on a contract basis. Along with its fixed resources the firm will employ varying quantities of **variable resources:** hourly paid production workers, electric power, raw materials, and component parts. These are called variable resources because their quantities can be adjusted fairly quickly, depending on the level of production required.

The length of the short run differs among firms. For some service companies the short run may be only a few weeks. Many service operations require only a small quantity of capital that can be readily increased. A city taxicab company, for example, can expand its operations rather quickly by increasing the number of cabs and by hiring additional office personnel. For a subway system the short run would obviously be much longer. It may take ten years to make the decisions, acquire the land, sign the contracts, and construct new subway lines. In the meantime the subway's equipment can be operated more or less intensively by running trains more or less frequently, by hiring or laying off nonsalaried personnel, and by using varying amounts of electric power.

In some industries the short run depends on the time it takes to hire and train skilled labor. Chemical engineers, aeronautical designers, and financial analysts must train for years before their skills are available to business. In small firms the most important limitation in the short run may be the time and ability of single entrepreneurs. A person who runs a small business may not want to take on heavier burdens or may lack the training to adapt to new developments easily.

Consider the following industries. Can you identify the resources that are likely to be fixed in the short run? How long do you think the short run would be?

steel production   coal production
soybeans   dental services
ladies' clothing   auto manufacture
college textbooks   catering services

We generally think of the short run as the time period required for *expanding* the firm's fixed resources. But the short run is important also in decisions to reduce fixed resources—or even to go out of business altogether. Reducing productive capacity takes time, although the duration may be different from the time required to expand. After the decision is made to contract operations, a firm may go on for a while operating its fixed resources until it is able to dispose of them on satisfactory terms. In the meantime it can increase or decrease output by changing the quantity of variable resources employed. For example, suppose Mother Muffin decides to retire but wants to sell her plant and equipment to someone else. While she looks for a successor and negotiates the terms, she will keep on operating the business. The length of the short run in this case is the time it takes her to arrange the sale.

Production decisions in the short run

Principle of diminishing marginal product

The Golden Sands Dune Buggy Company had a shop with capacity for operating five assembly lines. For several months business had been slow, and only two of the lines had been in use. But the economy started on an upswing, and the orders for dune buggies came in faster than they could be filled. The production manager took on another worker and put a third line into operation. Business continued to improve and soon the orders were piling up again. The production manager hired another worker. Then the sales manager of the company received an important order from a large amusement park. "We've got to fill it fast," the company president said, "I don't want to lose this customer."

The production manager pointed out that there was additional plant capacity not in operation. But the unused assembly lines included older and less efficient equipment. While it might be profitable to hire workers to operate these lines, each additional worker would add less to monthly output than those already working.

The company president thought it over and decided to go ahead. "The cost of filling this order will be higher than for our other orders, but the price will just cover it."

The principle we have been describing is the *principle of diminishing marginal product*. (This principle is also known as the law of diminishing returns.) *Marginal product* is the contribution to output of the last unit of a *variable* resource hired—in this case, the last worker hired. Beyond some quantity of output in the short run, the marginal product of a variable resource tends to decline. This is because of the limitations of the fixed resource. The product of the last worker at Golden Sands was smaller than that of the others because of the use of the least efficient machines. Most factories and shops have equipment of varying efficiency. As output increases, the less efficient machines will be pressed into service.

During the short run in any industry, the quantity of output from the use of variable resources follows a similar pattern. As variable resources are added to a firm's fixed resources, output can be said to move through stages. (1) Without some variable resources there can be *no output*. (2) When a small quantity of variable resources is employed, each unit adds more to total output than the one before. Marginal product increases. (3) Then over some range of production, marginal product may be *constant*. Each unit of the variable resource adds the same quantity to output as the one before. Production within this range is still within the design limitations of the fixed plant. (4) At some level of operation, however, total output will *increase by smaller amounts* as more variable resources are added. We say that marginal product diminishes. (5) Finally, total output reaches a maximum, and using more variable resources will *not produce any change* in total output. There are no more machines to be utilized, or the capacity of the fixed plant has been reached. Adding more variable resources after this point may even cause total production to decline. This might happen, for instance, if too many workers were hired to operate the assembly lines or if production were carried on continuously through the night. Problems of crowding and breakdowns might cause total output to fall. Within this range we say that marginal product is negative.

Total, marginal, and average products

The principle of diminishing marginal product is illustrated in Table 2. **Total product** (TP) is the level of output associated with any quantity of variable resources. *Total product* (column (2)) increases with every increase in the quantity of labor (column (1)) over the range of operation for which the plant and equipment are designed. Then total product reaches a peak and levels off. Beyond this point total product starts to decline if more labor is added.

Marginal product—the amount an additional unit of labor adds to total output—is given in column (3). (Each amount is shown between the lines, because it represents the difference between two amounts in column (2).) Beyond a certain level of operation, marginal product begins to decline. In Table 2 this point is reached when the fifth unit of labor is added: total product increases from 10 to 13, a smaller amount than when the fourth unit was added. If as many as eight units are employed, the eighth will add nothing to total product. And a ninth will cause total product to decrease.

The **marginal product** (MP) is defined as the change in total output which results from the addition of a unit of a variable resource. The algebraic formula is

$$MP = \frac{\text{change in total product}}{\text{change in variable resource}}$$

$$= \frac{TP_2 - TP_1}{QL_2 - QL_1} = \frac{\Delta TP}{\Delta QL}.$$

where the symbol Δ stands for "change in," TP stands for total product, and QL stands for variable resource (quantity of labor). Using the data in Table 2, the marginal product of the fourth worker is

$$\frac{10 - 6}{4 - 3} = \frac{4}{1} = 4 \text{ units of output.}$$

It is useful to know how much each unit of labor produces on the average—that is, the total product divided by the number of units employed. This is shown in column (4). Up to some level of employment, increasing the number of variable resources causes average product to increase. Average product reaches a peak and then starts to decline as more labor is added.

The **average product** (AP) is defined as output per unit of a variable resource employed. The algebraic formula is

$$AP = \frac{\text{total product}}{\text{units of variable resources}} = \frac{TP}{QL}.$$

Using the data in Table 2, the average product per worker when four workers are employed is

$$\frac{10}{4} = 2.5 \text{ units of output.}$$

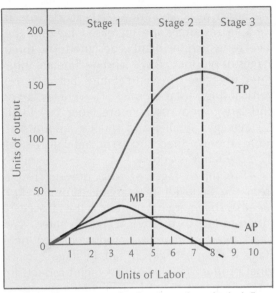

Figure 1 Short-run production for a hypothetical firm. The top curve shows total product (TP), while the lower two curves are average product (AP) and marginal product (MP). Stage 1 is characterized by rising AP; stage 2 begins where MP and AP intersect; stage 3 begins where TP starts to decline and MP moves below zero.

The data in Table 2 are graphed in Figure 1, with output on the vertical axis and units of labor on the horizontal axis. The three curves for total product, marginal product, and average product have characteristic shapes. These shapes result from the principle of diminishing marginal product in the short run. A typical total product curve rises steeply at first and then more slowly as output approaches the capacity of the fixed plant. Total product

Table 2
Production (per month) from the Use of Variable Resources with a Fixed Quantity of Plant and Equipment

(1) Quantity of labor (QL)	(2) Total Product (TP), dune buggies per month	(3) Marginal Product (MP), change in total product, $\frac{\Delta TP}{\Delta QL}$	(4) Average Product (AP), product per worker, $\frac{TP}{QL}$
0	0		0
		1	
1	1		1.0
		2	
2	3		1.5
		3	
3	6		2.0
		4	
4	10		2.5
		3	
5	13		2.6
		2	
6	15		2.5
		1	
7	16		2.3
		0	
8	16		2.0
		−1	
9	15		1.67

reaches a peak and then starts to decline if variable resources are increased beyond the level for which the plant is designed. The three stages of product growth and decline are indicated in Figure 1 by vertical lines. Between the vertical lines, total product (1) averages larger and larger amounts as more labor is added, (2) averages smaller and smaller amounts as more labor is added, and (3) actually decreases as more labor is added.

The three stages of total product result from the behavior of marginal product. Remember that marginal product is the change in total product as another worker is hired. We have seen that marginal product rises during stage 1. Then it begins to fall. In stage 2, marginal product falls below average product. In stage 3, marginal product becomes negative. The three stages of marginal product correspond to the three stages of total product.

There is also a special relationship between marginal product curves and average product curves. *The marginal product curve always lies above the average product curve over the range for which average product is rising.* This range corresponds to stage 1 of total product. Marginal product lies below the average product curve over the range for which average product is falling. This is because marginal product tends to pull up the average when it is above the average, and it tends to pull down the average when it is below the average. This is always true. An illustration may be helpful. Suppose you are recording track scores. Students run a measured mile and their time is recorded. The time of the last student to run is the marginal time. The average time is computed by adding all times and dividing by the number of students: average time = total time/number of students. A fast runner adds a small marginal time and pulls the team average down. A slow runner adds a larger marginal time and pulls the average up. If you plot all students' marginal times on a graph and calculate the average time at every point you will find this is always true.

There is another characteristic of marginal product and average product curves. *A mar-*ginal product curve will always cut its average product curve at the highest point.* Why is this? It is because when marginal product falls below average product it begins to pull average product down. This can also be seen in Table 1. Notice that marginal product is above average product over the range 1 to 5 units of labor and that average product is rising. But when a sixth worker is added, marginal product falls below average product and begins to pull the average down. Marginal product crosses average product at its highest value: AP = 2.6. The point at which MP intersects AP defines the end of stage 1 and the beginning of stage 2 in total product. The point at which MP becomes negative and total product begins to decline defines the beginning of stage 3.

Firms are not likely to operate within stage 3. But they will generally not operate in stage 1 either. This is because average product is increasing in stage 1. The firm would be wise to continue to add variable resources as long as average product is increasing. *This means that firms will prefer to operate in stage 2*, where average product is falling and marginal product is below average product.

Costs in the short run

Now we are going to change our language. Instead of talking about units of output, we are going to talk about cost. This isn't a change of subject. When we say that marginal product and average product decline beyond a certain point, it is really like saying that production costs increase. *Diminishing marginal product means increasing marginal cost.* From now on we will talk cost language instead of output language. As economists, we are concerned with cost because cost can be expressed in money terms and compared with selling price.

If you look at the data in Table 2 you will see that average product (column (4)) rises at first as more workers are hired. As this happens, average labor cost must be falling. As workers produce more units apiece, each unit costs less in labor time. Then when average product starts to fall, it must be true that average labor cost per unit of output starts to rise. As workers produce fewer units apiece, each unit costs more in labor time.

Table 3
Hypothetical Cost Data for Producing Dune Buggies (per month)

(1) Quantity of output, QP	(2) Fixed Cost, FC	(3) Variable Cost, VC	(4) Total Cost, TC	(5) Average Fixed Cost, AFC	(6) Average Variable Cost, AVC	(7) Average Total Cost, ATC	(8) Marginal Cost, MC
0	$5,000	0	$ 5,000	—	—	—	
1	5,000	$ 2,000	7,000	$5,000	$2,000	$7,000	$ 2,000
2	5,000	3,000	8,000	2,500	1,500	4,000	1,000
3	5,000	4,000	9,000	1,667	1,333	3,000	1,000
4	5,000	5,000	10,000	1,250	1,250	2,500	1,000
5	5,000	7,000	12,000	1,000	1,400	2,400	2,000
6	5,000	10,000	15,000	833	1,667	2,500	3,000
7	5,000	14,000	19,000	714	2,000	2,714	4,000
8	5,000	19,000	24,000	625	2,375	3,000	5,000
9	5,000	31,000	36,000	555	3,444	4,000	12,000
10	5,000	45,000	50,000	500	4,500	5,000	14,000

In fact, the average variable cost curve is simply a mirror image of the average product curve. Likewise, if we reverse the marginal product curve, we get the curve for marginal cost.

In Table 3 we present some figures to show the relationship among different cost concepts.

Total costs

The cost of a firm's fixed plant and equipment in the short run is called **fixed cost** (FC). It includes such fixed expenditures as rent, interest and repayment of debt, and depreciation of equipment. Moreover, larger firms usually include the salaries of top management as part of fixed cost. Fixed cost remains the same throughout the month regardless of the level of output. In Table 3 fixed cost is $5,000 all the way down column (2).

The cost of variable resources is called **variable cost** (VC). It includes total expenditures for labor, raw materials, fuel, and any other resources that are used in varying amounts along with the firm's fixed resources. Changes in marginal product cause changes in variable cost. For small quantities of output total variable cost rises slowly. This corresponds to the range of output over which marginal product is rising. At some level of output total variable cost begins to rise more rapidly. This corresponds to the range in which marginal product is falling. Can you find the point at which this starts to happen in column (3)?

The sum of fixed cost and variable cost is **total cost** (TC). This is shown in column (4). We can write the relationship in the following shorthand form:

$$TC = FC + VC.$$

Like variable cost, total cost rises slowly at first and then more rapidly. In fact, *since fixed cost must remain the same, any change in total cost must reflect a change in variable cost.*

Average costs

If we divide *fixed cost* (FC) by the *quantity produced* (QP), we get **average fixed cost** (AFC):

$$AFC = \frac{FC}{QP}.$$

Unlike all the other costs, *average fixed cost declines over the whole range of output,* as shown in column (5). This is because fixed cost is a constant amount; as total output increases, each unit of output bears a smaller portion of the cost of fixed plant and equipment. Business firms refer to this as "spreading the overhead" over a greater number of units.

The **average variable cost** (AVC) is calculated a similar way, by dividing total variable cost by the quantity produced:

$$AVC = \frac{VC}{QP}.$$

Over the smallest range of output, average variable cost declines as more units are produced. This corresponds to stage 1 when average product is rising. But when average product starts to decrease, average variable cost starts to increase. The AVC is shown in column (6); its value results from dividing column (3) by column (1).

The **average total cost** (ATC) is the sum of average fixed cost and average variable cost:

$$\text{ATC} = \text{AFC} + \text{AVC.}$$

Since ATC measures the average cost of production per unit of output, it can also be calculated by dividing total cost at every level of output by the quantity of output:

$$\text{ATC} = \frac{\text{TC}}{\text{QP}}.$$

Thus column (7) is the sum of columns (5) and (6), or it is column (4) divided by column (1). It combines unit fixed costs that decline as output increases and unit variable costs that first decline and then rise when average product starts to decrease.

Marginal costs

The last column of Table 3 gives the marginal cost associated with every level of output. **Marginal cost** (MC) is defined similarly to marginal product. It is the change in total cost resulting from a unit change in output:

$$\text{MC} = \frac{\text{change in TC}}{\text{change in QP}}$$

$$= \frac{\text{TC}_2 - \text{TC}_1}{\text{QP}_2 - \text{QP}_1} = \frac{\Delta \text{TC}}{\Delta \text{QP}}.$$

In Table 3, the figures for MC in column (8) are equal to the increases in TC in column (4). They are also equal to the increases in total variable cost in column (3). This is because, as we have already seen, the only cost that increases as production is stepped up is variable cost. In the short run, fixed cost doesn't change and total cost is the sum of FC and VC.

Marginal cost bears the same relationship to average cost as marginal product bears to average product. That is, over the range for which marginal cost is below average cost it pulls the average cost curve down; over the range for which marginal cost is above average cost it pulls the average cost curve up. It follows that marginal cost curves must always intersect average cost curves (AVC or ATC) at their lowest points.

We will hear a lot about marginal cost in the pages that follow. MC is one of the most important concepts in economic theory. It underlies many economic decisions because the decision-maker wants to know the cost of a change in a program or an activity. What will it cost to fill a new order for dune buggies? The company may have to hire an additional worker to use equipment that is not as efficient as that already in use. The contribution to output of the extra worker will be less than that of the others, and—another way of saying it—the unit cost of the additional output may be greater than the cost of the present output. Marginal cost is rising. Since the price at which it sells dune buggies will have to remain the same under perfect competition, the company's management must decide whether the cost increase is acceptable. If not, it will decide against filling the order. The customer will have to wait or else buy from another manufacturer.

To summarize, the behavior of marginal cost reflects the behavior of marginal product. When marginal product is increasing, MC declines along with average variable cost and average total cost. Over some range marginal product and marginal cost may be constant, as the firm operates within particular design characteristics of the plant. When marginal product begins to fall, marginal cost increases because each unit of output begins to cost more. In the short run, marginal cost always increases after a certain point as production approaches the limits of available resources or the capacity of the plant itself. By resorting to various makeshifts, production can be increased further. The company can rent more equipment and hire additional workers. Or alternatively, it can ask its present workers to put in more hours. But these makeshifts involve additional expenses or inefficiencies that

Extended Example
Production Costs in the Food Industry

You may have noticed as you grew older that birthdays have gotten more expensive. The suede jacket or typewriter that you want this year will cost substantially more than the chemistry set or drum you wanted as a child. Not only will your gifts be more costly but your birthday cake has risen in price too!

Prices of baked goods have risen along with the rising costs of ingredients and of the processing which goes into the finished product. Even when some costs have fallen, others have generally increased in greater proportion and final price has continued upward.

A layer cake selling for $1 yields the farmer only about 10¢. Furthermore, the "spread" between the supermarket price and what the farmer receives has been widening. The main ingredient provided by the farmer is wheat. Wheat prices fluctuate according to world supply and demand. A plentiful supply in one year may push price below average total costs of producing wheat, leaving the farmer with negative profit or loss in the short run. As a result, production may be cut back the next year and price will rise. It takes 2.3 bushels of wheat to make 100 pounds of flour. In 1977 wheat was selling for about $2.50 a bushel, or about 7¢ per pound of flour. This was about double the price on your birthday ten years ago. Wheat must be cleaned, ground, and sifted for an additional cost of 1¢ per pound. Sugar, shortening, and eggs add more costs and all these ingredients must be transported to bakeries. The flour must be shipped in special wax-coated rail cars so that the flour won't stick. Transport costs comprise about 30¢ of the price of your birthday cake.

Baking the cake requires human labor at almost every stage. Rising wage rates and worker fringe benefits have more than doubled in the last decade. Packaging costs have risen also, partly because of shortages and higher prices for paper and petroleum-based plastics. Between 1973 and 1975 alone, packaging materials costs rose about 35%. Of course, energy costs are another major part of baking the cake, and energy costs have soared.

Finally, transport costs to retail outlets claim a large part of the cake price. Delivery is highly fuel intensive and labor intensive, both scarce and costly resources. As a result of their high costs, bakers themselves receive less than 1¢ for each dollar's worth of cake sold. Retailers add a mark-up of about 20¢ to cover their overhead costs: rent, labor, utilities, taxes, and so forth.

All in all, family food budgets will continue to increase between 3 and 5% yearly, largely as a result of higher processing and marketing costs. The only hope for lower production costs seems to lie in labor-saving strategies along the entire chain of processing activities. Greater standardization of containers would also help to reduce average costs and permit more efficient arrangement of warehousing and trucking space. Improving techniques of production would cause average and marginal costs to fall, shifting supply curves to the right. Lower costs would help bakers to fill consumer demand at lower prices.

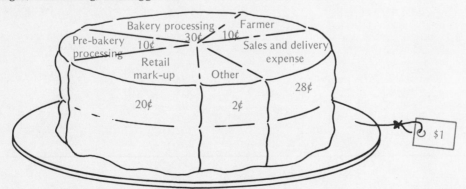

raise costs per unit. If the greater demand for dune buggies continues over a long term, the company may decide to build an addition to its plant. Then it will be able to move to a larger scale of output; but that is a subject for the next chapter on long-run production decisions.

Cost data summary

In the forgoing section we have presented a number of cost concepts that are important in economic theory. They may be summarized as follows:

Fixed cost (FC): Costs of plant, equipment, and management personnel are fixed in the short run.

Average fixed cost (AFC): Fixed cost per unit declines as output increases.

Variable cost (VC): Total cost of variable resources rises slowly at first with increases in output, then more rapidly.

Average variable cost (AVC): Unit cost of variable resources declines at first but rises as average product starts to decrease.

Total cost (TC): Total costs of fixed and variable resources (FC + VC) rise slowly as output increases at low levels of output, then more rapidly as output increases further in the short run.

Average total cost (ATC): Unit cost (AFC + AVC, or TC/QP) declines at first and then rises at higher levels of output.

Marginal cost (MC): Additions to total cost decline at first and then rise as output approaches the limit of fixed resources in the short run. If MC is below average cost, it pulls the average down; if MC is above average cost, it pulls the average up.

Profit maximization in the short run

Suppose you are the president of the Golden Sands Dune Buggy Company. You ask your economist to give you some figures on the firm's monthly production costs and economic profit at various levels of output. The economist brings you the data in Table 4.

Costs, revenue, and profit

Dune buggies sell at a price of $4,000. The marginal cost of producing dune buggies is different at different levels of output. Cost figures in Table 4 show that marginal cost (1) decreases as output is increased to the level of two dune buggies per month, (2) remains constant over a range of output, and then (3) increases by larger and larger amounts until a production level of ten dune buggies is reached. **Total revenue** (TR) increases by $4,000 for each dune buggy. Economic profit would be the difference between total revenue and total cost at any level of output:

economic profit = TR − TC.

Table 4
Monthly Data for Dune Buggies

(1) Output	(2) Total Cost	(3) Marginal Cost	(4) Total Revenue	(5) Marginal Revenue	(6) Profit
0	$ 5,000		0		−$5,000
1	7,000	$ 2,000	$ 4,000	$4,000	− 3,000
2	8,000	1,000	8,000	4,000	0
3	9,000	1,000	12,000	4,000	3,000
4	10,000	1,000	16,000	4,000	6,000
5	12,000	2,000	20,000	4,000	8,000
6	15,000	3,000	24,000	4,000	9,000
7	19,000	4,000	28,000	4,000	9,000
8	24,000	5,000	32,000	4,000	8,000
9	36,000	12,000	36,000	4,000	0
10	50,000	14,000	40,000	4,000	− 10,000

(Handwritten annotations: "FC" and "5000" above the Total Cost column; "VC" with values 2000, 3000, 4000, 5000, 7000, 1000; "AC" above the Marginal Cost column.)

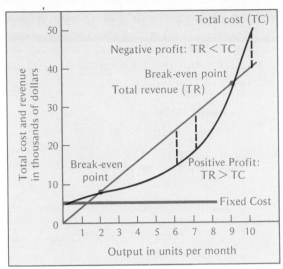

Figure 2 Comparison of total cost and total revenue curves shows economic profit. The vertical dotted lines show economic profit or loss. A loss (i.e., negative economic profit), shown at the top, results when TC is greater than TR.

Compare total cost with total revenue in Table 4. Economic profit is shown in column (6).

Production of fewer than three dune buggies per month would not be profitable. If the firm produces two a month it would just break even: total cost would equal total revenue, and economic profit would be zero. This is called the **break-even point**—that level of output at which total revenue just covers total cost. Increasing the level of production would increase revenue faster than cost, and profit would rise to a peak of $9,000. Beyond this point, however, increasing production would result in sharply higher costs. At nine units of output the firm would just break even, and for larger outputs it would incur heavy losses as costs would be rising faster than revenue.

Figure 2 shows a graph of total cost and total revenue for the dune buggy company. Fixed cost is the horizontal line at $5,000, and variable cost is added to fixed cost to produce the total cost line. Total cost rises slowly as the plant is used more efficiently. Beyond five units total cost rises faster.

Economic profit is the difference between the total cost line and the total revenue line. Because total revenue increases at a constant rate ($4,000 for each dune buggy), it is shown

in Figure 2 as a straight line beginning at the origin.

The firm's break-even point is the level of output at which the total revenue line crosses the total cost line. Notice that there are two break-even points. At every level of output economic profit is measured by the vertical distance between total revenue and total costs: Economic Profit = TR − TC. A production level of fewer than three dune buggies per month will result in *negative economic profit* (or loss) as total cost lies above total revenue. The same is true for a production level of more than nine units per month.

Average cost and average revenue

Another way of locating the firm's break-even point is to compare average total cost with the price (P) at which the product sells. This is the purpose of Figure 3, showing three average cost curves and the price line. Remember that average total cost (ATC) is the sum of two components: average fixed cost and average variable cost (ATC = AFC + AVC). In Figure 3, average fixed cost is shown as a curve which declines over the entire range of output. Average variable cost declines at first and then rises more and more rapidly. It is shown in Figure 3 as a U-shaped curve. Average total cost, which

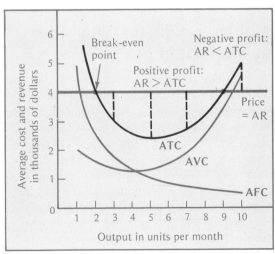

Figure 3 Average cost curves. Comparison of average total cost (ATC) and price (average revenue) shows economic profit: positive when AR > ATC; negative when AR < ATC. Average fixed cost (AFC) declines through short run.

is the sum of the other two curves, is also a U-shaped curve lying above them.

Price is shown as a horizontal line drawn at $4,000. The price is also called **average revenue** (AR). This is because

total revenue = price $\times$ quantity sold.

Rearranging terms,

$$\text{price} = \frac{\text{total revenue}}{\text{quantity sold}}$$

$$= \text{average revenue.}$$

Economic profit per unit is shown in Figure 3 as the difference between average total cost and price or average revenue. In order to break even the firm must produce at least two buggies per month and not more than nine.

Economic profit per unit is indicated by the distance between average revenue and average total cost at any level of output:

unit economic profit = AR − ATC.

Where average revenue lies above average total cost, unit economic profit is positive. Where average revenue lies below average total cost, unit economic profit is negative. Where the two are equal, at outputs of two and nine dune buggies, unit economic profit is zero and the firm is just breaking even.

Making production decisions at the margin

If we are given all the information in Tables 3 and 4, it is easy to locate the range of output over which the firm can earn economic profit. But not all this data may be available to the managers of the firm. It is not always possible to determine the variable costs associated with each level of output. Often the firm must base its decisions on cost data that are within its immediate range of operation. Management can estimate how much more it will cost to produce one more dune buggy per month, or one less. In short, it can tell what its marginal cost is. The firm also knows how much it can add to its total revenue by producing one more

dune buggy per month. The change in total revenue associated with a unit change in output is called **marginal revenue.** We can express marginal revenue (MR) in terms similar to those for marginal cost:

$$MR = \frac{\text{change in TR}}{\text{change in QP}}$$

$$= \frac{TR_2 - TR_1}{QP_2 - QP_1} = \frac{\Delta TR}{\Delta QP}.$$

By comparing changes in total revenue with changes in total costs, the firm decides on a level of output for maximum economic profit.

In competitive markets marginal revenue is the same as price. This is because a competitive firm is a price-taker; price is set in the competitive market. Thus under perfect competition P = MR = AR. Each additional unit sells for the same constant price; all units on the average sell for the same price. (In Table 4, it is simple to compare P with MR and AR. At a price of $4,000 the marginal revenue from sales of additional dune buggies is $4,000. At any level of sales average revenue is total revenue divided by units sold: AR = TR/QP. Thus at sales of 4 units AR = $16,000/4 = $4,000; at sales of 8 units AR = $32,000/8 = $4,000. Similarly at every level of sales AR = MR = P.)

The firm makes its production decision by comparing MC with P = MR = AR. *When marginal cost is less than marginal revenue, the firm will decide to expand production.* By doing so it will add more to revenue than to costs, and economic profit will increase.

The reverse is also true. When marginal cost is greater than marginal revenue, the firm will want to reduce its output. That is because a reduction in output will subtract more from costs than from revenue. Contracting production will allow economic profit to increase.

It follows that when marginal cost is just equal to marginal revenue, the firm will maintain its output at that level—where the last unit produced adds the same to total costs as its selling price. At this level of output the firm is earning maximum economic profit. In Table 4 the firm's maximum output consistent with maximum economic profit is seven dune buggies a month. The marginal cost of the seventh unit is $4,000. The seventh unit also adds $4,000 to total revenue.

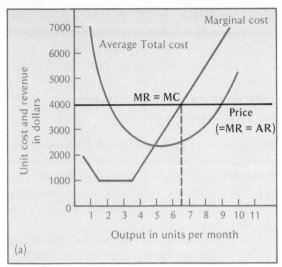

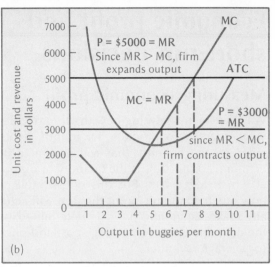

Figure 4 (a) Marginal cost and marginal revenue determine level of output for profit maximization. A firm seeks to produce Where MR = MC. Here that point means an output of seven dune buggies per month when price is $4,000. (b) When price changes, the firm will adjust output accordingly. When price rises to $5,000, our firm moves up its marginal cost (supply) curve to new equilibrium—output is now 8 dune buggies. When price drops to $3,000, our firm moves down the MC curve—output is now 6 dune buggies.

The rule of setting production at the point where MC = MR is a fundamental principle of microeconomics. When MC = MR, the firm is earning maximum economic profit. This holds true for all forms of competition—imperfect as well as perfect. We will see later how it applies to monopoly, oligopoly, and monopolistic competition.

Figure 4 illustrates these production decisions at the margin. Output per month is shown on the horizontal axis and marginal cost on the vertical axis. The marginal cost curve declines at first and then begins to rise. Market price is shown as a horizontal line drawn at a price of $4,000 (Figure 4a). This is also marginal revenue and average revenue, because under perfect competition the price is not affected by the level of the firm's output. Each unit sold adds the same amount to revenue.

Compare marginal cost with marginal revenue. Increasing production from four dune buggies to five adds $2,000 to costs and $4,000 to revenue. Because MC is less than MR, the firm will want to expand output beyond five units per month. At seven units MC becomes equal to MR, and this is the firm's profit-maximizing position. To go beyond seven units would add more to costs than to revenue. At a monthly output of seven units, therefore, the

firm will have no incentive to contract or expand its output.

Now suppose market price rises to $5,000. This can be shown in Figure 4b by drawing the marginal revenue (price) line at the level of $5,000. The firm will now decide to expand its production of dune buggies from seven per month to eight. How would the firm adjust its output if the price falls to $3,000? To $2,000?

Have you noticed that the quantity of output the firm will supply can be read from its marginal cost curve? In fact, a portion of a firm's MC curve constitutes its supply curve. In Figure 5 we have reproduced part of the rising portion of the firm's marginal cost curve and labeled it supply. This portion of the MC curve tells you the maximum quantities of output that the firm will supply at different prices. At every price, the quantity supplied can be read on the horizontal axis.

Economic profit and short-run decisions

Measuring economic profit

We have been analyzing how the firm decides what quantity to produce per month. It decides on the quantity that will maximize its economic profit. This is the quantity of output at which MC = MR. But this doesn't tell us how much economic profit the firm will actually make. Economic profit is determined by the difference between average cost and price (or average revenue).

The firm first calculates economic profit (AP) earned per unit of output. This is found by taking the difference between average total cost and average revenue: AP = AR − ATC. By multiplying unit economic profit AP by the number of units produced, the firm obtains the figure for total economic profit. If the firm is producing seven dune buggies per month, we have seen that its marginal cost is equal to its marginal revenue. Referring to Table 3, we find that the average cost of seven units is $2,714 (from column (7)). Since the buggies are selling at a market price of $4,000 each, unit economic profit is $4,000 − $2,714, or $1,286. Multiplying this by the number of units gives us

total economic profit: $1,286 × 7 ≈ $9,000. The firm at this point is paying all its costs of production including normal profit and clearing a maximum economic profit above that.

Firms may accept losses in the short run

But suppose business is bad. Consumer demand curves shift to the left and price falls. Now instead of making an economic profit the firm incurs losses. Total revenue minus total cost becomes a negative number. What should the firm do?

A glance at Figure 6 shows the situation of our dune buggy firm if market price falls to $2,000. Management compares its marginal cost with marginal revenue (price) and moves back down the marginal cost curve. Marginal cost is equal to marginal revenue at an output of five dune buggies per month. This level of output maximizes economic profit (or, rather, minimizes loss). Average total cost at this level of production is $2,400, which means that the firm is taking a loss of $400 on each dune buggy. Its total loss is $400 × 5 or $2,000.

How long will the firm continue to operate in the face of such losses? In the short run the answer depends on the relation between price and average variable cost. The firm's fixed costs are frozen in the short run and must be paid regardless of the level of operation. If the firm stops production altogether, it will still owe the entire amount of its fixed cost for the remainder of the short run. If it keeps on producing some quantity, it may earn enough to pay its variable cost and make some contribution toward payment of its fixed cost.

This is precisely the case for our dune buggy firm, as we can see from Figure 6. The price of $2,000 covers average variable costs of $1,400 (see Table 3) and leaves $600 to apply to payment of fixed cost. If the firm stopped production, it would still have to pay the fixed cost of $5,000 per month. By producing five dune buggies and selling them for $2,000 each, it obtains $600 × 5 = $3,000 to apply toward the fixed cost of $5,000. Thus the loss is held down to only $2,000 per month. The firm can

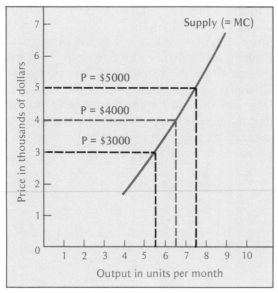

Figure 5 A part of the rising portion of the MC curve (where diminishing marginal product sets in) is identical to the firm's supply curve.

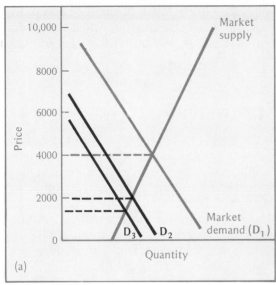

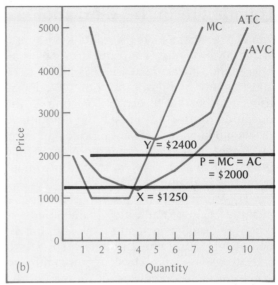

Figure 6 (a) As market demand declines to D_2 or D_3, price falls. (b) Intersection of the MC curve with ATC determines the point of minimal short-run losses. Intersection of MC curve with AVC determines the shut-down point, Price = $1250.

pay the cost of its labor, electric power, raw materials, and component parts—that is, all variable cost. The remainder will go toward paying fixed charges for plant and equipment, office space, and administrative staff. The $2,000 loss may be covered temporarily by borrowing or by selling other assets owned by the firm. This is better, in the short run, than stopping production entirely.

The shut-down point in the short run

The firm cannot produce at just any price. If demand keeps falling, market price may fall so low that the firm can't cover average variable cost. It will have to shut down. By shutting down the firm will incur a smaller loss than to go on producing with price lower than the cost of variable resources used in production. Losses will be limited only to fixed costs contracted for the short run. Thus when price falls as low as average variable cost, the firm reaches its **shut-down point.**

You can locate the shut-down point on Figure 6b by following the firm's marginal cost curve down to the point at which MC is equal to average variable cost. To produce and sell for a price lower than average variable cost

would add more losses to what the firm is already losing on its fixed cost. The lowest average variable cost of producing dune buggies is $1,250 when four units are produced each month. As long as price is at least $1,250 the firm minimizes losses by continuing to operate in the short run.

The shut-down point sets the minimum conditions for operating in the short run. Producing above this minimum helps the firm to fulfill its obligations over the period for which some resources are fixed. If the firm continues to incur losses over the short run it cannot remain in business indefinitely. At the end of the short run, a firm incurring losses must finally go out of business. The decision to enter or to leave an industry is a long-run decision. We will deal with long-run decisions in the next chapter.

Equilibrium in the short run

You will recall that market equilibrium is found at the level of price and output at which all buyers and sellers are satisfied with the price and quantity of their transactions. Producers have no incentive to expand or contract the operation of their fixed plant and equipment. At equilibrium, all firms are producing a level of output that yields maximum economic profit (or minimum loss). In short-run equilibrium, the following conditions hold:

(1) $MC = MR$. Firms are producing a quantity of output at which marginal cost is equal to marginal revenue. The last unit of output adds the same amount to costs as it adds to revenue. At this level of output the firm is maximizing economic profit (or minimizing loss). A portion of a firm's MC curve constitutes its supply curve.

(2) $MR = P = MC$. Under perfect competition, marginal revenue is equal to price. Equilibrium price is high enough to cover the marginal cost of the additional resources used to produce the last unit of output.

(3) $P \geq AVC$. The firm is covering its variable cost for the short run. In the short run, firms may earn revenues greater than total costs or they may experience losses. Nevertheless, in the short run firms will continue to operate as long as price is at least as great as average variable cost.

These features of short-run equilibrium are of considerable benefit to consumers and to business firms. Consumers are able to satisfy their demands at acceptable prices, and business firms are able to conduct their operations and pay their suppliers. But the short-run equilibrium may not be ideal. Total revenue may exceed total cost, or it may be less than total cost.

When total revenue differs from total cost, firms will be earning economic profit or loss. From the standpoint of the industry as a whole, the number of firms in the industry is either too small or too large. If there are too few firms to satisfy demand, price will be high and firms will collect economic profits. If there are too many firms for the existing market, price will be low and firms will suffer economic losses. In the short run nothing can be done about this. New plants cannot be built and old plants will not be torn down. In the long run, however, firms will respond to their economic profits or losses, and that is the subject of the next chapter.

Summary

In the short run, competitive firms make decisions to employ certain quantities of variable resources along with the existing stock of fixed resources. Opportunity costs are an important part of this decision. *Accounting costs* are shown on a firm's income and expense statement. But accounting costs measure only *explicit* costs, including costs of variable and fixed resources and depreciation of capital. Net income after taxes is the amount available for distribution to owners or for retained earnings (business saving). Besides explicit costs of the firm, *economic costs* also include *implicit* costs: the opportunity costs of using the firm's own resources in some way. Normal profit is a necessary return to entrepreneurship, and economic profit is an excess return. Economic profit rewards innovative firms and encourages resource mobility.

In the short run, the principle of diminishing marginal product governs production. Applying variable resources to a fixed resource causes total product first to increase at an increasing rate, then to increase at a decreasing rate, and finally to decrease. Marginal product first rises and then falls, pulling average product up when marginal product is greater than average product and pulling average product down when marginal product is less than average product. The reverse of product calculations is cost calculations. Total cost rises first at a decreasing rate and then at an increasing rate. Marginal cost first falls, then rises, pulling average cost down when marginal cost is less than average cost and pulling average cost up when marginal cost is greater than average cost.

A firm's break-even point is the level of output at which total revenue becomes greater than total cost. Over some range of output the firm may collect economic profit. The firm maximizes economic profit (or minimizes loss) by producing the quantity of output at which marginal cost is equal to marginal revenue: MC = MR. In perfect competition price equals marginal revenue: P = MR. At that level of output total economic profit is equal to the product of units of output times unit economic profit—the difference between price and average cost per unit. In the short run, a firm will produce at a loss as long as price is sufficient to cover average variable costs. After variable costs are paid, the firm can apply the remainder of revenues to fixed costs and minimize its loss. If price falls as low as average variable cost, the firm reaches its shut-down point. Firms may experience economic profit or loss in the short run. But in the long run, economic profit or loss will disappear through entry and exit of firms.

Key Words and Phrases

- **depreciation** the cost of wearing out of capital equipment during the course of business activity.
- **accounting costs** the out-of-pocket costs and depreciation which result from business activity over a particular time period.
- **explicit or historical costs** costs actually paid or allocated in the course of business activity; these costs are the same as accounting costs.
- **net income or accounting profit** the remaining revenue after paying all explicit costs and allocating depreciation expense.
- **opportunity cost** the real economic cost of using resources in a particular way.
- **implicit costs** the opportunity costs of a firm's own resources; these are costs the firm pays to itself.
- **normal profit** a necessary return in payment for entrepreneurial resources.
- **economic profit** a return greater than the necessary amount needed to reward ordinary entrepreneurial services.
- **short run** a period of time in which some resources are fixed in quantity.
- **fixed productive resources** resources such as a plant, equipment, and management staff, all of which are fixed in the short run.

- **variable resources** resources which are used together with fixed resources in the short run; some variable resources are fuel and energy, labor, and raw materials.
- **total product** level of a firm's output over a given time period for all the resources used by the firm.
- **marginal product** the change in total output that results from adding a unit of a variable resource; often, the quantity of output added by the last hired worker.
- **principle of diminishing marginal product** above some level of output, a firm's total output will increase by smaller amounts as variable resources are added; the amount produced by each additional unit of variable resource tends to decrease.
- **average product** total product for any particular period of time divided by the units of variable resources used in production.
- **fixed costs** the unchanging cost of a business firm's fixed resources in the short run.
- **average fixed costs** total fixed costs in a particular period of time divided by the number of units of output produced.
- **variable costs** the total cost of variable resources employed during a particular period of time.
- **average variable costs** total variable costs in a particular period of time divided by the number of units of output produced.
- **average total costs** total costs in a particular period of time divided by the number of units of output produced.
- **marginal cost** the additional cost of producing an additional unit of output.
- **break-even point** the level(s) of output at which revenue from sales will be just equal to *total* costs of production.
- **shut-down point** the level of output at which revenue from sales is just sufficient to cover a firm's *variable* costs of production.

Questions for Review

1. Distinguish between accounting costs and economic costs. What resource costs are considered in each case? How does economic profit differ from accounting profit?

2. State clearly the principle of diminishing marginal product. Does this principle apply over all ranges of output? Explain.

3. Use the hypothetical data below to construct a graph of revenue, costs, and profit at all levels of output.

Quantity	Price	Fixed Cost	Variable Cost
1	5	3	4
2	5	3	7
3	5	3	9
4	5	3	13
5	5	3	19
6	5	3	27
7	5	3	37

4. Use the data from question 3 to calculate average total cost and marginal cost. Plot on a second graph directly below your graph in question 3. Verify that MC = ATC at its lowest point. Verify that profit is maximum at the level of output at which MC = MR.

5. Use the data from questions 3 and 4 to demonstrate two ways of calculating profit at the maximum profit point.

6. What is the lowest price the firm in question 3 will accept in the short run? Suppose price does fall to this level. What is the total amount of the firm's loss? State clearly the conditions which would cause the firm to shut down in the short run.

7. Draw up a hypothetical income statement for a firm producing economics textbooks. Include all explicit costs and depreciation expense incurred during the period. Then modify your "bottom line" figure to allow for normal profit. Label the remaining figure "economic profit."

8. Define: Profit and Loss Statement, short-run losses.

9. We have defined a firm's supply curve as a portion of the rising part of its marginal cost curve. Why is only a *portion* of the curve involved in supply decisions? What part of the MC curve is *not* part of its supply curve?

28

Perfection Competition:
Costs and
Production Decisions in
the Long Run

The Golden Sands Dune Buggy Company had enjoyed several prosperous years. The market for dune buggies was excellent. At the going price of $4,000 the company earned economic profit of $1,286 on every vehicle it sold. But at the end of the year the president reported to the board of directors that competition was beginning to move into the market. The firm would have to expect declining sales in the years ahead and lower prices for each unit sold.

The president was right. Economic profits on dune buggies had led other firms to enter the industry. The following year dune buggies were selling for only $3,000. Figure 1 shows the marginal cost and average cost curves for Golden Sands. You will remember from the last chapter that the company had established its output at the level at which marginal cost was equal to marginal revenue (or to price, since there is perfect competition). At a price of $4,000 the firm was producing seven buggies per month. For each unit the firm made economic profit equal to the difference between price and average total cost. In Figure 1a economic profit on each dune buggy is the distance ab, and total economic profit is represented by the rectangle abcd.

But this is only the short run. Over the short run some resources are fixed. Adding variable resources to a firm's fixed resources allows production to take place. Output may sell for a price greater than total cost, providing economic profit. Or price may be less than total cost (while still covering variable cost) and economic profit may be negative. In either case firms will continue to produce in the short run. *Over the long run it is possible to change the quantity of fixed resources in the industry.* New firms may enter the industry in anticipation of earning economic profit; or old firms may leave the industry to avoid further loss.

As new firms entered the industry, the supply curve for dune buggies moved to the right (to S_1). A larger quantity of output was now supplied at every price level. This forced market price down to $3,000, as shown in Figure 1b. Golden Sands cut back its production, moving down its MC curve until MC was equal to MR at P = MR = $3,000. At output of six units per month, the firm is still able to earn total economic profit of $500 \times 6 = $3,000. Eventually, if supply were to increase still further, supply would shift to S_2. Price would continue to fall and Golden Sands would cut production again. At a market price of $2,400 Golden Sands would still be in business but producing only five units monthly, the quantity at which MC would be equal to an MR of $2,400. Economic profit would be zero. Golden

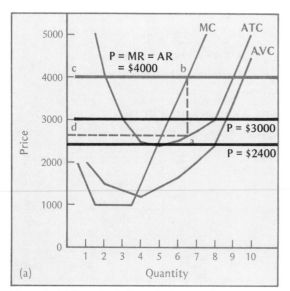

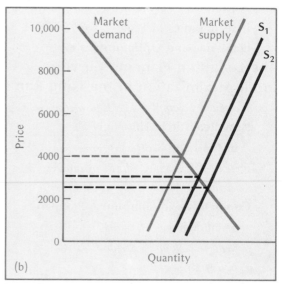

Figure 1 (a) Hypothetical marginal cost and average cost curves for producing Golden Sands dune buggies. The distance ab is the economic profit for producing seven buggies. (b) Supply and demand for the dune buggy market. As new firms enter the market, supply expands to S_1 and then to S_2.

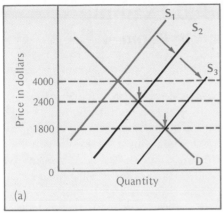
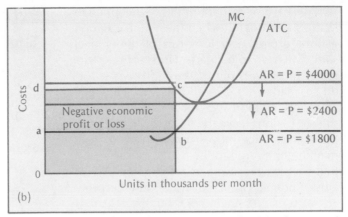

Figure 2 (a) As new firms are added to an industry, supply may expand—supply curves move to the right. (b) As supply expands, the price (average revenue) of each unit declines. Firms may experience negative economic profit.

Sands would still earn what economists call "normal profit"—enough to pay dividends to its stockholders—but the company's great days would be over.

Long-run competitive equilibrium

The decision to enter or leave an industry is a long-run decision. In the short run a firm may make economic profit or loss, but it will continue to operate as long as price covers variable costs. Over a longer period economic profit or loss encourages new firms to enter or old firms to leave an industry. In the long run under perfect competition economic profit approaches zero.

Figures 2 and 3 summarize the process by which an industry moves toward long-run equilibrium. In Figure 2a, as supply curves of new firms are added to the existing industry supply, the market supply curve shifts to the right, from S_1 to S_2. As supply increases, price falls. Consumers can buy larger quantities at lower prices. To an individual firm, the falling market price appears on Figure 2b as a downward shift in the horizontal line drawn at market price. The lower price means smaller economic profit. The firm moves down its marginal cost curve and produces a smaller quantity. Until market price falls to $2,400 there is still economic profit. But below this price the firm will take a loss. At a price of $1,800 the loss on each unit is the difference between price and ATC. Total loss is the rectangle abcd.

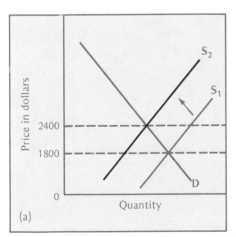
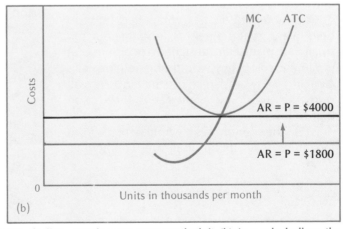

Figure 3 (a) As firms leave an industry, the supply may decline—supply curves move to the left. (b) As supply declines, the price (P = AR) of each unit increases.

We have seen that firms may accept losses in the short run. But when their short-run obligations expire, new long-run planning decisions will have to be made. Firms experiencing losses must drop out of the industry. As they do so, market supply will begin to fall. Figure 3a shows the industry supply curve shifting to the left as firms leave the industry. In Figure 3b, the market price moves up again until all remaining firms are producing for sale at a price that just covers average total cost. This includes normal profit but no economic profit.

At a market price of $2,400 the industry is said to be in **long-run competitive equilibrium.** There is no longer any incentive for new firms to enter. All firms are earning revenue sufficient to pay full costs, including normal profit, and there is no incentive for any of them to leave the industry.

For producers and consumers, this is an ideal arrangement. There are five reasons why.

(1) Consumers are satisfied; they are getting the product at minimum long-run price. There is enough output to fill demand at a price buyers are willing to pay.

(2) Producers are satisfied; they are not forced to leave the industry. Price is sufficient to cover the cost of the last unit produced: P = MC. Furthermore, the entry and exit of firms have stabilized price at a level that just covers average total cost, including normal profit: P = ATC. But there is no economic profit or loss for any firm.

(3) The number of firms in the industry is just enough to fill the market demand at existing market price. There is no overcapacity or undercapacity. No firm has an incentive to enter or leave the industry.

(4) Competition has compelled firms to build plants that are neither too large nor too small. All plants are designed to produce at minimum cost. They would not be more efficient if they were larger or smaller. (We will study the question of plant size in the section that follows.)

(5) The economy as a whole benefits from industries that are in long-run competitive

Extended Example
The Bicycle Boom

Until the 1970s, bicycle production in the United States was somewhat less than exciting. Between 6 and 7.5 million units were produced each year, mostly by eight small, family-held firms. But the relative tranquility changed in 1971 and the industry hasn't been the same since.

Suddenly, adult Americans began to buy bikes. Sales to adults account for more than half of all bikes sold in today's market and pushed industry sales to 15.2 million in 1973. The physical fitness fad was partly responsible. The energy crisis and the emphasis on the environment led many young adults to cycling for work and play.

The surge in demand caught bike manufacturers by surprise. Their frantic efforts to fill orders for 10-speed adult bikes led to sharply rising costs and falling quality. Limited to their fixed productive capacity, firms moved up their marginal cost curves and prices rose.

Foreign producers jumped at the chance to penetrate the booming U.S. market and to fill the gap left by inadequate domestic capacity. Imports rose 20% in one year, capturing 37% of the market in 1972. Foreign manufacturers still supply almost 30% of component parts, including all multispeed gear systems, 80% of tires, and 75% of bike chains.

Bike sales took a beating in the recession of 1973–1975. The adult market was saturated. Sales growth depends on replacements, and good 10-speeds can last up to ten years. Fortunately, the average child outgrows two or three bikes before reaching the 10-speed. And domestic firms are particularly adept at gauging the tastes of the young and capitalizing on new fads. The "Motorcross" bike became especially popular; it sports racing plates, an extra cross bar, and sometimes a fake fuel tank.

Industry prospects look favorable for the remainder of the 1970s. The Federal Highway Administration has appropriated $6 million for demonstration bikeways to supplement the 25,000 miles of bike routes now in use. With the greater area for bike riding, demand is expected to stabilize at about 16 million units per year.

Cyclists are adding accessories to their equipment and fueling a prosperous new industry. Some of the extras include locks and lights, pole banners that glow in the dark, snap-on baby seats, flower baskets, and duffel bags. Accessories add up to $100 million in sales a year. Growth in sales is expected to be about 8 to 10%, with industry revenues of $1 billion in 1977; and manufacturers will turn out 30,000 bikes a day.

Illustrate graphically changes in market conditions for bicycles. What is the effect of imports on the industry demand curve? What happens to profits as the industry approaches long-run competitive equilibrium?

equilibrium. Such industries produce at the lowest possible cost in terms of the scarce resources they use. They pay productive resources a return just sufficient to cover their opportunity costs—that is, they do not attract resources that could be employed better somewhere else.

Plant size and the long run

What about the size of plants in long-run competitive equilibrium? For maximum efficiency should plants be small or large? The answer is: It depends. As plants are built to produce greater output, their average costs often tend to fall. But beyond some level of plant size, average costs may start to increase.

Long-run average costs are all variable. There are no fixed costs in the long run. Variable costs in the long run include all costs of plant and equipment and administrative personnel, costs which are considered fixed in the short run. The shape of the long-run average cost curve depends on the behavior of these and other costs at various levels of plant size.

Economists refer to the size of plant as *scale*. In some industries the scale of plant may have no effect on unit costs. Then we say that production involves *constant returns to scale*, or *constant average costs* at every plant size. In the more usual case, however, larger plants experience increasing returns to scale, or lower average costs, up to some level of output. Beyond that optimum level of operation plants may have decreasing returns to scale, or higher average costs.

When average costs are lower in large plants, we say that production involves **economies of large scale.** When average costs rise with larger plant capacity, we call this **diseconomies of large scale.**

Economies of scale in the long run

Why do larger plants often have lower production costs? There are four basic advantages in large size, both technological and administrative.

(1) A large plant may be able to use more advanced and specialized equipment. Some equipment requires a large production run if it is to be efficient. Also, in larger plants the work force may become more specialized and may develop higher skills.

(2) With a larger operation, a firm may be able to buy its materials in larger quantities at a price discount.

(3) A large plant may make more profitable use of by-products. It may even develop subsidiary plants, using by-products to produce other goods. A large petroleum refinery, for instance, may produce chemicals derived from oil. A fish-packing plant may process the heads and tails and sell them as fertilizer.

(4) Large plants provide many opportunities to increase efficiency through better organization and administration. Production can be organized into specialized divisions so that less time is lost shifting workers from one operation to another. The flow of materials can be regulated more carefully so that less time is lost waiting for things to arrive. Staff members can be trained for particular functions such as production planning, market research, cost accounting, and finance.

In some industries there is almost no limit to the economies of scale. Long-run average costs continue to fall as plants increase in size. Figure 4a shows the *long-run average cost* (*LRAC*) *curve* for a transportation firm. By expanding its plant and equipment to a very large size, the transportation firm is better able to use modern technology to reduce its costs. Airlines or railroads can increase their capital stock greatly without encountering diseconomies of scale. Their average cost curves may continue to decline as capital and development costs are spread over more and more passengers or tons of freight. Automobile and steel factories are other examples of increasing returns to scale. In fact, the history of modern mass production is largely a story of increasing returns to scale in industries where vast amounts of capital investment have paid off through higher productivity and lower unit costs. Your Chevy could be made in a factory employing a few hundred workers, but not at a price that you would want to pay.

Some industries seem to be characterized by the curve in Figure 4b. Average costs drop at first and then remain about the same over a wide range of plant sizes. In many manufacturing industries, plants of quite different sizes manage to be competitive with each other. Some minimum size is often necessary in order to enjoy the available economies of scale. But beyond that point, whatever economies there may be from growing larger are offset by diseconomies—such as higher cost of management. As a result, small producers are not undersold by big ones. The printing industry furnishes a good example: a few giant firms exist side by side with a number of medium-sized and small firms. If you want to print a large metropolitan telephone directory you will go to one of the giants, but if you're the editor of a small magazine with a limited press run you may find that a small printer will give more individual attention to your order. A firm may find it more practical to establish a customer relationship with a supplying firm of roughly similar scale. This ensures that the resources of the supplying firm are adequate for the needs of the buying firm.

Diseconomies of scale

In some industries the long-run average cost curve rises after a certain size of plant has been reached. This may happen because of administrative problems: there may be too many employees for easy supervision, or there may be

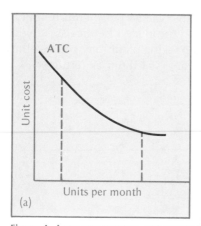
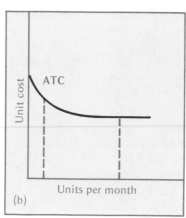
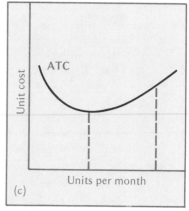

Figure 4 Long-run average cost curves show scale economies: (a) an industry with economies of scale, that is, declining costs as plant size increases; (b) an industry with initial economies of scale and eventual constant average costs; (c) an industry with initial economies of scale and eventual diseconomies of scale.

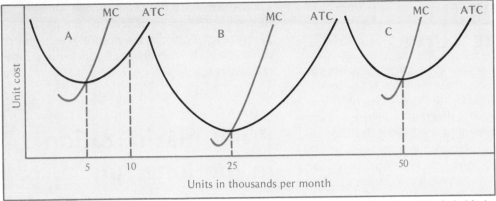

Figure 5 Short-run average total cost curves for ice-cream plants of different sizes. Plant A is desirable for small output: its minimum costs per unit occur when producing 5,000 gallons. Plant B operates "best" at an output of 25,000 gallons. Plant C operates best at 50,000 gallons; notice, however, that plant C has higher unit costs than plant B (that is, its lowest point is higher than plant B's lowest point).

so many supervisors that it is difficult to coordinate them all. As we saw above, some diseconomies may be offset by savings from large production runs. But one kind of diseconomy cannot easily be offset—the higher cost of having to use poor quality resources. For example, a coal mine may be able to expand only by working seams of coal that are less productive or more difficult to mine than those currently in operation. Or a farm, if it is to grow much larger, may have to start cultivating land that is less fertile or is farther away. Figure 4c shows a long-run cost curve for an industry that experiences decreasing returns to scale.

Plant size and optimum scale

If you were the president of an ice cream company and were thinking of building a new plant, how would you decide on its size? Which plant size would have the *optimum scale*—that is, the scale that offers lowest average total costs. Let us suppose that the long-run average cost curve for ice cream plants resembles the curve in Figure 4c. A small plant can supply its local area with ice cream, but a larger one may be able to supply the whole town at lower unit cost. Beyond a certain point the plant has to reach farther out for its customers, and this increases its advertising, transportation, and handling costs. Thus average costs will be higher for very large ice cream plants.

In Figure 5 we have drawn short-run average total cost curves for plants of different sizes. An ice cream plant of size A is designed to produce 5,000 gallons of ice cream per month. It could produce up to 10,000 gallons, but this would exceed its design capabilities and unit costs would increase. A plant of size B is designed to produce 25,000 gallons per month. Its unit costs are lower than those of plant A because of the economies of large scale. A plant could be built to produce 50,000 gallons per month, but it would have to sell to customers outside the metropolitan area, and that would increase its costs. It would experience diseconomies of scale.

You decide to build a plant of size B because you expect to operate within a range of output on both sides of 25,000 gallons per month. That is, you may sometimes produce as much as 35,000 gallons per month, but your unit costs will still be lower than if you were operating a plant of size C. And in slow times you may throttle down to 15,000 gallons, but your unit costs will be lower than if you were operating a plant of size A.

The long-run planning curve

Before you decided on the optimum scale, you had engineers prepare estimates for plants of various sizes. The picture they presented may have resembled the diagram in Figure 6. Plant A_5 is designed to produce 5,000 gallons of ice cream a month, plant A_{10} will produce 10,000 gallons, and so forth. An **envelope curve** has been drawn to enclose the individual plant curves. This envelope curve is the *long-run average cost curve* or *industry planning curve*.

The long-run average cost curve is *not* a separate, independent curve. It is drawn from short-run average total cost curves for plants of various sizes. Every point on the long-run curve represents the lowest average cost for which that quantity of output could be produced. An infinite number of short-run curves could be drawn and a single point taken from each to construct the long-run curve.

This is why the envelope curve *touches* (we say, *is tangent to*) the short-run average cost curves for plants of various size. But except for the B_{25} curve, it is *not* tangent to them at their lowest point. This is significant because it shows that a plant designed to produce exactly 25,000 gallons per month will achieve the low-est average cost for firms in the industry. It represents the *optimum* scale of plant. Smaller plants fail to enjoy all the potential economies of larger scale. Larger plants encounter diseconomies.

Profit maximization in the long run

In a perfectly competitive industry, firms in the long run will all tend to build plants of optimum scale. That is, their short-run average cost curve will be tangent to industry long-run average cost at its lowest point. In Figure 5, all firms would build plants of size B_{25}. When the industry is in long-run competitive equilibrium, price will have fallen to the point where no firm makes an economic profit—that is, price will also be tangent to the long-run average cost curve at its lowest point. We can abbreviate this statement to read:

$$P = AR = \text{minimum ATC} = \text{minimum LRAC}.$$

But each firm will also be in short-run equilibrium. As we saw earlier, this means that its marginal cost (MC) is equal to its marginal

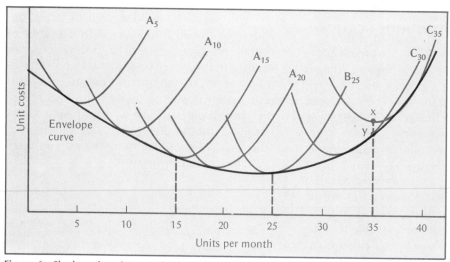

Figure 6 Single points from each short-run average total cost curve for plants of every different size constitute an envelope curve. The envelope curve is tangent to all the short-run curves. The envelope curve is called the long-run average cost curve.

Extended Example
The End of the Short Run

Nostalgia buffs know about them.

There aren't many left and soon they'll probably be extinct. But they used to be the favorite meeting place for teenagers after school, businessmen at lunch, and couples out for an evening stroll.

Of course, I'm referring to the drugstore soda fountain.

There was a distinctive odor about them—a combination of fizz-water and bubbly fudge sauce. And they served real honest-to-goodness milk shakes—poured thickly from metal shakers with beads of condensation running down the sides. For lunch, a crisp club sandwich or a slaw dog, so rich with filling that you had to eat it with a fork. And through it all a feeling of personal attention to your individual tastes.

They're almost all gone now. The short run has come to an end and they're dropping away. They've been victims of the inexorable force of supply and demand.

Demand first. Population growth has certainly increased the potential market. But the growth of the automobile and suburban sprawl and the faster pace of modern life have sent customers to the fast-food franchised eateries. The tastes of today's young adults have become accustomed to the standardized product, often ordered through a microphone and shoved at you through a slot!

As soda fountain customers drifted away demand curves shifted back, revenues fell, and normal profits changed to economic losses. Many establishments remained in business as long as revenues were sufficient to cover variable costs. Fixed costs were low for their aging capital equipment; losses at the soda fountain could often be subsidized by profits at the prescription counter.

What was happening to supply over these decades? Remember that a supply curve is the rising portion of marginal cost, above average variable cost. How have modern conditions affected the position and shape of marginal cost?

The answer requires a word about scale of plant. Optimum scale for drugstore lunch counters is rather small. This is just a fact of its character. Small scale limits the use of specialized labor, equipment, and management. The problem of scale is a real disadvantage in competition with the new forms of food service where optimum scale is very large. Mass techniques of organization, purchasing, and production in large volume have enhanced efficiency far beyond that possible at the lunch counter. The predictable result is a wide difference between the average and marginal cost curves for the two types of service. In terms of supply price, the old couldn't compete with the new.

To make matters worse, the industry was experiencing long-run diseconomies of growth—not offset by economies. The expansion of industry in general was increasing the cost of resources. Old drugstores are generally located on high-cost, highly taxed urban land. The opportunity costs are high, excluding all but the most profitable enterprises. Utility rates and materials costs have risen similarly. Furthermore, general wage inflation in urban areas has been especially hard on such a labor-intensive activity. Diseconomies of economic growth have shifted long-run average cost (LRAC) curves upward for the drugstore lunch counter.

For any business enterprise the end of the short run brings on the crucial question of long-run planning. One by one these old establishments have faced up to the economic facts of life. We are witnessing the sad demise of an American institution.

Often the decision to purchase food involves more than simple nutrition. What bundles of "characteristics" are included in purchases: at the soda fountain and at the fast-food eatery?

revenue (MR). Since average cost is at its minimum, marginal cost must be equal to average cost. The complete statement of the conditions of long-run equilibrium for a firm in perfect competition thus becomes

$$MC = MR = P = AR$$
$$= \text{minimum ATC} = \text{minimum LRAC.}$$

How realistic is this view of the long run?

The picture we have been presenting of firms in a state of perfect competition is not a photograph of firms in the real world. The theory of perfect competition is a model. It is a description of a theoretical world in which no firm has any control over the price at which it sells its product, and in which nothing prevents firms from entering or leaving an industry. Economists study this ideal world because it shows how resources would be allocated efficiently under perfect competition.

In most industries long-run adjustments are constantly taking place in response to competitive forces. Firms enter or leave an industry on the basis of profitability. Where demand is growing as it was in the computer and office copier industries in the 1960s, new firms will try to establish positions. Some will succeed. Others will fail and be forced to withdraw, or they may be absorbed by established firms.

Seldom, if ever, will an industry reach the point that we have called long-run equilibrium. This is because conditions in the economy keep changing. Market demand for each product changes, and prices change with it. New developments in technology and materials cause industry cost curves to move up or down. It would be quite remarkable if any industry were to reach long-run competitive equilibrium and remain there. Rather, an industry will move toward what would be a long-run equilibrium position *if no further changes were to occur;* it will not reach that position because *some change will occur* and send it off in another direction. In the computer industry, for example, a succession of technological changes have reduced production costs and opened up entirely different markets. Microcomputers are now being used

Extended Example
Market Changes in the Long Run

Sometimes changes in consumer demand can change a dying industry into a booming one. The ice for your beer keg was very likely the product of a $175 million a year industry—an industry which faced possible extinction only thirty years ago.

In the early 1800s ice was made in the United States by cutting natural ice from ponds and storing it in icehouses for use throughout the year. The first ice plants were built in 1869 and used the principle of ammonia absorption to freeze water. Output was about 50 million tons a year and the iceman was an important part of American life.

All this changed in the 1920s with the appearance of home refrigerators; ice-making companies began to go out of business. It looked as if market demand would never again be high enough to justify long-run plans to produce this very basic product.

Who could have predicted the tremendous changes in the United States social environment since World War II? Americans have been earning more and spending more. They've been partying and picnicking and stocking their freezers with processed foods. With no room for storing ice for peak needs they've turned to self-service dispensers, and the ice-making industry is off and running.

Small companies have combined into larger ones with greater capital for new fast-freezing equipment. The Turbo method freezes thin layers of water in sheets like plywood; the sheets are then broken into chips. The Voght method freezes ice around a metal tube which is then slipped out; the resulting ice cylinder is sliced into many circular pieces for a larger cooling surface. Both methods require only about 25 minutes. A total of about 5 million tons of ice is produced annually, with about two-thirds considered "social ice" and the remainder used to supplement mechanical refrigeration in railroad cars, trucks, and storage depots.

Increasing consumer demand provided the incentive for technological change in this industry. External economies of growth shifted long-run planning curves down. Supply has become more elastic over the long run.

Construct a series of graphs illustrating shifts in demand and supply over time. Show how supply curves reflect long-run average costs and how optimum scale has increased. What has happened to industry planning curves? What has happened to price?
How does this article illustrate the responsiveness of industry to consumer preferences: in the long run and in the short run? Why is it correct to say that industries seldom actually reach long-run competitive equilibrium?

for many industrial purposes that nobody thought of a few years back.

In some industries adjustments to changing conditions may be very slow because of *rigidities within the industry*. Long-run plans require large commitments of costly resources for a very long time period. The short run thus becomes very long, and firms may show economic profit (or loss) for long periods. This seems to be true of the steel industry in the United States. Because of heavy financial commitments made years ago, many mills operate equipment that is technologically obsolete. Technologically backward firms may suffer loss over many years before they finally leave the industry or update their capital equipment. In some other industries barriers to entry are high enough to keep out new firms, even when existing firms are earning substantial economic profit.

Competitive equilibrium: a standard of efficiency

Economists are interested in the theory of long-run competitive equilibrium because it offers a standard of economic efficiency. In long-run competitive equilibrium industries would be producing the goods most desired by consumers at the lowest possible prices. Firms would be building plants of optimum scale and operating them at minimum cost per unit of output. Moreover, they would be producing just the collection of goods and services that the market wanted—not too many of some things and too few of others—and there would be nothing left over that couldn't be sold. There would be no economic profit—only normal profit.

This state of affairs would be ideal in many ways. Consumers would get goods and services at the lowest possible prices. Any improvement or new discovery would be reflected quickly in lower prices and greater output. And no government board or planning authority would be needed to tell firms how to go about it. Of course, no economy in the world has ever attained this kind of efficiency and none ever will. *But economists often use long-run competitive equilibrium as a standard by which to judge the actual performance of an industry.* We can say, for instance, that an industry in

Extended Example
Sugar Elasticity and the Long Run

If you have a "sweet tooth" you may remember with horror the sudden increase in sugar prices in 1974. The price of raw sugar in the United States jumped from 11 cents to 60 cents per pound in only 10 months. Bakers, bottlers, and candy-makers all over the country passed on their higher costs to their customers.

Price has settled down now. By 1977 sugar was selling for less than 8 cents a pound. But the wide price gyrations of the past continue to make sugar producers and consumers nervous.

Sugar markets have been coping with problems of elasticity. Demand and supply curves have been going through a painful period of adjustment to new conditions in the world economy. Demand for sugar has been highly inelastic. This is because there are few substitutes, sugar purchases consume only a small portion of the budget, and more and more people are beginning to regard sugar as a necessity rather than a luxury. In 1973 Americans used an average of 103.5 pounds of sugar in processed foods and drinks for a total of 12.5 million tons. Consumption has been growing fairly steadily at a rate of about 2% a year. Rising affluence and population growth have increased appetites for luxury foods among the developing nations as well. This is particularly true in the newly rich Arab nations where sugar is clearly regarded as a "superior" good.

The worldwide inflation of 1973 also fed the demand for sugar. Many commodity speculators purchased salable products as a hedge against falling currency values in many countries. All these factors contributed to high and rising demand for raw sugar. Global demand was relatively price inelastic, and demand curves were shifting to the right as incomes and population increased.

The sudden surge in demand bumped up against the typical problem in agriculture: inelastic supply in the short run. The world's supply of raw sugar depends on production and investment decisions made months or years in advance. About a third of total production comes from sugar beets and the remainder from sugar cane. In 1973, the Soviet Union experienced a severe crop failure in its valuable sugar beet producing region. Supplies on the world market dropped sharply, and sugar producers throughout the world were able to raise prices repeatedly to ration out their limited supplies.

High prices should serve an incentive function as well, and supply curves should become more elastic as producers adjust their production plans. Unhappily, land suitable for sugar cane is in short supply. To increase output it is necessary to increase yields from existing acreage. Better irrigation systems and improved planting and harvesting techniques help, but such improvements are costly. New processing mills for the increased yield cost $30 to $50 million each. Sugar companies were slow to make these investment expenditures until the higher demand proved to be permanent. In the meantime, short-run supply curves remained inelastic and prices soared.

The long run provides time for changes in demand as well as supply. Users of a scarce commodity will seek out substitutes. Fortunately, there is a plentiful alternative to sugar beets and cane in—would you believe?—corn. The Japanese developed a technique for liquifying corn starch to produce a sugary syrup nearly twice as sweet as sugar. Under normal circumstances its high cost kept it from competing with sugar; but its cost was 10 to 15% below the high prices of 1974. Corn syrup became an especially attractive substitute for sugar in the production of jam and cola drinks. Americans reduced their average consumption of sugar to 91 pounds in 1975 and made up the difference by consuming about 10 pounds of the new sweetener.

Demand curves for sugar were becoming flatter at just about the time that expanded sugar production was finally hitting the market. The long-run supply curve became more elastic and prices dropped sharply. But the story doesn't end here. Once producers have expanded their productive capacity, they are back in their short run. When new capital improvements are in place, output again becomes fairly rigid, and suppliers are subject to wide price fluctuations.

These adjustments in sugar markets are typical in agriculture where demand and supply curves tend to be inelastic. Prices vary widely as farmers adjust production. But in agriculture the adjustments always come too late—a sad result of the growing cycle. The expected profitability of expanding output is true only for the very first farmers to bring increased supplies to market. For the rest, there may be losses and severe cutbacks, setting the stage for another boom and bust cycle in the future!

What other agricultural markets are subject to extreme fluctuations as a result of short-run supply inelasticity? What implications does this problem have for long-range food supplies? How has government helped farmers to deal with this problem?

which most of the output is produced by two or three large firms is rather far removed from our ideal of competitive equilibrium. In the following chapters, as we study monopoly and imperfect competition, we will see in what ways such an industry is likely to fall short of the competitive ideal, and why.

What determines the number of firms?

This is an important question for two reasons. First, *the number of firms will affect the level of competition in U.S. industry* and thus the power of firms to restrict output and to keep prices above average total cost. Consumers may suffer as a result.

Second, *the number will determine the efficiency of U.S. firms.* When there are many firms in competition, they will tend to construct plants of optimum scale and operate them at lowest average total cost. Without competition there is no necessary drive to maximize output per unit of scarce resources. Our society may suffer as a result.

In Table 1 we have listed some U.S. industries together with certain of their characteristics. Column (2) gives the number of firms in each industry in 1972. Column (3) gives the percentage of the market supplied by the 50 largest firms in each industry. Wherever the figure in column (3) is low, it means that the largest 50 firms supply only a small proportion

Table 1
Degree of Competition in Industry (1972)

Industry	(1) Number of firms	(2) % of market supplied by 50 largest firms
Motor vehicle parts	1,748	86
Newspapers	7,461	60
Plastic products	6,762	34
Radio and TV equipment	1,524	77
Bread and cake	2,800	62
Commercial printing, lithograph	8,160	24
Meatpacking	2,293	68
Sawmills	7,664	45
Milk	2,024	56
Machinery, except electrical	16,220	13
Soft drinks	2,271	44
Commercial printing, letterpress	13,040	35
Women's dresses	5,294	28
Food preparations	1,856	67
Special dies, tools	6,513	21
Paints and allied products	1,318	66

Extended Example

Franchises and Ray Kroc's Burger Stand

Most of us feel that we deserve a break—if not today, at least once in a while. Millions take their breaks at McDonald's and contribute to one of the nation's grandest success stories since World War II.

The "McDonald's Experience" is based on an image of fun and healthy, family-oriented food service. Fast feeding was a natural in the United States. Eating in defense plants and military camps during the war had accustomed Americans to standardized foods. New techniques of mass production and blitz media advertising had been developed in manufacturing industries and were waiting to be applied to food service. Moreover, the device of franchising was soon to revitalize marketing arrangements throughout consumer industries generally.

Ray Kroc didn't foresee all this when he began his selling career. He began with only a large share of persistence and determination and a fierce drive to be successful. Selling paper cups and later milkshake machines took him into restaurants around the country, where he gradually became acquainted with some of the problems of the fragmented food industry. But Kroc had the creative vision to conceive a better way. He saw the potential profitability of streamlining the process of serving food: eliminating waste and increasing efficiency through mass production; relieving dependence on temperamental cooks through prepackaged, premeasured foods; and providing food of consistent quality at lowest prices.

In 1954 Ray Kroc found the spot for beginning his venture. It was a hamburger stand in San Bernardino, California, and it caught his attention because it needed equipment for preparing 48 milkshakes at one time! The stand was the property of Maurice and Richard McDonald and already bore the distinctive golden arches trademark. It was located at the end of U.S. Route 66 and captured the bulk of east-west traffic in the area. The name was appealing, having the charm of a child's nursery rhyme. Kroc persuaded the brothers to sell all trademarks, copyrights, formulas, arches, and the name for $2.7 million. Then he launched into the sale of licenses entitling *franchisees* to share in the benefits of assembly-line methods in food service.

The word "franchise" comes from a French word meaning "to free." Franchising was intended to free enterprising workers from dead-end jobs and allow them to own and operate their own businesses. The first major franchisee in the United States was General Motors, which began to license dealers in 1898. The sale of dealer franchises helped to overcome some of GM's distribution problems. It was a source of financial capital for the manufacturer and a source of highly motivated salespeople who were working for their own interests. The drive to "be your own boss" accelerated in the 1950s, fueled by the growing production of cheap, mass produced goods. By 1967, total sales of all franchised businesses amounted to $90 billion and accounted for one-fourth of all retail sales.

Of course, franchising also created some problems. It was driving independent Mom and Pop enterprises out of business. It was also milking franchisees. Many enthusiastic newcomers provided their life's savings and the labor of their families to get their franchise outlet going, often to lose their entire investment if the business failed. A Congressional investigation into some shady franchising operations slowed the pace of growth in some industries during the 1970s.

Franchising was appropriate for hamburger sales because the product could be standardized, produced efficiently on a large scale, and sold through mass selling techniques. McDonald's franchisees were required to follow definite product standards and selling practices. They were instructed in all aspects of the industry at Hamburger University outside Chicago. Although antitrust legislation prohibits the franchisor from selling supplies to the franchisee, unwritten agreements were made for purchasing pre-measured, prepackaged supplies from approved suppliers. Franchisees pay $15,000 initially, to be returned without interest in twenty years. Many franchisees also rent their building and equipment from McDonald's for annual rent of 8.5% of gross revenues. They also pay a yearly franchising fee of 3%. In the 1970s McDonald's began gradually buying back its franchises and by 1973 was operating 30% of the stands itself.

In 1974 total sales were $2 billion with the average stand grossing $600,000. McDonald's is big business. The chain buys 1% of all beef wholesaled in the United States and provides more meals than the U.S. Army. Its stock trades on the New York Stock Exchange and in 1973 was considered a "glamour" stock along with A.T.&T., Polaroid, Xerox, and Sears.

At McDonald's the economies of large scale reduced costs through use of mass production technology. Production was streamlined from patty to patron, and price remained for years at only 15¢. Equipment is designed for maximum efficiency and operators are trained for maximum productivity. The norm is to serve a burger, fries, and shake within 50 seconds. New products are tested exhaustively before they are introduced. Every aspect of the business is carefully studied and standardized for psychological appeal. (Only the low nutritional value of the food is never subject to critical review.)

The drive to keep price low means low unit profits, so volume is important for maximum total profits. High volume depends on advertising, and McDonald's has been innovative here, too. The economies of large scale yield efficiencies in advertising budgets. Franchisees pay 0.75% of gross revenues into a central fund that supports McDonald's displays in parades and state fairs, and provides free hamburgers to various classes of customers (including victims of disasters—always well publicized). Advertisements stress McDonald's family-oriented image and point up associations with popular politicians, movie stars, and sports figures.

All has not been unmitigated success, however. In recent years McDonald's has redirected its growth away from the suburbs and back to central cities. The result has been exposure to some of the nation's problems of urban growth. For instance, complaints have arisen from groups who resist changes in neighborhood quality. Blacks have been critical of the small number of black franchisees. Nutritionists and environmentalists have campaigned against the massive influence of the chain. Unions resent the use of teenage labor at wages lower than the legal minimum wage.

Nevertheless, Ray Kroc is a multimillionaire as a result of his innovation. He owns 20% of the company's stock, worth almost half a billion dollars in 1977. In fact, McDonald's has made many millionaires. Kroc's secretary in the early years accepted stock instead of wages. Her share is now worth $70 million!

of the industry's output. Wherever the figures in column (3) are high, a few large firms dominate the industry.

From the standpoint of our competitive ideal, the best industries are those for which the figures in column (3) are low. Where there are many firms, competition will be greater. Firms will tend to construct plants of optimum scale and operate them at minimum average total cost. Where there are relatively few firms, they may use their market power to restrict output and keep prices above average total cost.

What determines the number of firms in the industry? One factor, of course, is *the quantity of output demanded by consumers*. If market demand is only ten units per month, one firm can usually satisfy it by operating a single

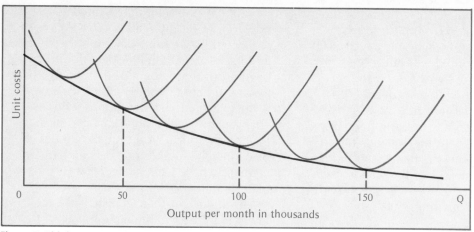

Figure 7 This long-run average cost curve slopes downward. This curve illustrates economies of scale over increasingly larger quantities of output.

plant. The plant will probably be smaller than the optimum and will operate at greater than minimum average cost. If market demand is 500 units per month, two firms operating two plants of optimum scale may suffice. If demand is 5,000 units per month, the market may require 20 plants of optimum scale operating at minimum cost. This would be closest to the competitive ideal and best in terms of consumers and society. In many U.S. industries large numbers of firms do exist, as Table 1 shows.

Another factor that determines the number of firms in an industry is the shape of the long-run average cost curve. In Figure 2 we saw that some industries have decreasing average costs as the scale of plant increases. In other industries average costs tend to be about the same for different sizes of plant or to increase for plants larger than a certain scale. Now suppose an industry has a long-run average cost curve that slopes downward over its entire length. In Figure 7 the long-run curve is drawn on the assumption of continuing economies of scale for plants of larger and larger size. Plants producing 500,000 units per month have lower average costs than plants producing 100,000. Plants producing 750,000 units have even lower costs. Thus even if market demand is for 750,000 units, only one plant will be needed for efficient production.

Something like this happens in industries requiring a great deal of capital equipment where fixed costs are very high. As output in-

creases, fixed costs are spread over a larger and larger volume. Industries that are characterized by economies of very large scale include steel, autos, aircraft, tires, and organic fibers. In these industries fewer than fifty firms supply almost the entire U.S. market.

Economies of scale have important consequences for consumers and for society. If larger and larger volumes can be produced for lower unit costs, then the ideal plant is one big enough to produce for the entire market—that is, a single monopoly firm. Industries that experience continuing economies of very large scale are often called *natural monopolies.* Technical conditions within such an industry lead to dominance by one firm. Examples of natural monopolies are utilities such as electric power and telephone service. It is easy to see why they are generally run as monopolies if you try to imagine several telephone companies competing for customers on the same block, each stringing its own lines. Natural monopolies are discussed in the next chapter along with ways of regulating them.

Economic Thinker
Alfred Marshall

Alfred Marshall (1842–1924) was born into a middle-class Victorian family in a London suburb. Marshall was probably the greatest microeconomist of the last one hundred years. His reputation rests mainly on his *Principles of Economics* (1890), which was used as a textbook in many English (and some American) universities for nearly fifty years. Even now, much of modern microeconomic theory can be described as "it's all in Marshall."

Alfred Marshall's skills were appropriate for the new wave of economic thought (the neoclassical theory) that occurred at the end of the nineteenth century. He was educated at Cambridge, England, and was a lecturer in political economy at Oxford. He was primarily a mathematical economist, able to think through economic relationships mathematically. Then he would express the results in clear and precise detail.

Marshall was especially interested in the subjective process through which consumers determine the *utility* of a good or service. Using calculus he was able to explain the *paradox of value:* that is, the paradox that diamonds are worth more than water even though water is essential to life. Marshall showed that value is determined by the *marginal* utility of a good and that the intensity of wants decreases with each unit acquired. Diamonds have great marginal utility because few units are owned. Water has less marginal utility because it is relatively more plentiful. The price of each depends on its marginal utility.

Marshall showed how demand curves are the result of many psychological factors and how production responds to consumer demand. Demand determines price and output in the short run, but in the long run firms change the mix of resource inputs so that price finally just covers "real costs" of production.

In the long run, industries would experience sufficient economies to offset the diseconomies of growth. Greater specialization, more efficient technologies, and improved capital would reduce the costs and prices of many products. Marshall introduced the concepts of demand elasticity and consumer surplus to economic theory.

Marshall's most important contribution to economic theory was in applying marginal analysis to income distribution. Whereas earlier economists had described diminishing marginal productivity of land, Marshall showed that the marginal product of *all* resources tends to diminish as variable resources are combined with fixed amounts of other resources. Business firms try to combine factors of production so as to achieve greatest profit. They compete in the market for a resource, causing its price to be bid up or down until price is precisely equal to the value of marginal product. This view gave support to the idealistic view of income distribution according to each resource's productivity in the free market system.

Marshall went on to develop a neoclassical view of the relationship between the quantity of money and the level of economic activity. The Cambridge theory of "cash-balances" eventually became an important part of much of today's business cycle theory.

Industry growth and changing costs

We have been discussing the pattern of costs *within* a firm for various scales of plant. We found that in long-run competitive equilibrium each firm will build plants that can be operated at minimum total cost. But sometimes as an industry grows, changes in costs occur that result from the actions of other firms. Changes come about as a consequence of the growth of the industry itself, and the changes affect the cost curves of all individual firms. For example, the available supply of skilled machinists may increase as an industry grows so that the individual firm's costs of hiring and training workers will fall. Or specialized firms may spring up that concentrate on supplying materials or parts the industry needs for lower costs; examples are piston rings for auto manufacturers and memory chips for producing pocket calculators.

Changes in costs associated with industry growth are called external economies and diseconomies. When such costs fall, we say that there are **external economies.** When they rise, we say there are **external diseconomies.**

External economies in the long run

External economies of growth may be of several kinds. We have already mentioned economies that come from the development of new supplying firms. Firms that make memory chips and piston rings may be able to supply these inputs at lower cost than if other firms made their own. Such specialized firms achieve economies of scale that are passed on to their customers in the expanding industry. Moreover, supplying firms may respond to industry growth by developing more advanced technology and improving their equipment. Thus in any industrial area we will find a growth of special warehousing, marketing, and transportation services that reduce costs for the firms using them.

When growth brings on external economies, industry long-run average cost curves shift downward. Downward shifting long-run average costs will permit construction of new plants at even lower costs at every scale. The entire array of cost curves will shift downward to reflect new cost patterns.

When production costs decline with growth in the number and size of firms, the industry is called a *decreasing cost industry*. With industry growth, larger quantities of output can be supplied at lower and lower prices. Over time, the industry long-run supply curve slopes downward. As consumer demand increases, price falls. (In terms of elasticity, price elasticity of supply has a negative sign over the long run.)

Decreasing costs in the long run are characteristic of young industries employing new technologies. In the earliest stages of industry development production costs are high. High cost, skilled labor, and primitive technology keep productivity per dollar low. As consumer demand increases, however, firms are encouraged to develop more complex technology, often operated by lower cost labor. Production is divided into specialized operations and product flow is regulated for maximum productivity per dollar. Supplying firms compete to provide materials and parts for lower prices. Finally, product price is forced down, to the benefit of the consuming public.

Probably the best recent example of a decreasing cost industry is the industry producing pocket calculators. From an initially high price and small quantity, industry output grew through the stages described above, until calculators are now available at much reduced prices.

The automobile industry was once a young industry. Autos were made largely by hand at extremely high cost. Henry Ford pioneered in the idea of mass production autos at low prices. He saw that a wider consumer market would encourage the development of external economies. So he raised the wages of his work force to an unheard of $5 a day! And he encouraged others to do the same. As spending increased generally throughout the economy, the auto industry was able to turn out a better quality product at prices which fell relative to other consumer prices.

External diseconomies in the long run

In some industries growing consumer demand may have the opposite effect on costs. A common type of external diseconomy is the unplanned, harmful effects on an entire industry that result from the expansion of individual firms. For instance, if lobster fishing increases off the Maine coast, a point may be reached at which overfishing reduces the supply of lobsters so severely that they become more difficult and more costly to find. That is why governments try to regulate fisheries so as to ensure plentiful supplies at reasonable costs.

External diseconomies may result from the limited supply of mineral resources, the overuse of transportation facilities, or from higher wage rates for certain types of skilled labor. When input prices rise, production costs and the prices of final product must also rise. There are other external diseconomies that may intervene to increase production costs in the long run. The community may require that firms install antipollution equipment to avoid depleting the area's scarce air and water resources. Or it may levy taxes or fines to remedy past offenses. All these changes will push long-run average cost curves upward with industry growth. New plants will operate with higher average cost curves.

When production costs increase with growth in the number and size of firms, the industry is called an *increasing cost industry*. Its long-run supply curve slopes upward as larger quantities are supplied at higher costs. As consumer demand increases, price rises. (In terms of elasticity, supply curves become less elastic over the long run.)

Increasing costs in the long run are characteristic of old industries employing obsolete technologies and using basic materials in increasingly limited supply. All opportunities for productivity gains have often been fully exploited. Entry of new firms has reduced revenues, so that research and development funds are scarce. Suppliers of resources charge higher prices for their inputs, which may be of poorer quality. Higher production costs must be passed on to the consumer in higher prices.

The most obvious recent examples of increasing cost industries are those which supply energy: the electric power generating industry and the petroleum industry. High-cost, low-quality coal and petroleum have raised unit costs of material inputs, and high capital costs aggravate the problem. Furthermore, environmental restrictions have complicated the cost picture, adding to the costs of new capital equipment for new or expanding firms.

Social economies and diseconomies

We have discussed external economies and diseconomies as if all cost changes from growth were actually paid by firms in the industry. This is not always the case. Long-run growth in one industry may produce benefits and costs outside the firm to the wider community. These economies and diseconomies are said to be external to the industry, and are often referred to as **externalities** (or social externalities). These externalities may either be *social benefits* or *social costs*.

Growth in one industry may produce technological benefits for other industries. New job skills and resource development may mean lower production costs for other industries. The entire community will benefit from social externalities. A fully employed labor force, buying from local merchants and paying higher taxes, contributes to the general prosperity of the community. Moreover, a prosperous and well-managed industrial expansion can attract other activities which give balance to the community's economic structure.

When industry growth yields external economies, the community receives benefits for which it does not have to pay. Many communities seek the social benefits of growth through tax incentives to industry and through government programs sympathetic to the needs of business.

Viewpoint
Global Economies and Diseconomies of Growth

How will global economic growth affect costs of production? What are the potential external economies and diseconomies of wide-ranging industrial growth?

One group of economists, planners, and philosophers is pessimistic about the problems of growth in coming decades. They believe the Malthusian prediction that population will outrun the world's supplies of resources. As nations grow wealthier, consumer demand increases. Demand for industrial materials will push up against scarce supplies. Prices must rise to ration out the limited quantities of scarce metals, energy, and even air and water. Long-run average cost curves will shift upward, making long-run supply curves less elastic. If the doomsayers are correct, the world's people will have to content themselves with more moderate life-styles are fewer improvements in living standards in years to come.

Another group of economists is more optimistic about the long-range effects of growth. They point to the advance of science which has helped to develop new resources and to wring more benefits from existing ones. Through the use of modern technology, wealthy economies actually consume a far smaller proportion of raw materials in producing their national output than do less developed ones. It is growing demand in *poorer* countries which is responsible for the excessive consumption of the earth's resources. As technology spreads, these nations should begin to experience growth economies which reduce their use of scarce resources and lower their production costs.

Professor Wilfred Malenbaum of the University of Pennsylvania's Wharton School has found evidence of declining resource use in developed nations. For instance, the U.S. share of the world's liquid fuel use fell from 58% in the early 1950s to 35% in the last decade; he predicts a further drop to 25% by the year 2000.

The U.S. government has taken steps to deal with other diseconomies of industrial growth. In 1969 Congress passed the National Environmental Policy Act, declaring a national policy to protect the environment. The Council on Environmental Quality was established to advise the President and Congress on environmental issues. One of the requirements of the new law was that any major federal action affecting the environment should be accompanied by an "environmental impact statement." An environmental impact statement is a detailed projection of all favorable and unfavorable environmental results of federal actions, any irreversible commitment of resources, and alternative courses of action which might be taken.

The law did not set penalties for violation of its provisions, but the environmental impact statements spotlighted the environmental costs of some projects. Conservationist groups used the courts to block actions judged to be in conflict with the intent of the law. Of 332 cases completed between 1970 and 1975, the courts agreed with the conservationists in two-thirds of the total.

Many states have also adopted procedures for evaluating the environmental impact of local projects. The effect of environmental restrictions will be to require firms to include environmental costs in their long-run average cost curves. For some firms the results will be higher costs and higher consumer prices. Consumers will restrict their purchases somewhat at the higher prices but will pay for all resources actually used in production. Where full production costs are excessive, production will not be carried on and industrial growth will slow.

Sometimes growth in one industry produces higher costs for other industries. This is often the case when two or more industries compete for a particular resource. The growing demand for scarce materials or labor can lead to higher production costs and higher prices for consumers.

When external diseconomies extend to the community as a whole, they are called social costs. Social costs occur when industry growth puts too much pressure on the resource capabilities of the community. The result is higher production costs for other industries, higher living costs for workers, and higher wage demands in a continuing upward spiral. This time the community pays a price greater than the benefits it enjoys from industrial expansion. The cost of growth may be a lower quality of life for local citizens. When growth reaches this stage, many communities act to restrain further expansion through higher business taxes and limits on new business licenses.

Internalizing externalities

One way of making industry aware of its social externalities is to require each firm to pay for its own social costs. This changes these costs from social to private costs so that firms see them as part of their costs of operation. In other words, the externalities are "internalized."

In recent years many communities have established regulations to limit the social costs of industrial growth. Firms have been required to install "scrubbers" in their smokestacks to remove injurious chemicals and to run their waste water through purification systems. Mining firms have been required to restore the topsoil where they have done strip-mining and to landscape the surface before they leave. Some communities require that entering plants be designed to fit into an established pattern of development.

Naturally, these restrictions increase costs for the firms involved. Consumers in turn must expect to pay higher prices for the products. The long-run average cost curves will shift upward to reflect the full costs of these industries. If consumers are unwilling to pay the increased prices, then sales will fall (or fail to increase). Internalizing externalities ensures that the price system can work efficiently to allocate all resources the way consumers want.

Summary

In the short run firms may receive economic profit when market price exceeds average total cost. Or a firm may operate at a loss when price is less than average total cost. But in the long run new firms can enter or old firms leave an industry until price is finally equal to average cost and only normal profit remains.

In long-run equilibrium the product is sold at minimum price, firms are earning adequate profit, and the number of firms is sufficient to fill market demand. Furthermore, plants are constructed of optimum scale: the scale of plant is large enough to enjoy all economies of large size but not so large as to experience diseconomies. At optimum scale, production can be carried on at minimum average total cost and maximum economic efficiency. Technological factors determine the optimum scale of plant and thus the optimum number of firms in an industry. This is important for maintaining a competitive industry structure.

A firm's long-run average cost (LRAC) curve is an envelope curve. It consists of points taken from short-run average total cost curves for different size plants. In long-run equilibrium the point of greatest profits occurs when $MC = MR = P = AR = $ minimum $ATC = $ minimum LRAC. In the real world long-run equilibrium is seldom actually achieved, because conditions in the economy keep changing. In addition, there are within some industries rigidities and barriers to entry that prevent long-run equilibrium.

The number of firms in an industry will determine the level of competition and the efficiency within that industry. The number of firms is determined by the level of output demanded by consumers and by the shape of the long-run average cost curve.

When an industry grows, it may cause changes in cost patterns for the individual firms. External economies of growth yield lower costs through improvements in the quality and use of resources. External diseconomies yield higher costs through excessive pressure on limited resources. Growth may yield social externalities which are not actually received or paid for by the growing industry.

Key Words and Phrases

- **long-run competitive equilibrium** a condition in which entry and exit of firms have eliminated all economic profit and have forced firms to produce at minimum average costs.

- **economies (and diseconomies) of scale** the decrease (and increase) in average total costs which results when plants are constructed of larger size.

- **optimum scale** the size of plant which achieves minimum average total costs.

- **envelope curve, or long-run planning curve** a graph which traces the lowest average total costs for producing any volume of output in plants of various sizes.

- **natural monopolies** industries in which economies of scale continue for plants of very large size.

- **external economies (and diseconomies) of industry growth** the decrease (and increase) in average total costs which results when industry growth causes resource prices to fall (or to rise).

- **externalities, or social benefits and costs** advantages or disadvantages which come to a community because of industry growth.

Questions for Review

1. List the factors in an industry which would tend to yield economies of scale in the long run. What circumstances would lead to diseconomies?

2. Suppose optimum scale of plant is 100 units of output per week, but the market will only absorb 75 units. You must choose to build either of the following plants: Plant A, designed to produce 60 units but operated beyond maximum efficiency; Plant B, designed to produce 75 units and operated at maximum efficiency; Plant C, designed to produce 90 units but operated at less than maximum efficiency. Which plant would you choose and why?

3. Refer again to question 2. Suppose the market would absorb 500 units. How would you describe long-run competitive equilibrium in the industry? Outline the process by which the industry would approach long-run equilibrium.

4. Explain the following:

$$MC = MR = P = AR = \min ATC = \min LRAC.$$

5. Cite examples from current news of external economies and diseconomies resulting from industry growth.

6. "The best cure for higher prices is high prices." Explain.

7. Explain precisely what is meant by "internalizing" external diseconomies of industry growth. Can *economies* also be "internalized"? Once they are internalized, can such benefits and costs be termed externalities?

8. How realistic is the theory of long-run competitive equilibrium? Cite examples from recent experience of industries whose movement toward long-run equilibrium was interrupted, causing a new series of market adjustments. One suggestion: digital watches.

9. Define: social benefits and costs.

29

Monopoly

Most of us think we know how monopoly works—after years of landing on Boardwalk and Park Place. In the game of Monopoly the idea is to accumulate property and then charge high rents to our customers. Under the rules of the game they have no choice but to pay our price.

Monopoly like this is hard to find in the real world. People don't have to stay at the Ritz or the Waldorf-Astoria unless they want to; there are other hotels that will be glad to accommodate them at a lower price. We don't have to buy Cadillacs—Mustangs may do as well. In our discussion of the economics of monopoly, therefore, we will be dealing with an extreme case. Pure monopoly, like perfect competition, seldom exists in the real world.

We are interested in monopoly, however, because by studying how monopolists behave we learn a good deal about how other firms behave. Later we will use the term "monopolistic competition" to describe an industry in which there are elements both of monopoly and of competition. As we shall see, most business firms fall between the two extremes of pure monopoly and perfect competition.

Defining monopoly

What is a pure monopoly? We define a **monopoly** as a firm that is the only producer of a product for which there are no acceptable substitutes. Consumers must purchase that company's product or go without. Examples of pure monopoly are public utilities such as electric, gas, water, and telephone companies, and many railroads and bus companies. Outside the public utility field it is hard to find a pure monopoly in this country. At one time the Aluminum Company of America had a monopoly in the production of aluminum, but there are now three large firms in that industry. Federal laws make it illegal for any firm to try to set up a monopoly. Even agreements among several firms to restrict competition are against the law.

Monopolies are of two kinds—natural and artificial. *Natural monopolies* result from certain technical conditions in the market, while *artificial monopolies* result from deliberate efforts to keep out competition.

Natural monopolies

Some markets lend themselves to monopoly because of their limited size. The dining car on a passenger train serves a limited market. It wouldn't be practical to have two competing cars on the same train. The same may be true of a tourist hotel on a small island or a television repairman in a rural community. When a market is small, a single supplier may be the *natural* result. In these situations a **natural monopoly** is formed.

Most communities in the United States have only one electric company, one gas company, and one telephone company. It would be very wasteful to have two or three electric companies competing in the same neighborhood, each with its separate power line. Once a public utility has become established in an area, there is no room for a competitor. Also, because of economies of scale, public utilities tend to have decreasing average costs for larger quantities of output. A big generating station or gas plant can easily provide service to a sizable community. As it expands its service, it spreads the cost of its fixed plant over more and more customers, and unit costs fall.

Even the entire United States may not be large enough to ensure competition in some industries. Largeness is a matter of technical requirements. If the optimum scale of production is very large relative to the size of the market, then the market may support only one giant producer. Once again, we have a situation where a natural monopoly results.

Artificial monopolies

There are other monopolies that are created as a matter of public policy. These legal monopolies are *artificial* in the sense that government declares them monopolies by its will. An **artificial monopoly** results from legal barriers or government policy. Many artificial monopolies are either government monopolies or government-regulated monopolies. For example, most governments, including ours, have made the postal service a government monopoly. Most local governments in the United States

Extended Example
Monopoly in Dolls

One U.S. toy company hired Muhammad Ali to knock out its competitors. Back in the 1960s Mego International, Inc., was just another merchant importing cheap dolls from factories in Hong Kong. It marketed low-priced counterparts of the G.I. Joe and Barbie dolls, only to find that its competitors were copying its copies and selling them at even lower prices. Looking around for something that couldn't be copied, the new young president, Martin B. Abrams, decided to acquire licenses to make dolls resembling famous TV personalities. One of the new creations was a Muhammad Ali doll that fought with an opponent in a miniature boxing ring. There were also Sonny and Cher dolls, Wizard of Oz dolls, and Superman dolls. The company paid $100,000 or more for the exclusive rights to each well-advertised name, along with 5% royalties. This strategy helped it climb into the top ten companies in the toy business within four years. Not only did its sales shoot up, but its prices went up along with them. One of the company's top executives pointed out what the rights to famous names had done for its products: "They can't be copied by others, so our prices—and our profits—are higher than otherwise."

operate their own water and sewer systems and often the trash and garbage collection as well. These services are all believed to be essential to the community. It is also felt that they should be provided at the lowest cost—with no monopoly profit. If we thought it would be more efficient, we might want our government to own the telephone, electric power, gas, and transportation systems, as is done in so many European countries. In the United States these are generally operated by privately owned firms that are given a legal monopoly. Government regulates their prices and output. When a railroad or a phone company wants to raise its rates, it must get approval from the appropriate public commission.

Another kind of legal artificial monopoly results from our patent system. A **patent** is a temporary monopoly granted by the federal government, giving an inventor the sole right to manufacture and sell a new invention. The word derives from "letters patent," a document used by kings in medieval times to confer a privilege or a right on someone. In order to patent an invention, you must show that it is a new and significant development in its field. A patent is property and can be sold or inherited during its lifetime (17 years in the United States). The purpose of patents is to encourage inventions and to encourage their use in production.

The most valuable patent ever issued in the United States was the one for Alexander Graham Bell's telephone. His patent was construed by the courts to cover not only the mechanical device he invented but the whole principle of speech transmission by electricity.

Companies such as Xerox (in photocopying), Hewlett-Packard (in electronics), Digital Equipment (in minicomputers), Polaroid (in instant photography), and IBM (in computers and typewriters) have used patents to protect themselves from competition while they established strong market positions in their industries. But a patent only provides a monopoly of a specific invention; it doesn't prevent competitors from producing substitutes for it.

Decision-making by the monopolist

We have all had fantasies of being the sole owner of something the world wants—a self-emptying mousetrap or the secret of changing lead into gold. We imagine ourselves becoming immensely rich, the money pouring in faster than we can spend it. Let's pursue this dream for a moment and ask ourselves how we could earn the greatest economic profit from our monopoly. "That's simple," you say. "Just charge all the traffic will bear." How much the traffic will bear depends on the monopolist's demand curve.

The monopolist's demand curve

How much will the traffic bear? If we set our price very, very high probably nobody will buy our product. People can live without our self-emptying mousetrap if need be. If we reduce the price to, say $100, we may sell one or two of our mousetraps to people who have everything. The money won't exactly be pouring in. We reduce it again and sell more. If we keep on reducing our price, we will sell more and more mousetraps until we reach a point where the additional revenue we get from selling another one won't cover the additional cost of making it. In economists' language, we have reached the point where *marginal cost equals marginal revenue.*

You'll observe that we have followed the same rule that sellers follow in a competitive market. We have expanded output to the point where MC = MR. The difference is that under competition price is not affected by the actions of a single seller. By contrast, in order for the monopolist to sell a larger output, price must be reduced. In effect, *the monopoly firm is the industry,* and like the industry it faces a downward sloping demand curve for its output. It must base its output decision on market prices which are different at every level of output. The monopoly firm can choose between selling a few units at a high price or many units at a low price.

For pure monopoly to exist there must be no acceptable substitute for the good in question. Without substitutes consumers cannot readily shift to another supplier if the price is high. For example, if the electric company raises its rates we can't change to another source of light and power. If the bus company's fares go up, not many of us will choose to walk or ride a bicycle. Of course, some consumers have the alternative of using less of these services, and if prices get very high some alternatives will be found. Natural gas may substitute for electricity in some cases (such as heating), and private autos can be used instead of buses or trains. Poor substitutability is also important when prices are low. Electric power and mass transportation are not themselves good substitutes for other services. Therefore, consumers will not increase their purchases significantly when prices are reduced.

Figure 1 shows two possible demand curves for a monopolist. For simplicity, the demand curves are shown as straight lines. The good with few substitutes has a steeply sloping demand curve, and the good with many substitutes has a curve with lower slope. In either case, the quantity the monopolist can sell is greater at lower prices. At any point on the demand curve average revenue is equal to price. Total revenue is the number of units sold times price or average revenue. Total revenue is represented by a rectangle drawn beneath the demand curve with base equal to quantity sold and height equal to price or average revenue.

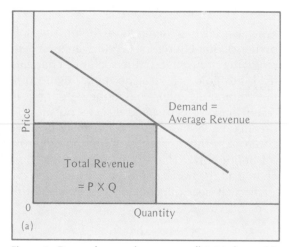

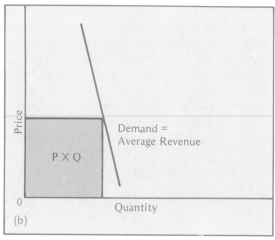

Figure 1 Demand curves for a monopolist: (a) demand for a good with many substitutes; (b) demand for a good with few substitutes.

Extended Example
Local Monopolies

When the history books are written about the last half of the twentieth century, one of the most significant economic developments will be said to be the shopping center. Ownership of automobiles has enabled us to live in suburbs, away from the urban centers of commerce. Business has responded by following the market to suburbia, building ever more lavish and more complete shopping malls for middle-income Americans.

Less noticed than the growth of shopping malls has been the boost they have given to local monopolies. The malls were generally built around a few big "anchor" stores. The large space occupied by these stores gave them the power to demand certain conditions in their lease arrangements. One important specification was that certain competitors not be allowed to rent space. Discount stores, for instance, and aggressive promoters of other kinds were to be excluded; small specialty shops were restricted to handling only a single line of merchandise—like clothing, or books, or jewelry, or food.

Exclusionary contracts like these have the effect of establishing a monopoly. They reduce the available supply of goods and services to only that amount provided by a single merchant. Customers are attracted to the mall by the convenience of one-stop, nearby shopping with ample parking. Their demand curves become highly inelastic when there are no substitute suppliers of particular items. A monopolist can move up consumer demand curves to the point at which marginal revenue is equal to marginal cost and profits are maximized. The result is higher prices and smaller quantities sold.

In the beginning exclusionary contracts were considered necessary by landlords and tenants alike. Landlords needed assurance of stable renters if they were to obtain long-term financing for the project. Tenants wanted a guaranteed market if they were to undertake the large investment and the risks involved in a new and unfamiliar marketing arrangement. To limit competition enabled a project to get on its feet financially and to become established as a viable institution in the community.

But by the 1970s, the Federal Trade Commission was charging that exclusionary contracts violate laws prohibiting restraint of trade. State attorneys-general and attorneys for small business firms also brought suit against mall developers. In most cases the complaints were settled through "consent decrees" which carry no penalties for past offenses. The consenting firm simply agrees to cease certain forbidden practices in the future or it will suffer heavy fines.

A major case was settled in 1976 with Sears Roebuck and Co. Sears operates 900 stores throughout the United States and is the major tenant in more than 265 shopping centers. Sears' contracts have excluded competitors and discounters from the centers and have limited competition from the other tenants. A consent decree settled in 1976 provided for fines up to $10,000 for any similar practices in the future.

What are other long-range effects of the movement to shopping malls? What are some benefits and costs? What has been the course of shopping-center development in your area?

What is the optimum level of output for the monopolist? What quantity and price will achieve maximum economic profit? Figure 1 doesn't give us enough information to determine optimum price and output. We need additional data for sales and costs, some of which are shown in Tables 1 and 2.

Suppose the firm is a seller of autographed T-shirts and the sole producer of its product. Perhaps it has signed agreements with the celebrities whose autographs are on the shirts, guaranteeing that no other firm can use their names. If the firm restricts production to one or two shirts it can sell them at high prices. But if the firm wants to sell more, it must reduce price. The total revenue it earns at every price level is shown in column (3). *Total revenue* is calculated by multiplying the *quantity sold* in column (1) by the *price* in column (2). The monopoly firm also wants to know how much is added to total revenue with each increase in the quantity sold. The change in total revenue from each change in sales is shown in column (4). Changes in total revenue constitute the firm's marginal revenue from sales and are shown between successive values of total revenue.

You will recall that under perfect competition marginal revenue is the same as average revenue or price. This is because the demand curve for the individual firm is horizontal. The perfectly competitive firm can continue to increase sales without affecting price. On the other hand, a monopoly firm can sell a larger quantity only if price is reduced. Average revenue falls with every increase in the quantity sold. Because price must fall with a larger volume of sales, *marginal revenue for the monopoly is always less than average revenue or price.* To sell the third unit requires a lower price on all units sold—on units one and two as well as on unit three. Marginal revenue for the third unit is not its price. Marginal revenue is the price of that unit *minus* the price reductions on units one and two. In Table 1 the marginal revenue of the third T-shirt is $5, which is its price, $7, minus the price reductions of $1 each on units one and two.

We have drawn the average and marginal revenue curves for T-shirts in Figure 2. Notice that the MR curve is always below AR and falls faster as quantity sold increases. Marginal revenue eventually becomes negative. This is because for the monopoly to sell six units requires a price reduction that yields less total revenue than was received for five units.

The monopolist's cost curves

We may assume that costs are the same for the monopolist as for the competitive firm. If the monopoly buys its labor and materials in the same markets as competitive firms, it will pay similar costs. In Figure 3 we have drawn the marginal and average cost curves just as we drew them in our earlier discussion of competition. The AC curve is *saucer shaped.* Marginal cost is large at small volumes but falls sharply. As output expands, however, MC eventually begins to rise and passes through the AC curve at the bottom of the saucer.

The monopoly is now faced with the same decision as the competitive firm. Assuming that management wants to maximize profit, it will continue to supply additional units of the good or service as long as each additional unit

Table 1
Hypothetical Sales Information for Autographed T-Shirts

(1) Quantity, Q	(2) Price	(3) Total Revenue, TR	(4) Marginal Revenue, MR
0	$10	$0	
			$9
1	9	9	
			7
2	8	16	
			5
3	7	21	
			3
4	6	24	
			1
5	5	25	
			−1
6	4	24	
			−3
7	3	21	

Table 2
Hypothetical Cost Data for Autographed T-Shirts

(1) Quantity, Q	(5) Total Cost, TC	(6) Average Cost, AC	(7) Marginal Cost, MC	(8) Profit
0	2	—		−2
			7	
1	9	9		0
			5	
2	14	7		2
			1	
3	15	5		6
			3	
4	18	4.5		6
			4.5	
5	22.5	4.5		2.5
			7.5	
6	30	5		−6
			19	
7	49	7		−28

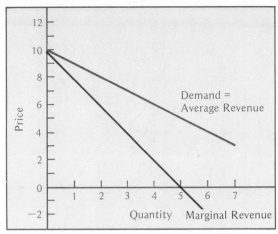

Figure 2 The average revenue and marginal revenue curves for our monopoly selling T-shirts. The MR curve is always below the AR curve.

sold adds more to revenue than it adds to cost. When marginal cost rises and is just equal to marginal revenue, the profit-maximizing level has been reached and the monopolist will not sell more. In Figure 3 the profit-maximizing level of output is four T-shirts. If the monopoly firm were to sell more than four T-shirts, marginal revenue would be less than marginal cost and profit would not be maximized. If the firm sells only three T-shirts, marginal revenue will be above marginal cost. Economic profit would be greater if sales were increased to four units.

Profit is maximized at sales of four units. But what price will the monopoly firm set? We find price by drawing a line up from the horizontal axis to the demand curve and reading price on the vertical axis. The four shirts can be sold at a price of $6. If the monopoly tries to sell more shirts, revenue will increase by less than costs. If it sells fewer shirts, revenue will fall by more than costs.

Economic profit for the monopolist

Economic profit for our T-shirt monopolist is shown in Figure 3 as the shaded rectangle with length equal to quantity sold and height equal to the difference between AC and AR. Given the cost structure shown in Figure 3, no other combination of price and output would yield greater economic profit. At any other output the area of the shaded rectangle would be smaller. Profits per unit might be greater at

some other level of output. But remember that the monopolist is seeking to maximize *total* economic profits, not *unit* profits. At some other level of output the difference between average revenue (AR) and average cost (AC) might be greater. But the total-profit rectangle is greatest at the profit-maximizing output.

The point of maximum economic profit is easy to see if you examine cost data for the firm. Table 2 lists the important costs on which the cost curves in Figure 3 are based. Average cost is calculated by dividing total cost by quantity of output. Marginal cost is the difference in total cost for each unit change in output.

The monopoly firm continues to expand output as long as marginal revenue is greater than marginal cost. To expand output to 5 units would add more to costs than to revenue. The profit-maximizing output must be four units per time period. Four units is the greatest level of output for maximum economic profit.* Total profit is shown in column (8). Economic profit is equal to total revenue less total cost: TR − TC = $24 − $18 = $6. Or profit is unit profit times quantity of output:

$$(AR − AC) \times Q = (\$6 − \$4.50) \times 4$$
$$= \$1.50 \times 4 = \$6.$$

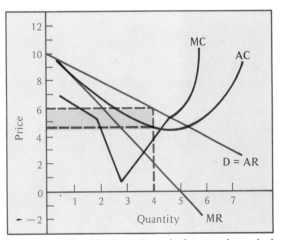

Figure 3 The intersection of marginal cost and marginal revenue curves determines the profit-maximizing point for our T-shirt monopoly.

* A more precise cost analysis would locate the profit-maximizing output between 3 and 4 units. This is because MC refers to the *process* of adding another unit. In an actual production decision the units of output might be stated in thousands and the maximum profit position would be 3.5 thousand units.

From the standpoint of the monopolist, this level of output is ideal. Since economic profit is at a maximum, the monopolist has no incentive to change. From the standpoint of the economy as a whole, however, the situation is not ideal. The reason is that T-shirts are not being produced at the lowest possible cost. From society's standpoint the point of maximum efficiency would be at 5 units of output, where MC = AC. This is because unit costs are lowest at that output. For the monopolist, economic profits are gained at the expense of efficiency in the use of productive resources.

The profit-maximizing rule holds true even when the monopolist doesn't make a profit beyond the normal profit that is included in the cost curves. Consider Figure 4. This monopolist maximizes profit at an output of Ox where marginal cost is equal to marginal revenue. This happens also to be the point at which average cost equals average revenue or price. Price just covers full costs, including normal profit, and there is no economic profit. This result resembles perfect competition in that only normal profit is earned. Unlike perfect competition, however, the minimum point on the AC curve has not been reached. Consumers have to pay a higher price for the product than they would under perfect competition.

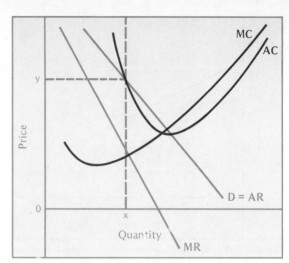

Figure 4 Cost curves for a monopolist. For this particular monopolist AC= AR = P. The profit-maximizing point occurs at output Ox, because this is where MC = MR. Price is determined by the intersection of the dotted line at x and the AR curve. Total revenue equals the area formed by the dotted lines.

Elasticity again

The market power of the monopolist depends in part on the shape of demand for the product. *When demand elasticity is low, the monopolist is in a very strong position.* This is the case when customers are willing to purchase roughly the same quantity of a product regardless of its price. When a good is essential and there are few substitutes, demand tends to be less elas-

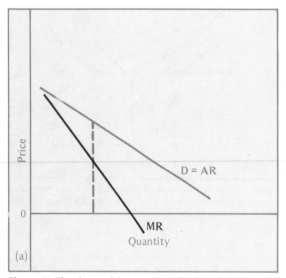

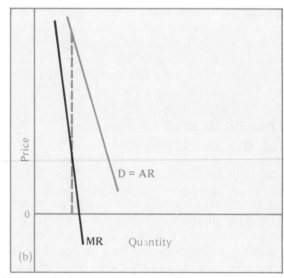

Figure 5 The demand for a monopolist here is (a) somewhat elastic and (b) inelastic. Compare the distances between MR and AR for (a) and (b). For inelastic demand marginal revenue is much lower than price (AR). Notice that output is less for (b) than for (a) while price is higher. This means higher profits for the monopolist with inelastic demand.

Viewpoint

Do Monopolies Really Maximize Economic Profits?

In this chapter we've analyzed the behavior of monopolies with the assumption that a rational monopoly will try to make as much economic profit as possible. This implies that top executives sitting in their offices are able to tell exactly where the point of maximum profit is. But when they are asked, most executives say they don't know where that point is. They may not even know what their demand and cost curves look like. To maximize profits all the time, executives would have to know exactly how many units they can sell at any given price. Of course, they have marketing departments that study the buying habits of consumers. But consumer preferences change from time to time, and market data may be obsolete by the time it gets to the decision-makers.

Information about a firm's cost conditions may be just as elusive. When a firm produces a variety of products, it is difficult to tell how much of the overhead costs belong to each one. It may also be difficult to predict how a change in the amount produced will affect costs. It is the job of cost accountants to figure out these things, but they often disagree over how best to go about it.

Let's suppose, however, that the firm making autographed T-shirts knows exactly what its demand and cost curves are. It still may not try to maximize economic profits. There are good reasons why. If the company does too well, it may encourage potential competitors to enter the field. History shows that monopolies don't last indefinitely. Sooner or later other firms make their way into the business, and the more profitable the business is, the harder they will try. Another reason why a monopolist may not pursue maximum profits is the fear of attracting public criticism which may lead to government investigations. Moreover, we have pointed out that very few pure monopolies exist in the real world. There are substitutes for almost everything.

In the next chapter, we will take a look at that very large segment of business activity that doesn't fit into the framework of either pure monopoly or perfect competition. We will see that monopolistic behavior is found to some extent in almost every industry. Most companies charge higher prices than they would if they were perfectly competitive. But in setting their prices they take into account the reactions of other companies in the same industry, as well as the antitrust laws and the general state of the market.

tic than for other goods. The demand for housing, electric power, and gasoline tends to be relatively less elastic than demand for non-essential goods. The price of gasoline doubled in 1973–1975 and although consumption did decline, the change was slight. Most motorists had no alternative but to pay the new price. Demand may also be less elastic if price is relatively low or if expenditure on the item is a small part of a household's total budget. The classic example of an essential good is salt.

When demand elasticity is low over the relevant price range, the demand curve will be steep and a monopolist will have greater power to raise price. The marginal revenue curve will fall more steeply than average revenue (demand) when demand is less elastic. The result may be high unit profit and high total profit even when the volume of sales is low. Figure 5 shows how the slope of the demand curve affects the distance between marginal revenue and average revenue.

The monopolist will have less power to set price when demand is more elastic. If there are many substitutes, or if the product is easily given up, consumers will cut their purchases sharply when price increases. Similarly, if price falls, they will buy significantly more. The availability of substitutes is especially important in limiting a monopolist's power. The Coca-Cola company has a monopoly upon the "Coke" formula, but if it were to double its price, most of its customers would switch to one of the other cola beverages.

Price discrimination

Sometimes a monopoly can increase economic profits by charging different prices to different classes of customers. This practice is called **price discrimination.** Price discrimination is possible only if markets can be separated in some way, so that buyers in the low-priced market aren't able to resell their purchases in the higher-priced market. By charging different prices in different markets a firm can take advantage of differing elasticities of demand. In markets where demand is less elastic, it can charge higher prices and reap larger profits. An airline company, let us say, may decide to charge different rates for adults and for children. Adult demand is less elastic, since many travelers on business or vacation will usually fly anyway, regardless of price. The demand for children's flights is relatively more elastic: children may or may not be brought along, depending on price. Figures 6a and 6b show how this difference affects pricing decisions.

How does the firm determine the price to charge the two different groups of customers? It will figure its marginal revenues in both markets and then determine the point where combined marginal revenue is equal to marginal

cost. This is shown in Figure 7. The AR and MR curves in Figure 7 are obtained by adding together those in Figures 6a and 6b: we simply add the quantities demanded at each price in 6a and 6b. There is no need to add marginal costs for the two markets, since there is only one marginal cost for the firm regardless of the market in which it sells. Figure 7 shows that marginal cost is equal to combined marginal revenue at output Q_1. From the vertical scale we see that MC and MR equal 10. But where will we set our prices? How will total sales be divided between the two markets? Return to Figures 6a and 6b. Price and quantity will be determined by a vertical line passing through the MR curves at the point where MR is equal to 10. The airline will sell OQ_2 tickets to adults at a price of OP_2, because that is where marginal revenue in that market is equal to marginal cost. It will sell OQ_3 tickets to children at a price of OP_3 because that is where marginal revenue in that market is equal to marginal cost. Notice that price is higher in the market in which demand is less elastic.

Some other examples of price discrimination include: lower-priced ladies' tickets at ball games; no cover charge for ladies in singles bars; special rates for nighttime phone calls; lower off-season prices at hotels and beach resorts. Quite often price discrimination is practiced without customers even knowing it. Large appliance manufacturers commonly sell part of their output to mail-order houses such as Sears Roebuck and Montgomery Ward, but under different brand names and at lower prices. Manufacturers of auto tires, storage

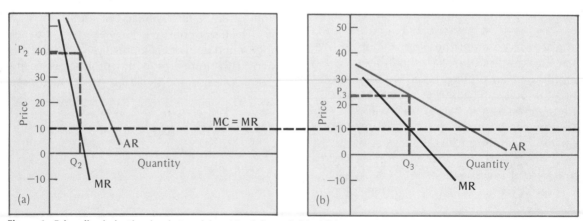

Figure 6 Price discrimination in air travel for: (a) adults and (b) children.

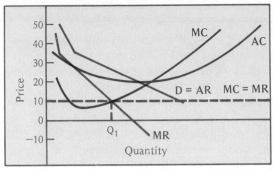

Figure 7 Combined demand for airline travel. The MR and AR curves are the sum of quantities for both markets.

batteries, and other products do the same. From the manufacturer's point of view this is efficient because it makes use of excess production capacity that would otherwise remain idle. One can even say that it is equitable, since higher prices charged to those who can afford to pay more make it possible to offer lower prices to others—as when a doctor charges a rich patient more than a poor patient for the same service.

When price discrimination is practiced by firms engaged in international trade, it is sometimes called **dumping.** The word has a negative sound, suggesting that the foreign producer is dumping goods on local markets in order to keep prices higher in the home country. Sometimes dumping is even used as a means to destroy competitors so that a monopoly in one nation will become an international monopoly. Dumping is possible because demand curves in distant markets are often more elastic. Customers are able to choose among several producers, substituting readily if price is high. From the point of view of local producers, dumping looks like unfair competition. U.S. companies don't like dumping when foreign companies do it here. Congress has passed legislation penalizing foreign manufacturers who sell at lower prices in the U.S. market than in their home markets. Not long ago Poland was fined for dumping golf carts in the U.S. market.

We've seen that the monopolist has to divide the market in order to discriminate successfully. Otherwise goods purchased in the low-priced market could be resold in the high-priced market. For simplicity's sake we've used only two markets in the foregoing examples. Actually, price discrimination may be practiced in several markets at the same time. Each additional segment increases the firm's economic profit. An airline may have market segments for businessmen, children, tourists (excursion fares), standby customers, and charter groups. At the very extreme, a seller may be able to treat each individual customer differently, thus dividing the market into innumerable segments. This is unusual, but doctors and lawyers have been known to do it. The country doctor who charges patients according to what they are able to pay, perhaps taking several bushels of apples instead of cash, is actually a highly discriminating monopolist.

Shortcomings of monopoly

How does monopoly affect us?

Economics is not an exact science. It is not possible to measure the precise effects of economic actions in the same way that a chemist measures a chemical change. Even so, an economist must not fall into a trap at the other extreme. An economist must be careful not to base conclusions on purely subjective standards of judgment. We must look for objective criteria on which to judge the effects of monopoly.

Two broad and important criteria have been discussed earlier in this text. They are *efficiency* and *equity*.

The need for efficiency is a result of the economic problem. Because our resources are scarce, we must use them wisely. We must produce the maximum output per unit of input. To the extent that resources are used for maximum production, we have achieved efficiency.

Equity is another important criterion. Recall that equity refers to the distribution of output among participants in the economic system. Distribution takes place according to

Extended Example
Taxing the Monopoly Firm

Suppose you've been elected mayor of a large industrial town. One of your campaign promises was to equalize the taxes on local manufacturers. At present each big company is taxed a certain amount per dollar of product. Business firms complain that the tax forces them to raise their prices and makes it difficult for them to compete with companies elsewhere. Citizens' groups feel that corporations aren't carrying a fair share of the tax burden and want the tax increased.

You call in your tax adviser who reports: "Your Honor, you've inherited a bad tax. It's just possible that if you do the right thing you'll be able to please business and make the citizens' groups happy at the same time."

Being a realistic politician, you doubt that it's possible to please everyone at the same time, but you're willing to try. Your tax adviser says, "The best tax in this situation would be a property tax—that is, a tax that remains fixed regardless of the company's

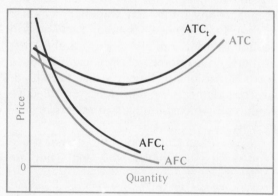

Figure 8 Effects of a fixed tax on a firm's costs. A fixed tax shifts cost curves upward by equal amounts. ATC_t and AFC_t are costs plus the fixed tax.

output. As you can see from the diagram in Figure 8, a fixed tax simply shifts a firm's fixed cost curve upward. Average fixed costs rise and average total costs rise also, but marginal costs remain the same as they were before. Because the fixed tax doesn't increase with output, the company's profit-maximizing behavior isn't affected by the tax. Now look at Figure 9. You'll observe that marginal cost is equal to marginal revenue at the same level of output and the same price as before the tax. The tax siphons off some of the company's economic profit without affecting the price of the product."

You can't quite believe him. A tax that doesn't raise the price? It sounds like a free lunch.

"It doesn't raise the price," your adviser explains patiently, "because the firm is already at its profit-maximizing point. If it changes output or price, economic profit will fall.

"Let's examine the tax you have now. When a tax is placed on each unit produced, it increases marginal costs. In Figure 10, you'll notice that both the MC and the ATC curves shift upward by the amount of tax on each unit. This changes the profit-maximizing output so that MC is equal to MR at a smaller quantity and a higher price. The community collects the tax revenues shown by the rectangle with base equal to Q_t and height equal to the tax on each unit: $ATC_t - ATC$. Because the firm's profit-maximizing output is less, total tax revenue is less than it would be with a fixed tax."

You say, "if we shift to a fixed tax (e.g., a property tax) on these big firms, then prices will be lower than with the present tax. Tax revenues will be higher, and both business and the general public will be happy. That should be good for a lot of votes."

You thank your tax adviser and promise that when you run for governor you'll get in touch.*

---

*There is a hitch here, of course. In the short run, business firms will pay your tax and suffer the loss of profits. However, in the long run they will assess the relative profitability of various plant locations. If other areas are less heavily taxed, they will move outside your jurisdiction—but you'll be out of office by then anyway.

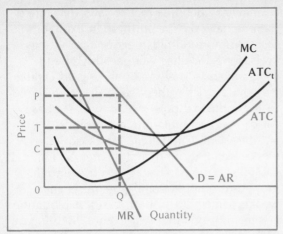

Figure 9 With a fixed tax ATC rises to ATC_t. MC and MR are unchanged so MC = MR at the same point as without the tax. Total revenue, which equals the rectangle OP × OQ, can be divided into three parts: (1) monopoly profits, equal to TP × OQ; (2) tax revenues, equal to CT × OQ; (3) costs of production, equal to OC × OQ.

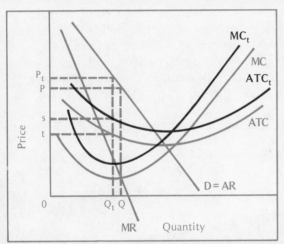

Figure 10 The effects of a per unit tax on monopoly output. MC is now changed to MC_t. Thus MC_t = MR at a smaller Q of output. The result is a higher price than before the tax.

the values and goals of the society. Values and goals may be primarily material or primarily ethical or a balance of both. Emphasis on material values will reward individuals on the basis of their material contributions to output. Emphasis on ethical values bases rewards on the particular ideology of the community.

Of the two judgment criteria, efficiency is more easily measured. A numerical value can sometimes be placed on the benefits and costs of various economic actions and their efficiencies compared. Judgment based on the equity principle would require first that there be agreement on values and goals. To advocate particular ethical positions is beyond the scope of a positive science.

With these qualifications in mind, let us summarize the harmful effects of monopoly on our economic lives. Later we will consider arguments in favor of bigness in industry.

Efficiency

(1) Monopoly violates the principle of efficiency by misallocating resources. This is easy to see by comparing costs and revenues at the monopolist's equilibrium level of output. The profit-maximizing monopolist produces the quantity of output for which MC = MR. But because MR is less than price, marginal cost is less than price. The price paid by the consumer is greater than the marginal cost of production. When price is higher than marginal cost, this should be a signal to increase output. Consumers are willing to pay the cost of additional output. The principle of efficiency would require that more resources be allocated to this industry. A monopoly will not do this. The monopoly must restrict output so as to maintain a high price and to maximize economic profit.

(2) Monopoly violates the principle of efficiency by charging a higher price than minimum average costs. In monopoly there is no competitive pressure to expand output to a level of production consistent with minimum average costs. When unit costs are not held to the minimum, society's scarce resources are used inefficiently.

A monopoly may attempt to protect its market power by restricting new technological development. When a monopoly controls pro-

Economic Thinker
Paul Sweezy

Paul Sweezy (born 1910) is one of the nation's most distinguished Marxist economists. His economic philosophy was strongly affected by the Great Depression of the 1930s. He saw monopoly capitalism as the principal basis for economic crises. As a Harvard professor (from 1934–1942), he wrote articles and books which applied Marxist theory to American economic institutions. He helped found the *Monthly Review,* the leading Marxist journal in the nation, and is still one of its editors.

Sweezy's most famous book, *Monopoly Capitalism* (1966), was coauthored by Paul Baran. In it Sweezy and Baran illustrate how the United States is *not* an effective capitalist economy where all productive resources receive their just rewards. Rather the authors argue that monopoly conditions prevail in much of the American economy. Giant corporations have captured increasingly large shares of business by employing monopoly strategies. These corporations also help influence American foreign policy toward militarism and imperialism.

An earlier work by Sweezy, *The Theory of Capitalist Development* (1942), is a notable restatement and updating of Marxist theory. Sweezy believes that events in today's world economy are proof of the dynamic processes Marx described. Marxist economists see social reality as a process of change. Economies go through a definite and predictable life-cycle. According to the Marxists, it is a mistake to take capitalism—or any other "ism"—as something immutable. An economic system is not fixed like the orbits of the planets but moves from one stage to another.

Change is taking place today in the relationships between fully industrialized nations and the less developed nations of the Third World. The causes of change are the same historical processes which produced—and will eventually destroy—capitalism.

Sweezy believes that today's developed nations have prospered through exploitation of other more primitive economic systems. Preexisting societies were destroyed and reorganized to serve the purposes of capitalist invaders. Then the wealth was transferred to the industrial powers to serve as a basis for capital accumulation and growth.

Just as individual capitalists exploited workers and accumulated greater capital, capitalist nations have achieved economic growth through imperialist ventures into weaker lands. But in both cases, exploitation creates tensions that will eventually bring on collapse of the dominant powers. The change may be gradual or it may be violent and abrupt. But it is inevitable.

Sweezy is doubtful that attempts at economic reform can actually reverse the inevitability of this historical process. This is because the economic system is part of the entire social context and cannot be repaired independently of the rest. Government is part of the social context and is the means by which capitalist rule is ensured. Total change will begin gradually with a series of socialist revolutions in separate countries. Finally, a worldwide socialist system will develop, capable of eliminating world capitalism in one final struggle.

ductive capital, strategic resources, and technical knowledge, it may limit their use for innovation. The result is prolonged inefficiency, wasting scarce resources for years to come.

Equity

(1) Monopoly violates the principle of equity by maintaining price higher than marginal cost. A high price for a monopolist's product reduces the real income of consumers. If buyers are to continue to consume the monopolist's product, they must reduce their spending for other goods and services. Demand curves in competitive markets must shift to the left. The result is distortion in incomes throughout the economy. Differences in income are based not on different contributions to production but on possession (or lack) of monopoly power. In addition, economic profit accumulated by monopoly owners further distorts income distribution.

(2) Finally, monopoly may seriously undermine the principle of equity by supporting political power in the hands of a few. Concentration of economic power represents a threat to equity, whether the basis of distribution is material or political.

Government and monopolies

Government regulation of monopolies

In the Extended Example on taxing the monopoly we've used the term monopoly a bit loosely. Most large firms aren't pure monopolies. In the next chapter we will examine that large gray area between pure competition and pure monopoly. Most pure monopolies are what we call "natural monopolies"—electric companies, telephone companies, railroads. The city you live in probably has just one electric company, one gas company, and one phone company. In the United States we call these firms *public utilities* and regulate their price and output policies. The economic advantages of large-scale production make mo-

nopoly the most efficient structure for providing these services. Capital costs are very high and unit costs to the consumer are lower if a single firm is able to spread its capital costs over a large volume of output. Once a firm is operating successfully others cannot easily enter the area because of the necessary heavy investment: in vehicles and rights of way; in telephone lines and switching equipment; in power plants and cables.

Local utilities in this country are regulated by *Public Service Commissions*. At the federal level the Interstate Commerce Commission (ICC) regulates interstate transportation by rail, bus, and truck. The Civil Aeronautics Board (CAB) regulates the airlines. The Federal Communications Commission (FCC) regulates telephone and radio service. The Federal Power Commission (FPC) regulates the price and output of electric power. The purpose of regulation is to prevent natural monopolies from exploiting their market position at the expense of consumers.

Regulated prices

Under regulation, utility prices are based on costs of production. Generally the firm is allowed to charge rates that cover full costs plus a reasonable rate of return on its capital investment. The rate of return must be high enough to compensate savers for the use of their funds—that is, the utility must be able to pay enough interest and dividends to induce people to buy its securities.

Often the actual rate of return depends on how much business the utility is doing. An airline may be permitted to charge fares that will enable it to earn 9% on its capital investment when its planes are operating at 60% of capacity. If planes are more than 60% full, allowed earnings will be greater than 9%. One difficulty here is getting everybody to agree on the value of the invested capital. What is the value of a five-year-old Boeing 707 or a two-year-old baggage cart? In times of inflation it is necessary to figure what it would cost to replace them at present

Viewpoint
Regulation or Strangulation?

It is said that your freedom to do as you please ends precisely at my nose! Government helps to protect your freedom—and my nose—particularly when the overwhelming strength of one adversary would give it unfair advantage over a weaker opponent.

John Kenneth Galbraith popularized the phrase "countervailing power" to illustrate the need for a strong government to balance the power of strong industrial corporations. It was for this purpose that regulation of private business firms began in the 1880s and 1890s.

The first regulatory agency was the Interstate Commerce Commission (ICC), established in 1887 to regulate operations of U.S. railroads. The ICC was set up to ensure fair conditions of freight service for all customers whether large or small. In 1914 the Federal Trade Commission (FTC) was set up to preserve competition among industrial firms and to protect consumers from deceptive advertising. In the 1930s the Securities and Exchange Commission (SEC) was established to prohibit fraud and unfair practices in the exchange of securities. These and many other federal agencies have worked to protect the interests of the individual consumer and the small business firm against an unfair use of power by large enterprises.

Since 1965 the number of major regulatory agencies has doubled from 12 to 24. Regulators, appointed officials, and civil servants now make 18 times more rules than the elected members of Congress: about 7,500 in 1974. Regulatory agencies consumed $3.8 billion of the federal budget in 1977 or $10.36 for every American citizen. The focus of the new agencies has been on environmental issues including health and safety.

In recent years the entire spectrum of regulatory agencies has come under attack. One basis for criticism has been the new emphasis on environmental safety and health. Probably the agency most hated by American businessmen is the Occupational Safety and Health Agency (OSHA). The purpose of OSHA was to set standards for employee health and safety and to fine employers if these guides were not followed. For strict compliance with OSHA standards, employers are planning to spend $3.6 billion in 1979.* This accounts for almost 3% of all planned capital investment in that year. Few deny that regulation of health and safety standards are needed. But many business and government administrators argue that the present arrangement is costly and unworkable and should be overhauled.

The Environmental Protection Agency (EPA) is also criticized for setting impossible or undesirable standards for industry. It has set maximum noise limits for newly produced locomotives, power saws, motorcycles, snowmobiles, and other noise polluters. And it is involved in setting noise standards for autos and commercial aircraft. Its air and water standards for the next ten years are estimated to cost $500 billion, or more than $230 a year for each American. About 350 foundries in the United States have been closed down over the years 1972–1976 for failure to meet environmental safety and health standards.

The Federal Energy Administration (FEA) was established in 1975 by the Energy Policy Conservation Act. The FEA adds another requirement to manufacturers of major appliances. The act calls for a 20% overall reduction in energy use by 1980. The change will require new appliance designs and materials and major retooling of factory equipment.

The immediate effect of environmental health and safety regulations has been to increase the uncertainties of private business firms. Without clear information on current and future requirements it is difficult for them to plan ahead. As a result, new investment may have been cut back so as to minimize exposure to agency pressure.

*Source: Office of Management and Budget

More importantly, improvements in industrial safety are costly, adding a hidden tax to every item produced. If consumers are to accept the higher priced products they must be convinced of the superior benefits they will receive. True benefit-cost analysis is necessary to justify the costs in higher prices, higher costs to business, and lower productivity. Some benefits include a one-third reduction in the American highway death rate following auto safety regulation. There has also been measurable progress in cleaning the nation's air and water of harmful chemicals. Sulfur dioxide in the air has declined about 25% since 1970, and new cars expel 83% less hydrocarbons and carbon monoxide than 1970 models. Benefits like these are difficult to measure against costs.

Other forms of regulation bear directly on customer costs. Regulation of transportation is the oldest and continues to add to the costs of freight and passenger travel. Trucking firms, for instance, are prohibited from serving any routes not authorized by the ICC. As a result, trucks travel many useless miles consuming thousands of gallons of gasoline, often empty of any cargo at all! The reason for such requirements is to protect the markets of many small trucking firms operating in local areas.

The Civil Aeronautics Board (CAB) has acted similarly in the market for air travel. Routes and fares are set for all airlines that fly interstate (between states). Fares are often double the fares on unregulated lines flying within a single state. The reason is the need to guarantee service to small isolated communities, which is possible only if airlines are allowed to make up their losses there on other routes. The frequent result is that too many flights are scheduled and capacity is underutilized, with wasted fuel and higher fares. In fact, some studies showed that high air fares and low profitability for airlines go hand-in-hand. Critics (including some airline management) claim lower air fares would bring greater volume and higher profitability. Early in 1977 President Carter called for deregulation of the airlines.

The question of regulation has increasingly occupied the minds of Congress, and proposals are being considered to change the current system. One idea, called the "Sunset Amendment," would require that agencies "self-destruct" after a certain specified period of time unless Congress makes a definite effort to continue them. Another would require the President to offer yearly plans to eliminate unneeded regulation; the President's recommendations would go into effect unless Congress acted to overrule them. In the area of transportation, current proposals would make route and fare rules more flexible. Environmental health and safety could be promoted by taxes levied on auto pollution, industrial injuries, and deaths.

It may be surprising that the chief opposition to some deregulation has come from the industrial firms themselves (like truck firms and airlines) and from organized labor. They argue that deregulation would bring ruinous competition with rate wars and bankruptcies. The result would be a decline in service and even no service for some markets. The public, too, is not convinced of the need for deregulation; a federally funded study shows that 56% of Americans want more regulation and only 35% want less. Other objections come from the regulatory agencies themselves, which provide jobs for more than 64,000 people.

Extended Example
Price Discrimination by a Regulated Monopoly

Some regulatory commissions permit a public utility to discriminate among customers in setting its rates. One reason for doing this is to permit the company to provide a larger quantity of service and to earn more total revenue than it could if it charged only one rate. Like the doctor who charges his patients according to how much they can afford to pay, the utility company tailors its rates to its customers. Figure 11 shows how this is done in the electric power industry.

Some users of electric power are willing to pay a high rate for small amounts of power. Their demand appears at the highest point of the curve. Some are willing to pay a moderate rate, and others would use more power if rates were very low. Their demand appears in the lower range of the curve. By setting different rates the power company is able to satisfy all these demands at the highest rate each class of user is willing to pay: high rates at the highest point of the demand curve and lower rates farther down. The firm's total revenues are shown as the entire shaded area under the demand curve.

Now look at the long-run average cost curve. You'll notice that it lies above the demand curve. No single user is willing to pay rates that will cover the full costs of providing individual units of service. But with its discriminatory rates the company will nevertheless be able to cover its costs at quantity OQ. This is not magic. It is because those who pay the higher rates will provide enough revenue to make up for those who pay the lower rates. Total costs are shown by the rectangle OCDQ with the base equal to quantity, OQ, and the height equal to average total cost, OC. Total revenues are shown by the entire area under the demand curve up to quantity OQ. The revenue area appears to be of about the same area as the cost rectangle. This means that total revenues are about equal to total costs. We can say that as long as the *triangle PCE* is at least as large as the triangle EDB, the regulated utility will be able to cover its costs.

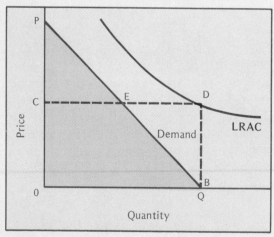

Figure 11 Price discrimination with a rate schedule. Total revenue equals the shaded area under the demand curve (line PEB). Total costs equal the area of the rectangle OCDQ.

prices. When prices are going up, the utility will ask the regulatory commission to let it increase the value of the base on which its rates are determined by enough to allow for the eventual replacement of its capital equipment.

Why the post office gets subsidies

There is more than one way of setting prices for public utilities. The lawmakers may decide that a service is of such value to the community that it should be provided at less than its full cost.

Figure 12 shows the market demand for first-class mail delivery in the imaginary country of Atlantis. You'll notice that demand is somewhat elastic over the range shown. When postage rates are reduced, people send a lot more letters. Business firms send out advertising circulars and politicians mail campaign literature. Furthermore, as the volume of mail increases, the average total cost of providing mail service declines. This is because of econ-

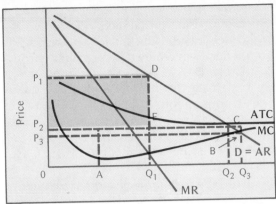

Figure 12 A regulated monopoly, such as the post office. Monopoly profits (= P_2P_1DE) are not permitted by the regulatory commission. At a price of P_2 the firm (post office) is covering only its full costs. At the maximum practical output, OQ_3, price does not cover full costs; a subsidy is necessary equal to the rectangle P_3P_2CB.

omies of large scale; the fixed cost of vehicles, sorting machines, and office space can be spread over many pieces of mail. Marginal costs drop sharply at first and average cost declines throughout the range shown.

If the postal service of Atlantis wants to maximize its profits, it will set its price at OP_1 and handle the volume OQ_1. At this point, $MC = MR$. Profits are shown by the rectangle P_1DEP_2.

A regulatory commission might say: "This is a public service, and the people of Atlantis don't want the post office to make economic profits. They want postal rates to cover full costs and no more." The price of first-class mail will be set at OP_2, where price is equal to average cost. The volume of mail will be OQ_2. Economic profits are eliminated.

However, at the price OP_2 the value of the postal service to each user is still greater than the cost of providing additional units of service. We know this because the demand curve for postal services lies above the marginal cost of producing postal service. Atlantis may decide to reduce price still further and provide greater service. At a price of OP_3 the volume of mail delivered will be OQ_3, and the price will cover the additional cost of the last unit of mail delivered ($MC = AR$). But the price OP_3

won't cover full costs, including the cost of the postal service's fixed equipment. You can see this by comparing total revenue (the rectangle OP_3BQ_3) and total costs (the rectangle OP_2CQ_3). The excess of costs over revenue (P_3P_2CB) must be paid by the government in the form of a subsidy to the postal service.

Government monopolies

We encounter many forms of government monopoly every day. As you leave your home in the morning, you give a letter to the national post-office monopoly. You may be carried to work or to school by a municipal transportation monopoly. Very likely, the price you pay does not cover the full costs of providing these services. You probably don't give this much thought until someone asks why the postal service and the bus and subway should be run by a public authority and subsidized by all the taxpayers.

The philosophy of these matters is not consistent. But a reasonable explanation would probably include *externalities*. When production of a service provides social benefits over and above the benefits purchased in the market, there may be justification for providing it at public expense.

Railroads have long been government monopolies in most countries. In the United States most are still privately owned, though heavily regulated by the federal government. If you've recently taken a long ride on a passenger train you've been a customer of Amtrak. Amtrak is a public corporation set up in 1970 to handle railroad passenger business after privately owned railroads found they could no longer provide the service. If Amtrak had not formed, nearly all intercity passenger rail service would have disappeared. Amtrak's passenger coaches still ride over privately owned rails and are repaired in the private shops of the railroad companies, in return for fees. Passenger service is still unprofitable, since most people prefer other modes of transportation. Congress underwrites Amtrak's deficits, which amount to about two-fifths of the total cost of carrying passengers.

Municipal and interurban transportation in the United States was once privately owned and subject to regulation as a public utility. In

Viewpoint
The U.S. Postal Service

Benjamin Franklin started it all. Then in 1847 the postal service became a federal responsibility when the Post Office Department was established. The objective of the coordinated postal service was to stimulate national communication and commerce and to aid national defense. It was felt that federal government subsidies should be used when necessary to further the process of integrating and strengthening a nation of diverse needs and concerns.

Postal service revenues increased regularly as the nation grew, but so did the deficits financed by federal subsidy. The growing volume of mail required substantial investments in new equipment and technology, raising unit costs. Even with substantial automation, labor costs continued to amount to 85% of costs. In the 1970s rising wage demands and rising gasoline costs (needed for postal vehicles) added to the problem of higher costs.

In order to protect the postal service from competition and encourage investment in modern equipment, the U.S. government gave the Post Office a legal monopoly on first-class mail delivery. The protected market in letter handling was an important advantage which permitted price discrimination in the mails. Markets could be separated easily: first-class letters, second-class bulk mail, and parcels. Price discrimination permits pricing on the basis of elasticity of demand: higher relative prices where demand is less elastic.

The U.S. Post Office monopoly on first class mail made demand highly inelastic. Because there is no suitable substitute, users will pay a high price to acquire the service. Business bulk mail and parcels may be sent by alternate means. In order to compete, package rates must be lower than rates of other carriers. The result is a *cross subsidy* within the postal service. High first-class letter charges help to pay the costs of carrying other mail at below cost rates.

In recent years there has been growing criticism of rising postal rates and deteriorating service. In 1971 the service was removed from federal government responsibility. The Post Office Department was abolished and the U.S. Postal Service established as a quasi-private corporation. It was to receive a temporary government subsidy to ease the transition, but it was assumed that the Postal Service would be self-supporting by the year 1984.

Unfortunately, other factors have intervened to worsen the financial plight of the sick service. Overtime demand has become more elastic. Rising mail charges led many business firms to develop substitute means of communication. The growth of private parcel carriers is the most obvious example, but electronic means of communication also compete with the postal service. Unhappily for the Postal Service, electronic means of communication are an acceptable substitute for the most profitable types of mail:
(1) Telephone communications are a substitute for business letters;
(2) Electronic funds transfer allows users to deposit checks and pay bills without use of the mails.
Some consumers have avoided higher postal rates by paying bills in person. Several publishing companies distribute magazines and advertising material door-to-door through independent companies or through subsidiaries. Other business firms insert their advertisements in newspapers for cheaper distribution. Greater elasticity of demand in these markets has meant lower volume and higher unit costs.

While the volume of mail has declined, the number of homes and business addresses the Post Office must serve has continued to rise. This increases unit costs further with the possibility that letter rates may reach 18 cents by 1980. The postal service's current deficit is running at a yearly rate of almost a billion dollars, or $3 million a day, but it could rise to two billion in only a few years.

Nobody seems to know the solution to the problems that plague the postal service. Raising rates again is apparently not the answer. Some people have suggested eliminating Saturday delivery service in order to reduce costs. In terms of the efficiency principle the postal service is a failure; the value of benefits purchased is less than the cost of providing the service.

Perhaps the postal service should be evaluated in terms of a third criterion. Production of many goods and services imparts benefits and costs to the society over and above the explicit benefits and costs for which a price is paid. We have referred to these unmeasured benefits and costs as *externalities:* the external benefits and costs that accrue to a society as a result of particular kinds of economic activity.

External benefits and costs are difficult, if not impossible, to measure correctly. Still, when production adds to a community's living standards or to its resource costs, an effort should be made to evaluate the full effects. Some of the external benefits of cheap postal service might include:

(1) integration of a diverse society into a coherent unit;
(2) dissemination of advertising information to increase the market for mass-produced goods;
(3) exposure to cultural and political information for isolated areas;
(4) employment for many low-skilled workers.

You may be able to add more external benefits and perhaps some external costs as well. The important question would be whether *total benefits* of cheap postal service exceed *total costs*. If this is indeed the case, then a strong argument could be made for continuing to subsidize the service from public funds. Like the public school system, the postal service would be operated as a service whose total benefits to the society as a whole justify making it a public responsibility.

the last few decades most of the systems have been sold to government and reorganized as public enterprises. Private companies found it difficult to obtain the high fare increases that became necessary to cover rising costs. It was easier for a municipally owned transit system to do this. Metropolitan Chicago has a Regional Transit Authority that doesn't own any of the interurban systems that it governs but subsidizes them from funds it receives from local taxes. This enables it to plan rail and bus services without regard to whether any particular service is profitable.

Socialists have traditionally favored turning large sectors of industry over to public ownership. In Britain, after World War II, the Labor government nationalized basic industries such as coal, railways, and trucking. In 1976, however, British socialists changed their minds about the benefits of nationalizing industry. Government monopoly has been found to work best in industries that were already monopolies under private ownership. Most West European socialists would probably agree with a leading British member of Parliament, R. A. S. Crosland, that industries should be nationalized only when this will improve them—that is, "where the existing industry is clearly performing poorly, when competition either cannot or is not permitted to enforce an improvement, where physical or fiscal controls are incapable of curing the situation, and where public ownership will not bring attendant disadvantages of its own."

Summary

A monopoly is the single supplier of a good or service without acceptable substitutes. Natural monopolies result from technical conditions of production; because of economies of large scale, a single producer is more efficient than competition among many firms. Some artificial monopolies are granted by government when the service is believed to be essential to the community; patents create artificial monopolies and help to encourage invention.

The demand curve for a monopolist slopes downward because it is the industry demand curve. The result is that a monopolist's marginal revenue is not the same as price. When

MR = MC, the level of output is lower and price is higher than under competition. The monopoly firm may continue to collect economic profit in the long run because of the absence of competition.

A monopoly firm has greater power to raise price when demand is relatively inelastic. Price discrimination is possible when elasticity differs among separate markets.

Monopoly violates the principle of efficiency by producing less output at higher resource costs than under competition and by limiting the capacity for innovation and communication of new technology. Monopoly violates the principle of equity by distorting the distribution of real income.

Monopoly profits can be taxed away through a fixed tax without altering the pattern of production and pricing in the economy. Natural monopolies are often regulated by government agencies. Regulated monopolies may expand the volume of service so that price covers marginal cost but not average total cost. When this happens, a subsidy must be paid. The postal system is an example of a regulated monopoly which may provide external benefits in return for the subsidy it receives.

A monopoly firm may not maximize economic profit if it wants to avoid the entry of new competition or the possibility of government investigation.

Key Words and Phrases

- **monopoly** a condition in which a single seller controls the entire output of an industry.

- **natural versus artificial monopoly** monopolies which result from technical factors within the industry versus those which result from a conscious act of government.

- **patent** a legal monopoly over the use of an innovation for a fixed period of time.

- **price discrimination** the use of different prices in different markets.

- **dumping** the practice in international trade of setting lower prices in distant markets than in the home country.

Questions for Review

1. List as many advantages and disadvantages of monopoly as you can think of. Be careful to state the conditions under which the advantages would exist.

2. Use the following hypothetical data to determine a monopoly firm's price and output. First you must calculate total revenue, marginal revenue, and marginal cost for every level of output. What is the monopolist's profit at the profit-maximizing output?

Quantity demanded	Price	Total cost
1	10	6
2	9	11
3	8	15
4	7	20
5	6	26
6	5	33

3. Refer again to the data in question 2. Assume the industry is competitive and new firms can enter the industry producing under the cost conditions given. What would a firm's price and output be?

4. The data in question 2 can also be used to illustrate price discrimination. If the firm is able to discriminate completely among buyers, what would be its total revenue? What would be its economic profit? On a graph of demand, what geometric space represents total revenue under conditions of perfect price discrimination?

5. The rising cost of oil imports has led many members of Congress to favor a tax on domestic production of petroleum. The aim would be to tax away a firm's "windfall profits." Would you recommend a fixed tax or a tax on every gallon produced? Why?

6. Define: patent, marginal cost pricing.

30

Imperfect Competition:
Monopolistic Competition and Oligopoly

We have studied two quite different forms of economic behavior: perfect competition and monopoly. In monopoly there is only one seller providing a unique good or service. In perfect competition there are many sellers—all producing identical products. The monopoly firm has control over the price at which its product sells, but producers in a perfectly competitive market have no such control.

There are few real monopolies in our economy and few markets in which perfect competition can be found. Most markets are in between; they are characterized by what we call *imperfect competition*. This is an odd name to use for everyday economic activities. It's like saying, "You understand what we mean by perfect competition, don't you? Well, this isn't it."

One reason we do this is that the theory of perfect competition was developed first, and for a long time was the only theory to explain economic behavior. Economists knew that perfectly competitive markets were few and far between. In analyzing the real world they didn't expect firms to behave exactly as in the world of economic theory. Only fairly recently did economists begin to develop a theory based on less-than-perfect competition. This proved to be a step forward in our understanding. The theory of imperfect competition helps to explain things that happen in real life. It explains such things as the tendency of prices in some industries to rise together in spurts, or the existence of four gas stations at one intersection, or the gigantic sums of money spent on advertising beer and pet foods.

Two kinds of imperfect competition may be distinguished: monopolistic competition and oligopoly. *Monopolistic competition* resembles perfect competition in that many firms compete with each other. It resembles monopoly in that each firm has some power to influence the price at which it sells. A firm in monopolistic competition affects price by trying to convince buyers that its product is the only one that will meet their needs. To the extent the firm succeeds in this it establishes a monopoly and can set a monopoly price. Henry's Delicatessen is the only Henry's Delicatessen around, just as Maude's dress shop is different from any other. If you're sold on Henry or on Maude, you'll patronize them rather than their competitors, even if their prices are somewhat higher.

Oligopoly (from Greek roots, meaning "few sellers") is a situation in which the market is dominated by a few firms. This is true for industries producing automobiles, steel, and soap, and for other large-scale industries. Oligopoly differs from monopolistic competition in that new companies find it difficult to enter these fields. Almost anybody can start a little shoe store or some other small business, but few people would think seriously of setting up a new auto company to compete with General Motors.

Monopolistic competition

Probably most U.S. firms could be characterized as monopolistically competitive. Typically, monopolistic competition develops in industries (1) having a simple technology and (2) requiring relatively small initial capital investment. This allows many small firms to enter, and vigorous competition may result. A classic example is the garment industry, where a worker who knows how to make women's gloves or dresses needs only a few sewing machines to open a new shop.

Because many firms are competing, each will try to differentiate its product from the products of others. Many good examples can be found among retail stores. Often there are real differences among them—not necessarily in the goods on their shelves but in the services they provide. No two stores are alike. They differ in their location or in the other services they provide. Some stores are open longer hours or sell a wider variety of items. Differences may even be intangible, existing largely in the mind of the customer: friendlier clerks, a cleaner store, a more reliable management. A store may appeal to people because their friends shop there, or those they would like to have as friends.

Economic Thinker

Joan Robinson

When Joan Robinson (born 1903) began studying economics in England during the early 1900s, there was substantial agreement among economists about the structure of the market system. It was assumed that markets were fundamentally competitive. Somewhere in the textbooks reference was usually made to monopoly, but this was "a hard, indigestible lump" which never quite fit in with the competitive analysis. The logical consistency of the competitive model was so attractive that economists tried not to notice that it didn't fit the real world.

The problem could not be ignored forever, and the modern theory of monopoly was eventually developed. Monopoly is different from competition because of a "gap in the chain of substitutes" for some good. When the output of a firm is bound on all sides by such gaps, the firm is a monopoly. If entry of new firms is restricted into this industry, profits may continue to be greater than normal for some time.

Joan Robinson was significant for her work in the theory of how monopoly firms behave. But she went much further than this. She saw that goods in real markets are often partial substitutes for other goods. They may not be perfect substitutes, but they are reasonably substitutable so that absolute monopoly is rare. The real world is characterized by monopolistic competition among firms selling similar but differentiated products.

It was her path-breaking work in the theory of monopolistic competition for which Joan Robinson is best known—especially in her book *The Economics of Imperfect Competition*. She also analyzed the effects of imperfect competition on income distribution. A firm in monopolistic competition restricts output in order to maintain price. The result is a lower level of plant operation than optimum and lower employment of factors of production. And finally the result of imperfect competition is a greater return to entrepreneurs relative to the incomes of other factors of production. The gap between industry's ability to *produce* goods and workers' ability to *consume* them will bring on periodic depressions. This conclusion led Robinson to accept Marx's analysis of the process of change in economic systems.

As a Reader of Economics at Cambridge, Joan Robinson has continued her work in the theory of imperfect competition, employment, capital accumulation, and economic philosophy, including Marxist economics.

If *product differentiation* fails—that is, if customers aren't convinced that one seller's product is different from another's—then the industry will be similar to a perfectly competitive one. All firms will receive the same price for a very similar if not actually identical product. To the extent that product differentiation succeeds, some firms will be able to get higher prices than others. Thus convenience food stores can charge more than other grocers; they offer longer hours of operation, and they operate many small outlets close to people's homes.

To take a different example, almost every city has its "class" stores—its own version of New York's Fifth Avenue or Chicago's Michigan Avenue or Los Angeles' Wilshire Boulevard. These include department stores, jewelry, clothing, and furniture stores, and restaurants. These stores sell many of the same products as do the mass merchandisers, but their prices are generally higher. Nevertheless, because customers believe added status is conferred by shopping there or because many hold the idea that "the more you pay, the more you get," or because of more personal attention—all are factors—the customers will "shell out" for steep prices.

Demand curves in monopolistic competition

Demand curves for firms in monopolistic competition slope downward. The steepness of the slope depends on the characteristics of the product. If a product is highly differentiated—that is, if it appears to consumers to be completely different from competing products—demand for it will be rather inelastic and the downward slope will be steep. Demand for the product will resemble the demand curve of a monopolist, since there are no close substitutes. A less differentiated product will have obvious substitutes and so its demand curve will be less steep—more nearly like a demand curve in perfect competition.

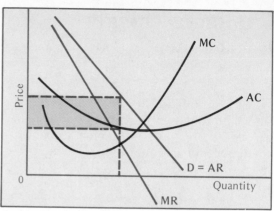

Figure 1 Market for the cola drink Pepto-Fizz. A firm in monopolistic competition faces a downward-sloping demand curve. Marginal revenue lies below average revenue. Total profit is shown by the shaded area.

Figure 1 shows a hypothetical demand curve for an imaginary cola drink, Pepto-Fizz. For many consumers Pepto-Fizz is a beverage that has no substitute. Others will substitute Coke or Pepsi if they can get it cheaper. The marginal revenue curve lies below the demand curve to show that each reduction in price produces a smaller increase in revenue.

Costs in monopolistic competition

Costs in monopolistic competition have the same characteristics as costs in other market structures. Short-run average cost curves are saucer-shaped, and marginal cost curves rise after some optimum level of production has been reached. The output that maximizes profit is at the point where MC = MR. Selling price is determined from the point on the demand curve directly above MC = MR. Profit per unit is the difference between price or average revenue and average cost: AR − AC. In Figure 1, total profit is the area of the rectangle whose base is the quantity sold and whose height is AR − AC.

Long-run equilibrium in monopolistic competition

The fact that firms are in monopolistic *competition* with each other has an important bearing on what happens to them over time. In the short run a firm may receive economic profit, as shown by the rectangle in Figure 1. But since the industry is competitive, this profit cannot last. Unlike the situation in monopoly, conditions in monopolistic competition permit free entry of other firms. The initial capital requirements are relatively low, encouraging people to set up in business on a small scale. Technical information is widely available. Even though the products are similar, there is often room enough in the market for one or two more firms producing slightly different versions of the same product.

As new firms enter, the industry moves toward long-run equilibrium. But long-run equilibrium under monopolistic competition lacks the ideal characteristics of perfect competition. As new firms enter they take away part of the market from existing firms. Each firm's demand curve shifts to the left, eliminating some economic profit. In Figure 2 the entry of new firms has reduced each firm's sales by half. There is still some economic profit, however, and new firms continue to enter.

When each firm's sales have fallen to the position shown in Figure 3, there is no longer any incentive for new firms to enter. The industry has reached long-run equilibrium.

What are the characteristics of long-run equilibrium under monopolistic competition?

(1) At equilibrium, *there are no economic profits*. There are only normal profits, which are not great enough to encourage other firms to enter the industry. There are no losses either, because firms with losses have withdrawn. Therefore, when MC = MR, average revenue must also equal average cost: AR − AC = 0. The price is just enough to cover full costs.

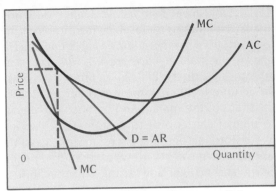

Figure 3 Long-run equilibrium under monopolistic competition. Economic profit is eliminated and firms operate at less than their lowest cost level of output.

(2) Because the demand curve slopes downward, the average cost curve must also be sloping downward at the point where AR = AC. That is the only way the two curves can just touch without crossing each other. This is significant. It means that *firms are not producing at their minimum-cost level of output*. If they produced more, AC would be lower. Remember that under perfect competition, firms are in equilibrium at the lowest point on the AC curve. To the extent that unit costs under monopolistic competition are higher than they might be under competition, the economy is using too many resources to produce each unit. Consumers are paying a higher price than they would under perfect competition.

(3) Since each firm is operating at less than the optimum level, *there are too many firms in the industry*. The same amount of output could be supplied by fewer firms. This means that more capital resources are being allocated to this industry than would be necessary under perfect competition. The illustration most often given of this is the highway intersection having three or four gas stations with several idle pumps. Other examples are the small stores in every community that seem to have barely enough customers to stay in business, or two barbers on opposite sides of the street where one barber wouldn't be kept busy full time.

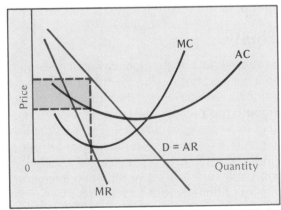

Figure 2 Economic profit attracts new firms into the industry. The individual firm's demand curve shifts to the left. Economic profit is reduced.

(4) Because their very existence depends on differentiating themselves from their competitors, *firms in monopolistic competition have to spend money making their products different* from all other products. Bill's Shoe Shop is anxious to acquire loyal customers in order to protect its share of the market and perhaps expand it. A retailer can appeal to customers in various ways: through better services, more accessible shelves, a greater variety of brands, special sales, and heavier advertising. In other industries the options are fewer. A manufacturer of electric drills for home carpenters may be selling a product that is practically identical with those of competitors. In order to carve out a place in the market this firm may have to use special merchandising techniques to get its products displayed so that customers will buy them. It will also advertise heavily. In terms of our model, all of these methods will help to shift an individual firm's demand curve to the right and to make it steeper.

The most common route to product differentiation is through *advertising*. Advertising can often persuade consumers of the uniqueness, the superiority, and the necessity of owning a product, regardless of what the facts may be. But if total market demand for the good is fixed, advertising can only shift customers from one product to another. A rightward shift in one firm's demand curve means a leftward shift in another's. A barrage of advertising from one producer must be countered by others with similar barrages. The result may go far beyond what could reasonably be considered informing the public. Much of the effort will be devoted to confusing the public, or to diverting it or entertaining it.

Advertising is expensive. It increases average cost curves and increases the price of the product. The final result of heavy advertising may be that total industry sales remain the same but unit costs rise for every firm.

Shortcomings of mon. competition

How does monopolistic competition affect us?

Monopolistic competition should be evaluated in terms of the principles of efficiency and equity. Because monopolistic competition is similar to monopoly in product uniqueness, it has some of the same disadvantages as monopoly (refer to the previous chapter). There are other disadvantages which grow out of particular features of monopolistically competitive markets.

Efficiency

Monopolistic competition violates the principle of efficiency because it allows too many producers in the industry. When initial capital requirements are low and technical information readily available, many firms can enter the market. The result is too many firms, each operating at less than its optimum level of output. At low levels of operation, unit costs are higher than necessary. Plant and equipment are underutilized and prices are higher than necessary. Productive resources are used wastefully, and efficiency is impaired.

In monopolistic competition some resources are used for nonprice competition: product differentiation and advertising. Using resources in this way may be a net benefit to society if the result is greater information, greater variety of products, and a wider range of qualities to choose from. However, if the result is false advertising claims, superficial product gimmickry, or rapid obsolescence of products, then there is a net loss.

Equity

Monopolistic competition may enhance equity in a society, but in a way which damages the principle of efficiency. The attraction of monopoly profits and the limited initial capital requirements encourage entry of small firms. Entrepreneurs seeking business opportunities find a wide range of possible activities. Regrettably the same factors which encourage entry make continued prosperity less sure, and many of these small enterprises soon succumb to market forces. Ultimately, the waste of human and capital resources may be substantial.

Oligopoly

Where have you heard these sayings before?

"You've come a long way, baby." "The quality goes in before the name goes on." "We're number two. We try harder."

If these slogans don't sound familiar, you must have been in a coma for the last five years. They're from advertisements for cigarettes, TV sets, and rental cars. These are quite different industries, but they have one thing in common: they are oligopolies. You'll remember that an oligopoly is an industry dominated by relatively few firms. They tend to be few because large amounts of capital are required to set up operations. There are other barriers that help to prevent new firms from entering these industries; exclusive patents and high marketing costs are examples.

Other industries that are characterized by oligopoly are steel, aluminum, petroleum refining, machinery, typewriters, and electric light bulbs, to mention only a few. An industry may be dominated by a handful of firms—aluminum and automobiles—or there may be so many firms that the situation is close to monopolistic competition. The steel industry has one very large firm, six or seven medium-sized firms, and a few even smaller firms producing for specialized markets. In aluminum there are just three large firms. In autos there are four large firms and a number of foreign firms which sell in the U.S. market. Petroleum has seven very large firms, a moderate number of medium-sized firms, and a host of small firms.

Oligopolies formed naturally in the auto and steel industries. In the beginning, many small firms competed for market shares. But the heavy costs of initial capital equipment made unit production costs high. Combining several firms through merger permitted capital costs to be spread over a larger combined volume. A merged firm could then undersell its rivals, drive them out of business, and sometimes buy them up at bargain prices. Eventually, the number of firms was reduced to a few large giants. In some industries the process of merging slowed when public attention was aroused. Now the large firms tolerate and even encourage the growth of small firms in order to avoid public pressure to break up the large ones.

Extended Example
Oligopoly in Chips?

When is a potato chip not a potato chip?

When it's stackable.

In the past, most potato chips were produced by about a hundred firms scattered around the United States. Total sales ran about $1.5 billion a year, primarily from small plants close to consumer markets. Chips break easily and packages are bulky, so they cannot be shipped very far. This kept production on a fairly small scale.

In 1969, however, Procter and Gamble, the large food and housewares firm, began to test-market its "new-fangled potato chips." P & G dehydrated its potatoes, ground them and pressed them flat, and then fried them. The finished "chips" were uniform in size and shape and could be stacked in sealed cans similar to tennis ball cans.

The new process had several advantages. It permitted substantial cost savings through large-scale processing and packaging. The compact containers could be shipped large distances, and the product had a shelf life of about a year. Whereas most markets for conventional potato chips were served by about five local firms, the new product could be provided economically by as few as three or four nationwide giants.

Fighting back, the traditional chip makers petitioned the Food and Drug Administration to prohibit the use of the term "potato chip" on any product not made in the conventional way. After much consideration, the agency finally ruled that the new packages could be labeled "potato chips made from dried potatoes." The ruling was a setback for the conventional chip producers, some of whom set out to develop a similar product of their own.

This case illustrates that some innovative drive can occur in oligopolistic industry. Large firms can afford outlays for product development, capital investment, and sales promotion. When they succeed, the result is a restructuring of the industry.

The unique thing about oligopoly is that what each firm does depends on what the others are doing. There are so few firms that no single firm can ignore the pricing and output decisions of the others. If Avery Company should reduce its price and take away part of the market from Bates Company and Clark Company, then Bates and Clark would be forced to follow suit. Soon the three companies would probably be back with the same share of the market as before, except that each would sell its product for less money and none of the firms would gain. Of course, in reality Avery knows that the others would match its lower price; so it doesn't reduce it. It won't raise price either. A higher price would mean the loss of its share of the market to competitors.

This testing of the market and backing down is fairly common in oligopolistic industries until firms learn how their rivals will probably respond. Then price tends to stabilize and firms decide it's better not to rock the boat. Where there are few sellers, every firm's price and output depends on the pricing and output policies of other firms. Oligopoly firms are interdependent. Each firm must base its decisions on the actions and reactions of others. If you have played bridge or poker or chess, you know what it means to base your decisions on the reactions of others: it means that you can't decide beforehand on the proper strategy to adopt, but must be prepared to follow several different strategies depending on what the others do.

It is understandable that interdependence among large oligopoly firms might lead eventually to agreements to fix price. To agree in advance on price is called **collusion.** Oligopolies certainly prefer collusion over ruinous price wars and industry-wide losses. Collusion might take place through industry trade associations. Member firms submit price lists to the association's trade journal; when members know what other firms are charging, they are likely to charge the same. In other industries rate schedules are readily available for making comparisons.

Price and output in oligopoly

Duopoly

Let's begin our discussion of oligopoly pricing with a case that is close to monopoly. Suppose there are two firms in an industry, both with long experience and loyal customers. They divide the market, behaving like monopolists in their own parts of the market. They don't do this by agreement or collusion but by long practice. Together, they will maximize their joint profits.

This form of oligopoly is called *duopoly*—the prefix *duo* meaning two. If the firms have identical cost curves they will equate MC with MR and each will produce half the total industry output. Each firm's profit is the difference between price and average cost at the profit-maximizing level of output. The existence of economic profit does not attract other firms to the industry because of the high capital investment needed to gain entry. The situation is diagrammed in Figure 4.

Duopoly has the same disadvantages as monopoly. Consumers pay a higher price than the competitive price and receive a smaller quantity. Costs of production are higher than the minimum, since MC = MR at a point where the average cost curve is still falling. This means that plants are operated at less than optimum scale. Resource allocation is distorted: inputs are not used as efficiently as they could be.

We have assumed that the duopoly firms have identical cost curves and that they have developed a practice of dividing the market between them. But if their cost curves are different, or if they haven't worked out a way of living together in peace and harmony, there is nothing to prevent one firm from deciding to reduce its price and go after a bigger share of the market. If the other firm responds by doing the same thing, then more goods would be produced at a lower cost. This would be fine for consumers, but the two firms would no longer be maximizing their profits.

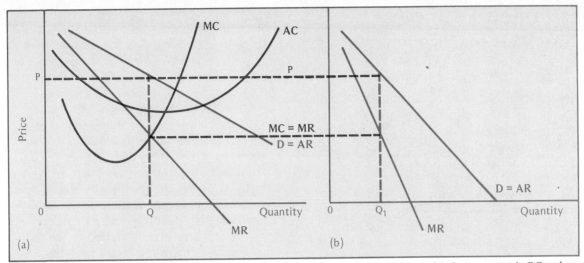

Figure 4   In a duopoly, market demand is shared by two firms. (a) Industry demand: total industry output is OQ, where MC = MR. (b) The firms' demand: each firm equates MC with MR and produces output OQ_1, one-half total industry output. Price P is read from the demand curve.

Kinked demand curves

When there are more than two firms, the problem of determining a firm's equilibrium price and output becomes more difficult. There is no method by which we can assign particular shares of the market to particular firms. Still, each firm is affected by the decisions of other firms. This means that each will consider what other firms will do when it decides on its price and output. The situation is shown by the peculiar looking demand curve in Figure 5. We call this a **"kinked" demand curve** because it is bent in the middle.

The kink in the demand curve occurs at the customary market price of $8. At prices higher than $8 demand is highly elastic. If a single firm raises its price, other firms will not follow; the high-priced firm will lose customers to them. If the firm raises its price as high as $10, it will lose all its customers. At prices below $8, on the other hand, demand is highly inelastic. Other firms in the industry will resist being undersold and will tend to match any price reduction by any single firm. Even a price reduction to $6 will gain only a few customers from other firms.

The existence of a customary market price discourages price competition in an oligopolized industry. Firms will consider the reactions of other firms and try to avoid spoiling the market.

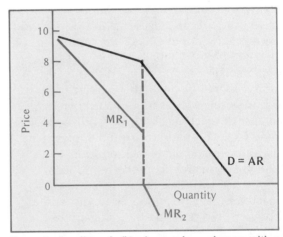

Figure 5   An oligopoly firm faces a demand curve with a kink. The kink occurs at the customary price. Above the kink, demand is elastic: a price rise will cause the firm to lose customers. Below the kink, demand is inelastic: a price reduction will gain few customers.

Extended Example
Price Wars in Oligopoly

The inflation of the 1970s and smaller than normal gains in productivity sent many firms scrambling for customers. This was especially true of large retail grocers. Several large food chains dominate the industry with A & P the leader. A & P was founded in the mid-1850s and until twenty-five years ago held at least one-tenth the total market. But between 1973 and 1975 the supermarket chain lost more than $200 million on sales of almost $7 billion.

Although food prices have been rising sharply in recent years, most of the increase has come from rising costs of packaging, transportation, taxes, depreciation, rent, and advertising. Food processing and distribution accounts for about 60% of the total food bill, adding substantially to the cost of supermarket operations. In 1973 the cost of eating soared by $14\frac{1}{2}$%, the greatest advance since 1947. Food prices increased almost as much again in 1974, but by that time recession had brought unemployment as well. Shoppers cut back on food, particularly high-cost processed foods.

A & P was hard hit. In 1972 the giant reacted by beginning a massive discounting program. The price-slashing slogan was WEO—Where Economy Originates. Trouble was, the old A & P stores could not handle the large volume of business and customers grew disgusted with the inconvenience. Worse yet, more efficient competing chains were able to match the low prices and A & P actually lost more than $50 million. Second-place Safeway Stores moved ahead to become the nation's largest chain.

The disastrous results of price cutting convinced A & P of the error of its ways. To revive sales the firm embarked on extensive remodeling and advertising to reshape its image. Inefficient and unprofitable operations were closed down, and it is hoped that the firm will once again earn a profit by the end of 1977.

Profit margins have always been thin in food retailing, leaving little room for price cutting. In 1973 industry-wide profits were only one-half cent per dollar of sales, and profits rose to only a penny per dollar in 1975. But over a year's time a supermarket turns over its stock more than a dozen times, earning that penny many times. As a result, average earnings per dollar of stockholders' equity is about eight percent—still about a third less than the average for all industries. Part of the problem is high labor costs which consume an increasing share of supermarket costs. Utility and paper costs and rents are also up. Furthermore, future sales growth is expected to be slow because of a leveling of the rate of population growth. The result will be increasing competition and greater efforts to improve efficiency. Economies of scale and the high costs of new electronic check-out equipment will continue to push small enterprises out of the market.

What does this account of A & P reveal about the firm's demand curve? How do the oligopoly firms in this industry use nonprice competition? What circumstances might cause the role of price leader to shift?

Price rigidity

The kink in the demand curve means that price will change infrequently. Prices which remain stable over long periods when demand and costs are changing are said to be "rigid." Figure 6 illustrates *price rigidity* in oligopoly.

When the demand curve is kinked, the marginal revenue curve has two parts. At a price below the customary price, marginal revenue drops sharply because the firm gains few customers. This leaves a broad gap at the point of the customary price. To the left of the gap in Figure 6, marginal revenue is greater than marginal cost; firms will have an incentive to expand output. To the right of the gap, however, marginal revenue is less than marginal cost; firms will want to contract output. The equilibrium output occurs at the customary price, since quantity sold at this price is the profit-maximizing quantity. Economic profit is the difference between price and average cost at this quantity.

The power to control prices is useful when demand falls throughout the market. In oligopoly a leftward shift in demand will mean cutbacks in production for all the firms in the industry. The kink will remain, however, at the customary oligopoly price. Firms will reduce output and employment, but price will remain rigid (see Figure 7).

An increase in industry demand could have the reverse effect. Firms may expand output and employment at constant prices for a time, each fearing a loss of customers if it is the

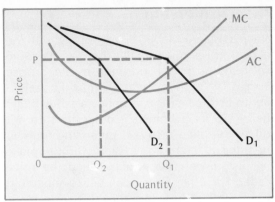

Figure 7 A leftward shift in demand (from D_1 to D_2) leaves price unchanged and only quantity falls (from Q_1 to Q_2).

only firm to raise prices. Finally, prices may rise together, with the result that oligopoly prices tend to move in spurts in response to higher demand.

At the customary price, firms have no incentive to change price or quantity. Even if their average cost curves shift, marginal cost is not likely to change enough to move it out of the gap shown in the diagram. A drop in costs will just add to economic profits at the normal level of operation. An increase in costs will be absorbed from economic profit. Figure 8 shows how costs can vary widely without affecting a firm's equilibrium point. The profit-maximizing output and price remain the same at all three levels of MC and AC. When cost curves shift up or down, only the amount of economic profit is affected. Price remains rigid.

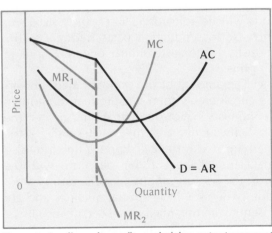

Figure 6 In oligopoly, profit-maximizing output occurs at the customary price and quantity. Because of the kink, the marginal revenue curve has a gap at the customary price.

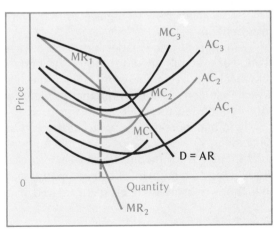

Figure 8 Wide shifts in AC and MC do not affect the profit-maximizing output. Prices tend to remain rigid.

Price leadership

When costs continue to rise throughout the market, prices must finally rise, too. Pressure will build up within the industry for a price change, but each individual firm will be reluctant to be the first to raise price. Each will fear the loss of its customers if other firms do not follow the price increase. Often the firms in the industry look to one leading firm to make the first move. This firm is called the **price leader.** The other firms don't get together and agree to follow the leader; the practice develops over the course of time. In the steel industry, for example, United States Steel is considered the price leader, and in tobacco the leader is R. J. Reynolds.

The price leader may be the largest firm in the industry, or the most aggressive firm, or the one having the lowest costs, or the firm with the longest experience in estimating costs. The leader can set its price as if it were a monopoly, at a point that maximizes its own profits. Other firms will then follow, though they may have to accept somewhat less than maximum profits for themselves.

Price leadership is most common among firms that sell undifferentiated products, such as many industrial commodities. Without some sort of coordination among them, individual price setting could disrupt the established pattern of market shares and lead to price wars—that is, to a cat-and-dog struggle over which firm is to get what share of the market. Formal agreements to set prices are illegal in the United States. But formal agreements are not really necessary as long as each firm understands how to behave so that every firm benefits.

Attempts at price leadership don't always work. For example, the Ford Motor Co. had to take back a price increase on its 1976 models when its competitors—principally General Motors—refused to go along.

Ford had increased its prices at the end of December, 1975 by 2.2% for cars, 2.8% for light trucks, and 3% for medium and heavy trucks. Henry Ford II, chairman of the company, said that the increase would be reconsidered if it had an adverse effect on sales or if the competition did not follow suit. On January 15, 1976, a Ford spokesman announced that the company was rolling back its average price by $97 in order "to keep Ford products competitive in the marketplace."

The price increases for medium and heavy trucks remained in effect, but those for passenger cars and light trucks were abandoned except for small increases in prices of optional equipment. The spokesman said that orders for new cars had fallen off since the price increase.

Mark-up pricing

A common practice in oligopoly is **mark-up pricing;** firms set price at a fixed percentage above average cost. Most business firms don't know enough about their costs and revenues to draw the neat diagrams we have presented here. In practice, many firms begin by estimating what their sales are likely to be in the upcoming period. From this it is possible to estimate the cost per unit. To the unit cost they add a percentage mark-up to arrive at their price.

For instance, suppose a firm makes metal rods for use in manufacturing. At the current level of operation unit costs include:

labor	$3.50
materials and power	1.50
fixed costs	.50
Total unit cost	$5.50

If firms agree on a standard mark-up of 10%, rods will be sold for $5.50 (1.10) = $6.05. An increase in production costs throughout the industry will lead to similar price revisions in all firms.

The amount of the standard mark-up varies considerably from one product to another. Economists have found that the greater the elasticity of demand the smaller will be the mark-up. For instance, suppose this firm also makes metal sheets to be sold along with the rods for use in various manufacturing processes. The rods have special qualities and are essential in the making of certain products. The sheets, on the other hand, are not essential; there are substitutes that will do just as well. The firm will be able to charge a higher mark-up on the rods, for which demand is less elastic. Demand conditions may justify only a 5% mark-up on sheets to maximize revenue.

When a company produces a large variety of products its market analysts must try to determine the relative elasticities of the different items. If the firm were to use the same mark-up for all its products, it would fail to maximize revenues. Some prices would be too low and others too high.

The use of standard mark-ups helps to explain why prices under oligopoly may remain stable over a long period. If average cost curves are fairly flat over a wide range of output, firms will not necessarily increase their prices when there are increases in demand. The result may be very different if there is a substantial drop in demand. In fact, *a drop in demand may lead to a price increase!* This is because unit costs are often higher at a low volume of output. As volume falls, the high fixed costs of capital equipment must be spread over a smaller number of units. To add a standard mark-up will mean higher prices—an especially serious problem at a time when consumer spending is already low. In 1975, one of the worst years in the recent history of the automobile industry, General Motors raised prices although unit sales were declining.

Cartels

If oligopolists were free to do as they chose, most of them would probably enter into formal pricing agreements. Then they would know exactly what to expect from each other. Such an arrangement is called a cartel. A **cartel** is a formal agreement among producers aimed at regulating prices and output and dividing markets. At one time steel production in the United States was cartelized and prices were regulated according to the **basing-point system.** All steel was priced at its production cost in Pittsburgh plus the cost of transportation to its destination. Judge Gary of the United States Steel Company held dinners at which the representatives of the leading companies decided

on a price. All such arrangements are now illegal in the United States except when they are believed to aid small competitors. For example, in many communities the price of milk is fixed by dairymen's associations, which are permitted under the law.

Cartels are legal in many other countries, however. One famous cartel is the Organization of Petroleum Exporting Countries (OPEC), which is led by the Arab oil-producing countries of the Middle East. In 1974–1975, OPEC was able to quadruple the price of oil in the world market. Cartels are usually set up to prevent what producers regard as ruinous competition. Members agree to live and let live; each firm is guaranteed a share of the market and promises to abide by common arrangements on pricing and selling.

As long as the members of a cartel stick together, they are able to function like a monopoly. This means that when demand is low they must restrict production. They must resist the temptation to cut price in order to sell more. Eventually, conflicts are likely to occur among the members of a cartel, and sooner or later some of them find it in their interest to leave the group. As a result, cartels are often short-lived. They flourish during good times when demand is high, but break apart when demand falls and each member prefers to go it alone.

The payoff matrix

In oligopoly, each firm must consider the reactions of other firms to a change in its price. A cut in price by one firm may be followed by a price cut by its competitors, with the result that all will end up with the same shares of the market as before but with lower profits. A payoff matrix, which may be used to illustrate this interdependence, is shown in Figure 9.

Suppose there are two firms in an industry. At a uniform price of $10, firm A's profits are $40,000 and firm B's are $60,000. If A reduces its price to $8 while B keeps its price at $10, A will gain some of B's customers and make profits of $60,000 while B's profits will fall off to $50,000. If A then reduces its price to $5 while B stubbornly maintains its price of $10, A will gain still more of B's customers. But the lower price will reduce A's profits to $50,000. The best possible solution for A would be the price of $8 provided B were to remain at $10.

But of course B won't let A take its customers away. B can always fight back by reducing its own price. If B follows A to a price of $8, A's profits will be only $30,000 as against B's profits of $40,000. This isn't satisfactory for A, which can raise its profits to $40,000 by going to a price of $5. At this price, B can't improve its profits by any price change.

Other approaches to pricing

The foregoing approach to pricing assumes that the firms want to live with each other. But in some markets one firm may decide to underprice the other until it has forced the rival out of business. For example, if A sets its price at $2, no pricing policy will enable B to earn more than $20,000. This relatively low level of profit may eventually convince B to leave the industry. In the meantime A may make up its losses from economic profits elsewhere.

Still another solution would be for the two firms to merge. Prices could then be set to maximize total profits. The merger would bring maximum returns if the A part of the new company sets its price at $8 and the B part sets its price at $10.

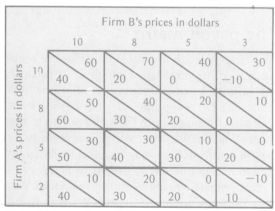

Figure 9 A payoff matrix. Firm A's profit is shown below the diagonal in each square. Firm B's profit is above the diagonal.

Nonprice competition

"It's the real thing"

There are other ways of competing than through price. In both oligopoly and monopolistic competition, most firms turn to advertising as a way of persuading customers that their products have something special about them. The simplest form of advertising is to put a label on the product to distinguish it from its competitors. Consumers who like Orchard Farm canned peaches will look for the label whenever they buy canned peaches; it saves them the trouble of choosing among perhaps half a dozen brands of different prices and qualities. The next step is to bring Orchard Farm products to the attention of the general public that reads newspapers, listens to the radio, or watches television.

The media used by advertisers vary with the kind of product. Producers of industrial equipment don't advertise in *Newsweek* or *Time*, and supermarkets don't advertise in *Fortune* or *Business Week*. Beer companies advertise on TV sports programs, soap companies on women's daytime programs, and deodorant manufacturers on the family hour. Hobby items are most often advertised in specialty magazines, and industrial commodities in trade journals. The introduction of an entirely new product is sometimes accompanied by tremendous advertising outlays, particularly if the industry depends heavily on advertising for consumer acceptance. Menthol-tipped cigarettes were popularized with heavy advertising. Substantial outlays may also be used to introduce an old product to a new market—as in selling cigars to women, for example.

Expenditures on advertising amount to between 2 and 3% of national income in the United States. The percentage falls slightly during periods of rising output and rises when output is falling. In some industries, notably cigarettes and soap, the sums spent on advertising are a substantial proportion of total costs.

Is advertising good or bad? It would be difficult to conceive of a modern capitalist economy without any advertising at all. Every business firm needs to tell the public about its products, and the defenders of advertising stress this information-giving function. People read grocery store ads to find out the specials of the week. But most advertising seeks to persuade rather than inform, like the ads for pain-killers that tell you Brand X works faster than Brand Y. Some ads tell you nothing at all; they use psychological tricks to make you feel favorably disposed toward their beer or their cigarettes so that you will unconsciously prefer those brands when you see them in the store.

Defenders of advertising say that beer, cigarette, or auto advertising helps support our communications system. *Newspapers, magazines, radio, and TV get most or all their revenue from advertising.* Thus advertising pays for much of our information and entertainment. This is true, reply the critics, but they point out that communications might be paid for in other ways. The new cable TV systems that are now spreading through the country charge their users a direct fee. If the entire communications system were supported directly by its users, the resources that now go into producing those expensive beer commercials could be devoted to producing quality programs. In short, say the critics, *advertising represents waste.*

Waste? Not so fast, reply the defenders. Advertising is beneficial to the economy in several ways that we haven't mentioned yet. *Advertising enables companies to expand their production.* Since under imperfect competition average cost curves decline with increases in

Extended Example
Nonprice Competition in a Regulated Industry

When firms are reluctant or unable to compete on the basis of price, they are likely to use other forms of competition. The airlines, whose fares are regulated by the Civil Aeronautics Board, provide many examples.

An airline may compete by offering more frequent service between certain points than its rivals. It tries to increase its market share by providing greater convenience to passengers. Some airlines paint their planes brilliant colors. All seem to believe that attractive flight attendants in fashionable uniforms and with a reputation for friendly service are a valuable asset!

When demand elasticities differ among markets, an airline may compete more aggressively in the market where demand is more elastic. For example, travelers between Atlanta and New York have several airlines to choose from. As a result, they are offered filet mignon to eat, perhaps with a little red wine on the side. The less fortunate traveler from Atlanta to Detroit may have to be content with hamburger or chicken salad.

output, firms could sell more products at lower prices—even after figuring in the cost of advertising. Figure 10 illustrates this result. Also, *advertising helps in the marketing of new products.* If a company couldn't acquaint the public with a new product, it couldn't sell enough to cover the costs of developing it. Defenders of advertising also argue that it actually stimulates the development of new products, since in order to advertise effectively a company needs to have something new and better to offer.

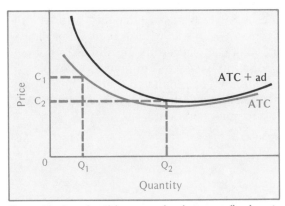

Figure 10 An advertising campaign increases fixed costs and shifts ATC up to ATC + ad. But advertising increases sales volume from Q_1 to Q_2 and unit costs fall. When firms set MC = MR, the result may be lower prices and higher volume as consumers move down their demand curves.

The critics don't buy these arguments either. They say that for *every company that reduces its costs and prices through advertising, there are probably others that raise their costs and charge the consumer more.* Certainly it would be hard to prove that automobiles would cost *more* if they weren't advertised! And in some industries each company's advertising is cancelled out by other companies' advertising. Cigarette advertising doesn't appear to sell more cigarettes; it only serves to keep the major producers from losing their shares of the market to other cigarette producers. Advertising may help to capture a share of the market for a new product or a new company, but this isn't necessarily beneficial to consumers. Perhaps the old product was just as good as the new one. Some critics, such as John Kenneth Galbraith, hold that *advertising stimulates people to want goods that they wouldn't want otherwise.* Thus advertising has helped to build up a transportation system based on the private automobile, a more costly form of transportation than commuter railroads and buslines.

The issues are complex and highly debatable. However the gains and costs of advertising may balance out, it's safe to say that advertising will be around for a long time. It's built into our capitalistic economy. Misleading or unethical advertising is prohibited under the Wheeler-Lea Amendment to the Federal Trade Commission Act. The Commission often issues orders to advertisers to cease and desist from advertising practices that it considers illegal. Not long ago, for example, the FTC ordered egg producers to stop claiming that eggs do not contribute to high blood cholesterol levels and heart disease. The manufacturers of Listerine and Wonderbread were ordered to broadcast commercials correcting claims made in previous advertising. And some years ago Geritol was fined $50,000 for advertising that its product cured "tired blood."

Even socialist and communist economies find a place for advertising. In 1966 the Soviet government set up an ad agency called Soyuztorgreklama (National Trade Advertising) to help create demand for new types of consumer goods. One of its clients is a factory in Minsk that produces TV sets. The factory has placed ads in trade magazines describing its latest models: "The novelty of the year—Horizon

Extended Example
The Rent-a-Car War

Life is never very quiet among the big car rental companies, but in the fall of 1975 the price discounts began flying like shrapnel. National Car Rental System announced in October that it was charging a plain flat rate for its subcompacts, without the usual separate charge for mileage. The rate was about $5 less than Hertz and Avis were charging.

Why did National cut its price? According to some industry people, National had been losing some of its market share to fourth-ranked Budget Rent-a-Car Corporation. In the previous three years Budget claimed to have increased its share of the important airport market from 5% to 11%, largely at National's expense.

National's price cut was soon met by its competitors. One industry spokesman said, "You've got to meet competition first and worry about profits later." The war raged in the subcompact sector, comprising about 10% of the market, with the losses being made up on the more profitable standard-size cars. The leading companies not only cut prices but raised their advertising budgets: the president of Hertz even declared that it was "an advertising war more than a price war."

Some of the bystanders shared in the casualties. The small independent car rental agencies were reportedly losing business to the heavily advertised price-cutters. The little agencies, with a third or more of their fleets in small cars, lacked the resources to compete. One harassed president, quoted by *Business Week,* predicted that in the course of the struggle "they are going to destroy a lot of small competitors."

107," or "Horizon 104—the only first-class TV set in the country." Some Soviet factories spend relatively large sums of money on multimedia campaigns in newspapers, magazines, movie-theater commercials, and television. Foreign companies including U.S. firms are also beginning to advertise in Soviet magazines. One enterprising firm in Hungary put up a window display in a Moscow department store showing a girl in a nightgown applying body lotion to her long, naked legs. Most of the advertising in communist countries so far is still of the informational type, designed to move goods that might not otherwise get sold, or to inform the consumer that the shortage in some good is over.

Trademarks

A trademark is a word, emblem, or symbol used to identify a product or a service. Because it identifies a product immediately as being associated with a particular company, a trademark is a type of advertising and a form of nonprice competition. Some trademarks are very old. The Nabisco trademark is based on an old religious symbol: the orb and cross. Shell Oil's trademark goes back to early nineteenth century London, when the man who founded Shell got his start selling shell-covered boxes to tourists. The Prudential Insurance Company's symbol, adopted in 1896, is the Rock of Gibraltar.

A trademark, like a patent, is property and may be sold or licensed. Manufacturers often license companies in other countries to use their trademarks, thus giving others the advantage of their own international reputation. A company may lose its right to a trademark if the mark becomes part of everyday language. Originally aspirin, cellophane, and thermos were trademarks, but they are now only words referring to types of products. The courts have held that a trademark ceases to be such when the public no longer recognizes it as belonging to a specific company.

Extended Example
How Sacred Is a Trademark?

One of the world's most valuable trademarks is the one owned by Britain's Rolls Royce, Ltd. The manufacturer of fine automobiles distinguishes its product through use of a unique radiator grill and "Flying Lady" hood ornament. The most famous Rolls Royce to bear this trademark is the Silver Cloud. In 1976 some new models were selling for $90,000.

An enterprising Florida manufacturer noticed the similarity between the Silver Cloud and old models of the Chevrolet Monte Carlo. The company began manufacturing and selling for $3,000 a customizing kit for use on the Chevrolet. The kit included a similar grill and hood ornament and was designated the Custom Cloud.

Rolls Royce was not amused. The firm brought suit in federal district court for trademark infringement. The court ruled against the Florida firm, barring further use of the distinctive emblem and name.

Oligopoly firms take their trademarks seriously!

Differentiated and nondifferentiated oligopoly

Oligopolies take different forms. They vary because they serve different kinds of markets. Some oligopoly firms produce industrial commodities to supply other manufacturing firms. Some produce goods or services for sale to final consumers. For these different markets, different selling techniques are appropriate and different forms of competition develop.

Firms producing for industrial markets often produce an undifferentiated product: aluminum, copper, steel, chemicals, construction equipment, and electrical apparatus. These commodities are fairly uniform among producers. A firm producing such products is known as a *nondifferentiated oligopoly*. Because these oligopolies are reluctant to engage in price competition, they compete by offering better service or more advanced research and development. They will work closely with customers to fill the needs of each more completely than rival firms.

Firms producing for final consumers have greater opportunities for nonprice competition. The product of one firm can be more easily distinguished from others. Oligopolies producing such products are known as *differentiated oligopolies.* Brand loyalty can be established through advertising and product differentiation. Product uniqueness helps to move a firm's demand curve to the right and protect its market share.

Oligopoly firms often spend vast sums of money to develop a corporate symbol appropriate to the firm's image. In recent years oligopolies like A & P, Exxon, and United Airlines have employed specialized research organizations to determine the most marketable company trademark or "logo." In one case, however, results of the corporate design campaign were somewhat ludicrous. In the mid-1970s, the National Broadcasting Company spent fourteen months and an estimated $750,000 to replace its old NBC emblem with a simple N composed of red and blue wedges. The design was believed to impart "the bold look of strength and modernity." It was flashed on television screens 1,150 times in the first month in an effort to implant the new image firmly in the consciousness of the viewing public. Too late, NBC learned that substantially the same design had earlier been adopted by the Nebraska Educational Television Network. To add insult to injury, the competing design had been developed in only one day at a cost of less than $100! Eventually, NBC made an out-of-court settlement to the Nebraska station in return for exclusive use of the trademark.

Positioning

Firms in oligopoly or monopolistic competition often compete for a "position" in the market. **"Positioning"** is a way of aiming a product at a particular market. In this way a product is differentiated from rival products aimed at consumers in general. Thus an aspirin tablet can be advertised as especially effective for arthritis pain, or for women, or for adults under particular stress. Cough medicines can

be billed as nighttime remedies or as especially effective for coughs with runny nose. The phrase, "We're number two. We try harder" was very effective for a car-rental firm that wanted the public to think of it whenever it thought of the number one firm. Some beer is sold for the sportsman, some for the family man, and some for sophisticates (though few people can tell one brand from another if they're blindfolded). In the same way, manufacturers of perfumes and hair colorings aim their products at the simple country lass, the career girl on the go, or the modern mom.

Apparently, it is more profitable for a firm to have an ensured position in one segment of a market than to compete over a wide range with all the other firms in the industry. If you can convince the modern moms that your hair preparation is necessary for them and that it is the only one worth buying, your firm's demand curve will shift rightward and become less elastic. This will enable your firm to make greater economic profits than it might otherwise.

Pros and cons of oligopoly

How does oligopoly affect us?

Oligopoly should also be evaluated in terms of the principles of efficiency and equity. To the extent that oligopoly firms behave as monopolists, the disadvantages of monopoly apply. There are other circumstances that bear on the results of oligopoly.

Efficiency

Oligopoly may improve efficiency in the economy. Oligopolized industries are often characterized by high initial capital requirements, effectively barring entry of new firms to the industry. But a few large firms may serve the entire market at lower unit costs by operating productive capital at a larger volume of output. Price may still be greater than minimum average costs, yielding economic profit. But oligopoly firms may compete for greater market share by investing profits in research and development. In this way oligopoly profits may finance technical progress, although sometimes there may be wasteful duplication of research efforts.

Over time oligopoly may have a worse effect on efficiency. Efficiency in the use of productive resources depends on steady growth in employment and output. When demand fluctuates, changes in prices will help to prevent sharp changes in resource use. In particular, a decline in demand should lead to a price decrease to stimulate sales and to maintain plant operation at optimum levels. This is not likely to happen in an oligopolized industry.

We have seen how a kinked demand curve encourages price stability. When demand falls, oligopoly firms are likely to reduce production and employment rather than price. The result is to aggravate the problem of reduced demand, increasing unemployment and intensifying a recession.

Cost-push inflation may lead to equally damaging effects in oligopoly industries. When prices rise independently of a rise in demand, the economy is said to be experiencing *cost-push inflation*. Cost-push inflation often originates in strongly unionized industries and in industries producing basic industrial commodities. Both are characteristics of oligopolized industries. The market power of oligopolies may allow them to pass on their high labor costs to their industrial customers. There is less incentive to resist labor demands and the demands of materials suppliers. Because all firms in the industry are equally affected by cost increases, they may be expected to follow closely the price changes of the industry price leader. Again, the effect is to aggravate the problem of cost-push inflation and worsen the tendency toward instability in output and employment.

Equity

The similarities with monopoly suggest damage to the principle of equity from oligopoly. There is an additional consideration among oligopoly firms in the United States.

The economic power wielded by large firms may have led to the development of offsetting power in labor unions and in government. Economist John Kenneth Galbraith coined the phrase "countervailing power" to describe the power of industrial unions and of government regulatory agencies. These giants may serve to hold down the power of each other. On the other hand, they may also overwhelm individual consumers who have no similar means of combining to achieve common goals.

Summary

Most imperfect competition is described as monopolistic competition or oligopoly. In monopolistic competition many firms compete to sell differentiated products. Demand is downward sloping but the easy entry of new firms pushes individual demand curves to the left. The result may be no economic profit in the long run. But still firms will be producing less than their optimum level of output and at higher than minimum costs. There will be too many firms for efficient operation and heavy expenditures for product differentiation.

Monopolistic competition violates the principle of efficiency by misallocation of resources. It may enhance the principle of equity by allowing small businesses to operate; but many will not be profitable and must fail.

In oligopoly a few large firms control industry output. Capital costs are high and technology is complex, impeding the entry of competing firms. The small number of firms means that pricing and output decisions in one firm depend strongly on decisions in the others. The result may be a degree of formal or informal collusion.

Duopoly is a condition where the market is divided between two large firms. When there are several firms, a firm's demand curve is kinked at the customary price. Firms resist price changes; price rigidity means that cost changes will affect profits only in the short run. Price changes ultimately depend on action by the industry price leader. Oligopolies sometimes practice mark-up pricing.

A cartel is a formal agreement to fix price and output among firms, but cartels are illegal in the United States. Oligopolies may compete through nonprice competition: advertising, trademarks, customer service, research and development, and positioning.

Oligopoly may improve efficiency by operating few plants at optimum volume. But oligopoly contributes to instability in resource use by maintaining prices in a time of falling demand and by aggravating cost-push inflation. Oligopoly violates the principle of equity by encouraging the growth of "countervailing power."

Key Words and Phrases

- **monopolistic competition** a condition in which many small sellers compete to sell differentiated products.
- **product differentiation** efforts to distinguish a product from another similar one.
- **oligopoly** a condition in which a few large sellers control most of the output of an industry.
- **merger** combination of the productive assets of two or more firms into a single larger firm.
- **collusion** an agreement among two or more firms to cooperate in setting price and output.
- **kinked demand curve** a demand curve for oligopolies with a bend (kink) at the customary price; demand above the kink is elastic while below it demand is inelastic.
- **duopoly** a condition in which two large firms share the market for a particular good.
- **price rigidity** a tendency for prices to remain constant in spite of the existence of a surplus or scarcity.
- **price leader** a firm which normally is the first to signal a price change in a particular industry.
- **mark-up pricing** a practice of adding a fixed percentage to the average total costs of producing a good or service.
- **cartel** a formal agreement among producers to regulate prices and output.
- **basing point** a geographic location used as the basis for setting price plus transportation charges to the point of delivery.
- **trademarks** distinguishing symbols used to promote identification of a particular firm and its product.

- **positioning** aiming a product at a particular segment of a larger market.
- **countervailing power** the development of organized power to offset power elsewhere in industry.
- **cost-push inflation** price increases that result from higher resource prices, often higher wage rates.

Questions for Review

1. Explain the process by which ease of entry in monopolistic competition eliminates all economic profits. Why is the final result zero economic profits, but still greater than minimum average total costs?

2. Discuss the advantages and disadvantages of monopolistic competition in terms of efficiency and equity. What policy is appropriate?

3. How is duopoly different from oligopoly? How does the difference affect demand curves?

4. Discuss the advantages and disadvantages of price rigidity. Why is price leadership important in oligopoly?

5. Use the following hypothetical data to calculate elasticity for every price change along the demand curve. What is the marginal revenue associated with every price change? What price will the firm set?

Price	Quantity demanded
20	0
15	50
10	100
5	125

6. How is a payoff matrix useful? Under what conditions can a firm avoid the uncertainties associated with a payoff matrix?

7. Define: collusion, differentiated oligopoly.

8. We have shown how price rigidity increases oligopoly profits when new technology reduces costs of production. Are there some benefits for consumers when the opposite takes place: that is, when inflation *increases* costs of production? How do oligopoly firms deal with this situation?

31

Market Power and Public Policy

Is big business good or bad? Americans tend to distrust big business, and we were the first country to pass laws restricting the growth of business firms. Our courts, acting upon the laws, have forced some big firms to break up and prevented others from merging. By limiting the power of big business, we have sought to prevent the growth of monopoly and oligopoly in the American economy.

Our contradictory attitudes

Still we have some of the world's largest corporations. Every year *Fortune* magazine publishes a list of the 500 largest corporations in the United States. These corporations control about two-thirds of the assets of American industry. In terms of employment, one percent of the country's business firms employ 60 percent of the business-employed workers. General Motors alone employs hundreds of thousands of workers; its total output is roughly equal to the gross national product of Belgium.

Some of our most important industries are dominated by just a few companies. In 1977 no more than four large companies accounted for at least 75 percent of total production in aluminum, light bulbs, flat glass, breakfast cereals, chewing gum, cigarettes, sewing machines, auto tires, and motor vehicles. One company produces about a third of the pig iron made in the United States and more than a quarter of the steel ingots.

Yet in a land of bigness we honor the little man. Most Americans have at some time in their lives had an ambition to go into business for themselves, and many of us have done so. Our government has a Small Business Administration to help small, struggling firms to survive. At the same time, we admire the executives who run large corporations and fly from city to city in company planes.

These contradictions are rooted deep in the history of our country. For our first hundred years the United States was a land of small farmers and tradesmen. Even the plantations of the South, worked by black slaves, were not very large by present standards. The political ideas of Americans reflected the con-

ditions of their economic life. But after the Civil War great changes began to take place in the U.S. economy. Railroads were laid from the Atlantic to the Pacific, bringing the grain of the Midwest to the growing cities of the East. New business firms began to consider the whole country their market. The wider market encouraged mass production using machines that could turn out a much faster flow of goods. At the same time a revolution was taking place in agriculture: the reaper, the combine harvester, and steam-powered threshing and husking machines increased output per farm worker. Americans began to leave the farms for the cities where they became industrial workers and consumers for giant manufacturing firms.

The first great merger movement

The late nineteenth century was a period of phenomenal industrial growth, particularly in the raw materials and transportation industries. In the 20 years after 1878, the volume of industrial production, the number of industrial workers, and the number of factories more than doubled. Railroad mileage increased from 93,262 miles in 1880 to 190,000 miles in 1900. A group of creative entrepreneurs developed who soon became famous for their aggressive pursuit of wealth and power. Among them were the oilman John D. Rockefeller, the steel magnate Andrew Carnegie, and railroad builders Cornelius Vanderbilt, Leland Stanford, Collis P. Huntington, Henry Villard, and James J. Hill.

The vehicle these men used to build their empires was the corporation. The corporate form enabled them to raise large amounts of capital through the sale of stock. It also made it easy for large enterprises to acquire small specialized firms and to build powerful market organizations. *Holding companies* enabled one individual or group to effectively control a number of separate corporations. A holding company produced no good or service. It was created solely for the purpose of owning a majority of the stock in each subsidiary company. A famous holding company was the Standard Oil Company of New Jersey, created by John D. Rockefeller to own many small operating companies producing petroleum products.

Another way of building large corporations was through *merger:* the combination of two or more independent corporations into one. In this way a large firm might acquire smaller firms. The American Tobacco Company and the American Sugar Refining Company were formed by mergers in 1890 and 1891. Mergers were of two kinds: *horizontal* when the firms were direct competitors, and *vertical* when one firm was the supplier or the customer of the other.

Horizontal mergers

Horizontal mergers were most common in railroading and in the telephone industry where it was important to have smooth coordination among different parts of the country. Furthermore, firms in these industries required large amounts of investment in capital equipment before they could begin to function. This made it advantageous for small firms to combine their resources to provide dependable service over a larger geographical area. Horizontal mergers also helped to reduce unneeded duplication of facilities. Two separate railroads serving the same route would be economically inefficient unless there was enough demand for their services to keep both of them operating at a sufficiently high level.

Horizontal mergers helped firms to reduce costs through economies of scale. Figure 1 shows the effect of market size on unit cost. Firms A and B provide service to a market in which the quantity demanded is 10,000 units per day. If the two firms divide the market equally, each will operate at a volume of 5,000 units and a unit cost of $2.

However, firm A by itself could satisfy the entire demand at a unit cost of only $1. This market is too small to enable both firms to operate at the most efficient, lowest cost level of output. A single firm providing a larger volume can spread the costs of capital equipment over many more units of service.

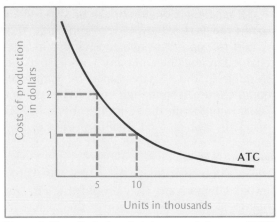

Figure 1 The effect of market size on cost. Suppose 10,000 units are to be produced and sold in one market. If firms A and B each produce 5,000 units, unit cost is $2; however, firm A alone could produce all 10,000 units at a unit cost of only $1.

The railroad builders were the first to take advantage of these economies of scale. Cornelius Vanderbilt established the first through-route from New York to Chicago. He acquired ownership or effective control of many railroad lines connecting the rich agricultural and manufacturing areas of the Northeast. Along routes where he faced competition he would reduce freight charges below costs and drive his weaker rivals out of business. Then he would make up his losses by charging higher freight rates on other routes. He bought the stock of failing roads at low prices: the New York and Harlem Railroad in 1862 and later its competitors, the Hudson River Railroad and the New York Central Railroad running from Albany to Buffalo. He tried unsuccessfully to take over the Erie Railroad, but his acquisition of the Lake Shore and Michigan Southern in 1873 extended his route to Chicago.

Price discrimination Vanderbilt was able to maximize revenues through a complex structure of discriminatory freight rates. Different rates were possible because of differences in the elasticity of demand along different routes and among different commodities. The elasticity of demand for rail service depended on (1) the availability of substitutes and (2) the value of the freight.

If customers could choose between competing rail lines or between rail and barge, they would be more sensitive to changes in rates charged by any one company. For instance, ore shippers in the Mesabi Range of Minnesota could choose to send their iron ore by lake and canal transport to the foundries in Pennsylvania. This kept railroad freight rates fairly low along this route. On the other hand, cotton growers in the deep South who needed to ship their cotton to textile mills in the North had fewer alternatives. They could be charged higher freight rates. Moreover, the high rates charged on northbound cotton made it possible for the railroads to reduce southbound rates on manufactured goods. This added insult to injury. It gave northern manufacturers a cost advantage over competitors in the South and held back the industrialization of the South.

The second factor in price discrimination, freight value, was equally important. Manufactured goods are more compact than bulky commodities like ore, grain, and other primary products; hence they tend to be higher in value per carload. Also, manufacturers could often create their own transportation services if they chose. For these reasons the rates for manufactured goods produced in the Northeast tended to be lower than for bulky raw materials from the West and South. Since the shipment of low-value, bulky commodities to eastern factories often left freight cars empty for the "back haul," it cost the railroads very little to carry manufactured goods southward and westward.

In all these ways discriminatory freight rates had significant effects on the prosperity and growth of industry in different regions of the country. The result was growing political pressure against horizontal railroad mergers among farmers of the South and Midwest.

Vertical mergers

Vertical mergers occurred in industries that required a dependable supply of inputs at every stage of processing. Steel-makers needed a steady supply of iron ore and coal for making pig iron and basic steel. The steel itself then had to be rolled or drawn into rods, sheets, beams, and other structural forms. Many small firms joined together to form vertically integrated concerns.

Andrew Carnegie was an industrial organizer in iron and steel who created and combined many different firms. He finally sold his interests to J. P. Morgan, the financier who formed the United States Steel Company. Carnegie began by investing in a firm that built railroad bridges. This led him into steel-making and the manufacture of locomotives. Carnegie and his associates soon acquired a leading position in the manufacture of steel. In 1870 with the building of the Lucy Furnace, they began turning out their own pig iron from which steel is manufactured. By 1877 the Carnegie mills were making about a seventh of the Bessemer steel in the United States. In 1882 the company acquired a major interest in the H. C. Frick Coke Company, which controlled deposits of good coking coal needed for blast furnaces. The final step in the process of vertical integration was taken in 1896 when Carnegie obtained a lease on iron ore fields in the Mesabi area of Minnesota. The ore was transported by company-owned boats and railroads to the coke ovens in Pittsburgh. The only stage of production not included in Carnegie's empire was the large-scale rolling of steel products such as tubes and wire.

John D. Rockefeller accomplished a similar feat with the Standard Oil Corporation. Rockefeller began as the operator of pipelines carrying crude oil from the oil fields to refineries. As an important supplier of pipeline services to well owners, he was able to buy crude oil at low prices. As an important supplier of crude oil to refiners, he was able to sell at high prices. High profits on pipeline operations enabled him to buy up oil wells, on the one hand, and refineries, on the other. By the early 1880s he had brought approximately 80% of the nation's refining capacity and 90% of the pipelines within the scope of his organization. Moreover, he had acquired a large interest in railway tank cars.

Trusts

In the earlier years of industrial combination, a common method of integration was the **trust.** The stockholders of several corporations turned their stock over to a small group of managers who held the stock as trustees, i.e., with the power to vote for the directors of each corporation. The trustees were thus able to manage the combination of firms as a single unit. John D. Rockefeller established the Standard Oil Company of Ohio as a trust in 1882. His example was widely followed, and by 1890 there were trusts in sugar, lead, whiskey, cottonseed oil, and salt. In 1892 the Supreme Court of Ohio declared trusts to be illegal. Rockefeller reorganized the company as a holding company under the more hospitable laws of New Jersey, naming it the Standard Oil Company of New Jersey.

Antimerger legislation

The great merger movement of the late 1800s aroused much public opposition, particularly from those who felt they had been treated unfairly by the giants. The farmers of the Midwest were especially angry about the discriminatory freight rates they had to pay on their grain shipments. The result was a populist movement demanding government control over the industrial giants. The farm vote was important to many members of Congress. Under populist pressure two important laws were enacted: the Interstate Commerce Act of 1887 establishing the Interstate Commerce Commission (ICC) with the power to control rates and practices of interstate railroads; and the Sherman Antitrust Act of 1890.

The Sherman Antitrust Act

Section 1 of the Sherman Act declared illegal "every contract, combination in the form of trust or otherwise, or conspiracy, in restraint of trade or commerce among the several States, or with foreign nations." Section 2 forbade any person to monopolize or to attempt, combine, or conspire to monopolize such trade.

The intention of the law was broadly to condemn all actions designed to achieve a monopoly structure in industry. But because the language was broad, it was also vague. The law failed to spell out exactly what actions were forbidden. It left to the courts the responsibility for interpreting the law, case by case, and applying it where market power was believed to be excessive. The courts have not been consistent. In one early decision the Supreme Court held that the first section of the act could not be read literally as outlawing "every contract . . . in restraint of trade" since any business contract might restrain the parties in some degree. That section, the Court declared, should be understood to prohibit only unreasonable restraint. This declaration came to be known as the "rule of reason." It left the way open for many more combinations and the growth of even greater market power.

Prosecution under the Sherman Act was uneven, and mergers continued. In 1899 the number of new mergers reached 1,208 and giants like International Harvester and National Biscuit Company were formed.

During the administration of Theodore Roosevelt (1901–1908), antitrust activity increased. Roosevelt moved against combinations in a number of industries and was supported by the Supreme Court. In 1911 the Court ordered Standard Oil of New Jersey and the American Tobacco Company to break up into smaller competing enterprises and to cease certain "unfair competitive practices."

The Clayton Antitrust Act

In 1914, during the administration of Woodrow Wilson, Congress passed new legislation defining certain business practices which were to be forbidden. The Clayton Act prohibited the following practices "where the effect may be to substantially lessen competition or tend to create a monopoly":

Discriminatory price cutting where rivals may be forced out of business leaving one firm in control of the market;

Extended Example
Giant of the Steel Industry

The nation's economy is built on iron and steel. We live in it, ride on it, and cook on it. Iron and steel form the building blocks of modern industry. Iron was produced in America as far back as colonial times. Forges turned out many of the plows, hammers, and machines needed by our developing nation. But production was small scale, using local ores and charcoal and serving local markets. Production costs were high because of heavy initial capital investment and the heavy use of labor. Labor was essential for pounding the pig iron to produce wrought iron. The Bessemer process and the open-hearth process, developed in the late 1800s, removed the impurities from iron through less costly methods and yielded finer grades of metal.

Andrew Carnegie grew up with the iron and steel industry. His family migrated from Scotland when he was a boy and settled near Pittsburgh. Pittsburgh was becoming an important center of iron production and rail traffic because of its location near the major coal fields. Carnegie quickly saw the potential profitability of combining the interests of the two industries. With his brother and some friends, he established firms for producing iron rails, railroad bridges, locomotives, and sleeping cars.

Carnegie was less interested in the purely technical aspects of production than in developing long-run strategy. He hired experts in the detailed operation of the enterprises so that he could concentrate on financial planning. His acquaintance with banker Junius S. Morgan introduced him to the world of finance.

The earliest Carnegie enterprises were partnerships; but in 1874 Pennsylvania passed a law authorizing "limited partnership associations" similar to corporations, and the firms were reorganized. Then followed expansion into production of raw materials: coking coal to fuel the new furnaces and limestone and ore mines on Lake Superior. The process of vertical integration was completed with the acquisition of ore shippers on the Great Lakes and firms producing all the major end products. Finally, the separate operating companies were brought together under New Jersey corporation law into the Carnegie Company.

In the meantime, competitors were also establishing fully integrated steel firms. One strong competitor was J. P. Morgan, son of Junius Morgan.

Under competition, production was highly unstable because of instability in manufacturers' demand for capital equipment. When sales dropped, overhead costs per unit of steel output soared. Firms tried to increase volume by drastically cutting price. But demand was inelastic in the short run, and the weaker firms were forced into bankruptcy. Informal pools were formed to allocate market shares, but these were not very successful.

Competition was worrisome to the steel giants, so in 1901 the three major steel producers joined to form the United States Steel Corporation, with outstanding capital stock worth more than a billion dollars and with control of three-fifths the nation's steel business. The goal of the new combined firm was, "a completely rounded system of coordinated plants adapted to the entire process of mining and transportation, and of transforming raw materials into . . . highly finished products . . . at the lowest cost." Plants were modernized and made more efficient; new technology was installed and a complete system of cost accounting was introduced. But perhaps most significant was the introduction of a bonus system for rewarding employees on the basis of merit.

The combination was more profitable than competition had been. By operating its facilities at full capacity the firm was able to supply 70% of the nation's steel output and to achieve substantial cost reductions. But it faced a delicate problem. Its dominance of the steel industry left it open to attack from the Antitrust Division of the Department of Justice. However, U.S. Steel Board Chairman, Elbert H. Gary, a lawyer, believed that the firm would not be dissolved if "the intentions of the managers are good, (and) . . . there is no disposition to exercise a monopoly or to restrain legitimate trade." Competitive *conduct*, not its monopoly *structure*, would justify U.S. Steel's existence.

U.S. Steel did not attempt to monopolize output completely but instead encouraged competition. By its pricing policies it aimed at securing stable and profitable revenues for all firms in the industry. When demand fell, it kept prices high to avoid bankruptcies among small firms. When demand rose, it avoided price increases so as to discourage new entry and excess capacity. Chairman Gary hosted a series of dinners for industry executives and established U.S. Steel as price leader. Identical prices were established through the basing-point system, which set all delivered prices in the nation at price plus freight charges from Pittsburgh.

The administration of President Theodore Roosevelt was notable for its vigorous prosecution of antitrust violations. U.S. Steel operated in the belief that responsible business giants should cooperate with government, turning over their records freely and justifying their policies. In this way, they believed they could counter the efforts of some groups to break up the large firms. In 1911, however, steel's anticompetitive practices were challenged by the Justice Department. The judgment went in favor of the company. The Supreme Court ruled that the Sherman Act could be used only against unreasonable restraints of trade. Standard Oil and American Tobacco Company were illegal under the law, but U.S. Steel had not abused its power to restrain competition.

During World War II, U.S. Steel continued as the nation's largest single producer of steel products. After the war, the firm diversified into chemicals, cement, natural gas, electric cable, and mining equipment. (In 1975 more than half the firm's profits came from its nonsteel divisions.)

After the war, the firm was slow to modernize, and imported steel gained a foothold in American markets. The peak year for imports was 1971 when foreign producers supplied 18% of the American market. U.S. Steel charged that Japan and Common Market countries were engaging in illegal trade practices to undercut American-made steel. Specifically, steel-makers abroad receive government subsidies for their exports so as to keep price low and maintain

Andrew Carnegie

employment in their local steel industry. But American-made steel must pay a tax when it is sold in their markets. The result has been falling profits at precisely the time when steel-makers critically need funds for new capital investment. During the 1970s, profits have been less than 3¢ per dollar of sales.

It is estimated that American steel producers must increase capacity by at least 20% by 1983 to keep up with rising demand. This amounts to about 30 million tons of new steel capacity at a cost of about 15 billion dollars. Five years are necessary for planning and constructing new steel capacity, during which expanding firms suffer substantial losses. Without new investment the market will be increasingly supplied by imports. Already Russia out-produces the United States and Japan is catching up fast.

The American steel industry wants government to prohibit imports from nations which have engaged in certain unfair practices. U.S. Steel has a suit in New York Customs Court against the Common Market for rebating taxes on their steel exports. A decision in favor of U.S. Steel would mean as much as a 20% increase in import tariffs on steel and substantially reduce competition in domestic markets.

Tying contracts under which buyers are required to purchase the entire line of a supplier's products, thus reducing competition among suppliers;

Interlocking directorates when the directors of one company serve on the boards of other firms in the same industry with power to direct pricing and output policies as if they were one firm;

Stock ownership in competing companies where this would enable the companies to be operated unfairly to competition.

The Federal Trade Commission

At the same time, Congress established the Federal Trade Commission (FTC) as a watchdog to seek out unfair methods of competition in interstate commerce. The FTC was given two powers: (1) to investigate trade practices and report its findings, and (2) to issue a complaint against any firm that it found to be practicing unfair competition. After considering testimony by those concerned, the commission might either dismiss the complaint or issue an order to cease and desist the unfair practice. Over the years the FTC developed a system of trade practice conferences through which members of an industry are guided as to what constitutes unfair competition.

In 1938 the FTC Act was amended by the *Wheeler-Lea Act* giving the commission power to forbid false or misleading advertising. Congress specifically made it illegal to publish false claims for food, drugs, cosmetics, and therapeutic devices.

The second great merger movement

Experience showed, however, that antitrust laws were unable to prevent the growth of market concentration. The Clayton Act specified certain actions as illegal, but this encouraged firms to find other ways to increase their size and power. Furthermore, the courts still clung to the "rule of reason" in deciding whether or not combinations were in restraint of trade. In 1920 a case was brought against

Extended Example
Menace at the Breakfast Table

"If the FTC can convince the courts of the validity of its shared monopoly theory, it can declare over half of all the industries in America—producing over two-thirds of our manufactured products—guilty and break all of them, and along with it the free market system," said William E. LaMothe, president of Kellogg Company.

It is natural that business firms should feel themselves in conflict with a government regulatory commission. In fact, *they are supposed to be adversaries.* Business firms have as their objective to serve the public by providing goods that can be sold at a profit. A regulatory commission has as its objective to serve the public by protecting consumers against unfair business practices. To determine the precise point at which business methods become unfair practices is not a simple task. Occasionally, it may seem that business firms are penalized for performing too well—for meeting too completely the needs of the market and for being too successful at earning a profit.

The issue then becomes: *At what point does success become a threat to competition?*

The question has become important in recent years because of the increasing size of the U.S. market and increasing opportunities for business diversification. With more efficient transportation and communication facilities, firms have been able to consolidate many operations under a single management. Centralization of financial decision-making, purchasing, and advertising has reduced unit costs and increased profits. When profits are re-invested in expansion or greater diversification, then success yields more success!

A 1976 case before the Federal Trade Commission illustrates the complexity of the problem. According to FTC and Justice Department lawyers, the breakfast cereal industry in the United States is a "shared monopoly." A few large companies use their market power to collect monopoly profits and to exclude competition. Through their diversified products, Kellogg, General Mills, General Foods, and Quaker Oats provide more than 90% of our breakfast cereals. The suit now before the Commission asks that the *three* largest firms be required to sell off one or more of the brands they now produce. If the courts agree, this will establish a significant new precedent in antitrust law. The precedent could then be used in other industries in which a few large firms produce a number of diversified products. Some possible targets might be autos, steel, and electrical goods.

Seven out of ten Americans consume cereals, at least occasionally. Industry sales grew from $165 million in 1950 to $2.67 billion in 1975. The largest firm is Kellogg, which supplies 56% of the U.S. market, including seven top-selling brands. Profits were $103 million in 1975 on sales of $1.2 billion. General Mills is next with 21% of the market and General Foods accounts for 16%. Quaker Oats supplies 9% and is not included in the suit.

The FTC claims that increased competition in the industry would save customers $128 million each year. The Commission charges that the firms maximize monopoly profits through tacit agreements not to cut price. Kellogg acts as the price leader. "Gentlemen's agreements" have also eliminated the use of package premiums and coordinated advertising budgets of cooperating firms. Firms have set up barriers to entry by brand proliferation, by control of supermarket shelf space, and by extensive advertising, $81 million in 1970. New firms in the industry would have to spend as much as $10 million to introduce a cereal to compete with the more than 100 well-known brands.

For instance, when small firms tried to introduce new granola cereals, the big four introduced their own nationally advertised brands and captured most of the market.

The President's Council on Wage and Price Stability is also interested in the outcome of the FTC suit. The Council believes that shared monopoly and administered pricing are partly responsible for the recent surge of price inflation. In fact, during the recession of 1973–1975, grain prices declined but the prices of cereals continued to rise.

What are the important characteristics of the cereal industry? What market structure does it resemble most closely? How can you explain rising cereal prices when grain prices were falling?

United States Steel, which then had 60% of the nation's iron and steel capacity. The court ruled that the company had not committed specific illegal acts. It found no reason to break up the corporation as long as it did not abuse its market power. *Bigness in itself was not illegal.*

The Clayton Act may even have encouraged mergers. The act prohibited a firm from acquiring control of a competing corporation through ownership of its stock, but it did not prevent the firm from buying it outright. The 1920s saw a new growth of industrial concentration. In 1929 the numbers of mergers reached a new peak of 1,245—largely in the young communications and automobile industries. Markets were becoming larger, increasing the need for large-scale industrial operations. Typical of the times was the growth of radio broadcasting and the stimulus this gave to nationwide advertising by the industrial giants.

The Great Depression antitrust action

The 1930s brought a wave of concern over the plight of small business firms, pushed to the wall by the depression and by the growing power of the giants. Franklin Roosevelt's New Deal tried to protect weak firms by encouraging industrial cooperation rather than competition. The *National Recovery Act* set up industry boards to stabilize business practices and keep prices at a level that would enable small operators to stay in business.

The *Robinson-Patman Act of 1936* amended the Clayton Act to forbid price cutting when used as a weapon to destroy competition. Chain stores had used their market power to cut prices and force small retailers out of business. The law forbade wholesale discounts to large retailers unless it could be shown that discounts were justified by savings in costs. The stated aim of the act was to preserve competition, but it may actually have protected inefficiency since many of the small firms could not have survived in competition against more efficient large-scale retailers.

The *Miller-Tydings Act of 1937* went still farther in the direction of regulating retail prices. It put the stamp of federal approval on state "fair trade laws." These laws permitted manufacturers of branded, trade-marked goods to set the prices at which distributors could sell their goods. The main purpose of a brand name was to shield the product from competition in the marketplace. Its effectiveness would be destroyed if retailers began cutting prices.

The movement favoring resale price maintenance had begun as far back as the 1880s among manufacturers trying to promote brand names for their products. In the 1930s most states passed laws requiring *all* dealers to sell at a manufacturer's recommended price if *some* dealers did. "Fair trade laws" applied mainly in drugs and pharmaceuticals, books, photographic supplies, liquor, some household appliances, radio and TV sets, watches, jewelry, and bicycles.

Post-World War II antitrust activity

In the 1950s and 1960s the fair trade laws became unpopular. The growth of discount stores increased the public's sensitivity to higher prices, as did the inflationary trend of the 1970s. Moreover, the whole principle of the fair trade laws ran counter to the traditional antitrust approach favoring price competition. A Department of Justice study of the question estimated that "fair trade" was costing consumers $2.1 billion a year. In 1976 Congress repealed the Miller-Tydings Act.

The strength of the second great merger movement led to another important piece of legislation in 1950, the *Celler-Kefauver Amendment* to the Clayton Act. The new law closed the loophole which had allowed firms to expand by buying the assets of competing firms. It forbade any acquisition or merger which would "substantially . . . lessen competition, or tend to create a monopoly."

The Celler-Kefauver Amendment seemed to focus antitrust law back toward the *structure* of an industry. Supporters of the law felt that to permit monopolistic *structure* would eventually bring on monopoly *conduct*. Therefore, they sought to prevent the growth of monopoly in its earliest stages. Horizontal mergers are now forbidden except where the merger of two very small firms will help them to compete more successfully against a dominant firm. Vertical mergers are examined closely and forbidden where the effect is to give one firm a substantial advantage and to close out competition from other firms.

A landmark in the fight against vertical mergers was the case of the Brown Shoe Manufacturing Company in 1962. The company had petitioned for approval of its acquisition of Kinney Shoe Stores, the eighth largest shoe retailer in the nation. Although neither firm was very large, the Supreme Court ruled against the acquisition. The decision was based on the belief that merger of these firms would be a start down the road toward greater concentration in the shoe industry.

The third great merger movement

Despite all this legislation, another period of mergers and acquisitions came in the 1960s. In the years 1948 through 1959 corporate mergers had averaged 428 per year, fewer by far than in the 1920s. But in the 1960s the average rose to more than 1,250. These new combinations took a different form, however; corporations expanded by acquiring firms in totally unrelated fields.

Conglomerate mergers

The name **conglomerate** was given to an industrial combination of firms in fields that might have no relation to one another. Thus Radio Corporation of America (RCA) bought the Hertz car rental agency, Columbia Broadcasting System bought Creative Playthings, and the Greyhound bus lines acquired the Armour meat-packing company. Of the 4,003 mergers in 1969, 90% were classified as conglomerates.

There were several reasons why companies branched out in this way. One was that the antitrust laws effectively prohibited horizontal and vertical mergers, but they did not prevent acquisitions in other fields. Another reason was that a corporation seeking to grow often found more profitable opportunities in other industries. A third reason was the development of computers and the scientific management techniques that they made possible. It became cheaper and easier to carry on planning, control, organizing, and other centralized functions of management, so that conglomerates were able to increase the efficiency of the companies they acquired.

Not all conglomerates were successful. A few mergers turned out to have been based on enthusiasm rather than real business prospects. Some of the firms used accounting techniques that made their earnings look larger than they really were. Afterward, of course, the new company was found to be less profitable than expected.

The goliaths

The most spectacular of the new conglomerates was the International Telephone and Telegraph Corporation (ITT) under Harold Geneen. Between 1955 and 1970, ITT's annual sales rose from $450 million to $6 billion. During this period it absorbed Sheraton Hotels, Avis car rentals, Bobbs-Merrill publishers, Levitt and Sons builders, Continental Bakeries, Smithfield hams, and other firms in the cellulose, vending-machine, and fire-protection fields.

Another famous conglomerate was Ling-Temco-Vought (LTV), founded by a World War II Navy electrician and school dropout, James J. Ling. Ling began with a small electrical contracting business in 1946. By 1967 he had acquired 80 companies in 18 industries including meat packing, sporting goods, airlines, and steel. LTV's total sales were $2.8 billion in 1968, making it 25th in the nation's top 500 industrial corporations. In 1969 the Department of Justice brought suit to force the company to divest itself of some of its acquisitions, and the firm's creditors got control of the board of directors. Ling left the company, but most of the structure he had created remained. By 1975 LTV had slipped to 37th among the country's top 500 industrial corporations.

Litton Industries began with $3 million in sales in 1953 and grew to $3.4 billion in sales in 1975. Litton is noted for its pioneering research and development, particularly in advanced military technology. It includes firms producing foods, missile guidance systems, business furniture and equipment, nuclear submarines, electronics, textbooks, and even economic development advice to foreign governments.

Textron began in 1923 as a textile firm, but it no longer produces any textiles. The company operates 27 divisions with 113 plants producing electronic equipment, aircraft, drugs, machine tools, marine engines, and helicopters.

Managing a conglomerate is a difficult job. The diversity of its operations requires special talents on the part of top management, all of which are costly and place heavy burdens on the firm's finances. But diversity is also an advantage, in that poor performance in one division may be offset by very good performance in another.

Extended Example
Merger Strategy in Japan

Big business in Japan is big by any standards. In 1967 the 100 largest companies had 36% of total manufacturing assets. Concentration was highest in iron and steel, shipbuilding, automobiles, electrical machinery, and home appliances.

After World War II, the U.S. Army of occupation brought American antitrust philosophy to Japan and broke up the big family-owned holding companies like Mitsui, Mitsubishi, Sumitomo, and Yasuda. In the early 1950s these conglomerates began to recombine and new industrial giants also appeared. Much of the impetus for their formations came from departments of the Japanese government, particularly the powerful Ministry of International Trade and Industry.

The recession of 1973–1975 hit hard in Japan and accelerated the trend toward combining many firms that were in financial trouble. Firms with excess capacity sought mergers that would permit them to lay off workers and shut down high-cost plants. Others sought agreements or cartel-like arrangements to control prices and output.

Some Japanese economists are opposed to the trend toward bigness, and the Fair Trade Commission which enforces the antitrust law has been investigating mergers to make sure they are legal. Most observers believe that the reorganization of industry will continue because otherwise many weak firms will simply go under.

Several different types of industrial reorganization have been taking place. One is in strategic industries such as computers. The government has played a leading role in the reorganization of computer manufacturers because the industry is felt to be of national concern and because it requires large capital outlays. A second group of industries, including petrochemicals and steel, has needed some sort of coordination to prevent the development of cutthroat competition. A third category of old, labor-intensive industries such as textiles, plywood, and fishing have been losing ground to competitors at home and abroad. Their reorganization has taken the form of shifting capital out of low-profit areas into new lines of production; it has involved agreements, mergers, and even bankruptcies.

A fourth category, overlapping with the third, consists of firms needing some kind of rescue operation to survive. Often the reorganization, requiring mergers and other strong measures, is led by banks. This category includes the small steel companies and the sugar industry.

Thus the government and the banks in Japan are playing an active part in guiding the development of industry. The laws may have been inspired by American antitrust philosophy, but the world of business is being run along Japanese lines.

Attacking the conglomerates

By the late 1960s the public was becoming alarmed about the power of the conglomerates. Pressures mounted in Congress for changes in the tax laws which had favored conglomerate mergers. The Department of Justice filed cases against several of the largest conglomerates testing whether the courts would find them in violation of the antitrust laws.

The case against ITT drew the greatest public attention. The Department of Justice petitioned the court to require ITT to divest itself of several recent acquisitions. Then reports appeared in the newspapers that ITT was applying political pressure to force the Department to settle the case in its favor. As a result of the publicity, ITT finally agreed to divest itself of all the recent acquisitions except the largest one—the Hartford Fire Insurance Company.

In recent years, antitrust actions have focused on *preventing* concentration in industry rather than attempting to break it up after it has developed. On balance, however, it would seem that the total effort at enforcing the antitrust laws so far has been quite small. One leading student of the problem wrote in 1959: "The total amount of money spent to enforce the antitrust laws over sixty-five years would not buy a medium-size naval vessel, and even if one adds to this figure the costs incurred by private parties in antitrust suits, the resulting sum probably would not finance a modern aircraft carrier."*

The changing philosophy of antitrust

We have seen how the courts have interpreted antitrust laws differently at different periods. They have focused either on the *structure* of an industry or on the *conduct* of firms in the industry. The early emphasis on *structure* led to the breakup of such firms as the Standard Oil Company of New Jersey and the American Tobacco Company.

Then followed a long period when the "rule of reason" was the guiding principle. A giant firm might avoid prosecution by refraining from specific acts of monopoly *conduct*. In 1945 the courts changed direction again. The Aluminum Company of America (Alcoa) was charged under the Sherman Act with monopolizing the manufacture of aluminum ingots and the sale of aluminum products. The firm had achieved market power through a basic patent and then expanded by reinvesting its profits. Its large and efficient operation discouraged the entry of other companies, and since the late 1930s Alcoa had supplied more than 90% of the market for aluminum.

Alcoa was not accused of unfair business conduct. Still, in 1945 the courts ruled against the firm on the grounds that the law prohibited the existence of so much market power. Structure, rather than conduct, was again to be the test of legality.

Recent rulings have continued to follow this principle. Some mergers have been prohibited in order to prevent monopoly "in its incipiency"—before monopoly structure can develop. Even small firms have been prohibited from merging. Brown Shoe Manufacturing Company produced only 4% of the nation's output of shoes. Kinney was the eighth largest retailer. But in 1962 the court ruled that a merger would give the combined firm power to exclude competitors and would be a start toward greater concentration in this fragmented industry.

If structure is to be the test, then what about industries in which most of the production is already in the hands of a few large firms? While the structure may not be precisely that of monopoly, the *performance* may resemble it. In industries characterized by oligopoly, firms may perform like monopolists without ever committing an illegal act. Because the firms are aware of their interdependence, they will base their price and output decisions on the expected reactions of other firms. Parallel performance among separate firms produces results similar to monopoly even without a formal agreement.

The courts have hesitated to tackle this problem. The only significant case was the one against the big three tobacco firms in 1946. American Tobacco, Liggett & Myers, and R. J. Reynolds were accused of monopoly performance because of their nearly identical prices. The court ruled that "conscious parallelism of action" is illegal and that "no formal agreement is necessary to constitute an unlawful conspiracy." Since then, the courts have retreated from the rigor of this decision, leaving the question of parallel performance still unsolved.

Regulation as an alternative

The aim of the antitrust laws is to maintain competition and prevent monopoly. In some industries, however, we accept monopoly and try to regulate it through public commissions. These industries include the public utilities—electricity, telephones, local transit, water, and gas. These are the natural monopolies we discussed earlier. There is another group of industries that aren't monopolies but are regulated because this is believed to be in the public interest. They include the following industries: railroads, oil pipelines, natural gas, motor carriers, airlines, and radio-TV communications.

* Donald J. Dewey, *Monopoly in Economics and Law* (Chicago: Rand McNally, 1959), p. 302.

Viewpoint
Today in Antitrust

Over the last several years Congress has been cooperating with the Justice Department and the Federal Trade Commission to draw up more powerful new antitrust legislation. Bills now under consideration would provide the means to: (1) block mergers before they take place so that investigation into their probable effects can be completed; and (2) give state attorneys-general power to file class action suits for triple damages in cases of price fixing or other monopolistic practices. Under the proposed law, penalties for disobeying an FTC order would rise to a maximum of $5,000 a day from the current $100 a day.

The new emphasis on antitrust action is probably an outgrowth of the inflation of the 1970s. Steadily rising prices in the face of declining demand have aroused suspicions of collusive pricing among large firms in concentrated industries. Food and fuel are among the main targets. Alleged price rigging in sugar, bread, coffee, beer, and breakfast cereal is currently under investigation. Manufacturers of drugs and hospital supplies have also been subject to complaints, along with professional associations and local real-estate boards.

In the mid-1970s the greatest attention of the trust busters was focused on allegations of monopolistic practices in the petroleum industry. In 1974 the FTC charged Exxon, Texaco, Gulf, Mobil, Standard Oil of California, Standard Oil Company (Indiana), Shell, and Atlantic Richfield with following a "common course of action" in production, transportation, and supply of crude oil to the "detriment of independent refiners."

The FTC complaint actually involved two subsidiary issues: Is competition among the majors—the "Seven Sisters"—really effective? And should the federal government continue to protect smaller independent refiners from competition with the majors?

Of the top ten U.S. corporations, five are oil companies. Exxon is the world's largest company, with revenues (in 1977) greater than many of the hundred countries in which it conducts operations. Still, it is not clear that the major firms have abused their market power, and profit rates are in line with profits in other manufacturing industries.

Under a bill introduced in Congress in 1976 the 22 largest companies would have to divest themselves of properties worth $28 billion. Each firm would be allowed to operate in only one of three areas: production, transportation, or refining and marketing. Another bill would require oil companies to dispose of their interests in competing energy sources. Oil companies account for about 18% of the nation's coal production and 32% of uranium production. Critics suspect that oil company investment in alternative energy sources is designed to slow the development of competing fuels which could undermine their oil monopoly.

Defenders of the petroleum industry claim that competition is vigorous with 10,000 companies producing oil and gas, 131 operating refineries, and 15,000 wholesaling and 200,000 retailing gasoline. Nevertheless, the major firms are interlocked into joint ventures which enhance their individual market power. They have combined their resources in major projects like the Alaska pipeline and offshore oil-producing leases. Small firms could not accumulate the funds or absorb the risks involved in such enterprises.

It is also claimed that a large vertically integrated firm can coordinate more efficiently the flow of oil to consumers. In this view, restructuring the industry would so disrupt production as to reduce supplies and force up prices. It would cause duplication of facilities and research efforts. It would reduce capital available for exploration of alternate energy sources. If these allegations are true, breakup would prevent the United States from achieving energy independence in the next decade and would be detrimental to the nation's security and defense.

The mammoth economic power of the major oil firms has been one of the reasons for the preferential treatment of small producers. The 123 independent petroleum companies are able to acquire oil cheaply under the present system. From 1959 to 1973 they were allowed favorable licenses to import crude oil under the import quota system. Then in 1974 the Federal Energy Administration adopted a cost-sharing "entitlements" program to guarantee low-priced domestic oil equally to all firms. The independents buy 46% of their crude oil from the major producers at controlled prices. The entitlements program helped independents to increase their market share from less than 20% in 1968 to almost 30% in 1975. Now the independents worry that if current arrangements are changed they will have to pay more for their oil and compete on less favorable terms.

Independents were also helped by favorable tax arrangements in recent years. The oil-depletion allowance encouraged major producers to construct surplus oil-producing capacity. When demand for oil fell, the majors would sell oil cheaply to independents. But when the energy crunch came in 1973, this supply was not available to the independents.

It seems safe to say that over the next decade pressure to break up the "Seven Sisters" will continue. An energy-conscious nation will be following almost their every move. As the oil firms move into the exploration and development of alternate energy sources, public pressure will increase. This is as it should be. Even if the oil firms are not broken up, their business is so central to our national interests as to deserve constant public scrutiny and accounting.

Do you think the "Seven Sisters" should be broken up? Will this increase efficiency? Would such an act lead to lower prices? Explain.

The problems of regulation are too complex to cover adequately in an elementary textbook. A look at the railroads will give you a very small bird's-eye view of what is involved.

The Interstate Commerce Commission

Even before passage of the Sherman Antitrust Act, state and federal governments had been regulating the railroads. The public had grown angry over collusive agreements among the railroad companies and their practice of discriminatory pricing. In 1887 Congress created the Interstate Commerce Commission (ICC) and directed it to prevent such practices. Other legislation in 1906 and 1910 strengthened the ICC, giving it more power. By the 1920s the ICC had taken over many of the functions of railroad management.

Until the 1930s the railroads were treated as if they monopolized transportation services. The original aim of the ICC was to protect the customers of the railroads from monopoly practices and to see that the roads earned no monopoly profit. But in the 1930s railroads began to face increasing competition from pipelines, highways, waterways, and air transport. By 1939 the railroads were carrying less than 63% of the intercity freight and 66% of the passenger traffic. Matters grew worse after World War II, and by the 1960s the railroads had only 40% of the intercity freight traffic and about 2.5% of the intercity passenger traffic.

The railroads found that progress had passed them by. Who was at fault? There was blame enough for everyone. The railroads were at fault for becoming rigid and bureaucratic; the unions for insisting on outmoded work rules that kept labor costs high; the ICC for preventing the railroads from adjusting their rates so as to compete with other forms of transportation; and Congress and the public for failing to see that a useful national asset was being squeezed out of existence.

Congress slowly took steps to rescue what was left. In 1964 it appropriated money to help state and local governments develop mass transit systems in urban areas. In 1970 it established Amtrak to take over the passenger business of the railroads. And in 1976 it set up

Extended Example
The Little Engine That Could?

On the first working day of 1973 President Nixon signed into law an act which revolutionized rail transportation in the United States. The Regional Rail Reorganization Act was designed to restructure the railroad industry in the nation's industrial heartland. By this Act, five bankrupt railroads operating in the East and Midwest were absorbed in 1976 into a single quasigovernment corporation known as Conrail.

Most of the new system (94%) represents lines formerly operated by the Penn Central Railroad. Penn Central operated 20,000 miles of routes and carried 228 thousand tons of coal, 65,000 tons of ores, 55,000 tons of food, 44,000 tons of pulp and paper, and 24,000 tons of grain *each day*. Other railroads in the new system are the Reading, Lehigh Valley, Central of New Jersey, Ann Arbor, and Lehigh and Hudson River lines. Although the new Conrail system is intended eventually to earn a profit, its first year of operation was highly unprofitable.

Not all the nation's railroads are losing money. The most profitable roads are those of the West and South which face less competition from barges, trucks, and other railroads. Roads carrying coal and grain to the West Coast and farm and industrial commodities among the middle Atlantic states and long-haul carriers of heavy industrial goods have remained profitable.

The railroads in the Northeast have been suffering from the movement of factories south and from the growth of service businesses and light industry which use less rail transport. Nowadays, coal is often transported by barges on the nation's rivers because costs are much lower than rail. The interstate highway system and St. Lawrence Seaway have drained off other profitable freight. Increasingly, railroads have suffered from stringent union work rules which have kept productivity low and maintained inefficient duplication of facilities. As an example, in the early 1970s, there were still 3,000 ways to route freight from Washington, D.C., to St. Louis. And yet, local governments and powerful shippers have insisted on continuation of many unprofitable lines.

Rail traffic is highly sensitive to economic recession because of the types of freight carried. Autos, auto parts, and coal account for about a third of railroad freight business. Major strikes in these industries and declines in consumer spending have a disastrous effect on revenues.

Another problem facing the railroads is deteriorating tracks, terminals, and other facilities. In years of declining revenues, railroads cut back on maintenance of equipment and improvement of facilities. Other forms of transportation often receive government subsidies from tax revenues. Commercial airlines use government-financed systems of airways; water freight uses rivers maintained by government; trucking companies use tax-supported highways; and users of private autos benefit from controlled gasoline prices.

On the other hand, the energy crisis may have benefited railroads. The recent revival of the coal industry has been a boon for railroads, still the prime movers of coal. The energy cost of moving a ton of freight by rail is one-fourth the cost by truck.

In 1972 the six failing Northeast railroad lines were operating 26,000 miles of track for gross revenues of $2.3 billion. To allow these firms to collapse would have choked industrial activity in the seventeen affected states and would have thrown 2.7 million railway employees out of work. Reorganization into the Conrail system will consolidate routes and permit roads to abandon unprofitable lines for greater efficiency.

The new corporation is formally known as Consolidated Rail Corporation. Conrail is to be financed by federal grants of at least half a billion dollars and sale of $1.5 billion worth of government-guaranteed securities. Existing lines will be bought outright or absorbed through exchanges of stock in

Conrail. At some time in the future the government might take over entirely all track and roadbed and allow Conrail to run the trains without bearing the financial burden of maintaining the track. More than 6,000 miles of unprofitable track will be abandoned or else subsidized by federal, state, or local governments. Workers displaced by reorganization will be eligible for financial support while out of work.

Passenger traffic is practically nonexistent in the Conrail system. In 1969 most of the nation's passenger rail traffic was placed under the quasigovernment corporation Amtrak. Amtrak continues to require annual subsidies to offset intercity operating losses—estimated at $325 million in 1975. The new rail act will provide $800 million additional expenditures to make tracks smoother and safer and to provide new cars, locomotives, and stations.

The railroad reorganization plan was designed to preserve competition by preventing the collapse of major roads. However, profitable roads continuing under private ownership resent having to compete with a road that can cover any losses with a federal subsidy. Other competing forms of transportation may also demand subsidies, leading to further government intervention into the private economy. Eventually, the entire industry may be nationalized.

In most of the world, railroads are already nationalized. Still, there is a high degree of innovation—the bullet trains in Japan are a prime example. In Britain, France, and West Germany there are plans for trains capable of speeds up to 150 miles an hour. Traffic is high along the nationalized systems, but deficits are common.

Conrail to absorb the freight lines of the failing northeastern railroads. None of these public enterprises was expected to show a profit; all would require government subsidies for many years.

Inherent weaknesses of regulation

Regulation of the railroads has not served the public interest as well as it might have. How well does regulation work in other industries? There are many critics. Some say that commissions set up to do the regulating often end by becoming captives of the interests they are supposed to control. Others say that regulation takes away the incentives of private enterprise. One leading authority, Clair Wilcox, has suggested that certain failings are inherent in regulation:*

"Regulation, at best, is a pallid substitute for competition. It cannot prescribe quality, force efficiency, or require innovation, because such action would invade the sphere of management. But when it leaves these matters to the discretion of industry, it denies consumers the protection that competition would afford. Regulation cannot set prices below an industry's costs, however excessive they may be. Competition does so, and the high-cost company is compelled to discover means whereby its costs can be reduced. Regulation does not enlarge consumption by setting prices at the lowest level consistent with a fair return. Competition has this effect. Regulation fails to encourage performance in the public interest by offering rewards and penalties. Competition offers both."

The debate over bigness

We saw at the beginning of this chapter that 500 large corporations control about two-thirds of the assets of American industries. This implies that much of the economy no longer fits the competitive model as described in eco-

* Clair Wilcox, *Public Policies Toward Business* (Homewood, Ill.: Richard D. Irwin, 1966), p. 476.

nomic theory. How serious is the problem? Is industrial concentration something to be feared? Is it increasing, as some people say, or is it staying about the same or even decreasing? What ought we to do?

Measuring concentration

Numerous efforts have been made to measure the degree of concentration in various industries and in the economy as a whole. Measurement is difficult because the structure of industry is so complex. Some firms produce a variety of goods for sale in many different markets. In one market a firm may face substantial competition, while in another it may have a degree of monopoly power. If it serves a large geographic area, it may meet heavier competition in one region than in another.

Concentration may be defined as the extent to which the largest firms dominate an industry. This is usually expressed as a *concentration ratio*. The concentration ratio measures the fraction of industry sales made by the largest firms (usually the four largest). For example, recent figures compiled by the Department of Commerce show that the four largest aluminum producers have 100% of the market. The four largest auto firms supply 92% of the domestically-produced market. The production of electric bulbs has a concentration ratio of 91%; of cigarettes, 81%; and of sewing machines, also 81%. On the other hand, the women's dress industry has a concentration ratio of only 7%; this is an industry of many small firms of which the largest four have only 7% of the market. The great majority of U.S. industries have concentration ratios less than 50%.

The important question is whether industry is becoming more or less concentrated. The evidence is not clear. Taking the country as a whole, the largest manufacturing firms have increased their share of total manufacturing output substantially since World War II. The largest 50 firms have shown the greatest increase in market shares. It is true, of course, that there has been a turnover in the membership of the top group. Nevertheless, results are similar when we compare a group of the same firms over the years.

If industry is indeed becoming more concentrated, what ought to be done about it? Even in the most concentrated industries there are still several firms, and the customer can choose among them. You aren't compelled to buy a car made by Ford or General Motors or Chrysler; you can buy a foreign car, as many people do, or one made by American Motors. It would be nonsense to say that there is no competition in an industry because it is dominated by a few large firms. There is also competition between industries, as between steel and aluminum, or glass and plastics.

Bigness defended

Large size is not universally condemned. Many other nations protect and encourage combinations of enterprises into giant firms. Some groups in the United States point to the advantages of large size and recommend relaxation of the antitrust laws.

One argument in favor of bigness stresses the international competitiveness of U.S. firms. Small firms may be less able to compete against giant firms in foreign markets. They should be allowed to develop the cost advantages of large scale. Furthermore, strong firms should be allowed to merge with weak firms, spreading their better management techniques, more dynamic production planning, and more efficient operations to other firms. Preventing mergers may actually discourage innovative and efficient management techniques.

Secondly, larger firms can better afford an aggressive research and development effort. In large firms the risks and costs of research and development can be spread over a greater volume of output. Large firms keep constant watch on their rivals' successes and work vigorously to keep costs down and to maintain their own market share. Their awareness of potential competition from new products keeps big firms on their toes. Government policy to restrict growth would thwart this stimulus to development.

Viewpoint
How Big Does a Company Have to Be?

One of the arguments for giant firms is that some goods lend themselves to large-scale production. Economic efficiency, it is said, requires a large output relative to the size of the market. Small firms will be unable to achieve the same economies of scale, and their costs will be higher than those of the giant firms. But how big does a firm have to be to achieve these economies?

In 1956 an important study was made of this question. Although that was 20 years ago, the fundamental conclusions are still significant. The research showed that there were only two industries in which 10 or more firms could not supply the market at lowest cost. Only in typewriters and cigarettes did a firm have to produce at least 10% of industry output in order to achieve maximum efficiency.

In each of the following industries, maximum efficiency was attainable with less than 10% of the market in sales volume.

Industry	Percent of market needed for efficiency	Number of firms needed for lowest costs
Steel	2–20	5 to 50
Soap	8–15	7 to 13
Cement	2–10	10 to 50
Rayon	4–6	17 to 25
Tires and tubes	$1\frac{3}{8}$–$2\frac{1}{4}$	approx. 50
Petroleum	$1\frac{3}{4}$	approx. 60
Distilled liquor	$1\frac{1}{4}$–$1\frac{3}{4}$	approx. 60
Canned fruits and vegetables	$\frac{1}{4}$–$\frac{1}{2}$	200 to 400

*From Joe S. Bain, *Barriers to New Competition: Their Character and Consequences in Manufacturing Industries* (New York: Cambridge University Press, 1965), pp. 80, 861.

Finally, the visibility of large firms helps to monitor their activity. Industry performance and methods of competition are more easily regulated among large firms, and steps can be taken to correct anticompetitive practice. Defenders of bigness hold that the important question is not "Is the firm big?" but "Is bigness in the public interest?" When bigness reflects greater efficiency, they would answer "Yes."

Living with bigness

Some economists believe that we must learn to live with big business and that the antitrust laws were bound to fail. A well-known economist of this school is John Kenneth Galbraith, whose books have had considerable influence among the general public. Galbraith sees bigness as an inevitable result of modern technology. Modern technology has made Adam Smith's competitive model obsolete. Today's large organizations can produce and sell goods more efficiently than small ones. Furthermore, instead of being controlled by the competitive market, large firms have used advertising and marketing techniques to take control of the market themselves. They are largely immune from antitrust laws since government lawyers are more likely to go after the small and medium-sized firms that cannot afford a strong defense. Galbraith says our current antitrust policy is like locking the barn door after the horse has been stolen.

Galbraith does not advocate breaking up large firms, however. He believes that dissolving large firms would sacrifice the benefits of modern technology which created bigness. Instead, he points to ways of balancing and controlling the power of big business for the benefit of society. He recommends government ownership, or *nationalization*, of highly concentrated industries so that they can be run in conformity with national policy. He would also build up the "countervailing power" of labor unions, consumer groups, and government regulatory bodies as a way of balancing the power of big business. In short, bigness doesn't worry Galbraith as long as other bigness grows up to offset it.

Economic Thinker
John Kenneth Galbraith

You may have seen John Kenneth Galbraith (born 1908) on his Public Television series "The Age of Uncertainty," a lively, 13-part history of economics. Galbraith is one of the two or three best-known economists of today. Besides writing many well-known economics books, Galbraith was a professor of economics at Harvard, has served as ambassador to India (during Kennedy's administration), and has even dabbled as a novelist.

John Kenneth Galbraith was born on a farm in Ontario, Canada. After studying at the universities of Toronto and California, he began his career as an agricultural economist. It was during the Great Depression of the 1930s and agriculture was suffering heavy losses. Farm prices were dropping sharply while the prices farmers paid for manufactured goods were rising. Galbraith concluded that the market economy of the United States is actually divided into two parts: the competitive sector of small farmers and shopkeepers and the monopoly sector of industrial giants. The giants are the major cause of inflation and of fluctuations in output and employment. Then the competitive sector has to bear the costs of depression. To break up the giants is not the answer. According to Galbraith this would only produce oligopoly, which is not much better. Furthermore, according to Galbraith, the system actually works rather well most of the time. Technical innovation by large firms has yielded unprecedented gains in real incomes, while the growth of unions has helped to spread these gains more equitably among working people. In fact, it was the power of the giants that brought on the development of union "countervailing power."

Galbraith believes that the power of large firms can best be checked by encouraging development of more forms of countervailing power. The nation should aim not to eliminate power but to increase the power of those groups which lack it: agriculture, consumers, and small business. Galbraith urges that we face up to the new realities of modern life—the technical and organizational benefits which bigness produces. Large-scale firms should not be broken up. When necessary, they should be regulated so that their policies cannot injure other groups in the economy.

Galbraith has also attacked American capitalism for what he believes is one of its greatest flaws: too little is allocated to the public sector. This idea, which has been present in his earlier works, emerged to form the core of his recent and controversial book *Economics and the Public Purpose* (1973). He sees the public sector—housing, education, public transportation, urban services, health services—underfunded and too much emphasis placed on private-sector activities. The private sector dominates, partly because of the power of the big corporation. However, Galbraith would do away with current antitrust laws in favor of nationalization of industries in the public sector and wage and price controls in much of the private sector.

Another viewpoint of big business was offered by the important economist and social thinker, Joseph A. Schumpeter (1883–1950). He showed how a capitalist society grows and develops through the work of entrepreneurs. He described economic development as a process of "creative destruction."

"The fundamental impulse that sets and keeps the capitalist engine in motion," Schumpeter wrote, "comes from the new consumers' goods, the new methods of production or transportation, the new markets, the new forms of industrial organization that capitalist enterprise creates." Every new creation *destroys* old ways and opens the door to progress. According to Schumpeter, it is innovation that provides the necessary competition to curb monopoly power. Even the strongest monopoly is vulnerable to this kind of competition; the constant threat of new competition is sufficient to discipline the large firm and keep it on its toes.

Bigness opposed

Monopoly and innovation One argument in favor of bigness involves the capacity of large firms for conducting research and developing new products. But there is some question whether large firms have actually promoted technological progress. In fact, of 61 important inventions made since 1900, only 11 came from research teams in large industrial laboratories. More than half were the product of independent inventors working alone: These include air conditioning, the automatic transmission, power steering, cellophane, the helicopter, the jet engine, streptomycin, insulin, and the continuous casting of steel. Several other inventions came from small or medium-sized firms: DDT, the crease-resistant process for fibers, the continuous hot-strip rolling of steel sheets, and shell molding. Many inventions came from university research.

Why have many large firms generally been slow to innovate? Why has their market power not been used for imaginative entrepreneurship? The answer lies partly in the large bureaucratic structures needed to run these firms. Bureaucracies are not often the source of crea-tive thinking. Furthermore, as Schumpeter noted, creation destroys—and a giant firm has a vested interest in continuing past products and processes. A small firm, on the other hand, may leap at a chance to adopt new techniques and products as a way to undersell its competitors and increase its share of the market.

Bigness and the market system Another school of economists wants to fight industrial concentration. One of the best known of these is Professor George J. Stigler of the University of Chicago. He acknowledges that large firms may be more efficient in the sense of lower production costs, but he maintains that their cost advantage comes from market power. Large firms are able to buy their materials for less than competitive market prices and to sell for higher than competitive market prices. In most industries, small and medium-sized firms produce at the same low costs as the giants. In fact, the giants are often composed of numerous divisions that operate independently, almost as separate firms. Each of them may be economically viable and efficient on its own.

Stigler fears the growth of economic power in the hands of big business. Economic power is a potential source of political power—power to undermine individual liberties and stifle participatory democracy. But Stigler also fears government regulation of business. His prescription is simple: bust the trusts. He would apply the Sherman Act vigorously to break up industrial concentration as well as to prevent it from developing. If the laws are enforced vigorously, a competitive structure would result. A competitive *structure* is better than regulating business *conduct*. With only small and medium-sized firms, the final result would be competitive *performance* in industrial markets.

Economic Thinker
George Stigler

In the economics profession disagreement is healthy. Economists have traditionally brought their ideas into the open to encourage debate. Vigorous debate is in some ways a substitute for the laboratory experiments which are not possible in a social science. When many active minds examine a question, they can expose the flaws in logic behind a particular conclusion.

There is probably no greater opponent of Galbraith's "acceptance" of big business than George J. Stigler. Stigler is one of the staunchest supporters of the free market, whose "invisible hand" works to the benefit of all. But the invisible hand works best in perfect competition. So the greatest enemy of our capitalistic system is not the opposing economic systems of other countries but the monopoly and oligopoly elements of our own economy.

Born in the state of Washington in 1911, George Stigler has taught economics at the London School of Economics, Columbia, and Brown Universities. He has been Professor of Economics at the University of Chicago since 1958. Stigler has observed the growing power of large manufacturing firms and finds it dangerous. Whereas small-scale competition is responsive to consumer demand, large firms are able to control output and prices, reaping monopoly profits. Whatever cost advantages there are in large size are generally a result of the use of monopoly power to force down the prices of material inputs. Under imperfect competition resources are misallocated and the community suffers a loss in efficiency. Stigler believes that equity is harmed, too, because of the dominance of powerful institutions in our political system.

Professor Stigler is opposed to the recent emphasis on monopoly *conduct* in enforcing antitrust laws. He believes that large firms can always discover new tactics to accomplish their monopoly purposes without ever being judged in violation of

the laws. The only effective remedy to their power is to attack monopoly *structure*; that is, to break up large-scale manufacturing firms and enforce competition throughout U.S. industry.

The military-industrial complex   Shortly before he left office, President Dwight D. Eisenhower spoke of "the conjunction of an immense military establishment and a large arms industry" which had developed after World War II and the Korean War. He urged the nation to "guard against the acquisition of unwarranted influence, whether sought or unsought, by the military industrial complex. The potential for the disastrous use of misplaced power exists and will persist . . . we should take nothing for granted."

President Eisenhower's message was all the more remarkable in coming from a five-star general and former Chief of Staff of the armed forces. He was thinking of the network of common interests that had developed among Pentagon officials, defense contractors, and certain members of Congress whose reelection often depends on defense contracts for their districts. The implication is that their common interests may at some times take precedence over the interests of the nation, particularly when it comes to deciding how big the military budget should be.

In reality, the size of military expenditures seems to depend on a number of factors, the most important of which is the international situation. Expenditures rose greatly during the Vietnam War, dropped in the early 1970s, and then began to rise in response to Soviet military spending. In 1973, about 30% of federal government outlays went for national defense, but the percentage fell to 25% in 1976.

Some critics say that corporations doing most of their business with the Department of Defense, such as General Dynamics, Lockheed, and others, are treated as extensions of the government and not as private firms. As Galbraith has pointed out, these firms often use plants belonging to the government, get their working capital from the government in the form of "progress payments," receive management guidance from the Defense Department, are required to follow detailed accounting rules, and are heavily staffed with former military personnel.* Their plants are regarded as a national defense resource. It has been charged that military contracts are awarded to the leading firms on the basis of available capacity rather than competitive bidding. One author analyzed the awarding of aerospace contracts in the years 1960–1972. He found that when a major production line was available it would receive a new military contract for a product resembling that of its previous contract. In this way all of the eight major aerospace production lines were kept busy from 1960 to 1972.**

What you think about the military-industrial complex is likely to depend on how you feel about national defense. If you feel that our international obligations require all the strength we possess and perhaps more, you will be less inclined to criticize the way it is achieved. If you feel, as some of the critics do, that the defense system is like any other big enterprise in wanting to grow as large as it can regardless of whether growth is needed, you will worry about how to control it. The question has been a key issue in several presidential elections. In 1960 John F. Kennedy and the Democrats charged that the United States was falling behind the Soviet Union in the production of nuclear missiles. In 1975 the administration of Gerald Ford was attacked both by some Democrats and some Republicans for "weakening" the country's military posture.

Summary

Advances in technology and the great size of the American market were factors in the trend toward industrial concentration. In the late nineteenth century firms combined through merger or acquisition and through holding companies or trusts. Mergers were horizontal or vertical. Monopoly power permitted price discrimination, particularly in railroads and petroleum pipelines. The first antitrust laws were aimed at regulating railroad monopoly—the Interstate Commerce Act—and at preventing monopoly structure—the Sherman Antitrust Act. The Clayton Antitrust Act of 1914 prohibited specific types of monopolistic conduct: discriminatory price cutting, tying contracts, interlocking directorates in the same industry, and stock ownership in competing companies. The Federal Trade Commission was established to investigate and to prosecute violations.

The "rule of reason" refers to lenient Court interpretation of antitrust legislation where only monopoly *conduct* was ruled illegal. The result was a new wave of mergers in the 1920s. Automobiles and communications were the major new industries. Antitrust laws of the 1930s aimed at protecting small business firms by prohibiting price discounting by large retailers—the Robinson-Patman Act and the Miller-Tydings Act. In 1950 the Celler-Kefauver Act amended the Clayton Act to prohibit acquisition of firms where the effect would be to lessen competition.

---

* John Kenneth Galbraith, *The New Industrial State* (Boston: Houghton Mifflin Company, 1967), p. 314.
** James R. Kurth, "The Political Economy of Weapons Procurement: The Follow-on Imperative," *American Economic Review,* May 1972.

Business firms of the 1960s turned to conglomerate merger: International Telephone and Telegraph, Ling-Temco-Vought, Litton, and Textron. But again the courts changed direction and began to focus on monopoly structure. The aim has been to prevent the formation of new monopolies by carefully investigating all new applications for merger. The most difficult problem facing the courts is parallel performance among firms where no formal agreement has taken place. Some large and concentrated industries are regulated by public commissions; the Interstate Commerce Commission regulates rail and water transport.

There are disagreements as to the relative merits of bigness versus small-scale competition in the United States. Some say bigness provides greater opportunities for research and development and enhances our competitiveness in international trade. They believe large-scale enterprises should be regulated in the public interest. Others claim large enterprises have been slow to innovate and should be broken up.

Some current problems in antitrust involve the military-industrial complex, price leadership in the cigarette industry, collusion among large equipment manufacturers, pricing and production in the petroleum industry, concentration in telephone communications, and reorganization of railroads.

Key Words and Phrases

- **holding company** a firm which is established for the purpose of holding voting stock in other operating firms, thus controlling production.
- **horizontal mergers** combinations of firms producing the same good or service.
- **vertical mergers** combinations of firms supplying raw materials, transportation of these materials, and production of finished products from the raw materials.
- **trusts** a combination of firms for the purpose of controlling production and pricing of a particular good.
- **tying contracts** contracts requiring the purchaser of a particular type of output to purchase an entire line of goods from the same supplier.

- **interlocking directorates** the practice of a single individual serving on the boards of several firms and influencing their market behavior.
- **fair trade laws** laws forbidding quantity discounts to large retailers as a means of protecting small retailers from price competition.
- **structure, conduct, and performance** alternative ways of judging the arrangement or behavior of firms in an industry.
- **conglomerate mergers** combinations of firms producing unrelated goods and services.
- **rule of reason** a court practice of judging only monopoly behavior without regard for monopoly structure in industry.
- **conscious parallelism** similar pricing practices resulting from similar market conditions rather than from actual collusion.
- **creative destruction** the process of innovation which destroys old processes and products.
- **concentration ratio** the percent of industry output produced by the four (or eight) largest firms.

Questions for Review

1. Outline three historical periods of significant merger activity. What were the characteristics of mergers in each? Show how the major antimonopoly legislation grew out of industry conditions in each period.

2. List examples of horizontal and vertical integration in existing business firms. What conditions gave rise to conglomerate integration?

3. Discuss the problems of legislating controls on conglomerate mergers. What are the advantages and disadvantages of conglomerates?

4. List important legislation by which government attempted to prevent monopoly price *reductions*. What is the long-term basis for forbidding price reductions, even if they reflect lower production costs? State your answer in terms of structure, conduct, and performance.

5. Discuss the major arguments pro and con on the question of industrial concentration.

6. Define: price discrimination, interlocking directorates.

Part Eight

Resource Markets

32

Allocation of Resources and Marginal Productivity

We have been looking at the ways in which firms price and sell their finished goods to consumers. Now we must turn to the beginning of the production process. We will examine how firms combine their resources to produce the final product.

An economic system, you will remember, has to answer three questions: What is to be produced? How is it to be produced? For whom is it to be produced? In the preceding chapters we saw how the first question is answered as consumers express their demand for goods and services in the marketplace. The second question is answered in the chapter before us now: How is production to be carried out?

In this chapter we will describe the markets where resources are exchanged for use in production. We will show how demand and supply interact to determine resource prices and the incomes of resource owners. In the next chapter we will examine separately the markets for the four classes of productive resources: land, labor, capital, and entrepreneurship.

Resource allocation: the background

Economic relationships play such an important part in our productive lives that it is not surprising to find a strong influence on our political lives as well. Certainly our political views influence and are influenced by our economic arrangements. This was never truer than in the early years of the Industrial Revolution, a time during which nations experienced the upheavals and distortions of fundamental change. Changing class structures made life insecure, and new learning shattered old beliefs. Philosophers tried to interpret the causes and predict the results of economic change.

Two of these philosophers had especially great impact on the societies they described. One was Adam Smith, whom we have already met. Adam Smith's theory of production was based on the economic relationships which developed during the Industrial Revolution. Smith saw that goods and services were created through the use of productive resources.

He divided these productive resources into our familiar classifications: land, labor, capital, and entrepreneurship. And he showed that production depends on the combined efforts of all four types of resources. This was particularly important because it showed that the profit received by the entrepreneur was actually *earned* income—income earned through directing the use of productive resources. In this view, the value of the finished product embodied the value of all resources used in production. Smith was optimistic about economic growth. He predicted that improvements in technology and greater division of labor would help to increase the productivity of all resources. Then a growing consumer market would help to speed economic development even further. In this system the prosperity of each group of resource owners was linked through interdependence with all other groups.

Adam Smith was optimistic about other results of the market system, too. He believed that free markets would allocate scarce resources efficiently toward the kinds of products people want. Business firms would strive to produce the greatest output of goods and services at the lowest cost. Moreover, rewards for production would be distributed to resource owners in fair proportion to their contribution to output.

The other giant of early economic philosophy was Karl Marx. He started writing his famous economic treatise *Capital* nearly seventy years after Smith wrote *The Wealth of Nations*. By the time Karl Marx was writing, the Industrial Revolution seemed to have caused more misery than good. Marx observed the suffering of working people and built a theory of class exploitation and a prediction of violent revolution to come. It appeared that labor was not receiving its fair share of output from production.

Marx started from an idea developed earlier by David Ricardo. The output of industry is entirely the result of labor; therefore, the value of goods and services is only the value of the labor required to produce them. This idea became part of Marx's **labor theory of value;** it was an outgrowth of the simpler times when production was indeed largely the result of human effort. But the new capitalist system had forced some changes in economic relationships. Workers were no longer individually responsible for planning production and marketing their output. In the industrial era they grew to be dependent on capitalists who owned the *means of production*—the factories and machines of the new technology. Naturally the capitalist owners of industrial plant and equipment used their productive property to serve their own interests and the interests of the capitalist class. Thus, according to Marx, the "propertyless proletariat" became subservient to the wishes of the owners of capital.

Without bargaining power relative to their employers, industrial workers were forced to accept wages barely above subsistence. Improvements in technology increased their productivity, but the growing surplus of goods and services was taken over by the capitalist owners. According to Marx, the final result would be a larger and larger imbalance between the incomes of these groups. Workers would have less to spend, but capitalists would have more savings to invest in productive equipment. In fact, the availability of funds for investment would worsen the position of workers as machines would gradually replace labor in production. A reserve army of unemployed workers would develop from which capitalist employers would draw workers at lower and lower wage rates.

Marx believed that all this was inevitable. It seemed to him that capitalism carried within itself the "seeds of its own destruction." Eventually, the great bulk of the working proletariat would rise up against these injustices and overthrow the capitalist class. Following violent revolution the means of production would be operated in the interests of the working class alone. Marx's influence on the politics of his era and of years since has been enormous.

The lot of the average worker improved from the time Marx was writing in the 1840s and 1850s. By the 1870s, followers of Adam Smith went on the counterattack. They became known as the *neoclassical economists*, and they were especially significant for developing a new theory of income distribution. They showed that income depends not on class conflict but on relative productivity. The economist Alfred Marshall analyzed the important relationships within resource markets more precisely than Smith had done. He and John Bates Clark went even further. They stressed the ultimate justice of a system that rewarded participants according to their contribution to work.

In fact, the ideas explored by the neoclassical economists are the basis for our theory of resource markets. We can now answer the question: How is production to be carried out?

Theory of marginal productivity

Suppose you are the production manager of a bicycle factory. You run an assembly line, and you employ workers who put together the bicycles. There are separate departments for making wheels and forging frames, and another where paint is sprayed and trim applied. As the production manager, you are responsible for getting everything together at a minimum cost. If sales of bicycles go up, you have to hire more workers, buy more materials, and perhaps even put in another assembly line. When you go out to buy more resources you do so because you need them for making bicycles. Your demand for resources stems from the technology of bicycle manufacture and depends on the demand for bicycles. We say that your demand for resources is a **derived demand** because it is derived from the demand for finished goods.

Much of the demand for industrial products is derived demand. Most primary products such as cement, steel, aluminum, and copper are purchased not for themselves but for use in making other products. Some of these other products may not be consumer goods either, but producer goods which in turn are used to make goods for final consumption. This is important to remember because changes in the demand for consumer goods sometimes cause much sharper changes in the demand for producer goods and for primary products.

Usually an enterprise owns a certain amount of plant and equipment. The bicycle company has its buildings and assembly lines and machines. It also has a staff of managers who run the business. These fixed resources do not change in the short run.

When the firm enters resource markets in response to a change in demand, it looks for *variable resources* to use in combination with its fixed resources. We call them variable resources because they are employed in varying quantities together with the firm's fixed resources.

Resource demand in perfect competition

Let us begin by examining derived demand for resources in a perfectly competitive market. This means that firms will be price takers. They will buy inputs and sell output at a constant price determined in the market.

Suppose your bicycle firm enters the market for labor resources. In this case labor is a variable resource to be used with the firm's fixed quantity of plant and equipment. We will assume that there is a range over which the firm can vary its output by varying the quantity of labor hired. (The firm also varies the amount of some other resources such as materials and energy, but for simplicity we will consider only labor.) Because plant and equipment are fixed, there is an upper limit to the output the firm can produce in the short run. This brings us to our old friend, the principle of diminishing marginal product.

You will remember the principle of diminishing marginal product: *when successive units of a variable resource are added to a fixed resource the result at some point will be smaller and smaller additions to total product.* Thus if we add more units of labor to a firm's fixed plant and equipment, the additions to total product will eventually decline.

Table 1 shows a hypothetical schedule of the *marginal product of labor.* The schedule is drawn up for a time period during which some of the firm's resources are fixed. For simplicity we have begun our computations at the point at which marginal product begins to decline. Actually, marginal product might increase as labor is added up to some point, then remain constant for a bit, and then start to decline. Marginal product, you will recall, is defined as the change in total product resulting from a change in the quantity of a variable input. In Table 1, the figures for marginal product, shown in column (3), are placed between the lines to show that they represent the differences in total product, listed in column (2).

Marginal revenue product

As the production manager of the bicycle company, you are interested in producing as many bicycles as you can sell at a price that covers the costs of production. You will hire another unit of labor if it contributes more to the value of total output than it adds to total costs. In Table 1, columns (3) through (6) help us to see how much each unit of labor (Q_L) adds to the value of the output. Because the

Table 1
Hypothetical Production Data for the Use of Labor Resources in a Firm in Perfect Competition

(1) Quantity of labor, Q_L	(2) Total Product, TP	(3) Marginal Product, MP	(4) Product price, P_P	(5) Total Revenue, TR	(6) Marginal Revenue Product, MRP	(7) Price of labor, P_L
1	10		$5	$50		$15
		10			$50	
2	19	9	5	95	45	15
3	27	8	5	135	40	15
4	33	6	5	165	30	15
5	38	5	5	190	25	15
6	41	3	5	205	15	15
7	42	1	5	210	5	15
8	42	0	5	210	0	15
9	40	−2	5	200	−10	15

product is sold in a perfectly competitive market, price remains the same no matter how many units the firm sells. The value of the marginal product in column (6) is called labor's **marginal revenue product** (MRP). It is calculated by figuring the *change in total revenue* that results from *adding one more worker:*

$$MRP = \frac{\text{change in TR}}{\text{change in Q}_L} = \frac{\Delta TR}{\Delta Q_L}.$$

Marginal revenue product declines because marginal product declines. If the firm hires three additional workers, the third will contribute $40 to the value of the firm's output. A fourth would contribute $30, and a fifth only $25. MRP for a seventh worker would be only $5.

The actual quantity of labor hired depends in part on how much it contributes to production. But it depends also on the cost of labor. The firm will keep hiring workers as long as the last one hired adds more MRP than the firm must pay in wages. Column (7) shows that the market price of labor is $15 for the given time period. It would pay to hire six workers, since the cost of the sixth is just equal to that worker's MRP of $15. Workers one through five add more MRP than their cost, and workers seven through nine add less. The sixth worker adds just enough revenue to justify hiring him or her.

The principle underlying the demand for a resource can be stated this way: *A firm will hire the quantity of a variable resource at which the marginal revenue product of the last unit hired is just equal to its price.* Glancing at Table 1 again, we can see that hiring seven workers would gain MRP of only $5, which would be less than the wage cost. The optimum number of workers to be added is six.

Demand curve for resources

Graphs of the data in Table 1 will help us to visualize the relationships between total quantities and marginal quantities. Figure 1 shows what happens to total product and marginal product as more workers are hired. Total product rises but by a smaller quantity for each additional worker. Total product levels off

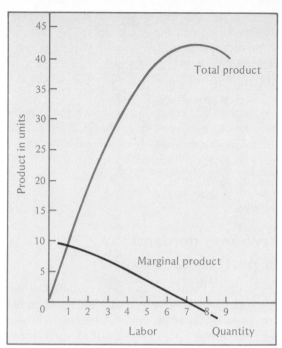

Figure 1 Production from the use of variable quantities of labor with a fixed quantity of other resources.

at eight workers and declines when more than that number are hired. The marginal product for each worker, shown by the lower line in Figure 1, declines throughout. If more than eight workers are hired, marginal product becomes negative.

Figure 2 is a similar graph for total revenue and marginal revenue product. As workers are hired, total revenue rises, reaches a peak, and then starts to decline. MRP declines continually. The curves in Figure 2 have exactly the same shape as those in Figure 1, since they are based on the same quantities of output multiplied by the price for which the product sells ($5).

Figure 3 shows the MRP curve by itself. We have drawn MRP separately to show that the MRP curve for a resource is the same as the firm's demand curve for this resource. The horizontal line at $15 represents the price of labor. At that price the firm will hire six workers. To hire fewer than six would sacrifice more revenue than the additional cost of labor. To hire more than six would add more to costs than the firm would receive in additional revenue.

If the wage rate rises to $25, the firm moves back up its MRP curve and hires only five workers. The value of the fifth worker's MRP is just enough to offset the higher wage rate. If the wage rate falls to $5, the firm moves down its MRP curve and hires eight workers. At every wage rate, the firm hires workers until MRP is equal to the wage rate.

We have been discussing the firm's demand for labor, but of course there are other variable resources: materials, fuel, and power, for instance. Exactly the same analysis applies to each of them. Each resource contributes its output and thus helps to increase the firm's total revenue. *Each resource has its MRP curve, which is the same as the firm's demand curve for that resource.*

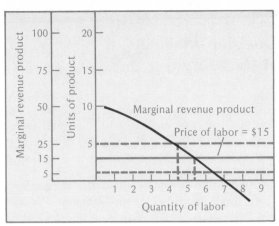

Figure 3   Demand for labor. A firm compares labor's marginal revenue product with its price and hires the quantity of labor at which MRP = P. At a labor price of $15, the firm will hire six workers.

Market demand for resources

No resource is used by just one firm. The market demand for any resource is the sum of the demands of all the firms using it. The bicycle company hires workers for its assembly line. So do other bicycle companies. Supermarkets, department stores, and the post office also hire workers in resource markets. The demand for workers of a particular kind will be the sum of the demands of all the firms employing them.

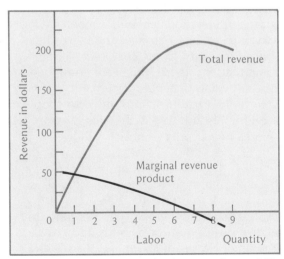

Figure 2   Revenue from the sale of output when variable quantities of labor are hired. Price of product = $5.

Determinants of demand

We have shown that demand for any resource reflects its contribution to output. In economic terminology a resource's contribution to output is its marginal revenue product. Marginal revenue product is determined by the marginal product of the resource and the price of output. This means that resource demand depends on (1) resource productivity and (2) consumer demand for output.

In a dynamic economy like ours, the demand for a resource is never constant. It changes over time depending on changes in productivity and in consumer markets. The more productive a resource becomes, the greater will be the demand for it. The greater consumer demand becomes, the greater will be the demand for resources used in production. Finally, the demand for any resource is affected by (3) changes in the availability and prices of other resources. Let's look at these three determinants in more detail.

Resource productivity   The more productive a resource is, the greater will be the demand for it and the higher will be its price. Its productivity often depends on its quality and on the quantity of other resources used with it.

Extended Example
Decision-Making at the Margin

"Natura non facit saltum." After having read this chapter you must surely agree this is true. It is an old Latin saying and it means, "Nature doesn't take leaps."

People do not take leaps either. People make small decisions a little at a time. They make decisions at the margin. They decide on a little more or a little less, and they balance off the benefits gained against the costs given up. This is what we mean by marginal analysis.

Marginal analysis is important to consumers as they allocate their budgets. Marginal analysis requires measurement one step at a time. Comparisons are made *incrementally:* the incremental change observed when one small step is taken. Consumers use marginal analysis to make buying plans; they compare the incremental change in utility with the price of one more unit. Because of diminishing marginal utility, the incremental change in utility is smaller with each additional unit purchased.

Marginal analysis is especially important to business firms as they make the decisions to allocate their budgets for producing output. Many U.S. retailers were faced with an interesting marginal question during the recession of 1973–1975. High unemployment and inflation had led to sharp cuts in consumer spending. Retailers began to accumulate unsold stocks of merchandise and their revenues fell. How could they encourage consumers to begin buying again?

Marketing departments hit on a revolutionary new idea: Sunday shopping for some, all-night shopping for others. It was hoped that the added convenience would stimulate sales and increase consumer loyalty to particular retail stores. Of course, once a single retailer in an area opened at odd hours, others were forced to follow or risk losing many of their own customers.

Retailers would have used marginal analysis to determine how many additional hours to offer. Each additional hour was expected to yield greater sales, but operating costs would rise, too. How many extra hours should the store provide?

To evaluate the profitability of longer hours, it would be necessary to compare the incremental *gains* with the incremental *cost* of each additional hour of operation. The first extra hour may indeed have brought in more customers: those whose work schedules prevented shopping during regular hours, families who enjoyed shopping together in the evenings, last minute gift buyers. Costs probably increased only slightly, as overtime rates were paid a few clerks and power usage continued in the late evening hours. The first few hours of operation may have added more to benefits than to costs.

But consider another possibility. Many, if not most, of the extra shoppers probably would have managed to do their shopping during regular hours if they had been forced to. Part of the late night shopping probably replaced shopping which would have been done anyway, and the marginal benefits to the store were probably slight. The same cannot be said of store costs. Much higher wage costs and utility bills and the added cost of security at night probably added significantly to operating expenses. The net result may actually have worsened the profitability of some firms.

Marginal analysis would require a cutoff at the point where incremental gains fall below increased costs. Unfortunately, other considerations entered a retailer's decision. Each retailer hesitated to change the policy for fear of losing customers. It is ironic that efforts like this were continued in spite of widely accepted agreement that they were futile. Customers continued to shop at odd hours and to pay the high costs in the form of higher prices on merchandise.

Actually, the late-night shoppers do not pay the full costs of their shopping. Who pays? How would you describe the equity of this result; that is, how would you describe the relative distribution of benefits and costs among all classes of shoppers? Why didn't the stores get together and agree to abandon the plan when profitability fell?

Workers in the advanced industrial countries are more productive than elsewhere. They have valuable resources with which to work. Furthermore, workers in many countries benefit from an educational system that stresses science and vocational training. Some nations like Sweden, Germany, Japan, and the United States reward individual achievement by providing achievers the opportunity to enjoy higher standards of living. Attitudes toward work are important too. People in the industrial countries believe that work is a good thing; they believe that if they sacrifice leisure in the present they will be able to enjoy higher income in the future.

Workers in the industrialized countries are fortunate also in the rich supplies of other resources for use in production. The advantages of fertile land, minerals, water power, and specialized capital equipment help them to be more productive. Even in nations like Japan, which must import most of its raw materials, the people have used initiative and entrepreneurial ability to develop highly productive economies. Human creativity is very important in raising a country's productivity; it leads to better products and processes so that a greater output can be obtained from a limited quantity of material resources.

In nonindustrial cultures productivity is much lower because the conditions mentioned above are lacking. Many people live from one day to the next or from one year to another. They lack capital equipment and other resources. Few are able to get the kind of training that is available in the industrialized countries. The economic conditions of masses of people are not much different from those of their ancestors hundreds of years ago.

Consumer demand Because the demand for resources is a derived demand, it depends on conditions in markets for consumer goods. When consumers' incomes are rising, the demand for many goods and services is likely to rise. As firms are able to sell a larger output, they are encouraged to hire more resources and to increase production. Thus the demand curve for a resource is likely to shift to the right over the course of time. The result is greater employment and sometimes higher pay as well.

Time doesn't always bring higher demand for a particular resource. Sometimes the demand curve for a resource may shift to the left. This may happen because the resource becomes less productive than other resources. Or it may be the result of a decline in consumer demand for the finished product. This can be a serious problem in a resort town, for instance, where the fading popularity of a certain tourist attraction leaves local workers without a livelihood. An oil spill on a beach may bring unemployment to workers in hotels and restaurants. Or the discovery that eggs contain harmful amounts of cholesterol may reduce the derived demand for resources in the poultry industry. Perhaps you can name other resources that have been displaced by declines in consumer demand.

Prices of other resources When we studied the demand for goods, we found that the demand for one good might be strongly influenced by a change in the price of some other good. For instance, an increase in the price of beef may cause consumers to eat more pork. Or an increase in the cost of vacations may cause a fall in the demand for beach wear. A similar relationship holds among resources: the demand for one resource is often related to the price of another.

The best-known relationship is that between the price of labor and the demand for labor-saving machinery. The mechanization and automation of U.S. industry over the past century were a direct result of the high cost of labor. In railroading, labor had been used to fire the coal boilers that produced the steam to run the locomotives. When wages rose among railroad workers, the railroads switched from steam power to electric or diesel-electric. The result was a decrease in demand for locomotive firemen. For years the railway unions sought desperately to hold back this decline in the demand for labor. In the same way, the development of television and, before that, the phonograph reduced the demand for live entertainers. These resources are substitutes; an increase in the price of one will encourage business firms to use its substitute.

Not all resources are substitutes. Quite often they are complementary; that is, they have to be used together. If sales of automobiles increase, the demands for steel, rubber, glass, and auto workers will increase together. If some new technical process reduces the price of steel, this might increase the demand for auto assembly-line workers. Can you see why?

Elasticity of demand for resources

The demand curve for a resource may slope downward very gradually or very steeply. The shape of the curve reflects the elasticity of demand for the resource. When demand is very elastic, a change in the price of the resource will have a more than proportionate effect on the quantity purchased. An increase in teenagers' wage rates would probably reduce their employment greatly. In contrast, consider the demand for skilled machinists who assemble bicycle transmissions. If the wages of such workers were to double, bicycle factories would still continue to employ them. In economists' language, the demand for the teenagers is elastic and the demand for the machinists is inelastic.

Elasticity of demand for a resource differs just as it does among consumer goods. For resources there are four basic factors affecting elasticity of demand: (1) the rate of decline in the marginal revenue product; (2) substitutability among resources; (3) elasticity of demand for final product; and (4) percentage of total costs paid for the resource.

MRP rate of decline   If the marginal productivity of a resource falls rapidly, demand will be inelastic. This can be seen from Figure 3, showing the demand curve for labor based on its marginal revenue product. The less rapidly the marginal revenue product falls, the more the demand curve will approach the horizontal and the more elastic will be the demand for the resource. Employers will hire substantially more workers if wage rates fall.

Extended Example
Trends in Productivity

The *quantity* of a nation's resources is limited. Growth in output depends largely on improvements in *quality*. Improved quality enables a single unit of resource to produce greater output. We say there has been a gain in *productivity*. In the United States productivity increased by an average of 3.1% yearly from 1950 to 1968. Since then, output per single worker hour has grown only 1.6% on the average each year.

Productivity gains shift marginal revenue product curves to the right and increase equilibrium prices of resources. Higher resource prices mean higher incomes for American households. Moreover, when productivity increases, the gains in spendable earnings are *real* gains. Higher productivity means more goods and services without inflationary pressures. *Real* incomes increase along with *money* incomes.

The United States may be experiencing a reversal in the trend toward higher productivity. If this is indeed the case, we may have to adjust our life-styles to a more or less stationary economy in the future. What is the reason for the change?

Advances in learning are the fundamental source of productivity growth. The

Substitutability   A second basis for a resource's elasticity of demand is the ease with which other resources can be substituted for it. A farmer may work his field with two men and two machines, five men and one machine, or ten men without a machine. His demand for workers or machines will depend on their prices. If the price of farm labor rises he will switch to machines; if the price of machines rises he may employ more workers. Thus the demand for both labor and machinery is relatively elastic in this case. On the other hand, if resources must be used in fairly rigid proportions, a change in their prices will bring no significant change in employment. Some machine tools must be operated with a constant

massive advances in technological knowledge of the postwar period may have been only a brief spurt in the long sweep of history. Furthermore, the major gains from extending basic education to all levels of the work force may already be behind us. Similarly, the gains from shifting large numbers of agricultural workers into manufacturing industries are not expected to be repeated.

The composition of U.S. industry is changing, too. The emphasis on service employment has reduced the potential for expanding productivity. This is because service industries use less capital equipment relative to the numbers of workers employed. Moreover, service industries and government services offer fewer opportunities for research and development of cost-saving technologies.

One basis for increasing productivity involves improvements in the way resources are combined for work. What are the potential advantages and limitations of combining resources in new ways?
Show how shifts in MRP affect the nation's production possibilities curve. How is the greater output distributed among households?
Service industries have experienced lower gains in productivity than manufacturing. Can you suggest ways in which jobs can be made more productive?

quantity of labor. Trucks and airplanes require crews of specific sizes. In these employments, technical factors limit substitutability and keep demand curves for labor inelastic.

Final-product demand elasticity A third basis for the elasticity of demand for a resource is the elasticity of demand for the final product. If an increase in the price of the product causes a sharp drop in sales, this will be reflected in the demand for resources to make that product. The demand for single family dwellings is relatively price elastic; this is because home ownership consumes such a large portion of a family's income. As a result, rising prices may cause severe cutbacks in production and throw many construction workers out of work.

Percentage costs A fourth determinant of elasticity of demand for a resource is the proportion of total costs accounted for by that resource. If labor is only a small part of total costs, a wage increase will have less effect on the price of the final product than if labor accounts for a large part of total costs. Suppose two firms each have to pay a wage increase of 5%. In one firm labor costs amount to only 10% of total costs, but in the other labor costs amount to 80%. The costs of one firm will increase by .05 × .10 or by only $\frac{1}{2}$%, while those of the other will increase by .05 × .80 or 4%. Product prices will rise accordingly and the effect on each firm's sales will be quite different. If elasticity of product demand is the same for both, one firm will lose more sales than the other, and so its demand for labor will be more elastic than the other's.

Demand under imperfect competition

We began by examining the demand for resources in perfect competition. In perfectly competitive markets sellers have no influence over price. Price is uniform throughout the market and for any quantity sold by an individual firm.

Actual markets, as we know, are likely to be less than perfectly competitive. In the chapter on monopoly we saw that when one firm controls the output of an industry, its demand curve is the demand curve for the entire industry. It can sell a small output at a high price or a larger output at a lower price. If it wants to increase its sales, the monopoly firm must reduce its price. This is true for all firms in imperfect competition.

The declining demand curve under monopoly and imperfect competition has important consequences for the firm's resource demand curve. When we calculate the marginal revenue product, we can't use the same price for additional units of output as we did for the firm in perfect competition. We must use a declining range of prices in calculating MRP.

Economic Thinkers
Frank and Lillian Gilbreth

Lillian Gilbreth

Good things come in pairs—and sometimes even in dozens!

It was a pair of industrial engineers around the turn of the century who pioneered in the development of techniques for increasing the productivity of labor. Frank and Lillian Gilbreth used scientific methods to analyze and improve work processes. They were the first "efficiency experts." The Gilbreths were marriage partners as well as professional partners. They produced twelve children, and their unusual family life was the subject of their son's book, *Cheaper by the Dozen.*

The Gilbreths called their industrial experiments Time and Motion studies. They saw that most industrial jobs could be performed in numerous ways. But, according to Frank, there was always "one best way." Scientific methods could be used to discover that one best way, the way most conserving of time and motion. Scientifically designed work methods would help workers to produce more than they could through individual ingenuity alone.

Their studies began simply. Small lights were attached to the hands of a worker performing a single task. The operation was photographed by a still camera with open shutter. The resulting picture would show a series of dots reflecting the speed and direction of hand movements. Then the analysts could study the picture for clues for improving the procedure and for training new operators to perform the job better.

After years of studying work, the Gilbreths developed a list of seventeen basic hand movements which are common to all human activity. They named the seventeen classifications "therbligs"—Gilbreth spelled backwards (roughly). Therbligs provided a framework for classifying and improving work procedures. Some of the classifications are pinch grasp, wrap grasp, and hold.

Each work activity was broken down into tiny units or therbligs and the series of actions recorded on a chart. Often the chart was divided into two columns and the actions of both hands recorded as they worked together. The chart helped to define and explain job requirements clearly and consistently.

The Gilbreths' objective was not to have workers work harder or faster, but to reduce wasted motion so that workers could produce more units of output per time period. Their experiments were especially useful in routine procedures where a large volume of units must be processed. The original studies were done in bricklaying, but the techniques soon spread to iron and steel, shoe manufacture, book binding and printing, and office work. Workers were shown how to place materials conveniently to minimize wasted motion. The order and arrangement of motions were simplified so that often the quantity of output increased by as much as four times.

Workers reacted favorably to the new procedures. They developed a healthy pride in their productive ability and often contributed suggestions from their own experience for further gains in productivity.

Industrial engineers continue to work toward improving the applications of technology to industrial jobs. Every gain in productivity reduces costs of production and helps to reduce long-run average cost curves. The result is lower prices for the consumer and larger output from the nation's scarce resources.

Table 2
Hypothetical Production Data for the Use of Labor Resources in a Firm Under Imperfect Competition

(1) Quantity of labor, Q_L	(2) Total Product, TP	(3) Marginal Product, MP	(4) Product price, P_P	(5) Total Revenue, TR	(6) Marginal Revenue Product, MRP	(7) Price of labor, P_L
1	10		$10	$100		$15
		10			$100	
2	19		9	171		15
		9			71	
3	27		8	216		15
		8			45	
4	33		7	231		15
		6			15	
5	38		6	228		15
		5			−3	
6	41		5	205		15
		3			−23	
7	42		4	168		15
		1			−37	
8	42		3	126		15
		0			−42	
9	40		2	80		15
		−2			−46	

Table 2 shows the data for a firm in imperfect competition. It is almost the same as Table 1, except that product price in column (4) decreases with greater output. Ten units of output can be sold for a price of $10 each. But if the firm is to sell 19 units, it must reduce price to $8. Total revenue at different prices is shown in column (5). Changes in total revenue give us the marginal revenue product, shown in column (6).

If we compare the MRP schedule for the firm under imperfect competition with that for the competitive firm in Table 1, we find that the imperfectly competitive MRP curve falls more steeply. This is because of the downward sloping demand curve under imperfect competition. Figure 4 shows the difference graphically. The competitive firm's MRP curve is shown in Figure 4a, coinciding with the MP curve because product price is constant. Figure 4b presents the same MP curve for a firm under imperfect competition. But the MRP curve declines more rapidly than in Figure 4a because larger outputs can be sold only if price is reduced. *Thus under imperfect competition the demand for resources is relatively inelastic.*

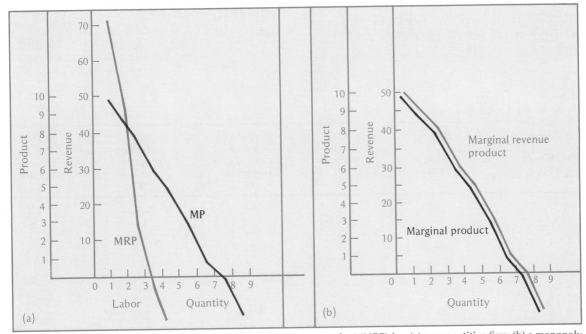

Figure 4 Comparing marginal product (MP) and marginal revenue product (MRP) for: (a) a competitive firm; (b) a monopoly firm. In (a), MP and MRP coincide. In (b), MRP declines more rapidly than MP because price must be reduced to sell more output.

Hiring resources for maximum profit

A firm can continue to hire variable resources up to the point at which the MRP of the last unit hired is just equal to its cost. In this way the firm maximizes economic profit from the use of a single variable resource.

The mainspring of a competitive economic system is profit. The hope of making a profit drives the firm to hire resources. A firm that wants to maximize profit will hire variable resources on the basis of marginal revenue product (MRP). The procedure it will follow can be seen from Table 3, which is drawn from the data used in Table 1. This time we have added column (8), showing total labor cost (VC), and column (9), giving the cost of fixed resources (FC) that the firm also uses. Column (10) is the total resource cost (TC), equal to the sum of columns (8) and (9): TC = FC + VC. Finally, the firm's economic profit is shown in column (11) as the difference between total revenue and total resource cost: Economic Profit = TR − TC.

The highest level of employment consistent with maximum economic profit occurs with 6 units of the variable resource. Total revenue at this point is $205. Total resource costs are $180. Economic profit is $250 − $180 = $25. The cost of hiring the sixth unit of labor is $15 (since labor costs are $15 per unit), and the MRP of the sixth unit is $15 (obtained by subtracting a total revenue of $190 from a total revenue of $205). If a seventh unit of labor were added, its MRP would be only $5 and the firm's economic profit would fall to $15. The optimum level of employment is that at which six units of labor have been hired.

The profit-maximizing quantity of labor is shown graphically in Figure 5a. As more units of labor are hired at $15 each, total variable cost rises along the diagonal line from the origin. The total resource cost curve (TC) is parallel to variable cost but higher because of fixed costs of $90 at every level of employment. Total revenue rises by varying amounts. The curve TR reaches a peak when seven units of labor have been hired, levels off, and then declines as the firm pushes against the limits of its fixed resources. The firm's economic profit is the difference between the TR curve and the TC curve at every level of employment. The difference is shown separately in Figure 5b. Economic profit is negative at low levels of employment, becomes positive over a middle range, peaks over the range 5–6 units of labor, and then declines. If the firm seeks to maximize its profit, it will choose to employ six units of labor.

Hiring more than one variable resource

The real-world decision is a little more complicated, of course, because production always

Table 3
Profit for the Competitive Firm

(1) Quantity of labor, Q_L	(5) Total Revenue, TR	(8) Total labor cost, VC	(9) Cost of fixed resources, FC	(10) Total resource cost, TC	(11) Economic profit, = TR − TC
1	50	$15	$90	$105	−55
2	95	30	90	120	−25
3	135	45	90	135	0
4	165	60	90	150	15
5	190	75	90	165	25*
6	205	90	90	180	25*
7	210	105	90	195	15
8	210	120	90	210	0
9	200	135	90	225	−25

*The two maximum profit points arise from the use of whole units of labor. Most resources can be used in fractions; even a single worker can be hired for part of a day. The unique profit-maximizing point for this firm would occur with $5\frac{1}{2}$ workers, and profit would be slightly greater than $25.

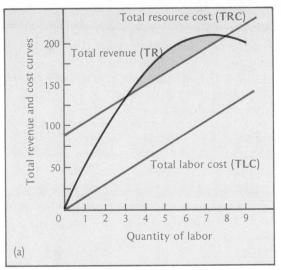

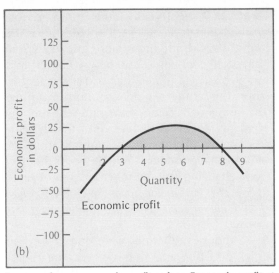

Figure 5 (a) Comparing the total revenue and total resource cost curves shows economic profit or loss. Economic profit at every level of employment is the vertical distance between total revenue and total resource cost. Positive profit is shown in the shaded area; the longer the broken line in the shaded area, the greater the amount of profit. (b) Only the economic profit is shown. When the curve is above the horizontal axis, positive profit results.

involves the use of several variable resources. The firm must select the proper combination of resources for lowest cost production. The optimum resource combination will be the one at which the firm produces the desired quantity of output at the lowest resource cost.

A farmer, for example, may use resources in various combinations. The farmer may combine labor, machinery, land, and fertilizer in different proportions to achieve the same amount of output. The decision is made on the basis of each resource's contribution to production together with its price.

The farmer begins by hiring the resource that produces the greatest output per dollar of cost. A hay reaper and binder may do the work of hundreds of hours of labor but may cost thousands of dollars. The farmer has to figure the addition each resource makes to total

product relative to its price. The numerical comparisons are shown in Table 4. Suppose the marginal revenue product of labor (MRP_L) is equal to $50—that is, one unit of labor adds $50 to total product. If it costs the farmer $15 to hire one unit of labor, then the contribution of labor per dollar is 50/15 or $3.33, as shown in column (4). In the same way, if one unit of capital equipment adds $100 to total production ($MRP_K = 100$) and costs $40, its contribution per dollar is 100/40 or $2.50, as shown in column (7).

In this example labor is a more productive resource than capital: its marginal revenue product per dollar is $3.33 compared to only $2.50 for capital. This farmer would want to hire more labor. *As a general principle, we can say that as long as one resource produces more output per dollar than other resources, more of it*

Table 4
Hypothetical Data for Labor and Capital Productivity

(1) Quantity of Resource	(2) MRP_L	(3) P_L	(4) $\dfrac{MRP_L}{P_L}$	(5) MRP_K	(6) P_K	(7) $\dfrac{MRP_K}{P_K}$
1	50	15	3.33	100	40	2.5
2	40	15	2.67	80	40	2.0
3	30	15	2.00	60	40	1.5
4	25	15	1.67	40	40	1.0
5	20	15	1.33	30	40	0.75
6	15	15	1.00	20	40	0.5

should be hired. If labor adds more to total product per dollar spent than machines, the farmer should hire more labor and fewer machines. If a dollar spent on machines adds more to total product than a dollar spent on labor, the farmer should use more machines. The farmer will continue to adjust the employment of variable resources until the marginal revenue product of every resource is the same. Only at that point can there be no further gain from changing the combination of resources used. *The last dollar spent on every resource should add an equal amount to the value of total product.*

Suppose the farmer were employing four units of labor and one unit of machinery. Looking again at Table 4, we see that the marginal revenue product per dollar of four units of labor is $MRP_L/P_L = 1.67$, while the marginal revenue product per dollar of one unit of machinery is $MRP_K/P_K = 2.50$. Clearly this is not the optimum combination of resources. If the farmer spends one dollar less on labor and one dollar more on machinery, the loss in output from the marginal dollar's worth of labor is $1.67 but the gain in output from the additional dollar's worth of capital is $2.50. It will pay to keep shifting dollars from labor to capital until $MRP_L/P_L = MRP_K/P_K$.

In Table 4, if the farmer reduces employment of labor from four units to three and increases employment of machinery from one unit to two, the result is the optimum combination of resources for that level of output. At three units of labor and two of machinery, the last dollar spent on each resource adds the same amount to total product. There is no way the farmer can gain by shifting expenditure from one resource to the other. At the optimum combination of resources, the farmer's output is produced at minimum cost.

But we need not stop here. Remember that a firm maximizes its profit by employing resources up to the point at which the MRP of each resource is equal to its price. The farmer in our example has not yet reached that point. Every dollar spent on both resources is return-

ing two dollars of MRP. The farmer can afford to keep on expanding employment up to the point where six units of labor have been hired and four units of machinery. At that point a dollar spent on labor will add a dollar's worth of output, and a dollar spent on machinery will also add a dollar's worth of output:

$$\frac{MRP_L}{P_L} = \cdots = \frac{MRP_K}{P_K} = 1.$$

When this condition is satisfied, (1) the farmer is then using the least-cost combination of resources and (2) is realizing a maximum economic profit from the use of all resources.

Resource supply

We have seen how the independent decisions of business firms determine the market demand for a resource. A firm employs every resource up to the point where its MRP is equal to its price.

What determines the equilibrium price of resources?

As in any other market, resource prices are determined by the interaction of supply and demand. The market for a resource reaches equilibrium where the quantity demanded is equal to the quantity supplied. The individual business firm then becomes a price taker. For a firm in perfect competition resource supply becomes horizontal at the market price. The competitive firm can hire any quantity at that price, but it is too small to affect market price. Later we will show how resource supply is different in imperfect competition.

A low market price for a resource is often the result of a bountiful supply, and a high price the result of a more limited supply. In our economy there is often an overabundance of particular resources. The most obvious examples are unskilled labor, which is usually in excess supply, and even skilled labor of types that are no longer needed. Certain kinds of capital are sometimes overabundant: office space or apartments in undesirable locations; or obsolete factory equipment that is still usable. An overabundance of resources relative to

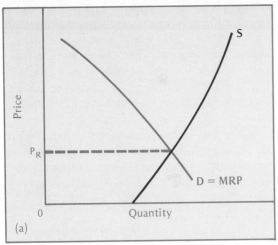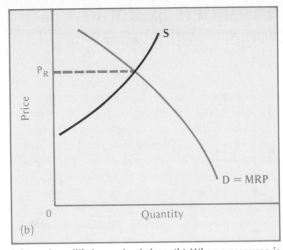

Figure 6 (a) When a resource is abundant, supply is far to the right and equilibrium price is low. (b) When a resource is scarce, the supply curve lies to the left and equilibrium price is high.

demand keeps their market supply curves far to the right, as shown in Figure 6a, holding price down.

An interesting example of a shifting resource supply is to be seen in the history of the teaching profession. Several generations ago, elementary- and high-school teaching were considered a woman's job. In many communities, in fact, it was the only acceptable employment for women. The steady flow of young women into this market and the stock of older women who were widowed, divorced, or otherwise unemployable kept supplies abundant and salaries low. All this changed in the period after World War II. Women began to find many new employment opportunities that were as challenging as the teaching profession. Supply curves for teachers shifted to the left in some areas and grew more slowly in others. At the same time the demand for teachers increased with the postwar baby boom and as adults began attending school for more years. Also, teachers formed unions and pushed for higher pay scales. Better pay made teaching an attractive career for both men and women and supply began to increase. The field seemed to be heading toward a high-employment, high-salary equilibrium.

Unfortunately for would-be teachers, derived demand began to shrink at the very time that more people were entering the profession. By the 1960s the birthrate had begun to fall, and by the 1970s there were empty classrooms in many elementary schools. Today many teachers have lost their jobs. Some cannot find teaching jobs and are retraining for new professions.

If teachers are overabundant, some other skills are in short supply. Labor-market forecasts for the 1980s suggest that there will be shortages of accountants, social workers, and health-care personnel. People having these skills may find that resource prices are high in those fields. Other scarce resources include capital equipment needed for energy development and for meeting environmental standards in production. Figure 6b illustrates price determination when resource supplies are low relative to demand.

Government subsidies for resource development

As our population grows and as we demand more and better goods and services, we must ensure that our supply of productive resources grows also. The federal and state governments have tried to encourage development of new resources in order to prevent bottlenecks and hold down costs of production. This aid often takes the form of *subsidies*. These subsidies can be grouped together as contributions to factors of production, especially land, labor, and capital.

Extended Example
Women in the Labor Market

Economics is the study of how a society uses its scarce resources to fulfill its unlimited wants. Labor is a scarce resource. In past years labor resources consisted chiefly of adult males, and production was limited as a result. But recently the United States is making use of another valuable source of labor resources: its women.

Women are entering the labor force in greater numbers than ever before. Early in this century about one-fifth of the female population worked outside the home, and these generally retired when they married. Following World War II, women's participation in the labor force rose to 46% of the female population. By 1975 women constituted 40% of the U.S. labor force of 92.6 million workers, up from only 30% in 1950. The great surge in demand for female workers is partly a result of the growing volume of clerical work required by government agencies and partly a result of changing technical requirements in many industries. The growth in supply is a result of smaller families and more female-headed families, as well as the need for two paychecks in many households.

Although their job opportunities have been improving, women continue to be employed principally in low-paying jobs. Forty percent of women workers are employed in primary or secondary education, 33% in clerical jobs, and 22% in service industries, including household workers. Women are poorly represented in the professions such as law, engineering, and medicine.

Their low job status helps to explain the low relative wages of female workers. Another reason in many cases is the part-time or temporary nature of their employment. Discrimination in pay and hiring continues to play a major part in low female earnings. While incomes of full-time working women rose from $2,827 in 1956 to $7,719 in 1975, their income relative to male workers actually dropped from 63% to 59%. Female-headed families constitute 13% of all families or 7.5 million families, and their numbers are increasing at a rapid rate. They make up almost half the nation's poverty population with median income of only $6,844 (1975). The average full-time male employee earned about $5,000 more than the average full-time woman.

The gap between earnings of white and black women has been narrowing. Black women in 1974 averaged 94% as much pay as white women. Black male workers averaged 73.4% of white male earnings: $9,082 compared to $12,343.

The problem of low female earnings is partly a result of the successful breakdown of social and economic barriers to employment. Because women have been seeking employment in greater numbers, more females are now in entry level jobs. More years are needed before women can build the job experience that leads to rising productivity. Educational and skill development for the professions and for technical jobs will qualify females for higher earnings. Still, it is important to continue efforts toward elimination of job discrimination and other barriers to use of this important resource.

Because of their low seniority women are often the first to be laid off in a recession. Some labor-market analysts contend that including females in the unemployment statistics overstates the actual problem of unemployment in the economy. They suggest that unemployed women should be left out of unemployment calculations—especially if they have working husbands. What is wrong with this proposal?

"It is ridiculous for upper-class wives to work just so they can buy a fancy new car." Evaluate this statement.

How can investment in human and material capital help to relieve the problem of low female earnings? Illustrate graphically.

Subsidies to land resources Agricultural scientists provide information to farmers, helping them to use land more efficiently. Government loans provide low-cost funds for irrigation and land reclamation. Emergency aid is available in the event of weather disasters, such as droughts or heavy frosts.

Subsidies to labor resources The government underwrites training programs for labor in several ways. It subsidizes vocational training. It gives tax credits to private employers who provide on-the-job training. Laws that prohibit discrimination in hiring on the basis of race or sex also help to enlarge the labor supply.

Subsidies to capital resources A number of government tax and spending programs are aimed at increasing the supply of capital. Corporations are allowed credits on their income taxes when they invest in new plant and equipment. Government agencies make low-interest loans in certain sectors of the economy: the Small Business Administration, the Federal National Mortgage Association, the Government National Mortgage Association, the Rural Electrification Administration, the Farmers Home Administration, Banks for Cooperatives, Federal Land Banks, and others.

Some federal funds go directly into construction of plant and equipment. When Congress appropriates money for research and development, it is spending money to create new capital. Other capital investments by the government include construction of docks and port facilities, power generation plants, and transmission equipment. Education loans (like the well-named National Defense Education Loans) are examples of government investment in human capital.

Activities such as these help to shift resource supply curves to the right, thus reducing resource costs and holding down the prices of final products.

Taxes to discourage resource employment

Governments may sometimes take steps to reduce the use of resources. One way is to tax resources, thus making their employment more costly.

The effort to stop water pollution is a case in point. Many local governments now impose a tax on firms that discharge industrial wastes into rivers and streams. Or they require the offending firms to install corrective equipment. The effect is to shift water supply curves upward and to the left, thus adding the cost of water purification to a firm's total costs of production.

The energy crisis of the 1970s provides another example of a government policy directed at reducing the use of a resource. The growing dependence on imported oil was seen to be a threat to the long-range security of the United States. In order to discourage the use of foreign oil and to encourage domestic producers to expand their output, President Ford imposed a tax on each barrel of imported oil. The effect was to raise production costs in industries using petroleum products. Unfortunately, because the demand for oil is relatively inelastic and the tax was small, the tax had no appreciable effect on oil consumption in the short run. President Carter proposed taxes on gasoline that would increase each year if Americans did not voluntarily cut the use of this precious resource. The plan was to increase taxes eventually to a point that would be high enough to discourage wasteful gasoline use.

Earnings of resource suppliers

Determining incomes

We have seen that the demand for productive resources is a derived demand. A firm hires resources according to their contribution to total revenue. It will hire a particular resource up to the point at which the contribution of the last unit is equal to its price. The price of the resource, in turn, is determined by demand and supply in the resource market. The chain of events is summarized in Figure 7.

All suppliers of resources—land, labor, capital, and entrepreneurship—receive incomes which depend on prices in their resource markets. The incomes of all resources add up to the total national income. Thus the share of total national income received by each resource supplier depends on (1) the productivity of the resource, (2) the price of the final product, and (3) the price of the resource as determined in the resource market. This is how a competitive economy answers the third fundamental economic question, *For whom is output to be produced?*

Consider Figure 7 again. The total amount a firm pays for a resource is given by the rectangle with sides OP_R and OQ_R. That is the price of the resource multiplied by the number of units hired. If we suppose that Figure 7 shows total market demand for the resource in question, then the rectangle shows the share of national income received by this particular resource.

We know that if all resource shares are added together, they must equal total national income. Each resource will be paid according to its contribution to total production. This is easy to see if we suppose that only two kinds of resources are employed. Figure 8 allows us to compare income shares for two kinds of resources: labor and capital. The demand for each resource reflects its marginal revenue product. Total income is the sum of the two rectangles: income to labor $= OP_L \times OQ_L$ and income to capital $= OP_K \times OQ_K$. But we know that the value of total output must be equal to the shaded area under each curve. How do we explain the difference between the rectangle and the whole shaded area under each curve?

Look at Figure 8a. Total product is equal to the entire shaded area. Of this total, the income paid to labor is represented by the rectangle. What is left over goes to the owners of capital. Now look at Figure 8b. Total product is again equal to the entire shaded area. Of this total, the income paid to owners of capital is represented by the rectangle. What is left over goes to labor. Thus each resource is paid according to its MRP, and the total payments add up to the value of the total product.

This is significant because it contradicts Marx's labor theory of value: income shares are paid to all resources according to their contribution to output. It shows that a perfectly competitive market system distributes income according to productivity. Resource owners are encouraged to cooperate to increase the size of the nation's "pie." Then they are rewarded by larger slices.

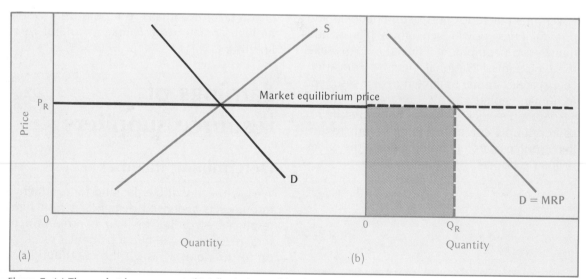

Figure 7 (a) The market for a resource. (b) A firm's demand for the resource. A firm compares the market equilibrium price, in (a), for a resource with its MRP; then it selects the quantity resource, in (b), for which P = MRP.

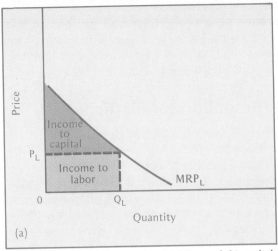 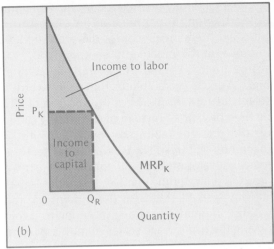

Figure 8 A firm's MRP curve for: (a) labor and (b) capital. Total product is the shaded area (both the blue and the brown) in each graph. Since each resource is paid the value of its marginal product, total product is being distributed according to each resource's contribution to output.

Marginal revenue productivity and incomes

The relative shares of resources do not remain fixed. They vary from time to time or from place to place, depending on resource productivity and on the value of the final product. Highly productive workers who have the advantage of specialized training or better equipment are likely to get a larger share of total output. This doesn't mean that they work harder or are better citizens; it means only that they have a higher MRP.

But workers may also have a higher MRP if the price of their finished product is high relative to other products. Auto workers have a higher MRP than garment workers, mainly because consumers are apparently willing to pay more for their cars than for their clothes. The average person may spend a thousand dollars or more per year on cars and only two hundred dollars per year on clothes. Many workers are aware of this, and their unions have devoted much effort to keeping the prices of their products high by fencing out low-priced competition. Labor unions have been among the strongest supporters of trade barriers against foreign manufacturers. Likewise, many resource owners in North Carolina who depend for their incomes on high consumer demand for tobacco are less than enthusiastic about advertising the harmful effects of smoking on people's health.

Changes in resource prices over time

How high a price can the owner of a resource charge? Of course, it depends partly on the MRP of the resource. But there are other factors that affect resource price. In the long run, prices of resources depend on the ease with which other resources can be substituted for them. Another way of saying this is that the *behavior of* resource prices over time depends on long-run elasticity of demand and supply.

When a resource is essential to an operation, it must be purchased with little regard for price. The result is relatively inelastic demand: a change in the price of the resource will have relatively little effect on the quantity purchased. But if a resource has many substitutes, the quantity demanded will vary widely with a change in price; demand will be relatively elastic.

When resource demand is inelastic in the short run, price may fluctuate widely. A temporary shortage may compel buying firms to bid vigorously, pushing the price up. An abundant supply will not lead to greater employment in the short run, and price will fall. Certain metals are essential in producing alloys for the manufacture of stainless steel. When supplies are interrupted for any reason, their prices may rise sharply. Certain specialized labor skills are essential in some manufacturing processes and can command high prices.

Demand may be inelastic in the short run. But in the long run, firms can develop substitutes and demand becomes more elastic. For instance, in the nineteenth century, labor was scarce in the United States and wage rates high. Workers were able to move westward in search of new horizons and opportunities to be their own boss. Instead of continuing to bid up the price of labor, employers substituted machines. The result was substantial technological development of our nation's industry. A more recent example involves the nation's new subway systems. Many of these trains are run without human operators, in order to avoid paying the rising wage scales of municipal employees.

The longer the time period, the easier it becomes to substitute resources. Business firms confronted with a rising wage trend can plan to develop alternative means of production. As a result, the demand for resources is likely to be more elastic over longer periods of time. This has been true of the demand for labor in the coal-mining industry. Following World War II, the high wages won by John L. Lewis and the United Mine Workers gave the owners an incentive to mechanize their mines wherever they could and to close those they couldn't. Employment in coal mining fell sharply in the postwar decades.

Inelastic supply may also cause wide variations in resource prices. If a given price increase causes quantity supplied to increase more than proportionately, we say that supply is elastic. If the change in quantity supplied is smaller in proportion than the change in price, we say that supply is inelastic.

Inelastic supply curves may be the result of restrictions in the labor market. The supply of workers may be limited by discriminatory hiring practices, by inadequate educational opportunities, or by restrictive job requirements. When supply is inelastic, wage rates may rise sharply without producing a significant increase in the quantity of labor supplied. The large pool of available labor may keep wages abnormally low in other markets.

The civil rights acts of recent years have helped to reduce discriminatory hiring practices, and to make labor supply more elastic. But many restrictions on educational opportunities remain. Furthermore, some employers still set unrealistic job qualifications, such as requiring a college diploma for jobs of relatively low skill. The result is to keep supply more inelastic and wage rates higher than they would be otherwise.

The politics of elasticity

The relative elasticity of demand and supply curves has important results in terms of the relative power of demanders and suppliers of resources. If a resource is essential to production, buyers of resources are often helpless to resist high resource prices. Its relatively inelastic demand makes its employment necessary without regard for price. If supply is also inelastic, resource owners can command high prices when demand shifts to the right. On the other hand, a drop in demand will reduce resource price sharply as the inelastic supply competes for the few available jobs.

During periods of growth in production, buyers have stronger positions when supply is relatively elastic. They can increase resource employment without offering substantial wage increases. Conversely, a strong union of resource suppliers is more powerful when demand is relatively inelastic. When buyers have rigid resource requirements, sellers can command higher resource prices for roughly the same quantity.

Elasticities in resource markets have significant macroeconomic effects as well. Relatively elastic demand and supply curves imply greater ease in allocation of resources among alternative employments. Quantities respond readily to small changes in price. As a result, incomes to resource owners remain fairly stable.

Summary

Employment of resources helps to determine income shares among owners of factors of production. The neoclassical economists developed the theory of marginal productivity to explain the hiring decision. Demand for a resource is a derived demand and depends on the marginal product and the marginal revenue product of the resource. A variable resource's MP and MRP decline because of the limitations of fixed resources; the resource's MRP is its demand curve. A firm will demand more units of a resource as long as its MRP is greater than its price.

The determinants of demand for a resource include: its productivity and the quantity and quality of other resources used with it; consumer demand for the finished product; and prices of substitute or complementary resources. Demand elasticity is affected by the rate of decline of MRP, the substitutability of the resource, elasticity of demand for the finished product, and the percentage of total costs represented by the resource. When the final product is sold in imperfect competition, resource demand is less elastic; this is because larger quantities of the finished good can only be sold at lower prices, reducing a resource's MRP more rapidly than in competition.

A profit-maximizing firm will hire resources up to the point at which MRP is equal to price. Price is determined by the interaction of resource demand with supply. The firm will choose among alternate resources so that the last dollar spent on every resource adds an equal amount to the value of total product. For example, a firm will choose labor and capital so that $MRP_L/P_L = MRP_K/P_K$. The profit-maximizing combination of all resources is the one at which $MRP_L/P_L = \ldots = MRP_K/P_K = 1$. Government helps to increase supplies of some resources by offering subsidies. Government attempts to reduce the use of some resources by taxing them.

The share of national income going to a particular resource is its price times the quantity hired. Income shares of all resources sum to the entire national income. Basing resource incomes on marginal productivity ensures that all resources are compensated according to their contribution to production. Shifts in demand and supply may cause changes in resource earnings over time.

Key Words and Phrases

- **labor theory of value** Karl Marx's theory that all value was fundamentally the result of the productivity of labor.
- **capitalists' surplus** according to Marx, this is the excess of value produced by labor that is kept by the capitalist.

- **neoclassical economists** economists who expanded the work of the classicists (Smith, Ricardo, Malthus, etc.) and gave it mathematical precision; they developed the theory of marginal productivity.
- **theory of marginal productivity** a theory in which resource owners are paid in proportion to their contribution to production.
- **derived demand** demand for a resource which results from consumer demand for the finished product.
- **fixed resources** a stock of resources which is fixed in the short run.
- **variable resources** resources which may be combined in varying amounts with an existing stock of fixed resources.
- **marginal product** the change in total product which results from employment of an additional unit of variable resources.
- **marginal revenue product** the change in total revenue that results from employment of an additional unit of variable resources.

Questions for Review

1. Discuss the important political debate which has centered around payment for productive resources. Who were the major contributors to the debate?

2. List the determinants of demand for a productive resource. Give examples showing how changes in these determinants affect demand elasticity.

3. When the telephone company began charging for information calls, the union representing information operators complained. Explain in terms of demand elasticities and shifts in demand.

4. The following equation is an important guide to the profit-maximizing use of resources: $MRP_L/P_L = \ldots = MRP_K/P_K = 1$. Explain why.

5. Explain why marginal revenue product (MRP) slopes more steeply when output is sold under conditions of imperfect competition.

6. Define: derived demand. Give some examples.

7. In 1977 Americans suddenly discovered that their homes were poorly insulated. Rising costs for heating and air-conditioning led many homeowners to increase insulating material in their attics. Was insufficient insulation ever an economically efficient decision? Explain in terms of MRP/P.

8. For years one of the few acceptable employments for young women was teaching. What did this mean in terms of elasticity of supply? What effect would you predict on pricing in this market?

33

How We Price and Employ Our Resources

Before a scoutmaster takes a troop on an overnight hike, he or she teaches the scouts how to read a compass. In the preceding chapters we have been preparing ourselves for a journey of our own, into the world of resource employment. For a compass we have the theory of marginal productivity. We will see how the theory can be of help in finding our way through the economic thickets of the world. In particular, we want to see just how wages, rent, interest, and profit are determined in our free market system. These are the shares of total income that go to labor, land, capital, and entrepreneurial ability. What determines the income share of labor? Of capital? Of the other resources?

Labor: the theory of wages

Labor receives the largest income share of the four classes of resources. In 1976 the U.S. labor force was almost 92 million people out of a total population of about 215 million. Economists use the term "labor" to include all persons who work for pay. The repairman who comes to your home is a member of the labor force. So are your dentist and your stockbroker. Your boss is a member of the labor force and his boss is too, all the way up to the company president.

Members of the labor force may be paid in various ways: wages, salaries, commissions, or bonuses. Whatever their pay is called, it is classified as **wages** because it is payment for labor resources. Wages do not include the returns that go to capital or land or entrepreneurship; we don't count interest or rent or profits as pay for labor. Naturally, people who own their own businesses may receive a salary for their labor, as well as profits from owning and managing the business. Top executives in a corporation may receive part of the profit in addition to their salary. In companies that have profit-sharing plans, the employees receive part of the profit in addition to their wages and salaries. In the pages that follow we will use the term "wages" to refer to payment for labor resources alone.

We will also distinguish between money wages and real wages. **Money wages** are the actual earnings in dollars and cents for any given time period—say a week or a day or an hour. **Real wages,** on the other hand, are the earnings expressed in terms of what they will buy. It is possible for your money wage to go up while your real wage is going down; this may happen during periods of inflation. If the boss gives you a 10% raise but prices go up by 15%, then your real wage has clearly fallen. In our discussion we will assume that prices remain the same unless we specify otherwise. When we speak of *wages*, we will mean *real wages.*

The marginal product of labor

By now you are aware that workers in the developed industrial countries live much better than workers in most parts of Asia or Africa. This is because total output in the developed countries is so much higher than in other countries, and there is more to be divided among those who work. We have seen that this is partly because workers in these countries are more productive: their health is better; they have better education and training; and they have acquired attitudes toward work that lead them to work more effectively. But beyond that, workers in the developed countries have much more to work *with,* in the form of capital equipment and advanced technology. The average worker in the United States or Germany, for example, uses machinery and equipment worth thousands of dollars.

You will see a number of these causes of higher productivity the next time you call someone to fix your refrigerator or washing machine. The repair person will drive up in a truck, carrying tools and spare parts; he or she will be someone with at least twelve years of schooling plus additional training in the field; and the worker will watch the time carefully so as not to waste it. Perhaps you will also sense other things that aren't as obvious, such as the existence of managers who organize the repair service and hire the workers, as well as a concern on the part of the manufacturer for earning the goodwill of customers. If you talk to the repair person you may learn that he or she used to do something else and moved into this work because of particular skills and because of the opportunity to earn a higher income.

The earnings of labor, by and large, depend upon productivity. If we look at a chart showing the trend in real earnings of American workers over the last 75 or 100 years together with the trend in output per worker, we find that the real earnings curve and the output curve practically coincide. In some periods output grew faster than real earnings and in others it grew more slowly, but over the long run their growth patterns have been very close.

We mentioned *output per worker.* If output per worker has risen, this means that total output has risen faster than the number of workers. Each of today's 92 million workers is more productive on the average than one of the 49 million workers of fifty years ago. How does this square with the principle of diminishing marginal product? Recall that our analysis of resource markets showed that adding larger and larger quantities of labor to a fixed quantity of land or capital will result in smaller and smaller additions to total product. When other resources are fixed in amount, the *diminishing marginal product of labor* will limit its employment and its earnings.

The marginal product of labor need not decline, however, if the quantities of other resources increase. For example, in the industrialized countries a growing population means more consumers, more producers, and larger consumer markets. Growing markets provide the incentives for business to invest in new capital equipment and new scientific technologies. Better education and training add more human capital to our stock of resources. More and better capital resources may offset the tendency toward diminishing marginal productivity of labor. As a result, output per worker can increase along with the growing labor force, and all can enjoy higher real wages.

Wage determination in labor markets

Even though the general level of real wages has risen over the years, what about wages for particular occupations and skills?

Typists enjoy higher real earnings now than they did 30 years ago. So do engineers, psychologists, and sanitation workers. Still, some occupations have gained more than others. What determines the rate of pay that any particular kind of labor can earn?

There is no simple answer to the question of how wages are determined in labor markets. There are a number of answers, depending on conditions in particular markets. We will first look at two basic types of labor markets: the competitive model and monopsony. Then we will study the effect of unions on wages.

The competitive model It is helpful to begin with a perfectly competitive labor market. The market for restaurant cooks is fairly competitive with many buyers and sellers. No buyer of labor (that is, no employer) is able to influence the wage rate. No seller of labor (that is, no worker) is able to influence the wage rate either. As a result, the wage rate in competition is determined in the market by the intersection of market demand and market supply.

Hypothetical market demand and supply curves for restaurant cooks are shown in Figure 1a. Market demand is the sum of all individual demand curves for labor. The demand curve slopes downward because of diminishing MRP in the short run. Market supply represents the quantities of labor that would be available in the market at different wage rates. The supply curve slopes upward, since more people would be drawn to that particular type of work at higher wage rates. Employers would have to pay a higher wage to hire more workers. The market equilibrium wage for this type of labor is shown as OW.

For any individual restaurant manager the demand for labor is the same as labor's marginal revenue product curve, the downward-sloping line in Figure 1b. Supply is a horizontal line drawn at the level of the market wage OW. Each employer will hire the quantity of labor for which marginal revenue product is equal to the market wage rate.

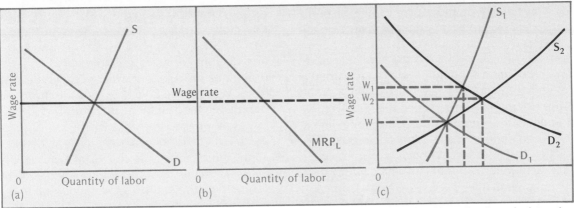

Figure 1 Hypothetical market supply and demand curves for restaurant cooks. (a) Market demand and supply determine industry wage rate. (b) The number of cooks hired is determined by the intersection of the wage rate with the marginal revenue product curve of labor. (c) Suppose industry demand for cooks rises from D_1 to D_2. This initially raises the wage rate from W to W_1. However, over time, the supply of cooks—drawn by higher wages—will rise from S_1 to S_2. Now there is a new—and lower—equilibrium wage, W_2.

Suppose there is an increase in consumer demand for restaurant meals. Prices rise and the marginal revenue product of labor increases. The result will be increased demand for cooks. The demand curve in Figure 1c shifts from D_1 to D_2. In the short run the supply of labor is fairly inelastic. The quantity of workers hired will rise only slightly, but the wage rate will rise sharply to W_1. The higher wage for short-order cooks will draw more people into that occupation, but it will require some time for them to learn the trade. As they do so, the supply of labor curve will shift to S_2. Employment will increase further and the wage rate will fall to W_2.

As everyone knows, wage rates differ for different kinds of work. Even under perfect competition we would expect some differences to exist. Work that is particularly unpleasant or dangerous, such as coal mining or working with explosives or building skyscrapers, would have to pay more in order to induce people to do it. Otherwise, if there is full employment, workers will be able to find more pleasant jobs. (If there is much unemployment, or if some workers are prevented from moving into other jobs, then they may be forced to work at anything they can find. But then the labor market is no longer perfectly competitive.) We would also expect to find higher

wage rates in jobs requiring more training; workers have to be compensated for the time and money invested in acquiring the necessary skills. Workers such as bricklayers or carpenters who can't work during bad weather will receive higher hourly rates to make up for the days when they are idle. Hard work or more responsible work may be paid more than easy work.

No theory will explain all the many differences in wage rates; some differences seem to be accidental. If you go around a large city checking the wages of janitors, for instance, you may find that they vary considerably. Some janitors earn more than others because their work is superior, allowing them to work in better buildings in the more fashionable parts of town. Others earn more because they have been on the job longer. A few may earn more because someone likes them.

Monopsony So far we have been assuming perfect competition in the labor market. There are many employers, and workers can choose among many employments. But quite often a worker has little or no choice; there may be only one possible employer for a certain kind of labor in a given town. A firm that is the single buyer of a resource is called a **monopsony**. *A monopsony is similar to a monopoly, except that it is on the buying side of the market.* It doesn't have to bid against other firms for the resource in question.

The effect of monopsony in a resource market is illustrated in Figure 2. The demand curve is downward sloping just as under competition, but this is where the similarity ends. In competition the equilibrium wage is determined at the point where market demand and supply curves intersect. Then the supply curve facing an individual firm is a horizontal line at the equilibrium wage. The individual firm under perfect competition is a *price taker:* it can acquire any amount of labor without affecting the market price. The result is different when the resource buyer is a monopsony. The monopsony firm is a single buyer, and therefore it faces the market supply curve. In Figure 2 the supply of labor curve slopes upward. If the monopsony firm hires more labor, it must offer a higher wage.

The monopsony firm bases its hiring decision on the additional cost of hiring an additional unit of a resource. The additional cost is called its **marginal resource cost** (MRC). In competition any quantity of labor can be hired for the same wage; therefore, marginal resource cost is equal to the wage rate. In monopsony additional quantities of labor must be paid a higher wage rate; therefore, marginal resource cost is greater than the wage.

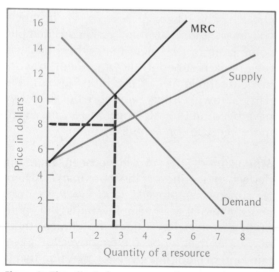

Figure 2 The effect of a monopsony in a resource market. As the only employer of labor, the monopsony's supply curve is its marginal resource cost (MRC) curve. Under this monopsony, quantity hired is three and wage rate is $8. However, the competitive market equilibrium would lead to more workers hired (here four) and a higher wage paid (around $9).

A numerical example will help to make this clear. Table 1 shows some hypothetical cost data for a monopsony firm. Suppose the firm decides to increase employment of labor from three units to four. The price rises from $8 to $9. What is the added cost to the firm? It is the higher price of $9 for the fourth unit plus the additional $1 for each of the other three units. The addition to total cost with each added unit of labor is shown in column (4), *Marginal Resource Cost.* MRC is calculated by subtracting the total cost of acquiring three units from the total cost of acquiring four units. Thus the MRC of the fourth unit is $12 and that of the fifth unit is $14.

In monopsony, the marginal resource cost associated with increasing employment is always greater than the supply price. This is different from perfect competition when firms are "price takers." In Figure 2, MRC is drawn above supply. To acquire more labor the monopsony firm must offer a higher price. But it must pay the higher price to all the units of labor it employs.

A monopsony firm will reach its equilibrium level of employment where its resource demand curve intersects MRC. At equilibrium the last worker hired adds the same to revenues and to costs. In Figure 2 this is the point at which the quantity of labor hired is three units and the wage rate is $8. The equilibrium level of employment is less than under perfect competition, and the equilibrium wage is lower. (Read the market price of three units of labor at a.) To hire more than 3 units would add more to costs than to the value of output; thus fewer workers will be employed than under perfect competition and for less pay. There is a similarity between the monopsonistic employer of labor and the monopolistic seller of goods. Just as the monopolistic seller is led to produce less than the competitive firm and to set a higher price, so the monopsonistic employer will tend to hire fewer workers and to pay lower wages.

Unions and the labor market

Monopsony illustrates imperfect competition on the demand side of the labor market. *Unions illustrate imperfect competition on the supply side.* One purpose of unions is to achieve wage

Table 1
Hypothetical Cost Data of a Monopsonist Acquiring Labor

Quantity of resource	Price	Total cost of resource	Marginal resource cost
0	$ 5	$ 0	
1	6	6	$ 6
2	7	14	8
3	8	24	10
4	9	36	12
5	10	50	14

rates and working conditions different from those provided by the intersection of supply and demand in a competitive market. When there is no union, each worker makes his or her own agreement with the employer in competition with other workers. But a union seeks to bargain on behalf of all the workers, giving them monopoly power over the sale of their labor. If employers refuse to meet union demands, the union can call a strike and withhold all labor from the job.

There are three ways a union can raise wage rates. *One is to raise the demand for labor.* If the union can cause demand to increase as in Figure 1c, the equilibrium wage for workers in the union will be higher. The number of workers hired will also increase. In some industries unions have tried to do this. These are primarily industries in which the demand for labor has been declining because of technological changes or because of competition from other industries. Garment workers' unions have tried to help their employers produce and sell more clothing; they have cooperated in increasing productivity and in helping to advertise the products. Unions of steelworkers have pressed for higher tariffs to keep out competing products from abroad and thus to increase demand for American workers. Railway unions were able for a long time to force their employers to hire workers who were no longer needed; firemen on diesel engines were a significant example. These efforts may have only limited success. In the long run the demand for labor depends on its MRP, which depends on technical progress, the growth of capital, and consumer demand for finished goods.

A second way that a union can raise wage rates is by restricting the supply of labor. This has been the approach used by the **craft unions**—organizations of workers having a particular kind of skill, such as bricklayers, carpenters, electricians, and plumbers. Craft unions have restricted their membership by requiring long periods of apprenticeship, by setting very high initiation fees, by admitting very few new members, or all of these. Figure 3 illustrates a typical market for skilled craftsmen. In the absence of restrictions, the competitive supply curve for labor would be S. The craft union, by restricting the supply of labor, succeeds in achieving the curve S_u and pushing the wage level up from W to W_u. It does this, of course, at the cost of fewer jobs and less output.

Unions have also tried more socially desirable ways of reducing the supply of labor. They have favored laws to limit child labor, to raise the school-leaving age, and to make it possible for workers to retire earlier. They even

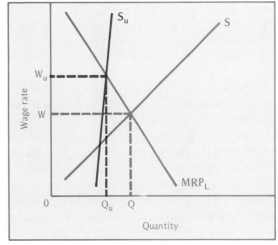

Figure 3 A craft union restricts supply to keep wage rates high. S represents free market supply, which leads to wage W and quantity of workers hired Q. S_u is the supply from a craft union. The union wage rate W_u is higher while the numbers of union workers hired (Q_u) is lower than in the free market.

agreed to *mandatory* retirement at age 65. (However, some now feel unions made a mistake and that retirement should be *voluntary* or optional at 65.) Unions have also favored shorter work weeks and longer vacations. All of these have helped to reduce the supply of labor below what it would otherwise be and to keep wage rates higher.

A third way that a union can raise wage rates is by getting employers to agree not to pay less than a certain wage. This can be done through legislation or through a labor-management contract spelling out what the union wages will be for particular kinds of labor. The effect on wage levels is shown in Figure 4. Under competitive conditions the wage would be W, determined by supply and demand. But the union contract sets the wage at W_u. Firms will hire the quantity of labor at which MRP equals the cost of an additional unit of labor. This is given by Q_u. The higher the union wage level, the less will be the quantity of labor hired.

Several things must be said about this. The diagram exaggerates the extent to which most unions are able to raise wages. Some, perhaps many, labor-management contracts set union wage rates that are about what the market would pay anyway. The union negotiators generally ask for more than they expect to get, and management responds by offering less than it is willing to settle for. The wage they finally agree upon will depend on the strength of the union and the aggressiveness of its leadership, as well as on the resistance of management. Often it is not very different from wages under competition.

But even when unions succeed in pushing up the *money* wage rate, their victory will not amount to much unless productivity increases, too. Without gains in productivity, the prices of finished goods may rise also. If a number of unions in basic industries sign agreements for excessive wage increases, the resulting price increases will spread throughout the economy and to the goods that workers buy. Their *money* wages will increase, but higher prices will mean that their *real* wages increase less or not at all.

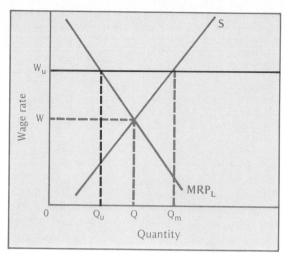

Figure 4 Unions bargain for some minimum wage W_u, which may be higher than the competitive wage, W. The industry demand curve is the MRP_L curve. Thus at W_u the supply of workers Q_m is much higher than the numbers hired, Q_u. In fact, the amount of workers hired Q_u is less than would be under competition (Q).

Again the result may be different when a union deals with a monopsony employer. The union may be able to raise wages without raising prices by forcing the employer to pay the wage that would be achieved under competition. Left to itself, the monopsonist would pay less than that rate, as we saw in Figure 2. Thus the union is able to achieve better terms for its members than they could get if they were left to bargain as individuals. This may often be the case in small towns or in industries where a few giant firms employ many semiskilled workers.

Sometimes unions help to raise the wages of some workers at the expense of others. For instance, if a craft union is able to achieve higher than average wages for its members by restricting its numbers, this means that those who are kept out of the craft will have to find other kinds of work and perhaps accept lower wages. In some industries powerful unions have been able to achieve wage increases that their employers then passed on in the form of higher prices to consumers. Workers in lower-wage industries do not necessarily benefit from the higher wages won by unionized workers. Like all consumers, they have to pay higher prices for the products of those industries. Something like this happened in 1975–1977; the net result was greater inequality in income between different types of jobs.

Extended Example
Minimum Wage Laws

Since 1938 the federal government has set minimum wage rates for workers outside agriculture. In 1976 the legal minimum wage for workers covered by the Fair Labor Standards Act was $2.30 an hour. The purpose of the law is to "put a floor" under the wages of the lowest paid workers. What is the effect of such a law?

If we assume a competitive labor market, the effect is to raise the wage of the lowest paid workers, as in Figure 4. But because employers equate wage with MRP, the result is a lower level of employment. Those who favor minimum wage laws disagree with this analysis. They argue that the labor market is not competitive for many workers. Many labor markets are characterized by monopsony so that employers can actually hold wages below the competitive level. To the extent that this is true, a minimum wage law can bring these workers up to the market level without any reduction in employment.

A number of statistical studies have been made of industries in which the law has forced employers to raise the wages of the lowest paid workers. These studies indicate that the minimum wage does lead to reductions in employment. The workers most affected by the federal minimum wage law are those in small-scale industries such as retailing, domestic service, cigars, fertilizers, sawmills, seamless hosiery, men's and boys' shirts, footwear, and canning. The minimum hits hardest in low-wage areas of the country, mainly in the South, while it has relatively little effect in other areas. The loss of employment is most severe among the unskilled, the nonwhite, and teenagers. Some economists have proposed excluding teenagers from the minimum wage law, or providing a lower minimum for them than for others, in the belief that this might reduce the high rates of unemployment among young people.

The highest wage gains have been achieved by coal miners, airline pilots, teachers, merchant seamen, and construction workers. Garment workers have strong unions, but they have not made big wage gains. Most union workers, however, are better paid than nonunion workers. Among the lowest paid workers are nonunionized farm laborers, domestic servants, store clerks, and laundry workers.

Unions have other purposes, of course, than to raise wages. One important function is to handle the complaints or *grievances* that arise on the job. In the labor-management contract there will be a section entitled *Grievance Procedure* setting up a system for handling a worker's complaint. A union representative, or *shop steward,* will usually discuss the complaint first with the immediate superior or foreman. If the worker and the union representative are not satisfied with the foreman's response, the union representative can then submit the grievance to the plant superintendent. Sometimes a grievance will be appealed all the way up to top management. If satisfaction is still not achieved, the grievance may be submitted to an *arbitrator*, jointly chosen by the employer and the union. Arbitrators are impartial specialists in industrial relations. If the arbitrator's decision is *binding,* this procedure is called *binding arbitration.*

Unions have also done much to eliminate unpleasant and dangerous working conditions, establish rules for promotions and layoffs, and prevent hard-driving employers from speeding up the work excessively.

The development of unionism

In the earlier years of the Industrial Revolution labor unions were treated as illegal conspiracies which interfered with normal trade. Nevertheless, they existed in the United States as early as the 1790s when the shoemakers, carpenters, printers, and other skilled craftsmen formed unions. Unionism as we know it began in the late nineteenth century. It probably developed then in response to the growth and abuses of big business. Craft unions were the predominant type of labor union until the 1930s, when industrial unions were organized in the new mass production industries such as steel and automobiles. **Industrial unions** included all workers, skilled and unskilled, in a particular industry or sometimes even a group of industries. For example, all auto workers, from sweepers to assembly-line workers to tool-and-die makers, were eligible to become members of the United Auto Workers. A wave of union organizing began, encouraged by the **National Labor Relations Act** of 1935 (Wagner Act). This law forbade employers from interfering with the right of workers to form unions and required employers to bargain in good faith with unions once they were established.

During the 1930s, the federal government encouraged the growth of unions in the belief that employers had too much power over wages and working conditions. But by the 1940s many people had come to feel that unions were getting too strong. There was widespread resentment against strikes and rising prices, as well as outrage over certain union practices that were regarded as unfair. This antiunion sentiment culminated in the **Taft-Hartley Act** of 1948, intended to regulate collective bargaining between labor and management. The Act contains provisions designed to prevent abuses of union power:

(1) It outlaws closed shop agreements among workers and employers engaged in interstate commerce. **Closed shop** would allow a firm to hire only workers who *already* belong to the union.

(2) The law permits **union shop** arrangements (requiring workers to join the union *after* they are hired) unless these are prohibited by state law. A number of states (21 in 1976) have passed so-called **right-to-work laws** making compulsory union membership illegal. In those states, mostly in the South and West, the **open shop** prevails; employers may hire union or nonunion workers as they please, and no worker is required to join a union. As a consequence, wage rates in these states tend to be lower than in the heavily unionized industrial states of the Midwest and Northeast.

(3) The Taft-Hartley Act was the basis for another important restriction on union power. This law granted the President power to issue an injunction against a strike when the strike is believed to be contrary to the national interest. An **injunction** is a court order to refrain from a certain specified action. A *labor injunction* forbids the union to strike for a 90-day "cooling off" period. To disobey an injunction would risk contempt of court charges, with heavy fines and possible imprisonment.

(4) Another limitation of union power has come under some attack in recent years. This is the prohibition of secondary boycotts. To *boycott* is to withhold cooperation from a business in order to pressure it to accept target demands. A **secondary boycott** is one where workers withhold cooperation from a business firm in order to pressure it to accept the demands of another union. It is a way of enforcing demands through worker solidarity. Secondary boycotts could seriously interfere with production in firms not directly involved in the particular dispute.

A bill to permit secondary boycotts was vetoed by President Ford in 1976; it failed to pass Congress again in 1977. The bill would have permitted "common situs" picketing on construction jobs. A union of electricians, for example, could surround a construction site with striking pickets. Then cooperating members of other unions (plumbers, floorers, and roofers) could refuse to cross the picket line and bring the entire operation to a halt. "Common situs" would give substantial new power to unions and is hotly denounced by business management. Secondary boycotts would be particularly damaging in the construction industry, which accounts directly for about one-tenth of annual national output and provides employment for additional millions of workers in steel, lumber, cement, transportation, and other industries.

Defenders of "common situs" argue that the principle of united action requires that workers be permitted to use all reasonable means of pressure. Otherwise employers could substitute nonstriking workers for strikers and win any dispute with the union.

In general, unions try to resolve their differences with management peacefully, without strikes. Through **collective bargaining** they draw up regular contracts which specify terms of employment: hours and wage rates, vacations and sick leave, seniority rights and retirement benefits, grievance provisions. If representatives of both groups are unable to agree on the terms of the contract, they may hire a mediator to attempt a compromise solution.

Contracts may run for as long as three years. During the life of a contract, disagreements may arise over interpretation of contract clauses. Minor disputes can be settled by the established grievance committee of workers and employers. Major disputes may be referred to a professional arbitrator for settlement.

The **strike** is a union's ultimate tool for advancing the interests of labor. When a reasonable period of collective bargaining fails to produce an agreement, the union may call for a strike. Sometimes the decision to strike is made by the local union, but more often today it is decided, or at least approved, by the national union of workers involved. When a contract is finally agreed on, the union guarantees not to call a strike for the life of the agreement. Sometimes a local union may disobey the no-strike provision. This is a **"wildcat" strike** and it is generally opposed by the national union.

Employers can use a form of strike, too. When employers close down an operation in defense of their position, this is called a **lockout.**

Unions of the 1970s

The 1970s have been hard on the labor-union movement. Two recessions have reduced job opportunities for union members. High wage demands have aggravated inflation and priced many workers out of the market. The public has grown hostile to many union wage demands, particularly the demands of public employees. Leaders of major unions are approaching retirement because of age or because of competition for top union offices. Even more serious for unions are the long-run problems of automation, the growing relative power of industrial conglomerates, and the shrinking share of organized labor in the work force.

There is no doubt that labor unions are changing; they must change to adapt to the new conditions of work in the United States. When Samuel Gompers founded the American Federation of Labor (AFL) in 1886 it was a loose organization of unions of cigar makers, harness makers, organ workers, and other unions which no longer exist. By the early 1900s railroad workers, construction workers, and miners made up the important unions of the AFL. Later, unions of mass-production workers pushed union membership to the highest levels ever achieved: 33.2% of all nonfarm workers in 1955. Total union membership is now estimated at 20,566,000, or about one-fourth of the nonfarm labor force. (See Table 2 for a list of the largest unions.)

Unions are still adapting, and now the major push comes from unions of public employees—government, education, and nonprofit institutions. Today more than a million federal government employees are covered by union contracts and the American Federation of State, County, and Municipal Employees (AFSCME) has an additional 750,000 members. Even teachers, farm workers, ballplayers, nurses, and doctors are joining unions. Only white-collar office employees have generally

Table 2
Major Unions in 1974

Union	Membership	Dues income
Teamsters	1,973,000	$ 52,096,860
Auto workers	1,545,000	116,660,772
National Education Association	1,470,000	—
Steelworkers	1,300,000	79,903,091
Brotherhood of Electrical Workers	991,000	57,325,795
Machinists	943,000	39,975,728
Carpenters	820,000	28,212,395
Retail clerks	651,000	—
Laborers	650,000	14,495,911
AFSCME	648,000	—

resisted unionization. They feel they will receive the same benefits as unionized employees without having to pay union dues.

Some unions are attempting to increase their power by merging. The two large federations of unions merged in 1955; the American Federation of Labor and the Congress of Industrial Organizations joined to form the AFL-CIO. For twenty years its president has been George Meany, a former plumber from the Bronx. George Meany is considered the granddaddy of unionism by many of the 14 million members of AFL-CIO affiliated unions. The only major challenge to his long reign was the withdrawal of the United Auto Workers union by its president Walter Reuther in the late 1960s. (In 1957 the AFL-CIO expelled the mammoth International Brotherhood of Teamsters for corrupt practices.)

What accounted for Meany's long dominance of the labor movement? In general, he was respected by representatives of labor, management, and government alike. He was often called a labor statesman, one who could perceive and defend the interests of his constituents in the broader context of the national interest. His rules of operation were: "Never beg, never threaten, never think you're right all the time." These rules and his philosophy of unionism helped him to achieve a degree of industrial peace while defending the interests of union members. And most important his influence helped to persuade wage earners of the futility of inflationary wage demands without gains in productivity.

Public employee unions

Today if you deal with a public employee, the odds are better than 50–50 you're dealing with a union member. And public employee unions are becoming more aggressive in their demands at a time when the public sector is starved for funds. Postal employees, air-traffic controllers, teachers, hospital employees, firefighters, police, and sanitation workers have been responsible for more and more work stoppages in recent years. Most of the strikes were illegal by local or federal law and some strikers were jailed.

Currently, the fastest growing union of all is the American Federation of State, County, and Municipal Employees (AFSCME). It is the fifth largest union in the AFL-CIO and the largest union of public employees. Its president is Jerry Wurf, a union organizer for twenty years. Wurf has impressed friends and foes alike with his aggressive support of policies favorable to labor.

Public support for unions of public employees waned during the recession of 1973–1975 and with the increasing financial problems of state and local governments. Public workers were accused of excessive wage demands, unwarranted strikes, and too little work. Wurf complains that many of the problems of state and local finances are the result of mismanagement by government officials. Many local government officials are inexperienced in the area of labor relations and are strongly influenced by local political considerations. When politicians promise lower taxes and better public services, they naturally create unreasonable attitudes in the minds of voters. Wurf believes that unions can help to plan government services and tax policies more systematically. They have the research staffs and the expertise in industrial relations to make decision-making more scientific in the public area. He favors collective bargaining and binding arbitration rather than strikes in unions like police and firefighters where strikes might result in death or serious injury. He believes that moderation in these areas would promote fair practices in other areas of public employment.

Labor issues for coming decades

Wages and hours have always been a primary concern of labor organizations. But efforts to raise the general level of wages will be self-defeating if wage gains exceed worker productivity. Over the first half of the 1970s hourly wages rose 39.4% while productivity increased only 6.5%. Excess wage increases can be paid in either of two ways: by the consumer in the form of higher prices or by the employer in the form of lower profits. Inflationary cost increases threaten the nation's economic health by distorting relative values and disrupting normal production relationships. And falling profits reduce the ability to invest in expanding productive plant and equipment.

There is another side to the issue of wage inflation. Unions argue that progressive income tax rates have actually reduced worker take home pay so that real wages are now no higher than in 1968. Many unions have demanded escalatory clauses keyed to changes in the *consumer price index* (CPI) in order to protect their purchasing power. These escalator clauses are known as *cost-of-living adjustments* (COLAs). Escalator clauses have the advantage of extending contracts over longer periods without risk of loss of purchasing power. But they have the disadvantage of validating inflation and the resulting loss of purchasing power for noncovered workers.

For many years, wage rates in the United States exceeded those of most other industrial nations. This was not a serious problem because output per worker in the United States was also higher. With high worker productivity, labor costs per unit of output were low. We could produce goods of high quality at prices that were competitive in world markets.

Accelerating wage inflation in the United States during the 1950s and 1960s and rising productivity in other nations changed all this, and the United States suffered a gradual weakening in world trade. Unions complained when corporations established plants abroad to take advantage of cheap foreign labor. The picture may be changing again. In fact, by 1975 increasing wages in other industrialized nations had overtaken U.S. wage rates. Table 3 illustrates the change.

Another important reason for the change in relative wage rates has been increasing fringe benefits for workers in other countries. Fringe benefits or indirect labor costs add about 26% to basic wages in the United States but more than 50% to wages in many European nations. *Fringe benefits* include paid holidays and vacations, pensions and health insurance, and unemployment benefits. The higher cost of these benefits in European nations has driven many foreign firms to seek cheap labor in the United States!

After wage negotiation, the next biggest issue of collective bargaining concerns the length of the work week. The current forty-hour week in manufacturing was an accomplishment of the 1940s. Now the thirty-two-hour week without a reduction in pay is an important goal of unions, particularly the United Auto Workers (UAW). Improvements in productivity, the increase in part-time employees, and the growth of service industries have already reduced average work weeks in nonfarm employment to about 36 hours. High unemployment during the recession of 1973–1975 spurred a new drive to reduce regularly scheduled hours in manufacturing. The hope was that shorter hours would help to put more people back to work. Of course, it might have the opposite result of increasing "moonlighting" or second jobs among persons already employed.

The labor contract between Ford Motor Company and the UAW in the fall of 1976 promised workers 40 paid days off a year, in effect reducing the average work week substantially. Whether the agreement adds to costs of production, and thus to auto prices, will depend on trends in worker productivity. Some auto workers prefer shorter hours to more pay. They see their wage gains eaten up by inflation and prefer to enjoy the gain of greater leisure instead.

Probably the most serious problem facing labor is growing unemployment. Every year

Table 3
Pay Scales, or Total Labor Costs per Hour (including fringe benefits)

Country	1970	1975
Sweden	$3.01	$7.12
Norway	2.49	6.56
Denmark	2.37	6.32
Canada	3.49	6.19
United States	4.25	6.06
Belgium	2.08	6.05
West Germany	2.43	5.64
Netherlands	2.12	5.54
Switzerland	1.99	5.03
Italy	1.87	4.36
Austria	1.54	4.07
France	1.74	4.01
Britain	1.68	3.70
Japan	1.10	3.45

Source: *U.S. News & World Report,* Feb. 2, 1976, taken from Swedish Employers' Confederation.

jobs are wiped out because of automation and increased efficiency. At the same time, more new jobs are needed to accommodate a growing work force. It has been estimated that the United States must create an average of 72,100 new jobs every week for the next ten years. This is twice as many jobs as the number generated weekly during the past decade.

To generate employment on this scale requires a high level of saving and investment in human and material capital for use in production. Tax and spending programs of the federal government can help to stimulate job-creating activities: (1) Business can be given tax incentives to invest in plant and equipment expansion and modernization, particularly in industries where demand is pushing against the ceiling of productive capacity. (2) Employment subsidies can be awarded to private firms which provide on-the-job training. (3) Government can subsidize public service jobs to provide employment for workers without industrial skills. (4) Government can sponsor skill development programs to prepare workers for productive employment.

Whatever the means employed, it is important that the nation solve the problem of unemployment. In the words of Charles L. Schultze, now President Carter's Chairman of the Council of Economic Advisors: "The single most important contribution toward solving the major social problems of this generation—deteriorating inner cities, inequality among the races and between the sexes, high and still-rising crime rates, poverty, insecurity, and hardship for a minority of our citizens— would be a high level of employment and a tight labor market."

Supply elasticity of labor

Workers differ from other resources, of course, in being human. They are free to sell their labor power in the market or not to sell it. We usually take it for granted that at higher pay levels the quantity of labor supplied will be greater. This is a reasonably safe assumption, especially in a modern economy. But in some economies where workers are not strongly motivated to increase their earnings, the supply curve of labor takes on a strange shape. Workers may be content to put in only a few hours for an in-

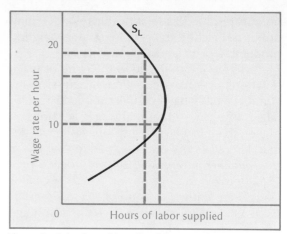

Figure 5 A backward-bending labor supply curve occurs when workers reach a point in wages where they prefer leisure to more work; at a high enough wage, they can afford not to work beyond a certain level and may even reduce the number of hours worked.

come which satisfies their basic needs. If their hourly wage is increased they may even work fewer hours and continue to receive the same total income as before.

When workers behave this way, the supply curve of labor may bend backward as in Figure 5. At higher rates of pay, *fewer* rather than *more* hours are worked. This is often true in some primitive economies, in the tropics, and in rural areas of developed economies. Something similar may happen at a very high level of affluence, when workers prefer leisure to working extra hours of overtime. Nevertheless, for most purposes of economic policy in the United States, we are safe in assuming that the supply curve of labor slopes upward to the right.

Land: the theory of rent

The earnings of land differ from those of labor because the supply of land is fixed. The total amount of land in the United States, for example, cannot be increased or decreased. The supply curve of land is vertical. This means that the value of land as a whole is determined by demand alone, as shown in Figure 6. The demand curve for land, like demand for other resources, slopes downward, reflecting the principle of diminishing marginal revenue product. As larger quantities of land are used in combination with certain fixed resources, output increases by smaller and smaller amounts.

Differences in the productivity of land resources or a change in the market price of output will cause a shift in demand and a change in the price buyers are willing to pay. In Figure 6, land yielding a MRP of MRP'_L will earn a price OR'. Land yielding MRP''_L will earn only OR''.

The classical economists referred to the price of land as **rent.** David Ricardo (1772–1823) observed that agricultural land would be cultivated up to the point at which the value of output from the poorest acre used just covered the nonrent cost of cultivation. On the most fertile acres the cost of cultivation per unit of output would be lower, and the difference would be collected by the landlord as rent. As demand for food rose, less fertile acreage would be brought into use. Less fertile land would cost more to cultivate, and the owners of the more fertile land would get higher rent. The least fertile acreage would earn no rent. The value of output would just cover nonrent costs of cultivation and there would be no surplus for the landlord.

The term *rent* is used broadly to mean *any payment to a resource over and above the amount necessary to keep the resource in use.* Since land is fixed in supply, all of the return paid to land is rent. The land is there anyway, and it would be available even if the price were zero.

From the standpoint of an individual user of land, its price is a cost just like the cost of any other resource. The renter must pay this price for its use. From the standpoint of society, the price of land is a surplus that accrues to owners because the supply of land is fixed.

Alternative uses for land

Resource prices normally perform two important functions: an incentive function and a rationing function. The first of these is not relevant in the market for land, since no amount of incentive can increase appreciably the quantity of land available. However, the second function is especially important. With a

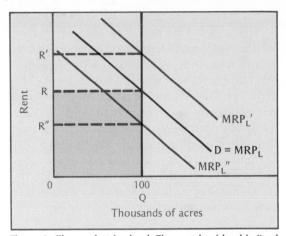

Figure 6 The market for land. The supply of land is fixed and the supply curve is vertical. But when supply is perfectly inelastic, the price is determined by demand alone. Once again, the demand curve equals the marginal revenue product (of land) curve. Thus for MRP'_L the rent equals R', while for MRP''_L the rent equals R''. The total amount of rent (R) is shown by the shaded area.

limited supply of land it is important to ration the existing quantity wisely among all possible uses. The fixed quantity of land must be allocated toward those types of production which produce the greatest value.

Although the total supply of land is fixed, the supply available for particular employments is variable. Land may be shifted from use as parking lots, to tennis courts, to condominiums. The quantity available for any particular employment varies with the rent paid.

Dividing land among many different uses allows renters to express their demand for land according to the value of its output in many different employments. And it allows owners of land to vary the quantity they supply in each of many different markets. The result will be a wide variety of rentals paid. Land suitable for growing a strain of grapes for fine wine will command a higher rental than useless swamp land. If the land is adjacent to a large amusement park, it may command even greater rentals as a parking lot. This suggests two reasons for high MRP and high rentals: the value of the output of land and its location. A favorable location allows land to deliver its good or service with a greater net gain to its user. The payment of rent serves to allocate land to its best uses in terms of productivity and location.

The possibility of alternative uses of land complicates our definition of rent. *When there are alternative uses, the payment necessary to keep land in its current employment is the amount it could earn in its next most productive use.* By this definition the payment to landowners includes an opportunity cost. The user of land must pay the land's opportunity cost in order to attract land for a particular use. Any excess rental over its opportunity cost is the landowner's surplus. In Figure 7 the landowner's surplus is FP, the excess earnings of land used as an amusement park over its productivity as a tree farm.

A tax on land

Since land rent is a surplus that the owner gets simply from being the owner, some people have been in favor of taxing the surplus away. The American economist Henry George (1839–1897) proposed that government tax away all the rent from land and use it to finance social programs. He pointed out that economic progress would lead to a growing scarcity of land. Owners of land would reap ever greater returns at the expense of labor and capital. *Because the supply of land is inelastic, a tax on land would not reduce the quantity supplied in the market.* George believed that the revenue from this source would be so great that no other tax would be necessary, and so he called his proposed tax the "single tax." Figure 8 illustrates the argument. The equilibrium rent is OR. If a tax OT is levied on rental income,

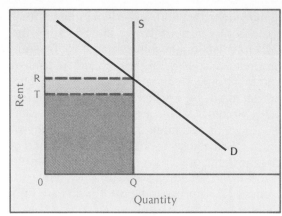

Figure 8 When supply is inelastic, it is possible to tax away the owner's surplus without reducing the quantity supplied in the market. If R is the rent, a tax of OT leaves only TR left for the owner.

landowners will continue to supply the same quantity of land but for a return of only TR.

A practical difficulty with the single-tax idea is that most landlords have had to pay a high price to acquire the land which now rents at high rates. It would not be fair to impose a tax on the owner of a lot in Manhattan equal to the difference between its rent and that of swamp land in Tennessee.

Our state and local governments depend on property taxes for a substantial proportion of their revenues. A number of urban economists have come to favor a tax on land, rather than the prevalent property tax, as a way of raising revenue. They point out that property taxes fail to distinguish between land itself and the buildings or improvements on it. Taxes on buildings discourage investors from building and improving them. High property taxes have been one cause of the deterioration of some central city areas. A tax on land alone does not have such negative effects because it does not affect resource allocation. The most profitable use of land before the tax is imposed remains the most profitable use afterward.

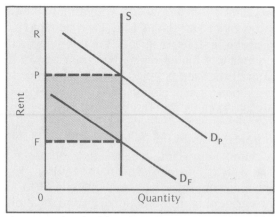

Figure 7 When land has alternative uses, a portion of the payment is an opportunity cost (OF). The excess payment over opportunity cost is the landlord's surplus (FP), or rent.

Viewpoint
Speculating in Urban Land

"I would not call owning land a good way to become wealthy; I would not call owning land the best way to become wealthy; owning land is the *only* way to become wealthy."

He may have overstated his case a little, but Chicago businessman Marshall Field accumulated a vast fortune by speculating in urban and suburban land.

The value of land is a result of supply and demand. Supply is fixed: "The Lord ain't making any more." And demand increases as population grows and as scientific advances increase land's productivity. The selling price of an acre of land reflects its earning capacity or rent. A seller must receive a price equal to the sum of expected future rentals, discounted by the rate of interest which could be earned in other employments. The formula for the price of land is:

$$\text{Price} = \Sigma \frac{R}{(1 + i)^t}$$

where R = expected rent, i = interest rate on other investments, and t = the number of periods in the future the rent is paid. Thus if the going rate of interest is 5%, a piece of property yielding a rent of $100,000 a year for five years should sell for

$$\frac{100,000}{1.05^1} + \frac{100,000}{1.05^2} + \frac{100,000}{1.05^3}$$
$$+ \frac{100,000}{1.05^4} + \frac{100,000}{1.05^5} = \$432,950.$$

Land differs from other resources in that its value may increase through no effort of its owner. Urban and suburban lands increase in value as a region develops economically. Many improvements made at the expense of all taxpayers actually increase the wealth of property owners. Streets, airports, schools, water systems, police and fire systems, civic centers, and sports arenas make land sites accessible and more valuable. These improvements constitute the city's *infrastructure*. The infrastructure is the city's stock of basic services. The New York Regional Plan Commission found that the city's infrastructure costs taxpayers more than $30,000 for every residential homesite in the metropolitan area. A land speculator can make substantial gains on sales of land acquired at low prices and sold after the city's infrastructure is complete.

The benefits of land speculation are likely to be inequitable. That is, benefits and costs are distributed among different groups of people. There is another disadvantage. Land speculation is destabilizing. Because land values are expected to continue to move in the same direction, speculators will tend to hold land longer for maximum gain. The effect is to reduce the supply of land available in the market and keep prices higher than otherwise. Then high land costs are built into the production costs of everything we buy, adding to price inflation. Furthermore, high land costs drive business and industry away from urban centers, contributing to urban sprawl. This adds to the community's costs of providing infrastructure.

Communities have been unable to correct the problems created by land speculation. In part, the reason is the type of taxes levied on property. Property taxes increase when the owner makes capital improvements on the land. This type of tax penalizes those who make investments for increasing the land's productivity. But it rewards those who hold land idle in anticipation of an increase in its price. In this way, property taxes may encourage land speculation and a resulting misallocation of resources. Some communities have tried to improve incentives by levying a tax based on the land's value in its most productive use. This has some unpleasant side effects, however. For instance, consider a farm located just outside the city limits of a growing city. If the land's best use is for an office building or a subway station, the use tax on the farm might exceed the annual output of the farm. For optimum resource allocation the farmer would have to move—a solution that may be politically unpopular. Moreover, the ultimate effect of such a tax might be a vast area of concrete and steel without trees and open spaces.

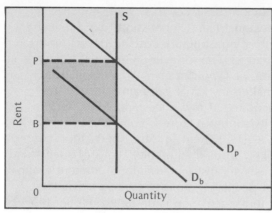

Figure 9 The demand for a baseball pitcher is D_p; the demand for this same fellow working as a bartender—his next most productive employment—is D_b. The wage OP breaks down to opportunity cost OB and rent BP; the total amount of rent is shown in the shaded area.

The rental component of wages

The word "rent" has more than one meaning. We commonly use it for the monthly payment on an apartment or the cost of hiring a car from an "auto rental agency." These payments are not rent in the economist's sense because they include elements of wages, interest, insurance premiums, and other costs. **Economic rent** is something else: it is the surplus over and above the amount necessary to keep a resource (any resource) in its current employment. If a potato farmer leases his land to a shopping center for a hundred thousand dollars a year, a portion of the payment is rent. It is economic rent because any payment above its value as a potato farm would be enough to persuade the farmer to give it up.

The same principle applies to prices paid for other resources, including labor. Economic rent to labor is any surplus over a worker's value in some other employment. For example, some workers have unique skills. The supply curve for their skills is perfectly inelastic (vertical), since their particular skills cannot be increased in quantity. Star quarterbacks, pitchers, or goalies are examples. Others are concert musicians, popular lecturers, and skilled glassblowers. Such workers may earn very high pay if the demand for their services is high. For

public figures like Muhammad Ali, Olivia Newton-John, or Robert Redford the limit is very high indeed.

The rental element in a pitcher's salary is shown in Figure 9. Total wage is OP. The pitcher's next most productive employment is bartending for a wage of OB. The pitcher's opportunity cost is OB and economic rent is BP, the surplus over and above the wage necessary to keep him in his next best employment.

There is also a rental element in the wages of most ordinary workers. This can be seen in Figure 10, showing market supply and demand curves for bartenders. The wage rate OW is determined by the intersection of supply and demand. The slope of the supply curve shows that some bartenders would be willing to work for a wage less than OW. They get a wage higher than the wage they would be willing to accept because employers have to bid more to get all the bartenders they need, OQ. All of the bartenders to the left of Q are receiving more than enough to keep them from working at something else. The difference between what they are actually paid and what they would accept is economic rent. The principle of rental surplus here is quite similar to the idea of consumer surplus.

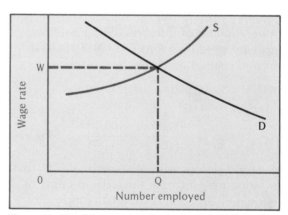

Figure 10 The labor market for bartenders. All the bartenders on the supply curve to the left of equilibrium are willing to work at less than market wage W; therefore, they are earning economic rent.

Capital: the theory of interest

A favorite novel among economists is Daniel Defoe's *Robinson Crusoe*. You may remember the story. A sailor is shipwrecked on a deserted island in the South Seas and gradually builds up his own economic system from almost nothing. Crusoe made his own tools and built his own house. But in doing so he had to take time off from other activities such as sleeping and gathering food. Eventually, he accumulated quite a lot of what we call capital.

Saving and investment

Capital includes all human-made resources. Capital is important in the economy because it magnifies the amount of work that can be done by a given amount of labor. But the process of creating capital is roundabout. It means that resources must be used first for producing tools before those tools can be used to produce the goods and services needed for consumption. In less developed countries this presents a problem, just as it did for Robinson Crusoe. Often most of the available labor and natural resources are needed just to produce the necessities of life.

The earliest pieces of capital equipment were simple tools made of stone. Later boats and sledges were built to make hunting and fishing easier. Eventually irrigation facilities, roads and bridges, and metal forges were constructed. The growing stock of capital increased worker productivity. More and more labor could be released from direct production of consumer goods and put to work in the roundabout process of making more capital goods—the means of even greater production. Factories were built to make steel, the steel was made into rails, and the rails were used to build railroads to carry grain from the Kansas prairies to the consumer markets of the East.

The process we have sketched is called *saving and investment*. To save is to refrain from consuming. Less consumption enables resources to move out of consumer goods production into capital goods production. The construction and installation of capital goods are called investment.

Compared to most of the world, the industrialized countries are rich in capital. They have been able to save and invest on a large scale. But capital, like other resources, is limited even in the wealthiest countries. It should be used carefully and not wasted. It must be allocated to its most efficient uses. In the United States and other countries where the market system predominates, prices are the mechanism through which investment capital is steered into its best use. The price of investment capital is the *interest* payment.

The demand for investment funds: capital budgeting

The process by which a business firm plans investment outlays is called **capital budgeting;** it is similar to the way a family budgets its income. Both the business and the family try to get the most for their money. They set up priorities and allocate their resources first for those things that have the greatest priority. This gives them the greatest benefit per dollar of investment expenditure.

Suppose a firm is considering the purchase of a fleet of delivery trucks. The initial outlay for the investment for one year is $100,000. At the end of the year the trucks can be sold for $75,000. Income from the use of the trucks during the year is estimated at $50,000. The cost of operating the trucks is expected to be $15,000, leaving a net income of $35,000. For an initial investment outlay of $100,000, the firm will realize $75,000 + $35,000 (the resale value of the trucks plus the net income from operations) = $110,000. This is a *benefit-cost relationship* of 110,000/100,000 = 110/100 = 1.10. The investment in the trucks returns an amount equal to the initial outlay plus 10 percent: 1 + 10%.

The company is also considering other, alternative investment projects. It could build a warehouse instead of renting space in some other company's warehouse, and this would provide a return of 4%. Or it could invest in a bookkeeping machine that would return 20%. We can arrange these investment projects in descending order according to their rates of return.

The *rate of return* is also called the **marginal efficiency of investment** (MEI). This is defined as the projected profitability of additional investment projects calculated as the expected rate of return on an investment expenditure. The marginal efficiency of investment (MEI) schedule in Table 4 serves as the firm's demand schedule for investment funds. It resembles the demand schedules for other resources, which are based on the marginal revenue product (MRP) of those resources. *The firm will demand the quantity of investment funds for which its marginal efficiency of investment is at least as great as the cost of borrowing those funds.*

The cost or price of borrowed funds for investment is the **interest charge.** If the funds cost 16% a year, the firm will borrow only the $10,000 needed for purchasing the bookkeeping machine. Why? This is the only investment that will yield a return sufficient to cover the cost of borrowing at 16%. The bookkeeping machine, in fact, earns a 20% rate of return. If the interest rate is only 8%, the firm will demand investment funds totaling $10,000 + $100,000 = $110,000. The firm will invest not only in the bookkeeping machine, but also in the fleet of trucks: both projects will yield rates of return greater than the interest rate paid. In short, the firm will demand the quantity of funds for which the expected rate of return on investment is at least as great as the cost of borrowing. At 8% it will undertake the two most productive investment projects on its MEI schedule.

The firm's demand curve for investment funds is shown in Figure 11. The horizontal lines at 16% and 8% mark off possible costs of borrowing and show the quantity of funds that will be borrowed at each interest rate.

If the firm uses its own funds instead of borrowing them in the capital market, it will follow the same principle. In this case, the firm will consider the interest rate its own cash

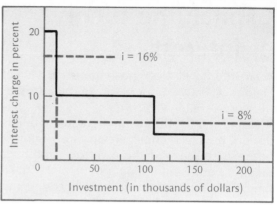

Figure 11 A firm's demand for investment funds is shown as the marginal efficiency of investment. The MEI for a single firm is a series of stair steps.

could earn if loaned to another firm. It would make no sense to invest the firm's own cash for a return of 4% if the interest return on loans is 8%. The alternative interest income the firm could earn by lending its own cash is an opportunity cost to the firm and must be considered in its budgeting process.

Business firms throughout the economy will calculate their investment priorities in this way. By combining their individual demand curves for funds we arrive at the market demand curve for investment capital. *The market demand curve reflects the MEI for the entire economy.* It resembles the demand curves for labor and other resources. Figure 12 shows a market demand curve for investment funds. All the individual curves of particular firms have been combined to make one smooth, downward-sloping curve.

Investments lasting more than one year

Our simple example involved investments lasting only one year. Most investments run for much longer. It is necessary to expand the preceding analysis to cover longer-term investments as well.

Table 4
Hypothetical Investment Projects

Project	Initial outlay	Rate of return over initial outlay
Bookkeeping machine	$ 10,000	20%
Fleet of trucks	100,000	10%
Warehouse	50,000	4%

The equation for calculating rate of return for one year is:

Net benefits over the year
Cost of one year's investment

$$= 1 + \text{rate of return over cost.}$$

Let us substitute in the equation as follows:
Net benefits over the year = R, the year's net income on the investment project;
Cost of one year's investment = P, the initial outlay for the investment;
Rate of return over cost = r, the marginal efficiency of investment.

The new equation reads $R/P = 1 + r$. Rearranging the terms, we get a more useful equation: $P = R/(1 + r)$. The term $(1 + r)$ is the quantity by which the income from the investment at year's end is "discounted," or divided, to equal its price. The income of the investment over one year, discounted by one plus the rate of return, is equal to its purchase price. Substituting the values of P and R, a firm can determine the rate of return over one year.

If the investment project is expected to last two years, it must yield an acceptable rate of return in the second year as well as in the first. In fact, it must yield the acceptable rate of return not only on the initial outlay for the investment alone. It must yield the acceptable rate of return on the *return* that was earned in the first year. Otherwise, there would be no advantage in holding the investment after the first year.

To be profitable, the investment will earn some rate of return, r, on the initial outlay in year one. At the end of the year, the investment will be worth $P(1 + r)$.

At the end of the second year the project must have earned the acceptable return on the total value of the investment after the first year. The investment should then be worth $P(1 + r)(1 + r)$. Multiplying the initial outlay by $(1 + r)^2$ gives the value of the investment at the end of the second year.

To earn a *return* on a *return* is known as **compounding.** Your return on your savings account is compounded. If you have $100 in your account and the interest rate is 5%, your account will grow by $5 the first year. During the second year it will grow by $5 *plus* 5% of $5,

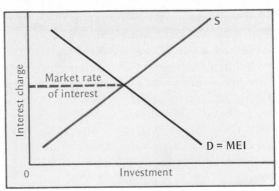

Figure 12 **The market for investment funds. Market demand is equal to the sum of all individual MEI curves (D = MEI).**

or a total of $5.25. At the end of the second year your account will be worth $100 $(1 + r)^2$ = $100(1.05)^2 = $100(1.1025) = $110.25. Each year your account grows by 5% times the original deposit plus 5% of 5% for each year the account is held. The formula for the value of your account after the second year is Final Value = Initial Deposit $(1 + r)^2$. The value after the third year is Initial Deposit $(1 + r)^3$.

An investment expenditure is similar to your bank deposit in that a certain amount is committed to it in the present. During the time it remains committed it earns a return for the owner. The equation for an investment which yields a return over several years is

$$P = \frac{R_1}{(1 + r)^1} + \frac{R_2}{(1 + r)^2} + \frac{R_3}{(1 + r)^3}$$
$$+ \cdots + \frac{R_n}{(1 + r)^n}$$

where R_1 is the income for the first year, R_2 for the second, and so forth. Substituting values for P and R, the firm can calculate the MEI for an investment which produces income for several years.

Nominal and real interest rates

Just as we distinguished between money wages and real wages, we must distinguish between the *nominal* and the *real* rate of interest. It often happens that the rate of interest charged on a loan does not represent the real interest cost to the borrower. The difference results from changes in the price level.

The **nominal interest rate** is the amount the borrower pays in terms of the cash payment made. The **real interest rate** is the cost in terms of actual purchasing power given up by the borrower. Suppose the interest rate is 12%, a rate high enough to discourage investors from borrowing under normal conditions. But if inflation is raising the price level at a rate of 9% annually, the real cost to the borrower is only 12% − 9% = 3%. The borrower will pay back the loan in dollars that have shrunk by 9% so that total repayment will be worth only 3% more in purchasing power than the loan.

The effect of moderate inflation is to *reduce* real borrowing costs and to encourage capital construction. Borrowers are able to pay back their loans in money that is worth less than the money they borrowed. Figure 13 illustrates the effect of this difference between the nominal and real rates of interest. Of course, inflation has this effect of stimulating investment only as long as the lenders of money take no action to protect themselves. If inflation is expected to continue, lenders will increase the nominal rate of interest sufficiently to make up for the loss in purchasing power during the period of the loan. If inflation continues and worsens, it may produce such fear among business firms that investment will finally be cut off, regardless of the rate of interest.

Tax credits

In recent years the federal government has tried to stimulate capital construction by raising the marginal efficiency of investment. Under a tax law passed in 1964, business firms were allowed to deduct 7% of the price of an investment from their income taxes. Again in the 1970s a tax credit of 10% was given in the hope of stimulating investment.

The effect of a tax credit is to raise the expected net income of an investment project. In our formula, this increases R, the expected income, for the year the initial outlay is made. When the capital budgeting equation is solved, the result is a higher value for r, the rate of return over cost. This causes a rightward shift in the MEI curve, since every investment project has a higher r. If the policy is successful, the result will be a larger quantity of investment demand at every interest rate. More new investment projects will be undertaken, and the nation's capital stock will increase.

The supply of investment funds: savings

We have been analyzing the demand for investment funds. What about the supply side? Who supplies the funds available for business borrowing?

Much of the supply of loanable funds comes from the personal savings of households. Many families set aside a portion of their incomes to provide for their long-range security. They may keep their savings in the form of cash, deposit some of it in savings accounts, take out insurance policies, or buy various kinds of securities. Little need be said at this point about holdings of cash because these are not used for investment. But other forms of saving find their way into the supply of loanable funds and are used for investment purposes. The amount actually available depends on the lending policies of banks and on the amount of borrowing by federal and state and local governments—since government competes with business firms in the money markets.

One way of supplying savings to business firms is through the purchase of corporate bonds. Households may buy corporate bonds through a broker. More often they buy bonds indirectly through banks, savings and loan associations, and insurance companies. These institutions are called *financial intermediaries* because they take savings that people have deposited with them and make them available for business loans.

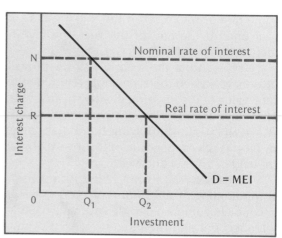

Figure 13 The effect of inflation on interest and borrowing. Inflation reduces the real cost of borrowing from ON to OR. Investment increases from OQ_1 to OQ_2.

As Figure 12 indicates, demand and supply determine the rate of interest charged on loans. The smaller the supply, other things being equal, the higher will be the interest rate. The larger the supply, other things being equal, the lower will be the interest rate.

We have been speaking of the rate of interest as if there were only one interest rate at any time. In fact, there is a whole range of interest rates for different kinds of bonds having different levels of risks. Government securities are the safest securities because they are backed by the U.S. government; however, because they are safe investments, they pay a low rate of interest. In 1976 new issues of U.S. Treasury bills maturing in three months were paying 5.5% interest. U.S. three- to five-year bonds were paying 7.5%. Highly rated municipal bonds were paying about 7%. Interest earned on municipal bonds is tax-free, so that an interest rate of 7% may be worth as much as 10% or more to lenders. Corporate bonds are not as safe as U.S. government securities and pay higher interest. The highest graded corporate bonds were paying 8.8%, and bonds of lower grade and carrying more risk were paying 10.35% in 1976.

Large investors like to diversify their holdings. They supply their funds in various types of money markets. They purchase not just one kind of bond but a variety so as to be sure of satisfying different financial needs. In doing so they take three things into account: the yield of a bond, the time to maturity, and its risk.

The **yield** of a bond is the percentage rate of return per dollar invested. Yield is sometimes the same as the interest rate on the bond, but often it differs because bonds are frequently bought at more or less than their face value. What counts is the percentage return received on the amount actually paid for the bond. Interest rates vary depending on the length of time until **maturity**—that is, the number of years and months before the investor receives face value of the bond. Long-term bonds generally pay higher interest rates than short-term. This is partly because a higher interest payment is necessary to induce lenders to wait longer for their money. Another reason for the higher interest on long-term bonds is the greater risk of the borrower defaulting over a longer period.

Lenders purchase a variety of securities to satisfy their need for the *highest possible yield* with the *lowest risk* and the *shortest length of time to maturity*. They will buy some short-term securities with low yields, some long-term securities with high yields, some risky securities with high yields, and some safe securities with low yields. They seek a balanced *portfolio* of securities rather than a specialized one. The result is different supply curves in different markets and different interest rates, too.

In summary, the demand for investment funds is based on the marginal efficiency of investment. A firm's MEI reflects the rates of return (r) on investment projects arranged from the highest to the lowest. The firm will continue to borrow for investment as long as the MEI of additional projects is greater than the interest on borrowed funds. Interest rates depend on the interaction between demand and supply in the money markets. The supply of investment funds is based on the actions of savers and the competing borrowing of governments. Savers supply their funds in a number of money markets so as to accumulate a diversified group of securities. Riskier and longer-term loans will normally be made only if interest income is higher.

When money markets are operating efficiently, the result is to allocate investment funds to those projects which are expected to yield the greatest return. More funds flow to safe investments and their interest cost is lower. Risky projects are allocated fewer funds and their interest cost is higher. New investment projects increase the nation's capital stock and help us to produce more goods and services.

Entrepreneurship: the theory of profit

We come now to the fourth kind of resource used in production, entrepreneurship. Just as other kinds of resources earn returns in the form of wages, rent, or interest, entrepreneurial resources earn a return in the form of **profit.** The term *profit* is probably the most controversial term in economics. Some people feel that profit-making isn't quite nice. According to public opinion polls, a large segment of the public thinks that business profits are too large. Many people in business, on the other hand, say that profits aren't large enough and that the federal income tax on corporations bites too heavily into them.

Whatever the truth may be, profit is in fact a *necessary* return to an important productive resource, entrepreneurial ability. The entrepreneur is the initiator, the creator, and the organizer of any productive enterprise. It is entrepreneurial talent that is responsible for combining other resources into a functioning organization.

Functions of profit

Profit serves two functions: (1) It is a regular return for performing entrepreneurial duties; and (2) it is a special return for exceptional services. In the first sense profit is similar to rent, wages, and interest payments. It is the opportunity cost of hiring entrepreneurial ability. In this sense profit is what we have called *normal profit*. It must be paid if the entrepreneur is to continue in any particular employment.

In the second sense, profit provides the incentive for new creative undertakings. Without the hope of profit, entrepreneurs would not take the risks involved in starting new businesses or moving existing firms along new paths. Profit has been the mainspring of modern capitalism, driving it along in its phenomenal growth and technological development. Without vigorous entrepreneurship, our resources might never have been used to their full potential. In this sense the returns earned for exceptional service are *economic profit*.

The development and application of a new product or process are called an innovation. In recent decades American entrepreneurs have been responsible for innovations in many areas: in production, the steam engine, computerized machine tools, mass production, and the assembly line; in communication, the telephone, telegraph, and transistors; in transportation, the internal combustion engine, the airplane, and diesel and rocket engines. The successful innovators reaped great profits and were followed by imitators. Economic profits gradually disappeared as prices were forced down by competition from the imitators. Still, the hope of new economic profits spurs on new innovators today.

A part of the innovator's responsibility is *to accept the uncertainty* that goes along with change. The new product or process may be technically a very good one and still turn out to be unacceptable to consumers. When that happens the whole investment may be lost. The Edsel automobile introduced by Ford in 1958 is the classic example of such a failure. Millions of dollars were spent in developing and testing the Edsel, but it failed. Quadraphonic sound seems to be another example of an innovation that didn't catch on. Condominium living was once believed to be the wave of the future in the housing industry, but consumers have been slow to give up the dream of single-family homes. Every failure means an entrepreneur who is losing money. But the successes are sometimes spectacular: (1) the Polaroid camera, which made fortunes for its developers; and (2) the new microcomputers that combine thousands of transistors on one silicon chip, enabling pocket calculators and digital watches to be produced inexpensively. Can you name others?

Some economic profit is a result of monopoly. In this respect the successful innovator enjoys a monopoly until imitators catch up and take over part of the market. That is one reason why dynamic firms keep trying to develop innovations, in order to enjoy the exceptional profits that go with them. *But monopoly payments are generally temporary.* They result from natural frictions in the marketplace, from a lack of complete and immediate response to market conditions. Eventually, rivals come in and the monopoly profits disappear.

Only when these natural frictions become institutionalized can monopoly profits persist. If competitors are prevented from entering the industry, an entrepreneur may continue to receive economic profit. A patent is one form of institutionalized monopoly. Inventors are ensured protection from competition for 17 years. The patent laws are intended to encourage innovation by giving the inventor a chance to

Extended Example
Profits

An important difference between our free market economy and a command economy is the use of profits. In our system, profits are a necessary return to a vital resource. Profits perform two functions: (1) they ration out scarce resources to the industries where need is most urgent; and (2) they provide the incentives to conduct enterprises in the interests of the consuming public. In a communist system, scarce resources are allocated according to a central plan, and incentives take the form of awards, bonuses, and public recognition of service.

In 1976, American corporations earned pretax profits of $118.7 billion. This was almost 7% of all income for that year. Federal, state, and local governments collected $64.7 billion in corporate profit taxes, and corporations paid out $35.1 billion in dividends. The remaining $19 billion was retained in corporations for reinvestment.

Since 1929, profits after taxes have averaged about 6% of national income, but the profit share has been declining in recent years. For manufacturing industries, the usual profit is about 5¢ for each dollar of sales or about 11.6¢ for every dollar of shareholder equity.

Is this too much? Are corporations collecting too great a share of output? The answer depends on the level of competition in U.S. industry. Where there is competition, it is not possible for a single firm to collect excess profits. Prices will be forced down to the competitive level and wages will be forced up to the going rate in the industry. This will leave firms with only normal profit for the entrepreneurial resources used in production.

profit from his work. This kind of temporary restriction on competition is probably desirable. There are other means of guaranteeing control of the market for early comers; certain property rights and leasing or franchising privileges are some examples. Not everyone can open a McDonald's or a Kentucky Fried Chicken restaurant.

Building human capital

Many of us make investments without going near the capital market. We invest in ourselves. We build up our entrepreneurial ability by going to school or taking special courses in business management. The decision to invest in human capital is similar to a decision to invest in any other kind of capital. In part, it rests on a comparison between what we hope to earn through different alternatives.

What is the price of an investment in human capital? Education requires expenditures for tuition, books, and extra living expenses. But the price also includes the opportunity cost of the student's time while in training—the money that could be earned by working instead of studying.

The expected return from an investment in human capital is higher income in the future. A prospective student might compare the average income for various occupations and calculate the flow of future earnings. Then the student would balance the income flows against the cost of the training to acquire the necessary skills. Of course, the decision that follows isn't just a matter of dollars and cents. Not all the benefits from developing skills can be measured that way. Some of the gains from having those skills are what economists call *psychic benefits*. Thus schoolteachers may draw certain satisfactions from their work over and above their paychecks—satisfactions they would not obtain from working as secretaries. Deep-sea divers and trail guides may value the thrills of their jobs above their actual incomes. On the other hand, some unpleasant jobs provide negative psychic income which should be deducted from the worker's paycheck to arrive at net benefits from work. Air-traffic controllers and marriage counselors probably fall in this category.

Summary

The marginal productivity theory helps to explain employment and price in all four resource classifications.

Demand for labor depends on labor's MRP when it is used along with certain fixed resources. In competitive labor markets employment and wages are determined by the intersection of demand and supply. Where there is a single monopsony buyer of labor, employment is determined by demand and marginal resource cost. Because MRC is greater than supply price under monopsony, employment and wages are lower than in competition.

Unions are a means of monopolizing the supply of labor and controlling its price. Unions attempt to raise wages by: increasing demand for labor, restricting the supply of labor, or establishing a minimum wage rate. Unions also arrange a grievance procedure for arbitrating disagreements between labor and management.

Unionism grew slowly in the United States until the 1930s with the development of mass production and with passage of the National Labor Relations Act. The Taft-Hartley Act of 1948 curbed some unfair practices of unions and gave the President power to issue an injunction against strikes. Collective bargaining is a means of establishing labor-management relationships without strikes. In general, union power has failed to grow significantly in the 1970s; the American Federation of State, County, and Municipal Employees is the nation's fastest growing union.

Demand for land depends on its marginal productivity, but unlike many resources the supply of land is fixed or inelastic. Rent is a surplus paid any resource in fixed supply. When supply is fixed, any payment is more than the amount necessary to keep the resource in production. Therefore, rent cannot serve an incentive function, but only an allocative or rationing function. Henry George proposed a single tax to collect the rental surplus from landlords, but it is important to tax only the land itself and not the *improvements* made on the land. Some types of labor may earn "economic rent" if their payment exceeds their opportunity cost in the next most productive employment.

Demand for financial capital depends on the marginal efficiency of investment, calculated as the rate of return over the initial outlay for investment projects. Capital budgeting is a means of comparing returns on alternative investments with the cost of borrowing. The capital budgeting decision can be influenced by inflation, which affects the real interest rate, and by tax credits, which affect the net income from a project. The supply of financial capital flows from business and personal savings. Savings are supplied in various money markets according to yield, time to maturity, and risk. The result is different interest rates for different types of securities. Interest rates help to allocate savings toward the most profitable uses.

Entrepreneurship earns profit for initiating, creating, and organizing a productive enterprise. Exceptional performance of entrepreneurial duties is rewarded with economic profit. Sometimes economic profit is the result of monopoly. Entrepreneurship may be developed by investment in human capital.

Key Words and Phrases

- **wages** payment made to households that supply labor resources for use in production.
- **real versus money wages** wages in terms of real purchasing power versus wages in terms of dollar amounts.
- **marginal product of labor** the change in total output that results from a unit change in employment of labor.
- **marginal revenue product of labor** the change in total revenue that results from a unit change in employment of labor.
- **monopsony** a condition in which a single buyer faces the entire supply of a resource.
- **marginal resource cost** the change in total cost that results from employing an additional unit of a variable resource.
- **craft unions** unions of workers having a particular skill or trade.
- **minimum wage** a legal limit on the lowest wage which can be paid.
- **grievance** a disagreement between a worker and management of a business firm.
- **shop steward** the union's representative within the work force of a particular business firm.

- **arbitrator** an impartial outsider who settles disputes between unions and management.

- **binding arbitration** a settlement by an impartial outsider that is binding to both unions and management.

- **industrial unions** unions of all workers within a particular industry.

- **closed shop** an agreement forbidding hiring of workers who do not belong to the union; closed shops are now illegal.

- **union shop** an agreement requiring all employees to join the union after they are hired; union shops are illegal in some states.

- **right-to-work laws** state laws forbidding union membership as a requirement for new employees; these laws make union shops illegal.

- **open shop** a condition in which union membership is not considered in hiring or employment.

- **injunction** a court order to cease a particular activity; a labor injunction forbids strikes within 90 days of the order.

- **secondary boycott** a withdrawal of support from a particular business firm because of that firm's dispute with another union.

- **collective bargaining** a process by which labor and management agree on wages and work practices.

- **strike** a union's most powerful tactic; the union halts work at target firms by having its members stop working indefinitely.

- **wildcat strikes** strikes called by a local union without consulting with the national office of the union.

- **lockout** a tactic of management to halt work as a means of pressuring a union to accept management's demands.

- **COLAs** cost-of-living adjustments that raise wages in line with increases in consumer prices.

- **fringe benefits** extra benefits provided labor over and above the established wage.

- **rent** payment to households that supply land resources for use in production.

- **single tax** a proposal to tax away the "unearned surplus" from land.

- **economic rent** payment to any resource over and above its opportunity cost.

- **capital budgeting** a process of establishing priorities in investment projects based on their expected profitability.

- **marginal efficiency of investment** the expected rate of return on investment projects.

- **interest** the annual return on capital; the cost of borrowed funds for investment.

- **discounting** dividing a future income payment by one plus rate of return to arrive at the current value of an investment.

- **compounding** earning a return on an investment plus a return on earlier returns from the investment.

- **real versus nominal rates of interest** the real cost of borrowing after deducting the rate of price increase versus the stated interest charge on a loan.

- **financial intermediaries** institutions which collect the savings of households and make them available to business for investment.

- **yield** the rate of return of an investment over the price actually paid.

Questions for Review

1. Explain the derivation of the marginal resource cost (MRC) curve. What is the MRC curve when a firm buys resources in a competitive market?

2. Use the following hypothetical data to determine equilibrium employment and wage. Then suppose unions impose a minimum wage of $15 per day. What is the result in terms of unemployment?

Quantity demanded	Wage/day	Quantity supplied
4	20	14
5	15	10
6	10	6
7	5	2

3. Refer again to the data in question 2. Suppose union members participate in technological progress which doubles their productivity. Show the results arithmetically and graphically.

4. List the major pieces of labor legislation and the important provisions of each.

5. Discuss the significant problems facing unions in the future.

6. State clearly the economic definition of rent, whether applied to land or any other resource. Show why rent can perform only a rationing function. How is this significant in levying taxes?

7. Distinguish between industrial unions and craft unions.

8. Distinguish between the real and nominal rates of interest. Show how a difference between the two can lead to a change in the level of investment in capital resources.

34

Poverty, Discrimination, and Public Assistance

In the previous two chapters we showed how resource owners receive their shares of national income. In a free market individual shares are based primarily on contributions to production. Although income shares may be "fair," they may still be too small to provide a decent life. Moreover, various structural problems prevent some people from earning anything at all: some are disabled and unable to work; others face educational or job discrimination. In addition, there are not always enough jobs for everyone who can work and there are problems in matching available jobs with the unemployed. The single worst result of these market imperfections is the existence of poverty.

Most of us have seen poverty. A few may have seen it firsthand. The rest of us have had only a passing acquaintance with it: we have distributed food baskets to poor families; we have played with deprived children in public schools and playgrounds; and we have driven along country roads past tar-paper shacks or through the slums of the larger cities.

In this chapter we will consider some important questions about poverty in the United States:

(1) Who are the poor?

(2) Why are they poor?

(3) What, if anything, can be done about poverty?

(4) How does poverty affect those of us who aren't poor?

Defining poverty

It is hard to say exactly what poverty is. We think of being poor as having to live in a shack, wear secondhand clothes, and eat cheap food. But this is not poverty of the sort suffered in much of the world. Many of the poor in the United States are only poor *relative* to the living standards the rest of us enjoy. We refer to this type of poverty as **relative poverty:** relative poverty is a condition of living substantially below the standards of others nearby. To a Pakistani or African Bushman, U.S. poverty would not be poverty at all. In fact, by modern American standards, most of the human race has been poor throughout most of its history. Our predecessors on this continent lived in huts made of birchbark or animal skins and survived on food consisting mainly of corn and a few wild animals. They were poor by our current standards—though they were not poor relative to those around them. Even the wealthiest medieval Europeans lived in unheated fortresses, ate black bread, and died of the plague.

To have no suitable home or food at all is **absolute poverty:** absolute poverty is a condition of living below a level currently acceptable as necessary for human health and existence. Most people in the United States do not face the problems of absolute poverty—of wondering where our next meal is coming from, or fearing the winter, or watching our brothers and sisters die in infancy.

People in much of the world are still poor not only in a relative sense, but also by absolute standards. One measure by which we can compare the poverty and wealth of nations is the amount of *annual output of goods and services* (GNP) *per person.* In the United States, output per capita is now about $6,000 a year (in 1973 dollars). Only Sweden and Switzerland rank higher (about $6,300). For West Germany the figure is about $5,600. For Britain it is about $3,100; for Greece, about $1,700; for Turkey, $600; for India, $100. See Table 1 for more comparisons.

Table 1
GNP per Capita for Selected Countries in 1974

United States	5,979	Jordan	286
Afghanistan	81	Kenya	172
Angola	492	Luxembourg	5,377
Australia	4,184	Mexico	870
Austria	3,858	Nepal	90
Belgium	4,873	Netherlands	4,557
Burma	82	Nigeria	250
Cambodia	81	Norway	4,872
Canada	5,487	Pakistan	126
Costa Rica	775	Portugal	1,339
Denmark	5,364	Spain	1,728
Finland	3,770	Sudan	135
France	5,002	Sweden	6,379
Germany (West)	5,615	Switzerland	6,297
Greece	1,691	Turkey	604
Iceland	4,930	Uganda	161
Ireland	2,174	United Kingdom	3,129
Israel	2,732	Venezuela	1,357
Italy	2,609	Zaire	147
Japan	3,687		

Source: *Statistical Abstract of the United States, 1975*; data from *Organization for Economic Cooperation & Development* and *World Almanac for 1976.*

Such figures are apt to be misleading. Levels of living can't always be measured in terms of dollars and cents. Many people in Asia, Africa, and Latin America live outside the market economy where output is not recorded or exchanged for money. They have fairly well-organized systems of sharing in production and distribution, through which those in need are helped and sustained by other members of their society. Still, it is fair to say that masses of them are poor by any objective standard—poor in terms of health, nutrition, and life expectancy; and poor also in being condemned to lives of unremitting struggle for survival.

The industrialized nations have been able to do away with most of the absolute poverty known by our ancestors. The Industrial Revolution brought a tremendous spurt in output and incomes, making it possible to invest in new capital that led in turn to still greater output.

Throughout most of the twentieth century in the United States the number and proportion of families living in absolute poverty have declined significantly. Better educational and job opportunities have improved the earning capacity of many workers. Furthermore, labor force participation has increased, as more wives have become wage earners. As a result, average per capita incomes have increased. Today the number of people living in the United States who can be said to live in absolute poverty is quite low—though not as low as it might be considering our national wealth.

The U.S. government has its own definition of poverty. According to the Social Security Administration, *an acceptable minimum level of income is three times what a family needs to buy essential food.* This government definition is known as the **poverty line.** In 1975 a family of four living in a city needed about $5,500 to meet this standard. Those earning below this minimum necessary for life were said to be living in absolute poverty (as well as poverty *relative* to the rest of us). In 1975 the federal government estimated 25.8 million Americans were poor. This means about 12.3% of the U.S. population was below the poverty line. The many forms of government assistance, however, help to move nearly all these families above the desperation of absolute poverty.

There are critics of this federally defined poverty line. Some feel it is too arbitrary. For instance, a family of four with a total income of $5,499 would be listed as poor, while another family earning $5,501 would not be classified as poor. In addition, the poverty level changes each year to reflect price inflation. Since most price indexes that measure inflation are based on the cost of an average market basket of items bought by a *middle-class family,* the dollar level of the poverty line may be incorrect. Others maintain that the poverty line measures only absolute poverty, that is, those barely able to survive. To these critics, relative poverty should be emphasized more. Being cut off from sharing in this country's wealth and from participating in this country's freedom of choice or being locked into a pool of unskilled labor is considered by these critics serious enough to warrant further government intervention and funds.

Who are the poor?

The poor in America are not easy to categorize. They include all ages and races of people, and they are poor for a variety of reasons. Studies have been made to find out the most common characteristics of the poor. The most common of all seems to be race. About a third of our poor families are nonwhite, even though nonwhites form only one-eighth (12%) of our population. A second major characteristic of the poor is that many of them live in rural areas. Another characteristic is that many poor families are headed by females.

A fourth common characteristic is that many of the poor are elderly and past the earning age. Their only regular income is from Social Security. A word of caution is necessary here because the statistics may be misleading. Many of the elderly own homes and other property. They may also be able to draw on savings or other assets, so they are not as poor as the level of their money incomes might suggest. But those who have nothing to fall back on aside from their Social Security are in dire straits indeed.

Table 2
Characteristics of the Poor (1974)

(1) Characteristic	(2) No. persons classified as poor	(3) Percent of total families*	(4) Percent of character- istic classified as poor*
Total	24.3 million	100.0%	11.6%
Male-headed families	12.5	77.1	7.1
White families	16.3	88.7	8.9
Nonmetro (rural families)	9.2	4.1	14.0
Over-65 families	3.3	19.9	15.7
Nonwhite families	8.0	11.3	29.5
Female-headed families	11.8	22.9	34.4

*Figures do not sum to totals because some persons are counted in more than one classification.
Source: *Statistical Abstract of the United States, 1975.*

Table 2 presents information about persons who have one or more of the four characteristics of poverty mentioned above. That is, they are nonwhite, live in rural areas, belong to families headed by females, and/or are old. Column (4) shows that in 1974 some 29.5% of nonwhite families were classified as poor, compared with 8.9% of white families. Of rural families, 14.0% were classified as poor. Of female-headed families, 34.4% were poor compared with 7.1% of male-headed families. Finally, 15.7% of families over 65 were poor.

Aiding the poor

To say that almost 26 million Americans live in poverty is to make a pretty startling statement. After all, we are the world's richest country. We seldom see beggars in our streets. Most of the poor, of course, aren't to be seen unless we go where they live—down into the black ghettos of the inner city, into the cheap rooming houses of the elderly, or out to the depressed areas of the countryside. The poor may not look any different from other people. Many, if not most, have refrigerators and washing machines and television sets. They live, after all, in a society where such things are standard equipment.

Programs for dealing with poverty take different forms, depending on the reasons why people are poor. We can distinguish several categories of poor people: those who are able to work but can't find employment; those who are employed but whose incomes are below the poverty level; and those who, for one reason or another, are mostly outside the labor market. The latter are sometimes called the "hard-core" group of the poor, because no matter how prosperous the national economy may become they will still be poor. **Hard-core poverty** includes the elderly, the disabled, the handicapped, and those who must stay home to care for dependent children; it also includes those lacking in human capital, that is, those who have received little education and are not prepared for work in available jobs.

Hard-core poverty

The hard-core group accounts for half or more of the poverty population. Their problems have to be handled on a case-by-case basis, usually through the welfare departments of their communities and states. Each poor family is assigned to a case worker who is responsible for investigating their circumstances and determining what kind of aid is needed and how much. There are a number of separate programs designed to help such families, using federal, state, and local funds. The largest program is called **Aid to Families with Dependent Children** (AFDC), which gave assistance to more than 11 million persons in 1975. Another program is the **Supplemental Security Income Program** (SSI), which helps the aged, blind, and disabled. There were over 4 million SSI recipients in 1975. The federal **Food Stamp Program** enables about 17 million people with low budgets to purchase food at reduced cost. Health care is also provided to welfare families under the **Medicaid** program that pays the cost of medical and hospital services.

Extended Example
Lyndon Johnson's War on Poverty

When Lyndon Baines Johnson became President, conditions were ripe for beginning new initiatives to attack old problems. Economic advisers in the executive branch of government, Walter Heller and Kermit Gordon, had been conducting research into the extent of poverty in the nation. Their findings and recommendations were to form the basis for a new poverty program.

There was a national commitment to act decisively, and Lyndon Johnson was uniquely prepared to lead the effort. He had been born in southern Texas and had grown up among poor blacks and Chicanos from across the Mexican border. As a public schoolteacher, he had seen how poverty and illiteracy stunted the lives of the poor. During the New Deal of the 1930s, he had served as state director of the National Youth Administration, providing training and jobs for disadvantaged young people. As Congressman and Senator, he had come to understand the importance of the government's role in setting policy to moderate the inequalities of the market system.

It was Johnson's aim not only to help the nation's thirty-five million poor people. His goal was also to strengthen the entire moral and economic fabric of the nation. While the economy was booming and jobs were plentiful, many poor people remained outside the system, trapped under circumstances which prevented them from participating in and contributing to a more productive economy. The President sought to focus government's creative efforts on preparing young people to move out of the poverty cycle and to provide the benefits of a "Great Society" to all Americans.

On January 8, 1964, President Johnson declared War on Poverty. He allocated a billion dollars from the current budget and appointed Sargent Shriver to direct the effort. Congress passed the Economic Opportunity Act establishing a wide array of programs to get at the causes and effects of poverty:

(1) The Community Action Program set up local agencies to organize the poor in planning and carrying out programs involving neighborhood education, health, and legal services.

(2) The Job Corps and the Neighborhood Youth Corps provided training and education for young adults and teenagers from poor families. Head Start and Upward Bound aimed at providing equal educational opportunities for preschool children and for potential college applicants. Operation Mainstream and New Careers were adult retraining programs, and the Work Incentive Program trained and placed welfare recipients.

(3) Other education programs provided special assistance to needy children, educationally deprived students, immigrant students, and handicapped students.

(4) In 1965 Medicare and Medicaid were passed, providing health insurance for the aged and for the poor. As demand for health services increased, funds were provided for increasing nurses' training, for aid to medical schools and medical students, and for hospital construction and modernization.

(5) The Housing and Urban Development Act of 1965 provided subsidized loans for building low-rent housing and gave rent supplements to poor families.

The War on Poverty differed from earlier, more generalized approaches which depended on the "trickle down" theory of aid for the poor. The old idea was that any federal spending would eventually "trickle down" to incomes of low-income families. The new approach emphasized service and "in-kind" programs, providing specific goods and services to particular groups of the disadvantaged. Between 1965 and 1969, federal welfare spending grew from $53.5 to 86.5 billion (in "real" dollars of constant purchasing power), an increase of 62% in four years.

In the Nixon administration the programs were continued with some changes; many were finally phased out as the nation returned to general assistance programs. Between 1970 and 1974 welfare spending grew from $93.7 billion to $139.6 billion (again in constant dollars), a 49% increase in four years. As a percentage of total national output, federal social welfare expenditures were 5.8% in 1965, 8.1% in 1970, and 11.2% in 1975. The percentage in 1975 would have been smaller if it had not been for the two recessions in the 1970s.

When President Johnson left office, the nation's poverty population had been reduced to 24.1 million—a 31% reduction in four years. The War on Poverty and a growing economy had been moving people out of poverty at a rate two and a half times faster than at any time in history. During the early 1970s, the poverty population stabilized at about 25 million, in part because of two recessions.

In the presidential election of November, 1964, the public had supported Lyndon Johnson's vision of the Great Society with the largest plurality in history—61% of the popular vote. But four years later distrust and fear had set in. Candidate Richard Nixon pointed to "an ugly harvest of frustration, violence and failure" and gained a narrow victory over Johnson's Vice President, Hubert Humphrey. The public seemed to renounce the philosophy of the Great Society.

Other factors were also sapping the nation's resolve to correct some of the inequalities of the market system. In the earlier period a growing economy had been providing the resources for new government programs. But by 1968 the Vietnam War was claiming more of the nation's resources and raising the cost of social welfare programs.

What were the net effects of the War on Poverty? Analysts have explored the benefits and costs of specific programs and found in general that results did not come up to expectations. This could mean that the programs themselves were failures or it could mean that the original expectations were not realistic. The conclusion that a program failed depends on the perspective of the examiner; the fact that change of any sort will benefit some groups more than others may label it a success in the eyes of one and a failure in the eyes of another. For blacks and many of the poor there was definite progress in education, employment, income, and civil rights in the 1960s.

The programs were costly, and some of the costs were the result of experimentation. The government operates in a fishbowl; its mistakes are widely labeled the result of inefficiency and waste. In the private sector high costs are often associated with superior quality and with progress in research and development; high costs are seen to be a necessary price for quality and growth. Also, many of the government's programs were interrelated so that it was impossible to separate the costs and benefits of a single enterprise. Unemployment, for instance, was attacked through education and vocational training, job counseling, improved work habits and attitudes, fair-hiring standards, transportation and placement services, and child care. No single program can have much impact without coordination among all programs. And often no single program will achieve benefits equal to the cost of that particular program.

Welfare programs have been widely criticized. They are complex and overlapping. Some people receive benefits under several programs, while others receive nothing at all. Benefit payments vary widely among states, usually being low in the poor states and higher in the richer states such as New York and California. A class of "welfare cheaters" has grown up, consisting of people who prefer to live on welfare rather than to work. Those cheating may draw benefits under multiple names, or from two different counties, or even from two different states. To combat cheating, the welfare agencies have to use administrative methods that are cumbersome, costly to the public, and humiliating to recipients. A bureaucracy is necessary to handle the paperwork and decide who is entitled to benefits and how large the benefits should be. In an effort to cut down on the number of "freeloaders," the system often denied aid to families with able-bodied men. One unfortunate result of this was that it gave fathers an incentive to desert their families, knowing that they would receive more aid without a man in the household. Many states now give benefits to families with able-bodied males and make efforts at the same time to guide recipients toward jobs.

There are two basic forms of public assistance for the elderly: Social Security and Medicare. **Social Security Insurance** is one of the oldest programs of public assistance, having been legislated during the depths of the Great Depression in the 1930s. Insurance benefits under the Social Security Act are paid by the federal government to workers and their dependents on the basis of their past contributions to the Social Security Trust Fund. Both workers and employers now pay 5.85% of a worker's paycheck up to $16,500 (for a maximum worker contribution of $965 a year). The fund makes transfer payments to retired workers and to dependent widows and children of deceased workers. Payments are minimal but they help to stave off abject poverty. Because insurance programs apply only to formerly employed workers, many needy families are not eligible for benefits. For these poor families there are welfare payments, financed primarily by federal funds and supplemented by state and local tax revenues.

Viewpoint
Have We Abolished Poverty?

How many poor people are there in the United States? According to the Bureau of the Census, there were 26 million poor people in September 1976, or 2.5 million more than the year before. Nonsense, responded some economists. "If poverty is a lack of basic needs, we have almost eliminated poverty in the United States," says Professor Sar A. Levitan of George Washington University.

The disagreement revolves upon the definition of poverty. The Census Bureau defines poverty in terms of money income. In 1975 a nonfarm family of four was counted as "poor" if its money income was $5,500 or less. But those were the very people who benefited from nonmoney forms of income such as food stamps, subsidized housing, and Medicaid. According to Professor Edgar K. Browning, these and other types of *income in kind* were enough to raise the average income of "poor" families well above the poverty line. Moreover, these forms of family assistance are not taxed as income and, therefore, provide poor families greater net benefits than an equal amount of income. A study by the U.S. Department of Health, Education, and Welfare, cited by Prof. Browning, concluded that the federal government channeled $11.1 billion of goods and services to poor families in 1973. The

The other important public assistance program for the elderly is **Medicare**, which was passed by Congress in 1965. Medicare helps pay the medical bills for the aged. This program became necessary because old people, who become ill more frequently than any other age group, were no longer able to bear the increasing costs of medical care.

total included benefits in the form of food, housing, education, health care, and job training programs. The value of these *"in-kind" transfers* amounted to $637 per poor person. "When in-kind transfers (exclusive of public education provided by state and local governments) are counted as income, the average poor family in 1973 had an income that was approximately 30 percent *above* the poverty line."*

This may be only a way of saying that the government's welfare programs are accomplishing what they were set up to do. The Census Bureau's figures are confusing because they count only the money benefits paid to people on welfare and not the non-money (in-kind) benefits. Either the Bureau should count benefits in kind, in which case there would have been almost no poor people in 1973, or it should leave out all welfare benefits, in cash as well as in kind, thus increasing the number of poor people in 1973 to more than 26 million.

An economist might prefer to define poverty to include all those who depend on welfare benefits for their support—that is, all those who are unable to earn their own way. A social worker or a nutritionist might prefer the other measurement, which shows that almost nobody in America has to go without food, clothing, and shelter. After all, there are many countries around the world where the living standards of U.S. welfare recipients must seem the height of luxury.

* Edgar K. Browning, "How Much More Equality Can We Afford?" *The Public Interest*, No. 43, Spring 1976, p. 92.

Cyclical poverty and jobs

The best remedy for poverty is a job. Most families with a working adult are above the poverty level. Those who aren't are people whose wage earners are in the very lowest-paid jobs, or who have unusually large families, or both. In 1967, a year of prosperity, only about 20% of poor families had adults working full time. About 30% were headed by people who were either unemployed or working only part time. The rest of the poor families had no one in the labor force. Thus most poor families have no working adults, either because they are unable to work at all or because they can't find jobs.

Finding and hanging onto a job is complicated by fluctuations in the output of the economy. Our capitalist economy passes through periods of recession, expansion and growth, booms, and contractions. Because of these changes during the business cycle, the level of employment is constantly changing, sometimes expanding and sometimes contracting. Poverty associated with cyclical changes in the nation's output is called **cyclical poverty.**

In the good years of the business cycle, employment opportunities are rising and many poor are able to find jobs that require only a low level of skills. It follows that in bad years unemployment has a devastating effect on workers who are just above the poverty level. Many of them are thrust back down into the poverty from which they had risen. In 1975 the average rate of unemployment for the country as a whole stood at 8.9%. But as in previous recessions, it was much more serious among teenagers (20.7%), nonwhites (14.4%), and low-skilled workers in general (12.8%). Among inner-city teenagers, unemployment reached as high as 40%. At the other extreme, among married men in general, it averaged only 5.1%.

Fortunately, many of the unemployed receive other income to help tide them over. Those whose unemployment is only temporary can be helped through **unemployment compensation.** In most states workers who lose their jobs can collect unemployment checks for a period of up to six months, and many states have extended the period by three or six months more. These payments are made to workers who have lost their jobs but who are still actively seeking work and are willing to accept a suitable offer. The payments are financed through a tax on employers. The amount of the individual benefit depends on how much the person was earning and the length of experience on the job. Benefits also vary among the states, being lowest in Mississippi and highest in Washington, D.C.

More than two-thirds of the unemployed received unemployment compensation in 1975. Others who were not eligible for unemployment compensation received public assistance and food stamps. Programs that help the unemployed are of great value, not only in preventing much hardship but also because they help to counteract the business cycle by putting purchasing power in the hands of spenders. In 1975 unemployment compensation, public assistance, and food stamps provided eligible families with about 90% of their previous after-tax incomes. As a result of these programs, real per capita disposable income fell only slightly during the recession.

Islands of poverty

We have discussed two kinds of poverty: hard-core poverty that afflicts those who are outside the labor market; and cyclical poverty that results from economic fluctuations. A third kind of poverty is caused by *structural* changes in the economy. When workers are unable or unwilling to respond to economic change, they may be left high and dry outside the mainstream of economic life. Such groups comprise **islands of poverty.**

Islands of poverty are the result of human immobility. If people were always able to change their work or their residence in response to changes in the economy, this kind of poverty would not exist. If a coal mine in Kentucky closed down, the miners would move somewhere else. If the demand for welders dropped off, welders would switch to bricklaying or carpentry. In actual life, of course, many people cannot change their locations or their skills. They may be reluctant to leave a place where they have lived all their lives, where they have friends and relatives. They are not likely to know of opportunities thousands of miles away. Parts of the southeastern United States and Appalachia have high levels of unemployment today because their traditional industries have declined while many of the workers have remained. Not all workers stay rooted, of course. Many workers do migrate— especially the younger ones. One famous example of poverty and migration was the Oklahoma dust bowl of the 1930s, when drought forced thousands of farmers to abandon the

Extended Example
An Island in Kentucky

Martin County, Kentucky, was once an island of poverty. In 1964 unemployment was more than 21% and the county had one doctor, two lawyers, no dentists, no drugstore, no newspaper, and no radio station. By 1977 there were twelve lawyers, nine doctors, two dentists, three drugstores, better roads, and unemployment of 3%. Weekly paychecks were averaging $350 and annual salaries from $15,000 to $20,000.

What brought on this miraculous transformation?

The first helpful change was the decision to build a 24-mile branch line of the Norfolk and Western Railway through the county. The railroad offered a means of moving the region's low-sulfur coal to market, coal that was increasingly in demand as the nation's energy crisis worsened. Cheap transportation facilities encouraged five coal producers to move in and invest $200 million in new facilities. Today the expected annual production is 13 million tons. Three thousand of the region's work force are now employed in ninety coal mines.

The growth in economic activity has stimulated development of financial intermediaries. Bank deposits have more than tripled, and a savings and loan association collects savings for local investment. Tax revenues have been increasing, too, providing the means for building a garbage collection system, water system, recreation park, and swimming pool.

The new prosperity has brought a few problems. One big problem is a lack of housing for the workers attracted to the area. Another is the strain on public services that normally result from heavy population inflows. Still, the county's residents are pleased with the turn their region has taken and are hopeful they can maintain a steady rate of growth in production and incomes.

land. John Steinbeck wrote of them in *Grapes of Wrath*, telling of one family's journey to California with all their belongings piled on an old truck.

Governments have tried to deal with this sort of poverty in a number of ways. One basic question is whether workers should be helped to move from a depressed area to locations where there are jobs, or whether new industry should be encouraged to move to the depressed area. There are difficulties in both approaches.

If workers are to be taken up by the roots and transplanted somewhere else, they must be assured of jobs, homes, and a welcome from their new neighbors. People in other communities may resent the arrival of poor groups who compete with them for existing jobs and services. And it is difficult for any government agency to guarantee workers permanent jobs in private industry in some distant part of the country.

The usual approach is for governments to try to bring industry into areas where it is needed. This has been tried in a number of counties with varying results. In theory, a region having surplus labor should be attractive to outside firms because wages will be lower there. But the very fact that industry is lacking in an area suggests that business opportunities may be limited. If profits were there for the taking, companies would already have moved in. There may be a mismatch between the area's resources and the needs of industry: lack of the necessary job skills, lack of industrial capital, or lack of transportation facilities. If government is to encourage the movement of industry, it must help to train workers, give tax credits for investment, and enable firms to borrow money more cheaply. A number of state governments in the United States use these incentives to attract industry, and they are helped in this by the federal government. The Economic Development Act of 1965 and the Appalachian Regional Development Act of 1966 were passed by Congress in an effort to encourage area redevelopment. A danger is that the government may be asking taxpayers to subsidize unprofitable enterprises in one part of the country that will compete with businesses elsewhere. Then one region's gain might be another's loss. The hope, of course, is that the new enterprises will create jobs without taking them away from other workers, and that eventually the subsidies can be discontinued.

New approaches

Welfare programs have become very expensive, amounting to about 10% of all government outlays (not counting Social Security). The high administrative costs and a growing belief that the present system of public aid has been a failure have led to a search for a new approach.

Direct grants

In 1975 federal and state governments spent more than $43 billion on public welfare and housing assistance. If this amount had been distributed directly to the nation's estimated 25.8 million poor, it would have amounted to $1,666 for each of them, or $6,664 for a family of four. Much of it did not go directly to the poor, of course, since administrative costs had to be covered—salaries for government employees, particularly the thousands of case workers engaged in deciding who is to get public assistance and how much.

It might be cheaper to support the poor directly at public expense rather than channeling funds through public welfare programs. One objection to this idea is that giving money to the able-bodied poor might destroy their incentive to work. Low-skilled workers might receive more in welfare grants than they could earn on the job. Also, there are some people who don't mind living off public funds rather than supporting themselves, and perhaps there are others who would come to accept that way of life.

A negative income tax

A widely discussed proposal would channel funds directly to the poor while preserving work incentives. It would use the federal income tax system to set a *negative* income tax for poor families. Just as people above a certain level of income pay taxes to the government, those below a certain level of income would receive payments *from* the government. The amounts they would receive would depend on the size of their earned incomes.

Suppose the government set $5,500 as the amount of income needed to enable a family of four to subsist in today's economy. A family with no income at all would receive a negative tax of the entire $5,500. If the family began to have earned income, the negative tax payment would decrease—*but not by as much as the earned income.* The purpose of this provision is to give people an incentive to work at paying jobs rather than staying home and collecting money from the government. There would obviously be no monetary advantage to the head of the family in accepting a part-time job paying, say, $1,000 if the government reduced its negative tax payments by the same amount.

Most versions of the proposal begin by setting a minimum income that will be guaranteed, such as $5,500. If the family has additional earned income it will be taxed a certain percentage, say 50%. For example, a family with earned income of $1,000 might be required to pay a tax of .50($1,000) = $500, giving it a total income of $5,500 + $500 = $6,000. The family would still be better off than if it had no earned income. Likewise, a family earning $3,000 would pay a tax of .50($3,000) = $1,500, giving it a net income of $5,500 + $1,500 = $7,000. When its earned income reached $11,000, its positive income tax would be .50($11,000) = $5,500. This would just offset its negative income tax, and the government would no longer be paying the family a direct subsidy: $5,500 + $5,500 = $11,000. Income of $11,000 would be the cutoff point at which families stop receiving a negative payment from government and begin paying a positive tax.

The chief drawback to the negative income tax idea is that it would cost more than direct grants, and probably more than the existing system of public welfare. The cost would be high for two reasons. First, the minimum income guarantee would have to be high enough to provide for families in which no one is able to work at all. Second, the tax rate on earned income would have to be low enough

to give able-bodied people an incentive to look for jobs. The lower the tax rate, the higher would be the cost of the program. That is because the payments would taper off at a higher level of family income. In the example above, reducing the tax rate would increase work incentives. If the tax on earned income were reduced to 25%, the family would pay only .25($11,000) = $2,750. Its tax bill would not completely offset its negative tax until earned income reached .25($22,000) = $5,500. At such a high level of income, perhaps three-quarters of the families in the country would be receiving negative income tax payments. Of course, nobody is proposing such an extensive program as that.

The negative income tax would have the advantage of being simple to administer. The negative tax payments could be made through the existing Internal Revenue system—the government would mail out checks on, say, a monthly basis. It would collect its positive tax on earned income in the same way it does now, at the end of each year. This would probably require a larger Internal Revenue staff, but it would eliminate the need for social workers and the present public welfare bureaucracy.

Another advantage to the negative income tax proposal is that it might encourage individual initiative. Many of those benefiting from the negative tax would be given a sense of personal control over their family budgets and an incentive to look for some sort of earned income.

Leaders of both the Democratic and Republican parties have at times given support to the negative income tax. President Nixon went farthest with it when in 1969 he asked Congress to enact a modest "workfare" plan calling for a guaranteed minimum of $2,320 a year (including about $850 in food stamps). Opposition in Congress held back the proposal and eventually the administration dropped it.

One of the chief arguments against it was that people would be able to get money without working. Even with the system of incentives, the critics argued, there would be many who would refuse to work. This objection was tested in some interesting experiments begun in New Jersey and Pennsylvania in the late 1960s and continuing into the 1970s. A number of welfare families were given income guarantees of varying amounts and were also taxed at various rates on their earned incomes. The behavior of these families over a period of several years was compared with that of families not receiving income guarantees. The main employment effect of the income guarantees was on some working wives, who took advantage of the extra money to spend more time at home. Little effect was observed on husbands, who continued to work about as much as before. Even more significant was the effect on family spending habits; recipients of income guarantees tended to spend more for basic nutrition, for health and education services, and for upgrading their living standards.

Discrimination

Racial discrimination

Discrimination on the basis of race continues to be a serious cause of poverty. Slightly more than a third of the poor are nonwhite. Nonwhites find it harder to get jobs than other people, and the jobs they do get tend to pay less. They are among the last to be hired and the first to be fired. They may have difficulty finding housing at a fair price or in an area of their choice. As a result, the poverty rate among nonwhites is three or four times as high as among whites.

Poverty among nonwhites can be shown to have several causes. Many nonwhites come from rural farming backgrounds in the South; rapid mechanization since World War II has forced them to migrate to the cities at a time when the demand for unskilled workers has been decreasing and when even semiskilled workers are finding it difficult to get jobs. Many unions have set up barriers against blacks—unions of construction workers such as electricians, carpenters, and bricklayers are examples. Relatively fewer nonwhites make it into office jobs, and relatively more are forced into service occupations that pay low wages. In 1974 half of white workers were in professional, administrative, or selling jobs while only 32% of non-white workers were. Fewer than one-third of white workers were in unskilled or service occupations, while more than half of nonwhite workers were. And as we have already noted, unemployment is much higher among nonwhites.

Sex discrimination

Sex discrimination may explain the incidence of poverty among female-headed families. Throughout most of history women have generally been assigned different jobs or received lower pay for the same tasks as men. In Western society, the movement to a more industrialized economy brought increasing demand for unskilled labor and led women toward greater participation in the labor force. This trend toward ever-increasing numbers of women working outside the home continues.

Economic discrimination against women is no longer legally or culturally acceptable. Income differentials based on sex, though they have narrowed over the last twenty-five years, still persist in many areas of employment. In 1975 women were earning an average of only 57% of male earnings for full-time work. The gap is not the result of present discrimination alone. Some of the difference is probably the result of lack of continuity or experience in the job market, a possible result of past discrimination. Still, there is evidence that among males and females of comparable experience the wages of male workers tend to rise more steeply than those of females. In addition, a greater percentage of men than women are working, due to childbearing responsibilities and the preference of many women for the role of housewife. For these reasons, some percentage difference in favor of men will probably continue.

Dual markets

Discrimination affects more than just the money incomes of the poor. To a great extent, minority families live and work and consume in a different economy from that of the majority. Discrimination forces them to sell their labor within the occupations and industries that are open to them. And what is open to blacks and women is a labor market smaller and at times separate from that for white males. Because the jobs they can get are limited and a large number of workers are competing for these jobs, wage rates tend to be lower. Figure 1a illustrates price and quantity determination in labor markets for the general population; Figure 1b shows what happens to those who are forced to sell their labor in a more restricted market. In 1b demand is relatively low and supply is relatively large, resulting in a lower equilibrium price. The restricted workers are condemned to low wages or unemployment.

But that is not all. There are also dual markets for consumers. Nonwhites often pay more for housing, health services, and education than their white counterparts. This is true even when we take into account the lower rents in slum areas, because overcrowding and poor quality are likely to more than offset the lower rents. The prices of groceries are often higher in ghetto areas, insurance rates are higher, and bank credit for business and real estate is often sharply limited. Figure 1c shows how a large demand for the limited housing available can keep housing costs high.

Government policies against discrimination

A number of federal and state laws have been passed in recent years in an effort to end discrimination in the job sector. The Civil Rights Act of 1964 made it unlawful for an employer, labor union, or employment agency to discriminate against workers because of race, color, religion, sex, or national origin. It authorized the Equal Employment Opportunity Commission (EEOC) to enforce the law. One problem facing the EEOC was how to define discrimination, since discrimination or bias may take many subtle forms. Under the law, persons who feel they are victims of discrimination can file complaints with the commission and even take legal action in the courts. The commission issued the following warning to employers:

If a statistical survey shows that minorities and females are not participating in your work force at all levels in reasonable relation to their presence in the population and the labor force, the burden of proof is on you to show that this is not the result of discrimination, however inadvertent.

An example of the complex forms discrimination can take is to be seen in a case involving the U.S. Steel Company. In its Birmingham mill it had a dual seniority system, under which some lines of work were reserved for whites and others for blacks. If a job was open in the white seniority line, it had to be filled by the white worker who had been there

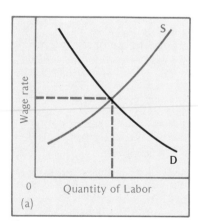
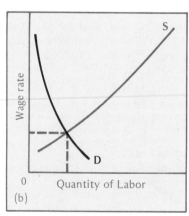
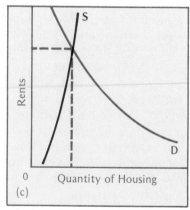

Figure 1 (a) General market for labor. (b) Dual or restricted market for labor. The quantity of labor demanded is less and supply is greater; wages are therefore lower. (c) A dual market for housing available to the poor. As the supply is restricted, the supply curve moves to the left; rents therefore increase.

Table 3
Money Income of Families (1974)

	Percent Distribution						
	Under $3000	$3000 to $4999	$5000 to $6999	$7000 to $9999	$10,000 to $14,999	$15,000 and over	Median
White families	3.8	6.5	8.0	12.7	24.7	44.3	$13,816
Black families	12.7	13.5	16.2	16.2	20.1	21.1	8,255
All families	4.7	7.5	8.5	13.0	24.3	40.9	12,836

longest. The same was true for the black seniority line. A black could not be put in a white job no matter how long he or she had been employed or how qualified he or she might be. Likewise, white workers could not fill jobs that were in the black seniority line. A federal district court held that this was against the law and ordered the company to establish a single seniority system under which any worker could fill a job if he or she had the proper qualifications and had been there long enough.

Another way of overcoming job discrimination is the **Affirmative Action** approach. This requires the employer to make a special effort to find minority-group employees who are eligible for higher positions or can be moved into departments where minorities are underrepresented. The federal government has applied the Affirmative Action approach to companies and other organizations above a certain size having federal contracts, including universities.

Affirmative Action has its critics. They say that employers are pressured to hire less efficient workers than they otherwise would, resulting in a decline in work standards. The use of quotas has come under the heaviest fire: quotas are said to involve "reverse discrimination"—that is, discrimination against nonminority groups such as white males. These men grumble, "You have to be either black or a woman in order to get ahead." Much of the criticism has been over the issue of job security. Because blacks and women are often the last hired, they tend to be the first fired when production is cut back. But if an employer must maintain a quota, it may be necessary to fire other workers with longer seniority instead. Minority leaders reply that even if reverse discrimination occurs, this doesn't begin to make up for all the past injustices to minorities.

Inequality

We are slowly wiping out absolute poverty in the United States. If we consider the food and housing aid given to people on welfare, hardly anybody in the United States is unable to maintain a minimum standard of living. Clearly, poverty as it was known throughout human history and is still known in much of Asia and Africa today, no longer exists in the United States. Many people, however, are relatively poor: although they do not live below a standard consistent with physical well-being, they live at levels substantially below those of most of us.

This can be seen by comparing different family incomes with the median for the whole United States. *The median family income is in the middle of all incomes*—that is, half the families have incomes that are higher and half have incomes that are lower. In 1974 the median family income was $12,836. About one-fifth of the families had incomes that were less than half the median—that is, about 13 million families or 37.4 million people had family incomes less than $6,418. This shows that there is a fairly wide spread of incomes down the lower end of the income range; they are not bunched together near the median. Table 3 shows the numbers of families falling into various income categories.

Reading a complicated table of numbers may be difficult. That is why economists use the Lorenz curve shown in Figure 2. A **Lorenz curve** shows at a glance just how equally or unequally incomes are distributed. Here is how it works. On the horizontal axis we measure percentages of families. On the vertical axis we measure percentages of total income. If the income distribution were perfectly equal—that is, if every family received exactly the same income—it would be measured by the diagonal line connecting opposite corners of the square. This is because the first 20% of families would receive 20% of the total income, the first 40% of the families would receive 40% of the total income, and so on up to 100%. We call this diagonal the reference line. By comparing actual curves of income distribution with the reference line we can see how unequally income is distributed.

The Lorenz curve in Figure 2 illustrates income distribution in the United States in 1950. It tells us that the lowest 20% of families received about 5% of income. The lowest 80% of families received slightly more than 50% of income. This means that the top 20% of families received more than 40% of income. Putting it another way, the top 20% of families received more than eight times as much income as the bottom 20% of families.

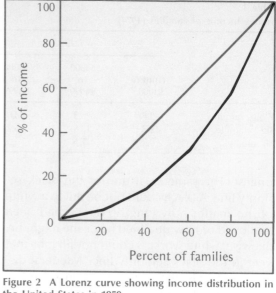

Figure 2 A Lorenz curve showing income distribution in the United States in 1950.

Figure 2 shows moderately unequal distribution in 1950. Changes since then are shown in Figure 3, which gives Lorenz curves for the years 1960 and 1972. The curves have become a little flatter over this period of time, but their basic shape has remained the same.

Table 4 provides the percentage data from which the curves are drawn. The Bureau of the Census makes the figures available annually. They are based on incomes of all kinds, in-

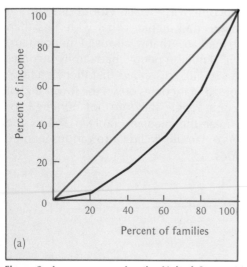

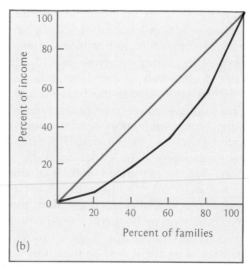

Figure 3 Lorenz curves for the United States: (a) in 1960; (b) in 1972. Notice their similarity. This indicates income distribution has changed very little.

Table 4
Share of Aggregate Income Before Taxes Received by Each Fifth of Families, Ranked by Income

	1947	1950	1960	1966	1972
Lowest fifth	5.1%	4.5%	4.8%	5.6%	5.4%
Second fifth	11.8	11.9	12.2	12.4	11.9
Third fifth	16.7	17.4	17.8	17.8	17.5
Fourth fifth	23.2	23.6	24.0	23.8	23.9
Highest fifth	43.3	42.7	41.3	40.5	41.4
Top 5 percent	17.5	17.3	15.9	15.6	15.9

Source: *Economic Report of the President,* February 1974.

cluding Social Security, public welfare, and other transfer payments. Without those transfer payments the income distribution would have been much more unequal. The major shifts in income distribution actually occurred before 1948. Since then, the share of the lowest fifth has stabilized at slightly more than 5%, and the share of the highest fifth at 40%. The share of the top twentieth of the population declined slightly from 17.5% in 1947 to 15.9% in 1972. These are not great changes. We may conclude that although absolute levels of living have improved, *there has been no significant gain in income equality in recent decades.*

Most economists who have studied the facts of income distribution do not expect any great change to take place in the foreseeable future. This is because the forces making for more equal distribution are offset by forces that work for less equal distribution. Among those that tend toward less equality are: the tendency of labor unions to win benefits for middle-income workers rather than lower-income workers; an increasing tendency for wives of middle- and higher-income men to enter the labor force, thus raising their family incomes substantially; and the fact that low-income men are retiring at earlier ages.

Among the forces working in the opposite direction, toward greater equality, are: the continuing migration of farm workers to the city, where their incomes are likely to be at least a little higher than in rural employment; a reduction of income differences between whites and nonwhites; more equality for women; and further increases in welfare benefits for the poor. On balance, it seems likely that the forces working toward equality may be somewhat stronger than those working against.

Some people look to taxation as a way of reducing inequality. Politicians sometimes speak of "closing the tax loopholes" through which people with high incomes are often able to reduce their federal income tax bill. But as it stands, the present tax structure probably has little effect on income shares. Some taxes are progressive—that is, they take a larger fraction of higher incomes, as the federal and state income taxes do; others, such as sales taxes and the Social Security tax, are regressive in that they weigh more heavily on lower incomes. Taken altogether, it appears that people at the lower end of the income distribution pay about the same proportion of their income in taxes as do people in the middle and upper-middle range. Only when we get to the $100,000-a-year level and above do we find people paying a significantly greater proportion of their income to the tax collector.

Americans could choose to restructure the tax system, if we wished, to make it more progressive. But tax reform is politically very difficult to accomplish. There are literally hundreds of special interests that bring pressure to bear upon legislators to get favorable treatment for themselves, and the result may be a tax law that is different but not much better than before. The tax reform bill of 1976 was 1,500 pages in length and so complex that even tax lawyers were not certain what some of the provisions meant.

Of course, an important part of any program to relieve the problem of poverty is a strong commitment to economic growth. A growing output of goods and services enables more families to enjoy rising living standards without reducing the living standards of others. A democracy like ours must be responsive to the needs of the people. If those needs become intense and widespread, voters will

Economic Thinker
Arthur Okun

When economists serve in government, they can influence policy in ways that they believe will improve our economic system. This is a valuable opportunity, but it also implies an obligation to state clearly the basis for their policy recommendations.

Arthur M. Okun (born 1928) had wide experience in academic economics before becoming a part of policymaking. He was Professor of Economics at Yale University before becoming economic adviser and Chairman of the Council of Economic Advisers under President Lyndon Johnson. In recent years he has served as economic consultant to private corporations and as senior fellow at Brookings Institution in Washington

Dr. Okun's primary concern in economic policymaking involves government's role in promoting greater equality. Under the market system, free competition in the marketplace will mean inequality of income distribution. We permit these inequalities to continue because we believe they help our system to operate efficiently. We believe that increasing equality would involve a cost in terms of efficiency; that is, there is a tradeoff which prevents us from moving too far toward perfect equality.

Other nations have taken more extreme positions. Socialist governments have reduced inequality but have suffered a massive cost in efficiency as a result. Dictatorial systems may achieve maximum efficiency but only at tremendous costs in terms of equality and human liberties.

Democratic capitalism has followed a third route, through an "uneasy compromise" between equality and efficiency. The United States has established what Okun calls a "split-level society." On one level our social and political system grants equal rights to all citizens. Equality of rights guarantees our personal freedoms against any move by government to take them. It protects us from total dominance by the market; there are some values which just don't have a price tag. But equality of rights is most important for another reason. It ensures that individuals are treated fairly—that human beings are treated with dignity simply because they are human beings.

This last reason for rights is the basis for tension in our society. For, as Okun points out, dignity and starvation do not mix well. The second level of our split-level society is our economic institutions. Our economic system is characterized by the free market where individuals must "succeed or suffer"—and suffering is certainly damaging to human dignity.

The market has its place; its power is decentralized and efficient. But the market must be kept in its place; it must not be allowed to erode other human values.

This is where the "uneasy compromise" in our system experiences strains. Okun is surprised that the strains are not more disruptive. In spite of the fact that the lowest half of income earners in the United States have only one-fourth of income and one-twentieth of wealth, still there is little pressure for change. Apparently we fear the excess use of power to achieve equality more than we would value the greater equality.

There are ways to achieve the one without the other, however. And Okun believes that movement toward greater equality would increase efficiency as well. To provide greater opportunities for human development would tend to increase our nation's productive capacity and improve living standards for all of us. Progressive income taxes are a substantial move in this direction, and federal outlays for the disadvantaged are also important. In-kind aid, including education and health care, job counseling and training, and housing, should be directed toward those in need. All these efforts would help to narrow the disparities which now shut off some groups from contributing to our economic system.

Okun is not seeking absolute equality, because efficiency would decline so much that there would be less to redistribute. After some point, as the slices of our "economic pie" became more equal, the pie—our national output of goods and services—would decline in size, or at least fail to grow. Okun explains this tradeoff in his book *Equality or Efficiency: The Big Tradeoff.* Our system can be healthy and continue to have substantial differences in income. What is not healthy is the sharp "contrasts in civilization" which exist between the rich and the poor. Okun looks forward to a society with "fewer races, and more dances that feature cooperation and fraternity"—a society in which interdependent groups prosper through the prosperity of others, rather than through dominance over others.

demand redistribution from the haves to the have-nots. To avoid excessive political pressure in support of greater equality, it is important to increase the size of the economic pie, encouraging all to contribute to production and allowing all to share in its distribution.

Urban poverty and crisis

In the past, we thought of poverty as primarily a rural problem. In 1930 nearly half the U.S. population was rural, and many rural families lived lives of hardship—especially the sharecroppers and hired farmhands. But since 1940, our rural population has been declining fairly steadily, while city population has been increasing by about 3 million a year. By 1950 the urban population had reached 64%, and by 1970 the ratio was 74%.

Many of the rural migrants came seeking the greater opportunities the city promised: escape from drudgery and relief from the uncertainties of a life dependent on the vagaries of nature and the fluctuations of the agricultural market. But all too often they found that city life had its own drudgery and uncertainty. They came to the city with serious disadvantages: low education, few skills, poor health, and little understanding of their new surroundings. The city, for its part, was no longer able to absorb vast tides of unskilled migrants as it formerly had. The number of industrial jobs for such people had declined as technological progress put increasing emphasis on training and skill. Add to this the higher living costs in cities, and it is not surprising that 9.3% of central-city whites and 29.6% of central-city blacks were reported in 1973 as having incomes below the poverty line.

These circumstances combine to create a giant cancer in our cities: overcrowded and decaying housing, poor nutrition, low standards of health care, inadequate education, lack of industrial skills all working upon each other to produce still worse conditions for future generations of city dwellers. The cities are faced with increasing problems while their resources for solving them are dwindling. The reasons are easy to see, but solutions are elusive.

Urban finance

Cities get their money from taxes and from funds turned over to them by state and federal governments. The mayor of a large city has to make regular pilgrimages to the state capital to plead for help and to Washington to add another voice to the national chorus of mayors imploring Uncle Sam to be more generous.

The ability of any city to raise money through its own taxes is limited. Taxpayers can easily move outside the city to avoid paying while continuing to enjoy many of the benefits of city services. Thus the cities are caught between the need to collect more revenue and the tendency of higher tax rates to drive away people and business. Cities must keep their tax rates low and adjust them to fit different elasticities of supply and demand: that is, set high tax rates on activities that must be located in cities and lower rates on activities that may be carried on elsewhere. This leads to a heavy dependence on property taxes. In 1973 taxes on property accounted for about a quarter of all city revenues.

The property tax has been with us since the days of ancient Rome. In the modern city, however, it is an unsatisfactory way of raising revenue. For one thing, the area of land in the city is practically fixed and cannot be expected to grow. If the city tries to increase its revenues from the property tax to meet increasing needs, it must tax individual property owners more heavily. This may not be feasible unless the value of their property has risen. Higher property values depend on rising levels of economic activity; the city's economy must first prosper if the revenues from property taxes are to grow to any great extent.

Second, while the supply of land is relatively inelastic, the quantity of improvements that can be made on the land is relatively elastic. Owners can choose to make capital investments on their urban properties, or, on the other hand, to invest somewhere else. If improvements are taxed too heavily, investment funds are likely to flow elsewhere—taking people, business, and jobs along with them. The city can't prosper if its tax policies drive enterprises away or discourage new enterprises from coming in.

Third, property taxes are thought to fall more heavily on people with lower incomes than on those with higher incomes, at least where housing properties are concerned. The reason is that the cost of their dwellings is a larger portion of the incomes of poorer families; this is true whether the family buys or rents its housing. Heavy property taxes thus tend to reduce the purchasing power of the very families whom public services are intended to help.

For all these reasons, property taxes are an inadequate source of revenue for city governments. Between 1960 and 1973, city expenditures in the United States more than tripled while revenue from property taxes barely doubled. The gap was filled largely by federal and state funds—about two-thirds of the amount coming from the states.

At the same time their taxing capabilities were approaching a limit, cities were faced with increased demands for public services. Growing concentrations of poor people in the central cities increased the need for welfare assistance, child-care facilities, low-cost housing, mass transportation, health services, schools, and public safety.

Welfare assistance The cities depend heavily on federal help for their welfare programs. Federal grants finance from half to three-quarters of the public assistance programs administered by state and local governments. Washington distributes its help on the basis of per capita incomes in the different states, with New York State receiving 50% of its welfare funds from the federal government and Mississippi 78%. This still leaves some large cities with the problem of paying for part of their welfare costs; New York City, for example, pays 75% of its welfare burden. This is why the growth in numbers of the urban poor has worsened the financial problems of our large cities, particularly those in the industrial areas of the Northeast.

One possible solution would be to let the federal government pay the entire welfare bill, on the grounds that the problem of urban poverty is not really a local problem. A large proportion of those on welfare rolls in northern cities did not live there originally but came to escape even worse conditions somewhere else.

Under this proposal, federal income tax revenues would replace state and local taxes as a means of financing welfare. Then state and local governments could concentrate their efforts on other public services related to their local needs. This would have the added advantage of making it easier to standardize procedures and benefits nationally. If the negative income tax idea were adopted, most of the city and state welfare bureaucracies would no longer be needed.

Housing Since World War II, the housing of the urban poor has deteriorated. Very little new housing has been built that poor families can afford. While metropolitan areas have grown tremendously, the new housing has been in the suburbs or in luxury high-rise apartments in the cities, leaving the poor to crowd together in older dwellings.

Some low-rent housing has been provided for poor families through public housing projects; that is, housing built by local governments with the help of federal funds. This approach has not gone very far. One reason is that few neighborhoods want a public housing project built nearby, bringing in hundreds or thousands of poor people of different racial or ethnic backgrounds. Moreover, some public housing developments in central cities have become giant concrete boxes, breeding crime and violence to such a degree that poor families have refused to move into them. One development in St. Louis remained largely empty for years until it was finally torn down.

A better approach might be to give poor families direct payments to spend on housing. It would then be up to each family to decide where they wanted to live. The housing market might be expected to respond to the demand from low-income groups as it would to any other group of buyers. In one respect, this would place the poor on the same footing as other groups. Middle-income and upper-middle-income homeowners now receive indirect housing subsidies: the federal government permits them to deduct the interest payments on their mortgages from taxable income when figuring their income taxes. Low-income families aren't able to get mortgages. Giving them a housing subsidy would help to offset this inequity.

Health, education, and public safety Welfare and housing are not the only financial problems the cities have had to wrestle with. The costs of standard services such as police and fire protection, schools, and hospitals have shot up in recent years. Public-service costs tend to rise faster than costs in manufacturing because there is no way of increasing output per person. The public still wants a policeman on the block and a fire station close at hand, small classes in the schools, and adequate medical facilities. The workers who provide these services are just as concerned with the rising cost of living as other workers are, and they are determined not to be treated as second-class citizens. Their unions have grown stronger and more militant in recent years. The upward climb of these costs has added greatly to the financial problems of the cities.

The three E's

You will remember the three E's. We have mentioned them often in this text: Efficiency, Externalities, and Equity. They will help us to gain perspective on the complex issues of urban poverty.

Efficiency Economic decisions are made by many different individuals and groups. They make decisions after comparing benefits and costs. Consumers compare the benefits they expect to get from their purchases with the prices they will have to pay. Business firms make benefit/cost comparisons when they hire resources. Savers make benefit/cost comparisons when they decide where to put their investment funds so as to obtain the highest yields. When all individuals and groups are maximizing their benefits and minimizing their costs, we say an economy is efficient. It is efficient because it is channeling resources into employments where they will produce the greatest benefits; it is obtaining maximum output at the least expenditure of scarce resources.

Externalities Sometimes we receive benefits or costs that nobody intended. We call them externalities because they are outside the decision-making process of the individual consumer, business firm, or investor. They represent added benefits or costs to the community as a whole. Some examples of external costs are: the discharge of gases that results when a consumer purchases a polluting automobile; the hazard to fish when business firms pour dangerous chemicals into rivers; the deterioration of the landscape when investors underwrite strip-mining or unattractive factory construction. Some examples of external benefits are: the increase in human capital when the labor force develops new skills; the improvement of our social environment when jobs are plentiful; and the larger tax revenues generated by greater economic activity.

If we are to judge the efficiency of an economy completely, we should include the externalities it produces along with the rest of its output. If the community enjoys external benefits from a particular activity, then it makes sense to channel more resources toward that activity. If an activity results in external costs, we may want to move fewer resources in that direction.

Of course, it is difficult to measure external benefits and costs precisely. They are outside the market system. It is the job of government to estimate them and to include them in its analyses of the benefits and costs of public services. In this way we may hope to achieve a more efficient allocation of resources toward those activities which yield the *greatest total benefit* at the *lowest total cost.*

Equity Finally, the principle of equity involves the fair distribution of benefits and costs among our population. A free market system by itself, if it functioned perfectly, would distribute its private benefits only to those willing to pay for them. The ability to pay would be measured by a person's contribution to the system through his or her own production, resulting in a corresponding amount of income. One can argue that the market system is "fair" if it rewards persons strictly according to their contribution to output. But most modern industrial societies feel that this is not enough. For one thing, it takes no account of people's actual needs—which may have little to do with their earnings. Our system of taxes and transfer payments helps to deal with this by taxing some groups more heavily than others and by paying income supplements to poor families.

A second point against the distribution of benefits provided by a free market system is one that we have already touched on: the fact that it creates externalities which may be distributed in a quite random fashion, giving benefits to some and imposing costs on others.

The three E's and urban problems

The problems of the cities are a reflection of the efficiency of our market system, the externalities that it sometimes creates, and the equity (or inequity) with which it distributes benefits and costs. The free market was allocating resources efficiently when it encouraged the great migration of workers to the cities in recent decades. Without knowing it, workers were responding to a long-term decline of jobs in agriculture and an increase of opportunities in industry. But the system didn't distribute the costs and benefits of this process equitably. The private benefits of industrial development went disproportionately to highly skilled workers who eventually moved to more pleasant surroundings in the suburbs. The social costs fell disproportionately on low-skilled workers, members of minority groups, and others who were unable to escape from the external costs of growth: the slums, traffic congestion, air and noise pollution, and crime.

The result was what now appears to have been excessive investment in goods and services which provide private benefits: urban high-rise buildings and luxury apartments, highway systems rather than mass transit, and sprawling suburbs. At the same time too few resources seem to have flowed into activities for which costs are high but private benefits are low. One can argue that public housing, health, and education have been underfunded although their costs would have been justified by the external benefits they could bring to society as a whole. We can also argue that income-support payments and welfare benefits are too small to meet the needs of the poor and to provide the additional external benefits of greater equality in our communities.

In the last analysis, it is the general public that must decide. Efforts to correct inequities depend on the support of voters. Cities and localities, as we have seen, find it difficult to shoulder an additional tax burden for this purpose. If the nation as a whole is willing to undertake the commitment, it can do much to make our system more equitable. If efficiency is defined to mean the maximum output of *all* benefits relative to costs, then perhaps the final result will be to make our system operate more efficiently, too.

We can no longer afford poverty

Great inequality in incomes may have made some sense when our economic system was younger. Poverty at one end of the scale made wealth possible at the other end. A large class of rich people were able to save much of their income and thus make funds available for business to invest. The existence of poverty enabled capitalists to accumulate the resources through which they built up the means of production. A parallel to this can be seen in the twentieth century history of the Soviet Union, where incomes are also very unequal and where the masses of the population have been kept to a very low standard of living so as to make resources available for industrial development.

In a modern developed economy like ours high rates of saving are less important. The necessary rate of new investment often declines as an economy develops, and it becomes important to ensure a high level of consumption instead. This requires a broad base of secure, middle-income families. Poor families do not purchase new automobiles, buy new homes, or take expensive trips to vacation resorts. They provide little market for the fruits of technological advance, and they pay few personal taxes.

Although poor people spend little to boost our economy, they add significantly to its costs. The costs include increased crime, ill health, and urban blight. These costs are borne by the rest of the population through higher taxes and the loss and deterioration of property.

Probably the greatest cost of poverty is in underdeveloped productive resources. Unhealthy, poorly trained, and badly motivated workers are unable to make much of a contribution to national output. Instead, they represent a drain upon it. No modern nation can afford a large poor population.

Summary

Poverty can be characterized as *relative* poverty if living standards are below the levels of others in the community, or *absolute* poverty if living standards are below those considered necessary for human health. The productivity of the U.S. economy means that few families live in absolute poverty. The poverty line refers to a level of income three times the cost of a nutritional diet: $5,500 for an urban family of four in 1975.

The poverty population in the United States includes disproportionate numbers of rural families, nonwhites, and female-headed families. Elderly people also receive low incomes, but many are saved from poverty by past savings and investments.

Poverty programs aim at filling particular needs of certain poor groups. Hard-core poverty is treated through Aid to Families with Dependent Children, Supplemental Security Income, the Food Stamp Program, and Medicaid. The elderly are aided through Social Security and Medicare. Cyclical poverty is treated through unemployment compensation, welfare assistance, and food stamps. Islands of poverty are treated through encouragements to industry to move into depressed areas.

Current proposals involve significant changes in the present welfare system. Direct grants would channel funds directly to the poor with less administrative waste. A negative income tax would have similar advantages, but its cost would be high. Other positive programs aim at reducing racial and sexual discrimination in hiring. Since 1950, there has been little change toward greater equality of income distribution in the United States.

In recent years poverty has become more an urban problem than a rural problem. The in-migration of the poor and the out-migration of the affluent have left cities unable to finance their necessary services: welfare assistance, housing, health, education, and public safety. Proposals to deal with urban poverty should be based on the concepts of efficiency, externalities, and equity. When all external benefits and costs are considered, the principle of efficiency may justify allocating more resources toward solution of urban problems. Correcting the problem of poverty can help to increase the prosperity of our entire economy.

Key Words and Phrases

- **relative poverty** a condition of living far below the level of others nearby.
- **absolute poverty** a condition of living below standards currently considered necessary for human health.
- **output per capita** the nation's total output divided by its population.
- **poverty line** the Social Security Administration's definition of poverty based on three times the cost of a normal nutritional diet.
- **"in-kind" programs of aid** nonmoney grants or assistance to the poor; food stamps are an example.
- **hard-core poverty** poverty that results from conditions which make an individual unsuited for work in the modern economy; includes the elderly, disabled, the handicapped, and the unmarried parent who must take care of dependent children.
- **cyclical poverty** poverty which results from a low level of total production and employment in the nation's economy.
- **unemployment compensation** payments intended to relieve the harmful effects of temporary unemployment.
- **islands of poverty** poverty which results from structural changes, such as the decline or disappearance of an industry in a particular region.
- **direct grants** outright payments to poor people.
- **negative income tax** payments to poor people based on negative tax rates on incomes below some particular level of income.
- **dual markets** separate labor markets to which most blacks and women are restricted.

- **Affirmative Action programs** government-imposed guidelines or quotas that force employers to reach out and employ members of groups which may have suffered discrimination in hiring.
- **Lorenz curve** a graph that illustrates the degree of income inequality in the nation.

Questions for Review

1. Under what circumstances is the following statement correct? "There will always be relative poverty."

2. Distinguish between "in-kind" programs to aid the poor and general assistance programs. What are the major advantages and disadvantages of each?

3. Discuss the problem of islands of poverty and the difficulty of developing solutions. Cite specific examples from current affairs.

4. Discuss the pros and cons of Affirmative Action programs.

5. Outline the major causes for the problems facing American cities. What are the advantages and disadvantages of suggested solutions?

6. Use current statistical publications to draw up a table showing the proportions of various populations classified as poor: that is, rural, elderly, nonwhite, and female-headed families.

7. Distinguish between a negative income tax and direct grants to the poor.

Index